MANAGEMENT FOR PRODUCTIVITY

To the Student: A Study Guide for the textbook is available through your college bookstore under the title Study Guide to Accompany *Management for Productivity*, 1st edition by John R. Schermerhorn, Jr. The Study Guide can help you with course material by acting as a tutorial, review and study aid. If the Study Guide is not in stock, ask the bookstore manager to order a copy for you.

THE WILEY SERIES IN MANAGEMENT

MANAGEMENT FOR PRODUCTIVITY

JOHN R. SCHERMERHORN, JR.

SOUTHERN ILLINOIS UNIVERSITY AT CARBONDALE

JOHN WILEY & SONS

**NEW YORK
CHICHESTER
BRISBANE
TORONTO
SINGAPORE**

Copyright © 1984, by John Wiley & Sons, Inc.

All rights reserved. Published simultaneously in Canada.

Reproduction or translation of any part of
this work beyond that permitted by Sections
107 and 108 of the 1976 United States Copyright
Act without the permission of the copyright
owner is unlawful. Requests for permission
or further information should be addressed to
the Permissions Department, John Wiley & Sons.

Library of Congress Cataloging in Publication Data:

Schermerhorn, John R.
    Management for productivity.

    Includes indexes.
    1. Management.   I. Title.
HD31.S3326 1984   658   83-21576
ISBN 0-471-87140-0

Printed in the United States of America

10 9 8 7 6 5 4 3 2

Cover and Text design— Sheila Granda
Cover Photo— Paul Silverman
Production Supervisor— Jan M. Lavin
Copy Editor— Joan Knizeski
Photo Researcher— Teri Stratford
Photo Editor— Kathy Bendo

To my sons John Christian and Charles Porter

While you played
I wrote.
But always,
I was listening
and loving
you.

ABOUT THE AUTHOR

JOHN R. SCHERMERHORN, JR., is Professor of Administrative Sciences and Associate Dean of the College of Business and Administration at Southern Illinois University at Carbondale, where he teaches graduate and undergraduate courses in management. He earned a Ph.D. in Organizational Behavior from Northwestern University and previously taught at Tulane University and the University of Vermont. Highly concerned with helping the discipline of management serve the needs of practicing managers, he has written *Management for Productivity* to help others bridge the gap between the theory and practice of management.

Dr. Schermerhorn has prior work experience in business and hospital administration and re-mains professionally active in management training and consultation with a variety of organizations in the United States. He has international experience in Egypt, the Philippines, Poland and Tanzania, as well as several countries in South America. A member of the Academy of Management where he currently serves as chairperson of the Management Education and Development Division, Dr. Schermerhorn is known to educators and students alike as senior co-author of *Managing Organizational Behavior* (John Wiley & Sons, 1982). His published research appears in the *Academy of Management Journal*, *Academy of Management Review*, *Journal of Management*, and *Group and Organization Studies*, among other scholarly journals.

PREFACE

Managers in today's dynamic and ever-changing world are challenged to help organizations and their members make worthwhile performance contributions to contemporary society. *Management for Productivity* directly addresses the need to achieve high productivity through good management. For the student, this book presents the essentials of management theory in a systematic and thorough way, while keeping the discussion interesting and practical. For the instructor, it offers complete coverage of the basic functions of management, with special attention to decision making and problem solving in an environment where productivity improvement is a major concern. Within this framework, the student's exposure to the full scope of management theory and management skills as specified by AACSB accreditation guidelines is ensured. Chapters on production and operations management, managerial ethics and social responsibility, labor-management relations, budgets and management information systems, management in an international arena, and organization conflict, change, and development add depth to the traditional, functional coverage. Many concrete examples throughout the book increase its relevancy and value to students seeking managerial careers in a wide variety of occupational settings.

The writing style of *Management for Productivity* is designed to appeal to the student's interests without sacrificing rigor or substance. The book is thoroughly researched and current in both the theory and practice of management.

Over 50 reviewers from U.S. colleges and universities have helped create an intellectually sound textbook, as well as one that is a pleasure for students to use. Several special features help make this the most timely, substantive, and exciting textbook now available to serve the needs of students and instructors in an introductory principles of management course.

SPECIAL FEATURES

The first goal of this textbook is to cover the right topics in sufficient depth and breadth that the student gains a solid exposure to the fundamentals of management theory as they apply in the contemporary environment. The second goal, and one that is a necessary condition for the first to succeed, is for the book to attract and hold the reader's interest. The following unique features of *Management for Productivity* combine to offer just such a pleasurable and captivating reading experience:

- *State-of-the-art design* The design format of the book communicates a professional character most appropriate to the practice of management. The format creates a stimulating visual orientation to the subject matter that is not only attractive in design, but also mature and professional in its approach.

- *Creative and custom-designed illustrations*

Incorporated in the book are over 300 illustrations, photographs, and tables that highlight major topics, concepts, and issues in a way that further communicates the substance of the book to the reader. These illustrations complement text explanations to facilitate student understanding of key points.

- *Lively and conversational writing style* The text is written by an experienced and successful author who gives careful attention to making the material captivating for the reader. This writing style has proved highly successful in the past, and reviewers of this book enthusiastically report that the author has once again been able to transform the substance of an academic discipline into an interesting and applied perspective of great appeal to the career-oriented student.

- *Numerous real-world examples* Frequent examples are used to communicate how theories and concepts apply to the real world of management as practiced in actual situations. The book does more than merely relate examples to the reader, however, it presents them in an interactive way that causes the reader to think seriously about how he or she would act in the situation depicted. *Newslines* offer excerpts from newsmagazine and newspaper reports relevant to topics under consideration. They enhance the professional quality of the book by encouraging the reader to stay abreast of the news and become an informed manager conversant in day-to-day current events.

- *Thorough coverage of management in all types of organizations in domestic and international settings* Throughout the book, examples relate the practice of management to organizations of all types and sizes operating in a wide variety of environments. The *illustrative cases* interspersed throughout provide the reader with an exposure to management in small businesses, large businesses, not-for-profit organizations, and international businesses. In-text examples further illustrate how chapter material applies in the various organizational settings within which a student's career orientation may lie.

- *Fully integrated emphasis on careers* The book requires students to think seriously about their future careers. Examples and special features present management applications in a full spectrum of occupational choices including marketing, finance, accountancy, personnel, and production. Each chapter concludes with a *Career Perspective,* a special segment that helps the reader to think seriously about his or her career aspirations and consider how chapter topics relate to career opportunities and success.

A PROFESSIONAL LEARNING INSTRUMENT

Management for Productivity is a professional learning instrument that uses basic principles of learning theory to offer an integrated and effective educational experience for the student. The overall learning potential of the book is enhanced by:

- *Part and Chapter Openers* Highlight provocative real-world experiences or situations that set textbook topics in the context of day-to-day management practice.

- *Planning Ahead* Introduces the major topics covered in the chapter and establishes a framework for targeted reading.

- *Chapter Summary* Immediately follows the last section of a chapter and reminds the reader of major chapter themes.

- *Thinking Through the Issues* Ten questions that stimulate the reader to ponder major issues relating to chapter content.

- *The Manager's Vocabulary* Lists key terms of the chapter.

- *Career Perspective* A short vignette that depicts a career application or opportunity relevant to material covered in the chapter and asks the reader to relate to the material in terms of its personal career implications.

- *Case Application* A real-world experience or situation that requires the student to apply chapter materials to solve a managerial problem or explore a managerial opportunity.

- *Class Exercise* A quick-hitting in-class exercise that engages students in a learning situation requiring personal reflection, sharing with others, and general but focused class discussion.

- *References* Notes directing the reader's attention to sources used by the author in developing chapter topics.
- *Part Integrating Cases* Two comprehensive cases at the conclusion of each book part that require students to apply in an integrated fashion their learning from all chapters in the part.
- *Glossary* A list of important definitions that cross references key terms with the chapters in which they are first presented.

As you can see, *Management for Productivity* offers a comprehensive variety of chapter and part materials as ways of enriching the learning experience. The Career Perspectives, Case Applications, Class Exercises, and Part Integrating Cases, in particular, make the book a largely self-contained instructional instrument.

ORGANIZATION OF MATERIAL

Management for Productivity is organized in a part and chapter sequence consistent with the traditional treatment of management principles. However, this traditional coverage is grounded in today's complex and dynamic environment. It also clearly focuses attention on productivity as a basic criterion of managerial and organizational success. The book thus develops the fundamentals of management within the contemporary real-world setting in which the reader will be asked to function as a manager. Although traditional in substance, *Management for Productivity* is both provocative and current in its treatment of the fundamentals of management.

Part 1 of the book sets the stage for a directed study of management. It contains three chapters whose topics introduce management as a scientific discipline, the history of management thought, and the basic challenges of managerial decision making and problem solving. The next four parts of the book follow the traditional sequence: Part 2—*Planning* for Productivity, Part 3—*Organizing* for Productivity, Part 4—*Leading* for Productivity, and Part 5—*Controlling* for Productivity. Within each part, the initial chapter

introduces the fundamentals of the management function under study. Subsequent chapters develop aspects of the function in greater depth and are designed to be used in any order or combination at the instructor's discretion.

Part 6 examines the fundamentals of management in the context of major issues representative of the contemporary environment. Separate chapters address the application of management theories in an environment that challenges the modern manager to achieve success in managing organization change, conflict, and development; managing labor-management relations; managing in an international arena; and, managing with ethics and social responsibility. For the instructor's convenience, these chapters are written for use in any sequence or combination. They may also be separately assigned in conjunction with chapters from other parts of the book.

Part 7 of the book provides a futuristic look at management. It highlights a fast-changing modern world of complex social trends, advanced technology, high stress, and dynamic career opportunities. The final chapter encourages students to look ahead into the exciting world of the late 1980s and 1990s, and to move into this world with the desire and confidence to meet successfully the great challenges which it will surely present to us all.

The Appendix provides an additional opportunity for students to become acquainted with basic quantitative decision techniques. Use of this appendix will round out the introduction to the field of management science/operations research presented in the chapter discussions.

COMPLETE INSTRUCTIONAL SUPPORT PACKAGE

There is always more to creating a motivating and enthusiastic learning environment than any textbook alone can provide. *Management for Productivity* is supported by a comprehensive learning package. This package of supplementary resources has been developed by a number of experienced educators. It offers a variety of easy and creative ways for the instructor to provide students with an innovative and complete learning experience. The specially designed instructional support package contains these items.

- *Student Learning Guide* Specifically developed by Patrick Kroll of the University of Minnesota to complement the substance and pedagogical style of *Management for Productivity,* this study guide assists students in assimilating the subject matter and in identifying its practical applications. Included for each text chapter is a set of learning objectives, a chapter overview, a programmed learning drill, and a self-test procedure. Available for each book part are career applications, simulation exercises, personal assessments, and supplementary readings. The learning guide is a comprehensive resource that we recommend for the student.

- *Advanced Instructional Modules* (AIM) This unique supplement assists the instructor in bringing five areas of advanced study to the special attention of students. A highly innovative package prepared by subject-matter experts, *AIM* allows the instructor to accent any of the following topics in a manner complementary to text coverage.

1. *Women in Management,* by V. Jean Ramsey, Western Michigan University
2. *Microcomputers in Management,* by Edward M. Knod, Jr., Western Illinois University
3. *Mangement and the Quality of Working Life,* by Michael A. Gurdon, University of Vermont
4. *Management in the Not-for-Profit Sector,* by Curtis P. McLaughlin, University of North Carolina at Chapel Hill
5. *Small Business Management,* by Harold K. Wilson, Southern Illinois University at Carbondale

AIM is designed to provide one week of hands-on teaching material in each of these five advanced study areas. The authors have prepared for each topic two supplementary class lectures, individual and group student project assignments, class exercises and case assignments, additional readings, and test items.

- *Color Transparency Acetates* This creative instructional supplement provides over 100 multicolor transparency acetates ready for classroom use. Developed by professional media designer Dale Brown of Southern Illinois University at Carbondale in consultation with the author, these acetates highlight key features and concepts from the text. They are an engaging means of presenting major topics in class lectures and discussion.

- *Transparency Master Book* Over 200 transparency masters are contained in a separate booklet. These include masters for 100 key figures from the text as well as 100 masters also designed by Dale Brown to augment textbook illustrations for unique classroom presentations. Many masters have separate lecture notes to guide the instructor. They are also accompanied by companion masters that can be used to prepare student handouts, and which include a small reproduction of the figure and room for taking notes as each transparency is shown.

- *Profiles of Managers and Management Scholars* This series of profiles introduces contemporary managers and scholars who have made important historical contributions to the field of management. Bound in one volume, these profiles can be used as handouts or as lecture supplements to enrich topics being studied.

- *Instructor's Resource Manual* Prepared with the assistance of Patrick Kroll, this manual is a comprehensive resource for the instructor that provides alternative course syllabi and chapter teaching outlines, suggested testing and grading procedures, tips and ideas on teaching methods and techniques, student assignments and projects for individuals and groups, answers to questions in Thinking Through the Issues, responses to Career Perspective and Case Application questions, procedures for utilizing Class Exercises to full advantage, analyses of Part Integrating Cases, plus many other instructional support items and opportunities.

- *Test Bank Booklet* Over 2,000 multiple-choice and true/false questions and answers are available in a separately bound test bank.

- *Microtest* The entire test bank is available on MICROTEST—floppy disks for Apple II and

IBM PC microcomputers. The disks make it possible to produce computer-generated tests in a fast and user-friendly fashion.

- *Autotest* This test bank is also available, on request, on magnetic tape for mainframe application of the computerized testing program.

Management for Productivity with its package of instructional supplements clearly offers the instructor a way to create an exciting, interesting, and in-depth learning experience for students. A truly comprehensive and self-contained learning instrument, this book was written for today and tomorrow, and for both instructor and student. Use it with enthusiasm and great success!

ACKNOWLEDGMENTS

Management for Productivity was made possible through the extraordinary support provided me by many fine people. My gratitude first goes to John Lawler of the University of Illinois, Ron Teichman of the Pennsylvania State University, and Greg White of Southern Illinois University at Carbondale who served as subject matter experts on chapters in their areas of special interest—labor-management relations, budgets and management information systems, and production/operations management and management science, respectively.

Special thanks are also due to the persons whose efforts led to the exceptional package of supplementary instructional materials that accompany the text: Patrick Kroll (University of Minnesota) whose outstanding contributions to the text and the instructional support package are deeply appreciated; Dale Brown (Southern Illinois University at Carbondale) whose expertise resulted in the fine transparency package; and Michael A. Gurdon (University of Vermont), Edward M. Knod, Jr. (Western Illinois University), Curtis P. McLaughlin (University of North Carolina at Chapel Hill), V. Jean Ramsey (Western Michigan University), Harold K. Wilson (Southern Illinois University at Carbondale) the co-authors of the unique *Advanced Instructional Modules (AIM)*. Jo-Anne Naples, Shirley Moore, Judy Bleicher, Beverly Pavler, and Joyce Miller at Naples Editing Services also gave expert help.

There are four persons without whom I absolutely could not have created *Management for Productivity*—Gary South, Cam McClelland, Gale Lukat, and Lisa Stearns. To Gary, my graduate assistant, I again say thank you. For both Gary and I, special acknowledgement goes to Cam, who must be the finest word processor operator in the whole world, and also to Gale and Lisa, who provided the additional typing and administrative support necessary to the task. I am further indebted to Clif Andersen for his outstanding support while serving as Acting Dean of the College of Business and Administration, Southern Illinois University at Carbondale.

Of course, this book and the entire learning package are the result of the efforts of my editor Rick Leyh and his excellent support group at John Wiley & Sons. Rick first said it could be done. He then proceeded to encourage and support the project throughout. The commitments of Rick and the Wiley staff to excellence and discipline receive my highest personal respect. Special thanks go to the following superb group of Wiley personnel who worked tirelessly on the project: Susan Ahlstrom (administrative assistant), John Balbalis (illustration), Kathy Bendo (photo research), Sheila Granda (design), Rosamond Dana, Joan Knizeski, and Rosemary Wellner (editing), Jan Lavin (production), and Bill Kellogg (supplements).

A special acknowledgement goes to my wife, Ann, for being willing to put up with the demands, absences, and peculiarities of a husband who once again decided to write a book. Perhaps she and our sons, Christian and Porter, will now benefit from a husband and father whose attention shifts back to the lawn, the house, the car, evenings, mornings, weekends . . . and fun!

While speaking about the sacrifices of textbook writing, there's another person who unknowingly helped me along the way—Willie Nelson. I don't know how good a manager you are, Willie, but there have been days when it took "Little Things," "Good times," "Yesterday's Wine," and many others to keep me going. If there's a little nostalgia in all this, it's real. Writing a book is lonely work that entails many "Sweet Memories"—some of lost moments . . . others of those to be found again.

Finally, I am proud to recognize and publicly thank the many colleagues from colleges and universities around the country whose thorough reviews and suggestions helped create the finished product. My greatest appreciation goes to the following management educators.

Raymond Alie
WESTERN MICHIGAN UNIVERSITY

Robert Bjorkland
RIDER COLLEGE

Allen Bluedorn
UNIVERSITY OF MISSOURI

Dale Brown
SOUTHERN ILLINOIS UNIVERSITY AT CARBONDALE

Edward Brown
SINCLAIR COMMUNITY COLLEGE

Bob Bulls
J.S. REYNOLDS COMMUNITY COLLEGE

Joe Byrnes
BENTLEY COLLEGE

Charles Cole
UNIVERSITY OF OREGON

Robert Dennehy
PACE UNIVERSITY

Lincoln Deihl
KANSAS STATE UNIVERSITY

Dan Farrell
WESTERN MICHIGAN UNIVERSITY

Edward Giermak
COLLEGE OF DUPAGE

John Gelles
VENTURA COLLEGE

James Genseal
JOLIET JUNIOR COLLEGE

Michael Gurdon
UNIVERSITY OF VERMONT

Theodore Hansen
SALEM STATE COLLEGE

Alan Hollander
SUFFOLK COUNTY COMMUNITY COLLEGE

David Holt
JAMES MADISON UNIVERSITY

Ed Knod
WESTERN ILLINOIS UNIVERSITY

Reuben Krolick
CALIFORNIA STATE UNIVERSITY

Patrick Kroll
UNIVERSITY OF MINNESOTA

James McElroy
IOWA STATE UNIVERSITY

Curtis McLaughlin
UNIVERSITY OF NORTH CAROLINA

Joe Michlitsch
SOUTHERN ILLINOIS UNIVERSITY AT EDWARDSVILLE

Donald Nelson
MERRIMACK COLLEGE

Joseph Paolillo
UNIVERSITY OF WYOMING

John Pierce
UNIVERSITY OF MINNESOTA AT DULUTH

Phil Quaglieri
NORTHERN ILLINOIS UNIVERSITY

V. Jean Ramsey
WESTERN MICHIGAN UNIVERSITY

Richard Randall
NASSAU COMMUNITY COLLEGE

Elizabeth Redstone
CUYAHOGA COMMUNITY COLLEGE

M. J. Riley
KANSAS STATE UNIVERSITY

Klaus Schmidt
SAN FRANCISCO STATE UNIVERSITY

Richard Schoning
CALIFORNIA POLYTECHNIC UNIVERSITY

Charles Strain
OCEAN COUNTY COLLEGE

Laurence Stybel
BABSON COLLEGE

Jim Swenson
MOOREHEAD STATE UNIVERSITY

Shiela Teitelbaum
KINGSBOROUGH COMMUNITY COLLEGE

Donald Warrick
UNIVERSITY OF COLORADO

Harold K. Wilson
SOUTHERN ILLINOIS UNIVERSITY AT CARBONDALE

Charles Yauger
ARKANSAS STATE UNIVERSITY

**JOHN R. SCHERMERHORN, JR.
CARBONDALE, ILLINOIS**

CONTENTS

CHAPTER 3   The Manager as Decision Maker and Problem Solver

PART 2 PLANNING FOR PRODUCTIVITY

CHAPTER 4   Fundamentals of Planning

CHAPTER 5 Strategic Planning and Organizational Objectives   135

PART 3
ORGANIZING
FOR
PRODUCTIVITY   171

CHAPTER 6 Fundamentals of Organizing   175

PART 4 LEADING FOR PRODUCTIVITY

299

Perspective: The Work Ethic Is Underemployed   300

CHAPTER 10   Fundamentals of Leading

303

CHAPTER 11   Leading Through Communication

335

CHAPTER 12 Leading Through Motivation 369

CHAPTER 13 Leading Through Group Dynamics 399

PART 5
CONTROLLING FOR PRODUCTIVITY

PART 6 PRODUCTIVITY IN THE CONTEMPORARY ENVIRONMENT

CHAPTER 17 Managing Conflict, Change, and Organization Development

CHAPTER 18 Managing Labor-Management Relations

CHAPTER 19 Managing In an International Arena 621

CHAPTER 20 Managing With Ethics and Social Responsibility 655

PART 7
CONCLUSION

MEMORANDUM

TO: The Reader
FROM: John Schermerhorn
SUBJECT: *Management for Productivity*

This book is written for you, someone who now is or one day will be a manager. Being a manager is a special type of challenge because it involves working in a position of supervisory responsibility. The field of management offers a body of scientific knowledge that can help you fulfill this responsibility successfully and in a way that benefits you, the persons with whom you work, the organization for which you work, and society as a whole. The many learning opportunities contained in this book should help prepare you to be an effective manager in each of these respects.

THE BOOK IN PERSPECTIVE

Two points about this book and my goals in writing it for you are especially important. First, managers exist in all types of organizations. The issues, concepts, theories, and insights of this book are useful no matter where you plan to work—in business, education, government, health services, or social services. Second, my personal commitment has been to provide an active learning opportunity filled with practical insights and useful knowledge that will benefit you in the work setting. Although there is a lot of theory in this book, the theory is explained, illustrated, and applied in ways that should help you perform more effectively in a managerial capacity.

To take full advantage of the book, however, you must read carefully and stay involved each step of the way. Keep in mind that *Management for Productivity* is written

1. To apply management theory to the practice of management in all types of organizations and occupational settings.

2. To emphasize the practical application of theory and help you perform more effectively as a manager.

3. To make you an active participant in a self-contained experience as a way of increasing your learning.

KEY FEATURES OF THE BOOK

Special features make this a reader-oriented book. They are briefly introduced here so you can use them as they appear throughout the text. The features are of two types: (1) practical reference points and (2) study aids.

Practical Reference Points

It is important for you to know what is happening in the real world of management. My task is to acquaint you with a knowledge base that you can use to analyze work situations and systematically choose and implement good responses. This decision-making and problem-solving capability requires you to be familiar with many management concepts and theories that most textbooks simply present to the reader. *Management for Productivity* does more. It explains and applies them with the assistance of the following features.

Part-Opening Headlines Newspaper or newsmagazine headlines that reflect the real-world significance of the central theme of chapters in each part of the book.

Part-Opening Perspectives Portions of speeches, essays, or newspaper accounts of a managerial perspective appropriate to the major theme addressed by chapters in each part of the book.

Chapter Openers Short vignettes at the beginning of each chapter to provoke your interest in topics to be presented.

Newslines Excerpts from newspaper and newsmagazine articles that show how text material is reflected in the day-to-day "problems" and "opportunities" of practicing managers.

Illustrative Cases, Examples, and Activities Practical examples, summary guidelines and principles, or activities which can help you consider the meaning of key terms and concepts.

Career Perspectives Career-related situations for you to think about and respond to as part of your developing familiarity with the field of management.

Case Applications Short cases that ask you to step into management situations and take and defend appropriate managerial actions based on an application of chapter content to the case situations.

Class Exercises Exercises designed to examine your perspectives on chapter content and relate them to the perspectives held by others in the class.

Part Integrating Cases Cases at the end of each major part of the book that offer an opportunity to apply the theories and concepts to actual management situations in an integrated way.

When you encounter these features in your reading, consider them carefully. All are representative of the realities of day-to-day management practice.

Study Aids

This book has an important academic side. You must read about and study the field of management if you are to expand your knowledge in a way that will be of true benefit when facing the wide variety of problems and opportunities that occur in managerial situations. To help you achieve this understanding, *Management for Productivity* provides these additional study aids.

Planning Ahead Specific statements at the beginning of each chapter that highlight the key topics to be discussed.

Summary An overview at the end of each chapter that briefly outlines the major themes introduced in the reading.

Thinking Through the Issues Ten end-of-chapter questions that stimulate your thinking on major issues relating to chapter content.

The Manager's Vocabulary A list of key terms introduced in the chapter.

Glossary A list at the end of the book that defines all key terms referenced in each Manager's Vocabulary and notes the chapter in which each was originally introduced.

These features were chosen to help you learn more when reading this book. Planning Ahead, for example, should be especially useful when you read a chapter for the first time. The Summary, Thinking Through the Issues, and the Manager's Vocabulary are additional chances to review chapter material and consider whether or not you have covered it sufficiently. Finally, the Glossary of key terms and definitions combines with the other features to help you study for exams and maximize your learning about management.

A FINAL COMMENT BEFORE YOU BEGIN

Management for Productivity will actively involve you in a learning process. Think seriously as you read. Think about yourself, the work experiences you have had, and your career aspirations. Think about other people, their feelings, and how their work experiences compare with your own. *Management for Productivity* is important and relevant to your education and your career. Read enthusiastically and enjoy reading as you learn!

MANAGEMENT FOR PRODUCTIVITY

PART

1

INTRODUCTION

Chapters in This Part of the Book

PRODUCTIVITY GAINS ARE PAYING OFF ON MANY FRONTS

A New Era for Management

"Productivity" has been the great buzz-word of the 1980s. This measure of overall performance success in producing the goods and services necessary to everyone's day-to-day existence is a most important social and economic issue. Indeed, as individuals, organizations, and even nations seek to survive and prosper in a world of great economic and social complexity, "productivity improvement" is the common hue and cry. The above news headlines are signs of our times.[1] They reflect both the unprecedented attention that productivity issues are currently receiving and the resulting challenges placed on managers.

Such headlines will introduce each new part of this book. Their purpose, as demonstrated here, is to call to your attention important challenges facing modern managers. Each set of headlines will be followed by a "Perspective." This will be a short, provocative statement further highlighting the real-world significance of the headlines' themes in special respect to the chapters that follow. Drawn from domestic and international sources, these part opening perspectives should stimulate your thinking about the relationship

between managerial success and productivity in today's world.

The productivity challenges of the 1980s focus more and more on the manager as a person whose efforts can result in performance gains or losses depending on how well organizational resources are utilized. Indeed, productivity improvement involves fundamental changes in both organizations and in the jobs of the managers who make them work. Good management and high productivity go hand-in-hand. This is the issue that should maintain your interest and desire to learn about the theories and practice of management as presented in this book.

With the challenge clearly in mind, let's begin with some thoughts on the demands you will face in the process of becoming a successful manager. We'll examine two viewpoints— one of a first-line supervisor and the second of a chief executive officer. Both points of view reflect the perspective that "change" is a sign of the times for managers.

Perspective: The Traditional Manager is on the Way Out

Chances are that most people begin their managerial careers as first-line supervisors. In an article entitled "Twilight of the First-

Line Supervisor?" Peter Drucker, a noted management author and consultant, states[2]

"No job is going to change more in the next decade than that of the first-line supervisor in both factory and office. And few people in the work force are less prepared for the changes and less likely to welcome them."

An interesting insight into the role of this first-line supervisor about whom Drucker speaks is found in the *Business Week* article from which the second of our introductory headlines—"A New Era for Management"—was taken. The following excerpt gives you added feel for some of the factors that may have prompted Drucker to take the position he did.[3]

"At Ford Motor Company's Edison (New Jersey) plant, workers on the trim-assembly line move back and forth between storage bins and the conveyor, picking up parts and installing them on freshly painted body shells that soon will become Ford Escorts and Mercury Lynxes. Each worker has about a

[1] The headlines are from *Business Week* (May 16, 1983), p. 16; (April 25, 1983), p. 50.

[2] Peter F. Drucker, "Twilight of the First-Line Supervisor?" *The Wall Street Journal* (June 7, 1983), p. 32.
[3] "The Old Foreman Is On the Way Out, and the New One Will Be More Important," *Business Week* (April 25, 1983), p. 74. Used by permission.

minute to do a job, putting on headlights, door locks, or headliners (ceiling fabric) before starting the cycle again. Repetition dulls the senses, and the setting is perfect for the old, bull-of-the-woods manager who stalks up and down the line, berating workers for omitting a bolt or failing to tighten a screw.

"Supervisor Donald R. Hennion used to do just that: He was a 'hard-nosed, loudmouthed disciplinarian,' he says of himself. But now he chats with the workers, solicits their ideas, and even encourages them to use recently installed buttons to stop the line if a defect prevents them from correctly doing their job. The thought of an hourly worker stopping the line would have made old Henry Ford apoplectic. But the 'stop concept' is one aspect of a worker participation program that has improved quality, reduced absenteeism, and lessened hostility between bosses and workers at Ford's Edison plant. Its success depends on first-line supervisors: They must listen to what workers have to say, use the workers' ideas, and focus on problemsolving rather than meting out discipline."

Times have changed at the Edison plant, as in organizations throughout the United States and the rest of the world. The traditional "hard-nosed" or "bull-of-the-woods" manager *is* on the way out. What is demanded now is a manager with the capacity to lead in an atmosphere of participation and human respect, as well as in a work environment increasingly characterized by high technology, complex industrial relations, and continuing pressures for productivity enhancement. Supervisor Hennion seems

to have succeeded in this participatory and modern approach to management. In his own words, Hennion describes the end result:[4]

"You're more *productive* in the long run. People on the line seem happier. You still have the same boredom, but the attitude is changing. We're working as a team."

These thoughts should stimulate you to ask what it takes to succeed in a managerial career. Consider this list of personal capabilities offered by H. B. (Bruce) Atwater, Jr., chairman and executive officer of General Mills, Inc.[5]

- *Intelligence* "You don't have to be a genius, but an individual in a large, multidivision organization needs to have a relatively high level of intelligence. The problems we deal with are tremendously complex, and it does take a reasonable amount of mental horsepower to deal effectively with them."
- *Decisiveness* "With intelligence must go decisiveness. There are a number of people who see 67 sides to a question and can never reach a conclusion. You have to know what kind of facts to get, when to stop getting them, and how and when to make a decision. Too often managers miss out on an opportunity because they are still 'checking the facts.' "
- *Ability to handle conflict well* "What we are talking about here is the ability to get an issue out in the open and up for useful discussion even

under difficult circumstances. Many people simply cannot overcome conflict and will do almost anything to avoid it. It is my experience that the person who shies away from disagreement and who takes criticism personally will not be a good manager."
- *Mental agility and conceptual thinking* "Can you take a very complex situation, sort it out, put it back together, and make the necessary—and correct—decision? You've got to be able to develop and see clearly a single broad picture that's made up a whole series of ambiguous and divergent facts."
- *High tolerance for stress* "Business demands extensive travel, but even in your office the day deals almost entirely with the difficult, the troublesome, and with conflict. Most of the time your plate is piled high with these kinds of situations—the successful business executive has to know how to handle them all. A high energy level and good physical wellbeing are essential."

Management for Productivity is written to help you develop these and other personal capabilities. If you are serious about a career that sooner or later will entail managerial responsibilities, this book is for you! Read and study it with enthusiasm and with these final words of advice from Bruce Atwater in mind.[6]

"It's very important to have a commitment to whatever it is you choose to do. I don't necessarily mean a commitment to the specific company, but a commitment to the job and to doing it as well as you possibly can.

---

[4] Ibid., p. 75.
[5] Herbert Blanchett, "Debunking Management Myths," *Stanford GSB*, Vol. 51 (Summer 1983), p. 9.

[6] Ibid., p. 10.

1

MANAGERS, MANAGEMENT, AND PRODUCTIVITY

WE HAVE BECOME A SOCIETY OF ORGANIZATIONS

Society in this century has become a society of organizations. Social tasks—from providing goods and services to education and care of the sick and the elderly—that only a century ago were done by the family, in the home, in the shop, or on the farm, are increasingly performed in and through large organizations. These organizations—whether business enterprises, hospitals, or schools and universities—are designed for continuity and are run by professional managers. Managers have thus become the leadership groups in our society. The leadership groups of old—whether landed aristocracy, business tycoons, or priests—have disappeared or become less significant.

The first job of the manager is to make the organization perform.[1]

The prior excerpt from the *Wall Street Journal* is by the noted author and management theorist Peter F. Drucker. His comments clearly point out the tremendous importance of organizations and their managers in today's society. Chapter 1 will introduce you more specifically to the challenges of being a good manager. Key topics in the chapter include:

Managers
Organizations
Managers in Organizations
Productivity and the Manager
The Management Process
The Nature of Managerial Work
Managerial Skills
The Study of Management

Work is an activity that produces value for other people.[2] Most people, whether they like it or not, have to work for a living. That is, they must produce goods or provide services of value to others if they are to obtain the basic requirements of life and a few luxuries as well. Some alternative life-styles do downplay such economic necessity: people join communes, others just "drop out," while some rely on the goodwill of parents or friends for their support. But the large majority of people spend a significant part of their lives working.

The subject of work and the need for it to be done well enough that individuals and society as a whole may prosper and grow is what makes the material covered in the following pages meaningful. This book is about managers and other people at work in organizations. Reading and learning from this book should help you understand the many events that will give meaning to your future work experiences and career.

MANAGERS

A **manager** is a person in an organization who is responsible for the work performance of one or more other persons. People are a basic resource of organizations. As the **human resources** of organizations, people use **material resources** such as information, equipment, and facilities to produce a good or service. If the people perform well, the organization performs well; if the people don't, the organization can't. The **manager's job** is to help the organization achieve a high level of performance through the utilization of its human and material resources. More simply, a manager's job is "to get things done through other people."

Managers are therefore universal. They are essential to organizations of all types and sizes. Schools, hospitals, social agencies, small retail businesses, hotels, and large corporate enterprises all have managers working toward the same general goal of improved performance for the organization.

Thus you should agree with Drucker's statement in the chapter opener. Organizations are essential to society, and the basic task of every manager is to help the organization perform. This is not easy, but it is achievable. As we begin the study of management together, keep the following thought in mind; it nicely sets the stage for what follows in this book.[3]

No job is more vital to our society than that of the manager. It is the manager who determines whether our social institutions serve us well or whether they squander our talents and resources. It is time to strip away the folklore about managerial work, and time to study it realistically so that we can begin the difficult task of making significant improvements in its performance.

ORGANIZATIONS

Managers work in organizations. But what is an organization, really? The term *organization* is one that we all use and understand . . . that is, until we are asked to define it. How would you define the concept of organization?

Consider, for example, what differentiates a collection of 50 people milling around an airport from 50 others who comprise a professional football team.[4] The 50 people in the airlines terminal share little in common and produce nothing more than what is represented by their individual efforts. Their collective meaning is as simple as 50 × 1 = 50. We run into such collections of people everywhere—in museums, parking lots, supermarkets, sporting events, and even neighborhoods. They are *not* organizations.

An "organization," like a football team, represents something more than the mere presence of a number of individuals. Sporting teams, business firms, health clinics, schools, social agencies, political parties, and fraternal groups *are* organizations. They are organizations, in part, because the people who comprise them work on individual tasks to help achieve a collective purpose. Formally defined, an **organization** is a collection of people working together in a division of labor to achieve a common purpose.

Table 1.1 Some Organizations and Their Outputs

Organizations	Outputs
Hospitals Nursing homes	Health services
Restaurants Hotels	Hospitality services
Government agencies Community groups	Social services
Universities High schools	Educational services
Libraries	Cultural services
Manufacturers Publishers	Consumer products

There are many types of organizations. Some, like the Ford Motor Company and the Xerox Corporation, produce consumer goods; others, like schools and hospitals, produce services. Examples of organization settings within which managers work are shown in Table 1.1. Other examples may be added to the list to reflect your personal career interests.

Organizations also come in various sizes. The names of very large ones such as General Motors, Exxon, and the IBM Corporation are familiar to most everyone, and the impact on society of such "colossal giants" is certainly great.

(Left) A collection of people milling around a shopping area does not constitute an organization. (Right) An organization is a collection of people working together in a division of labor for a common purpose.

apple computer inc.®

At the age of 26, Steven Jobs heads a billion-dollar company that has revolutionized the computer industry. Jobs is chairman of the board of Apple Computer, Inc., which he founded in 1976 with his friend Stephen Wozniak. Both have since become wealthy. Jobs now runs the company; while Wozniak remains a major shareholder in the business.

It all began in 1976 when Jobs and Wozniak raised $1300 by selling a VW microbus and a scientific calculator, and began building a typewriter-sized computer in a garage. Jobs, who had worked one summer in the orchards of Oregon, christened the computer "Apple."

After early interest in microcomputers became apparent, Jobs and Wozniak sought professional assistance to obtain venture capital sufficient to expand their production capabilities rapidly. The rest of the story is history. Sales in 1977 were $2.7 million; in 1980 they were $117 million; by 1983 they were expected to reach over $900 million. Apple is the first company to join the ranks of *Fortune* magazine's 500 largest U.S. corporations after only five years of operation. During this time the company changed from a small two-person enterprise to a multinational corporation employing over 3000 people.

Apple now faces competitive pressures from IBM and others who have since offered their brands of microcomputers to the public. As things stand, the following comment from a recent *Time* magazine article sums up the situation quite well.

> Jobs, who had the vision to build one of America's foremost companies from a hobbyist's toy, must show that he has the foresight and ability to guide a major corporation.

Source: Information from "The Seeds of Success," *Time* (February 15, 1982), pp. 40–41; "The Apple Millionaires," *Management Today* (October 1982). pp. 42, 43; and, Peter Nulty, "Apple's Bid to Stay in the Big Time," *Fortune* (February 7, 1983), pp. 36–41.

Let's not forget the many smaller enterprises that also characterize society, however. The local retailer, grocery store, gas station, and laundry are perhaps small in size, but they do impact our daily lives. Like IBM, and other corporate giants, small organizations also depend on managers for their performance success. Whether your career goals favor large or small enterprise, the importance of developing your managerial capabilities remains high.

Illustrative Case: Apple Computer, Inc.

Organizations perform tasks that are beyond individual capabilities alone. This is the basic reason for their existence. One of the most talked-about new products of the 1980s—the personal or microcomputer—helps to illustrate this fact.

Some time ago two men, working at home and in their spare time, created a computer of compact size and considerable power. *Newsline 1.1* describes how Stephen Wozniak and Steven Jobs turned that idea into a revolutionary new product, a major new company, and a multimillion-dollar success story. Although the technological breakthroughs and financial success of both young men are commanding subjects in their own right, we can usefully speculate now on the emergence of the organization known as Apple Computer, Inc.[5]

In the Beginning Jobs and Wozniak first produced Apple Computers in a makeshift production facility located in a garage. Their organization most likely resembled that shown in Figure 1.1. The two entrepreneurs probably hired one or more production workers to help assemble the computers. As owner-managers, they probably did everything from purchasing raw materials to helping in the production process to selling the finished computers.

Later As the demand for computers increased, Jobs and Wozniak needed to expand their production capabilities and turn their personal attention to more strategic concerns. They needed to hire assembly workers, salespersons, and purchasing agents, among others, and they needed to hire other people to help manage *them*! As the company grew, the two had to rely on the other people to do work they had previously done themselves. This reallocation of work to these other people, and the coordination of their individual efforts, constitutes the essence of "organization." The task for the original entrepreneurs and the other new managers in the company was to ensure that the performance potential of Apple Computer, Inc. became a reality. *Newsline 1.1* reports their success in this quest. Figure 1.2 shows just how complex the company's organization became along the way.

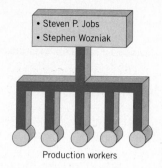

FIGURE 1.1 Apple Computer, Inc.—The way it may have looked in the beginning.

Production workers

Three Ingredients of Organizations

Organizations begin with people. Beyond that, they involve three ingredients: a common purpose, a division of labor, and a hierarchy of authority. Let's take a detailed look at each of these ingredients as a special characteristic of organizations as the settings in which managers work.

Purpose

The **purpose of an organization** is to produce a good or service. This emphasis on production is evident in the Apple Computer example and in each of the organizations listed in Table 1.1. It applies regardless of whether the organization's output is a physical product or a service. Businesses produce consumer goods and services such as recreational opportunities, gourmet din-

FIGURE 1.2 Apple Computer, Inc—The way the top management staff looks today. (*Source:* Developed from information provided in Apple Computer, Inc., *Annual Report*, 1982, p. 33.)

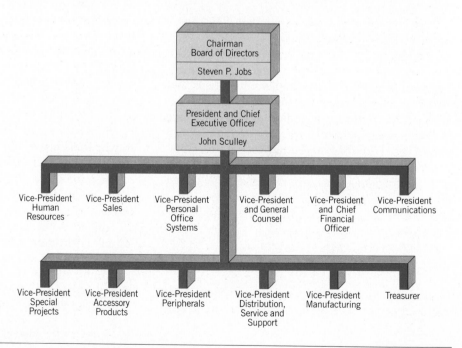

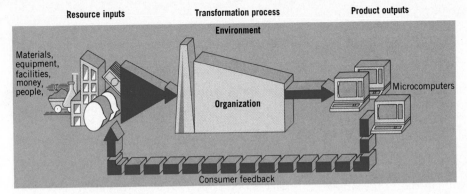

Resource inputs   Transformation process   Product outputs

Environment

Materials, equipment, facilities, money, people,

Organization

Microcomputers

Consumer feedback

FIGURE 1.3 An open-systems view of Apple Computer, Inc.

ing, and accommodations. Organizations in the nonprofit sector produce services such as health care, education, welfare and public assistance, judicial processing, and highway maintenance.

One way to analyze any organization is to view it as an **open system;** that is, a system that interacts with its environment and transforms resource inputs into outputs. As open systems, organizations transform human and material resource inputs from their environment into product or service outputs that are returned to the environment for consumption. The final good or service produced from the resource-transformation process represents the organization's purpose. The production of this good or service is made possible by the direct interaction of the organization with its environment.

Figure 1.3 depicts Apple Computer, Inc. as an open system. Apple's employees are human resource inputs that combine in the transformation process with various material resource inputs to create microcomputers as finished products. Both the material and human resources are obtained from the external environment, which in turn consumes Apple computers and provides continuing justification for the company's existence.

Division of Labor

All organizations require individual efforts. A combination of the work of many people is what allows organizations to overcome the human limitations of their members. The founders of Apple realized at a certain point in the growth of their firm that they could not do all the required work by themselves. Other people had to be hired to

assist in accomplishing essential tasks. The final result was a collection of many people performing jobs that, when added together, resulted in the production of microcomputers. This process of breaking the work into smaller components and allocating them as individual or group tasks designed to fit together in service of the organization's purpose is called the **division of labor.**

A division of labor is indicated by the different job titles in Figure 1.2. It is apparent in all organizations, including colleges and universities. The work of your instructor, for example, differs from that of others teaching accounting, marketing, history, or biology. Their work, in turn, differs from that performed by the director of university housing, the dean of students, and the manager of the student bookstore. The effort of each person is necessary, however, if the university is to achieve its educational purpose. Indeed, your education would probably suffer dramatically if all of these tasks were performed solely by your instructor. The division of labor is everywhere, and it works!

Hierarchy of Authority

The division of labor also creates a basic problem for organizations. When work is divided into many parts, something must be done to make sure that the separate work efforts accumulate to create the desired end result. For organizations to achieve performance success, the division of labor must be coordinated. Managers bear the responsibility of seeing to it that this occurs.

One of the ways in which a manager coordinates the division of labor is through **formal authority.** Think of this as the right to "command" other persons. Although you might find the notion of "command" a bit uncomfortable, it is descriptive. Organizations give managers the authority to require that other persons contribute work activities relevant to the organization's purpose. This authority is an important basis for managerial action, and some managers are better at using it than others. Surely, for example, you respond quite differently to the work directives of your various instructors. For some you do everything asked, and then more; for some you do just what is asked, and no more; for others you don't do what is asked, and you don't care. Given that all instructors in your school have the same formal authority, how can we explain this variation in your responses? One explanation is that some instructors are using their formal authority better than others, perhaps by supplementing it with other ways of influencing your behavior.

When many managerial positions exist in one organization, they also require coordination. This is accomplished by giving some managers formal authority over other managers. The result is a **hierarchy of authority** in which work positions are arranged in order of increasing formal authority. In Figure 1.2, the chairman of the board is the highest level of formal authority for Apple Computer, Inc. A hierarchy of authority has been created, though, by the delegation of authority from this position to managers at lower levels. That is, some of Steven Jobs's previously held right of command over company employees has been delegated to the president, vice-presidents, and the managers who work for them.

MANAGERS IN ORGANIZATIONS

Now that we share an appreciation of the organization as a manager's work setting, let's speak more precisely about what it means to be a manager. This involves a look at various levels and types of managers, as well as the basic challenge that all managers share.

Managerial Levels

It is common to differentiate managers according to level or relative standing in an organization's hierarchy of authority. This distinction is shown in Figure 1.4.

Top Managers

Job titles common to the highest level of management include chief executive officer, chief operating officer, president, and vice-president. Persons at the highest level of management ensure that goals are set and accomplished in accord with the organization's purpose, and they monitor the environment to identify potential problems and opportunities associated with this purpose. Going back to the example of Apple Computer, Inc., it is the task of Steven Jobs (chairman of the board) and John Sculley, (president) to stay abreast of trends in the microcomputer market and formulate ways for the company to stay ahead of its rapidly growing competition. By the late 1980s, for example, Apple's success will depend on how well the top management team does in mobilizing the orga-

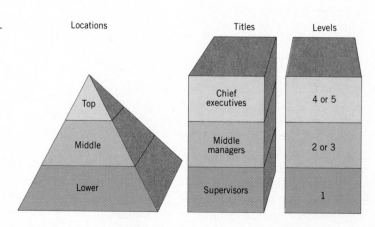

FIGURE 1.4 Ways of Classifying managers by hierarchical levels.

Table 1.2 Sample Compensation Packages for Higher Managers in Major U.S. Industries

	Chief Executive Officer	Division Manager
Base salary	$300,000	$100,000
Annual bonus	50% of base	40% of base
Capital accumulation	$25,000 stock options	$7500 stock options
Life insurance	3 times base salary	1½ times base salary
Perquisites	Car, luncheon club, country club	Possibly: car, luncheon club, or country club

Source: Adapted from Jill Bettner, "Executive Pay Raises Likely to be Less in 1981; Bonuses and Perks Keyed to Job Performance," *Wall Street Journal* (November 17, 1980), p. 46. Adapted by permission of the *Wall Street Journal.* Copyright © 1980 Dow Jones & Company, Inc. All rights reserved.

nization to meet the challenges of IBM, Tandy, Wang, Osborn, Zenith, and other major entries in the microcomputer market.

Middle Managers

Middle managers constitute the second or third level in an organization's hierarchy of authority. They report to managers at the top level, while lower-level managers report to them. Middle managers in a hospital are department heads, in a university they are deans, and in a business they might be division managers, plant managers, regional sales managers, district controllers, or personnel directors, among others.

Middle-level managers are crucial to organizations. They interpret directions set by higher managers into plans and action guidelines for lower-level personnel. In turn, they are conduits through which information flows upward in the hierarchy and keeps top managers informed about lower-level concerns. This middle level of responsibility is a testing ground from which many organizations fill top management appointments. Table 1.2 shows some of the incentives for middle managers in the corporate sector to excel at their jobs and to seek promotion. Perhaps this table captures one or more of the goals to which you aspire in a managerial career.

Lower Managers

Job titles such as supervisor, unit head, team leader, and foreman are common to persons at the first-line or supervisory level of management. These are the people to whom operating and production employees report. They implement the plans and directives of middle and upper management levels on a day-to-day basis.

Most persons enter management at the supervisory level. Your first job after graduation may be of this type. Or you may be employed as a technical specialist—for example, in sales, personnel, finance, or accounting—and report to a first-line supervisor. Sooner or later, however, the likelihood is that your initial appointment will lead to new positions of direct managerial responsibility.

Lower-level managerial jobs are demanding. Supervisors can experience a lot of stress when the expectations of workers and higher managers come into conflict. Think of the supervisor whose superior clamors for overtime work to meet a special order at the same time that subordinates complain they are overworked and need time for their families. Such situations demand considerable judgment and interpersonal skill on the manager's part.

Types of Managers

It is convenient to classify the types of managers found in organizations. Three of the more common distinctions are between staff managers and line managers, between functional managers and general managers, and between administrators and managers. First, recall that any manager is a person in an organization who is responsible for the work performance of one or more other people. This definition holds equally well for each of the following managerial types.

Line Managers and Staff Managers

Line managers have responsibility for work activities that make a direct contribution to production of the organization's basic product or service. Their efforts clearly influence the process whereby resource inputs are transformed into product or service outputs. The president, production manager, and production supervisors in Figure 1.5 all have line responsibilities. **Staff managers,** by contrast, use their special technical expertise to support the production efforts of line personnel. Looking again at Figure 1.5, the personnel manager and controller have staff responsibility. Although neither one directly impacts the production function, each provides essential support services. One ensures that proper cost and financial data are accumulated, while the other ensures that personnel are recruited and hired to fill vacant positions. Other titles common to staff managers are legal counsel, senior auditor, strategic planning analyst, and public-relations manager.

Your managerial career may lead you in a line or staff direction—or both. The two "help-wanted" ads here demonstrate career opportunities in both directions.[6]

Help Wanted: Line Manager

Plant Manager A leader in the manufacture of computer-related systems requires a seasoned professional with a proven record of accomplishment in a high-technology product. The successful candidate will be an aggressive, systems-oriented, degreed individual with strong communication skills and capable of managing a work force of up to 1000 employees. Production management experience of 8–10 years in a facility with some exposure to industrial/manufacturing engineering background would be a definite plus.

Help Wanted: Staff Manager

Accounting Manager One of the world's fastest-growing manufacturers of digital electronic instrumentation has an immediate opportunity for

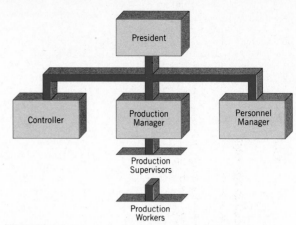

FIGURE 1.5 A typical manufacturing organization.

an Accounting Manager. Reporting to the Controller, this position will be responsible for the general ledger, cost accounting, credit management, and will assist in budget preparation. The person selected for this position will also be responsible for ongoing accounting activities. Requirements include a BBA in accounting and at least 5 years of experience in a manufacturing setting.

Functional Managers and General Managers

Another useful distinction in business firms is between functional managers and general managers. **Functional managers** have responsibility for a single area of activity such as finance, marketing, production, personnel, accounting, or sales. Note that these functional areas directly correspond to course titles found in college and university programs of study in business and administration.

General managers are responsible for more complex organizational subunits that include many functional areas of activity. The general manager of a department store, for example, oversees many separate functions, including purchasing, warehousing, sales, personnel, and accounting. As you progress through your academic program of study, courses in the various functional areas may well be integrated in a final capstone course on strategic planning and business policy. This course typically offers a general manager's view of the corporate enterprise.

NEWSLINE 1.2

CLASSIFIED ADVERTISING

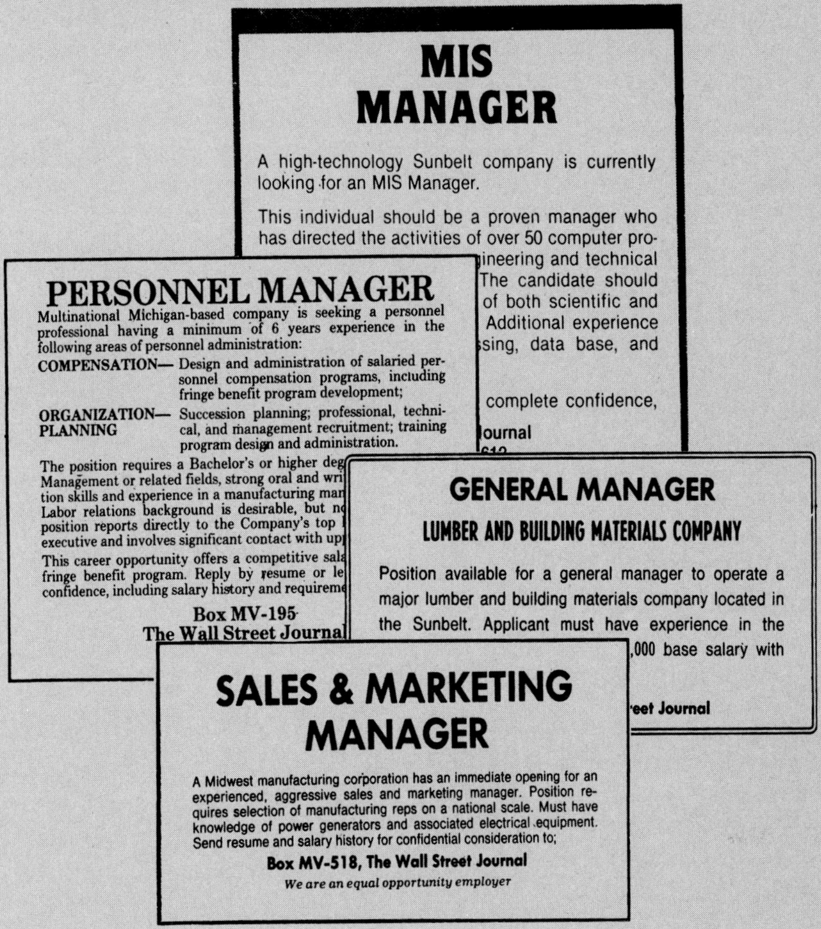
MIS
MANAGER

A high-technology Sunbelt company is currently looking for an MIS Manager.

This individual should be a proven manager who has directed the activities of over 50 computer pro-
...ineering and technical
The candidate should
of both scientific and
Additional experience
...sing, data base, and

complete confidence,
...ournal

PERSONNEL MANAGER

Multinational Michigan-based company is seeking a personnel professional having a minimum of 6 years experience in the following areas of personnel administration:

COMPENSATION— Design and administration of salaried personnel compensation programs, including fringe benefit program development;

ORGANIZATION— PLANNING Succession planning; professional, technical, and management recruitment; training program design and administration.

The position requires a Bachelor's or higher deg... Management or related fields, strong oral and wri... tion skills and experience in a manufacturing ma... Labor relations background is desirable, but n... position reports directly to the Company's top ... executive and involves significant contact with up...

This career opportunity offers a competitive sal... fringe benefit program. Reply by resume or le... confidence, including salary history and requirem...

Box MV-195
The Wall Street Journal

GENERAL MANAGER

LUMBER AND BUILDING MATERIALS COMPANY

Position available for a general manager to operate a major lumber and building materials company located in the Sunbelt. Applicant must have experience in the ...,000 base salary with

...eet Journal

SALES & MARKETING MANAGER

A Midwest manufacturing corporation has an immediate opening for an experienced, aggressive sales and marketing manager. Position requires selection of manufacturing reps on a national scale. Must have knowledge of power generators and associated electrical equipment. Send resume and salary history for confidential consideration to;

Box MV-518, The Wall Street Journal

We are an equal opportunity employer

Source: These ads are from the *Wall Street Journal* (May 3, 1983), pp. 21–23; (May 24, 1983), p. 26; (May 25, 1983), p. 19. Reprinted by permission of the Wall Street Journal. Copyright © 1983 by Dow Jones & Company, Inc. All rights reserved.

Newsline 1.2 presents a collage of help-wanted ads from a newspaper. Note the job opportunities for functional managers in various fields of specialization, as well as for the general manager position. Although these jobs require qualifications that probably lie beyond your present capabilities, they do represent the opportunities sure to be available to you sometime in the future.

Administrators and Managers

A third distinction in the vocabulary of management is between people called administrators and those called managers. In fact, the terms are basically equivalent, with the one distinction that **administrators** are managers who work in public or nonprofit organizations as opposed to business concerns. This is the source of job titles such

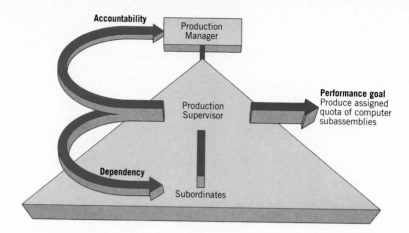

FIGURE 1.6 A production supervisor's basic challenge.

as hospital administrator, public administrator, city administrator, and human-service administrator.

An earlier point emphasized that managers are universal ingredients of organizations. They are found in organizations of all types and sizes in both the private and public sectors. Whatever the job title, if an "administrator" is held accountable for the performance of one or more subordinates, he or she is also a manager.

The Manager's Challenge

Most managers are simultaneously subordinates and superiors. Think about this statement and what it can mean. As subordinates, managers are held accountable by their superiors (or "bosses") for the performance of their work units. Herein lies every **manager's challenge**: to fulfill an accountability to superiors for work-unit performance, while depending on the efforts of subordinates to make this performance possible.

Assume you are the supervisor of a work group assembling components for Apple Computer, Inc. The diagram in Figure 1.6 depicts your basic manager's challenge. At the same time that you are held accountable by higher management for the production of a daily quota of computer subassemblies, you depend on the contributions of five subordinates to make this performance possible. In the final result, you are responsible for work that is in large part produced by someone else. This reality will be most evident on those days when the unit fails to meet its quota. When this happens, the production manager

won't ask your subordinates what went wrong; she or he will come directly to you and ask that question! You can't avoid responsibility by saying, in return, "My subordinates are the ones who didn't do the work."

It is the manager's job to ensure the performance of the work unit. This book is designed to help you master this basic manager's challenge, regardless of the level or type of managerial position you hold, and whether you work in a business or a nonprofit organizational setting.

PRODUCTIVITY AND THE MANAGER

Somewhere near a Ford Motor Company plant in Dearborn, Michigan, a tavern displays this sign.[7]

> I Spend Forty Hours a Week
> Here—Am I Supposed
> to Work, Too?

The sign epitomizes the manager's challenge about which we just spoke. It is one thing for people to affiliate with an organization as employees; it is quite another for them to make a useful performance contribution as well! The ultimate criterion of managerial success is the performance accomplishment or "productivity" of the group of people reporting to the manager. That is, work-unit productivity is the manager's bottom line.

What Is Productivity?

Productivity is a summary measure of the quantity and quality of work performance with resource utilization considered.[8] The traditional economic definition of productivity focuses on the ratio of physical outputs to resource inputs. Sample productivity indices are output per person-hour (business), clients served per staff member (social agency), and student credit hours taught per full-time equivalent faculty member (university). From a managerial perspective, however, productivity reflects a broader performance measure that identifies success or failure in producing goods and services in quantity, of quality, and with a good use of resources. The following example puts the concept into a manager's action perspective.[9]

> When 20 units were produced by one person in one hour last month and 22 identical units are produced by one person in one hour today, productivity has risen 10 percent. If 20 units were produced last month and 20 units of higher quality are produced today, productivity has also risen.

Yes, productivity is a broad performance factor that applies a criterion of work achievement to individuals, groups and organizations. Figure 1.7 shows the three levels of productivity with which all managers are concerned. Managers are in a position to influence directly the productivity of individuals and groups under their supervision. They are also in a position to help integrate these performance contributions into the organization as a whole. Only when such integration occurs is high organizational productivity possible.

A major part of every manager's job, therefore, is to establish and maintain the conditions for productivity. High productivity, in turn, requires more than appropriate technology and skilled workers. It requires their creative and successful combination into a well-functioning total performance system.

High-performing individuals and groups are the foundations of organizational productivity. Facilitating individual and group performance, accordingly, is the ultimate test of managerial competence. As *Newsline 1.3* shows, true productivity in this comprehensive performance sense is only achieved when all resources—hu-

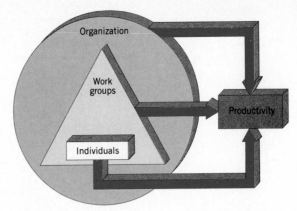

FIGURE 1.7 Three levels of productivity in organizations.

man as well as material—are well utilized to produce the goods and services of the organization.

Performance Effectiveness and Performance Efficiency

Two criteria measure a manager's success in the quest for productivity and personal competency. **Performance effectiveness** is a measure of task output or goal accomplishment. If you are the production supervisor depicted earlier in Figure 1.6, performance effectiveness simply means meeting the daily production quota for your work unit. True productivity, however, requires more comprehensive performance accomplishment. After all, you might meet your production quota, but waste resources in the process. Thus a second criterion of productivity is also used as an indicator of managerial success: efficiency.

Performance efficiency is a measure of the resource cost associated with goal accomplishment—that is, outputs realized compared to inputs consumed. This is most obvious in the cost of labor (e.g., in terms of employee wages), but it also includes the cost of all resources used in the production process. Measures of equipment utilization, facilities maintenance, and returns on capital investment are all efficiency criteria. Going back to the example of the production supervisor, the most efficient manager is the one who meets the daily production quota at minimum cost with respect to resource utilization.

Figure 1.8 shows various combinations of

NEWSLINE 1.3

THE PSYCHOLOGICAL COMPONENT IN PRODUCTIVITY

Recent issues of the *Wall Street Journal* tell of administration plans for rejuvenating the economy: tax cuts, business investment credits, pruning the federal fat, stabilization of the securities markets, lower interest rates, less regulation, and so forth. These measures, we are told, eventually will result in higher productivity. Nicholas. A Bond, Jr., a professor of psychology at California State University in Sacramento, says the following.

As an industrial psychologist, I am surprised that so many people believe that higher productivity will result directly from the financial remedies proposed. Productivity usually depends on relations between the producing technology and the people operating the system. Though complex, these relations are fairly well known. For instance, quality and quantity of production are influenced by the goals which people set for themselves. The information system which supervises the production must be perceived as fair and reliable; it must have "teeth," so that inadequate output can be tied to specific behaviors of specific people, and so that exceptional performance can be quickly recognized. Intragroup social relations can play a part. Some of the most productive work groups in the world are made up of people who have strong shared work values and commitments. Often, special techniques can be used: reinforcement schemes, job enrichment, and providing the challenge that comes from encouraging workers to develop a new method, product, or service.

When Japanese management took over an electronics plant in Chicago, output was nearly doubled and quality rejects declined 96 percent, to near-zero. These gains had nothing to do with tax credits or the state of the bond market; they had everything to do with the way the work force was treated, motivated, and monitored.

Source: Wall Street Journal (March 10, 1981), p. 23. Reprinted by permission of the *Wall Street Journal*. Copyright © 1981 Dow Jones & Company, Inc. All rights reserved.

performance effectiveness and efficiency. A manager can be effective but inefficient, efficient but ineffective, ineffective and inefficient, or both effective and efficient. The latter case is optimum from a productivity standpoint. True managerial success entails both effectiveness in goal attainment and efficiency in resource utilization.

Productivity and Quality of Working Life[10]

The issue of resource utilization highlights another facet of productivity that is of great significance in today's world of strong social and humanistic values. This deals with human-resource utilization in the performance process. Productivity is ideally achieved through high performance (effectiveness and efficiency) *and* with a sense of personal satisfaction by the people doing the work. Both performance and satisfaction should result from every manager's efforts to work with individuals and groups to achieve high productivity.

This concept of personal satisfaction is reflected in the **quality of working life**, a term that

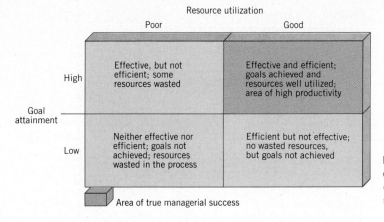

Resource utilization

	Poor	Good
High	Effective, but not efficient; some resources wasted	Effective and efficient; goals achieved and resources well utilized; area of high productivity
Low	Neither effective nor efficient; goals not achieved; resources wasted in the process	Efficient but not effective; no wasted resources, but goals not achieved

Goal attainment

Area of true managerial success

FIGURE 1.8 Performance effectiveness and efficiency—and managerial success.

has gained deserving prominence of late as an indicator of the overall quality of human experiences in the workplace. Just as machines that are poorly maintained break down and eventually wear out altogether, so too do the human resource suffer from neglect and adverse working conditions. Over the long term, the human resources of organizations must be well maintained if their continued performance contributions are to be ensured. Managers are increasingly expected, and rightfully so, to facilitate productivity for the organization while maintaining the quality of working life for its members.

This expanded view of productivity is a consistent theme throughout the book. As you move on, keep in mind that a high quality of working life is one that offers the individual such things as

- Adequate and fair compensation for a job well done.
- Safe and healthy working conditions.
- Opportunity to use and develop personal capabilities.
- Opportunity to grow and progress in a career.
- Integration into the social framework of the organization.
- Protection of rights to privacy, freedom of speech, equitable treatment, and due process.
- A healthy balance of work demands and non-work responsibilities and opportunities.
- Pride in the social relevance and value of the work itself and the organization.

THE MANAGEMENT PROCESS

If productivity is the ultimate measure of managerial success, the management process is the means employed to achieve it. In this respect, "management" is something managers do in their quest for productivity. Accordingly, the **management process** is defined as the process of planning, organizing, leading, and controlling the utilization of resources to accomplish the organization's purpose. Success in implementing the management process requires a capability to make decisions, solve problems, and take action to use resources effectively and efficiently in support of the organization's purpose.

This book is devoted to the study of management as a body of knowledge that offers insight into this process. Thus **management** is also a term representing a field of academic inquiry that is based on scientific foundations and that is an important action foundation for any manager. The reason is straightforward. Managers study "management" to improve the management process.

So far we have used the term *management* in two separate but complementary ways. It refers (1) to a body of knowledge and (2) to a process. Our attention now turns to clarifying the four functions or activities that constitute the management process.

Four Functions of Management

Planning, organizing, leading, and controlling are the four basic **management functions**. Al-

A line manager plans, organizes, leads and controls the activities of persons directly involved in the production of an organization's goods or services.

though Parts 2, 3, 4, and 5 of this book are devoted to each of these functions respectively, consider for the moment their basic definitions with examples set in the context of Apple Computer, Inc.

Planning Determining what is to be achieved, setting goals, and identifying appropriate action plans. Planning centers on determining goals and the means to achieve them.

> *Example* Apple's president anticipates a technological breakthrough in microcomputers; he determines that a new version of the current line needs to be developed within two years.

Organizing Allocating human and material resources in appropriate combinations to implement action plans. Organizing turns plans into action potential by defining tasks, assigning personnel, and supporting them with resources.

> *Example* A special task force on new product development is established; people are assigned, meeting facilities are made available, and necessary technical support is established.

Leading Guiding the work efforts of other people in directions appropriate to action plans. Leading

involves encouraging work efforts that support goal attainment.

> *Example* At the first task-force meeting the president clarifies the need for a new computer, helps the group to establish a reasonable timetable for action, and identifies the rewards that can be expected from goal accomplishment.

Controlling Monitoring performance, comparing results to goals, and taking corrective action. Controlling is a process of gathering and interpreting performance feedback as a basis for constructive action and change.

> *Example* The president stays in touch with the committee to monitor its progress over time; a special meeting is called to discuss problems when it appears the timetable may be slipping; appropriate adjustments in the timetable and task-force activities are made.

Each of the management functions will be examined in detail in separate parts of this book to ensure that you have the proper foundations for achieving success in the management process. For now, another way to keep the four functions of management clear is to think of them as a series of task-related decisions made by managers in the course of their work. These decisions are the following.

Planning   Deciding what is to be done.

Organizing   Deciding how it is to be done and who is to do it.

Leading   Deciding how to make sure it gets done.

Controlling   Deciding if it is or is not getting done, and what to do if it isn't.

Management Functions at Three Managerial Levels

Responsibility for the four management functions universally applies to managers working in all types of organizations. Research does indicate that the relative emphasis on each of the functions tends to vary across the three managerial levels.[11] As shown in Figure 1.9, time allocated to planning and organizing tends to increase at higher management levels; time spent on controlling is proportionately greater at lower management levels; time spent on leading is relatively similar at each management level.

In summary, managers implement the four management functions in the process of utilizing resources to support the organization's purpose. As we turn now to look further into the nature of managerial work, remember that planning, organizing, leading, and controlling are basic activities in the action framework through which successful managers achieve productivity.

THE NATURE OF MANAGERIAL WORK

So, you want to be a manager! Have you ever thought seriously about what this means? That is, have you thought seriously about what managers actually do on a day-to-day basis?

A Day in the Life of a Manager

Henry Mintzberg is a management researcher who has thought seriously about the prior questions. In fact, his 1973 book, *The Nature of Managerial Work,* has become a classic in the field. The book reports his in-depth examination of the daily activities of corporate chief executives. One interesting excerpt from his observations regard-

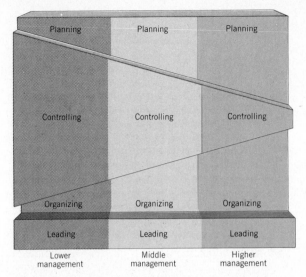

FIGURE 1.9 Relative time spent on the management functions at each managerial level. (*Source:* Based on Thomas A. Mahoney, Thomas H. Jerdee, and Stephen J. Carroll, "The Job(s) of Management," *Industrial Relations,* Vol. 4, No. 2, February 1965, pp. 97–110.)

ing an executive's workday follows.[12]

There was no break in the pace of activity during office hours. The mail (average of 36 pieces per day), telephone calls (average of five per day), and meetings (average of eight) accounted for almost every minute from the moment these executives entered their offices in the morning until they departed in the evenings. A true break seldom occurred. Coffee was taken during meetings, and lunchtime was almost always devoted to formal or informal meetings. When free time appeared, ever-present subordinates quickly usurped it. If these managers wished to have a change of pace, they had two means at their disposal—the observational tour and the light discussions that generally preceded scheduled meetings. But these were not regularly scheduled breaks, and they were seldom totally unrelated to the issue at hand: managing the organization.

Thus the work of managing an organization may be described as taxing. The quantity of work to be done, or that the manager chooses to do, during the day is substantial, and the pace is unrelenting. After hours, the chief executive (and probably many other managers as well) appears to be able to escape neither from an environment that recognizes the power and status of his position nor from his or her own mind, which has been well trained to search continually for new information.

Why do managers adopt this pace and workload? One major reason is the inherently open-ended nature of the job. The manager is responsible for the success of the organization. There are really no tangible mileposts where one can stop and say, "Now my job is finished." The engineer finishes the design of a casting on a certain day; the lawyer wins or loses a case at some moment in time. The manager must always keep going, never sure when he or she has succeeded, never sure when the whole organization may come down because of some miscalculation. As a result, the manager is a person with a perpetual preoccupation. The manager can never be free to forget the job, and never has the pleasure of knowing, even temporarily, that there is nothing else to do. No matter what kind of managerial job, managers always carry the nagging suspicion that they might be able to contribute just a little bit more. Hence they assume an unrelenting pace in their work.

Clearly, a manager's job in any organizational setting will be busy and demanding. You should read and think about the prior description of chief-executive work as it relates to your personal goals and aspirations. It no doubt reflects some of the reasons there is increasing concern for "job stress" and "job burnout" in managerial ranks. We will discuss these topics in more detail in later chapters. For now, though, recognize that to be a manager means to face considerable pressure. This book contains many insights that should help you to handle this pressure successfully and to achieve satisfaction in your work.

Overall, managerial work on a day-to-day basis is well characterized as involving the following.[13]

1. *Long hours* A workweek of at least 50 hours is typical, and up to 90 hours is not unheard of. Length of workweek tends to increase as one advances to higher managerial levels.

2. *Intense activity* The busy day of a manager includes up to 200 separate incidents or epi-

Table 1.3 11½ Minutes in a Supervisor's Workday

Time	Description
2:15 P.M.	Pat checks with scheduler S. Looks at hourly report of number of cars coming through body shop.
2:16	Walks over to R on pickup line and checks to see if earlier repair trouble was corrected.
2:17	Calls over inspection foreman to show him a hole missing in a piece. Inspection foreman acknowledges he will notify the trim department.
2:19	Pat tells R to locate the hole by eye until it comes through all right.
2:19½	Pat has a drink.
2:20	Pat walks over to station 5 and asks how many operators he still has to relieve.
2:20½	Moves along the line—stations 5, 6, 7—checking visually on the quality of work.
2:21	Checks a loose nut on a fixture at station 7. Speaks with operator.
2:22	Operator at station 3 calls for materials.
2:22¼	Pat tells operator at subassembly bench E to make up more material.
2:23	Walks over to MH to note the line is getting low on hinges. They discuss the number short and agree there is enough for tomorrow.
2:25	Pat walks from MH to station 1 and makes visual inspection of the car body to check on the hole discussed earlier at the pickup line.
2:26	Pat sees foreman from preceding section and tells him about the missing hole.
2:26½	A hand signal from welder W.

Source: Adapted by permission of the publisher from pp. 25–31 of "Foremen Relationships Outside the Work Group" by Robert Guest and Frank Jasinski, *Personnel*, Vol. 36 (1959), © 1959 by AMACON, a division of American Management Association. All rights reserved.

Table 1.4 Ten Managerial Roles

Role	Description	Example
Interpersonal		
Figurehead	Symbolic head; performs routine duties of a legal or social nature	Greeting visitors; signing legal documents
Leader	Responsible for motivation of subordinates and for staffing and training	Most activities involving subordinates
Liaison	Maintains network of outside contacts	Processing mail, phone calls, meetings, etc.
Informational		
Monitor	Seeks and receives information to understand organization and environment	Processing mail; maintaining personal contacts; reading periodicals and reports
Disseminator	Transmits information to other organization members	Forwarding reports and memos; making phone calls; holding meetings
Spokesperson	Transmits information to outsiders	Forwarding reports and memos; making phone calls; holding meetings
Decisions		
Entrepreneur	Initiates organizational improvement projects	Holding strategy sessions; identifying new responsibilities and new product ideas
Disturbance handler	Responsible for corrective action when organization faces unexpected crises	Resolving subordinate conflicts; adjusting to environmental crises
Resource allocator	Responsible for allocation of human and other resources	Scheduling; budgeting; giving rewards
Negotiator	Responsible for representing the organization in negotiations	Negotiating and union contracts; making sales

Source: Abridged and adapted from pp. 92–93 in *The Nature of Managerial Work* by Henry Mintzberg. Copyright © 1973 by Henry Mintzberg. Adapted by permission of Harper & Row, Publishers, Inc.

sodes in an eight-hour period at supervisory levels and 20–30 for chief executives. Take the example of Pat, a typical supervisor in an automobile plant. Table 1.3 depicts this high level of activity observed in only 11½ minutes of one of Pat's workdays.

3. *Fragmentation and variation* Interruptions are frequent in managerial work; tasks are completed quickly and involve many different types of activities ranging from scheduled meetings and telephone calls to answering mail and writing reports.

Managerial Roles

Other research findings shed additional light on the nature of managerial work. Henry Mintzberg,

whose study of chief executives has served as a landmark in studies of managerial behavior, views managerial work as characterized by:[14]

1. *Interpersonal relationships* Most of a manager's time is spent interacting (through oral and written communications) with other persons inside and outside of the work unit.

2. *Information processing* A major part of any manager's job is information processing, that is, managers can spend up to 50 percent of their time giving and receiving information.

3. *Decision making* Managers ultimately use information to make decisions that solve problems and/or take advantage of opportunities.

Mintzberg associates these characteristics

with a set of 10 action roles that managers must be prepared to play. Each role falls into one of the three categories listed and derives from the formal authority underlying a manager's position of work responsibility in the organization. Essentially, a manager's formal authority creates interpersonal roles, informational roles, and decisional roles.

The 10 managerial roles falling into these three categories are listed in Table 1.4 along with appropriate examples. They represent things you should be prepared to do as a manager. They are, in turn, the things for which you need appropriate mangerial skills.

MANAGERIAL SKILLS

A **skill** is an ability to translate knowledge into action that results in the desired performance.[15] Truly important skills for managers are those that help them to help others become productive in their work. The field of management offers a knowledge base for the initial development of these managerial skills.

The Essential Skills

Robert L. Katz classified the essential skills of managers into three categories—technical, human, and conceptual.[16] They are described in Table 1.5 along with examples of each.

A **technical skill** is an ability to use a special proficiency or expertise relating to a method, process, or procedure. Accountants, engineers, and attorneys, for example, possess technical skills acquired through formal education. Most jobs have technical skill components. Some require preparatory education (e.g., the staff accountant), while others allow skills to be learned through appropriate training and job experience (e.g., a salesperson).

Human skill is the ability to work well in cooperation with other persons. It emerges as a spirit of trust, enthusiasm, and genuine involvement in interpersonal relationships. A person with good human skills will have a high degree of self-awareness and a capacity to understand or empathize with the feelings of others. Given the highly interpersonal nature of managerial work, human skills are critical for all managers.

All good managers ultimately have the ability to view the organization or situation as a whole and solve problems to the benefit of everyone concerned. This is a **conceptual skill** that draws heavily on one's mental capacities to identify problems and opportunities, gather and interpret relevant information, and make good problem-solving decisions that serve the organization's purpose.

Essential Skills at Three Managerial Levels

Although all three skills are essential at each managerial level, their relative importance tends

Table 1.5 Essential Managerial Skills

Skill	Description	Examples
Technical	Ability to use tools, techniques, and specialized knowledge	■ Accountant doing an audit ■ Engineer designing a machine
Human	Ability to work effectively in interpersonal relationships	■ Accounting manager supervising a group of accountants during an audit ■ Manufacturing manager resolving conflict with a design engineer
Conceptual	Ability to see the organization as a whole and solve problems to the benefit of the total system	■ Analysis of a possible merger with another firm ■ Analysis of employee absenteeism and turnover

Source: Adapted by permission of Harvard Business Review. From ''Skills of an Effective Administrator by Robert L. Katz, *Harvard Business Review*, Vol. 52 (September-October 1974), p. 94. Copyright © 1974 by the President and Fellows of Harvard College; all rights reserved.

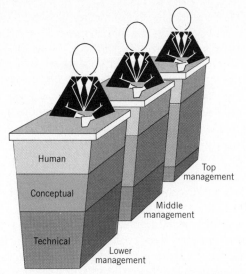

FIGURE 1.10 Essential managerial skills at various management levels.

manager's concerns at higher levels, where conceptual skills gain in relative importance. As the figure shows, human skills remain fairly consistent in their importance across the managerial levels.

Learning Managerial Skills

Now is the time to assess the status of these skills in your personal repertoire of capabilities and ask what you should do to ensure over the long run that you acquire and maintain the skills required to achieve managerial success. This brings us to the subject of learning.

Learning is any change in behavior that occurs as a result of experience. In effect, learning is also a skill—one that reflects a special capability to take advantage of experience and to grow and develop personally as a result. Learning is therefore an important and continued managerial responsibility that begins for you right now as a management student.

Figure 1.11 shows how the various aspects of a typical management course facilitate learning.[17] The basic learning sequence involves initial experience and subsequent reflection. Theory

to vary across levels. Figure 1.10 shows that technical skills are relatively more important at lower management levels where supervisors are dealing with concrete problems. Broader, more ambiguous, and longer-term decisions dominate the

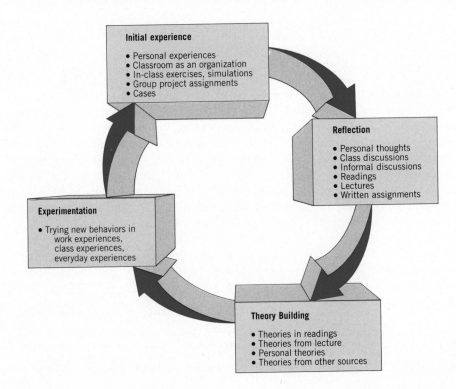

FIGURE 1.11 Experiential learning in a management course. (*Source:* John R. Schermerhorn, Jr., James G. Hunt, and Richard N. Osborn, *Managing Organizational Behavior* (New York: Wiley 1982), p. 25. Used by permission.)

building follows to explain what took place. The theory is then tested through personal experimentation at the next opportunity.

The many activities in Figure 1.11 assign you substantial responsibility for learning the essential managerial skills. Your instructor and this book can offer special cases, examples, and exercises to provide the initial experience. We can even stimulate reflection and theory building by presenting various management theories and discussing their practical implications. You and only you, however, can do the active experimentation required to complete the learning process.

THE STUDY OF MANAGEMENT

With the prior points in mind, let's overview the way *Management for Productivity* is organized for you as a learning instrument. The book contains seven major parts. Part 1 introduces the field of management and its significance to the practicing manager. It consists of the present chapter plus two others—"Historical Perspectives on Management" (Chapter 2) and "The Manager as Decision Maker and Problem Solver" (Chapter 3).

The next four parts cover each of the managerial functions: Part 2, Planning for Productivity; Part 3, Organizing for Productivity; Part 4, Leading for Productivity; and Part 5, Controlling for Productivity. Note that each of the part titles includes "productivity" as the ultimate focus of a manager's efforts. The individual chapters are written, accordingly, to help you develop an action capability with each function. Although you will study theories and concepts throughout, the thrust of every chapter will be to apply them to solve real managerial problems.

Part 6, Productivity in the Contemporary Environment, introduces the setting within which managerial decision making and problem solving occurs. Separate chapters in this part of the book introduce you to the challenges of implementing the management functions in respect to conflict, change, and organization development (Chapter 17), labor-management relations (Chapter 18), the international arena (Chapter 19), and ethics and social responsibility (Chapter 20).

By the time the book concludes in Part 7 with Chapter 21, titled "Management for Productivity: A Career Perspective," these various components of management should be clear in your mind. By that time, also, you will have learned many things to help you achieve success as a manager.

SUMMARY

A manager is a person in an organization who is responsible for the work performance of one or more other persons. An organization is a collection of people working together in a division of labor to achieve a common purpose. Managers are the very heart of organizations; they are the "glue" that holds the components of organizations together. Through the efforts of managers organizations fulfill their production or service purposes. Every manager's goal is to ensure high performance in that part of the organization for which he or she is responsible.

A manager's basic challenge, therefore, is to fulfill this performance accountability while depending on subordinates to do the required work.

Figure 1.12 summarizes the central theme of Chapter 1. Managers at all levels in organizations draw on "management" as a knowledge base to develop the essential skills (technical, human, conceptual) that allow them to implement successfully the management functions (planning, organizing, leading, and controlling) while fulfilling various roles (interpersonal, informational, and decisional). The desired end result is high productivity for individuals, groups, and the organization as a whole. Productivity, in turn, is an overall measure of the quality and quantity of work performance with resource utilization considered.

As we move further into the study of management, remember that the goal of this book is to help you

- Understand the essence of managerial work.
- Learn a basic vocabulary shared and used by managers.
- Establish proper knowledge foundations for

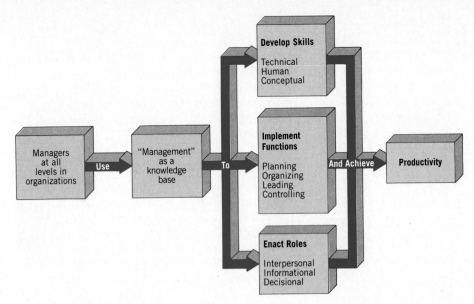

FIGURE 1.12 A comprehensive view of management.

developing the essential managerial skills.

■ Become familiar with each of the four basic management functions.

■ Anticipate some of the major challenges faced by managers who must enact their roles in today's dynamic environment.

Finally, remember that management is a part of your everyday experiences. In part, the job of this book is to help you learn to recognize this and then learn from your experiences. The field of management is an exciting area of study, and the opportunities for learning are simply unsurpassed.

THINKING THROUGH THE ISSUES

1. What is a manager? What is an organization?

2. Why are managers important to organizations?

3. Diagram each of the following organizations as open systems according to Figure 1.3: a local hospital, a department store, the fire department, a restaurant.

4. Explain the basic differences between (a) line managers and staff managers, (b) functional managers and general managers, (c) administrators and managers.

5. Diagram the manager's basic challenge for persons holding each of the following positions using Figure 1.6 as an example: hospital administrator, high-school principal, fire chief, restaurant owner.

6. Why is "productivity" a criterion of managerial success?

7. For two of the persons diagrammed in response to question 5, give examples of possible managerial accomplishments that would fall in each cell in Figure 1.8.

8. List the four managerial functions and give examples of how they would be used by the remaining two persons listed in response to question 5.

9. Review the 10 managerial roles listed in Table 1.4. Show exactly how these roles might be found among the activities of one of the persons listed in response to question 5.

10. Look at the syllabus provided for your management course. How does it help you fulfill the learning cycle shown in Figure. 1.11?

THE MANAGER'S VOCABULARY

Administrator
Conceptual skill
Division of labor
Formal authority
Functional manager
General manager
Hierarchy of authority

Human resources
Human skill
Learning
Line manager
Management
Management functions
Management process

Manager
Manager's challenge
Manager's job
Material resources
Open system
Organization
Performance
effectiveness

Performance efficiency
Productivity
Purpose of an
organization
Quality of working life
Skill
Staff manager
Technical skill
Work

CAREER PERSPECTIVE: PERSONAL RÉSUMÉ OF TERRY LEE

Permanent Address
116 Fairview Avenue
Dover, PA 17315

Temporary Address
304 West Main
Carbondale, IL 62901

Professional Objective   To enter a supervisory position that will utilize my technical and management capabilities and establish challenging opportunities for advancement.

Education   Southern Illinois University at Carbondale; G.P.A. 3.1/4.0; B.S. Marketing Management (May 1984)

Employment Experience

Present   College of Science, Dean's Office, Student receptionist

Summer 1983   Sun Oil Company, Oklahoma City. Roustabout
Summer 1982   Retail sales clerk, Two Guys Department Store, York, Pa.
1979–1981   Sales work, receiving, inventory
                        Summer jobs while attending high school and college

Hobbies   Swimming, photography, backgammon, and music

Personal Data   Date of Birth: May 4, 1963   Marital Status: Single
                              Health: Excellent   Willing to relocate

References   Available on request.

Questions

1. Based on the résumé, do you feel Terry Lee is a good candidate for an entry-level managerial position? Why or why not?

2. If you were a personnel interviewer, what questions would you ask Terry to gain more information than that provided in the résumé? Why are these questions appropriate to ask a candidate for a management job?

3. Compare your personal résumé to Terry's. What should you be doing to establish the strongest job credentials possible by your date of graduation?

CASE APPLICATION: TOM CORONADO[18]

True to form, Tom Coronado—manager of employee relations for Huse Manufacturing Company—pulled into his reserved company parking space early. It was 7:30 Monday morning—usually the most hectic day of the week, with more than its share of problems. But first the good news: Friday had been payday. Now the bad news: Monday of every week turned up Friday's payroll errors. With new hires, overtime work, and different wage-rate categories, there always seemed to be mistakes in figuring wages and paychecks.

To make matters worse, in recent weeks these errors had been on the increase. Reason: a new computerized payroll system. Long live progress, Tom thought. He was also thinking—with concern—about a 10 o'clock meeting scheduled with the executive vice-president on this very subject. Tom would have to report on how the new system was working out. Right now, though, he needed to find at least an hour of quiet to get his report together.

Fortunately his office was quiet, and Tom was able to review a couple of computer printouts. But shortly after 8 o'clock the phone began to ring. His secretary wasn't in yet, so Tom had to take six calls personally in 20 minutes. The first five were about errors in the payroll checks: two calls were from shop supervisors, one was from a worker on the night shift, one from the production superintendent, and one from the local union president. This last was the most sweat; the union leader's parting shot was "When in blazes are you going to straighten out this payroll mess?" The sixth call was from Tom's secretary. She wouldn't be in today.

Over the next hour Tom was able to correct most of the payroll errors—with a little help from his friends. These included payroll clerks, the production superintendent, a junior systems analyst, and one hourly paid worker. By 9:30 Tom thought he was ready to stick his phone in a filing cabinet and sit down with his materials for a last review before the 10 o'clock meeting. Five minutes later the phone started

ringing. It was Ted Brokenshire, president of the Metropolitan Personnel Association. Would Tom be willing to give a talk at the association's next meeting?

By the time he hung up the phone, Tom realized he had talked away the rest of his prep time before the meeting. It was 9:57. Quickly he pulled together his notes and materials and walked into the two corridors to the vice-president's office. The secretary waved him right in to a meeting that lasted two hours. But they were two hours well spent, Tom thought. The problems and the progress of putting in the new payroll system were taken apart, analyzed, gone over, and put together again. And despite the recent increase in mix-ups, implementation was actually two weeks ahead of schedule.

Tom came out of the meeting feeling good and ready to go ahead on the assignment. As he entered his office it also occurred to him that he had a few more ingredients for that talk he had agreed to give to Metro Personnel. Then his eye caught the clock: 12:20. Now for some lunch, he thought. He remembered that he hadn't had breakfast, and how he felt like having a big plate of shrimp lo mein. Then the phone rang.

Tom finally left for lunch at 2:30. As he pulled into the parking lot of the Shanghai Dynasty, he recalled that they were closed on Mondays.

Questions

1. Is this description of Tom Coronado's workday consistent with the ideas on managerial work advanced in Chapter 1? Why or why not?

2. Based on the case description, is Tom a line or staff manager? A functional or general manager? Explain your answers.

3. Which of the essential managerial skills are being used by Tom? Give examples from the case description.

CLASS EXERCISE: WHAT MANAGERS DO

Managers maintain a complex set of relationships with other persons in the work setting. These interpersonal relationships involve, at a minimum, contacts with subordinates, peers elsewhere in the organization, and superiors. They may also include contacts with outsiders such as clients and resource suppliers.

1. Think about the questions that follow. Record your answers in the spaces provided.

   A. How would you estimate a typical manager would allocate time to these various relationships?

   _____ percent with subordinates

   _____ percent with boss

   _____ percent with peers and outsiders
   100 percent = total time in interpersonal contacts

   B. How many hours do managers work per week?

   C. What amount of a manager's time is spent in the following?

   _____ percent at scheduled meetings

   _____ percent at unscheduled meetings

   _____ percent at desk work

   _____ percent on telephone

   _____ percent on organization tours

2. Talk over your responses with a nearby classmate. Explore similarities and differences in your answers. Try to understand each other's reasoning.

3. Be prepared to participate in class discussion led by your instructor.

REFERENCES

[1] From Peter F. Drucker, "We Have Become a Society of Organizations," *Wall Street Journal* (January 9, 1978), p. 12. Reprinted by permission of the *Wall Street Journal*. Copyright © 1978 Dow Jones & Company, Inc. All rights reserved.

[2] *Work in America: Report of a Special Task Force to the Secretary of Health, Education and Welfare* (Cambridge: MIT Press, 1973), p. 3.

[3] Reprinted by permission of the Harvard Business Review. Excerpt from "The Manager's Job: Folklore and Fact" by Henry Mintzberg, *Harvard Business Review*, Vol. 53 (July-August 1975), p. 61. Copyright © by the President and Fellows of Harvard College; all rights reserved.

[4] Jay R. Galbraith, *Organization Design* (Reading, Mass.: Addison-Wesley, 1977), p. 2.

[5] For information see "Striking It Rich," *Time* (February 15, 1982), pp. 36–44, and "The Apple Millionaires," *Management Today* (October 1982), pp. 42, 43.

[6] Adapted from ads in the *Wall Street Journal* (February 9, 1982), pp. 17, 19.

[7] Justin Gooding, "Blue-Collar Blues on the Assembly Line," *Fortune* (July 1970), p. 69.

[8] See Richard A. Bobbe and Robert H. Schaffer, "Productivity Improvement: Manage It or Buy It?," *Business Horizons*, Vol. 26 (March-April 1983), pp. 62–69; Jon English and Anthony R. Marchione, "Productivity: A New Perspective," *California Management Review*, Vol. XXV (January 1983), pp. 57–65.

[9] Robert A. Sutermeister, *People and Productivity* (New York: McGraw-Hill, 1976), p. 5.

[10] Adapted from Richard E. Walton, "Quality of Working Life: What Is It?" *Sloan Management Review*, Vol. 15 (Fall 1973), pp. 11–21.

[11] See, for example, the work of Mintzberg (1975), op. cit.; also, Thomas A. Mahoney, Thomas H. Jerdee, and Stephen J. Carroll, "The Job(s) of Management," *Industrial Relations*, Vol. 4 (February 1965), pp. 97–110.

[12] Abridged and adapted from p. 30 in *The Nature of Managerial Work* by Henry Mintzberg. (New York: Harper & Row, 1973), p. 30. Copyright © 1973 by Henry Mintzberg. Reprinted by permission of Harper & Row, Publishers, Inc.

[13] Summarized from Morgan W. McCall, Jr., Ann M. Morrison, and Robert L. Hannan, *Studies of Managerial Work: Results and Methods*, Technical Report #9 (Greensboro, N.C.: Center for Creative Leadership, 1978) pp. 7–9.

[14] Mintzberg (1973), op. cit., p. 46.

[15] Robert L. Katz "Skills of an Effective Administrator," *Harvard Business Review*, Vol. 52 (September-October 1974), p. 94.

[16] Adapted by permission of the Harvard Business Review. From "Skills of an Effective Administrator" by Robert L. Katz, *Harvard Business Review*, Vol. 52 (September-October 1974), p. 94. Copyright © 1974 by the President and Fellows of Harvard College; all rights reserved.

[17] See David A. Kolb, "On Management and the Learning Process," in David A. Kolb, Irwin M. Rubin, and James M. McIntyre, *Organizational Psychology: A Book of Readings*, Second Edition (Englewood Cliffs, N.J.: Prentice-Hall, 1974), pp. 27–42.

[18] From Lawrence J. Gitman and Carl McDaniel, Jr., *Business World* (New York: Wiley, 1983), p. 98. Used by permission.

2

HISTORICAL
PERSPECTIVES ON
MANAGEMENT

AN EARLY
MANAGEMENT CONSULTANT

The manager's challenge is almost as old, it seems, as time itself. Consider the following excerpt from the book of Exodus in the Bible.[1] It relates how Moses benefited as a manager from the wise counsel of his father-in-law Jethro.

Some time after leading his people out of Egypt, Moses camped at the base of the Mountain of God. His days were consumed by making the many decisions required to maintain the tribe. Moses was the one who made sure that the flock had proper food and clothing. He listened to their concerns, settled their disputes, and responded to all of those who came before him inquiring about God. Moses was a manager and his responsibilities were enormous.

Moses was fortunate to be joined in this camp by his father-in-law, Jethro. After observing Moses' daily routine, the wise counsel Jethro commented, "Thou wilt surely *wear away,* both thou and this people that is with thee; for this thing is *too heavy* for thee; *thou are not able to perform it thyself alone."*

Jethro went on to give Moses the following advice. He counseled Moses to select other persons to assist him in these many managerial chores. He further suggested that these people be given the responsibility to rule over groups of thousands, hundreds, fifties, and tens. Finally, he encouraged Moses to let them judge the small matters for the people under their control and to bring the large matters only to him.

Moses listened to his father-in-law and did everything he said. He chose capable men from all Israel and made them leaders of the people, officials over thousands, hundreds, fifties and tens. They served as judges for the people at all times. The difficult cases they brought to Moses, but the simple ones they decided themselves.

PLANNING AHEAD

Jethro's advice gave Moses a way to organize his people. In the process Moses learned how to perform better as a manager. People have systematically thought about and practiced management throughout the ages. In Chapter 2 you will become acquainted with various historical perspectives on the study of management. Key topics include:

Perspectives on Management
The Evolution of Management Thought
Classical Approaches to Management
Behavioral Approaches to Management
Quantitative Approaches to Management
Modern Approaches to Management

A **theory** is a set of concepts and ideas that systematically explains and predicts physical and social phenomena. A **management theory** explains and predicts the behavior of organizations and their members. Managers use management theories to make good decisions in their day-to-day efforts to plan, organize, lead, and control for productivity.

In the chapter opener, for example, Moses had a problem. His father-in-law Jethro offered advice that in essence reflected sound management theory. This advice was to reorganize Moses' tribe in the form depicted in Figure 2.1, where Moses assumed a position of leadership over other managers at four levels of authority— rulers of thousands, hundreds, fifties, and tens. This new framework for organization and management presumably benefited all concerned by freeing Moses to make the truly important decisions needed to lead his tribe successfully.

Managers of today have the benefit of the organized body of knowledge we call "management" as a source of theories to guide their decisions and actions. Although Jethro didn't have access to the same body of knowledge, his experience, insight, and wisdom still led him to develop a workable theory of management. Other persons throughout history have also thought systematically about management and organization practices. The result of their accumulated efforts is contained in the pages of this book. To understand what follows, it is helpful to understand these historical "roots" of contemporary management thought. This chapter discusses the various historical perspectives on management and closes with an overview of the approach used to integrate these perspectives in the rest of this book.

PERSPECTIVES ON MANAGEMENT

J. Paul Getty is a successful businessman. He is also one of the richest men in the world. Some time ago Getty was interviewed for Playboy magazine. The interview includes his views on the "fine art of being the boss" and begins with the following story.[2]

> I had occasion to choose one person from a list of five candidates for promotion to a top executive position. Accompanying the mass of reports and documents concerning the five was a covering roster that listed them according to the length of their experience. The first on the list was far and away the most experienced, in the sense that he'd held executive positions nearly five years longer than his closest rival. Had I been content to use amount of experience as the sole yardstick, he would have been my choice. According to legend, the Roman emperor Hadrian once found himself in an analogous position. One of his generals, the story goes, felt overdue for promotion. He took his case to the emperor and cited his long service as justification. "I am entitled to a more important command," he declared. "After all, I'm very experienced— I've been in ten battles."
>
> Hadrian, a shrewd judge of men and their abilities, did not consider the man qualified for higher

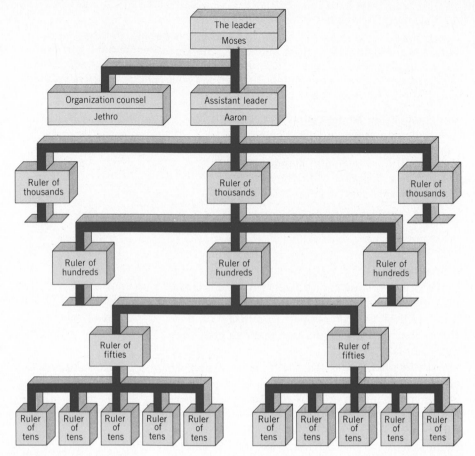

FIGURE 2.1 Moses' organization. *Source:* From *New Ways of Managing Conflict*, by Jane G. Likert and Rensis Likert. Copyright © 1966. Used with permission of McGraw-Hill Book Company.

rank. He waved a casual hand at some army donkeys tethered nearby. "My dear general," Hadrian said dryly, "take a good look at those donkeys. Each of them has been in at least *twenty* battles—yet all of them are still donkeys."

Getty's point is that experience alone is not a good indicator of managerial ability. He further implies that formal education alone (such as reflected in a college degree) may not be a good predictor of eventual managerial success either. Getty states that management is something that "cannot be systematized, learned by rote nor practiced according to formula. It . . . is an art—even a creative art." Think about this statement. Is management an art? Or is it something more—perhaps a science as well?

Management as an Art

An **art** is something a person practices based on skills applied to achieve a desired result. We ad-

mire, for example, painters, writers, actors, and dancers. When good, they are "artists" in the true sense of the word. Can we say, as J. Paul Getty would, that the successful manager is every bit the "artist," too?

History is replete with examples of persons who achieved managerial success without formal training. One of these is Kathrine Graham, former owner of the *Washington Post*. Her experience is briefly profiled in the Career Perspective at the end of this chapter. Persons such as Katharine Graham rely on something innate for their success—a special ability to learn quickly from experience. Like Jethro, they can look at situations, formulate appropriate theories, and make good decisions as a basis for action. They arrive at useful management theories through intuition and experience, not by formal preparatory education. This is something we should all take advantage of to the full extent that our capabilities allows.

Management as a Science

Good management, however, is based on something more than an artistic talent that a few lucky people possess. It has sure and strong scientific foundations as well.

A **science** is a body of knowledge systematically created via the scientific method. Table 2.1 lists the steps in the scientific method and shows how managers in one company applied them to solve a particular problem. The scientific approach to problem solving is further discussed in Chapter 3. For now, recognize that science is an action foundation available to each of us in our everyday lives. You study the sciences of mathematics, psychology, sociology, physics, and chemistry to learn basic principles that help you to deal with events, decisions, and people. You are fortunate that management also has the characteristics of a science. It can be studied, learned, and then practiced accordingly with an increased probability of success.

The field of management draws on other sciences to establish insights for managerial practice. Figure 2.2 shows the major roots of management as a scientific field of inquiry. They include the behavioral and social sciences as well as mathematics. The influence of these scientific roots on the study of management will become clear as you read further in the present chapter.

FIGURE 2.2 The Field of Management and its scientific roots.

Generally, we can say that management as a science does the following.[3]

1. *Provides managers with a way of thinking systematically about the behavior of people at work in organizational settings.* The scientific method has helped researchers to examine experiences and to establish cause-effect relationships among var-

Table 2.1 The Scientific Method

Steps	Managerial Example
1. Observations are made regarding real-world events and occurrences.	*Example* Company officials become convinced that productivity in a manufacturing plant could be higher.
2. An explanation for the events and occurrences is formulated.	*Example* The officials agree that productivity improvement could result from increased worker involvement in quality control.
3. Statements are made that use the explanation to predict future events and occurrences.	*Example* Company officials and a team of researchers predict that the implementation of periodic work-group meetings to discuss quality control will increase commitment to quality and that productivity gains through quality improvement will result.
4. The predictions are verified by an examination conducted under systematic and controlled conditions.	*Example* Two groups of workers are selected for study and their existing levels of productivity measured. In one group, meetings are held once a week to discuss quality; in the other, no such meetings are held. Productivity is measured again for both groups. The prediction that regular work-group meetings to discuss quality control will improve productivity is tested against the data.

Table 2.2 Management as a Profession?

The Case For	Professional Characteristic	The Case Against
A growing number of today's managers have degrees from uniformly accredited colleges of business.[a]	1. Formal education in a specialized body of knowledge	The ranks of management include those with no formal higher education and those with nonbusiness degrees.
Socially responsible managers have become trustees of the public welfare.	2. An unselfish service motive	Occasional convictions for price fixing, collusion, and antitrust violations have eroded the public's confidence in management's unselfish service motive.
A college degree is usually required for a position in management today.	3. Controlled entry	Managers are not licensed to practice like doctors, lawyers, dentists, and other professionals. Entry into management ordinarily depends on the right combination of ability and opportunity.[b]
Many professional and trade organizations have formally written codes of ethics and conduct for managers.	4. Universal ethical code	Unlike the traditional professions of law and medicine, not all managers have or adhere to a common code of ethics.
Trade organizations (such as the National Association of Manufacturers and the U.S. Chamber of Commerce), professional and academic organizations (such as the Academy of Management), and educational organizations (such as the American Management Association) guide, direct, and encourage responsible and ethical management.	5. A sanctioning organization	There is no equivalent of the American Medical Association or the American Bar Association in the field of management. Today's managers are not subject to censure by a single professional organization.

Source: Robert Kreitner, *Management: A Problem-Solving Process* (New York: Houghton-Mifflin, 1979), p. 16. Used by permission.

[a] Originally formed in 1916, the American Assembly of Collegiate Schools of Business imposes strict curricular standards on its member institutions.

[b] It is interesting to note that at least one well-known management writer has taken a firm stand against the licensing of managers. Peter Drucker has stated in *The Practice of Management* (p. 10) that "no greater damage could be done to our economy or to our society than to attempt to 'professionalize' management by 'licensing' managers, for instance, or by limiting access to management to people with a special academic degree." Drucker feels that performance and achievement are the only valid criteria for determining who stays or goes on the field of management.

ious work outcomes and the conditions that give rise to them. The field of management doesn't have all the answers. But it does offer a logical approach that should help you find answers that will solve the real problems in your work situations.

2. *Provides managers with a "vocabulary" of terms and concepts that allow work experiences to be clearly analyzed, shared, and discussed.* Although you may not like to learn new terms and their definitions, it is important to your managerial future. With concepts specified, managers can verbalize their impressions of work situations, share them with one another, and better understand their experiences. All organized activities depend on a vocabulary. Sports are a good example. It is far easier to play and learn to play a game such as soccer when you can converse with other players about critical issues in a common vocabulary. Managers need to converse with one another for similar purposes. The field of management provides the vocabulary.

3. *Provides managers with "techniques" for dealing with many of the problems that commonly occur in the work setting.* There is good theory behind the present state of management knowledge. The theories discussed in this book have been carefully selected for their practical applications. There is no "theory for theory's sake"! Without an ability to turn "theory" into "practice," the study of management would not have much personal value. Keep this in mind and carefully consider the applications as we discuss them along the way.

Management as a Profession

Some people refer to management as a "profession" and to managers as "professionals." The essence of any **profession** involves elements of both art and science, plus something more. That something is reflected in the characteristics of professions listed in the center column of Table 2.2. The table summarizes the basic points in a continuing debate whether or not managers are professionals in the true sense of the word.

Being a manager clearly satisfies some but not all of the basic criteria of professionalism. Even though the field of management may not represent a true profession, the practice of man-

agement is a career path of high social importance. Managers are in position to have a positive impact on the society in which we live. To be good as a manager, whether a true professional or not, is something to be proud about.

The professional character of management is enhanced by the presence of a basic body of knowledge, or scientific foundation, from which you and others can draw insight. Everyone is fortunate to have access to this body of knowledge as it comes to us through the efforts of many management scholars, past and present. Let's now turn to put the evolution of modern management theory into a historical frame of reference.

THE EVOLUTION OF MANAGEMENT THOUGHT

One of the delightful aspects of contemporary society is a reawakening of interest in our past. People everywhere are investigating their ancestors, or "roots," trying to learn as much as possible about the experiences of their forebears. Some people, myself included, feel that understanding our roots helps to understand better who we are at present. *Newsline 2.1* shows how some companies are also profiting from research of their histories. The same logic can be applied to the body of knowledge we now refer to as management. To understand better what management is today, it is useful to identify its roots from the past.

There are many roots in the history of management thought. In the chapter opener we cited the Bible as a source of insight. Although this example may have caught you by surprise, the essence of management thinking began long before that.

Early Management Thinking

Table 2.3 presents several of the earliest sources of systematic management thinking. The list begins with 5000 B.C. and the ancient Sumerian civilization. It includes the efforts of early Egyptians to construct the great pyramids that remain today one of the seven wonders of the world. The list goes on through the Babylonians, Ro-

NEWSLINE 2.1

PROFITING FROM THE PAST

For years Polaroid's W-3 plant in Waltham, Mass., was a model of efficiency—the sort of small, collegial shop that the photography firm loved to boast about. But relations with workers slowly soured, productivity slumped—and by the time fifteen years had passed, no one could remember the reasons why. Enter Phelps Tracy, corporate historian. By interviewing employees and examining old records, the consultant, a trained social scientist, pieced together the puzzle: as the plant's employment and output had increased over the years, managers had imposed ever tighter controls that gradually sapped the workers' morale. Employees and management pored over Tracy's findings. Soon they discovered the source of the plant's troubles—and took the steps needed to solve them.

Company histories were once chiefly public-relations ploys, crafted to enshrine their subjects in a free-enterprise Hall of Fame. But along with Polaroid, firms like AT&T, International Harvester, Consolidated Edison and Wells Fargo Bank are now asking serious scholars like Tracy to research their pasts. One hope is that company executives will acquire a longer-term perspective as they become more familiar with the past history of their companies. A corporate vice-president notes, "It's beneficial to know your corporate roots."

Source: "Profiting from the Past," *Newsweek* (May 10, 1982), pp. 73, 74. Used by permission.

mans, and Machiavelli to more recent history, and then to more familiar times.

The Industrial Revolution and Beyond

Picture the world of the 1700s. It was a time of social revolution when 13 colonies separated from England to become the United States of America. It was a time when the growth in population necessitated a tremendous leap forward in the manufacture of basic staples and consumer goods. During this time of industrial revolution, Adam Smith established the management principles we now know as specialization and the division of labor. These principles, which revolutionized the world of work, are clarified in one timeless example of the making of common pins, taken from his treatise *Wealth of Nations*.[4]

> One man draws out the wire, another straights it, a third cuts it, a fourth points it, a fifth grinds it at the top for receiving a head; to make the head requires two or three distinct operations! To put it on, is a peculiar business, to whiten the pins is another; it is even a trade by itself to put them into the paper; and the important business of making a pin is in this manner divided into about eighteen distinct operations, which in some manufactories are all performed by distinct hands, though in others the same man will sometimes perform two or three of them. . . . . Ten persons, therefore, could make among them upward of forty-eight thousand pins a day. Each person, therefore . . . . might be considered as making four thousand eight hundred pins in a day. But if they had all wrought separately and independently. . . . . they certainly could not each of them have made twenty; perhaps not one pin in a day; that is . . . . perhaps not the four thousand eight hundredth part of what they are at present capable of performing, in consequence of a proper division and combination of their different operations.

While Adam Smith's ideas ushered in the industrial revolution, we know its legacy best through Henry Ford, whose efforts in the mass production of automobiles also reflect these basic

Table 2.3 Early Examples in the Evolution of Mangement Thought

Approximate Dates	Source	Major Contribution
5000 B.C.	Sumerians	Used written records to assist operation of governments and commerce
4000–2000 B.C.	Egyptians	Organized efforts of 100,000 people for constructing pyramids
2000–1700 B.C.	Babylonians	Code of Hammurabi set standards for wages, obligations of parties, and penalties
300 B.C.–300 A.D.	Romans	Ran empire using effective communication and centralized control
1300	Venetians	Established legal framework for commerce
1500	Machiavelli	Developed guidelines for use of personal power
1776	Adam Smith	Used division of labor as a key to private enterprise
1800	Eli Whitney	Used interchangeability of parts as basis of mass production
19th century	Many	Employed various management techniques in the formation of productive large-scale corporate enterprises

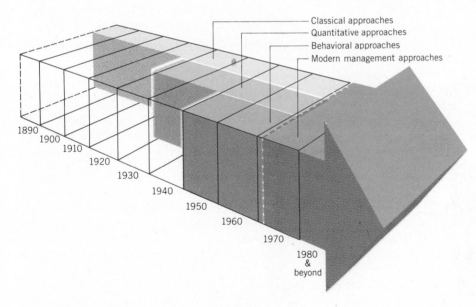

Classical approaches
Quantitative approaches
Behavioral approaches
Modern management approaches

1890 1900 1910 1920 1930 1940 1950 1960 1970 1980 & beyond

FIGURE 2.3 Major approaches to management.

principles. Fortunately, while Ford and other industrial pioneers of the late 1800s and early 1900s were employing specialization and division of labor with great success, other persons were systematically thinking about the world of work and its managerial implications. They began to study management as a science that once developed could help managers learn how to achieve productivity in the workplace.

The result is a series of schools of thought or approaches to management. As shown in Figure 2.3, the classical, quantitative, and behavioral approaches are the predecessors of the modern approach to management used today.

CLASSICAL APPROACHES TO MANAGEMENT

There are three branches of the classical approach to management: (1) scientific management, (2) administrative principles, and (3) bureaucratic organization. Figure 2.4 associates each of these branches with a prominent person in the history of management thought. The classical approaches generally share the assumption that people are rational and economic in their orientations toward work.

Assumption: People Are Rational

Every manager makes assumptions about the people with whom he or she works—be they subordinates, superiors, peers, customers, or suppliers. One assumption that could be maintained is that people are most responsive to economic incentives; that is, they will rationally consider opportunities made available to them and do whatever is necessary to achieve the greatest economic gain.[5] Each branch of classical management theory reflects this assumption.

Scientific Management

In 1911 Frederick W. Taylor published *The Principles of Scientific Management*. This interesting book became a cornerstone of the scientific management approach and is still provocative (and quick) reading today.

Taylor's Contributions[6]

Early in his book, Taylor makes the following statement: "The principal object of management should be to secure maximum prosperity for the employer, coupled with the maximum prosperity for the employee." He goes on to offer managers four principles of **scientific management** to meet this responsibility.

1. Develop a "science" for every job; this includes rules of motion, standardized work implements, and proper working conditions.
2. Carefully select workers with the right abilities for the job.
3. Carefully train these workers to do the job; offer them proper incentives to cooperate with the job science.
4. Support these workers by planning their work and by smoothing the way as they go about their jobs.

Taylor viewed these principles as a stark contrast to the ordinary management practices of his day. They were an attempt to bring rational and scientific practices into a world of work with the following characteristics.

- Jobs performed by rule-of-thumb methods, with no standard times, methods, or motions.
- Training, at best, was under an apprentice system.
- Almost all of the work and most of the responsibility rested with workers.
- The idea of management as a group performing unique duties was not widespread.

The four principles of scientific management were Taylor's suggestions for maximizing individual productivity. He felt that most workers of his day performed below their true capacities. He also felt that a scientific approach to management

FIGURE 2.4 Major branches in the classical approach to management.

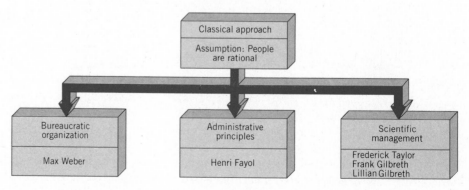

resulting in proper direction and monetary incentives could correct the problem. Instead of relying on tradition, hear say, guesswork, or rules of thumb, managers should act on the basis of facts proved through research and experimentation.

Contributions of the Gilbreths

While Taylor is often called "the father of scientific management," Frank Gilbreth and Lillian Gilbreth are the acclaimed pioneers of motion study in industry.[7] **Motion study** is the science of reducing a job or task to its basic physical motions. As they are still used today motion studies analyze how a person performs a task. Performance improvement is sought by such means as eliminating wasted movements and

One of the Gilbreth's contributions to management theory was an emphasis on the study and improvement of motions as a way of increasing job performance.

substituting smooth sequences of movement for jerky ones.

The Gilbreths' work with motion study established the foundations for later advances in the areas of job simplification, work standards, and incentive wage plans. Their most popularized study dealt with bricklaying. In at least one case, motion study reduced the number of motions used by bricklayers and tripled their productivity at the task.

Lessons from Scientific Management

Taylor, the Gilbreths, and their contemporaries used scientific techniques to try to improve the productivity of people at work. Their early efforts remain influential in modern approaches to management and will be reflected throughout this book. In particular, the significant lessons of scientific management relate to

- The role of compensation as an incentive for increased production.
- The design of jobs, specification of methods, and identification of necessary support for their accomplishments.
- The proper selection of individuals to work in these jobs once they are designed.
- The training of individuals to perform according to task requirements and to the best of their abilities.

Administrative Principles

Another classical approach to management evolved from systematic attempts to document and understand the experiences of successful managers. There are several important names in this administrative-principles school of thought, including Mary Parker Follett, James D. Mooney, and Lyndall Urwick.[8] Among them, Henri Fayol stands out as a successful manager as well as a scholar and writer.

Fayol's Principles of Management

Henri Fayol was a high executive in French industry. In 1916 he published *Administration ·Industrielle et Generale* outlining his views on the proper management of organizations and the people within them.[9] His book offered the five "rules" of management that follow. As you can see, these rules closely resemble the four functions of management identified in Chapter 1 as planning, organizing, leading, and controlling.

1. *Foresight*   To complete a plan of action; to prepare a scheme for the future.
2. *Organization*   To provide the resources needed to implement the plan; to mobilize effort in support of the plan.
3. *Command*   To get the best out of people working toward the plan; to lead; to select and evaluate workers properly.
4. *Coordination*   To ensure that the efforts of subunits fit together properly; that information is shared and any problems solved.
5. *Control*   To verify progress; to make sure things happen according to plan; to take any necessary corrective action.

Listed in Table 2.4 are 14 principles of management that Fayol specified as particular ways of implementing the prior rules. You will find many of these principles underlying our review of contemporary management concepts and theories throughout this book. Significant, too, is that one of Fayol's most forceful appeals was that the rules and principles of management could and should be taught to persons who intended to become practicing managers. A statement in one part of his book reflects such concern for the process of management education in which you are now engaged.[10]

> Everyone needs some concept of management; in the home, in affairs of State, the need for managerial ability is in keeping with the importance of the undertaking, and for individual people the need is everywhere greater in accordance with the position occupied. Hence there should be some generalized teaching of management; elementary in the primary schools, somewhat wider in the post-primary schools, and quite advanced in higher educational establishments. . . . . It is chiefly a matter of putting young people in the way of understanding and using the lessons of experience. At present the beginner has neither management theory nor method, and in this respect some remain beginners all their lives. Hence an effort must be made to spread management ideas throughout all ranks of the population.

Lessons of the Administrative-Principles Approach

It is from the work of Fayol and his contemporaries such as Follett, Mooney, and Urwick that management theory derives its present emphasis on the processes of planning, organizing, leading, and controlling. Their legacy is well summarized in the 14 management principles in Table 2.4. Proponents of the administrative-principles approach believe that managers using the general principles of management will achieve productivity.

Contributors to this approach are often criticized for being too willing to generate management principles from case histories and individual experiences without subjecting them to rigorous scientific scrutiny. In addition, they are criticized because the principles sometimes break down when scientific scrutiny is applied. Indeed, part of the richness of modern management theory lies in its ability and willingness to use scientific research to establish precisely when and under what conditions various principles operate to best advantage—and what to do when they don't. We must credit Henri Fayol and his colleagues for having the wisdom to initiate these principles in the first place and thus giving later management scholars a chance to extend and modify them creatively.

Bureaucratic Organization

Max Weber was a German intellectual whose life and work paralleled those of Taylor and Fayol. Weber's contribution to management can be summed up as follows: managers using proper organizational structures will achieve productivity. At the heart of Weber's thinking lies his concept of "bureaucracy."

Bureaucracy

Perhaps your image of a bureaucracy is of long registration lines, red tape, and the like. For Max Weber, by contrast, a **bureaucracy** was an ideal, intentionally rational, and very efficient form of organization founded on principles of logic, order, and legitimate authority. Weber described it as follows.[11]

Table 2.4 Fayol's General Principles of Management

1. *Division of work*   The object of division of work is to produce more and better work with the same effort. It is accomplished through reduction in the number of tasks to which attention and effort must be directed.
2. *Authority and responsibility*   Authority is the right to give orders, and responsibility is its essential counterpart. Whenever authority is exercised responsibility arises.
3. *Discipline*   Discipline implies obedience and respect for the agreements between the firm and its employees. Establishment of these agreements binding a firm and its employees from which disciplinary formalities emanate should remain one of the chief preoccupations of industrial heads. Discipline also involves sanctions judiciously applied.
4. *Unity of command*   An employee should receive orders from one superior only.
5. *Unity of direction*   Each group of activities having one objective should be unified by having one plan and one head.
6. *Subordination of individual interest to general interest*   The interest of one employee or group of employees should not prevail over that of the company or broader organization.
7. *Remuneration of personnel*   To maintain the loyalty and support of workers, they must receive a fair wage for services rendered.
8. *Centralization*   Like division of work, centralization belongs to the natural order of things. However, the appropriate degree of centralization will vary with a particular concern, so it becomes a question of the proper proportion. It is a problem of finding the measure that will give the best overall yield.
9. *Scalar chain*   The scalar chain is the chain of superiors ranging from the ultimate authority to the lowest ranks. It is an error to depart needlessly from the line of authority, but it is an even greater one to keep it when detriment to the business ensues.
10. *Order*   A place for everything and everything in its place.
11. *Equity*   Equity is a combination of kindliness and justice.
12. *Stability of tenure of personnel.*   High turnover increases inefficiency. A mediocre manager who stays is infinitely preferable to an outstanding manager who comes and goes.
13. *Initiative*   Initiative involves thinking out a plan and ensuring its success. This gives zeal and energy to an organization.
14. *Esprit de corps*   Union is strength, and it comes from the harmony of the personnel.

Source: Abridged from Henri Fayol, *General and Industrial Administration* (New York: Pitman, 1949), pp. 20–41. Used by permission.

The purely bureaucratic type of administrative organization . . . . is, from a purely technical point of view, capable of attaining the highest degree of efficiency. . . . . It is superior to any other form in precision, in stability, in the stringency of its discipline, and in its reliability. It thus makes possible a particularly high degree of calculability of results for the heads of the organization and for those acting in relation to it. It is finally superior both in intensive efficiency and in the scope of its operations and is formally capable of application to all kinds of administrative tasks.

Several special characteristics identify the Weberian notion of bureaucracy.

1. A *division of labor* in which authority and responsibility are clearly defined.

2. Every employee's work *duties and responsibilities explicitly defined.*

3. Standard *rules and procedures.*

4. Offices or positions organized in a *hierarchy of authority.*

5. Organizational members selected for their *technical competence.*

6. *Career managers* working for fixed salaries.

The anticipated advantages of bureaucracy are shown in Figure 2.5 as efficiency in the utilization of resources and fairness or equity in the treatment of employees and clients. The possible disadvantages of bureaucracy are also shown in Figure 2.5. These include a preponderance of red tape, rigidity in handling problems, resistance to change, and employee apathy. Surely your experience includes examples of both the advantages and disadvantages of bureaucratic features of organizations.

Weber's work has a major impact on management as a scientific field of inquiry today.

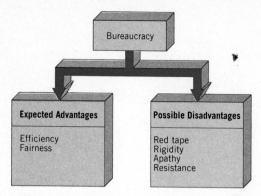

FIGURE 2.5 Advantages and disadvantages of Weber's ideal bureaucracy.

Researchers still examine the characteristics of bureaucracy to determine for what size organizations and under what environmental conditions they work best.

BEHAVIORAL APPROACHES TO MANAGEMENT

Using the assumptions of individual rationality and economic motivation, classical theorists developed technical approaches to management. Given proper job designs, management practices, and organizational structures, Taylor, Fayol, Weber, and others assumed that a rational person would respond to appropriate economic incentives and contribute to the productivity of the enterprise.

The 1930s, however, saw the emergence of an alternative approach to management that included a greater emphasis on the human factor. Major branches in this behavioral approach to management are shown in Figure 2.6. They in-clude the famous Hawthorne studies and Maslow's theory of human needs, as well as theories generated from these foundations by Douglas McGregor and Chris Argyris.

Assumption: People Are Social and Self-Actualizing

The various branches of the behavioral approach generally reflect a shared belief in the social and self-actualizing nature of people. People at work are assumed to act on the basis of (1) desires for satisfying social relationships, (2) responsiveness to group pressures, and (3) the search for personal fulfillment. This basic assumption has its roots in the Hawthorne studies and the seminal theory of human needs developed by Abraham Maslow.

The Hawthorne Studies[12]

In 1924 the Western Electric Company initiated a study of individual productivity in the company's Chicago plant known as the Hawthorne Works. The company was interested in examining Taylor's first principle of scientific management by studying the effects of physical working conditions on individual work outputs.

The Illumination Studies

Between 1924 and 1927 a series of studies were conducted to determine how various levels of illumination affected output. The intensity of light for different work groups was varied, changes in output measured, and the results analyzed. The researchers were disappointed, however. They failed to find any relationship between

FIGURE 2.6 Major branches in the behavioral approach to management theory.

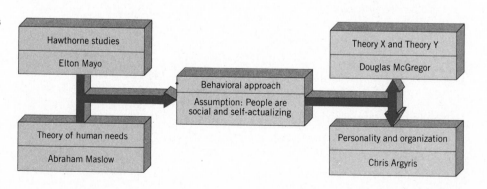

level of illumination and production. In some groups output "bobbed" up and down at random; in others it increased steadily; in one group it increased even though illumination was reduced to the level of moonlight! Perplexed by these results, the researchers concluded that unforeseen "psychological factors" somehow interfered with the experiments.

The Relay-Assembly Test-Room Studies

Western Electric remained persistent in its desire to learn more about the effects of physical working conditions on productivity. In 1927 a group of researchers from Harvard University led by Elton Mayo began a new series of studies to examine the effect of worker fatigue on output. Care was taken to design a test that would be free of the "psychological effects" thought to have confounded the earlier illumination studies.

Six workers who assembled relays were isolated for intensive study in a special test room. They were subjected to various rest pauses, lengths of workday, and lengths of workweek while their production was regularly measured. Once again, researchers were unable to find any direct relationship between these changes in physical working conditions and output. Productivity of the test workers increased regardless of the changes made.

This time the results were not dismissed as inconsequential. Mayo and his colleagues concluded that the new "social setting" created for research purposes in the test room accounted for the increased productivity of the workers. Two factors were singled out as having special importance. First was the group atmosphere in the test room. The workers shared good social relations with one another and the desire to do a good job. Second, supervision was more participatory. Test-room workers were made to feel important, were given a lot of information, and were frequently consulted for their opinion on what was taking place. This was not the case in their normal work situations. •

These conclusions led to a focus by managers and management theorists on the social dimensions of work and their potential impact on productivity. They also led to an identification of what is now known in social-science research as the **Hawthorne effect.** This is the tendency of persons who are singled out for special attention to perform as anticipated merely because of the expectations created by the situation. In the case of the test-room studies, the operators may have improved their productivity simply because they thought increased output was what the company and researchers wanted.

Further Studies

The relay-assembly test-room studies ended in 1929. From then until worsening economic conditions forced termination in 1932, Mayo's studies continued at Hawthorne. During this time, interest focused specifically on such things as employee attitudes, interpersonal relations, and group relations. In one of the studies, an almost unbelievable 21,126 employees were interviewed to learn what they liked and disliked about their work environment. "Complex" and "baffling" results led the researchers to conclude that the same things (e.g., work conditions, wages) can be sources of satisfaction for some workers and dissatisfaction for others. In other words, people are different! This same viewpoint was advanced by Frederick Taylor.

The final Hawthorne study was conducted in the bank wiring room, once again centered on the work group. One of the "surprises" of this study was the finding that people would restrict their output in order to avoid the displeasure of the group even if it meant sacrificing pay that could otherwise be earned by increasing output. This finding pointed out that the work group can have strong negative as well as positive influences on individual productivity.

Lessons of the Hawthorne Studies

The Hawthorne studies shifted the attention of managers and scholars away from the physical and technical aspects of work emphasized by the scientific management approach, and toward social and human behavior factors as keys to productivity. In sum, the Hawthorne researchers would argue: managers using good human relations will achieve productivity. Obviously this is a lesson Mr. Dithers in the *Blondie* cartoon has yet to learn!

"Blondie" by permission of King Features.

Abraham Maslow: A Theory of Human Needs

A **need** is a physiological or psychological deficiency a person feels the compulsion to satisfy. From a managerial perspective, this is a significant concept because needs create tensions that affect a person's work attitudes and behaviors. Abraham Maslow was an eminent psychologist who identified five levels of human needs: physiological, safety, social, esteem, and self-actualization. Maslow's **hierarchy of needs** is shown in Figure 2.7.

FIGURE 2.7 Maslow's hierarchy of needs.

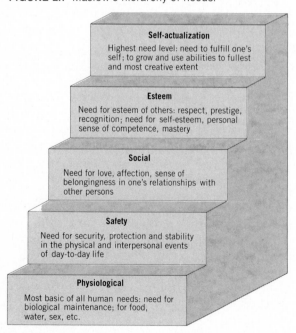

The Theory[13]

Maslow's theory of human needs is based on two fundamental principles.

1. *The deficit principle* A satisfied need is not a motivator of behavior; people act to satisfy "deprived" needs—that is, needs for which a satisfaction "deficit" exists.

2. *The progression principle* The five needs exist in a hierarchy of prepotency; a need at any level only becomes activated once the next lower-level need has been satisfied.

These two principles view people as seeking to satisfy sequentially the five levels of need in their work. A deprived need dominates individual attention and determines behavior. Once this deficit is satisfied, the next higher-level need is activated and progression up the hierarchy occurs. When the level of self-actualization is reached, the deficit and progression principles cease to operate. The more this need is satisfied, the stronger it grows.

Lessons from Maslow's Theory

Maslow's theory sensitizes everyone to the basic human needs that people bring with them to their work. It suggests that a manager's job is to (1) provide avenues for individual need satisfaction that also support essential organization and work-unit goals, and (2) remove any obstacles blocking need satisfaction and causing frustration, negative attitudes, or dysfunctional behavior. In general, the managerial implication of Maslow's theory has much in common with the Hawthorne studies: managers who satisfy human needs will achieve productivity. This humanistic orientation remains a major influence on management theory and practice today. It will be discussed more critically in our examination of motivation theories in Chapter 12. Maslow's efforts directly influenced the theories of Douglas McGregor and Chris Argyris, to be discussed next.

Douglas McGregor: Theory X and Theory Y

Douglas McGregor was heavily influenced by both the Hawthorne studies and Maslow's work. His classic book, *The Human Side of Enterprise*, advanced the thesis that managers could benefit greatly by giving more attention to the social and self-actualizing needs of people at work.[14] McGregor felt that managers must shift their view of human nature from a perspective he called "Theory X" to one called "Theory Y." These are classic terms in the vocabulary of management. Even today, you will hear people referred to as either Theory X (bad!) or Theory Y (good!) managers.

Theory X and Theory Y

According to McGregor, a manager of the **Theory X** model views his or her subordinates as by nature

- Disliking work.
- Lacking in ambition.
- Irresponsible.
- Resistant to change.
- Preferring to be led than to lead.

Theory Y, by contrast, involves an alternative set of assumptions. A manager operating under a **Theory Y** perspective views subordinates as naturally

- Willing to work.
- Willing to accept responsibility.
- Capable of self-direction.
- Capable of self-control.
- Capable of imagination, ingenuity, creativity.

Lessons from Theory X and Theory Y

Theory X assumptions can cause managers to be directive, narrow, and control-oriented in their approach to people at work. These supervisory behaviors, in turn, were felt by McGregor to foster passive, dependent, and reluctant subordinates.

A Theory Y perspective encourages managers to allow subordinates more participation, freedom, and responsibility in their work. McGregor felt they would respond accordingly with individual initiative and high productivity. Theory Y managers delegate authority, allow subordinates to participate in decisions, and offer them greater job autonomy and task variety. This creates more opportunities for the satisfaction of esteem and self-actualization needs through work.

It is easy to see the humanistic appeal of McGregor's work. This is the legacy left by Douglas McGregor—one of the most prominent names in the vocabulary of any informed manager.

Chris Argyris: Personality and Organization

Chris Argyris is a productive scholar who continues to make significant contributions to management thinking. His early work on personality and organization is consistent with the belief in a higher order of human nature advanced by Maslow and McGregor.

The Theory[15]

Argyris argues that certain management principles found among the classical management approaches are inconsistent with the mature adult personality. The resulting incongruence between individual personality and the organization causes conflict, frustration, and failure for people at work. Consider the following examples of classical management principles and the unfortunate results predicted by Argyris.

Task specialization Assumes people will behave more efficiently as tasks become specialized.

Result Inhibits self-actualization.

Chain of command Assumes efficiency is increased by a strict hierarchy where top directs and controls bottom.

Result Creates dependent, passive, and

WORKERS AREN'T THE PROBLEM, THEORIST ASSERTS; BOSSES ARE

Here's fresh evidence for what every employee secretly knows: workers are smart and managers are dumb.

Well, maybe not dumb. But certainly not very bright when it comes to organizing companies to get the most out of employees. The problem, according to social psychologist Jay Hall, is that managers tend to assume workers are incompetent when, actually, the reverse is true.

"We exalt technology and management expertise when things go well, but when things go wrong, we blame the people who do the work," says Hall. He thinks that is a bum rap.

"We are good at what we do," writes Hall in *The Competence Process*, a book published by the company he heads. Incompetents don't build sturdy bridges and skyscrapers, he says or land men on the moon. But for every space shuttle there are thousands of new cars that rattle and countless appliances that burn out the first time they are plugged in. Are workers to blame? No, says Hall. "The answer is management. Management has discouraged competence."

Managers are the culprits, says Hall, because people are capable by nature. Not only that, people actually *need* to work, and to do well at their jobs, for their mental health.

But listen to the managers. "People don't want to work any more." "It's hard to get good help these days." Companies don't expect much from their work force, and often, not much is what they get.

Source: Excerpted from Eugene Carlson, "Workers Aren't the Problem, Theorist Asserts; Bosses Are," *Wall Street Journal* (May 8, 1981), p. 25. Reprinted by permission of the *Wall Street Journal.* Copyright © 1981 Dow Jones & Company, Inc. All rights reserved.

subordinate workers with little control over their work environments.

Unity of direction   Assumes efficiency will increase when work is planned and directed by one supervisor.

Result   Creates ideal conditions for psychological failure; psychological success requires that individuals define their own goals.

Span of control   Assumes efficiency will increase when a supervisor's responsibility is limited to five or six employees.

Result   Creates dependent, passive, and subordinate workers with little control over their work environments.

Lessons from the Theory

Argyris predicts that when people suffer incongruence between their mature personalities and management practices, they will be prone to absenteeism, turnover, aggression toward higher levels of authority, apathy, alienation, and a focus on compensation as the ever-increasing trade-off for their unhappiness. His advice to managers, in turn, is to accommodate the mature personality by expanding job requirements to include more task variety and responsibility and adjusting supervisory styles to include more participation and better human relations. In sum, Argyris, suggests that managers using responses to "mature" personalities will achieve productivity.

Newsline 2.2 shows that this theme still receives deserved attention today.

QUANTITATIVE APPROACHES TO MANAGEMENT

About the same time that the Hawthorne studies were prompting some theorists to develop behavioral approaches to management, other scholars were creating quantitative techniques to facilitate managerial decision making. This latter thrust developed into a discipline we now know as **quantitative analysis, management science,** or **operations research.** These interchangeable terms describe a scientific approach to management that uses mathematical techniques to analyze and solve problems.[16]

Illustrative Case: Emergency Snow Removal[17]

Let's introduce the quantitative approaches to management by example. Turn back the clock to February 1969, when Mayor John V. Lindsay of New York City faced a fall reelection campaign. An overpowering snowstorm had just dumped massive amounts of snow on the city.

The Problem For the first few days after the snowstorm, residents of New York enjoyed their new, beautifully white recreation wonderland. Skiers could be seen everywhere. By midweek, however, the city's citizens were no longer enjoying the snow, and John Lindsay was wondering if he would be mayor this time next year. Little progress was made in clearing the streets and removing the snow. Residents of the boroughs of Queens and Brooklyn complained that Manhattan was getting better service. Sanitation workers suggested that more recruits were needed, owners of snow-removal equipment suggested that more equipment was needed, and almost every special-interest group had some type of solution that would directly or indirectly benefit them. Mayor Lindsay asked his quantitative analysis (QA) unit to find a solution to the problem.

After carefully considering the situation, the QA unit concluded that four basic questions had to be answered:

1. How much snow falls in New York City?
2. How much work has to be done to clean it up?
3. What is the city's capacity for performing this work?
4. What improvements are needed in the system?

The Answers

Question 1 After searching U.S. Weather Bureau records, the analysts determined that a similar storm, with a snow depth of about 15 inches, occurred about once every 12 years. The number of times that a storm of this intensity would hit New York City when there was a small snow-fighting force on duty, such as on a Sunday, was about once in 87 years. The chance of this happening during an election year was even less. They also found that the city averages slightly over 30 inches of snow a year, that there are approximately six storms per year with 1 inch or more of snow, and that there are only two storms per season with more than 4 inches of snow.

Question 2 For any snow cleanup, three sequential procedures are required: (1) spreading salt, (2) plowing, and (3) snow removal. Collecting data on cleanup, the analysts decided that new priority areas should be developed for snow removal. These areas included about 1600 miles of streets near parkways, bus routes, police stations, and hospitals.

Question 3 Since the principal snow-fighting equipment was plows and spreaders, the main emphasis was on this equipment's capacity and mobilization. After making an analysis of downtimes, the QA unit determined that only 134 spreaders and 1050 plows would be available. Applying QA techniques, the analysts learned that it would always be possible to keep the high-priority areas plowed. While there was adequate plowing equipment, the number of salt spreaders was found to be inadequate.

Question 4 Even though the number of plows was adequate, their deployment was not.

Since most of the plowing vehicles were refuse-collection trucks, they were distributed according to needs of refuse collection and not snow removal. Because Manhattan was more densely populated, it ended up with more plows per mile than other areas. Thus the complaint that Manhattan was receiving superior snow removal was probably correct. In addition, the analysts determined that the spreaders were not correctly located and that new garage areas were needed. In order to improve weekend and holiday mobilization, they suggested that the actual plow mechanisms be placed on about one-fifth of the trucks and that salt be placed in some of the salt spreaders before the weekend of a holiday. To avoid flat tires, the salt had to be removed from the spreaders after the weekend or holidays.

Implementing the Suggestions

The results of this quantitative analysis of the snow-removal problem were presented to Mayor Lindsay as his reelection campaign started. The suggested solutions were implemented, and a major press conference was called to release the findings. The city's residents were assured that a snowstorm of a magnitude like the one that brought the city to its knees in February could now be quickly and effectively handled. The QA unit happened to be at the right place, at the right time, and with the right answers. Mayor Lindsay, by the way, was reelected.

Foundations, Techniques, and Applications

The previous case illustrates how a quantitative approach to management can work. A problem is encountered, it is systematically analyzed, appropriate mathematical computations are made, and an optimum solution is selected as a result. This is a truly scientific approach to managerial decision making and problem solving.

Foundations

The essence of any quantitative management approach is found in the following characteristics.

1. *Primary focus on decision making*   The end result of problem analysis will include direct implications for managerial action.
2. *Based on economic decision criteria*   Final actions are chosen on the basis of such criteria as costs, revenues, and rates of return on investment.
3. *Use of formal mathematical models*   Possible solutions to problems are specified as mathematical equations and then analyzed according to mathematical rules and formulas.

Quantitative approaches to management use computers to process information and perform statistical analyses of data.

Table 2.5 Applications of Quantitative Approaches in Various Jobs

Job Title	Use of Quantitative Analysis
Operations researchers	Address issues such as location of new plants, deciding which factory to close, development of corporate planning models, and scheduling of projects.
Financial analysts	Develop models to evaluate cash flows and financial positions, select portfolios, and answer questions regarding lease-purchase problems.
Production analysts	Address issues involving quality control, demand forecasting, plant layout, and inventory control.
Marketing researchers	Evaluate consumer preferences, market demand, market-share conditions, product acceptance, and marketing strategies via surveys or statistical sampling.
Systems analysts	Turn management ideas into logical flows of data that can be automated; for example, a systems analyst might be asked to develop an automated payroll system—one that flows from worker time sheets to computer inputs to outputs of computer-written paychecks and payroll reports.

Source: Adapted from Barry Render and Ralph M. Stair, Jr., *Quantitative Analysis for Management* (Boston: Allyn and Bacon, 1982), pp. 15, 16. Used by permission.

4. *Frequent use of computers* Heavy reliance is placed on electronic computers and their advanced processing capabilities.

Techniques

Several basic quantitative techniques are listed here. Linear programming, simulation, and queuing theory are but a few of the more common names you might recognize. The list also gives a brief example of each technique as it applies to actual management practice. These techniques are discussed in greater detail in Chapter 16 on production and operations control and in the Appendix, "Quantitative Decision Techniques: An Introduction to Management Science."

Forecasting Making projections into the future through mathematical calculations.

Inventory modeling Controlling inventories by mathematically establishing how much to order and when.

Linear programming Calculating how best to allocate scarce resources among competing uses.

Queuing theory Computing the number of service personnel or stations that will minimize customer waiting time and service cost.

Network models Breaking large and complex tasks into smaller components that can be separately analyzed and controlled (e.g., PERT, program evaluation and review technique and CPM critical path method).

Simulation Making a model of a problem and using a computer to solve the problem many times under various decision circumstances.

Regression analysis Predicting relationships among two or more variables (e.g., the impact of increased advertising on sales).

Applications

One way to view applications of quantitative approaches to management is in a career perspective. Table 2.5 lists a number of job titles for persons specializing in applied quantitative analysis. Perhaps you aspire to one of these or similar positions that depend on expertise in various quantitative decision techniques.

Quantitative Analysis Today

The methods of quantitative analysis offer special value in addressing the technical problems faced by organizations. The perspective shared by these approaches is that managers using quantitative decision techniques will achieve productivity. Success in the application of quantitative techniques, however, depends on both the technical expertise of the scientist and the willingness of other persons to implement the recommended problem solutions. Quantitative management specialists are sometimes criticized for their lack of sensitivity to this additional human factor. A well-rounded and truly comprehensive view of problems, including both technical and human-resource considerations, is the ideal direction advocated by modern management approaches.

MODERN APPROACHES TO MANAGEMENT

Today there is a convergence of management thinking. Modern approaches to management recognize that the prescriptions of the classical, behavioral, and quantitative schools do not apply universally in every situation, or to the exclusion of one another. Instead, current approaches recognize a need for managers to know what will work best in any given situation. Because modern management approaches constitute the substance of this book, they will only be very generally introduced here. As you read further and learn about them in more detail, you will find that modern management concepts and theories try to balance the rational/economic assumptions of the classical school with the social/self-actualizing assumptions of the behavioral school. Instead of assuming one or the other, or assuming everyone has similar needs, personalities, or orientations toward work, the modern approaches build from a base of **contingency.** No longer is there "one best way" to manage. Modern theorists ask when and under what conditions various assumptions and their associated management guidelines hold. In so doing, the goal is also to identify the best elements of other management approaches and clarify in a comprehensive sense their practical implications. Figure 2.8 summarizes this logic and helps you to prepare for the coming introduction to modern management approaches.

Assumption: People Are Complex

An alternative to the assumptions that people are basically rational/economic or social/self-actualizing in their nature is the following viewpoint: people are complex and variable.[18]

- They attend to multiple and varied needs.
- They change these patterns of needs, action tendencies, and desires over time.
- They respond to a wide variety of organizational demands and managerial strategies.

This is the guiding assumption of modern management approaches. It recognizes that people are different and change over time. Managers must be able to understand these differences and respect them when making decisions and taking action. Two important concepts in this regard are systems and contingency. As you read on, keep this summary perspective of the modern management approaches in mind: managers using systems and contingency thinking will achieve productivity.

The Systems View of Organizations

In Chapter 1 we defined the term *organization*. It was further described as an open system that

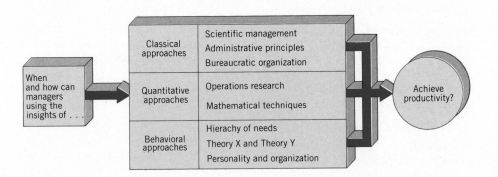

FIGURE 2.8 The basic thrust of modern management theory.

When and how can managers using the insights of . . .

Classical approaches
Scientific management
Administrative principles
Bureaucratic organization

Quantitative approaches
Operations research
Mathematical techniques

Behavioral approaches
Hierachy of needs
Theory X and Theory Y
Personality and organization

Achieve productivity?

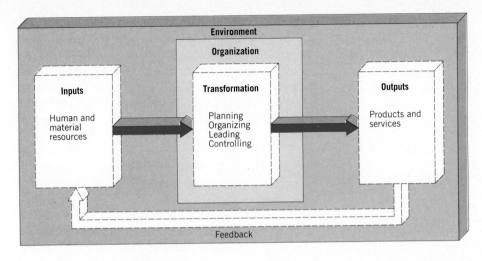

FIGURE 2.9 An open-systems view of organizations.

receives resource inputs from the environment and transforms them into product or service outputs, which are returned to the environment for consumption. Formally speaking, a **system** is a collection of interrelated parts that function together to achieve a common purpose. An open system, as you should recall, is one that interacts with its environment; a **closed system** does not.

An open system's view of organizations is once again shown in Figure 2.9. Note the central role of the management functions in facilitating the transformation of system inputs into outputs. The significance of this managerial contribution to the organization as a well-functioning system traces, in part, to the insights of Chester Barnard.

Chester Barnard and Cooperative Systems

Chester Barnard served for many years as chief executive officer of the New Jersey Bell Telephone Company. His book *The Functions of the Executive* is a highly respected account of management theory viewed from the perspective of the practicing manager.

For Barnard, the essence of any organization was "cooperation"—that is, a willingness of people to communicate and interact with one another to serve a common purpose. Something larger than the individual—a "system"—resulted from this willingness to cooperate. The "system" allowed people to accomplish far more together than they could acting as individuals alone. Barnard described a cooperative system as:[19]

A complex of physical, biological, personal, and social components which are in a specific systematic relationship by reason of the cooperation of two or more persons for at least one definite end.

It was the function of the executive or manager to make this cooperation possible. In so doing, the vitality of the organization as a total system would be ensured.

Ludwig von Bertalanffy and General Systems Theory

Perhaps the best known of the system theorists is Ludwig von Bertalanffy.[20] In the 1940s and 1950s he proposed a theory of general systems that would explain the behavior of all levels of science from that concerned with a single cell to the study of society. His work largely focused around the interconnections among the components of systems and the dynamic relationship between open systems and their environments. Although his ideas have proven cumbersome as a universal model of scientific inquiry, they have contributed to the emphasis on a "systems" viewpoint of organizations and their management. Within the vocabulary of management, for example, these systems terms are frequently used.

Subsystem A smaller component in a larger system.

System boundary The point of separation between a system and its external environment.

Feedback Information about system performance that can be used by a system for purposes of adaptation, control, and constructive change.

Equifinality The ability of a system to achieve the same end state from a variety of paths.

Negative entropy The tendency toward system continuity and survival; a reversal of the entropic process that is a universal tendency of all living systems to move toward death.

Open Systems and the Environment

The environment is a critical element in the open-systems perspective on organizations. Because it is a source of resources and feedback, it has a significant impact on organizations. As the environment changes over time, for example, it is the manager's job to stay informed and help the organization respond in a productive way. The crisis of the U.S. auto industry during the late 1970s and early 1980s illustrates what can happen when managers fail to remain in contact with dynamic environments and help their organizations respond to them. In this particular case, foreign auto makers did a better job of recognizing petroleum shortages and changing consumer tastes, and responded to them with appropriate products.

Within the total system represented by any organization, many separate subsystems will operate in interdependence with one another to create the desired outputs. Figure 2.10 illustrates how various subsystems of the Mid-Ohio Electric Company interact with one another and the relevant environment to serve the utility's customers. The manager of each subsystem component must ensure that the subsystem integrates well with other subsystems in order to achieve high productivity for the total system or organization as a whole. This figure is a good visual representation of the organization as a complex open system.

The significance of the external environment is evidenced by dramatic increases in prices over the last decade of petroleum products.

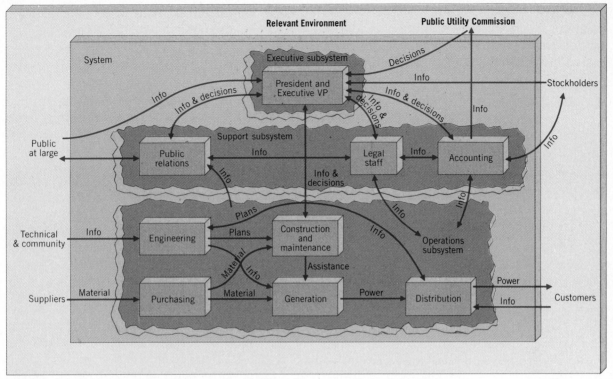

FIGURE 2.10 Mid-Ohio Electric Company as a functional system. *Source:* H. Randolph Bobbitt, Jr., Robert H. Breinholt, Robert H. Doktor, and James P. McNaul, *Organizational Behavior: Understanding and Prediction,* © 1974, p. 219. Reprinted by permission of Prentice-Hall, Inc., Englewood Cliffs, New Jersey.

Feedback is also central to an open system. It reflects the environment's evaluation of an organization or a subsystem. Through feedback, managers learn how well the organization's or subsystem's products or services are being received. This is reflected in the willingness of the environment to continue providing important resource inputs in exchange for them. Based on feedback, constructive action can be taken by managers to maintain or improve organizational productivity. When properly used, feedback helps ensure the survival and longer-term prosperity of the enterprise.

The open-systems view highlights the environment as a critical influence on organizations. The contingency theories have done an especially good job of extending the implications of this organization-environment relationship for managers.

Contingency Theories

Contingency approaches to management theory emphasize environmental differences and the need for managers to respond appropriately to them. This is a clear departure from the "one-best-way" appeals characteristic of earlier management approaches and toward management guidelines that vary to fit the demands of various situations. The essence of the contingency perspective is to help managers analyze and understand situational differences and choose responses that best facilitate productivity in each circumstance.

Recent advances in management theory draw heavily on this contingency viewpoint. You will encounter them at key points throughout the chapters to come. Their substance and ultimate practical value will also become clear as they are examined in detail along the way. For now it is sufficient to introduce the basic ideas of four important contingency viewpoints that will be discussed in later chapters.

- Organization structure must match environmental demands.
- Organization structure must match technological demands.
- Structures of organizational subsystems must match the unique demands of their respective environments.
- Leadership behaviors must be appropriate to the situational demands of various work groups.

The contingency approaches advocate that managers carefully analyze the unique characteristics of situations and respond accordingly in their decision-making and problem-solving efforts. Depending on such things as environmental demands, technological factors, and workgroup characteristics, the manager's actions will vary from one situation to the next. What is a good managerial response for one type of situation may be a poor one for another, and vice versa. This is a major insight brought to management practice by contingency theorists. It is used to guide your learning throughout the remainder of this book.

The Approach of This Book

The modern approach to management we will use is diagrammed in Figure 2.11. As shown in the figure, managers have basic decision-making and problem-solving responsibilities. They draw on personal skills and the knowledge base offered by the field of management to implement each of the basic management functions—planning, organizing, leading, and controlling. Furthermore, these functions are implemented in a contemporary environment that requires contingency and systems thinking to achieve productivity. Among the important environmental forces in this action framework are conflict, change and organization development, labor-management relations, the international arena, and ethics and social responsibility.

Figure 2.11 encompasses both the systems view of organizations and the contingency views of management, while respecting insights from the classical, behavioral, and quantitative approaches. There is no one best way to manage. A manager must decide how to act in any given circumstance based on careful analysis of the unique characteristics of the situation. System interdependencies and the contingencies of differing but always dynamic environmental forces will demand differing strategies for implementing the four basic functions of management. Our

FIGURE 2.11 A framework for studying management.

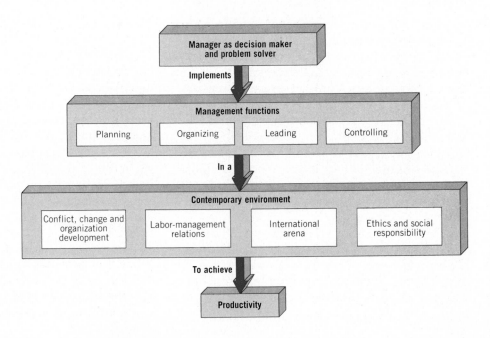

goal in the rest of this book is for you to understand these functions and the nature of the contemporary work environment so that your managerial decisions and actions will always be sound and successful.

SUMMARY

This chapter examined management as an art, science, and profession. It went on to trace the evolution of management as a field of scientific inquiry from early civilizations through the emergence of four basic approaches or schools of thought—classical, behavioral, quantitative, and modern. Each approach builds from an underlying assumption regarding human nature, and each leads managers to focus attention on somewhat different action alternatives.

Classical management approaches emphasized the rational/economic side of people. The works of Taylor, Fayol, and Weber suggested ways of structuring tasks, organizations, and managerial actions to take advantage of this tendency. The behavioral approaches, in contrast, focused on the social and self-actualizing tendencies of people at work. The Hawthorne studies and a new generation of theorists including Maslow, McGregor, and Argyris emphasized the importance of good human relations, group dynamics, and supervisory styles in the workplace.

The quantitative approaches specify mathematical techniques for solving management problems. Given that an optimum problem solution can be implemented, these approaches offer managers ways to solve problems subject to quantitative measurements.

Ultimately, a modern and comprehensive approach to management has emerged from these historical roots. It offers an expanded view of people at work that recognizes the complex and variable nature of every human being. The modern approach also views organizations as complex open systems and it seeks to define situational contingencies under which various managerial strategies are most appropriate.

This book uses a modern viewpoint centering on the manager's basic responsibility to act as a decision maker and problem solver. Chapter 3 reviews this latter responsibility in detail. It is an important prelude to your study of the four management functions and the contemporary environment within which they will be implemented as part of your career. In summary, recall that managers implement the management functions in the contemporary environment to achieve productivity!

THINKING THROUGH THE ISSUES

1. Can management be considered an "art" and/or a "science"? Is management a "profession"? Why or why not?

2. How did the industrial revolution influence the evolution of management thought?

3. What were Taylor's four principles of scientific management? How did they differ from the prevailing management wisdom of his day?

4. What major parts of this book relate most closely to the work of Fayol? Justify your answer.

5. Is Weber's concept of an ideal bureaucracy valid today? Explain your answer.

6. How did Maslow's theory of human needs influence McGregor's notions of Theory X and Theory Y?

7. Explain how Argyris's theory of personality and organization is critical of certain classical management principles.

8. What is the major limitation to utilization of the quantitative management approach in actual organizational situations?

9. Choose an organization with which you are familiar. Explain its "system" characteristics.

10. Explain the role of "contingency" in modern management theory. Give an example of typical contingency behavior on the part of a subsystem manager in the organization used in your response to Question 9.

THE MANAGER'S VOCABULARY

Art	Hierarchy of needs	Operations research	System
Bureaucracy	Management science	Profession	System boundary
Closed system	Management theory	Quantitative analysis	Theory
Contingency	Motion study	Science	Theory X
Equifinality	Need	Scientific management	Theory Y
Feedback	Negative entropy	Subsystem	
Hawthorne effect			

CAREER PERSPECTIVE: KATHARINE GRAHAM[21]

Until her retirement, Katharine Graham was one of the most important executives in the United States. Both the size and influence of Graham's Washington Post Company are impressive. The company has three divisions. Its newspaper division consists of the *Trenton Evening Times*, the *Sunday Times Advertiser*, and the *Washington Post*, one of the nation's foremost newspapers. The magazine and book division is made up of *Newsweek* and Newsweek Books. The broadcasting division has four television stations, in Jacksonville and Miami, Florida, Hartford, Connecticut, and Detroit, Michigan.

When the company came suddenly into her possession upon her husband's death in 1963, Katharine Graham had to learn to be a topnotch manager through experience. Despite her inexperience in business—she had devoted the years after her marriage to her family—she set out to become an effective manager after deciding to carry on rather than sell the organization.

While developing her expertise, Graham depended on Frederick Beebe, the family attorney, to guide the Washington Post Company as chairman. Still, her influence as owner seemed to grow with her confidence in her management talents. After Beebe's death in 1973, she assumed the chairmanship of the firm.

Effective planning and dynamic leadership allowed Graham to transform her company from a loosely structured family enterprise to a business with "good controls, good planning, timely reporting," in the words of one director. Her objective was to raise profit margins to the level of those for industry leaders while maintaining editorial quality.

When a recession led to a need for tighter financial controls, it was her decision not to cut editorial budgets at the *Post* and *Newsweek*. Instead, she chose to pursue a vigorous policy of cutting production and distribution costs. Graham cut personnel and moved toward automation of the production process, despite union protests and threatened strikes.

Katharine Graham also recognized the importance of an effective organization. When people did not produce the results she required, she saw that they left the company. On the other hand, when she had confidence in people, she was willing to delegate authority, allowing them to function relatively autonomously. Such was the case with Benjamin Bradlee, executive editor of the *Post,* who succeeded in restyling the paper into an innovative and news-packed publication with first-rate investigative reporting. As publisher of the paper—a leadership role she assumed in addition to that of chairman of the company—Graham kept close tabs on it but did not intervene unless she found some aspect consistently distasteful.

When the Washington Post Company went public in 1977, Graham's emphasis on planning and close financial control increased still further. More strenuously than ever, she stressed the value of long-range plans and market studies to indicate new opportunities for profit. Nothing, however, caused her to waver from her insistence on quality. As Graham put it, "I have to do an endless song and dance about how excellence and profitability go hand in hand—which isn't an act. I really think they do." At the time of her retirement, Katharine Graham was recognized as one of the most effective contemporary managers.

Questions

1. Did Katharine Graham succeed in the "art" or "science" of management? Defend your answer.
2. Did Graham have a better chance at managerial success than you would, for example, if you were to take over a similar company 20 years from now? Why or why not?

CASE APPLICATION: CHINA'S NEW MANAGEMENT CADRE[22]

In 1980 China made a dramatic step forward in management education by inviting William Dill, then Dean of the New York University's Graduate School of Business Administration, to lead an effort to organize a national management faculty in the country. Up until this time, China had no real tradition of management education. Furthermore, that which did exist had suffered from the cultural revolution of the 1960's when untrained workers suddenly replaced their experienced predecessors in industrial management positions and higher education itself came to a virtual standstill.

The China of today faces serious shortages of management talent at the very time when industrial and economic development is a major national priority. Dill's task was to help solve this problem by establishing The Chinese National Center for Industrial Science and Technology Management at the Dalian Institute of Technology, Dalian, Manchuria. The Center's goal is to update management professors and participate in the training of the next generation of managers. One result has been the increased availability of short courses or training seminars for practicing managers. These opportunities are designed to upgrade the knowledge and skills of people like Zhen Wen Hui.[23]

Zhen Wen Hui is director of Shanghai factory 18 which manufactures The Flying Leap Forward brand of black-and-white TV sets. Because his family was poor, he did not finish primary school. Instead, at the age of 14 Zhen went to work as an apprentice in a radio-repair store. Later he enlisted in the Chinese army. Upon discharge he went to work at Radio Factory No. 4 but attended middle-school and high-school classes in the evenings. After completing high school, he took university evening courses in enterprise organization and management.

Now 52, Zhen runs a plant that employs 1850 people and produces some 200,000 TV sets. He recently attended a three-month management training program run by the city of Shanghai.

Questions

1. What could China's managers learn from management courses that discuss the theories of (a) Max Weber, (b) Abraham Maslow, (c) Douglas McGregor and (d) Chris Argyris?

2. What topics would you like people like Zhen Wen Hui to cover in a three-month management-training course? Write a sample syllabus for the course, assigning one topic for each week of instruction and defend your choices.

CLASS EXERCISE: THE GREAT MANAGEMENT HISTORY DEBATE:

It's time for a debate! The *key question* is "What is the best thing a manager can do to ensure high productivity for his or her organization?"

1. The instructor will assign you (individually or as part of a group) to one or more of the following positions to be argued in response to the key question. Think about the question and make notes on how you will respond. Be prepared to argue and defend your response before the entire class.

Position A: "Frederick Taylor offers the best insight into the question. His advice would be to . . ." (advice to be filled in by you or the group).

Position B: "Max Weber's ideal bureaucracy is the best answer to this question. His advice would be to . . ." (advice to be filled in by you or the group).

Position C: "Henri Fayol is the best source of insight into this question. His advice would be to . . ." (advice to be filled in by you or the group).

Position D: "The Hawthorne studies are the true source of insight into this question. They suggest that a manager should . . ." (advice to be filled in by you or the group).

2. Await further instructions on the conduct of the class debate.

REFERENCES

[1] Adapted from "The Second Book of Moses, Called Exodus," Chapter 18, *Holy Bible* (Philadelphia: A. J. Homan, 1942), p. 88–89.

[2] Slightly abridged from J. Paul Getty, "The Fine Art of Being the Boss," *Playboy* (June 1972), p. 143. Reprinted by permission.

[3] Based on Larry L. Cummings, "Towards Organizational Behavior," *Academy of Management Journal*, Vol. 3 (January 1978), pp. 90–98.

[4] Adam Smith, *An Inquiry into the Nature and Causes of the Wealth of Nations*, Fifth Edition (Edinburgh: Adam and Charles Black, 1859), p. 3.

[5] See Edgar H. Schein, *Organizational Psychology*, Second Edition (Englewood Cliffs, N.J.: Prentice-Hall, 1970), pp. 55–58.

[6] References to Taylor's work are from Frederick W. Taylor, *The Principles of Scientific Management* (New York: W. W. Norton, 1967), originally published by Harper & Brothers in 1911. See Charles W. Wrege and Amedeo G. Perroni, "Taylor's Pig-Tale: A Historical Analysis of Frederick W. Taylor's Pig-Iron Experiments," *Academy of Management Journal*, Vol. 17 (March 1974), pp. 6–27, for a stinging criticism; see Edwin A. Locke, "The Ideas of Frederick W. Taylor: An Evaluation," *Academy of Management Review*, Vol. 7 (1982), p. 14, for an excellent treatment of the contemporary significance of Taylor's work.

[7] See Frank B. Gilbreth, *Motion Study* (New York: Van Nostrand, 1911).

[8] See Henry C. Metcalfe and Lyndall Urwick (editors),

The Collected Papers of Mary Parker Follett (New York: Harper & Brothers, 1940); James D. Mooney, *The Principles of Administration,* Revised Edition (New York: Harper & Brothers, 1947); Lyndall Urwick, *The Elements of Administration* (New York: Harper & Brothers, 1943).

[9] Available in the English language as Henri Fayol, *General and Industrial Administration* (London: Pitman, 1949); much subsequent discussion is based on M. B. Brodie, *Fayol on Administration* (London: Pitman, 1949).

[10] Ibid., pp. 14–16.

[11] A.M. Henderson and Talcott Parsons (editors and translators), *Max Weber: The Theory of Social Economic Organization* (New York: The Free Press, 1947), p. 337.

[12] The Hawthorne studies are described in detail in F. J. Roethlisberger and William J. Dickson, *Management and the Worker* (Cambridge, Harvard University Press, 1966); and G. Homans, *Fatigue of Workers* (New York: Reinhold, 1941). Both sources were used in preparing the synopsis.

[13] This discussion on Maslow's theory is based on Abraham H. Maslow, *Eupsychian Management* (Homewood Ill.: Richard D. Irwin, 1965) and Abraham H. Maslow, *Motivation and Personality,* Second Edition (New York: Harper & Row, 1970).

[14] Douglas McGregor, *The Human Side of Enterprise* (New York: McGraw-Hill, 1960).

[15] This section is based on Chris Argyris, *Personality and Organization* (New York: Harper & Row, 1957).

[16] See, for example, C. West Churchman, Russel L. Ackoff, and Leonard Arnoff, *Introduction to Operations Research* (New York: Wiley, 1957).

[17] This case is originally reported in E. W. Savis, "The Political Properties of Crystalline H$_2$O: Planning for Snow Emergencies in New York," *Management Science,* Vol. 20, No. 2 (October 1973), pp. 137–145. The present version is from Barry Render and Ralph M. Stair, Jr., *Quantitative Analysis for Management* (Boston: Allyn and Bacon, 1982), pp. 4, 5. Used by permission.

[18] Schein, op. cit., p. 70.

[19] Chester I. Barnard, *The Functions of the Executive* (Cambridge: Harvard University Press, 1938), p. 65.

[20] See Ludwig von Bertalanffy, "The History and Status of General Systems Theory," *Academy of Management Journal,* Vol. 15 (December 1972), pp. 407–426; see also the discussion of his work in Daniel Katz and Robert L. Kahn, *The Social Psychology of Organizations,* Second Edition (New York: Wiley, 1978), pp. 8, 9.

[21] Adapted frm Louis E. Boone and David L. Kurtz, *Principles of Management* (New York: Random House, 1981), pp. 4, 5. Used by permission.

[22] See "Overcoming China's Management Gap," *NYU Business,* Vol. 1 (Winter 1982), pp. 26–27, 48; "Teaching Management to Marxists," *Fortune* (March 23, 1981), p. 102; A. J. Robinson, "Interviewing China's Bureaucratic Managers," *Wall Street Journal* (March 9, 1981), p. 16.

[23] "China Seeks a New Management Cadre," *Business Week* (June 16, 1980), pp. 142–147. Used by permission.

3

THE MANAGER AS DECISION MAKER AND PROBLEM SOLVER

THE MISADVENTURE
OF THE CHAIRMAN'S MOLEHILL

This really happened.[1]

Here's how a simple misunderstanding sent some $4 million gurgling away.

The molehill materialized in the executive dining room. Between sips of lobster bisque, the chairman wondered aloud, "Why don't we have a distribution facility in Springfield, Missouri? Isn't our biggest customer there?"

Ever alert for a possible whim of iron, an executive vice-president anxiously promised to look into the matter. The chairman's attention returned to his bisque. This was the last he would hear of Springfield for the next 16 months.

The word was passed. By afternoon, the chairman's remark was a tidal wave sweeping through executive country, swelling as it inundated successively lower levels.

"The chairman wants to know how come we don't have a distribution center in Springfield" became "Whose fault is it we don't distribute out of Springfield?" became "The chairman wants the Springfield operation set up pronto!"

So, of course, it was done. Not that anyone believed the investment was sound. A complete company distribution center, operating comfortably under capacity, already existed in nearby Kansas City. In fact, central Missouri was extremely well covered; Springfield would be absolutely redundant.

Land was bought at Springfield, a large structure was erected, an expensive inventory was installed, a crackerjack staff was assembled. The important local customer was flattered by the attention but puzzled as well. It had been perfectly content with overnight deliveries from its supplier's Kansas City depot. The Springfield facility opened without fanfare and, it was evident almost immediately, without business.

Cobwebs grew at Springfield. Anxiety grew even faster at headquarters. "The chairman's pet project is headed up the creek and so are we!" wailed the brass. "Make it work no matter what you have to do!" Failing and sometimes contradictory orders bombarded Springfield. Space was expanded, the stagnant inventory increased, a staff already developing gin-rummy addiction was beefed up.

As you'd expect, matters grew steadily worse. . . . Losses became so massive that the chairman would soon learn of the Shame of Springfield. Wrath was expected momentarily; titled heads would be a farthing to the bushel.

Actually, denoucement was a bit of a letdown. "Seen the Springfield numbers, Bill?" the chairman inquired.

"Uh, I have, Chief."

"Close it. Dumb idea in the first place. Somebody down there didn't do his homework. And Bill . . .?"

"Chief?"

"Keep me posted next time Operations is dreaming up a stunt like this. Looks like I'll have to filter the whole organization's thinking personally. . . ."

PLANNING AHEAD

The "Misadventure of the Chairman's Molehill" illustrates sincere managerial efforts gone astray. In fact, it appears that decisions and actions resulting from the president's dinner-table remarks created a problem where there originally was none! This chapter introduces key aspects of managerial decision making and problem solving. Key topics include:

Choice Making, Decision Making, Problem Solving
Managerial Problem Solving
The Problem-Solving Process
Finding and Identifying Problems
Formulating and Analyzing Alternative Solutions
Choosing Among Alternatives: Making the Decision
Implementing the Solution and Evaluating Results

Good managers locate problems to be solved, make decisions about appropriate solutions, and take action to utilize organizational resources to implement these solutions. This statement reflects an active approach to the managerial role. We might add an additional caveat that good managers solve the *right* problems. In the chapter-opening example, the executive vice-president and other subordinate managers took action to resolve what they mistakenly thought was a problem for the company—the absence of a distribution facility in Springfield, Missouri. It turns out the result was an error of costly proportions.

As a manager you will need problem-solving and decision-making skills. Furthermore, the organization context in which these skills are applied will challenge you in at least the following special respects.[2]

1. *Managers make decisions within the organization's hierarchy of authority.* The types of problems to be solved and decisions to be made will vary by managerial level.

2. *Managers make decisions for which other persons often have necessary and relevant information.* Managers will often become involved with groups of people in their decision-making and problem-solving efforts.

3. *Managers make decisions that often affect many or all elements of the organization as a total system.* Managers must be sensitive to different and sometimes conflicting priorities, and to prob-

lem definitions that may vary from one part of the system to another.

4. *Managers make decisions that are implemented by other people.* Managers typically depend on subordinates and other persons in the organization to implement their decisions; accordingly, the human dynamics associated with each and every decision made must be clearly understood.

The rest of this chapter introduces you to the key elements of decision making and problem solving in this special managerial context.

CHOICE MAKING, DECISION MAKING, PROBLEM SOLVING

Figure 3.1 identifies the range of managerial activities encompassed by three action terms—*choice making, decision making,* and *problem solving.* Because these terms are critical to managers' day-to-day activities and to the developing logic of this chapter, they should be clearly differentiated.

Choice Making

Choice making is the narrowest activity depicted in Figure 3.1. It is the process of evaluating and selecting among alternatives representing potential solutions to a problem. Managers make choices in various ways. Two of these, the eco-

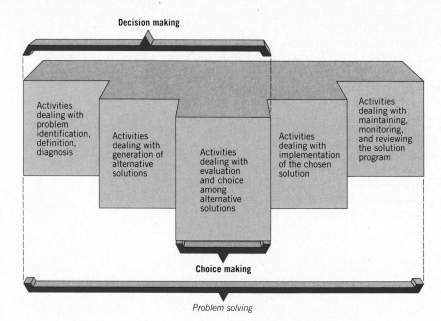

Decision making

Activities dealing with problem identification, definition, diagnosis

Activities dealing with generation of alternative solutions

Activities dealing with evaluation and choice among alternative solutions

Activities dealing with implementation of the chosen solution

Activities dealing with maintaining, monitoring, and reviewing the solution program

Choice making

Problem solving

FIGURE 3.1 Choice making, decision making, and problem solving. (*Source:* From *Managerial Decision Making* by George P. Huber. Copyright © 1980, Scott, Foresman and Company, p. 8. Reprinted by permission.)

nomic/rational and "satisficing" models of choice making, will be discussed in some detail in this chapter. Also to be explored are the differences between making the final choice in any given situation by individual, consultative, and group approaches.

Decision Making

Of the three terms, **decision making** may be the most familiar to you. Figure 3.1 shows that decision making is a more encompassing concept than choice making, but less encompassing than problem solving. It includes all activities ranging from the identification of a problem through the actual choice of a preferred solution. We will treat decision making in its broader context as part of the essential problem-solving process.

Problem Solving

Problem solving is the process of identifying a discrepancy between an actual and desired state of affairs and then taking action to resolve the discrepancy. Creativity is a major element in problem solving. It takes creativity to locate or find the right problems; it takes creativity to choose good solutions; it takes creativity to implement these solutions in a productive way.

Every manager's action responsibilities require a continued ability to solve problems through decision making and effective choices. Creativity, insight, and skill are required every step of the way.

MANAGERIAL PROBLEM SOLVING

A **problem** exists whenever there is a difference between an *actual* situation and a *desired* situation.[3] A checkbook that fails to balance at the end of the month represents a problem, given that a balanced checkbook is a desired state of affairs. Similarly, a problem exists when turnover or absenteeism increases in a manager's work unit, when performance falls for a particular subordinate, or when one's superior communicates dissatisfaction with something the manager has said or done. Each of these circumstances represents a less than totally desirable situation.

The challenge to the manager in each of the prior cases is to proceed with effective problem solving. The quality of managerial problem solving in the context of planning, organizing, leading, and controlling directly influences organizational productivity. Any manager's decisions impact the organization, and as a manager you should feel a sense of responsibility for the or-

CUBIST PROFITS
Ideal Toy Rebounds with Rubik

Lionel A. Weintraub, 61, chairman of Ideal Toy Corp., has yet to figure out the solution to Rubik's cube. But he's having no trouble figuring out the bottom-line effect of the cube, which has put his company squarely in the black. Ideal Toy, headquartered in Hollis, New York, expects to sell more than ten million cubes in the fiscal year that ends on January 29, 1982, boosting revenues by $40 million to an estimated $210 million. Earnings will reach an all-time high of at least $9 million, a wide swing from a net loss of $15.5 million in the previous fiscal year.

Ideal Toy stumbled onto its salvation. Weintraub picked up the U.S. rights to manufacture Rubik's cube (named for its inventor, Erno Rubik, a Hungarian architecture professor) two years ago, after several big American toy makers turned it down. He hasn't always been so lucky. His company's Evel Knievel line of toys bombed when the stuntman was jailed for beating a former press agent with a baseball bat.

Source: "Cubist Profits: Ideal Toy Rebounds with Rubik," Fortune (January 11, 1982), pp. 7, 8. © 1982 Time Inc. Courtesy of Fortune Magazine.

LAKER'S MAYDAY
An Upstart Airline Crashes

Freddie Laker is a British entrepreneur whose ideas regarding transatlantic air travel led to a great success in the beginning. Then problems set in and Laker made a key miscalculation. *Time* captures the story in its essential detail.[2]

Launched in 1966 as a charter carrier, Laker Airways jolted competitors in 1977 with its Skytrain round-trip service between New York and London for $236, or almost $200 less than the best excursion fare available on regularly scheduled airlines. Beamed Laker: "This puts transatlantic air travel in the pocket of the workingman." Later many other carriers matched his low prices.

. . . The Skytrain was so popular and profitable that in the next two years Laker, who owns 90 percent of the airline, borrowed $359 million to expand his fleet of DC-10s and Airbus A300s with the intention of adding new services between European and Asian capitals. Then trouble struck. Fuel prices surged, recession in the U.S. and Europe cut into passenger traffic, and the rise of the dollar's value against the pound upset Laker's balance sheet. Much of his revenue was in pounds, but he had to make debt payments in dollars.

. . . Sir Freddie, who was knighted by Queen Elizabeth in June 1978, tried in vain to get help. He phoned Iain Sproat, Britain's Under-Secretary for Trade, to warn that without government aid, his airline would crash. Later that day Prime Minister Margaret Thatcher discussed Laker's plight with several Cabinet members, but chose not to bail out the carrier. Early next morning, at a tense meeting with his board of directors at Gatwick, Laker called it quits.

Source: "Kerosene's Rising Sun," Time (February 1, 1982), p. 60; "Laker's Mayday," Time (February 15, 1982), p. 51. Used by permission.

ganization's success. *Newsline 3.1* demonstrates the full weight of this responsibility as it affected Lionel Weintraub and Freddie Laker—two managers whose decisions affected their companies in quite different ways.

Problem-Solving Skills

Managers must be skilled at both finding and solving problems that threaten to impair productivity in the workplace, or that offer opportunities to improve productivity in the future. There are two good reasons for you to develop these problem-solving skills. First, people vary in their responses to problem solving as a basic managerial responsibility. Managers can fall into three categories of action.[4]

1. *Problem avoiders* Those whose need for certainty leads them to ignore information that would otherwise signal the presence of a problem.
2. *Problem solvers* Those who act to solve problems when they arise—that is, who are good at reacting to a defined problem.
3. *Problem seekers* Those who look for problems to solve or opportunities to exploit as a matter of routine—that is, who are proactive in anticipating and solving problems before they occur.

Although there will be times when problem avoidance is an appropriate managerial response, managers must be able to react well and solve problems when they arise. Ultimately, too, success at problem seeking may well distinguish the exceptional managers from the merely good ones. Problem seekers are forward-thinking managers who anticipate problems and opportunities and take appropriate action, rather than wait for problems to develop and suddenly present themselves. Robert Taylor, president of Minnetonka, Inc., recognized in the early 1970s that its Village Bath product line might reach its maximum potential in the mid-1970s. Village Bath toiletries include soap balls, bubble baths, bath oils, and shampoos sold primarily through gift shops and drugstores. Taylor realized that he needed a new product line to serve as a vehicle for growth. The result was Softsoap, a pump-dispensed liquid hand soap. By 1981 Softsoap was one of the best-selling hand soaps in the world.[5]

The second reason to develop your problem-solving skills is that the results of any decisions you make can have a direct impact on your career. Problems well solved can bring special reward and recognition that includes higher salary, promotions, special privileges, and other career advancement opportunities. Poor problem-solving decisions, by contrast, can cause personal dissatisfaction and the loss of such benefits.

Problem-Solving Styles

Managers differ in their problem-solving styles. Two extremes are the systematic and intuitive thinker. Although each style can be successful in a given situation, there are basic differences between the two. A **systematic thinker** approaches problems in a rational and analytical fashion. This person is able to break a complex problem into smaller components and then address them in a logical and integrated fashion. An **intuitive thinker** is more flexible and spontaneous. This person is likely to respond imaginatively to a problem, based on a quick and broad overview of the situation and possible alternative courses of action. How about you? Are you more systematic or intuitive in problem solving?[6]

Systematic Thinkers Tend To

Make a plan for solving a problem.

Be very conscious of their approach.

Define the specific constraints of the problem early in the process.

Discard alternatives only after careful analysis.

Conduct an ordered search for additional information.

Complete any discrete step in analysis that they begin.

Intuitive Thinkers Tend To

Keep the overall problem continuously in mind.

Rely on unverbalized cues, even hunches.

Defend the solution in terms of fit.

Which problem-solving style works best with Rubik's cube—systematic or intuitive thinking?

Consider a number of alternatives and options simultaneously.

Jump from one step in analysis or search to another and back again.

Explore and abandon alternatives very quickly.

There is growing research evidence that a person's strength in each of these problem-solving styles relates to the utilization of the right and left hemispheres of the brain.[7] The right hemisphere is now recognized to control intuition. It is the center for creative thinking and artistic talents. The left hemisphere, by contrast, controls the more analytical and logical thought processes associated with systematic problem solving. Since the evidence also suggests most people are left-brain dominant, and therefore stronger in systematic or analytical thinking, special care may have to be exercised to develop one's intuitive-creative capabilities to their fullest potential.

We will return to this issue of creativity and intuition at other times in the book. It is some-thing you should think seriously about in an effort to maximize your potential for managerial success. Think, too, about the possibility that you may be right- or left-brain dominant. As a manager there will be times when you will have to and want to react quickly to problems on the basis of intuition alone. There are other times when only the power of systematic problem-solving can accomplish the job. True success in meeting the manager's challenge in today's dynamic and complex environment depends on an ability to use both problem-solving styles well. Personal discipline and self-development efforts may be required to enhance your capabilities with the style associated with your less dominant side.

Each problem-solving style has advantages and disadvantages. As you consider moving back and forth between them, remember:

1. **Intuitive problem solving** tends to be quick and less complex in terms of the number of people involved in decision making, but it runs the risk of good solutions being ignored and failure to consider all aspects of the problem.

2. **Systematic problem solving** tends to be thorough and more balanced as the ideas of many persons are taken into account, but it can be time consuming and costly in terms of the number of persons involved.

Problem Solving and the Managerial Functions

Figure 3.2 shows the centrality of the problem-solving process to each of the four basic managerial functions. No manager can avoid making decisions that address day-to-day problems which arise in each of these contexts. In fact, a useful way to approach this book is to ask what you can learn about these functions and the environment of management in order to do well when the inevitable problems actually occur. Table 3.1 gives examples of problem-solving decisions you should be prepared to make in the process of planning, organizing, leading, and controlling for productivity. Later parts of the book allow you to examine these and other issues in detail.

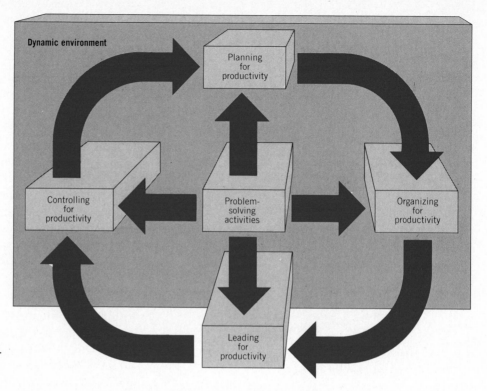

Dynamic environment

Planning for productivity

Controlling for productivity

Problem-solving activities

Organizing for productivity

Leading for productivity

FIGURE 3.2 Problem solving and the management functions.

Table 3.1 Some Problem-Solving Decisions Faced by Managers

Planning for Productivity

What is the mission of my organization or work unit?
What should our objectives be?
What are my objectives?
What changes are occurring in the environment?
How should our strategy be revised to achieve future success in this environment?

Organizing for Productivity

How should the organizational division of labor be accomplished?
How can coordination among multiple parts of the organization be accomplished?
What decisions can be made at each managerial level?
What staffing needs exist for the various jobs?
How can we train people to function best with new technologies?

Leading for Productivity

What can be done to achieve higher levels of individual and group task performance?
What can be done to reduce turnover and absenteeism?
What needs do my subordinates have?
Why has satisfaction decreased among my subordinates?
How can I help to resolve conflicts among my subordinates?

Controlling for Productivity

How can performance be measured?
Who should measure performance and how often?
What information systems are needed?
Why haven't we achieved our objectives?
What can be done to increase performance in the future?

THE PROBLEM-SOLVING PROCESS

Forthcoming ideas and guidelines apply the more technical elements of problem solving in the managerial context just described. We begin with the five major steps in the problem-solving process diagrammed in Figure 3.3.

Steps in Problem Solving

The problem-solving process underlies all managerial behavior. It encompasses continuing responsibility for gathering information that may indicate the presence of an actual or potential problem. The process includes specific responsibility for

1. Problem identification.
2. Generation of alternative solutions.
3. Selection of a preferred solution.
4. Implementation of the preferred solution.
5. Evaluation of results.

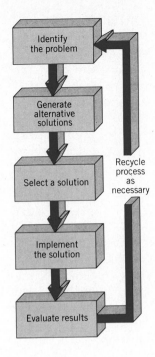

FIGURE 3.3 The problem-solving process.

Step 1

Identify the problem. In the first stage of the problem-solving process the manager is concerned with finding and identifying the problem. Questions to be asked include: "What is the *actual* situation? "What is the *desired* situation?" "What is the *cause* of the difference?" This is a stage of information gathering, information processing, and deliberation. It often begins with the appearance of *symptoms* indicating the presence of a problem. The manager's goal is to assess a situation properly and look beyond symptoms to find out what is wrong. In so doing, special care must be taken not to confuse symptom and problem. A crucial mistake is to solve a symptom while ignoring the true problem. Merely reprimanding a subordinate for absenteeism, for example, might never solve the real problem of dissatisfaction with a new job assignment.

Step 2

Generate alternative solutions. Once the problem is identified, it is possible to formulate one or more potential solutions. Creativity is extremely important in this stage of problem solving. Information is gathered, data analyzed, and the pros and cons of possible alternative courses of action

established. Additional information is gathered where appropriate. This effort to identify, clarify, and evaluate alternative solutions is critical to any problem-solving effort. The end result can only be as good as the quality of the alternative solutions generated in this step.

Step 3

Select a preferred solution. This is the point of choice. Given the alternatives, along with the pros and cons of each, a manager can choose a preferred course of action. The questions of how and by whom this final choice is made must be successfully resolved in each problem situation. In some cases the manager alone should make the choice; in others a group approach might be best. In some cases, the best alternative may be selected on a cost-benefit criterion; in others, additional criteria may enter into play. These issues will be examined in some detail shortly.

Step 4

Implement the solution. Given the preferred solution, appropriate action plans can be established for its implementation. This is a point of action initiation and direction setting. It is also a time when the manager must have the support of other key persons whose efforts will actually implement the solution as chosen. People will be more diligent and thorough in helping to implement decisions they accept—and therefore to which they are committed. Thus the degree to which these persons have or have not been involved in the prior steps may substantially affect the success of the total problem-solving process. A good alternative that is arrived at improperly may end up poorly implemented and ineffective in the final result!

Step 5

Evaluate Results. The problem-solving process remains incomplete unless the manager checks to ensure that after the intended actions are taken, the desired and actual situations are finally one and the same. That is, true problem solving includes establishing an information system to evaluate results and allow for the process to be recycled as necessary.

Illustrative Case:
Columbia Decides to Go Coed[8]

During the 1970s, many of America's institutions of higher education turned coed for the first time in their histories. Columbia University was one that long held out as a school for men only. But the president of Columbia, Michael Sovern, identified a problem: in recent years applicants had drastically fallen off from the desired levels. Columbia's drawing power was down. Finally, it broke with tradition and Sovern announced that the college would begin accepting female students in 1983. His steps in reaching this decision may have proceeded as follows.

Step 1

Identify the problem. Actual number of applicants increasingly less than desired number; fewer high-school graduates seeking college educations.

Step 2

Generate alternative solutions. Many things could be done, including:

A. Lower admission standards.
B. Open admissions to female applicants.
C. Reduce tuition and fees.

Step 3

Select a preferred solution. Of the alternatives, B seems most consistent with institutional constraints and offers substantial chance of impact on the problem.

Step 4

Implement the solution. Sovern announces that the necessary changes in admissions policy will be in place by fall 1983.

Step 5

Evaluate results. Some system must be established to compare what happens to the applicant pool once female admissions are allowed (i.e., determine if original problem successfully resolved).

Clearly, President Sovern of Columbia recognized the existence of a problem and instituted the steps necessary to attempt its resolution. The final solution reflects more systematic than intuitive thinking. Sovern doesn't appear to be a problem avoider; instead, he seems to have acted well as a problem solver. But we still might argue that he could have been more proactive in anticipating the problem of enrollment declines and acting to avoid them before the actual trend set in. Then and only then could he be considered a true problem seeker.

FINDING AND
IDENTIFYING PROBLEMS

Problem finding involves identifying gaps between actual and desired states and determining their causes. These gaps may represent performance deficiencies or unexplored opportunities. The manger who is good at finding problems to be solved is continually searching and scanning the work environment for indicators of potential problems or opportunities. This is an ongoing information-gathering and processing responsibility. Four of the methods that assist managers in this essential stage of the problem-solving process are:[9]

1. *Examining deviations from past experience* When a previous and satisfactory pattern of performance is interrupted, the manager has a good signal that a problem might exist.

Table 3.2 Problem Finding: The Case of Laker Airways

Newsline 3.1 discusses the failure of Laker Airways, a failure based in part on Freddie Laker's decision to purchase new planes in a declining world economy. Laker might have been able to anticipate the problems before they occurred by acting as follows.

1. He could have examined deviations from past experience.	Laker Airways surely maintained historical data on costs, passenger usage, and revenues. Trends could well have been detected in these data that showed increasing costs, decreasing revenues, and declining transatlantic customers.
2. He could have examined deviations from plans.	If Laker Airways had specific objectives for such things as passenger loads and revenues, actual performance could have regularly been compared to these objectives. As soon as a gap between objectives and actual performance appeared, steps could have been taken to answer the question "Why?"
3. He could have listened to other people.	When deciding whether or not to make a major investment in new planes, Laker could have been extra diligent in gathering reactions to his proposals. A special task force could have been established to act as devil's advocate arguing against the investment; customer surveys of future travel plans could have been taken.
4. He could have better analyzed the competition.	Other airlines surely faced similar economic pressures. By carefully watching their behavior, Laker might have realized that he should move more cautiously with capital investments in new planes—or not at all.

2. *Examining deviations from plans* When results are falling short of projections, the chances are that one or more problems might exist.

3. *Speaking with other people* Peers, subordinates, or higher-level managers within the organization, as well as outsiders such as customers and resource suppliers, can be the source of problem-identifying information.

4. *Watching the performance of other organizations or subunits* The performance of other organizations, especially competitors, can be a good indicator of how well the organization is doing. By the same token, the performance of other subunits within an organization can provide similar insight to the manager regarding his or her subunit's achievements.

These four aids to managerial problem finding are further described in Table 3.2. The example is based on the failure of Laker Airways, a popular cut-rate air service between the United States and Europe, which we first introduced in *Newsline 3.1*.

Types of Managerial Problems

Managers face problems of both personal and organizational foundations. *Newsline 3.2* is a reminder that the "personal" problems of employees often have organizational implications. Most problems can also be classified as routine or nonroutine and as expected or unexpected.

Routine and Nonroutine Problems

Routine problems arise on a regular basis and can be addressed through standard responses. Called **programmed decisions**, these responses implement specific solutions determined by past experience as appropriate for the problem at hand. Good examples of programmed decisions are to reorder inventory automatically when on-hand stock falls below a predetermined level, to place students on probation when they fall below a certain grade-point average, or to initiate an IRS audit when charitable contributions reported on an income tax return exceed a certain limit.

Nonroutine problems are unique and new. Because standard responses are not available, they call for a creative process of problem solving specifically tailored to the situation at hand. Because they have not been encountered before, nonroutine problems have no set solutions. They involve **nonprogrammed decisions** implementing a creative solution. Considerable attention will be devoted in the sections that follow to this nonroutine side of problem solving.

NEWSLINE 3.2

PROBLEMS OF DUAL CAREER PROFESSIONAL FAMILIES AFFECT ORGANIZATIONS

Six months after he joined the major Chicago bank, the 31-year-old banker was offered the kind of job that could make his career: the chance to start and head the brand-new European branch of his department.

Regretfully, he turned it down.

He explains that his wife has a top professional post with a "Big Eight" accounting firm, a job that would be hard, if not impossible, to duplicate in London. "It came down to my wife and her job. I would have gone if it wasn't for that," he says.

He admits to having second thoughts, especially since he hopes to head the department someday. While superiors "talked a good story and said, 'we'll think of you again,' I do wonder, if anything else comes up, would they offer it to me?" he says.

Source: Excerpted from Liz Roman Gallese, "Manager's Journal," *Wall Street Journal,* July 23, 1979, p. 16. Reprinted by permission of the Wall Street Journal. Copyright © 1979 Dow Jones & Company, Inc. All rights reserved.

Expected and Unexpected Problems

Another way to view managerial problems is as expected or unexpected. **Expected problems** are anticipated as situations that will require decisions sometime in the future. For example, a typical manager may be expected to make decisions periodically on staff salary and promotion recommendations, vacation-request approvals, and committee assignments. It may be less easy to plan ahead for decisions arising from an unexplained employee absence, equipment breakdown, or a raw-materials shortage. These **unexpected problems** are, rightly or wrongly, not anticipated. They are addressed by reaction after their occurrence.

Astute managers can often establish programs or decision routines that handle "unexpected" problems falling into categories of events that really can be anticipated to some extent. Among the prior examples, consider the unexpected employee absence. Although it might not have been predicted that a specific employee would be absent on any given day, it might be anticipated that at times various employees may be absent. A procedure or rule could be established to handle these "unexpected" but now "anticipated" absences when they occur. In the example, a standby list of temporary substitute workers might be maintained for use as needed.

Newsline 3.3 describes an unexpected problem that can't be anticipated—crisis! Crises occur by surprise, and crisis decisions must be made under considerable stress, pressure, and often unusual circumstances. It may well be that the ability to handle crisis successfully is the ultimate test of a manager's problem-solving capabilities. Continental Airlines's president Alexander Damm, as described in the newsline, used a group approach to the crisis. He might have just as easily opted to respond on his own. This important choice of who should be involved in the decision is one we will consider shortly.

Problems at Various Managerial Levels

It is helpful to recognize that the types of problems faced by managers can vary somewhat across levels in the hierarchy. Higher-level man-

CATASTROPHE DEMANDS RAPID DECISION MAKING

Unforeseen events have a way of cropping up and undoing the best-laid plans of management. An example is the May 25, 1979, crash of an American Airlines DC10. Diagnosing the cause to be cracks in the engine pylons, the Federal Aviation Administration (FAA) ordered all 137 of the nation's DC10s grounded. The *Wall Street Journal* reported the plight of one major U.S. Airline as follows.

A look at Continental gives a glimpse of the problems that have had to be considered by all the airlines with DC10 fleets. Among the topics demanding urgent decisions: how to reroute aircraft to fill the service gaps left by the idled jumbos; how to help stranded ticket holders; what advertisements to kill; what employees to lay off; and who, if anyone, could be sued to recover the huge damages resulting from the lost business.

There were no precedents to follow; never before had the government taken such sweeping action. The grounding came without warning.

Continental president Alexander Damm summoned his top executives to a 5 A.M. meeting; chairman Robert Six was abroad. In shirtsleeves (at that early hour the air conditioning hadn't kicked on), the executives considered Continental's plight.

The grounding put Continental in special jeopardy. Over the years it has reduced its fleet to two planes, 15 DC10s and 55 Boeing 727s. Due to their larger size, the DC10s have some 41 percent of Continental's seats.

Until the crisis, the Continental fleet had been considered a model of streamlining; suddenly the asset of greater efficiency turned into a liability. United Airlines, for instance, still has jumbo Boeing 747s in its fleet, and Western Air Lines has Boeing 707s operating.

So, although both these competitors had lost their DC10s, they still could run long-range flights. The Continental executives immediately had to acknowledge the obvious: Service from the West Coast to Hawaii and the South Pacific had to be halted. The 727s don't have the range for such flights.

Contributing to the drain are painful personnel problems. The shutdown had idled almost 400 pilots of the airline's wide-body jets. These tend to be senior men, earning up to $80,000 and more a year, and they can't be laid off.

Source: Excerpted from Roy J. Harriss, Jr., "Winging It," *Wall Street Journal,* June 15, 1979, p. 1. Reprinted by permission of the Wall Street Journal. Copyright © 1979 Dow Jones & Company, Inc. All rights reserved.

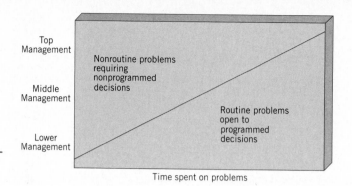

FIGURE 3.4 Types of problems at various management levels.

Top Management

Middle Management

Lower Management

Nonroutine problems requiring nonprogrammed decisions

Routine problems open to programmed decisions

Time spent on problems

agers generally spend a greater proportion of their time on nonroutine problems, while lower-level managers are more involved with routine problems open to more programmed decisions. The nonprogrammed decisions of higher-level managers typically have a major impact on the organization's overall performance potential. Figure 3.4 summarizes how problems vary in general across managerial levels in organizations.

Barriers to Accurate Problem Identification

The chapter opener, "The Misadventure of the Chairman's Molehill," offers a classic example of problem misidentification. What the chairman's assistants defined as the problem was in error. They viewed the problem as the lack of a distribution center in Springfield, Missouri. As a result, the alternative of not opening a center in Springfield was never considered.

The way a problem is originally defined has a major impact on the success of the later steps in the problem-solving process. Some problems need to be considered vis-à-vis the possibility of simply doing nothing at all. The test to be applied is: "What would happen if nothing whatsoever were done?" In the case of the Springfield distribution center, this indeed would have been the best course of action. Unfortunately, the way the problem was originally defined prevented it from being recognized as a bona fide alternative.[10] What follows are three common sources of error with special potential to interfere with problem identification as the initial stage of the problem-solving process.

Defining the Problem Too Broadly or Too Narrowly

It is easy to jump into a situation and define the problem too broadly or too narrowly. To take a classic example, the problem stated as "build a better mousetrap," might better be defined as "get rid of the mice." The latter definition opens a variety of alternative ideas otherwise eliminated by the objective of modifying or simply improving existing mousetraps. Another informative example is found in the case of large-scale tomato farmers.[11]

> Plagued by an unacceptably high rate of damage to the delicate fruit by mechanical harvesters, tomato farmers defined their problem as a deficiency in the design of the harvesters. Unsuccessful years of improving the harvesters went by before someone redefined the problem as lying, not with the harvesters, but with the tomato itself. The result: Horticulturists came up with a new hybrid tomato that was easier to pick and that had tougher skin, thus greatly reducing harvester damage to the tomato.

Focus on Symptoms Instead of Causes

Symptoms alert managers to problems. They are indicators of underlying causes, but should not be construed as the causes themselves. Managers who are good problem solvers know what symptoms to look for in work situations and how to understand what they find. For example, physicians are carefully trained in this process. During a physical exam the doctor systematically asks questions and is quick to note where one symptom (e.g., a recurrent sore on a finger) may be indicative of a true problem that requires further medical attention (e.g., treatment for a small skin cancer). Further diagnostic work and possible medical treatments follow.

Managers need similar diagnostic and action abilities. Instead of sores and headaches, the manager's problem indicators include such things as absenteeism, turnover, tardiness, negative attitudes, poor-quality work, and declining work quantity on the part of employees. These problem symptoms are among the many issues encompassed in the study of management. Just as every qualified physician has been schooled in the medical sciences, so too should the practicing manager be schooled in management as a basis for rigorous and systematic problem finding and diagnostic efforts.

Selective Perception

Persons in organizations have a tendency to define problems from their own points of view. We call this **selective perception.** Unfortunately, selective perception can lead to biased or only partial problem definitions. It often occurs, for example, when persons of various technical or functional backgrounds tackle the same problem. The likelihood in a business setting is that marketing, production, and finance specialists may define a problem in terms of their respective areas of expertise. This is one reason why good managers always take steps to test alternative points of view on a given problem situation to ensure that the best definition of the problem is achieved.

GENERATING AND ANALYZING ALTERNATIVE SOLUTIONS

Once a problem is identified, problem solving requires the formulation and analysis of alternative potential solutions. This is a time for creativity in generating ideas or possible solutions and in determining which of them offer solutions most likely to solve the problem.

As a manager you will be especially challenged in this step by nonroutine problems–ones that appear unexpectedly and with unique characteristics. These are the problems that test your right-brain and intuitive/artistic capabilities. Finding a good solution to them will always require something extra on your part. That something extra is **creativity,** an application of ingenuity and imagination that results in a novel approach or unique solution to a problem.

Before investigating creativity as something that helps managers formulate and analyze alternative solutions to problems, take a little test.

Some consultants and consulting firms specialize in seminars designed to enhance the creativity of managers and business executives.

Each of the following puzzles actually symbolizes a familiar word or phrase. Solving each requires you to be creative in looking at things with a fresh and unrestrained eye. See how well you do–the answers will come later.[12]

1	SAND	2	MIND	3	O	4	DICE
			MATTER		M.D.		DICE
					PH.D.		
					D.D.D.		

Creativity in Problem Solving

The greater the creativity that can be brought to bear on a problem, the more alternative solutions of potential value that are likely to be considered and the greater the likelihood that they will be rigorously evaluated. A lack of creativity constrains problem solving and can compromise the quality of any solutions achieved. Table 3.3 lists some of the things managers can do to ensure creative problem solving. The list includes ideas to prevent going off on the wrong track and to help get back on the right track once this has already happened.

Individual Creativity

Let's look back to your earlier problem-solving efforts with the word and symbol puzzles. The correct answers are (1) "sandbox," (2) "mind over matter," (3) "three degrees below zero," and (4) "paradise." Just as the puzzles now look easier

in retrospect, creativity is something that can be enhanced through discipline and good managerial judgment. To stimulate individual creativity one must overcome[13]

1. *Perceptual blocks*   The confusion of important and insignificant data; an inability to "see the forest through the trees."
2. *Cultural blocks*   Taboos and traditions that guide thinking.
3. *Emotional blocks*   Internalized fears of making a mistake or being criticized if "wrong."
4. *Intellectual blocks*   Language or symbolic inadequacies.

Blocks such as these can impair individual creativity in the problem-solving process. As a result good alternatives may fail to be discovered or considered, and poor ones may be selected for implementation merely because they are readily available. The precepts in Table 3.3 can help you avoid such blocks and improve individual creativity. A willingness to take advantage of the group as a problem-solving resource can help as well.

Group Techniques to Improve Creativity in Problem Solving

Groups can be of great help to managers in the alternative-generation phase of the problem-solving process. Two useful approaches for bringing the capabilities of groups to bear on problems are

Table 3.3 Precepts for Creative Problem Solving

To Prevent Going Off on the Wrong Track

Run over the elements of the problem in rapid succession several times until a pattern emerges.

Suspend judgment; don't jump to conclusions.

Explore the environment; vary the temporal and spatial arrangement of the problem's elements.

To Get Back On the Right Track

Produce another solution after the first has been found.

Critically evaluate your own ideas; constructively evaluate those of others.

When stuck, change your representational system (e.g., if you have been thinking about a problem in verbal terms, try using graphs instead).

Take a break when you are stuck.

Talk about your problem with someone.

Source: Ray Hyman and Barry Anderson, "Solving Problems," *Science and Technology* (September 1965), pp. 36–41. Used by permission.

the brainstorming and nominal group techniques.

In **brainstorming**, groups of five to ten members meet to generate ideas. Four rules typically govern the process.[14]

1. *All criticism is ruled out.* Judgment or evaluation of ideas must be withheld until the idea-generation process has been completed.
2. *"Freewheeling" is welcomed.* The wilder or more radical the idea, the better.
3. *Quantity is wanted.* The greater the number of ideas, the greater the likelihood of obtaining a superior idea.
4. *Combination and improvement are sought.* Participants should suggest how ideas of others can be turned into better ideas, or how two or more ideas can be joined into still another idea.

By prohibiting evaluation, brainstorming reduces fears of criticism or failure on the part of individuals. Typical results include enthusiasm, involvement, and a freer flow of ideas. Researchers consider brainstorming techniques superior to open group discussions as a basis for creative thinking and the generation of possible solutions to identified problems.[15]

There will be times when the persons whose help is needed in problem solving have differing opinions and goals such that antagonistic argument can be predicted for a group meeting. In such cases, a nominal group technique could be more appropriate than brainstorming. In a **nominal group** the following rules apply.[16]

1. Participants work alone and respond in writing with alternative solutions to a stated problem.
2. These ideas are then read aloud in round-robin fashion without any criticism or discussion.
3. The ideas are recorded on large newsprint as they are read aloud.
4. The ideas are then discussed individually in round-robin sequence for purposes of clarification only; evaluative comments are not allowed.
5. A written voting procedure is followed; it re-

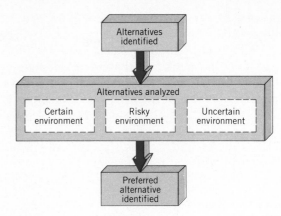

FIGURE 3.5 Three environmental conditions under which problem alternatives can be analyzed.

sults in a rank ordering of the alternatives in terms of priority.

6. Steps 4 and 5 are repeated as desired to add further clarification to the process.

The final voting procedure allows alternatives to be explicitly evaluated under the nominal group technique, without risking the inhibitions, hostilities, and distorted outcomes that may accompany antagonistic or more open and unstructured meeting formats. Thus nominal grouping can aid problem solving by improving the processes of both generating and evaluating alternative solutions.

Problem Conditions or Environments

Figure 3.5 describes three different conditions or environments under which problem-solving decisions are made—certainty, risk, and uncertainty. The degree of certainty associated with the expected outcomes of various alternatives has a definite impact on the manager's problem-solving efforts. Ultimately, a manager's problem-solving decisions are made under each of these environmental conditions. As managers tackle the more complex and nonroutine problems characteristic of higher levels of responsibility, the degree of uncertainty associated with decision making increases.

Certain Environments

Certainty exists in the problem environment when information is sufficient to predict the results of each alternative in advance of implementation. When one invests money in a savings account, absolute certainty exists as to the interest that will be earned on that money in a given period of time. Certainty is an ideal condition for managerial problem solving. The challenge is simply to locate the alternative offering a satisfactory or even ideal solution. Unfortunately, certainty is the exception instead of the rule in the managerial decision environment.

Risky Environments

Risk involves a lack of complete certainty regarding the outcomes of various courses of action, but an awareness of the probabilities associated with their occurrence. A **probability,** in turn, is the degree of likelihood that an event will occur. Probabilities are usually expressed as percentages, or as a number of chances out of ten. It is common, for example, to hear students estimating the probability of getting an A on their exams. One student might refer to an 80 percent probability of an A; another calls the same likelihood an eight-out-of-ten chance.

Probabilities can be assigned through objective statistical procedures or through managerial intuition. Statistical estimates of quality rejects in various size production runs can be made; a senior production manager, on the other hand, can make similar estimates based on past experience. Risk is a fairly common decision environment faced by managers. *Newsline 3.4* describes how Ford Motor Company executives faced a risky environment in their decision to solve a sales problem by offering a new compact car to American consumers.

Uncertain Environments

When managers are unable even to assign probabilities to the outcomes attached to various problem-solving alternatives, **uncertainty** exists. This is the most difficult of the three environments. Uncertainty forces managers to rely heavily on individual and group creativity to succeed in problem solving. It requires unique, novel, and often totally innovative alternatives to existing patterns of behavior. Responses to uncertainty are based on intuition, educated guess, and

hunch. When the Ideal Toy Company purchased marketing rights for the unusual puzzle we now know as Rubik's Cube, a "hunch" paid off handsomely!

Techniques for Analyzing Alternatives

Each of the three decision environments poses a different challenge to managers. Problem solving under certainty is the best of all worlds. Use of a basic inventory of alternatives can ensure that all pertinent issues are considered. Risky and uncertain environments demand more complex treatment. Decision trees and decision matrices or payoff tables can assist in these more difficult problem-solving conditions.

Inventory of Alternatives

Let's work with a case.[17] You are the manufacturing manager for a small company. Tracing a problem of increasing quality rejects leads you to a faulty machine. Four alternatives are now before you.

1. Repair the machine.
2. Replace the machine with a reconditioned one.
3. Replace the machine with a new but identical model.
4. Replace the machine with a new, more modern model.

This is a problem for which you can gather and analyze alternatives with a lot of certainty. The major challenge is to make sure that all possible issues are considered and that the facts are accurate. An **inventory of alternatives** lists each alternative and summarizes favorable and unfavorable points of each, including anticipated costs and benefits. Then **cost-benefit analysis** can be applied to compare the costs and benefits of all alternative courses of action with one another.

The inventory of alternatives shown in Table 3.4 (which appears on page 84) was prepared for the prior problem. With the information displayed in such form, your decision as the manufacturing manager in this case should be made with greater confidence that all relevant things have been considered.

NEWSLINE 3.4

FORD AWAITS THE PAYOFF ON ITS 4-YEAR GAMBLE ON NEW COMPACT CAR

All across the continent Ford Motor Co. is gearing up for the May 26 launching of its new compact car.

The activity is a last-minute flurry in the long and complicated process of introducing a new car. Ford, in fact, has been hard at work for more than four years on the new model, to be sold as the Ford Tempo and the Mercury Topaz, with little difference between the two versions. The undertaking has involved thousands of people and an investment of more than $1 billion.

During these tumultuous years, Ford engineers, designers, and marketing experts have made countless decisions about what they expect consumers to want in a compact car for the rest of this decade. They won't know for at least six months after the Tempo and Topaz go on sale whether their decisions were essentially correct.

"The risks we take are huge," says Erick Reickert, the Ford executive responsible for planning the Tempo. "There are thousands of decisions that go into a car, and we're trying to predict a market that's years away."

Ford and other auto makers, of course, do everything they can to minimize the risks. They analyze sales statistics to see what features are popular with consumers, and they tear apart competitors' cars to see how they work. They also talk to consumers, using market-research tools such as "focus groups," panels of people asked to bare their innermost thoughts about cars.

But for all that, a look at some Ford decisions during the four-year gestation of the Tempo and how the new cars will be presented to the public shows that the process isn't always especially scientific. Executives often are forced to trust their instincts. Top executives sometimes reverse subordinates' decisions on a seeming whim. And while some disputes are settled through compromise, other decisions are based on which department has the most clout. In the end, the decisions will mean the difference between success and failure of the new cars.

Source: Excerpted from Douglas R. Sease, "Dealer's Turn: Ford Awaits the Payoff on its 4-Year Gamble on New Compact Car," *Wall Street Journal* (May 4, 1983), p. 1. Reprinted by permission of the *Wall Street Journal*. Copyright © 1983 Dow Jones & Company, Inc. All rights reserved.

Decision Trees

A **decision tree** graphically illustrates the alternatives available to a manager attempting to solve a problem. It assists in the careful analysis of multiple courses of action. Consider another example.[18] The president of Emperor Products Corporation has a problem. The firm is experiencing increased sales. The director of marketing wants to add additional production capacity to keep pace with demand; the company treasurer is more cautious and wants to meet demand for the short term by increased overtime. Neither the alternative of the marketing director nor the one of the company treasurer offers entirely certain outcomes. What should the president do?

In actual fact, she called the treasurer and marketing director to a meeting. They discussed the recent rise in sales and discussed what might

Table 3.4 Inventory of Alternatives: Case of the Faulty Machine

	Alternative	Time Required to Implement	Estimated Costs	Favorable Points	Unfavorable Points
A	Repair machine.	15 days	$2000	Workers are familiar with the machine; it has proved itself.	Might break down again soon; not as fast as new machine; takes longer to fix.
B	Replace with reconditioned machine.	8 days	$4500	Same as old machine; no training necessary.	Reconditioned machine may not last as long as new one; not as fast as some new ones.
C	Replace with new but identical machine.	5 days	$6000	Same as old machine; no training necessary; likely to last a long time.	Relatively expensive.
D	Replace with new, modernized machine.	5 days	$7000	Fastest machine available; likely to last a long time.	Most expensive; operator will require some training.

Source: Leslie W. Rue and Lloyd L. Byars, *Supervision: Key Link to Productivity* (Homewood, Ill.: Richard D. Irwin, 1982), p. 67. Used by permission.

happen in the future. They agreed that while there was a 60 percent likelihood sales would rise, there was a 40 percent chance they would stabilize or even drop. To help analyze the implications of these assumptions, the decision tree shown in Figure 3.6 was diagrammed. It focused attention on four outcomes associated with the two alternative courses of action.

The relevant managerial question in this case became, "What can happen if we (1) add equipment and sales rise, (2) add equipment and sales fall, (3) add overtime and sales rise, (4) add overtime and sales fall?" Working further, the treasurer made some computations that estimated net cash flows for each of these four possible

future conditions. These cash flows are noted at the end of each branch of the decision tree in Figure 3.6.

Although the decision-tree analysis doesn't solve the problem for the president, it does help clarify the potential outcomes associated with the two alternative courses of action. Decision trees are valuable managerial tools for this very reason.

Decision Matrices or Payoff Tables

Looking at the decision tree in Figure 3.6, you might be tempted to conclude that adding equipment is the best bet because it offers the highest potential net cash flow—$460,000 . . . if sales rise. The *if* in the last statement, though, is the trick. You don't know with complete *certainty* that sales will rise. At best, you have assigned a probability of 60 percent that they will rise, and, there is a 40 percent chance sales will fall.

A **decision matrix** or **payoff table** extends decision-tree analysis by displaying the various outcomes for each alternative course of action while taking the probabilities of their occurrence into account. This typically involves calculation of an **expected value** for each alternative course of action—that is, the dollar value of the predicted outcomes for an alternative multiplied by the probability of its occurrence.

Let's go back to Emperor Products. After analyzing the decision tree, the president con-

FIGURE 3.6 Decision-tree analysis of the emperor products case.

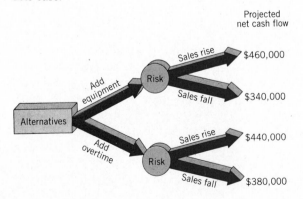

Table 3.5 Decision Matrix or Payoff Table for Emperor Products Example

Possible Future Conditions	Decision Alternatives	
	Add Equipment	Add Overtime
Sales rise ($P = 0.6$)	$EV = \$276,000$ ($\$460,000 \times 0.6$)	$EV = \$264,000$ ($\$440,000 \times 0.6$)
Sales fall ($P = 0.4$)	$EV = \$136,000$ ($\$340,000 \times 0.4$)	$EV = \$152,000$ ($\$380,000 \times 0.4$)
Total expected value	$412,000	$416,000

P = Probability.
EV = Expected value.

structed the decision matrix shown in Table 3.5. Each cell in the table shows the expected values (EV) of each outcome as income produced times the probability of its occurrence. It also shows that total expected values can be calculated for each alternative—adding equipment or adding overtime—by summing the expected values for each if sales rise or drop. In the example, the total expected value of adding equipment is $412,000; for adding overtime it is $416,000.

At this point the president and her advisors are better prepared to make a decision under the conditions of risk associated with this problem. They would most likely choose to add overtime since it has a higher expected value.

CHOOSING AMONG ALTERNATIVES: MAKING THE DECISION

Once alternatives are formulated and analyzed, a final choice among them must be made. At this point in the problem-solving process, a manager must answer three questions.

1. Is a choice really required?
2. How should the choice be made?
3. Who should be involved in the choice?

Deciding to Decide

Managers are too busy and have too many valuable things to do with their time to respond personally to every problem situation that comes their way. Thus the effective manager will know when to delegate decisions to others, how to set priorities, and when not to act at all. When presented with a problem, it is recommended that managers ask themselves the following questions.[19]

1. *Is the problem easy to deal with?* Small and less significant problems should not get as much time and attention as bigger ones. Even if a mistake is made, the cost of error on small problems is also small.

2. *Might the problem resolve itself?* Putting problems in rank order leaves the less significant for last . . . if any time remains. Surprisingly, many of these will resolve themselves or be solved by others before the manager gets to them. One less problem to solve leaves time for other uses. *Newsline 3.5* reports how one manager benefited from a postponement strategy.

3. *Is this my decision to make?* Many decisions can be made by persons at lower levels. These decisions should be delegated. Others can and should be referred to higher levels. This is especially true for decisions that have consequences for a larger part of the organization than any under a manager's immediate control.

Deciding How to Decide

Decisions made by managers can be divided into those made under the assumptions of classical decision theory and those made under more behavioral assumptions. Under the former, managers make **rational choices**—that is, those that are logical and optimal based on economic decision criteria. Under the latter, managers make

NEWSLINE 3.5

DECIDING WHEN NOT TO MAKE DECISIONS

One morning Bob Kemper, the western regional manager of United Airlines, was faced with a contingent of black cabin cleaners. A white supervisor, they claimed, was consistently assigning them to the less attractive cleanup tasks. Kemper, six supervisory levels removed from the employees, had no obligation (other than the airline's open-door policy) to deal with the problem. Yet the complaint was potentially explosive.

He reflected on how his predecessor had handled a similar problem several years before. Conducting an on-the-spot tribunal, he had phoned the supervisor, established the facts, and, determining that the supervisor was wrong, settled the matter then and there. The aggrieved party in that instance was much impressed and delighted. However, supervisory morale sank and for a time discipline deteriorated. Nonetheless, the manager in question had created a legend through such displays as a man of action who could cut through red tape and get results. This had undoubtedly contributed to his subsequent promotion.

Kemper chose a different course. He listened carefully to the complaint, assured the cabin cleaners that justice would be done, but postponed action. Kemper, in effect, "decided not to decide." His belief was that in buying time, he could make pointed inquiries and probably stimulate those below him to take corrective action. This did indeed occur and the basis for the grievance was corrected. In the process, the supervisor saved face and, in Kemper's view, the supervisor learned more by solving the problem himself than by Kemper's solving it for him.

Source: Excerpted from Richard T. Pascale and Anthony G. Athos, "Deciding When Not to Make Decisions," *Wall Street Journal* (January 4, 1982), p. 22. Reprinted by permission of *Wall Street Journal*. Copyright © 1982 Dow Jones & Company, Inc. All rights reserved.

choices that involve adequate but not necessary optimal satisfaction of decision criteria.

Classical Decision Theory

Classical decision theory views the manager as acting in a world of complete certainty. The manager faces a clearly defined problem, knows all possible action alternatives and their consequences, and then chooses the alternative giving the best or "optimum" resolution of the problem. Classical theory is often used as a model for how managers ideally should make decisions. The prior analysis of the faulty machine problem sets the stage nicely for a decision to be made from a classical perspective.

Behavioral Decision Theory

Behavioral scientists question the assumptions underlying classical decision theory. They recognize that the human mind is a wonderful creation, capable of infinite achievements. But they also recognize cognitive limitations, or limits to our information-processing capabilities. These limitations compromise the ability of managers to make decisions according to the classical model. They impair abilities to define problems, identify all possible action alternatives, and choose alternatives with ideal and predictable consequences. As a result, behavioral decision theory is offered as a more accurate description of how people make decisions in actual practice.

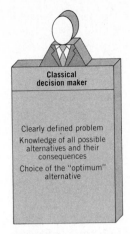
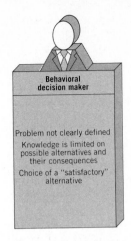

FIGURE 3.7 Differences between classical and behavioral decision makers.

Behavioral decision theory assumes that people act only in terms of what they perceive about a given situation. Because such perceptions are frequently imperfect, the behavioral decision maker acts with limited information. This is especially applicable to managers making decisions about ambiguous problems. They have only partial knowledge about the available action alternatives and their consequences. They consequently choose the first alternative that appears to give a satisfactory resolution of the problem. Herbert Simon, who won a Nobel Prize for his work, calls this a **"satisficing"** style of problem solving and decision making—choosing the first satisfactory alternative that comes to your attention.[20]

Figure 3.7 summarizes the basic differences between the classical and behavioral decision-making approaches.

Deciding Who Should Decide

The actual choice of a particular problem solution can be arrived at through individual, consultative, or group methods. In practice, these methods result in decisions of the following types.

1. *Individual decisions* The manager makes the final choice alone, based on information he or she possesses, and without the participation of other persons. This choice often reflects the manager's position of formal authority in the organization.

2. *Decision via consultation* The manager solicits inputs on the problem from other persons. Based on this information and its interpretation, the manager then makes a final choice.

3. *Group decisions* The manager not only consults with other persons for information inputs, but also asks them to participate in problem-solving discussions and in making the actual choice. Although sometimes difficult, the group decision is the most participative of the three methods of final choice. Guidelines for facilitating group decisions are given in Table 3.6.

Good managers use each of these approaches to making a final choice in the problem-

Table 3.6 Facilitating Group Decisions

1. Avoid blindly arguing for your own individual judgments. Present your position as clearly and logically as possible, but listen to other members' reactions and consider them carefully before you press your point.
2. Avoid changing your mind just to reach agreement and avoid conflict. Support only solutions you are able to agree with at least to some degree. Yield only to positions that have objectives and logically sound foundations.
3. Avoid "conflict-reducing" procedures such as majority vote, tosssing a coin, averaging, or bargaining in reaching decisions.
4. Seek out differences of opinion. They are natural and expected. Try to involve everyone in the decision process. Disagreements can help the group's decision because a wide range of information and opinions improves the chances for the group to hit on more adequate solutions.
5. Do not assume that someone must win and someone must lose when discussions reach a stalemate. Instead, look for the next most acceptable alternative for all members.
6. Discuss underlying assumptions, listen carefully to one another, and encourage the participation of all members.

Source: These guidelines are found in "Decisions, Decisions, Decisions," *Psychology Today* (November 1971), pp. 55, 56. Used by permission.

solving process. The key is to know *when* to use each method. Chapter 10 examines these options in detail as part of a manager's approach to leadership. For now it is sufficient for you to recognize that both assets and liabilities are associated with the use of group as opposed to individual problem-solving approaches. The assets of group problem solving include[21]

1. *Greater sum total of knowledge and information* The involvement of more than one person increases the information that can be brought to bear on the problem.

2. *Increased acceptance of final decision* Participants in group problem-solving processes are more inclined to accept the final decision or feel a sense of responsibility for making it work.

3. *Better understanding of final decision* Because participants in group problem solving are involved in all stages of discussion, comprehension of the decision is high.

Overall, these assets suggest that use of more group-oriented methods of problem solving can increase acceptance, understanding, and quality of the final decision. However, there are potential liabilities to group problem solving as well. They include

1. *Social pressure to conform* The desire to be a good member and go along with the group can lead people to conform prematurely to poor decisions.

2. *Individual domination* A dominant individual may emerge and control the group's choice.

3. *Time requirements* Groups are frequently slower to reach decisions than individuals acting alone; furthermore, groups can delay their final choice while individual members "play games" and/or "fight" with one another.

IMPLEMENTING THE SOLUTION AND EVALUATING RESULTS

The final challenges in the problem-solving process are to implement the chosen solution and evaluate results. Implementation is a day-to-day managerial responsibility that speaks for itself.

Nothing new can or will happen unless action is taken. Managers not only need the courage and creativity to arrive at a decision, they also need the ability and willingness to take action to implement the decision. Take, for example, what happened a few days before one Christmas when a regional manager for United Parcel Service (UPS) learned that the railroad had left a flatcar carrying two UPS trailers on a siding in central Illinois.[22]

> The regional manager paid for a high-speed diesel that whipped the flatcar into Chicago ahead of an Amtrak passenger train, and he ordered two of UPS's fleet of 24 Boeing 727s diverted to Chicago to get the contents of the trailers to their destinations in Florida and Louisiana in time for Christmas. In spite of the extraordinary expense, the manger neither asked permission nor even informed UPS headquarters in Greenwich, Conn., until weeks later.

The regional manager in this case took quick and positive action to solve the problem; he received high praise from his superiors as a result.

A common managerial error is to overlook the need to communicate solution details successfully to others—and to gain their commitment to follow through with all necessary action. Figure 3.8 is a classic portrayal of how poor communication in problem solving can cause implementation breakdowns. One major advantage of group problem-solving methods is that they increase understanding of final decisions among all those participating in deliberations. They also facilitate commitment to complete implementation of the chosen solution.

Evaluation is an often neglected but still essential component in problem solving. It is necessary to compare actual results to the desired outcomes to see if the problem really has been resolved. Evaluation also frequently reveals where modifications can be made in the original solution to improve its results over time. Both the positive and negative consequences of the chosen course of action should be evaluated. If the original solution appears less than entirely desirable, it may require a return to earlier steps in the problem-solving process to generate a modified or new solution. In this way problem solving becomes a dynamic and ongoing activity.

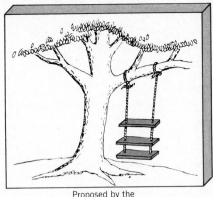

Proposed by the
production manager

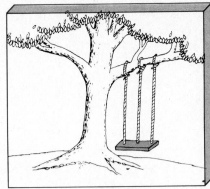

As specified in the
production request

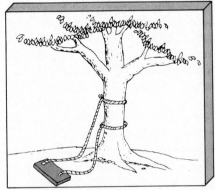

As designed by
research and development

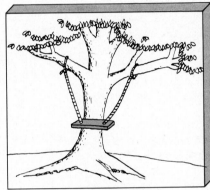

As manufactured
by production

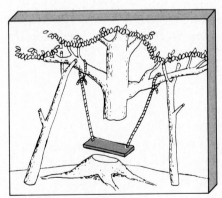

As installed at
the buyer's site

What the
buyer wanted

FIGURE 3.8 Poor communication makes implementation of solutions difficult.

SUMMARY

Managers spend enormous amounts of time attempting to solve problems that occur in the day-to-day process of planning, organizing, leading, and controlling. This book is written to help you achieve success in this action framework, as summarized in Figure 3.9. Use this figure as a frame of reference as you look ahead to the learning opportunities that follow.

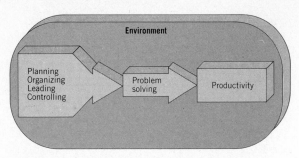

FIGURE 3.9 The manager as problem solver.

Problem solving is a process of identifying discrepancies between actual and desired states of affairs and taking action to resolve those discrepancies. The five general steps in this process are to (1) identify the problem, (2) generate alternative solutions, (3) select a preferred solution, (4) implement the solution, and (5) evaluate results and take corrective action when necessary. As part of our review of these steps, we examined

- The various types of problems faced by mangers and how these problems vary by managerial level.

- Creativity as a necessary element in problem solving.

- Decision aids for problem solving in certain, risky and uncertain environments.

- The need to know when to, how to, and who should make the decisions required in problem solving.

Our review also addressed a host of issues spanning a range of individual and group techniques for increasing creativity, economic versus behavioral decision models, the use of inventories of alternatives, decision trees, decision matrices and payoff tables in analyzing alternatives, and the logic of choosing when problems should be addressed through individual, consultative, or group decision methods.

All managers must be good at looking for and finding problems toward which to direct attention. This is the final test of the manager as a problem solver. True managerial success will depend on your ability to identify performance gaps and opportunities in sufficient time to resolve them to the benefit of the individuals involved and the productivity of the organization.

THINKING THROUGH THE ISSUES

1. Explain the difference between choice making, decision making, and problem solving.

2. Identify the five steps in the problem-solving process and give examples of each step as they might be followed by a manager in an organization with which you are familiar.

3. Explain how the types of problems faced by managers may vary among top, middle, and lower management levels.

4. Identify three barriers to accurate problem identification. Explain steps that can be taken by managers to avoid each barrier.

5. What is creativity? How can it be fostered in individuals?

6. What is the difference between brainstorming and nominal grouping as ways to increase creativity through the use of groups?

7. Show how a decision matrix is a more advanced way of analyzing alternatives than the decision tree.

8. State three assets and three liabilities of group problem solving.

9. When should a manager choose not to solve a problem of which he or she is aware?

10. What is a major reason that implementation difficulties often accompany even the best of problem solutions?

THE MANAGER'S VOCABULARY

Behavioral decision theory	Certainty	theory	Decision making
Brainstorming	Choice making	Cost-benefit analysis	Decision matrix
	Classical decision	Creativity	Decision tree

Expected value	Nonprogrammed decisions	Problem finding	Satisficing
Expected problems	Nonroutine problems	Problem solving	Selective perception
Intuitive thinker	Payoff table	Programmed decisions	Systematic thinker
Inventory of alternatives	Probability	Rational choices	Uncertainty
Nominal group	Problem	Risk	Unexpected problems
		Routine problems	

CAREER PERSPECTIVE: EXECUTIVE'S CRISIS[23]

BLOOMINGTON, Minn.—The day is etched into Jerald H. Maxwell's memory.

His family will never forget it, either. To them, it is the day he started weeping in his room, the day his exuberant self-confidence ended and his depression began, the day his world—and theirs—came tumbling down.

It was October 23, 1979, the day Maxwell was fired in disgrace as chairman and chief executive of Med General Inc. The high-flying medical-products company, its growth fueled by risky sales tactics that over extended it financially, was on its way down. It would end up in bankruptcy proceedings seven months later.

Maxwell was the son of a construction foreman, he aspired to success even as a youth. "Horatio Alger rags-to-riches was built into me, it drove my whole life," says Mr. Maxwell, who breaks into a grin when talking about the good days gone by. At the University of Oregon he was the president of his fraternity house and vice-chairman of the Young Republicans. After college came management jobs in the construction business, his own consulting firm and, in 1970, Med General, which he helped start.

Med General was just another obscure little company until 1974, when it introduced a device designed to control chronic pain by stimulating nerves. The company's sales spurted to $6.9 million in 1978 from just $539,445 in 1973, and it was ranked in the top 10 of *Inc.* magazine's list of fast-growing small companies.

Maxwell's ego grew with Med General. The license plates on his company Cadillac carried his nickname, "Big Max," and his business cards carried the title of "field general." He was a celebrity in Twin Cities business circles by mid-1979. When Med General stock hit a high of $16.50 a share in over-the-counter trading (up from less than $1 in the early 1970s), Maxwell's 238,635 shares were worth nearly $4 million.

Then it ended. To meet Maxwell's overly optimistic sales goals, Med General extended easy credit terms to its customers. And some salesman simply shipped out goods that hadn't been ordered. As a result, sales were overstated and Med General didn't have enough money coming in to pay its bills. Maxwell says he wasn't aware of the questionable sales practices. "I gave the marching orders, and things got distorted at the other end," he says, softly adding, "But it was still my responsibility. I was in charge."

Whether to blame or not, he began showing the emotional strain and went into a hospital suffering physical and mental exhaustion in early

October 1979. "I couldn't get through a staff meeting without crying," he recalls. Maxwell came out of the hospital a week later and tried to revive Med General, but it was too late. Med General's bankers demanded that the board dismiss Maxwell and another top executive because of the precarious financial condition. The ax fell on October 23.

Questions

1. Jerald Maxwell paid a high price for the failure of his decisions as chief executive officer of Med General. Did he overreact to the company's problems? Why or why not?

2. Are you prepared to accept both the success and failure of your future decisions as a manager? Explain your answer.

CASE APPLICATION: TOUGH DECISION AT INDAL ALUMINUM[24]

On December 31, 1981, the Indal Aluminum Company decided to close down its Murphysboro, Illinois, plant. There were 172 employees six months prior to the closing, but by December market conditions were forcing layoffs, and the company could not find a buyer for the local plant. Some employees had been with the company 18 years, others as little as six months. All were to get severance pay equal to one week per year's service.

But Indal also did more. The company ran an ad in the local newspaper in an attempt to find new jobs for its displaced employees. This ad began as follows.

Indal Skill Bank

Because of an imminent plant shutdown, Indal Aluminum, Murphysboro, has a sizable group of qualified, dedicated, and well-motivated employees with a wide variety of skills and experience. It is our intent to help match our demonstrated talents and abilities with your needs. . . . These employees commute from within the circle of Chester, Percy, DuQuoin, Benton, Pittsburg, Anna & Grand Tower. If an interested employer would like to explore possibilities & opportunities, including frank evaluation, please call.

For over 15 days this ad was run by Indal at a cost exceeding $2600. The plant's industrial relations manager, John Hogan, said, "I've been very pleased with the results of the ad. It was designed to try to relocate laid-off Indal employees in new jobs in the southern Illinois area."

Questions

1. Use the five steps of the problem-solving process to recreate how you think Indal top management arrived at the decision to run this special advertising campaign. What do you think they identified as the problem, what alternatives may have been considered, how was the choice made, and how it was implemented and evaluated?

2. Do you think the decision to initiate the placement campaign was a good one for Indal? Why or why not?

CLASS EXERCISE: DOTS AND SQUARES PUZZLE:

1. Shown below is a collection of 16 dots. Study the figure to determine how many "squares" can be created by connecting the dots.

2. Draw as many squares as you can find in the figure while making sure a dot is at every corner of every square. Count the squares and write

this number in the margin to the right of the figure.

3. Share your results with those of a classmate sitting nearby. Explain the location of squares missed by either one of you.

4. Based on this discussion, redraw your figure to show the maximum number of possible squares. Count them and write this number to the left of the figure.

5. Await further class discussion led by your instructor.

REFERENCES

[1] From Thomas W. Steiger, "The Misadventure of the Chairman's Molehill," *Business*, Vol. 31 (September-October 1981), pp. 39, 40. Used by permission.

[2] David A. Kolb, Irwin M. Rubin, and James M. McIntyre, *Organizational Psychology: An Experimental Approach*, Second Edition, © 1974, pp. 42–43. Reprinted by permission of Prentice-Hall, Inc., Englewood Cliffs, New Jersey.

[3] George P. Huber, *Managerial Decision Making* (Glenview, Ill.: Scott, Foresman, 1975).

[4] Michael J. Driver, "Individual Decision Making and Creativity," in Steven Kerr (Editor), *Organizational Behavior* (Columbus, Oh.: Grid Publishing, 1979), pp. 59–91.

[5] Lawrence J. Gitman and Carl McDaniel, Jr., *Business World* (New York: Wiley, 1983), p. 104.

[6] Adapted from "How Managers' Minds Work," by James L. McKenney and Peter G. W. Keen, *Think* (May-June 1974), p. 83.

[7] See, for example, William Taggart and Daniel Robey, "Minds and Managers: On the Dual Nature of Human Information Processing and Management," *Academy of Mangement Review*, Vol. 6 (April 1981), pp. 187–195.

[8] Adapted from "Columbia Decides to Go Coed," *Time* (February 1, 1982), p. 63.

[9] William F. Pounds, "The Process of Problem Finding," *Industrial Management Review*, Vol. 11 (Fall 1969), pp. 1–19.

[10] Steiger, op. cit., p. 40.

[11] These two examples are from Tom Taliaferro, *Instructor's Film Guide for Creative Problem Solving: "How to Get Better Ideas"* (Del Mar, Cal.: CRM McGraw-Hill Films) p. 2.

[12] From "Out of Mind-Set Experiences," *Manager*, No. 1 (1979), p. 22. Used by permission.

[13] Taliaferro, op. cit., pp. 5, 6.

[14] Huber, op. cit.

[15] D. W. Taylor, P. C. Berry, and C. H. Block, "Does Group Participation When Using Brainstorming Facilitate or Inhibit Creative Thinking?" *Administrative Science Quarterly*, Vol. 3 (June 1958), pp. 23–47.

[16] See Andre L. Delbecq, Andrew H. Van de Ven, and David H. Gustafson, *Group Techniques for Program Planning* (Glenview, Ill.: Scott, Foresman, 1975).

[17] Leslie W. Rue and Lloyd L. Byars, *Supervision: Key Link to Productivity* (Homewood, Ill.: Richard D. Irwin, 1982), p. 66.

[18] This example is from Edward A. McCreary, "How to grow a Decision Tree," *Think* (March-April 1967), pp. 13–18.

[19] James A. F. Stoner, *Management*, Second Edition (Englewood Cliffs, N.J.: Prentice-Hall, 1982), pp. 167–168.

[20] For a sample of Simon's work, see Herbert A. Simon, *Administrative Behavior* (New York: The Free Press, 1947); James G. March and Herbert A. Simon, *Organizations* (New York: Wiley, 1958).

[21] See Norman R. F. Maier, "Assets and Liabilities in Group Problem Solving: The Need for an Integrative Function," *Psychological Review*, Vol. 4 (1967), pp. 239–249.

[22] "Behind the UPS Mystique: Puritanism and Productivity," *Business Week* (June 6, 1983), p. 66. Reprinted from the June 6, 1983 issue of Business Week by special permission, © 1983 by McGraw Hill, Inc., New York, NY 10020. All rights reserved.

[23] Excerpted from Lawrence Ingrassia, "Executive's Crisis: Aftermath of a Failure," *Wall Street Journal* (March 12, 1982), pp. 1, 20. Reprinted by permission of the *Wall Street Journal*. Copyright © 1982 Dow Jones & Company, Inc. All rights reserved.

[24] Based on Ben Gelman, "Indal Finds Jobs for Some of its Laid-Off Employees," *Southern Illinoisan* (January 31, 1982), p 2.

Part 1

INTEGRATING CASES

DAVID BERTINI

David Bertini was an outstanding salesman. He was promoted to branch manager of his sales branch when the former branch manager left the company. As branch manager, David was responsible for planning, organizing, leading, and controlling his salespeople.

He was pleased with the promotion, although he was not sure how a manager should behave. He assumed that because he received the promotion for being such a good salesman, this was the key to being a good branch manager—being a model salesman.

He started officially as branch manager on Monday morning. Tuesday, one of his salespeople, Sally Chapin, told him that one of his old accounts was considering going to the competition. David told Sally not to worry. "I'll find out what's going on." He leaned over his desk and began dialing the customer's number before Sally had a chance to finish her explanation as to why she thought the customer was considering the competition. Within 15 minutes, David discovered that price was the problem and made a special

Source: Adapted from Richard E. Boyatzis, *The Competent Manager* (New York: Wiley, 1982), pp.36–39. Used by permission.

deal with the customer. He confirmed the sale. After he finished the telephone call, David smiled at Sally and said, "Any time you need help, come right in and ask!"

Two months later, David was talking to Bill Rinehart, the regional sales manager, and asked him, "How do I get my salespeople to come and ask me for help? They seem to stay away, and I know that some of them are having problems." Bill offered to visit David's branch and help him find out what the problem was.

After spending several hours at the branch office, Bill sat down with David. Bill had been surprised to find out that David was making his salespeople feel incompetent because he always interfered with their sales efforts. At least, that's how they saw it. Bill knew that David had sound coaching skills; that was why he had received the promotion. The conversation was enlightening to David. He discovered that he got the promotion because of skills he had shown in helping some new salespeople from another branch a year earlier, not because of his own sales record. As he and Bill discussed the situation, David began to see that the branch manager is supposed to guide, coach, and help his salespeople. He should be helping each of them figure out why

a customer was backing down or why a customer ordered less than the month earlier.

David had many of the appropriate skills to be branch manager. Bill had known that good sales managers have some different skills than good salespeople and had considered this in making the promotion. David's problem had been that his self-image and social role had not changed when his job demands changed (i.e., when his job changed). Bill felt that the talk, reviewing his image of the branch manager's responsibilities with David, and giving David several books on sales management would take care of the problem. David called Bill several weeks later and said, "Being a manager is tough, but I like it. Thanks for the talk, Bill."

Bill thought the problem had been solved until eight months later when he noted that sales at David's branch had dropped continuously for three months. Bill was concerned because this represented the first quarter that the branch had been operating under sales goals and plans that were developed while David was branch manager. Bill called David and said, "I noticed that sales are down. What's going on?"

"Well, Bill, this damn recession has people cautious. They're afraid of getting caught with too much inventory." replied David.

Bill was not satisfied with that answer. "But you have been down each of the past three months. Are you sure that's all due to inventory concerns?"

David added, "Actually, it's a combination of things. One of them I could use your help with. Some of my salespeople don't seem to be working as hard as they have before. It's like they never came back from vacation."

Bill decided it was time for another trip to David's branch. What Bill discovered was complicated. At first it seemed that several of David's key salespeople were still angry at David for having fired Sally Chapin a number of months previously. He asked David if he had considered discussing why he had fired Sally at one of his staff meetings. David did not like the idea because it meant that he would have to hold a staff meeting. Bill was again surprised that David did not have regular staff meetings. He asked David, "How do you know what's going on with your people?" David told him that he met with each person individually and discussed various issues at least once a month. David tried to explain to Bill that it allowed him to develop a more personal relationship with each one. The story unfolded like an onion. Soon Bill learned that David had never met with his staff to discuss the branch's sales goal and plan of action. Some of the salespeople did not even know what the branch's overall goal was.

"David, how can you get people to pull together if they don't even know their shared sales goal?" Bill was feeling frustrated with David and began pushing his questions at David faster. David attempted to explain. "I have always felt that individual sales goals are important. The branch goal is only meaningful for me."

Questions

1. How does David Bertini define his responsibilities as a manager? Explain your answer.

2. What criticisms of David's managerial performance would most likely be offered by (a) Abraham Maslow, (b) Douglas McGregor, and (c) Chris Argyris? Defend your answer.

INDUSTRIAL CONTROLS, INC.

Franz Bauer had been a respected executive in a larger and successful conglomerate. He rose to the position of group vice-president, and his career in the company appeared promising. After all, he had an undergraduate degree in mathematics, a Harvard MBA, a good deal of experience in a large firm, and a history of success. Yet approximately 12 years ago, Bauer elected to acquire a small firm engaged in manufacturing controls for a wide range of industrial machines, doing about $200,000 worth of business annually.

Bauer intended from the very beginning to expand his firm from a small company to a medium-size enterprise. He wanted to accomplish this through retained earnings and occasional loans in order not to dilute his ownership and control. In fact, Industrial Controls, Inc. did grow at an average rate of 20 percent per year until 1974, when the company had sales in excess of $5 million and employed 89 people (79 full-time and 10 part-time).

Evolution of the Firm

Stage 1

After acquiring Industrial Controls, Bauer hired a production manager. He selected John Dooley, who had been a foreman in Bauer's former division at the conglomerate and was known to him as a hard worker. Dooley did not have a college degree but had some electronic training in the U.S. Navy and took several evening courses at a local university.

Four years after acquiring Industrial Controls, Bauer acquired another small firm (a four-person operation) owned and operated by Thomas Cotton, an engineer who held several patents on equipment similar to that manufactured by Industrial Controls, but more sophisticated. Prior to forming his own company, Cotton had been employed as a sales engineer in a large firm in a similar line of business. Bauer also hired Cotton as the chief engineer and salesman. Cotton

Source: This case was prepared by Donald W. Scotton, chairman of the Departments of Marketing and General Administration, and Jan P. Muczyk, Department of Management and Labor, the Cleveland State University. It is slightly adapted and used here with their permission. Copyright © Donald W. Scotton and Jan P. Muczyk.

was given the opportunity to purchase a small interest in the firm and took advantage of it.

As long as the firm was small, these three individuals and the sales manager were able to manage the operations quite well. They worked out of the same office in a small building, saw each other frequently, remembered important matters without writing them down, and informally coordinated all of the details of day-to-day operations with a minimum of policy, procedures, and paperwork. There was no need for an organizational chart or for formal job descriptions.

Stage 2

There was nothing unique in what Industrial Controls was making and doing that could not be provided by any number of large corporations in the machine-controls field. In fact, Industrial Controls was in competition with the larger companies when it came to producing and selling machine controls that had standard applications. Consequently, Industrial Controls had elected to carve out for itself a niche: machine controls custommade to the specification of a client and personalized service that the large suppliers of more standardized equipment were not interested in providing.

Business continued to expand as the result of development of new and more complex lines of machine controls, and the operation was moved to a new and larger facility with individual offices for all corporate officers. Growth was further accelerated by the acquisition of several additional lines of related machine controls.

Up to this time, Bauer had been able to orchestrate the entire operation; that is, he was the glue that held everything together and gave it direction. At this juncture of the company's evolution, Bauer became involved in a number of community affairs that took more and more of his time.

When the sales manager resigned, Cotton, because he liked selling above all else, was made the vice-president of sales and marketing. Peter Daren, the chief development engineer who had reported to Cotton, was elevated to the position of chief engineer in charge of research and development as well as application engineering. Daren earned this promotion primarily on the basis of being a brilliant circuit designer. He also sought the position and might have left the organization if it were denied him. Daren continued to do a considerable amount of research and development and application engineering after his promotion. Dooley remained as the production manager but had a much larger operation.

It must be kept in mind that in a company producing sophisticated industrial equipment to customer specifications that are at times incomplete because the customer isn't certain about what is wanted, the interdependence between sales, production, and engineering is considerable.

At this point of the company's evolution, a number of problem areas required attention. The inventory of components increased from $400,000 to $1,200,000 in one year. Although some of the increase was justified by greater volume of business, the latter figure was deemed excessive. Engineering complained that it was not receiving accurate customer specifications from sales as well as receiving late modifications of the specifications. Production was complaining that it was receiving inadequate engineering releases and not enough lead time for assembling and testing the equipment. Furthermore, Dooley argued that because most orders were customized, production inefficiencies and delays were inevitable. Dooley and Daren felt that sales was not developing markets for more standardized items in larger quantities, which in turn would ease the workload for engineering and production. Sales and production felt that engineering was not giving them the support that was essential in this type of operation. When the customer service personnel needed assistance on a major equipment problem in the field, engineering was reluctant to drop development and application work to assist with the problem. Customer service personnel complained that engineering was designing equipment that was difficult to service in the field. Sales believed that engineering preferred to develop new product lines than to perfect existing equipment. Manufacturing personnel complained that they were not getting the amount of assistance from engineering required to assemble a product either designed or modified by the Engineering Department. Customer complaints also started arriving at an increasing rate.

Stage 3

In light of rapid growth and increased complexity of the product lines, Bauer decided to reorganize. As a first step, he hired Sharon Cline as an assistant to the president in order to augment his time. Cline had considerable experience in several manufacturing plants, in a consulting firm, and in teaching marketing courses part-time at a local university. Soon after, Bauer assigned Cline the responsibility for corporate planning. He also separated the marketing functions from sales and put Cline in charge of the former.

Bauer then hired a controller to assist in managing the accounting and financial aspects of the firm. Although Juan Paves was a Certified Public Accountant and had accounting experience, he was new to financial

planning and control. Consequently, Bauer retained these responsiblities.

Because the product line had become more sophisticated and because the work load was now greater, Bauer appointed Leroy Hinds, who had formerly worked in the Engineering Department and had half-time responsibility for quality control, as a full-time quality-control manager reporting directly to him. Irving Affermon was hired as a part-time personnel manager to establish personnel policy and handle personnel problems, which had increased to the point that they were consuming a considerable amount of time of the operating personnel, including Bauer. Although Affermon had personnel administration experience in a larger firm, he was out of a job at the time he was hired by Industrial Controls. Dooley was given the title of vice-president of manufacturing. Figure P.1 reflects the current organization.

After brief experience with the reorganization, Bauer con-

Figure P.1 Partial organization chart of Industrial Controls, Inc.

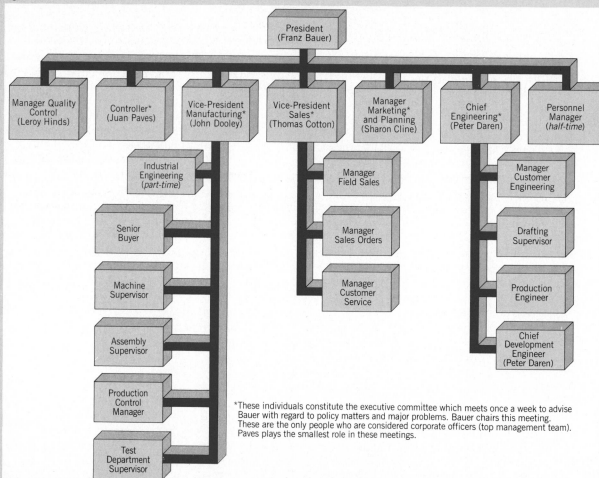

*These individuals constitute the executive committee which meets once a week to advise Bauer with regard to policy matters and major problems. Bauer chairs this meeting. These are the only people who are considered corporate officers (top management team). Paves plays the smallest role in these meetings.

cluded that something more fundamental had to be done in order to prepare his organization for future growth and to deal with the problems that were occupying his time.

Bauer believed, as did his fellow corporate officers, that a computer would aid them in a number of areas, such as processing sales orders, compiling an accurate bill of materials, controlling inventory, and billing customers accurately. The responsibility of integrating the new computer into company operations was given to Cline.

Bauer contemplated his future and that of the company. He concluded that he had the following choices:

1. He could sell his firm to one of the companies that in the past expressed an interest in buying Industrial Controls, Inc.

2. He could become chairman of the board and leave the operating decisions to someone else. But who?

3. He could stay with the same management team and get more personally involved in the operations of the firm by divesting himself of his outside interests.

4. He could hire a new cadre of managers and remain as chief executive officer or become chairman of the board.

Bauer had a strong sense of loyalty to his present key personnel who played a large role in building the company. Consequently, he opted for the third alternative but decided to seek outside help to aid him in overcoming the present problems and preparing the company for future growth.

Bring in Consultants

Bauer contacted two consultants who suggested performing a needs analysis first and a general approach to solving the firm's problems that would be made more specific after the needs analysis was completed. James Muzak and Ellen Ragu accepted the assignment and found that the motivation level of the managers and supervisors was very high. The managers worked long hours (including Saturdays and Sundays), but were still getting behind. They were seldom in their offices because of the day-to-day crises that came up. Cotton was on the phone with customers, manufacturer's representatives, and factory salesmen. Daren was designing and testing several pieces of equipment in order to make delivery dates. Dooley was on the shop floor helping the production people with their problems and expediting rush orders. Cline instead of Affermon was dealng with a number of personnel problems in addition to her other duties. Nobody had time to train subordinates. Few people understood fully what Cline was doing, and no one knew what Affermon was doing.

Meetings were held frequently, but the consensus was that they were too long and at times unproductive. Personal conflicts were apparent between some people in sales, engineering, and production who needed to interact in order to get the job done. A number of procedures that Bauer initiated were frequently ignored. In addition, some procedures that could have been routinized remained unnecessarily complex. Hinds proved to be an irritant to engineering and production, and even his subordinate questioned his competence in the job.

In spite of the problems that have been identified, the company experienced rapid growth and was profitable every year of its existence.

During the needs analysis, two things left a special impression on the consultant. First, when the managers were asked by Bauer sometime earlier to formulate action plans for next year, most of them had trouble beginning and completing them. Second, all of the managers genuinely wanted to improve their effectiveness.

The consultants concluded that they should present Bauer with a list of major problems, their priorities, and a concrete action program for dealing with these problems.

Questions

1. What do you consider to be the major problems at Industrial Control, Inc.?

2. What problems are of most immediate significance and why?

3. What do you recommend Bauer should do to address these problems and improve the performance effectiveness and efficiency of the company?

PART
2

PLANNING
FOR
PRODUCTIVITY

Chapters in This Part of the Book

PARTICIPATORY PLANNING ENDS FINANCIAL CHAOS

Luck, Planning Bring Success to Small Firm

The prior headlines[1] convey the importance of the planning function to large and small organizations as they try to survive and prosper in a dynamic and sometimes threatening environment. "When to plan?" "How to plan?" and "Who should plan?" are essential questions every manager should be able to answer.

Look again at the first headline. It contains a theme of participation. In fact, the associated article goes on to describe how an organization benefited when its planning process was revised to allow greater employee input. This was a strategic move by the organization's management; it is also a move that has pros and cons. Chapters 4 and 5 will examine this among many other planning issues.

One issue deals with the relationship between planning and intuition. The role of both in the success of at least one smaller firm is the story behind the second introductory headline. Coming discussion will help you to understand these and other aspects of planning viewed from a managerial perspective. Your capability to perform successfully as a manager should be enhanced as a result.

Before we begin, though, let's take a look at Japanese management and organization practices for a point of international comparison. Among all nations of the world, the productivity achievements of the 1970s and early 1980s belong to this small but industrious nation. Yoshi Tsumuri, an international scholar and expert on Japanese management practices, observes:[2]

"What one sees today in Japanese manufacturing and service industries is the result of conscious, cumulative efforts since World War II on the part of business, labor, and government to rebuild a war-torn economy and reverse the shoddy image of goods 'made in Japan.' Products of superior quality and their acceptance in the world market have become the two key elements in the business strategy of Japanese firms. . . ."

What follows is an excerpt from a *Wall Street Journal* article by Kenichi Ohmae, a director of McKinsey and Company, and manager of the consulting firm's Tokyo and Osaka offices. Ohmae's remarks about the importance of *both* short-term and long-term planning should stimulate your thinking on the guiding theme for Part 2—planning for productivity!

Perspective: The Long and Short of Japanese Planning[3]

One of the myths that enshrines Japanese business executives is that they are long-term planners. In contrast, American managers are thought to be obsessed with maximum short-term results. This view is particularly popular among American academics and journalists who have never been privy to Japanese decision making.

In fact, Japanese managers focus by and large on the short term. The stunning Japanese successes in the auto, semiconductor, and consumer electronics markets have taken place over the long haul, but have occurred primarily because of a determined focus on short-term, incremental gains.

Japanese businesses pay close attention to performance

---

[1] These headlines are from the *Wall Street Journal* (May 27, 1981), p. 1; (April 14, 1982), p. 27.

[2] Yoshi Tsurumi, "Productivity: The Japanese Approach," *Pacific Basin Quarterly* (Summer 1981), p. 7.

[3] Slightly adapted from the *Wall Street Journal* (January 18, 1982), p. 18. Reprinted by permission of the *Wall Street Journal*. Copyright © 1982 Dow Jones & Company, Inc. All rights reserved.

on a monthly and sometimes weekly basis—performance measured not against a three-year or five-year plan, but against budget, against return on sales, against competitor accomplishments.

In many industries where Japanese business has been most successful, companies have been motivated less by long-term strategies than by a mania to keep up with the competition. A "me-tooism" mind-set is common in Japanese companies, the notion that "whatever the competition does, we *must* do, too."

Consider the portable electronic calculator story, where four Japanese manufacturers—Sharp, Casio, Canon, and Toshiba—turn out 50 million sets annually and dominate the world market. What many foreigners fail to realize is that these four manufacturers barely survived a reciprocal head-on competition that has wiped more than 40

Japanese companies from the calculator market in the past five years and seriously eroded the profitability of the industry. Many Japanese companies entered the industry simply because their competitors did, and they plunged into aggressive wars for market share.

By no definition can this fierce rivalry, deeply rooted in the Japanese character, be construed as rational, long-term planning. Even the winners look less like planners driving down the experience curve than participants in a demolition derby.

One reason Japanese companies are considered such far-sighted planners is that they often succeed by sticking with products or work forces longer than short-term logic would suggest they should. But their success often results from sheer persistence, not a vision of the future.

Like communes or villages,

Japanese companies have a strong survival instinct. Consider Omron, one of the casualties in the hand-held calculator war that refused to say die or be sold off. Instead, it bore heavy internal losses while it redeployed its work force, plant, and basic technology—microprocessor, keyboard, display, printer—to become a major factor in the electronic cash register industry and the dominant force in automated control systems for traffic, banking, and continuous-process industries. "Today," says Takao Tateishi, Omron's president, "the very plant that once built calculators now produces cash registers!"

What are the lessons of these examples? Perhaps the truism that a short-term focus is a prerequisite for a long-term focus, that they do not have to be incompatible, certainly that differences between Japan and the United States are much more subtle than these broad labels, and, finally, that the right kind of shortsightedness and stubbornness characterize winners everywhere.

Japanese companies play for the season championship in an increasingly international contest, but one day at a time. Strategy for them is a fast and real game played within the restraints and strengths of a distinctive team according to principles that make excellent companies everywhere and according to rules that change as fast as technology and luck. Short term or long term; lucky or good? Maybe both.

4

FUNDAMENTALS
OF
PLANNING

THIS BOOK'S FOR YOU, GEORGE ALLEN!

A wonderful book is available—*The Executive's Illustrated Primer of Long Range Planning.* Dick Levin, the author begins with a story about how the book is written with George Allen, ex-coach of the Washington Redskins football team, in mind. Levin's statement follows.[1]

George Allen is a personal hero of mine even though he doesn't know me from a goalpost. From 1971 through 1977, George's over-the-hill gang, a.k.a. the Redskins, transformed my Sundays. His contrary wisdom in trading his first-, third-, fourth-, and eighth-round draft picks for Billy Kilmer and assorted superannuated Rams that first year made me a genius in hindsight two years later. When winning through geriatric intimidation became his trademark, I considered dying my hair gray to show my devotion. By the end of the glory that was the 1972 season, my hero had proved himself a turnaround artist extraordinaire at Washington, and I suddenly knew that I could be one too—if there was just an NFL franchise I could afford. I identified.

There is only one point on which we ever disagreed. His critics used to say, "George, you're mortgaging your future for the present. This trading youth for age is like living on your capital. It has to stop." I paid no attention, blinded by loyalty. The day the scales fell from my eyes was the day George Allen said, "Hell, the only future I'm interested in is this Sunday afternoon."

I'm here to tell you, George, that as surely as the sun will rise, Monday morning comes. And beyond Monday, next year, next season. I believe that even in pro football and politics there is a long term beyond the next game, the next election. I think that you are one hell of a strategist, George Allen, but your time horizon is too short. Out of my admiration and my debt for those good Sundays, this book, George Allen—everything I know and can tell about planning for the other side of Sunday—is for you.

George Allen was famous in football circles for his focus on the short term. He wanted to win football games next week, not next year. He planned for the short term and acted accordingly. This chapter is written for managers who are also concerned for the longer-term success of their organizations. Key topics in the chapter include

Do Managers Really Plan?
Planning as a Management Function
The Planning Process
Forecasting
Benefits of Planning
Making Planning Effective

The process of management involves looking ahead. Good managers are able to assess the future and make provision for it. Planning, the first of the four basic managerial functions, is how this responsibility is carried out. To become good as a manager requires that you become a good planner. Henri Fayol, a key figure in the history of management thought, goes so far as to consider planning the most important managerial function.

Planning is formally defined as a process of setting objectives and determining what should be done to accomplish them. It is a decision-making activity through which managers act to ensure the future success of their organizations and work units, as well as themselves. As such, planning has three action characteristics that present special challenges to the manager. Planning is[2]

1. *Anticipatory in nature*   Through planning managers decide what to do and how before it must actually be done.

2. *A system of decisions*   Planning involves making decisions that define desired future states and the actions required to achieve them.

3. *Focused on desired future states*   Planning targets efforts to facilitate the accomplishment of important organizational objectives; it is a means of ensuring arrival at desired future states.

DO MANAGERS REALLY PLAN?

Given that planning is one form of decision making in which managers should engage, the next question is whether or not they really plan at all in actual practice. The two sides to the debate over this question can be summarized as follows.

Argument: Managers Are Too Busy to Plan

Chapter 1 introduced Henry Mintzberg's work on managerial behavior. You should recall his point that managers are busy people who spend most of their time solving immediate problems while being frequently interrupted by a variety of written and oral communications. As a result, Mintzberg argues that managers are too busy to plan. The very nature of managerial work makes it difficult for managers to do planning as a systematic and reflective activity. Instead, Mintzberg concludes,[3]

> When managers plan, they do so implicitly in the context of daily actions, not in some abstract process reserved for two weeks in the organization's mountain retreat. The plans of the chief executives I studied seemed to exist only in their heads—as flexible, but often specific, intentions. The traditional literature notwithstanding, the job of managing does not breed reflective planners; the manager is a real-time responder to stimuli, an

individual who is conditioned by the job to prefer live to delayed action.

Argument: Managers Plan All the Time

The other side to this debate can be illustrated by a case. This case was observed by researchers investigating Mintzberg's suggestion that most managers are too busy to plan, no matter how good their intentions may be.

Illustrative Case:
The Hospital Administrator[4]

The hospital administrator was undertaking a three-year building-expansion program that would result in a 25 percent increase in the size of the hospital. A great deal of time was spent dealing with physicians, staff members, architects, the hospital board, and other concerned persons in planning how to construct the addition. During the period observed by the researchers, 13.8 percent of the administrator's telephone conversations related specifically to planning the best way to meet the needs of the hospital. Scheduled and unscheduled meetings were also frequently used for planning the expansion program. During these meetings, various people sat down and studied each alternative and their potential impact on the entire hospital. Overall, approximately 37 percent of the administrator's available time was devoted to the identification of alternatives and a determination of their feasibility. This and uncounted additional time was spent on planning for this one single event.

Current Thinking

This example shows how one hospital manager planned to meet the challenges of a special situation. While we can agree with Mintzberg that managers are busy people—and this hospital administrator certainly was busy, like the chief executive of any organization—the evidence overwhelmingly suggests that they do in fact plan. Some managers, of course, plan more than others, some do it better than others, and some neglect planning on occasion for any one or more of the following reasons.

- They just don't think about the future.

- They are impatient and act before thinking.
- They view planning as an activity to be done by someone else.

Still, the reality of the situation is that planning, while sometimes neglected and even done poorly, is an essential managerial responsibility. *Newsline 4.1*, for example, gives testimony to how good planning facilitated prosperity for a small manufacturing firm in a dynamic industry. It suggests that managerial success entails a bit of two ingredients—good planning and good luck.

PLANNING AS A MANAGEMENT FUNCTION

As a special form of managerial decision making, planning is of ever-increasing importance. Organizations in contemporary society are facing increasing challenges from even more complex technologies, greater environmental uncertainties, and the sheer magnitude of investments required in capital, labor, and other supporting resources. To succeed in the midst of such forces, managers at all levels in organizations are challenged to plan well.

Figure 4.1 depicts the relationship of planning to the other management functions in the ultimate quest for productivity. What is sometimes called the primary principle of planning recognizes that planning is the first and most basic of all the managerial functions. It is a decision-making activity that is the foundation of

FIGURE 4.1 Planning as a management function.

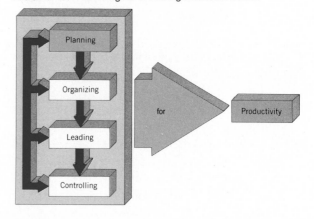

NEWSLINE 4.1

QUAKER STOVE CO. PROSPERING ON GOOD PLANNING, GOOD LUCK

Cast-iron stoves may seem quaint relics of another time, but the cast-iron stove *business* is alive and fiercely competitive. The U.S. has a small army of modern-day stove makers, building by hand in garage corners or on assembly lines with the help of venture capital.

To most of these entrepreneurs, the market has been less than kind. Many have gone out of business, burned by high interest rates and burdened by stocks of unsold merchandise. Some built stoves for the masses, only to see the infatuation wane. Hundreds more failed for other reasons, experts say. "The failure rate is verging on a depression this year," says Andrew B. Shapiro, president of Wood Energy Research Corp., Camden, Maine.

Quaker Stove Co. is bucking the trend. Owners Cyril and Lenore Rennels, who started the business in 1976, expect a pretax profit of $600,000 this year on sales of $5 million. Last year, the Trumbauersville, Pa., company earned $420,000 before taxes on $3.5 million in sales. Quaker will make and sell about 8,000 stoves this year; last year, the volume was 6,000.

Luck was on Quaker's side. When other stove-making companies rushed to expand, only to go broke, Quaker "grew small," Mr. Rennels says. "We grew steadily without borrowing." Steady growth wasn't always voluntary, however. Until two years ago, when Continental Bank in Philadelphia granted them a $300,000 credit line, the Rennelses couldn't get any commercial loans. They simply didn't have the money to enlarge their operations.

The Rennelses also have a knack for spotting trends and adapting to them by developing new stove models. "Quaker has succeeded in staying abreast," says Wood Energy's Shapiro. "They were in the vanguard of fireplace inserts when it was important to get into that field. They developed a coal stove. I think they've shown imagination."

Source: Virginia Inman, "Quaker Stove Co. Prospering on Good Planning, Good Luck," *Wall Street Journal* (August 17, 1981), p. 17. Reprinted by permission of the *Wall Street Journal.* Copyright © 1981 Dow Jones & Company, Inc. All rights reserved.

the management process. Planning helps managers set the stage for further decisions on how to

Organize Design and staff an appropriate structure.

Lead Motivate the human resources, ensure their interpersonal compatibilities, and maintain high levels of task accomplishment.

Control Monitor performance accomplishments and take corrective action where necessary.

What Is a Plan?

A **plan** is a statement of the intended means for accomplishing a desired result. Plans are action statements created by planning, a process of thinking before taking action. Because a plan describes an intended course of action, it should answer the questions of "what?" "how?" "when?" "where?" and "who?" The "what" and the "how" are clearly in evidence in this excerpt from one of the Evans Products Company's plans.[5]

We will strive to maintain our strong consumer image as the "building materials specialist" by stocking ranges of merchandise which allow the customer to choose quality products at a variety of price levels.

Every good plan is also an action statement that includes a clear-cut objective. This **planning objective,** in turn, is the desired future state or end result to be accomplished· through implementation of the plan. For example, Evans Products states a 1985 planning objective for its retail group as "operating 450 stores and a near doubling of revenues."

Dimensions of Plans

Figure 4.2 shows four dimensions for classifying the plans with which you will become involved as a manager. The dimensions are time, scope, use, and level.

Time

It is common to differentiate plans according to the time horizons they represent—short, intermediate, or long term. A rule of thumb is that **short-range plans** cover one year or less, **intermediate** or **medium-range plans** cover one to five years, and **long-range plans** cover five years or more.

In actual practice it is sometimes hard to make such precise distinctions. It is even harder to specify that plans of any one length are to be preferred over others. Rumor has it that Abraham Lincoln was once asked how long he thought a man's legs should be. "Long enough to reach the ground," Lincoln replied. Plans should be considered in the same manner. They should reach far enough into the future to adequately cover the subject under consideration.

Figure 4.2 Four dimensions of organizational plans.

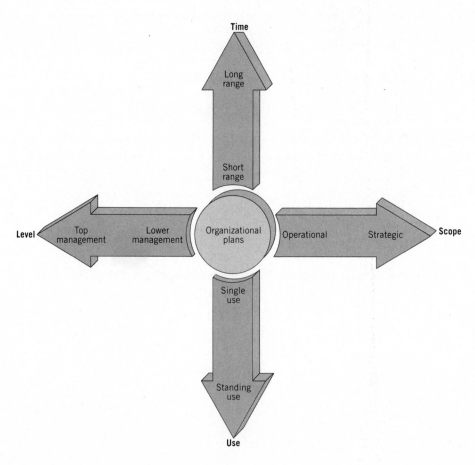

Scope

Another useful perspective on plans is the scope or breadth of activities they represent. **Strategic plans** are comprehensive in scope and reflect longer term needs and directions of the organization or subunit. Planning of this scope involves determining where the organization should go in terms of overall objectives, and then deciding what strategies and resources are required to enable this to happen. **Operational plans,** by contrast, are more limited in scope and address those activities and resources required to implement strategic plans. Because of this activating or energizing nature, operational plans are sometimes referred to as tactical plans. Tactical or operational planning, accordingly, deals more with the allocation of resources and scheduling of actual work activities than with the selection of strategies. Operational plans typical to a business firm include

Production plans Dealing with the methods and tools needed by people in their work.

Financial plans Dealing with the obtaining of money required to support various activities (e.g., capital acquisition) and with the management of money available to the organization at any given point in time.

Facilities plans Dealing with facilities and facilities layouts required to support appropriate task activities.

Marketing plans Dealing with the sales and dis-tribution of an organization's products or services.

Personnel plans Dealing with the recruiting, selection, and placement of personnel appropriate to the various jobs and tasks within the organization.

Remember, planning that is longer range and comprehensive in scope is generally strategic planning. Strategic plans, themselves, establish an action framework within which operational plans can be specified and implemented to the benefit of the organization as a whole. A hierarchy of strategic and operational plans should always complement one another.

As Figure 4.3 suggests, the hierarchy of strategic and operational plans is a significant coordinating device for the organization. Ideally, it helps to ensure that task activities on the part of each individual and group within the organization interrelate and help accomplish overall organizational objectives. Many of the topics covered in later chapters relate to additional means for managers to ensure that such hierarchical coordination between strategic plans, operational plans, and work efforts of individuals and groups is achieved.

Use

Plans also differ according to frequency or repetitiveness of use. A **single-use plan** is used only once. It is designed to meet the needs of a unique situation and will probably not be used again in

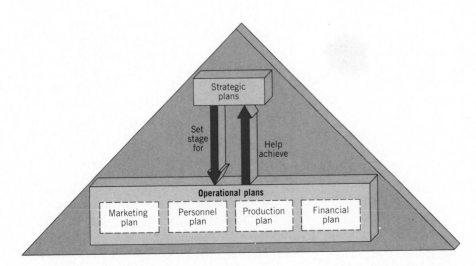

FIGURE 4.3 A hierarchy of strategic and operational plans.

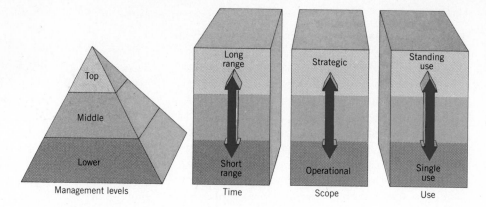

FIGURE 4.4 Levels of management planning in organizations.

Management levels

Time

Long range

Short range

Scope

Strategic

Operational

Use

Standing use

Single use

its exact form. Budgets are good examples of typical single-use plans. They are designed to fit a specific project or time period and are discontinued when the project is completed or the time has expired.

Standing-use plans, on the other hand, are designed to be used again and again. They exist in the form of organizational policies, procedures, and rules. These different types of plans will be discussed shortly in greater detail.

Level

Plans vary, too, by the level of management at which they originate. In fact, it is useful to view planning responsibilities as shown in Figure 4.4. Plans established by higher-level managers establish the action framework within which plans at middle and lower management levels become defined. When it comes to the planning function,

1. *Top-level managers* spend greater proportions of their time on long range and strategic planning that results in the establishment of standing-use plans applicable to the organization as a whole.

2. *Middle-level managers* focus their planning on intermediate-range objectives that pertain more to their functional or departmental areas of subunit responsibility.

3. *Lower-level managers* are concerned with specific and short-range plans that link their subunits with the planning objectives of middle and upper management levels.

Strategic Plans

The four planning dimensions just described allow us to talk in more detail about the types of plans with which managers become involved. A strategic plan is comprehensive in scope and establishes the action framework through which an organization intends to survive and prosper in its environment. Figure 4.5 shows how strategic and operational plans combine to facilitate achievement of organizational objectives.

Strategic plans are long range in orientation. They are usually formulated by top management and put into action by middle-level and lower-level managers. As the foundations on which operational plans are based, they constitute an important interface between operational plans and organizational objectives. Strategic plans and the process of strategic planning are so important that a substantial portion of the next chapter is devoted to these topics. In 1981 Edgar Griffiths was fired as RCA's chairman because of a lack of strategic long-range planning. One RCA executive noted, "While Griffiths was chairman, long-range planning meant: 'What are we going to do for lunch'?" Griffiths's emphasis had been strictly on short-term earnings.[6]

Operational or Tactical Plans

Operational plans, in turn, can be divided into those of a standing-use nature and those of a single-use nature. Let's take a brief look at each of these types of plans as they are significant to managers. Policies, procedures, and rules are all standing-use operational plans. They address problems or situations that tend to be repetitive in nature. Once in place, they are relatively stable and serve to direct the actions of organization members time and time again.

Policies

A **policy** is a plan that communicates broad guidelines for making decisions and taking action. Policies are found in all aspects of an organization. Some policies typical to most types of organizations are shown in Table 4.1. In general, policies tend to focus a manager's thinking on broad means through which organizational objectives are to be accomplished. They are specific enough to be somewhat constraining, but general enough to allow the manager considerable discretion in day-to-day actions. For example, one organization's employment policy states that it is an affirmative-action employer and will not discriminate in hiring by race, creed, or color. As a broad guideline for action, this policy sets a

Table 4.1 Examples of Organizational Policies

Ethics	To conduct organizational affairs by high human and moral standards, with an ultimate sense of social responsibility.
Working conditions	To maintain clean, safe, and technically superior working conditions for all employees.
Compensation	To provide the best remuneration for all contributions rendered to the organization, while remaining fair and equitable in relation to labor market demands and general economic conditions.
Employment	To employ people without regard to race, sex, religion, or national origin.

framework for hiring practices throughout the organization.

Policies commit managers to general action directions or constraints, and they increase the predictability of everyone's actions in the subject

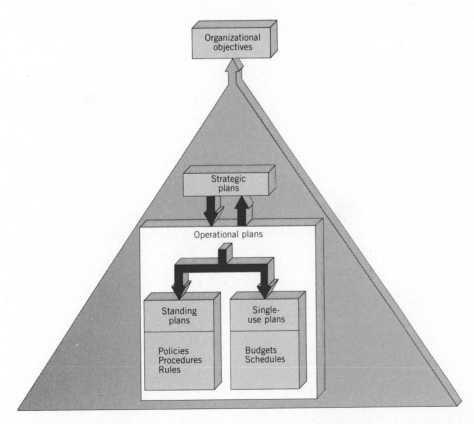

FIGURE 4.5 Types of organizational plans.

Organizational objectives

Strategic plans

Operational plans

Standing plans — Policies Procedures Rules

Single-use plans — Budgets Schedules

areas. Policies are essential to organizations in that they ensure that day-to-day decisions are consistent with the strategies and objectives of the organization as a whole. They help organizations to[7]

1. *Coordinate multiple activities.* The broad guidelines for actions established by policies help to interrelate various people and work groups around a common theme. This helps to ensure that they pull together toward the common goal, even though performing separate and very different tasks.

2. *Achieve efficiency in operations.* By specifying action guidelines, policies tend to limit decision alternatives and help conserve managers' time. Policies also reduce the time spent by higher-level managers in answering questions on recurring topics at lower levels because a policy contains the standing answer to such questions.

3. *Develop future managers.* By setting broad guidelines that still allow some discretion in their implementation, policies allow managers to experience responsibility and take some risk in their decision making.

4. *Establish a desired image.* By being available as formal statements, policies are easily communicated to external public and organization members. As such they help to clarify an image of what the organization is and/or intends to be.

In summary, we can look at the managerial significance of policies in the following light. Policies guide decisions and actions and help implement strategic plans. A good policy, in turn, is one that is

1. *Communicated to all concerned.* A policy cannot guide anyone's actions if people don't know of its existence.

2. *Clear and understandable.* A policy cannot guide anyone's actions if people don't understand its intentions.

3. *Stable but not inflexible.* A policy should have continuity over time since one that changes frequently will cause confusion; however, policies do need to change over time as circumstances change.

Procedures and Rules

Procedures and rules are more specific in their action implications than organizational policies. **Procedures and rules** are standing-use plans that precisely describe what actions are to be taken in specific situations. They emphasize details in specifying things people are expected to do and not to do in the course of their work. Whereas policies are broad guidelines for action that permit considerable discretion, procedures and rules communicate precise guidelines for action. They permit little or no individual discretion. Procedures and rules are often found in employee handbooks or manuals that outline what are commonly called SOPs—standard operating procedures.

Let's return to the prior example of an organization's employment policy. Under this policy, the organization wants to ensure that all job applicants receive fair, equal, and nondiscriminatory consideration during the application process. Table 4.2 illustrates how this policy is supported by a series of precise procedures and rules for supervisors to follow when interviewing job applicants. Note that the table includes both "do's" and "don'ts." This is the essence of any rule or procedure—the communication of a precise and relatively strict plan of action for handling recurring situations in the work setting.

Procedures and rules help ensure the attainment of organizational objectives. Overall, they act along with policies to help channel the decisions and actions of organization members in common directions that are consistent with the strategies and objectives of the total system. They provide predictability by clearly defining behavior appropriate to various situations.

Remember, procedures and rules are necessary ingredients of a successful planning package for the manager. They are found at all levels and in all parts of organizations. In particular, they specify actions to support policies.

Budgets

Single-use plans are developed for a specific circumstance or time frame. They include both budgets and schedules. **Budgets** are plans that commit resources to activities, projects, or programs. Managers become involved with three ba-

Table 4.2 Employment Interviewing Procedures

On the Subject of	Do *Not* Ask	Okay to Ask
Age	Questions showing preferences for specific age group	Date of birth, proof of true age
Family	About family planning, family size, children's ages, child-care plans, spouse's employment, or salary	Freedom to travel if job requires, meeting work schedule requirements. *All* applicants for a position must be asked the same questions
Handicaps	General questions that bring out information that is not job related	Whether person has sensory, mental, or physical handicaps that relate to ability to perform job
Marital status	Whether person is married, single, separated, divorced, engaged	Nothing
National origin	About ancestry, birthplace of applicant, parents, or spouse	Ability to speak, read, or write English or a foreign language if the job requires
Religion	About religion	Anticipated absences from the job

sic types of budgets—fixed, flexible, and zero-base. A **fixed budget** allocates resources on the basis of a single estimate of costs. The estimate establishes a fixed pool of resources that can be used, but not exceeded, in support of the specified purpose. A **flexible budget,** in contrast, allows the allocation of resources to vary in proportion with various levels of activity. Thus a manager operating under a flexible budget can expect a base increment in resource allocations when activity increases from one estimated level to the next. Fixed and flexible budgets are compared in Table 4.3 using the examples of a nursing unit in a community hospital.

The intent of zero-based budgeting is for managers to totally reconsider their priorities, objectives, and activities at the start of each new budget cycle. Under a **zero-based budget,** a project or activity is budgeted in terms of resource allocations as if it were brand new. Managers are not allowed to assume that resources previously allocated to a project or activity in the past will simply be continued in the future. Instead, all projects must compete anew for available funds. Zero-based budgeting is used by businesses, government agencies, and other types of organizations to help ensure that only the most desirable programs receive funding. It is especially useful in inflationary times, when the need exists to respond to changing trends and avoid budgeting on the basis of historical precedent instead of present-day realities.

Budgets are powerful management tools which allocate and commit the resources of an enterprise. They distribute resources across multiple and often competing uses. In so doing, budgets help clarify and reinforce action priorities, maintain coordination, and facilitate evaluation of ultimate results. Good managers anticipate the future well enough to bargain for and

Table 4.3 Fixed versus Flexible Budgets for the Director of Nursing Services in a Community Hospital

Resources Needed	Fixed Budget Allocation	Flexible Budget Allocations		
		50 Patients	75 Patients	100 Patients
Full-time personnel	$60,000	$45,000	$60,000	$80,000
Part-time personnel	12,000	8,000	12,000	20,000
Supplies and support	18,000	14,000	18,000	24,000

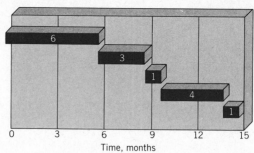

Activities

1. Complete research and development work

2. Complete engineering design

3. Prepare budgets

4. Build prototype

5. Test prototype

FIGURE 4.6 A sample schedule for developing the prototype for a new computer.

obtain an adequate budget. These managers then prove able to achieve performance objectives while remaining within the confines of the budget. Poor managers fail to anticipate the future properly, accept inadequate budgets, and/or are irresponsible in expending their resources and overrunning their budgets. Because of their managerial significance, we will deal more extensively with budgets in Chapter 15 as part of our review of controlling as a basic managerial function.

Schedules

Schedules are single-use plans that tie activities to specific time frames or targets. Most typically they commit time and labor to an organizational project or activity. We use schedules every day in the form of calendars, appointment books, and simple reminders or "do lists" of things to be done and when. An important part of any schedule is the assignment of priorities to activities. Good schedules not only denote what needs to be done, they also identify what needs to be done first.

IBM, for example, is working today to develop new and more sophisticated personal computers for the future. Schedules such as the one shown in Figure 4.6 might well be used to specify the sequence of work activities that must be completed if various efforts are to accumulate properly over time and result in prototypes for new products. Later in Chapter 16 we will examine *Gantt charts* as formal ways of graphically depicting work schedules for the production of the goods and services of organizations.

Scheduling is a challenging as well as important managerial activity. Previously we took special note that managers are busy people. They are bombarded each day by a multitude of tasks

and demands that can be hard to balance in the face of frequent interruptions, crises, and unexpected events. The result is that managers easily fall prey to what R. Alex MacKenzie, noted author and consultant on the subject of time management, identifies as some of the leading "time wasters."[8]

- Telephone interruptions.
- Visitors dropping in without appointments.
- Meetings.
- Crisis situations.
- Lack of objectives, priorities, and deadlines.
- Cluttered desk and personal disorganization.
- Involvement in routine and detail that should be delegated to others.
- Attempting too much at once and underestimating the time it takes to do it.
- Failure to set up clear lines of responsibility and authority.
- Indecision and procrastination.
- Inability to say "no."
- Fatigue.

It is of little surprise, therefore, that managers are more and more seeking expert advice on how to schedule and manage their time. The time-management seminar is one personal-development opportunity that managers are increasingly taking advantage of to improve their skills at scheduling personal time. These seminars advise executives to schedule and more aggressively manage their time in response to daily work pressures. *Newsline 4.2* describes some of the advice typically offered. Think about this issue and ask yourself whether or not personal planning through better time management can help in your work, educational, and even leisure activities.

NEWSLINE 4.2

DON'T WASTE TIME

Among the advice offered to managers by time management experts are the following "do's" and "don'ts."

- Don't face your desk toward an open door because it invites interruptions.
- Don't eat a lot or drink booze at lunch because you'll become sleepy.
- Do cut down the number of meetings by 10 to 15 percent because meetings are notorious time-wasters.
- Do hire a good secretary who can screen your mail and phone calls.
- Do learn how to say no to people (including the boss) who want to divert you from the work you should be doing.
- Don't waste time regretting failures or the things you didn't accomplish.
- Don't let subordinates manipulate you into doing their thinking for them on jobs you've delegated to them.
- Do learn both how to concentrate intently and how to relax.

Source: Adapted from John A. Prestbo, "Don't Waste Time," *Wall Street Journal* (December 11, 1978), p. 28. Reprinted by permission of the Wall Street Journal, © 1978 Dow Jones & Company, Inc. All rights reserved.

THE PLANNING PROCESS

We have been talking about plans—what they are, their dimensions, and the various types of plans with which managers become involved. Plans, though, are outcomes; they are the results of planning—the process of deciding what needs to be done to accomplish objectives. As a process, planning involves deciding in advance of action[9]

- *What* is to be done.
- *When* it is to be done.
- *Where* it is to be done.
- *By whom* it is to be done.
- *How* it is to be done.

Earlier in this chapter we reviewed the case of a hospital administrator to verify that managers do in fact plan. Whether or not managers plan well, of course, is quite another matter. Have you ever heard of the Edsel automobile? In 1952 the Ford Motor Company introduced the first prototype of the Edsel. It was heralded as the car of the future. By the time Edsels came off the assembly line in the late 1950s, however, they were a $350 million flop. They just didn't sell.

The failure of the Edsel could reflect a planning breakdown at the highest executive level in Ford Motor Company. Why, for example, didn't top-level managers recognize the changes in consumer tastes that were occurring during the 1950s and plan accordingly? Or did they recognize the changes, but fail to assess them properly and incorporate their implications into decision making? Perhaps the Ford managers could have benefited from more systematic attention to the steps in a formal planning process.

Steps in Formal Planning

Like problem solving, planning can formally be thought of as a series of steps. As shown in Figure 4.7, these steps are as follows.

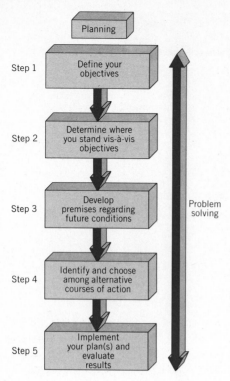

FIGURE 4.7 Steps in the formal planning process.

Step 1

Define your objectives. This establishes where you want to go. Ideally, objectives are specific enough that you will know you have arrived when you get there or how far off the mark you are at various points along the way.

Step 2

Determine where you stand relative to the objectives. This step evaluates current status vis-à-vis the desired future state. It includes an analysis of current strengths and weaknesses in terms of being able to accomplish your objectives in the future.

Step 3

Develop your premises regarding future conditions. This step involves analyzing the situation for external factors that may inhibit goal accomplishment, and forecasting future trends as they relate to these same factors. Sometimes this is called the *generation of future scenarios.*

Step 4

Identify and choose among alternative courses of action. This step is the point of actual decision. Here you list and evaluate alternative courses of action for resolving any discrepancy between where you are and where you want to be. Then you choose one or more alternatives to formulate a course of action appropriate to the achievement of your objectives. This course of action becomes the plan.

Step 5

Implement the plan and evaluate results. This is the action stage where actual results are determined. To achieve your objectives you must both establish a plan and implement it well. True implementation also involves evaluation of results to ensure accomplishment of objectives. When actual results are less than planned objectives, corrective action should be taken in terms of modifications to the original plan and/or the actions through which it is implemented.

Thus the planning process is really a special application of the more general problem-solving process examined in Chapter 3. This relationship between problem solving and planning is also highlighted in Figure 4.7. You may clarify it further by reference back to Figure 3.3 and related discussion.

Different Approaches to Planning

The steps in the planning process can be approached in different ways. Some of the more common approaches are compared and contrasted below.

Inside-Out versus Outside-In Planning[10]

Inside-out planning involves focusing your efforts and energies on doing what you already do, but trying to do it as best as can be done. Planning from the inside out is not going to make dramatic changes in organizations' services or product outputs, but it can result in maximum effectiveness and good human and material resource utilization. Dick Levin, the specialist on long-range planning whose advice to George Allen appeared in the chapter opener, tells of a friend to illustrate this approach.

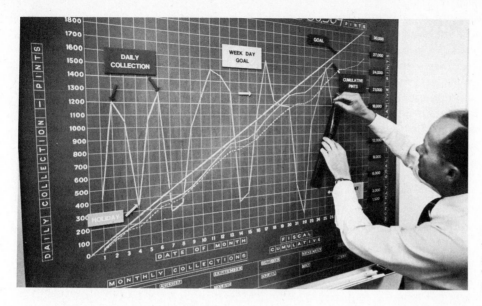

Planning involves the identification of desired goals and the actions through which they can be accomplished.

My good friend Jim is president of a very successful miniconglomerate in the communications industry in Chapel Hill. Jim says the measure of an organization's success is its "humpability factor." (And I've never seen an organization the size of his—250 persons—in my experience with more humpability than Jim's.) Humpability is Jim's term for sheer work, output, effort, push, drive—Jim says once he established absolute, unflagging humpability in his organization, the firm found that it could be anything better than the competition. (It's a fact. His company is in eight separate businesses, and all do well.) Jim's focus is on the inside—keeping up the humpability of the troops. "Whatever comes through the door, we can probably make money at it," he says. He probably can; the financial health of his diverse holdings attests to it.

Levin has another friend, Sid, who operates in the highly competitive corrugated box business. He once made boxes used in department stores for dresses, hosiery, and the like. But the demand slipped as stores stopped including boxes with material purchases. Sid looked around at his options in the corrugated box industry. He saw large and established firms waging wars with one another for this market. Instead of competing with them, Sid decided to serve the market niche they were avoiding—the small special-order business.

Sid uses **outside-in planning;** that is, he analyzes the external environment and makes the internal adjustments necessary to exploit the opportunities and minimize the problems it offers. Levin's description of the success experienced by Sid with this approach speaks for itself.

> The big boys are ecstatic; here is this little guy, relieving them of those cost-ripping, production-line wrenching setups for 213 boxes. He takes their *nuisance* business. Put him out of business? Are you insane? They love Sid. And Sid prospers—a beautiful example of looking outside to see opportunities even in a grossly overcrowded market.

In summary, the managerial implications of these two planning approaches are as follows.

1. *Use inside-out planning* when you want to do what you and/or other people are already doing, but want to do it better. The planning objective in this case is to determine "how" to do it better. Jim did this well.

2. *Use outside-in planning* when you want to find a unique niche for your activities—that is, to do something no one else is doing. The planning objective here is to find the available niches and select the one(s) you are likely to exploit to best advantage. Sid was superb at this approach to planning.

Top-Down versus Bottom-Up Planning[11]

An important dilemma in planning relates to the choice of where the process should begin. **Top-**

down planning** is where top management sets the broad objectives and then allows lower management levels to make plans within these constraints. **Bottom-up planning** begins with plans that are developed at lower levels without such constraints. They are then sequentially passed up the hierarchy to top management levels.

The inevitable managerial question becomes: should planning start at the very top of the organization and then filter down, or should it begin at the bottom and build up to the top? We can explore this question with the help of another of Dick Levin's classic examples: this one involves the University of North Carolina at Chapel Hill, where he works.

> My university sets a terrible example of bottom-up long-range planning. At Chapel Hill we're comprised of 14 colleges and schools, enrolling 21,000 students. Periodically, the chancellor puts out a memo to the vice-chancellors and provost calling for a long-range plan, and the vice-chancellors and provost put out a memo to all the schools and colleges calling for a long-range plan, and the deans of the schools and colleges put out a memo to all the department heads calling for a long-range plan, and the department heads put out a memo to their faculties calling for a long-range plan. Then the faculty members send their long-range plan to their department heads, and the department heads edit, condense, and retype the plans, put them into a common binder, and send them to their deans who edit, condense, and retype all the department plans, put them into a common binder, and send them to the vice-chancellors or provost, who edit, condense, and retype them, put them into a common binder, and send them to the chancellor's planning assistant who edits, retypes, and condenses them and adds a bit of editorial glue before putting them in a common binder and giving them to the chancellor. End of tale. End of plan too.

A person of never-ending experiences, Levin goes on to speak of another case taken from his university. This one involved a new dean who decided to make a plan and then unveil it to his faculty, an extreme top-down approach. This didn't work either; Levin reports that "the dean got stomped (Southern expression for 'after serious reflection, returns to full-time teaching and research')."

Both bottom-up and top-down planning ap-

proaches have disadvantages. When followed to the extreme, bottom-up planning may fail to result in an integrated overall direction for the organization as a whole. This occurs when multiple plans from various subsystems reflect uncoordinated or even conflicting action directions. But a major advantage of this approach is a strong sense of commitment and ownership among those involved in the planning at lower levels. Pure top-down planning, on the other hand, sometimes fails on just this latter point. It may not satisfy the needs of lower levels to participate in and influence the planning process through which future directions guiding their actions become set.

Levin ultimately suggests that the best planning *begins* at the top, but then proceeds in a way that allows serious inputs from all levels. Managers are thus advised to combine the best elements of both the top-down and bottom-up planning approaches. That is, to

- Communicate to all concerned the basic planning assumptions (who we are, what we want to be, and what the future is expected to hold).
- Seek inputs on these and related planning issues from all levels in the organization.
- Lay out various action alternatives, but let all levels comment on their relative merits and demerits.
- Work hard all along the way to get commitment to the final choice of action direction from all levels.

Planning with Precise versus Imprecise Objectives

Most of the planning literature leaves the impression that all planning involves precise and concrete objectives. Peter Drucker, the famous management theorist and consultant, unequivocally states, for example, that planning starts with objectives and answers the question, "What do we have to do to attain our objectives tomorrow?"[12] The implication of this perspective is that planning can and should be accomplished with precise objectives. This approach is illustrated in the set of interrelated business objectives that follow.

Overall objective Make a return on investment of 15 percent after taxes within five years.

Table 4.4 Planning with Precise and Imprecise Objectives

Planning with Precise Objectives	Planning with Imprecise Objectives
Characteristics	*Characteristics*
Specific missions	Diffuse missions
Specific and measurable goals	Diffuse goals that are difficult to measure
Rational, analytic, and quantitative	Intuitive, nonquantitative
Focused, narrow perception of task	Broad perception of task
Lesser need to process novel information	Greater need to process novel information
More efficient use of energy	Possible redundancy, false leads
Separate planning and acting phases	Planning and acting not separate phases
Contingencies	*Contingencies*
People prefer well-defined tasks	People prefer variety, change, complexity
Relatively stable external environment	Relatively unstable external environment
Rigid organizational structure	Flexible organizational structure

Source: Adapted from Michael B. McCaskey, "A Contingency Approach to Planning: Planning with Goals and Planning Without Goals," *Academy of Management Journal*, Vol. 17, No. 2 (June 1974), p. 290. Used by permission.

Subobjective Increase sales to $1 million within five years.

Sub-Subobjective Increase market share, increase advertising expenditures, penetrate new markets, redesign products, and develop new products.

While this is a useful approach to the planning process, there will be times when the organization's or subunit's objectives cannot be as precisely specified. This may occur, for example,[13]

1. Early in an organization's life, before its overall mission is clearly established.
2. When the external environment is unstable and uncertain.

3. When members of the organization don't trust one another well enough to decide on common goals.

When conditions like these exist, managers must be prepared to proceed with the planning process without clear-cut objectives. Michael McCaskey, a professor at the Harvard Business School, calls such planning with imprecise objectives *directional planning*. His comparison of the characteristics and situational contingencies of each planning approach is summarized in Table 4.4.

Planning and Controlling

As the first of the four basic management functions, planning sets the stage for the others. This point was made earlier in the chapter. Figure 4.8 further highlights the special interconnection between planning and controlling.

Control involves responsibility for the measurement and evaluation of action results, and the reformulation of plans where appropriate. When plans are working well, control results in a continuation of past actions. When plans are less successful than desired, corrective action must be taken. This may include the modification of existing plans and/or the creation of entirely new ones.

Planning and controlling, therefore, are forever interrelated in the process of management.

FIGURE 4.8 Thg planning, action, and control cycle in management.

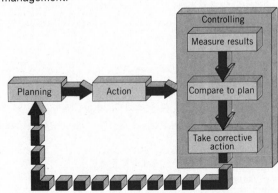

Without control, planning lacks follow-through; without plans, controlling lacks a guiding frame of reference. Simply put, planning leads to controlling, which leads to further planning. This essential relationship of planning and controlling in the management process will be discussed again in Part 5—"Controlling for Productivity."

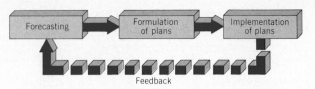

FIGURE 4.9 Forecasting and planning.

FORECASTING

Forecasting is an attempt to predict outcomes that will happen in the future. All good plans involve forecasts, as shown in Figure 4.9; but forecasting, in itself, is not planning. Planning is a more comprehensive activity that involves deciding what to do about the implications of forecasts once they are made.

A forecast is a vision or perspective on the future that managers can use as a planning premise. Forecasts thereby involve assumptions about what will happen in the future. When properly performed, they are a major resource to the manager in the planning process. Unfortunately, this task is not as easy as it may seem. Could you, for example, have foreseen the technological advances that enabled the manufacture of the cheap reliable pocket calculators readily available today? Could you have predicted the advent of the digital watch and the micro- or personal computer? Do you believe that by the late 1980s capable computers will be available at reasonable cost and in a size just slightly larger than the pocket calculators of today?

Types of Forecasts

As a manager you will encounter various types of forecasts. Table 4.5 describes some of the more obvious ones as economic, technological, competitive, and consumer forecasts. Less obvious but still very important are forecasts of new laws and government regulations, resource availabilities, labor supplies, and political events. In each of these cases, the forecast addresses a critical factor with the potential to seriously impact the planning process.

Forecasting Techniques

There are also types of forecasting methods or techniques. Some forecasting is based solely on guesswork, hunch, or intuition. Consider Ideal Toy's early success with the Rubik's Cube. Was it just a good hunch that led Lionel Weintraub to anticipate the tremendous market potential of the cube, even after other companies had turned the project down? Or was there something more systematic involved? Even if it was just a good guess, not every manager can survive over the long run on pure guesswork alone. There are many times when planning can benefit from the more systematic qualitative and quantitative forecasting techniques currently available.

Qualitative Forecasting Techniques

Qualitative forecasting techniques use expert opinions to predict the future. In some cases a single person of special expertise or reputation may be consulted. For example, it is common for ex-secretaries of State of the United States to advise large corporations on international affairs and the risks associated with doing business

Table 4.5 Types of Forecasts Useful to Managers

1. *Economic forecasts* Predict the economic well being of the region, nation, and/or world.
2. *Technological forecasts* Predict what new technologies will be developed in the future and how current technologies will change.
3. *Competitive forecasts* Predict the actions of similar types of organizations.
4. *Consumer forecasts* Predict trends in consumer tastes and demands.

abroad. Their job is straightforward—to analyze political and economic events and forecast the risks associated with various operating strategies.

A sophisticated way of gathering and synthesizing the expert opinions of many persons is the **delphi technique**.[14] In this approach, experts respond independently to a survey questionnaire on a topic. After the responses are analyzed, the results are distributed in anonymous fashion back to the experts along with another round of follow-up questions. The experts have the chance to modify and/or expand their original responses based on the new data summarizing the viewpoints sent in by other members of the delphi panel. This process is repeated through enough cycles that a consensus position or forecast finally emerges from the panel of experts.

The Institute for the Future (IFF), a small but prestigious think tank, is one of the leading practitioners of the delphi technique. It was commissioned in the early 1970s by DuPont, Scott Paper, Lever Brothers, and Monsanto to project important events in the 1980s. This assignment was called "Project Aware." Among other things, a delphi forecast projected that the 1980s would see[15]

1. Decline in the quality of life with continued urban decay, depersonalization of activities,

and distrust of major institutions, but continued increase in the economic standard of living.

2. Resolution of the energy crisis by market forces as rising prices changed energy use and provided incentives for the development of new energy sources.

3. Intensified worker discontent despite improvements in working conditions.

4. Other developments such as use of computers in elementary schools and production of cold vaccines.

How do you assess the accuracy of this forecast after more than a decade? Generally, it seems to speak well for the delphi technique.

Quantitative Forecasting Techniques

Quantitative forecasting techniques use statistical analyses and mathematics to predict future events. Among the more popular ones are time-series analysis, econometric modeling, and statistical surveys. Because such techniques require more sophisticated training, managers often rely on staff experts or outside consultants to perform and even interpret quantitative forecasts for them. The essence of each method follows.

Could you have predicted even just five years ago that children would be attending computer camps in the summertime?

Table 4.6 Some Historical Forecasting Errors

George Templeton Strong (1865)—On Manhattan

By the year 1900, Brooklyn undoubtedly will be the city, and Manhattan will be the suburb. Brooklyn has room to spread; Manhattan has not. The New Yorker uptown on 35th Street already finds it a tedious and annoying job to commute to his business downtown and home again. Can you imagine him fighting his way all the way up to the pig farms on 100th Street 40 years hence?

Daniel Webster (Senate speech, 1848)—On the West

I have never heard of anything, and I cannot conceive of anything more ridiculous, more absurd, and more affrontive to all sober judgment than the cry that we are profiting by the acquisition of New Mexico and California. I hold that they are not worth a dollar!

Simon Newcomb (astronomer, 1903)—On Aviation

The demonstration that no possible combination of known substances, known forms of machinery, and known forms of force can be united in a practical machine by which man shall fly long distances through the air, seems to the writer as complete as it is possible for the demonstration of any physical fact to be.

Henry Adams (1903)—On World Collapse

My figures coincide in fixing 1950 as the year when the world must go to smash.

Admiral William D. Leahy to President Truman (1945)—On the Atomic Bomb

That is the biggest fool thing we have ever done. . . . The bomb will never go off, and I speak as an expert in explosives.

Source: Reprinted from "It'll Never Fly, Orville: Two Centuries of Embarrassing Predictions," *Saturday Review* (December 1979), p. 36.

Time-series analysis This forecasting method makes predictions by projecting trends of the past and present into the future. Through statistical routines such as regression analysis, historical comparisons are made and trends are extrapolated into the future.

Econometric modeling This forecasting technique builds complex computer models to simulate future events based on probabilities and multiple assumptions. Predictions are statistically made based on the relationships discovered to exist among variables included in the models. General economic trends are typically forecasted via econometric models.

Statistical surveys Opinion polls and attitude surveys such as those reported in newspapers and on television are examples of statistical surveys used to forecast events. They are often used to predict consumer tastes, employee preferences, and political choices for the future. The forecast itself is based on statistical analysis of the answers respondents provide to survey questions. Such surveys vary greatly in their confidence fac-

tors according to the rigor underlying the survey and research designs, as well as the strength of the statistics used to analyze results.

Forecasting Errors

In the final analysis, forecasting always relies on human judgment. Even the most sophisticated quantitative approaches still require interpretation in order to complete the actual forecast. Forecasting is thus a good example of where "art" and intuition enter into management practice. As such, forecasts are subject to error and should always be treated cautiously. Some classic examples of historical forecasting errors are presented in Table 4.6. Read and enjoy them, but don't neglect this potential for error as you make plans based on premises established by the forecasts of yourself or other persons.

BENEFITS OF PLANNING

This chapter has so far posed and answered several questions regarding the fundamentals of

NEWSLINE 4.3

KAWASAKI OFFERS CITY ITS WORKERS

LINCOLN NEB., October 23—The concern traditionally shown by Japanese management about the fate of loyal workers has emerged in Nebraska.

Ten production workers are no longer needed at the Kawasaki Motor Corporation's plant here because of a slowdown in sales. Instead of being laid off, however, on Monday they will become temporary employees of the city of Lincoln. But the workers will be paid by the Japan-based company.

Steve Eicher, assistant personnel manager at Kawasaki, said the innovative idea of lending workers to the municipal government instead of terminating their employment came up in a brainstorming session of executives early this month. "It kind of evolved," he said. The company then approached the city with the idea.

Together with a part-time supervisor from Kawasaki, the 10 workers are to receive an average of about $280 a week plus all their usual fringe benefits. If the workers were laid off, their unemployment compensation would be about $106 a week.

This is not entirely a result of generosity on Kawasaki's part. Robert C. Summers, personnel manager at the 200,000-square-foot plant just north of Lincoln, said that Kawasaki wanted to make sure the workers would return to the assembly line when sales went up again, as expected. The company's philosophy is that it is cheaper to keep paying experienced workers than to break in new employees later.

Source: Excerpted from "Kawasaki Offers City Its Workers," *New York Times* (October 24, 1981), p. 23. © 1981 by the New York Times Company. Reprinted by permission.

planning. These questions include, "What is a plan?" "What is planning?" "Do managers plan?" and "How do managers plan?" Now the question is, "Why should managers plan?" Three important answers to this question follow.

Stability, Adaptability, and Contingency

Managers plan for various circumstances. They may plan for stability—that is, to ensure continuation of existing success in a fairly stable environment. They may plan for adaptability to ensure successful reaction to frequent changes in a more dynamic and uncertain environment. They may also plan for contingency in the sense that they anticipate events that may occur in the future and identify appropriate actions that may be taken should they do so.

The purpose of planning, whether it be for stability, adaptability, or contingency, is to keep management the master of the organization's fate.[16] Effective planning benefits organizations by helping them achieve these results through an active and forward-thinking—rather than reactive and passive—posture. When done well, planning can serve the needs of organizations on both a short-run and long-run basis. *Newsline 4.3,* for example, shows how Kawasaki Motor Corporation handled a short-term problem in a manner that was carefully planned ahead to best serve its long term interests.

Clarified Means-Ends Chains

A **means-ends chain** links the work efforts of individuals and groups at various levels of the

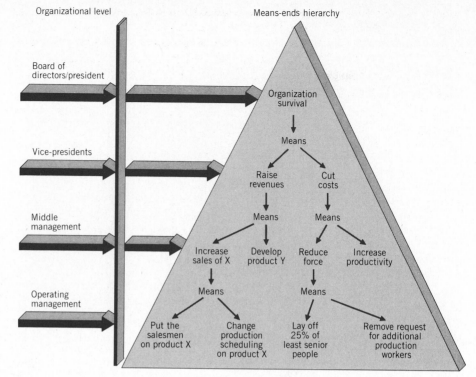

Organizational level

Board of directors/president

Vice-presidents

Middle management

Operating management

Means-ends hierarchy

Organization survival

↓

Means

↙ ↘

Raise revenues   Cut costs

↓   ↓

Means   Means

↙   ↓   ↙   ↘

Increase   Develop   Reduce   Increase
sales of X product Y force   productivity

↓   ↓

Means   Means

↙   ↘   ↙   ↘

Put the   Change   Lay off   Remove request
salesmen   production   25% of   for additional
on product X scheduling least senior production
           on product X people   workers

FIGURE 4.10 Sample means-ends chains in an organization. (*Source:* Adapted from Arthur G. Bedeian, p. 90 of *Organizations: Theory and Analysis* by Arthur G. Bedeian. Copyright © 1980 by Dryden Press, a division of Holt, Rinehart and Winston, Inc. Reprinted by permission of Holt, Rinehart and Winston, CBS College Publishing.)

organization to a common purpose. Through strategic and operational plans, higher-level objectives become the ends toward which lower-level objectives are directed as means. Planning is one way of linking ends and means at each step. In Figure 4.10, for example, a vice-president's objective of raising revenues is the end toward which a middle manager's objective of increasing sales becomes a means. By clarifying means-end chains, planning facilitates unity of purpose and helps managers coordinate the organization as a complex system of people, tasks, structure, and resources.

Performance Improvement

A number of research studies document a positive relationship between planning and organizational performance.[17] The importance of planning for improved organizational performance may well trace to the following additional advantages of a well-executed planning program.

1. *Planning focuses managers' attention on objectives* that can generate results; it gives a perfor-

mance-oriented sense of direction to the organization.

2. *Planning helps managers set priorities* and focus their energies on the most important problems first.

3. *Planning helps managers emphasize organizational strengths* and minimize or overcome weaknesses.

4. *Planning helps managers cope with ever-changing external environments* by helping to anticipate problems and opportunities.

5. *Planning facilitates control.*

MAKING PLANNING EFFECTIVE

Planning isn't all that managers can and should do, but it is extremely important. Good planning can go far in helping managers organize, lead, and control organizations to achieve productivity. Bad planning can also have just as dramatic, but negative, effects on productivity. Before leaving this chapter, it is appropriate to review some helpful planning guidelines. Let's preface this review with a short case.

Illustrative Case: Ento International[18]

After many years of success as a supplier to basic processing industries, top managers at Ento International began to see that its future profitability was being threatened. New steel-industry processes were slowing the growth of demand for Ento's products, and it was widely believed that present developments in the aluminum industry would soon have a similar effect.

Ento's top managers watched these developments with growing concern and finally concluded that the company could no longer afford the luxury of concentrating only on production improvements. They decided that what Ento needed in order to prepare for a less certain future was a formal strategic planning program.

Ento's management made what it considered a good start on the program. They created a central planning department to develop the planning system and put the executive vice-president in charge. The vice-president hired a prestigious consulting firm, and with its help the planning department staff was soon hard at work on Ento's first strategic plan. Planning procedures recommended by the consultants were adopted, and guidelines were issued to the company's divisional managers for gathering planning data. The department also developed sophisticated mathematical techniques to help in analyzing and evaluating alternatives and instructed the divisional managers in their use. Each manager was also given a planning manual with step-by-step instructions for producing a long-range plan for his or her division.

All this activity kept a lot of people busy, and top management was at first very impressed. However, after two years it became clear that strategic planning was not succeeding in clearing up some of Ento's major problems. Sales and profits had not improved, and the implementation of the long-range plan had not been effective. Furthermore, people throughout the organization were frustrated about having to complete complex forms and carry out elaborate procedures as part of the planning activities each year.

What went wrong at Ento International? The answer to this question involves both the limits of planning and the proper organization of the planning process itself. With the case as background, an examination of these issues can help you to put the fundamentals of planning into a final managerial perspective.

Limits of Planning

Planning has its limits as well as potential benefits. Among the many factors that may cause planning to fail are the following pitfalls. They deserve your attention as things which can be avoided by the informed manager. Plans may fail because

- Top management fails to incorporate formal planning into the organization's routines.
- Those who plan are not knowledgeable about or skilled in each step of the formal planning process.
- Poor information is used as the basis for planning.

Managers sometimes overemphasize details and lose sight of the broader purposes of planning.

"THEN IT'S SETTLED. WE'LL MAKE 7 MILLION WITH BLUE HANDLES, 5 MILLION WITH RED HANDLES, 4 MILLION WITH PURPLE HANDLES AND 2 MILLION WITH GREEN HANDLES."

- There is a lack of necessary internal support for plans.
- Unforeseen events occur and disrupt plans.
- There is an unwillingness to modify or cancel poor plans.
- Managers overemphasize the details as opposed to the purpose of planning.
- Managers are unwilling to give up established objectives and replace them with more appropriate new ones.
- Resistance to change by organizational members inhibits the implementation of plans.

Organizing for Planning

Although planning is a responsibility of every manager, organizations benefit from well-planned and well-coordinated planning systems. In general, the need for more comprehensive formal planning systems increases as organizations grow in size. These systems may involve the designation of certain persons to act as staff or corporate planners, and they certainly involve clarification of supervisory, middle-manager, and chief-executive roles in the planning process. Consider this example of the well-organized corporate planning effort spearheaded by Chairman Charles F. Knight at Emerson Electric Company.[19]

> The centerpiece of Emerson's planning process is an annual conference that brings together top division management with Knight, Corporate Planning Chief Joseph J. Adorjan, Vice-Chairman William A. Rutledge, and President E. L. Keyes, Jr. For two days managers hammer out broad, one- and five-year objectives designed to achieve 15% annual corporate earnings growth. Then, through a series of monthly and quarterly meetings, top divisional and corporate executives keep close tabs on both short- and long-range strategies.

Staff Planners

As the planning needs of organizations grow, there is a corresponding need to increase the sophistication of the overall planning system itself. This can be done by designating or hiring **staff planners,** persons who take responsibility for leading and coordinating the planning function for the total organization or one of its major subsystems. A staff planner is usually expected to

- Assist line managers in preparing plans.
- Develop special-purpose plans at the request of higher management.
- Gather information and maintain data files appropriate to all types of planning.
- Assist in communicating plans to organization members.
- Monitor in-use plans and suggest corrective action where necessary.

Organizations may invest even more heavily in the planning function by forming *staff planning groups.* These are formal work units assigned to promote planning throughout the organization. They bring together persons of special expertise, allow them to focus efforts on specific planning tasks, and go a long way toward helping the organization as a whole coordinate multiple planning efforts. The sophistication of staff planning activities tends to be greater in larger and more complex organizations, and where executives deemphasize planning in their personal work efforts.

Supervisory Planning

Figure 4.11 summarizes planning responsibilities typically encountered by supervisors in organizations. Planning at this first level of management is more short run in nature and based on guidelines established by higher-level plans. It is also heavily oriented toward time scheduling and resource distribution to achieve high performance for a work unit.

Planning by Middle Managers

Middle managers should be at the interface between higher-level planning and the supervisory planning just described. A middle manager will largely be concerned with establishing for a division or major subsystem the policies, procedures, budgets, and schedules through which the organization's strategic plans are implemented. These plans allocate resources to work units. They are also action frameworks within which lower-level managers and supervisors

Table 4.7 Planning Responsibilities at Three Management Levels

Level	Planning Focus	Time Horizon	Planning Activities
Top management	Total organization	Long range	Set strategies, allocate resources
Middle management	Divisional or major subsystem	Long- and Medium range	Set policies, procedures, budgets; allocate and employ resources
Supervisory management	Work unit or department	Short range	Set schedules; operate under policies, procedures, budgets; employ resources

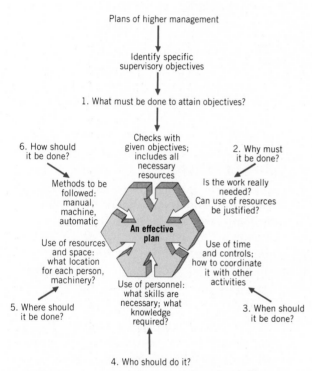

FIGURE 4.11 Planning at the supervisory level. (*Source:* Leslie W. Rue and Lloyd L. Byars, *Supervision: Key Link to Productivity* (Homewood, Ill.: Irwin, 1982), p. 45. Used by permission.)

must plan to distribute and employ their allocated resources to best advantage.

Top Management Planning

Managers at the top or executive level center their attention on longer-range strategic issues. These responsibilities center on establishing overall organizational objectives and identifying the strategies capable of ensuring their achievement. The net result is a strategic focus that provides a sense of identity and integration for planning activities at the other management levels. Top management planning is the pinnacle of an organization's means-ends chain. It helps middle-level and lower-level planning achieve a sense of integration around a common purpose.

Table 4.7 contrasts the differences in planning at the three basic levels of management. It helps clarify the planning responsibilities you will encounter at various career stages.

SUMMARY

A plan is a statement of the intended means for accomplishing a desired objective. Planning is the process through which managers select objectives and then decide what must be done in order to attain them. As such, planning is one of the basic management functions. It is an essential responsibility of any manager, but it demands a capability to plan well in a complex and often dynamic environment.

Managers become involved with plans that vary in terms of time horizon (short, intermediate, and long term), scope (strategic and operational), use (single use and standing use), and level of attention (top, middle, and lower management). Important special types of plans include policies, procedures or rules, budgets, and schedules.

The planning process can be considered as a

series of steps including (1) defining objectives, (2) determining where things stand relative to the objectives, (3) developing premises regarding future conditions, (4) identifying and choosing among alternative courses of action, and (5) implementing the plan and evaluating results. Forecasting is a planning aid of particular importance in Step 3. It can be accomplished through both qualitative and quantitative techniques.

The potential benefits of planning are numerous. They include opportunities for greater integration of means-ends chains and improved performance, as well as establishing action foundations for stability, adaptability, and contingency in day-to-day operations.

Ultimately, planning is done by managers at all levels in the organizational hierarchy. It can also be done by persons or groups specially designated to act as staff planners for the organization as a whole.

The next chapter investigates in greater detail the process of strategic planning and the role of organizational objectives as means of ensuring coordination of activities across all levels and subsystems in organizations. Before moving on, however, consider the following exchange of quotations by W. E. Henly and author Dick Levin, whose thoughts on planning were introduced earlier in the chapter.[20] They are a nice conclusion to this initial look at the fundamentals of planning.

I am the master of my fate,

I am the captain of my soul.
W. E. Henly

Not without a plan, you're not.
R. I. Levin

THINKING THROUGH THE ISSUES

1. Define *plan* and *planning*. Explain the differences between the two terms.

2. State and explain three reasons why managers might not plan *as much as* they should.

3. State and explain three reasons why managers might not plan *as well as* they should.

4. List the five steps in the formal planning process and give examples of each.

5. Demonstrate how planning is critical for successful accomplishment of the other management functions.

6. Why are means-ends chains important to organizations, and how does planning relate to them in actual practice?

7. How does forecasting become a part of the planning process?

8. Assume you are (a) manager of a local health-food store and (b) president of a bank. In each case will you be more inclined to plan outside-in or inside-out? Top-down or bottom-up? Why?

9. What types of contingency plans should a university have? How about a bank? A hospital? An automobile dealership?

10. When would a staff planner and/or staff planning group benefit an organization and be worth the required dollar investment?

THE MANAGER'S VOCABULARY

Bottom-up planning	Intermediate-range plans	Planning	Schedules
Budgets	Long-range plans	Planning objective	Short-range plans
Delphi technique	Means-Ends chain	Policy	Single-use plans
Fixed budget	Operational plans	Procedures	Staff planners
Flexible budget	Outside-in planning	Qualitative forecasting	Standing-use plans
Forecasting	Plan	Quantitative forecasting	Strategic plans
Inside-out planning		Rules	Top-down planning
			Zero-based budget

CAREER PERSPECTIVE:
HELP WANTED—CORPORATE PLANNER[21]

A $2.5 billion meat and food processing corporation located in the Southwest is currently seeking a Senior Corporate Planning Executive, who will report directly to the CEO.

The individual selected will head a professional staff and will direct all strategic, long-range, and annual planning activities as well as marketing research projects. As a member of Senior Management, the successful candidate will have the opportunity to develop an integrated planning system which will focus the future growth and direction of the corporation.

The ideal candidate will have solid experience in all types of planning activities and a proven track record in designing and implementing successful planning functions. We offer exciting professional opportunities and an outstanding benefits package. Compensation will be commensurate with your experience and accomplishments. If you are this type of individual, we invite you to send your resume and salary history in complete confidence to:

Box 00-123

The Wall Street Journal

Questions

1. Assume you meet the experience requirements for this job. What would you include in a letter of application to explain your viewpoint on what an "integrated planning system" should entail?

2. What do you think would be appropriate prior experience and education for a person applying for this position? Why?

CASE APPLICATION: COLUMBIA'S CREATIVE IRRITANT[22]

Columbia University's Graduate School of Business named a new dean. He is John C. "Sandy" Burton, a person who likes to think he has been "a creative irritant" in his own fields of accounting and finance. The question is whether or not Burton will be a similar "creative irritant" for his business school as a whole. He comes to the Columbia deanship at a time when applications remain strong and MBAs from top schools are commanding very high salaries. However, there is evidence that the demand for MBAs will decline dramatically in the near future as industry and other employers tighten their hiring practices in response to the economic pressures of the present times.

American business is also criticizing the business schools as contributing to some of their current productivity ills. For example, businessmen complain that graduates don't know enough about foreign cultures, science and technology, politics, and related issues to help their businesses compete effectively in the world and national marketplace.

Burton replies, "I don't think the goal of business schools should be to make up for the deficiencies of the total educational system. It's not up to business schools to train students in foreign languages or basic math; and there are reasons to debate whether we should be teaching communication skills such as writing. The comparative advantage of business schools is in providing students with analytical techniques and frameworks for thinking about the business problems they will confront in the future." When asked about the charge that U.S. companies are too short-term in their planning horizons, and that the techniques taught in business schools are partly to blame for this effect, Burton replies as follows. "There may be something to that, but the real problem is not with the techniques, it's with the high inflation and, even more important, the high uncertainty about inflation rates. With the kind of economic environment the U.S. has in recent years, a short-term focus may well be rational."

The largest proportion of Columbia's graduates go into the New York financial world of banks, investment houses, and brokerage firms. When asked whether he hoped to change that pattern, and encourage more students, for example, into manufacturing firms, he replied as follows. "Columbia is a general business school, and will continue to be. We offer good preparation for students going into manufacturing or any area of business. But Columbia has drawn its strength historically from the fact that it is in the center of the financial world. That's where the largest market for our students is, and I think it is appropriate for us to serve market needs."

Questions

1. Do you think Burton needs to engage his business school in a rigorous planning activity? Why or why not?

2. If he is to plan for the future, what approach should Burton take to ensure that the best plans will be defined *and* that they will be well implemented?

CLASS EXERCISE: TIME MANAGEMENT

One purpose of planning is to help managers allocate their time and that of others most efficiently. Think of your current time schedule. How well do you allocate your time? What can you do to plan better for your time utilization?

1. Complete the time log below for a recent schoolday by describing your activities during each time block. Include as much detail regarding your work, leisure, and student activities as possible.

Morning 7–8 8–9 9–10 10–11 11–12

_____

_____

Afternoon 12–1 1–2 2–3 3–4 4–5

_____

_____

Evening 5–6 6–7 7–8 8–9 9–10

_____

_____

2. Carefully analyze your time log in Part 1 to identify "time wasters". These are the things that represent a non-productive use of your time. Circle them on the time logs.

3. Discuss your list of "time wasters" with those of a nearby classmate. Discuss, too, how these time wasters can be eliminated. Await further class discussion.

4. Read (in your spare time!) James T. McCay, *The Management of Time* (Englewood Cliffs, N.J.: Prentice-Hall, 1959), or Alan Laekin, *How to Get Control of Your Life* (New York: Signet, 1973), for many helpful tips on time management.

REFERENCES

[1] Dick Levin, *The Executive's Illustrated Primer of Long Range Planning*, © 1981, pp. 2, 3. Reprinted by permission of Prentice-Hall, Inc., Englewood Cliffs, New Jersey.

[2] Based on Louis E. Boone and David L. Kurtz, *Principles of Management* (New York: Random House, 1981), p. 89.

[3] Reprinted by permission of the Harvard Business Review. Excerpt from "The Manager's Job: Folklore and Fact," by Henry Mintzberg, *Harvard Business Review* (July-August 1975), p. 51. Copyright © 1975 by the President and Fellows of Harvard College; all rights reserved.

[4] This case is adapted from William F. Glueck, *Management*, Second Edition (Hinsdale, Ill.: The Dryden Press, 1980), pp. 242–243.

[5] From Evans Products Company's *1980 Annual Report*.

[6] Lawrence J. Gitman and Carl McDaniel, Jr., *Business World* (New York: Wiley, 1983), p. 104.

[7] Based on Robert L. Trewatha and M. Gene Newport, *Management*, Third Edition (Dallas: Business Publications, 1982), pp. 145–148.

[8] R. Alex MacKenzie, *The Time Trap* (New York: AMACON, American Management Associations, 1972).

[9] George Steiner, "Making Long-Range Company Planning Pay Off," *California Management Review*, Vol. IV (1962), pp. 28–41.

[10] This section is based on a discussion by Levin, op. cit., pp. 80–88. The quotes from pp. 81, 83 are used by permission.

[11] This section is based on a discussion by Levin, op. cit., pp 93–97; The quote from these pages are used by permission.

[12] Peter F. Drucker, *Management: Tasks, Responsibilities, Practices* (New York: Harper & Row, 1973), p. 126.

[13] Michael B. McCaskey, "A Contingency Approach to Planning: Planning with Goals and Planning Without Goals," *Academy of Management Journal*, Vol. 17 (June 1974), pp. 281–291.

[14] See Andre L. Delbecq, Andrew H. Van de Ven, and David H. Gustafson, *Group Techniques for Program Planning* (Glenview, Ill.: Scott, Foresman, 1975).

[15] *Business Week* (August 25, 1973), pp. 70–71.

[16] Levin, op. cit., p. 15.

[17] See, for example, Delmar Karger and Zafar Malik, "Long Range Planning and Organizational Performance," *Long Range Planning*, Vol. 8 (December 1975), pp. 60–64; Zafar Malik and Delmar Karger, "Does Long Range Planning Improve Company Performance?" *Management Review*, Vol. 8 (September 1975), pp. 27–31; and Stanley Thune and Robert House, "Where Long Range Planning Pays Off," *Business Horizons*, Vol. 13 (August 1970), pp. 81–87.

[18] Adapted from Kjell A. Ringbakk, "Why Planning Fails," *European Business* (Spring 1971), pp. 15–27. Used by permission.

[19] "Emerson Electric: High Profits from Low Tech," *Business Week* (April 4, 1983), p. 61. Reprinted from the April 4, 1983 issue of Business Week by special permission, © 1983 by McGraw-Hill, Inc., New York, NY 10020. All rights reserved.

[20] Levin, op. cit., p. 14. Used by permission.

[21] *Wall Street Journal* (February 16, 1982), p. 16. Reprinted by permission of the *Wall Street Journal*. Copyright © 1982 Dow Jones & Company, Inc. All rights reserved.

[22] Adapted from Adam Meyerson, "Sandy Burton, Columbia's Creative Irritant," *Wall Street Journal* (March 8, 1982), p. 18. Reprinted by permission of the *Wall Street Journal*, © 1982 Dow Jones & Company, Inc. All rights reserved.

5

STRATEGIC PLANNING AND ORGANIZATIONAL OBJECTIVES

OVERDRIVEN EXECS

To hear some middle managers there tell it, the pressure cooker atmosphere at Pittsburgh's H. J. Heinz Co. wasn't confined to the concern's steamy food-processing plants.

"When we didn't meet our growth targets, the top brass really came down on us," recalls a former marketing official at the company's huge Heinz U.S.A. division. "And everybody knew that if you missed the targets enough, you were out on your ear."

In this environment, some harried managers apparently resorted to deceptive bookkeeping when they couldn't otherwise meet profit goals set by the company's top executives. Invoices were misdated and payments to suppliers were made in advance—sometimes to be returned later in cash—all with the aim, insiders say, of showing the sort of smooth profit growth that would please top management and impress securities analysts.

Today Heinz officials won't comment on the profit-juggling practices or on what led to them until an investigation is completed by the board of directors' audit committee. However, what began as an attempt to satisfy superiors undoubtedly has tarnished the image of one of the country's corporate stalwarts. The Heinz annual meeting has been delayed; and the outside auditors' opinion of the company's fiscal 1979 report has been withheld until the juggling scheme's precise effect—currently estimated at a cumulative $8.5 million—on previously reported Heinz earnings is determined.

Whether at Heinz or at any of thousands of other U.S. companies, pressure to achieve goals is, of course, an everyday fact of life. Properly applied, such pressure can motivate employees to turn in their maximum performance. Sometimes, though, corporate goals are set too high or are simply unreasonable. Then an employee often confronts a hard choice—to risk being branded incompetent by telling superiors that they ask too much, or to begin taking unethical or illegal shortcuts.

"A certain amount of tension is desirable," explains Paul Lawrence, professor of organizational behavior at the Harvard Business School. "But at many companies the pressures to perform are so intense and the goals so unreasonable that some middle managers feel the only way out is to bend the rules, even if it means compromising personal ethics."[1]

PLANNING AHEAD

Managers at all levels in organizations are responsible for performance contributions to the achievement of organizational objectives. Managers at top levels set the broad objectives, while those at middle and lower levels carry them out in operational terms. This chapter will prepare you for all three levels of managerial responsibility. It should also help you avoid the pitfalls described in the opening example. Key topics in the chapter include

The Concept of Strategy
Organizational Objectives
Strategic Planning and Organizational Objectives
Major Elements of Strategic Planning
Strategic Planning and the Manager

Battling Bell	*Aiming High*	*Financial Forays*
GTE Runs Big Risks As It Strives to Enter Complex New Markets	American Greetings Cares Enough to Try Its Very Hardest	Sears Expansion Brings Increased Competition To Bankers and Brokers
It Faces Unregulated AT&T And Many Other Rivals; Management Overhauled	No. 2 Card Maker Is Turning To TV, New Technology To Best No. 1 Hallmark	But Some Doubt the Success Of Retailer in Ventures; Sears's Internal Problems

Question What do the above headlines share in common?[2]

Answer Each conveys the strategy employed by an organization in its attempt to ensure operating success in a challenging environment.

The articles that accompany these headlines report on organizations taking or about to take certain risks by anticipating the future and then acting on the basis of this anticipation. American Greetings is aggressively pursuing a new marketing strategy in an attempt to replace Hallmark Cards as the nation's largest greeting-card manufacturer; Sears is diversifying into the new business realm of financial services; GTE is reaching out to explore opportunities created by court rulings deregulating a telephone industry previously dominated by AT&T. The managers who guide these organizations are also taking risks. Many careers are on the line as the quality of "strategic" decisions is put to the test of achieving organizational success.

The chapter-opening example shows how the pressures of high performance objectives affected middle managers in one company. Consider also the case of RCA, a company that had six chief executive officers between 1976 and 1981.[3] One CEO lasted only five months in 1981. This turnover in the executive ranks reflects dramatic declines in RCA's operating success over the period–reduced corporate credit ratings, losses in its financial-services division, and poor ratings with its television network, NBC. Table 5.1 summarizes the cost of such performance failures in terms of executive turnover and compensation settlements. Such "sweet deals" are expensive for the company and probably have a negative effect on some executive careers as well.

Underlying such organizational problems as those encountered at RCA, one often finds errors of strategic thinking. This chapter focuses on strategy, strategic planning, and organizational objectives to help develop your capabilities in this regard and to help you understand strategic issues challenging the organizations for which you work. The importance of these topics cannot be overemphasized. The following example shows how even the most famous of U.S. entrepreneurs, Henry Ford, was deficient in this respect.[4]

Surely You Have Heard—

■ That Henry Ford, starting with nothing in 1905,

Table 5.1 The Sweet Deals at RCA

Coming In	Position	Contract Term	Compensation
Jane C. Pfeiffer	Chairman of NBC	10/78–9/81	$225,000 per year + total incentive compensation for three years of $600,000
Edgar H. Griffiths	Chairman and CEO	12/79–11/82	$450,000 per year
Maurice R. Valente	President and chief operating officer	1/80–12/82	$400,000 per year + total incentive compensation for two years of $400,000 + stock option of 25,000 shares + the differential between former employer's bonus and $180,000 for 1979
Walter S. Holmes Jr.	Chairman, CIT	2/80–1/83	$400,000 per year
Donald B. Smiley	Director	8/80–7/81	$250,000 consulting fee
Thornton F. Bradshaw	Chairman and CEO	7/81–6/86	$450,000 per year + five-year total incentive compensation of $1.5 million + cash value of 6,500 participation units valued at a minimum of $29 each + stock option of 50,000 shares

. . . and Going Out	Termination Date	Settlement
Maurice R. Valente	6/80	$1.25 million
Jane C. Pfeiffer	7/80	$705,000
Edgar H. Griffiths[a]	6/81	Five-year consulting contract of $1.25 million

Source: "RCA: Still another Master," *Business Week* (August 17, 1981), p. 84. Reprinted from the August 17, 1981 issue of *Business Week* by special permission, © 1981 by McGraw-Hill, Inc., New York, NY 10020. All rights reserved. [Data from exhibits filed with SEC by RCA.]
[a] Remains a member of RCA's board.

had 15 years later built the world's largest and most profitable manufacturing enterprise.

- That the Ford Motor Company, in the early 1920s, dominated and almost monopolized the American automobile market and held a leadership position in most of the other important automobile markets of the world.

- That Ford had amassed, out of profits, cash reserves of a billion dollars or so.

But Did You Also Know—

- That, only a few years later, by 1927, this seemingly impregnable business empire was in shambles? Having lost its leadership position and barely able to stay a poor third in the market, it lost money almost every year for 20 years or so, and remained unable to compete vigorously right through World War II.

- That in 1944 the founder's grandson, Henry Ford III, then only 26 years old and without training or experience, took over, ousted his grandfather's cronies two years later in a palace coup, brought in a totally new management team and saved the company?

THE CONCEPT OF STRATEGY

A **strategy,** in the sense communicated by the introductory headlines, is a comprehensive plan or action orientation that sets critical direction and guides the allocation of resoures for an organization. It is a focus for action that represents a "best guess" regarding what must be done to ensure longer-run prosperity for the organization or one of its subsystems. Thus any strategy begins with decision making; every strategy, in turn, has the capability to guide the behavior and direction of an organization in its environment.

Strategy and Environment

In essence, strategy defines the direction in which an organization intends to move and establishes the framework for action through which it intends to get there. Strategy is a choice made by an organization's decision makers that specifies how they plan to match the organization's strengths and weaknesses with problems or opportunities in the external environment. Strategy, we can say, is the means through which an organization intends to come to terms with its environment.

The external environment is a dynamic and complex force with which organizations and their managers must contend. We will have more to say about the environment later in this chapter and at many times throughout the book. For now, though, note that varying environmental conditions can have different implications for strategy formulation and implementation. In particular,

1. *Stable environments lend themselves to more programmed strategies.* When there is little change in the environment, strategies can be programmed because the organization's needs are likely to remain fairly constant over time. Programmed strategies are specified in great detail and implemented with precision and under strict control over time.

2. *Dynamic environments require more flexible strategies.* When the environment is changing, programmed strategies can inhibit the organization's adaptation to new circumstances. Flexibility is necessary to allow for variation of strategic emphasis to keep abreast of changing environmental conditions over time.

3. *Uncertain environments call for contingency strategies.* When the environment is highly unpredictable, the strategic challenge moves beyond even the advantage that flexibility provides. Uncertainty requires contingency in the sense that a set of alternative strategies exist, each ready for implementation whenever a specific change of circumstances makes it appropriate.

Types of Strategies

We will draw on the work of William Glueck, one of the foremost scholars and writers in the area of strategy, throughout this chapter. Table 5.2 depicts four basic types of strategies available to managers—stability, growth, retrenchment, and combination. As different means for an organization to achieve success in various environments, each of these strategies can be approached from a programmed, flexible, or contingency perspective. The four grand strategies are briefly described here.[5]

Stability Strategy

A **stability strategy** maintains the present course of action. Glueck believes this is the most frequent of all grand strategies used by organizations. Reasons for using this strategy include

- The organization is already perceived to be performing well.
- It is less risky as a course of action.
- It is easier and more comfortable as a course of action.

Table 5.2 Four Types of Strategies

Strategy	Frequency of Use	Success
Stability	Most frequent	When industry is mature, environment is slow in changing, and/or firm is successful now
Growth	Second most frequent	Mixed results
Retrenchment	Least frequent	Mixed results
Combination	Used mainly by large firms; used more often than retrenchment	In periods of economic transition (recession, recovery) and/or periods of change in main product-service life cycle

Source: Adapted from *Business Policy: Strategy Formulation and Management Action,* Second Edition, by William F. Glueck, p. 121. Copyright © 1976 by William F. Glueck. Used with the permission of McGraw-Hill Book Company.

BETHLEHEM TO STAY WITH STEEL WHILE COMPETITORS DIVERSIFY

BETHLEHEM, PA.—Despite a depressed market for its major product, Bethlehem Steel Corp. will continue to put its money in the steel business for at least the next couple of years.

That's how Donald H. Trautlein, chairman, sees the near-term course for the nation's second largest steelmaker. Bethlehem's strategy seems to contrast with that of some of its competitors, who are aggressively diversifying into nonsteel business. U.S. Steel Corp., the No. 1 steelmaker, has made a $6.4 billion bid for Marathon Oil Co., National Steel Corp. has entered the savings and loan business, and Armco Inc. has bought an insurance company.

"Our intention today isn't to look outside the business we are in now," Trautlein said in an interview. In 1980, steel and steel-related operations accounted for 83% of Bethlehem's $6.7 billion sales. The rest came from shipbuilding, plastics and coal operations. Underscoring Bethlehem's commitment to steel is the company's $750 million modernization, announced last July, of four steel plants over the next four years.

Trautlein believes the company's efforts to become "'the lowest cost" steelmaker in the industry—where low productivity has been a major cause of poor earnings—will pay off when demand picks up. Longer term, however, Bethlehem isn't discounting the possibility that it might be forced to go outside steel, as others have done, to improve financial performance. The company's return on sales was a dismal 1.8% in 1980, down from 3.9% in 1979.

Trautlein is more certain about the short term that steel demand can go nowhere but up. After seeing months of depressed steel demand, with November and December "nothing short of a disaster," Trautlein said, "we've got to believe that we aren't going to be in this kind of recession forever." The chief executive officer thinks that the economy will begin to recover gradually in spring or early summer and that orders for steel then will pick up quickly because of pent-up demand and low inventories at the customer level.

Source: From Amal Nag, "Bethlehem's Near-Term Tactic is to Stay with Steel while Competitors Diversify," *Wall Street Journal* (January 15, 1982), p. 10. Reprinted by permission of the *Wall Street Journal*. Copyright © 1982 Dow Jones & Company, Inc. All rights reserved.

■ The organization needs a "breathing spell" after time spent on one or more other strategies.

Choice of a stability strategy doesn't necessarily represent a "do-nothing" posture for an organization or its managers. Instead, it is a continuation of an existing operating pattern or action agenda. It is most appropriate for successful organizations in relatively stable environments. An example of a well-known firm's decision to pursue a stability strategy in the face of competitive moves to the contrary is shown in *Newsline 5.1*. What do you think? Is this a "do-nothing" move on the part of Bethlehem Steel? Or is it just a wise choice by the chief executive officer?

Growth Strategy

The **growth strategy** stands in direct contrast to the stability strategy just described. Growth in-

WHAT BLEW THE HEAD OFF MILLER'S PROFITS

In 1969 Philip Morris paid $130 million for controlling interest in Miller Brewing Company. Miller proceeded to offer its "Lite" beer to the market and pursue very aggressive (and creative) advertising campaigns. By 1981 Miller's moved from seventh to second place in the highly competitive brewing industry.

As an investment for Philip Morris, however, Miller's has not been such a star. In 1980 the company's management raised prices just when the U.S. economy was going flat. Its competitors did not follow suit. Miller's sales leveled off after gaining substantially in prior years. This was all complicated by Miller's heavy spending during the mid to late 1970s on capital expansion to keep up with rising sales. Sales growth failed to keep pace with capacity expansion and profits suffered as a result.

"Overcapacity is a key ingredient hurting their earnings," says analyst Emanuel Goldman of Sanford C. Bernstein & Co. And with marketing expenses remaining high, "the growth in volume did not keep up with the spending to get the volume," says industry consultant Robert S. Weinberg.*

Source: Information on Miller Brewing Co. is found in *Fortune* (June 29, 1981), pp. 62–63, *Time* (April 26, 1982), p. 50, and *Business Week* (February 15, 1982), p. 39.
* The quotes are from *Business Week*, op cit.

---

volves expansion of the organization's current operations. It can occur through a pattern of planned expansion of existing services or products, or it can occur through diversification and the addition of new products or services. In either case, growth is a more risky strategy to pursue than stability, and the pressures on executive decision makers are great. *Newsline 5.2* describes how Philip Morris, Inc., Miller beer's parent company, struggled in 1982 to overcome problems encountered when growth was pursued at an inopportune time.

Glueck gives five reasons why organizations adopt growth strategies.

1. Growth is necessary for long-run survival in volatile industries; stability can mean short-run success but long-range death.

2. Many managers equate growth with effectiveness.

3. Some people believe that society benefits from growth strategies.

4. Many managers wish to be remembered—to leave a monument to themselves in the workplace. Thus managerial motivation encourages them to gamble and choose a grand strategy of growth; risk is less with a stability strategy, but so are the rewards and recognition.

5. Growth companies become better known and may be more capable of attracting quality employees as a result.

Retrenchment Strategy

A **retrenchment strategy** implies a decision to slow down, cut back, and seek performance improvement through greater operating efficiency. Glueck considers retrenchment the less frequent and least popular of all the grand strategies. The reason is simple. To pursue retrenchment is, on the surface at least, an admission of failure. Thus it is viewed as a strategy of "last resort" by most managers.

Combination Strategy

Finally, we have the **combination strategy**—that is, the simultaneous use of more than one of the other strategies. The combination of strategies can involve the organization as a whole, or it may reflect the differences among strategies employed by major subunits. For example, a company might pursue stability overall, but attempt to do so by pursuing growth in certain major internal divisions and retrenchment in others. Combination strategies are most common to larger, more complex organizations and are employed more frequently during volatile and distressed economic times.

ORGANIZATIONAL OBJECTIVES

Ideally, there is a one-to-one relationship between strategy and organizational objectives. Simply, good strategy helps achieve organizational objectives.

Organizational objectives are "those ends which the organization seeks to achieve by its existence and operations."[6] They are concrete ends or goals that symbolize the ultimate purpose of organizations. Strategies, in turn, represent the means through which these ends are pursued at any given point in time.

Types of Organizational Objectives

Theorists generally discuss official and operating objectives of organizations. **Official objectives** constitute the organization's formal purpose or mission such as would be stated in a report to shareholders, article of incorporation, or other similar official documents. Chesebrough-Pond's states its official objective as serving as "a diversified worldwide manufacturer of branded consumer products for the health and well-being of the entire family." CBS Inc. states its objective as being "a broad-based entertainment and communications company." Apple Computer Inc. views its official objective as "bringing technology to individuals through personal computers."[7]

The official objectives of organizations serve five basic purposes. They help organizations to achieve[8]

1. *Identification* Clarity of purpose. This includes internal agreement and commitment, as well as a clear-cut identity in the eyes of suppliers, customers, clients, and other outsiders.

2. *Integration* Overlap between the objectives and aspirations of members and the needs of the organization as a whole. This involves linking the satisfaction of individual needs with the accomplishment of organizational objectives.

3. *Collaboration* Mechanisms for resolving the inevitable conflicts among organization members. This involves providing a sense of overall agreement within which specific conflicts can be handled in a constructive rather than destructive fashion.

4. *Adaptation* Ability to respond quickly and positively to environmental changes that place different demands on the organization and its members. This includes the wherewithal to keep abreast of such changes and incorporate them into key problem-solving and decision-making processes.

5. *Revitalization* Ability to renew the basic energy and potential of the organization over time. This involves not change per se, but continued provision for self-renewal and the avoidance of decay in the organization's resource potential.

Operating objectives, by contrast, are specific ends toward which organizational resources are actually allocated. They are more tangible than official objectives and represent key results that organizations pursue in their day-to-day activities. A list of common operating objectives follows.[9] Overall, such operating objectives relate to the productivity achieved by the organization in fulfilling its official objectives and basic purpose.

- *Profitability* Producing goods or services at a net profit in the business sector or within budget allowances in the public sector.
- *Market standing* Proportion of market in providing goods or services served by the organization versus its competitors.
- *Resources* Obtaining and maintaining human

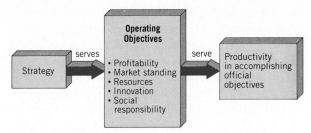

FIGURE 5.1 Strategy and organizational objectives.

and physical resource inputs of adequate quality and quantity.

- *Innovation* Achieving the level of new product, service, or process development required to keep the organization competitive over time.

- *Social responsibility* Serving the public good by making a positive contribution to the environment and overall quality of life.

Figure 5.1 shows the working relationship between strategy, operating objectives, and official objectives. The causal sequence is linear in logic. A good strategy facilitates achievement of operating objectives. Satisfaction of the operating objectives serves the official objectives, which should represent fulfillment of the organization's basic purpose.

Hierarchy of Objectives

Chapter 4 introduced the concept of a means-ends chain. Defined as the linkage between the work efforts of individuals and groups to the overall purpose of the organization, the means-ends chain actually represents a functional interrelationship among operating objectives at various levels.

A **hierarchy of objectives** is a series of objectives linked to one another at the various levels of management such that each higher-level objective is supported by one or more lower-level ones. Figure 5.2 presents a hierarchy of objectives for a sample business firm in the consumer-goods industry. The existence of a hierarchy of objectives is important to any organization for several reasons.

1. It helps to ensure the proper alignment of all organizational levels with the organization's purpose.

2. It helps to coordinate decisions at all levels around this sense of purpose.

3. It provides a basis for establishing standards facilitating performance measurement at all management levels.

4. It helps to avoid **suboptimization**—that is, having some subunits accomplish their objectives at the expense of the other subunits in the organization.

5. It helps to prevent **displacement of objectives** wherein means become more important than the ends they were originally intended to serve.

Management by Objectives

In Chapter 14 we will discuss **management by objectives,** usually referred to as MBO, as a management technique that assists in clarifying and implementing an organization's hierarchy of objectives. MBO is a process of joint objective setting between a superior and subordinate. It involves managers working with their subordinates to clarify performance objectives that are consistent with the objectives of the work unit and

FIGURE 5.2 A sample hierarchy of objectives.

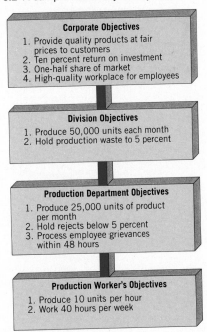

organization as a whole. When this process is followed throughout the organization, MBO clarifies the hierarchy of objectives as a series of well-defined and integrated means-ends chains.

The roots of MBO lie in the work of Peter Drucker. His logic goes something like this.[10] In an organization, each person contributes something different. But everyone's efforts must be coordinated to produce the goods or services of the organization as a whole. The task performance of each individual and group must somehow be linked through means-ends chains to the organization's purpose, objectives, and strategy. Every manager at every level in an organization is a key link in this process. Managers bring life to the hierarchy of objectives by linking objectives at one level (i.e., the means) to those at the next higher level (i.e., the ends). As a system or

FIGURE 5.3 Evan Products Company's strategic plan. *Source:* Evans Products Company's 1980 Annual Report. Reprinted by permission.

Strategic Plan 1981-1985

The primary objectives of Evans' long-term strategic planning are to (1) identify and anticipate trends in our major businesses, (2) explore opportunities within the expected market environment, and (3) evaluate alternative investments. Some of the key trends, strategies and operating plans developed in 1980 to achieve profitable and consistent growth over the plan period are summarized here.

Key Trends

More homes are being fixed up these days than are being built. There are several good reasons why this is happening. High new home prices and mortgage rates are making remodeling existing homes the more attractive financial alternative... Turnover in the nation's 87 million housing units is spurring improvements by new owners... Rising energy costs are continuing to prompt installation of energy conservation products... Old homes in inner cities are being restored at a record rate.

"Do-It-Yourselfers" spur growth in home improvement product sales

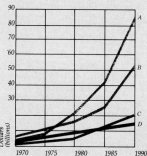

Home improvement product sales by types of retailers:

A Home centers ("Do-It-Yourselfer" sales exceed 80% of total sales.)

B Contractor-oriented lumber & building materials (L&BM) dealers ("Do-It-Yourselfer" sales are less than 30% of total sales.)

C Consumer-oriented L&BM dealers ("Do-It-Yourselfer" sales are between 50% and 80% of total sales.)

D Hardware stores

Source: National Home Center News and Frost & Sullivan

Basic Strategy

Emphasize marketing directly to the consumer through retail building materials stores and the sale of affordable, custom-built homes. Focus manufacturing activities on specialty products and products used by the growing remodeling market.

Operating Plans

Retail Stores:

By 1985 our *Retail Group* anticipates operating 450 stores and a near doubling of revenues. •

The percentage of sales to the growing "Do-It-Yourself" market should increase due to:

1. The above-average growth rate inherent in the market.
2. Emphasizing cash-and-carry stores in the new store program.
3. Enlarging and remodeling dual yards, which serve both the consumer and contractor, to accommodate increased consumer sales. Dual yards will continue to be operated where substantial contractor business is available.

We plan to expand our market penetration in the 20 states we now serve, and to expand into additional states.

Existing stores will be continually evaluated in terms of the need to remodel, relocate or remerchandise. The primary goal is to improve our return on investment.

We will strive to maintain our strong consumer image as the "building materials specialist" by stocking ranges of merchandise which allow the customer to choose quality products at a variety of price levels. Equally important is customer assistance from free literature and knowledgeable sales personnel.

Personnel training programs will be intensified to enhance customer service, as well as to provide management for our increasing number of stores.

Custom-Built Homes:

Through increased penetration of existing markets and entering into new market areas, our *Homes Group's* output is expected to approach its current rated capacity by 1985.

Evans Financial Corp. will continue to develop innovative loan programs that are responsive to home loan market conditions and to maintain reliable external investment sources to fund such programs.

Manufacturing:

Our *Shelter Products Group* plans to increase the portion of its building product sales to the remodeling market. The Group plans to enter new market areas, as well as to serve existing sales areas more efficiently by opening additional plants for the manufacture of aluminum doors and windows and kitchen cabinets.

Our *Forest-Fiber Products Group* anticipates improved profitability from its wood products activities as higher operating rates and improved efficiencies are attained in more favorable markets. Additional offshore markets will be developed.

The Group's battery separator business is expected to strengthen its market position primarily by capitalizing on technological advances as its markets expand.

procedure for joint objective setting between a superior and subordinate, MBO helps managers do just that. The basis for this observation will become more apparent when MBO is reviewed in more detail in Chapter 14 as an integrated planning and controlling system.

STRATEGIC PLANNING AND ORGANIZATIONAL OBJECTIVES

Let's move back one step in this discussion of organizational objectives to the action sequence through which strategy is formulated and ultimately mobilized to help achieve organizational objectives. It is time to talk about strategic planning in the following sense of the term: strategic planning creates strategy that serves organizational objectives.

Strategic Planning Defined

Chapter 4 defined a strategic plan as one that is comprehensive in scope and reflects the overall direction of the total organization or one of its subunits. Figure 5.3 presents the strategic plan for Evans Products Company for 1981–1985. Note that it provides a good picture of how the organization intends to operate as a consumer-products company for a five-year period. **Strategic planning,** accordingly, is defined by George Steiner, another leading scholar in this field, as the process of determining the major objectives of an organization and defining the strategies that will govern the acquisition and utilization of resources to achieve those objectives.[11]

The Purpose of Strategic Planning

Strategy is an organization's way of maintaining a positive relationship with its external environment. Strategic planning helps make this happen. It clarifies for the members of the organization and relevant outsiders

- The goods or services the organization intends to provide.
- The methods it will use to produce them.
- The performance targets underlying these efforts as a whole.

Each of these features is evident in the strategic plan for the Evans Products Company shown in Figure 5.3. The reason for doing all this is made clear by Peter Drucker.[12]

> The future will not just happen if one wishes hard enough. It requires decision—now. It imposes risk—now. It requires action—now. It demands allocation of resources, and above all, of human resources—now. It requires work—now.

A major element of the "work" with which Drucker is so concerned is strategic planning!

Steps in Strategic Planning

Figure 5.4 summarizes the major steps in systematic strategic planning as a basis for managerial action. The essence of the approach is for management to assess seriously current strategy vis-à-vis organizational objectives, select a strategy, and then implement it through medium-term and short-term action plans.

Note in Figure 5.4 that strategic planning begins with organizational or enterprise objectives. They set a frame against which strategists begin a formal process of performance review and planning. Step 1 in the process is one of appraisal. In this step both the environment and organization are carefully assessed for their future implications. An actual strategic choice is made in Step 2. The strategy is implemented in Step 3 and evaluated in Step 4.

Take a good look at Figure 5.4 and talk yourself through each of the strategic planning steps. Although strategic planning, in the sense of actually implementing this process for the organization as a whole, is largely a top management responsibility, managers at all levels must be prepared to participate in various phases of the strategic planning process. It is also true that every manager should be able to lead the strategic planning process for his or her work unit.

Strategic Questions for the Manager

It is helpful to put strategic planning in a managerial perspective by thinking of it as a process of answering a series of questions about an organization and its environment. Thinking strategically about your organization or one of its

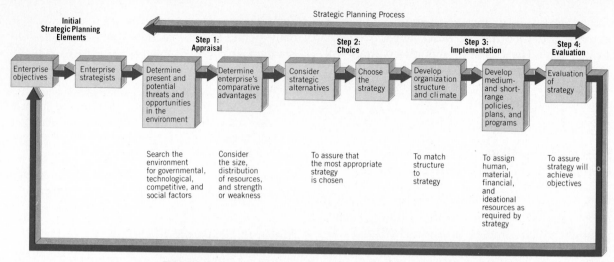

FIGURE 5.4 A model of strategic planning. *Source:* From *Business Policy: Strategy Formulation & Executive Action*, Second Edition by William F. Glueck, p. 5. Copyright © 1976 by William F. Glueck. Used with the permission of McGraw-Hill Book Company.

subunits, for example, would mean seeking answers to at least five basic questions.

1. Where are we now?
2. Where do want to be in the future?
3. How can we get there?
4. What route is best for us?
5. How and when can we implement it?

Illustrative Case: Report of the Chairman of the Board

The logic of these questions parallels the problem-solving/decision-making process discussed in Chapter 3. Indeed, strategic planning, as all planning, is a problem-solving activity. The recent history of the American Telephone and Telegraph Company (AT&T) is a case in point. Deregulation of the communications industry has resulted in dramatic changes in the environment in which the company had achieved success during the recent past. Along with the 1980 annual report, shareholders received the following letter from the chairman of the board. It presents chief executive officer C. L. Brown's viewpoint on the strategic planning challenge faced by one of the largest and most successful companies in the world.[13]

Dear Share Owner:

In the following pages of this report you will find an accounting of the Bell System's performance in the year just past—the service we provided, the improvements in technology and operating methods we introduced, the earnings we achieved.

Here I propose to address what seems to me made the year unique: in the course of it we crossed the threshold of a new era in Bell System history. It is an era that affords us—albeit not without risks—opportunities no less challenging than those our business faced at its founding more than a hundred years ago. In short, I believe that 1980 was in a number of significant ways Year One of the Bell System's future. It was a year in which the shape of that future—at least in broadest outline—came clear.

It was a year in which—to meet the requirements of that future and to fulfill its opportunities—we took the first steps toward a restructuring of the Bell System that, once it has been accomplished, will make ours an organization vastly different from the one we know today.

And, finally, it was a year in which we redefined the scope of our business and raised our marketing horizons. No longer do we perceive that our business will be limited to telephony or, for that matter, telecommunications. Ours is the business of information handling, the knowledge business. And the market we seek to serve is global. . . .

On August 20, the Board of Directors approved a realignment of AT&T's general departments that separates those departments whose responsibilities relate mainly to regulated activities from those dealing with prospectively deregulated markets. At the same time, we moved toward establishment of a relatively small corporate staff to provide overall strategic and financial direction to the enterprise as a whole. . . .

More fundamentally, we shall be transforming a business that for more than 60 years has been structured to meet the requirements of a highly regulated environment to one that matches the dictates of a day and age that looks mainly to the marketplace to decide what products and services the public will be supplied, who will supply them and at what price. That means that not only must we change our business's structure; we must change many cherished policies and practices—ways of doing business—that, while proven over generations of Bell System management, no longer fit today's circumstances. . . .

But what will most distinguish the management of the future from that of the past is the varying degrees of risk we will confront. Consequently one of our first priorities as we go about reshaping our business is the development of criteria to help guide resource allocation between and within its principal sectors. Certainly, as we are permitted to venture in unregulated markets, it will be our aim to seek returns to investors commensurate with the risks involved. In this connection, it appears to be widely recognized that it would not be fair to investors to permit regulators to use profits earned in unregulated markets as an offset to revenue requirements in regulated markets.

Why—in view of the complexities it confronts—has the Bell System chosen to anticipate change rather than await it?

The answer in a word: opportunity.

What creates that opportunity is the scope of the market and the unique resources and skills the Bell System can bring to bear on meeting its needs. . . .

Finally, what further changes the future will bring is beyond knowing. Indeed, how the Bell System will be configured ten years from now I can't predict. But I can say what standard we mean to apply to the decisions we'll be called upon to make on the way to that unknowable destination. It is the standard of excellence. Our purpose is to seek—at every point of decision—the highest and best use of the organizations and resources we call the Bell System. The highest and best. With that as our standard, I have not the least doubt that, unknowable as the future is, it will be a great future.

C. L. Brown

C. L. BROWN

February 6, 1981

Brown's letter informs shareholders that AT&T is taking action to ensure a successful future for itself, even in a time of great environmental challenge and change. To Brown, such challenge and change offer opportunities for the company. Good strategic planning is his way of taking best advantage of them.

MAJOR ELEMENTS OF STRATEGIC PLANNING

Figure 5.5 presents four major elements in the appraisal stage of strategic planning. These include an analysis of (1) the organization's mission and objectives, (2) threats and opportunities in the external environment, (3) managerial values and the corporate culture, and (4) internal strengths and weaknesses of the organization. This framework helps define four strategic planning principles useful to managers at all organizational levels—regardless of whether their responsibilities are to lead, to participate in the process, or merely to implement the results. The four principles will be introduced in discussion. As a prelude to further study, though, consider two illustrations of strategic planning in action.

Chase Manhattan Goes Competitive[14]

Chase Manhattan Bank had a long-term history of comfortable success. During the mid-1970s, however, Chase experienced a sharp decline in earnings that led its chairman, David Rockefeller, and other chief executives to reassess the bank and its strategic orientation.

The executives decided that the first step was to define clearly what the bank should be. A three-page mission statement that outlined the company's preferred business mix was drawn up early in 1977. The statement said in part, "We will only do those things we can do extremely well and with the highest level of integrity." This mission statement led Chase to take a hard look at some of the more unprofitable aspects of its business. Many low-volume branches were closed, and questionable loan business that might have been accepted before was turned away. The mission statement also detailed spe-

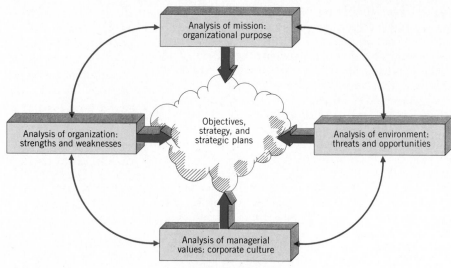

FIGURE 5.5 The major elements in strategic planning.

cific financial targets such as return on equity and debt to capital ratio goals.

Chase also initiated major efforts to improve communications between top management and the rest of the employees. The participation created a sense of "ownership" of the new program that many consultants consider essential to establishing any long-lasting change. The company promoted managers considered to be appropriate role models, replaced many existing executives by outsiders, overhauled salary and incentive programs, and started an advanced management course for promising young managers.

In the final result, this effort by Chase resulted in a shift from a focus on style to a focus on performance.

Michigan Sees Robot-Making as a Solution to its Troubles[15]

Governor William G. Milliken felt victimized by the recent economic recession. His three terms as the Republican governor of Michigan may well have been the toughest of any state chief executive. Michigan's problems were extreme in an economy that slid into recession with a great accompanying decline in the automobile industry. The state's 16 percent unemployment rate was the highest in the nation. Predictably, Governor

Milliken was looking to the future and working hard to find a new strategy to lower Michigan's dependency on the automobile industry in the longer run.

What was on the governor's mind? Robots. He decided to make Michigan the robot capital of the world. His strategy rested on two assumptions. First, the automobile industry had fundamentally changed in recent years. Even if the industry did bounce back quickly from recession, many skilled workers would probably remain unemployed. Second, robots are expected to enjoy an enormous market in future years.

Milliken felt that Michigan was well equipped to take advantage of the robot boom. Residents had the skills robot-makers needed, and the state had a fine college system that could serve the high technology aspect of the manufacturing challenge.

On the negative side, Michigan's highly unionized labor force earned the highest average wage rate in the United States outside of Alaska. Some existing robot manufacturers complained that these pay scales were above what they would consider to be normal industrial wages. Thus debate started—and continues—over whether or not Michigan, in the long run, would succeed in its quest for a substantial segment of the robot manufacturing industry.

Analysis of Mission: What Is the Organization's Purpose?

Very early in this book we singled out *purpose* as one of the basic ingredients of organizations. We defined purpose simply as an intention to produce a specific good or service. Now, it is appropriate for us to extend this discussion and examine how, under what conditions, and with what result the organization's purpose is served.

What does the name "IBM" mean to you? The firm's founder, Thomas J. Watson, Sr., once stated his desire that the corporate identity among employees, customers, and outsiders convey a belief in[16]

1. *Respect for the individual*   Respect for the dignity and the rights of each person in the organization.
2. *Customer service*   To give the best customer service of any company in the world.
3. *Excellence*   The conviction that an organization should pursue all tasks with the objective of accomplishing them in a superior way.

Watson's desires are the basis for a series of principles that still guide IBM employees in their work.

- To give intelligent, responsible, and capable direction to the business.
- To serve our customers as efficiently and as effectively as we can.
- To advance our technology, improve our products, and develop new ones.
- To enlarge the capabilities of our people through job development and give them the opportunity to find satisfaction in their tasks.
- To provide equal opportunity to all our people.
- To recognize our obligation to stockholders by providing adequate return on their investment.
- To do our part in furthering the well-being of those communities in which our facilities are located.
- To accept our responsibilities as a corporate citizen of the United States and in all the countries in which we operate throughout the world.

The essence of organizational or corporate purpose as conveyed by the IBM example is to serve as a guiding philosophy or "superordinate goal" from which all members of the organization can find direction. A **superordinate goal** is useful in that it conveys and represents the overall purpose of the organization to its members and interested outsiders. It lends a sense of unity and direction to an enterprise.

Researchers have placed increased emphasis on the role of superordinate goals in facilitating organizational performance. Successful companies in both Japan and the United States are identified as having clear superordinate goals that create shared action guidelines for employees. Such superordinate goals focus attention on[17]

- *The company as an entity*   The whole organization is reinforced as something one should identify with and belong to, and which deserves admiration and approval from employees and society.
- *The company's external markets*   The emphasis is on the value of the company's products or services to humanity, and on those factors important in maintaining this value—that is, quality, delivery, service, and customers' needs.
- *The company's internal operations*   Attention is focused on such things as efficiency, cost, inventiveness, problem solving, and customer attention.
- *The company's employees*   Attention is paid to the needs of people with respect to their productive function and as valued human beings in a larger social context.
- *The company's relation to society and the state*   The values, expectations, and legal requirements of the surrounding larger community are explicitly honored.
- *The company's relation to culture*   The underlying beliefs about "the good" in the culture are honored, including such things as beliefs about honesty and fairness.

Strategic Planning Principle No. 1

Strategy and objectives must direct effort toward accomplishment of the organization's basic mission and overall purpose.

The first strategic planning principle recognizes

that analysis of basic mission and clarification of superordinate goals are important elements in the strategic planning process. As the earlier case of the Chase Manhattan Bank points out, a clear mission helps managers to make essential operational decisions. This sense of mission can lend continuity to the organization over time by serving as a focal point for strategy formulation and the application of individual and group work efforts. Finally, a clear mission helps an organization communicate its identity to the environment.

Lately the trend has been to capture corporate identities in the form of symbolic images or logos. Three logos are shown here. What do they suggest to you in terms of the mission and superordinate goals of the organizations they represent? Compare your image for the middle logo with images summarized in *Newsline 5.3*. Clearly, organizational identities are not always without controversy in the broader competitive and social environments within which they exist.

Analysis of the Environment: What Are the Threats and Opportunities?

Once the organization's mission is clarified and its meaning established in the form of superordinate goals, the next strategic planning element is analysis of threats and opportunities in the organization's environment. Given the intended direction for the enterprise, it is necessary to assess the potential influence of the environment on that desired end state.

Four major components of the external environment, as shown in Figure 5.6, are economic, political, social, and technological forces. Managers must consider these forces for the threats and opportunities posed to the organization.

Good judgments must then be made during the strategic planning process. Each environmental component is especially important for its potential to impact essential resource inputs and the consumption of product or service outputs. In general,

1. *The* **economic environment** Consists of customers, suppliers, and competitors whose actions have the potential to affect demand for goods or service and resource availabilities.
2. *The* **political environment** Includes governmental units at regional, state, national, and international levels; special-interest groups and other political entities; and the legal-judicial framework of society.
3. *The* **social environment** Consists of the value systems, sociodemographic characteristics, and other basic characteristics of persons comprising the society.
4. *The* **technological environment** Includes the available technologies and the related capability of society to develop or acquire appropriate technologies in the future.

Factors such as these combine at any point in time to create stable, dynamic, or uncertain environments. They also combine to create environments that are more or less bountiful in the support they offer organizations. Table 5.3, for example, shows how environmental factors might impact the strategic planning activities of a university and an energy company.

Other things being equal, the richer the environment in terms of support provided to the organization on economic, political, social, or technological grounds, the better off the organization will be in operational terms. Whether the external environment is richer or poorer in nature, however, it must always be properly identified and interpreted as an input to the planning process. This puts great weight on the manager's ability to gather appropriate information on the

FIGURE 5.6 The role of environmental appraisal in strategic planning.

MOBIL'S STYLE STRIKES SOME BOSSES AS ARROGANT, OTHERS AS ADMIRABLE

As the second largest U.S. oil company, Mobil has a habit of doing things its own way, pugnaciously defending its profits and its practices in advertisements, public statements, and open challenges to the press.

Mobil is accustomed to offering huge sums to acquire other companies. In the mid-1970s, it bought Marcor, Inc., the parent of Montgomery Ward and Container Corp. of America. In the past three years, it has bid about $5 billion for oil companies on the auction block. Now Mobil is trying to outbid Seagram Co. and E. I. du Pont de Nemours in the fight for Conoco Inc.

Against this backdrop, *Wall Street Journal* reporters asked several business executives if they thought Mobil was arrogant, overaggressive, or simply a competitor. (A Mobil spokesman says the company won't respond to characterizations of its style by others.)

> Mobil's bid for Conoco is frightful. I think it risks the public at large losing respect for big companies when they throw around big resources, as we've seen in the past couple of months.
>
> —Charles N. Barber, chairman, Asarco Inc., New York

> Mobil is a very orthodox large company. I don't think it's arrogant, and I don't think Mobil would be funding programs for public television if it didn't care about the public.
>
> —Andrew Ippolito, chairman and chief executive, Discovery Oil Ltd., Los Angeles

> I would say Mobil is aggressive, not arrogant. Their attitudes are strong and their points of view are well made, especially in advertisements.
>
> —Frank W. Considine, president and chief executive, National Can Corp., Chicago

> They're just wasting their money if they're trying to build an image through those ads. And I can't see using pricing as a weapon against government. It smacks of immaturity, like a little kid striking out in all directions.
>
> —Phil R. North, chairman, Tandy Corp., North Worth, Texas

> I don't think Mobil's aggressiveness is any different from Seagram's, Du Pont's or other industries, and I have no objection whatsoever to a merger of Mobil and Conoco.
>
> —John A Kocur, president, Apache Corp., Minneapolis

Source: "Mobil's Style Strikes Some Bosses as Arrogant, Others as Admirable," *Wall Street Journal* (July 28, 1981), p. 27. Reprinted by permission of the *Wall Street Journal.* Copyright © 1981 Dow Jones & Company, Inc. All rights reserved.

Table 5.3 An Analysis of Environmental Components

Environmental Components	Environment Implications for State-Supported University	Implications for Energy Company
Economic		
The state of the economy of different nations; relationships with customers, suppliers and competitors	Increasing education cost; declining enrollments; relationships with private foundations and other universities	Increasing production costs; gas allocations; varying customer needs
Political		
The general political climate of society; public image and attitudes toward product and services	Funding levels from the state; tenure restrictions; faculty unionization	Divestiture and regulation; oil embargo; nationalization by foreign countries; OPEC
Social		
The general sociological and cultural changes in society	Questions concerning the value of a college degree; continuing education programs; internal personnel policies	Attitudes toward high gas prices, price fixing, and kickbacks; concerns over pollution and destruction of natural resources; eliminating employment discrimination
Technological		
The availability of resources and constraints facing organizations; the level of technology	Availability of quality instructors; teaching innovations such as computers, videotape, etc.	Declining raw material sources (e.g., crude oil); availability of alternative sources (e.g., solar, nuclear, coal)

Source: Andrew D. Szilagyi, Jr., *Management and Performance* (Santa Monica, Cal.: Goodyear Publishing, 1981), p. 57. Reprinted by permission of Scott, Foresman and Company.

environment and to spot and interpret important trends. Forecasting as discussed in Chapter 4 is an important managerial tool in this regard. Indeed, all planning, whether done for an entire organization or a subcomponent, must be consistent with environmental challenges as experienced and as predicted for the future.

Strategic Planning Principle No. 2

Strategy and objectives should target effort on specific results that will solve key problems and exploit key opportunities in the organization's external environment.

Analysis of the Organization: What Are its Strengths and Weaknesses?

Through analysis of the external environment, managers gain perspective on what an organization's strategy *might* be. It is necessary to probe further, however, and analyze the strengths and weaknesses of the organization in order to determine precisely what the strategy *should* be. The role of this internal appraisal of the organization in strategic planning is depicted in Figure 5.7.

An internal appraisal clarifies actual organizational capabilities and establishes a realistic basis for strategic planning. Several internal factors are important to most organizations in this regard. Some questions that should be asked address the following.

1. *Human resources* To what extent are technical and managerial personnel available in appropriate quality and quantity?

2. *Material resources* To what extent does the organization have access to other essential resources, including facilities, money, equipment, and supplies?

3. *Technology* To what extent does the organization have access to technical improvements and/or have the capability to develop or access them in the future?

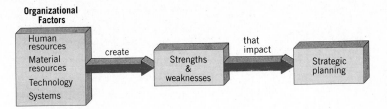

FIGURE 5.7 The role of internal appraisal in strategic planning.

4. *Systems* To what extent is the organization supported by appropriate systems for processing information, ensuring quality control, maintaining resource flows, distributing final products or services, and the like?

A sample analysis of weaknesses in the marketing area of one growing company, along with their strategic implications, follows.[18]

Marketing weaknesses Eighty percent of profits emanate from one product; market declining at 5 percent per year; market share constant.

    Strategic implications Reduce single-product dependence; change market strategy to improve performance.

With this example in mind, consider the third strategic planning principle.

Strategic Planning Principle No. 3

Strategy and objectives should build on strengths and minimize weaknesses in the organization.

Analysis of Managerial Values: What Is the Corporate Culture?

A manager's decisions and actions will always be affected in part by **values**—broad beliefs about what is or is not appropriate. Values that affect a manager's behavior derive from two distinct sources: the individual and the organization.

Managerial Values

A person's values develop from experience as a result of education and external influence. Broadly stated, values and their orientations can be classified as follows.[19]

- *Theoretical* Oriented toward truth and knowledge.

- *Economic* Oriented toward practical and useful aspects of work.
- *Aesthetic* Oriented toward form, grace, and harmony.
- *Social* Oriented toward people and human relations.
- *Political* Oriented toward power and competition.
- *Religious* Oriented toward unity in the universe.

Values influence what people want or intend to do. For example, managerial values may impact results in a strategic planning situation. Consider the potential strategic implications of the predispositions of executives who believe that[20]

- To be successful, a firm must attack in the marketplace, versus others who believe you "go along to get along."
- To succeed, a firm must innovate, versus others who prefer to "let others make the mistakes first."
- One treats employees so they know who is boss, versus others who believe cooperation comes from a participative approach to employees.
- The government and consumers, unions, and other groups in society are enemies, versus others who believe cooperation is possible and desirable.
- Their firms should be socially responsible, versus others who feel they are there to make a buck and let the buyer beware.

Corporate Culture

Corporate culture is the predominant value system for the organization as a whole. The values of individuals in organizations are subject to the

Delta Airlines is a company whose corporate culture encourages everyone to work hard to attain high performance and maintain positive work attitudes.

working style, but they are expected to articulate and support their activities with evidence of progress.

4. *Delta Air Lines Inc.* A focus on customer service produces a high degree of teamwork; employees will substitute in other jobs to keep planes flying and baggage moving.

A book by Terrence Deal and Allen Kennedy, *Corporate Cultures: The Rites and Rituals of Corporate Life,* stresses the important impact corporate culture can have on an organization's success.[22] By codifying and symbolizing for all to see "the way we do things here," they argue, corporate culture can set a performance tone for the organization. In organizations with strong cultures, everyone knows and supports the organization's objectives; in those with weak cultures, no clear sense of purpose exists. Deal and Kennedy also point out that corporate culture is subject to considerable influence by company founders, such as Thomas J. Watson, Sr., of IBM, or the chief executives of the moment. *Newsline 5.4* is one example of how a new top manager's past experiences and values had an early and substantial influence on the Ralston-Purina Company.

Corporate culture complements the sense of mission and superordinate goals we discussed earlier. It ultimately affects not only the process of strategy formulation, but also the behaviors and working environments of all employees. Consider, for example, the description of the basic principles, beliefs, and values of one very large firm that follows.[23] What does the description suggest about this company as a consumer goods manufacturer? . . . as an employer? Would you be inclined to buy the firm's products? Would you work for it as an employee?

influence of corporate culture. This can occur through selection—where people are hired because their personal values are consistent with corporate culture—and by socialization—where newcomers learn values and ways of behaving that are consistent with those of the organization.

Organizations benefit from consistent corporate cultures properly matched with strategies. Some examples of successful companies that have achieved a good match of culture and strategy are[21]

1. *International Business Machines Corporation* Marketing drives a service philosophy that is almost unparalleled; the company keeps a hotline open 24 hours a day, 7 days a week, to service IBM products.

2. *International Telephone & Telegraph Corporation* Financial discipline demands total dedication; to beat out the competition in a merger, an executive once called the [former] chairman Harold S. Geneen at 3 A.M. to get his approval.

3. *Digital Equipment Corporation* An emphasis on innovation creates freedom with responsibility; employees can set their own hours and

Basic Business Principles

To recognize our responsibilities as industrialists, to foster progress, to promote the general welfare of society, and to devote ourselves to the further development of world culture.

Employees' Creed

Progress and development can be realized only through the combined efforts and cooperation of each member of our company. Each of us, therefore, shall keep this idea constantly in mind as we devote ourselves to the continuous improvement of our company.

NEWSLINE 5.4

NEW RALSTON CHIEF SAYS HE'LL SACRIFICE SALES TO KEEP COMPANY'S PROFIT MARGINS HIGH

ST. LOUIS—William P. Stiritz, the new head of Ralston Purina Co., learned a lesson in the early 1960s that helped mold his approach to business.

In those days, he was a brand manager in Pillsbury Co.'s grocery products division. As Mr. Stiritz tells it, "a bright young manager" figured out a way to increase sales of angel food cake mix. Prices were cut 20 percent in the Denver area. Volume doubled. The ebullient manager persuaded Pillsbury to use the marketing strategy nationwide. Competitors, however, also cut prices. As a result, profits plunged—and the manager was fired.

The episode taught Mr. Stiritz to respect profit margins, even at the expense of market share. And in this first interview since being named president of Ralston last January, Mr. Stiritz makes it clear that improving profit margins will be a priority. "The end isn't just selling goods," Mr. Stiritz stresses, but rather to "earn an adequate return. That goal sometimes gets lost."

Source: From David P. Garino, "New Ralston Chief Says He'll Sacrifice Sales to Keep Company's Profit Margins High," *Wall Street Journal* (July 2, 1981), p. 19. Reprinted by permission of the *Wall Street Journal*. Copyright © 1981 Dow Jones & Company, Inc. All rights reserved.

The Seven "Spiritual" Values

1. National service through industry
2. Fairness
3. Harmony and cooperation
4. Struggle for betterment
5. Courtesy and humility
6. Adjustment and assimilation
7. Gratitude

The firm is Matsushita of Japan. It is best known elsewhere in the world as the manufacturer of Panasonic products. This example provides a good frame of reference for our fourth and final strategic planning principle.

Strategic Planning Principle No. 4

Strategy and objectives should be consistent with prevailing managerial values and the corporate culture.

STRATEGIC PLANNING AND THE MANAGER

So far in Chapter 5 we have discussed the concept of strategy, strategic planning and organizational objectives, and the major elements in the strategic planning process. Now it is time to link them together in a broad managerial context.

Strategic Management Versus Operating Management

Strategic management is the managerial responsibility for formulating and implementing strategies that lead to longer-term organizational success. Any manager, at any level in an organization, is responsibile for strategic management as it pertains to his or her immediate work unit. For the organization as a whole, strategic management is ultimately a top management responsibility. Still, managers at all levels must support the process if it is to succeed.

Table 5.4 A Comparison of Operating Management and Strategic Management

	Operating Management	Stategic Management
Concern	Operating problems, strategy support	Longer-term survival, strategy development
Focus	Present results	Future results
Constraints	Present resources and environment	Future resources and environment
Problem solving	Reactive, based on past experience	Anticipatory, finds new approaches
Decisional context	Low risk	Higher risk

Source: Adapted with permission from *Long-Range Planning*, Vol. 8, No. 4 (August 1975), p. 38, Bernard Taylor, "Strategies for Planning". Copyright 1975, Pergamon Press, Ltd.

Table 5.4 compares strategic management and operating management responsibilities. Note the contrast in the table between a focus on present versus future results, reactive versus anticipatory problem solving, and low- versus high-risk decision contexts. Note, too, that strategic management cannot succeed without the support of effective operating management. By the same token, effective strategic management establishes the framework for mobilizing the efforts of operating management in ways that best serve organizational objectives.

Top Managers as Strategists

The chief executive officer (CEO) of an organization must initiate and monitor the strategic planning process, see to it that good strategic choices are made, and ensure that these choices are implemented, evaluated, and revised as necessary over time. CEOs surely have help in this task. Other top managers help, staff planners often help, and even outside consultants may be hired to help as well. Still, the CEO is most often the one in charge, and who thereby reaps the benefits of good strategic management and pays the price when it is done poorly. A *Business Week* article—"Goodbye, Archie: Pink Slip for the Boss"—tells the fate of Archie McCardell, a former CEO of the International Harvester Company.[24] He resigned under pressure in 1982 while being held accountable by the board for the company's inability to extract itself from a state of financial chaos. Whether personally to blame or not, McCardell was penalized for the strategic management failures of the firm.

Some reasons for top management failure in strategic management include[25]

1. *A power-hoarding strategist creates overambitious, incautious strategies that ignore environmental signals.* These strategists have not developed adequate strategic planning systems.

2. *A power-hoarding strategist refuses to change an existing unsuccessful strategy.* These strategists do not accept advice from subordinates and don't search the environment themselves for relevant developments.

3. *The chief strategist creates no strategy at all.* These strategists expect the organization to run itself without a strategy.

4. *The strategist creates a strategy that is overambitious given the resource base of the organization.* These strategists have not adequately analyzed the organization's strengths and weaknesses.

Multilevel or Comprehensive Strategic Planning

Even though top managers are usually the strategists, and even though strategic management and operating management have their fundamental differences, each level of management needs the other in order to do its own job well. Strategic management sets the guidelines or action framework for operating management. It provides the sense of direction and cohesion that helps the many diverse parts of the organization work together. Operating management, in turn, uses resources to do the things necessary to implement strategy and realize its impact on organization objectives. Without the applied efforts of operating managers, strategies would remain well-intentioned ideas that never achieve their desired results.

Thus true strategic management requires an integrated and comprehensive organization-wide approach to planning, action, and evaluation, just as we discussed in the last chapter. Figure 5.8 shows how such multilevel strategic planning involves all layers of management in a major company. This figure is a good one to think about. It shows how your task responsibilities might fit into the strategic planning process early in a managerial career, when you will typically work at a lower management level with operational concerns stressing strategy implementation, as well as later when you assume middle and upper management responsibilities reflecting greater emphasis on strategy formulation.

Strategic Planning and Managerial Intuition

Throughout this chapter we have examined strategic planning as a rational and systematic managerial activity. To do strategic planning well, the implication goes, you should proceed step-by-step as suggested in Figure 5.4. But, as important as it is to grasp the logic of strategic planning in this systematic sense, there is another side to strategic planning that can't be neglected.

Formal Planning Versus Planning by Intuition

Henry Mintzberg, based on his pragmatic view of managerial behavior discussed in Chapter 1, claims that the reality of a manager's day-to-day work often results in more informal or intuitive planning approaches. In support of this position he offers three observations.[26]

FIGURE 5.8 The strategic planning process in a large diversified company. *Source:* Adapted by permission of the *Harvard Business Review*. Exhibit from "Strategic Planning in Diversified Companies" by Richard F. Vancil and Peter Lorange, January–February 1975, pp. 85–85. Copyright © 1975 by the President and Fellows of Harvard College; all rights reserved.

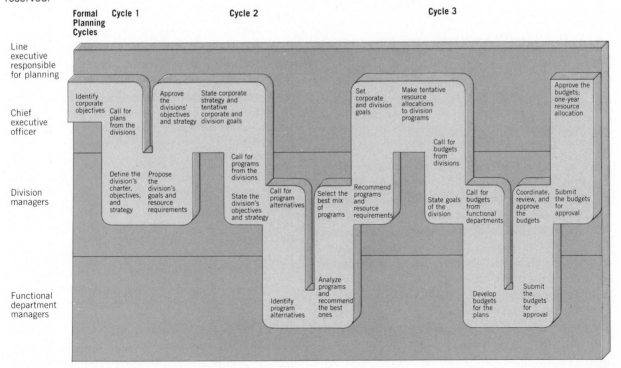

1. *Managers favor verbal communications.* This suggests relational or interactive means of gathering planning data, rather than ordered and sequential ones.

2. *Managers frequently deal with impressions, speculations and feelings.* This suggests they are more likely to "synthesize" than "analyze" data in their search for the "big picture."

3. *Managers work at a fast pace, perform a wide variety of duties, and are subject to frequent interruptions.* This suggests they will be denied quiet time alone to think and plan in a systematic fashion.

This reasoning leads Mintzberg to argue that actual planning in the manager's workday world may become planning via intuition. Such planning is highly dependent on the person or persons involved. "Hunch," "judgment," "synthesis," and "intuition" are the key words determining success or failure of the planning effort.

Logical Incrementalism

Another emerging view of strategic planning complements the work of Mintzberg to some extent. James Brian Quinn begins one of his articles with the following quote, which conveys his theme of strategic planning through logical incrementalism.[27]

> When I was younger I always conceived of a room where all these [strategic] concepts were worked out for the whole company. Later I didn't find any such room. . . . The strategy [of the company] may not even exist in the mind of one person. I certainly don't know where it is written down. It is simply transmitted in the series of decisions made.

Quinn's article goes on to argue that strategic shifts in organizations rarely occur in the singular and clear-cut fashion that the emphasis on formal strategic planning suggests. Instead, his ideas on **logical incrementalism** view strategies emerging over time as a series of incremental changes to existing patterns of behavior. These incremental changes, in turn, presumably reflect a good deal of intuition on the parts of responsible managers.

As both Mintzberg and Quinn suggest, strategic planning can be considered an incremental-intuitive process as well as a systematic-formal one. Within any given set of broad strategy guidelines, any manager will likely proceed incrementally to adjust actual behavior to problems and opportunities of the moment. Successful strategic planning therefore requires both a familiarity with the process and elements of formal strategic planning plus the capability to make day-to-day decisions of strategic significance in dynamic and intuitively challenging settings.

Making Strategic Planning Effective

There are pitfalls to be avoided and guidelines to be followed by managers trying to do a good job of strategic planning. Let's look at the pitfalls first.

Pitfalls to Avoid

Strategic planning failures fall into two general categories. Failures of substance reflect inadequate attention to the major planning elements previously discussed—analysis of mission, environment, organizational strengths and weaknesses, and managerial values and corporate culture. Either the elements were neglected or improper conclusions were drawn. Our discussion of these elements gives you a sensitivity to the issues and should help you attend to them more systematically in actual planning situations.

Failures of process, on the other hand, reflect poor handling of the processes through which the elements of strategic planning were addressed. Process failures often involve key persons being excluded from the planning effort, with the result that their commitment to eventual action follow-through suffers accordingly. This may result from overcentralization of planning in top management, or from too much delegation of planning activities to staff planners or separate planning departments. Another process failure to guard against is getting so bogged down in details that the planning process becomes an end in itself, instead of a means to an end. Management can succeed only when good strategies actually result from the time and other resource investments made in strategic planning.

Guidelines to Follow

A set of basic guidelines on how to make strategic planning effective can be developed from the literature. They include the following words of advice.

1. *Use a checklist for minimizing errors of substance.*
Dick Levin calls this ''six ways to know when you've got the right plan.''[28]

Check One: Is the strategy consistent with the environment?

Check Two: Is the strategy internally consistent?

Check Three: Is the strategy appropriate to available resources?

Check Four: Is the risk in the strategy the appropriate risk?

Check Five: Does the strategy have an appropriate time horizon?

Check Six: Is the strategy workable?

2. *Get the right people involved.* Avoid process pitfalls by what Quinn calls total posture planning. An example follows.[29]

Shortly after becoming CEO of General Mills, James McFarland decided that his job was ''to take a very good company and move it to greatness,'' but that it was up to his management group, not himself alone, to decide what a great company was and how to get there. Consequently he took some thirty-five of the company's topmost managers away for a three-day management retreat. On the first day, after agreeing to broad financial goals, the group broke up into units of six to eight people. Each unit was to answer the question, ''what is a great company?'' from the viewpoints of stockholders, employees, suppliers, the public, and society. Each unit reported back at the end of the day, and the whole group tried to reach a consensus through discussion.

On the second day the groups, in the same format, assessed the company's strengths and weaknesses relative to the defined posture of ''greatness.'' The third day focused on how to overcome the company's weaknesses and move it toward a great company. This broad consensus led, over the next several years, to surveys of fields for acquisition, the building of management's initial ''comfort levels'' with certain fields, and the acquisition-divestiture strategy that characterized the McFarland era at General Mills.

3. *Don't be afraid to conclude that an existing strategy is good or even the best one.* Here's advice from Dick Levin again.

It isn't always necessary to change strategy in order to succeed. Many companies and organizations operate for years with the same strategy.

Analysis of opportunities, risks, and trends in the environment is the foundation upon which strategic planning is built. Going through the process keeps the organization alert even when the outcome is no change for now. If your product is Lifesavers, Hershey bars, or Ivory soap, don't fiddle with the formula. Do glance around periodically; if you don't spot any alligators, you can still enjoy the view.[30]

4. *Approach strategic planning with responsibility for the total process in mind.* Look back to Figure 5.4, which identifies four stages of management responsibility—appraisal, choice, implementation, and evaluation. We have focused our examination on appraisal. True strategic management, however, doesn't stop with appraisal or even with the choice of a strategy. It includes responsibility for implementation and follow-through evaluation as well.

5. *Use strategic planning as a stepping-stone for success in the other management functions.* When done well, strategic planning helps managers fulfill their organizing, leading, and controlling responsibilities. When these are done well in return, they help in the implementation and evaluation stages of strategic planning highlighted in No. 4.

6. *Remember that a good strategy alone will not ensure organizational success.* A strategy merely sets the stage for action. The action, in turn,

will only be as good as the ability of the rest of the organization and its members to implement strategy in a coordinated manner. This requires a clear hierarchy of organizational objectives that is well integrated in a multilevel planning framework.

SUMMARY

Strategy is a comprehensive plan that sets critical direction and guides the allocation of resources for an organization or subunit. Through stability, growth, retrenchment, and combination strategies, organizations seek to prosper in the face of environmental challenges. The process through which strategies are formulated, implemented, and evaluated is strategic planning.

Strategic planning identifies organizational objectives and determines the strategies that govern the use of resources to achieve these objectives. It can be viewed as a formal planning approach involving four interrelated steps—appraisal, choice, implementation, and evaluation. The major elements underlying the appraisal stage of strategic planning are:

1. *Analysis of mission* What is the organization's purpose?

2. *Analysis of the environment* What threats and opportunities does it hold?

3. *Analysis of the organization* What are its strengths and weaknesses?

4. *Analysis of managerial values* What is the corporate culture?

Throughout our discussion of strategic planning, numerous examples were used to illustrate the concepts and ideas being presented. You had a chance to view strategic planning through the eyes of great companies like AT&T, IBM, and Matsushita. These examples should help you develop a practical feel for this important managerial activity—both as a leader of the strategic planning process at the work-unit level, and as a general participant in the process as it relates to the organization as a whole.

Eventually we focused on the managerial implications of strategic planning. Top managers were singled out as the major enterprise strategists, but managers at all levels were shown to have responsibility for strategic management. All managers are also responsible for helping the organization benefit from truly comprehensive, multilevel strategic planning. Finally, we recognized the roles of intuition and logical incrementalism in any planning activity, and discussed pitfalls to be avoided and several gudelines to be followed for doing effective strategic planning in organizations.

THINKING THROUGH THE ISSUES

1. What is strategy? Define and give examples of strategies based on growth, stability, retrenchment, and combination.

2. Why are strategy and objectives so important to one another in organizations?

3. List and describe the five continuing objectives common to all organizations. Would these apply equally well to your local bank and community hospital? Why or why not?

4. How do operating and official objectives differ from one another?

5. What is the relationship between an organization's means-ends chains and its hierarchy of objectives?

6. What major questions can be asked to guide the process of strategic planning?

7. List and clarify the four steps in strategic planning. How, if at all, do these steps correspond to the steps in formal planning detailed in Chapter 4 and the steps in the problem-solving process detailed in Chapter 3?

8. What is "corporate culture"? What is its significance to top-, middle-, and lower-level managers in an organization?

9. What role does intuition play in strategic planning? Explain your answer.

10. List the four strategic planning principles identified in this chapter. Explain the managerial significance of each.

THE MANAGER'S VOCABULARY

Combination strategy
Corporate culture
Displacement of
objectives
Economic environment
Growth strategy
Hierarchy of objectives

Logical incrementalism
Management by
objectives (MBO)
Official objective
Operating objective
Organizational
objectives

Political environment
Retrenchment strategy
Social environment
Stability strategy
Strategic management
Strategic planning
Strategic planning

principle No. 1,2,3,4
Strategy
Suboptimization
Superordinate goal
Technological
environment
Values

CAREER PERSPECTIVE: BACK TO THE OVERDRIVEN EXECS

Many experts consider middle managers to be the ones most prone to ethical dilemmas caused by extraordinary pressures to meet organizational objectives. Unlike top executives, middle managers often have little say in how the objectives are set, but they are held accountable for results, and their careers often hang in the balance. Consider the following incident from the Dorsey Corporation's glass container plant in Gulfport, Mississippi, as reported by the *Wall Street Journal*.[31]

> Manager William Tate, aware that the aging facility's output was falling behind that of other company plants, began to fear that Dorsey would close his plant and throw him and 300 other employees out of work. According to the company, Mr. Tate secretly started altering records and eventually inflated the value of the plant's production by about 33 percent.
>
> The overreporting was discovered when a janitor, ignoring Mr. Tate's order to burn the actual records, instead hid the documents behind a chicken coop and showed them to company auditors visiting on an inspection tour. Mr. Tate was fired, and Dorsey Corporation was forced to restate downward its 1977 and 1978 earnings to reflect the production discrepancy.
>
> Mr. Tate refuses to discuss the matter. But his wife, Gayle, says her husband was under "constant pressure" to raise the plant's production. "Bill knew that as long as he kept production up, he and his men had a job. But when it fell, that was it," she says.

Questions

1. Do you feel Tate's actions can be justified?
2. Should Tate have been fired? Why or why not?
3. What can/will you do in your future career to avoid such "mistakes" when driven by top management pressures for performance?

Two U.S. retailers with names easily recognized by consumers are PepsiCo, Inc. and the J. C. Penney Company. Each company also has a major competitor with a similarly strong consumer identity—for PepsiCo the competitor is Coca-Cola, for Penney's it is Sears, Roebuck. An inside look at PepsiCo and J. C. Penney's, however, shows major differences in their approach to operations in a highly competitive environment. Consider these glimpses of life within each firm.

At PepsiCo[32]

Once the company was content in its No. 2 spot, offering Pepsi as a cheaper alternative to Coca-Cola. But, today, a new employee at PepsiCo quickly learns that beating the competition, whether outside or inside the company, is the surest path to success. In its soft-drink operation, for example, Pepsi's marketers now take on Coke directly, asking consumers to compare the taste of the two colas. That direct confrontation is reflected inside the company as well. Managers are pitted against each other to grab more market share, to work harder, and to wring more profits out of their businesses. Because winning is the key value at Pepsi, losing has its penalties. Consistent runners-up find their jobs gone. Employees know they must win merely to stay in the place—and must devastate the competition to get ahead.

At J. C. Penney's[33]

Life at J. C. Penney Co. is another matter. The business style of the company's founder espouses not taking unfair advantage of anyone with whom the company does business. This style still dominates the company. Customers know they can return merchandise without question; suppliers know Penney's won't haggle over terms; employees are comfortable in their jobs knowing that Penney's will avoid layoffs at all costs. A quick victory is far less important at J. C. Penney than building customer and employee loyalty. A Penney store manager, for example, was once severely rebuked by the president for making too much profit. Hard to believe, but that excess profit was considered unfair to customers whose trust Penney's seeks to win. Penney's personnel policies reflect concerns for employment security and consensus management. Its chairman and chief executive, Donald V. Siebert, allows his managers to participate in almost all major decisions. His goal is to "create developmental opportunities by helping people understand what happens at different levels of the organization."

Questions

1. Analyze the corporate cultures of PepsiCo and J. C. Penney. What are their implications for strategic planning in each company? Explain your answer.

2. Which of these companies would you most prefer to work for if your only job choice was to become employed by one or the other? Why?

CLASS EXERCISE: WHAT'S THE STRATEGY?[34]

Examples of organizational strategies are regularly reported in newspapers and other various news media.

1. Read the following descriptions of corporate strategies as summarized from recent newspaper reports.

2. Test yourself by identifying each strategy as stability, growth, retrenchment, or combination. Write your responses in the spaces provided.

3. Refer back to the chapter to clarify your understanding of these four types of strategies as necessary.

4. Share your responses with a nearby classmate, reconcile any differences, and await further class discussion.

Polaroid   Once the darling of Wall Street, Polaroid Corporation has had some tough times of late. The company has sought to diversify itself from its mainstay market of instant photography. It is open to acquisitions and plans to introduce new products in the near future.

Strategy:_____

Firestone   Firestone has been hit hard by cutbacks in the automobile industry. But, the Number 2 tire maker is fighting to get back on track. John Nevin, the company's president, has led an attempt to rebound by cutting back on the number of factories and employees. All this is based on forecasts that tire sales will remain at reduced levels in the foreseeable future.

Strategy:_____

Stroh Brewing   As foreign beer companies continue their success in U.S. markets, American brewers are suffering in the slower-growing market for domestic beers. Stroh's is a regional, family-held Detroit company. Its survival strategy is to go national by acquiring Schlitz, the nation's third-largest beer company. The offer is $500 million in cash.

Strategy:_____

General Electric Chairman John F. Welch, Jr. intends to continue moving the company into high technology products and services. In a two-year period GE spent $1 billion on acquisitions, new businesses and joint ventures. It also sold off 71 businesses that didn't match up to Welch's expectations.

Strategy:_____

REFERENCES

[1] Excerpted from George Geschow, "Overdriven Execs," *Wall Street Journal* (November 8, 1979), p. 1. Reprinted by permission of the *Wall Street Journal*. Copyright © 1979 Dow Jones & Company, Inc. All rights reserved.

[2] These headlines are from the *Wall Street Journal* (March 18, 1982), p. 1; (March 17, 1982), p. 1; and (October 12, 1981), p. 1.

[3] "RCA: Still Another Master," *Business Week* (August 17, 1981), pp. 80–86.

[4] From Peter F. Drucker, *Management: Tasks, Responsibilities, Practices* (New York: Harper & Row, 1973), pp. 380, 381.

[5] This section is based on William F. Glueck, *Business Policy: Strategy Formulation and Management Action*, Second Edition (New York: McGraw-Hill, 1976), pp. 120–147.

[6] Ibid., p. 35.

[7] As stated in Chesebrough-Pond's 1982 Annual Report, CBS's Annual Report for 1981, and Apple Computer, Inc.'s 1982 Annual Report.

[8] Warren G. Bennis, *Organizational Development* (Reading, Mass: Addison-Wesley, 1969).

[9] Modified from Peter Drucker, *The Practice of Management* (New York: Harper & Bros., 1954), p. 62.

[10] Drucker, op. cit.

[11] Adapted from George Steiner, *Top Management Planning* (New York: Macmillan, 1969), p. 34.

[12] Drucker (1973), op. cit., p. 122.

[13] Excerpted from "AT&T '80," *American Telephone and Telegraph Company 1980 Annual Report*, pp. 2, 3. Used by permission.

[14] Information from "Corporate Culture," *Business Week* (October 27, 1980), pp. 158–160. Reprinted from the October 27, 1980 issue of *Business Week* by special permission, © 1980 by McGraw Hill, Inc., New York, NY 10020. All rights reserved.

[15] Adapted from Eugene Carlson, "Michigan Sees Robot-Making as a Solution to its Troubles," *Wall Street Journal* (March 23, 1982), p. 29. Adapted by permission of Wall Street Journal, Copyright © 1980 Dow Jones and Company. All rights reserved.

[16] Cited in Richard Tanner Pascale and Anthony G. Athos, *The Art of Japanese Management: Applications for American Executives* (New York: Simon & Shuster, 1981), pp. 184, 185.

[17] Pascale and Athos, op. cit., pp. 179–180.

[18] Adapted from David E. Hussey, "The Corporate Appraisal: Assessing Company Strengths and Weaknesses," *Long Range Planning*, Vol. 1 (December 1968), pp. 19–25.

[19] See G. Allport, P. Vernon, and G. Kindzey, *Study of Values* (Boston: Houghton-Mifflin, 1960).

[20] Glueck, op. cit., p. 23.

[21] See *Business Week*, op. cit., p. 148.

[22] Terrence E. Deal and Allen A. Kennedy, *Corporate Cultures: The Rites and Rituals of Corporate Life* (Reading, Mass.: Addison-Wesley, 1982); see also Roger Ricklefs's book review in *Wall Street Journal* (July 28, 1982), p. 16.

[23] From Pascale and Athos, op. cit., p. 51.

[24] *Business Week* (May 17, 1982), p. 57.

[25] Adapted from Glueck, op. cit., p. 45.

[26] Henry Mintzberg, "Planning on the Left Side and Managing on the Right," *Harvard Busines Review*, Vol. 54 (July-August 1976), pp. 51–53.

[27] James Brian Quinn, "Strategic Change: Logical Incrementalism," *Sloan Management Review*, Vol. 20 (Fall 1978), p. 7.

[28] Adapted from Dick Levin, *The Executive's Illustrated Primer of Long Range Planning* pp. 98–100. Reprinted by permission of Prentice-Hall, Inc., Englewood Cliffs, New Jersey.

[29] Quinn, op. cit., p. 16.

[30] Levin, op. cit., p. 23.

[31] Geschow, op. cit. Reprinted by permission of the *Wall Street Journal*. Copyright © 1979 Dow Jones & Company, Inc. All rights reserved.

[32] The description of PepsiCo is from "Corporate Culture," *Business Week* (October 27, 1980), p. 48. Used by permission.

[33] Information on Penney's is from ibid. and "Teamwork Pays Off at Penney's," *Business Week* (April 12, 1982), p. 107, from which the quote is taken.

[34] Based on reports in the *Wall Street Journal* (April 22, 1982), p. 16; (November 19, 1980), p. 33; *Fortune* (May 17, 1982), p. 11, and (April 18, 1983), p. 6.

THE CASE OF THE MISSING TIME

It was 7:30 Tuesday morning when Chet Craig, general manager of the Norris Company's Central Plant, swung his car out of the driveway of his suburban home and headed to the plant in Midvale, six miles away. The trip to the plant took about 20 minutes and gave Chet an opportunity to think about plant problems without interruption.

The Norris Company operated three printing plants and did a nationwide business in quality color work. It had about 350 employees, nearly half of whom were employed at the Central Plant. The company's headquarters offices were also located in the Central Plant building.

Chet had started with the Norris Company as an expeditor in its Eastern Plant 10 years ago, after his graduation from Ohio State. After three years he was promoted to production supervisor, and two years later was made assistant to the manager of the Eastern Plant. A year and a half ago he had been transferred to the Central Plant as assistant to the plant manager; one month

Source: Copyright © 1971, Northwestern University. All names and organizational designations have been disguised. Northwestern University cases are reports of concrete events and behavior prepared for class discussion. They are not intended as examples of good or bad administrative or technical practices.

later, when the manager retired, Chet was promoted to general plant manager.

Chet was in good spirits this morning. Various thoughts occurred to him as he said to himself, "This is going to be the day to really get things done." He thought of the day's work, first one project, then another, trying to establish priorities. He decided that the open-end unit scheduling was probably the most important—certainly the most urgent. He recalled that on Friday the vice-president had casually asked him if he had given the project any further thought. Chet realized that he had not been giving it any attention lately. He had been meaning to get to work on his idea for over three months, but something else always seemed to crop up.

"I haven't had time to really work it out," he said to himself. "I'd better get going and finish it off one of these days." He then began to break down the objectives, procedures, and installation steps in the project. It gave him a feeling of satisfaction as he calculated the anticipated cost savings. "It's high time," he told himself. "This idea should have been completed a long time ago."

Chet had first conceived the open-end unit scheduling idea almost two years ago, just prior to leaving the Eastern Plant. He

had talked it over with the general manager of the Eastern Plant, and both agreed that it was a good idea and worth developing. The idea was temporarily shelved when Chet had been transferred to the Central Plant a month later.

His thoughts returned to other plant projects he was determined to get under way. He started to think through a procedure for the simpler transport of dies to and from the Eastern Plant. He thought of the notes on his desk: the inventory analysis he needed to identify and eliminate some of the slow-moving stock items, the packing controls that needed revision, and the need to settle on a job printer to do the outside printing of simple office forms. There were a few other projects he could not recall offhand, but he felt sure that he could tend to them sometime during the day. Again, he said to himself, "This is the day to really get rolling."

When he entered the plant, Chet was met by Al Noren, the stockroom foreman, who appeared troubled. "A great morning, Al," said Chet, cheerfully.

"Well, I don't know, Chet; my new man isn't in this morning," said Noren morosely.

"Have you heard from him?" asked Chet.

"No, I haven't."

"These stock handlers take it for granted that if they're not here, they don't have to call in and report. Better ask Personnel to call him."

Al hesitated a moment. "Okay, Chet," he said, "but can you find me a man? I have two cars to unload today."

Making a note of the incident, Chet headed for his office. He greeted some workers discussing the day's work with Marilyn Benton, the office manager. As the meeting broke up, Marilyn took some samples from a clasper and showed them to Chet and asked if they should be shipped that way, or if it would be necessary to inspect them. Before he could answer, Marilyn went on to ask if he could suggest another clerical operator for the sealing machine to replace the regular operator, who was home ill. She also told him that Gene, the industrial engineer, had called and was waiting to hear from Chet.

Chet told Marilyn to ship the samples and made a note of the need for a sealer operator and then called Gene. He agreed to stop by Gene's office before lunch and started on his routine morning tour of the plant. He asked each supervisor the volumes and types of orders they were running, the number of people present, how the schedules were coming along, and the orders to be run next; he helped the folding room supervisor find temporary storage space for consolidating a carload shipment; discussed quality control with a pressman who had been running poor work; arranged to transfer four people temporarily to different departments, including two for Al in the stockroom; talked to the shipping supervisor about pickups and special orders to be delivered that day. As he contin-

ued through the plant, he saw to it that reserve stock was moved out of the forward stock area; talked to another pressman about his requested change of vacation schedule; had a "heart-to-heart" talk with a press helper who seemed to need frequent assurance; approved two type and one color okays for different pressmen.

Returning to his office, Chet reviewed the production reports on the larger orders against his initial projections and found that the plant was running slightly behind schedule. He called in the folding room supervisor and together they went over the lineup of machines and made several changes.

During this discussion, the composing room supervisor stopped in to cover several type changes, and the routing supervisor telephoned for approval of a revised printing schedule. The stockroom supervisor called twice—first to inform Chet that two standard, fast-moving stock items were dangerously low; later to advise him that the paper stock for the urgent Dillon job had finally arrived. Chet telephoned this information to the people concerned.

He then began to put delivery dates on important inquiries received from customers and salespersons. (The routine inquiries were handled by Marilyn.) While he was doing this he was interrupted twice—once by a sales correspondent calling from the West Coast to ask for a better delivery date than originally scheduled; once by the vice-president of Personnel, asking Chet to set a time when she could hold an initial induction interview with a new employee.

After dating the customer

and sales inquiries, Chet headed for his morning conference in the executive office. At this meeting he answered the vice-president of Sales' questions in connection with "hot" orders, complaints, the status of large-volume orders, and potential new orders. Then he met with the vice-president and general production manager to answer "the old man's" questions on several production and personnel problems. Before leaving the executive offices, he stopped at the office of the purchasing agent to inquire about the delivery of some cartons, paper, and boxes, and to place an order for some new paper.

On the way back to his own office, Chet conferred with Gene about two current engineering projects. When he reached his desk, he lit a cigarette, and looked at his watch. It was 10 minutes before lunch—just time enough to make a few notes of the details he needed to check in order to answer knotty questions raised by the vice-president of Sales that morning.

After lunch Chet started again. He began by checking the previous day's production reports; did some rescheduling to get out urgent orders; placed delivery dates on new orders and inquiries received that morning; consulted with a foreman on a personal problem. He spent about 20 minutes going over mutual problems with the Eastern Plant.

By midafternoon Chet had made another tour of the plant, after which he met with the vice-president of Personnel to review a touchy personal problem raised by one of the clerical employees, the vacation schedules submitted by his supervisor, and the pending job evaluation program. Following this conference, Chet hurried back to his office to complete the special statistical report for Universal Waxing Corporation, one of Norris's biggest customers. When he finished the report he discovered that it was 6:10, and he was the only one left in the office. Chet was tired. He put on his coat and headed for the parking lot. On the way out he was stopped by the night supervisor and the night layout supervisor for approval of type and layout changes.

As he drove home, Chet reviewed the day he had just completed. "Busy?" he asked himself. "Too much so—but did I accomplish anything?" The answer seemed to be "Yes, and no—there was the usual routine, the same as any other day. The plant kept going and it was a good production day. Any creative or special work done?" Chet winced. "I guess not."

With a feeling of guilt Chet asked himself, "Am I an executive? I'm paid like one, and I have a responsible assignment and the authority to carry it out. My supervisors at headquarters

think I'm a good manager. Yet one of the greatest returns a company gets from an executive is innovative thinking and accomplishments. What have I done about that? Today was just like other days, and I didn't do any creative work. The projects I was so eager to work on this morning are no further ahead than they were yesterday. What's more, I can't say that tomorrow night or the next night they'll be any closer to completion. This is a real problem, and there must be some answer to it.

"Night work? Yes, sometimes. This is understood. But I've been doing too much night work lately. My wife and family deserve some of my time. After all, they are the people for whom I'm really working. If I spend much more time away from them, I'm not meeting my own personal objectives. I spend a lot of time on church work. Should I eliminate that? I feel I owe that as an obligation. Besides, I feel I'm making a worthwhile contribution in this work. Maybe I can squeeze a little time from my fraternal activities. But where does recreation fit in?"

Chet groped for the solution. "Maybe I'm just rationalizing because I schedule my own work poorly. But I don't think so. I've studied my work habits and I think I plan intelligently and delegate authority. Do I need an assistant? Possibly, but that's a long-time project and I don't believe I could justify the additional overhead expense. Anyway, I doubt whether it would solve the problem."

By this time Chet had turned off the highway into the side street leading to his home. "I guess I really don't know the answer," he said to himself as he pulled into his driveway. "This morning everything seemed so simple, but now. . . ."

Questions

1. Is Chet a good planner? Why or why not?

2. Why can't Chet get his job done?

3. How should a general manager like Chet actually spend his or her day?

4. What should Chet do in this case?

DELTA AIRLINES

Over the years Delta has been one of the most successful airlines. Analysts who follow the airline attribute its success to

Source: Information from "Delta Airlines," *The Economist* (September 26, 1981), p. 68; "Delta: The World's Most Profitable Airline," *Business Week* (August 31, 1981), pp. 68–72; "Slow Growth Help," *Industry Week* (June 14, 1982), pp. 118–120; "Delta Is Ready," *Forbes* (September 15, 1980), p. 81.

good planning, employee support, and a unique "hub-and-spoke" scheduling system. Together these factors help Delta achieve a record of productivity among the highest in the industry.

A *Business Week* article reports that Delta's secret is simple. It combines good planning—15 years ahead for flight equipment and support facilities—with a massive effort to motivate employees. The net result is the

highest productivity in the airline industry.

A vice-president of one of the investment firms that tracks the airline industry says, "Delta is one of the very few airlines in the industry that can afford the luxury of developing long-range plans and sticking to them." When events happen that are beyond Delta's control—for example, a fuel shortage or the air controllers' strike of August 1981—cause operations to deviate from projections, Delta sticks as closely as possible to its original plans. Delta's unwillingness to alter its long-range plans is exemplified by the airline's unwillingness to cut back its load capacity even during poor economic times. Delta's president, David C. Garrett, Jr., states, "We still try very hard to stick to our plan."

One reason for Delta's profitability is its innovative scheduling procedure. Using a "hub-and-spoke" routing system, Delta funnels traffic from smaller cities through the large Atlanta airport for connections. Careful planning results in an arrangement of timetables such that passenger interconnections occur with a minimum of delay.

Delta also benefits from employee loyalty and high labor productivity. The company tries to avoid layoffs, but also expects employees to remain flexible and positive in approaching their jobs. The same employee checking passengers in at the gate, for example, may handle baggage or move the jetway ramp to the airplane doors.

Another aspect of Delta's operations is an exceptionally efficient communications policy. Top managers meet all employees in groups of 25 to 30 at least once every 18 months. The meetings start with a formal briefing of what Delta has done lately. Then the group's supervisor is excused and the floor is opened up for questions, complaints, and suggestions. Delta's top management also maintains an open door for those who want to talk privately.

Finally, Delta's planning also involves maintaining and improving its aircraft fleet. It pursues these long-term plans regardless of external conditions. Robert Openlander, senior vice-president of finance, says that because Delta is consistent, it is always poised to attack the next growth period for the airline industry. Delta is in such a position, while the rest of the industry may well have laid off a lot of people and restricted its fleet-improvement program because of financial limitations. Delta jumped in strength after the recession in 1971; it did it again in 1975, and again in 1981 when things began to return to normal after the air traffic controllers strike.

Questions

1. Is Delta's strategy of sticking to its long-range plans regardless of the ebbs and flows in economic prosperity correct or incorrect? Explain your answer.

2. Does it appear that Delta plans from the inside-out or the outside-in? Does it appear that Delta plans from the top-down or the bottom-up? With what net result in each case?

3. As you read and think about Delta Airlines as it is described in this case, do you see the company as being in a good strategic position for the future? Why or why not?

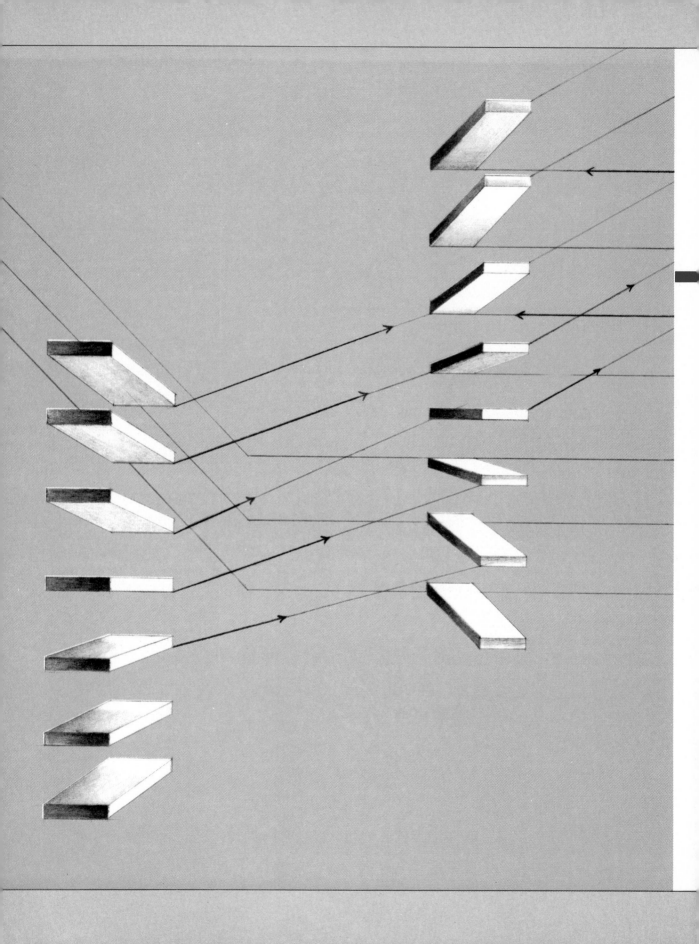

PART
3

ORGANIZING FOR PRODUCTIVITY

Chapters in This Part of the Book

BUREAUCRATIC TIE-UPS DELAY STUDENT AID

A&P Reorganizes Top Management for Better "Balance"

"Bureaucracy" and "bureaucrats," the need for "reorganization"—virtually the scourge of modern society. Wherever we go, wherever we turn, it seems that organizational problems must be solved if we are to make our way. The preceding headlines[1] are but two of an infinite number of examples that communicate this theme.

Do you remember the brief discussion of bureaucracy in Chapter 2? It's important now that you do. When originally described by Max Weber, "bureaucracy" was an organization known for its fairness, continuity, and efficiency. He felt it was an ideal way to organize the work of many people to serve a purpose. It is now time to learn more about the organizing function of management and about how it helps managers achieve productivity.

As you read and study Part 3, you will learn about various structural forms of organizations, the nature of bureaucracy and its alternatives, job designs for individuals and groups, and the challenges of staffing these jobs with capable human resources. The four chapters covering these topics contain many insights that will help you as a manager begin the process of turning plans into performance results. After plans are set, organizational resources must be prepared for action. This is the manager's responsibility of organizing for productivity.

We'll begin our new avenue of study with a perspective on organizations contained in a short but provocative book, *The Art of Japanese Management,* written by Richard Pascale and Anthony Athos. They discuss the role played by organization structure in the success of Matsushita, a giant of Japanese industry (its products are sold under the brand names National, Panasonic, Quasar, and Technics) and a company that ranks as one of the 50 largest corporations in the world. Pascale and Athos introduce Matsushita as[2]

"A great corporation that makes more than money, and is likely to go on doing so, for it has become an organizational system that meets the needs of its society, its customers, its executives, and its employees, and it is "programmed" to adapt as may be necessary to changes that may come. This is an extraordinary achievement."

They go on to point out how founder Konosuke Matsushita was able to "organize" his company for success in a sometimes threatening and always challenging environment. As it turns out, this example nicely introduces the various topics covered in Chapters 6 through 9.

Perspective: The Successful Organization[3]

Founder Konosuke Matsushita was a commoner who started as an apprentice in a bicycle shop, earning 25 cents a day. As the news of Thomas Edison's remarkable discoveries got to Japan, Matsushita was inspired by the possibilities of a new industry. He left his secure job and set out on his own. His first product was a double-outlet adapter, molded in his living room. The product screwed into light sockets, permitting the one-outlet Japanese houses to double their

---

[1] These headlines are from the *Chronicle of Higher Education* (March 24, 1982), p. 1; and the *Wall Street Journal* (April 8, 1982), p. 22.

[2] Richard Tanner Pascale and Anthony G. Athos, *The Art of Japanese Management* (New York: Simon & Schuster, 1981), p. 28. Used by permission.

[3] Ibid., pp. 32, 33.

6

FUNDAMENTALS
OF ORGANIZING

STREAMLINING HEW:
A NOVEL APPROACH

Joseph A. Califano, Jr., served as secretary of the Department of Health, Education, and Welfare during the Carter administration. As a manager, he was held accountable by President Carter for a large, complex organization. Many people, including the secretary, felt that HEW needed to be streamlined as an organization. One cartoonist's view of Califano's organizing problems is shown here.[1]

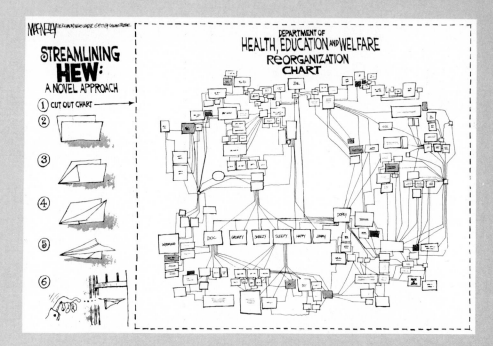

The cartoon speaks for itself. Organizing, the process of dividing and coordinating the work of many people, is one of the most challenging tasks performed by managers. At times, such as the cartoon suggests, the task seems all but impossible. In fact, we know a lot about organizing as the second of the four basic management functions. This chapter contributes to your understanding of management by introducing the following topics.

Organizing as a Management Function
Organization Structure
Structure from a Manager's Perspective
Departmentation
Vertical Coordination
Horizontal Coordination

"We live in a society of organizations. . . . The first job of the manager is to make the organization perform." These words of Peter Drucker introduced you to the study of management in Chapter 1. It is now time to develop a more fundamental understanding of organizations as (1) instruments of work that produce essential goods and services for society, and (2) work settings within which managers and other persons apply their efforts.

Our study begins by revisiting the concept of organization itself. In Chapter 1, an *organization* was defined as a collection of people in a division of labor working together to achieve a common purpose. The four basic elements in this definition are the foundation for this and the next three chapters in Part 3. These elements are

1. *Collection of people* The very reason for organizations to exist at all is to combine the efforts of many people to accomplish more than they are otherwise capable of doing. This is called **synergy,** the creation of a whole that is greater than the sum of its individual parts. Synergy occurs in organizations when people work together in such a way that one another's performance effectiveness is increased.

2. *Division of labor* The work of the organization must be subdivided and allocated as specialized work tasks to individuals and groups. Through specialization people are able to develop skills and expertise appropriate to their assigned tasks, and thereby gain in performance effectiveness.

3. *Working together* The separate and specialized activities of many people must be coordinated if synergy is to be achieved. Unless people work together, their accomplishments will fail to benefit the organization's overall performance objectives.

4. *Common purpose* This is the superordinate goal of the organization. It constitutes the point of unity around which the division of labor is implemented and coordinated.

ORGANIZING AS A MANAGEMENT FUNCTION

Organizing is the second management function. Once plans are created, the manager's task is to "organize" the human and physical resources properly to carry them out. There is an important difference, though, between the thing we call "organization" and the management function called "organizing." *Organization* (the noun) results from or is created by the efforts of managers to *"organize"* (the verb). **Organizing,** therefore, is a process of dividing work into manageable components and coordinating results to serve a purpose. It follows planning as an essential management responsibility and basically arranges or mobilizes organizational resources for action.

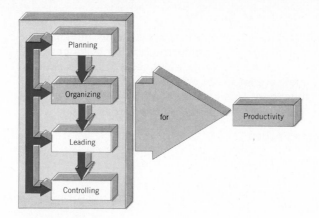

FIGURE 6.1 Organizing as a management function.

Figure 6.1 depicts this critical role of organizing as one of the managerial functions. Organizing helps turn plans into performance results. It is the basis for defining tasks, allocating resources to them, and arranging resources and tasks in productive combinations.

The Importance of Organizing

The benefits of good organizing efforts by managers are many. When done well, for example, organizing[2]

- Clarifies the flow of work.
- Provides guidelines for individual performance.
- Aids planning and control by creating a framework for these efforts.
- Establishes channels for communication and decision making.
- Avoids duplication of work and conflict over tasks.
- Focuses effort by relating activities to objectives.

The cartoon introducing this chapter suggests the federal government is one of any number of large and extremely complex organizations that may find these benefits elusive. You should wonder, in turn, if such failures are due to the sheer impossibility of the task, or just to poor management. The first point of view, that large and complex institutions can't be well run because they are impossible to organize, is hard to support. Substantial insights in management theory provide the basis for effective organizing to

be accomplished in any setting—public or private, large or small, simple or complex. It is up to the manager to recognize these insights and take advantage of them in management practice.

Illustrative Case: A Secret Organization

At times it helps to think of an unusual example to help clarify a term or concept. One such illustration for the organizing function of management is the Mafia. Albeit an illegal organization, the Mafia may also be the world's largest business with a net income estimated by the Federal Bureau of Investigation to be in the $10 to $12 billion range. This would place it Number 1 in the Fortune 500 Directory if it were a legitimate corporation. All of this requires successful organization and management, as well as criminal activity. What follows is a description of certain parallels that have been observed between the Mafia and legitimate organizations.[3]

> The Mafia operates similarly to a political party or a giant corporation, especially a conglomerate. The Mafia combines the wealth, complexity, and organizational skills of a conglomerate such as ITT with the secrecy, efficient brutality, and amorality of the Russian secret police. It is centralized in some aspects (utilizing an enforcement department to maintain discipline), but decentralized in execution of business ventures. Departmentalization is used in the Mafia like any good business or political machine. It has vice-presidents in charge of operations such as gambling, loan sharking, narcotics, prostitution, labor racketeering, nightclubs, hijacking, and legitimate businesses. Each of these branches is expected to help the

other. The Chicago Mafia is further divided into three geographic areas headed by district managers. Under each of the district managers is a third level of top lieutenants. On the next level in each geographic area are aides to the lieutenants.

Bosses primarily engage in crimes of conspiracy and avoid involvement in crimes such as loan sharking and labor racketeering. Just as with big business, management of the Mafia acts on a very different level and often miles away from operations. The boss of each family passes down his decisions to an underboss, who is responsible for keeping the family running smoothly. The underboss chooses the lieutenants to be in charge of a particular group of illegal activities. These lieutenants, also called *caporegimes*, are next in the chain of command and supervise a regime or squad of soldiers. The soldiers, in turn, are responsible for fulfilling orders passed on to them by the lieutenants. Frequently, the soldiers are allied with non-Mafia associates who take orders from them.

A staff position of *consigliere*, or counselor to the family head, operates as a horizontal offshoot from the chain of command. The consigliere, often a partly retired member who commands much respect, provides advice to the family boss. This position also serves a morale function by providing an appearance of due process for members. The consigliere is much like a special assistant to the president.

Lieutenants have about 20 soldiers under their command. The line manager or underboss supervises from 10 to 25 lieutenants, depending on the size of the family and the specialized enterprises the family operates. The consigliere reports directly to the boss of the family.

Some large American corporations have as many as 10 levels of management. In the Mafia, a soldier is separated from top management by only three levels. This structural arrangement allows for problems to be handled more quickly and results in better human relations.

The Mafia is an organization that copes with change and reacts quickly to change. Donald Cressey illustrates the flexibility of the Mafia in the following quotation.

In about three months, New York Cosa Nostra members in the spring of 1965 organized and then operated a multimillion-dollar cigarette-smuggling operation which involved purchase of huge quantities of untaxed cigarettes in North Carolina, truck transportation of the cigarettes to New York, a network of warehouses and wholesalers, and a huge system of retail sellers. Managers of a legitimate firm dealing in legitimate merchandise could not have organized such an enterprise in less than three years.

After finishing this chapter, these basic means through which the Mafia has organized itself will become even clearer to you. You will also find that the terms used in the preceding description—such as structure, chain of command, centralization and decentralization, among others—apply to organizations of all types. The purpose now is to learn the terms and concepts, and examine their potential applications in the *legitimate* organizational settings within which you might work.

Organizing as a Decision Process

The basic elements of the Mafia organization emerged and accumulated over time as a series of decisions made by Mafia leaders in response to the many problems and opportunities present in the environment. It is useful to view organizing as a decision process such as the one depicted in Figure 6.2. Given the existence of strategies or other plans that identify what needs to be done, organizing is a process of deciding how to

- Divide the required work into smaller tasks.
- Assign these tasks to capable individuals and/ or groups.
- Allocate the necessary supporting resources.

FIGURE 6.2 Organizing as a decision process.

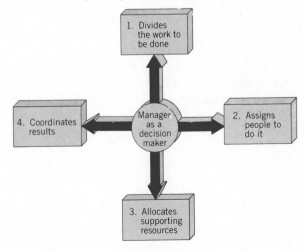

- Coordinate these multiple tasks to achieve the desired collective result.

In the vocabulary of management, this decision process addresses two fundamental questions.

1. How should work efforts and workers be *specialized* in a division of labor; that is, how should the multiple components of the organization be differentiated from one another?

2. How should work efforts and workers be *coordinated* in return; that is, how should the multiple components of the organization be integrated to ensure a common result?

Underlying these two seemingly straightforward questions lies a perplexing dynamic. The differentiation of work tasks creates a corresponding need for integration if a common purpose is to be served. As differentiation increases, however, integration becomes ever more difficult. Thus managers are continually challenged to achieve both differentiation and integration in order to properly organize the material and human resources under their control.

ORGANIZATION STRUCTURE

The **structure** of an organization is the formal system of working relationships that both divide and coordinate the tasks of multiple people and groups to serve a common purpose. High productivity depends on both resources and structure being appropriate to the task at hand. One without the other will be insufficient to ensure performance success. Structure helps the human resources of organizations work together in productive task combinations.

Remember, structure and resources support the performance efforts of individuals and groups in organizations. This relationship is summarized in Figure 6.3. It is also present in the justification for the large-scale restructuring of the Monsanto Company announced by its president, Richard J. Mahoney. He remarked that the new structure wasn't a panacea, but he also said, "While organization by itself doesn't get anything done, at the very least we ought to improve the odds and remove the impediments to success."[4]

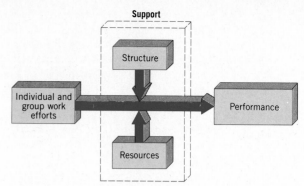

FIGURE 6.3 Structure as a support element in organizations.

Organization Charts and the Formal Structure

You know the concept of structure best in the form it is shown in Figure 6.4, an organization chart for a major U.S. corporation. An **organization chart** is a diagram that describes the basic arrangement of work positions within an organization. Charts such as the one in Figure 6.4 convey useful information about an organization's basic structure. From an organization chart, one can typically determine

1. *The division of work* The basic components into which work is divided are shown as boxes on a typical organization chart. Each box represents an office or position to which work is assigned and individual or group staff assignments are made.

2. *Supervisor-subordinate relationships* The solid lines between boxes represent authority relationships linking managers and their subordinates. The typical organization chart shows who reports to whom in the hierarchy of authority.

3. *Type of work performed* The position titles on the boxes in organization charts convey the nature of the work assigned to the position holder.

4. *Subunit groups or components* A good organization chart shows how various positions are grouped together under common managers to form subunits. These subunits are often called departments.

5. *The levels of management* A complete organi-

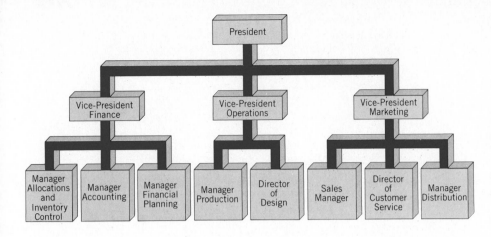

FIGURE 6.4 Organization chart of a women's sportswear company. *Source:* Lawrence J. Gitman and Carl McDaniel, Jr., *Business World* (New York: Wiley, 1983), p. 125. Used by permission.

zation chart shows management levels in the entire hierarchy of authority. Successive layers of superior-subordinate relationships are clarified as if in a map.

A typical organization chart, in summary, shows the various components in an organization's basic division of labor and the lines of formal authority linking them to one another. Because of this, these charts are said to represent the **formal structure** of the organization. This is the structure of the organization in its pure or ideal state—it depicts the way the organization is intended to function. But organization charts don't always depict the way the organization actually operates. There is often a difference between what is described in the formal structure and the ways things really get done in day-to-day practice.

The Informal Structure

Behind every formal structure typically lies a shadow organization. In my college, for instance, faculty members officially report to department chairpersons. Everyone knows, though, that on matters pertaining to typing service the department secretary is the key person to have on their best side. Without the secretary's support, for example, it is very easy to get backlogged in the typing pool while the work of more "preferred" faculty gets done first. This is the shadow organization in operation. We could almost go so far as to say that on matters relating to typing services, faculty members report to the secretaries.

This "structure behind the structure"—this set of unofficial but critical working relationships, this pattern of actual day-to-day work activity—is the **informal structure** of an organization. Sometimes referred to as the informal organization, it is the undocumented and officially unrecognized structure that coexists with the formal structure depicted by an organization chart.

No manager can succeed without understanding both the formal and informal structures through which his or her work setting is organized. Consider the following example.[5]

> When Bill Smith graduated from engineering school and joined the laboratory of a large manufacturing company, he was assigned the task of supervising four laboratory technicians who checked production samples. In some ways he did supervise them, but in other ways he was restricted by the group itself, which was quite frustrating. He soon found that each technician protected the others so that it was difficult to fix responsibility for sloppy work. The group appeared to restrict its work in such a way that about the same number of tests were made every day regardless of his urging to speed up the work. Although Bill was the designated supervisor, he observed that many times the technicians, instead of coming to him, took problems to an older technician across the aisle in another section. Bill soon realized that these situations were evidence of an informal organization and that he had to work with it as well as the formal organization.

Figure 6.5 contrasts the formal and informal structures present in this case. Note that although the technicians formally report to Bill,

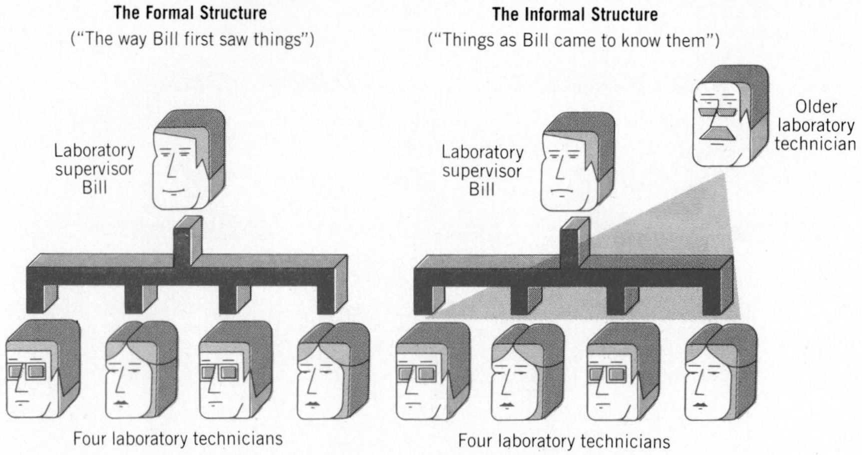

The Formal Structure
("The way Bill first saw things")

The Informal Structure
("Things as Bill came to know them")

Laboratory supervisor Bill

Laboratory supervisor Bill

Older laboratory technician

Four laboratory technicians

Four laboratory technicians

FIGURE 6.5 Contrasts in formal and informal structures.

they informally defer to an older technician in another unit for guidance. Bill must learn to work with both the informal structure that includes this external person as well as the formal structure that does not, if he is to succeed in his position of managerial responsibility.

Potential Benefits of Informal Structures

Informal structures can offer very positive support to formal structures. For example, no formal structure, no matter how well conceived, can anticipate and thereby program itself to solve all future problems. Especially in new or unusual situations and/or during times of rapid change, informal structures can benefit the organization by helping its members to

- Accomplish their work.
- Overcome gaps in the formal structure.
- Communicate with one another.
- Support and protect one another.
- Satisfy social needs.
- Gain a sense of identification and status.

Potential Costs of Informal Structures

Potential costs or disadvantages are also associated with informal structures. Because they exist outside the formal authority system, informal structures can be independent and at times prone to act contrary to the best interests of the organization as a whole. Among the liabilities that

may result when individuals interrelate in informal structures separate from the authority and communication channels of the formal organization are

- Resistance to change.
- Diversion of managerial attention from other issues.
- Diversion of efforts from organizational objectives.
- Susceptibility to rumor.

STRUCTURE FROM A MANAGER'S PERSPECTIVE

Structure represents two things to a manager. First, structure is something within which a manager must work. In this sense, the structure is the surrounding organization of which the manager and his or her work unit are smaller component parts. Second, structure is something managers create. Middle-level or lower-level managers are responsible for properly structuring work units to accomplish their tasks and thereby contribute to organizational objectives; top managers are responsible for creating comprehensive structures for the organization as a whole. In both these cases, structuring is synonymous with organizing. "To structure" or "to organize" is to create an appropriate organization for accomplishing intended results through work.

A Characteristic of the Work Setting

Let's first consider structure as a characteristic of the manager's work setting. The shaded area in Figure 6.6 represents the external structure of the organization within which a manager and the work unit, represented by the triangle, are embedded.

A basic responsibility of every manager is to interface the work unit properly with other components in the total organizational system. This requires an ability to understand the formal and informal components of the surrounding structure and to be able to work well within them. "To work well" in this case means to obtain the resource support necessary to maintain work-unit productivity on a day-to-day and longer-term basis. If the triangle in Figure 6.6 was, for example, the purchasing department of a small manufacturing company, the purchasing manager would have to work closely with other units of the company as well as higher management for the purchasing group to do its job well.

In the first instance, structure is something "out there." It is a part of the total work setting that the manager must comprehend and successfully work within if the work unit is to receive adequate support and fulfill its objectives as part of the total organizational system.

Something to Be Created

Figure 6.6 also depicts structure from a second managerial perspective. Look at the triangle as it encompasses the manager in working relationship with other members of the work unit. In this case the manager's organizing task is to ensure that the structure of the work unit does the best possible job of facilitating high performance. Now, structure becomes more susceptible to managerial influence and control. In fact, it is part of a manager's job to evaluate the work-unit structure regularly and initiate any changes necessary to modify it constructively over time.

Creating a proper structure is a major challenge whether it is a structure for the organization as a whole or for one of its smaller components. We will approach this challenge from two directions in the remainder of this chapter and in Chapters 7 and 8. First, we will examine the determinants of structure—the things with which a structure must prove congruent if the organization or work unit is to succeed in the longer run. Second, we will clarify the components of structure—that is, those things such as jobs, job groupings, and authority relationships that are the basic building blocks of structure itself. Whereas the determinants establish the constraints a structure must fit, the components are

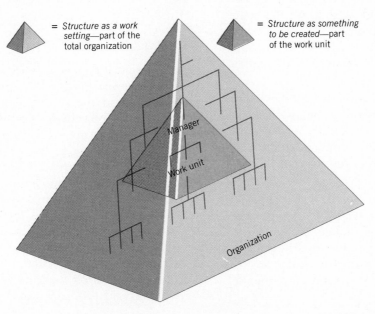

= Structure as a work setting—part of the total organization

= Structure as something to be created—part of the work unit

FIGURE 6.6 Two managerial perspectives on structure.

Manager

Work unit

Organization

the building blocks that must be configured properly to form an appropriate structural response to them.

Determinants of Structure

There are five major determinants of structure: strategy, technology, environment, people, and size. Chapter 7 is devoted to a review of these determinants and their managerial implications. It addresses how, why, and with what implications such factors should and do impact managerial decisions that create structure for an organization or one of its subunits. In the meantime, several basic propositions regarding the ideal relationship between structure and its determinants can be stated.

1. *Structure should follow strategy.* An organization's structure should be consistent with and support the overall objectives of the organization and its strategy for achieving them.

2. *Structure should be appropriate to the basic technology of the organization.* Mass production of automobiles requires a different type of structural support than the process of refining oil. Likewise, the service intensity of a hospital emergency room requires a different structure than the service routines of a bank.

3. *Structure should be appropriate to the external environment.* Environments pose different challenges to organizations depending on the complexity, variability, and uncertainty of their major components. Structures appropriate to one type of environment may not work well in alternative ones.

4. *Structure should accommodate the people within the system.* People vary in their skills, interests, needs, and personalities. These individual differences must be accommodated by organization structures to maximize support for individual work efforts.

5. *Structure should accommodate organizational size.* As organizations grow they tend to become more complex in terms of people, technologies, functions, and even environments. These complexities, along with sheer pressures of size, create additional need for structural accommodations.

Components of Structure

When it comes to configuring the various components of the organization into an appropriate structure, managers must do a good job of both specialization and coordination. Figure 6.7 depicts these two action components in relationship to one another and offers a comprehensive view of the manager's role as organizer.

Specialization

Specialization is the process through which multiple work tasks are defined in a division of labor. Managers are concerned with two levels of specialization: (1) by job design and (2) by departmentation.

Specialization by **job design** is the allocation of specific work tasks to individuals and groups. Chapter 8 is devoted exclusively to this topic. It is essential for a manager to know what choices are available in establishing appropriate job designs for individuals and groups in the organization.

Specialization by **departmentation** is creation of work units or groups by placing several jobs under the authority of a common manager. The resulting work units are called departments, which, when grouped together in hierarchical levels, form the total organizational system. There are many alternative ways to form departments. Several will be discussed shortly.

Coordination

Once specialization has been accomplished, steps must be taken to integrate the resulting division of labor toward the accomplishment of overall organizational objectives. **Coordination** is the process of linking the specialized activities of individuals and groups to one another and ensuring that a common purpose is served. It provides for proper communication among organizational components, enables them to understand one another's activities, and helps them to work well together in the general work flow.

There are two dimensions of coordination to be accomplished: (1) vertical and (2) horizontal. **Vertical coordination** coordinates the activities of individuals and groups up and down the hier-

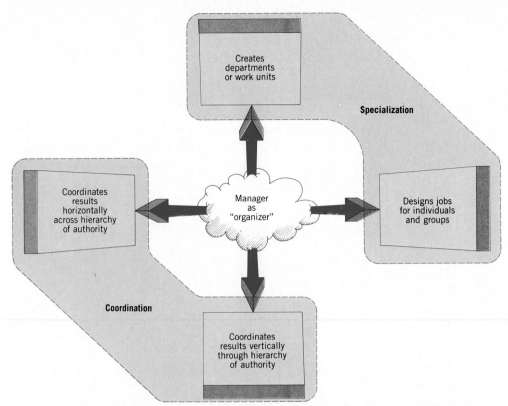

FIGURE 6.7 Major elements in the specialization and coordination of work in organizations.

archy of authority. **Horizontal coordination,** in contrast, cuts across the organization to coordinate the activities of individuals and groups working at or close to the same level in the hierarchy. Both dimensions of coordination will be discussed in this chapter after the various forms of departmentation are examined. Remember, an effective manager does both specialization and coordination well in fulfilling the organizing responsibility. Figure 6.7 should help you keep this challenge in mind as you read on.

DEPARTMENTATION

Departmentation is a process of grouping people and activities together under the supervision of a common manager. Many choices are available regarding the types of departments one can create.[6] We will discuss them in three categories—functional, divisional, and matrix forms. Each form has special advantages and disadvantages

that make it more appropriate for some situations than others. When departmentation is done well—that is, when a good match between form and situation is achieved—it contributes to organizational success by[7]

- *Clarifying authority relationships* by specifying who does what work and who reports to whom.
- *Facilitating communication and control* by grouping together people with related job responsibilities.
- *Increasing decision quality* by helping to ensure that decisions are made at the points where appropriate information and competence are located.

Departmentation by Function

Departmentation by function groups together in a common organizational unit people performing similar or closely related activities. Functional de-

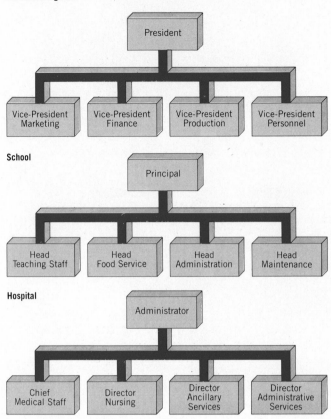

FIGURE 6.8 Functional forms of departmentation.

partments are common in business organizations. The example in Figure 6.8 shows the functional departments of marketing, finance, production, and personnel, all headed by vice-presidents and reporting to the company president. In this structure, all production problems are the responsibility of the production vice-president, marketing problems are the province of the marketing vice-president, and so on. Figure 6.8 also shows how functional departmentation may occur in other types of organizations such as schools and hospitals.

Table 6.1 summarizes the major advantages and disadvantages of a functional form of departmentation. The advantages derive from having people of similar technical expertise, interests, and responsibilities grouped together in one unit. They tend to have similar training and professional development needs, and functional departments provide good opportunities for these specialized interests to be developed to the maximum. This tends to create work groups high in colleagueship and good at solving technical problems.

Functional departmentation has potential disadvantages as well. Because the same good or service passes through the hands of many separate departments in the production process, it is sometimes hard to pinpoint responsibilities for error. Personnel in functional departments can also develop overly narrow and technical viewpoints that lose the total system perspective. The result can include failures to communicate across department lines and a lack of responsiveness to interdepartmental issues as each department refers problems up its hierarchy for resolution. Functional department heads, as a result, may spend too much time working on problems that should actually be resolved at lower levels in the hierarchy.

Functional structures are best suited for stable environments and stability-oriented strate-

Table 6.1 Advantages and Disadvantages of Functional Departmentation

Advantages	Disadvantages
Allows task assignments to be made consistent with technical training	May result in reduced accountability for total product or service delivery
Allows greater specialization in technical areas of expertise	Overspecialization may occur
Supports in-depth training and professional development	Communication across functions can break down
Promotes high-quality technical problem solving	Too many interdepartmental problems may be referred upward in the hierarchy for solution
Reduces technical demands on the supervisor	Narrow, self-centered perspectives can develop within functions
Provides career path within areas of technical expertise	May be slow in responding to complex multifunctional problems

gies. They also tend to work well in smaller and less complex organizations. Even in these cases, though, precautions must be taken to guard against or minimize the possible disadvantages summarized in Table 6.1.

Departmentation by Division

What should an organization do when pursuing a strategy of rapid and diversified growth, or when facing an unstable environment requiring quick responses to rapidly changing problems and opportunities? **Departmentation by division**—that is, the formation of departments based on product, client, territory, time, or project differences—can respond to such demands. The structure of Matsushita as introduced in the Part 3 opener is a good case in point.

Figure 6.9 shows divisional departmentation in various types of organizations. In each case attention is directed to the special focus of the division, be it product, territory, client, or time. In the product organization, for example, managers have responsibility for specific product lines. Costs, profits, problems, and successes can thus be attributed to a central point of responsibility for each product. This not only facilitates accountability, but also creates product managers who are more likely to remain sensitive to product needs and changing consumer tastes.

Organizations using a divisional focus hope to gain the advantages listed in Table 6.2. These include having departments that are more responsive to change, more sensitive to total system problems and opportunities, and more accommodating of the special needs or require-

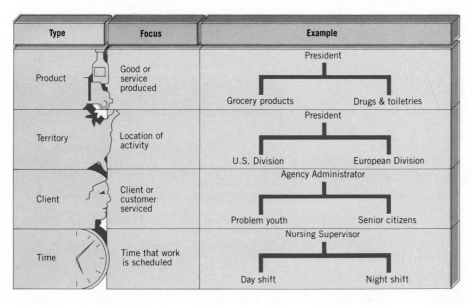

FIGURE 6.9 Basic forms of divisional departmentation.

Type	Focus	Example
Product	Good or service produced	President — Grocery products / Drugs & toiletries
Territory	Location of activity	President — U.S. Division / European Division
Client	Client or customer serviced	Agency Administrator — Problem youth / Senior citizens
Time	Time that work is scheduled	Nursing Supervisor — Day shift / Night shift

Table 6.2 Advantages and Disadvantages of Divisional Departmentation

Advantages	Disadvantages
Flexible in response to environmental developments	May not allow for sufficient depth of technical expertise
Concentrates functional attention on a common task; improves coordination among the functional activities	May lead to duplication of efforts as personnel assigned to separate divisions work on similar problems
Promotes cross-functional performance accountability	May result in overemphasis on division versus organizational objectives
Facilitates growth through the addition of new divisions to handle additional products or services	May result in destructive competition among divisions to acquire resources and meet performance targets

ments of the persons, projects, or products represented in the divisional focus. As a result, the divisional form of departmentation is popular among large organizations with diverse operations cutting across many products, territories, and customers.

There are also potential disadvantages to departmentation by division. Table 6.2 indicates that the divisional focus may lead to duplication of certain functions common to all divisions, may deny the organization sufficient depth in certain functional areas of expertise, and may overemphasize division objectives to the detriment of the total system. As with departmentation by function, divisional departmentation must be well managed to maximize its advantages and minimize its disadvantages to the organization.

Matrix Departmentation

A third basic form of departmentation is known as **matrix departmentation** or *matrix organization*. As diagrammed in Figure 6.10, it combines functional and divisional forms to take best advantage of each. Personnel are still employed in a standard functional hierarchy and report up this hierarchy to a functional department head. In addition, however, they are assigned to cross-functional teams focusing on specific projects or

programs. These personnel represent the technical function on the team, but with a special focus on program objectives as well. Members of the teams thus have a dual allegiance to higher authority: (1) to their respective functional managers, and (2) to the program manager. A design engineer, for example, would report to the engineering manager on functional matters as well as to a program manager on matters applying functional expertise to a program. This "two-boss" system exemplifies the basic matrix concept.

Who Uses a Matrix?

The matrix form grew out of developments during the late 1950s and early 1960s in the U.S. aerospace industry. As *Newsline 6.1* shows, it has now gained a strong foothold in American industry. The matrix organization has been successfully used in such settings as manufacturing (e.g., aerospace, electronics, pharmaceuticals), service (e.g., banking, brokerage, retailing), professional (e.g., accounting, advertising, law), and nonprofit (e.g., city, state, and federal agencies, hospitals, universities). There is also growing awareness that matrix departmentation can help manage the complexity of multinational corporations. The flexibility offered by the matrix struc-

FIGURE 6.10 Matrix departmentation in a business firm.

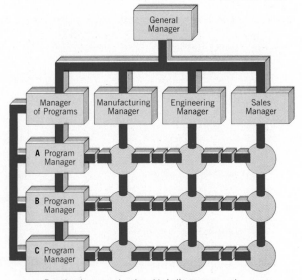

Functional personnel assigned to both programs and their respective functional departments

NEWSLINE 6.1

HOW TO STOP THE BUCK SHORT OF THE TOP

Traditionally, American business has been built around the organization chart, on which clear-cut hierarchies of power are defined: Orders are handed down while decisions are passed upward, until the buck stops with the chief executive. But as businesses diversify and market environments grow more complex, top-level executives are discovering that the old functional and product-line hierarchies, despite their straightforwardness, are bogging down. Executives are swamped with data while the company languishes, awaiting orders.

Now, in an effort by upper management to get out from under the paper crush and speed up decision making, growing numbers of companies are trying a still-evolving organizational form, commonly called matrix management.

Source: From "How to Stop the Buck Short of the Top," *Business Week* (January 16, 1978), pp. 82–83. Reprinted from the January 16, 1978 issue of *Business Week* by special permission, Copyright © 1978 by McGraw-Hill, Inc., New York, N.Y. 10020. All rights reserved.

ture helps accommodate cross-national differences as well as multiple product, program, or project orientations.

Why Is a Matrix Used?

The following example illustrates the conditions under which management might consider shifting to a matrix form of departmentalization.[8]

> Let us assume we are managing a medium-sized ($50 million sales) growing firm in the specialized electronic instrument field. To be successful in this field one must stay at or close to the edge of the rapidly advancing technology and also stay in close touch with the specialized and changing needs of approximately 100 companies who are potential customers. The firm grew up with a conventional functional organization with each of the major functions of manufacturing, sales, and research and development headed up by one of the original founders. Now all of this original group have retired except the present board chairman. The present CEO advanced to the presidency through the ranks because of his conspicuous executive ability and now has become the center of all-important decision making in the firm. And that is the rub. Until recently, because of the rich informal ties forged during the founding years, the management system operated smoothly and quickly around the central figure of the CEO. But now the proliferation of product lines and the problems of size have erected a pile-up of issues awaiting the attention of the overworked CEO. Furthermore, there are increasing signs of bickering and fault finding between the functional departments, much of which are coming up around unexpected delays in the introduction of the new products that are essential for keeping a competitive advantage. The senior managers are aware that their most successful new product introduction of the past three years was a direct result of an informal cross-functional team that grew up around a middle-level sales manager who seemed to have the right kind of leadership touch. It is in this context that the top management team has begun to explore the matrix idea.

The matrix form provides a mechanism for handling diverse products or services in a balanced manner, while still making it easy to change or grow in new product or service directions. The customer or client of a matrix organization always has a program manager available to respond to questions, provide status reports, address problems, or serve as a consultant. By the same token, chief executives such as the general manager in Figure 6.10 have similar access to both program and functional managers. This helps them know what is going on, right or wrong, and why. The matrix is designed to force decision making down to the lowest operating level where the necessary information exists. It does this by creating permanent cross-functional teams for decision making and problem solving. One resulting advantage of a matrix organization is that it frees top managers from many routine day-to-day problem-solving chores. As more decisions are made at the program level, higher managers have more time to devote to strategic planning and the many external factors of organizational significance. Thus the matrix is suited for organizations pursuing growth strategies in dynamic and complex environments.

The matrix also has limits. Some disadvantages of the matrix structure follow.[9]

1. *Power struggles* The "two-boss" system of the matrix can set up power struggles between functional and program managers as each strives to attain maximum advantage for personal perspectives.

2. *Anarchy* Unless great care is taken to clarify the workings of the "two-boss" system, employees may become confused when unable to identify appropriate higher authority.

3. *"Groupitis"* Program teams may become too focused on themselves and the group process; they may lose sight of action requirements and production goals.

4. *Excessive cost* Because of the dual form of departmentation, the matrix adds overhead in extra salaries for program managers; this creates problems when the need for a matrix is not well established and/or a matrix operation is made more complex than necessary.

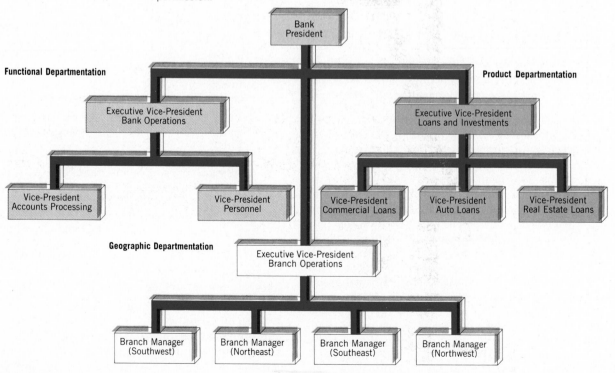

FIGURE 6.11 Mixed forms of departmentation in a multinational firm. *Source:* Lawrence J. Gitman and Carl McDaniel, Jr., *Business World* (New York: Wiley, 1983), p. 131. Used by permission.

Mixed Forms of Departmentation

Many organizations use the different forms of departmentation in various combinations. Figure 6.11, for example, shows a multinational firm mixing functional, product, and geographic forms of departmentation in different facets of its operations.

VERTICAL COORDINATION

Arranging people and resources into departments is only one part of the manager's organizing responsibility. It is also necessary to coordinate results if the organization's purpose is to be adequately served. Multiple and separately functioning parts must somehow be combined into a functioning whole. The central element in this coordination process is authority.

Authority, you should recall from earlier chapters, is the right of command. It represents a right to take action and a right to expend resources. Formal authority is vested in managerial positions, and managers are legitimated to act in the organization's behalf and exercise authority over one or more other persons. The upward and downward flow of authority from one managerial level to the next constitutes the organization's hierarchy of authority. Vertical coordination is the process of using the hierarchy of authority to help integrate the separate and specialized components of an organization.

What follows is an introduction to four fundamental elements in vertical coordination: (1) chain of command, (2) span of control, (3) delegation, and (4) centralization-decentralization. Each of these elements has received considerable attention throughout the history of management thought. The result is a series of classic principles of organization that are defined and critiqued in coming discussion.

Chain of Command

Let's use Figure 6.12 as a point of reference. The solid line shows the formal line of authority between workers A, B, and C at the lowest level of the organization and the general manager at the highest level. This **chain of command** is an unbroken line of authority that vertically links all

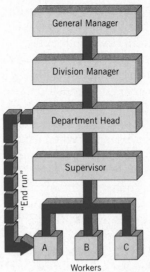

FIGURE 6.12 The chain of command.

persons in an organization with successively higher levels of authority. Two principles convey classic views on how the chain of command should operate in any organization: the scalar principle and the unity-of-command principle.

Scalar Principle

There should be a clear and unbroken chain of command linking every person in the organization with successively higher levels of authority up to and including the chief executive officer; this chain of command should be followed when orders are conveyed from higher to lower levels of authority.

The reason for the scalar principle is to ensure that all persons know to whom they report and therefore also know from whom they can expect to receive directions. Violation of the scalar principle occurs when a higher-level manager bypasses someone's supervisor to give orders directly to that person. This situation is depicted by the dotted line in Figure 6.12 between the Department Head and Worker A. Such "end runs" can confuse the employee and undermine the authority of the employee's supervisor.

Unity-of-Command Principle

Each person in an organization should report to one and only one supervisor.

This is one of the oldest of the classic principles and complements the scalar principle just described. By recommending that each subordinate report to only one supervisor, the principle's intention is to ensure clarity in the transmission of orders through the chain of command and continuity in the completion of work assignments. A person can experience considerable conflict and frustration, for example, when asked to do different things by two higher-level managers and/or when asked to do too much for the time available when the requests of many managers are added together. The unity-of-command principle advises against creating multiple reporting relationships in organizations.

Think back, though, to the matrix organization. One of its central tenets is a "two-boss" or dual-authority system. That is, it systematically and intentionally violates unity of command. Although it does stand contrary to classic advice, the matrix concept is a legitimate violation of the unity-of-command principle. In those situations where the matrix is an appropriate structure, the potential advantages to be gained outweigh such risks as the confusion and conflict just mentioned. Furthermore, knowing full well that the matrix violates unity of command, matrix managers can take special precautions to avoid such problems. Working to ensure good communication between program managers, functional managers, and program team members is but one example of what can be done in this regard.

Span of Control

Span of control is the number of subordinates reporting directly to a manager.

Span-of-Control Principle

There is a limit to the number of persons one manager can effectively supervise; care should be exercised to keep the span of control within manageable limits.

There was a time in the emergence of management theory when people searched for the ideal span of control. V. A. Graciunas, a French management consultant, even sought a sophis-

ticated mathematical formula to determine the ideal span of control.[10] Although the magic number was never found, his work and that of others has pointed out that limited spans of control can increase vertical coordination by allowing managers to spend more time with each subordinate.

Factors Influencing Spans of Control

Even though an exact or ideal span of control can't be calculated, there are certain factors which set limits on how large or small spans of control should be in various situations. They include[11]

1. *Similarity of functions supervised* Span of control should decrease as the number of different functions to be supervised increases.
2. *Physical proximity of functions supervised* Span of control should decrease as the physical distance between functions supervised increases.
3. *Complexity of functions supervised* Span of control should be smaller for subordinates performing more complex tasks than for those performing simpler tasks.
4. *Required coordination among functions supervised* The more interrelated the tasks to be supervised, the smaller the appropriate span of control.
5. *Required planning for functions supervised* The more time a manager is required to spend planning for the functions to be supervised, the smaller the appropriate span of control.

Span of Control and Levels in the Hierarchy

Span of control and the number of levels in an organization's hierarchy of authority are interrelated. Organizations with generally larger spans of control tend to be *flat*—they have few levels of management. Organizations with generally small spans of control tend to be *tall*—they have many levels of management. These differences are illustrated in Figure 6.13.

Whenever spans of control are reduced, the likelihood is that new management personnel will be added. Before making such a change, therefore, serious thought should always be given to both the cost of the added supervision and the potential consequences of having more

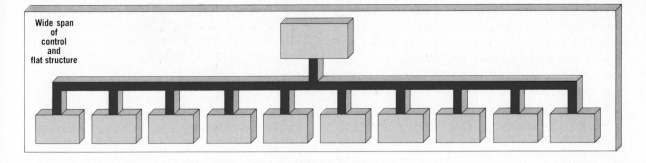

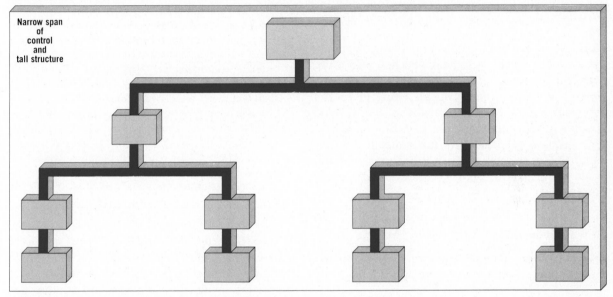

FIGURE 6.13 Flat and tall structures with same number of positions. *Source:* Lawrence J. Gitman and Carl McDaniel, Jr., *Business World* (New York: Wiley, 1983), p. 128. Used by permission.

levels in the chain of command. For example, some recent cost-cutting efforts in U.S. industry have been aimed at reducing the number of management levels. This suggests that many firms are willing to live with larger spans of control in order to keep the number of vertical levels in the chain of command to a minimum.

Delegation

All managers must decide how much work they should do themselves and what should be assigned to others. **Delegation** is the process of distributing and entrusting work to other persons. There are three steps in this process.[12]

1. *The manager assigns duties.* The person who is delegating indicates what work the subor-

dinate is to do and that he or she will then be held accountable for results.

2. *The manager grants authority to act.* Along with permission to proceed with the assigned work, certain rights (such as to spend money, direct the work of others, use raw materials, represent the organization to outsiders, or take other steps necessary to fulfill the new duties) are transferred to the subordinate.

3. *The manager creates an obligation to act.* In accepting an assignment, a subordinate takes on an obligation or assumes responsibility to the boss to complete the job as requested.

Accountability, authority, and responsibility are the foundation elements of vertical coordination in the delegation process. **Accountability** is the requirement for a subordinate to answer to the supervisor for results accomplished in the performance of any assigned duties. *Authority* is what is delegated by the superior to provide the subordinate with sufficient rights of command and action capabilities to carry out the assigned tasks. **Responsibility** is the obligation to perform that results from accepting assigned tasks; it is a commitment by the subordinate to the supervisor to carry out duties as agreed.

Another classic principle of organization warns managers not to ask things of subordinates for which they lack sufficient authority to perform. If an instructor comes to you and says that you are being held accountable for how well your student work group does on a class project, the charge is really unfair. You are being given responsibility and held accountable for the work of people over whom you have no authority. When the authority delegated is not equal to the responsibility created, the risk is reduced subordinate performance, confusion, and conflict—or all three.

Authority-and-Responsibility Principle

Authority should equal responsibility when work is delegated from supervisor to subordinate.

Centralization-Decentralization

One of the continuing debates in management theory is over the question: "Should authority for most decisions be concentrated at the top levels of an organization, or should authority to make decisions be dispersed by extensive delegation throughout all levels of management?" The former is referred to as the process of **centralization;** the latter is called **decentralization.** A practical view of both sides of the argument about the two follows.[13]

> In favor of the decentralizers, it can certainly be said that excessive centralization is a common error that can do extreme damage to an organization. Most people are familiar with the pattern: the ever-lengthening delays while head office makes up its mind, the futile attempts to lay down universal laws and procedures however inappropriate to the special circumstances of those affected, the top people growing more and more

out of touch with the day-to-day realities, the people who work close to the products or customers having to refer decisions which they have the knowledge and experience to make correctly up to people who have neither, the stillbirth of enterprising ideas because of the frustration of waiting for the go-ahead until it's too late, or getting it in time but hedged in with reservations and modifications which make success almost impossible.

> But, of course, the dangers of excessive decentralization are just as damaging: production schedules being drawn up without consulting a sales forecast, two representatives—one from the region and one from the product division—trying to sell the same product to the same customer while telling conflicting facts about it, sales drives aimed at a volume of orders which the factories cannot in fact meet, good young managers bottled up in inadequate jobs because their bosses will not release them for promotion in other departments and have no vacancies in their own, and the general state of affairs where the planning department is an expensive joke and the firm has as many policies as managers.

There is no classic principle governing centralization-decentralization. The debate, in fact, is one that can easily take emotional and even value-laden overtones. There are those, for example, who feel that only decentralization is consistent with the values found in free and democratic societies. Others feel that with knowledgeable people at the top of organizations there is no need to take important decisions out of their hands. Centralization-decentralization, however, is not an "either/or" choice. Each has its place in the overall process of vertical coordination. It is a matter for the effective manager to decide when each is most appropriate to maintain desired coordination, and then to be able to implement the decision well.

HORIZONTAL COORDINATION

The final topic for this chapter is horizontal coordination, the process through which activities are integrated across levels instead of up and down the chain of command. The matrix form of departmentation is one example of how organizations can be structured to distribute authority in a way that improves coordination among sub-

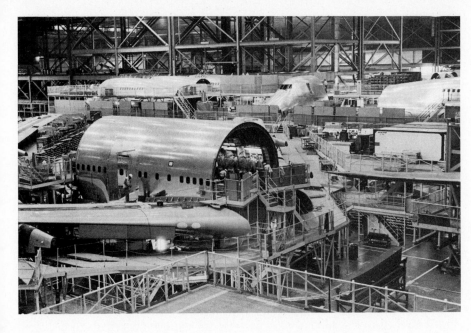

The complexity of the aerospace industry lends itself to matrix organization structures.

units. Other related means of facilitating horizontal coordination through the creation of effective lateral relations will be examined in Chapter 7. These include the formation of cross-functional teams, task forces, and liaison personnel. When it comes to horizontal coordination in organizations, though, our attention must first be given to functional authority and line-staff relationships as important organizing devices.

Functional Authority

Horizontal coordination requires authority to act across instead of between hierarchical levels. **Functional authority** is authority to act in relation to the activities of other persons or units lying outside the formal chain of command. It typically rests on specialized expertise or the possession of technical information and extends only over matters to which these apply. Managers affiliated with such technical departments as accounting, personnel, legal, finance, and engineering frequently use functional authority to fulfill their roles in an organization's division of labor.

A good example of functional authority in most organizations is found with the personnel department. As the location of technical expertise on such matters as selection criteria, legal employment procedures, and organizational record

keeping, the personnel department is often in a position of functional authority over other departments. To ensure compliance with federal laws and internal policies, the director of personnel often has the functional authority to set standard formats for job descriptions, screen applicants for affirmative-action requirements, and ensure that salary offers fall within organizational guidelines.

Line and Staff Relations

Another means for achieving horizontal coordination is through a clear designation of line and staff units. Chapter 1 described the role of staff managers as supporting the activities of line managers by providing advice and technical assistance in their areas of expertise. When this staff role is effectively done throughout an organization, it helps ensure uniform and coordinated action with respect to relevant technical matters. In a large retail chain such as K-Mart or J. C. Penney, for example, line managers in each store make day-to-day operating decisions directly connected with the sale of merchandise. Staff specialists at the corporate or regional levels, though, provide direction and support so that all stores operate with the same credit, purchasing, employment, and advertising procedures. In this

NEWSLINE 6.2

A NEW TARGET: REDUCING STAFF AND LEVELS

Managers, especially presidents and chief executive officers, are frequently on the lookout for ways to cut costs and increase operating efficiency within their organizations. Among the many alternatives, reducing the size of corporate staff and number of management levels in the hierarchy of authority are two popular targets of these efforts, as the following illustrations show how two major corporations have been affected by these considerations.

Acme-Cleveland Corporation   When B. Charles Ames became chief executive of Acme-Cleveland Corp., he was appalled to find that although the machine tool maker's earnings had plunged to $2.3 million in fiscal 1981's first quarter from $4.2 million in first-quarter 1980, its corporate overhead was remaining constant, topping $23 million per year. "I reached the conclusion early," says Ames, "that there were way too many people—the bulk in middle management and corporate structure." Ames quickly chopped his headquarters staff to 50 people from the 120 he inherited. "We need to operate with fewer people who are given broader responsibilities," he explains.

Ford Motor Company   At Ford Motor Company, thee are 11 layers of management between the factory worker and the chairman, while Toyota Motor Company makes do with six. Now Ford's management has come to the uncomfortable conclusion that this excess layering has had two negative results: high overhead and a morass of red tape.

The company recently increased by several million dollars its plant managers' spending authority in order to push decision making further down the hierarchy. And Ford is starting to disband some of the corporate subcommittees that traditionally had reviewed divisional decisions. "We've had Big Brother syndrome, looking over each others' shoulders, checking and rechecking," admits William J. Harahan, Ford's director of technical planning. "I suggest that we can no longer afford these layers of manufacturing management."

Source: Acme-Cleveland Corporation example from "A New Target: Reducing Staff and Levels," *Business Week* (December 21, 1981), p. 67; Ford Motor Company example from "Trust: The New Ingredient in Management," *Business Week* (July 6, 1981), p. 104. Both reprinted by permission. Copyright © 1981 by McGraw-Hill, Inc., New York, N.Y. 10020. All rights reserved.

way, staff activities facilitate horizontal coordination across the many geographically dispersed stores.

The distinction between line and staff is not always clear-cut, however, and conflict in the working relations between line and staff personnel sometimes causes problems. Take the case of one company that experienced rapid growth. Confusion emerged in the relationships between line personnel and the corporate treasurer. A consultant's confidential report to the president contained the following recommendations for eliminating the problem by clarifying areas of line and staff authority.[14]

> The treasurer has line authority over and is responsible for directing activities of such personnel as he requires to establish system policies and procedures for the functions under his jurisdiction and to administer system treasury and accounting functions reserved for his department. He has no direct line authority over the day-to-day activities of accounting personnel in the divisions and regions except as specifically delegated by the president. He is responsible for developing and interpreting budgeting, accounting, and financial policies to the divisions and regions, for assisting these organizations in carrying out such policies, and for satisfying himself that such policies are correctly and ably administered in the field.

> At the request of division managements, or voluntarily when system welfare is materially concerned, the treasurer shall make recommendations concerning the employment, promotion, dismissal, or change in compensation of supervisory personnel engaged in activities within his functional responsibility. Final action on such matters shall be taken by division managements when mutual agreement has been reached with department heads concerned.

Staff Authority vis-à-vis the Line Manager

The authority of staff in relationship to line personnel varies along a continuum. At the one extreme, staff is purely *advisory* in its authority. A staff person can be consulted at a line manager's discretion, and staff advice can be accepted or rejected at the line manager's discretion. At the other extreme is *functional* authority as discussed in the preceding section. Here, staff is able to direct the line manager on matters defined as

falling within the staff's technical expertise. A personnel department may *advise* a line manager on desired qualifications for hiring new workers; the personnel department may *require* the manager to follow equal-employment-opportunity hiring guidelines. In the example of the company treasurer reported earlier, the treasurer had functional authority in developing and interpreting budgeting and financial policies for the line operating divisions. He had only advisory authority to recommend on personnel hired by the divisions to carry out these policies.

Personal Staff versus Specialized Staff

Staff assignments can be made on either a personal or specialized basis. **Personal staff** appointments are "assistant-to" positions that provide special administrative support to higher-level positions. They help the higher managers extend time by assuming administrative details and other more routine matters. In Figure 6.14, the assistant to the president is acting in a personal staff capacity.

Specialized staff performs a technical service or provides special problem-solving expertise for other parts of the organization. Specialized staff can be a single person such as the corporate attorney shown in Figure 6.14, or a complete unit such as the personnel department also shown in the figure. Note, however, that line relationships will still exist within staff units. For example, Figure 6.14 shows that those persons assigned to the personnel staff unit are under the personnel director's formal line of authority. Other specialized staff assignments you can expect to find in organizations include those concerning legal matters, personnel practices, public relations, planning, accounting, and labor relations.

Guidelines on the Use of Staff

The staff components of organizations support line managers with both administrative assistance and specialized technical expertise. *Newsline 6.2*, however, indicates that staff assignments can be overdone, and at times they become prime targets for cost-cutting efforts.

There is really no one best way of dividing the work between line and staff in an organiza-

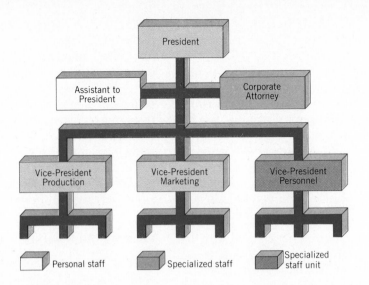

FIGURE 6.14 Personal and specialized staff in an organization.

Personal staff Specialized staff Specialized staff unit

tion. What *is* best for any given organization is a staff component that satisfies its needs for specialized technical assistance. At TRW Systems, the approach that works best is "don't let them ever get too large." TRW has fewer than 500 people on its corporate staff out of a total employment of nearly 100,000 employees. IBM, on the other hand, seems to work well on the principle of "don't let them ever stay too long in one place." The company rotates managers between line and staff positions. At one point, no staff person at IBM had been away from a line-management job for more than 18 months.[15]

SUMMARY

This chapter concludes your first in-depth look at organizing as a management function. Organizing is a process of dividing work into manageable components and coordinating results to serve the organization's purpose. Underlying this process is managerial authority, the right to command, the right to act, the right to allocate resources. Authority sets the stage for managerial decisions that initially create an appropriate division of labor and then coordinate results.

Two basic elements in specialization, or the process through which the organizational division of labor is established, are: (1) forming work units or departments, and (2) designating specific jobs for individuals and groups. The latter topic is the subject of Chapter 8. The former involves departmentation, which can be accomplished through functional, divisional, and matrix forms.

The need for coordination among the multiple and specialized components of organizations can also be viewed as a two-dimensional managerial responsibility. In respect to vertical coordination, the goal is to establish appropriate authority relationships through the chain of command, span of control, delegation, and centralization-decentralization. Each issue is the subject of a classic principle of organization that still merits consideration by the modern manager.

Horizontal coordination, on the other hand, cuts across the vertical hierarchy of authority. In most organizations, achieving horizontal coordination begins with use of functional authority and the maintenance of good line-staff relations. Other approaches include the matrix form of departmentation and additional ways of creating effective lateral relations, to be discussed in Chapter 7.

The next chapter will take a dynamic view of organizations and inquire into how they should be designed to best advantage. As you put the present chapter in perspective, remember that managers must divide and then coordinate work to accomplish organizational objectives. This is what "organizing" is all about.

THINKING THROUGH THE ISSUES

1. Explain the importance of organizing relative to the other management functions.

2. Draw an organization chart for an organization with which you are familiar. Explain the hierarchy of authority as it applies to this organization.

3. What is the difference between the formal and informal structure of an organization? Give examples of each in a work situation with which you are familiar.

4. What does it mean to say that, for a manager, structure is both (a) a characteristic of the work setting, and (b) something to be created?

5. How does specialization by job design differ from specialization by departmentation?

6. State four different ways an organization can use a divisional form of departmentation. Give examples of each.

7. How does a matrix organization combine the advantages of both the functional and divisional forms of departmentation?

8. State four classic principles of organization.

9. Give a reason why each of the prior principles is valid for the modern manager. Also give an example of when it might be legitimately violated.

10. Clarify the difference between personal and specialized staff in an organization.

THE MANAGER'S VOCABULARY

Accountability	Departmentation by division	Job design	Span-of-control principle
Authority-and-responsibility principle	Departmentation by function	Matrix departmentation	Specialization
Centralization	Formal structure	Organization chart	Specialized staff
Chain of command	Functional authority	Organizing	Structure
Coordination	Horizontal coordination	Personal staff	Synergy
Decentralization	Informal structure	Responsibility	Unity-of-command principle
Delegation		Scalar principle	Vertical coordination
Departmentation		Span of control	

CAREER PERSPECTIVE: GETTING CONTROL OF CORPORATE STAFF WORK

Peter Drucker, noted author and management consultant, offers managers the following advice on hiring staff personnel and ensuring their performance contributions to the enterprise.[16]

> Don't ever put anyone into a staff job, for example, unless he or she has successfully held a number of operating jobs, preferably in more than one functional area. For if staff people lack operating experience, they will be arrogant about operations, which always look so simple to the "planner." And unless staff people have proven themselves in operations, they will lack credibility among operating people and will be dismissed as "theoreticians."

This is so elementary a rule that even the most extreme proponent of "staff supremacy," the Prussian army of the 19th Century, strictly observed it. An officer had first to get promoted twice in troop command—from second to first lieutenant and then to captain—before he could sit for the general exam.

But today, in government even more than in business, we put young people fresh out of business or law school into fairly senior staff jobs as analysts or planners or staff counsel. Their arrogance and their rejection by the operating organization practically guarantee that they will be totally unproductive. By contrast, no one in Japan—whether in business or government—gets into staff work of any kind until he has had seven—or, more usually, ten—years of successful performance in three or four operating assignments.

With rare exceptions, staff work should not be a person's "career" but only a *part* of his or her career. After five or seven years on a staff job, people ought to go back into operating work, and not return to a staff assignment for five years or so. Otherwise, they will soon become behind-the-scene wirepullers, "gray eminences," "king makers" like those brilliant mischief makers, the staff officers of the Prussian army. Staff work, by definition, has great authority, the authority of knowledge. But it has no responsibility; it is advice, plan, forecast rather than decision, execution, results. And it is the oldest adage of politics that authority without responsibility corrupts.

Above all, the true results of staff work are most effective, more productive operating people. Staff is support for operating people and not a substitute for them.

Questions

1. Do you anticipate a staff job early in your managerial career? If so, do you plan to take it with or without the operating experience advocated by Drucker? Defend your choice.

2. Do you agree with Drucker's viewpoint as expressed in his last sentence? What can a staff person do to avoid this pitfall?

CASE APPLICATION: FULLFEDER PEN COMPANY[17]

The Fullfeder Pen Company was organized about 10 years ago by Ludwig Fullfeder, an engineer who simultaneously became its president and general manager of all operations. Initially the firm had about a dozen employees engaged in the manufacturing and assembly of a full line of high-quality ball-point and felt-tip pens that Ludwig designed and patented. As sales expanded, Ludwig kept adding both additional plant facilities and employees to handle the increased business that resulted, mainly from customers seeking specialized pens for advertising purposes.

In 1973, Fullfeder Pen was purchased by

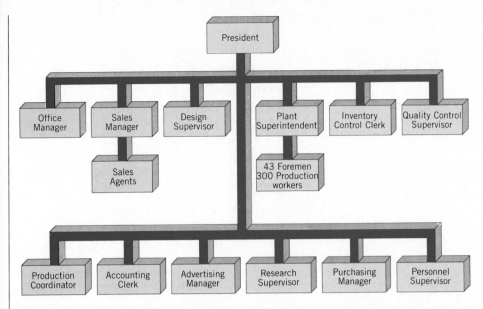

FIGURE 6.15 Fullfeder Pen Company.

Macro Pen Industries. Fullfeder was thereupon reorganized and Ludwig elected president of the new company. At the time, Macro Pen also recommended that he develop an organizational structure. Fullfeder never felt one was necessary. "I've always done the thinking here," he remarked to a friend. Ludwig, a stolid individual accustomed to managing his own shop on an informal basis, nevertheless grudgingly set up the organization chart in Figure 6.15 without consulting the Macro Pen management.

This organizational structure was put into effect and seemed to work satisfactorily for about a year. During this period, "Mad Ludwig," as the production workers nicknamed him after a television program on Bavarian King Ludwig II, labored frantically to make the chart work. He worked 12 to 14 hours each day, much of the time in the plant supervising the production line. And when not supervising the manufacturing process, he would move from department to department solving one problem after another.

On one such typical day, Ludwig:

1. Told purchasing to change suppliers of the basic plastic stock for pen barrels.
2. Hired a new accounts receivable clerk to work in the office.

3. Reviewed and made corrections on advertising copy for a trade journal.
4. Expedited a shipment of pens for a long-time account.

After a year of this kind of managing, Ludwig realized that his structure was not functioning properly. There were continual production breakdowns, sales were down, and profits were off; to complicate things, his family physician gave him orders to slow down.

The problem, Ludwig felt, was the friction between the department heads. They were just not cooperating. Ludwig felt there was only one solution—dismiss the "troublemakers" in charge of several of the departments and hire new and more cooperative ones.

Questions

1. Would dismissing the "troublemakers" remedy the situation for Ludwig? Why or why not?
2. What *is* the problem in this case?
3. Would a reconfiguration of the organizational structure be appropriate? If so, what would you recommend and why?

CLASS EXERCISE: THE ORGANIZATION CHART

1. Study the following set of positions found at the upper management level of a business firm.

Sales	Vice-President Engineering	Quality Assurance
Production	Controller	Vice-President Research and Development
President and Chairman of the Board	Legal Counsel	Vice-President Manufacturing
Advertising	Board of Directors	Secretary Treasurer

2. Draw an organization chart that arranges these positions in a logical fashion.

3. Identify those positions representing (a) staff appointments and (b) line appointments.

4. Decide if your organization chart basically uses a functional, divisional, matrix, or mixed form of departmentation.

5. Share your results with a nearby classmate. Discuss any differences of opinion. Await further class discussion.

REFERENCES

[1] Cartoon by Jeff MacNelly of the Richmond *News Leader.* Copyright © Chicago Tribune. Used by permission.

[2] Adapted from Howard M. Carlisle, *Management: Concepts, Methods and Applications,* Second Edition (Chicago: Science Research Associates, 1982), p. 478.

[3] Based on Radie G. Bunn and Anthony J. Tasca, "Mafia: Parallels with Legitimate Business," from the November 1974 issue of the *University of Michigan Business Review,* published by the Graduate School of Business Administration, the University of Michigan. Portions reprinted by permission. The final quote is from Donald Cressey, *Theft of the Nation* (New York: Harper & Row, 1969), p. 245.

[4] David Nicklaus, "Monsanto Recombines," *St. Louis Post-Dispatch* (July 4, 1982), p. 6E.

[5] Keith Davis, *Human Relations at Work* (New York: McGraw-Hill, 1967), p. 212.

[6] For a discussion of departmentation, see H. I. Ansoff and R. G. Bradenburg, "A Language for Organization Design," *Management Science,* Vol. 17 (August 1971), pp. B705–731; Mariann Jelinek, "Organization Structure: The Basic Conformations," in Mariann Jelinek, Joseph A. Litterer, and Raymond E. Miles (eds.), *Organizations by Design: Theory and Practice* (Plano, Texas: Business Publications, 1981), pp. 293–302.

[7] Adapted from David R. Hampton, *Contemporary Management,* Second Edition (New York: McGraw-Hill, 1981), p. 260.

[8] Adapted from p. 7 of *Matrix* Stanley M. Davis and Paul R. Lawrence, Copyright © 1971, by permission of Addison-Wesley Publishing Company, Reading, MA. This source offers a good overview of matrix organizations.

[9] Ibid., pp. 129–144.

[10] See, for example, V. A. Graciunas, "Relationships in Organizations," in L. Gulick and L. Urwick (eds.), *Papers on the Science of Administration* (New York: Institute of Public Administration, 1937), pp. 181–187.

[11] See C. W. Barkdull, "Span of Control—A Method of Evaluation," *Michigan Business Review,* Vol. 15, No. 3 (May 1963), pp. 27–29.

[12] William H. Newman, Kirby E. Warren, and Jerome E. Schne, *The Process of Management Strategy, Action, Results,* Fifth Edition (Englewood Cliffs, N.J.: Prentice-Hall, 1982), p. 221.

[13] From Anthony Jay, *Management and Machiavelli* (New York: Holt, Rinehart & Winston, 1967), pp. 58–59.

[14] Harold Koontz, Cyril O'Donnell, and Heinz Weihrich, *Essentials of Management,* Third Edition (New York: McGraw-Hill, 1982), p. 242.

[15] Robert M. Tomasko, "Subbing Division, Line Work for Corporate Staff," *Wall Street Journal* (March 28, 1983), p. 14.

[16] Excerpted from Peter F. Drucker, "Getting Control of Corporate Staff Work," *Wall Street Journal* (April 28, 1982), p. 24. Reprinted by permission of the *Wall Street Journal.* Copyright © 1982 Dow Jones & Company, Inc. All rights reserved.

[17] Case reprinted by permission from *Contemporary Management Incidents* by Bernard Deitzer and Karl A. Shilliff, Grid Publishing, Inc., Columbus, Ohio; 1977, pp. 29–31.

7

ORGANIZATIONAL DESIGN

BUREAUCRACY AT ITS BEST: AWARDS OF MONEY, ACCLAIM

WASHINGTON—Everybody knows about bureaucrats.[1] They are lazy, overpaid, and indifferent to the public that pays them. They live in Washington and have no idea what's really important to the rest of the country. They are partners in the big three of What's Wrong With Government: Waste, Fraud, and Abuse.

Politicians love them because they make such easy targets. Ronald Reagan as a candidate made campaign points by seizing on a nationwide dislike for bloated government. Reagan the president declared war: "We are going to follow every lead, root out every incompetent, and prosecute any crook we find who's cheating the people of this nation," he said.

That shouldn't prove difficult in a government with a civilian payroll of 2.9 million. But along the way the investigators might stumble across some good guys, because among the lazy, the incompetent, and the crooked, there also are the efficient, the dedicated, and the conscientious.

C. Dale Forst got a job as laundry plant manager in a Veterans Administration hospital, and his experienced eye told him things could be better. He eliminated a rinse cycle, fiddled with different kinds and amounts of soap and bleach, turned down the water temperature, and, lo, the government saved $23,400 the first year.

Kenneth P. Boehne, working for the U.S. Railroad Retirement Board in Chicago, changed accounting practices. The results: $9.4 million in one-time savings and more than $7 million in increased investment income. Boehne has a habit of such things. Another time, while working for the General Accounting Office, he criticized the railroad board's investment practices. They were changed and investment income increased $50 million.

Such stories fall in the good-news category and seldom make headlines.

Just as the chapter opener implies, it is easy to find headlines critical of bureaucracies. The fact of the matter is they can and do work when designed and implemented well. In this chapter we take a closer look at bureaucracy, alternatives to it, and a variety of ideas for the structural design of effective organizations. Key topics in the chapter include

Bureaucracy
Mechanistic and Organic Organizations
Strategic Factors in Organizational Design
Environment
Organizational Context
Subsystem Design

Every organization is different. Rarely, if ever, will you find one organization whose character and needs are the exact replicas of another's. This means that organizations will require different structures as well. What works for one organization may not work for another. Chapter 6 examined the fundamentals of organizing in terms of alternative forms of departmentation, and in respect to the various means of achieving horizontal and vertical coordination. This chapter introduces you to a body of knowledge concerned with helping managers decide the best way to structure an organization or one of its subsystems. This process of choosing and implementing an appropriate structural configuration is called **organizational design.** Good organizational design, in turn, is based on the examination of relationships between structure and environment, technology, size, strategy, and people.

We will approach organizational design from a problem-solving perspective.[2] Whenever a manager observes a difference between what the organization is capable of achieving and what is actually happening in terms of performance results, efforts to redesign the organization (i.e., to change the structure) may be called for. Figure 7.1 depicts how organizational design serves a problem-solving purpose in such circumstances. Note, as is shown in the figure, that the causes of poor or substandard performance may be something other than a deficient structure. In such cases managerial responses discussed elsewhere in the book may be needed. At the very least, structure should always be considered as a possible cause of performance problems. When it turns out to be all or part of the problem, organizational design is an appropriate response for correcting any structural deficiencies that may exist.

As you read on, recall that structure is significant to any manager from two perspectives. As described in Chapter 6,

1. *Managers must understand the structure of the total organization as a work setting.* Managers are responsible for serving as good interfaces or liaisons between their subunits and the other components of their parent organizations. This is greatly facilitated when they understand how the rest of the system is structured and the logic of any organizational design efforts that occur over time.

2. *Managers must have the capability to make good choices regarding the structures of those portions of organizations under their direct control.* The president of a company, for example, must be sure the total organization is structured properly; a department manager, on the other hand, is concerned about work-unit structure. Both must be prepared to lead the process of organizational design in their areas of managerial responsibility.

BUREAUCRACY

No discussion of organizational design is complete without a thorough look at bureaucracy. A *bureaucracy,* as described in Chapter 2, is a form

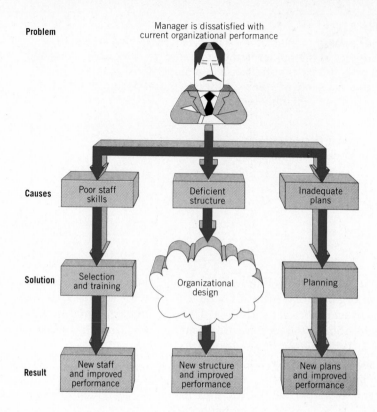

Problem — Manager is dissatisfied with current organizational performance

Causes — Poor staff skills | Deficient structure | Inadequate plans

Solution — Selection and training | Organizational design | Planning

Result — New staff and improved performance | New structure and improved performance | New plans and improved performance

FIGURE 7.1 Problem-solving approach to organizational design.

of organization described by the German sociologist Max Weber.[3] Many people, perhaps even yourself, view bureaucracy in a negative sense. See, for example, the Sidney Harris cartoon, "An employee's view of bureaucracy." For Weber, though, a bureaucracy was a desirable form of organization—and bureaucrats were the people who made it work.

Bureaucratic Features of Organizations

As first introduced in Chapter 2, the characteristics of an ideal bureaucracy include:

1. *A clear-cut division of labor* Each position has well-defined authority and responsibility.

2. *Positions arranged in a hierarchy of authority* Each lower-level position is supervised by a higher-level one.

3. *Positions staffed on the basis of technical competence* Appointments and promotions are based on expertise and competence.

4. *A system of impersonal rules and standards* Uniformity and coordination in performance are

ensured by consistent application of rules and standards.

You can see that the ideal bureaucracy is based on logic, order, and legitimate authority. Organizations adopting these bureaucratic features are supposed to be rational, fair, and efficient as a result. Notwithstanding these intentions, bureaucracies rarely function in the intended fashion. The classic bureaucratic form of organization is prone to the following limitations in practice.

1. *Bureaucratic structures can be too rigid and formal.* Because they rely heavily on rules and procedures, bureaucracies are not well suited for rapidly changing and uncertain environments. It is difficult to change formal procedures to adapt to new conditions as they arise.

2. *Bureaucratic structures can become unwieldly as organizations grow in size.* As the number of levels in the hierarchy of authority increases, persons at higher management levels can grow increasingly out of touch with lower-level operations. Top management decisions may fail to

An employee's view of bureaucracy. (© Sidney Harris.)

reflect operational realities as a result.

3. *Overspecialization in bureaucratic structures can reduce employee initiative.* As jobs become narrower in scope and well defined by procedures, individuals sacrifice autonomy and independence. Reduced creativity and problem-solving potential may result as people conform to established rules instead of reaching out in new directions.

Indeed, there are times when highly bureaucratic organizations seem nothing more than sources of endless lines, red tape, insensitivity to unique problems, and resistance to change. Although the ideal bureaucracy is supposed to create order and efficiency, its critics point out that such dysfunctions as those just discussed can create inefficiency and disorder instead.[4] *Newsline 7.1* indicates that the problems of managing bureaucracy are worldwide—as far away in both miles and culture as China. Interestingly, the Chinese are looking to American management practices to help correct inefficiencies in their organizations.

Radical Prediction: The Coming Death of Bureaucracy

In 1966 Warren Bennis, a well-known and provocative management theorist, published an article entitled "The Coming Death of Bureaucracy." The following excerpts from the article represent the essence of Bennis's radical prediction.[5]

The bureaucratic "machine model" was developed as a reaction against the personal subjugation, nepotism, cruelty, and capricious and subjective judgments that passed for managerial practices during the early days of the industrial revolution. Bureaucracy emerged out of the organizations' need for order and precision and the workers' demands for impartial treatment. It was an organization ideally suited to the values and demands of the Victorian era. And just as bureaucracy emerged as a creative response to a radically new age, so today new organizational shapes are surfacing before our eyes.

I shall try to show why the conditions of our modern industrialized world will bring about the death of bureaucracy. There are at least four relevant threats to bureaucracy.

1. *Rapid and unexpected change.* Bureaucracy's strength is its capacity to efficiently manage the routine and predictable in human affairs. Its nicely defined chain of command, its rules and its rigidities, are ill-adapted to the rapid change the environment now demands.

2. *Growth in size.* While, in theory, there may be no natural limit to the height of a bureaucratic pyramid, in practice the element of complexity is almost invariably introduced with great size.

3. *Complexity of modern technology.* Today's activities require persons of very diverse highly specialized competence. These changes break down the old, industrial trend toward more and more people doing either simple or undifferentiated chores. Hurried growth, rapid change, and increase in specialization pit these three factors against the pyramid structure. We should expect the pyramid of bureaucracy to begin crumbling.

4. *A basically psychological threat springing from a change in managerial behavior.* There is, I believe, a subtle but perceptible change in the philosophy underlying management behavior; a new concept of the human being, based on in-

NEWSLINE 7.1

PEKING TO ACT ON BLOATED BUREAUCRACY AND "LOW EFFICIENCY, ENDLESS HAGGLING"

PEKING—One encouraging thing about China today is official awareness of the problems the country faces and a determination to overcome them. Though the problems may be gigantic and the solutions elusive, identifying problems is the essential first step toward eradicating them.

One such problem was pinpointed by Premier Zhao Ziyang in his speech to the National People's Congress. "Bureaucratic tendencies," he said, "are an important obstacle to our new approach to economic development and the realization of our modernization program." To ensure the effective leadership that China needs, Zhao said, "the State Council is determined to adopt firm measures to alter the intolerably low efficiency resulting from overlapping and overstaffed administrations with their multitiered departments crammed full of superfluous personnel and deputy and nominal chiefs who engage in endless haggling and shifts of responsibility."

Just how serious the problem is at the highest levels was disclosed by Xie Bangyuan, deputy of Government Offices under the State Council. According to Xie, there are about 1000 ministers and vice-ministers in the central government with some ministries having as many as 20 or more vice-ministers. Such a ponderous bureaucracy makes decision making a slow and painful process, as each of the many high officials involved in effect has veto power. When approval for anything is sought, documents are passed from one official to another, and anyone may, for whatever reason, raise questions that require months of "further study."

The bureaucratic morass is aggravated by the Chinese practice of each level asking the next higher level for instructions before making a decision. The process often is continued up the bureaucratic ladder to the very top. In a way, this practice accounts for the current need to have so many vice-ministers and vice-premiers, as petty matters often require their personal attention.

In recent months, Chinese officials have been impressed by American management specialists who have lectured on the necessity for each official to be given a certain amount of authority and also to have the limits of that authority clearly defined. "In the past, we thought, we were showing respect to our superiors by referring each matter to them for instructions," one Chinese official said. "But now we see that we are really adding to their burden by doing so, while not assuming responsibility ourselves."

Source: Excerpted from Frank Ching, "Peking to Act on Bloated Bureaucracy and 'Low Efficiency, Endless Haggling,'" *Wall Street Journal* (January 11, 1982), p. 24. Reprinted by permission of the *Wall Street Journal.* Copyright © 1982 Dow Jones & Company, Inc. All rights reserved.

creased knowledge of complex and shifting needs; a new concept of power, based on collaboration and reason; and a new concept of organizational values, based on humanistic-democratic ideals.

Bennis's ideas have received a great deal of attention from theorists and practitioners alike. But it is more important to put this radical prediction in perspective and examine its implications than to reject the essence of bureaucracy out of hand. In the end, you'll find there is a place in organizational design for both bureaucracy and what lies beyond.

Bureaucracy and Beyond

Modern theory, instead of viewing all bureaucratic structures as inevitably flawed—that is, assuming a bureaucratic form of organization is dysfunctional whatever the circumstance—takes a "contingency" perspective on the issue. The term *contingency* implies "it all depends," and this notion well characterizes the *contingency approach to organizational design*. As a key element in modern management theory, this approach addresses the questions:

1. When and under what conditions is a bureaucratic form the appropriate structural design for an organization?
2. What alternatives to the bureaucratic form can be applied in those situations when it is not a good choice?

The contingency direction of organization theory, as represented in the preceding questions, has foundations in important research conducted in England during the early 1960s by Tom Burns and George Stalker.[6] Their pioneering study helps us to think about what lies "beyond bureaucracy" without committing to its "death" in the process. The action framework for the contingency approach to organizational design, accordingly, includes "mechanistic" and "organic" structures as two extreme but equally bona fide options available to managers and their organizations.

MECHANISTIC AND ORGANIC ORGANIZATIONS

The research developments offered by Burns and Stalker had roots in the open-systems view of organizations again depicted in Figure 7.2. The external environment is an important variable in this perspective on organizations. It is both the source of resource inputs and the consumer of product outputs. When theorists first recognized this input-output interdependency between the organization and its environment, they introduced a dynamic element into thinking about organization structures. Attention shifted away from seeking principles of organization that would universally apply in all situations, to seeking contingency guidelines for achieving the best fit between structure and a wide variety of environmental conditions that might exist.

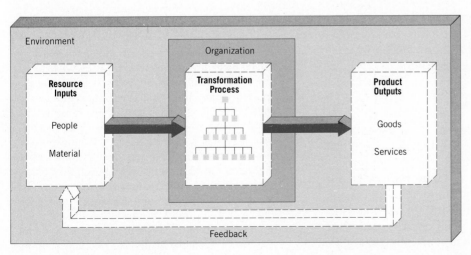

FIGURE 7.2 Organization-environment interdependency in the open-systems view of organizations.

Burns and Stalker, for example, investigated 20 manufacturing firms in England and Scotland and concluded that two quite different organizational structures could be successful, depending on the nature of a firm's environment. The bureaucratic form of organization thrived when the environment was stable, but experienced difficulty when the environment was rapidly changing and uncertain. In the latter environments, successful organizations used a structure that contrasted markedly with the traditional bureaucracy. This alternative emphasized horizontal relations, flexibility, and managerial discretion. Each of these factors seemed to help the organization solve problems and explore opportunities as the environment changed over time. Burns and Stalker called the two different but equally successful structures "mechanistic" and "organic" organizations, respectively. Figure 7.3 portrays them as opposite extremes on a continuum of organizational design strategies.

Later studies in the United States and elsewhere confirmed the general findings of Burns and Stalker. As researchers recognized that the specific problems and opportunities of different situations call for different organizational structures, their efforts increasingly adopted the "contingency" perspective. Contingency theories of organization and organizational design still dominate the literature of modern management theory. There are many ways to run an organization, not just one. For any organization to survive and prosper over time, informed managers must continuously adapt structures to explore the opportunities and solve the problems that emerge with an ever-dynamic environment. Broadly speaking, the correct choice of structure for an organization or subunit ranges from mechanistic at one extreme to organic at the other.

Mechanistic Structures

Mechanistic structures are highly bureaucratic in form. As shown in Figure 7.3, they involve more centralized authority, many rules and procedures, a precise division of labor, narrow spans of control, and formal and impersonal means of coordination. Decision making in mechanistic structures adheres to the chain of command. The *New Yorker* cartoon picks up on this theme to

FIGURE 7.3 A continuum of organizational design strategies.

communicate a cynical view of life within a mechanistic organization. Although the cartoon is humorous, don't let it mislead you. A mechanistic structure is a good design for organizations operating under basically stable environmental conditions.

Organic Structures

Warren Bennis's radical criticism of bureaucracy is largely predicated on bureaucracies being unable to adapt to ever-increasing complexity and change in society. He suggests that to survive and prosper in contemporary society, organizations must achieve adaptability by seeking alternatives to the mechanistic structure. Bennis's key word for these new organizations is *temporary*. Once again, a direct quote gives you the flavor of his thinking.[7]

> The social structure of organizations of the future will have some unique characteristics. The key word will be *temporary*. There will be adaptive, rapidly changing temporary systems. These will be task forces organized around problems to be solved by groups of relative strangers with diverse professional skills. The groups will be arranged on an organic rather than mechanical model; they will evolve in response to a problem rather than to programmed role expectations. The executive thus becomes a coordinator or "linking pin" between various task forces. . . . People will be evaluated not vertically according to rank and status, but flexibly and functionally according to skill and professional training. Organizational charts will consist of project groups rather than stratified functional groups. . . . Adaptive, problem-solving, temporary systems of diverse specialists, linked

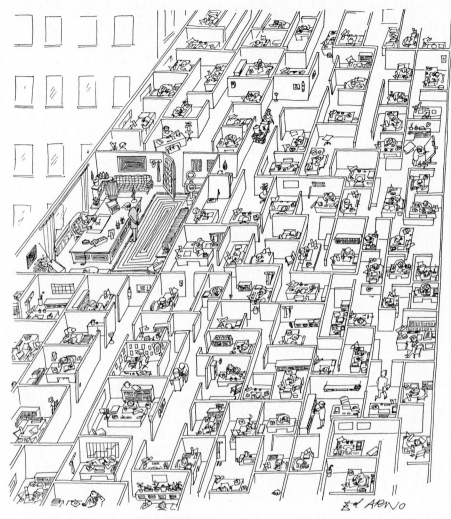

"I'm afraid a raise is out of the question, Benton, but in view of your sixteen years of service we are advancing you two spaces."

A mechanistic organization (Drawing by Ed Arno: © 1977 The New Yorker Magazine, Inc.)

together by coordinating and task-evaluating executive specialists in an organic flux—this is the organization form that will gradually replace bureaucracy as we know it.

The organic organization identified by Burns and Stalker has much in common with this temporary system envisioned by Bennis. Figure 7.3 summarizes the basic characteristics of **organic structures** as decentralized authority, few rules and procedures, less precise division of labor, wider spans of control, and informal and personal means of coordination. Whereas mechanistic structures tend to work best under stable

conditions, organic structures do better when environmental conditions are changing.

Organizational Design Implications

In summary, mechanistic and organic structures are opposite ends on a continuum of organizational design strategies. A preliminary guideline for choosing between the two can be stated as: stable conditions call for more mechanistic structures, while changing conditions call for more organic structures. This general guideline is only an initial point of departure from which more specific principles of organizational design are continually evolving. Before we examine these current directions, keep the following points in mind.

1. *No organization or subunit is likely to be purely mechanistic or purely organic in structure.* Structures will vary from dimension to dimension in Figure 7.3 and develop unique profiles of mechanistic and organic characteristics. Although a given structure will typically end up being "more" organic or "more" mechanistic in nature, it will rarely be totally one or the other.

2. *Any organization or subunit, whether it uses a mechanistic or organic structure, will still reflect the fundamentals of organizing described in Chapter 6.* At both the mechanistic and organic ends of the design continuum organizations require some sort of specialization in the form of job designs and departmentation, and both vertical and horizontal coordination must still be achieved through appropriate mechanisms.

STRATEGIC FACTORS IN ORGANIZATIONAL DESIGN

The ultimate goal in organizational design is to provide structures that help organizations and their subunits achieve high productivity in fulfilling their basic purposes. The contingency approach to organizational design taken by modern management theory assists managers to meet this responsibility.

A Contingency Approach to Organizational Design

The research of Burns and Stalker and that which followed in the contingency tradition argues against the search for a single and best-for-all-circumstances organizational structure. Managers are advised to choose structures appropriate to specific operating situations. This choice, furthermore, depends on the strategic factors introduced on a preliminary basis in Chapter 6 as important influences on structure—environment, strategy, technology, size, and people.

Figure 7.4 integrates the strategic factors into a contingency model of organizational design.

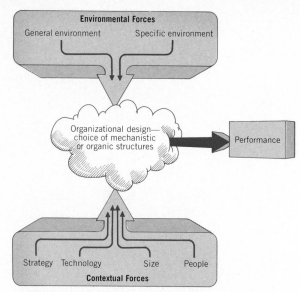

FIGURE 7.4 Contingency model of organizational design.

The model groups the strategic factors into two sets of situational forces—environmental and contextual. Environmental forces will shortly be defined to include general and specific factors in the external environment of the organization. Contextual forces include strategy, technology, size, and people. This approach to organization design thus moves a step beyond the preliminary suggestions of Burns and Stalker, and into the more comprehensive view that structure must fit the situation as defined by environment and context.

Information Processing as an Integrating Concept

Table 7.1 summarizes basic questions that can be asked relative to these strategic factors. Answering the questions for a given organization provides a useful description of the environmental and contextual contingencies that bear important implications for organizational design. Although the answers will describe the situation facing an organization, they won't specify the preferred choice of organizational structure. To help managers get to this point, existing theory must be pushed one step further into the realm of information processing. The logic follows.

Organizations are information-processing systems.[8] In order for plans to be set, actions

Table 7.1 Strategic Questions in Organizational Design

Strategic Factors	Strategic Questions
Environmental forces	
General & specific	What are the significant elements in the environment, and what do we know about them?
Contextual forces	
Strategy	What are the purpose, objectives, and basic strategy of the organization? What does management really want to achieve?
Technology	What are the basic tasks of the organization? What work methods or technologies are used to accomplish these tasks?
Size	How many people does the organization employ, and what growth in size is likely to occur?
People	What kinds of people work in the organization; what needs and expertise do they have?

taken, results evaluated, and corrective measures instituted, people must (1) have access to pertinent information and (2) process and interpret it properly as a basis for problem solving, decision making, and action. Information processing, in turn, becomes more difficult as the uncertainty present in the situation increases.

A brief review of research on communication networks will help you clarify this developing argument. Figure 7.5 depicts two basic communication networks, the wheel and the all-channel. The center column in the figure summarizes research concluding that the all-channel network does a better job on complex tasks—that is, on diverse tasks with a large number of component elements. This success of the all-channel network results when high interaction among members makes it easier to process the greater amounts of information required to solve complex problems. The wheel network, with more restricted information-processing capabilities, performs better at simple tasks.[9]

Look now at the right column in the figure. It equates the wheel network to a mechanistic

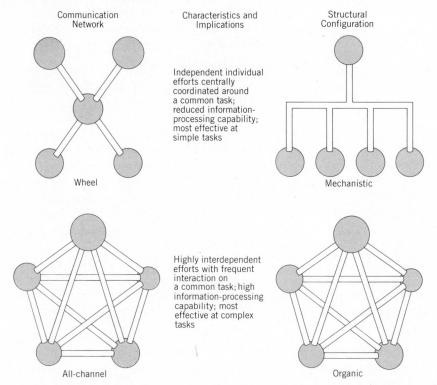

Communication Network

Characteristics and Implications

Structural Configuration

Independent individual efforts centrally coordinated around a common task; reduced information-processing capability; most effective at simple tasks

Wheel

Mechanistic

Highly interdependent efforts with frequent interaction on a common task; high information-processing capability; most effective at complex tasks

All-channel

Organic

FIGURE 7.5 Communication networks and their organizational design implications.

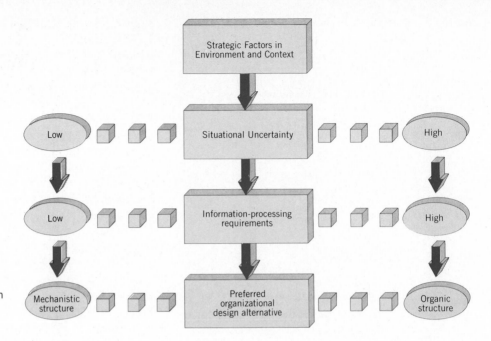

FIGURE 7.6 An information processing view of organizational design.

structure that emphasizes the vertical hierarchy of authority as a basis for communication and problem solving. The all-channel network, by contrast, emphasizes lateral as well as vertical communication and interaction. It is more characteristic of an organic structure.

The two ends on the continuum of organizational design strategies therefore offer different information-processing capabilities. This makes both mechanistic and organic structures more appropriate for some situations than others. Generally stated, organic structures better satisfy the information-processing requirements of complex problems more common to uncertain situations; mechanistic structures better satisfy the information-processing requirements of simpler problems more common to certain situations.

Extending this point further, those environmental and contextual forces considered strategic factors in organizational design are so identified *because* they influence situational uncertainty. We can now summarize the underlying argument of the contingency approach to organizational design as follows.

1. Organizations and subunits should be designed so that their structures are consistent with the information-processing requirements of major problems facing decision makers.

2. Information-processing requirements of successful problem solving increase as the amount of uncertainty in the situation increases.

3. The degree of situational uncertainty is determined by strategic factors in the external environment and organizational context.

Figure 7.6 puts this logic of organizational design into schematic form. In order to employ the logic to advantage, however, managers need the capability to analyze strategic factors in the environment and context of their organizations, determine the implications of these factors for information processing and problem solving, and apply the resulting insights to design and implement appropriate structures. Our attention now shifts toward providing you with a means for analyzing environment and context to determine their organizational design implications.

ENVIRONMENT

The external environment is an important strategic factor in organizational design. Its influence is summarized in the following organizational design guideline.

Organizational Design Guideline No. 1

When environmental uncertainty is high, a more organic structure is best; when environmental uncertainty is low, a more mechanistic structure is best.

Two questions logically follow from this guideline: (1) What determines environmental uncertainty? (2) What are the key elements in the external environment of organizations? Let's take first things first.

Environmental Uncertainty

Environmental uncertainty is the rate and predictability of change associated with important environmental elements. Table 7.2 shows a certain environment composed of stable and relatively predictable elements. A more uncertain environment will have more dynamic and less predictable elements.

When you think of organizations operating in certain environments, picture them as facing little or no change in the actions of competitors, customers, resource suppliers, economic factors, political events, and the like. As a result, few changes in the goods or services produced by this organization, or in the manner of production itself, are necessary over time. Even when changes in the environment do occur, they are usually known far enough in advance that the organization has adequate time to respond. One example is the Internal Revenue Service, affectionately known as the IRS. Protected by laws, regulations, and an enduring purpose, the IRS knows what it has to do, to whom, and how—year after year. As a result, the IRS is and should be primarily mechanistic in its structural design.

Now, think of another quasi-governmental organization, the National Aeronautics and Space Administration. NASA is responsible for the U.S. space program. Its successes include landing astronauts on the moon and developing the space shuttle. These weren't accomplished in a world of great certainty. NASA's environment has been highly uncertain as a result of forces ranging from questionable funding and political instabilities on the one hand, to sheer scientific unknowns on the other. NASA is and should be primarily organic in its structural design.

Organizations in uncertain environments experience changing demands that occur on a sudden and unpredictable basis. These organizations will frequently modify their outputs and/or means of production in response. They require the adaptability and creative problem-solving capabilities offered by more organic structures if they are to succeed under such conditions. This was exactly the situation experienced by the General Electric Company when it decided in 1981 to enter the highly uncertain field of biotechnology. It did so by trying to provide an entrepreneurial character for the new business unit. "Some people are stifled in a corporate environment," said Terence E. McClary, a GE vice-president, "We want to get them into one where they can be more creative." A similar effort in different product areas by Xerox uses "strategic business units," small teams of engineers that take ideas from the concept stage to feasibility models, for similar purposes.[10] In each case, the objective is to respond to uncertain conditions by establishing unique structures with more organic than mechanistic characteristics.

To deal with both certain and uncertain environments effectively, however, managers must

Table 7.2 Components of Environmental Uncertainty and Their Organizational Design Implications

Type of Environment	Rate of Change	Degree of Predictability	Design Implication	Example
Certain	Stable	High	Mechanistic	IRS
↕	↕	↕	↕	↕
Uncertain	Dynamic	Low	Organic	NASA

NEWSLINE 7.2

A PUSH FOR BETTER ENGINEERS

NEW YORK—More than 50 government, higher-education, and industry leaders agreed here last week on a plan of action to decrease the shortage of engineering faculty members and increase the number of engineering doctoral students who choose teaching careers.

Edward E. Davis, Jr., president of Exxon Research and Engineering Company, who chaired the meeting, said the leaders were "unified" in their belief that a critical problem exists in engineering education and must be solved to improve the country's economy and defensive strength.

He said the recommendations approved by the participants would be given to universities, professional societies, industrial groups, government officials, and Congress in an effort to develop a coordinated response to the problem.

Source: From "Leaders Agree on Plan to Cut Shortage of Engineering Professors," *The Chronicle of Higher Education* (April 14, 1982), p. 9. Used by permission.

first know what is in them. They must know what to look for when scanning environments and analyzing results to establish their implications for organizational design. Management theory divides the external environment into general and specific components.

The General Environment[11]

The **general environment** consists of the cultural, economic, legal, political, and educational conditions in the locality within which an organization operates. These general environment components are important background influences on the entire management process, and we will refer to them on occasion throughout the remainder of this book. They are briefly highlighted here.

Cultural Values

Cultural values indicate what actions are important, right, proper, and desirable from a societal perspective. They change slowly over time, vary widely across national and ethnic boundaries, and represent background social influences of significance to organizations. Organizations that operate in more than one country are particularly influenced by variations in cultural values. This issue is thoroughly reviewed in Chapter 19, "Managing in an International Arena." Even within a country, however, the cultural system may vary from one region and/or point in time to the next. An energy company operating in the United States faced quite different social values relating to the use of natural resources during the 1950s and 1960s than it does now. Surface coal mining is a good example. A strip mine operates today under tight government restrictions reflecting emerging public values on land reclamation.

Economic Conditions

The economic prosperity in a region substantially influences the amount of resources available to help organizations grow and develop. At the same time, it affects the capability of consumers to buy the goods and services organizations produce. Adverse changes in the economic health of a country or region can have a dramatic impact on the performance of even very large firms. In the early 1980s, for example, the American economy was sluggish and interest rates were exceptionally high. We suffered the highest rate of bankruptcies since the Great Depression. Chrysler came close to failure; Braniff Airways went out of business in 1982. On the more positive side, economic prosperity encourages the growth of organizations and makes a wider range of products and services available to a country or region. This happened in mid-1983 as the world economy began improving and organizations of all types reflected the benefits.

Educational Conditions

Organizations need qualified employees. Very few organizations can afford to train individuals fully for all jobs. Thus they rely on secondary schools, vocational centers, colleges, and universities to provide a pool of skilled job applicants. High-technology firms, in fact, tend to locate in close proximity to universities with strong

engineering and computer science programs—Silicon Valley in the San Francisco Bay area of California is a good example. Undoubtedly, the educational conditions of a region can have a major impact on an organization's operations. *Newsline 7.2* shows how a shortage of engineers hampered U.S. industrial productivity in the 1980s.

Legal and Political Conditions

The fourth component of the general environment is the prevailing legal and political system. Governments influence organizations through laws and regulations that restrict certain freedoms of action. Business firms within the United States must not only understand today's regulations on environmental pollution, they must also anticipate how these will change in the future. As we will discuss in Chapter 20, "Managing with Ethics and Social Responsibility," the legal-political system of a country is a major constraint

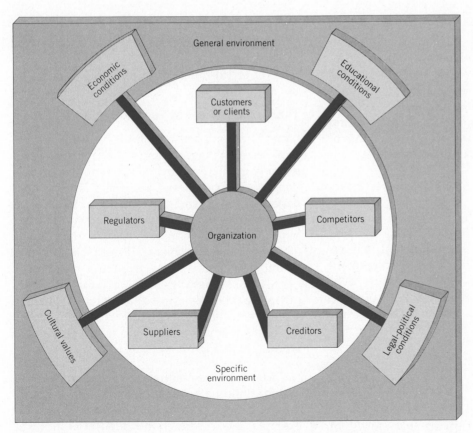

FIGURE 7.7 Elements in the general and specific environments of organizations.

within which both individuals and organizations must operate. A well-developed legal-political system can provide important services for organizations. U.S. corporations, for instance, benefit directly from federal economic forecasts, a national banking system, and international economic treaties. Stability in the legal-political system is also helpful. Organizations need to know the rules of the game and be assured they will not change dramatically from one point in time to the next.

The Specific Environment

The **specific environment** consists of the actual organizations, groups, and persons with whom an organization must interact in order to survive and prosper. It represents the resource suppliers, regulators, clients, and consumers, among others depicted in Figure 7.7.

Sometimes called the task environment, the specific environment consists of people and other organizations of immediate consequence. The general environment is broader in nature and constitutes a background set of forces. For example, the U.S. trucking industry is regulated to some extent by federal legislation. This is a general environment force common to the entire industry. In Missouri, however, a citizen's group called PATH (People Associated for Tomorrow's Highways) actively lobbies for state laws to restrict the size and weight limits of trucks using state highways. PATH is a specific environmental force with which the trucking industry must contend in Missouri.[12]

ORGANIZATIONAL CONTEXT

In addition to the external environment, a manager must be prepared to analyze the **organizational context** for action. This includes its technology, size, strategy, and people. Each of these contextual elements is an additional strategic factor that may influence an organization's structure and performance.

Technology

Technology is the combination of equipment, knowledge, and work methods that allows an organization to transform inputs into outputs. Technology represents the tools, techniques, and know-how necessary for effective task performance. When you think of technology in the workplace, the advent of the computer is one of the most dramatic technological developments of the recent past. *Newsline 7.3* shows the growing impact of this particular technology on managerial jobs.

The availability of proper technology is a major element in efforts to increase productivity. It is a necessary form of support for the efforts of people in their jobs. The following headline from a continuing series of ads by the Motorola Company, entitled "Meeting the Japanese Challenge," communicates this message well.[13]

> Give American Workers
> the Right Tools
> and They Can
> Outperform Anybody
> in the World

Technologies are classified in various ways. Two of the schemes more commonly used by theorists and managers to describe the technologies of organizations follow.

Thompson's View of Technology

James D. Thompson classifies technologies as intensive, mediating, or long-linked.[14] In **intensive technology** there is uncertainty as to how to produce desired outcomes, and there is high interdependence among the members of the work force. People must be brought together to combine a variety of techniques and information creatively to solve problems. Examples include a hospital emergency-room team and members of a research and development laboratory. Standard operating procedures are difficult to define for an intensive technology. Coordination is achieved by mutual adjustments among those persons working together on a task.

Mediating technology links together parties seeking a mutually beneficial exchange of values. It is common in service industries. Banks, for example, link creditors and depositors in a way

ADAPTING TO COMPUTER AGE SENDS EXECUTIVES TO SCHOOL

It's galling to an executive when the computer wizards who work for him rattle off their jargon—"input," "byte," "software," and so on—and the boss has only the faintest notion of what is being said.

Many executives are taking the obvious remedy: schooling in computers. There are increasing reasons for doing that. Computers, once the province of corporate data-processing staffs and a mystery to others, are becoming an almost mandatory discipline for a growing number of managers. . . .

Many executives went through college and business school before working with computers became an integral part of education. Now they are rushing to night-school courses, management seminars, and corporate education sessions to try to fill the gaps in their understanding.

"More and more people are finding it necessary to find out about computers," says Alicia Evereklian, senior program director for information systems in the American Management Association's Center for Management Development.

She says that because of growing demand the association's course, "Fundamentals of Data Processing for the Non-Data Processing Executive," is run more than 80 times a year around the country. That is more than twice as often as it was run only two years ago. Other of the association's three-day courses in the field, all priced at around $550, also are soaring in popularity. "It's either fear of being left behind or the desire to learn, but they all seem to be coming," Evereklian says.

Source: From William M. Bulkeley, "Adapting to Computer Age Sends Executives to School," *Wall Street Journal* (January 28, 1981), p. 23. Reprinted by permission of the *Wall Street Journal*. Copyright © 1981 Dow Jones & Company, Inc. All rights reserved.

that pools their reliance on one another. If one creditor defaults on a loan, no one depositor is injured. Stockbrokers, real estate firms, employment agencies, retailers, and insurance companies are further examples of organizations using a mediating technology.

An automobile assembly line is a classic example of **long-linked technology.** This is a mass-production process relying on highly specialized jobs performed in a closely controlled sequence to create a final product. The long-linked technology is relatively inflexible and is most appropriate for very standardized tasks.

Woodward's View of Technology

Joan Woodward classifies technology into three categories: small batch, mass production, and continuous process.[15] Each of these is illustrated by the photographs in Figure 7.8. In **small-batch production,** such as the stained-glass-window shop, a variety of custom products are tailormade to fit customer specifications. The machinery and equipment used are generally not elaborate, and considerable individual craftsmanship is often needed. In **mass production** the organization produces a large number of one or a few products with an assembly-line type of system. The work of one group is highly dependent on others. The equipment is often mechanically sophisticated and accompanied by detailed instructions for workers. Mass production is the equivalent to Thompson's long-linked technology and is well represented by the automobile assembly line. Organizations using **continuous-process technology** produce a few products through the contin-

FIGURE 7.8 Small-batch stained-glass window shop (top). Continuous process oil refinery (center). Mass production of automobiles (bottom).

The Technological Imperative

In the early 1960s Joan Woodward conducted a study of technologies and structures in English manufacturing firms. Among some 100 manufacturing plants, she observed that structure varied systematically as technology changed from small batch to mass production to continuous process. Even more significantly, she concluded that having the right combination of structure and technology was critical. Successful small-batch and continuous-process plants had flexible structures, while their more rigidly structured counterparts were less successful. Successful mass-production operations, by contrast, were rigidly structured. Their counterparts with flexible structures were less successful.

The summary implications of Woodward's research have become known as the **technological imperative;** that is, that technology is a major influence on organizational structure. Woodward's work also contained the contingency theme that structure should vary in accordance with the nature of the prevailing technology. The more complex the technology in terms of its problem-solving requirements, the more organic the appropriate structure; the less complex the technology, the more mechanistic the appropriate structure. This general relationship can now be stated as another organizational design guideline. Its action implications are depicted in Figure 7.9.

Organizational Design Guideline No. 2

When technological complexity is high, such as in small-batch, continuous-process, and intensive technologies, a more organic structure is best; when technological complexity is low, as in long-linked, mass-production, and some mediating technologies, a more mechanistic structure is best.

Size

Size, typically measured by number of employees, is also an important strategic factor in organizational design. Although the categories are broad and somewhat arbitrary, organizations of 1–250 employees are generally considered small,

uous feeding of raw materials into a highly automated production system. Classic examples are automated chemical plants and oil refineries.

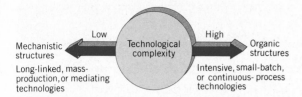

FIGURE 7.9 Organizational design implications of the technological imperative.

251–1000 employees = medium, and 1000+ employees = large. It is also common to talk about organizational size in terms of assets, sales, and revenues, but such measures have been found to be generally equivalent to number of employees for research purposes.[16]

As the size of an organization increases, the number of its separate components typically multiplies as well. Growth creates pressure to increase specialization and differentiation by adding departments, management levels, and even personnel with new types of expertise. With the added complexity of greater numbers of employees, many internal components, and increased diversity among people and components, managers of larger organizations face increased coordination problems.

A large amount of research has sought to determine precisely how the problems and pressures of increased size relate to organizational structures. Although it is clear that larger organizations tend to have more mechanistic structures than smaller ones, it is not at all clear that this *should* be the case.[17]

Newsline 7.4 shows, for example, that larger firms often try to find ways to diminish the impact of increasing size by creating smaller and more independently functioning subcomponents that may well have strongly organic characters. Smaller organizations, in turn, appear to operate well with either mechanistic or organic structures, depending on other strategic factors of environment and context.

It is precisely the latter point—the apparent overshadowing of size-structure relationships by the influence of other strategic factors—that makes it difficult for researchers to be more definitive in their conclusions. Accordingly, our third organizational design guideline is somewhat guarded.

Organizational Design Guideline No. 3

Organizations tend to adopt more mechanistic structures as they increase in size; however, organizations of any size may find the advantages of organic or mechanistic structures desirable, depending on the influence of other strategic factors of organizational design.

Strategy

Chapter 6 made the point that strategy influences structure. Research on strategy-structure relationships largely originates with the pioneering work of Alfred Chandler, Jr.[18] He analyzed the histories of Du Pont, General Motors, Sears, and Standard Oil of New Jersey in depth and concluded that structure must support strategy if desired results are to be achieved.

Chandler's work and the research that has followed can be interpreted in this fashion. When an organization pursues a stability strategy, this choice should be based on the premise that little external change will be occurring. Accordingly, the organization's structure should provide for great certainty in the relationship between operations and plans. Success with stability strategies therefore is associated with more mechanistic structural configurations. When strategy is growth oriented, however, the situation as a whole becomes more complex and uncertain. Operations are likely to require considerable change and adaptation over time. The appropriate structure is one that can adapt to and support the inevitable modifications, even major changes, that will subsequently occur in both the strategy and operations. This structure will be more organic in configuration.

Structure helps organizations implement strategy. When necessary, managers should adjust structure to be congruent with any changes in strategy. This logic is summarized as a fourth organizational design guideline.

Organizational Design Guideline No. 4

Stability strategies will be more successful when supported by mechanistic structures; growth strategies will be more successful when supported by organic structures.

NEWSLINE 7.4

SOME FIRMS FIGHT ILLS OF BIGNESS BY KEEPING EMPLOYEE UNITS SMALL

ST. PAUL, MINN.—For a company with some 87,000 employees and annual sales in excess of $6 billion, Minnesota Mining & Manufacturing Co. spends a lot of time "thinking small."

"We are keenly aware of the disadvantages of large size," says Gordon W. Engdahl, the company's vice-president for human resources and its top personnel officer. "We make a conscious effort to keep our units as small as possible because we think it helps keep them flexible and vital," he says. "When one gets too large, we break it apart. We like to say that our success in recent years amounts to multiplication by division."

Increasingly, however, blame for the laggard performance of many large corporations is focusing on their structures and entrenched ways of doing things. A growing body of opinion has it that the "economies of scale" made possible by bigness often are more than nullified by organizational rigidities and bottlenecks.

"More companies seem to be showing concern that their neat organization charts don't always reflect reality and certainly don't, in themselves, overcome the tensions between autonomy and control that get worse with size," says Larry E. Greiner, a professor of organizational behavior at the University of Southern California's School of Business Administration.

Indeed, few companies anywhere have attacked bigness more ferociously than 3M has. Its 52,000 U.S. employees are divided among 37 divisions and nine subsidiaries. "We create a new one when we feel an existing one is too large," Engdahl says.

3M has manufacturing plants in 91 communities around the United States, and only five of them employ 1000 persons or more. Although the average company installation employs 270, the median number is 115. Most of the plants produce many different products, and that variety helps cushion downturns in any one product line. It also allows workers to change assignments from time to time.

The same principles are applied to the company's managerial and technical employees. Work is thought of in terms of "project," which can be a product or a market segment. Projects rarely involve more than a dozen managers and professionals.

"One consistent request we get from our people is that they be allowed to run a business of their own," says Robert M. Adams, 3M's vice-president for research and development. "Our project system gives a lot of them the chance to do just that."

Source: Excerpted from Frederick C. Klein, "Manageable Size: Some Firms Fight Ills of Bigness by Keeping Employee Units Small," *Wall Street Journal* (February 5, 1982), pp. 1, 14. Reprinted by permission of the *Wall Street Journal.* Copyright © 1982 Dow Jones & Company, Inc. All rights reserved.

People

The fourth strategic factor in organizational context is *people*, the human resources that staff the organization for action. The characteristics of individuals staffing the organization become variables of additional importance to organizational design.

An initial word of caution is appropriate as you consider the relationship between people and organizational structure. People are different, and they vary greatly in their reactions to organizational situations of all types. What we refer to here about the *general* tendencies of people may or may not prove true for any one *individual*. Still, it is helpful to have a basis for thinking about appropriate people-structure relationships in a general sense.

Research on this subject involves a search for congruency. That is, it is recognized that organizational design should provide the human resources of organizations with the supporting structures they need to achieve both high performance and satisfaction. Chapter 2, for example, introduced Chris Argyris as a contributor to the behavioral school of management thought. He feels that the needs of a healthy and mature person are inconsistent with the constraints imposed on them by mechanistic structures. This "incongruency" thesis implicitly argues for all organization structures to be more organic and less mechanistic in nature.

Modern theory moves beyond Argyris's viewpoint to address people-structure relationships in a contingency fashion. The prevailing argument is that because mechanistic structures are stable and well defined, they appeal to people wanting task direction and more routine in their work. Because organic structures are flexible and less defined, they appeal to people wanting task discretion and more variety in their work.

Good examples of persons preferring to work in organic structures are scientists and other professionals. They have high skill levels and expertise that result in considerable job knowledge and problem-solving capabilities. As a result, these persons often prefer to work with more freedom at complex and uncertain tasks. The discipline and routine of a mechanistic structure most probably would *not* support these people well in their work. At the other extreme we might find persons working in a manufacturing or assembly-line situation and depending more on external guidance for technical problems to be solved. They will receive better support from a mechanistic structure with its clearly defined tasks and more predictable authority relationships.

As we move into later chapters of this book, the human resource, in both its individual and group forms, will become more and more a focus of attention. For now recognize that people do represent another strategic factor in organizational design. People and structure are generally related in accordance with our fifth organizational design guideline.

Organizational Design Guideline No. 5

People with greater technical skills and expertise will prefer working in more organic structures; people with lesser technical skills and expertise will prefer working in more mechanistic structures.

SUBSYSTEM DESIGN

A *subsystem* was defined in Chapter 2 as a single department or work unit headed by a manager and representing a smaller part of a larger organization. A comprehensive approach to organizational design provides appropriate structures for each subsystem in an organization as well as proper coordination among them.

The Lawrence and Lorsch Study

A key study of organizational subsystems was reported in 1967 by Paul Lawrence and Jay Lorsch of Harvard University. They studied ten firms in three different industries—plastics, consumer foods, and containers.[19] The firms were chosen because they varied in their performance success; the industries were chosen because they represented different levels of environmental uncertainty. The plastics industry faced a highly uncertain environment composed of many diverse, changing, and unpredictable elements. The container industry operated at the other extreme in a very certain environment. In between was the consumer-goods industry in an environment of moderate uncertainty.

This research study was unique in that it examined both the relationship between external environment and total system structure, and the relationship between the structures of subsystems and specific subcomponents of the firm's external environment. Key subsystem-environment relationships were: sales and market subenvironment, production and technoeconomic subenvironment, and research and scientific subenvironment.

The results of the Lawrence and Lorsch study can be summarized as follows:

1. *The overall structures of successful firms in each industry matched their respective environmental challenges.* Successful plastics firms in uncertain environments had more organic structures; successful container firms in certain environments had more mechanistic structures.

2. *Subsystems in a given firm faced subenvironments whose characteristics differed from one another.* The scientific subenvironment in the plastics firms, for example, was substantially higher in uncertainty than the firms' market and technoeconomic subenvironments.

3. *Subsystems in the successful firms had structures that matched the challenges of their respective subenvironments.* Because the characteristics of subenvironments faced by subsystems tended to vary, different subsystems within a firm had to assume different structures to accommodate the special problems and opportunities of their respective subenvironments.

4. *Subsystems in the successful firms were well integrated with one another.* Subsystems were well integrated even though they maintained different structures.

Differentiation and Integration

Use of the word *contingency* in the vocabulary of organizational design highlights the fact that there is no one best way for organizations to structure themselves. As we have said several times, organization structure must match strategic factors in environment and context. Lawrence and Lorsch sensitize us to the fact that even within an organization, differences among subsystems will emerge as each subunit tries to position itself best to meet the special demands of its subenvironment. Indeed, the five organizational design guidelines already discussed apply equally well to the choice of subsystem structures. A given subsystem may be more mechanistic or organic in orientation, depending on the strategic factors in *its* environment and context.

This point highlights both differentiation and integration as issues of major significance in the organizational design of subsystems and in the maintenance of relationships among them.

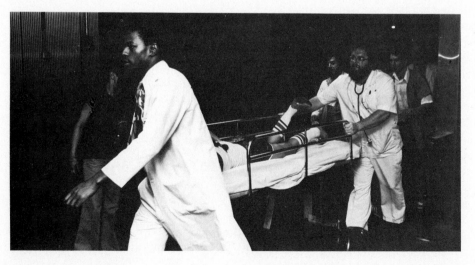

A hospital emergency room requires a structure that can accommodate intensive and often complex activities in a team setting.

As subunits in organizations adopt different structures in response to their unique needs, they will and should become differentiated from one another. This differentiation, in turn, creates a need for integrating mechanisms that ensure proper coordination with the rest of the system. Organizational design at the subsystem level thus involves the selection of both differentiated structures and appropriate integrating mechanisms.

Differentiation

Differentiation is a term used to represent the degree of difference that exists among the structures and managerial orientations of various departments or other subsystems of an organization. Lawrence and Lorsch identify four dimensions of differentiation that become important for managers seeking to understand and manage differences among organizational subunits.[20]

1. *Differences in time orientation* The planning and action horizons of managers vary from short to long term. Sometimes these differences in time orientation become characteristic of work units themselves. In a business firm, for example, the manufacturing subsystem may be more short term in orientation than the research and development group. These differences can make it difficult for personnel from the two units to work well together.

2. *Differences in goal orientation* The specific tasks assigned to a subunit can result in subsystem personnel focusing on different and possibly contradictory operating objectives. Production managers, for example, tend to be cost conscious, while marketing managers are volume conscious. When such goal differences exist, it is harder for managers from different subunits to agree on solutions to common problems.

3. *Differences in interpersonal orientation* To the extent that patterns of communication, decision making, and social interaction vary from one unit to the next, it may be harder for personnel from different subsystems to work together. Interpersonal relationships in work units can vary from the one extreme of an all-channel communication network, such as might be found in a

research and development unit, to the wheel network, perhaps common to a production operation. The interpersonal "style" of the unit manager may also vary on such broad dimensions as strong "task" orientation to strong "people" orientation.

4. *Differences in structure* The structure of subsystems will vary in the specialization of labor as well as in their overall tendencies toward a mechanistic or organic configuration. Structure affects the behavior and expectations of unit personnel. It may inhibit working relationships between units as a result. A manager from a mechanistic unit may well be bound by strict rules and procedures that limit his or her discretion in interunit negotiations. This could be quite frustrating for someone from a more organic unit who is used to flexible problem solving and is willing to make an on-the-spot decision.

In general, the Lawrence and Lorsch study suggests the following organizational design guideline regarding levels of subsystem differentiation.

Organizational Design Guideline No. 6

Organizations facing more uncertain external environments will require greater internal differentiation among subsystems than will organizations facing more certain external environments.

Integration

It is one thing for managers to allow for appropriate differentiation in subsystem design; it is quite another to achieve coordination among these differentiated units in return. The problem is that increased differentiation creates a need for increased coordination. Furthermore, coordination becomes more difficult as differentiation increases.

Integration is a term used to represent the level of coordination achieved among subsystems in an organization. Among the mechanisms for achieving subsystem integration through effective lateral relations are[21]

1. *Rules and procedures* Clearly specify required activities and behaviors between departments.

Table 7.3 Mechanisms for Creating Effective Lateral Relations Among Subsystems in an Organization

Mechanism for Lateral Relations	Information-Processing Capacity	Integration Potential
Rules and procedures	Low	Low
Hierarchical referral	↑	↑
Planning		
Direct contact among managers		
Liaison roles		
Task forces		
Teams	↓	↓
Matrix organizations	High	High

Source: Developed from Jay Galbraith, *Organizational Design* (Reading, Mass.: Addison-Wesley, 1977).

People know that when certain situations arise, specific rules are to be followed.

2. *Hierarchical referral* When rules and procedures are inadequate, coordination problems are referred upward to a common superior.

3. *Planning* Goals and targets are set to keep everyone headed in the same direction.

4. *Direct contact among managers* Individual managers from separate units work together across departmental boundaries to coordinate activities.

5. *Liaison roles* Persons or positions specially assigned to provide communication and coordination between departments.

6. *Task forces* Members of separate units are selected to form a task force to coordinate intergroup activities for a specific period of time.

7. *Teams* Teams are similar to task forces, but are more permanent and have more decision-making authority.

8. *Matrix organizations* Formal structures that create permanent interunit coordination through the matrix form of departmentation.

These integrating mechanisms are further summarized in Table 7.3.

The goal in subsystem design is to use the mechanism for lateral relations that accomplishes the required level of integration. When subsystem differentiation is low, an organization can rely on integrating mechanisms more common to a mechanistic structure—rules and procedures and hierarchical referral. High differentiation requires more elaborate means for achieving effec-

tive lateral relations. These include cross-functional teams or task forces and eventually a matrix structure. Each of these mechanisms for creating lateral relations is consistent with an organic structure. Our seventh and final organizational design guideline follows accordingly.

Organizational Design Guideline No. 7

The greater the need for and difficulty of achieving integration among highly differentiated subsystems, the more an organization's mechanisms for creating lateral relations must shift toward task forces, teams, and the matrix, and away from rules, procedures, and hierarchical referral.

Managing Subsystem Design

Throughout most of this chapter we have viewed organizational design from a top manager's perspective. Mechanistic and organic structures—and the guidelines for matching them with strategic factors in the external environment and organizational context—have largely been analyzed from a total system frame of reference. But it is also legitimate to view organizational design at the subsystem or work-unit level where the same general guidelines apply. A basic responsibility of every manager is to ensure that the subsystem he or she supervises is properly designed to achieve high productivity as an important component in the total organization.

The process of subsystem design requires fulfillment of two basic responsibilities—differentiation and integration. The action steps a manager can use to double-check the desirability of a given subsystem design at any point in time are the following.

1. Analyze the subcomponents of the organization's external environment that are most important to the affairs of the subsystem.
2. Configure subsystem structure to match these environmental demands and opportunities, as well as the size, technologies, strategies, and people that form the operating context of the subsystem itself.
3. Examine the degree of differentiation between the subsystem and others in the organization.
4. Choose a mechanism for creating effective lateral relations that is consistent with the existing degree of differentiation.
5. Repeat each of these steps at regular intervals to ensure that constructive modifications in subsystem design are made over time.

SUMMARY

This chapter on organizational design introduces the strategic factors important to managers striving to solve problems tracing to inadequate or inappropriate organizational structures. The basic goal of organizational design is to match structure with environment and context in a way that facilitates high productivity. The environment includes both general and specific elements; context includes size, technology, strategy, and people. Two primary alternatives constitute the basic continuum of organizational design strategies. At one extreme the mechanistic structure closely adheres to the bureaucratic model of organization described by Max Weber. At the other extreme lies an organic form that is more flexible and less hierarchical in nature.

A contingency model of organizational design includes situational uncertainty and information processing as critical elements. Strategic factors that increase or decrease situational uncertainty similarly affect an organization's information-processing requirements. Any organization must maintain a structural configuration capable of handling its information-processing needs over time. When the match between structure and information processing needs is a good one, the organization's chance for performance success is increased; when a mismatch occurs, it will be harder for the organization to succeed.

The contingency approach to organizational design includes a series of guidelines that take meaning at two levels of management responsibility—the total-system and subsystem. Top managers are responsible for ensuring that the structural configuration of the organization as a whole is compatible with its environment and context and that subsystem relationships are adequately differentiated and integrated. At the subsystem levels, middle and lower managers must act in similar fashion to ensure that work-unit structures meet the needs of their special situations and circumstances. By analyzing work-unit environment and context and by being aware of a subsystem's relationships with other units, the manager will be better prepared to master this ongoing challenge.

THINKING THROUGH THE ISSUES

1. Identify five characteristics of an ideal bureaucracy. Give examples of an organization other than the Internal Revenue Service that seems to satisfy these characteristics.
2. What is Bennis's basic argument regarding "the coming death of bureaucracy"? Why *won't* this death occur?
3. Describe three basic differences between mechanistic and organic structures.
4. What roles do situational uncertainty and information processing play in organizational design?
5. Distinguish between elements in the general and specific environments as factors of importance in organizational design.
6. State an organizational design proposition

summarizing the basic contingency relationship between environment and organizational structure.

7. What is the "technological imperative"? What is its organizational design implication?

8. Why is strategy an important variable to consider in organizational design?

9. Explain how the concepts of differentiation and integration apply to subsystem design in organizations.

10. Among the alternative mechanisms for creating effective lateral relations among subsystems, which are more appropriate in mechanistic organizations? In organic organizations? Why?

THE MANAGER'S VOCABULARY

Continuous-process technology
Differentiation
Environmental uncertainty
General environment

Integration
Intensive technology
Long-linked technology
Mass production
Mechanistic structures

Mediating technology
Organic structures
Organizational context
Organizational design
Size (of organization)
Small-batch production

Specific environment
Technological imperative
Technology

CAREER PERSPECTIVE: DO YOU PREFER A JOB WITH A BIG OR SMALL COMPANY?[22]

A friend's son who last June graduated with an art history degree couldn't find a job until now. After a diligent search, he finally turned up two offers: one with a giant corporation, the other with a small enterprise. When he asked for my opinion on which offer to accept, I shared thoughts from Barry Nathanson, president of Richards Consultants Ltd., an executive recruiting firm based in New York City.

1. How important is risk versus relative security? A large company with a record of stability obviously is going to offer more security than the most innovative newcomer. You're putting your career at risk in a small company if things don't work out; but if they do, you'll probably move up faster and have a chance at obtaining equity in the company.

2. In a smaller company, you'll get greater exposure to senior management and more opportunities to become involved in overall corporate goals and directions. In a big company, you'll probably be responsible for one piece of business. In a small company, you can work across functional lines and set up more corporate goals as opposed to division goals.

3. How important is self-fulfillment and the chance to express your creativity? The opportunities will be greater in a small company than in a big company with a rigid structure of many layers of management. But you'll be under pressure to produce quickly, and your failures will become readily apparent.

4. If you're a new graduate, consider the advantages of working for a

large company for a few years. You'll get superior standardized training, be taught how to look at situations from different perspectives, and have contact with leading experts in your field. You'll also be given greater support, while in a small company you'll be expected to do more things yourself.

5. To whom will you report? In a large company, you'll be responsible to many supervisors, while in a small enterprise, you might report directly to the top person. Will your efforts be rewarded with recognition or will you be an anonymous functionary?

6. What are your lifetime goals? Are you willing to pursue patiently a steady upward course in a big company eventually to become a captain of industry and something of a celebrity who is quoted in newspapers and interviewed on talk shows? Or do you lust for high visibility early in life and accept the need for risky maneuvers to reap big payloads?

When settling on a job, Nathanson says, ask yourself what you're looking for beyond mere salary.

Questions

1. What are you looking for beyond mere salary in a first job after graduation?

2. Do you intend to seek this position with a large or small organization? Why?

CASE APPLICATION: PUBLIC POWER'S NUCLEAR-RESOURCES STAFF[23]

The nuclear-resources staff of the Public Power Company is a group of 21 engineers operating out of Public's central office. In 1975 Public had only two nuclear generators in operation, both at the Green Point facility, and the resources staff consisted of only eight engineers. Federal regulations governing their operation were relatively straightforward, and the resources staff enjoyed a cooperative working relationship with the federal Nuclear Regulatory Commission (NRC). Staff members had little difficulty understanding what was expected of them or their relationships to other staff and management personnel.

Problems began to emerge when Public Power decided to add a third nuclear unit at a new site, Rolling Hill. Although senior officials

at the company thought the nuclear-resources staff would be able to adapt to the new situation, it wasn't going to be that simple. To begin, the new site required staff to travel more. The Green Point site was located 28 miles south of corporate headquarters. Many nuclear-resources staff members and their families lived in a pleasant residential area between Green Point and headquarters, making the drive to either location convenient. Rolling Hill, however, was over 100 miles north of Public Power's main offices and roughly a 2½-hour drive from the Green Point facility. Addition of the Rolling Hill site therefore had the immediate effect of vastly increasing nonproductive travel for the nuclear-resources staff.

In spite of the increased staff size, the engineers felt they could no longer handle their workload without more assistance. Written communication began replacing informal, face-to-face conversations, and staff members began using detailed tracking systems to make sure they obtained the information they requested. One member of the resources staff went so far as to initiate a formal "request for staff assistance" system with standardized forms and a detailed log. The staff manager now requires monthly reports from all staff members listing all projects worked on in a given month and their percentage of completion. The staff manager uses these reports to compile a monthly work report to Public's management. There was no requirement for monthly reporting in 1975.

Hearing complaints about paperwork and noticing declining productivity of the group, management decided to redistribute some of the nuclear-resources staff's responsibilities to other departments. This redistribution has created even more formalized systems for information exchange and documentation. Memos and meetings now characterize interdepartmental relationships that were once informal. What was once a purely technical orientation for resources staff has become burdened in documentation as reporting requirements increase. Most of the staff's engineers are uncomfortable with this new development.

Increased government regulation has further complicated matters for the staff. The number of "action items" from the Nuclear Regulatory Commission has quadrupled since 1975, due in large part to public outrage over the Three Mile Island incident. The technical arguments of 1975 no longer satisfy the NRC, which has chosen to deal with issues on a case-by-case basis without reference to precedent or economic arguments. NRC staff reviewers have exhibited a willingness to bypass management and appeal directly to outside forums such as Congress, the news media, and private anti-nuclear groups. NRC managers, in an effort to avoid controversy, have passed the burden of proof directly to Public Power.

The company's staff decisions made on a purely technical basis are now routinely challenged by an emotional public aided and abetted by a powerful government agency. Staff engineers have had neither the time nor the guidance to think through the political issues that have emerged in the nuclear-power field. Regulatory agencies are routinely advised that more time is needed by the staff to respond to various issues. This tendency on the staff's part to request more time has begun to erode its credibility with the NRC, with the result that the regulators are less willing to grant extensions or to listen to technical arguments once they are submitted. Important work is postponed by staff members in an effort to avoid hasty solutions to regulatory issues, and the solutions that are developed are seldom acceptable to the NRC.

The hiring of additional resources staff members has failed even to approximate the pace of an increasing workload. Staff personnel have had to work longer and longer hours to maintain a semblance of control. There is less time for technical problem solving, less time for socializing at work, and less time to participate in personal-improvement courses. A relaxed social atmosphere has been replaced by a high-pressure, formalized one. There has been a loss of group cohesiveness, a general decrease in staff motivation, and symptoms of severe stress exhibited by nearly all staff members who were with Public in 1975. Recently, two senior staffers have resigned and several others have made no secret of their displeasure with the staff's current state of affairs.

Questions

1. What are the sources of situational uncertainty for the nuclear-resources staff?

2. Which organizational design guidelines are relevant to this case and why?

3. What would be the advantages and disadvantages of an organic structure for Public Power Company?

CLASS EXERCISE: ORGANIZATIONAL DESIGN

1. Circle the characteristics from each list below that suggest good matches with the structure identified in the column heading.

2. In the space to the right of each circled characteristic, indicate which strategic factor of organizational design it represents—general environment, specific environment, technology, strategy, size, or people.

3. Share your responses with a nearby classmate. Defend your choices by reference to appropriate organizational design guidelines. Discuss any differences among your answers. Await further class discussion.

Organic Structure
Mass-production process   _____
Professional employees   _____
Turbulent economy_____
Few employees_____
Orientation toward stability_____

Mechanistic Structure
Unskilled employees_____
Orientation toward growth_____
Political instability_____
Continuous processing_____
Many employees_____

REFERENCES

[1] Excerpted from "Bureaucracy at Its Best: Awards of Money, Acclaim," *Today in Southern Illinois* (April 28, 1982), p. A1. Used by permission.

[2] Henry L. Tosi and Stephen J. Carroll, *Management,* Second Edition (New York: Wiley, 1981), p. 259.

[3] Max Weber, *The Theory of Social and Economic Organization,* translated by A. M. Henderson and H. T. Parsons (New York: Free Press, 1947).

[4] See, for example, Robert K. Merton, *Social Theory and Social Structure* (New York: Free Press, 1957); Alvin Gouldner, *Patterns of Industrial Bureaucracy* (New York: Free Press, 1954).

[5] Excerpted from Warren G. Bennis, "The Coming Death of Bureaucracy," *THINK,* Vol. 32 (November-December 1966), pp. 32–33. Reprinted by permission from *THINK* magazine, published by IBM. Copyright © 1966 by International Business Machines Corporation.

[6] Tom Burns and George M. Stalker, *The Management of Innovation* (London: Tavistock, 1961).

[7] Bennis, op. cit.

[8] Jay Galbraith, *Organizational Design* (Reading, Mass.: Addison-Wesley, 1977); Michael L. Tushman and David A. Nadler, "Information Processing as an Integrating Concept in Organizational Design," *Academy of Management Review,* Vol. 3 (July 1978), pp. 613–624.

[9] See the research summary in Marvin E. Shaw, *Group Dynamics* (New York: McGraw-Hill, 1971), pp. 137–153.

[10] "Big Business Tries to Imitate the Entrepreneurial Spirit," *Business Week* (April 18, 1983), p. 84.

[11] This section is based in part on John R. Schermerhorn, Jr., James G. Hunt, and Richard N. Osborn, *Managing Organizational Behavior* (New York: Wiley, 1982), pp. 327–333. Used by permission.

[12] "Heavier Trucks Run Into a Roadblock," *Business Week* (April 26, 1982), p. 36.

[13] *Wall Street Journal* (March 16, 1982), p. 9.

[14] James D. Thompson, *Organizations in Action* (New York: McGraw-Hill, 1967).

[15] Joan Woodward, *Industrial Organization: Theory and Practice* (London: Oxford University Press, 1965).

[16] David S. Pugh, David J. Hickson, C. R. Hinings, and C. Turner, "Dimensions of Organizational Structure," *Administrative Science Quarterly,* Vol. 13 (1968), pp. 65–105; Peter M. Blau and R. A. Schoennerr, *The Structure of Organizations* (New York: Basic Books, 1971).

[17] See Richard L. Daft, *Organization Theory and Design* (St. Paul: West, 1983), pp. 127–133.

[18] Alfred D. Chandler, Jr., *Strategy and Structure* (Cambridge, Mass.: MIT Press, 1962).

[19] Paul R. Lawrence and Jay W. Lorsch, *Organization and Environment* (Boston: The Division of Research, Graduate School of Business Administration, Harvard University, 1967).

[20] Ibid.

[21] Based on Galbraith, op. cit.

[22] Joyce Lain Kennedy, "Do You Prefer Job With a Big or Small Company?" *The Plain Dealer* (January 3, 1982). Used by permission.

[23] This case was prepared by Daniel Robey in collaboration with Todd Anthony and Michael Schoppman. From Daniel Robey, *Designing Organizations: A Macro Perspective* (Homewood, Ill.: Richard D. Irwin, 1982), pp. 238–240. Used by permission.

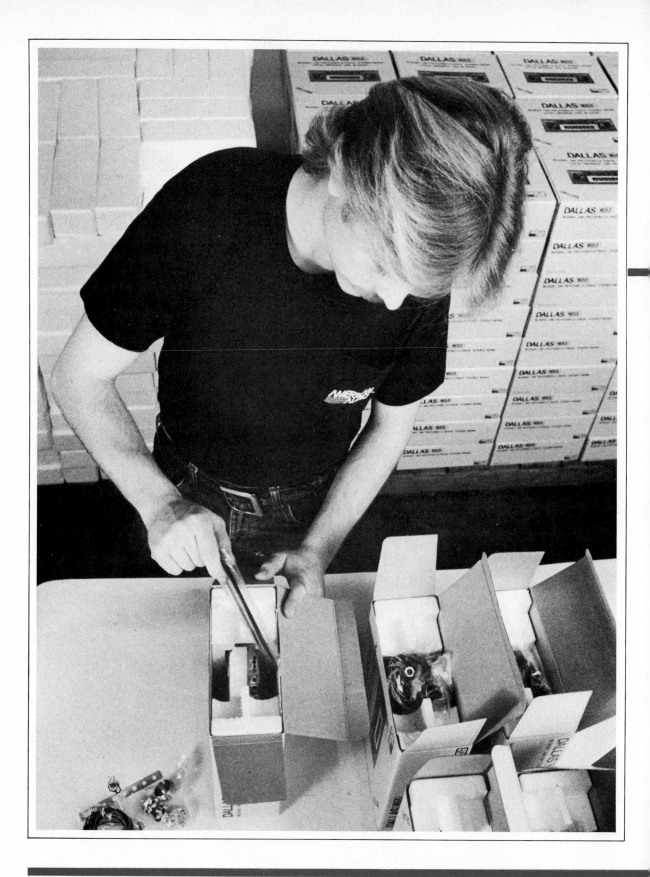

8

DESIGNING JOBS FOR INDIVIDUALS AND GROUPS

ARTIST EXPLORES ESSENCE OF THE DAILY GRIND BY PUNCHING IN EVERY HOUR FOR A YEAR

NEW YORK—Don't tell Sam Hsieh about the nine-to-five grind. For a year he punched a time clock not just twice a day, but every hour on the hour, day and night.[1]

"I wanted to express the artist's life and work," explains Hsieh, a 30-year-old immigrant from Taiwan who considers himself a "performance" artist. "One year is my symbol for life. Punching a time clock is my symbol for work. Most working people do the same boring things over and over again."

At the end of Hsieh's year-long "performance," about 70 people gathered in his Manhattan loft to watch him "punch in" for the final time. (The performance lasted from April 11, 1980, at 5 P.M. until April 11, 1981, at 6 P.M.) Dressed in a gray worker's uniform with his name sewn above the pocket, the five-foot-two Hsieh appeared in the time-clock room at 5:59:30. He stood solemnly for 30 seconds, took four steps forward and punched in.

The applause and cheering seemed to embarrass Hsieh. He turned to his guests, grinned shyly, and said, "Thank you. I like to show my film now."

Hsieh had made the film of himself by exposing one 16-mm frame after each punch of the clock. To dramatize the time lapse of one year, he shaved his head before punching in the first time.

The film shows the hands of the time clock whirling around while Hsieh's hair grows out in six minutes from stubble to shoulder length. Because he didn't stand in exactly the same place for each frame, he appears to be having convulsions.

Besides tolerating an ever-increasing sense of fatigue, Hsieh put up with frequent bad dreams—dreams he says were being interrupted constantly. "I dreamed I wanted to stop punching the time clock and stop being an artist."

Leo Castelli, a New York art gallery owner, said he respects Hsieh, who is "obviously very serious about what he's doing and very committed." But Castelli isn't sure that Hsieh's performance can be considered avant-garde. Performance art (expressing ideas by using the body rather than by creating an object) became a legitimate art form in New York in the 1960s, he says, as exemplified by such people as Chris Burden, who had himself shot in the arm.

The clock-punching effort wasn't Hsieh's first attempt at performance art. His other undertakings have included "Year in a Cage," in which he locked himself in a cage for a year and didn't speak, read, or write; "Leap," in which he jumped from a second-story window; "Half Ton," in which he let a half ton of sheetrock fall on his body, and "Horse Manure," in which he jumped into a large vat of horse manure.

PLANNING AHEAD
Sam Hsieh's dedication to his work as an artist is obvious. The nature of work in general, though, as symbolized by his hourly punching of the time clock for a year, should give you cause to wonder. When does work become a source of satisfaction for the individual, as well as a performance contribution to the organization? Can it be both? This chapter explores these questions as they relate to job design as part of a manager's organizing responsibilities. Key topics include

The Meaning of Work
Satisfaction and Performance
Job Design in Concept and Practice
A Diagnostic Approach to Job Enrichment
Creative Work-Group Designs
Alternative Work Schedules

A fundamental part of the organizing process in any work setting is designing jobs for individuals and groups. Once jobs are designed and tasks assigned, it is possible to staff them with human resources, form departments, delegate authority, and establish the mechanisms for coordination. In many ways the job is the building block of organizations. Jobs combine into departments or work units that together create organizations.

A **job** is a collection of tasks performed in support of organizational objectives. In practice most jobs are supported by a formal **job description,** a written statement that details the duties and responsibilities of any person holding the job. A good job description specifies the tasks the person staffing the job is expected to perform and thus helps ensure that individual efforts serve organizational objectives. Figure 8.1 shows how each job or position on a typical organization chart can be backed up by a written job description. These positions are staffed by people, the human resources of organizations, who are expected to fulfill the responsibilities detailed in the formal job descriptions.

This chapter, as symbolized by the opening example of Sam Hsieh punching a time clock every hour on the hour for a year, is about people at work and the jobs they perform. Specifically, the goal is to acquaint you with various strategies for designing jobs that facilitate productivity for individuals and groups. Let's begin with the meaning of work itself.

THE MEANING OF WORK

Work was defined in Chapter 1 as an activity that produces value for other people. What, though, do you think about when you see or hear the word "work"? A hit song of 1981, for example, describes it as follows.

> *Working 9 to 5; what a way to make a living,*
> *Barely getting by; it's all taking and no giving.*
> *They just use your mind, and they never give you credit,*
> *It's enough to drive you crazy if you let it.*
>
> "9 to 5" by Dolly Parton[2]

Is this what "work" means to you—"9 to 5 . . . all taking and no giving . . . never give you credit . . . drive you crazy if you let it"? Or is there something more that one can get from work? Some sense of accomplishment and satisfaction, if you will?

The following excerpt is from an article that appeared in the *Wall Street Journal.* It introduces the world of work as perceived by members of a steno pool at Chevron corporate headquarters.[3]

SAN FRANCISCO—It's only midmorning, but the fancy electric typewriters and other machines are already pounding with the sound and rhythm of muffled jackhammers. Another boss in a vest enters the room, clips a blue work order to the six-page penciled memo he is carrying, and—without a word or an expression—piles it on to the stack of paper on a supervisor's desk.

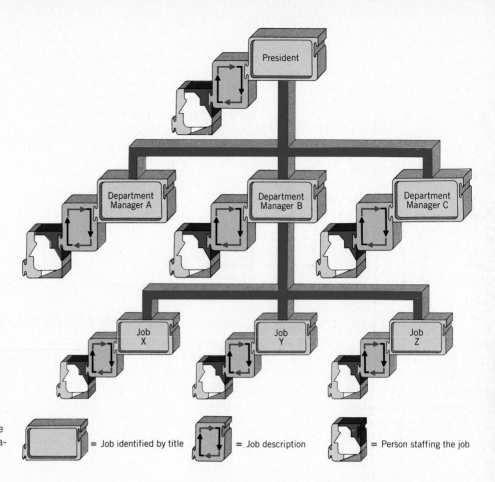

FIGURE 8.1 Jobs, job descriptions, and people—the building blocks of organizations.

= Job identified by title

= Job description

= Person staffing the job

The man in the vest doesn't mean much to Teresita Clamucha, Jean Hill, or Mimi Tong, one of whom will soon be typing his memo. He is just another contributor to the paper flood that constitutes daily life in the government-affairs stenography pool of Chevron USA, Inc.'s public-affairs department.

Life in the pool—seven hours of typing and filing, broken up by occasional dictation duties—is clean, safe, and fairly well paid. It is also dull, according to stenographer Jean Hill. "If I could possibly earn my living any other way, I'd do it," she says. "Sheer necessity and lack of education, that's why I'm here."

The pool is crowded and stuffy; rows of file cabinets eat up one-third of the space, and two fans with aqua blades push the stale air around. There aren't any windows; a mural with a forest scene provides the only "view."

Each member of this Chevron pool harbors some fantasy about working elsewhere. On most corporate ladders, the steno pool remains only a rung or two above the bottom. Few aspire to it, and it still is almost exclusively the province of women. They are as likely to be former teachers as they are to have barely finished high school. Some hope the pool will be the first step toward becoming an executive's personal secretary—as in the movies—but many more regard it simply as a steady paycheck. The most common gripe is that management doesn't appreciate the work and rarely says thank you.

Work can and should be more than a source of economic livelihood. But, the preceding quote typifies how work sometimes fails to achieve a broader meaning for the people who do it. Indeed, one frequently hears concern expressed for what some call the prevalence of "white-collar woes" and "blue-collar blues" in our society. Ideally, work should involve a give-and-take, a positive and mutually beneficial exchange of values between the individual and the organization.

The Psychological Contract

You are probably familiar with the word *contract* as it is used to describe a formal written agreement between labor unions and organizations on such matters as employee pay, work hours, vacation privileges, and seniority rights. But there is another "contract" that links individuals to their work organizations. This **psychological contract** is the shared set of expectations held by the individual and the organization, specifying what each expects to give to and receive from the other in the course of their working relationship.[4]

A psychological contract represents the exchange of values expected to result from an individual's decision to work for the organization and the organization's decision to employ the individual in return. Figure 8.2 depicts this exchange in terms of inducements and contributions. An individual offers **contributions** or work activities of value to the organization. These contributions, such as time, effort, creativity, and loyalty, make the individual a productive resource for the organization. **Inducements** are things of value that the organization gives to the individual in return for such contributions. They include pay, fringe benefits, training, and other opportunities.

When the exchange of values between the individual and the organization is fair, a state of inducements-contributions balance exists, and a positive or healthy psychological contract results. In a sense, the rest of this chapter seeks to increase your ability to successfully manage the psychological contracts of subordinates. Both the organization and the individual can benefit when the "fit" between the individual and the job is a good one. A high quality of work life for the individual and productivity for the organization are the ideal results.

Work and the Quality of Life

The quality of life is everyone's concern, and the quality of work is an important component in the quality of life for most of us. This reality makes the manager's responsibility a most important one from a *social* as well as organizational perspective. You might remember this through the following words of a steelworker.[5]

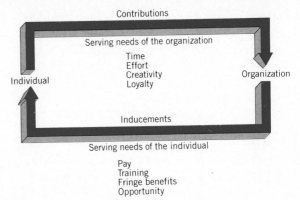

FIGURE 8.2 Inducements and contributions in the psychological contract.

When I come home, know what I do for the first twenty minutes? Fake it. I put on a smile. I got a kid three years old. Sometimes she says, "Daddy, where've you been?" I say, "Work." I could have told her I'd been in Disneyland. What's work to a three-year-old kid? If I feel bad, I can't take it out on the kid. Kids are born innocent of everything but birth. You can't take it out on your wife either. That is why you go to a tavern. You want to release it there rather than do it at home. What does an actor do when he's got a bad movie? I got a bad movie every day.

Clearly, the experiences people have at work can spill over to affect their nonwork lives, just as nonwork experiences can affect their working lives. Every employee of every organization, including yourself, clearly pursues two overlapping lives—a work life and a nonwork life. The environment that managers help create for people at work may have consequences extending far beyond the confines of the actual work setting. Poor management practices can decrease someone's quality of life, not just the quality of work life. Good management has the opportunity to increase both! Good managers, accordingly, are able to organize work and design jobs such that high levels of both job satisfaction and task performance result.

SATISFACTION AND PERFORMANCE

Job satisfaction is the degree to which an individual feels positively or negatively about various aspects of the job, including assigned tasks, the work setting, and relationships with co-workers. Both Dolly Parton's lyrics in the song "9 to 5" and the example of Chevron's steno pool suggest the presence of considerable job *dis*satisfaction. They imply that people in general may not be satisfied with their jobs on any one or more of these facets. This issue is of great interest to researchers. At best, though, results indicate that people in general are neither extremely satisfied nor extremely dissatisfied with their jobs.

Performance is the quantity and quality of task contributions from the individual or group doing a job. Job or task performance is the reason for creating a particular job in the first place, and it is a cornerstone of overall organizational productivity. Performance, as is commonly said, is the "bottom line" for people at work.

Although the continuing debate over whether or not people are generally satisfied with their jobs is interesting, a manager's concerns are much more immediate and specific. The most important thing for the manager to recognize is that some workers achieve a sense of personal satisfaction from their jobs, while others do not, and some achieve high levels of task performance, while others do not. The test of a manager's skill is to discover what work means to individual subordinates and then create a work environment that helps them achieve both performance and satisfaction.

Herzberg's Two-Factor Theory[6]

Frederick Herzberg is a psychologist who has studied job satisfaction in detail. His two-factor theory is one of the most frequently praised and criticized of all management theories. After examining almost 4000 responses of people to questions about their work, Herzberg and his associates noticed that different things were identified as sources of job satisfaction and job dissatisfaction. A summary of the actual data is presented in Table 8.1.

Hygiene Factors

Items causing feelings of *job dissatisfaction* are most often associated with *job context;* that is, they related more to the work setting than the nature of the work itself. Sources of job dissat-

Table 8.1 Sources of Job Satisfaction and Job Dissatisfaction

Factors that Led to Extreme *Dissatisfaction*	Factors that Led to Extreme *Satisfaction*
Company policy and administration	Achievement
Supervision	Recognition
Relationship with supervisor	
Work conditions	Work itself
Salary	
Relationship with peers	Responsibility
Relationship with subordinates	Advancement
Status	
Security	Growth

Source: Adapted by permission of the *Harvard Business Review.* Excerpt from "One More Time: How Do You Motivate Employees?" by Frederick Herzberg, *Harvard Business Review,* Vol. 46 (January-February 1968), p. 57. Copyright © 1968 by the President and Fellows of Harvard College; all rights reserved.

isfaction are called **hygiene factors** and include such things as working conditions, interpersonal relations, organizational policies and administration, supervision, and salary. Look at the newspaper excerpt that follows.[7] You may find it somewhat shocking, but the example shows how poor hygiene in the job context can leave people dissatisfied in their work.

> IMLAY CITY, MICH. (AP)—Hamill Manufacturing Co. has agreed to stop requiring assembly-line workers to raise their hands for permission to go to the bathroom, a union spokeswoman said Wednesday.
>
> Ruth Union of United Auto Workers Local 481 said the company also agreed to pay back wages to workers who were suspended for refusing to follow the rule.
>
> The company's four hundred employees make seat belts for Ford Motor Company. Employees recently staged a one-day work stoppage to protest the rule and a mass of unresolved grievances.

Hygiene factors in Herzberg's theory only affect job dissatisfaction. Improving them, such as changing the rules on bathroom privileges in the example, can make people less dissatisfied. It will not, however, contribute to improved job satisfaction. Remember, hygiene factors exist in a job context and affect job dissatisfaction.

Satisfier Factors

To improve *job satisfaction,* Herzberg argues that a manager's attention must shift away from hygiene and toward **satisfier factors.** As shown on the right side of Table 8.1, satisfiers are part of *job content* and relate to what people actually do in their work. They include such things as a sense of achievement, recognition, responsibility, advancement, and personal growth experienced as a result of task performance. The two-factor theory argues that improvements in job content (i.e., adding satisfier factors to a job), can increase satisfaction. In contrast to the hygiene factors, satisfier factors exist in job content and affect job satisfaction.

Two-Factor Dynamics

Two principles summarize the managerial implications associated with the two-factor theory.

1. Improvements in hygiene factors can prevent and/or help eliminate job dissatisfaction; they will not improve job satisfaction.
2. Improvements in satisfier factors can increase job satisfaction; they will not prevent job dissatisfaction.

Because job satisfaction and job dissatisfaction are separate dimensions in Herzberg's theory, people at work may fall into any of the combinations shown in Table 8.2. The most positive result is the shaded combination of high satisfaction and low dissatisfaction. Faced with any of the other cases, the manager's goal should be to correct poor hygiene to eliminate any sources of job dissatisfaction and to build satisfier factors into job content to maximize opportunities for job satisfaction.

Implications

Even though management scholars debate the merits and faults of the two-factor theory,[8] it is still useful. Most managers allocate considerable time, attention, and other resources to improving things that Herzberg would consider hygiene factors. Special office fixtures, piped-in music, attractive lounges for breaks, and even high base salaries are examples. The two-factor theory cautions against expecting too much from these in-

Table 8.2 Combinations of Job Dissatisfaction and Job Satisfaction

Job Dissatisfaction	Job Satisfaction
High	Low
Low	Low
High	High
Low	High

vestments alone. Herzberg's distinction between job context and job content reminds managers that there are two important aspects of all jobs: (1) what people do in terms of job tasks—job content, and (2) the work setting in which they do it—job context. We will use both dimensions in our discussion of job design as a managerial responsibility.

The Satisfaction-Performance Relationship

One offshoot of the two-factor theory is a controversy illustrated by the following conversation.[9]

> As Ben walked by smiling on the way to his office, Ben's boss remarked to a friend: "Ben really enjoys his job and that's why he's the best damn worker I ever had. And that's reason enough for me to keep Ben happy." The friend replied: "No, you're wrong! Ben likes his job because he does it so well. If you want to make Ben happy you ought to do whatever you can to help him further improve his performance."

The central question in the conversation is whether or not a satisfied worker will also be a high performer. Will managerial efforts designed to increase a person's job satisfaction cause that person's performance to improve as well? Will a decline in job satisfaction cause a corresponding decrease in performance? The possible answers to these questions involve three alternative points of view, each with different managerial implications.

1. Satisfaction causes performance ($S \rightarrow P$).
2. Performance causes satisfaction ($P \rightarrow S$).
3. Rewards cause both performance and satisfaction ($R \rightarrow P, R \rightarrow S$).

Argument: Satisfaction Causes Performance (S → P)

If this argument is true, managers should strive to improve the job satisfaction of subordinates as a means of increasing their work performance. Job satisfaction alone, however, is not a good predictor of individual work performance. Seeking to increase performance simply by increasing satisfaction is not a good managerial decision.

Argument: Performance Causes Satisfaction (P → S)

If this second argument is true, managers are advised to focus their attention directly on performance. When high performance is achieved, the reasoning goes, job satisfaction will naturally follow. The key to this relationship is that the performance must be properly rewarded. Performance followed by valued rewards creates satisfaction.

Argument: Rewards Cause Both Performance and Satisfaction (R → P, R → S)

The third argument suggests that when rewards are properly allocated, both job satisfaction and high performance will result. The managerial implications of this perspective are straightforward. If you are only interested in creating high job satisfaction, pass out high rewards. If you are interested in high work performance as well, allocate rewards contingent on performance—that is, give greater rewards to high performers and smaller rewards to low performers.

Modern management theory builds from this third approach to the satisfaction-performance relationship. It emphasizes performance *and* satisfaction as two key results of people's efforts at work. Throughout the remainder of this book we will be discussing managerial strategies for facilitating both.

High-performing individuals are the cornerstone of high productivity for work groups and organizations. The performance side of this strategic orientation therefore speaks for itself. And, even though it may not cause performance, job satisfaction is also a significant object of managerial attention. Table 8.3 lists a number of consequences of high and low job satisfaction. High satisfaction, for example, will generally result in better attendance, reduced turnover, and an overall receptivity to ideas and directions. Job satisfaction is also of recognized psychological importance to the individual and is surely a component in the quality of work life. Thus it is easy to argue that managers should seek to create job satisfaction among their subordinates as something desirable in and of itself, even if there can be no guarantee that the highly satisfied worker will be a high performer as well.

Consistent with the theme of the present chapter, we begin by examining how effective implementation of job design as part of a manager's organizing responsibilities can serve the manager's goal of achieving productivity by facilitating both high performance and satisfaction among subordinates.

Table 8.3 Possible Consequences of High and Low Job Satisfaction

Job Facets	High Satisfaction	Low Satisfaction
Work itself	Come early; stay late; stay on job	Seek transfer; be absent or late; quit
Supervision	Approach; accept advice from; stay on job	Avoid; complain and argue with; reject advice, quit
Co-workers	Approach; conform to; stay on job	Avoid; argue with; be absent; quit
Promotion	Increase effort; raise aspirations; stay on job	Decrease effort; lower aspirations; quit
Pay	Increase effort; stay on job	Complain; solicit competing offer; decrease effort; quit

Source: Adapted from A. E. Locke, "Job Satisfaction and Job Performance: A Theoretical Analysis," *Organizational Behavior and Human Performance*, Vol. 5 (1970), p. 496. Used by permission.

JOB DESIGN IN CONCEPT AND PRACTICE

Most of us spend 40 or more hours a week, 50 or more weeks a year, for the bulk of our adult lives, in jobs at work. We said earlier that a job is the collection of tasks a person performs in support of an organization's production purpose. The key word in the definition is *tasks*. When a job is properly defined, both task performance and job satisfaction should be facilitated. Figure 8.3 shows performance and satisfaction as key results managers should strive for in their efforts to create good jobs for subordinates.

Job Design

Job design was defined in Chapter 6 as the process through which specific work tasks are allocated to individuals and groups. A manager's efforts in job design will be directed toward both job content and job context. That is, job design encompasses both the specification of task attributes (job content) and the creation of a work setting (job context) whose attributes help these tasks to be accomplished with high levels of performance and satisfaction. Figure 8.3 clarifies the manager's job-design responsibility as well as its intended benefits. Additional thoughts on each aspect of job design follow.

Work-Setting Attributes

Job context, as represented by work setting attributes, is important to job design. Think, for example, about physical facilities, location, and even office layout. *Newsline 8.1* reminds us that such things are of continuing concern to informed managers in progressive organizations. This chapter later focuses, in particular, on work schedules as key aspects of the work setting.

Task Attributes

The design of task attributes involves determining appropriate **job scope**—that is, the number and combination of tasks an individual or group is asked to perform. At issue is the degree of specialization desired in the division of labor. Do you remember the work of Adam Smith introduced in Chapter 2? He contributed to the industrial revolution by breaking the manufacture of pins into a series of sequential steps, each very narrow in scope. His guiding principle of job design, in effect, was that productivity will increase as specialization in the division of labor increases. By narrowing job scope in this manner, the range of skills needed to perform a given job is also reduced. Presumably, it is easier to hire persons for the narrower task and help them become highly skilled and expert in its implementation.

Specialization, however, can be overdone. Jobs can become so narrow that they lose challenge for some people. When boredom, alienation, and dissatisfaction result, productivity is often sacrificed. The machine-paced assembly line is an example that may come to your mind. Consider life on the line as conveyed by a headline.

Assembling computers means that happiness doesn't come till 4:30

The article from which this headline is taken reads as follows.[10]

> SAN ANTONIO—At 9 A.M. the assembly line has been moving for only one hour, but already the day is dragging.
>
> In position five on line four, Annette Fullbright catches the next circuit board crawling down the line. At the current pace, one board passes her

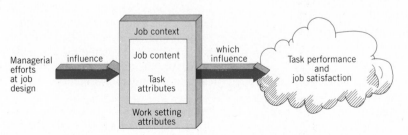

FIGURE 8.3 Managerial responsibilities in job design.

NEWSLINE 8.1

DESIGNERS MODIFY THE OPEN OFFICE TO MEET COMPLAINTS OF WORKERS

The open office, which has been growing in popularity since its introduction in the United States about 12 years ago, is taking on a new look. For one thing, it is less open. It is also becoming more sophisticated, with designers viewing offices as urban planners do cities—analyzing transportation patterns, setting up neighborhoods, and varying the landscapes.

But there have been plenty of problems. Employees complain that the open office strips them of privacy and that the din from their neighbors, especially with the advent of high-speed computer printers, make concentration impossible. They say that the endless rows of cubicles are boring. "It's also a question of status," says Joseph Intonato, a facilities planner for Chemical Bank in New York. "People like that traditional image—the good solid look."

Some people have worked out their own solutions. At Digital Equipment Corp. in Maynard, Mass., employees have pilfered panels from storage rooms, adding extra walls to their offices, says James Gebo, manager of interior planning. Gebo tells of a privacy seeker at the company who slid a five-foot-high file cabinet in front of the opening to his office; he jumps over it to enter and leave.

Armco and other companies also are departing from the "rat's-maze" look of the early open offices and are creating what some designers call "cityscapes." At Digital Equipment's New Hampshire office, for instance, designers have tried to "set up a bunch of neighborhoods," according to Gebo. By using different panel heights and an array of colors, and breaking up groups of employees with coffee areas and high-walled conference rooms, Bego says, the company has "turned a sea of open panels" into "different communities."

Source: Excerpted from Lawrence Rout, "Designers Modify the Open Office to Meet Complaints of Workers," *Wall Street Journal* (November 5, 1980), p. 29. Reprinted by permission of the *Wall Street Journal.* Copyright © 1980 Dow Jones & Company, Inc. All rights reserved.

work station every minute and a half. Forty down, 280 left to go today.

Over in quality control, Ismael Hernandez puts his soldering gun back in its holster, fidgets with his left shirt sleeve, and steals a quick glance at his watch. Thirty more minutes before coffee break. Two and a half hours to lunch. Seven and a half hours more until quitting time.

Two aisles over to the right, Delta Pena checks the dates on a calendar hanging near her work station. A smile flashes across her face. Tomorrow is payday.

On the Datapoint Corp. assembly line here, where desk-top office computers take shape, everybody, it seems, has a special way of marking time. Prisoners of a relentless, mechanized dictator, these workers toil over long workbenches like bees, repeating the same tedious task hundreds of times a day. From the moment they enter the hive at 8 A.M. until 4:30 P.M. when the assembly line creeps to a halt, their lives are as programmed as the computers they're assembling.

"Sometimes I could just scream and rip the line apart," grumbles Mary Martin, unwinding after work at a bar called the Pressure Cooker. "Boring? You don't know boring until you've done this."

Astute managers are sensitive to this push-and-pull dynamic between the potential benefits and pitfalls of increased job specialization. There are situations where specialized job designs are best; there are others where an expanded job scope is much more appropriate. Before exploring the guidelines for making such job design choices, the alternative strategies of job design should be understood in some detail. Let's introduce them by example.

Illustrative Case: Designing a Job for Jackson White

Think back to Datapoint Corporation and the computer assembly process just described. Assume Jackson White is a competent person who enjoys interpersonal relationships. He likes to participate in interesting conversations, and he feels good when being helpful or stimulating to others. Assume, too, that Jackson has just been employed by Datapoint. How do you think he will react to each of the following job designs?

The Assembly-Line Job Jackson reports to a work station on the computer assembly line. A partially assembled circuit board passes in front of him on a conveyor belt every 1½ minutes. He adds two pieces to each board and lets the conveyor take the unit to the next work station. Everyone gets a 10-minute break in the morning and afternoon. There is a ½-hour lunch period. Jackson works by himself in a quiet setting.

Prediction No. 1

Note your predictions for White's performance and satisfaction in this work setting.

Job satisfaction:	Low	Moderate	High
Job performance:	Low	Moderate	High

The Modified Assembly-Line Job Jackson works on the same assembly line. Now, however, a circuit board comes to his station every 12 minutes, and he performs a greater number of tasks. He adds several pieces to the board, adds a frame, and installs an electric switch. Periodically, Jackson changes stations with one of the other workers and does a different set of tasks with the same circuit board. In all other respects, the work setting is the same as in the first job described.

Prediction No. 2

Mark your predictions for White's performance and satisfaction.

Job satisfaction:	Low	Moderate	High
Job performance:	Low	Moderate	High

The Team-Assembly Job Jackson is part of a team responsible for completely assembling circuit boards for the computers. The team has a weekly production quota, but makes its own plans for the speed and arrangement of the required assembly processes. The team is also responsible for inspecting the quality of the finished boards and for correcting any defective units. These duties are shared among the members and are discussed at team meetings. Jackson has been selected by the team as its plant liaison. This means that, in addition to his other duties, he works with people elsewhere in the plant to ensure a smooth supply of component parts to his team and a smooth flow of completed circuit boards to later stages in the assembly process.

Prediction No. 3

Make a final set of predictions for White's performance and satisfaction.

Job satisfaction:	Low	Moderate	High
Job performance:	Low	Moderate	High

A Continuum of Job-Design Strategies

A continuum of the job-design strategies implied in the case is shown in Figure 8.4. The strategies are job simplification, job enlargement and rotation, and job enrichment. Each strategy varies in degree of specialization and has merits and faults. Managers must learn when and how to

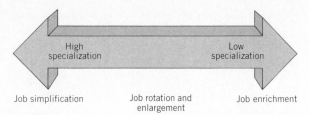

FIGURE 8.4 A continuum of job-design strategies.

Table 8.4 Expected Advantages and Potential Disadvantages of Job Simplification

Expected Advantages	Potential Disadvantages
Increased productivity because of	*Reduced productivity because of*
Lower skill requirements	Absenteeism
Greater ease of training	Turnover
Less difficult supervision	Boredom
Greater ease of replacement	Dissatisfaction
Use of specialized equipment	Inefficiency

employ each to its proper advantage. You should be able to associate each job design strategy with its application in the case. Go back and note which job design strategy—simplification, enlargement and rotation, enrichment—best describes each of Jackson White's jobs. Read on to verify your answers.

Job Simplification

Job simplification involves standardizing work procedures and employing people in clearly defined and very specialized tasks. Jackson White's first assembly-line job was simplified. It had a very narrow scope, as did the jobs of Datapoint's computer assemblers described earlier in the newspaper excerpt. The most extreme form of job simplification is, of course, complete **automation**—the total mechanization of a job. While our concern here is with forms of job simplification that still involve the human element, we will deal with automation and its growing contemporary significance at other points in the book. This is a timely issue for you to begin thinking about, as *Newsline 8.2* suggests.

Table 8.4 summarizes potential advantages and disadvantages of job simplification. Although jobs narrow in scope appeal to some people, disadvantages emerge when a simplified job is inconsistent with what people really desire from their work. This issue can be analyzed from the perspective of Maslow's hierarchy of human needs introduced in Chapter 2. In the case of Jackson White, for example, an important social need is thwarted in his assembly-line job, which prevents interaction with co-workers. Thus we would predict that his job satisfaction would be low and that he might even frequently be absent from work. Boredom may lead to a high error

rate; his overall performance could be just adequate to prevent him from being fired!

Job Enlargement and Job Rotation

Job enlargement and job rotation are strategies of job design that increase the number and variety of tasks performed by a worker. The expanded job scope is assumed to offset some of the disadvantages of job simplification and thereby increase job performance and satisfaction for the individual.

Job enlargement increases task variety by combining into one job two or more tasks that were previously assigned to separate workers. The only change in the original job design is that a worker does more different tasks than previously. **Job rotation** increases task variety by periodically shifting workers among jobs involving different task assignments. Job rotation can be done on almost any time schedule, such as an hourly, daily, or weekly basis.

Jackson White's second job on the modified assembly line is an example of job enlargement with occasional job rotation. Instead of doing only one task in circuit-board assembly, he now does three. Furthermore, he occasionally changes jobs with another worker to complete a different phase of the assembly process.

Because job enlargement and rotation can reduce some of the monotony of highly simplified jobs, we would expect an increase in White's satisfaction and performance. Satisfaction should remain only moderate, however, since the job still doesn't respond completely to White's social needs. Although his work quality should in-

NEWSLINE 8.2

STEEL-COLLAR JOBS: AS ROBOT AGE ARRIVES, LABOR SEEKS PROTECTION

LOUISVILLE, Ky.—Two men in T-shirts and work pants chat as they casually aim paint sprayers at clothes-dryer doors moving along an assembly line. Across the hall, in another glassed-in booth at General Electric Co.'s Appliance Park here, a robot silently sprays enamel on washing-machine lids at a consistent, careful pace.

The robot, essentially a large, computer-controlled mechanical arm, "doesn't talk back and it doesn't take breaks," observes Clarence Engle, a fabrication manager at the giant manufacturing complex. It doesn't draw a paycheck, either. By year-end, the two men's $8.14-an-hour jobs "will be taken by robots," Engle says, and the employees will be transferred to other work here.

Industrial robots are rapidly moving into the U.S. labor force as manufacturers accelerate automation in order to hold down costs, boost sagging productivity, and compete better in world markets.

Source: Excerpted from Joann S. Lublin, "Steel-Collar Jobs," *Wall Street Journal* (October 26, 1981), p. 1. Reprinted by permission of the *Wall Street Journal*. Copyright © 1981 Dow Jones & Company, Inc. All rights reserved.

crease as boredom is reduced, some absenteeism associated with the incomplete satisfaction is likely to keep job performance at a moderate level as well.

Job Enrichment

Frederick Herzberg, as reflected in his two-factor theory, considers it illogical to expect high levels of satisfaction and performance from persons whose jobs are designed according to the rules of simplification, enlargement, or rotation. "Why," he asks, "should a worker become motivated when one or more 'meaningless' tasks are added to previously existing ones or when work assignments are rotated among equally 'meaningless' tasks?"[11] Thus he recommends **job enrichment** as the practice of building satisfier factors into job content.

Job enrichment differs from other job design strategies in that it seeks to expand job depth, not just job scope. **Job depth** involves the extent of planning and evaluating duties performed by the individual worker rather than the supervisor. Changes designed to increase job depth are sometimes referred to as "vertical loading." Remember that job enlargement and rotation expand only job scope, while job enrichment also increases job depth.

Jackson White's team-assembly job contains elements of job enrichment. The team is now responsible for doing some planning and evaluation duties, as well as actual product assembly. White should respond well to the challenges of this arrangement. It also provides the opportunity to satisfy his strong social needs. He should get added satisfaction from acting as the team's plant liaison because of the regular contact with other people it involves. High performance and satisfaction are the predicted results.

Seven principles guiding Herzberg's approach to job enrichment are listed in Table 8.5. Note that each principle is an action guideline designed to increase the presence of satisfier fac-

Table 8.5 Herzberg's Principles of Job Enrichment

Principle	Job Content Factors Involved
1. Remove some controls while retaining accountability	Responsibility and achievement
2. Increase the accountability of individuals for own work	Responsibility and recognition
3. Give a person a complete natural unit of work (module, division, area, and so on)	Responsibility, achievement, and recognition
4. Grant additional authority to an employee, provide job freedom	Responsibility, achievement and recognition
5. Make periodic reports directly available to worker instead of to supervisor	Recognition
6. Introduce new and more difficult tasks not previously handled	Growth and learning
7. Assign individuals specific or specialized tasks, enable them to become experts	Responsibility, growth, and advancement

Source: Reprinted by permission of the *Harvard Business Review*. Excerpt from ''One More Time: How Do You Motivate Employees?'' by Frederick Herzberg, Vol. 46 (January-February, 1968). Copyright © 1968 by the President and Fellows of Harvard College; all rights reserved.

tors in job content. Note, too, that the job-enrichment principles reflect increased job depth, or vertical loading, by allowing subordinates to share in work planning and evaluating responsibilities as well as in actual task accomplishment.

A DIAGNOSTIC APPROACH TO JOB ENRICHMENT

Modern management theory takes job enrichment a step beyond the work of Frederick Herzberg. Most important, it recognizes that job enrichment is not for everyone. *Newsline 8.3,* in fact, demonstrates that jobs that just by title may seem dull to you and me—assembly-line worker, elevator operator, toll collector—aren't disliked by everyone who does them. Some people, for reasons ranging from capabilities to work-related needs, prefer simplified jobs to enriched ones. The diagnostic approach to job enrichment developed by Richard Hackman and Edward Lawler recognizes this fact. It offers an approach to job design that is useful to managers.

The Theory[12]

The diagnostic approach to job enrichment is shown in Figure 8.5. Five core job characteristics represent the task attributes of special impor-

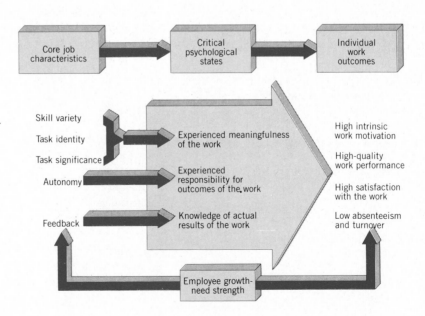

FIGURE 8.5 Core job characteristics and individual work outcomes. *Source:* Adapted from J. Richard Hackman and Greg R. Oldham, ''Development of the Job Diagnostic Survey,'' *Journal of Applied Psychology,* Vol. 60, 1975, p. 161. Used by permission.

THOSE "BORING" JOBS—
NOT ALL THAT DULL

Every 12 seconds, Donald Clay assembles four tiny parts, places them on a chain moving past his chair in an auto plant near Detroit—and then does it again, all day long.

In a state office building in Springfield, Ill., Hattie Cobb pushes buttons on a self-service elevator, doing work that the passengers could perform for themselves.

And at the 22-lane tollgate to Lincoln Tunnel on the New Jersey Turnpike, Ronald T. Sorrentino does nothing but make change for hurried motorists—about 1200 of them in a typical day.

To many Americans, these jobs would appear to be the epitome of boredom. The work is repetitious, devoid of much variety, and confining.

Yet these workers say boredom is not an everyday problem for them. In each instance, they've found reward in what would seem to be a dull task. . .

Sorrentino, the toll collector, remarks: "It's just the type of job that you have to accept for what it is, and enjoy it. I'm always moving in and out of the booth, meeting people, and just keeping busy."

When traffic slows up at the Lincoln Tunnel gate, he and other toll collectors converse over their intercom phones. Some bring small radios to work. Sorrentino sings to himself, and might even whip a harmonica from his pocket at idle moments.

Incidents, big and little, break the monotony. There's a bus driver who gives candy to the collector each time he passes through. Police ask that they be on the lookout for a particular car. Motorists ask directions, or voice complaints. Jacqueline Onassis occasionally goes by on the way to her New Jersey horse farm, and sports figures are often recognized—and are asked for their autographs.

No such distractions visit the workplace of Clay, who assembles pieces of electrical regulators for Ford automobiles, beginning at 5:30 each weekday morning. It's not really a boring job," insists Clay. "The bad thing is that you have to sit in one spot for so long. I guess you could say it's boring from that standpoint."

To occupy his mind, Clay converses with other assemblers working nearby. Often he practices singing the compositions that his country-music band, "North Country Grass," performs on weekends around the Detroit area.

Pushing elevator buttons hour after hour is hardly a challenging chore, but 65-year-old Cobb insists it is neither dull nor demeaning. She sees herself performing a personal service. "I feel useful here," she says, "I go out of my way to be courteous and helpful. Without this work, I would be on relief. There aren't many jobs I could handle with my leg troubles."

Source: Reprinted from "Those 'Boring' Jobs—Not All That Dull," *U.S. News & World Report* (December 1, 1975), pp. 64, 65. Copyright 1975 U.S. News & World Report, Inc.

tance. A job that is high in the core characteristics is considered enriched. These core characteristics and their definitions are

Skill variety   The degree to which a job requires a variety of different activities in carrying out the work and involves the use of a number of different skills and talents of the individual.

Task identity   The degree to which the job requires completion of a "whole" and identifiable piece of work—that is, one that involves doing a job from beginning to end with a visible outcome.

Task significance   The degree to which the job has a substantial impact on the lives or work of other people elsewhere in the organization or in the external environment.

Autonomy   The degree to which the job gives the individual substantial freedom, independence, and discretion in scheduling the work and in determining the procedures to be used in carrying it out.

Feedback (from the job itself)   The degree to which carrying out the work activities required by the job results in the individual obtaining direct and clear information on the results of his or her performance.

Hackman and his colleagues believe that the presence of these core characteristics in a job results in three critical psychological states that promote job satisfaction and high performance for the worker: (1) experienced meaningfulness in the work, (2) experienced responsibility for the outcomes of the work, and (3) knowledge of actual results of the work activities. The theory also recognizes that the core characteristics don't affect all people in the same way. The key variable in this latter regard is **growth-need strength**— that is, the individual's desire to achieve a sense of psychological growth in his or her work. A person high in growth-need strength seeks higher-order need satisfaction, using the terminology of Maslow's hierarchy-of-needs theory. These include needs for ego fulfillment and self-actualization.

The diagnostic approach predicts that people with strong growth needs will respond positively to enriched jobs, while people low in growth-need strength will have negative reactions and find enriched jobs a source of anxiety. This is the logic behind the location of growth-need strength in the model shown in Figure 8.5.

Illustrative Case: Travelers Insurance Company[13]

To help you apply the diagnostic approach as a practicing manager, let's work through an example. Travelers Insurance Company depends heavily on computerized information processing. This information is generated from keypunched cards that serve as input to the computer. The keypunch operator's job is to transfer data onto punched cards from printed or written documents supplied by user departments.

Requests for keypunching come from many departments within the company. These requests are received in the keypunch unit by assignment clerks who review the requests for accuracy, legibility, etc. Rejected requests are sent to the unit supervisor, who corrects the problems through direct contact with the user departments. Accepted requests are parceled out to keypunch operators in batches requiring approximately one hour of punching time.

The operators are supposed to punch exactly the information on the input documents, even when obvious coding mistakes exist. A verifier then checks all punching for accuracy as measured against the supporting documents. Any punching errors are randomly assigned back to the operators for correction.

Prediction No. 1

1. Use the scale below to assess the keypunch operator's job on each of the five core job characteristics.

Skill variety:	Low	High
Task identity:	Low	High
Task significance:	Low	High
Autonomy:	Low	High
Feedback:	Low	High

2. Based on your analysis of the job, what do you predict in terms of an operator's job performance and satisfaction?

Job performance:	Low	Moderate	High
Job satisfaction:	Low	Moderate	High

Continuing on with the Case Top managers in the company became concerned because the keypunch operators were apathetic and sometimes hostile toward their jobs. Error rates were high and absenteeism was frequent. If you predicted low performance and satisfaction, you were right!

The company next hired professional consultants to look into the situation. The consultants identified the following weaknesses in the core characteristics of the keypunch operator's job.

Skill variety There was none. Only a single skill was involved, the ability to accurately punch the data recorded on input documents.

Task identity It was virtually nonexistent. Keypunch batches were assembled to provide an even work load in the unit, but did not create whole and identifiable jobs for the operators.

Task significance None was apparent. The keypunching operation was a necessary step in providing service to the company's customers. The individual operator, however, was isolated by an assignment clerk and a supervisor from any knowledge of what the operation meant to the user department, let alone its meaning to the ultimate customer of the company.

Autonomy There was none. The operators had no freedom to arrange their daily tasks to meet production schedules, or to resolve problems with the user departments, or even to correct, while punching, information that was obviously wrong.

Feedback There was none. Once a punching batch left the operator's hands, he or she was not guaranteed feedback on its quality, since punching errors were randomly assigned back to the operators for correction.

The consultants decided to enrich the keypunch job design for some of the operators. Actual changes included the following.

1. (   ): The random assignment of work batches was discontinued. Instead, each operator was assigned continuing responsibility for certain accounts—either user departments or specific recurring jobs. Now all work for a given account goes to the same operator.

2. (   ): Some planning and evaluating duties were included along with the central tasks of keypunching. These changes are elaborated upon as we discuss additional changes later.

3. (   ): Each operator was allowed direct contact with keypunch clients. The operator, not the assignment clerks, now inspects input documents for correctness and legibility. When problems arise, the operator, not the supervisor, takes them up with the client.

4. (   ): The operators are provided with a number of additional sources of data about their performance. The computer department now returns incorrect cards to the operators who punched them; operators correct their own errors. Each operator also keeps a personal file of punching errors. These can be reviewed to determine trends in the frequency and types of errors being made. Each operator receives a weekly computer printout summarizing errors and productivity. This report is sent directly to the operator not to the supervisor.

5. (   ): Operators now have the authority to correct obvious coding errors on input documents. They also set their own punching schedules and plan their daily work, as long as they meet deadlines. Some competent operators have been given the option of not having their work verified.

These changes illustrate the five implementation concepts depicted in Figure 8.6 as ways to modify core characteristics and accomplish job enrichment. The implementation concepts are combining tasks, forming natural work units, establishing client relationships, vertical loading, and opening feedback channels.

Prediction No. 2

Look back to the changes made by the consultants. Each change represents one of the implementation concepts just described. Write the name of the appropriate implementation concept in the space to the left of each of the consultants changes, as described earlier.

The correct answers in the preceding prediction are (in scrambled order): (2) task combina-

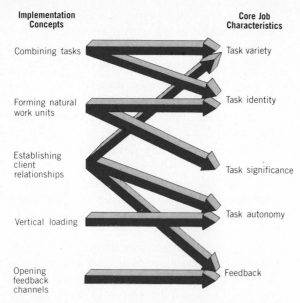

Implementation Concepts

Combining tasks

Forming natural work units

Establishing client relationships

Vertical loading

Opening feedback channels

Core Job Characteristics

Task variety

Task identity

Task significance

Task autonomy

Feedback

FIGURE 8.6 Implementation concepts and core job characteristics. *Source:* Copyright 1975 by the Regents of the University of California. Adapted from J. R. Hackman, et al., "A New Strategy for Job Enrichment," *California Management Review*, Vol. XV, No. 3, 1975, pp. 96 and 97, by permission of the Regents.

tion, (4) feedback, (1) natural unit of work, (5) vertical loading, (3) client relationships. Think about these implementation concepts. They represent concrete actions managers may take to modify the design of jobs under their control.

Questions and Answers on Job Enrichment

There are a number of other questions you should be asking in regard to job enrichment. Answering these questions gives us a way of summarizing previous discussion.

Question: "Is it expensive to do job enrichment?"

Job enrichment can be costly. It is unlikely that the enrichment of the keypunch operator's job cost very much. But only one phase of a job-enrichment project at AT&T cost over $25,000 because of required facility rearrangements. The cost of job enrichment will increase as the required changes in the work flow technology and physical characteristics of the work setting increase.

Question: "Will people demand more pay for doing enriched jobs?"

Herzberg argues that if employees are being paid truly competitive wages (i.e., if pay dissatisfaction does not already exist), the satisfactions of performing enriched tasks will be adequate compensation for the increased work involved. But one study reports that 79 percent of the people whose jobs were enriched in one company felt that they should have been paid more.[14] A manager must be cautious on this issue. Any job-enrichment program should be approached with due recognition that pay may be an important issue for the people involved.

Question: "What do the unions say about job enrichment?"

It's hard to speak for all unions. Suffice it to say that the following comments of one union official sound a note of caution.[15]

> Better wages, shorter hours, vested pensions, a right to have a say in their working conditions, the right to be promoted on the basis of seniority, and all the rest. That's the kind of job enrichment that unions believe in. And I assure you that that's the kind of job enrichment that we will continue to fight for.

Question: "Should everyone's job be enriched?"

No, not everyone's job should be enriched. The informed manager will make careful decisions when considering job enrichment as a way of promoting satisfaction and performance among individuals in the work unit. Cost, technological constraints, and union opposition among other factors, may make it difficult to enrich some jobs. The people most likely to respond favorably to job enrichment are those seeking higher-order or growth-need satisfactions at work, who are not dissatisfied with hygiene factors in the job context, and who have the levels of training, education, and intelligence required to do the enriched job.

CREATIVE WORK-GROUP DESIGNS

Job-design principles can be applied at the group as well as individual level of attention. Thus it is appropriate to shift our attention to examine emerging ideas for creative work-group designs. Many innovations are taking place in this area—a large number of them in Europe, where some of the more provocative attempts to utilize teams of workers as a means of breaking up the monotony of assembly lines have been tried. We'll focus on one example—automobile assembly in Sweden.

Autonomous Work Groups

Let's start by comparing and contrasting the accompanying photographs. One photograph is of automobile assembly in the United States; the second is taken in an automobile manufacturing plant in Sweden. Given a choice, which work setting would you prefer?

It has been said that the automobile assembly line "epitomizes the conditions that contribute to employee dissatisfaction: fractionation of work into meaningless activities, with each activity repeated several hundred times each work-

A General Motors automobile assembly line in Baltimore, Maryland (above). Inside the Kalmar plant in Sweden where teams of workers perform a variety of tasks while assembling the various components of Volvo automobiles (below).

day, and with the employees having little or no control over work pace or any other aspect of working conditions."[16] Indeed, the basic principles underlying the automobile assembly line, as depicted in the General Motors plant, have changed little since introduced by Henry Ford in 1913.

What are the alternatives? What can we do to protect workers from the alienation and frustration that often accompany work in such settings? One answer to this question is to apply job enrichment at the group level. This is currently being attempted in the form of **autonomous work groups,** self-managed work teams responsible for accomplishing defined performance objectives. They have the discretion to decide how tasks will be distributed among individuals and at what pace work will progress in order to meet these objectives. Members of autonomous work groups may go so far as to establish pay grades and train and certify members in required job skills.

The physical arrangement of workers and partially finished autos in the Kalmar plant suggests the presence of autonomous work groups. This photo was taken in a facility that produces Volvo cars. This innovative plant was specially built to accommodate autonomous work-group principles. The result of the Kalmar experience is described by one observer as follows.[17]

- The basic idea of Kalmar is flexibility—now people can choose the way they assemble a car. The facility has fewer supervisors than a normal auto plant.

- Whereas assembly-line workers would be rooted in position doing a single specialized chore all day, Kalmar's workers are grouped in about 25 teams of 15 to 25 persons each. Each team handles a general area, such as door assembly, electric wiring, or fitting upholstery.

- Members of teams can exchange jobs or change teams when they wish. They can also vary the pace of the work, keeping up with the general flow of production by speeding up or pausing as they wish—because the car-carrying trolleys can be delayed for a while both before entering and after leaving each team's work area.

- While conventional assembly-line workers must perform operations on the undercarriage by the tiring method of working from beneath, the Kalmar worker presses a button and the trolley rolls an auto

90 degrees on its side so the work can be done from a comfortable position.

- The resulting building differs markedly from conventional plants. While they tend to be large rectangles, Kalmar consists of four six-sided structures—three of them two stories tall and the others a single story—that fit together, forming the general shape of a cross.

- The windows are big, and the workshop is compartmented so the workers, located along the outer walls, have natural light and the sensation of being in a comfortably small workshop.

As the exterior photograph of the Kalmar plant suggests, it would be an expensive facility to replicate throughout the United States. Literally all of the existing assembly-line facilities would have to be abandoned and new ones constructed. The benefits and costs are controversial. Kalmar, for example, can produce only 30,000 cars per year; a typical U.S. plant produces 200,000. To build a Kalmar-style plant capable of producing 60 cars per hour (a standard U.S. goal), a 10-mile-long facility might be required!

The disadvantages of the Kalmar approach to autonomous work groups thus include reduced production rates, increased space requirements, and the need for radically new physical plants. On the other hand, designing the assembly process around autonomous work group principles is observed to offer advantages such as

- Ease of covering absent workers.
- Improved quality of output.
- Lower staff turnover.
- Improved worker attitudes.
- Reduced numbers of supervisory personnel.

Many experiments are currently underway to evaluate autonomous work groups and their potential impact on productivity and satisfaction in a variety of other settings. These are typically called "quality of work-life projects." One is described here.

Illustrative Case: General Foods Corporation in Topeka[18]

In 1968 General Foods Corporation was planning to construct a new dry dog-food plant in Topeka,

Kansas. The company's existing plant was experiencing problems. Employees were indifferent and inattentive to their work, waste was high, shutdowns frequently occurred, and there were even acts of worker violence and sabotage. General Foods wanted to avoid such problems in the new plant. Richard Walton, a noted social scientist, was asked to serve as a special consultant and evaluator.

Topeka Plant in 1971 Autonomous work groups were created in the new plant. Six teams of from 7 to 14 workers were formed. Each included "operators" and a "team leader." These teams were responsible for a large part of the production process. Within each team individuals were assigned work tasks by group consensus. Tasks were also rotated and shared. The team was responsible for handling problems with other teams, covering absentees, training members in equipment maintenance, ensuring product quality control, and maintaining the work area. Pay levels and raises for team members were based on the principle of job mastery; the guiding concept was "pay for learning." Individuals first mastered all jobs within their team and then within the plant. As they did so, their pay levels increased accordingly.

Some difficulties were in evidence as workers adjusted to the ways of the new plant. The compensation scheme caused problems. Decisions regarding job mastery were sometimes controversial, and tensions appeared as team members began to qualify for different pay levels. Not all workers liked the increased responsibility of team membership and the atmosphere of mutual help. Some team leaders found their roles difficult.

Still, Walton viewed the experiment positively as of 1971. Product quality and plant safety were high, employee attitudes were generally positive, and absenteeism was low. Prospects looked good for autonomous work groups at the Topeka facility. What would you say?

Topeka Plant Six Years Later Walton revisited the Topeka plant and reassessed the situation in 1977. Once again, he observed advantages in terms of positive employee attitudes, good safety, and reduced absenteeism and turnover. But certain problems also existed. Group dynamics were a key force in the plant. Some teams developed as working entities more quickly and positively than did others. Different levels of group "skills" among the teams accounted for at least part of this variance. In addition, a growing minority of

An exterior view of the Kalmar plant in Sweden where Volvos are produced.

NEWSLINE 8.4

FOUR-DAY WORKWEEK? EXPERTS DISAGREE SHARPLY ON WHETHER IT HAS A FUTURE

Once hailed as the wave of the future, the compressed workweek (four days, 40 hours) has run up against union opposition, restrictive overtime laws, and employer scheduling problems. The Labor Department says only 27 percent of U.S. workers are on the job fewer than five days a week. And only 2 percent of employers surveyed by Georgetown University professor Stanley Nollen and consultant Virginia Martin were considering adopting a compressed workweek.

A study by the University of Michigan and the Society of Manufacturing Engineers points the other way. In a survey of 125 manufacturing managers, 65 percent thought that a four-day week would be in effect at 50 percent of the nation's major industries in the future. They varied on how soon; the median year was 1987.

Source: Wall Street Journal (July 25, 1978), p. 1. Reprinted by permission of the *Wall Street Journal.* Copyright © 1978 Dow Jones & Company, Inc. All rights reserved.

workers appeared dissatisfied with the position of "team leader," the use of peer evaluations, ways of making pay decisions, levels of interteam cooperation, and plantwide coordination.

The General Foods experience shows that the success of such creative work-group designs depends to a considerable extent on the ability of managers and other personnel to facilitate group effectiveness under innovative conditions. Still, the various experiments to improve productivity and the quality of work life via autonomous work groups in many ways represent the cutting edge of innovative job-design strategies for the future. Although we have a lot to learn about implementing such creative work-group designs, there is much to be gained from continuing to try.

ALTERNATIVE WORK SCHEDULES

In 1978 a book with the title *Ten Thousand Working Days* appeared on the American literary scene. Its author, Robert Schrank, has spent most of his 60-plus years working as a laborer, farmhand, machinist, union organizer, business executive, and city official. He is aptly described as "one of the few experts on manual labor who has actually done very much of it." Schrank says at one point in his book:[19]

> I am skeptical of people who tell factory workers their jobs can become creative, autonomous, challenging and self-actualizing. . . . A production worker simply cannot decide on his own that the engine coming down the line should have four cylinders instead of eight or that a car body should be red instead of blue.

Schrank is obviously not enthusiastic about job enrichment and autonomous work groups. After observing one European experiment where people worked in pairs to assemble entire engines, he commented, "I was wondering, if I assembled 100 or 200, maybe 400 engines, what would the challenge be?" His suggested alternative is to provide workers with some of the amenities usually reserved only for managers and professional workers. One example is letting more workers have flexibility in setting their work schedules. In effect, Schrank is redirecting our attention back to job context and work-setting attributes as important, even if sometimes unrecognized, components of effective job design. Let's pursue the work schedule issue further.

Table 8.6 A Sample "4-40" Work Schedule

Employee	Mon.	Tues.	Wed.	Thurs.	Fri.	Sat.	Sun.
Evans	On	On	On	On	*Off*	*Off*	*Off*
White	*Off*	On	On	On	On	*Off*	*Off*
Vicars	*Off*	*Off*	On	On	On	On	*Off*

There are at least three alternatives to the traditional eight hours per day, five days per workweek schedule: the compressed workweek, flexible working hours, and job sharing. These approaches share a concern for making the workday and its time requirements more compatible with the needs of individuals and the pressures of nonwork responsibilities and interests they face.

The Compressed Workweek[20]

A **compressed workweek** is any work schedule that allows a full-time job to be completed in less than the standard five days of eight-hour shifts. Its most common form is the "4-40"—that is, 40 hours of work accomplished in four 10-hour days. A 4-40 schedule for a work unit of two employees is presented in Table 8.6. As the table shows, one advantage of the 4-40 schedule is three consecutive days off from work each week. This added time off benefits the individual in the form of more leisure time and lower commuting costs. The organization should benefit from lower absenteeism and any higher performance that may result.

Newsline 8.4 points out that the compressed workweek may have disadvantages as well. These include such things as the possibility of increased fatigue and family adjustment problems for the individual, as well as increased scheduling problems, possible customer complaints, and union-opposition problems for the organization.

Flexible Working Hours[21]

Flexible working hours is a term used to describe any work schedule that gives employees some choice in the pattern of daily work hours. A sample flexible working-hour schedule is depicted in Figure 8.7. Employees on this particular system are required to work five hours of "core" time—

that is, time they *must* be present at work. They are then free to choose their other three hours of work from the remaining "flextime" blocks.

Flexible working hours, or "flextime," gives the individual greater autonomy in work scheduling. Early risers may choose to come in earlier and leave earlier, while still completing an eight-hour day; late sleepers may choose to start later in the morning and leave later. In between these two extremes are opportunities to attend to personal affairs such as dental appointments, home emergencies, and bank visits. Advocates of this scheduling strategy argue that the increased discretion also encourages workers to develop positive attitudes and increased commitment to the organization. The resulting benefits to the organization may include reduced absenteeism, tardiness, and turnover, as well as higher individual performance on the job.

Job Sharing

Job sharing is a work schedule wherein one full-time job is split between two persons. Job sharing often occurs where each person works one-half day, although it can also be done on such bases as weekly or monthly sharing arrangements. When it is feasible for jobs to be split and then shared, organizations may benefit by being able to employ talented people otherwise unable to work. An example is the qualified specialist who is also a parent. This person may feel unable to stay away from home for a full workday, but be able to work a half-day. Job sharing allows two such persons to be employed as one.

FIGURE 8.7 Sample flexible working-hours schedule.

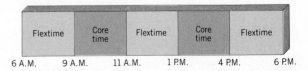

6 A.M.   9 A.M.   11 A.M.   1 P.M.   4 P.M.   6 P.M.

SUMMARY

This chapter has examined job design—the process of arranging work tasks for individuals and groups. Job design is a part of the manager's basic organizing responsibility. Along with departmentation, the formation of work groups, it creates the division of labor through which tasks get accomplished and overall organizational objectives are pursued.

Jobs are the basic interface between people and their work organization. A psychological contract forms around the job to exchange work contributions of individuals for inducements offered by the organization. True balance of inducements and contributions is an ideal state for a psychological contract. It is a balance you should always strive to maintain for yourself in future jobs; it is also one you should try to maintain for any subordinates you might have.

Jobs have the potential to produce two key work results: task performance and job satisfaction. Although we cannot say that a satisfied worker will always be a high performer, we can say that both high performance and high satisfaction are important goals to strive for in any job situation. High performance on the part of individuals and groups is a necessary prerequisite for high organizational productivity. Job satisfaction, in turn, helps reduce the costs of turnover, absenteeism, and low morale. It carries an important social relevance. After all, work is a major time-consuming activity for most adults and the quality of people's work lives can have an important impact on their nonwork lives. A manager who is successful at designing jobs that result in both high performance and job satisfaction for the individuals and groups involved is therefore fulfilling an important social as well as managerial responsibility. Effective management of job designs can result not only in direct productivity enhancement, but also in an improved quality of life for all concerned.

Major job design strategies are simplification, enlargement rotation, and enrichment. We reviewed a diagnostic approach to job enrichment that carefully analyzes task attributes as part of any job-design process. It was pointed out, too, that job enrichment is most appropriate for persons actively seeking higher-order or growth-need satisfactions in their work. Autonomous work grouping is a related technique for enriching job content at the group level. The General Foods plant in Topeka exemplifies one application of this approach, which has been extensively employed in Europe.

The work setting is another important job-design element. Work schedules are a good example of attributes in the job context that also play important parts in job design. Compressed workweeks, flexible working hours, and job sharing were presented as alternative ways of arranging work schedules to accommodate individual preferences.

Job design is an important managerial task. Good decisions in this regard can help managers maintain a high-quality work environment that is also productive. When you think of this aspect of your organizing responsibilities, consider how one person described the role of stenographers in her office at the Chevron Corporation: "It reminds me of a dinner party." "The executives are giving it, and we're the kitchen help."[22] Surely, things don't have to be that way. Do they?

THINKING THROUGH THE ISSUES

1. What is a psychological contract? Describe the psychological contract for a job you have recently held. Describe the implications of the balance or imbalance you felt existed between your inducements and contributions.

2. Define the concept of job satisfaction. Identify some of the facets of a job you might be more or less satisfied with.

3. Which is more important for managers to emphasize for persons under their supervision—high task performance or high job satisfaction? Why?

4. Describe the difference between hygiene factors and satisfier factors in Herzberg's two-factor theory. Give examples of each.

5. Do you agree or disagree with Herzberg's argument that job satisfaction and job dissatisfaction are separate dimensions—that is, that improvements or declines in one do not affect the other? Why or why not?

6. How does job enlargement differ from job rotation? Give an example of how each might operate in practice.

7. How does job simplification differ from job enrichment? Give an example of how each might operate in practice.

8. Describe the diagnostic approach to job enrichment advocated by Hackman and Lawler.

9. Define autonomous work grouping. Would it be correct to call this job enrichment for groups? Why or why not?

10. Is flextime something you would advocate as a policy in your organization? Why or why not?

THE MANAGER'S VOCABULARY

Automation	Flexible working hours	Job design	Job simplification
Autonomous work groups	Growth-need strength	Job enlargement	Performance
Autonomy	Hygiene factors	Job enrichment	Psychological contract
Compressed workweek	Inducements	Job rotation	Satisfier factors
Contributions	Job	Job satisfaction	Skill variety
Feedback (from job)	Job depth	Job scope	Task identity
	Job description	Job sharing	Task significance

CAREER PERSPECTIVE: JAPAN'S INVENTIVE ICONOCLAST[23]

Soichiro Honda's philosophy on people in a manufacturing enterprise flows directly out of his life and personality. Having received little education, he is skeptical about the value of learning that takes place in a classroom.

He believes that people learn best by doing and that the growth of expertise is of great mutual value to worker and company. Since 1968 Honda Motor Co. has maintained the "expert system." The system is based on a specific path of qualification that eventually allows a worker to be certified as an expert. All workers keep personal notebooks chronicling their work experience and creative contributions as means of tracking their own routes to expertise.

Soichiro Honda's company bestows vast amounts of responsibility in its workers. "There is a limit," Honda says, "to what can be thought out by big shots sitting at their desks. Where 100 people think, there are 100 powers; if 1000 people think, there are 1000 powers."

Honda not only leaves improvements in workfloor design and methods to the workers, but goes further. Supervisors, many in the early 30s, often play the central role in designing and building factories. "They get really enthusiastic when they are told to design a factory," says Honda. "After all, they are to build their own workshop. They discuss such matters as what type of equipment is to be used for transporting and processing heavy components, or decide that major engine components should be processed by hand. By this means the factory can be human oriented."

Above all, Honda's view of managing flows from his sense of the purpose of the workplace. "The workshop," he says, "should be a place where everybody finds joy in working and earns a living. An organization that enforces monotonous labor and deprives the workers of the right to think may work well for a while but is bound to get decayed in the long run. I noticed at auto factories in the United States that the working environment is bad. Decent people don't want to work at such places, and as a result the quality of labor at those workshops is poor."

Questions

1. Which job-design strategies seem most consistent with Soichiro Honda's philosophy? Would you like to work in an organization governed by this philosophy? Why or why not?

2. Suppose that you actually end up working in just the opposite type of system from the one Honda described. What could you do, if anything, to achieve a sense of job satisfaction as well as high performance from your work?

CASE APPLICATION: AN AMERICAN LOOK AT THE SWEDISH WAY[24]

Some time ago, Arthur Weinberg of the School of Industrial Relations, Cornell University, led a team of six U.S. auto workers to Sweden to see how laborers trained on the conventional production line would take to "industrial democracy." The Ford Foundation put up $50,000 to pay expenses and worker salaries for the four-week "worker exchange program," as it was called.

The group went to Sodertalje, about 25 miles south of Stockholm, to a Saab auto engine plant where three-person teams assemble the entire engine. As in the Kalmar Volvo plant, much is left to the team as to how to operate—individually or together. Their only obligation is to meet a production schedule of 14 engines per assembler daily.

Only one, a 31-year-old Cadillac worker named Ruth Russell, was really enthusiastic.

"In Detroit, my job is to insert 10 head bolts and a thermal plug at the rate of 88 an hour, but here I can put the whole engine together," Russell said. "I feel I'm accomplishing something."

Others were cool to the demands of the job. "It doesn't look as if people are working hard at all," said William Cox, 33, from Plymouth. "But when you go to work on the engines yourself, you find out, wow, these people are working their butts off." Another of the auto workers discerned the same boredom at Saab as in Detroit. "My job in Detroit is monotonous," he said, "but it's more relaxed."

The U.S. workers found much they admired: relaxed relationships between workers and supervisors, and close attention to safety and working conditions such as good light and low noise levels. "The first day on the job the women in my team asked why I talked so loud," said William Cox. "I was just talking the way I do in Detroit—it's so noisy you have to shout to make yourself heard." The fact that workers wash up on company time and attend to union matters on company time also impressed the Americans, as did the general informality. "Some people here bring plants and flowers in and out to brighten the place," said one American. "If that happened in my plant, they'd think you were stealing."

Questions

1. How do you explain the fact that only one out of the six American workers was really enthusiastic about job designs in the Saab plant?

2. What do these reactions imply on a more general basis for managers considering job-design changes in their areas of work responsibility?

CLASS EXERCISE: IMPLEMENTING FLEXTIME

1. Read the following memo describing an organization's new policy for handling flextime work schedules.

   Flextime is intended to ensure that work gets done in an orderly and efficient manner and at the same time permit employees and their supervisors, within certain limits, to establish work schedules which recognize individual needs.

   a. *Flextime schedules may be approved for employees with permanent positions of employment.*

   b. *Employees must work 40 hours per week.*

   c. *Offices must be open from 8:00 A.M. to 5:00 P.M.*

   d. *A minimum of one-half hour is required for each person as a lunch period.*

   e. *Individual work schedules are approved in advance by the department head for a minimum of*

   one week. Work schedules must conform to the needs of the department. Supervisors may require a change in work schedules to meet the needs of the department.

2. Use the charts below to show how three employees in one office could work flextime schedules. Remember that the requirements set forth in the memo must be fulfilled.

3. Share your ideas with a nearby classmate. Check one another's conformance to the organization's policy as well as the degree to which flextime has been used to each employee's advantage. Discuss any differences and await further instructions.

Employee A *(likes to sleep late)*

6:00 A.M.	7:00	8:00	9:00	10:00	11:00	12:00	1:00	2:00	3:00	4:00	5:00	6:00 P.M.

Employee B *(likes to exercise at midday)*

6:00 A.M.	7:00	8:00	9:00	10:00	11:00	12:00	1:00	2:00	3:00	4:00	5:00	6:00 P.M.

Employee C *(likes to be home to meet kids after school)*

6:00 A.M.	7:00	8:00	9:00	10:00	11:00	12:00	1:00	2:00	3:00	4:00	5:00	6:00 P.M.

REFERENCES

[1] Excerpted from Kathleen A. Hughes, "Artist Explores Essence of the Daily Grind by Punching in Every Hour for a Year," *Wall Street Journal* (April 24, 1982), p. 25. Reprinted by permission of the *Wall Street Journal*. Copyright © 1981 Dow Jones & Company, Inc. All rights reserved.

[2] Lyrics from "9 to 5" by Dolly Parton. Published by Velvet Apple/Fox Fanfare Music, Inc. Used by permission.

[3] Excerpted from Kathryn Christensen, "Life on the Job: Steno Pool's Members, Buried by Paper Flood, Yearn for Other Things," *Wall Street Journal* (May 6, 1981), pp. 1, 23. Reprinted by permission of the *Wall Street Journal*. Copyright © 1981 Dow Jones & Company, Inc. All rights reserved.

[4] Modified from John P. Kotter, "The Psychological Contract: Managing the Joining Up Process," *California Management Review*, Vol. 15 (Spring 1973), pp. 91–99.

[5] Studs Terkel, *Working* (New York: Avon Books, 1975), p. 7.

[6] The complete two-factor theory is in Frederick Herzberg, Bernard Mausner, and Barbara Bloch Synderman, *The Motivation to Work*, Second Edition (New York: Wiley, 1967); Frederick Herzberg, "One More Time: How do You Motivate Employees?" *Harvard Business Review*, Vol. 47 (January-February 1968), pp. 53-62. This discussion is based on both sources.

[7] Associated Press, "No More Hands Up on the Assembly Line," *Burlington Free Press*, Burlington, Vt. (July 7, 1977). Reprinted by permission.

[8] See Robert J. House and Lawrence A. Wigdor, "Herzberg's Dual-Factor Theory of Job Satisfaction and Motivation: A Review of the Evidence and a Criticism," *Personnel Psychology*, Vol. 20 (Winter 1967), pp. 369–389; Steven Kerr, Anne Harlan, and Ralph Stogdill, "Preference for Motivator and Hygiene Factors in a Hypothetical Interview Situation," *Personnel Psychology*, Vol. 27 (Winter 1974), pp. 109–124.

[9] For a complete discussion of this controversy, see Charles N. Greene, "The Satisfaction-Performance Controversy," *Business Horizons*, Vol. 15 (October 1972), pp. 31–41; Charles N. Greene and Robert E. Craft, Jr., "The Satisfaction-Performance Revisited," in Kirk Downey, Don Hellriegel, and John Slocum (eds.), *Organizational Behavior: A Reader* (St. Paul, Minn.: West Publishing, 1977), pp. 187–201. The quote is from Greene, p. 31.

[10] Excerpted from Roger Thurow, "Life on the Job: Assembling Computers Means that Happiness Doesn't Come till 4:30," *Wall Street Journal* (June 1, 1981), pp.

1, 20. Reprinted by permission of the *Wall Street Journal*. Copyright © 1981 Dow Jones & Company, Inc. All rights reserved.

[11] Herzberg, op. cit

[12] This presentation is adapted from John R. Schermerhorn, Jr., James G. Hunt, and Richard N. Osborn, *Managing Organizational Behavior* (New York: Wiley, 1982), pp. 181–186. Used by permission. The summary of the diagnostic theory is developed from J. Richard Hackman and Greg R. Oldham, "Development of the Job Diagnostic Survey," *Journal of Applied Psychology*, Vol. 60 (April 1975), pp. 161–162; J. Richard Hackman, Greg Oldham, Robert Janson, and Kenneth Purdy, "A New Strategy for Job Enrichment," *California Management Review*, Vol. XVII (1975), pp. 51–71; Greg R. Oldham, J. Richard Hackman, and Jone L. Pearce, "Conditions Under which Employees Respond Positively to Enriched Work," *Journal of Applied Psychology*, Vol. 61 (1976), pp. 395–403.

[13] From Hackman, et al. (1975), op. cit.

[14] Paul J. Champagne and Curt Tausky, "When Job Enrichment Doesn't Pay," *Personnel*, Vol. III (January-February 1978), pp. 30–40.

[15] William W. Winipsinger, "Job Enrichment: A Union View," in Karl O. Magnusen (ed.), *Organizational Design, Development and Behavior: A Situational View* (Glenview, Ill.: Scott, Foresman, 1977), p. 222.

[16] William F. Dowling, "Job Redesign on the Assembly Line: Farewell to Blue-Collar Blues," *Organizational Dynamics* (Autumn 1973), p. 51.

[17] Bowen Northrup, "Auto Plant in Sweden Scores Some Success with Work Teams," *Wall Street Journal* (March 1, 1977), p. 1. Reprinted by permission of the *Wall Street Journal*. Copyright © 1981 Dow Jones & Company, Inc. All rights reserved.

[18] See Richard E. Walton, "How to Counter Alienation in the Plant," *Harvard Business Review* (November-December 1972), pp. 70–81; Richard E. Walton, "Work Innovations at Topeka: After Six Years," *Journal of Applied Behavior Science*, Vol. 13 (1977), pp. 422–431.

[19] Robert Schrank, *Ten Thousand Working Days* (Cambridge: MIT Press, 1978); this review adapted from Roger Ricklefs, "The World of Work as Seen by a Worker," *The Wall Street Journal* (May 26, 1978), p. 19; Robert Schrank, "How to Relieve Worker Boredom," *Psychology Today* (July 1978), pp. 79-80.

[20] See Allan R. Cohen and Herman Gadon, *Alternative Work Schedules: Integrating Individual and Organizational Needs* (Reading, Mass.: Addison-Wesley, 1978), p. 125.

21 Ibid., pp. 54–64; Robert T. Golembiewski and Carl W. Prehl, Jr., "A Survey of the Empirical Literature on Flexible Work Hours: Character and Consequences of a Major Innovation," *Academy of Management Review,* Vol. 3 (October 1978), pp. 853–873.

22 Christensen, op. cit., p. 23.

23 Excerpted from John B. Schnapp, "Soichiro Honda, Japan's Inventive Iconoclast," *Wall Street Journal* (February 1, 1982), p. 16. Reprinted by permission of the *Wall Street Journal.* Copyright © 1982 Dow Jones & Company, Inc. All rights reserved.

24 *MBA Magazine* (March 1975), p. 42.

9

STAFFING THE HUMAN RESOURCES

MORE COMPANIES LOOK WITHIN FOR MANAGERS

An increasing number of companies are looking more intently into their own ranks for future management leaders.[1]

Several factors are involved. Some of the "fast-track" outsiders hired in the past have proved to be disappointments. Recruiting from outside involves huge relocation expenses and other costs. Promoting from within benefits morale. And corporations are placing more emphasis on old-fashioned experience and performance.

Managers also are expecting a reduced number of younger, first-level managers in the years to come, as the postwar population bulge eases off. Identifying talented managers is "a major strategic issue for the 1980s," says Howard V. Knicely, vice-president of human relations at TRW Inc.

Knicely anticipates "a real shortage of and intense competition for middle and senior managers." TRW has just developed a new management planning program to acquire, develop, motivate, and maintain talented managers.

Performance, not promise, or a glittering resume, is the old-fashioned but chief criterion for advancement at an increasing number of companies. That favors the insider, the person who has established a visible record of results obtained over years of employment.

"At the root of the whole process of identifying good managers is a superior's evaluation of a person's performance—that's still the bread and butter of American business," says Eugene Jennings of Michigan State.

The evaluation process is getting an outside assist from so-called assessment centers. These administer tests to weight candidates for promotion under simulated conditions. American Telephone & Telegraph Co., probably the biggest user of the centers, will spend about $40 million this year to evaluate some 40,000 of its employees.

"There's no question it's effective," says Lowell Fowble, manager of AT&T's assessment program. He says the tests are "more objective" than evaluations by superiors and have a greater success than the traditional annual reviews in predicting success at higher levels.

The chapter opener highlights the need to staff organizations with high-quality talent in order to complete the organizing process and set the stage for organizational objectives to be achieved. This applies not only to managerial talent as discussed in the example, but also to people in all jobs constituting an organization's division of labor. Chapter 9 examines the full range of staffing responsibilities you will face as a manager, and contains many insights that should benefit your career development. Specific topics of study include

The Staffing Process
Human-Resource Planning
Recruitment
Selection
Orientation
Training and Development
Replacement

The announcement in *Business Week* was matter-of-fact: "Christie Hefner, the 29-year-old daughter of Hugh M. Hefner, founder and chairman of Playboy Enterprises, Inc., was named president of the publishing and cable TV company. She succeeds Derick J. Daniels, 53, who resigned."[2] *Time* magazine was a bit more sensational in its reporting.[3]

Family Affair: Dad and Daughter at
Playboy

Marrying the boss's daughter has been one route to the top in American business. Last week Christie Hefner, 29, got to the top by being the boss's daughter. Hugh Hefner, 56, founder and chairman of the board of Playboy Enterprises, Inc., announced that he was promoting his daughter to president. Said the proud papa: "Christie's promotion is a natural transition. She has certainly been well prepared for this move."

With two Hefners running Playboy, there was no more room for Derick J. Daniels, 53, who resigned as president.

Look again at the excerpt from *Time*. Notice that the magazine reporter says Christie Hefner "got to the top by being the boss's daughter." Hugh Hefner, by contrast, states, "Christie's promotion is a natural transition. She [is] . . . well prepared for this move." The former implies promotion via family ties; the latter suggests promotion via competency. Beneath it all runs still another theme, the replacement of Derick Daniels as president.

"Selection" and "replacement" are two elements among several that comprise the staffing process. Once plans are made, and appropriate structures and jobs designed, the organization must be properly staffed with human resources if it is to achieve high productivity. Finding and maintaining a competent work force is the crux of the staffing challenge. Without proper human resources, even the best-designed organization guided by well-made plans can't achieve its performance potential.

THE STAFFING PROCESS

Staffing is the process of filling jobs with appropriate persons. As shown in Figure 9.1, staffing is an integral part of a manager's organizing responsibilities. It is the act of putting qualified and enthusiastic people into a well-designed work setting. The ultimate aim of the manager, of course, is to staff the organization with persons capable of achieving high performance.

Staffing and Performance

Major influences on individual task performance can be specified in an equation:

$$Performance = ability \times support \times effort$$

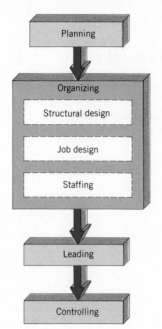

FIGURE 9.1 Staffing as part of the management process.

support. The capable person who is well supported but unwilling to exert the necessary effort won't be a high performer.

Figure 9.2 indicates that each element in the individual performance equation is addressed through different managerial initiatives. Support is achieved, in large measure, through proper design of organization structures and jobs. Effort is influenced via leadership, the subject of the four chapters in Part 4. Ability is a staffing issue. As such, proper staffing is an essential ingredient in the total management process. A recent headline sums the point up well.[4]

> Productivity Is:
> Learning How to Hire the
> Person Who Is *Right* for the
> Job

The logic of this equation follows. High performance is possible *only* when the organization's human resources have the ability to do the work, are willing to exert the necessary effort, and have proper support. Take away any one of these elements and performance will suffer. A hard-working person with great support can't perform without the required abilities. A capable person willing to work hard can't perform without good

Major Staffing Responsibilities

The basic objective in the staffing process is to match people and jobs in a manner that facilitates performance. The staffing process itself involves maintaining an appropriate work force by planning for and implementing appropriate recruitment, selection, orientation, training and development, and replacement activities. Briefly, the

FIGURE 9.2 Managerial initiatives to facilitate performance.

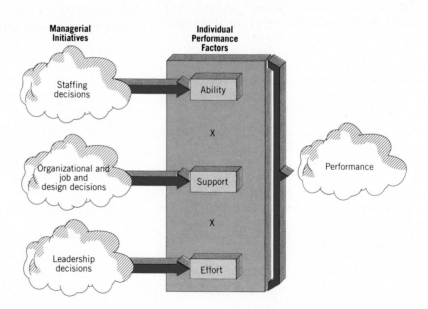

managerial significance of the major elements in the staffing process includes:

1. *Human-resource planning* Good planning identifies staffing needs and ensures they are met through ongoing analysis of performance objectives, job requirements, and available personnel.
2. *Recruitment* Once staffing needs are identified, effective recruiting is needed to establish a pool of qualified candidates for open jobs.
3. *Selection* Candidates in the recruiting pool must be carefully evaluated relative to job and organizational requirements; capable and interested people must be matched with jobs for which they are well suited.
4. *Orientation* New personnel must be properly introduced to their jobs, the organization as a work setting, co-workers, organizational policies and procedures, and supervisory expectations.
5. *Training and development* Orientation should be followed by ongoing training and development opportunities that maintain appropriate job skills and enhance individual capabilities for assuming increasing responsibilities over time.
6. *Replacement* There will be times when persons must be separated from their jobs and replaced by other job candidates; replacement includes promotions, transfers, and retirements that usually occur on a voluntary basis, as well as involuntary separations in the form of terminations.

Figure 9.3 summarizes these six elements in the staffing process. Taken together they focus managerial attention on the acquisition and maintenance of the human resources necessary to staff organizations for productivity.

The Role of the Personnel Department

One response of organizations to the importance and complexity of these staffing elements is to employ personnel specialists to assist in their implementation. It is common on an organization chart, for example, to find a personnel department headed by a personnel professional. This department would employ persons with special expertise in all aspects of the staffing process, as well as in performance evaluation, career planning and development, compensation and employee benefits, and labor relations—areas of managerial responsibility discussed later in this book.

You may pursue advanced education and a career in one or more of these personnel specialities. Even as a manager working in other functional areas, you must be prepared to work closely with counterparts in personnel to satisfy the organization's staffing needs. As we move on to examine specific staffing responsibilities in more detail, remember that in a typical organization a line manager and personnel specialist may work together, as suggested in Table 9.1.

FIGURE 9.3 The staffing process as a managerial responsibility.

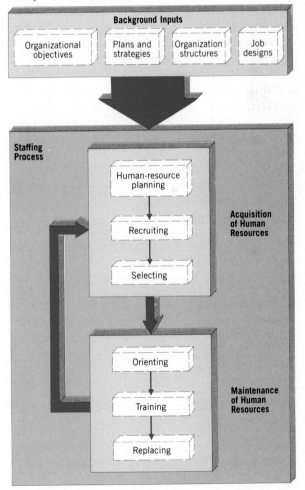

Table 9.1 Possible Division of Labor in the Staffing Process Between Line Manager and Personnel Specialist

In Respect to . . .	The Line Manager . . .	While the Personnel Specialist . . .
Recruiting	Requests filling a vacancy according to certain job specifications	Advertises the vacancy; develops candidate pool; ensures advertising meets government regulations
Selection	Interviews candidates and chooses most qualified	Screens applicants; ensures hiring is consistent with organizational policies and government regulations
Orientation, training, and development	Orients new employee to job and co-workers; monitors training needs; does on-job training	Processes paperwork associated with new employee; orients employee to organization as a whole; conducts organization-wide training program
Replacement	Recommends promotions, transfers, separations	Reviews such decisions for consistency with organizational policies and government regulations; processes related paperwork

HUMAN-RESOURCE PLANNING

Human-resource planning, sometimes called personnel planning, involves identifying staffing needs, forecasting the available personnel, and determining what additions and/or replacements are required to maintain a staff of the desired size and quality. Resulting personnel plans may be short, medium, or long range in orientation. Shorter-term plans deal more with existing needs; longer-range plans relate to future staffing considerations.

Why Human-Resource Planning Is Important

Without question, good human-resource planning can provide the following direct benefits to organizations and their managers.[5]

Helps management anticipate personnel shortages and surpluses and develop ways to avoid or correct problems before they become serious.

Permits forecasts of recruitment needs in terms of both numbers and types of skills sought.

Helps focus recruitment efforts on the most likely supply sources.

Provides for the identification of potential replacements or "backup" staff from either inside or outside the organization.

Integrates personnel plans with other strategic and operating plans.

Increasingly, the complexity of modern organizations and the challenges of managerial work require effective planning if results such as those in the list are to be achieved. Edgar Schein, a highly respected management educator and consultant, argues as follows.[6] Today's organizations are becoming more dependent upon people. They are increasingly involved in more complex technologies and are attempting to function in more complex economic, political, and sociocultural environments. As a result, the organization is more vulnerable to critical shortages of the right kinds of human resources. Furthermore, the more complex organizations become, the more they will be vulnerable to human error. The price of poor staffing will be high. It thus becomes a matter of *economic necessity* to improve human resource planning. As a manager you must be prepared to answer this challenge.

What Human-Resource Planning Involves

A comprehensive scheme of human-resource planning is shown in Figure 9.4. The process begins with a review of organizational strategies and objectives. This establishes the practical frame of reference against which personnel requirements and the internal supply of personnel can be forecast. Ultimately, the process should

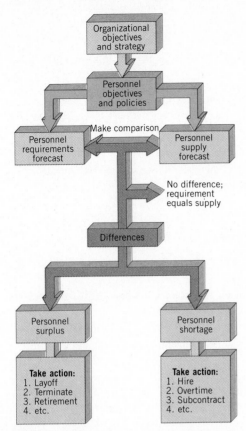

FIGURE 9.4 The human-resource planning process. *Source:* Lawrence J. Gitman and Carl McDaniel, Jr., *Business World* (New York: Wiley, 1983), p. 180. Used by permission.

produce action plans capable of correcting any staffing surplus or shortage that may exist.

Achieving a proper match between job requirements and staff capabilities is critical at all levels of management and for all types of jobs in organizations. Human-resource planning must complement strategic planning to ensure that organizations have the right number of people with the right skills available to do the required jobs. At its very core, human-resource planning involves establishing staffing needs and forecasting human-resource availabilities.

Establishing Staffing Needs

Job analysis is the orderly study of job requirements and facets that can influence performance results. It is a beginning point in any systematic effort to identify staffing needs. Correctly done, a job analysis will cover[7]

Work activities Exactly what is done.

Work tools The machines, tools, and other work aids used.

Job-related tangibles and intangibles The knowledge applied, materials processed, and products or services performed.

Job context Work schedules, physical conditions, social relations, compensation.

Performance standards Expected output in quantity and quality.

Personal requirements Requisite education, training, skills, experience, and other attributes.

Many organizations employ persons with specialized skills as job analysts. The job description for a job analyst working in the personnel department of one company is shown in Figure 9.5. Whether job analysis is performed by a manager or job analyst, the information on which it is based can be collected by a variety of methods. These include observation of the job and job occupant, interviews of the job occupant and/or the supervisor, questionnaire surveys of the occupant and/or supervisor, job diaries kept by the occupant, and recordings of job activities on videotape or film.[8] The final result should determine exactly *what* is done *when, where, how, why,* and *by whom.*

Job analysis is the basis for creating job descriptions and specifications that, in turn, provide a basic point of departure for the rest of the staffing process. Chapter 8 introduced the *job description* as a written statement detailing the duties and responsibilities of a job. A **job specification** is a list of the qualifications required of any job occupant. Such specifications usually include education, experience, and skill requirements for the job. With a good job description and job specification in hand, a manager can begin the search for people with the right qualifications to do the job well.

Human-Resource Forecasting

Forecasting the supply of human resources involves projecting future staffing needs and the

JOB TITLE: Job Analyst   DEPARTMENT: Personnel
IMMEDIATE SUPERVISOR: Director of Personnel
CLASSIFICATION: 09

Summary:
Under the guidance of the director of personnel: collects, analyzes and develops occupational data concerning jobs, job qualifications, and job requirements. Prepares job descriptions, job specifications, and job classification systems.

Duties:
1. Studies jobs being performed and interviews workers and supervisory personnel to ascertain physical and mental requirements.
2. Analyzes work flow and develops task statements relating to the job. Describes all duties and tasks performed.
3. Reviews the supervision received and supervision given as part of the job.
4. Analyzes unusual conditions in the work environment, such as temperature extremes, fumes, requirements for travel, etc.
5. Prepares job descriptions and job specifications.
6. Evaluates the comparative difficulty of jobs and establishes job classifications.
7. Develops recommendations for redesign of jobs as appropriate.

Job Specification:
Experience: Three years of employment in personnel work, with at least one year relating to activities associated with duties 1 through 7 above.

Education: College degree required, preferably in business administration, industrial psychology, or industrial engineering.

Skills: Must have a thorough knowledge of personnel work, especially that relating to job design and performance. Must be effective in oral and written communication.

FIGURE 9.5 Sample job description and job specification for the position of job analyst in a personnel department. *Source:* Howard M. Carlisle, *Management: Concepts and Situations*, Second Edition. (Chicago: Science Research Associates, 1982) p. 455. Used by permission.

anticipated supply of appropriate personnel. It is important to know, for example, how many people of what qualifications will be required by the organization, how many currently are in place, and how gaps between the two will be handled. A forecast that future needs will be greater than the present supply calls for an active recruiting strategy; a forecast that future needs will be less than present supply may require a strategy of planned terminations and/or nonreplacement. Factors to consider in each regard include the following.[9]

1. *When forecasting the need for human resources,* consider such things as

- Growth of the organization.
- Budget trends.
- Turnover because of resignations, terminations, transfers, and retirements.
- Introduction of new technology.

2. *When forecasting the supply of human resources,* consider such things as

- Promotable employees from within.
- Availability of required talent in external labor markets.
- Competition for talent within the industry.
- Population trends.
- Enrollment trends in training and education programs.

An important component in human-resource forecasting is the identification of promotable employees within the organization. This is greatly facilitated by the maintenance of a **human-resource audit** or systematic inventory of the strengths and weaknesses of existing personnel. A good audit helps managers plan promotions and career enhancement activities for personnel

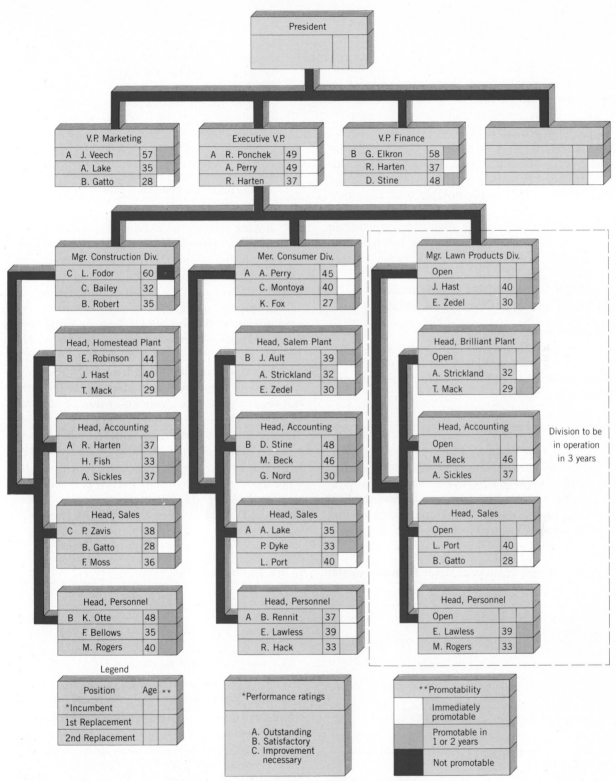

FIGURE 9.6 Human-resource inventory chart. *Source:* Henry L. Tosi and Stephen J. Carroll, *Management,* Second Edition (New York: Wiley, 1982), p. 327. Used by permission.

in their areas of responsibility, and plan for appropriate training, development, or replacement where weaknesses exist.

Figure 9.6 shows a comprehensive **human-resource inventory chart.** Sometimes called a replacement chart, it records the promotability of persons in key positions and is useful in planning future staff actions. Take the example in Figure 9.6. A new division must be adequately staffed three years down the road. Plans to satisfy this staffing need must be prepared in advance of the startup date. A nonpromotable and poor-performing head of sales should probably be replaced. Other persons on the chart are ready to move into higher responsibilities immediately; some others could do so given proper training.

External Constraints: Government Regulations and Organized Labor

Human-resource planning, like all planning, must be sensitive to key forces in the environment. Among these, two important external constraints are posed by government regulations and organized labor.

Government Regulations

Every manager is affected to some extent by federal laws governing the selection, employment, and replacement of employees. The following remarks by W. L. McMahon, vice-president of Corning Glass, testify to the complications that may accompany even well-intentioned govern-

ment regulations.[10]

Recruitment of personnel in today's organization requires careful consideration of federal laws. This has greatly increased the complexity of selecting qualified personnel at all levels in the company. We must comply with several equal employment opportunity laws often without a clear understanding of how to comply. Compliance is further complicated by the fact that guidelines may have been issued from different sources. The guidelines are often presented in different formats and may provide information that is inconsistent or difficult to implement.

A long history of federal legislation in the United States affects decision making in all matters pertaining to human-resource planning and personnel management. Table 9.2 highlights the legal impact of just a few pieces of legislation of recent importance. Of these, equal employment opportunity and affirmative action are regulatory issues of special significance in today's environment.

Equal employment opportunity is the right of people to employment and advancement without regard to race, sex, religion, color, or national origin. EEO, as it is commonly known, is federally enforced by the Equal Employment Opportunity Commission (EEOC) and generally applies to all public and private organizations employing 15 or more people. Virtually everyone is accorded this legal protection. When discrimination is encountered, legal charges can be filed and court action taken to resolve complaints.

Table 9.2 Legal Impacts of Major Federal Legislation on the Staffing Process

Major Legislation	Legal Impact
Title VII, Civil Rights Act (1964) and Equal Employment Opportunity Act (1972)	Prohibits employment discrimination based on race, color, religion, sex, or national origin
Equal Pay Act (1963)	Prohibits wage discrimination on the basis of sex; requires equal pay for equal work regardless of sex
Age Discrimination in Employment Act (1967; amended in 1978)	Prohibits employment discrimination based on age; specifically protects persons 40–70 years of age
Occupational Safety and Health Act (1970)	Established mandatory safety and health standards in organizations
Mandatory Retirement Act; Employee Retirement Income Security Act (1974)	Prohibits mandatory retirement before age 70; provides certain pension vesting rights for employees
Privacy Act (1974)	Gives employees the legal right to examine letters of reference about them

NEWSLINE 9.1

UNITED AIR TOLD TO REINSTATE UP TO 1800 FEMALE ATTENDANTS FORCED OUT BY SEX BIAS

CHICAGO—In a decision that could cost United Airlines millions of dollars, a federal judge ordered immediate reinstatement for as many as 1800 female flight attendants who lost their jobs when they married in the 1960s.

Judge James B. Moran's ruling stemmed from a 12-year-old class-action suit charging that the UAL Inc. unit violated federal sex-discrimination law by enforcing a no-marriage rule for the flight attendants between Oct. 27, 1965, and Nov. 7, 1968.

"Like any other employer who has engaged in unlawful employment discrimination, United may expect to suffer certain economic consequences," Judge Moran wrote in the ruling.

Source: Excerpted from John Curley, "United Air Told to Reinstate Up to 1800 Female Attendants Forced Out by Sex Bias," *Wall Street Journal* (January 13, 1982), p. 46. Reprinted by permission of the *Wall Street Journal*. Copyright © 1982 Dow Jones & Company, Inc. All rights reserved.

Sex discrimination in employment is a key target of the EEO. Consider the following announcement, which appeared one day in the *Wall Street Journal*.[11] It relates to a sex-discrimination case against United Airlines that was brought to the courts under EEO legislation. *Newsline 9.1* shows that the case was resolved in favor of the stewardesses, at great cost to the airline.

> If you were a stewardess for United Airlines and lost your employment as a stewardess between July 29, 1965, and November 7, 1968, because of United's no-marriage policy, you may be eligible to share in any relief obtained in a class action suit now pending in the federal court in Chicago. In this case, United's no-marriage policy has previously been ruled to be illegal sex discrimination, and former United stewardesses are seeking reinstatement and back pay.

> If you have not already received notice of the case and you fit the above description, please write to the Clerk of Court for more information. Inquiries must be received no later than April 1, 1981.

Equal employment opportunity legislation helps guarantee everyone's rights as an employee. It will also require you, as a manager, to act consistent with EEO guidelines in your human-resource planning and staffing efforts.

Whereas equal employment opportunity laws prohibit discrimination in recruitment, hiring, and promotion, **affirmative-action programs** are designed to increase employment opportunities for women and other minorities including veterans, the aged, and the handicapped. Based on two Executive Orders originally issued by President Lyndon B. Johnson, affirmative-action requirements apply to all organizations doing business with the federal government. The intent of the program is to ensure that women and other minorities are represented in the work force in proportion to their actual availability in the area labor market. Organizations that fail to meet these proportions must pursue assigned affirmative-action goals to increase the hiring and/or advancement of minorities. Failure to comply with affirmative-action guidelines can result in loss of federal funding and contracts.

Organized Labor

A second major external influence on human-resource planning and the staffing process is organized labor. Many industries employ a work force that belongs in whole or part to one or more unions. These unions are bargaining agents that negotiate contracts with employing organizations that can affect many areas of staffing and human-resource management. The provisions of a typical union contract, for example, relate to job specifications, seniority rules, compensation practices and benefits, grievance procedures, and working conditions.

One of the best continuing examples of how organized labor influences the personnel practices of organizations is found in the U.S. automobile industry. For years representatives of Ford, General Motors, and Chrysler have bargained with the strong, demanding leadership of the United Auto Workers (UAW). The contracts negotiated during the 1960s and 1970s were complex in terms of work rules and expensive in compensation and benefit packages. The result was an average wage for auto workers of $19.95 per hour in 1981. Any human-resource planning accomplished in this industry had to take the UAW and its desires into account.

Starting with the oil shortage of 1974, however, the U.S. auto industry suffered a crisis. By 1982, the automakers and the UAW were working more closely together to reduce production costs while still maintaining basic worker rights and benefits. Each side recognized that the productivity and future survival of the industry depended on cooperation and mutual adjustment to new and challenging times. At GM in 1982, labor and management negotiated an 18-month agreement that would keep GM's hourly wage and benefit costs at or below the existing average of about $19.55. The contract eliminated as many as 19 paid time-off days over a 16-month period, reduced the yield of the union's cost-of-living adjustment (COLA) provision, and skipped a straight wage increase normally paid in September. GM, in turn, promised to translate this $375-per-car savings into a price cut of $650 to $700 by reducing compensation for salaried employees and pressuring suppliers for price relief.[12]

You may become employed by an organization whose work force is represented in whole or part by a labor union. In such a setting, your plans and actions will have to be consistent with constraints set forth in the governing labor con-

tracts and any associated federal legislation. Chapter 19, "Managing Labor-Management Relations," addresses this and related topics in more detail.

RECRUITMENT

Recruitment is a set of activities designed to attract a qualified pool of job applicants to an organization. Emphasis on the word *qualified* is important. Effective recruiting brings employment opportunities to the attention of persons with abilities and skills appropriate to job specifications. Then and only then will recruiting facilitate the accomplishment of organizational objectives and fulfill its function as an essential ingredient in the total staffing process. In this process, human-resource planning leads to recruiting, which sets the stage for selection.

The Recruitment Process

The three steps in the recruitment process are: (1) advertisement of a job vacancy, (2) preliminary contact with potential job candidates, and (3) initial screening to create a pool of qualified applicants. You may know the process best in your response as an applicant to newspaper ads or word-of-mouth advertisements of job openings. Most probably you will become involved with the recruiting process when interviewing representatives of organizations visiting your campus in search of new employees.

Figure 9.7 shows separate events in the collegiate recruiting process as they involve line managers and recruiters from the organization, and the student as potential job applicant. Project yourself into this situation. You are near graduation and want a full-time job that relates to your major field of study. What will the three steps in the recruiting process look like from your side of things? Probably the following.

1. *Job advertisement* The organization advertises its job vacancies by posting short job descriptions at the campus placement center and/or in the campus newspaper.

2. *Preliminary contact* You sign up for an interview with a recruiter on campus; during a short (20–30 minute) interview you present a

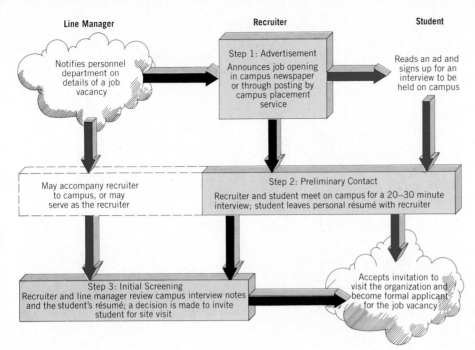

Notifies personnel department on details of a job vacancy

Step 1: Advertisement
Announces job opening in campus newspaper or through posting by campus placement service

Reads an ad and signs up for an interview to be held on campus

May accompany recruiter to campus, or may serve as the recruiter

Step 2: Preliminary Contact
Recruiter and student meet on campus for a 20–30 minute interview; student leaves personal résumé with recruiter

Step 3: Initial Screening
Recruiter and line manager review campus interview notes and the student's résumé; a decision is made to invite student for site visit

Accepts invitation to visit the organization and become formal applicant for the job vacancy

FIGURE 9.7 A successful episode in the college recruiting process.

written résumé of your background and explain your job qualifications.

3. *Initial screening*   The recruiter discusses interview results and your résumé with appropriate line managers; based on their knowledge of job specifications, you are among the candidates selected for a formal visit to the organization.

This is the recruitment process through the applicant's eyes. Figure 9.7 may also be used to clarify these aspects of recruiting from the perspectives of line managers and of recruiting specialists from a personnel department.

External and Internal Recruitment

There are two basic categories of job candidates toward whom recruiting efforts can be directed— qualified employees ready for promotion or transfer from within the organization, and persons from the outside. **Internal recruitment** involves making employees aware of job vacancies through job posting and personal recommendations. Most organizations have a procedure for announcing vacancies through newsletters, bulletin boards, and the like. They also rely on man-

agers to recommend subordinates who are good candidates for advancement. A history of serious internal recruitment can be very encouraging to employees. It demonstrates internal opportunities to advance in one's career by working hard and achieving high performance at each point of responsibility. This point is well conveyed in the chapter-opening example of increased emphasis in U.S. industry on internal recruiting on a performance basis.

External recruitment involves the attraction of job candidates from sources external to the organization. Newspapers, employment agencies, colleges, technical training centers, personal contacts, walk-ins, referrals, and even persons in competing organizations are among the sources of external recruits.

Each of these recruitment strategies offers potential advantages and disadvantages to the organization. Internal recruitment is usually the least expensive, deals with persons of known performance records, and leads to a pool of candidates who are already familiar with the internal workings of the organization. Because it also provides for advancement within the organization, internal recruiting encourages hard work among those desiring such opportunities. External re-

Part of a student's responsibility in the collegiate recruiting process is to review job postings at the campus placement center. This photo was taken at the Harvard Business School.

cruiting, on the other hand, brings in outsiders with fresh perspectives who are not biased or emotionally entangled in existing organizational practices. It also represents a source of specialized expertise or work experience that is not otherwise available from insiders. Overall, a good strategy is to maintain a mixture of external and internal recruiting. This allows the manager and organization to gain the best advantage of each as circumstances allow.

Realistic Recruitment

Two contrasts can be found in prevailing recruitment philosophies.[13] Traditional recruitment often seeks to "sell" the organization to outsiders. During the recruitment process only the most positive features of the job and organization are communicated to potential candidates. At the extreme, bias may even be introduced as these features are exaggerated while negative features are concealed. This form of recruitment is designed to attract as many candidates as possible. The problem is that the approach tends to create unrealistic expectations by the newly hired person. In terms used in Chapter 8, the individual's psychological contract becomes distorted as initial

expectations are left unfulfilled on the job. A decision to terminate employment is one possible result.

Premature turnover caused by unmet job expectations costs the organization because any investments in recruiting and training the new employee are lost and must be made again with someone else. There may also be emotional and financial costs to the individual. These include the emotional drain of "quitting" as well as the efforts required to find new employment elsewhere.

Realistic recruitment tries to provide the job candidate with all pertinent information and without distortion *before* the job is accepted. Instead of "selling" the organization by communicating only positive features, this approach tries to be fair in depicting actual job and organizational realities. While positive features are not ignored, the candidate is also told about potential negative features. As a result of this more complete view of the job and organization, new employees should have more realistic job expectations at the time of initial entry. Higher levels of job satisfaction and less premature turnover are the anticipated benefits. Research tends to confirm this viewpoint.

SELECTION

Selection is the process of choosing from a pool of applicants the person or persons best meeting job specifications. Events in a typical selection process are (1) completion of a formal application form, (2) further interviewing, (3) testing, (4) reference checks, (5) physical examination, and (6) final analysis and decision to hire or reject.

Elements in the Selection Process

Briefly highlighted here, the elements in the selection process are also shown in Figure 9.8, along with sample reasons why applicants might be rejected in each stage.

Job-Application Forms

Among the elements in the selection process, the job-application form declares the individual a formal candidate for the job vacancy. It summarizes the applicant's personal history and qualifications. The personal résumé is often included with the job application. This important document should accurately summarize an applicant's special qualifications. You, for example, should exercise great care in preparing your résumé for job searches. As a manager, you should also learn how to screen the applications and résumés of other persons for facts that can help you make a good selection.

Interviews

Formal interviews allow job candidates and key persons from within the organization to learn more about one another than the application form and résumé make possible. The interview is an extremely important part of the selection process because of the information exchange it allows. Thus it is important for both the job, candidate and the managers serving as interviewers to fulfill the interviewing task well.

Some things to remember when being interviewed as a job candidate follow.[14]

Preparation is essential. Answer questions fully and concisely. This requires preparation to find out all you can about the organization, the job, and the person doing the recruiting.

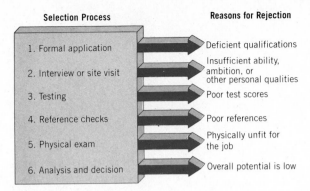

FIGURE 9.8 Steps in the typical selection process.

Think before answering. Use words well and give organized and focused answers. Before answering a question, pause—think about how to answer—then speak. Don't blurt out the first answer that comes to mind.

Appearance and enthusiasm are important. Present a total picture of yourself. Remember that such things as choice of clothing, good grooming, a firm handshake, and enthusiasm will convey a desirable image.

When you are the one doing the interviewing, keep the following points in mind. They are ways of maximizing what you learn about a job applicant.[15]

Plan for the interview. Review the job specifications and job description, as well as the candidate's application.

Create a good climate. Try to establish a friendly, open rapport with the applicant.

Allow sufficient time for an uninterrupted interview. Choose a quiet place, hold all phone calls, and give the candidate sincere and individual attention.

Conduct a goal-oriented interview. Direct your efforts toward gathering the information actually needed to make a good employment decision.

Screen your questions beforehand to avoid those that may imply discrimination. The Civil Rights Act restricts what can and cannot be asked in an interview; see Table 9.3 for tips on interviewing do's and don'ts distributed to all supervisors in one organization.

The formal interview between one or more representatives of an organization and a job applicant is an important screening process in job recruitment.

Press for answers to all questions and check for inconsistencies. Know what has been said on the application form and/or résumé; listen and probe politely to expand on the information provided.

Write notes on the interview immediately upon completion. Don't risk forgetting the details or your impressions; make good notes that can be reviewed later for purposes of deliberation and decision making.

Employment Tests

Employment tests are used to screen applicants on the basis of intelligence, aptitudes, skills, and personality. They generally fall into four major groups.[16]

1. *Intelligence tests* are designed to measure mental capacity and test memory, speed of thought, and ability to see relationships in complex problem situations.

2. *Proficiency and aptitude tests* are designed to discover interests, existing skills, and potential for acquiring skills.

3. *Vocational tests* are designed to identify a candidate's most suitable occupation.

4. *Personality tests* are designed to reveal personal characteristics and the way they may affect others.

Table 9.3 Employment Interviewing Guidelines for Supervisors

Subject	Do *Not* Ask	*Okay* to Ask
Age	Questions showing preference for specific age group	Date of birth, proof of true age
Family	About family planning, family size, children's ages, child-care plans, spouse's employment, or salary	Freedom to travel if job requires, meeting work schedule requirements if *all* applicants asked the same questions
Handicaps	General questions that bring out information that is not job related	Whether person has sensory, mental, or physical handicaps that relate to ability to perform job
Marital status	Whether person is married, single, separated, divorced, engaged.	Nothing
National origin	About ancestry; birthplace of applicant, parents, or spouse	Ability to speak, read, or write English or a foreign language if the job requires
Religion	About religion	Anticipated absences from the job

NEWSLINE 9.2

MORE EMPLOYERS ATTEMPT TO CATCH A THIEF BY GIVING JOB APPLICANTS "HONESTY" EXAMS

"Honesty" tests are an increasingly popular, and controversial, preemployment check for businesses from retailing to exterminating. The theory is that those who associate with the dishonest tend to be dishonest. And, although no single question can determine honesty, test makers say that an entire exam can.

They cover a variety of topics, from off-track betting to homicide, posing questions that job interviewers might neglect or be too embarrassed to ask. What's your favorite alcoholic drink? Which drugs have you tried? Did you ever make a false insurance claim?

Essay questions also provide more information than an ordinary job application could. "I only steal merchandise, not cash," one applicant wrote. Another commented: "I only smoke pot at lunch, not at breakfast."

Source: Excerpted from Susan Tompor, "More Employers Attempt to Catch a Thief by Giving Job Applicants 'Honesty' Exams," Wall Street Journal (August 3, 1981), p. 13. Reprinted by permission of the Wall Street Journal. Copyright © 1981 Dow Jones & Company, Inc. All rights reserved.

The goal of any employment test is to gather information that will help predict the applicant's eventual performance success on the job. To do so, a test must be both valid and reliable. A **valid test** measures exactly what it intends to relative to the job specification—for example, intelligence or manual dexterity. A **reliable test** yields approximately the same results over time if taken by the same person.

Because invalid and/or unreliable tests can create bias in selection decisions, the testing process is often controversial. It is also subject to legal constraints. Under Equal Employment Opportunity (EEO) legislation, any employment test used as a criterion of selection must be defensible on the grounds that it actually measures an ability required to perform the job. Testing must clearly relate to job specifications. Thus testing is an aspect of the selection process that should be carefully administered by persons with special training in testing theory and practice. This expertise is often present in the personnel staff of an organization.

Newsline 9.2 offers a final thought on one of the more recent controversies in employment testing. What do you think of "honesty exams" as standard employment practice?

Reference Checks

Reference or background checks are inquiries to prior employers, academic advisors, family members, and/or friends regarding the qualifications, experience, and past work records of a job applicant. Although they may also be biased, such as when friends are prearranged "to say the right things if called," reference checks can be helpful to both the potential employer (e.g., when a prior employer points out a hidden problem) and the applicant (e.g., when the list of suggested references is obviously legitimate or even prestigious).

Physical Examinations

Some organizations ask job applicants to take a physical examination. This health check helps ensure that the person is physically capable of fulfilling job requirements. It may also be used as a

Table 9.4 Sample Assessment Center Schedule

Day 1	Orientation of a dozen candidates
	Break up into groups of four to play a management game (observe and assess organizing ability, financial acumen, quickness of thinking efficiency under stress, adaptability, leadership)
	Psychological testing (measure and assess verbal and numerical abilities, reasoning, interests, and attitudes) and/or *depth interviews* (assess motivation)
	Leaderless group discussion (observe and assess aggressiveness, persuasiveness, expository skill, energy, flexibility, self-confidence)
Day 2	*In-basket exercise* (observe and assess decision making under stress, organizing ability, memory and ability to interrelate events, preparation for decision making, ability to delegate, concern for others)
	Role playing of employment or performance appraisal interview (observe and assess sensitivity to others, ability to probe for information, insight, empathy)
	Group roles in preparation of a budget (observe and assess collaboration abilities, financial knowledge, expository skill, leadership, drive)
Day 3	*Individual case analyses* (observe expository skill, awareness of problems, background information processed for problems, typically involving marketing, personnel, accounting, operations, and financial elements)
	Obtainment of *peer ratings* from all candidates
	Staff assessors meet to discuss and rate all candidates
Later	Candidates discuss assessments with staff assessors and receive counseling regarding career paths and areas of needed personal development

Source: Edwin B. Flippo and Gary M. Munsinger, *Management,* Fourth Edition (Boston: Allyn and Bacon, 1978), p. 237. Used by permission.

basis for enrolling the applicant in health-related fringe benefits such as life-, health-, and disability-insurance programs.

Final Analysis and Decisions to Hire or Reject

Final responsibility for analysis of all the data and making decisions to hire or reject job applicants rests with the manager. This may be done with or without the counsel of the personnel department or other persons with or for whom the job applicant would work. It is generally best to allow as many other relevant persons as possible to offer their inputs. This ensures that all possible factors are considered before a decision to reject or hire is made.

Assessment Centers

The **assessment center** is a special technique often used in selecting people for management jobs. A typical assessment center engages job candidates in a series of experiential activities over a one- or two-day period. These activities require participation in role playing, simulations, case analyses, and the like. A panel of experts evaluates the individual's performance during the exercise. This evaluation then becomes an additional information input to the selection process. Assessment centers are also used to help design appropriate training and development programs for high-potential employees.

A schedule for one company's assessment center is presented in Table 9.4. You can see that they are rigorous, well-planned exercises. Although they can be costly to run, they are valuable tools in the selection process. The chances are good that you will pass through an assessment center someday, perhaps as part of initial selection for a job with an organization, or as part of an evaluation of your readiness for internal advancement during a later career stage.

ORIENTATION

Newsline 9.3 introduces you to life at IBM, a company often talked about for the amount of loyalty

NEWSLINE 9.3

LIFE AT IBM: RULES AND DISCIPLINE, GOALS AND PRAISE SHAPE IBMERS' TAUT WORLD

When Thomas J. Watson, Sr. died in 1956, some might have thought the IBM spirit of the stiff white collar was destined to die with him. But indications are that the founder's legacy of decorum to International Business Machines Corp. still burns bright. For, besides its great success with computers, IBM has a reputation in the corporate world for another standout trait: an almost proprietary concern with its employees' behavior, appearance, and attitudes.

What this means to employees is a lot of rules. And these rules, from broad, unwritten ones calling for "tasteful" dress to specific ones setting salesmen's quotas, draw their force at IBM from another legacy of the founder: the value placed on loyalty.

What it all amounts to is a kind of IBM culture, a set of attitudes and approaches shared to a greater or lesser degree by IBMers everywhere. This culture, as gleaned from talks with former as well as current employees, is so pervasive that, as one nine-year (former) employee puts it, leaving the company "was like emigrating."

Source: Excerpted from Susan Chance, "Life at IBM: Rules and Discipline, Goals and Praise Shape IBMers' Taut World," *Wall Street Journal* (April 8, 1982), p. 1. Reprinted by permission of the *Wall Street Journal.* Copyright © 1982 Dow Jones & Company, Inc. All rights reserved.

and conformity asked of its employees. The underlying issue is **socialization,** the process of systematically changing the expectations, behavior, and attitudes of a new employee in a manner considered desirable by the organization. The intent of socialization is to achieve the best possible match between the individual and the job and between the individual and the organization. At risk is overconformity and loss of creativity on the employee's part.

Socialization of newcomers begins with initial orientation and continues during later training and development activities, as well as in day-to-day supervisor-subordinate relationships. **Orientation** is a set of activities designed to familiarize new employees with their jobs and coworkers, as well as with the policies, rules, objectives, and services of the organization as a whole. Done well, orientation enhances individual understanding of the organization. Higher

performance and satisfaction and increased commitment are the anticipated results. In addition, good orientation

1. *Reduces startup costs and time* Orientation helps a newcomer reach performance standards in minimum time by learning about the job, supervisory expectations, and organizational facilities and work routines.

2. *Reduces anxiety* The information made available during orientation helps reduce fears of failure and builds the newcomer's job confidence and competence.

3. *Reduces turnover* Like realistic recruiting, proper orientation helps reduce premature turnover otherwise caused by high anxiety and unmet expectations.

The unfortunate fact is that orientation is frequently neglected as a managerial responsibility. Newcomers are often left to fend for themselves and learn job and organizational routines on their own or through casual interactions with co-workers. Otherwise well-intentioned and capable persons may learn inappropriate attitudes and/or behaviors as a result. Over time this may detract from, not add to, their commitment, performance, and satisfaction.

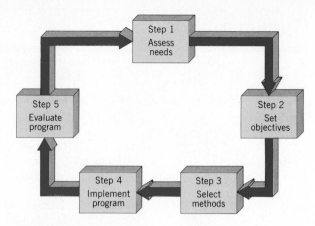

FIGURE 9.9 Model of the training process.

TRAINING AND DEVELOPMENT

Training is a set of activities that provides learning opportunities through which people acquire and improve job-related skills.

What Constitutes Good Training?

Good training is implemented by the steps shown in Figure 9.9. Each step of this systematic training process is an action responsibility of managers interested in the continued training and development of subordinates.

Step 1
Assess needs.   Good training begins with a careful analysis of actual training needs. This may range from one extreme of reviewing training needs on an organization-wide basis, to the other extreme of reviewing training needs specific to a single job or individual.

Step 2
Set objectives.   A needs analysis helps specify training objectives or desired end results for the training program. This should include the criteria or standards against which final results are to be measured.

Step 3
Select methods.   Training objectives establish a frame of reference for choosing appropriate instructional methods. A number of these will be reviewed here shortly.

Step 4
Implement program.   Actual training activities can then be made available in accordance with choices made in Steps 2 and 3.

Step 5
Evaluate program.   Training outcomes should always be compared to desired results as a measure

of actual performance success. As part of this attempt to determine whether or not a training program meets its objectives, participants can and should be queried for their personal assessment of the program, including both its technical content and the quality of instruction.

Speaking more generally, good training can only occur when managers establish an overall climate within which

- *Trainees want to learn.*   There is no substitute for training a person who wants to learn and improve. Indeed, willingness to learn is an important criterion that should be carefully considered when selecting persons to fill job vacancies.

- *Trainees are reinforced for learning.*   Training accomplishments and the willingness to learn through active participation in future training opportunities must be maintained. This requires reinforcement and reward for individual learning efforts and realized results.

Types of Training

The design of training programs varies between on-the-job or off-the-job training locations and among the alternative instructional methods that may be used.

On-the-job training occurs in the work setting and during actual job performance. The basic instructional approaches include job rotation, formal and informal coaching, apprenticeship, and modeling. *Job rotation* was discussed as a job design strategy in Chapter 8. As a training device, it offers opportunities for persons to spend time in different jobs and expand the range of their job capabilities. **Coaching** is the communication of specific technical advice to an individual. It can be done on a formal and planned basis by a supervisor or co-workers. It can also occur more spontaneously or on an informal basis as help offered by other persons when the need arises. **Apprenticeship** involves an assignment to serve as understudy or assistant to a person already having the desired job skills. Through this relationship an apprentice learns the job over time and eventually becomes fully qualified in his or her own right. Although most common to technical trades such as welding or machining, apprenticeship training is becoming more common for persons moving into new managerial jobs for the first time. **Modeling,** as a process of demonstrating through personal behavior what is expected of others, is also an influential means for building appropriate job skills. When persons in supervisory capacities work for good managers, for example, their managerial skills can be enhanced by simply practicing those things practiced on them.

Off-the-job training is accomplished away from the work setting. It may be done within the

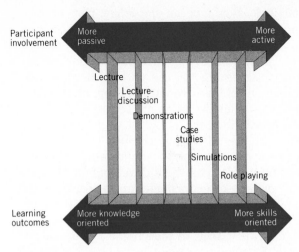

FIGURE 9.10 Instructional techniques and their training implications.

organization but in a separate training room or facility, or it may be done at a location remote from the organization. Examples of the latter include attendance at special training programs externally sponsored by universities, trade or professional associations, and consultants.

Figure 9.10 summarizes some of the instructional methods that are employed in off-the-job training: lectures, discussions, demonstrations, case studies, simulations, and role playing. You are probably familiar with most of them through your educational experiences. From a training perspective, two special features about these alternative techniques are worth highlighting. First, the role of the trainee becomes increasingly active as one moves away from lectures and toward role playing. This reflects a more active involvement of the learner and probably offers a greater chance for realizing more skills-oriented learning effects. Lecture methods, by contrast, involve a more passive role for the learner but can do a good job at content delivery.

Management Development

Training specifically targeted to improve a person's knowledge and skills in the fundamentals of management is referred to as **management development.** If you are truly serious about a managerial career, management-development

Organizations use a variety of instructional methods in the off-job training of employees. Here a videotape replay is used in the training of an insurance salesperson.

activities should be an important part of your continuing personal agenda. Although some organizations do a better job than others of providing management-development opportunities, this is something you can always attend to personally by taking advantage of programs or short seminars available in the marketplace.

Mentoring, the act of sharing experiences and insights between a seasoned executive and junior manager, is another increasingly important form of management development. It sets a new or early-career manager up as protégé to the senior person who then coaches and assists the junior person in efforts to develop his or her management skills to their highest potential. At Jewel Company, a large Chicago-based food retailer, for example, three MBAs are recruited each year. They are rotated through a series of job assignments in different Jewel divisions. Each trainee is assigned to a seasoned upper-level manager who acts as advisor and sounding board, that is, as an all-around mentor. This mentor system is applauded by past and present executives as having aided their careers and for helping attract bright people to Jewel.[17]

REPLACEMENT

The several steps in the staffing process both conclude and recycle with **replacement,** the act of removing a person from an assigned job. As a staffing responsibility, replacement relates to the management of promotions, transfers, terminations, layoffs, and retirements as depicted in Figure 9.11. The need for replacement, for example, can arise when

- A selection error results in a poor match of job requirements to personal ability.
- A person outgrows a job over time.
- A person is assigned to another job.
- A person violates a policy, rule, or procedure.
- There is not enough work.
- A person decides to quit.
- Illness or death prevents a person from working.
- A person decides to retire.

Any replacement situation offers potential benefits and costs. To restaff a position, the entire selection process must often begin anew. Although costly, this is also a great opportunity to review human-resource plans, update job analyses, job descriptions, job specifications, and make sure the best people are selected to perform the required tasks. Thus a manager must be ever vigilant in monitoring jobs under his or her control to recognize when replacement actions should be initiated. The human-resource inventory chart referenced earlier in this chapter is a tool that helps managers monitor the replacement possibilities in their work units.

Promotions and Transfers

One set of replacement decisions retains persons for employment within the organization, but moves them out of their present jobs. **Promotion** is movement to a higher-level position; **transfer** is movement to a different job at the same or similar level of responsibility.

Promotion ideally occurs on a performance basis; that is, a person is advanced in responsibility because of demonstrated capabilities for the new job. Some organizations promote by seniority, either by preference or because of union rules. Promoting by seniority eliminates ambiguity regarding why a particular person is chosen for advancement, and it does encourage people to remain on the job in the expectation that their "time will come." However, it can result in the promotion of persons who are less competent than others available—or who may even be incompetent.

Job transfers can be growth opportunities for the persons involved. They offer chances to broaden one's work experience, learn new skills, and become more familiar with other parts of the organization. In this sense the transfer is a personal development, opportunity given as a reward for a job well done. Managers can also use the transfer to get rid of a poor performing employee. In order for such "problem-solving" transfers to work out well for all concerned, a proper match between the transferred person's capabilities and the new job requirements must be found.

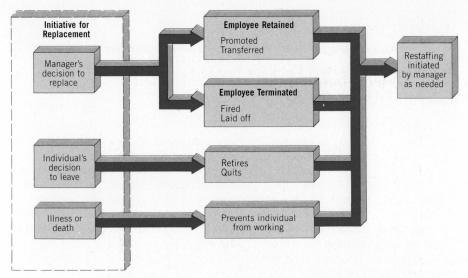

FIGURE 9.11 Replacement as a managerial responsibility.

Retirements

Retirement is something most people look forward to . . . until it is actually close at hand. Then the prospect of being retired can raise many fears and apprehensions. Still, retirement is inevitable, and many organizations are taking action to help their employees prepare for it. Pitney Bowes, Inc., the manufacturer of postal and office equipment, is a case in point. Concerned that its employees too often reached retirement adrift and without guidance, the company started a program wherein employees who are at least 50 years old are reimbursed up to $300 a year to help defray the costs of preparing for a second career. The employees can take courses until an aggregate total of $3000 is reached. Since the program was instituted in 1978, nearly 500 employees and spouses have availed themselves of the financial assistance by taking a wide range of courses in areas such as business management, real-estate appraisal, ceramics, sewing, and cooking. Counseling and just being a good listener are also among many things that managers can do to facilitate the successful retirement of subordinates.

Terminations

Newspapers and television newscasts of the early 1980s were full of reports on plant closings and employee layoffs. One week, for example, Cat-erpillar Tractor Company announced the layoff of 8000 (yes, eight *thousand*) employees—almost one-third of its entire work force!

Layoffs are always difficult, and organizations seem increasingly sensitive to the need to treat their employees fairly under such circumstances. A growing number of organizations provide outplacement services to terminated employees. These services range from personal counseling to direct assistance in seeking alternative employment. The Indal Aluminum Company, as discussed in the case application to Chapter 3, did just that. When hard economic times forced one of its plants to close, Indal set up an outplacement service and advertised in local papers to help departing employees find new jobs.

The most extreme form of termination is **firing,** the involuntary and permanent dismissal of an employee. Firing someone will always be painful to both parties, but there are times when employees should be dismissed from their jobs. When the dismissal is based on a true mismatch between what a job requires and what a person wants to and/or is capable of delivering, both the dismissed employee and the organization should benefit from correcting the mismatch. Such seems to have been the case of Ford Motor Company and its ex-president Lee Iacocca, as reported in *Newsline 9.4.* You probably know Iacocca much better as the person who went on in the early 1980s to lead the Chrysler Corporation

NEWSLINE 9.4

TWO WORDS THAT ARE TOUGH TO SAY: YOU'RE FIRED

"I just don't like you very much!"

Thus, according to biographer Victor Lasky, did Henry Ford II bluntly explain to a startled Lee Iacocca, a 30-year veteran at Ford Motor Co. who had worked his way right up to the presidency, why he was being summarily ousted.

Call it hard; call it insensitive; call it despotic, but Ford was far more honest in his encounter with Iacocca than are many chief executive officers today in their handling of high-level corporate sackings. Ford, at least, had the courage to own up to a basic fact of life in the executive suite: Incompatibility rather than incompetence is the trigger for the majority of upper-echelon firings in U.S. business. That fact makes it harder, not easier, for most company presidents to say, "You're fired!"

According to popular stereotype, top corporate executives are terrible-tempered tyrants, spring-loaded to fire anyone within range at the drop of a paper clip. But during two decades of counseling board chairmen and corporation presidents on sensitive matters of management organization, we have found the reverse problem. At least a third of them are unable, or unwilling, to present subordinates directly with the judgment that they must leave the company. In too many instances, the act is too long postponed—usually to the disadvantage of both parties. When time finally does run out, the CEO often assigns the unpleasant chore to someone else.

Source: Excerpted from Byrant and Carole R. Cushing, "Two Words That Are Tough to Say: You're Fired," *Wall Street Journal* (September 14, 1981), p. 26. Reprinted by permission of the *Wall Street Journal*. Copyright © 1981 Dow Jones & Company, Inc. All rights reserved.

from the brink of bankruptcy into a brighter future.

It may help to share some thoughts on this issue from the perspective of both the person being dismissed and the person doing the dismissing. Exploring these ideas should increase your sensitivity to this difficult part of the staffing process.

Questions the Dismissed Employee May Ask

Accepting the fact of being terminated is difficult. Often the notice of dismissal is a surprise. It catches the person off-guard and without any preparation for either the personal or the financial shock. The expert's advice, though, is for the dismissed employee to brace up and stay rational. It's time for them to ask some tough questions of their ex-boss.[18]

1. *Why am I being fired?* They have a right to know why. Knowing why can help them decide what to do next. Knowing why can also help them avoid a similar fate in the future.

2. *What are my termination benefits?* These benefits can help immeasurably. They range from severance pay and vested pension rights to the outplacement services mentioned earlier.

3. *Can I have a good reference?* A good reference can help in the coming job search. A direct personal recommendation might help place the person quickly with an appropriate employer.

What to Do When an Employee Has to Be Dismissed

Certain basic rules should be kept in mind by the manager who must do the firing. A good deal of common sense is called for. In addition, the manager should remember that[19]

- There is more to firing than giving condolences and severence pay.
- Firing should always be handled delicately and in full recognition that it can be as personally devastating as divorce or death of a loved one.

- Firing should always be done in complete compliance with organizational policies and in a manner defensible under government legislation.
- Firing should not be postponed; it is best done as soon as the inevitability of the dismissal is known.
- It is best to be clear, frank, and short in communicating the dismissal.
- There should always be some offer of assistance to help the fired employee reenter the labor market.

SUMMARY

This chapter on staffing concludes our coverage of organizing, the second of four basic managerial functions. Organizing involves the design of appropriate structures to guide and coordinate work activities, the design of jobs to ensure the accomplishment of essential tasks by individuals and groups, and the staffing of these jobs with qualified human resources. The staffing process itself is a responsibility often shared by line managers and members of personnel departments. Its basic elements include human-resource planning, recruitment, selection, orientation, training and development, and replacement.

Good staffing begins with a human-resource-planning program. Such programs maintain awareness of labor-market trends and organizational needs. Recruitment involves communicating job vacancies and attracting a pool of qualified candidates. Whether done inside or outside the organization, recruiting is best accomplished by being as realistic as possible with potential applicants. Good recruiting, in turn, creates a foundation for the selection of candidates whose capabilities best match job specifications. These new employees require an orientation to their jobs and continued training and development to further improve and/or expand job skills. The informed manager will be diligent in assessing training needs and then providing on-the-job and off-the-job training opportunities to satisfy them. Management development is a special case of training that is concerned with the growth of managers to their highest potential. As a manager, you will want to take advantage of management-development opportunities to maintain personal growth, as well as to make sure that such opportunities are available to persons working under your supervision.

Replacement is the final stage in the staffing process. When the need to replace arises through promotion, transfer, firing, layoff, retirement, illness, or death, the staffing process is recycled again. Although there will always be times when you regret losing a valued employee, replacement is an opportunity as well. It is a chance to reanalyze jobs to ensure that they are appropriately designed and that the job specifications are correct. It is a chance to fill jobs with persons whose abilities offer maximum performance potential.

In summary, remember that staffing is the process of matching individual abilities and job requirements. Thus it responds directly to the ability variable in the individual performance equation: performance = ability × support × effort. If staffing helps ensure ability, and organizational and job design help ensure support, what is now left to study is how the manager ensures effort. That is a leadership question that is the subject of the four chapters in Part 4.

THINKING THROUGH THE ISSUES

1. State the individual performance equation. Give an example of how a manager can influence each of the key variables in the equation.

2. Draw a diagram showing the interrelationships among the major elements in the staffing process.

3. What is job analysis and how does it relate to human-resource planning?

4. Explain how a personnel department often becomes involved in human-resource planning and the rest of the staffing process.

5. What is realistic recruiting? How can it benefit organizations?

6. Explain how an assessment center might be used to screen applicants for a vacant management position.

7. How does orientation differ from training as a managerial responsibility?

8. Is on-the-job training preferable to off-the-job training? Why or why not?

9. Describe why replacement should be considered an opportunity for the manager who must now fill a job vacancy.

10. What advice would you give to a manager who has to fire someone? Why?

THE MANAGER'S VOCABULARY

Affirmative-action programs
Apprenticeship
Assessment center
Coaching
Equal employment opportunity
External recruitment
Firing
Human-resource audit

Human-resource-inventory chart
Human-resource planning
Internal recruitment
Job analysis
Job specification
Management development

Reliable test
Replacement
Selection
Socialization
Staffing
Training
Transfer
Valid test

Mentoring
Modeling
Off-the-job training
On-the-job training
Orientation
Promotion
Realistic recruitment
Recruitment

CAREER PERSPECTIVE: ROBERT C. TOWNSEND—A MANAGERIAL PROFILE[20]

Robert C. Townsend is a top corporate executive whose humorous but insightful book, *Up the Organization,* became a popular bestseller. Most prominent for his success in revitalizing Avis, Inc., the rental car company, Townsend's staffing principles as set forth in his book include the following.

1. Most managements complain about the lack of able people and go outside to fill key positions. Nonsense. . . . I use the rule of 50 percent. Try to find people inside the company with records of success (in any area) and with appetites for the job. If these look like 50 percent of what you need, give them the job. In six months they'll have grown the other 50 percent and everybody will be satisfied.

2. The only way I know to get somebody trained is on the job.

3. Firing people is unpleasant, but it really has to be done occasionally. . . . Purging the bad performers is as good a tonic for the organization as giving sizable rewards to the star performers.

4. Fairness, justice, or whatever you call it—it's essential and most companies don't have it. Everybody must be judged on performance, not on looks or manners or personality or who they know or are related to.

Questions

1. What do you think of the "50 percent rule" as a basic staffing guideline? Why?

2. Overall, do you agree with Townsend's principles? Is this good advice for you or anyone else to follow as a practicing manager?

CASE APPLICATION: ED'S STORY[21]

Ed went east to get an MBA, after graduating with a psychology major from a state university in the Midwest. In graduate school he majored in management and marketing. During his second year of the MBA program, Ed interviewed with six different companies on campus and was invited back to three of them for further assessment. Prior to the campus interviews he had gone to a couple of "crash courses" the school offered on how to prepare for job interviews. He was given pointers on what to wear, what questions to expect, what questions to ask, and what information about the company he should obtain. At the end of the courses, he participated in a "mock interview" before a videotape machine. He saw himself on television for the first time and carefully listened to the "pointers" given him by the instructor. By the time Ed went to his first interview, he felt prepared. He had talked with other students about their experiences, read the three most recent annual reports for each company, and rehearsed answers to the "open-ended" questions he anticipated.

Two companies offered Ed a job as a "management trainee." There were differences between the two positions in terms of geographic location, starting salary, general reputation as a desirable place for the new college graduate,

and initial job assignment. Ed accepted a position with a large, multinational corporation that sold business machines as its main product. His long-term goal was to enter general management, not to spend his whole career in sales. However, in this particular company, going into sales was regarded by most as the fastest route to district-level management.

The initial training period lasted about three months and was held in a special campuslike location devoted to "corporate training and management development." Although the program was well conceived, organized, and interesting, Ed felt that he still hadn't learned "how things really work" in the company. The next six months of initial field sales experience helped to correct this deficiency. During this period Ed was placed under the mentorship of an experienced sales representative.

After the nine-month mark and a formal appraisal by his mentor, Ed was on his own in the field. For the first nine months, Ed had been on a straight salary. Now he was on a small base salary plus sales commission. The formula for computing it was fairly complicated and had one striking feature. If a company decided not to renew a machine rental contract, a portion of the lost revenue was "charged back" to the sales division and subtracted from Ed's commission.

This was designed to force sales personnel to give good, attentive service to their customers. In practice, however, some decisions to terminate rentals were completely out of the control of the salesperson, and Ed's income was not as predictable as it had been. Further, Ed soon learned that the charge-back system was considered a threat by many new sales representatives and was resented by others. The full impact of this compensation system was completely unanticipated by Ed. The previous explanation given to him had seemed abstract at the time—living with the system was another matter altogether.

After about six months in the field, Ed left for another company. Before leaving he had made a few small deals, but did not generate more han $3000 a month—barely enough to "cover" what he had been paid up to that point. When he quit the company was out over $30,000 it had spent in the first nine months to recruit, hire, and develop him as an employee. At least another $30,000 would have to be spent on his replacement—with no guarantee to the company that there would be a solid return on the next "human capital" investment.

Questions

1. Analyze "Ed's Story" from the perspective of each element in the staffing process. What mistakes did the company make?

2. What could Ed have done to ensure a better person-job match in his first employment after graduation?

CLASS EXERCISE: THE (UN)LAWFUL INTERVIEW

1. Assume you are interviewing a candidate for a job vacancy in your work unit. Mark in the space provided whether or not it is legal for you to ask the listed questions.

Interview Questions	Legal	Illegal
How old are you?	—	—
Are you married or divorced?	—	—
Do you have any dependents?	—	—
What was your last job?	—	—
Why did you leave it?	—	—
Do you have a criminal record?	—	—
Are you a citizen of the United States?	—	—
What is your educational background?	—	—
Why do you want this job?	—	—
Do you own a home?	—	—
Who are your personal references?	—	—
How long do you plan to stay on this job?	—	—
Will any health problems interfere with your job performance?	—	—

2. Share your responses with those of a nearby classmate. Discuss and resolve any discrepancies. Await further class discussion.

REFERENCES

[1] Excerpted from John Curley, "More Companies Look Within for Managers," *Wall Street Journal* (October 28, 1980), p. 17. Reprinted by permission of the *Wall Street Journal.* Copyright © 1980 Dow Jones & Company, Inc. All rights reserved.

[2] "Changes at Playboy," *Business Week* (May 10, 1982), p. 46.

[3] "Family Affair: Dad and Daughter at Playboy," *Time* (May 10, 1982), p. 96.

[4] *Wall Street Journal* (March 23, 1981), p. 3.

[5] Adapted from Lewis E. Albright, "Staffing Policies and Strategies," *ASPA Handbook of Personnel and Industrial Relations,* Dale Yoder and Herbert G. Heneman (Eds.), Vol. 1 (Washington, D.C.: Bureau of National Affairs, 1974), pp. 4–21.

[6] Edgar H. Schein, "Increasing Organizational Effectiveness Through Better Human Resource Planning and Development," *Sloan Management Review,* Vol. 19

(1977), pp. 1–20.

[7] See Ernest McCormick, "Job and Task Analysis," in Marvin Dunnette (Ed.), *Handbook of Industrial and Organizational Psychology* (Chicago: Rand McNally, 1976), pp. 651–696.

[8] William F. Glueck, *Management*, Second Edition (Hinsdale, Ill.: Dryden, 1980), p. 106.

[9] Adapted from Robert Kreitner, *Management: A Problem-Solving Process* (Boston: Houghton-Mifflin, 1980), p. 328.

[10] Quoted in Wayne R. Mondy, Robert E. Holmes, and Edwin R. Flippo, *Management: Concepts and Practices* (Boston: Allyn and Bacon, 1980), p. 198.

[11] *Wall Street Journal* (March 13, 1981), p. 24.

[12] Information from "Labor: A Pact That May Make History," *Business Week* (February 8, 1982), p. 81.

[13] This section based on John P. Wanous, *Organizational Entry: Recruitment, Selection, and Socialization of Newcomers* (Reading, Mass.: Addison-Wesley, 1980), pp. 34–44.

[14] Adapted from Gary Dessler, *Management Fundamentals*, Third Edition (Reston: Va.: Reston Publishing, 1982), p. 253.

[15] Adapted from the *ASPA Handbook of Personnel and Industrial Relations*, op. cit., pp. 152–154.

[16] Harold Koontz, *Management: A Book of Readings*, Third Edition (New York: McGraw-Hill, 1972), p. 336.

[17] "How Jewel Resets Its Crown," *Business Week* (October 27, 1980) pp. 178–183.

[18] See Robert Coulson, "Questions You Hope You'll Never Have to Ask," *Wall Street Journal* (January 25, 1982), p. 18.

[19] See Ronald Alsop, "Some Basic Rules for Managers to Follow When an Employee has to be Dismissed," *Wall Street Journal* (October 23, 1980), p. 25.

[20] Excerpted from Robert Townsend, *Up the Organization* (New York: Knopf, 1970), pp. 61, 63, 155, 188.

[21] This section based on pp. 34–44 of *Organizational Entry: Recruitment, Selection, and Socialization of Newcomers*, by John P. Wanous. Copyright © 1980, by permission of Addison-Wesley Publishing Company, Reading, MA.

Part 3
INTEGRATING CASES

NORTHSIDE CHILD HEALTH CARE CENTER

A few years ago comprehensive health-care facilities for children from low-income families were established by grants from the federal government. While the primary objective of the program was the provision of health care

Source: The original source for this case could not be identified. The version presented here appeared in Ross A. Weber, *Management: Basic Elements of Managing Organizations,* Revised Edition (Homewood, Ill: Richard D. Irwin, 1978), pp. 436–438.

to children, individual centers had the prerogative of adding other activities. Table P3.1 summarizes the objectives for the Northside Center at its founding. The government required that the agency supply one-third of the funds and that the center director be a board-certified pediatrician. No administrative experience was required.

The Northside Center was organized to provide a facility and extend services to an esti-

mated 5000 children in one area of the city. Figure P3.1 illustrates the organization structure. The center director, Dr. Regina Neal, is an extremely intelligent, aggressive pediatrician who is totally dedicated to improved health care for children. She sees health as including education, housing, employment of parents, day care, and the many other variables that affect the physical and mental health of children. She had been in private practice for a number of years and was actively engaged in the health rights movement.

Dr. Neal has definite opinions regarding ways in which services could be improved. She states that patient care is a team effort of pediatrician, nurse, and paraprofessional workers. For staff members who are accustomed to traditional health-care systems, she provides a stimulating environment in which to work. For example, she maintains that nurses can assume many of the responsibilities of well-child care, which comprises 80 percent of a pediatrician's workload. Costs could be reduced by hiring fewer pediatricians and adding paraprofessional workers to take on the routine managerial and technical duties.

Dr. Neal insists on treating patients two or three days a week in the pediatric care walk-in clinic. In effect, she acts as

Table P3.1 Initial Objectives of Northside Child Health Care Center

A. Objectives established by federal government:
   1. Comprehensive health care to children and youths from low-income families in major cities, to include:
      a. Promotion of health.
      b. Medical care.
      c. Case finding.
      d. Preventive health services.
      e. Diagnosis.
      f. Treatment.
      g. Correction for defects and aftercare.
      h. Dental care.
      i. Emotional care.
   2. Better methods for delivery of care.
   3. Improved quality of health services.
   4. Reduction of preventable and disabling illness.
   5. More efficient coordination of health services to children.

B. Subobjectives established by the center:
   1. To develop better procedures and mechanics for the delivery of comprehensive medical care.
   2. To coordinate existing health services for children, to bridge gaps, and to avoid duplication.
   3. To increase efficiency of the delivery of service.
   4. To reexamine concepts of pediatric care—can excellence and continuity reside in a health team, instead of in a doctor-oriented service?
   5. To determine to what extent medical-health professionals or other newly defined health workers can provide services traditionally given by the physician.

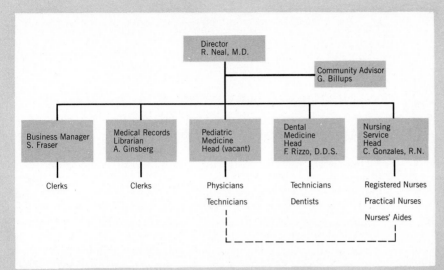

FIGURE P3.1 Organization chart of Northside Child Health Care Center before mission expansion.

center director, pediatric section head (because this position was never filled), and physician. She is a whirlwind of energy and an inspiring person. Nonetheless, some staff complain about her tendency to utilize favored personnel rather than those on duty. For example, she will bypass the duty nursing supervisor to communicate normal doctor's orders directly to the director of nursing services. Some registered nurses especially complain that Dr. Neal treats them according to the old stereotype of the nurse as doctor's handmaiden rather than as professional colleagues.

The center has been quite successful in treating children brought to the clinic. However, many staff are dissatisfied for two reasons: (1) they aren't seeing all the children they should because some aren't being brought in and (2) some illness is so family related that treatment of the child requires family treatment (for example, one child was treated several times for an infection of unknown origin; in fact, it was caused by a chronic disease af-

flicting her mother of which the center knew nothing).

Consequently, the center decided to expand its services to include adult care. Dr. Leonard Warren, an internist, recently left a lucrative suburban practice to accept a position as adult-care center. He in turn is engaging various physicians and staff technicians. A walk-in adult clinic service is to be provided (although it has not been decided yet whether or not this should be physically separate or integrated with the child-care director and co-director of the clinic). In addition, the staff feels they must do more than just wait for patients to come in; they want to get out into the community; therefore, a new section of social work and community services is being established. Social workers and psychologists from the new section, along with nurses from the nursing services section, are supposed to cooperate to locate illness and encourage treatment. More important, they hope to educate families to modify conditions and behavior that support illness.

A government community-medicine consultant suggests that the center organize family-health teams composed of a physician, a community-health nurse, a family social worker, and several paraprofessional aides. These teams could become intimately familiar with specific families and their problems. They could draw on specialized physicians, psychiatrists, and dentists when necessary. Many staff physicians don't like this proposal because they fear they will waste much precious time traveling outside the clinic center. The medical-records administrator wonders if she must maintain records for the new adult-care section and family-care activities without new clerks. The dental section director is similarly concerned. The director of nursing services is worried about whom the proposed teams would report to, how they would be controlled, and how she could supply nurses to the teams as well as the new adult-care clinic. Dr. Neal feels that the teams could simply report directly to her, so

she would be sure of cooperation from the physicians.

Questions

1. What are the organizational
    problems of the center?

2. Are there any special advan-
    tages to a matrix structure in
    this situation?

3. What structure do you pro-
    pose to meet the extended
    mission requirements? Why?

4. What are the staffing implica-
    tions of your proposed
    change in organizational
    structure?

HOVEY AND BEARD COMPANY

The Hovey and Beard Company
manufactured a variety of wood
toys including animals, pull toys,
and the like. The toys were manufactured by a transformation
process that began in the wood
room, where toys were cut,
sanded, and partially assembled.
Then the toys were dipped into
shellac and sent to the painting
room.

In the past, the painting was
done by hand, with each employee working with a given toy
until its painting was completed.
The toys were predominantly
two-colored, although a few required more than two colors.
Now, in response to increased
demand for the toys, the painting
operation was changed so that
the painters sat in a line along
an endless chain of hooks. These
hooks moved continuously in
front of the painters and passed
into a long horizontal oven. Each
painter sat in a booth designed
to carry away fumes and to back-
stop excess paint. The painters
would take a toy from a nearby
tray, position it in a jig inside the
painting cubicle, spray on the
color according to a pattern, and
then hang the toy on a passing
hook. The rate at which the

hooks moved was calculated by
the engineers so that each
painter, when fully trained, could
hang a painted toy on each hook
before it passed beyond reach.

The painters were paid on a
group bonus plan. Since the operation was new to them, they
received a learning bonus that
decreased by regular amounts
each month. The learning bonus
was scheduled to vanish in six
months, at which time it was expected that they would be on
their own—that is, able to meet
the production standard and to
earn a group bonus when they
exceeded it.

By the second month of the
training period, trouble developed. The painters learned more
slowly than had been anticipated, and it began to look as
though their production would
stabilize far below what was
planned. Many of the hooks were
going by empty. The painters
complained that the hooks
moved too fast, and that the engineer had set the rates wrong. A
few painters quit and had to be
replaced with new ones. This further aggravated the learning
problem. The team spirit that the
management had expected to
develop through the group bonus was not in evidence except
as an expression of what the engineers called "resistance." One
painter, whom the group regarded as its leader (and the
management regarded as the

ringleader), was outspoken in
taking the complaints of the
group to the supervisor. These
complaints were that the job was
messy, the hooks moved too fast,
the incentive pay was not correctly calculated, and it was too
hot working so close to the
drying oven.

A consultant was hired to
work with the supervisor. She
recommended that the painters
be brought together for a general discussion of the working
conditions. Although hesitant,
the supervisor agreed to this
plan.

The first meeting was held
immediately after the shift was
over at four o'clock in the afternoon. It was attended by all eight
painters. They voiced the same
complaints again: the hooks
went by too fast, the job was too
dirty, and the room was hot and
poorly ventilated. For some reason, it was this last item that
seemed to bother them most.
The supervisor promised to discuss the problems of ventilation
and temperature with the engineers, and a second meeting was
scheduled. In the next few days
the supervisor had several talks
with the engineers. They, along
with the plant superintendent,
felt that this was really a
trumped-up complaint, and that
the expense of corrective measures would be prohibitively
high.

The supervisor came to the

Source: Abridged and adapted from
George Strauss and Alex Bavelas,
"Group Dynamics and Intergroup Relations," in William F. Whyte (ed.),
Money and Motivation, Ch. 10. Copyright © 1955 by Harper & Row Publishers, Inc.

second meeting with some apprehensions. The painters, however, did not seem to be much put out. Instead, they had a proposal of their own to make. They felt that if several large fans were set up to circulate the air around their feet, they would be much more comfortable. After some discussion, the supervisor agreed to pursue the idea. The supervisor and the consultant discussed the idea of fans with the superintendent. Three large propellar-type fans were purchased and installed.

The painters were jubilant. For several days the fans were moved about in various positions until they were placed to the satisfaction of the group. The painters seemed completely satisfied with the results, and the relations between them and the supervisor improved visibly.

The supervisor, after this encouraging episode, decided that further meetings might also be profitable. The painters were asked if they would like to meet and discuss other aspects of the work situation. They were eager to do this. Another meeting was held, and the discussion quickly centered on the speed of the hooks. The painters maintained that the engineer had set them at an unreasonably fast speed and that they would never be able to fill enough of them to make a bonus.

The discussion reached a turning point when the group's leader explained that it wasn't that the painters couldn't work fast enough to keep up with the hooks, but that they couldn't work at that pace all day long. The supervisor explored the point. The painters were unanimous in their opinion that they could keep up with the belt for short periods if they wanted to. But they didn't want to because if they showed they could do this for short periods then they would be expected to do it all day long. The meeting ended with an unprecedented request by the painters: "Let us adjust the speed of the belt faster or slower depending on how we feel." The supervisor agreed to discuss this with the superintendent and the engineers.

The engineers reacted negatively to the suggestion. However, after several meetings it was granted that there was some latitude within which variations in the speed of the hooks would not affect the finished product. After considerable argument with the engineers, it was agreed to try out the painters' idea.

With misgivings, the supervisor had a control with a dial marked "low," "medium," and "fast" installed at the booth of the group leader. The speed of the belt could now be adjusted anywhere between the lower and upper limits that the engineers had set.

The painters were delighted and spent many lunch hours deciding how the speed of the belt should be varied from hour to hour throughout the day. Within the week the pattern had settled down to one in which the first half hour of the shift was run on a medium speed (a dial setting slightly above the point marked "medium"). The next two and a half hours were run at high speed, and the half hours before and after lunch were run at low speed. The rest of the afternoon was run at high speed with the exception of the last 45 minutes of the shift, which was run at medium.

The constant speed at which the engineers had originally set the belt was actually slightly below the "medium" mark on the control dial. The average speed at which the painters were running the belt was on the high side of the dial. Few, if any, empty hooks entered the oven, and inspection showed no increase of rejects from the paint room.

Production increased, and within three weeks (some two months before the scheduled ending of the learning bonus) the painters were operating at 30 to 50 percent above the level that had been expected under the original arrangement. Naturally, their earnings were correspondingly higher than anticipated. They were collecting their base pay, earning a considerable piece-rate bonus, and still benefiting from the learning bonus. They were earning more now than many skilled workers in other parts of the plant.

Questions

1. How would you describe the job design of the painting operation before any changes were made?

2. What aspect of the job design did the introduction of the ventilating fan change? Was the impact on job performance and satisfaction what you would have expected? Why or why not?

3. After all changes in the job design were made, which ones affected job performance and satisfaction the most? Why?

4. What staffing implications are associated with the changes in job design? Explain your answer.

PART

4

LEADING FOR PRODUCTIVITY

Chapters in This Part of the Book

NEW WICKES HEAD IS HARD-NOSED MANAGER WITH REPUTATION FOR RESCUING COMPANIES

Wal-Mart Chief's Enthusiastic Approach Infects Employees; Keeps Retailer Growing

The above headlines suggest that the chief executives of these two major companies have special qualities that should enhance the success of their companies.[1] What both executives share is a capacity for leadership—that is, a capacity to activate, energize, and ensure that the work of the organization gets done. What they apparently don't share is the personal style through which the leadership act is actually carried out. The headlines characterize the Wal-Mart chief as "enthusiastic"; the resulting picture is of a warm and people-oriented leader. The new Wickes head, by contrast, is characterized as "hard-nosed"; the resulting picture is a more impersonal leader with a strong task orientation.

Both the substance and the complexity of this part of the book are found in the two headlines. Our topic is leadership and, just as the headlines suggest, the ingredients of successful leadership may vary from one work situation to the next. As a result, we need to examine a number of alternative leadership theories, the subject of Chapter 10, as well as the processes through which leadership is carried out. These include communication, motivation, and group dynamics—the subjects of Chapters 11, 12, and 13.

We are fortunate to begin this new part of the book with some provocative thoughts expressed by Daniel Yankelovich, whose opinion polls regularly "take stock of America" on a wide range of subjects. In the statement that follows, Yankelovich discusses the work ethic as it relates to productivity in the United States and Japan. Instead of attributing productivity problems among U.S. workers to a deterioration of the work ethic, Yankelovich reports that the work ethic is as strong as ever. What we lack, he argues, are capable and sensitive leaders who can mobilize the ethic and encourage others to apply their efforts in productive and satisfying ways.

Perspective: The Work Ethic is Underemployed[2]

"Americans hold two beliefs about why the Japanese are outdoing us in autos, steel, appliances, computer chips, and even subway cars. The first is that our productivity has become stagnant. The second is that this has happened because our work ethic has deteriorated badly.

"The first belief is, alas, true. Since 1965, the country's productivity has improved at ever smaller rates. It now shows no growth at all, and may even be falling. But despite these signs and additional evidence that people are not working as hard as they once did, it is emphatically not true that our work ethic has become weaker. If by work ethic—a very slippery term—we mean endowing work with intrinsic moral worth and believing that everyone should do his or her best possible job irrespective

---

[1] The headlines are from the *Wall Street Journal* (April 20, 1981), p. 19; (March 31, 1982), p. 25.

[2] Excerpted from Daniel Yankelovich, "The Work Ethic Is Underemployed," *Psychology Today* (May 1982), pp. 5–8. Used by permission.

of financial reward, then recent survey research shows the work ethic in the United States is surprisingly sturdy, and growing sturdier.

"A 1980 Gallup study for the U.S. Chamber of Commerce shows that an overwhelming 88 percent of all working Americans feel that it is personally important to them to work hard and do their best on the job. (This should not be confused with Gallup findings that fewer Americans are enjoying their work—a separate issue.) The study concludes that a faulty work ethic is not responsible for the decline in our productivity; quite the contrary, the study identifies 'a widespread commitment among U.S. workers to improve productivity' and suggests that 'there are large reservoirs of potential upon which management can draw to improve performance and increase productivity.'

"In principle, most Americans are willing to work harder and turn out a higher-quality product; indeed, their self-esteem demands that they do so. That they are not doing it points directly to a serious flaw in management and in the reward system under which they perform their jobs. Why should workers make a greater effort if (1) they don't have to and (2) they believe that others will be the beneficiaries of such efforts? It is ironic that a political administration so finely tuned to encouraging the business community should pay such scant attention to stimulating the average American to work harder.

"As our competitive posture in traditional industries such as steel and automobiles grows ever more grim, workers and trade unions are starting to pay more attention to productivity. But in many labor circles productivity is still regarded as a code term for speedups that benefit management and threaten job security. The mismatch between the national goal of improved productivity and the inadequate system of rewards now in operation could hardly be more obvious.

"Perhaps more to the point is the Japanese experience in this country. The Japanese distinguish between the 'soft' factors of production (the dedication of the work force) and such 'hard' factors as technology, capital investment, and research and development. They recognize that the soft factors are just as important as the hard ones and that, indeed, the two are interdependent. It is this understanding that underlies the spectacular success of the Japanese not only in their homeland but also in the plants they own and manage in the United States. One Japanese strategy, for example, is to bring together both workers and managers to solve the problem of how new technology can be introduced to the advantage of both. Such participation does not just assure workers of job security; it enables them to devise with management a system that also provides job satisfaction. The Japanese success in this country is evidence that the American belief in the work ethic is not just rhetoric. Without the work ethic, the Japanese would have had to rely solely on the hard factors, by themselves not enough to spur productivity.

"Ironically, the Japanese seem to have a better grasp of how to capitalize on our work ethic than we do. In the American approach to work, the relevant institutions—business management, labor unions, government, professional economists—do not have a firm grasp of the soft factors and how they interact with the hard ones. Unwittingly, most 'experts' hold an obsolete image of the work force as a pool of 'labor' responsive solely to economic imperatives, driven by the fear of unemployment, and inspired by the promise of consumer goods—the familiar carrot-and-stick psychology that worked in the past when workers and work were different. The leaders who run our institutions do not really understand today's work force: tens of millions of well-educated Americans, proud of their achievements, jealous of their freedoms, motivated by new values, with substantial control over their own production, and ready to raise their level of effort if given the proper encouragement."

10

FUNDAMENTALS
OF LEADING

UNION RANK AND FILE TALK BITTERLY OF THEIR BOSSES

"It's dog eat dog between hourly workers and salaried employees. If management had its way, we would all be robots tomorrow. Like that," Donald Ance says, snapping his fingers to emphasize his point.[1]

Ance's view of American labor relations is simple; it is "us-against-them." Ance is a 42-year-old, blue-collar union member who works in a Milwaukee factory. Experts can expound on reindustrialization as the solution to America's business woes, but Ance's attitude points to a problem that doesn't get a lot of attention—many workers feel a great animosity toward their employers.

The workers speak angrily of the indignities of factory life. These are little things but they mean a lot. "Let's say you goofed up something pretty bad. You could be there 25 years later, and they'll remind you, 'Hey, don't goof this job up like you did back in 54.' Do you ever see them come out and say, 'You're doing a good job?' You don't hear that," says John Plazek, 58, a gruff, heavyset man who works a brake press at a Caterpillar Tractor Co. factory.

Indeed, many workers consider factory foremen to be the enemy. "The more grievances filed against a foreman [by union workers]," says James Kloss, 32, who was laid off by Allis-Chalmers Corp. last April, "the better the foreman looks in the company's eyes." Another Allis-Chalmers employee, Douglas Zahn, tells about the monthly meetings attended by a friend who was made a foreman. "At the first meeting, they said, 'What can we do to really rile these guys [workers] up?' The second meeting was the same: 'You guys [foremen] got any ideas, like can we write them up for going to the coffee machine too many times?' " Zahn says his friend quit.

Management no doubt has its own view of these stories. The real question isn't who is right or wrong, but whether this rift can somehow be bridged.

With all the differences between management and labor, it could take years to get them pulling in the same direction. The result could be to improve productivity more than any consultant armed with a clipboard could.

Although certainly on the extreme side, the thoughts expressed in the open-ing example highlight once again the challenges faced by managers in their work. A manager is a person forever in the middle—someone caught between the often conflicting demands of subordinates and superiors. Surviving and prospering in this environment demand a capability for leadership. This chap-ter introduces you to leadership through the following topics.

Leadership Concepts
Power: A Leadership Resource
Approaches to the Study of Leadership
Fiedler's Contingency Theory
House's Path-Goal Theory
The Vroom-Yetton Leader-Participation Theory
Leadership in a Managerial Perspective

Leading is one of the most talked about of the four management functions shown in Figure 10.1. Acting as a leader, it is a manager's respon-sibility to ensure that work efforts of other per-sons are directed toward the accomplishment of organizational objectives. **Leading** is just that. It is the process of directing human-resource efforts toward organizational objectives. To succeed as a leader, therefore, a manager requires knowl-edge and skills in all aspects of interpersonal re-lations, including communication, motivation, and group dynamics.

This chapter focuses on the essence of **lead-ership** as the manager's use of power to influence the behavior of other persons in the work setting. **Power,** in turn, is the ability to get someone else to do something you want done; said differently, it is the ability to make things happen the way you want. As leaders, managers should be good at using power in ways that influence others to work hard and apply their efforts toward the accomplishment of organizational objectives.

LEADERSHIP CONCEPTS

Leading and being a manager are not one and the same thing. To be a manager means to act effectively in the comprehensive sense of plan-ning, organizing, leading, and controlling. Lead-ership success is a necessary but not sufficient condition for managerial success. A good man-ager is always a good leader, but a good leader

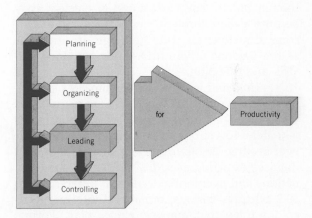

FIGURE 10.1 Leading as a management function.

is not necessarily a good manager. Success in the latter respect requires that the capacity to lead be complemented by the capacity to plan, organize, and control.

Our job in this chapter is to acquaint you with the full range of leadership concepts and theories. This will help you include the capacity to lead within your repertoire of essential man-agement capabilities. We'll begin by looking at the concepts of formal and informal leadership.

Formal and Informal Leadership

Formal leadership occurs when a manager leads through the exercise of formal authority. This right to command or to act derives from the manager's official position within the organization's hierarchy of authority. Anyone appointed to the job of "manager" has the opportunity to exercise formal leadership in relationships with subordinates. Some people, however, do a much better job than others at taking advantage of this opportunity. They are more influential in ensuring that subordinates' work efforts are productive over time. This chapter offers a knowledge base that will help you to perform well in any formal leadership capacity.

Informal leadership arises when a person without formal authority proves influential in directing the behavior of other persons. We know informal leaders best as the people who spontaneously take charge in a group situation. Although not formally appointed or elected, they become leaders through their actions and/or personal attractiveness. They "emerge" in situations as the persons others turn to for guidance, advice, and direction.

Formal and informal leadership coexist in almost every work situation. There are many times when managers have to work with subordinates who defer to a strong informal leader within their peer groups. At other times, managers may find themselves acting as formal leaders in some situations and as informal leaders in others. Figure 10.2 portrays various formal and informal leadership roles that managers may play. Formal leadership follows the chain of command and flows downward in the hierarchy of authority from superior to subordinate. Informal leadership, by contrast, emerges outside of the chain of command. Successful managers are capable of exercising informal leadership in a wide variety of relations with persons inside and outside the organization. This also includes, as shown in Figure 10.2, the capacity to influence one's superior. Remember, formal leadership is based on formal authority, while informal leadership is not.

Illustrative Case:
The Leadership Dilemma[2]

Speaking of leadership capabilities, let's get down to the real world. The following short case presents a typical leadership dilemma. Read the case and think about what you would have done.

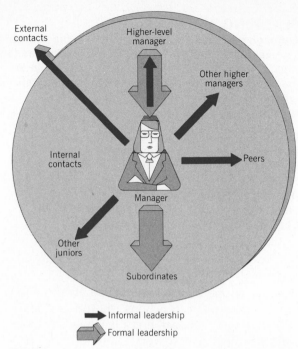

FIGURE 10.2 A manager's formal and informal leadership roles.

Even better, think about what you *will* do when faced with similar problems in the future!

The Manager's View of the Situation Here's one side of the problem. The manager has received a rush assignment late on Friday afternoon. It requires that certain difficult engineering drawings be completed as soon as possible so that the model shop can begin construction of a new device that may impress a valued customer. The only drafter she feels can do this complex task—and do it so there will be no likelihood of problems—is Phil Firenzi, her most senior, experienced employee. She knows Firenzi is somewhat of a prima donna, smug in his competence, independent, and outspoken. The job will require at least 5 hours of work, and, since it's almost 3 P.M., that means 3 hours of overtime. (Overtime is not compulsory, and Friday overtime is especially unappealing.)

The Subordinate's View of the Situation Here's the other side of the problem. If Firenzi is approached by the supervisor with a request for overtime, he will be outraged. Instead of feeling rewarded to be chosen the most able and most senior employee, he senses it as a "damn curse." He sees this "crazy" company and "inefficient" middle management as so poor at planning that they are always late, always coming up with emergencies and crises that "can't wait." The last thing he wants is more overtime just before a weekend—and particularly this weekend. He has promised his wife he would be home early to go to an important family function (his daughter's wedding rehearsal). He's sick and tired of being asked, "for the good of the company," to sacrifice his personal life for job requirements—and unnecessary ones at that. The company just isn't managed sensibly. As further evidence of management ineptitude, he notes that his boss has never taken the time or had the foresight to train one of her more junior colleagues to handle the complex drawings. The company is either too cheap to invest in training or too foolish.

The Manager's Possible Responses Basically, the manager wants Firenzi to do something that is, in part at least, above and beyond the explicit duties of the job. Further complicating the situation, although she may not realize this, is the fact that the employee is already in a negative frame of mind. As a result, we can almost predict that the manager will flatly make the request, get refused, and then become upset by the threat posed to her managerial position. She probably will ask herself, "What will *my* boss say if I don't get this job out after having been told how critical it is?" In response, she may try to pressure Firenzi to comply by resorting to one of the following strategies.

Threats She could say: "Remember how much I've done for you—extra time off when you wanted it, and high merit increases. Is this how you pay me back? How much do you think I'll feel like asking for another raise or giving you your way when *you* want something?"

Rewards She could say: "I know this is rough on you, but do a good job and I'll use this when I talk with the superintendent to get you a much bigger raise than you expected at salary-review time," and/or, "I'll try to get you better vacation time, new office space, double time instead of time-and-a-half, or one of a dozen other things if you do what I ask."

Dominance Detecting the unwillingness of her subordinate, the manager may launch into a long speech about the importance of the drafting assignment: "It will show your skill—only you are

Formal leadership occurs when a manager leads through the exercise of formal authority.

good enough to do it and that's why I turn to you," she might say. Or, "It's for the good of the company; it could mean an important new order, lots of new jobs, and more job security for everyone."

The Problems Created   A number of obvious problems are created by this situation, and by the manager's various responses. First, Firenzi is almost certain to be frustrated. He is placed in a position where he is torn between what he wants to do and feels is his "right" and the pressures of the boss. If he gives in, there will be resentment; if he doesn't, the boss-subordinate relationship has been injured. Even if he changes his mind, there is bound to be anger and a lingering feeling that the all-powerful boss has manipulated the weak subordinate.

Second, the boss spent a lot of time seeking to influence Firenzi based on what she *assumed* his needs to be—money, admiration, pride, a good relationship with supervision. She never uncovered what Firenzi *really* may have needed—for example, assurance that this repeating problem would be solved by training someone else to do the work in the future.

Third, Firenzi received no message suggesting that the boss cared about him as a person. He appeared only to be an instrument through which she could accomplish her goal of looking good to the superintendent.

The tragedy in all this is that the manager in this case would not only be failing as a formal leader, she probably would also end up distrusting her "unresponsive," "too-independent" subordinate as a result. From her point of view, the blame for missing the order would be his, not hers. Obviously, many things are at issue here. Trust, commitment, ego, and responsibility are but a few. Also at issue is *power*, something that has been called "America's last dirty word."[3] It is time to examine and study power for its leadership implications.

POWER: A LEADERSHIP RESOURCE

Power is an essential leadership resource. Managers use power to achieve the interpersonal influence through which leadership is ultimately exercised. Power is a force or capability that, when successfully activated, makes things happen. For many people, though, the word power carries a negative connotation that includes undertones of manipulation or political action. Isn't this your reaction to the impression conveyed in the following headline?[4]

> William Small Quits
> as NBC News Chief
> Amid Power Struggle

There is another side to the story. Most people, for example, like to work for someone who has "clout." In practice this term identifies someone who is successful at getting things done, and able to get support for the people and work unit he or she represents. "Clout" in this sense is "power." A manager with clout gets such things as[5]

- Good jobs for talented subordinates.
- Approvals for expenditures beyond budget.
- Above-average salary increases for subordinates.
- Items on the agenda at higher-level meetings.
- Preferred access to top decision makers in the organization.
- Early information about decisions and policy shifts in the organization.

Thus power is a very "good" thing when used properly by the manager. Recent research even goes so far as to suggest that a need for power is essential for executive success.[6] But this need for power is defined not as a need to control for the sense of personal satisfaction, as suggested in the Blondie cartoon, but as a desire to influence and control others for the good of the organization as a whole! This latter perspective is the essence of power as an essential leadership resource.

With power viewed in a positive way, the stage is set for you to learn more about leadership. To begin, we should answer three questions regarding how power becomes a leadership resource of managers.

1. What sources of power are available to the manager?

© 1979 King Features Syndicate.

2. What are the limits to a manager's power?
3. What managerial guidelines exist for acquiring and using power?

Sources of Power[7]

Figure 10.3 divides the sources of power into those based in the position and those based in the person of the manager. Effective managers acquire and use power from both sources to achieve influence over others in the work setting.

Position Power

Three bases of power relate to a manager's official position in a hierarchy of authority—reward, coercive, and legitimate power. They are defined as follows.

Reward power The capability to offer something of value, a positive outcome, as a means of controlling other people. Examples of such rewards include raises, bonuses, promotions, special assignments, and verbal or written compliments. To mobilize reward power, a manager says, in effect, "If you do what I ask, I'll give you a reward."

Coercive power The capability to punish or withhold positive outcomes as a means of controlling other people. A manager may attempt to coerce someone by threatening them with verbal reprimands, pay penalties, and even termination. To mobilize coercive power, a manager says, in effect, "If you don't do what I want, I'll punish you."

Legitimate power The capability to control other people by virtue of the rights of office. Legitimate power is formal authority, the right to command and to act in the position of managerial responsibility. To mobilize legitimate power, a manager says, in effect, "I am the boss and therefore you must do as I ask."

Any person appointed to a managerial position in an organization theoretically has legitimacy and access to both rewards and punishments. How well this position power is used, however, will vary from one person to the next. Leadership success will vary as well.

FIGURE 10.3 Power sources.

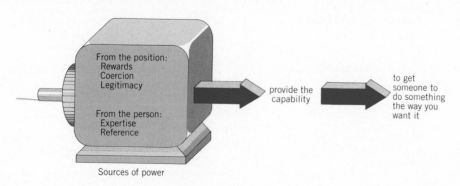

Personal Power

Another source of power is the person and what he or she brings to the situation in terms of unique personal attributes. Two bases of personal power are expertise and reference.

Expert power The capability to control other people because of specialized knowledge. Expertise derives from the possession of technical know-how or information pertinent to the issue at hand, which others do not have.

Reference power The capability to control other people because of their desires to identify personally and positively with the power source. Reference is a power derived from charisma or interpersonal attractiveness.

A Power Inventory

Table 10.1 summarizes the basic characteristics of these five sources of position and personal power. To maximize power in any leadership situation, a manager should take full advantage of power available in the position—that is, power based on legitimacy and access to rewards and punishments, as well as personal power based on expertise and reference. A basic equation serves as a reminder of these two components of managerial power.

$$\frac{\text{Managerial}}{\text{power}} = \frac{\text{position}}{\text{power}} + \frac{\text{personal}}{\text{power}}$$

The Limits to Power

Power is the potential to control the behavior of other people. But we all know that persons who have access to position and/or personal power don't always get their way. Almost every manager from the president of the United States to the head teller at your local bank or the instructor in your classroom has, at one time or another, given an order that wasn't obeyed. The question is, "Why?"

The Acceptance Theory of Power

Figure 10.4 shows that one of two things can happen when a manager issues a directive or makes a request of someone else. The person either responds as desired or doesn't respond at all. When a manager issues the directive or makes the request, he or she is attempting to exercise power. The power is only realized when the other person responds as desired—that is, when he or she "accepts" the directive or request.

This logic constitutes the acceptance theory of power as developed by Chester Barnard, an important contributor in the evolution of management thought whose ideas were introduced in Chapter 2.[8] Barnard argues that the ultimate control of power in any situation rests with the person who is the object of a manager's influence

Table 10.1 Characteristics of Various Power Sources

Power Source	How Accessed by Managers	Practical Considerations
Rewards	Control over rewards	Continued reward necessary to maintain influence; temporary effects
Coercion	Control over punishments	Continued punishment or threat of punishment necessary to maintain influence; temporary effects
Legitimacy	Position of formal authority	Limited by extent of others' respect for the position
Reference	Possession of appealing personal traits	Dependent on interpersonal attractiveness; more lasting effects
Expertise	Possession of knowledge, control over useful information	Limited by extent to which expertise is real or credible; more lasting effects

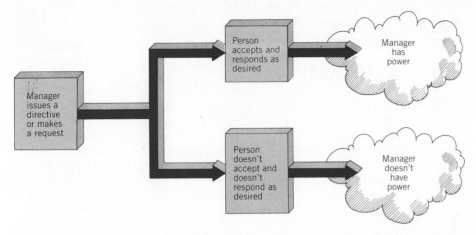

FIGURE 10.4 The acceptance view of power.

attempt. If the person complies, the manager's power is confirmed; if not, the manager's power is denied. Acceptance therefore establishes the limits to power.

Barnard developed the acceptance theory of power based on his many years of experience as an executive. This experience also helped him identify four conditions that determine whether or not acceptance will occur. A manager's orders are most likely to be accepted when,

- The subordinate truly understands the directive or request.

- The subordinate feels capable of carrying out the directive or request.

- The subordinate believes the directive or request to be in the best interests of the organization.

- The subordinate believes the directive or request to be consistent with personal values.

The Zone of Indifference

Power in organizations is also limited to the range of directives and requests that people consider appropriate to their basic employment or psychological contracts with the organization. This range defines a **zone of indifference.** Managerial directives and requests falling within this zone tend to be accepted and followed automatically; those falling outside the zone are more likely to be rejected. Take Firenzi, the drafter in the case mentioned earlier in this chapter. He probably considered the manager's request to

work special overtime as falling outside his zone of indifference.

Figure 10.5 diagrams the zone of indifference as it relates to various requests made of a secretary. Note that the action requests lying outside the zone of indifference require extraordinary initiatives by the supervisor, probably ones based on personal power. Inside the zone, position power sources are normally sufficient to achieve compliance. As this example shows, there is much to be gained when a manager recognizes the limits to position power and is able to access supplementary personal power when the need arises.

Disobedience: Saying "No" to Higher Authority

This discussion of the acceptance theory of power and the zone of indifference takes the viewpoint of a manager striving to influence someone else. As employees and subordinates in their own rights, however, managers will also be on the receiving end of influence attempts from their supervisors and other personnel. *Newsline 10.1* describes how executives of Phillips Petroleum describe life within the firm. If you read the newsline carefully, you'll detect an undercurrent of strain between company expectations and personal ethics. Key words in the discourse include *loyalty, cooperation,* and *conformity,* among others. The implication is that success in the company is based on a willingness to do as one is asked and on whatever terms.

NEWSLINE 10.1

"THE CORPORATION"

CBS News journeyed to the Bartlesville, Oklahoma, headquarters of the Phillips Petroleum Corporation, with a proposal guaranteed to leave even the most adventurous public-relations man breathless. CBS wanted to "look at the Phillips Corporation from the viewpoint of the executive suite . . . to explore the so-called corporate mind . . . what loyalties are demanded?—and where is the dividing line between loyalty to one's own self and loyalty to corporate objectives?"

"The Corporation," the television documentary that resulted; is a journalistic foray, made timely by the course of events, into the age-old discipline of ethics. In broad terms, it suggests that as corporations grow larger, more aggressive, and encompass more functions in our society, their demands on employees also grow. Corporations can become the focal point of life for many people, if they have not done so already. Employee loyalty may be transformed into an unhealthy, even dangerous, blind allegiance.

Phillips officials concede they run a disciplined business. Dissent is permitted, but once corporate policy is established it must be adhered to. Loyalty is required, greater loyalty rewarded. Attitudes are screened carefully before an employee is hired. Some clerks, once on the payroll, even have their performance monitored by computers. Everything is geared toward making the employee part of the overall corporate profit-making effort. "The worst thing that can happen," says company president William Martin, "is to have an employee that doesn't fit." A corporation has to have regimentation in order to run.

Phillips personnel say forthrightly that they like the life they lead for its security and monetary compensation. Ethics isn't a problem. "It's a simple trade-off," says employee Henry Fox, "If you want them to feed, clothe, and maintain you and keep you with all the sustenance of life that you want, you simply have to cooperate with them and conform with their rules and conform with their politics."

Source: Excerpted from Michael J. Connor, "CBS Brings in a Lucky Gusher," *Wall Street Journal* (December 6, 1973), p. 14. Reprinted by permission of the *Wall Street Journal.* Copyright © 1973 Dow Jones & Company, Inc. All rights reserved.

History, however, is replete with examples of loyal subordinates who failed to say "no" and were then led to commit socially undesirable acts. The "Watergate" crimes are but one example of questionable acts committed by people who felt they were "just following orders." Someday you may face the situation of being asked to do something outside your zone of indifference, perhaps in violation of personal ethics and/or even the law. Can you . . . will you . . . when will you . . . say "no"?

Newsline 10.2 conveys the great difficulty and the potential cost of saying "no" to a higher authority in the work setting. You can't be expected to know when, how, or even why you may act similarly by refusing to follow orders. But we would be sorely remiss in failing to recognize this flip side of the power coin. There will probably be times when you can and should say "no." Think about it. We'll have more to say on this in a related discussion of managerial ethics and social responsibility in Chapter 20.

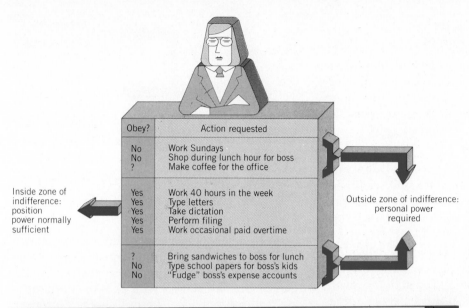

Obey?	Action requested
No No ?	Work Sundays Shop during lunch hour for boss Make coffee for the office
Yes Yes Yes Yes Yes	Work 40 hours in the week Type letters Take dictation Perform filing Work occasional paid overtime
? No No	Bring sandwiches to boss for lunch Type school papers for boss's kids "Fudge" boss's expense accounts

Inside zone of indifference: position power normally sufficient

Outside zone of indifference: personal power required

FIGURE 10.5 A secretary's zone of indifference. *Source:* Slightly adapted from John R. Schermerhorn, Jr., James G. Hunt and Richard N. Osborn, *Managing Organizational Behavior* (New York: Wiley & Sons, 1982), p. 481. Used by permission.

NEWSLINE 10.2

BOWEN SUPERINTENDENT RESIGNS

The superintendent of the A. L. Bowen Developmental Center resigned Monday, saying he could not "in good conscience" go along with orders to support closing the center near Harrisburg. Wayne Kottmeyer resigned from the $38,000-a-year job effective immediately.

But the man Kottmeyer says threatened to fire him, regional administrator Ron Bittle, denied ordering Kottmeyer to support the closing or lose his job.

Kottmeyer, 38, says he has "no plans at all" for future employment. The decision, Kottmeyer said, "was one of the hardest things I've ever done in all my life." Emotion choking his voice at times, Kottmeyer said he decided to end a 17-year career with Bowen Monday afternoon following a meeting in Anna with Bittle, regional administrator for the Illinois Department of Mental Health and Developmental Disabilities.

He said Bittle told him he could keep his job if he publicly supported Gov. James Thompson's decision to close Bowen at a legislative mental health task force hearing scheduled for this afternoon in Harrisburg.

Bittle said today he did ask Kottmeyer to "support the game plan," but he denied he threatened Kottmeyer would lose his job if he didn't. Kottmeyer's role as a department executive "was to assist us in carrying out our obligations," not to question the action, Bittle said.

Kottmeyer said Bittle told him he would be kept on staff if he would publicly support closing Bowen. Kottmeyer decided to resign, he said, because "I don't know any other way to show my displeasure for this thing. The staff worked so hard out here. It's not fair to the children. They're not going to get the education they're getting here anywhere else." "I won't tolerate it any longer," he said. "It's enough. It's all got to stop somewhere."

Source: Excerpted from Cathy A. Monroe and Evan M. Davis, "Bowen Superintendent Resigns," *Southern Illinoisan* (February 23, 1982), p. 1. Used by permission.

Managerial Guidelines for Acquiring and Using Power

Managers need power to succeed in both their formal and informal leadership roles. Leadership, in turn, depends on an ability to acquire and use power from both position and personal sources. Things to keep in mind include[9]

1. *Don't deny your formal authority.* Good managers use their position power well. They act as the "boss," but with discretion and sensitivity for the feelings of others. Rewards, punishments, and legitimacy are not guaranteed to work, but they are necessary and important power resources based in the manager's formal authority.

2. *Don't be afraid to create a sense of obligation.* Some managers are highly skilled at doing favors that cost very little but that other people appreciate a lot. The manager's power expands as a result.

3. *Create feelings of dependence.* The more people perceive themselves as dependent on the manager, the more inclined they will be to cooperate with his or her wishes. The best way to maintain dependency is to do a good job of finding and acquiring the resources other persons need.

4. *Build and believe in expertise.* Managers gain power by building reputations for technical expertise. Concrete and visible achievements in areas of task and/or organizational relevance are the foundations on which such reputations are established.

5. *Allow others the opportunity to identify with you as a person.* When others know and respect a manager as a person, they tend to behave and act consistent with the manager's desires. This requires regular interpersonal contact and good interpersonal skills to create the sense of positive identification.

APPROACHES TO THE STUDY OF LEADERSHIP

For centuries people have recognized that some persons serve well as leaders, while others do not. The inevitable question is "Why?" A correct answer to this question could greatly assist man-

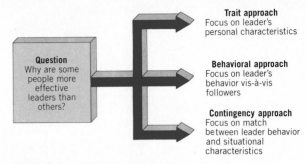

FIGURE 10.6 Three approaches to the study of leadership.

agers in developing personal leadership capabilities to their maximum potential—and would help ensure that all supervisory positions in organizations are staffed with people of appropriate leadership skills. These desirable outcomes, in fact, nicely state the ultimate goal of all leadership theories and research.

Management theory includes the three major approaches to the study of leadership presented in Figure 10.6—the trait, behavioral, and contingency approaches. Each takes a slightly different focus in an attempt to understand and predict leadership success. In general, leadership theories have become more sophisticated as attention shifted over time from leader traits to leader behaviors to situational contingencies.

The Search for Leadership Traits

The earliest research on leadership focused on personal traits or characteristics of the leader. The trait approach involves the following assumption: a leader's personal characteristics determine leadership success.

Sarge in the Beetle Bailey cartoon is using a trait approach to leadership. He seems to consider only one trait of any importance—a person's height! Actual trait research has studied height along with other physical characteristics (e.g., age or appearance), personality factors (e.g., tendencies toward dominance or cooperation), and intelligence as potential indicators of leadership success. The goal of trait research was to find a set of personal characteristics that separate effective and ineffective leaders. Given such a list, it would then be easy to select for leader-

© 1975 King Features Syndicate.

ship positions only those people whose characteristics matched the profile and who would therefore surely succeed.

Overall, researchers have been unable to isolate a definitive profile of leadership traits. The best that can be said now was first said in 1948 by the late Ralph Stogdill, a famous leadership researcher.[10]

> These findings are not surprising. It is primarily by virtue of participating in group activities and demonstrating the capacity for expediting the work of the group that a person becomes endowed with leadership status. . . . A person does not become a leader by virtue of the possession of some combination of traits, but the pattern of personal characteristics of the leader must bear some relevant relationship to the characteristics, activities, and goals of the followers.

Keeping Stogdill's words of caution in mind, it is useful to reflect on findings from one of the more recent and respected trait studies. It concluded that qualities important to effective leadership are[11]

1. *Supervisory ability* Ability to perform the basic functions of management, including planning, organizing, leading, and controlling the work of others.
2. *Need for occupational achievement* Desire for responsibility and success.
3. *Intelligence* Creative and verbal abilities, including judgment, reasoning, and thinking capacities.
4. *Decisiveness* Ability to make decisions and solve problems.

5. *Self-assurance* Feeling of personal competency in coping with problems.

The trait approach has given way to newer theories that take a broader perspective on leadership. More recent behavioral and contingency approaches are less concerned with who the leader is as a person. They are more concerned with how the leader acts and how well those actions fit the needs of the situation.

Focus on Leader Behaviors

The inability of researchers to isolate a set of personal traits uniquely characteristic of successful leaders led to a subsequent focus on actual leader behaviors. This leadership approach emphasizes the assumption: a leader's behavior vis-à-vis followers determines leadership success.

Central to leader-behavior research is the notion of **leadership style,** a term used to describe a recurring pattern of behaviors exhibited by a leader. Although all leadership involves the use of power to exert influence over others, leaders vary in the "style" they use to accomplish this result. The various components of leader-behavior research attempt to both identify various leadership styles and determine which style works best.

Basic Leadership Styles

Underlying most leader-behavior research is a focus on the degree to which a leader's behavior vis-à-vis followers evidences (1) concern for the task to be accomplished and/or (2) concern for the people doing the work. The terminology used by researchers to describe these two dimensions of leader behavior varies. Concern for task is sometimes addressed under the labels of initiating structure, job-centeredness, and task orientation; concern for people is also referred to as consideration, employee-centeredness, and relationship orientation. Regardless of the terminology used to label each of these basic orientations,

1. *A leader high in concern for task emphasizes behaviors that:*

- Plan and define work to be done.
- Assign task responsibilities.
- Set clear work standards.
- Urge task completion and monitor results.

2. *A leader high in concern for people emphasizes behaviors that convey:*

- Warmth and social rapport with subordinates.
- Respect for the feelings of others.
- Sensitivity to others' needs.
- Mutual trust.

In practice, leaders emphasize concerns for task and people in any of the combinations shown in Figure 10.7. Note the labels used to identify the leadership style resulting from each combination. Some may be common to your everyday vocabulary. You may, for example, describe managers or leaders with whom you come into contact as "autocratic" or "democratic" in style. We can give these styles more specific descriptions.

Directive or autocratic leadership A person showing a high concern for the task and low concern for people. A manager with this style would make most decisions for the work unit, issue orders, and expect them to be carried out.

Supportive or human-relations leadership A person showing a high concern for people and low concern for task. A manager with this style would focus on warm, interpersonal relationships, avoid conflict, and seek harmony in decision making.

Participative or democratic leadership A person showing a high concern for both people and

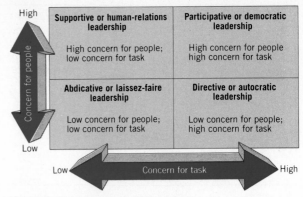

FIGURE 10.7 Four leadership styles.

task. A manager with this style would share decisions with the group, encourage participation, and support the task efforts of others.

Abdicative or laissez-faire leadership A person showing a low concern for both people and task. A manager with this style would turn most decisions over to the group and show little interest in the work process or its results.

Remember, these labels are used to describe the styles through which people attempt to exercise leadership in work situations. Behind each style are actions directed toward tasks and/or people. These actions give the styles meaning in the eyes of persons on the receiving end. Consider the following thoughts expressed by a corporate vice-president about the autocratic style of his boss and what it meant to him.[12]

> "I'm feeling like hell, that's why I look like hell! [My CEO] had me in this morning, and he ranted and raved and stomped around, and banged his desk, and called me a stupid son-of-a-bitch, and threatened to reduce my bonus, and told me the investment he had made in my project was worthless and . . . he said I belonged as a *schoolteacher* someplace. *God!* I'll be glad to get the hell out of here [referring to his upcoming retirement] and once I do I hope I never see that madman again."

Research on Leadership Behaviors

Research into leadership behaviors generally sought to determine which style was best. This was an important new initiative for management theory. If one best style could be identified, it would be possible to train people to adopt appropriate behaviors and achieve leadership success.

Beginning in the 1940s, the work of scholars at Ohio State University and the University of Michigan was especially important in examining these provocative research directions.[13] The results of their efforts at first suggested that subordinates of more people-centered leaders would be more productive and satisfied than those working for more task-oriented leaders. Successful leadership was associated with a supportive or human-relations style of behavior. Later results, however, suggested that truly effective leaders combined both task and people orientations into a more participative or democratic leadership style. This finding had great popular support. After all, it seems to make sense that good leaders are both task oriented and considerate in their relationships with other persons. It is also reassuring to think that people can be trained to adopt this style of behavior and thereby ensure themselves leadership success.

One of the more popular leadership models emerging from this latter perspective is the managerial grid concept described by Robert Blake and Jane Mouton.[14] They developed a capability to measure a person's concern for people and task and plotted the results on the managerial grid shown in Figure 10.8. Once it is determined where you, for example, would fall on the grid, an appropriate training program can be designed to help shift your leadership style in the preferred direction of high concern for task and high concern for people. In Blake and Mouton's terminology, this "9–9" leader is a person whose behavior is that of a team manager—one who is able to integrate task and people concerns to the benefit of the organization and its members.

Blake and Mouton's managerial grid is an intuitively appealing summary of the directions reflected in leader-behavior research. Unfortunately, it is now recognized that there is no consistent relationship between participative or democratic leadership and leadership success. The best that can be said is that these styles tend to result in high follower satisfaction. Productivity, however, is a more complex factor that depends on things other than leadership style alone. Simply put, the style observed to work well in some circumstances doesn't always work well in

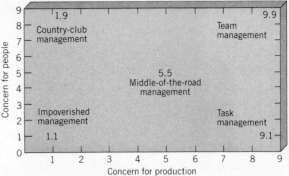

FIGURE 10.8 The managerial grid. *Source:* Robert R. Blake and Jane Srygley Mouton, "The Developing Revolution in Management Practices," *Journal of the American Society of Training Directors*, Vol. 16, No. 7 (1962), pp. 29-52. Reproduced with permission.

others. Indeed, most leadership theorists now recognize that the critical question is no longer "which is the *best* style?" but really "when and under what circumstances is a given style preferable to the others?" This question underlies an approach to leadership that emphasizes situational differences or contingencies.

Recognition of Leadership Contingencies

Listed here are a series of statements made by managers.[15] What do they have in common?

- "I put most problems into my group's hands and leave it to them to carry the ball from there. I serve merely as a catalyst, mirroring back the people's thoughts and feelings so that they can better understand them."

- "It's foolish to make decisions oneself on matters that affect people. I always talk things over with my subordinates, but I make it clear to them that I'm the one who has to have the final say."

- "Once I have decided on a course of action, I do my best to sell my ideas to my employees."

- "I'm being paid to lead. If I let a lot of other people make the decisions I should be making, then I'm not worth my salt."

- "I believe in getting things done. I can't waste time calling meetings. Someone has to call the shots around here, and I think it should be me."

The answer to the question is "success." Each of these behaviors proved effective in its situation. This is the major point underlying the contingency leadership theories we will now investigate—Fiedler's contingency theory, House's path-goal theory, and the Vroom and Yetton leader-participation theory.

Contingency theories recognize that there is no one best way to lead. What works well in one situation will not necessarily work well in another. The basic contingency assumption is that the match of leadership style and situation determines leadership success.

To clarify this notion, Figure 10.9 presents a range of leader behaviors managers may use for making decisions. At one extreme, boss-centered leadership prevails and decisions are made by the manager alone; at the other extreme, subordinate-centered leadership exists and subordinates participate in decision making. These extremes, and the approaches to decision making that lie between them, can each be successful if used in the right way and in the right situations. This is the essence of the contingency approach to leadership. Instead of searching for the one best way to behave in all situations (as the leader-

behavior researchers have done), contingency researchers try to determine when a particular behavior is the most appropriate way to achieve leadership effectiveness. They seek this knowledge by examining the proper match between situational needs or demands and the leader's action capabilities.

FIEDLER'S CONTINGENCY THEORY[16]

The first of the contingency theories was developed by Fred Fiedler in response to what he considered basic deficiencies in the leader-behavior approach. His theory is that successful leadership depends on a good match between the style of the leader and the demands of the situation. Specifically, a leader's basic task or relationship orientation should be consistent with situational demands in terms of the amount of control offered the leader. **Situational control** is defined as the extent to which a leader can determine what a group is going to do and what the outcomes of its actions and decisions are going to be. In situations of high control, leaders can predict with a high degree of certainty what will happen when they want something done; in situations of low control, uncertainty exists.

FIGURE 10.9 A continuum of leader behavior in decision making. *Source:* Reprinted by permission of the Harvard Business Review. Excerpt from "How to Choose a Leadership Pattern," by Robert Tannenbaum and Warren H. Schmidt, May–June 1973, p. 166. Copyright © 1973 by the President and Fellow of Harvard College, all rights reserved.

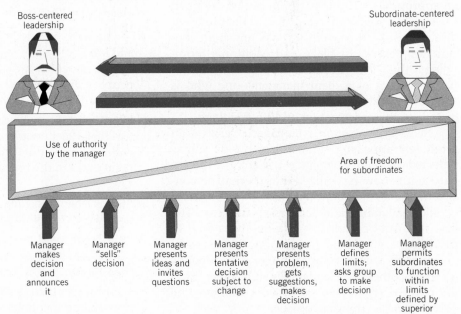

The essence of Fiedler's extensive research can be summarized in two propositions.

Proposition No. 1 A task-oriented leader will be most successful in situations of either high or low control.

Proposition No. 2 A relationship-oriented leader will be most successful in situations of moderate control.

You can readily see the contingency logic now being pursued. Neither the task-oriented nor relationship-oriented leadership style is predicted most effective all of the time. Instead, each style is effective when used in the right situation. Fiedler's challenge to the manager or aspiring leader is threefold: (1) to understand one's predominant leadership style, (2) to diagnose situations in terms of the amount of control offered the leader, and (3) to achieve a good match between style and situation.

Understanding Leadership Styles

Before reading on, complete the questionnaire presented in Table 10.2. This Least-Preferred Co-worker Scale, or the LPC scale, is used by Fiedler to determine a person's leadership style. Score the instrument as follows. Write the numbers you checked for each adjective pair in the space to the right of the page. Add these up to get a total LPC score.

If your LPC score is 64 or higher, you are a *high LPC leader* who tends to view even your least-preferred co-worker in relatively favorable

terms. Fiedler equates this tendency to a *relationship-oriented leadership style*. A score of 57 or lower depicts a *low LPC leader* who views the least-preferred co-worker in less favorable terms. This equates to a *task-oriented leadership style*. If you scored in the 58–63 range, Fiedler leaves it to your best judgment as to which direction your leadership style is weighted.

Diagnosing Leadership Situations

The next step in applying Fiedler's leadership theory is to diagnose the amount of control a situation allows the leader. Three situational variables are important in this regard: (1) **leader-member relations** (good or poor)—the degree to which the group supports the leader; (2) **task structure** (high or low)—the extent to which task goals, procedures, and guidelines are clearly spelled out; and (3) **position power** (strong or weak)—the degree to which the position gives the leader power to reward and punish subordinates.

Figure 10.10 shows that any given leadership situation can be diagnosed as falling into one of eight combinations of these variables. The figure also clarifies the best match of leadership style for situations of each combination. Let's further clarify by example the diagnosis of leadership situations.

Assume you are the supervisor of a group of bank tellers. Your subordinates seem highly supportive. The teller's job is well defined in respect to what tasks need to be done when and how. You have the authority to evaluate the tell-

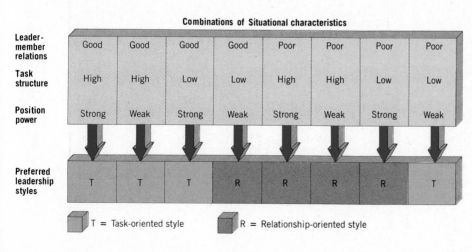

Combinations of Situational characteristics

Leader-member relations	Good	Good	Good	Good	Poor	Poor	Poor	Poor
Task structure	High	High	Low	Low	High	High	Low	Low
Position power	Strong	Weak	Strong	Weak	Strong	Weak	Strong	Weak
Preferred leadership styles	T	T	T	R	R	R	R	T

T = Task-oriented style   R = Relationship-oriented style

FIGURE 10.10 Predictions from fiedler's contingency theory of leadership. *Source:* John R. Schermerhorn, Jr., James G. Hunt and Richard N. Osborn, *Managing Organizational Behavior* (New York: John Wiley & Sons, 1982), p. 524. Used by permission.

Table 10.2 Least-Preferred Co-worker Scale

Throughout your life you will have worked in many groups with a wide variety of different people—on your job, in social groups, in church organizations, in volunteer groups, on athletic teams, and in many other situations. Some of your co-workers may have been very easy to work with in attaining the group's goals, while others were less so.

Think of all the people with whom you have ever worked, and then think of the person with whom you could work *least well*. He or she may be someone with whom you work now or with whom you have worked in the past. This does not have to be the person you liked least well, but should be the person with whom you had the most difficulty getting a job done, the *one* individual with whom you could work *least well*.

Describe this person on the scale by placing an X in the appropriate space.

Look at the words at both ends of the line before you mark your X. *There are no right or wrong answers.* Work rapidly; your first answer is likely to be the best. Do not omit any items, and mark each item only once.

Now describe the person with whom you can work least well.

			Scoring
Pleasant	8 7 6 5 4 3 2 1	Unpleasant	____
Friendly	8 7 6 5 4 3 2 1	Unfriendly	____
Rejecting	1 2 3 4 5 6 7 8	Accepting	____
Tense	1 2 3 4 5 6 7 8	Relaxed	____
Distant	1 2 3 4 5 6 7 8	Close	____
Cold	1 2 3 4 5 6 7 8	Warm	____
Supportive	8 7 6 5 4 3 2 1	Hostile	____
Boring	1 2 3 4 5 6 7 8	Interesting	____
Quarrelsome	1 2 3 4 5 6 7 8	Harmonious	____
Gloomy	1 2 3 4 5 6 7 8	Cheerful	____
Open	8 7 6 5 4 3 2 1	Guarded	____
Backbiting	1 2 3 4 5 6 7 8	Loyal	____
Untrustworthy	1 2 3 4 5 6 7 8	Trustworthy	____
Considerate	8 7 6 5 4 3 2 1	Inconsiderate	____
Nasty	1 2 3 4 5 6 7 8	Nice	____
Agreeable	8 7 6 5 4 3 2 1	Disagreeable	____
Insincere	1 2 3 4 5 6 7 8	Sincere	____
Kind	8 7 6 5 4 3 2 1	Unkind	____

Total_____

Source: Adapted from Fred E. Fiedler, Martin M. Chemers, and Linda Mahar, *Improving Leadership Effectiveness* (New York: Wiley, 1976), p. 7. Used by permission.

ers' performance and make pay and promotion recommendations. Plotting this high-control situation of good leader-member relations, high task structure, and high position power on Figure 10.10 shows that a task-oriented leader will be most effective.

Take another example. Suppose that you are appointed chairperson of a temporary committee charged with responsibility to improve labor-management relations in a manufacturing plant. Although the goal is clear, task structure is low because no one can say for sure what activities will actually result in "improved labor-management relations." Because the other committee members are free to quit anytime they want, you have little position power as chairperson. Furthermore, you perceive poor leader-member relations because some members resent your appointment as chairperson. Figure 10.10 shows that this low-control situation also calls for a task-oriented leader.

Finally, assume you are the new head of a retail unit in a large department store. Being new and selected over one of the popular sales clerks you now supervise, the result is poor leader-member relations. Task structure is high because the clerk's job is well defined, but your position power is low because the clerks work under a seniority system with a fixed wage schedule. Figure 10.10 shows that this moderate-control situation requires a relationship-oriented leader.

Matching Style and Situation

Clearly, Fiedler's position is that effective leadership results from a proper match of style and situation. He thus argues that prospective leaders should actively seek situations for which their predominate style, i.e. a task-oriented or relationship-oriented approach, is most appropriate. When a mismatch is recognized, it should be corrected by either of the two following strategies:

1. Try to change situational characteristics to better align them with one's leadership style.
2. Change one's leadership style to better fit the requirements of the situation.

Since Fiedler believes that leadership style is strongly tied to basic personality factors and is therefore not easy to change, he advocates option one as first priority. Through appropriate "situational engineering," he suggests, the characteristics of situations can often be modified to increase or decrease situational control to achieve a "best fit" with the individual's leadership style.

Managerial Implications

As with many other management theories, there is controversy surrounding Fiedler's work, and it is easy to find research that is both pro and con. Nevertheless, Fiedler's theory is an important turning point in the history of leadership studies. For the first time situational factors are recognized for their potential to influence the success of alternative leadership styles. Even as other theorists build on Fiedler's ideas and try to develop more refined contingency theories, the implications of Fiedler's situational thinking remain useful points of reference for managers interested in maximizing their leadership effectiveness.

HOUSE'S PATH-GOAL THEORY

A second contingency approach to leadership theory is the path-goal model advanced by Robert House.[17] This theory argues that effective leadership clarifies the paths through which subordinates can achieve both work-related and personal goals, assists them to progress along these paths, and removes any barriers on the paths that may inhibit goal accomplishment. To do this, House feels a leader must vary his or her behavior among the following four basic choices depending on the nature of the situation.

1. *Directive leadership.*

- Letting subordinates know what is expected.
- Providing specific guidance as to what should be done and how it should be done.
- Making his or her part in the group understood.
- Scheduling work to be done.
- Maintaining definite standards of performance.

2. *Supportive leadership.*

- Showing concern for the status, well-being, and needs of subordinates.
- Doing little things to make the work more pleasant.
- Treating members as equals.
- Being friendly and approachable.

3. *Achievement-oriented leadership.*

- Setting challenging goals.
- Expecting subordinates to perform at their highest level.
- Continuously seeking improvement in performance *and* showing a high degree of confidence that subordinates will assume responsibility, put forth effort, and accomplish challenging goals.
- Constantly emphasizing excellence in performance and simultaneously displaying confidence that subordinates will meet high standards of excellence.

4. *Participative leadership.*

- Consulting with subordinates.
- Soliciting subordinate suggestions.
- Taking these suggestions seriously into consideration before making a decision.

Predictions from the Theory

As Fiedler does, House suggests there is no one best way to lead. Path-goal theory advises leaders to match style or behavior with the demands of the situation. For House, though, the contingencies in a work situation are defined in terms of subordinate characteristics and task demands. In respect to subordinate characteristics, a leadership style will be effective in a path-goal sense if it satisfies needs and accommodates personal abilities. In respect to task demands, a leadership style will be effective if it complements rather than contradicts the degree of job structure that exists.

House's theory is summarized in Figure 10.11. The research version is quite complex in elaborating a number of possible contingency variables on the one hand and the four leadership

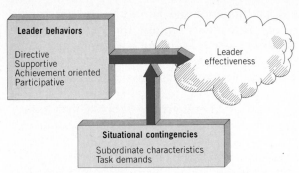

FIGURE 10.11 Path-goal theory of leader effectiveness.

behaviors on the other. Briefly, some of the theory's basic predictions building on the path-goal framework are

- Supportive leadership complements structured tasks.
- Directive leadership complements unstructured tasks.
- Achievement leadership complements achievement-oriented workers.
- Participative leadership complements highly capable workers.

Note in the predictions that the leadership styles are *complementing* subordinate characteristics or task demands. This means that the leadership style combines with situational contingencies to create a positive performance path for the individual. House's theory is also interesting because it recognizes that using an inappropriate leadership style can inhibit subordinate work efforts and interfere with the performance path. Leaders are specifically advised to avoid redundant behaviors—that is, trying to add to a work situation things that already exist. For example, a capable person may react unfavorably to a highly directive leadership style; because of this person's expertise, outside direction is unnecessary. Instead of complementing the situation, directive leadership behavior would confound it and most likely prove ineffective.

Managerial Implications

The essence of path-goal theory is that leaders should select from among the four leadership styles ways of behaving that complement the characteristics of followers and the demands of their tasks. A proper match will enhance leadership effectiveness. Research on this relatively new theory is just beginning to accumulate. The path-goal theory remains a promising extension of the contingency approach to leadership.

THE VROOM-YETTON LEADER-PARTICIPATION THEORY

Victor Vroom and Phillip Yetton offer another contingency theory that centers on how a leader makes decisions.[18] This theory builds on the premise that various problems have different characteristics and should therefore be solved by different decision methods.

Alternative Decision-Making Methods

As highlighted throughout this book, decision making is a key activity for managers. The way decisions are made is an important element in a manager's leadership style. Figure 10.12 depicts the three decision methods originally introduced in Chapter 3—the individual or authority decision, the consultative decision, and the group or consensus decision. The figure also relates each decision method to a continuum of leadership styles ranging from autocratic at the extreme where all decisions are made by the manager, to democratic or participative at the other extreme where decisions are made by the group as a whole.

The differences among the three decision-making methods portrayed in Figure 10.12 are important. We'll define them in the action context of a manager and members of his or her work unit. An **authority decision** is made by the manager and then communicated to the group. No input is asked of group members other than to provide specific information on request.

A **consultative decision** is one in which the problem is shared with each group member who is then asked for information, advice, or opinion to be used by the manager when making a final decision on behalf of the group. Consultative decisions take one of two forms. In one form group members are consulted individually; in the other,

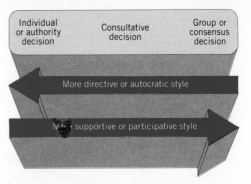

FIGURE 10.12 A continuum of decision methods and related Leadership Styles.

consultation occurs in a meeting of the group as a whole.

In a **group decision** all group members participate with the manager and finally agree by consensus on the course of action to be taken. The group-decision process is successful to the extent that each member is ultimately able to accept the logic and feasibility of the final group decision. Complete unanimity is not the goal. Instead, consensus is achieved when any dissenting member is able to say,

> I understand what most of you would like to do. I personally would not do that, but I feel that you understand what my alternative would be. I have had sufficient opportunity to sway you to my point of view but clearly have not been able to do so. Therefore, I will gladly go along with what most of you wish to do.[19]

Choosing a Decision-Making Method

The central proposition in the Vroom-Yetton model is that effective leadership results when the decision method used in problem solving matches problem characteristics. This means there will be times when authority, consultative, and group forms of decision making are each appropriate. As a leader and manager, therefore, your challenge is twofold:

1. To know when each decision-making method is the best approach for the problem at hand.
2. To know how to implement each decision-making method well when required.

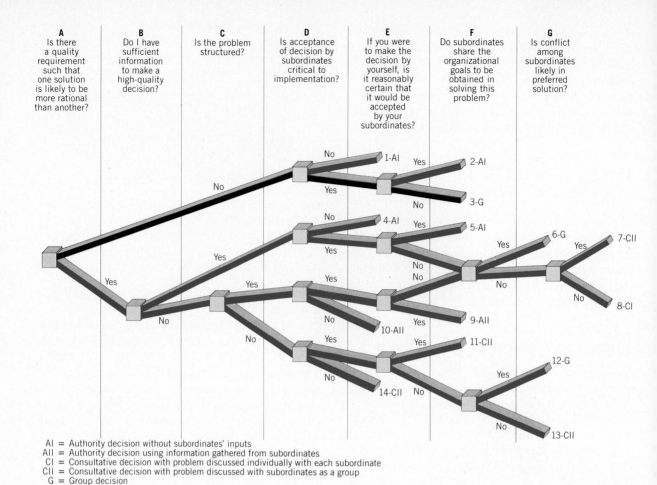

A Is there a quality requirement such that one solution is likely to be more rational than another?	**B** Do I have sufficient information to make a high-quality decision?	**C** Is the problem structured?	**D** Is acceptance of decision by subordinates critical to implementation?	**E** If you were to make the decision by yourself, is it reasonably certain that it would be accepted by your subordinates?	**F** Do subordinates share the organizational goals to be obtained in solving this problem?	**G** Is conflict among subordinates likely in preferred solution?

AI = Authority decision without subordinates' inputs
AII = Authority decision using information gathered from subordinates
CI = Consultative decision with problem discussed individually with each subordinate
CII = Consultative decision with problem discussed with subordinates as a group
G = Group decision

FIGURE 10.13 The Vroom-Yetton decision tree. *Source:* Slightly adapted and reprinted, by permission of the publisher, from "A New Look at Managerial Decision-Making," Victor H. Vroom, *Organizational Dynamics,* Spring 1973, pp. 69–70. Copyright © 1973 by AMACOM, a division of American Management Associations. All rights reserved.

Let's work on your ability to handle the first of these challenges. Take a moment to solve the following problem.

Problem[20]

Assume you are supervising the work of 12 engineers. Their formal training and work experience are similar, permitting you to use them interchangeably on projects. Yesterday your manager informed you that a request had been received from an overseas affiliate for four engineers to go abroad on extended loan for a period of six to eight months. For a number of reasons, the manager argued and you agreed that this request should be met from your group.

All your engineers are capable of handling this assignment, and from the standpoint of present and future projects there is no particular reason why any one should be retained over any other. The problem is somewhat complicated by the fact that the overseas assignment is in what is generally regarded in the company as an undesirable location.

How should this decision be made? Circle one.

authority?   consultation?   group?

Your response to the problem is a "gut" reaction. It represents how you would act in this leadership situation without any special guidance. The Vroom and Yetton leadership model, however, offers a way of more systematically approaching this and other problem situations.

According to Vroom and Yetton, a good decision is high in quality, accepted by the people who have to implement it, and time efficient. Furthermore, they have identified problem attributes that influence the capability of the decision maker to achieve these outcomes through each decision method. Listed across the top of Figure 10.13 are seven diagnostic questions. By asking and answering these questions in sequence for any problem situation, you can systematically proceed through the decision tree also presented in the figure. According to Vroom and Yetton, this decision tree will identify the ideal decision method to use in any problem situation.

Figure 10.13 highlights Vroom and Yetton's answers to the diagnostic questions for the problem situation to which you responded earlier. They feel a group decision is best in this case. To use the decision tree, begin at the extreme left and then answer the questions in sequence. Follow the developing path as you go. Go back to the original problem statement and compare your answer to theirs. Work through the decision-tree analysis to understand how Vroom and Yetton arrived at this conclusion.

Managerial Implications

The Vroom and Yetton model has been criticized as complex and cumbersome. You will probably agree after working through the diagnostic questions and following full details of the decision tree in Figure 10.13. Obviously, you aren't expected to do this for every problem you face as a manager. Yet there is a basic discipline to the approach that is most useful. When confronted by future problems, the model can help you recognize where time, quality requirements, information availability, and subordinate acceptance are critical issues affecting the choice of decision method. Furthermore, the model reinforces the contingency approach to leadership by helping you understand that each of the three alternative decision methods is important and useful. The key is to use each method only in those problem situations for which it represents the best leadership response.

LEADERSHIP IN A MANAGERIAL PERSPECTIVE

There is no getting around it. To be successful as a manager, it is necessary to be an effective leader. At the bottom of it all, management is the act of facilitating work by other persons. A successful manager is one who is able to direct the activities of other people so that both high performance and personal satisfaction result. Leadership is the use of power to achieve these results.

Figure 10.14 summarizes the essence of leadership from this managerial perspective. A good manager uses power and contingently applies a variety of leadership behaviors to facilitate performance and satisfaction. In the three chapters that follow we will examine how communication, motivation, and group dynamics enter into this leadership process. Before leaving the present chapter, though, let's reflect further on the fundamentals of leading as a managerial responsibility.

Contingency Leadership

We have reviewed three main branches of contingency leadership theory—Fiedler's contingency theory, House's path-goal theory, and the Vroom-Yetton leader-participation theory. They are now compared in summary fashion in Table 10.3. You should understand the differences among these theories, while still recognizing that

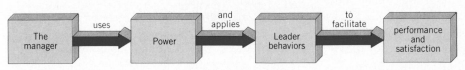

FIGURE 10.14 The essence of leadership from a managerial perspective.

Table 10.3   A Comparison of the Three Major Contingency Leadership Theories

Point of Comparison	Fiedler's Approach	House's Approach	Vroom-Yetton Approach
Focus	Situational control	Situational characteristics	Problem attributes
Diagnostic focus	Task structure Position power Leader-member relations	Subordinate characteristics Task characteristics	Seven questions on quality, acceptance, information, time
Leadership styles	Task motivated Relationship motivated	Directive Supportive Participative Achievement oriented	Authoritative Consultative Participative
Managerial implication	High- or low-control situations require task orientation; moderate control requires relationship orientation	Best leader chooses style to complement situational characteristics	Best leader chooses authority, consultative, or group-decision method according to nature of problem at hand

they share a common premise: there is no one best way to lead; what is best depends on the situation!

Questions and Answers on Leader Participation

Of the various leader behaviors, participation is one that seems especially prone to cause managers discomfort. Three questions managers often raise about letting subordinates participate in decision making follow. The accompanying answers should alleviate any similar concerns you may have about the use of participation as a key leadership behavior.[21]

Question   "If I let my subordinates participate in decision making, won't they come up with recommendations I can't live with?"

Yes, there will be times when subordinates come up with recommendations different from your own. However, there will also be times when their recommendations are the same as yours or better ones that you had not thought of. Just because subordinates have been allowed to participate in the decision-making process doesn't mean that every one of their recommendations must be accepted. When you do disagree, however, they should always be thanked for their assistance and given reasons for the decision that is finally made.

Question   "If I let my subordinates participate in decision making some of the time, won't I then have to check with them every time I make a decision?"

No, the extent to which subordinates are involved in decision making can be varied at your discretion. In fact, there are many decision-making and problem-solving matters in which subordinates have little or no desire to participate. Use good judgment in determining when matters are significant enough that subordinates will want to participate and/or when the subject is such that inputs from subordinates will substantially increase the probability that a good decision will be made.

Question   "If I let my subordinates participate in decision making, won't they lose respect for me and my position as manager?"

Decision making is an important responsibility of every manager. Always, too, the primary goal is to ensure that good decisions are made. Thus, when subordinates are allowed to participate in decision making in areas where they have expertise and interests, the likelihood is that better decisions will be made and that they will be better implemented. Your reputation as a competent manager who is concerned enough to value what subordinates have to say on important matters will be maintained and even enhanced as a result.

Participative leadership requires the ability to encourage group discussion and involvement in decision making.

Final Advice to the Leader

There is no one hard and fast rule that can be followed to achieve leadership success. A leader certainly requires the capabilities to show support, provide direction, and allow participation. A leader must be able to influence other persons through power based on personal sources and in the managerial position itself. And, a leader must be able to understand situational contingencies and act accordingly. This leaves a lot of responsibility up to you. It also encourages you to take maximum advantage of insights made available by each leadership theory reviewed in this chapter.

SUMMARY

Power is a foundation for leadership. It is a capacity to control or influence the behavior of other persons. Power becomes available to the manager through position (legitimacy, rewards, punishments) and through personal attributes (reference, expertise). Leadership is the use of power to direct the behavior of others toward organizational objectives.

Leadership research historically traces from an early emphasis on personal traits to more recent concerns for leader behaviors and situational contingencies. Trait researchers have generally been unable to find one profile of personal characteristics that universally separates effective from noneffective leaders. Leader-behavior researchers, likewise, have been unable to determine that one style or pattern of leader behaviors is consistently superior to others. As a result, three contingency theories have achieved recent prominence for their attempts to provide leadership guidance to managers: Fiedler's contingency theory, House's path-goal theory, and the Vroom-Yetton leader-participation theory. Each of these theories shares the common point of view that there is no one best way to lead. However, each offers a slightly different approach for achieving the best match between personal leadership style and situational demands. Once again, you are referred to Table 10.4 for a comparison of the three theories.

You have much to gain by reflecting on the tradition of leadership research. Underlying all successful leaders is probably the capability to be task-oriented and/or people-oriented as the situation requires. This demands that you know not only *when* to use various styles, but also *how* to use them. Many ideas are found throughout this chapter on the relative advantages of various leadership styles. What remains to be learned are the basic concepts and issues that affect a manager's ability to use them well in the interpersonal context of the work setting. This is the substance of the three chapters to follow.

THINKING THROUGH THE ISSUES

1. What is leadership? How does leadership differ from management?

2. What is the difference between a formal and informal leader? Is a manager only one or the other? Explain your answer.

3. Name five sources of power available to managers. Give an example of each power source and explain whether it is a source of personal or position power.

4. Of what significance to would-be leaders is the zone of indifference and the acceptance theory of power?

5. Why have scholars \shifted away from trait-leadership theory?

6. How have we benefited most from research into leadership behaviors?

7. Explain the general theme common to all contingency-leadership theories.

8. How do the contingency theories of Fiedler and House differ in their managerial implications?

9. Can the Vroom-Yetton model help managers to handle real problem situations successfully? Why or why not?

10. Identify and critically discuss two reasons why managers are sometimes reluctant to allow subordinates the opportunity to participate in decision making.

THE MANAGER'S VOCABULARY

Abdicative leadership
Authority decision
Autocratic leadership
Coercive power
Consultative decision
Democratic leadership
Directive leadership
Expert power

Formal leadership
Group decision
Human-relations
  leadership
Informal leadership
Laissez-faire leadership
Leader-member
  relations

Leadership
Leadership style
Leading
Legitimate power
Participative leadership
Position power
Power
Reference power

Reward power
Situational control
Supportive leadership
Task structure
Zone of indifference

CAREER PERSPECTIVE: HOW TO WIN THE CORPORATE GAME, OR AT LEAST TIE THE SCORE[22]

Bob Cressor was a vice-president of one of the largest corporations in America when he retired at 62. He admits he was a game player. "I played the corporate game for many years and left the field with a smile on my face," Cressor says. The smile indicated he'd won. Oh, he didn't pitch a shutout or go undefeated. He didn't demoralize the opposition with one slam-dunk after another.

"I suffered my share of interceptions, fumbles, strikeouts, and roughing-the-wrong-guy penalties," Cressor says candidly, "but I hung tough and gained the eventual victory by discovering very early that it's how you play the game that determines whether you win or lose."

When he trotted away early this year from Sun Co., after 34 years in the game, he was vice-president for constituency relations. By some yardsticks, Cressor would be measured a success. He didn't simply survive; he prospered. He became a company star principally because he kept telling himself it wasn't life or death, only a game, and that there were other games on other fields in which he could play. "You might say I played relaxed, recognizing I'd do okay if I learned the rules and could discipline myself to stay within them," Cressor explains.

A lot of the rules Cressor ad-libbed. Don't work for the boss is one of them. "I had 27 bosses in 34 years," he explains. A lot of them were great, but a few were so intimidated by their bosses they became monuments to inertia. A couple were plain incompetent.

"I have a gut feeling that a great many bosses are sitting one level above their competence quotient. You can't work for the boss; you must work for the company. The boss will pass; the company won't."

Cressor makes it clear he's not suggesting it's possible to fight your boss and survive. "There's no way a subordinate can help himself by taking on the boss. Who's right or wrong isn't important. The boss has the power and power wins every time. Help him; educate him; humor him; play gofer for him—but don't fight him. It's his ball."

Cressor warns it's a mistake to focus on the boss from one end of the day to the other, ignoring everyone else in the organization. "The world turns," he says, "and when it does the boss falls off, leaving you without any support at all from others in the game."

It's important to build an influence network, Cressor emphasizes—a network that includes persons in top management, your peers, and those on lower levels. "At some point, you are going to be dependent on someone up above—with muscle. But it's essential that you have support laterally and from below," he says.

Cressor started his business career as salesman, and though he did very well for himself, he didn't get rich. "Too many young people see stories about six-digit executive salaries and decide to go for it. Don't. One look at the organization chart should convince you the odds are stacked heavily against you. You'll make a living—but a winter place in Palm Beach? Hardly."

Questions

1. What are the leadership implications of Bob Cressor's comments about the "bosses" he had over the years?

2. Where does power fit into the managerial survival skills advocated by Cressor?

3. Do you think the "rules of the game" as described by Bob Cressor apply to most organizations? Why or why not?

Sherry Lansing was only 36 years old when appointed president of the movie-production division of Twentieth-Century Fox Film Corporation in 1980. After three years in that position, she went on to form a major independent film-production company with Stanley R. Jaffe. What follows is a glimpse of her leadership style as reported by a *Wall Street Journal* article.[23]

> When Twentieth Century-Fox Productions released "Nine to Five," the comedy about three working women, it grossed more than $38 million at the box office in its first 24 days. The movie owes much of its success to a fourth working woman whose name appears nowhere in the credits. The film project was already under way when Sherry Lansing arrived to head the film studio. She had the right the cancel the movie. Instead, she read the script and loved it.
>
> For many studio bosses, that would have been the extent of involvement until a final edited version of the film was ready to be screened. But Lansing, who was the first woman to head a major motion-picture studio, chose a more persistent and "hands-on" approach—an approach she applied to other aspects of her job.
>
> Every day, Lansing went to the set of "Nine to Five." She screened the daily shootings and talked frequently with producer Bruce Gilbert and director Colin Higgins, who also collaborated on the screenplay. "She warned us that she was a great meddler," says Higgins. "But she was terrifically supportive during the whole project." She helped edit the first three "cuts" of the movie, for example, and attended the first preview at the studio.
>
> In today's Hollywood, the intangible qualities of personality and style matter a great deal in studio management. Creative talent isn't under the yoke of long-term, exclusive contracts, so every studio mogul has to do some hand holding, ego massaging, and alliance building to get first crack at as many projects as possible.
>
> Insiders at Fox are impressed by the speed with which Lansing, who rose from a $5-an-hour scriptreader to the production-executive level before leaving Columbia Pictures, caught on to these subtleties and took charge. She installed a top-notch production team, attracted industry heavyweights, and nearly doubled the studio's feature-film production schedule.
>
> One of Lansing's strongest management assets is her personableness, says Richard D. Zanuck, who was ousted a decade ago as a Fox executive and later returned as a producer. "In this business, associations and friendships are of immense importance," he says. Adds Higgins, the director: "I wish all studio heads were as creative—and as much fun to be around."
>
> Zanuck and partner David Brown (the team responsible for "Jaws" and other big hits) say Lansing distinguished herself from other studio heads by her accessibility and her speed in making decisions. Other executives might take a week to return a call, but Lansing's typical 10- to 12-hour working day didn't end until she returned or had otherwise taken care of all the business calls received that day (usually 200 or more). She also read about a dozen scripts a week.

Questions

1. What is Sherry Lansing's leadership style? Support your conclusion based on facts presented in the case.

2. Does Lansing appear to practice contingency leadership? Why or why not?

3. Do you agree with the apprehensions expressed in the last paragraph of the case? Why or why not?

CLASS EXERCISE: MANAGING THE OUTPATIENT CLINIC

1. Analyze the situation that follows. Choose, from your point of view, which decision method would be the best approach to the problem at hand.

Case Situation[24]

You are the manager of an outpatient clinic in a large hospital. The hospital's management has always been searching for ways of increasing efficiency. They have recently installed a new computerized record-keeping and billing system, but to the surprise of everyone, including yourself, the expected increase in efficiency was not realized. In fact, efficiency and effectiveness have both fallen off (i.e., lost records, late billings, incorrect charges, etc.), and the extent of employee turnover has risen.

You do not believe there is anything wrong with the system. You have had reports from other hospitals who are using it, and they confirm this opinion. You have also had representatives from the firm that built and installed the system and machines go over them and they report that they are operating at peak efficiency.

Among your immediate subordinates (three first-line supervisors, each in charge of a shift, and your administrative assistant), the drop in production has been variously attributed to poor training of the operators, lack of an adequate system of financial incentives and poor morale. Clearly, this is an issue about which there is considerable depth of feeling and potential disagreement between your subordinates.

This morning you received a phone call from your manager. He had just received your figures for the last six months and was calling to express his concern. He indicated that the problem was yours to solve in any way that you think best but that he would like to know within a week what steps you plan to take.

You share your manager's concern with the falling productivity and know that your subordinates are also concerned. The problem is to decide what steps to take to rectify the situation.

What is the best decision method to use in approaching this problem?

Authority?   Consultative?   Group?

2. Now analyze the situation using the Vroom and Yetton decision tree presented in Figure 10.13. Compare their suggested decision method to yours.

3. Share your original choice and your version of the Vroom and Yetton solution with a nearby classmate. Analyze and reconcile any differences in these solutions. Await further class discussion.

REFERENCES

[1] Excerpted from Lawrence Ingrassia, "Union Rank and File Talk Bitterly of Their Bosses," *Wall Street Journal* (April 12, 1982), p. 24. Reprinted by permission of the *Wall Street Journal*. Copyright © 1982 Dow Jones & Company, Inc. All rights reserved.

[2] This case and subsequent discussion slightly adapted from *Leadership* by Leonard Sayles, pp. 46–49. Copyright © 1979 by Leonard Sayles. Used with permission of the McGraw-Hill Company.

[3] Rosabeth Moss Kanter, "Power Failure in Management Circuits," *Harvard Business Review*, Vol. 47 (July–August 1979), pp. 65–75.

[4] *Wall Street Journal* (March 1, 1982), p. 26.

[5] Adapted from Kanter, op. cit., p. 67.

[6] David C. McClelland and David H. Burnham, "Power is the Great Motivator," *Harvard Business Review*, Vol. 54 (March–April 1976), pp. 100–110.

[7] See John R. P. French, Jr. and Bertram Raven, "The Bases of Social Power," in Darwin Cartwright (ed.), *Group Dynamics: Research and Theory* (Evanston, Ill.: Row, Peterson, 1962), pp. 607–613.

[8] Chester Barnard, *The Functions of the Executive* (Cambridge: Harvard University Press, 1938), pp. 165–166.

[9] Adapted by permission of the Harvard Business Review. Excerpt from "Acquiring and Using Power," by John P. Kotter, Vol. 55 (July–August 1977), pp. 130–132. Copyright © 1977 by the President and Fellows of Harvard College; all rights reserved.

[10] Ralph M. Stogdill, "Personal Factors Associated with Leadership: A Survey of the Literature," *Journal of Psychology*, Vol. 25 (1948), p. 65.

[11] E. E. Ghiselli, *Explorations in Management Talent* (Santa Monica, Cal.: Goodyear, 1971).

[12] Comments by a senior executive of a *Fortune* 500

Company to A. G. Athos, July 26, 1975. As quoted in Richard Tanner Pascale and Anthony G. Athos, *The Art of Japanese Management* (New York: Simon & Schuster, 1981), p. 155. Used by permission.

[13] See Rensis Likert, *New Patterns of Management* (New York: McGraw-Hill, 1961); Chester C. Schriesheim and Steven Kerr, "Theories and Measures of Leadership: A Critical Appraisal of Current and Future Directions," in James G. Hunt and Lars Larson (eds.), *Leadership: The Cutting Edge* (Carbondale, Ill.: SIU Press, 1977), pp. 9–45, 51–56.

[14] Robert R. Blake and Jane Srygley Mouton, *The New Managerial Grid* (Houston: Gulf Publishing, 1978).

[15] Reprinted by permission of the Harvard Business Review. Excerpt from "How to Choose a Leadership Pattern," by Robert Tannenbaum and Warren H. Schmidt, Vol. 51 (May–June 1973), pp. 162–175, 178–180. Copyright © by the President and Fellows of Harvard College; all rights reserved.

[16] For a good discussion of this theory see Fred E. Fiedler, Martin M. Chemers, and Linda Mahar, *The Leadership Match Concept* (New York: Wiley, 1978).

[17] See, for example, Robert J. House, "A Path-Goal Theory of Leader Effectiveness," *Administrative Sciences Quarterly*, Vol. 16 (1971), pp. 321–338; Robert J. House and Terence R. Mitchell, "Path-Goal Theory of Leadership," *Journal of Contemporary Business* (Autumn 1974), pp. 81–97.

[18] See Victor H. Vroom, "A New Look in Managerial Decision-Making," *Organizational Dynamics* (Spring 1973), pp. 66–80; Victor H. Vroom and Phillip Yetton, *Leadership and Decision-Making* (Pittsburgh: University of Pittsburgh Press, 1973).

[19] Edgar H. Schein, *Process Consultation: Its Role in Organization Development* (Reading, Mass.: Addison-Wesley, 1969), p. 56.

[20] This case is from Vroom and Yetton, op. cit.

[21] Based on Marvin Karlins, *The Human Use of Human Resources* (New York: McGraw-Hill, 1981), pp. 102–104.

[22] Excerpted from Robert E. Finercane, "How to Win the Corporate Game, or at Least Tie the Score," *Sun Magazine* (Spring 1982), pp. 27, 28. Used by permission.

[23] Excerpted from Stephen J. Sansweet, "Fox Studio's Woman Chief Smashes Mogul Stereotype," *Wall Street Journal* (January 13, 1981), p. 23. Reprinted by permission of the *Wall Street Journal*. Copyright © 1981 Dow Jones & Company, Inc. All rights reserved.

[24] This case is from Irwin M. Rubin, Ronald E. Fry, and Mark S. Plovnick, *Managing Human Resources in Health Care Organizations* (Reston, Va.: Reston Publishing, 1978), pp. 138, 139. Used by permission.

11

LEADING
THROUGH
COMMUNICATION

HYATT HOTELS' GRIPE SESSIONS HELP CHIEF MAINTAIN COMMUNICATIONS WITH WORKERS

CHICAGO—On a recent afternoon, 14 Hyatt Hotel employees are sitting around a table, griping about their jobs.[1] A concierge complains that the hotel does little to aid handicapped guests; a maid protests her boss's order to change light bulbs while cleaning rooms.

Patrick Foley, Hyatt Hotels Corporation's president, sits at the head of the table, listening.

For the past eight months, Foley has listened to the complaints of employees at about a dozen Hyatt hotels. Sometimes he hears of serious problems that require immediate attention. More often, he hears seemingly trivial complaints—but they concern matters that can make day-to-day life miserable.

"Every time I do one of these meetings, I realize it's the little things that most often affect morale," Foley says. "This is a way to make the employee feel like we care."

It's a method that an increasing number of companies are thinking about using. Homer Hagedorn, manager of organization development at Arthur D. Little Inc., says that some 15 companies have asked him about it in the past year. "Managers are looking for affordable, credible, simple ways to strengthen communications," he says. "This is one of the most obvious."

Hagedorn cautions, however, that it doesn't always work. He knows of a chief executive who undercut the authority of lower-level supervisors by responding "from the hip" to employees' questions. In other companies, top officers lost credibility by refusing to answer any questions. And some executives have dropped the program, Hagedorn says, because they grew bored or found it too time consuming.

It's still early to judge Hyatt's program. A few middle-level supervisors say they resent being criticized by underlings in front of the president. But the program gets praise from some other employees. "I think it's a great idea," says James Dobbins, a cook at Hyatt's downtown Chicago hotel. Dobbins has never been to one of the sessions, but he hears "they really respond to our problems."

A range of those problems were brought up at the recent meeting at the hotel near Chicago's O'Hare Airport. Fourteen of the hotel's 1000 employees were invited, and they were just finishing lunch when Foley arrived.

The president begins by explaining to the eight men and six women that "this isn't a witch hunt. I'm not here to cause any problems." He promises to look into every complaint, and write a letter to each person afterward explaining his position.

PLANNING AHEAD

Patrick Foley is a leader who obviously works hard to maintain good communications with his workers. Without an ability to communicate, it is difficult for any manager to succeed in a leadership capacity. This chapter reviews the basic principles of interpersonal and organizational communication. Key topics include

Communication and the Manager
Communication as an Interpersonal Process
Barriers to Effective Communication
Perception and Communication
Organizational Communication
Guidelines for Effective Communication

A plumber from New York developed what he thought was an excellent method for cleaning drains. He wrote the Bureau of Standards to tell them that he was using hydrochloric acid and to ask them if it was harmless. The bureau replied, "The efficacy of hydrochloric acid is indisputable, but the chlorine residue is incompatible with metallic permanence."

The plumber wrote back, thanking the bureau for agreeing with him. Alarmed by his response, the bureau wrote another letter, saying, "We cannot assume responsibility for the production of toxic and noxious residues with hydrochloric acid, and suggest that you use an alternative procedure." The plumber wrote again, explaining how happy he was to learn that Washington still agreed with him.

At this stage, the bureau put the problem in simple terms: "Don't use hydrochloric acid. It eats the hell out of the pipes." Finally, the plumber understood.[2]

Although a bit extreme, this example points out that the thing we call "communication" is not always easy. In fact, if Patrick Foley of Hyatt Hotels Corporation isn't any better at communicating than the people at the Bureau of Standards were, his well-intentioned program of regular gripe sessions with workers will surely run into trouble. **Communication** is an interpersonal process of sending and receiving symbols with meanings attached to them. Many facets of communication are important to you as a manager. We'll begin our discussion by reviewing the centrality of communication to the managerial role.

COMMUNICATION AND THE MANAGER

Ask someone what lies at the root of most problems in their organizations. Nine times out of ten, the answer will be poor or insufficient communication. This popular response is tied to the fact that it is through communication with others that managers get the information they need to make decisions and solve problems. When poor decisions are made and the organization falters, bad communication is frequently to blame. The *New Yorker* cartoon is one of many examples of how this theme finds its way into contemporary humor.

Communication and the Managerial Role

One way to view the managerial role is as a nerve center of information flows. Figure 11.1 portrays the manager as center point in a complex information-processing system. Success in this role depends on a manager's ability to send and receive information while acting as a monitor, disseminator, spokesperson and decision maker. To fulfill these basic managerial responsibilities, a person must be good at gathering appropriate information from sources inside and outside the work unit (monitor role), distributing information within the work unit (disseminator role) and through external contacts (spokesperson role), and using information to solve problems and explore opportunities (decision-maker role).

Breakdown in communication. *Source:* Drawing by Ziegler; © 1982 The New Yorker Magazine, Inc. Used by permission.

Any manager's job, therefore, builds around the need to communicate. It is through communication that vital information for decision making is gained and the results of those decisions conveyed to others. Communication makes other people aware of a manager's desires and intentions and thereby sets the foundation for influence to take place. Leadership, in a word, is impossible without communication.

Research indicates that up to 80 percent of a manager's time is spent in oral communications.[3]

Figure 11.2 shows how executives studied by Henry Mintzberg distributed their time among various communication activities: scheduled and unscheduled meetings (69 percent), telephone calls (6 percent), desk-work reading and writing (22 percent), and walk-around tours (3 percent). Only 22 percent of their time was spent doing desk work. Obviously, this group of executives spent most of their time on the telephone or in direct face-to-face communications with other persons.

FIGURE 11.1 The manager as nerve center in an information-processing system. *Source:* Abridged and adapted text from chart on p. 72 in *The Nature of Managerial Work* by Henry Mintzberg. Copyright © 1973 by Henry Mintzberg. Reprinted by permission of Harper & Row Publishers, Inc.

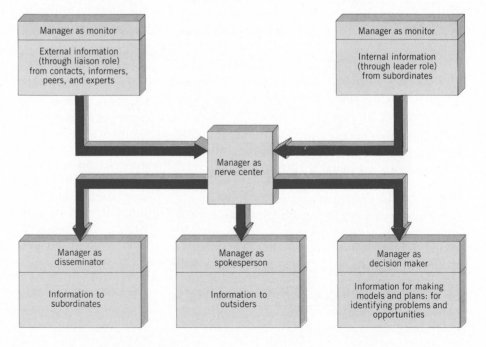

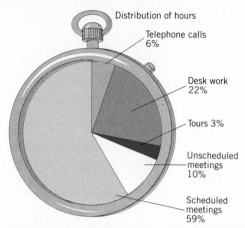

Distribution of hours

Telephone calls
6%

Desk work
22%

Tours 3%

Unscheduled
meetings
10%

Scheduled
meetings
59%

FIGURE 11.2 The distribution of managers' time among various forms of communication. *Source:* Abridged and adapted text from chart on p. 39 in *The Nature of Managerial Work* by Henry Mintzberg. Copyright © 1973 by Henry Mintzberg. Reprinted by permission of Harper & Row Publishers, Inc.

Communication and the Management Functions

Communication is essential to each of the four basic management functions. In order to plan, organize, lead, and control, managers must be able to communicate with other persons—and communicate well. Information from others helps formulate plans; information provided to others defines job assignments and helps organize work; information on standards, progress, and personal factors fulfills the leadership function; while information in the form of written and oral progress reports is a fundamental element in controlling. Communication is a linking process that enables each of the basic management functions to be carried out.

COMMUNICATION AS AN INTERPERSONAL PROCESS[4]

Communication is one of those words like *organization*. Everyone knows what it means until asked to define it precisely. Earlier we defined communication as an interpersonal process of sending and receiving symbols with meanings attached to them. Now it is time to look in detail at this very important process, which is supposed to result in the exchange of information and the achievement of shared understanding among people.

Elements in the Communication Process

The key elements in the communication process are diagrammed in Figure 11.3. They include a sender, who is responsible for encoding an intended meaning into a message and sending it through a channel to a receiver, who then decodes the message into a perceived meaning. Feedback from receiver to sender may or may not be given. Another way to view the communication process is as a series of questions. "Who?" (sender) "says what?" (message) "in what way?" (channel) "to whom?" (receiver) "with what result?" (perceived meaning).

To communicate with the receiver, the sender translates his or her intended meaning into symbols. This translation is an encoding process that results in a message that may consist of verbal (such as written) or nonverbal (such as gestures) symbols, or some combination of both. The receiver decodes the message into perceived meaning. This process of interpretation may or may not result in the assignment of the same meaning intended by the sender.

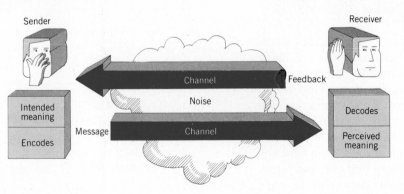

Sender

Receiver

FIGURE 11.3 The interpersonal communication process.

Channel / Feedback

Noise

Intended meaning

Encodes

Message

Channel

Decodes

Perceived meaning

Frequently, the intended meaning of the sender and the meaning as perceived by the receiver differ. How would you react, for example, to this well-intentioned roadside sign advertising a combination diner and gasoline station?[5]

```
EAT HERE AND GET GAS
```

Don't let the humor in this example fool you. Managers, like owners of roadside diners, often make mistakes in their communication attempts.

Effective versus Efficient Communication

Effective communication occurs when the intended meaning of the sender and the perceived meaning of the receiver are one and the same. This should be the manager's goal in any communication attempt, but it is not always achieved. Even now, I worry whether or not you will interpret these written words as I intend. My confidence would be higher if I were together with you, face-to-face in class, and you could ask clarifying questions. The opportunity to question (i.e., offer feedback to the source) is one advantage of face-to-face communication as opposed to the use of written memos, letters, posted bulletins, or reports.

Efficient communication occurs at minimum cost in terms of resources expended. Time is an important resource in the communication process. Picture your instructor taking the time to communicate individually with each student. It would be virtually impossible to do, and, even if possible, it would be costly. For similar reasons, managers sometimes choose to write memos rather than visit their employees personally, or choose to hold group rather than individual meetings.

Efficient communications are not always effective. A low-cost communication such as a posted bulletin may save time for the sender, but it doesn't always achieve the desired results in terms of having the intended meaning equal the perceived meaning. Similarly, an effective communication may not be efficient. For a manager to visit each employee and explain a new change in procedures may guarantee that everyone truly understands the change. It may also be very expensive in terms of the required time expenditure.

Good managers know how to maximize the effectiveness of their communications while still maintaining reasonable efficiency in the process.

BARRIERS TO EFFECTIVE COMMUNICATION

Noise, as suggested in Figure 11.3, is anything that interferes with the effectiveness of the communication process. Six major sources of noise that can threaten communication in work settings are semantic problems, the absence of feedback, improper choice or use of channels, physical distractions, cultural differences, and status effects. Noise threatens the success of any communication attempt, and each possible source should be recognized and subjected to special control.

Semantic Problems

Semantic barriers to communication occur as encoding and decoding errors and as mixed messages. Symbols, such as the words "Eat Here and Get Gas," are selected by the source and interpreted by the receiver. Communication will only be effective to the extent that the source makes good choices and encodes messages into symbols easily and clearly understood by the receiver. This is a semantic challenge.

We generally don't realize how easily encoding and decoding errors occur. They abound, however, as the following examples illustrate. Consider this sign appearing in a nightclub.

```
CLEAN AND DECENT DANCING
EVERY NIGHT EXCEPT SUNDAY
```

The unsolicited addition was: "You must do a big business on Sundays!" Or, how about this classified ad from a newspaper?[6]

```
For sale:
Large Great Dane.
Registered pedigree.
Will eat anything.
Especially fond of children.
```

In each of these examples the source chose poorly when encoding the intended meaning into words. Managers must be careful in this regard, especially in respect to their written communication. A vice-president in a large U.S. corporation, for example, was having trouble with his division managers, who occasionally responded inappropriately to his memos.[7] He hired a consultant for a training session that was held from 9:00 A.M. until lunch on a regular workday in the staff meeting room.

Before the meeting, several memos from the vice-president to the division managers were selected to be shown on a screen via a projector. After reading each memo on the screen the division managers were asked three questions: (1) What do you think the message says? (2) What priority would you give to the message: (a) *high*, take care of the matter immediately; (b) *medium*, take care of the matter relatively soon; or (c) *low*, take care of it when I can get to it. (3) What action would you take?

After everyone wrote their answers to the three questions, they were asked to read their responses to the total group. Numerous differences occurred among the managers. Later, the vice-president explained what he meant the memo to say, what priority he desired, and what action he wanted. As might be expected, a number of misunderstandings were corrected.

The Absence of Feedback

One-way communications, such as letters and posted notices, allow no feedback from receiver to source. Two-way communications, such as interactive conversations, allow for feedback. Because of this feedback opportunity, two-way communication is typically more accurate and effective than one-way. One-way communication, by contrast, is usually more time efficient. Many student interactions with instructors are frustrating because of one-way communications. Examinations are a good example. How often have you labored over the interpretation of a question and wished you could get clarification from the instructor? Sometimes you can't even ask; sometimes you can ask, but still don't get clarification. One-way communications are frequent in work settings. Sometimes they protect the source from the threat or discomfort that may accompany feedback; most always they result in the receiver being somewhat unsure as to the actual intentions of the source.

Poor Choice or Use of Communication Channels

A **communication channel** is the medium through which a message is conveyed from sender to receiver. Managers typically use oral, written, and nonverbal channels of communication. Some basic considerations pertaining to the various channels are summarized in Table 11.1. Because each has certain advantages and disadvantages, effective communication depends on a manager being able to choose the right channel for a given situation, and then to implement it well.

Oral and Written Channels

Oral communication takes place via the spoken word. Examples are telephone calls and face-to-face meetings. It takes skill to communicate orally. When done well, though, oral communication allows for feedback and spontaneous thinking and conveys personal warmth. Written communication also takes skill. We all know how hard it can be to write a good concise letter, or to summarize our thoughts in a formal report. When done well, the written message can be advantageous. It provides a historical record, can reach a large number of people simultaneously, and appears formal and authoritative. When done poorly, a written message can easily be misunderstood. This risk is confounded when there is no immediate opportunity for the receiver to react to the message via feedback. *Newsline 11.1* shows that many employers are concerned about a lack of good written communication skills in their management ranks.

A key choice you will routinely make as a manager is whether to communicate orally or in writing, or both, in a given circumstance. Some ideas on making these choices follow.[8]

1. *Oral communication by itself is most effective:*

- To reprimand an employee for poor work.
- To settle a dispute among employees.

NEWSLINE 11.1

SHORTCOMINGS IN BUSINESS WRITING PROMPT REMEDIAL STEPS BY SOME FIRMS

About 95 percent of 200 executives polled by Communispond, New York consultants, find business correspondence they get is "wordy" or "unclear." And 72 percent of those surveyed dislike writing letters and memos themselves. So Quaker State Oil Refining prints this command on its memo stationery: "Be complete but brief." Quaker State's president avoids writing memos by writing notes on others' memos.

An SCM tax official decided to try to write more clearly after one of his complex memos elicited "cloudy stares or puzzlement." Levi Strauss's president once kept a month's worth of memos to prove there were too many and most were too long. To correct poor English and boring memos, a U.S. Leasing vice-president conducts writing sessions for 15 top managers.

Some companies offer executives more formal business-writing training. They include: AT&T, International Paper, and Bank of New York.

Source: "Shortcomings in Business Writing Prompt Remedial Steps by Some Firms," *Wall Street Journal* (October 19, 1982), p. 1. Reprinted by permission of the *Wall Street Journal*. Copyright © 1982 Dow Jones & Company, Inc. All rights reserved.

2. *Written communication by itself is most effective:*

- To communicate information requiring future action.
- To communicate information of a general nature.

3. *Oral communication, then written communication, is most effective:*

- To communicate information requiring immediate action.
- To communicate a directive or order.
- To communicate an important policy change.
- To communicate with an immediate supervisor about work problems.
- To commend an employee for good work.

Nonverbal Channels

Nonverbal communication takes place through body language, voice intonations, and physical appearance. It can be a powerful means of trans-mitting messages. Eye contact or voice intonation can be intentionally used, for example, to accent special parts of an oral communication. The astute manager also observes body language unknowingly expressed by other persons. Watch how people behave in a meeting. A person who feels under attack may move his or her chair back, or lean away from the presumed antagonist; a person pleased with what is taking place is prone to lean forward, smile, and nod agreement. All of this is done quite unconsciously, but it still sends a message to those quick enough to pick it up. A **mixed message** occurs when a person's words communicate one message while actions, body language, or appearance communicate something else.

The physical layout of an office is an often overlooked form of nonverbal communication. As the two accompanying photographs show, various office arrangements convey quite different things to an office visitor. Check the layouts in the photos against those in your office, your instructor's office, or other offices with which

Table 11.1 Communication Channels Available to the Manager

Channel	Examples	Advantages	Disadvantages
Oral communication	Telephone calls, personal contacts, mass meetings	Allows immediate feedback; more personal; chance for spontaneous ideas, questions, solutions to arise	Give and take can be time consuming and cause conflict; no formal record of transaction; distortion can occur as message is passed on from one person to the next.
Written communication	Letters, memos, formal reports, posted notices, newsletters, policy manuals	Formal record exists; can be widely distributed; can save time when many persons must be contacted; can appear formal or authoritative	Interpretations can vary; no feedback opportunity; very dependent on writing skills; can be time consuming to prepare more lengthy reports
Nonverbal communication	Eye contact, facial expressions, gestures, intonation of voice, office layouts and appearance, personal dress	Can enhance what is being said orally; may reduce need for other communications	Not always consistent with the oral message; may be accomplished without the sender knowing or desiring it

The placement of furniture in a manager's office can communicate a nonverbal message to visitors.

you are familiar. What do these layouts "say" to the visitor?

Physical Distractions

Any number of physical distractions can interfere with the effectiveness of a communication attempt. Some of these distractions are evident in the following conversation between an employee, George, and his manager.[9]

> Okay George, let's hear your problem [phone rings, boss picks it up, promises to deliver a report "just as soon as I can get it done"]. Uh, now, where were we—oh, you're having a problem with your secretary. She's [manager's secretary brings in some papers that need immediate signature, so he scribbles his name where she indicates; secretary leaves] . . . you say she's depressed a lot lately, wants to leave . . . I tell you what, George, why don't you [phone rings again, lunch partner drops by] . . . uh, take a stab at handling it yourself. . . . I've got to go now.

Besides what may have been poor intentions in the first place, the manager in this example suffered from a number of physical distractions that created information overload; too many things were occurring at once. The communication with George suffered as a result. This problem can easily be corrected by setting priorities and planning. If George has something important to say, the manager should set aside adequate time for the meeting. Additional interruptions such as telephone calls and drop-in visitors should be avoided by issuing appropriate instructions to a secretary. Such distractions can be avoided or at least minimized through proper managerial attention.

Cultural Differences

Differences in cultural backgrounds between senders and receivers can also cause communication breakdowns. Managers operating in arenas where cultural differences are extreme must be most cautious in this regard. When messages cross cultural boundaries, the effectiveness of a communication attempt can be compromised. This can occur, for example, when communications involve persons of different ethnic backgrounds or national origins, or even from different geographic regions within a country. Consider the communications problems that could arise from just a couple of differences in business practices between the United States and elsewhere in the world.

In the United States   Assigning a deadline to something is accepted practice.

    Elsewhere   Establishing a deadline may convey rudeness.

In the United States   Punctuality is important; being late is rude.

    Elsewhere   Being late may be expected; being early or even on time may be rude.

Cross-cultural communication problems often include a language factor. The most obvious example is in the international arena where managers may experience difficulty when a message that works well in one language is translated into another. The following advertising miscues are good illustrations of this pitfall.[10]

Coca-Cola Company lost sales in some Asian markets when consumers were confused over the ad, "Coke Adds Life." They translated the message to mean—"Coke Brings You Back from the Dead."

General Motors' "Body by Fisher" label translates in Flemish to "Corpse by Fisher"—not something conducive to car sales!

Status Effects

The hierarchy of authority in organizations creates another potential barrier to effective communications. The result of noise created by such status effects can be disastrous. Consider the following examples of "corporate cover-ups" reported by the *Wall Street Journal*.[11]

Example 1   The president of a large machinery producer ordered work to begin on a new kind of photocopying machine. Though those with direct responsibility for the machine knew the job would take two years, a report to the president stated that the machine could be developed in a matter of months. The reason: each layer of management shaved a few weeks off the original estimate to please superiors. Working day and night, the staff managed to construct a prototype to meet the truncated timetable. The president inspected it and left with assurances it was "ready to roll." Hardly had he left the lab when the prototype burst into flames and was destroyed.

Example 2   The chief executive of an electronics company on the West Coast discovered that shipments were being predated and papers falsified to meet sales targets that his managers knew were unrealistically high. At least 20 persons in the organization cooperated in the deception, but it was months before the top found out.

Status differentials can create special barriers between managers and their subordinates. Given the authority of their positions, managers may be inclined to do a lot of "telling," but not much "listening." Subordinates, on the other hand, may be willing to tell only what they expect the boss wants to hear. The "Backing Off" cartoon offers a parody on the day-to-day consequences of status effects. Whether the reason is a fear of retribution for bringing bad news, an unwillingness to identify personal mistakes, or just a general desire to please, the end result in all cases is the same! The manager receiving distorted communications ends up making poor decisions because of a biased and inaccurate information base.

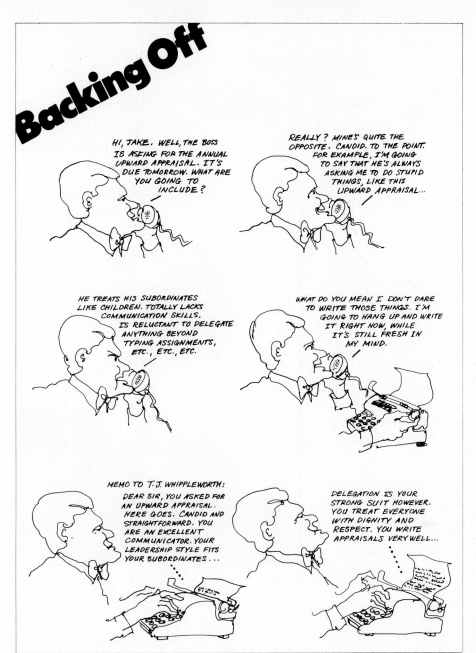

Status effects in upward communication. *Source:* Reprinted by permission from *Mgr. Magazine.* AT&T Long Lines.

PERCEPTION AND COMMUNICATION[12]

A word that has been used in this chapter and elsewhere in the book without anything specific said about it is *perception*. Actually, perception is an extremely important element in communication and other interpersonal relationships. **Perception** is the process through which people receive and interpret information from the environment. It is the way we form impressions about ourselves, other people, and day-to-day life experiences. It is also the way we process information into the decisions that ultimately guide our actions.

Figure 11.4 depicts perception as a screen or

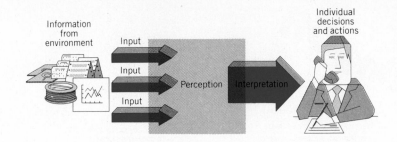

FIGURE 11.4 The perception process.

filter through which information must pass before it impacts individual decisions and actions. Depending on individual values, needs, cultural background, and other circumstances of the moment, information will pass through this screen with varying interpretations and degrees of accuracy. Thus perception introduces another form of potential noise into the communication process.

Understanding Different Perceptions

People can perceive the same situation quite differently. Do you see the young woman or the old woman in Figure 11.5? Check your perception by looking again to find both faces in the picture. Better yet, let's have a quiz.

Quiz: The Robbery[13]

The lights in a store had just been turned off by a businessman when a man appeared and demanded money. The owner opened a cash register. The contents of the cash register were scooped up, and the man sped away. A member of the police force was notified promptly.

Answer the following questions about the story by circling T for true, F for false, or ? for unknown.

1. A man appeared after the owner turned off his store lights.   T F ?
2. The robber was a man.   T F ?
3. The man who appeared did not demand money.   T F ?
4. The man who opened the cash register was the owner.   T F ?
5. The store owner scooped up the contents of the cash register and ran away.   T F ?
6. Someone opened a cash register.   T F ?

FIGURE 11.5 What do you see in this portrait? The young lady or the elderly lady?

7. After the man who demanded money scooped the contents of the cash register, he ran away.   T F ?
8. While the cash register contained money, the story does not state how much.   T F ?
9. The robber demanded money of the owner.   T F ?
10. A businessman had just turned off the lights when a man appeared in the store.   T F ?
11. It was broad daylight when the man appeared.   T F ?

Table 11.2 Perceptual Differences Between Managers and Their Subordinates

Source of Recognition	Frequency Supervisors Feel Given "Very Often"	Frequency Subordinates Feel "Very Often" Received
"Gives privileges"	52%	14%
"Gives more responsibility"	48	10
"Gives a pat on the back"	82	13
"Gives sincere and thorough praise"	80	14
"Trains for better jobs"	64	9
"Gives more interesting work"	51	5

Source: Developed from Rensis Likert, *New Patterns of Management* (New York: McGraw-Hill, 1961).

12. The man who appeared opened the cash register.   T F ?
13. No one demanded money.   T F ?
14. The story concerns a series of events in which only three persons are referred to: the owner of the store, a man who demanded money, and a member of the police force.   T F ?
15. The following events occurred: someone demanded money, a cash register was opened, its contents were scooped up, and a man dashed out of the store.   T F ?

Before scoring the quiz, a basic point must be restated. Through perception, each of us forms impressions about the world in which we live. These impressions affect our decisions and actions. Inaccurate impressions can lead to biased decisions and inappropriate actions.

Now, let's see how well you did on the quiz. Look back at your responses. Only three questions have a factual frame of reference: (3) false, (6) true, and (13) false. All other questions should be marked ?. Rereading the story will help you understand why this scoring is correct. A critical question remains—as a manager, can you afford to make perceptual errors when dealing with events and other persons in the work setting?

The manager's task is made even more complicated by the fact that different people will perceive the same situation differently. Thus not only must you be on guard to make your own perceptions as accurate as possible, you must also anticipate, recognize, and be prepared to react to the potential perceptual biases of others. Look, for example, at the data in Table 11.2. They show differences in how managers and subordinates perceived the same situation. At issue is the frequency with which recognition is given as a reward for work performance. Managers were asked: "How frequently do you give recognition for good work done by employees in your work group?" Subordinates were asked: "How frequently does your supervisor give recognition for good work done by employees in your work group?" As the table shows, the managers *perceived* they gave recognition frequently; subordinates *perceived* recognition as less frequently available as a work reward.

Avoiding Perceptual Distortions

Four common perceptual distortions that can have a significant impact on the quality of a manager's decisions and actions are stereotypes, halo effects, selective perceptions, and projections.

Figure 11.6 places each in a managerial perspective. Because these distortions can prevent managers from drawing an accurate impression of a person or situation, they can cause problems in the communication and problem-solving processes.

Stereotypes

A **stereotype** occurs when an individual is identified with a group or category, and then the attributes associated with the group or category

FIGURE 11.6 Perceptual distortions in a managerial perspective.

are assigned to the individual in question. Common stereotypes are those of young people, old people, teachers, students, union members, males, and females, among others. The phenomenon, in each case, is the same. A person is classified into a group on the basis of one piece of information—age, for example. Characteristics commonly associated with the group (i.e., "young people dislike authority") are then assigned to the individual. What is generalized about the group as a whole may or may not be true about the individual. Thus stereotypes tend to obscure individual differences.

Age and sex create two common stereotypes that may complicate work situations. *Newsline 11.2* plays on the reversal of a classic sex-role stereotype that secretarial jobs are for women only. "Management," by contrast, has traditionally been viewed as the work domain of men. Although these barriers are falling and women increasingly are able to assume any job to which they might aspire, women may still encounter job biases that trace back to traditional sex-role stereotypes.

Age stereotypes also exist in the workplace. The following example shows how the inappropriate use of age stereotypes by managers may place older workers at a disadvantage in various work situations.[14]

Problem Individual work performance is observed to be declining.

> *Impact of stereotype* Manager assumes older workers are resistant to change and reassigns the older worker, instead of encouraging improvement in the present job.

Problem Someone must be promoted to fill an important challenging job.

> *Impact of stereotype* Manager assumes older workers lack creativity, are cautious, and tend to avoid risk; the older worker is not selected for promotion.

Problem An older individual requests reassignment to a job requiring substantial physical strength.

> *Impact of stereotype* Manager assumes older workers are weak because their physical strength has declined with age; the older worker is asked to withdraw the request for transfer.

The use of stereotypes of any type can prevent a manager from accurately assessing individual differences at work. Because they can compromise managerial decisions and reduce the effectiveness of communications, stereotypes are a perceptual distortion that should be closely disciplined and controlled. Sex and age stereotypes are most unfortunate in a day and age when equal employment opportunity for all persons is not only the law, but a positive social value as well.

Halo Effects

A **halo effect** occurs when one attribute is used to develop an overall impression of a person or situation. This involves generalization from only one attribute to the total person or event. When meeting a new person, for example, the halo effect may cause one trait such as a pleasant smile to result in a positive first impression. By contrast, a particular hairstyle or manner of dressing may create a negative reaction.

Halo effects cause the same problem for managers as do stereotypes—individual differences become obscured. This is especially significant in respect to a manager's views of subordinates' work performance. One factor, such as a person's punctuality, may become the "halo" for a total performance evaluation. Just as it is not enough to assume that anyone who comes to work early is a good performer, occasional

NEWSLINE 11.2

SECRETARY OF YEAR NEVER EVEN WEARS A DRESS TO WORK

CHICAGO (AP)—Ellsworth Filhe, Jr. has broken a women's barrier. He is Chicago's 1982 Secretary of the Year.

Filhe is the first male member of the Professional Secretaries International's Chicago Lake Shore Chapter, and on Monday night at an awards ceremony he became the first man to win the honor since it was originated in 1950.

He received a plaque and typewriter-topped loving cup.

The 48-year-old bachelor, who has had five women bosses, is a confidential secretary at the Legal Assistance Foundation of Chicago and has been doing office work for 30 years.

He says he types 75 words a minute and takes shorthand even faster.

Filhe, who attended Wilson Junior College in Chicago, said he was a civilian clerk-typist for the Army when his boss was promoted and needed a secretary.

"He wanted to promote me, but I couldn't take dictation. He urged me to learn it at night school. I did and got the job." said Filhe, who joined Legal Assistance 11 years ago. "I'm self-motivated, and the people I've worked for don't structure my job too much. They give me a lot of freedom . . . as long as the results are there."

Filhe said he doesn't mind making coffee in the office, but he doesn't have to do it at Legal Assistance. "We've got a coffee machine."

Filhe draws praise from his superiors.

"He's clearly the best secretary I ever had," said Rita McClennon, director of development for Legal Assistance. "He's very direct; always clear about what I can and cannot expect from him. And he's very controlled, even when we're running a fund raiser and things get hectic."

Source: Quoted from "Secretary of Year Never Even Wears a Dress to Work," *Daily Egyptian* (January 28, 1982), p. 10. Copyright © 1982 Associated Press. Used by permission.

lateness may not equate with poor overall performance. Even though the general conclusion seems to make sense, it may or may not be true in a given circumstance. The manager's job is to get true impressions and not allow halo effects to result in biased performance evaluations.

Selective Perception

Selective perception, introduced in Chapter 3, is the tendency to single out for attention those aspects of a situation or attributes of a person that reinforce or appear consistent with one's existing beliefs, values, or needs. Like the other perceptual distortions, selective perception can

bias a manager's views on situations and individuals. One way to check this is to gather additional opinions from other people. This adds multiple perceptions to the single perception of the manager. When such perceptions prove contradictory, efforts should be made to check the original impression and determine which alternative is a most appropriate basis for decision making and action.

Projection

Projection is the assignment of personal attributes to other individuals. A classic projection error is the manager who assumes that subordinates want or desire the same from their work as the manager does from his or her own job. Suppose, for example, that you enjoy a lot of responsibility and challenge in your work. Suppose, too, that you are the newly appointed supervisor of persons whose work seems dull and routine. You might move quickly to start a program of job enrichment to help your subordinates experience more responsibility and challenge. Why? Because you want them to experience those things that you personally value. This may not be a good decision. Instead of designing the subordinates' jobs to best fit *their* needs, you have designed their jobs to fit *yours.* In fact, they may be quite satisfied and productive doing jobs that, to you, seem dull and routine. Your error was to project your desires to them, and then change a situation from good to bad as a result.

Projection is another perceptual distortion that compromises a manager's ability to respond to individual differences in the work setting. It can be controlled through a high degree of self-awareness and by a willingness to empathize with other persons and try to see things through their eyes.

Managing the Perception Process

Successful managers understand the importance of perception in the communication process and as an influence on behavior, and they act accordingly. They are aware of perceptual distortions, and they know that perceptual differences are likely to exist in any situation. As a result they try to make decisions and take action with a true understanding of the work situation as it is viewed by all persons concerned. A manager who is skilled in the perception process will[15]

1. *Have a high level of self-awareness.* Individual needs, experience, and expectations can all affect perceptions. The successful manager knows this and is able to identify when he or she is inappropriately distorting a situation because of such perceptual tendencies.

2. *Seek information from various sources to confirm or disconfirm personal impressions of a decision situation.* The successful manager minimizes the biases of personal perceptions by seeking out the viewpoints of others. These insights are used to gain additional perspective on situations and the problems or opportunities they represent.

Our nonverbal behavior often communicates messages to other persons. What is the man on the left in the photo communicating nonverbally?

3. *Be empathetic—that is, be able to see a situation as it is perceived by other people.* Different people will define the same situation somewhat differently. The successful manager rises above personal impressions to understand problems as seen by other people.

4. *Influence the perceptions of other people when they are drawing incorrect or incomplete impressions of events in the work setting.* People act in terms of their perceptions. The successful manager is able to influence the perceptions of others so that work events and situations are interpreted as accurately as possible and to the advantage of all concerned.

5. *Avoid common perceptual distortions that bias our views of people and situations.* These distortions include the use of stereotypes and halo effects, as well as selective perception and projection. Successful managers are self-disciplined and sufficiently self-aware that the adverse impacts of these distortions are minimized.

ORGANIZATIONAL COMMUNICATION

Organizational communication is the specific process through which information is exchanged in interactions among persons inside the organization. We noted in Chapter 7 that organizational structures are communication networks formally linking people and groups to one another. The networks may be arranged in different configurations—the wheel or all-channel networks, for example—depending on the information/processing requirements of the tasks or problems at hand. Now it is time to examine the channels or routes through which messages flow in these networks of organizational communication. These channels can be formal or informal, and the direction of information flows can be downward, upward, or lateral.

Formal and Informal Communication Channels

Formal communication channels follow the chain of command established by an organization's hierarchy of authority. An organization chart, for example, indicates the proper routing for official messages passing from one level or part of the hierarchy to another. Because formal communication channels are recognized as official and authoritative, it is typical for written communications in the form of letters, memos, policy statements, and other announcements to adhere to them.

Informal communication channels exist outside of the formal channels and do not adhere to the organization's hierarchy of authority. They coexist with the formal channels, but frequently diverge from them by skipping levels in a hierarchy and/or cutting across vertical chains of command. Figure 11.7 shows the informal channels that developed alongside the formal communication system of an advertising agency. Note that the informal channels do not coincide with working relationships formally specified by the agency's hierarchy of authority.

The importance of informal communication channels in organizations is highlighted in the recent best-selling book *In Search of Excellence.*[16] Thomas J. Peters and Robert H. Waterman, Jr., the book's authors, report their study of successful companies found: "The excellent companies are a vast network of informal, open communications. The patterns and intensity cultivate the right people's getting into contact with each other." Some of the interesting examples they cite include

Walt Disney Productions Everyone from the president on down wears a tag with only his or her first name on it.

Levi Strauss Calls its open-door policy the "fifth freedom."

Corning Glass Installed escalators instead of elevators in a new engineering building to increase opportunities for face-to-face contact.

3M Sponsors clubs for groups of 12 or more employees in hopes of increasing the probability of spontaneous problem-solving sessions.

One informal channel we all know about is the "grapevine." Among the advantages of grapevines are their abilities to transmit information quickly and efficiently. Every experienced manager knows that a message well placed in a

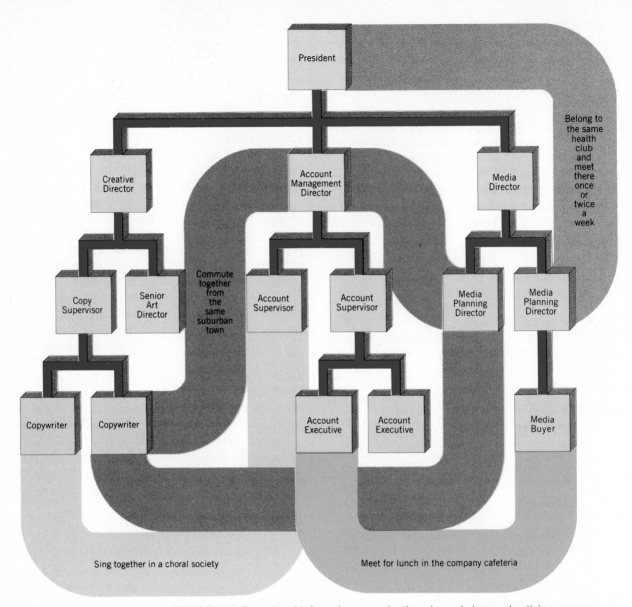

Labels within the figure:
President
Creative Director
Account Management Director
Media Director
Belong to the same health club and meet there once or twice a week
Copy Supervisor
Senior Art Director
Commute together from the same suburban town
Account Supervisor
Account Supervisor
Media Planning Director
Media Planning Director
Copywriter
Copywriter
Account Executive
Account Executive
Media Buyer
Sing together in a choral society
Meet for lunch in the company cafeteria

FIGURE 11.7 Formal and informal communication channels in an advertising agency. *Source:* Lawrence J. Gitman and Carl McDaniel, Jr., *Business World* (New York: John Wiley & Sons, 1983), p. 113. Used by permission.

grapevine can travel faster and often with greater impact than the same message passed along through formal channels. Grapevines also help fulfill needs for people involved in them. Being part of a grapevine, for example, can lend a sense of security by ensuring that you will "be in the know" when important things are going on. A grapevine can also provide social support through the variety of interpersonal contacts involved in the give and take of information.

The primary disadvantage of grapevines occurs when they transmit incorrect or untimely information. There is no doubt that rumors and prematurely released information can hurt an organization. Managers should come to know the grapevines operating in their work settings and use them as complements to formal channels. Instead of trying to eliminate grapevines, the advice is to make them work for you. After all, one of the best ways of avoiding incorrect rumor is to make sure they key persons in a grapevine get the right information to begin with.

Downward Communication

Figure 11.8 depicts organizational communication as it takes place in downward, upward, and lateral directions. **Downward communication** flows from higher to lower levels in the hierarchy. As indicated in Figure 11.8, one function of downward communication is to be informative. Lower-level personnel have the need to know what higher levels are doing and to be regularly reminded of key policies, strategies, objectives, and technical developments. When such information is shared, it can help minimize fears and suspicions regarding the intentions of higher-level personnel. Informative downward communication also increases the sense of security for receivers who feel they know the whole story.

Other, and perhaps more difficult, sides to downward communication are its directive and evaluative functions. Managers are responsible for communicating job instructions, standards, and other work expectations to subordinates. This information defines roles and assists subordinates in knowing what is expected of them and in what time frame. Ultimately, too, downward communications carry evaluations of past behavior and performance. This information further clarifies new expectations and becomes an essential part of a manager's controlling function.

Upward Communication

Upward communication involves messages flowing from lower to higher levels in an organization's hierarchy of authority. Figure 11.8 shows that organization members should and do engage in upward communication for a variety of reasons. These include keeping superiors informed about lower-level activities, sharing feelings and needs, reporting progress, and requesting resource support.

What Should Be Communicated Upward[17]

A task force at the Johnson & Johnson company concluded that upward communication should keep higher-level managers informed about

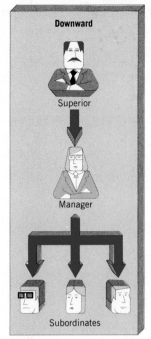
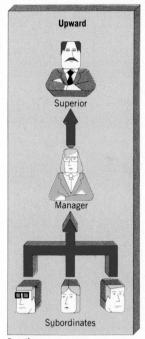

Function
Inform, direct work, evaluate results

Function
Inform, report progress, request support

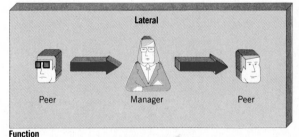

Function
Inform, request support, coordinate activities

FIGURE 11.8 Three directions of organizational communication.

1. *What subordinates are doing*   Highlights of their work, achievements, progress, and future job plans.
2. *Unsolved work problems*   Outlines of ongoing problems, and the aid subordinates may need to resolve them at present and/or in the future.
3. *Suggestions for improvements*   Ideas on ways to do things better at individual, work-unit, and/or organizational levels.
4. *How subordinates think and feel about their jobs, their associates, and the organization*   Personal feelings and attitudes relating to the emotional and interpersonal qualities of the work setting.

Table 11.3 Important Questions to Stimulate Upward Communication Regarding Subordinates' Feelings

Areas of Concern	Key Questions a Manager Can Ask of Subordinates
Feelings about the job	Are they satisfied with their pay?
	Are working hours and shift rotations reasonable?
	Is the workload fairly distributed?
	How adequate are tools, equipment, and office furniture?
	Do they feel that all possible candidates for promotion from within are given full and honest consideration?
Feelings about associates; superiors, subordinates, equals	What do they think of the efficiency of the boss, the department, the organization?
	Do they feel that the boss has favorites?
	Do they feel prepared to grow and advance?
	Do they feel that superiors resist new ideas?
	Are they afraid to present honest complaints to the boss?
	Do they feel that you understand their needs and desires?
Feelings about the organization	What do they think about the organization's integrity and fairness as an employer?
	What do they think of the organization's financial strength and ability to maintain its competitive position?
	What is the organization's reputation in the community?
	What do their families and associates think of the organization?
	Do they know and accept personnel practices regarding illness, vacations, etc.?
	Do they understand and take full advantage of all benefit programs, such as health, insurance, and retirement programs?

Source: Excerpted from Earl G. Planty and William Machaner, "Stimulating Upward Communication," Johnson & Johnson Company Report, undated. Used by permission.

The first three items on the list are work centered. They are things about which the Johnson & Johnson people felt the "alert" manager would normally try to stay informed. But the fourth item dealing with personal feelings and attitudes was one that seemed to receive less attention. It also appeared of equal and perhaps greater importance to the others. The task force thus went on to identify a number of questions that can be used by managers to learn valuable things about subordinates' feelings. A sample of these questions is given in Table 11.3. When questions such as these are answered, the manager ends up with additional information on which to make subordinate-related decisions. And, the subordinate has added opportunity to satisfy basic human needs and release emotional stress as a result of expressing ideas and feelings to a higher level of management.

Facilitating Upward Communication

Status effects were discussed earlier for their potential to limit the effectiveness of communication between subordinates and superiors. *Newsline 11.3* introduces "management by wandering around" as one strategy managers adopt to help overcome such problems. The basic objective is to break down status barriers, increase the frequency of interpersonal contact, and get better and more information from appropriate lower-level sources.

Other organizations try to structure opportunities for upward communication to occur on

NEWSLINE 11.3

WANT TO FIND OUT WHAT'S GOING ON? TAKE A WALK

There are basically two ways for a chief executive to find out what's happening in his organization: The first is to rely on the chain of command; the second is to find out for himself.

John C. Teets of Greyhound tries to spend a day or more each week in the field talking to plant managers, supervisors, and production people, asking questions of everyone he meets. He credits the practice with solving a major quality problem in a food division and contributing to a much healthier management climate.

"You can't follow the chain of command and know what's really going on in your company," insists Teets. "The information that comes in monthly reports has been screened several times; it often doesn't get to the core of problems." Moreover, he says, "lots of people who surround the boss operate from the assumption: 'If he doesn't ask, don't tell him.' They know nobody likes surprises."

The executives who practice "management by wandering around" try to avoid asking unfocused questions (e.g., "How are things going?") and instead find it more productive to ask focused questions (e.g., "What's going particularly well?" "What isn't going well?" "What are your biggest worries these days?"). Observes one CEO: "You don't always get honest answers the first time you come around, because people may be nervous or may think you don't really want to know. By the second or third time you come around, some will start to speak up."

Making people feel at ease in the presence of the "big boss" isn't always easy. But the comfort level can be enhanced by emphasizing that you want to know what ideas they have for making the company better. As a general rule, questions should be work, not personality, oriented, and have a clear business purpose.

How much a boss can learn from wandering around depends on the ability to establish a trusting relationship with those spoken with—and the knowledge of the people spoken with. Says one executive: "You find some people who've been waiting years to be asked for their ideas, and others who never gave it a thought."

Source: Excerpted from George H. Labovitz, "Want to Find Out What's Going On? Take a Walk," *Wall Street Journal* (December 20, 1982), p. 12. Reprinted by permission of the *Wall Street Journal.* Copyright © 1982 Dow Jones & Company, Inc. All rights reserved.

a more formal basis. One hospital reports a comprehensive approach that involves[18]

Open office hours The hospital director holds open office hours every Wednesday afternoon from 4:00 to 5:00 P.M. Any employee wishing to speak in private with the director may do so at that time.

Employee meetings Each week, the hospital director holds a 60-minute morning meeting and a 90-minute evening meeting for 25–30 hospital employees who are selected at random from departments and divisions throughout the hospital. These meetings have a fairly structured format that includes reports from the director on current and future programs to improve services. Most of the time is given to employees who wish to ask questions or talk about their concerns or ideas.

Employee advisory council An employee advisory council is composed of 30 employees who are elected by their fellow employees. The council acts in an advisory capacity to the hospital director. The hospital director holds monthly meetings with the group's executive committee to discuss issues raised by the council. He also asks for reactions to policies or programs currently being developed by top management that will affect hospital employees.

Suggestion box Employees are encouraged to submit their ideas to the director's office. Employees who identify themselves receive a letter of acknowledgment. Staff then review ideas that seem promising. Employees whose ideas for improving service are implemented are given public recognition, and when these ideas lead to savings in dollars or to increased revenues, the authors may receive cash awards.

Lateral Communication

Lateral communication occurs among persons working at the same level in the hierarchy of authority, but typically representing different departments or work units. Figure 11.8 shows the function of lateral communication as frequently to inform, but also to request support and coordinate activities. Common mechanisms for achieving lateral communication through formal channels are direct contact, cross-departmental committees, teams or task forces, and the matrix organization. These were discussed in Chapter 6 as ways for facilitating horizontal coordination among those organizational components whose activities are important to one another.

Informal channels are also important in the context of lateral communications. Given its ability to cut across vertical hierarchies, the grapevine typically emerges as a key element in this regard. Since lateral communications fall outside the formal chain of command, they tax the full extent of a manager's interpersonal and communication skills.

Communication of Roles

The term *role* has often been used in this book. A **role** is a set of activities expected of a person in a particular job or position within the organization.[19] One of the most important of a manager's communications is sending and receiving role expectations. On the sending side, the manager's responsibility is to define what he or she expects of subordinates. On the receiving side, the manager must be able to understand what his or her immediate supervisor is expecting as well.

Breakdowns or ineffectiveness in the communication of roles can result in role ambiguity and/or role conflict. **Role ambiguity** occurs when the person in a role is uncertain about what others expect in terms of his or her behavior. To do a job well, a person needs to know what is expected. Sometimes job expectations may be unclear because the manager has not even tried to communicate them to the subordinate. Other times the manager may have tried, but done so inadequately. Role ambiguity may also result from a failure of the subordinate to listen to what the supervisor is saying.

Role conflict occurs when the person in a role is unable to respond to the expectations held by one or more others. In this case, the role expectations are understood; that is, effective communication has taken place. But, for one reason or another, all of the expectations cannot be fulfilled. A common form of conflict is **role overload,** when too many role expectations are being communicated to a person at a given time. There is too much work to be done and too little time to do it. Managers who rely on one-way communications are especially prone to create role overload for their subordinates. Cut off from valuable feedback, it is hard for these managers to learn when or why a subordinate is being asked to do too much.

Role dynamics in the form of ambiguities and conflicts can create tensions that have adverse effects on work attitudes and performance. As a manager, you can be the cause of these tensions in others. You may also experience them yourself. In either case, good communication skills can help resolve any difficulties in the resulting role dynamics.

GUIDELINES FOR EFFECTIVE COMMUNICATION

The following item appeared quite some time ago in the London *Times*.[20] Although addressed to anthropology buffs, it holds a lesson for all managers interested in becoming effective communicators.

EASTER ISLAND—Mr. Thor Heyerdahl, the Norwegian scientist of Kon Tiki fame, declared here last night that the mystery of the great stone statues of Easter Island is a mystery no longer. Mr. Heyerdahl has just led another archeological expedition into the South Pacific, including several weeks on Easter Island.

Easter Islanders engaged by Mr. Heyerdahl and his party transported and erected one of the giant statues in what Mr. Heyerdahl is convinced is the same manner in which their forebears did. The team of 180 Easter Islanders had no difficulty in towing the statue over level grass from the quarry where it lay. On the selected site it was raised by levering the other side similarly. When the base of the statue reached the height of the plinth the levering and wedging process was applied only to the upper portion of the statue, which was thus raised gradually to a position from which it could be hauled vertically by ropes.

With 12 hired islanders Mr. Heyerdahl raised the 30-ton statue to the vertical in 18 days by this ancient method. This statue now ornaments the island skyline as the only one of the great monoliths standing as in ancient days. . . .

Mr. Heyerdahl and his fellow archeologists have a modest explanation of their discovery of the system by which ancient monuments were raised without mechanical aids. Previous expeditions to Easter Island have returned without the answer. Mr. Heyerdahl sought the opinion of the island's mayor on the methods used by ancient Islanders to erect their statues, and the answer was immediately forthcoming. "Why did you not tell this to previous expeditions?" asked Mr. Heyerdahl. "They never asked me," vouchsafed the phlegmatic old mayor.

Managers, as did the archeologists who preceded Heyerdahl to Easter Island, may sometimes fail to get accurate information from other persons simply for failure to ask. Other times, the manager may ask and still not find out!

Effective communication, facilitated by good listening, helped Thor Heyerdahl unlock the mystery of the Easter Island statutes.

Being an effective communicator is a skill. Part of the skill lies in recognizing and overcoming communication barriers we have already discussed. Another lies in encouraging a flow of accurate and sufficient information in your direction—that is, being the "active listener." One more lies in being able to give constructive feedback or criticism to others in a nonthreatening way. Through these interpersonal skills the manager can take full advantage of effective two-way communication with other key persons in the work setting.

Active Listening

Active listening is a term popularized by the work of Carl Rogers and advocated by counselors and therapists.[21] The concept recognizes that when people "talk," they are trying to communicate something; that "something" may or may not be what they are saying. It means taking action to help the source of a message say what he or she really means. There are five guidelines to becoming an active listener.

1. *Listen for message content.* Try to hear exactly what is being said in the message.
2. *Listen for feelings.* Try to identify how the source feels in terms of the message content.
3. *Respond to feelings.* Let the source know that his or her feelings, as well as the message content, are recognized.
4. *Note all cues, verbal and nonverbal.* Be sensitive to the nonverbal messages as well as the verbal ones; identify mixed messages that need to be clarified.
5. *Reflect back to the source, in your own words, what you think you are hearing.* Restate or paraphrase the verbal and nonverbal messages as feedback to the source; allow the source to respond with further information.

The latter guideline is one of the most powerful of the active listening techniques. It helps the listener avoid passing judgment or giving advice, and encourages the source to say more about what is really the trouble. The following *listener responses* to someone's direct *questions* illustrate this aspect of active listening.[22]

Question Just whose responsibility is the tool room?

Listener's response Do you feel someone is challenging your authority there?

Question Don't you think able people should be promoted before senior but less able ones?

Listener's response It seems to you that they should, I take it?

Question What does the supervisor expect us to do about these broken-down machines?

Listener's response You're pretty disgusted with those machines aren't you?

The listener in these examples possesses active listening skills and responded to questions in a way that encouraged further communication. The listener should end up receiving important information that can be put to constructive use. The other person should also feel better after having been able to say what he or she felt, and being heard!

Table 11.4 lists 10 additional rules for good listening. Note that good listening begins and ends in the ability to stop talking!

The Art of Giving Feedback

Feedback is the process of telling other people how you feel about something they did or said, or about the situation in general. Managers regularly give feedback to other people. Frequently this is performance feedback given in the form of evaluations and appraisals. There is an art to giving feedback so that it is accepted and used by the receiver. Feedback that is poorly given can be threatening and cause resentment instead of constructive change.

The first requirement in giving feedback is to recognize when it is truly intended to benefit the receiver and when it is purely an attempt to satisfy a personal need. A manager who berates the secretary for typing errors, for example, may actually be mad about personally failing to give clear instructions in the first place.

Figure 11.9 identifies the foundations for effective feedback. Assuming that one's original intention is correct—that is, to give feedback helpful to the receiver—a manager should also recognize that constructive feedback is[23]

Table 11.4 Ten Rules For Good Listening

Rule Listening	Reasoning Behind the Rule
1. Stop talking	You cannot listen if you are talking
2. Put the person at ease	Help a person feel free to talk; create a permissive environment
3. Show the person you want to listen	Look and act interested; listen to understand, not to oppose
4. Remove distractions	Don't doodle, tap, or shuffle papers; shut the door if necessary to achieve quiet.
5. Empathize	Try to see the other person's point of view
6. Be patient	Allow plenty of time; do not interrupt; don't start for the door or walk away
7. Hold your temper	An angry person takes the wrong meaning from words
8. Go easy on argument and criticism	Don't put people on the defensive and cause them to "clam up" or become angry; do not argue—even if you win, you lose
9. Ask questions	This encourages a person and shows that you are listening; it helps to develop points further
10. Stop talking	This is first and last, because all other guides depend on it; you cannot do an effective listening job while you are talking

Source: Adapted from *Human Behavior at Work,* Fifth Edition, by Keith Davis. Copyright © 1977 by Keith Davis. Used with the permission of McGraw-Hill Book Company.

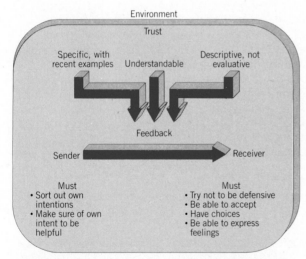

FIGURE 11.9 A model for giving and receiving feedback. *Source:* Joe Kelly, *Organizational Behavior: Its Data, First Principles and Applications,* Third Edition (Homewood, Ill.: Richard D. Irwin, 1980), p. 328. Used by permission.

- Given directly and with real feeling, and based on a relationship of trust between the giver and the receiver.
- Specific rather than general, with good, clear, and preferably recent examples.

- Given at a time when the receiver appears to be in a condition of readiness to accept it.
- Checked with others to be sure they support its validity.
- Concerned with things the receiver might be expected to be able to do something about.
- Not more than the receiver can handle at any particular time.

Newsline 11.4 puts this advice in even more practical terms. Note that active listening is one of the techniques for making criticism sessions more productive.

Ten Commandments of Good Communication

Effective communication is a two-way process that requires effort and skill by both sender and receiver. As a manager you will at times assume each of these positions in the communication process. This demands an ability to establish good interpersonal rapport with others, to empathize with them and understand the situation from their points of view, and to know yourself well enough to recognize where personal biases may be interfering with what is taking place.

NEWSLINE 11.4

HOW TO MAKE CRITICISM SESSIONS PRODUCTIVE

Criticizing a subordinate can be a real test for even the most seasoned manager. To often what is supposed to be a constructive session turns into a futile confrontation, with mutual gripes and hard feelings, but no solution of the problem.

Five simple suggestions can help the manager make criticism sessions more productive and problem solving.

Step 1. Get to the point. Don't evade the issue. Skip the small talk and go straight to the target: "Bob, I want to talk to you about your late reports," or "Barbara, I called you in to discuss your personality conflict with the director of sales."

Step 2. Describe the situation. Use a descriptive opening that is specific, not general. Avoid evaluative openings at all costs. Evaluative: "Bob, I can no longer deal with your late, sloppy reports." Descriptive: "Bob you've been late on three reports in the last two weeks. That caused us two shipping delays and cost us $5000."

Step 3. Use active listening techniques. Encourage the subordinate to tell his or her side of the story. It will reduce defensiveness, clarify the situation, and provide both parties with an opportunity to think the problem through. It helps to ask open-ended questions that invite discussion and cannot be answered with a simple "yes" or "no." Begin questions with *what* or *how,* or sometimes *tell me* or *describe.* Bad: "Do you like our new computer system?" Good: "How do you feel about our new computer system?"

Step 4. Agree on the source of the problem and its solution. It's essential that the subordinate agree that there is in fact a problem. If not, there's little likelihood the problem will be solved. Once you and the subordinate have identified and agreed on the problem, work together to identify the source, and let the subordinate get involved in coming up with a potential solution.

Step 5. Summarize the meeting. Have the subordinate synopsize the discussion and the agreed solution. Both subordinate and manager should leave the session with the same understanding of what was decided. Establish a follow-up date that allows the subordinate reasonable time to correct the situation.

Source: Excerpted from J. Stephen Morris, "How to Make Criticism Sessions Productive," *Wall Street Journal* (October 12, 1981), p. 24. Reprinted by permission of the *Wall Street Journal.* Copyright © 1981 Dow Jones & Company, Inc. All rights reserved.

The American Management Association published the following "ten commandments of good communication." If you will put these commandments together with your basic understanding of the communication process itself, you will have a good foundation for building and maintaining an effective set of interpersonal communication skills. The ten commandments of good communication are[24]

1. *Clarify your ideas before communicating.* Good communication requires good planning. Think through the message and consider who will be receiving and/or affected by it.

2. *Examine the true purpose of each communication.* Ask yourself what you *really* want to accomplish—obtain information, initiate action, or influence someone's behavior. Then prepare your message around the objective.

3. *Consider the total physical and human setting.* Meaning and intent are conveyed by more than words. Take into account not only what is to be said, but also the timing, physical setting, and social climate involved.

4. *Consult with others in planning communications.* Allowing others to participate in planning and developing facts can yield useful insights. Those who have helped you plan a communication are also likely to give it their active support.

5. *Be aware of the overtones as well as the basic content of your message.* Your tone of voice, expression, body language, and apparent receptivity to the receiver have a tremendous impact on those you wish to reach.

6. *Take every opportunity to communicate something of help or value to the receiver.* Get in the habit of looking at things from the other person's point of view. People respond best to managers whose messages take their interests into account.

7. *Follow up your communication.* Ask questions and encourage questions to learn if you have succeeded in expressing your true meaning and intentions. Allow for feedback in all communications.

8. *Communicate for tomorrow as well as today.* Plan communications to serve immediate needs as well as long-run interests and goals. Remember that postponing disagreeable communications makes them more difficult.

9. *Be sure your actions support your words.* The most persuasive communication is not what you say but what you do. Don't let your actions contradict your words.

10. *Be a good listener.* When we start talking, we often cease to listen. Listening demands that you concentrate on what is being said, and to recognize overtones as well as basic content.

SUMMARY

Communication is fundamental to organizations and to the activities of managers. Without an ability to communicate with others successfully, a manager will be unable to give and get the information needed to fulfill planning, organizing, leading, and controlling responsibilities. Especially when acting in a leadership capacity, the manager depends on communication to make his or her performance desires known and to provide support to the persons who must satisfy them.

Communication is an interpersonal process of sending and receiving symbols with meanings attached. These symbols can be verbal or nonverbal, and they can be transmitted as messages through written, oral, or nonverbal communication channels. It is up to the manager to choose wisely among possible symbols and channels to ensure that effective communication occurs. This is achieved only when the intended meaning of the sender and the meaning perceived by the receiver are one and the same.

Noise is anything that interferes with the effectiveness of communication. The potential sources of noise are many, and the concerned manager is always on guard to minimize their negative consequences for his or her communication attempts. One potential source of noise is perception, the process through which people receive, organize, and interpret information received from their environments. Because people tend to perceive the same situation differently, the manager must try to understand the perceptions of others and take them into account in all communication attempts. Among the perceptual distortions that tend to operate in work settings are stereotypes, halo effects, selective perceptions, and projections.

Organizational communication involves downward, upward, and lateral channels through which people in organizations transmit and receive information in interactions with one another. This includes both formal channels representing the chain of command and officially sanctioned by it, and informal channels such as the grapevine.

In the final result, effective communication

depends on both a sound framework for organizational communication and strong interpersonal communication skills among the organizational members. As a manager you will have to take the lead in demonstrating these skills and helping your subordinates develop them as well. Foremost among these are active listening and the art of giving feedback.

THINKING THROUGH THE ISSUES

1. Describe and give examples of why communication is essential to the management functions of planning, organizing, leading, and controlling.

2. Draw a diagram of the communication process and label the key components.

3. State five possible sources of noise in the communication process. Give an example of each type of noise as it might impact communications between you and (a) your course instructor and (b) your boss in a past or present job.

4. What is perception? How does perception influence communication?

5. What is a communication grapevine? How can the grapevine work to a manager's advantage and disadvantage in the work setting?

6. In organizational communication, what are the special demands on a manager as *sender* of downward and upward communication? What are the special demands on a manager as *receiver* of each type?

7. Explain "management by wandering around" as it relates to the communication process.

8. What is "active listening"? Can it really be used to advantage by a manager? Why or why not?

9. State four guidelines for giving feedback.

10. Which of the "ten commandments" of good communication are the *most* important? Why?

THE MANAGER'S VOCABULARY

Active listening	Efficient	Noise	Role overload
Communication	communication	Organizational	Selective perception
Communication	Feedback	communication	Stereotype
channel	Formal channels	Perception	Upward
Downward	Halo effect	Projection	communication
communication	Informal channels	Role	
Effective	Lateral communication	Role ambiguity	
communication	Mixed messages	Role conflict	

CAREER PERSPECTIVE: SO YOU'RE AFRAID TO CRITICIZE YOUR BOSS[25]

"Criticize my boss? I don't have the right to."
"I'd get fired."
"It's his company, not mine."
Many executives recognize that it's important to encourage criticism from their subordinates. Walking about United Airlines, Ed Carlson solicited criticism, both as a source of information and as a way of conveying

respect to middle managers. At ITT, Harold Geneen was well known for the way he bawled out subordinates, but he also structured the organization to encourage criticism of superiors, including himself. Geneen felt that criticism of superiors would enable problems to surface more quickly, so they could be nipped in the bud. Konosuke Matsushita built his company with a philosophy stressing criticism as a form of self-discipline necessary to the growth of the individual and the company.

Unfortunately, not everyone has the good fortune to work in such companies. George Steinbrenner, owner of the New York Yankees, is said to have given a Yankee manager, Billy Martin, a contract specifically prohibiting him from criticizing his superiors. And the business sections of newspapers and magazines are filled with examples of criticism of top executives with the source consciously being kept anonymous.

Questions

1. There will surely be times when you are convinced that things could be improved in the organization for which you work. There will also be times when you won't be quite sure how your boss will respond to criticism. What problems do you see associated with situations that require criticism of your boss?

2. What guidelines will you follow in communicating such criticism to a future boss?

CASE APPLICATION: MY DOOR IS ALWAYS OPEN[26]

Setting:	The Production Manager's Office
Participants:	Gilbert Steiner, Manager
	Harold Terry, Scheduler
Time:	Monday morning

Steiner: Good morning, Hal. Have a nice weekend?

Terry: Great, Mr. Steiner . . . took the family to the beach.

Steiner: Fine weekend for it . . . bet your kids enjoyed it.

Terry: They certainly did. My oldest boy loves the ocean.

Steiner: Billy!

Terry: (surprised) Yes, Billy. I didn't know you knew his name.

Steiner: You probably told me once.

Terry: You have a good memory.

Steiner: Thank you. Frankly, it's something I developed a long time ago. It's good management practice to get to know a little about your employees . . . their families . . . it brings you closer to them.

Terry: I can't argue with that.

Steiner: Sounds a little phony at first. . . . I mean a person could sound like a fool overplaying the concerned boss and carrying on about an employee's arthritic dog, Jasper . . . but I mean real interest and concern in the man and his family.

Terry: I'm sure it pays dividends in employee loyalty and productivity.

Steiner:	It certainly does. When you become a supervisor, I'm sure you'll realize it even more. . . . (pause) Well, we'd better get started before the week is over.
Terry:	Right. I've already checked the Final Assembly Department, and we should be able to ship the Fedderson order by Wednesday and the A-B-N Industries order by Thursday or Friday.
Steiner:	Good. I'll hold you to that. . . .
Terry:	We do have a couple of problems, though, which I want to talk to you about.
Steiner:	Yes?
Terry:	We can't ship to Ellis Industries as planned this week because . . .
Steiner:	(angrily) What?
Terry:	The parts we need still haven't arrived.
Steiner:	Dammit, man! You told me that last week didn't you?
Terry:	Yes, I did but . . .
Steiner:	And do you recall what I told you?
Terry:	You said it was my responsibility to make sure the parts came in.
Steiner:	And you blew it!
Terry:	Well, I did review the problem with Purchasing and they suggested . . .
Steiner:	To hell with Purchasing! Those paperwork clerks only help foul up things worse. You should have contacted the vendor directly and . . . (pausing and composing himself). Look, Hal, you're a big boy. I don't have to do your job, do I?
Terry:	Of course not, Mr. Steiner.
Steiner:	Then you will get those parts this week won't you?
Terry:	Yes, I'll get the parts.
Steiner:	And you'll ship by Friday?
Terry:	We'll ship by Friday.
Steiner:	(smiling) Good. Management by results is the only thing that counts . . . don't you agree?
Terry:	Yes, sir.
Steiner:	(serious) Look, Hal, I guess I come down hard on you sometimes but it's because I expect a lot from you. How can you grow without challenge . . . without difficult objectives to reach?
Terry:	I suppose you're right.
Steiner:	I know I'm right. It's a philosophy I learned from my father years ago . . . results count, not words.
Terry:	True.
Steiner:	Anything else I should know? I don't care for lots of detail, but, at the same time, a person can easily get cut out of the communications loop by getting too far from the action. And I don't like to get cut out of the loop.
Terry:	Not really. Everything else is moving according to schedule. (pauses) The people in Shipping are a little upset, though, over the late Friday afternoon shipping schedules and were asking me if we in Manufacturing might not work out a more sequential shipping schedule. I thought that was information we could use, particularly with the planned production increase for next quarter . . .
Steiner:	Ignore them. Those people are always complaining, and they'll bend your ear all day if you let them. That's not information, Hal, that's *noise* you're getting. When the shipping clerks stop complaining it means they're dead.
Terry:	Yes sir.
Steiner:	Anything else?
Terry:	No. As far as I know we've covered everything.
Steiner:	Hal, you know I like you. You've got tremendous potential in this department. I want to help you learn this business inside and out . . . I want to see you grow and develop.
Terry:	Yes?
Steiner:	Well, what I mean is . . . don't be reluctant to come to me if you have any problems which I can help you with . . . anything that you want to sit down and talk about . . . my door is always open.
Terry:	Thank you, Mr. Steiner. (turns to leave)
Steiner:	About that Ellis order . . . you did hear me didn't you?
Terry:	Yes, sir, I heard you. We'll ship by Friday.

Questions

1. Is Steiner's "open-door policy" effective? Why or why not?
2. Where do upward, downward, and lateral communication responsibilities impact Terry's role?
3. What would you do in this situation if you were Terry? Why?

CLASS EXERCISE: TRANSLATIONS FROM THE BAFFLEGAB:

We frequently talk about the need to improve our written communication skills. Rarely, however, does anyone force us to practice. It's time for a change.

1. Read each of the following statements. They are "executive communications" that can otherwise be termed "bafflegab."[27] In the space following each statement, write a brief but accurate translation, putting it the way you feel the message should be stated as part of a letter or memo.

   A. "We solicit any recommendations that you wish to make, and you may be assured that any such recommendations will be given our careful consideration."

   *Translation:*_____

   B. "This is our second request for reply to our delinquent-invoice notice date June 4, a copy of which is attached for your reference. It is imperative that we have your early reply to this communication."

   *Translation:*_____

   C. "Consumer elements are continuing to stress the fundamental necessity of a stabilization of the price structure at a lower level than exists at the present time."

   *Translation:*_____

   D. "The finance director claimed that substantial economies were being effected in his division by increasing the time interval between distribution of data-eliciting forms to business entities."

   *Translation:*_____

2. Share your translations with a nearby classmate. Discuss whose approach is clearest and most succinct, and why.

3. Modify your original translations as necessary to improve them. Await further class discussion led by your instructor.

REFERENCES

[1] Excerpted from Lawrence Rout, "Hyatt Hotel's Gripe Sessions Help Chief Maintain Communications with Workers," *Wall Street Journal* (July 16, 1981), p. 21. Reprinted by permission of the *Wall Street Journal*. Copyright © 1981 Dow Jones & Company, Inc. All rights reserved.

[2] Edgar F. Huse, *Management*, Second Edition (St. Paul, Minn.: West Publishing, 1982), p. 454.

[3] Henry Mintzberg, *The Nature of Managerial Work* (New York: Harper & Row, 1973).

[4] Portions of this section are adapted from John R. Schermerhorn, Jr., James G. Hunt, and Richard N. Osborn, *Managing Organizational Behavior* (New York: 1982), pp. 441–448. Used by permission.

[5] William J. Haney, *Communication and Interpersonal Communication: Text and Cases*, Fourth Edition (Homewood, Ill.: Richard D. Irwin, 1979), p. 315.

[6] These examples are from ibid., pp. 316, 317.

[7] This incident is reported in W. Warner Burke and Warren H. Schmidt, "Management and Organization Development: What is the Target of Change?" *Personnel Administration* (March-April 1971), pp. 44–57.

[8] Dale Level, Jr., "Communication Effectiveness:

Method and Situation," *Journal of Business Communication*, Vol. 10 (Fall 1972), pp. 19–25.

[9] Richard V. Farace, Peter R. Monge, and Hamish M. Russell, *Communicating and Organizing* (Reading, Mass.: Addison-Wesley, 1977), pp. 97–98.

[10] Andrew D. Szilagyi, Jr., *Management and Performance* (Santa Monica, Cal. Goodyear Publishing, 1981), p. 391; and, Edward M. Mazze, "How to Push a Body Abroad Without Making It a Corpse," *Business Abroad* (August 10, 1964), p. 15.

[11] Adapted from John and Mark Arnold, "Corporate Coverups," *Wall Street Journal* (June 5, 1978), p. 18. Reprinted by permission of the *Wall Street Journal*. Copyright © 1982 Dow Jones & Company, Inc. All Rights Reserved.

[12] Portions of this section are adapted from Schermerhorn, et al., op. cit., pp. 417–427. Used by permission.

[13] William V. Haney, *Communication and Interpersonal Relations: Text and Cases*, Fourth Edition. (Homewood, Ill.: Richard D. Irwin, 1979), pp. 250–251. Copyright © Richard D. Irwin, Inc., 1960, 1967, 1973, 1979. All rights reserved. Used by permission.

[14] Benson Rosen and Thomas H. Jerdee, "The Influence of Age Stereotypes on Managerial Decisions," *Journal of Applied Psychology*, Vol. 61 (1976), pp. 428–432.

[15] Some of these ideas are in Sheldon S. Zalkind and Timothy W. Costello, "Perception: Some Recent Research and Implications for Administration," *Administrative Science Quarterly*, Vol. 7 (September 1962), pp. 218–235.

[16] Thomas J. Peters and Robert H. Waterman, Jr., *In Search of Excellence* (New York: Harper & Row, 1983).

[17] This section is based on Earl G. Planty and William Machaner, "Stimulating Upward Communication," Johnson & Johnson Company Report, undated.

[18] Adapted from Robert B. Smith, "Bridging the Management Employee Gap," *Health Care Management Review*, Vol. 2 (Spring 1977), p. 910.

[19] See Robert L. Kahn, Donald M. Wolfe, Robert F. Quinn, and J. Diedrick Snoek, *Organizational Stress: Studies in Role Conflict and Ambiguity* (New York: Wiley, 1964).

[20] "An Easter Island Mystery Solved," *Times* (London) (August 1, 1956). Used by permission.

[21] This discussion is based on Carl R. Rogers and Richard E. Farson, "Active Listening" (Chicago: Industrial Relations Center of the University of Chicago).

[22] Haney, op. cit., p. 165.

[23] Adapted from John Anderson, "Giving and Receiving Feedback," in Paul R. Lawrence, Louis B. Barnes, and Jay W. Lorsch, *Organizational Behavior and Administration*, Third Edition (Homewood, Ill.: Richard D. Irwin, 1976), p. 109.

[24] Adapted, by permission of the publisher, from "Ten Commandments of Good Communication," *Management Review*, Vol. 44 (October 1955), pp. 704–705. © 1955 by AMACOM, a division of American Management Associations. All rights reserved.

[25] Excerpted from "So You're Afraid to Criticize Your Boss," *Wall Street Journal* (May 3, 1982), p. 26. Reprinted by permission of the *Wall Street Journal*. Copyright © 1982 Dow Jones & Company, Inc. All rights reserved.

[26] From Robert D. Joyce, *Encounters in Organizational Behavior: Problem Situations* (New York: Pergamon Press, 1972), pp. 2–5. Reprinted by permission of the publisher.

[27] The statements are from *Business Week* (July 6, 1981), p. 107.

12

LEADING THROUGH MOTIVATION

PSYCHIATRIST'S PATIENTS LOVE WORKING—SOME OF THEM TOO MUCH

NEW YORK—Jay Rohrlich has only a vague notion of the difference between a floating-rate debenture and a Treasury bill. But he is a Wall Street insider.[1]

Dr. Rohrlich is one of the few psychiatrists practicing in the downtown financial district. It's a singular place. Hardly anybody lives there, but hundreds of thousands work there—in high-pressure, high-risk occupations.

"If there's one problem that brings people to my office," he says, "it's that they like their work too much." In fact, he adds, "The intoxication of it obliterates whatever else they used to find enjoyable—they don't need to read books; they don't need to go to the theater; they sometimes don't even need to have sex."

Dr. Rohrlich believes that when it comes to work, most psychiatrists focus almost exclusively on the "negative side," on such things as stress and job dissatisfaction. He takes the opposite tack. "I was interested in people who enjoyed their work so much they couldn't enjoy anything else," he says.

Dr. Rohrlich used to practice on Manhattan's Upper East Side. There he noticed that his patients from the financial community "derived a kind of intoxication from their work that was missing from other patients." Wall Street he found, offers a clear-cut standard of success—"money, numbers, very undiluted kinds of objectives."

The catch is that work addicts usually don't recognize themselves as that. They come to an analyst with complaints of family troubles or of strains in some other areas of their personal lives. Dr. Rohrlich muses that most of his patients are "tremendously productive and interesting people," but "utterly lost in their personal lives."

PLANNING AHEAD

The chapter opener offers an interesting contrast to the lack of "motivation" often attributed to members of today's work force. Although "workaholism" may not be good in itself, managers are responsible for creating work environments within which people develop the desire to work hard as well as find opportunities to satisfy needs and achieve high-performance results. Chapter 12 addresses this leadership challenge.[2] Key topics include

The Concept of Motivation
Motivation and Rewards
Understanding Individual Needs
Equity Theory
Expectancy Theory
Reinforcement Theory
An Integrated Approach to Motivation

Why do some people outperform others in their work? What can be done to ensure that maximum performance is achieved by each and every employee? These questions have been asked for centuries. You must answer them if you are to master the manager's challenge as it was originally described in Chapter 1. Figure 12.1 reminds you once again that the basic challenge for anyone serving in a managerial role is to satisfy a performance accountability to a higher level of authority while being dependent on subordinates to produce the desired performance results. This chapter contains many ideas on how to exercise leadership in ways that encourage high performance on the part of other people. The concept of motivation is central to our investigation.

THE CONCEPT OF MOTIVATION

Suppose that a manager is fortunate enough to have subordinates whose abilities closely match task demands. Suppose, too, that these people have all the support required to do their jobs well. Can we predict that the subordinates will be high performers, and that the manager's challenge will therefore be satisfied? If the answer to this question were yes, your job as a manager would be greatly simplified. To ensure performance results, the advice would go, select per-

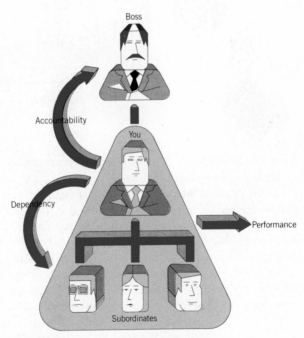

FIGURE 12.1 The manager's challenge.

sons of ability for the jobs to be done and make sure they get the necessary resource support.

Unfortunately, a manager's job isn't quite so easy. The reason traces to the variable implied as absent for the drill-press operator in the cartoon—work effort! You should remember effort as a critical variable in the individual performance

Source: Reprinted from *Mgr. Magazine,* 1977. Used by permission.

"What puzzles me is how he's gotten four weeks behind in his work when he's only been here two days."

equation introduced in Chapter 9: performance = ability × support × effort.

Our present interest in effort as a variable in the performance equation is based on the following logic. In order to achieve high performance, even people with ability and support must *try* to perform. That is, they must put forth adequate work effort. Willingness to exert effort, in turn, reflects **motivation to work.** This term is used in management theory to describe forces within the individual that account for the level, direction, and persistence of effort expended at work. A highly motivated person works hard in his or her job to support the production purposes of the work unit and the organization. An unmotivated person exerts minimum or no effort in this regard.

This chapter will help you learn more about leading through motivation. In order to enhance other people's motivation to work, you must be able to establish a work environment that makes such motivation possible. This environment will be one that makes the right kinds of rewards available to persons whose work efforts contribute to the achievement of organizational objectives.

MOTIVATION AND REWARDS

A **reward** is formally defined as a work outcome of positive value to the individual. Many types of rewards are available to people at work, and a manager is in a position to influence their allocation. Some of these rewards are listed in Table 12.1. They include such things as pay, praise, promotion, special work assignments, recognition, time-off, training opportunities, and privileges. Although we typically focus on pay as *the* key reward in the workplace, the other things in Table 12.1 count, too.

Table 12.1 Examples of Work-Related Rewards

Pay	Office fixtures
Promotion	Special assignments
Praise	Time off
Recognition	Special privileges
Fringe benefits	Enriched job
Feedback	Training opportunities

Rewards and Performance

Rewards are a means of paying attention to people and their work. Any reward, if used well, can assist the manager in establishing a motivational climate for persons within the work unit. The key phrase in the prior sentence is *if used well*. The manager's basic goal in this regard is to achieve a proper match between available rewards and workers' personal needs. The following parable suggests that this isn't always easy.

A Parable[3]

Once upon a time there was a donkey standing knee-deep in a field of carrots, contentedly munching away. A wise farmer wanted the donkey to pull a loaded wagon to another field, but the donkey would not walk over to the wagon. So the wise farmer stood by the wagon and held up a bunch of carrots for the donkey to see. But the donkey continued to munch contentedly on carrots in the field.

"But what," you ask, "do donkeys and carrots have to do with my goal of learning how to man-

Source: Reprinted from *Mgr. Magazine*, 1977. Drawing by Bill Basso. Used by permission.

age motivational dynamics?" The question is valid. Look at the carrot-and-stick cartoon, which appeared on the cover of a magazine distributed by the American Telephone & Telegraph Company to all of its supervisory personnel. The implied message is that managers use a variety of rewards or "carrots" in day-to-day attempts to encourage subordinates to put forth maximum efforts in their work.

Unfortunately, these attempts by managers are often no more successful than were the farmer's efforts in the parable. To allocate rewards successfully, that is, to achieve maximum motivational impact, it is necessary to:

1. Understand clearly what people need from their work activities.
2. Know how to distribute rewards so that these needs are met at the same time that the organization's interests are served.

Fortunately, managers have access to a number of motivation theories that offer insights relevant to both of these objectives. Each theory is largely grounded in the field of psychology and the philosophical tradition of hedonism. The latter asserts that people act to minimize pain and maximize pleasure in their lives. The motivation theories developed out of this tradition offer considerable assistance to the manager who wants to create a work environment within which people can achieve job satisfaction while facilitating high productivity for the organization.

Types of Motivation Theories

We will examine the managerial implications of three types of motivation theories in more detail—content, process, and reinforcement theories. Each of these theories offers its own special explanation of individual behavior at work.

Content theories of motivation offer ways to profile or analyze individuals to identify their needs. **Needs**, in turn, were first defined in Chapter 2 as physiological or psychological deficiencies that an individual feels some compulsion to eliminate. Content theories lend insight into various human needs and how they vary among people at work. The theories of Abraham Maslow and David McClelland are singled out in this chapter as two of the better-known examples of this orientation in motivation theory.

Process theories address the thought processes through which individuals give meaning to rewards and allow them to influence their behavior. They provide guidance on the actual allocation of rewards in specific work circumstances. We will discuss the equity and expectancy theories within this managerial frame of reference.

Reinforcement theory examines how people learn patterns of behavior based on environmental reinforcements. Using principles developed by B. F. Skinner, reinforcement theorists suggest ways of improving performance by clarifying goals, providing performance feedback, and properly administering rewards.

The content, process, and reinforcement approaches to motivation theory complement rather than compete or contradict one another. We will ultimately draw together the major insights of each into an integrative view of motivation that will prove useful to you as a practicing manager. As we turn to examine this carefully selected group of motivation theories, remember that you must not only master the elements of each theory, but also understand their managerial implications.

UNDERSTANDING INDIVIDUAL NEEDS

Content theories of motivation use individual needs to explain the behavior and attitudes of people at work. Because needs reflect physiological or psychological deficiencies that people are driven to satisfy, you will sometimes find the terms *needs, motives,* and *drives* used interchangeably. Although each theory discusses a slightly different set of needs, all agree that managers must be able to understand individual needs because needs cause tensions that influence attitudes and behavior.

Maslow's Hierarchy-of-Needs Theory[4]

Chapter 2 introduced Abraham Maslow's theory of human needs as a foundation element in the behavioral approach to management. His theory includes the hierarchy of needs depicted once

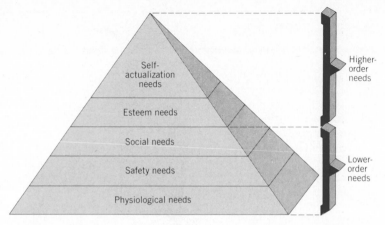

FIGURE 12.2 Maslow's hierarchy of human needs.

again in Figure 12.2. The five needs fall into two general categories. **Lower-order needs** include physiological, safety, and social concerns; **higher-order needs** include esteem and self-actualization concerns. The higher-order needs are placed in a separate category because they represent desires for psychological development and growth, as opposed to lower-order concerns for social and physical well-being. As already identified in our discussion of Herzberg's two-factor theory and job enrichment in Chapter 8, the motivational implications of higher- and lower-order needs are quite different.

You should recall from prior discussion the essence of each of the five needs in Maslow's hierarchy. Identify the correct term for the need described in the following list. Make sure you have the right answers before proceeding.

1. Need for love, affection, sense of belonging in one's relationships with others.

2. Need for respect, prestige, recognition in the eyes of others; need for sense of personal respect and competence.

3. Need for biological maintenance—food, water, etc.

4. Need for protection and stability in the events of life.

5. Need for fulfillment of one's potential, to use personal abilities to their fullest and most creative extent.

Answers: 1. Social; 2. Esteem; 3. Physiological; 4. Safety; 5. Self-actualization.

The Deficit and Progression Principles

The deficit and progression principles are central to Maslow's theory. For review purposes, we can summarize the two principles as follows.

1. **The deficit principle**. Holds that a satisified need is not a motivator of behavior. People are expected to act in ways that satisfy deprived needs—that is, needs for which a "deficit" exists. In the parable, for example, the farmer failed to recognize the deficit principle. He was offering a reward (carrots) that appealed to an already satisfied need (hunger).

2. **The progression principle**. Holds that the five needs exist in a strict hierarchy of prepotency such that a need at one level doesn't become activated until the next lower-level need is already satisfied. People are expected to advance step by step up the hierarchy in their search for need satisfactions.

In summary, Maslow's theory suggests that managers should recognize that deprived needs will dominate the attention of people at work and determine their attitudes and behavior. Furthermore, once a need is satisfied, the individual's attention progresses up to the next higher level in the hierarchy. Only when the level of self-actualization is reached do the deficit and progression principles cease to operate. The more self-actualization needs are satisfied, the stronger they are predicted to grow. According to Maslow, an individual should continue to be motivated by opportunities for self-fulfillment as long as the other needs remain satisfied. *Newsline 12.1* offers

NEWSLINE 12.1

LIFE ON THE JOB

LOS ANGELES—The breathtaking panorama, sweeping from the blue Pacific past the downtown office towers to the distant peaks of the San Gabriel Mountains, is wasted on Dave Brown.

Instead of the scenery, Brown, who is perched on a steel girder at the 18th-floor, penthouse level of the future Regency Wilshire luxury condominium, eyes the construction crew of the future Evian condominium nearby. He says with dissatisfaction: "They're going faster than we are."

The husky, 36-year-old Brown feels considerable pride in "hanging iron," perhaps the most chilling—and definitely among the better-paying—of construction jobs. Sometimes he is even taken with the history of it all: he signs the beams and columns he bolts together, drawing little flowers on them with a yellow marking pencil. "They'll cover them over," he says with a smile, "but they'll always be there."

Source: Roy J. Harris, Jr., "Life on the Job," *Wall Street Journal* (May 11, 1981), p. 1. Reprinted by permission of the *Wall Street Journal.* Copyright © 1981 Dow Jones & Company, Inc. All rights reserved.

an example of one person's self-fulfillment in an unusual job setting.

Managerial Implications

Table 12.2 shows how each of the five needs in Maslow's theory translates into things people want out of their work. Managers can try to provide these things in response to the needs of subordinates. Maslow's ideas, therefore, are helpful for understanding the needs people bring with them to their work and determining what can be done to satisfy them.

Research has not been able to verify the strict deficit and progression principles central to Maslow's theory. There is no consistent evidence, for example, that the satisfaction of a need at one level decreases its importance to the individual and increases the importance of the next higher need. Scholars, therefore, are continuing their efforts to modify Maslow's theory and improve its application to day-to-day individual behavior.

Alderfer's Modification

One of the most promising efforts to build on Maslow's work is the ERG theory of Clayton Al-

defer.[5] His theory differs from Maslow's in three basic respects. To begin, ERG theory collapses Maslow's five need categories into three. The first letters of each need identified by Alderfer label the theory itself—ERG. **Existence needs** pertain to people's desires for physiological and material well-being; **relatedness needs** represent desires for satisfying interpersonal relationships; **growth needs** are desires for continued psychological growth and development. Second, ERG theory does not assume that lower-level needs must be satisfied before higher-level needs become activated. Finally, ERG theory includes a unique "frustration-regression" principle whereby an already-satisfied lower-level need becomes reactivated when a higher-level need cannot be satisfied.

Alderfer's personal research demonstrates support for the ERG theory. When used in conjunction with Maslow's ideas, the theory offers an additional means for understanding and talking about the needs of people at work. The growth-need concept is especially useful; in fact we have already used it earlier in this book. One way to summarize prevailing job-enrichment guidelines, for example, is to state that job en-

Table 12.2 Things People May Want from Work

Needs	What a Person Wants
Higher-order needs	
Self-actualization	Creative and challenging work
	Participation in decision making
	Flexibility and autonomy
Esteem	Promotion to higher-status job
	Praise and recognition from supervisor
	High-performance evaluation and merit-pay increase
Low-order needs	
Social	Friendly co-workers
	Sponsored social activities on and off the job
	Compatible supervisor
Safety	Safe working conditions
	Job security
	Good base salary/wage and fringe benefits
Physiological	Food and water
	Shelter and comfort from weather
	Minimum salary/wage

richment is most appropriate for persons with strong desires for growth-need satisfaction at work. These ideas were expressed in our discussion of job design in Chapter 8.

McClelland's Acquired-Needs Theory[6]

Another useful theory of human needs was developed by David McClelland. In the late 1940s, McClelland and his co-workers began experimenting with the Thematic Apperception Test (TAT) as a way of examining individual needs. The TAT procedure is to ask people to view pictures and write stories about what they see. The stories are then content analyzed for themes representing three specific needs.

1. **Need for Achievement (nAch).** The desire to do something better or more efficiently, to solve problems, or to master complex tasks.

2. **Need for power (nPower).** The desire to control other persons, to influence their behavior, or to be responsible for other people.

3. **Need for affiliation (nAff).** The desire to establish and maintain friendly and warm relations with other persons.

The basic theory views these three needs as being acquired to varying degrees over time and as a result of individual life experiences. People, in turn, are motivated by the needs. McClelland encourages managers to learn how to recognize nAch, nAff, and nPower in themselves and in others, and to be able to create work environments responsive to the actual need profiles. Specific work preferences associated with each need are shown in Table 12.3.

Two applications of McClelland's acquired needs theory are especially relevant to managers. First, nAch, nAff, and nPower complement the needs identified in the theories of Maslow and Alderfer. Thus they add to your ability to understand people in their work settings. Acquired-needs theory is especially useful in this respect because each need is directly associated with the set of individual work preferences shown in Table 12.3. Second, if these needs are truly acquired, it may be possible to teach people to adopt the need profiles required to be successful in various types of jobs. McClelland reports some success in stimulating people's needs for achievement, and he is currently working on a program to help managers adopt profiles of nPower and nAff that he has found to be associated with executive success. More specific reference to these interesting aspects of McClelland's research follow.

Table 12.3 Work Preferences of Persons High in Need for Achievement, Power, and Affiliation

Individual Need	Work Preferences	Example
High need for achievement	Individual responsibility, challenging but achievable goals; feedback on performance	Field salesperson with challenging quota and opportunity to earn individual bonus
High need for affiliation	Interpersonal relationships; opportunities to communicate	Customer-service representative; member of work unit subject to group wage-bonus plan
High need for power	Control over other persons; attention; recognition	Formal position of supervisory responsibility; appointment as head of special task force or committee

Source: John R. Schermerhorn, Jr., James G. Hunt, and Richard N. Osborn, *Managing Organizational Behavior* (New York: Wiley, 1982), p. 113. Used by permission.

Need for Achievement (nAch)

Figure 12.3 presents a scene commonly used in TAT research. What story would you write about it? McClelland once asked three executives to respond to the same question. The first wrote of an engineer who was daydreaming about a family outing scheduled for the next day. Another described a designer who had picked up an idea for a new gadget from remarks made by his family. The third saw an engineer who was intently working on a bridge-stress problem that he seemed sure to solve because of his confident look.[7] Compare your response to those of the executives. What similarities and differences do you detect?

The nAch scores assigned to the stories of the three executives were

- Person dreaming about family outing — nAch = +1
- Person pondering new idea for gadget — nAch = +2
- Person working on bridge-stress problem — nAch = +4

A person high in nAch is most likely to prefer explicit and challenging goals, feedback on performance, and individual responsibility for results. These insights can be used when dealing with subordinates who are high need achievers.

FIGURE 12.3 Man looking at desk photo.

They can also be personally useful if you meet the criteria of a high need achiever. McClelland argues that a person high in nAch should seek opportunities for individual responsibility, specific goals, and performance feedback. A situation of diffused group responsibility, ambiguous goals, and little or no feedback would not respond well to the needs of a high achiever.

Need for Power (nPower)

It doesn't follow from McClelland's research that high need achievers make the best managers. Our discussion of leadership in Chapter 10 highlighted the centrality of power to the managerial role. It only makes sense, therefore, that a high need for power should appear in the profiles of successful executives. Successful executives are comfortable with the exercise of power and enjoy the ability and responsibility to influence other persons' behaviors. But they do so in a socially responsible way that is directed toward organizational rather than personal objectives. The successful high nPower manager exercises control on behalf of the work group and organization, not for the sake of being personally manipulative. A person high in need for power should be given opportunities to exercise control over others and to receive sufficient attention and recognition for supervisory performance results.

Need for Affiliation (nAff)

The need for affiliation is essentially the same as Maslow's social need and Alderfer's relatedness need. The most significant of McClelland's ideas in this respect is the suggestion that people high in nAff alone may not make good managers. Because desires for social compatibility and friendship are fundamental to nAff, McClelland argues that the desire to preserve satisfying affiliations can interfere with managerial decision making. There are times when managers must decide and act in ways that other persons are likely to disagree with and even resent. To the extent that high nAff interferes with someone's ability to make these decisions, managerial effectiveness will be sacrificed. The successful executive in McClelland's view is likely to possess a high nPower that is greater than nAff.

Questions and Answers on Individual Needs at Work

The content theories focus on human needs as a way to understand and predict the attitudes and behaviors of people at work. Even though the terminology differs, there is a substantial similarity in what the theories offer as an action frame of reference for managers. By way of summary, let's answer some questions you may have regarding the content theories and their managerial implications.[8]

"How many different individual needs are there?" Research has not yet determined the complete listing of work-related individual needs. Each of the needs previously discussed has been found useful by management scholars and practitioners alike. As a manager, you can use the ideas of Maslow, Alderfer, and McClelland as a point of departure for understanding the various needs that people may bring with them to the work setting.

"Can a work outcome or reward satisfy more than one need?" Yes, work outcomes or rewards can satisfy more than one need. Pay is a good example. It is a source of performance feedback for the high need achiever. It can also be a source of personal security, as well as a way to satisfy physiological and social needs.

"Is there a hierarchy of needs?" Research does not support the precise five-step hierarchy of needs postulated by Maslow. It seems more legitimate to view needs operating in a flexible hierarchy, such as the one in Aldefer's ERG theory. However, it is useful to distinguish between the motivational properties of lower-order and higher-order needs.

"How important are the various needs?" Research is inconclusive as to the importance of different needs. Individuals vary widely in this regard. They may also value needs differently at different times and at different ages or career stages. This is a major reason why managers should take advantage of all the content theories in attempts to understand the differing needs of people at work.

"What is the manager's responsibility from the perspective of the content theories?" Although the de-

tails vary, each content theory considers managers as responsible for allocating rewards in such a way that individuals find opportunities to satisfy important needs on the job. To the extent that some needs are acquired, the manager's responsibility also includes stimulating those needs to which the work setting is best able to respond in a positive manner.

EQUITY THEORY

Do you remember the first parable? It said something about farmers, donkeys, and carrots. Let's spin the parable around in another version.

A Second Parable

Once upon a time there were six donkeys hitched to a wagon pulling a heavy load up a steep hill. Two of the donkeys were not achievement oriented and decided to coast along and let others do most of the pulling. Two others were relatively young and inexperienced, and had a difficult time pulling their share. One of the remaining two suffered from a slight hangover from consuming fermented barley the night before. The sixth donkey did most of the work.

The wagon arrived at the top of the hill. The driver got down from his seat, patted each of the donkeys on the head, and gave six carrots to each. Prior to the next hill climb, the sixth donkey ran away.

An equity dynamic operates in the second parable. From a donkey's perspective, the moral of the story is to never be the sixth donkey if everyone gets six carrots! From a manager's perspective, the point is that equity problems in the allocation of rewards can affect behavior in the work setting. How would you like to lose your best worker under conditions such as those described in the parable? Motivation theory offers guidance that can help managers avoid such undesirable consequences.

The Equity Comparison

Equity theory is a process theory of motivation known best through the work of J. Stacy Adams.[9] The essence of the theory is that felt inequity is

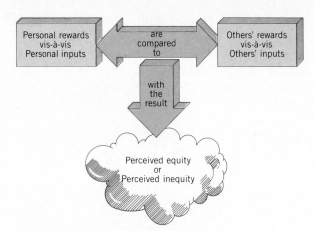

FIGURE 12.4 The equity comparison.

a motivating state. That is, when people feel they have been inequitably treated, they will try to remove the sources of discomfort and achieve a sense of equity. Inequities occur whenever people feel the rewards received for their work inputs are unequal to the rewards other persons appear to have received for their work inputs.

The equity comparison is shown in Figure 12.4. When perceived inequity results, Adams predicts one or more of the following ways of behaving to resolve the sense of inequity.

- Change work inputs.
- Change rewards received.
- Change the comparison points.
- Psychologically distort the comparisons to achieve a more favorable perspective.
- Leave the situation.

The research of Adams and others, largely accomplished in laboratory settings, lends tentative support to this prediction. People who feel overpaid—that is, who perceive felt *positive* inequity—have been found to increase the quantity or quality of their work. Those who feel underpaid—that is, who perceive felt *negative* inequity—reduce their work efforts to compensate for the missing rewards. The research is most conclusive in respect to felt negative inequity.

Managing Equity Dynamics

An equity comparison typically intervenes between a manager's allocation of rewards and the

NEWSLINE 12.2

MERIT-PAY PROGRAM DRAWS GRIPES FROM LOSERS—AND WINNERS

MILLERSVILLE, PA.—Last month, Penn Manor paid $1000 bonuses to 25 of its 233 teachers. The eight-school district, which has its headquarters in this Susquehanna Valley town, joined the few school systems in the country that tie teacher pay to classroom performance.

The Penn Manor board's decision to make public the names of the 25 merit-pay recipients didn't help matters. The daily paper in nearby Lancaster published the names in a page-one story that quoted a Penn Manor school official as hoping "that these people will serve as models" for other teachers.

The report hurt a science teacher who failed to qualify for a bonus, even though his principal regards him as a meritorious teacher. The teacher keeps a carefully mounted copy of the newspaper story in his desk drawer; it's clear from the underlined sentences and paragraphs that he regards his failure to make the bonus list as a personal rebuke. He bitterly recalls that on the day the list was published, his wife and a fellow member of his church choir asked why his name was missing. The science teacher is convinced the questions meant, in effect, "I'm not excellent in my field."

The merit plan also put on the spot the principals and department heads assigned to select the award winners. Penn Manor High, for instance, was allotted only 10 merit awards to distribute among the 45 of its 94 teachers who competed for the bonuses. As a result, many worthy teachers were disappointed, says the school's principal, Robert King.

Source: Excerpted from Burt Schorr, "School's Merit-Pay Program Draws Gripes from Losers—and Winners," *Wall Street Journal* (June 16, 1983), p. 23. Reprinted by permission of the *Wall Street Journal.* Copyright © 1983 Dow Jones & Company, Inc. All rights reserved.

impact of the rewards on the work attitudes and behavior of subordinates. Rewards perceived as equitably given can foster job satisfaction and performance; rewards perceived as inequitable can inhibit these key work results. The burden lies with the manager to take control of the equity dynamics in a situation and make sure that any negative consequences of the equity comparison are avoided or at least minimized when rewards are allocated. To do this, a manager should:

1. Recognize that equity comparisons are likely to be made whenever especially visible rewards such as pay or promotions are being allocated.

2. Anticipate the presence of felt negative inequities.

3. Carefully communicate to each individual an evaluation of the reward being given, an appraisal of the performance on which it is based, and the appropriate comparison points.

Remember too that feelings of inequity are determined solely by the individual's perceptions or interpretations of the situation. It is not how a manager feels about the allocation of rewards that counts; it is how the individuals receiving the rewards feel or perceive them that will determine the motivational outcomes of the equity dynamic. *Newsline 12.2* shows one example of how a well-intentional merit-pay plan experienced difficulties, some of which were the result of equity comparisons among those who received merit-pay increases and those who did not.

EXPECTANCY THEORY

A 1964 book by Victor Vroom introduced an expectancy theory of work motivation and made an important contribution to the management literature.[10] The theory seeks to predict or explain the task-related efforts expended by people at work. It asks the central question: What determines the willingness of an individual to exert effort on tasks that contribute to the production purposes of the work unit and the organization? This question, of course, constitutes the heart of a manager's interest in any motivation theory.

The Theory

Expectancy theory argues that work motivation is determined by individual beliefs regarding effort-performance relationships and the desirabilities of outcomes associated with various performance levels. The theory is based on the logic: "People will do what they can do when they want to.[11] It helps to keep expectancy theory in a proper managerial perspective by remembering that, in general, people exert work effort to achieve task performance and receive valued rewards.

Recall that the theory inquires as to when and under what conditions people will decide to put forth maximum work efforts in support of organizational objectives. To answer such a question in any given circumstance, Vroom suggests that a manager must know three things.

1. **Expectancy.** The person's belief that working hard will enable various levels of task performance to be achieved.

2. **Instrumentality**. The person's belief that various work-related outcomes will occur as a result of task performance.

3. **Valence.** The value the individual assigns to these work-related outcomes.

Multiplier Effects

Expectancy theory further posits that motivation (M), expectancy (E), instrumentality (I), and valence (V) are related to one another in a multiplicative fashion.

$$M = E \times I \times V$$

In words, this equation states that motivation is determined by expectancy times instrumentality times valence. In practice, this means that the motivational appeal of a reward offered as a work outcome to the individual is drastically reduced whenever expectancy, instrumentality, or valence—alone or in any combination—approaches zero. For a reward to have a high and positive motivational impact, expectancy, instrumentality, and valence must all be high and positive.

Suppose, for example, that a manager is wondering whether or not the prospect of earning a promotion will be motivational to a subordinate. Expectancy theory predicts the subordinate's motivation to work hard in the prospect of earning a promotion will be *low* if

1. *Expectancy is low* A person feels that he or she can't achieve the necessary performance level.

2. *Instrumentality is low* The person is not confident that a high level of task performance will result in being promoted.

3. *Valence is low* The person places little value on receiving a promotion; the promotion is not perceived as a valued reward.

The multiplier effect in the expectancy theory has important managerial implications. It clearly points out that managers must take action to maximize all three motivational components—expectancy, instrumentality, and valence—when seeking to create high levels of work motivation among subordinates by the allocation of work rewards. A zero at any location on the right side of the expectancy equation ($M = E \times I \times V$) will result in zero motivation. Figure 12.5 depicts the significance of the three expectancy-theory terms in such a managerial frame of reference.

Multiple Outcomes

Expectancy theory also recognizes that more than one outcome can be associated with a given work path. Again, take the possibility of promotion as an example. Even though promotion as a result of high performance may be considered both possible to achieve and highly desirable for the individual, the high performance accomplishment may also result in less desirable or even negative

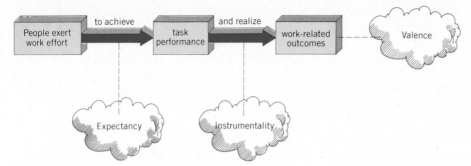

FIGURE 12.5 Expectancy theory in a managerial perspective. *Source:* John R. Schermerhorn, Jr., James G. Hunt, and Richard N. Osborn, *Managing Organizational Behavior* (New York: Wiley, 1982), p. 117. Used by permission.

outcomes. A good example in this case might be a loss of leisure time caused by the need to spend extra time at work. When such multiple outcomes are considered, the motivational appeal of the valued outcome (e.g., being promoted) may be nullified by the negative consequences of a companion outcome (e.g., lost leisure time). The informed manager will always try to identify and understand multiple outcomes from the other person's point of view, and adjust the use of rewards in his or her motivational strategy accordingly.

Illustrative Case: Money as a Motivator

A typical assumption made by managers is that people will be motivated to work hard if given the prospect of earning higher or "merit" pay as a result. Let's work through an example that puts this assumption to the test from an individual's perspective. For purposes of the example, the question is: Will a person work hard to achieve

high performance in response to the offer of higher pay as a reward?

Look at this example as diagrammed in Figure 12.6. The individual in the case faces a decision of how much effort to expend in his or her work. The decision may be to work hard to achieve a high performance level (follow path A), or working less hard and achieve a low performance level (path B). A manager would obviously like to encourage (that is, motivate) this person to apply work efforts on the high-performance path. We'll assume the manager chooses to do so by offering higher pay as a reward for high performance.

Expectancy theory predicts that the first question the individual will ask is, "Can I achieve the high performance level as a result of my work efforts?" The answer to this expectancy question will depend on the individual's perception of his or her ability, and the amount of support available from the supervisor and organization for achieving high performance. Given a positive re-

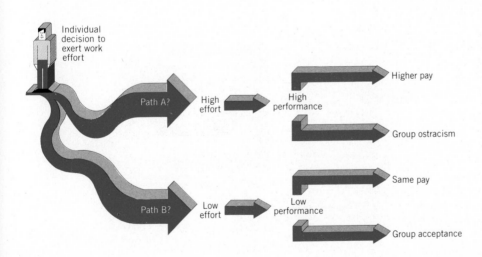

FIGURE 12.6 An example of applied expectancy theory. *Source:* John R. Schermerhorn, Jr., James G. Hunt, and Richard N. Osborn, *Managing Organizational Behavior* (New York: Wiley, 1982), p. 117. Used by permission.

sponse to this question, attention will shift to instrumentality and the outcomes that may be associated with each performance level. In the example in Figure 12.6, higher pay and social ostracism by co-workers might both result if high performance is achieved. By contrast, a lower performance level results in continuation of present pay and complete social acceptance from the group of co-workers. To evaluate these alternative consequences, valences must be assigned to each outcome on each path. Higher pay may seem very desirable (positive valence) and social ostracism very undesirable (negative valence).

The degree of motivation to exert effort along a given work path (e.g., the high-effort path A) is determined by the combined value of all effort-performance-outcome chains found on that path. Figure 12.7 depicts the two effort-performance-outcome chains for path A: a merit pay chain and a group ostracism chain. Sample numerical values are assigned to the actual expectancies, instrumentalities, and valences. They are indicated in parentheses.

Under the logic of expectancy theory, the individual's motivation to exert high effort will equal the total value of the merit pay chain plus the total value of the group ostracism chain, with all expectancies, instrumentalities, and valences respectively considered. When applied to the example, this means that individual motivation to pursue the high-performance path is zero. The reasoning follows. Even though merit pay is highly valued as a reward (valence = +1) and considered certain to follow high performance

(instrumentality = +1) that the individual is perfectly confident of achieving (expectancy = +1), its motivational power is canceled by the negative effects of also being socially ostracized by co-workers (valence = −1). The arithmetic under the basic expectancy equation can be expressed as follows:

$$M_{\text{high effort}} =$$
$$(E \times I \times V)_{\text{pay}} + (E \times I \times V)_{\text{ostracism}}$$
$$M_{\text{high effort}} =$$
$$(1 \times 1 \times 1)_{\text{pay}} + (1 \times 1 \times -1)_{\text{ostracism}}$$
$$M_{\text{high effort}} = (1)_{\text{pay}} + (-1)_{\text{ostracism}}$$
$$M_{\text{high effort}} = 0$$

One advantage of expectancy theory is its ability to help managers take into account multiple effort-performance-outcome chains when trying to determine the motivational value of various rewards potentially made available to subordinates. In the example we have been working with, a perceptive manager would expect the individual to work on the low-effort path unless something is done to alter the negative effects of the group ostracism anticipated to result along with higher pay on the high-performance path.

Managerial Implications

Expectancy theory basically advises managers to try to understand individual thought processes and then actively intervene in the work situation to influence them in a positive fashion. This in-

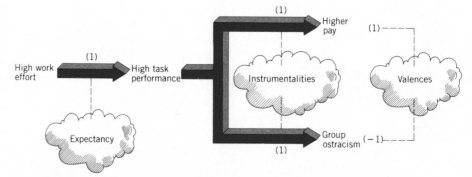

FIGURE 12.7 The high-effort work path from the expectancy example. *Source:* John R. Schermerhorn, Jr., James G. Hunt, and Richard N. Osborn, *Managing Organizational Behavior* (New York: Wiley, 1982), p. 117. Used by permission.

( )—Numbers in parentheses represent values assigned in the example to expectancy, instrumentalities, valences.
The ranges are: expectancy and instrumentality (0 to +1), valence (−1 to +1).

Table 12.4 The Managerial Implications of Expectancy Theory

Expectancy Term	Individual's Questions	Managerial Implications
Expectancy	"Can I achieve the desired level of task performance?"	Select workers with ability Train workers to use ability Support ability with resources Clarify performance goals
Instrumentality	"What work outcomes will be received as a result of the performance?"	Clarify psychological contracts Communicate performance → outcome possibilities Confirm performance → outcome possibilities by making actual rewards contingent on performance
Valence	"How highly do I value the work outcomes?"	Identify individual needs Adjust available rewards to match these needs

Source: John R. Schermerhorn, Jr., James G. Hunt, and Richard N. Osborn, *Managing Organizational Behavior* (New York: Wiley, 1982), p. 113. Used by permission.

cludes trying to maximize expectancies, instrumentalities, and valences that support the organizational objectives. Said differently, a manager should strive to create a work environment within which task contributions serving the organization's needs are also viewed by the individual as paths toward highly desirable rewards. This argument should sound familiar to you! It is perfectly consistent with House's path-goal theory of leadership described in Chapter 10.

Table 12.4 shows that a manager can influence expectancies by selecting individuals with proper abilities, training them to use these abilities, supporting them with appropriate resources, and clarifying performance goals. Instrumentality can be influenced by clarifying expectations and responsibilities in the psychological contract, by communicating performance-outcome possibilities specific to a given situation, and by confirming desirable performance-outcome expectations through direct action—that is, by rewarding high performance once it occurs. Finally, managers can influence valence by being sensitive to individual needs. This is where the content theories of motivation are of great benefit. They help managers to understand individual needs. Once these needs are understood, rewards can be adjusted to respond more adequately to them.

REINFORCEMENT THEORY

All of the prior motivation theories use cognitive explanations of behavior. That is, they are concerned with explaining "why" people do things in terms of satisfying needs, resolving felt inequities, and/or pursuing positive valences. Reinforcement theory, by contrast, views human behavior as determined by its environmental consequences. It avoids looking within the individual and examining thought processes, and focuses instead on the external environment and the consequences it holds for the individual.

Consider the following example.[12] A person walking down the street finds a $10 bill. Thereafter this person is observed to spend more time looking down when walking. The question is, "Why is the person so motivated?"

Cognitive explanation The person continues to look down frequently because of the high value held for money. Because the person reasons that more money may be found by looking down, he or she has decided to look down more frequently when out walking in the future. The observed behavior—"looking down"—follows a conscious decision to do so by the individual.

Reinforcement explanation When the initial behavior of looking down occurred, it was reinforced by the presence of a $10 bill. Having once been reinforced by this environmental consequence, the behavior becomes more likely to occur in the future.

The Law of Effect

The preceding example shows how the reinforcement orientation avoids making assumptions about individual though processes in order to explain behavior. Instead of looking at "values," "reasons," and "decisions," reinforcement theory views present behavior (e.g., looking down while walking) as determined by environmental responses to past behavior (e.g., finding a $10 bill after having once looked down while walking). The basis for the argument and the ultimate foundation for reinforcement theory is Thorndike's **law of effect**.

Law of Effect

Behavior that results in a pleasant outcome is likely to be repeated; behavior that results in an unpleasant outcome is not likely to be repeated.[13]

Organizational Behavior Modification

Operant conditioning, a term popularized by the noted psychologist B. F. Skinner,[14] is the process of controlling behavior by manipulating its consequences. You may think of operant conditioning as learning by reinforcement. It is learning that occurs via the law of effect. **Organizational behavior modification** ("OB Mod" for short) is a term that describes the application of operant conditioning techniques to influence human behavior in work settings. Its basic purpose is the

NEWSLINE 12.3

QUAKER PAYS ITS EMPLOYEES TO STAY WELL

CHICAGO (AP)—For employees at Quaker Oats Co., staying healthy pays in more ways then one.

Seeking to control the rising cost of employee health benefits, the company has adopted a stay-well program that offers its healthy workers cash bonuses.

For example, Edward Hirschland, 34, could wind up the year with an extra $300 if he doesn't plug into his medical benefits. He is a manager in the Chicago-based cereal giant's corporate planning group.

The bonus is available either as a taxable cash payment or a tax-exempt benefit to pay for a physical exam, eyeglasses, or other medical expenses not covered by the company's insurance program.

In addition, any of the 6000 employees enrolled in the new plan will get dividends of $100 or more if they keep their claims below a budgeted target.

The traditional, no-deductible insurance program that Quaker scrapped January 1 gave doctors "a blank check" to run up costs without challenge by employees or the company, said Quaker employee benefits director Robert Penzkover.

Penzkover estimated that about 70 percent of employees would profit from the new "health incentives plan."

In addition, he said, the bonus plan is expected to cut the growth in Quaker's annual medical costs from "an uncontrolled 25 percent inflation to a more modest 6 or 8 percent inflation."

Source: Associated Press wire service as appearing in the *Southern Illinoisan* (January 24, 1983), p. 5. Used by permission.

"systematic reinforcement of desirable organizational behavior and the nonreinforcement or punishment of unwanted organizational behavior."[15] An interesting example of rewards being used in a creative way for such reinforcement purposes is presented in *Newsline 12.3*.

There are four basic OB Mod strategies: positive reinforcement, negative reinforcement, punishment, and extinction.

1. **Positive reinforcement.** Increases the frequency of or strengthens behavior by making a desirable consequence contingent on the occurrence of the behavior.

   Example A manager nods to express approval to a subordinate making a useful comment during a staff meeting.

2. **Negative reinforcement**. Increases the frequency of or strengthens behavior by making the avoidance of an undesirable consequence contingent on the occurrence of the behavior.

   Example A manager who has been nagging a worker every day about tardiness doesn't nag when the worker comes to work on time one day.

3. **Punishment**. Decreases the frequency of or eliminates an undesirable behavior by making an unpleasant consequence contingent on the occurrence of the behavior.

   Example A manager docks the pay of an employee who reports late for work one day.

4. **Extinction**. Decreases the frequency of or eliminates an undesirable behavior by making the removal of a desirable consequence contingent on the occurrence of the behavior.

   Example A manager observes that a disruptive employee is receiving social approval for these acts from co-workers. The manager counsels co-workers to stop giving this approval.

The four OB Mod strategies are illustrated in Figure 12.8. Note how the supervisor uses each of the strategies to influence employees toward desirable quality-assurance practices. Note, too, that both positive and negative reinforcement are used to strengthen desirable behavior when it occurs; punishment and extinction are used to decrease the frequency of undesirable behaviors. Because positive reinforcement and punishment are so fundamental to any manager's motivational strategy, we'll single them out for further attention.

Positive Reinforcement

Positive reinforcement is an OB Mod strategy highly advocated by Skinner and his followers. To apply positive reinforcement well in the work setting, you must first be aware of the many things in organizations that have potential reward value. A number of these were presented earlier in Table 12.1. In addition, though, you need to know how to allocate these rewards in ways that achieve the desired performance effects. Two laws should guide your actions in this latter regard: the **law of contingent reinforcement** and the **law of immediate reinforcement**.[16]

Law of contingent reinforcement

In order for a reward to have maximum reinforcing value, it must be delivered only if the desired behavior is exhibited.

Law of immediate reinforcement

The more immediate the delivery of a reward after the occurrence of a desirable behavior, the greater the reinforcing value of the reward.

Taken together, these two laws suggest that managers should give rewards as immediately as possible, and contingent on desired behavior. Only then will they serve to maximum advantage as positive reinforcers in the work setting. Try your hand at following this advice in the following example.

Illustrative Case: The Assembly-Line Supervisor[17]

A new young manager was in charge of a group of workers on an automobile assembly line. This work unit was expected to produce components at a standard rate of 72 per hour. Actual performance was running around 45 per hour, and the

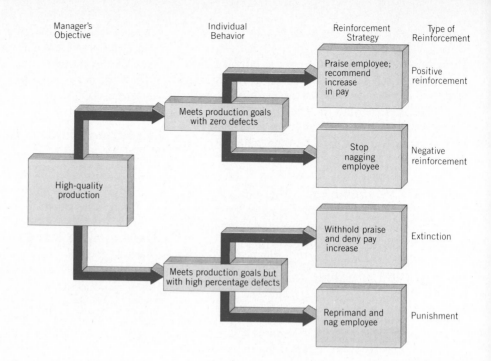

Manager's Objective	Individual Behavior	Reinforcement Strategy	Type of Reinforcement

High-quality production

Meets production goals with zero defects

Meets production goals but with high percentage defects

Praise employee; recommend increase in pay — Positive reinforcement

Stop nagging employee — Negative reinforcement

Withhold praise and deny pay increase — Extinction

Reprimand and nag employee — Punishment

FIGURE 12.8 Using reinforcement strategies.

manager's boss was holding her accountable for the production discrepancy.

The manager called her subordinates together and asked them what could be done to get production up to standard. They decided that an extra "break" might justify the increased effort. A deal was made. *If* the workers produced 72 units within an hour's time, they could use the remaining time in the hour as a break. The results were immediate and positive. Within a week the work unit was producing up to standard and taking a 25-minute break every hour!

Sometime after these results were realized, however, it became obvious to both the manager and her subordinates that the situation couldn't continue. Higher management and the other work units would not tolerate this group taking a 25-minute break every hour. Another deal was made. When the group reached 90 units an hour, the remaining time in the hour could be used as a break. As a result of this agreement, the work unit was soon able to take a 10-minute break almost every hour.

This manager used her reinforcement theory well. She was able to associate a desirable consequence—the work break—with behavior appropriate to organizational objectives—the desired per hour production rate. It is also

significant that the break was only one of a number of possible rewards the manager might have tried to use as a positive reinforcer. She wisely obtained information from the workers before choosing among the alternative rewards. The break was highly valued by the workers and proved a powerful positive reinforcer as a result.

Shaping

The supervisor in the previous example could have used another version of positive reinforcement to achieve the desired results. **Shaping** is the creation of a new behavior by the positive reinforcement of successive approximations to the desired behavior. Recall that the work unit in the example originally produced only 45 units per hour when 72 per hour was the goal. A shaping strategy would have rewarded subordinates with verbal praise and recognition each time they produced more than 45 units in an hour. As production continued to increase, reinforcement would be given only when production surpassed the previous high level. Once production reached 72 units, continued positive reinforcement would then be used to stabilize behavior at this new performance level.

Scheduling Reinforcement

Positive reinforcement can be given according to continuous and intermittent schedules. To succeed with a shaping strategy, for example, reinforcement should be given on a continuous basis until the desired behavior is achieved. Then an intermittent schedule should be used to maintain the behavior at the new level. **Continuous reinforcement** administers a reward each time a desired behavior occurs. **Intermittent reinforcement** rewards behavior only periodically.

Although there is some controversy in the research on reinforcement schedules, a manager can expect:[18]

1. Continous reinforcement draws forth a desired behavior more quickly than intermittent reinforcement, but is more costly in terms of the consumption of rewards.

Workers, like this forklift operator, must be encouraged, trained and reinforced to perform jobs safely.

2. Behavior acquired under an intermittent schedule will last longer after discontinuance of reinforcement than behavior acquired under a continuous schedule.

Guidelines for Positive Reinforcement

To use operant conditioning properly and to ensure that the allocation of rewards has the desired positive reinforcement effects, a manager should:[19]

1. *Clearly identify the desired behaviors*—that is, determine what specific behaviors will result in the desired performance contributions.
2. *Maintain an inventory of rewards* that have the potential to serve as positive reinforcers.
3. *Recognize individual differences* as to which rewards will actually have reinforcement value for subordinates.
4. *Let subordinates know exactly what must be done to receive a reward*—that is, set clear targets and give performance feedback.
5. *Administer the rewards contingently and immediately upon the appearance of the desired behaviors*—that is, make sure the reward is given only if the desired behavior occurs.

Punishment

Punishment is a means for eliminating undesirable behavior by administering an unpleasant consequence upon the occurrence of that behavior. To punish an employee, a manager may deny the individual a valued reward such as verbal praise or merit pay, or the manager may administer an adversive or obnoxious stimulus such as a verbal reprimand or pay reduction.

It is just as important to understand punishment as an OB Mod strategy as it is to understand the principles of positive reinforcement. Like the other reinforcement strategies, punishment can be done poorly or it can be done well. Your goal, of course, is to know when to use this strategy, and then to know how to do it well.

Problems with the Punishment Strategy

Let's look first at the problems that may accompany a manager's use of punishment. Three deserve special mention.[20]

1. *Although a behavior may be suppressed as a result of punishment, it may not be permanently abolished.* An employee, for example, may be reprimanded for taking unauthorized work breaks. The behavior may stop, but only when the manager is present. As soon as the threat of punishment is removed from the situation, such as when the manager is no longer present, the breaks may occur once again.

2. *The person who administers punishment may end up being viewed negatively by others.* A manager who frequently punishes subordinates may find that he or she has an unpleasant effect on the work unit even when not administering punishment. This manager has become so associated with punishment that his or her very presence in the work setting is an unpleasant experience for others.

3. *Punishment may be offset by positive reinforcement received from another source.* A worker may be positively reinforced by peers for the same behavior that is punished by a supervisor. The positive value of such peer support may sometimes be strong enough to cause the individual to put up with the punishment. Thus the undesirable behavior continues. As many times as a student may be verbally reprimanded by an instructor for being late to class, for example, the grins of classmates may well justify the continuation of tardiness in the future.

Does all of this mean you should never punish? No; the important things to remember are to do punishment selectively, and then to do it right. Consider the following case.

Illustrative Case: Warehouse Safety[21]

Peter Jones was employed as a forklift operator in a warehouse. He was the highest-paid non-supervisory employee in the firm, and his job was considered of high status. It took Pete 5½ years to work himself into the position. Unfortunately, he was prone to "show off" by unsafe driving that violated federal safety codes. Pete's supervisor chewed him out regularly, but the unsafe driving continued.

Finally, the supervisor analyzed the situation from a reinforcement perspective and tried to identify the environmental consequences associated with Pete's unsafe driving habits. As you may have predicted, the undesirable behavior was typically followed by laughter and special attention from the other warehouse workers.

The next time Pete was observed to drive unsafely, Pete's boss took him off the forklift truck and reassigned him to general warehousing duties for a period of time. When allowed back on the forklift, Pete drove more safely. Finally, a true punishment had been found.

Guidelines for Punishment

The following guidelines should be followed by managers when using punishment as an OB Mod strategy.[22]

1. *Tell the individual what is being done wrong* Clearly identify the undesirable behavior that is the reason for being punished.

2. *Tell the individual what is right* Desirable behavior (i.e., the preferred alternative to the behavior that is being punished) should be clearly established.

3. *Punish in private* Avoid publicly embarrassing people by punishing them in front of others.

4. *Follow the laws of contingent and immediate reinforcement* Make sure the punishment is contingent on the undesirable behavior and follows its occurrence as soon as possible.

5. *Make the punishment match the behavior* Be fair in equating the magnitude of punishment with the degree to which the behavior is truly undesirable.

Punishment and Positive Reinforcement

Remember that punishment can also be combined with positive reinforcement. In the warehouse safety case, Pete should be positively reinforced in the future when observed to drive safely. He will then know exactly what is wrong and the unpleasant consequences associated with it, and know what is right and the pleasant consequences that may be associated with it. This combined punishment and positive reinforcement strategy is advantageous in that it may help avoid the first problem of punishment identified earlier: having an undesirable behavior suppressed for but not permanently abolished.

Accolades, Criticisms, and Value Dilemmas

You have now been introduced to reinforcement theory, its supporting concepts, and its possible work applications through the concept of OB Mod. Testimony to the potential payoffs associated with the use of reinforcement techniques in work settings is shown in Table 12.5. Note that the "success stories" include some substantial corporations. Still, critics of the OB Mod approach to motivation argue that such positive results may well be due only to the fact that specific performance goals were clarified and workers held individually accountable for results.[23] Even as research continues, however, the power of operant conditioning techniques seems confirmed. Future research will probably tell managers how to use reinforcement theory better. That they should be using it already seems established.

The history of reinforcement theory is also replete with debates over the ethics of controlling human behavior. From the manager's stand-

Table 12.5 Results of Positive Reinforcement Programs in Selected Companies

Organization	Participants	Program Goals	Reinforcers Used	Results
Michigan Bell— Operator Services	2000 of 5500: employees at all levels in operator services	a. Decrease turnover and absenteeism b. Increase productivity c. Improve union-management relations	a. Praise and recognition b. Opportunity to see oneself become better	a. Attendance performance improved by 50% b. Productivity and efficiency has continued to be above standard
Michigan Bell— Maintenance Services	220 of 5500: maintenance workers, mechanics, first- and second-level supervisors	Improve a. Productivity b. Quality c. Safety d. Customer-employee relations	a. Self-feedback b. Supervisory feedback	a. Cost efficiency increased b. Safety improved c. Service improved d. No change in absenteeism e. Satisfaction with superior and co-workers improved f. Satisfaction with pay increased
B. F. Goodrich Chemical Co.	100 of 420: manufacturing employees at all levels	a. Better meeting of schedules b. Increase productivity	a. Praise and recognition b. Freedom to choose one's own activity	Production increased over 300%
General Electric	1000: employees at all levels	a. Meet EEO objectives b. Decrease absenteeism and turnover c. Improved training d. Increase productivity	Social reinforcers (praise, rewards, and constructive feedback)	a. Cost savings can be directly attributed to the program b. Productivity has increased c. Worked extremely well in training minority groups and raising their self-esteem d. Direct labor cost decreased

Source: Reprinted, by permission of the publisher, from "Behavior Modification on the Bottom Line," W. C. Hamner and E. P. Hamner, *Organizational Dynamics*, Vol. 4 (Spring 1976). Copyright © 1976 by AMACOM, a division of American Management Associations (pp. 12–14). All rights reserved.

point, there is concern that a use of operant conditioning principles ignores the individuality of people, restricts their freedom of choice, and ignores the fact that people can be motivated by other than externally administered rewards.

Advocates of OB Mod attack the problem straight on. They agree that it involves the control of behavior. But they argue that behavior control is an irrevocable part of every manager's job. Our view of managerial work reflects a similar view. It's inevitable that managers influence the behavior of other people. In fact, this influence must be done well if the manager's challenge is to be met successfully. The real question may be not whether it is ethical to control behavior, but whether it is ethical *not* to control behavior well enough that the goals of both the organization and the individual are served. Reinforcement theory can and should be used with both of these ends firmly in mind.

AN INTEGRATED APPROACH TO MOTIVATION

Figure 12.9 integrates the logic of the expectancy, equity, and reinforcement theories into one model of individual motivation. In the figure, performance is determined by individual ability, work effort, and organizational support. Motivation, in turn, influences performance through its impact on work effort.

From a manager's perspective, the key to leading through motivation lies in an ability to allocate rewards in a manner that responds positively to individual needs and goals. Motivation

should be directly enhanced when rewards are administered according to reinforcement principles. Motivation should also be indirectly enhanced by the satisfaction that results from such reinforcement and perceptions that rewards are equitably distributed. Figure 12.9 thus includes a key role for equity theory, highlights reinforcement principles in the allocation of rewards, and recognizes task performance and job satisfaction as separate, but equally important, work results. Content theories enter the model for their value to the manager as a basis for understanding individual needs and the values they lend to various work-related rewards.

When applied systematically and in an integrated fashion, the ideas contained in this chapter can be of great assistance as you seek success at managing motivational dynamics in the work setting. As our final example, it seems most appropriate to close with another parable. The moral of this one should now be perfectly clear to you!

A Final Parable

Once upon a time a farmer had six donkeys and a barn full of carrots, which she kept under lock and key. At the end of a day of wagon pulling, the farmer looked back over the day's performance of each donkey. To one of the donkeys she said, "You did an outstanding job; here are six carrots." To four of the others, she said, "Your performance was average; here are three carrots." To the remaining donkey she said, "You didn't pull your share of the load; here is one carrot." Another day of wagon pulling dawned. The

FIGURE 12.9 Motivational dynamics: an integrated approach.

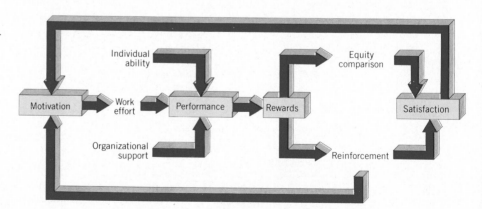

top donkey, having been properly rewarded, began the day in high spirits. The thoughts of the remaining donkeys were consumed with how they might earn more carrots through their efforts that day. The farmer had carrots available, but they had to be earned.

SUMMARY

A major part of any manager's leadership role is to enhance the willingness of people to exert work efforts to help accomplish organizational objectives. One approach to this goal is through the concept of motivation, a term defined as forces within the individual that account for the level, direction, and persistence of effort expended at work.

To help others experience a sense of motivation, part of a manager's leadership responsibility is to provide a work environment within which individual needs become satisfied through efforts that also serve organizational objectives. A major element in any work environment is the set of potential rewards available to the individual in return for work contributions and accomplishments. We have adopted the perspective of a manager who wishes to allocate rewards in such a way as to promote high levels of motivation among members of the work unit. To do this, we recognize the manager's need to (1) understand individual needs and (2) know how to allocate rewards so that these needs are satisfied and high levels of task performance result.

Three types of motivation theories were reviewed—content, process, and reinforcement theories. Although the theories differ, each offers useful implications for management practice. They are most useful when integrated and applied through the comprehensive viewpoint summarized in Figure 12.9.

The management of motivational dynamics begins with an ability to identify and understand individual needs. The content theories of Maslow, Alderfer, and McClelland are helpful in this regard. The process theories offer still further insight by helping us understand how people interpret various rewards and make decisions regarding the application of work efforts to achieve them. Equity theory introduces the important dynamic of social comparison in an individual's perceptions of rewards received for efforts contributed. Expectancy theory gives attention to how expectancies, instrumentalities, and valences affect motivation to work. Finally, reinforcement theory offers ideas on how to administer rewards contingent on performance and with maximum positive impact on individual behavior.

In the final result, the individual performance equation and the logic of these several theories nicely combine into the integrated motivation model presented in Figure 12.9. The insights of this model should help you predict individual behavior in future managerial situations and allocate rewards so that high levels of task performance and job satisfaction are achieved among members of your work unit.

THINKING THROUGH THE ISSUES

1. What is "motivation," and how does it relate to the individual performance equation?

2. Will a highly motivated worker necessarily be a high performer? Why or why not?

3. What is the key difference between the approaches taken by the content and process theories concerning their explanations of motivation to work?

4. Suppose you are a manager and find yourself with one group of subordinates who apparently seek higher-order need satisfactions at work, and another group that seems concerned only with lower-order needs. What would you do to motivate each group of subordinates? Why?

5. Give an example of how the equity dynamic has affected your behavior as a student. What should your instructors do to minimize the negative consequences potentially associated with this equity dynamic?

6. Name and define three key terms in expectancy theory. How do these terms interrelate

to explain the level of motivation that a person may display at work?

7. How does reinforcement theory explain individual behavior?

8. State four guidelines for positive reinforcement. Give an example of how positive reinforcement could be used to increase the performance of a person in a work situation familiar to you.

9. Do you agree with the statement, "Managers will sometimes have to punish people; the challenge is knowing when to punish and then being able to do it well. Why or why not?

10. Explain the managerial significance of the final parable.

THE MANAGER'S VOCABULARY

Content theories
Continuous reinforcement
Deficit principle
Existence needs
Extinction
Expectancy
Growth needs

High-order needs
Instrumentality
Intermittent reinforcement
Law of contigent reinforcement
Law of effect
Law of immediate reinforcement
Lower-order needs

Motivation to work
Need
Need for achievement
Need for affiliation
Need for power
Negative reinforcement
Operant conditioning
Organizational behavior modification
Positive reinforcement

Process theories
Progression principle
Punishment
Reinforcement theory
Relatedness needs
Reward
Shaping
Valence

CAREER PERSPECTIVE: JOB BURNOUT[24]

Jack works long hours, but his department's productivity is low. Everybody else, he says, is to blame. Jack dropped out of college at the age of 20 because of financial problems. When he first started work as a salesman, he worked harder to get ahead than his college-educated peers. He was spotted as bright and aggressive. He kept getting promotions until he became a regional sales manager. He earns a salary that permits him to pay for a suburban home, membership in a country club that his wife uses for tennis and bridge, and college for his two children.

But he's blocked in this job and he knows it. The national sales manager, whom Jack once stood a chance of succeeding, won't retire. So far as he's concerned, Jack's peers, the other regional sales managers, some of them younger and more aggressive, are getting the pick of new salespersons hired by the company. Jack looks on his own staff as the culls. He knows that it's only a matter of time before the "baby-boom brighties" in his company are going to force him out. He has high blood pressure.

Jack is a victim of "job burnout," a newly recognized syndrome that is thought to be costing employers a large if unmeasured amount of time and effort—and thus productivity. Sufferers generally show symptoms of chronic fatigue, low energy, irritability, and a negative attitude toward themselves and their jobs. Burnout is a specific set of symptoms brought on by severe or chronic stress directly related to the job rather than to personal difficulties such as divorce, death of a spouse, money problems, or aging. Burnout more often affects employees who deal extensively with other people on the job.

Christina Maslach, associate professor of psychology at the University of California at Berkeley, says burnout has three phases. In the first, she says, "There is emotional exhaustion, a feeling of being drained, used up, of having nothing more to give. Second, there is a cynicism, a callous, insensitive regard for people, a 'don't-knock-yourself-out-anymore-for-others' attitude." Finally, the burnout victim comes to believe that he or she has been unsuccessful and all job effort has been fruitless.

Questions

1. Burnout may be the flip side of too little motivation; that is, highly motivated people may run the risk of burning themselves out over time in their work. What is your potential for job burnout? Why?

2. What specific steps are you willing to take to avoid burnout in your career? How do you plan to balance personal needs and organizational demands along the way?

CASE APPLICATION: LOGGERS TIE PAY TO PRODUCTIVITY[25]

Since January 1983, the Crown Zellerbach Corporation has pursued a program to increase productivity and reduce labor costs. About 500 of the company's loggers in Washington and Oregon agreed to abandon their traditional wage scale, averaging $12 per hour, for a new program that pays them according to how much is produced. The new system eliminates some previous distinctions among logging crafts, reduces the number of restrictive work rules, and allows workers more say in how they actually manage their jobs.

The incentive to be more productive under the new plan is that pay, excluding pension and health insurance benefits, is now tied entirely to how much a wood crew produces each day. Performance is measured in units of 100 cubic feet of production as loggers fell trees, section them into logs, and then haul the logs to a sawmill. The new plan provides for all workers in a crew to earn the same pay based on the overall performance of the entire crew. Al-though the company decides where the crews are to log, each crew sets its own hours and task assignments. Since they are being paid by the amount they produce, the assumption is that the crews will be motivated to do the most efficient logging possible. The company also believes that the increased involvement of the loggers in decision making will help improve productivity.

The International Woodworkers of America (IWA), the union to which the loggers belong, sees some potential drawbacks to the incentive system. Workers may be tempted to ignore safety rules to produce more, and production quotas will be set with the average logger in mind. This means that 50-year-old workers may have to push themselves much harder to keep up with the 20-year-olds in the crew. On the other hand, there are potential gains involved as well. For example, the union is happy because more efficient logging "secures our jobs in the future."

Questions

1. Does this seem like a good motivational program from the perspective of: (a) expectancy theory? (b) reinforcement theory? Why or why not?

2. How could the insights of the content theories of motivation help managers implement this in a way that best fits the needs of individual crews under their supervision?

3. What problems do you foresee with this plan based on the insights of one or more motivation theories?

CLASS EXERCISE: BUSINESS, BEHAVIORISM, AND THE BOTTOM LINE

This exercise is based on the film, "Business, Behaviorism, and the Bottom Line." The film begins with a interesting interview with B. F. Skinner. Then Edward Feeney, vice-president of Emery Airfreight, explains how reinforcement theory was successfully applied to improve productivity in his company.

1. Before the movie begins, make sure you can define each of the following terms.

■ Operant conditioning.

■ Positive reinforcement.

■ Reinforcement schedule.

■ Shaping.

2. View the film. Take notes on your reactions to Skinner's ideas and their application at Emery Airfreight.

3. After the film is over, discuss your reactions briefly with a nearby classmate and await further class discussion.

REFERENCES

[1] Excerpted from Tim Carrington, "Psychiatrist Says His Wall Street Patients Love Working—Some of Them Too Much," *Wall Street Journal* (December 18, 1980), p. 27. Reprinted by permission of the *Wall Street Journal.* Copyright © 1980 Dow Jones & Company, Inc. All rights reserved.

[2] Portions of this chapter are adapted from John R. Schermerhorn, Jr., James G. Hunt, and Richard N. Osborn, *Managing Organizational Behavior* (New York: Wiley, 1982), pp. 107–126, 138–156. Used by permission.

[3] This and subsequent parables are adapted from Dale McConkey, "The 'Jackass Effect' in Management Compensation," *Business Horizons*, Vol. 17 (June 1974), pp. 81–91. Copyright 1974 by the Foundation for the School of Business at Indiana University. Used by permission.

[4] This discussion on Maslow's theory is based on Abraham H. Maslow, *Eupsychian Management* (Homewood, Ill.: Richard D. Irwin, 1965); Abraham H. Maslow, *Motivation and Personality,* Second Edition (New York: Harper & Row, 1970).

[5] See Clayton P. Alderfer, *Existence, Relatedness, and Growth* (New York: Free Press, 1972); Clayton P. Alderfer, Robert E. Kaplan, and Ken A. Smith, "The Effect of Variations in Relatedness Need Satisfaction on Relatedness Desire," *Administrative Science Quarterly,* Vol. 19 (1974), pp. 507–532.

[6] Sources pertinent to this discussion are David C. McClelland, *The Achieving Society* (New York: Van Nostrand, 1961); David C. McClelland, "Business Drive and National Achievement," *Harvard Business Review,* Vol. 40 (July-August 1962), pp. 99–112; David C. McClelland, "That Urge to Achieve," *Think* (November-December 1966), pp. 19–32; David C. McClelland and David H. Burnham, "Power is the Great Motivator," *Harvard Business Review,* Vol. 54 (March-April 1976), pp. 100–110.

[7] George Harrison, "To Know Why Men Do What They Do: A Conversation with David C. McClelland," *Psychology Today,* Vol. 4 (January 1971), pp. 35–39.

[8] This section is based, in part, on a discussion by Edward E. Lawler, III, in *Motivation in Work Organizations* (Monterey, Cal.: Brooks/Cole Publishing, 1973), pp. 30–36.

9 See, for example, J. Stacy Adams, "Toward an Understanding of Inequity," *Journal of Abnormal and Social Psychology,* Vol. 67 (1963), pp. 422–436; J. Stacy Adams, "Inequity in Social Exchange," in L. Berkowitz (ed.), *Advances in Experimental Social Psychology,* Vol. 2 (New York: Academic Press, 1965), pp. 267–300.

10 Victor H. Vroom, *Work and Motivation* (New York: Wiley, 1964).

11 Gerald R. Salancik and Jeffrey Pfeffer, "A Social Information Processing Approach to Job Attitudes and Task Design," *Administrative Science Quarterly,* Vol. 23 (June 1978), pp. 224–253.

12 Edward L. Deci, *Intrinsic Motivation* (New York: Plenum Press, 1975), pp. 7–8.

13 E. L. Thorndike, *Animal Intelligence* (New York: Macmillan, 1911), p. 244.

14 For some of B. F. Skinner's work see *Walden Two* (New York: Macmillan, 1948); *Science and Human Behavior* (New York: Macmillan, 1953); *Contingencies of Reinforcement* (New York: Appleton-Century-Crofts, 1969).

15 Fred Luthans and Robert Kreitner, "The Role of Punishment in Organizational Behavior Modification (OB Mod)," *Public Personnel Management,* Vol. 2 (May-June 1973), p. 157.

16 Both laws are stated in Keith L. Miller, *Principles of Everyday Behavior Analysis* (Monterey, Cal.: Brooks/Cole Publishing, 1975), p. 122.

17 Adapted from Harry Wiard, "Why Manage Behavior? A Case for Positive Reinforcement," *Human Resource Management* (Summer 1972), pp. 15–20.

18 Stephen F. Jablonsky and David L. Devries, "Operant Conditioning Principles Extrapolated to the Theory of Management," *Organizational Behavior and Human Performance,* Vol. 7 (April 1972), pp. 340–358.

19 Adapted in part from W. Clay Hamner, "Using Reinforcement Theory in Organizational Settings," in Henry L. Tosi and W. Clay Hamner (eds.), *Organizational Behavior and Management: A Contingency Approach* (Chicago: St. Clair Press, 1977), pp. 388–395.

20 See Jablonsky and Devries, op. cit., p. 345.

21 Adapted from Fred Luthans and Robert Kreitner, *Organizational Behavior Modification* (Glenview, Ill.: Scott, Foresman, 1975), pp. 127–129.

22 Adapted in part from Luthans and Kreitner, op. cit., 1973; and Hamner, op. cit.

23 Edwin A. Locke, "The Myths of Behavior Mod in Organizations," *Academy of Management Review,* Vol. 2 (October 1977), pp. 543–553.

24 Adapted from Jerry E. Bishop, "The Personal and Business Costs of Job Burnout," *Wall Street Journal* (November 11, 1980), p. 31. Reprinted by permission of the *Wall Street Journal.* © 1980 Dow Jones & Company, Inc. All rights reserved.

25 Information from *Business Week* (November 29, 1982), p. 35; *Wall Street Journal* (June 14, 1983), p. 1.

13

LEADING THROUGH GROUP DYNAMICS

THE ABILENE PARADOX

The July afternoon in Coleman, Texas (population 5607) was particularly hot—104 degrees as measured by the Walgreen's Rexall Ex-Lax temperature gauge.[1] In addition, the wind was blowing fine-grained West Texas topsoil through the house. But the afternoon was still tolerable—even potentially enjoyable. There was a fan going on the back porch; there was cold lemonade; and finally, there was entertainment. Dominoes. Perfect for the conditions. The game required little more physical exertion than an occasional mumbled comment, "Shuffle'em," and an unhurried movement of the arm to place the spots in the appropriate perspective on the table. All in all, it had the makings of an agreeable Sunday afternoon in Coleman—that is, until my father-in-law suddenly said, "Let's get in the car and go to Abilene and have dinner at the cafeteria."

I thought: What, go to Abilene? Fifty-three miles? In this dust storm and heat? And in an unair-conditioned 1958 Buick? But my wife chimed in with, "Sounds like a great idea. I'd like to go. How about you, Jerry?" Since my own preferences were obviously out of step with the rest I replied, "Sounds good to me," and added, "I just hope your mother wants to go." "Of course I want to go," said my mother-in-law. "I haven't been to Abilene in a long time."

So into the car and off to Abilene we went. My predictions were fulfilled. The heat was brutal. We were coated with a fine layer of dust that was cemented with perspiration by the time we arrived. The food at the cafeteria provided first-rate testimonial material for antacid commercials.

Some four hours and 106 miles later we returned to Coleman, hot and exhausted. We sat in front of the fan for a long time in silence. Then, both to be sociable and to break the silence, I said, "It was a great trip, wasn't it?" No one spoke. Finally my mother-in-law said, with some irritation, "Well, to tell the truth, I really didn't enjoy it much and would rather have stayed here. I just went along because the three of you were so enthusiastic about going. I wouldn't have gone if you all hadn't pressured me into it."

I couldn't believe it. "What do you mean, 'you all'?" I said. "Don't put me in the 'you all' group. I was delighted to be doing what we were doing. I didn't want to go. I only went to satisfy the rest of you. You're the culprits."

My wife looked shocked. "Don't call me a culprit. You and Daddy and Mama were the ones who wanted to go. I just went along to be sociable and to keep you happy. I would have had to be crazy to want to go out in heat like that."

Her father entered the conversation abruptly. "Hell!" he said. He proceeded to expand on what was already absolutely clear. "Listen, I never wanted to go to Abilene. I just thought you might be bored. You visit so seldom I wanted to be sure you enjoyed it. I would have preferred to play another game of dominoes and eat the leftovers in the icebox."

After the outburst of recrimination we all sat back in silence. Here we were, four reasonably sensible people who, of our own volition, had just taken a 106-mile trip across a godforsaken desert in a furnacelike temperature through a cloudlike dust storm to eat unpalatable food at a hole-in-the-wall cafeteria in Abilene, when none of us had really wanted to go. In fact, to be more accurate, we'd done just the opposite of what we wanted to do.

Individuals and groups are the human-resource foundations of organizations. Up to this point in our discussion of leadership, we have focused mainly on the individual. Now it is time to study individuals as they act collectively in the form of groups. The term *group* causes both positive and negative reactions in the minds of most people. Although it is said that "two heads are better than one," we are also warned that "too many cooks spoil the broth." "A camel is a horse put together by a committee," admonishes the true group skeptic!

Against this somewhat humorous background lies a most important point. Groups offer advantages and disadvantages for their members and for the organizations in which they exist. As far back as the historic Hawthorne studies, discussed in Chapter 2, researchers have noted that employees can develop strong group attachments and that these attachments may prove functional or dysfunctional for the organization. The purpose of this chapter is to examine the multiple and complex dynamics of group behavior in work settings and establish their managerial implications.

TYPES OF GROUPS IN ORGANIZATIONS

Suppose there is an automobile accident and you join a number of other people gathered around the wreck. Or suppose you are among several persons waiting for an elevator. Are these "groups"? No, they are not, at least in the way most social scientists define the term. A **group** is a collection of people who regularly interact with one another over time and in respect to the pursuit of one or more common goals. The key elements in this definition are interaction, time, and common goals. Neither the people standing around the wreck nor those waiting for the elevator meet all of these requirements. At best they are aggregations or collections of people.

Groups appear in various forms within the organization. Three of these forms— formal groups, informal groups and psychological groups—are especially important to you as a manager.

Formal Groups

A **formal group** is created by formal authority within an organization to transform resource inputs (such as ideas, materials, and objects) into product or service outputs (such as a report, decision, service, or commodity).[3] The work group, consisting of a manager and immediate subordinates, is the formal group with which we have been most concerned throughout this book. Indeed, it is appropriate to view organizations as interlocking networks of work groups such as shown in Figure 13.1. Note the "linking-pin" function served by the managers in this network. Because each manager acts as a superior in one work group and as a subordinate in another, all work groups become interconnected across the organization's hierarchy of authority. This helps

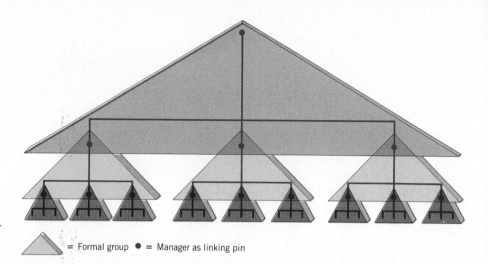

FIGURE 13.1 The organization as an interlocking network of formal groups.

△ = Formal group ● = Manager as linking pin

integrate the many separate components in an organization and thus serves as a basic building block of organizational structure.

Formal groups may be permanent or temporary in nature. **Permanent groups** retain their presence over time and often appear in organization charts as the work groups referred to as departments (e.g., market research department), divisions (e.g., General Motors Oldsmobile Division), or units (e.g., editorial unit). Managers are the formally designated leaders of permanent work groups. Such groups can vary in size from as small as two or three members to as large as several hundred members, and the manager's supervisory responsibility varies accordingly.

Committees and task forces are examples of **temporary groups.** They are created for a specific purpose and typically disband with its accomplishment. Temporary work groups usually have a designated chairperson or formal leader who is accountable for results. They can be important in facilitating task performance in the complex organizations and environment of today. Consider this problem faced by a national company.[4]

> With offices across the country, the company offers starting salaries that very from place to place. Management is concerned about possible inequities in gauging the cost of living and measuring the labor supply and demand in each location. This problem affects more than than one department, and no single person can handle it. The issues need to be carefully explored before making recommendations, and the plan will require a broad base of support for implementation.

This problem calls for a task force, a temporary and interdependent group that can solve the problem and make appropriate recommendations to management. To ensure good results, any task force must be properly prepared and function with good leadership. Basic guidelines for setting up and leading a task force include:[5]

1. *Select appropriate task-force members.* Select members who will be challenged by the assignment, who have a vested interest in the result, and whose skills and views complement one another.

2. *Clearly define the purpose and goal(s) of the task force.* Make sure task-force members and important outsiders know what is expected, why, and on what timetable.

3. *Carefully select the person who will serve as task-force leader.* Make sure this person has appropriate interpersonal skills, can respect the ideas of others, is and will remain prepared for the work that needs to be done.

4. *Periodically review progress.* Make sure task-force members feel a sense of accountability for results, review progress at regular intervals, and provide performance feedback.

In summary, formal groups share the common characteristic of being created within the hierarchy of authority to make performance contributions to the organization's objectives. It is the highest-level manager within a permanent group or the chairperson of a temporary group who is held accountable for this contribution. In both cases, the group must be well managed to achieve effectiveness. Elsewhere, we have labeled this leadership responsibility "the manager's challenge."

Informal Groups

In Chapter 6 we discussed the informal structure that exists as a companion or "shadow" to the formal structure of an organization. Just as the organization's formal structure may be viewed as an interlocking network of formal groups, so may the informal structure be viewed as an interlocking network of **informal groups**. These groups emerge within organizations without being formally designated by someone in authority for a performance purpose. They are found as the spontaneous subgroups or cliques that develop within formal groups. You may find, for example, that the same people eat together, go on breaks together, or engage in other spontaneous activities on the job. Informal groups also develop across, as well as within, formally designated groups. For instance, secretaries from one department may eat lunch with those from another. Informal groups also have leaders, but they emerge spontaneously, whereas their counterparts in formal groups are designated by authority.

There are reasons why informal groups emerge to coexist with formal groups in organizations. First, they help people get their jobs done. Informal groups offer a network of interpersonal relationships with the potential to "speed up" the work flow or "gain favors" in ways that formal lines of authority fail to provide. Organizations can benefit by the added fluidity and flexibility informal groups thereby bring to the performance effort. Informal groups also help individuals satisfy needs that are thwarted or left unmet by formal group affiliations. Among the things informal groups provide their members are:

- *Social satisfactions* Opportunities for friendships and pleasing social relationships on the job.
- *Security* Opportunities to find sympathy for one's feelings and actions, especially as they relate to friction with the formal organization;

opportunities to find help or task assistance from persons other than one's superior.
- *Identification* Opportunities to achieve a sense of belonging by affiliating with persons who share similar values, attitudes, and goals.

Informal groups are inevitable in organizations. Because they help satisfy individual needs, they can also serve an important function for the organization as well as individual members. *Newsline 13.1* shows one example of how informal groups can serve this dual purpose.

Instead of acting in fear of informal groups that may exist in their areas of responsibility, managers should seek out these groups, come to understand them, and identify the influential informal leaders. Given this foundation, informal groups can be incorporated into an overall management strategy and thereby serve to the organization's net advantage, not disadvantage.

Psychological Groups

There is another useful perspective on groups in organizations. Some groups are **psychological groups**[6] in the sense that group members are truly aware of one another's needs and potential resource contributions, and achieve high levels of interaction and mutual identification in pursuit of the common purpose. Just as we noted that not all aggregations of people are groups, not all groups are psychological groups. Most informal groups qualify as psychological groups, but many formal groups do not. Just because people are assigned to work together in the same department, for example, does not mean that they will share and work toward common goals. Think of group projects you have worked on in your college courses. Each project was designated as a formal group effort by an instructor. But did all of these groups meet the criteria of a psychological group as just defined? Surely they did not. Unfortunately, each group's performance success and your satisfaction as a member might have been higher if they had.

Managers often wish that their formal work groups would act as psychological groups. Our study of group behavior in organizations should aid you, as a manager and leader, to help your groups make this transition.

NEWSLINE 13.1

HOW WOMEN MANAGERS CAN USE INFORMAL GROUPS

Women managers can benefit from informal systems of relationships to support, inform, and advise one another within an organization.

- *Why this is necessary* Informal groups within an organization usually help their members become useful and productive and find opportunities that lead to promotions. But these relationships in management are generally dominated by men; there are usually more men and they have typically been there longer.

- *What the women's group can do* Provide information about available jobs in various parts of the company; locate and seek assistance from male managers who encourage and support women.

- *Obstacles to overcome when forming a group* Limit damaging competition among women; competent women can all move ahead, but the assistance of other women may be crucial.

A manager must be able to delegate work, to be dependent on other people to do their assigned jobs, and to assign those jobs in such a way that the person clearly knows what must be done. A manager must be able to provide assistance and support to subordinates. A manager must be able to coordinate and lead other people, to inspire confidence and trust by being confident of and trusting toward them. The informal women's group is a means of helping each woman manager succeed in those skills.

Source: Adapted from *Boardroom Reports*, July 15, 1977, p. 10, *Management's Source of Useful Information*, 500 Fifth Avenue, New York, NY 10036. Used by permission.

UNDERSTANDING GROUPS IN ORGANIZATIONS

Figure 13.2 portrays several action settings in which managers find themselves involved with groups. In both formal groups and in task forces or committees managers can be either formally appointed leaders or regular members. Managers also become involved as group members in a variety of informal networks. In each of these action settings, the manager is challenged to help the group achieve success and thereby contribute to the achievement of organizational objectives.

Usefulness of Groups

Newsline 13.2 conveys a concern one often hears expressed by people about their work—the amount of time wasted in meetings. This concern is significant since managers can spend over 40 percent of their time in meetings. Notwithstanding the problems they can pose, meetings in particular and groups in general are not only necessary—they are good for organizations and their members. They can make important task contributions to organizational objectives, and they can influence individual work attitudes and behaviors.

One of the "hot" management techniques the Japanese have popularized is the "quality circle," a special form of group meetings used to facilitate quality control. We will examine this idea in Chapter 16. For now, though, one organization's experience with quality circles helps illustrate the usefulness of groups as vehicles for organizational task accomplishment and individ-

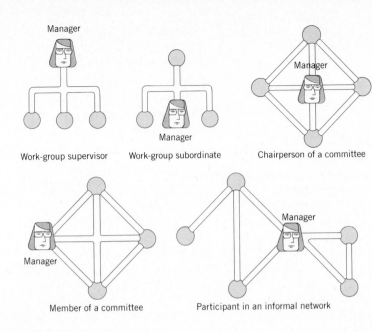

Manager

Work-group supervisor

Manager

Work-group subordinate

Manager

Chairperson of a committee

Manager

Member of a committee

Manager

Participant in an informal network

FIGURE 13.2 Possible group involvements of managers. *Source:* John R. Schermerhorn, Jr., James G. Hunt, and Richard N. Osborn, *Managing Organizational Behavior* (New York: Wiley, 1982), p. 218. Used by permission.

NEWSLINE 13.2

TIME WASTED IN MEETINGS IRKS BUSINESS

In the past, the weekly executive meeting at Dayton-Hudson Corporation, the Minneapolis-based retailer, sometimes lasted until 6:30 p.m. That made a long day for Richard Schall, vice-chairman and chief administrative officer, who often began the day with a breakfast meeting.

Now Shall rarely has breakfast meetings, and the weekly executive meeting may end as early as 4 P.M. Dayton-Hudson has taken the advice of a company team charged with helping executives cut endless and wasteful meetings.

Most executives can rattle off the rules for efficient meetings, such as starting on time, sticking to an agenda—and sticking to the point. But the rules often go by the board in actual meetings. Robert Levinson, a veteran of many corporate meetings, says most executives "waste time, don't come to concise conclusions, and cause confusion among their employees."

"When our people are in a meeting, they aren't making money," says Albert Hellwig, vice-president for administration of Scot Lad Foods Inc. So he sits next to speakers with his wristwatch at the ready to remind long-winded talkers when their time is up. He used to rely on a buzzer, but "it wasn't too popular," he says.

Dayton-Hudson also sets time limits for speakers to curb what Schall calls "the great need to tell more than others really care to know." And the company requires its executives to prepare a one-page summary in advance for each item on the agenda.

Source: Excerpted from Laurel Sorenson, "Time Wasted in Meetings Irks Business," the *Wall Street Journal* (September 24, 1980), p. 17. Reprinted by permission of the *Wall Street Journal.* Copyright © 1980 Dow Jones & Company, Inc. All rights reserved.

ual satisfaction. After a look at the case, we will address these two important uses of groups in more detail.

Illustrative Case: Quality Circles at a Shipyard[7]

On Wednesday afternoons shipwrights in Shop 64 at the Portsmouth Naval Shipyard set aside their tools and gather in a conference room to talk about their work. They are members of a quality circle, a group of 9 to 11 workers who meet for an hour each week to share ideas on ways to eliminate job-related problems and improve productivity. "It's enjoyable. We have a laugh now and then. But no way is this a one-hour coffee break," says Paul Blanchette of Berwick, who credits the meetings with improving morale and promoting a team spirit among the shipwrights.

All circle members are volunteers. They go through several weeks of training at the time their circle is formed. They then agree on what workplace problem they plan to address. "The circles first get after the things that aggravate and frustrate them the most. Then after that, they start looking at product quality," says Gene Foster, "chief facilitator" of the quality-circles program. He contends that dealing with workplace aggravations winds up being a money saver.

Groups and Organizational Task Accomplishment

Many tasks are beyond the capabilities of one person. It takes group efforts, for example, to build a jet airplane or a multistory office building. It takes a group to play basketball and to act out a television soap opera. And it takes a group to make a "quality circle." The common element to each of these examples is the benefit group synergy can bring to task accomplishments.

Synergy, you should recall, is the creation of a whole that is greater than the sum of its parts. When synergy occurs in groups, groups accomplish more than the sum total of their members' individual capabilities. Research shows that[8]

1. When the presence of an "expert" is uncertain (that is, you don't know if you have an expert

or not on a specific topic or problem), groups make better judgments than the average individual would make.

2. When problem solving can be handled by a division of labor and the sharing of information, groups are typically more successful than individuals.

3. Because of their tendencies to make more risky decisions, groups can be more creative and innovative than individuals in their task accomplishments.

Additional reasons why groups are sometimes superior to individuals in problem solving include: (1) groups have greater resources, (2) team membership includes a higher level of motivation to complete the task, (3) arguments of others force group members to examine their own beliefs more carefully, and (4) competition among individuals can produce more creative outcomes.

Groups will always be necessary to accomplish tasks important to the organization. Part of a manager's job is to know *when* a group is the best way to apply human resources to a given task. Then the manager must know *how* to achieve the full benefits of group synergy.

Groups and Individual Satisfaction

Another important function of groups is their ability to satisfy the needs of members. Both formal and informal groups provide for obvious social interactions and interpersonal fulfillments. They can be sources of individual security in the form of direct work assistance and technical advice, or emotional support in times of special crisis or pressure. Groups also give their members a sense of identification and offer opportunities for ego involvement by assisting in group activities.

Individuals can find in their group involvements the full range of need satisfactions discussed in Chapter 12. Those needs left unfulfilled by the formal work group may be met in the informal group. Whether or not the net result of group influence on the individual is positive or negative for the organization, however, depends on many factors. This is the issue that makes our study of groups in organizations so interesting.

Groups are often a successful way of stimulating creative problem solving in organizations.

Be thinking, as you read further in this chapter, of how you will act to maximize the satisfaction potential of groups in your future managerial assignments. The following example shows how groups were mobilized in a hospital to the benefit of both the organization and its members.[9]

In the spring of 1973, Rutland (Vermont) Hospital undertook a program to deter the depersonalization among employees that so often accompanies institutional growth. Having just completed a 100-bed addition, the once-small community hospital now boasted 300 beds and more than 600 employees. Specifically, the management was worried that the increase in both size of physical plant and number of employees would lead to a lack of employee identification with the hospital and that patients might pick up this depersonalization to their detriment.

After a series of discussions on the problem, it became apparent that in order to accomplish the goal, the hospital's administrative staff would actually have to get out into the hospital and meet with all of its employees, no matter how unwieldy such a system might seem on the surface.

The name of the program finally devised was as simple as the underlying concept: Employee Group Meeting Program. The mechanics of the program called for the executive vice-president and personnel director to meet on an informal basis with two groups of employees each week, joined in each instance by the appropriate department head and/or administrative officer. One meeting would be held in a nursing service area and the second in one of the other departments. The meetings were scheduled to allow for personal contact with every employee at least twice a year, for the express purpose of hearing problems, ideas, and requests for information.

Many of the early meetings were taken up with grievance-based items, such as wages, benefits, and other economic factors, and in all cases these were responded to properly. However, today's meetings are more likely to center around well-thought-out suggestions by well-prepared participants who frequently arrive with lists of concerns for consideration.

Group Effectiveness

As is evident in the prior discussion, task performance and member satisfaction are two key results of group activity. In the group context, satisfaction relates to the broader concept of **human-resource maintenance,** an ability of the group to maintain its social fabric and capabilities of its members to work well together over time. High member satisfaction suggests a greater capability for human-resource maintenance in a group. An **effective group** can therefore be defined as one that achieves and maintains high levels of *both* task performance and human-resource maintenance over time.

The Group as an Open System

Ideally, every manager and group member should work hard to promote group effectiveness. This requires an ability to understand and influence many variables with the potential to affect group behavior. Figure 13.3 portrays the

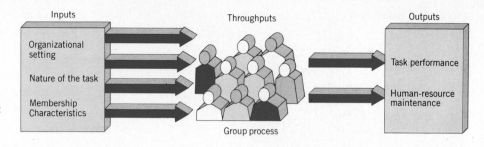

FIGURE 13.3 The work group as an open system. *Source:* John R. Schermerhorn, Jr., James G. Hunt, and Richard N. Osborn, *Managing Organizational Behavior* (New York: Wiley, 1982), p. 223. Used by permission.

group as an open system that transforms various inputs into the two key outputs—task performance and human-resource maintenance—representing our ultimate criteria of group effectiveness.

A group's ability to be effective depends, in part, on how well it transforms resource inputs into group outputs. We refer to this transformation or throughput stage as the **group process**—the means through which multiple and varied resource inputs are combined and transformed into group outputs. Stated in other terms, group process transforms resource inputs into group outputs.

Another important influence on group effectiveness is the nature of the inputs themselves. Even the most positive group process will fail to yield effective results when inadequate or inappropriate inputs are the only ones available. Among the basic inputs having the potential to impact group effectiveness are the organizational setting, nature of the task, and membership characteristics. Research results relevant to each of these input factors are summarized in Table 13.1.

Stages of Group Development

Because the behavior patterns of newly formed groups can be different from mature ones, it is helpful for you to be able to recognize the stage of development of groups in which you participate. Armed with this knowledge, you should be better able to predict what is likely to occur and take action to improve group functioning. A synthesis of the research on small groups suggests that there are four distinct phases of group development: (1) forming, (2) storming, (3) initial integration, and (4) total integration.

Forming Stage

The forming stage involves the initial entry of individual members into a group. At this point individuals ask a number of questions as they begin to identify with other group members and the group itself. These include: "What can or does the group offer me?" "What will I be asked to contribute?" "Can my needs be met while my efforts serve the task needs of the group?"

Table 13.1 Research Insights on Group Input Factors

Input Factor	Research Insight

Organizational setting
    Resources
    Space
    Structure
	Affects the degree to which members get close to one another; influences their basic capacity to apply skills and work together

Nature of the task
    Simple
    Complex
	Complex tasks place greater demands on the group process; membership satisfaction generally increases with greater task complexity

Membership characteristics
    Competencies
    Personalities
    Group size
	Competency is a necessary ingredient of performance success; heterogeneity and greater size increase a group's resource potential, but also place greater demands on the group process

In the forming stage, people are concerned to discover what is considered acceptable behavior and what the real task of the group is. Defining group boundaries and group rules is important. This identification process can be especially complicated in a work group. The setting may consist of individuals who have been in the organization for substantial time periods. Such things as multiple group memberships and identifications, prior experience with group members in other contexts, and individual impressions of organization philosophies, goals, and policies may all affect how well members initially come together in newly formed work groups.

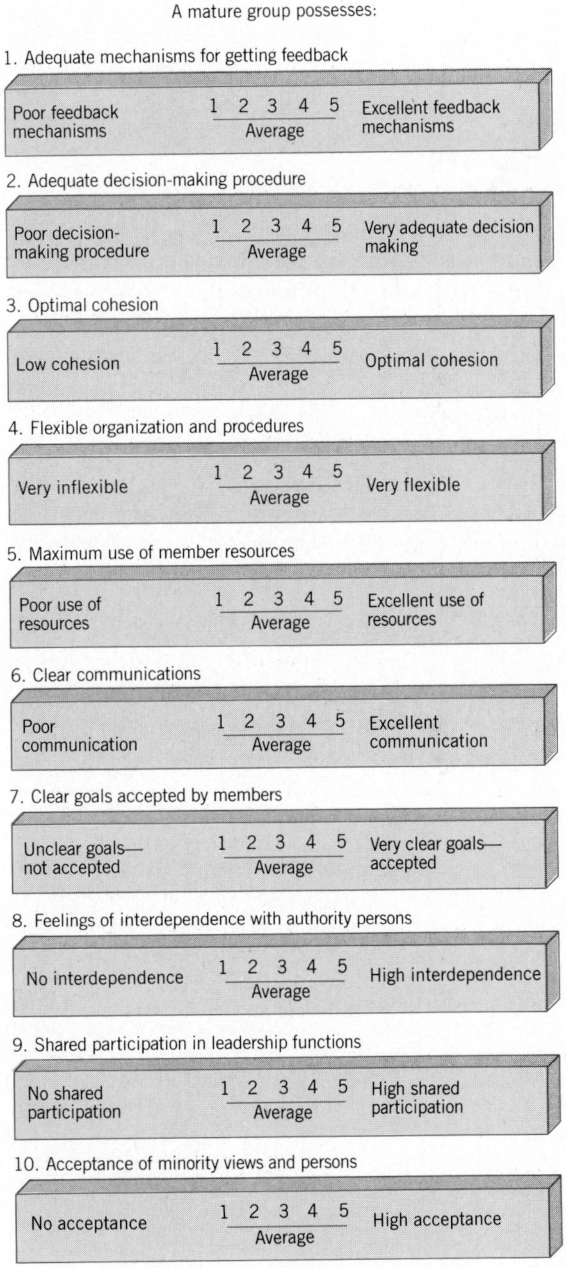

Storming Stage

The second stage of group development, the storming stage, is a period of high emotionality. Typically, the storming stage involves relatively high tension among the members, and there may be periods of overt hostility and infighting. Changes occur in the group, required activities are further elaborated, and attention is shifted toward obstacles standing in the way of group goals. People begin to clarify one another's interpersonal styles. Efforts are made to find ways to accomplish group goals while also satisfying individual needs.

Outside demands create pressures during the storming stage. Coalitions or cliques may form as subgroups emerge on an informal basis. Conflict may develop over authority as individuals compete to impose their preferences on others and achieve their desired position in the group's status structure.

Initial Integration

Whereas the storming phase is characterized by differences among group members, the initial integration stage stresses integration. Here, the group begins to become coordinated as a working unit. The interpersonal probes and jockeying for position that occur in the storming phase give way to a precarious balancing of forces. Group members strive to maintain this balance and to regulate individual behavior toward this end. Members are likely to develop a sense of close-

FIGURE 13.4 Criteria of group maturity. *Source:* Edgar H. Schein, *Process Consultation,* Copyright © 1969, Addison-Wesley Publishing Company, Inc., Chapter 6, p. 62, Figure 6.1, "A Mature Group Process." Reprinted with permission.

A mature group possesses:

1. Adequate mechanisms for getting feedback

| Poor feedback mechanisms | 1   2   3   4   5 Average | Excellent feedback mechanisms |

2. Adequate decision-making procedure

| Poor decision-making procedure | 1   2   3   4   5 Average | Very adequate decision making |

3. Optimal cohesion

| Low cohesion | 1   2   3   4   5 Average | Optimal cohesion |

4. Flexible organization and procedures

| Very inflexible | 1   2   3   4   5 Average | Very flexible |

5. Maximum use of member resources

| Poor use of resources | 1   2   3   4   5 Average | Excellent use of resources |

6. Clear communications

| Poor communication | 1   2   3   4   5 Average | Excellent communication |

7. Clear goals accepted by members

| Unclear goals— not accepted | 1   2   3   4   5 Average | Very clear goals— accepted |

8. Feelings of interdependence with authority persons

| No interdependence | 1   2   3   4   5 Average | High interdependence |

9. Shared participation in leadership functions

| No shared participation | 1   2   3   4   5 Average | High shared participation |

10. Acceptance of minority views and persons

| No acceptance | 1   2   3   4   5 Average | High acceptance |

ness (albeit superficial), a division of labor, and a sense of shared expectations. All this is designed to protect the group from disintegration. Holding the group together may become more important then successful task accomplishment.

During initial integration, harmony is emphasized and minority viewpoints may be strongly discouraged. This stage is perhaps descriptive of the family that went to Abilene in the chapter-opening example even though no one really wanted to go. A group may feel a sense of integration, but the sense may be more superficial than genuine.

Total Integration

Total integration characterizes a mature, organized, and well-functioning group. The group is able to deal with complex tasks and to handle membership disagreements in creative ways. This is a capability for constructive disagreement, which the family that went to Abilene sorely needed. Group structure is stable, and members are motivated by group goals. The primary challenges of this stage are to continue working together as an integrated unit, to remain coordinated with the larger organization, and to adapt successfully to changing conditions over time. A group that has achieved total integration will score high on the criteria of group maturity presented in Figure 13.4.

GROUP DYNAMICS

Group dynamics are forces operating in groups that affect task performance and membership satisfaction. Table 13.2 lists a number of characteristics that research has associated with effective work groups. The list offers good insight into group dynamics. As you read the list, try to anticipate the challenges experienced by managers who seek to create work groups that match each of the items.

Group dynamics represent the group-process part of the open-systems model of groups depicted in Figure 13.3 They enact the transformation process through which resource inputs are turned into task performance and human-resource maintenance as group outputs. When they fail in any way, group effectiveness is compromised. Naturally, an informed manager will want to encourage and facilitate group dynamics that become positive influences on group effectiveness.

One classic view of group dynamics is offered by George Homans, who feels that it is useful to distinguish among the activities, sentiments, and interactions of group members, and to examine the required and emergent forms of each. Because Homan's model can help you better conceptualize what goes on within groups, we briefly outline it here as an introduction to group dynamics.[10]

Table 13.2 The Nature of Highly Effective Groups

1. The members of the group are attracted to it and are loyal to its members, including the leader.
2. The members and leaders have a high degree of confidence and trust in each other.
3. The values and goals of the group are a satisfaction, integration, and expression of the relevant values and needs of its members.
4. All the interaction, problem-solving, and decision-making activities of the group occur in a supportive atmosphere. Suggestions, comments, ideas, information, and criticisms are all offered with a helpful orientation.
5. The group is eager to help members develop to their full potential.
6. The group knows the value of "constructive" conformity and knows when to use it and for what purposes.
7. There is strong motivation on the part of each member to communicate fully and frankly to the group all the information that is relevant and of value to the group's activity.
8. Members feel secure in making decisions that seem appropriate to them.

Source: Excerpted from *New Patterns of Management* by Rensis Likert, pp. 166–169. Copyright 1961 by Rensis Likert. Used with the permission of McGraw-Hill Book Company.

Required and Emergent Behaviors

Required behaviors are what the organization requests from group members by way of job performance and in return for the right of continued membership and support. Required behaviors fall in the "contributions" side of the psychological contract. They may include such things as being punctual, treating customers with respect, and being helpful to co-workers. **Emergent behaviors** are what group members do in addition to or in place of what is asked by the organization. Examples include helping out someone who is ill, taking extra time for breaks, and engaging in social activities.

Whereas the required behaviors are formally designed to benefit the performance goals of the group and organization, emergent behaviors arise from individual and group choice. They represent a spontaneous, instead of formal and planned, element in group behavior. In practice, both required and emergent behaviors can have both functional and dysfunctional implications for group effectiveness.

It may help you to think of the system of emergent behaviors as the "shadow" or informal aspect of any required group behaviors. This shadow effect is shown in Figure 13.5 which modifies the open-systems model of groups presented earlier. Ideally, the emergent system will

function in support of the required operations, enhance a group's process, and be a positive influence on overall group dynamics.

Activities, Interactions, Sentiments

Homans identifies activities, interactions, and sentiments as three basic elements of group dynamics that have both required and emergent forms. These concepts help managers understand groups.

Activities are verbal and nonverbal behaviors in which group members engage. They are things people do in groups and include efforts directed toward the group task, social activities, and other forms of physical movement. The required activities of a work group are often specified by job descriptions and organizational rules and policies. They formalize what the organization expects individuals to accomplish as group members and in return for the inducements offered. Both required and emergent activities will be found in any group.

Interactions are behaviors that group members direct toward other persons. The essence of any interaction is communication and information exchange. Interactions also occur in both required and emergent forms, and they can be both positive or negative influences on group effectiveness.

Sentiments are feelings, attitudes, beliefs, or values held by group members. They may be brought into a group from the outside by individual group members, or they may be learned from other group members. A new employee, for example, may value hard work and the concept of a "fair day's work for a fair day's pay." To maintain harmonious working relations with the group, however, this person may learn that it is important to avoid outperforming other members.

Group sentiments are especially subject to emergent forces. Although it may be easy to require formal positive attitudes toward work such as a respect for authority and belief in company rules and procedures, it is difficult to achieve these results in practice. When the goals of the emergent system support the required system, the likelihood for this match is greatly increased.

FIGURE 13.5 Emergent behaviors as a "shadow" for required behaviors in the group process. *Source:* John R. Schermerhorn, Jr., James G. Hunt, and Richard N. Osborn, *Managing Organizational Behavior* (New York: Wiley, 1982), p. 244. Used by permission.

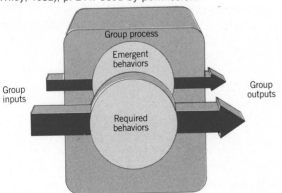

Managerial Implications

Homans's concepts of required and emergent group behaviors, and of activities, interactions, and sentiments as key elements in group dynamics, are useful ways of describing what takes place in groups. To the extent that a group's required and emergent behaviors complement instead of contradict one another, and to the extent that the activities, interactions, and sentiments of group members support organizational objectives, the group process is likely to be more harmonious. Higher group effectiveness is likely to result.

It is important to remember that supportive emergent behaviors are necessary for almost any group or organization to achieve true effectiveness. Rarely, if ever, can the required behaviors be specified so perfectly that they meet all the demands of the work situation. This is especially true in dynamic environments where job demands change over time. Indeed, there are times when the informal or emergent work behaviors are much more efficient than those required by the rules. We can illustrate very well in the reverse—that is, by giving an example of what happens when postal workers and police officers work strictly by the rules and do *only* what is required.[11]

> The U.S. postal system has many formal rules and policies that route delivery workers are supposedly required to follow. None of these men and women can perform their work satisfactorily while following all of these rules to the letter. Complete conformity is so ridiculous that postal employees have chosen to follow rules perfectly only when they wish to "strike" in opposition to federal law against "strikes." In such cases the "strike" is called a "work-by-the-rules strike." The deliverers leave in the morning, park on the opposite side of the street from their postal box (a rule), unlock their trucks, get their bags out, lock the trucks (a rule), go across the street, come back, unlock the trucks, put the mail in, lock their trucks, etc. Thus by following rules perfectly the deliverers come in late from their daily activities with only half the mail delivered, and free from any possible prosecution.

> Similarly, when New York City police officers wish to register a grievance about pay and working conditions, they simply ticket every car in New York City that they see in violation of the law. New York traffic and activities come to a screeching halt. Again, it is made clear that perfectly formal ways of working without emergent behavior are not satisfactory.

GROUP NORMS AND COHESIVENESS

Two key aspects of group dynamics that relate to the sentiments described in Homans' model are group norms and group cohesiveness. Let's introduce the concepts through the following incident. It involves Frank Jackson, someone who was full of ability and motivation when he joined a new work unit. Soon, however, he was influenced by the group to restrict work effort and achieve lower performance accomplishments than he was capable of. The factors affecting his decision include group norms and cohesiveness.

Illustrative Case: Frank Jackson[12]

Frank Jackson deftly soldered his last wires in the interconnection. That was 18 for the morning—not bad, he thought. He moved on to the next computer and began to string out the cable for the next job.

"You're new here, aren't you?" The man was standing beside Frank, soldering iron in hand.

"Yeah. I came over from Consumer Products Division—been with the company for 10 years."

"I'm Jim Miller. Been working here in computer assembly for five years."

The men shook hands. Jim walked back to the last job Frank did and looked it over. "Pretty good, Frank, pretty good." He looked back down the assembly floor. "How many have you done this morning?"

"Eighteen."

"Hey, you're quite a rate-buster, aren't you?" Jim laughed. "Most of us here figure 15 interconnections a day is about par for the course."

"Well, these I'm doing are pretty easy."

Jim frowned. "Yeah, but look what happens. You do 20, maybe 25 easy ones, and the boys stuck with the hard jobs look bad. You wouldn't want that to happen, would you?"

"Well, no, of course not."

"That-a-boy! You know, the boys here have a bowling team—kind of a company deal. Not everybody is on it—just the interconnection group. Even a few of them don't make it. You know, we like to keep it a friendly bunch." Jim paused. "Like to come next Wednesday?"

"Why, OK. Sure. Jim, what does the foreman think about the number of jobs a day?"

"Him? He don't know the difference, and if he did, what difference would it make? You can't find good interconnection men right off the street. He goes along—the boys upstairs don't know how fast the work should go, and they don't bother him. So he don't bother us."

Frank looked over his next job. He was doing the toughest kind of interconnection, and he knew that any reasonably skilled man should be able to do at least 40 jobs a day on most of the other interconnections. Boy, this was going to be a relaxing job. He didn't like to goof off, but these people were going to be working with him every day—and he wasn't about to get off on the wrong foot with them. Besides, he liked to bowl.

"It's all cost plus anyhow," Jim said. "The company gets plenty from the government for the work. They've got nothing to worry about. Hey, come over to the lounge with me—we can have a smoke. We got plenty of time."

Norms

A group **norm** is a behavior expected of group members. Norms are often referred to as "rules" or "standards" of behavior that apply to group members. When violated, they may be enforced with reprimands and other group sanctions. In the extreme, a violation of group norms can result in expulsion or social ostracism. This concern probably caused Frank Jackson in the preceding case to adopt the group norm of restricted performance.

Norms are among the sentiments that develop as group members interact with one another. They serve the group by allowing members to predict one another's behavior and to select appropriate behaviors for themselves. Norms help a group avoid chaos as the inputs of many individuals are organized into collective action. There are many types of norms. In a student study group, for example, there may be norms regarding attendance at meetings, social behaviors, preparedness for meetings, willingness to challenge one another's ideas, and so on.

One of the most important norms in any group relates to the level of work effort and performance that members are expected to contribute to the group task. This **performance norm** is a key characteristic of work groups, and it can have positive or negative implications for group and organizational productivity. Work groups with more positive performance norms tend to be more successful in accomplishing task objectives than groups, such as Frank Jackson's, with more negative performance norms.

The point of key managerial significance is whether or not a group norm has positive or negative implications for the organization. For example, compare and contrast the positive and negative versions of the norms shown in Table 13.3. Any manager would clearly prefer to have a work unit in which the positive versions of pride, teamwork, performance, leadership, and profitability norms prevailed. Other norms that emerge as important sentiments in work groups include relationships with supervisors, colleagues, and customers, as well as honesty, quality of work, security, personal development, and change.

Cohesiveness

Norms vary in the degree to which they are accepted and adhered to by group members. Conformity to norms is largely determined by a group's cohesiveness. Group **cohesiveness** is the degree to which members are attracted to and motivated to remain part of a group.[13] Persons in a highly cohesive group value their membership and strive to maintain positive relationships with other group members. They tend to conform to group norms as a result. Frank Jackson's work group was highly cohesive. Other members of the team rallied together to withhold their work efforts and adhere to the restricted performance norm. This sense of group belongingness apparently had a strong attraction for Frank. Perhaps it was a need for social affiliation that led him to accept this norm, instead of breaking it and running the risk of being ostracized from the group.

Table 13.3 Positive and Negative Versions of Group Norms

Norms	Positive Form	Negative Form
Organizational and personal pride	It's a tradition around here for people to stand up for the company when others criticize it unfairly.	In our company they are always trying to take advantage of us.
Performance/excellence	In our company people always try to improve, even when they are doing well.	Around here there's no point in trying harder—nobody else does.
Teamwork/communication	Around here people are good listeners and actively seek out the ideas and opinions of others.	Around here it's dog-eat-dog and save your own skin.
Leadership/supervision	Around here managers and supervisors really care about the people they supervise.	In our company it's best to hide your problems and avoid your supervisor.
Profitability/cost effectiveness	Around here people are continually on the lookout for better ways of doing things.	Around here people tend to hang on to old ways of doing things even after they have outlived their usefulness.

Source: Quotes in table reprinted by permission of the publisher, from "Confronting the Shadow Organization: How to Detect and Defeat Negative Norms," by Robert F. Allen and Saul Pilnick, from *Organizational Dynamics* (Spring 1973), pp. 6–10. Copyright © 1973 by AMACOM, a division of American Management Associations. All rights reserved.

Sources of Cohesion

Group cohesiveness is affected by a variety of personal and situational variables. Cohesion tends to be high in groups whose members share similar attitudes, socioeconomic backgrounds, needs, and other individual attributes. When members respect and hold one another's competencies in high esteem, cohesiveness is also likely to be high. Situational factors that enhance group cohesion include agreement on group goals, small size of membership, tasks requiring a high degree of interdependence, physical isolation from other groups, performance success, and performance failure or crisis.

Cohesion, Satisfaction, and Performance

Cohesive groups are good for their members. Members of highly cohesive groups are concerned about their group's activities and achievements. They tend, as opposed to persons in less cohesive groups, to be more energetic in working on group activities, to be less likely to be absent,

to feel happy about performance success, and to be displeased about failures. Cohesive groups generally have stable memberships and foster feelings of loyalty, security, and high self-esteem among their members. Thus they satisfy a full range of individual needs.

A critical question that remains, however, is whether or not cohesive work groups are always good for their organizations. Research answers: "It all depends on the group's performance norm!" A basic rule of group dynamics is that the more cohesive the group, the greater the conformity of members to group norms. When the performance norm of a work group or informal group is positive, high conformity has a very beneficial effect; when the norm is negative, however, high conformity can have undesirable results.

Figure 13.6 predicts productivity levels for various combinations of group cohesion and performance norms. Productivity is likely to be highest in a highly cohesive group with positive performance norms. In this situation, competent

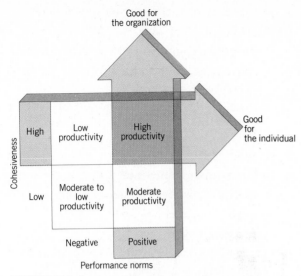

FIGURE 13.6 Group productivity for various combinations of group cohesiveness and performance norms.

group members can work hard and reinforce one another's performance efforts while experiencing satisfaction with the group affiliation. This situation is highlighted in the shaded cell of Figure 13.6.

The worst situation for a manager is a highly cohesive work group with negative performance norms. Here, members are once again highly motivated to support one another and conform to norms. They are also likely to be satisfied with this experience because of the cohesiveness of the group. But organizational productivity will

probably suffer as group members collectively restrict individual work efforts to levels consistent with the group's negative performance norm.

Between these two extremes are mixed situations. Moderate productivity is likely to result from groups with low cohesion under both positive performance norms; moderate to low productivity is likely when low cohesion is accompanied by negative performance norms. In each case, the lack of cohesion fails to rally complete member conformity to the guiding norm.

Influencing Norms and Cohesiveness

The norms and cohesiveness of any group, formal or informal, interrelate with one another to affect the behavior of group members. Managers should therefore be skilled at influencing norms and cohesion in ways that support high levels of both task performance and member satisfaction. Group effectiveness will be enchanced as a result.

Building Positive Norms

Table 13.4 shows that appropriate focus for norm-building efforts varies with each of the four stages of group development. In the forming and storming stages, norms relating to membership issues such as expected attendance and levels of commitment are important. By the time a group reaches the stage of total integration, growth-oriented norms relating to adaptability and

Table 13.4 Typical Sequence of Norm Development in Work Groups

Stage of the Group	Focus of Group Norms	Illustrative Behaviors Addressed
Early	Membership	Who is and who is not a member; attendance at group meetings; punctuality, commitment
	Influence	Leadership roles, strategies for doing the work of the group; status and dominance relations among members
	Affection	Patterns of intermember liking and disliking; balance between task work and interpersonal relationships
Late	Growth	Experimentation with new behaviors; adaptation of group norms and processes to a changing environment.

Source: David Nadler, J. Richard Hackman, and Edward E. Lawler III, *Managing Organizational Behavior* (Boston: Little, Brown, 1979), p. 124. Copyright © 1979 by David A. Nadler, J. Richard Hackman, and Edward E. Lawler III. Reprinted by permission of the authors and Little, Brown and Company.

change become most relevant. Groups that are unable to build norms consistent with the operating problems typical to each stage of development may fail to achieve effectiveness.

Because group norms are largely determined by the collective will of group members, it is difficult for a manager or designated group leader simply to dictate which norms a given work group will adopt. Instead, the concerned manager or leader must use a knowledge of group dynamics to help and encourage group members to adopt norms supportive of organizational objectives. Among the things a manager can do are the following.[14]

- Act as a positive role model.
- Reinforce the desired behaviors via rewards.
- Control results by performance reviews and regular feedback.
- Train and orient new members to adopt desired behaviors.
- Recruit and select new members who exhibit the desired behaviors.
- Hold regular meetings to discuss group progress and ways of improving task performance and member satisfaction.
- Use group decision-making methods to reach agreement on appropriate behaviors.

Influencing Cohesion

As was pointed out earlier, there are advantages and disadvantages to high group cohesiveness. It is good in combination with positive group norms; it can be very troublesome in combination with negative norms. Thus there will be times when a manager will want to build cohesiveness in work groups—for example, when trying to increase conformity to a positive performance norm. There may also be times when the objective is to break down cohesiveness, such as when group members exhibit high conformity to a negative performance norm. A number of things managers can do increase and decrease group cohesion follow.

1. In order to *increase* cohesion a manager can:

    - Induce agreement on group goals.
    - Increase membership homogeneity.

- Increase interactions among members.
- Decrease group size.
- Introduce competition with other groups.
- Allocate rewards to the group rather than individuals.
- Provide physical isolation from other groups.

2. In order to *decrease* cohesion a manager can:

    - Foster disagreement on group goals.
    - Increase membership heterogeneity.
    - Restrict interactions among members.
    - Increase group size.
    - Allocate rewards to individuals rather than the group as a whole.
    - Remove physical isolation.
    - Introduce a dominating member.
    - Disband the group.

"Groupthink"

There is another, more subtle side to group cohesion that can work to a group's disadvantage. Recall the Abilene paradox introduced in the chapter-opening example? Here's another look at the paradox as it operates in the business world.[15]

The Ozyx Corporation is a relatively small industrial company whose managers have embarked on a trip to Abilene. The president of Ozyx has hired a consultant to help discover the reasons for the poor profit picture of the company in general, and the low morale and productivity of the research and development division in particular. During the investigation, the consultant becomes interested in a research project in which the company has invested a sizable proportion of its R&D budget.

When asked about the project by the consultant in the privacy of their offices, the president, the vice-president for research, and the research manager each describe it as an idea that looks great on paper but will ultimately fail because of the unavailability of the technology required to make it work. Each also acknowledges that continued support of the project will create cash-flow problems that will jeopardize the very existence of the total organization.

Furthermore, each individual indicates he or she has not told the others about his or her reservations. When asked why, the president says he can't reveal his "true" feelings because abandoning the project, which has been widely publicized, would make the company look bad in the press. In addition, it would probably cause his vice-president's ulcer to kick up or perhaps even cause her to quit, "Because she has staked her professional reputation on the project's success."

Similarly, the vice-president for research says she can't let the president or the research manager know her reservations because the president is so committed to it that "I would probably get fired for insubordination if I questioned the project."

Finally, the research manager says he can't let the president or vice-president know of his doubts about the project because of their extreme commitment to the project's success.

All indicate that in meetings with one another, they try to maintain an optimistic facade so the others won't worry unduly about the project. The research director, in particular, admits to writing ambiguous progress reports so the president and vice-president can "interpret them to suit themselves." He says he tends to slant them to the "positive" side, "given how committed the brass are."

Symbolically, the participants in this boardroom meeting have just taken a ride to Abilene. Groups falling prey to the Abilene paradox have difficulty managing agreement. Members may publicly agree with courses of action while privately having serious personal reservations. Group cohesion is a key force in these situations. It sometimes results in a loss of willingness and ability among group members to evaluate one another's ideas and suggestions critically. Desires to retain cohesion, hold the group together, and avoid unpleasant disagreements lead to an overemphasis on agreement and an underemphasis on the critical appraisal of ideas or alternative courses of action.

Irving Janis is a social psychologist who has studied this group tendency in detail. He calls attention to the phenomenon of **"groupthink,"** a tendency for highly cohesive groups to lose their critical evaluative capabilities.[16]

Janis ties a variety of well-known historical blunders to groupthink, including the lack of pre-

Table 13.5 Symptoms of Groupthink

Illusions of group invulnerability   Members of the group feel it is basically beyond criticism or attack.
Rationalizing unpleasant and disconfirming data   Refusal to accept contradictory data or to consider alternatives thoroughly
Belief in inherent group morality   Members of the group feel it is "right" and above any reproach by outsiders.
Stereotyping competitors as weak, evil, and stupid   Refusal to look realistically at other groups.
Applying direct pressure to deviants to conform to group wishes   Refusal to tolerate a member who suggests the group may be wrong.
Self-censorship by members   Refusal by members to communicate personal concerns to the group as a whole.
Illusions of unanimity   Accepting consensus prematurely, without testing its completeness.
Mind guarding   Members of the group protect the group from hearing disturbing ideas or viewpoints from outsiders.

Source: See Irving Janis, *Victims of Groupthink* (Boston: Houghton Mifflin, 1972).

paredness of the U.S. naval forces for the 1941 Japanese attack on Pearl Harbor, President Kennedy's handling of the Bay of Pigs, and the many roads that led to the United States' involvement in Vietnam. Groupthink can occur anywhere. It may even have led to President Nixon's downfall in the Watergate fiasco.

Table 13.5 lists a number of symptoms of groupthink. Do you recognize any of these signs in groups which you are familiar? When and if a group ever does experience groupthink, Janis suggests the following action guidelines to avoid its negative consequences.

1. Assign the role of critical evaluator to each group member; encourage a sharing of viewpoints on all matters facing the group.

2. Avoid, as a leader, seeming partial to one course of action.

3. Create subgroups to work on the same problems and then share their proposed solutions.

4. Have group members discuss issues with outsiders and report back on their reactions.

5. Invite outside experts to observe group activities and react to group processes and decisions.

6. Assign one member to play a "devil's advocate" role at each meeting of the group.

7. Hold a "second-chance" meeting after consensus is apparently achieved on key issues to test the consensus once again.

GROUP TASK AND MAINTENANCE ACTIVITIES

Activities in Homans's model of group dynamics represent the action contributions of members to the group process. Research on the social psychology of groups identifies two types of activities that are essential if group members are to work well together over time: task and maintenance activities.[17]

Task Activities

Task activities contribute directly to the group's performance purpose. They include efforts to define and solve problems and apply work efforts in support of task accomplishment. Without relevant task activities, groups will have difficulty accomplishing their objectives. Performance success depends on group member's willingness to contribute activities such as the following.

Initiating   Setting agendas, giving ideas, defining problems, suggesting solutions.

Information giving and seeking   Offering information pertinent to task, asking for ideas of others, seeking facts.

Summarizing   Pulling ideas together into summary perspective, restating where the group appears to be in its task agenda.

Elaborating   Clarifying ideas by example, seeking to ensure that meanings and perspectives are shared.

Opinion giving   Evaluating ideas, suggestions, and proposed solutions.

Maintenance Activities

Maintenance activities support the emotional life of the group as an ongoing social system. They help strengthen and perpetuate the group as a social entity. When maintenance activities are performed well, good interpersonal relationships

Offering information and opinion is a task contribution to group dynamics.

are achieved and the ability of the group to stay together over the longer term is ensured. The maintenance activities listed here can help enhance member satisfaction and thereby contribute, along with the task activities, to group effectiveness.

Gatekeeping   Allowing another member to gain "talking time," that is, helping to make sure everyone has a change to speak.

Encouraging   Being warm and receptive to others, drawing forth contributions.

Following   Going along with the group, agreeing to try out the ideas of others.

Harmonizing   Reconciling differences, bringing conflicting parties to points of compromise and agreement.

Reducing tension   Drawing off emotions by changing the subject temporarily to a humorous or broader context.

Group Task and Maintenance Leadership

Both task and maintenance activities are required for groups to be effective over the long run. They stand in distinct contrast to the dysfunctional activities described in Table 13.6. Activities of this latter type are usually self-serving and detract from rather than enhance group effectiveness. Unfortunately, as you have probably observed, very few groups are immune from the display of such dysfunctional behavior by members.

Task and maintenance activities are leadership skills. They can and should be learned by all persons, especially managers who wish to be successful in helping groups perform to their highest potential. It is important to remember, though, that any member can assist a group by performing these functions. Although a person with formal authority, such as chairperson or supervisor, will often do them, the responsibility for task and maintenance activities should be shared and distributed among all group members. This means that everyone in a group has both opportunity and responsibility to participate in the leadership role by helping the group satisfy its task and maintenance needs. This *distributed leadership* responsibility in group dynamics includes the need for every member to:

1. Correctly diagnose group dynamics and recognize when task and/or maintenance activities are needed.
2. Respond appropriately by providing or helping others provide these activities.

TEAM BUILDING: MANAGING GROUP EFFECTIVENESS

When we think of the word *team*, sporting teams come to mind, such as the Dallas Cowboys, New York Yankees, and the U.S. Olympic team. We know that sporting teams have their problems. Members slack off or become disgruntled, and some are retired or traded as a result. Even world champion teams have losing streaks; the most highly talented players are prone to lose motivation at times, quibble among themselves, and go into slumps. When these things happen, the owners, managers, and players are apt to examine their problems and take corrective action to "rebuild the team" and restore what we have been calling group effectiveness.

Work groups are teams in a similar sense. Even the most mature work group is likely to experience problems over time. When difficulties arise from pressures of competition or normal work routines, team-building activities can help. **Team building** is a sequence of planned activities to gather and analyze data on the functioning of a group and implement constructive changes to increase its operating effectiveness.

There are many approaches to team building, but they generally share the steps shown in Figure 13.7. The cycle begins with sensitivity that a problem may exist or might develop in the future within the group. Group members then

Table 13.6 Dysfunctional Activities of Group Members

1. *Being aggressive* Working for status by criticizing or blaming others, showing hostility against the group or some individual, deflating the ego or status of others.
2. *Blocking* Interfering with the progress of the group by going off on a tangent, citing personal experiences unrelated to the problem, arguing too much on a point, rejecting ideas without consideration.
3. *Self-confessing* Using the group as a sounding board, expressing personal, nongroup-oriented feelings or points of view.
4. *Competing* Vying with others to produce the best idea, talk the most, play the most roles, gain favor with the leader.
5. *Seeking sympathy* Trying to induce other group members to be sympathetic to one's problems or misfortunes, deploring one's own situation, or disparaging one's own ideas to gain support.
6. *Special pleading* Introducing or supporting suggestions related to one's own pet concerns or philosophies, lobbying.
7. *Horsing around* Clowning, joking, mimicking, disrupting the work of the group.
8. *Seeking recognition* Attempting to call attention to self by loud or excessive talking, extreme ideas, unusual behavior.
9. *Withdrawal* Acting indifferent or passive, resorting to excessive formality, daydreaming, doodling, whispering to others, wandering from the subject.

Source: Based on J. William Pfeiffer and John E. Jones, *1976 Annual Handbook for Group Facilities* (La Jolla, Calif.: University Associates, 1976), p. 137. Used by permission.

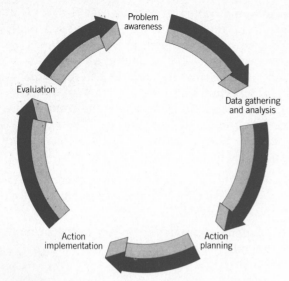

FIGURE 13.7 A typical team-building cycle. *Source:* John R. Schermerhorn, Jr., James G. Hunt, and Richard N. Osborn, *Managing Organizational Behavior* (New York: Wiley, 1982), p. 288. Used by permission.

work together to gather and analyze data such that the problem is finally diagnosed. Plans are made and corrective action implemented. Results are then evaluated, and any difficulties or new problems that are discovered can serve to recycle the team-building process.

You can see that team building is a data-based way of assessing a work group's functioning and taking corrective action to improve group effectiveness. This can be done with or without consulting assistance, and it can become a regular part of a group's continuing work routine. Team building can also be a very creative process. The following example shows this in the ways used to stimulate reflexive thinking in a group.[18]

A Team-Building Strategy. After preliminary remarks by the manager, group members can be asked: In order for us to get a picture of how you see our group functioning, would each of you take a few minutes to describe our group as a kind of animal or combination of animals, a kind of machine, a kind of person, or whatever image comes to mind? Some groups in the past have been described as:

1. *A hunting dog—a pointer.* We run around

and locate problems, then stop and point and hope somebody else will take the action.

2. *A Cadillac with pedals.* We look good on the outside, but there is no real power to get us moving.

3. *A Rube Goldberg device.* Everything looks crazy and you can't imagine anything will ever happen, but, in some way, for some reason, we do get results at the end.

4. *An octopus.* Each tentacle is out grasping anything it can, but doesn't know what the other tentacles are doing.

As people share these images and explain what elicits the image, some questions are asked. What are the common elements in these images? Do we like these images of ourselves? What do we need to do to change our image? The answering of these questions becomes the major agenda item of subsequent group meetings to carry out the team-building process.

Data gathering and analysis are key elements in the team-building cycle. To be successful in this stage, group outcomes in terms of task performance and member satisfaction must be carefully assessed. How input factors and the group process influence these results must then be determined. This allows decisions to be made regarding the constructive modification of group inputs and/or group processes to enhance future effectiveness.

There are many ways to gather data on group functioning. Structured and unstructured interviews, questionnaires, group meetings, and written records are all examples. Regardless of the method used, the principle of team-building requires that a careful and collaborative assessment be made. All group members should participate in the data-gathering process, assist in the data analysis, and collectively decide to take action to resolve and/or prevent problems that interfere with group effectiveness. We will further examine this set of responsibilities in our discussion of organization development in Chapter 17.

INTERGROUP DYNAMICS[19]

As groups mature and take control of their internal processes, attention eventually shifts to working relationships with other groups in the external environment. Intergroup relations are an important element in organizations, which we have already described as complex networks of interlocking groups. Organizations require good coordination among the activities of many groups in order to achieve productivity.

Think back to the linking-pin model of organizations shown in Figure 13.1. Within this network of work groups, any breakdown in intergroup relationships can cause problems for the organization as a whole, one or more of its subunits, and the managers of these subunits. As the following comments from the marketing and manufacturing departments in one company show, disagreements and conflict leading to breakdowns in intergroup relations can easily occur.[20]

Issue Breadth of product line.

> *Marketing says* "Our customers demand variety."

> *Manufacturing says* "The product line is too broad—all we get are short, uneconomical runs."

Issue Capacity planning.

> *Marketing says* "Why don't we have enough capacity?"

> *Manufacturing says* "Why didn't we have accurate sales forecasts?"

Issue Delivery and distribution.

> *Marketing says* "Why don't we ever have the right merchandise in inventory?"

> *Manufacturing says* "We can't keep everything in inventory."

Issue New products.

> *Marketing says* "New products are our life blood."

> *Manufacturing says* "Unnecessary design changes are prohibitively expensive."

Another good example of ever-present intergroup dynamics is in colleges and universities where numerous separate departments are responsible for teaching specialized subjects. It would be impossible for a student to get a degree if the course offerings and program requirements weren't well coordinated. But we all know that coordination occasionally does break down at considerable inconvenience to students!

"Groupthink" is the tendency for highly cohesive groups to lose their critical evaluative capabilities.

Intergroup Competition

The working relationships among groups in organizations should be such that each group achieves maximum productivity *and* that the accumulated results of all group accomplishments make a maximum contribution to organizational objectives. Unfortunately, the prior examples indicate there is a tendency for groups to develop rivalries and even antagonisms with one another that detract from this goal of intergroup cooperation and coordination. The net result is a sense of competition that can have negative consequences for the organization.

Groups in organizations compete with one another for rewards, status, resources, and special privileges, among other things. The following may be observed of groups in competition.

1. *Within* each competing group—

   ■ Members become closer knit and evidence increased group loyalty; group cohesion increases.

   ■ Concern for the accomplishment of the group's task grows; members become more task oriented.

   ■ Group members become more willing to accept a single leader; authority becomes more centralized.

   ■ Activities become more tightly organized; structure assumes a more mechanistic form.

2. *Between* the competing groups—

   ■ Each group views the other as an enemy.

   ■ Each group tends to develop positive images of itself and negative images of the other; one's own group strengths are overestimated while those of the other are underestimated.

   ■ Hostilities increase and communications decrease between the groups.

   ■ When forced into interaction with the other group, members listen only to what reinforces their original predisposition toward one another.

You can imagine the organizational difficulties that result from these competitive inter-group dynamics. Although competition between groups can be productive for the organization because of the increased cohesion and task orientation that may result, it can detract from productivity because of the distorted communications and coordination problems that may also result. Managers thus walk a thin line as they try to realize some of the advantages of intergroup competition while minimizing its disadvantages. *Newsline 13.3* suggests just how difficult this may be.

Managing Intergroup Competition

There are two approaches to managing intergroup competition. One is to deal with the competition after it occurs; the second is to prevent its occurrence in the first place.

Controlling Existing Competition

Strategies for minimizing the negative consequences resulting from groups already in competition include:

1. Identifying a common enemy (for example, another company to be outperformed).

2. Appealing to a common goal (for example, profits or customer satisfaction).

3. Bringing representatives of the groups into direct contact with one another (for example, setting up face-to-face negotiations).

4. Training members of the competing groups in group process and interpersonal skills (for example, engaging them in planned exercises to increase interpersonal awareness and promote greater work harmony).

Preventing Future Competition

Action guidelines that managers may follow to prevent destructive intergroup competition from occurring in the first place include:

1. Rewarding groups on the basis of their performance contributions to the organization as a whole.

2. Rewarding groups for the help they give one another.

3. Stimulating frequent interaction between members of various groups.

NEWSLINE 13.3

PITTING WORKERS AGAINST ONE ANOTHER OFTEN BACKFIRES

To prod branch managers to perform better, a European bank encouraged them to compete against one another to produce the most improved results.

The winner was promised a bonus. But the outcome was disappointing. The bank discovered that a greedy officer had steered a customer to a rival bank rather than help another branch manager win the bonus.

Chase Manhattan Bank hoped to create healthy competition between divisions by linking employees' bonuses to the fees their divisions generated. But the bonus plan encouraged employees to aim for high-volume customers instead of good credit risks. One group built a huge portfolio with a tiny new company called Drysdale Government Securities, Inc. In May Drysdale defaulted on interest payments on securities it had borrowed through Chase. Chase forecasts it will take an after-tax write-off of $117 million in the second quarter as a result.

Sales contests, a widespread form of competition, have also produced some awkward situations for the companies that sponser them. Data General Corp., a Westboro, Mass. computer maker, caught its salesman for the Texas area poaching on Oklahoma's turf. An office-copier salesman for another company asked a Lawrence, Kansas, customer to sign up for a copier even though the customer wasn't going to go through with the purchase. The salesman "just wanted to win his trip to Hawaii," says the customer, who refused to help out.

Source: Excerpted from Heywood Klein, "Pitting Workers Against Each Other Backfires, Firms Are Finding," the *Wall Street Journal* (July 15, 1982), p. 29. Reprinted by permission of the *Wall Street Journal.* Copyright © 1982 Dow Jones & Company, Inc. All rights reserved.

4. Avoiding tendencies for groups to withdraw and become isolated from one another.

5. Rotating members among groups whenever possible.

6. Avoiding win-lose competition among groups to obtain desired organizational rewards.

7. Emphasizing the sharing of resources for the maximum benefit of the organization as a whole.

This is a point where the managerial functions of organizing and leading come together. Organizational structures should be well designed to encourage cooperation. They should also be staffed with persons whose attitudes, goals, and interpersonal skills support cooperation. Then, good leadership should ensure that people, individually and in groups, fulfill the opportunity to achieve synergy through cooperative efforts.

SUMMARY

Groups differ from simple aggregations or collections of people. The key difference is that a group involves regular interactions over time among persons with shared commitments to a common purpose. Groups are an essential human resource of organizations. In their formal or work-group forms, they exist in interlocking networks in which managers serve a linking-pin function. Formal work groups can be permanent, such as departments or divisions, or temporary, such as committees and task forces. Informal groups spontaneously arise from the work setting. They exist in any organization and help satisfy the individual needs of members. Informal groups can also be functional or dysfunctional in respect to the accomplishment of organizational objectives. Some groups become psychological groups. In them, members are truly aware of one another's needs and potential resource contributions, share a strong sense of group commitment, and regularly interact on its behalf.

An effective group achieves high levels of task performance and human-resource maintenance over time. Managers must be concerned to increase and/or maintain effectiveness in groups where they are the formally designated leader or general participant. This requires an understanding of group-development stages and the essence of group and inter-group dynamics.

Group dynamics are those forces within groups that affect task performance and membership satisfaction. They are the components of the group process that help transform inputs into outputs. George Homans describes group dynamics in terms of required and emergent behaviors, as well as activities, interactions, and sentiments. Using this framework, group norms and cohesiveness emerge as important to any group process. Norms refer to the behaviors expected of other group members. Cohesiveness refers to the degree to which members are attracted to and motivated to remain part of the group. In combination, these two concepts can have a substantial positive or negative influence on group effectiveness. A key capability for any manager is to know how to influence norms and cohesion in ways that increase the productivity potential of formal and informal groups.

Effective groups depend on their members, both formal leaders and general participants, to share responsibility for important task and maintenance activities. Task activities directly facilitate performance accomplishment; maintenance activities help maintain the social fabric of the group over time.

To succeed over the long term, any group must periodically take stock of itself and make constructive modifications in its manner of operations. Teambuilding is a data-based approach that can help in this assessment and change process. Thus an additional leadership challenge for any manager is to facilitate teambuilding to ensure group effectiveness.

Finally, remember that groups in organizations must work cooperatively together in order to achieve the synergy necessary to accomplish organizational objectives. In any organization, natural tendencies can result in intergroup competition that assumes destructive proportions and increases the difficulty of achieving the necessary coordination. Successful managers act in ways to minimize the destructive potential of intergroup competition, while still taking advantage of its potential benefits.

THINKING THROUGH THE ISSUES

1. Define and give examples of formal and informal groups as they might exist in a work setting.

2. List and explain some of the advantages and disadvantages of informal groups for (a) their members and (b) their host organizations.

3. When does a formal group become a psychological group? Should every manager want his or her work unit to become a psychological group? Defend your answer.

4. What is group effectiveness? Explain how it differs from the concept of human-resource maintenance in the group setting.

5. Explain the difference between group norms and cohesiveness.

6. Suppose you are the manager of a work group that displays a negative performance norm. What can be done to overcome its negative effects?

7. List the four stages of group development. Why is it that groups often mistake the third stage—initial integration—for the fourth stage—total integration?

8. What is "groupthink"? How can it be prevented?

9. Explain the manager's role as a "linking pin" between interlocking groups in an organization.

10. What is team building and how can it help managers fulfill their responsibilities for supporting and maintaining high levels of work-unit productivity?

THE MANAGER'S VOCABULARY

Activities	Group dynamics	Interactions	Required behaviors
Cohesiveness	Group process	Maintenance activities	Sentiments
Effective group	Groupthink	Norm	Task activities
Emergent behaviors	Human-resource	Performance norm	Team building
Formal group	maintenance	Permanent groups	Temporary groups
Group	Informal group	Psychological groups	

CAREER PERSPECTIVE: THE ACID TEST[21]

Picture the setting. In a locked room high up in the Manhattan headquarters of International Telephone and Telegraph Corporation, 50 executives sit around two long, felt-covered tables. There from all over the world, they are reporting to Harold Geneen, chief executive officer of ITT. He sits at the center of a table.

"John," says Geneen, speaking to one of the executives, "what have you done about that problem?"

John speaks into the microphone in front of him. "Well, I called him, but I couldn't get him to make a decision."

"Do you want me to call him?"

"Gosh, that's a good idea. Would you mind?"

"I'll be glad to," says Geneen. "But it will cost you your paycheck."

"Never mind," says a flustered John. "I'll call him again myself."

Altogether, Geneen and his top executives spend over three months each year in meetings. Why so many? Might not the same results have been achieved by reports? Not in Geneen's view—for it was the pressure-cooker atmosphere of the face-to-face sessions that sifted out the unshakable facts and distilled them into sound and implementable decisions.

Questions

1. Are you prepared to work for a manager who runs meetings in the style of Harold Geneen? Why or why not?

2. Is Geneen's approach to managing groups a good one? Why or why not? Explain your answer.

The following incident describes a group of men working in an electroplating department of a plant.

The Sarto group invariably ate lunch together on the fire escape near Aisle 1. On those Saturdays and Sundays when overtime work was required, the Sarto group operated as a team, regardless of weekday work assignments, to get overtime work completed as quickly as possible. Off the job, Sarto group members often joined in parties or weekend trips. Sarto's summer camp was a frequent rendezvous.

Sarto's group was also the most cohesive one in the department in terms of its organized punch-in and punch-out system. Since the workers were regularly scheduled to work from 7:00 A.M. to 7:00 P.M. weekdays, and since all supervision was removed at 5:00 P.M., it was possible almost every day to finish a "day's work" by 5:30 and leave the plant. What is more, a worker who stayed until 7:00 P.M. could punch the time cards of a number of workers and help them gain free time without pay loss. (This system also operated on weekends, at which times supervisors were present, if at all, only for short periods.) In Sarto's group the duty of staying late rotated, so that no worker did so more than once a week. In addition, the group members would punch someone in the morning who was unavoidably delayed. However, such a practice never occurred without prior notice from the worker who expected to be late and never if the tardiness was expected to last beyond 8:00 A.M., the start of the day for the supervisor.

A Sarto spokesperson explained the logic behind the system.

> You know that our hourly pay rate is quite low, compared to other companies. What makes this the best place to work is the feeling of security you get. No one ever gets laid off in this department. With all the hours in the week, all the company ever has to do is shorten the work week when orders fall off. We have to tighten our belts, but we can all get along. When things are going well, as they are now, the company is only interested in getting out the work. It doesn't help to get it out faster than it's really needed—so we go home a little early whenever we can. Of course, some guys abuse this sort of thing—like Herman—but others work even harder, and it averages out.
>
> Whenever an extra order has to be pushed through, naturally I work until 7:00. So do a lot of the others. I believe that if I stay until my work is caught up and my equipment is in good shape, that's all the company wants of me. They leave us alone and expect us to produce—and we do.

Questions

1. Fully discuss and critique the Sarto group using the Homans model of group dynamics discussed in this chapter.
2. How would you feel about this group as a manager?
3. What changes would you suggest?

CLASS EXERCISE: THE TASK-MAINTENANCE GRID

1. Look at the task maintenance grid depicted in Figure 13.8. Then think about how you act as a member of groups. Think, in particular, about how you try to influence other members in directions supporting group goals.
2. Now respond to the following statements to get a precise picture of your behavior in groups. Respond frankly and quickly in a way that best describes how you are most likely to behave in a group problem-solving situation. Circle your responses according to the following scale.

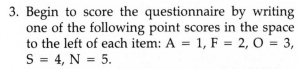

A = Always
F = Frequently
O = Often
S = Sometimes
N = Never

3. Begin to score the questionnaire by writing one of the following point scores in the space to the left of each item: A = 1, F = 2, O = 3, S = 4, N = 5.

4. Compute your task-behavior and maintenance-behavior scores by totaling your scores for all items falling in the following two sets.
   A. Task-behavior score = total score for odd-numbered items: 1 + 3 + 5 + 7 + 9 + 11 + 13 + 15 + 17 + 19.
   B. Maintenance-behavior score = total score for even-numbered items: 2 + 4 + 6 + 8 + 10 + 12 + 14 + 16 + 18 + 20.

5. Plot your task and maintenance behaviors on the grid in Figure 13.8. Mark the intersection of your task and maintenance scores by "X."

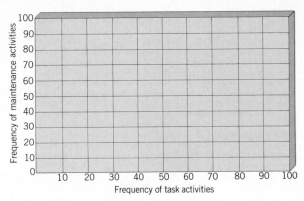

FIGURE 13.8 The task-maintenance grid.

Consider the accuracy of this profile of your task and maintenance behaviors in comparison with your initial self-evaluation.

6. Share your task-maintenance profile with a nearby classmate. Discuss the profile and its implications. Comment on your classmate's profile. Await further class discussion.

When I am a member of a problem-solving group,[23]

A F O S N   1. I offer facts, give my opinions and ideas, and provide suggestions and relevant information to help the group discussion.

A F O S N   2. I warmly encourage all members of the group to participate, giving them recognition for their contributions, demonstrating receptivity and openness to their ideas, and generally being friendly and responsive to them.

A F O S N   3. I ask for facts, generally being friendly and responsive to them.

A F O S N   4. I try to persuade members to analyze constructively their differences in opinions and ideas, searching for common elements in conflicting or opposing ideas or proposals, and trying to reconcile disagreements.

A F O S N   5. I propose goals and tasks in order to start action within the group.

A F O S N   6. I try to relieve group tension and increase the enjoyment of group members by joking, suggesting breaks, and proposing fun approaches to group work.

A F O S N   7. I give direction to the group by developing plans on how to proceed with group work and by focusing members' attention on the tasks to be done.

A F O S N   8. I help communication among group members by showing good communication skills and by making sure that what each member says is understood by all.

A F O S N 9. I pull together related ideas or suggestions made by group members and restate and summarize the major points discussed by the group.

A F O S N 10. I ask members how they are feeling about the way in which the group is working, and about each other, as well as share my own feelings about group work and the way the members interact.

A F O S N 11. I coordinate group work by showing relationships among various ideas or suggestions, by pulling ideas and suggestions together, andby drawing together activities of various subgroups and members.

A F O S N 12. I observe the process by which the group is working and use my observations to help in examining the effectiveness of the group.

A F O S N 13. I determine why the group has difficulty in working effectively and what blocks progress in accomplishing the group's goals.

A F O S N 14. I express group standards and norms and the group goals in order to make members constantly aware of the direction in which the work is going—the progress being made toward the group goal—and in order to get continued open acceptance of group norms and procedures.

A F O S N 15. I energize the group by stimulating group members to produce a higher quality of work.

A F O S N 16. I listen to and serve as an interested audience for other group members, weighing the ideas of others, and going along with the movement of the group when I do not disagree with its action.

A F O S N 17. I examine how practical and workable the ideas are, evaluate the quality of alternative solutions to group problems, and apply decisions and suggestions to real situations in order to see how they will work.

A F O S N 18. I accept and support the openness of other group members, reinforcing them for taking risks, and encouraging individuality in group members.

A F O S N 19. I compare group decisions and accomplishments with group standards, measuring accomplishments against goals.

A F O S N 20. I promote the open discussion of conflicts between group members in order to resolve disagreements and increase group togetherness.

REFERENCES

[1] Reprinted, by permission of the publisher, from "Managing Agreement in Organizations: The Abilene Paradox," by Jerry Harvey, *Organizational Dynamics* (Summer 1974). Copyright © 1974 by AMACOM, a division of American Management Associations, pp. 63–80. All rights reserved.

[2] Portions of this chapter are adapted from John R. Schermerhorn, Jr., James G. Hunt, and Richard N. Osborn, *Managing Organizational Behavior* (New York: Wiley, 1982), pp. 213–223, 242–251, 261–267, 275–279, 281–287. Used by permission.

[3] David M. Herold, "The Effectiveness of Work

Groups," in Steven Kerr (ed.), *Organizational Behavior* (Columbus, Ohio: Grid Publishing, 1979), p. 95.

4 From Susan D. Van Raalte, "Preparing the Task Force to Get Good Results," *S.A.M. Advanced Management Journal,* Vol. 47 (Winter 1982), pp. 11–16.

5 Adapted from Ibid.

6 See, for example, Edgar H. Schein, *Organizational Psychology,* Second Edition (Englewood Cliffs, N.J.: Prentice-Hall, 1970), p. 81.

7 Excerpted from the *Lubbock Avalanche Journal* (September 4, 1982), p. A–9. Used by permission.

8 See Marvin E. Shaw, *Group Dynamics: The Psychology of Small Group Behavior,* Second Edition (New York: McGraw-Hill, 1976).

9 Excerpted from Robert F. Lagasse, "Hospital Puts Employees in the Management Team," *Hospitals,* Vol. 51 (December 1, 1977), pp. 89–90.

10 This discussion is based on George C. Homans, *The Human Group* (New York: Harcourt, Brace, and World, 1950).

11 Burt Scanlan and J. Bernard Keys, *Management and Organizational Behavior,* Second Edition (New York: Wiley, 1983), p. 294.

12 This incident was obtained from Dorothy N. Harlow and Jean J. Hanke, *Behavior in Organizations* (Boston: Little, Brown, 1975), pp. 244–245. The original source cannot be located.

13 For a good summary of research on group cohesiveness see Shaw, op. cit.

14 Robert F. Allen and Saul Pilnick, "Confronting the Shadow Organization: How to Detect and Defeat Negative Norms," *Organizational Dynamics* (Spring 1973), pp. 13–17.

15 This case is reported in Harvey, op. cit.

16 See Irving L. Janis, "Groupthink," *Psychology Today* (November 1971), pp. 43–46; *Victims of Groupthink* (Boston: Houghton Mifflin, 1972).

17 The following discussion is based on Schein, op. cit., pp. 39–41; Rensis Likert, *New Patterns of Management* (New York: McGraw-Hill, 1961), pp. 166–169.

18 From William D. Dyer, *Team-Building* (Reading, Mass.: Addison-Wesley, 1977), pp. 55, 56.

19 This discussion is based on Edgar H. Schein, *Organizational Psychology,* Second Edition (Englewood Cliffs, N.J.: Prentice-Hall, 1970), pp. 96–103.

20 Benson S. Shapiro, "Can Marketing and Manufacturing Coexist?" *Harvard Business Review,* Vol. 55 (September-October, 1977), pp. 104–114.

21 Richard Tanner Pascale and Anthony G. Athos, *The Art of Japanese Management* (New York: Simon & Schuster, 1981), p. 70. Used by permission.

22 From Paul R. Lawrence, Louis B. Barnes, and Jay W. Lorsch, *Organizational Behavior and Administration* (Homewood, Ill., Richard D. Irwin, 1976); excerpts from the Slade Company Case, p. 134; as used in Scanlan and Keys, op. cit., pp. 301–302. Used by permission.

23 David W. Johnson and Frank P. Johnson, *Joining Together,* © 1975, pp. 19, 20. Reprinted by permission of Prentice-Hall, Inc., Englewood Cliffs, New Jersey.

Part 4

INTEGRATING CASES

MacGREGOR

My encounter with MacGregor came about during the course of a study of the extent to which operating managers actually use participative management techniques in their dealings with subordinates. MacGregor, who at the time was manager of one of the largest refineries in the country, was the last of more than 100 managers I interviewed in the course of the study. Although the interview had been scheduled in advance, the exact time had been left open; I was to call MacGregor at his office early in the week that I would be in the vicinity and set up a specific date and time.

Here's how that phone call went. The switchboard operator answered with the name of the refinery. When I asked for MacGregor's office, a male voice almost instantly said, "Hello." I then asked for MacGregor, whereupon the voice responded, "This is he." I should have recognized at once that this was no ordinary manager; he answered his own phone instantly, as though he had been waiting for it to ring. To my question about when it would be convenient for me to come see him, he replied, "Anytime." I said, "Would today be all right?" His response was, "Today, tomorrow, or Wednesday would be O.K.; or you could

come Thursday, except don't come between 10:00 A.M. and noon; or you could come Friday or next week—anytime." I replied feebly, "I just want to fit in with your plans." Then he said, "You are just not getting the message; it makes no difference to me when you come. I have nothing on the book except to play golf and see you. Come in anytime—I don't have to be notified in advance, so I'll be seeing you one of these days," and he then hung up. I was dumbfounded. Here was a highly placed executive with apparently nothing to do except play golf and talk to visitors.

I took MacGregor at his word and drove over immediately to see him without any further announcement of my visit. MacGregor's office, in a small building at one corner of the refinery, adjoined that of his secretary—who, when I arrived, was knitting busily and, without dropping a stitch, said to me, "You must be Mr. Carlisle; he's in there," indicating MacGregor's office with a glance at a connecting door.

MacGregor's office was large and had a big window overlooking the refinery, a conference table with eight chairs arranged around it (one of which, at the head, was more comfortable and imposing than the rest), an engi-

neer's file cabinet with a series of wide drawers, two easy chairs, a sofa, a coffee table with a phone on it, and a desk. The desk had been shoved all the way into a corner; there was no way a chair could be slipped in behind it, and it was covered with technical journals. A lamp stood on the desk, but its plug was not connected to an outlet. There was no phone on the desk. MacGregor, a tall, slender man with a tanned face, stood by the window peering absently into space. He turned slowly when I entered his office and said, "You must be Carlisle. The head office told me you wanted to talk to me about the way we run things here. Sit down on the sofa and fire away."

MacGregor's Modus Operandi

"Do you hold regular meetings with your subordinates?" I asked.

"Yes, I do," he replied.

"How often?" I asked.

"Once a week, on Thursdays between 10:00 A.M. and noon; that's why I couldn't see you then," was his response.

"What sorts of things do you discuss?" I queried, following my interview guide.

"My subordinates tell me about the decisions they've made during the past week," he explained.

"Then you believe in participative decision making," I commented.

"No—as a matter of fact, I don't," said MacGregor.

"Then why hold the meetings?" I asked. "Why not just tell your people about the operating decisions you've made and let them know how to carry them out?"

"Oh, I don't make their decisions for them and I just don't believe in participating in the decisions they should be making, either; we hold the weekly meeting so that I can keep informed on what they're doing and how. The meeting also gives me a chance to appraise their technical and managerial abilities," he explained. "I used to make all the operating decisions myself; but I quit doing that a few years ago when I discovered my golf game was going to hell because I didn't have enough time to practice. Now that I've quit making other people's decisions my game is back where it should be."

"You don't make operating decisions any more?" I asked in astonishment.

"No," he replied. Sensing my incredulity, he added, "Obviously you don't believe me. Why not ask some of my subordinates?"

Peterson's View of MacGregor

I picked Peterson who, when phoned to see whether he was available, said that he had nothing to do. So I went to Peterson's office.

Peterson was in his late twenties. He asked me what I thought of MacGregor. I said I found him most unusual. Peterson replied, "Yes, he's a gas." MacGregor refused to make decisions related to the work of his subordinates. When Peterson got into a situation he could not deal with, he said he called one of the other supervisors, usually Johnson, and together they worked it out. At the Thursday meetings, he reported on the decision and gave credit to his helper. "If I hadn't," he added, "I probably wouldn't get help from that quarter again."

In reply to a query on what the Thursday meetings were like, he said, "Well, we all sit around that big conference table in MacGregor's office. He sits at the head like a thinned-down Buddha, and we go around the table talking about the decisions we've made, and if we got help, who helped us. The other guys occasionally make comments—especially if the particular decision being discussed was like one they had to make themselves at some point or if it had some direct effect on their own operations." MacGregor had said very little at these past few meetings, according to Peterson, but he did pass on any new developments that he heard about at the head office.

Johnson's View of MacGregor

I also walked over to Johnson's unit and found him to be in his early thirties. After a couple of minutes of casual conversation, I discovered that MacGregor and all eight of his subordinates were chemical engineers. Johnson said, "I suppose MacGregor gave you that bit about his not making decisions, didn't he? That man is a gas."

"It isn't true though, is it? He does make decisions, doesn't he?" I asked.

"No, he doesn't; everything he told you is true. He simply decided not to get involved in decisions that his subordinates are being paid to make. So he stopped making them, and they tell me he plays a lot of golf in the time he saves," said Johnson.

Then I asked whether he tried to get MacGregor to make a decision and his response was: "Only once. I had been on the job for only about a week when I ran into an operating problem I couldn't solve, so I phoned MacGregor. He answered the phone with that sleepy 'Hello' of his. I told him who I was and that I had a problem. His response was instantaneous: 'Good, that's what you're being paid to do, solve problems,' and then he hung up. I was dumbfounded. I didn't really know any of the people I was working with, so because I didn't think I had any other alternative, I called him back, got the same sleepy 'Hello,' and again identified myself. He replied sharply, 'I thought I told you that you were paid to solve problems. Do you think I should do your job as well as my own?' When I insisted on seeing him about my problem, he answered, 'I don't know how you expect me to help you. You have a technical problem and I don't go into the refinery anymore. Ask one of the other managers. They're all in touch with what goes on out there.'

'I didn't know which one to consult, so I insisted again on seeing him. He finally agreed—grudgingly—to see me right away, so I went over to his office and there he was in his characteristic looking-out-the-window posture. When I sat down, he started the dirty-shirt routine—but when he saw that I was determined to involve him in my problems, he sat down on the sofa in front of his coffee table and, pen in hand, prepared to write on a pad of paper. He asked me to state precisely what the problem was and he wrote down exactly what I said. Then he asked what the conditions for its solutions were. I replied that I didn't know what he meant by that question. His response was, 'If you don't know what conditions have to be satisfied for a solution to be reached, how do you know when you've solved the problem?' I told him I'd never thought of approaching a problem that way and he replied, 'Then you'd better start. I'll work through this one with you *this* time, but don't expect me to do your problem solving for you because that's *your* job, not mine.'

I stumbled through the conditions that would have to be satisfied by the solution. Then he asked me what alternative approaches I could think of. I gave him the first one I could think of—let's call it *X*—and he wrote it down and asked me what would happen if I did *X*. I replied with my answer—let's call it *A*. Then he asked me how *A* compared

with the conditions I had established for the solution of the problem. I replied that it did not meet them. MacGregor told me that I'd have to think of another. I came up with *Y*, which I said would yield result *B*, and this still fell short of the solution conditions. After more prodding from MacGregor, I came up with *Z*, which I said would have *C* as a result; although this clearly came a lot closer to the conditions I had established for the solution than any of the others I'd suggested, it still did not satisfy all of them. MacGregor then asked me if I could combine any of the approaches I'd suggested. I replied I could do *X* and *Z* and then saw that the resultant *A* plus *C* would indeed satisfy all the solution conditions I had set up previously. When I thanked MacGregor, he replied, 'What for? Get the hell out of my office; you could have done that bit of problem solving perfectly well without wasting my time. Next time you really can't solve a problem on your own, ask the Thursday man and tell me about it at the Thursday meeting.''

I asked Johnson about MacGregor's reference to the Thursday man.

'He's the guy who runs the Thursday meeting when MacGregor is away from the plant. I'm the Thursday man now. My predecessor left here about two months ago.''

''Where did he go? Did he quit the company?'' I asked.

''God, no. He got a refinery of his own. That's what happens to a lot of Thursday men. After the kind of experience we get coping with everyone's problems

and MacGregor's refusal to do what he perceives as his subordinates' work, we don't need an operating superior any more and we're ready for our own refineries. Incidentally, most of the people at our level have adopted MacGregor's managerial method in dealing with the supervisors who report to us, and we are reaping the same kinds of benefits that he does. The supervisors are a lot more self-reliant, and we don't have to do their work for them.''

MacGregor's "Thursday Man"

I went back to the refinery with a few last questions for MacGregor. His secretary had made considerable progress on her knitting and her boss had resumed his position by the refinery window.

''Let me ask you a couple of questions about the Thursday meeting,'' I continued. ''First of all, I understand that when you are away, the 'Thursday man' takes over. How do you choose the individual to fill this slot?''

''Oh, that's simple. I just pick the man who is most often referred to as the one my subordinates turn to for help in dealing with their problems. Then I try him out in this assignment while I'm off. It's good training and, if he proves he can handle it, I know I have someone to propose for any vacancies that may occur at the refinery manager level. The head-office people always contact me for candidates. As a matter of fact, the Thursday-man assignment is sought after. My subordinates compete with each other in helping anyone with a problem because they know they'll get credit for their help at the Thursday meeting. You know, another development has been that jobs on the staff of this refinery are highly prized by young people who want to get ahead in the corporation; when junior management positions open up here, there are always so many candidates that I often have a tough time making a choice."

Questions

1. How do you describe Mac-Gregor's leadership style in terms of Fiedler's contingency theory, House's path-goal theory, and Vroom and Yetton's leader-participation theory?

2. Is MacGregor's leadership style effective? Why or why not?

3. Does MacGregor make good use of motivation, group dynamics, and communication in his leadership efforts? Explain your answer.

4. Is MacGregor a good manager? Would you like to work for him? Why or why not?

Source: Adapted from Arthur Elliott Carlisle, *Organizational Dynamics,* Vol 5 (1976), pp. 50–62. Used by permission.

TWO HEAD NURSES: A STUDY IN CONTRAST

In external features Floor A and Floor B are very similar. Each has about 30 private and semiprivate beds. On each floor medical patients and surgical patients are cared for by graduate nurses, student nurses, nurses aides, and maids.

Floor A

On Floor A, people speak in hushed voices. Conversation is at a minimum. Marilyn Smith, the head nurse, spends almost all her time at her desk. She gives instructions firmly and unambiguously. The nurses go from room to room caring for patients in a businesslike impersonal manner, and there is little give-and-take between them and the patients.

A. The Head Nurse

Smith's supervisor said of her: "Marilyn Smith is of the old school. She's really very stern and rigid. She runs an excellent floor from the standpoint of organization and system. It's beau-

Sophisticated equipment in the nursing station of a hospital in-patient care unit.

tifully organized. She has all her supplies in perfect condition, but she can't handle human relations. Her graduates claim that she treats them like students, watches everything they do, checks up on them all the time,

and won't allow them any responsibility. The students claim that Miss Smith gives them only routine duties, only the small details."

It is generally agreed that Smith is fair and not arbitrary.

433

For example, she makes a conscious effort to grant nurses' requests for time off whenever possible, but is strict and uncompromising with nurses who violate regulations. She is uniformly courteous in a formal manner. The following conversation with a member of the dietary department is typical: "I am calling for Myra Wilson, a patient in Room 413, a diabetic case. She would like coffee with every meal. Is that all right? Thank you."

She observes the same starchy courtesy whether the pressure of work is relaxed or at its height, and expects the same formal courtesy from her subordinates.

B. The Assistant

Smith delegates almost no authority to Brenda Green, her assistant. When Smith is on the ward, Green shares floor duty with the other nurses and does not work at the desk. When Green is in charge, there is a marked change in the atmosphere. People talk to each other more naturally and sit around when the work is slack. There is also considerable confusion on the ward.

C. Graduate Nurses

The attitude among the younger graduates toward Smith's supervision is expressed in the following quotations:

Miss Smith runs a very strict floor, and the nurses resent her because she treats them like students.

When I came here, Miss Smith checked up on everything I did, and that was hard to adjust to. You felt you were a student all over again.

When Miss Smith is off the floor, the doctors come here in a more sociable frame of mind. The whole atmosphere seems to relax. Often we have a nurses' aide mix up a pitcher of lemonade and we have it sitting right down at the desk. If you tried that in the daytime, Miss Smith would have a stroke. When Miss Smith is on, she absolutely does not tolerate any smoking. But when she's off, we all stop and smoke and have coffee.

I don't pay any attention to Miss Smith any more, and I don't think the other nurses do either. You just let what she says go in one ear and out the other. At first it bothered me, and I think it annoyed most of the others that she treated us like students. All I say is, "Yes, Miss Smith," and go ahead and do what I would have done anyway. We sit around and talk to each other when the work is done, and if Miss Smith asks us to be a little quieter we lower our voices, but we don't attempt to slink around or anything. There was a tendency to do that for a while, but you soon get over that.

The attitude of the older nurses is different, as the following quotations show.

I like working with Miss Smith. I know a lot of the nurses complain about her because she's fussy and checks on them. Personally I'd rather work on this floor than anywhere else for exactly that reason. Everything here is done properly. The doctors prefer this floor because this is where the patients get the best care. The other nurses aren't impressed by that. They insist they wouldn't work here because Miss Smith is a fussbudget. They don't seem to care whether the patients get good care or not.

I picked this floor because I liked the supervision here. I've worked with Miss Smith while I was a student and I knew what to expect. I honestly feel I still need a responsible person nearby to supervise. I need guidance, and therefore I prefer to work on a floor where there is a fairly strict supervisor. On some of the other floors things are too slipshod. Everything is hodgepodge, and it drives me crazy. I like things done in an orderly fashion, and it bothers me very much when everything is slipshod. I don't mean the atmosphere; I mean Miss Smith. She doesn't believe in relaxation at all. As for myself, I prefer to work hard and get it done with and then relax. I can see Miss Smith's point. After all, you have these sick people here and they have to be taken care of. She's got to lay down the law to us to a certain extent. I keep telling my husband how lucky he is to be in his kind of work. Everything in his place is buddy-buddy. But I guess in hospitals it just can't work that way. The head nurse has to be strict in order to get the work done. Isn't that right?

Some of the nurses are lovely to work with, but others just aren't good at supervising. They don't know how to express themselves. Now when Miss Smith is on, it is altogether different. She knows how to get things done the first time.

D. Student Nurses
Smith keeps her students under rigid discipline, and they complain to their supervisors that she gives them only routine work and doesn't allow them to take any responsibility. They feel they learn much less than on the floors. The students ask few questions either of Smith or of the graduate nurses. They rarely talk to anyone.

E. Relationships Among Workers
All relationships on Floor A tend to be formal and impersonal. There is very little give-and-take or development of camaraderie. Nurses' aides complain that the nurses never teach them anything. Smith divides up the work equitably and assigns it clearly, and there is no complaint that some members of the group are slack in carrying out their duties. Yet when Smith is off the floor there is evidence of antagonism among the different workers. The aides say that if they had problems they would take them up with their housekeeping supervisor.

F. Patient Care
The relationship between nurses and patients is formal and distant. Patients remain in their rooms, and very few walk about on the floor. Requests by patients and visitors are taken care of promptly and efficiently. The charts are in excellent order, but there is some evidence of slip-ups in nursing care. In one case, a patient was given the wrong drug and had a severe reaction. During the period when the ward was observed there were three instances of postoperative fever. Once when an intern removed a drainage catheter and forgot to replace it, the error was not corrected for five hours.

Floor B
The atmosphere on Floor B is warm and informal. There is a good deal of gossiping and good-natured horseplay, and the nurses discuss their problems with one another.

A. The Head Nurse
Tricia Rogers, the head nurse, spends only about two-thirds of her time at her desk, and the rest of the time she is on the ward helping with patient care and chatting informally with workers and patients. She often consults individual nurses or the entire nursing staff about problems and changes. She expressed her attitude toward supervision as follows.

> The hospital has changed since I graduated. At that time it was just losing the old military discipline and becoming more reasonable in its approach. The present

way is much better on the whole than the old. I find that if you give people a break, they are more likely to pitch in and help you when you're in a jam. I never could stand this old military discipline stuff.

Rogers is informal in her relationship with her subordinates. Her way of giving an order is typified in this quotation.

> Do you want to go to the pharmacy for me? Gee, that would be swell.

When telephoning central supplies, Rogers will say:

> Is this you, Betty? Listen you poor kid, this is me again. I'm sorry, but we've got to have two sets of trays. I thought I'd tell you because if I send the aide down, the poor kid won't get it right.

On the other hand, when the ward is under pressure, Rogers tends to give her answers in an offhand, somewhat distracted way.

B. The Assistant
Rogers deliberately divides authority with her assistant, giving her the jobs of ordering drugs and supplies and supervising the cleaning. She consults her when making decisions. When she is absent, the assistant carries on supervision much as Rogers does. There is little difference in the atmosphere on the ward whether Rogers or her assistant is in charge.

C. Graduate Nurses
One of the graduate nurses on

Rogers's floor said: "On this floor anybody can speak up whenever she feels like it, and we get along together fine. The nurses on this floor are very good to work with. Miss Rogers is an excellent head nurse, and there is good spirit."

This is typical of the attitude of the younger nurses. The older nurses feel somewhat different.

Miss Rogers is a very nice person, and all the nurses have been lovely to me. But I don't think the organization is as careful as it used to be, and that's why a lot of mistakes are made. It's very easy to forget to give medicine, for instance. It happened to me. Since each nurse is responsible for her own patients, nobody checks up to see whether you've actually given a patient what he's supposed to have. Nobody tells you how you're getting along. I don't know whether I'm doing a good job or not. Maybe I'm forgetting things. Maybe patients complain about me. If so, I never hear of it. I just have to guess that I'm doing all right. I wish that sometimes somebody would come along and check up, and let me know when I do things wrong and how I can improve myself. I feel that being out so long, I must have plenty of room for improvement.

Sometimes I work down on Miss Rogers's floor. I was down there last week, and it was exasperating. I had to go down to the drug room myself twice during the morning, and I know that some of the other nurses had to do that too. Well, that's foolish. If the drugs were checked properly in the first place, all the drug orders would have gone down at the same time. That would never happen on Miss Smith's floor because she runs it in a very orderly and systematic way. I don't get any joy out of working on Miss Rogers's floor because things are done just too sloppily.

D. Student Nurses
Rogers said that she enjoys teaching, but has some problems in maintaining discipline. Students seem to be accepted as an integral part of the social group. They take part in informal discussions and are free to ask any questions they wish.

E. Relationships Among Workers
The relationships among the different groups of workers on Rogers's floor is easy and informal. Some of the nurses' aides address Rogers by her first name, and she calls them by nicknames. There is strong spirit of camaraderie throughout the ward. On the other hand, Rogers does not assign tasks to each worker in a clear-cut, specific way, and consequently there is some tendency to shirk certain tasks. As one nurses' aide put it:

They just expect all of us to get the work done. If one person lies down on the job, it would mean that the other person does that much more. Evidently they don't stop to think who does what. We've got a little bit of jealousy. A good boss could straighten it out.

The nurses' aides on Rogers's floor say that if they had a problem they would first take it up with her.

F. Patient Care
The relationship between the patient and workers on the ward is easy and informal. The patients are part of the social group. They wander in and out of their rooms. At times they join in the chatting of a group of nurses, and even run small errands for the nurses. The nurses call them by their first names.

When the work is heavy, however, Rogers and the nurses tend to be brusque with the patients. They do not always meet the patients' requests or those of their visitors promptly. Charts are not maintained with scrupulous care.

Although some of the older nurses feel that the loose supervision is likely to result in slip-ups in nursing care, none were noted during the period of observation.

Patients who once have been on Floor B not infrequently ask that they be sent there again at the time of a second admission. Some doctors also request that their patients be admitted to this floor because of the good psychological care they receive.

Questions

1. Use the leadership theories introduced in Chapter 10 to

analyze and explain the different leadership approaches of Rogers and Smith.

2. How well do Rogers and Smith use basic concepts of (a) communication, (b) motivation, and (c) group dynamics as part of their leadership approaches? Explain your answer.

3. Who is the more effective leader—Rogers or Smith? Why?

Source: I am indebted to Professor George Strauss for this case. Used by permission.

PART
5

CONTROLLING
FOR
PRODUCTIVITY

Chapters in This Part of the Book

QUALITY: EVERYBODY TALKS ABOUT QUALITY, FORD PEOPLE MAKE IT HAPPEN

Auto Workers Can Only Do as Well as Head Office Permits

When we think of the word *control* from a productivity standpoint, "quality control" immediately comes to mind. Indeed, quality and productivity are perpetual interests of managers and consumers. As the above headlines[1] suggest, the automobile industry often bears the brunt of these concerns. The first is an obvious attempt by Ford Motor Company to advertise to consumers that it really is concerned for quality. The second reflects one auto worker's perspective on quality and performance deficiencies in the industry—it suggests the fault lies with management!

Martin Douglas is a U.S. auto worker who was laid off in 1980 after 16 years with General Motors. He wrote the article from which the second headline is taken. In the article he writes:[2]

David Suter

[1] These headlines are from the *Wall Street Journal* (February 18, 1982), p. 7.; *Albuquerque Journal* (July 24, 1980, p. A5.
[2] Martin Douglas, "Auto Workers Can Only Do as Well as Head Office Permits," *Los Angeles Times;* reprinted from *Albuquerque Journal* (July 24, 1980), p. A5. Used by permission.

"I am—or was—an American auto worker. I built General Motors cars for 16 years. Then, in March, I was laid off indefinitely. Although I don't think the major cause of the layoff was consumers' perceptions of my work ability, I believe that it was a factor.

"When we lament the lack of quality in television programming, we don't fault the writers or cameramen; we blame the producers and network executives who put the shows on the air. By the same token, it is not the worker who determines the quality of a car but the executives in Detroit and the plant supervisors. . . .

"The worker who performs a certain task 32 times a day, 5 days a week, knows more about the specifics of his particular job than anyone else. Yet, in 16 years, I have never been consulted or seen any other assembly-line worker consulted on how to improve a job qualitatively or quantitatively. There are 'suggestion programs,' but their main concern is always how to save the company's money.

"I don't believe it is inherent in human nature to do a lousy job. Man innately wants to do good work, but he needs to be involved. He needs to know how his job relates to the work as a whole. Nothing is as frustrating as not to be able to do your job properly because a job earlier down the line was omitted. To instruct a worker in such a case to go ahead and do his job anyway is absurd. Yet, this happens, because the basic operating philosophy is to get the job done at any cost. . . .

"The auto worker can only build as good a car as he is instructed or permitted to build. Quality is not something to be concerned with only when there is a slack in production. We on the line take our cue from those in the head office. If they don't really care about quality, they can't expect us to either."

Douglas clearly suggests that adequate control in the U.S. auto industry suffers from an overemphasis on production and poor management. Now that you've heard his perspective, I'd like to challenge you by turning once again to the recent Japanese experience for some contrasting ideas. The source is Harvey C. Bunke, editor of the management journal, *Business Horizons.* His thoughts after a recent trip to Japan follow.

Perspective: A Japanese Pilgrimage[3]

"From a distance, we watched the entrance of the foreign car into the American market. First the Volkswagen, for those who wanted something different, then the Mercedes, which we reluctantly admired, and finally the Japanese entries. Initially we were unconcerned—really, how could these funny looking foreign cars compete seriously with our American chariots—but as foreign imports grew we became uneasy—then concerned. By 1980, when imports accounted for more than 25 percent of the American market, we went from asking, 'What happened?' to 'What is to be done?'

"In late 1980 I was invited to visit Japan. Since my host headed a firm in the Toyota group, I looked forward to learning firsthand what, if anything, we had to fear from the Japanese car makers. . . . Anyone visiting a Japanese plant must be struck by two things—worker commitment and the level of technology: worker commitment that is drawn from the past, technology that belongs in the future. In my bewildered state I wondered how the Japanese did it.

"Where once the marking 'made in Japan' signaled a shoddy product, today it is taken as a sign of quality and reliability. Japanese cars, Americans increasingly say, are more dependable and of higher quality than American. Before its success in heavy manufacturing areas such as steel, autos, and earth-moving equipment, Japan was successful in making watches, cameras, radios, TVs, electronic products,

[3] Excerpted from Harvey C. Bunke, "A Japanese Pilgrimage," *Business Horizons,* Vol. 24 (1981), pp. 2–7. Copyright 1981 by the Foundation for the School of Business at Indiana University. Reprinted by permission.

and motorcycles. Today Japan is moving into the machine tools, semiconductor, and aircraft parts markets. Even the mighty Xerox and the invincible IBM are facing stiff competition from the Japanese. . . .

"Surprising to the western mind are the Japanese quality-control circles which are composed of perhaps a dozen workers and are devoted to improving efficiency and product quality. Picture eight workers gathered around a table on which sits a tiny, exquisite bonsai tree that epitomizes Japanese patience, persistence, and attention to detail. The meeting has been called in response to an assembly workers' discovery of a slight unevenness, smaller than a centimeter, between the door and the sill of one of the Toyota Corolla bodies passing down the line. Subsequently, bodies with a similar defect were observed. The error rate is very small, less than one defect in 100 car bodies. Still the fault is undeniably there.

"A flawed sample has been pulled off the line and the eight men volunteer opinions on the source of the problem. Fourteen suggestions are listed on the blackboard. After an hour nothing is decided, but these workers meeting here and in other interlocking quality-control circles will, through a number of exchanges of opinions, narrow down the possibilities and do the equivalent of a month of engineering detective work. This effort is duplicated again and again in Japanese industry. In this way workers not only help improve the product, they also draw satisfaction from participation, from feeling that they can influence and make a contribution to the production process."

14

FUNDAMENTALS OF CONTROLLING

Conserve Paper Please Circulate

MANAGEMENT IN GENERAL
A Newsletter for Management from Corporate Personnel-Akron

April 1976

MALICE IN BLUNDERLAND

Thomas L. Martin wrote a book published in 1973 called
<u>Malice in Blunderland</u>. If you haven't read it, you might
want to obtain it from your local library or the Corporate
Research Library. The following are some excerpts:

"MURPHY'S LAWS"

First Law: If something can go wrong, it will.
Second Law: When left to themselves, things always go from bad to worse.
Third Law: Nature always sides with the hidden flaw.

"REVISION OF MURPHY'S FIRST LAW"

If anything can go wrong (with a mechanical system),
it will, and generally at the moment the system becomes
indispensable.

"COROLLARIES TO MURPHY'S FIRST LAW"

It is impossible to make anything foolproof because fools
are so ingenious.

Any wire or tube cut to length will be too short.

Interchangeable parts won't.

Identical units tested under identical conditions will not
perform identically in the field.

After any machine or unit has been completely assembled,
extra components will be found on the bench.

Components that must not and cannot be assembled improperly,
will be.

All constants are variables.

In any given computation, the figure that is most obviously
correct will be the source of the error.

The book goes on and on with other laws as well. The thought hit us that
you might have your own contributions. So, if you have corollaries to
"Murphy's First Law," send them to us and we will publish them in a later
issue of Management in General.

The most infamous of "Murphy's Laws"—if anything can go wrong, it will—is a classic introduction to a chapter on controlling as a management function.[1] After all, control is something managers do to prevent things from going wrong in the first place, and/or to identify and correct errors that have already occurred. Key topics to be covered in this chapter are

Controlling as a Management Function
Organizational Control Systems
Performance Appraisal Systems
Pay and Reward Systems
Employee Discipline Systems
Management by Objectives: An Integrated Planning and Control System
Making Controls Effective

Control is one of those words like *power*. If you aren't careful when it is used, it leaves a negative connotation. While this value judgment may be quite appropriate in certain contexts, (e.g., control that is malicious), control plays a positive and necessary role in the management process. To have things "under control" at work is good; for things to be "out of control" is bad. This chapter overviews controlling as an essential management function. It considers effective control an important means for coordinating the multiple and varied activities of people in organizations and ensuring that organizational objectives are served as a result.

CONTROLLING AS A MANAGEMENT FUNCTION

Controlling is a process of monitoring performance and taking action to ensure desired results. Its purpose is to make sure that actual performance is consistent with plans. Its basis is information well used by managers for decision making and problem solving.

The Importance of Controlling

Figure 14.1 depicts controlling in relation to the other management functions. Simply put, control is a means for making sure actual performance is consistent with intentions and that organiza-

tional objectives are thereby achieved. Planning sets the directions and allocates resources. Organizing brings people and material resources together in working combinations. Leading directs people in the utilization of these resources. Controlling sees to it that the right things happen, in the right way, and at the right time as a result. In other words, proper controls help managers make sure that people in organizations do *what* is necessary, *when* it is necessary, and in the *way* it is required.[2]

The importance of control in this latter respect is further enhanced by the following forces common to work situations.

1. *Uncertainty* Plans and objectives deal with the future, and the future is always uncertain. Especially in today's world of rapid and sometimes unpredictable change, there is a need for control points and control systems that allow for constructive adjustments in activities, plans, and even the objectives themselves over time.

2. *Complexity* As organizations grow in size and diversity, they become increasingly complex. Adequate controls are required to help coordinate activities and accomplish integration in the face of such complexity.

3. *Human limitations* People make mistakes. Forecasting errors are common in complex and unpredictable environments; errors of judgment also occur whenever decisions

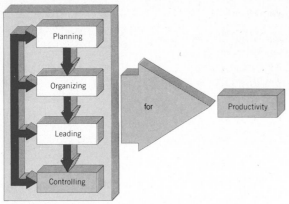

FIGURE 14.1 Controlling as an essential management function.

move out of the quantitative and into the more intuitive realms. Control helps spot such mistakes.

4. *Delegation and decentralization* Delegation and decentralization increase the decision-making authority and discretion of lower-level managers. As authority to act moves down the hierarchy, control mechanisms are required to ensure that accountability for results flows back up. Controls help managers delegate authority and decentralize decision making, while retaining a means to monitor and ensure performance results.

Controls thus fulfill at least three purposes in organizations. First, proper control helps make sure overall direction is consistent with short-, intermediate-, and long-range plans. Control provides a means for monitoring performance under plans as time passes. Second, control helps ensure that action objectives and performance accomplishments at various levels and among various units in an organization are consistent with one another in proper means-ends fashion. Objectives pursued at one level (e.g., individual), for example, should be the means to achieving ends represented by objectives at the next higher level (e.g., group). Finally, control helps ensure compliance with basic organizational rules and policies. This involves not only direct task requirements such as attendance and work hours, but also basic rules of propriety and respect for individuals. Many organizations, for example,

have issued formal policies protecting employees from sexual harassment at work.

Elements in the Control Process

The emphasis of control is on action designed to prevent problems, correct problems, and/or explore opportunities. The classic example, and the purest form of the control process, is a home thermostat. We set the thermostat to a desired temperature. When actual conditions in a room deviate from the setting, the thermostat senses the difference and takes corrective action (in winter adding warm air; in summer adding cool air). The thermostat then continues to function as a control device. These airflows are maintained only as long as the actual and desired temperatures differ. Once the desired temperature is achieved, the thermostat automatically turns off the heating or cooling system. It remains off until another deviation is sensed, and the cycle begins anew.

A thermostat represents a **cybernetic control system,** one that is self-contained in its performance monitoring and correction capabilities. Rarely is such an ideal state achieved in management practice. Instead, it is up to the manager to establish a mechanism for implementing the four basic elements in the **control process** that follow.

1. Establish performance objectives and standards.
2. Measure actual performance.
3. Compare actual performance with objectives and standards.
4. Take necessary action.

Figure 14.2 puts the four elements of the control process in a summary perspective. Underlying the process is an action framework that we can represent through a basic control equation:

Need for action =
desired performance − actual performance

The greater the variance between actual and desired performance, the greater the need for action. When actual is less than desired, the need

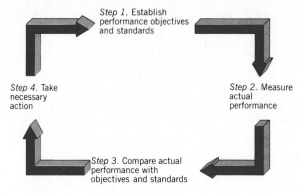

Step 1. Establish performance objectives and standards

Step 4. Take necessary action

Step 2. Measure actual performance

Step 3. Compare actual performance with objectives and standards

FIGURE 14.2 The control process.

for corrective action exists. When actual performance is greater than desired, a need exists to understand why this is so and learn how to maintain this high level of accomplishment in the future. Both of these premises are foundations for the control process.

Establishing Objectives and Standards

The control process begins with planning and the clarification of performance objectives. In our discussion of planning in Chapters 4 and 5, we devoted considerable attention to objectives as desired end states. From a control standpoint, any objective should be associated with a standard or criterion of measurement for determining when the desired end state has been reached. Managers become involved with two basic types of standards. **Output standards** measure performance results in terms of quantity, quality, cost, or time. Some examples include percentage error rate, dollar deviation from budgeted expenditures, and the number of units produced or customers serviced in a time period. **Input standards**, by contrast, measure the work efforts that go into a performance task. They are used in situations where actual performance outputs are difficult or expensive to measure. Examples include conformance to rules and procedures, efficiency in the use of resources, and even work attendance and punctuality.

Some standards are historical and use past performance as the target for future performance. They can also be comparative—that is, based on how performance measures up to that achieved

by other persons, work units, or organizations working on similar tasks and under similar circumstances. Finally, standards can be engineered. Through such methods as time and motion studies, for example, jobs can be precisely analyzed to determine what outputs are possible and/or what inputs are most appropriate. The work of Frederick Taylor and the Gilbreths, reviewed in Chapter 2, is the precursor of sophisticated engineering techniques used today for purposes of setting performance standards.

Measuring Actual Performance

Objectives and standards set performance targets and the means for evaluating results. In the measurement stage of the control process, the task is to measure actual performance outputs and/or inputs accurately. The emphasis in the last sentence should be the word *actual*. Measurement must be done well enough to spot deviations or variances between what actually occurs and what is desired. This, again, is the central logic of the control equation advanced earlier.

Comparing Actual Performance with Objectives and Standards

You may have heard the term **management by exception.** This involves focusing managerial attention on situations where deviations between actual and desired performance are substantial.

As shown in Figure 14.3, two outcomes are possible when actual performance is compared with objectives and standards. First, performance may equal the standard. This maintenance situation requires no corrective action. However, managerial effort should still be sufficient to maintain the desired performance in the future. Second, performance may differ from the standard. This is the "exception" case, and it deserves immediate attention and a decision as to what action should be taken in response to the observed exception.

Taking Necessary Action

Management by exception allows managers to conserve valuable time and energy by focusing

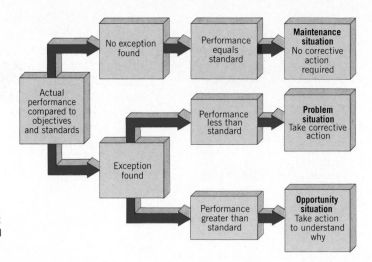

FIGURE 14.3 Management by exception in the control process.

[Figure labels: Actual performance compared to objectives and standards → No exception found → Performance equals standard → **Maintenance situation** No corrective action required; Exception found → Performance less than standard → **Problem situation** Take corrective action; Performance greater than standard → **Opportunity situation** Take action to understand why]

attention on areas of primary need. This need takes two forms: problem and opportunity. The problem situation is the most obvious; here actual performance is less than standard. As Figure 14.3 shows, effective control in a problem situation requires that corrective action be taken to restore performance to the desired level. Equally important, though, is the exception signaled by actual performance exceeding standard. This is an opportunity situation that calls for efforts to learn why performance expectations were exceeded and how such levels can be maintained in the future. It is also a chance to reevaluate the existing standards to determine whether or not they should be revised upward.

Internal and External Control

There are two ways in which the control process influences behavior in organizations: internal and external control.[3] **Internal control** occurs through self-discipline and the personal exercise of individual or group responsibility. **External control** occurs through direct supervision or the application of administrative systems such as rules and procedures. Effective control, as *Newsline 14.1* suggests, involves a good blend of both.

Internal Control

Internal control is really self-control. It occurs when the individual determines how things

should be done and exercises personal discipline in accomplishing performance results. The potential for internal control is enhanced by the presence of clear performance objectives, appropriate skills and abilities, and necessary resource support. Given good directions and standards, work proceeds on the assumption that capable persons will do the work and be diligent in monitoring and correcting their performance to ensure compliance with standards. Douglas McGregor's Theory Y perspective, introduced in Chapter 2 as part of behavioral management theory, includes a willingness for people to exercise self-control in their work.[4] Of course, he also notes that people will do this only for those matters to which they are truly committed. Thus, managers who expect others to exercise internal control should be willing to allow them to participate in the decisions through which the objectives and standards are initially set.

Reliance on internal or self-control also requires a high degree of trust on the part of managers. When people are left to perform on their own, the manager must trust them to fulfill this obligation. Douglas McGregor would probably argue, and we should agree, that managers are well advised to trust others to exercise self-control wherever possible. When and if the trust is proved unjustified, alternative measures can be taken. Unfortunately, many managers begin with the assumption that others *can't* be trusted. This is a limited view of human nature that may well inhibit the personal growth of subordinates.

NEWSLINE 14.1

ONE-TIME HARVARD TEACHER BUILDS GROUPS OF FIRMS BY LEAVING HIS MANAGER'S ALONE

CONCORD, MASS.—"Street smarts," says Charles M. Leighton, "will beat the hell out of analytical smarts any time."

He once taught management at Harvard Business School, but Charlie Leighton doesn't believe in ponderous corporate procedures. As chairman of the holding company called CML Group, he lets the managers of the 11 subsidiaries operate by "gut feeling," he says.

It's an interesting case study in decentralized management. Headquarters consists of nine people, including three secretaries (one of whom Leighton shares with a colleague). His office is on the second floor of an old railroad depot, and trains noisily rattle by.

Business consultants say many holding companies exert too much control when they acquire a number of concerns. "They feel they should be managing, but they don't know much about the individual businesses," says Robert H. Waterman, a director of McKinsey & Co., a New York-based management consulting firm. "What they're really doing is interfering."

CML tries to avoid that. Heads of subsidiaries set financial goals, handle internal differences, and even start new product lines without CML's approval if substantial capital outlays aren't required.

Hands-off is the CML strategy, but CML isn't a passive parent and Leighton gets his message across. At a Carroll Reed store, for example, he was annoyed by cigarette butts littering the doorway. After his suggestions that a receptacle be placed outside were ignored, he took a broom, swept the stoop, and emptied the butts into a container. A pail was outside the next day, he says.

Source: Excerpted from Christopher Grisanti, "One-Time Harvard Teacher Builds Group of Firms by Leaving His Managers Alone," *Wall Street Journal* (July 12, 1982), p. 15. Reprinted by permission of the *Wall Street Journal*, Copyright 1982 Dow Jones & Comapny, Inc. All rights reserved.

Many of our thoughts on enriched job designs in Chapter 8 are based on this element of self-control. They also require an element of managerial trust in order to succeed.

External Control

External control works through the formal authority system of the organization. A manager exercises external control through the direct supervision of subordinates. Extended throughout the hierarchy of authority, these superior-subordinate supervisory linkages provide for an ex-change of control and accountability that helps integrate the activities of an organization's multiple components.

An organization's administrative system formalizes control in a background or structural sense. These systems include the set of rules, procedures, policies, and written instructions established to guide the behavior of organization members in preferred directions. In relatively certain environments, administrative systems can be established to control anticipated operations and predictable problems. This frees the manager from some supervisory responsibilities and

Table 14.1 Four Types of Controls Applied in a Brewery

Control Type	Central Question	Brewery Example
Precontrol (or feed-forward)	What needs to be done before we begin?	All ingredients for the beer are carefully selected for quality
Steering (or concurrent)	What can we do to improve performance while things are in process?	Fermentation is monitored to ensure it takes place at proper rate
Yes/no	How well have we done before moving on to the next stage?	Hops are tested for quality after roasting before being added to the brew
Postaction (or feedback)	Now that we've finished, how well did we do?	Final brew is batch tested for quality before being bottled

leaves more time to focus on exceptions and other aspects of the management process.

Types of Controls

Managers use four basic types of external controls: precontrols, steering or concurrent controls, yes/no controls, and postaction controls.[5] Table 14.1 introduces them in the context of a brewery example. As we turn now to examine each type in more detail, remember that managers most often use the various controls in combination with one another.

Precontrols

Precontrols, sometimes called *feed-forward controls,* are initiated before the start of a production or service activity. They include the specification of appropriate output and/or input factors. Basically, precontrols act to ensure that performance objectives are clear and that the correct resources are in place to accomplish them.

Steering Controls

Steering controls focus primarily on what occurs during the work process. They act in anticipation of problems and are sometimes called *concurrent controls.* The key feature of any steering control is the capability to take corrective action *before* final results are achieved. Guided missiles operate on steering controls that make in-flight corrections to ensure that a target is reached. Similar steering controls can be exercised over a wide range of activities in any work setting.

Yes/No Controls

Yes/no controls specify formal checkpoints that must be successfully passed before an activity proceeds further. They are common in work situations where a product passes sequentially from one work unit to another with improvements being added at each stop along the way. A series of yes/no controls can be used to check performance at each stop point to determine if work should proceed to the next one. One common cause for rejection would be a quality deficiency, the subject of the headlines section introducing this part of the book. Good use of yes/no controls helps spot errors or deviations before they become compounded. Cost savings and better quality assurance are the hoped-for results.

Postaction Controls

Postaction controls, sometimes called *feedback controls,* take place after an action is completed. Restaurants ask how you like a meal . . . after it is eaten; a final course grade tells you how well you performed . . . after the course is over; a final budget summary informs managers of any cost overruns . . . after a project is complete. Postaction controls are most useful in helping plan future activities of a similar nature, formally documenting current performance results, and setting a baseline for distributing performance-contingent rewards to those participating in the activity.

ORGANIZATIONAL CONTROL SYSTEMS

Figure 14.4 specifies basic components of organizational control systems. Each component has the potential to increase or ensure the predictability of performance when well utilized by managers. The figure divides these components into two groups. Controls in the first group derive from planning, organizing, and leading as management functions. The second group of comprehensive controls are new directions for study.

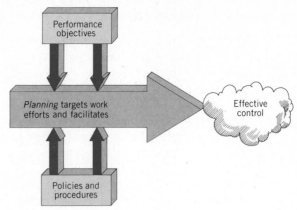

FIGURE 14.5 Good planning facilitates control.

Planning and Controlling

Planning gives direction to the organization as a whole and to the individuals and groups that are its working components. Figure 14.5 shows how good planning facilitates control. Control via performance objectives occurs when work behaviors are directed toward the right end result. When goals are clear to begin with, deviations caused by a lack of direction in one's work efforts are less likely to occur.

Control via policies and procedures occurs in somewhat similar fashion. Policies and pro-

cedures set guidelines for behavior and include specified rules for solving anticipated problems. By ensuring that people act and make decisions uniformly and respond in the same ways to defined problem situations, control is facilitated. Reflecting on past experience and then planning ahead by specifying policies and procedures to guide future behavior in similar circumstances are important aspects of control in any organization.

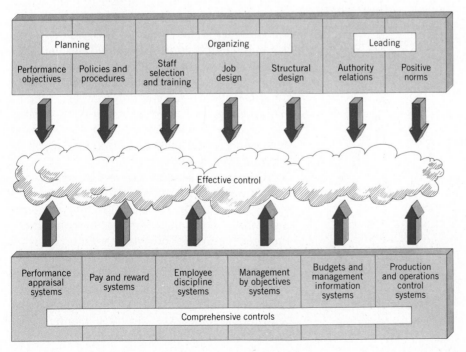

FIGURE 14.4 Components of organizational control systems.

Organizing and Controlling

Throughout this book we have emphasized the necessity of providing adequate support for people's work efforts in organizations. Two essential types of support are making sure that people of ability are employed, and that jobs and structures match the tasks to be accomplished as well as the people who are asked to do them. Figure 14.6 summarizes how the organizing function facilitates control by serving these purposes.

Control via staff selection and training involves the maintenance of a qualified work force. This means that staffing activities are sufficient to ensure a continued influx of qualified personnel and to provide them with adequate training opportunities to enhance their skills over time. The closer the match between skills and job requirements, the greater the probability that work efforts will be appropriate to performance objectives. This reduces the need for external controls and increases the potential for internal or self-control.

The design of organizational structures and jobs is also an important component in an overall control system. Control via structural and job design occurs when a good match is achieved between the tasks to be accomplished, the people who do them, and the structure within which the work takes place. The contingency approaches to organizational design discussed in Chapter 7 and the diagnostic approach to job enrichment covered in Chapter 8 capture this logic well. When

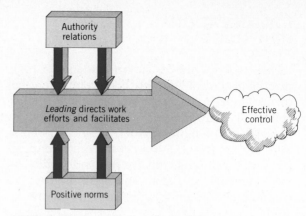

FIGURE 14.7 Good leadership facilitates control.

structures and jobs are right, control is facilitated and organizational performance made more predictable.

Leading and Controlling

Leadership is a use of power to influence other people to act in ways that serve organizational objectives. Figure 14.7 shows that leadership acts as another basic component of control in organizations. Control via authority relations occurs when a person of formal authority (i.e., a manager) directly supervises the work activities of someone else. This is one of the external forms of administrative control discussed earlier. By formally overseeing work, deviations from standard can be prevented and/or corrected through direct superior-subordinate communications. When a manager's power extends beyond the position and into personal sources—namely reference power and expert power—this control capability expands even further.

Control via positive norms also acts to constrain individual behaviors. Our examination of group dynamics in Chapter 13, however, suggests that norms may support or contradict a manager's efforts. The best condition is when group norms support the organization's performance objectives. When effective leadership is exercised through the development of positive norms, individual behavior is directed toward organizational objectives. In this manner good leadership also facilitates control.

FIGURE 14.6 Good organizing facilitates control.

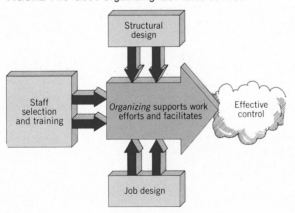

Comprehensive Controls

Each of the prior aspects of organizational control builds directly from one of the other management functions. As you can see, these topics have been covered elsewhere in this book. It is time to shift our attention to the other six comprehensive controls previously identified in Figure 14.4. Performance-appraisal systems, pay and reward systems, management-by-objective systems, and employee-discipline systems will be reviewed in the present chapter. Control by budgets and management information systems is covered in Chapter 15; production and operations controls are covered in Chapter 16.

PERFORMANCE APPRAISAL SYSTEMS

Performance appraisal is a process of formally evaluating performance and providing feedback on which performance adjustments can be made. Figure 14.8 shows the interrelationship of performance appraisal with the four elements in the control process. The initial clarification of objectives and standards sets the stage for performance appraisal. The performance-appraisal process, in turn, facilitates the identification of discrepancies between objectives and results, as well as the determination of what actions may be necessary. It is unlikely that any organizational control system can be effective in a comprehensive sense unless it includes a good performance appraisal system that is well implemented.

Performance appraisal can be done at the individual, group, or total organization level. We'll restrict our attention to the appraisal of individual performance. Many of the issues, problems, and principles that can be identified at this level of action also apply to the others.

Purposes of Performance Appraisal

Two basic purposes are served by good performance-appraisal systems: evaluation and development. Table 14.2 identifies that these purposes are served by managers fulfilling judgmental (serving evaluation purposes) and counseling (serving development purposes) roles. Both roles are thus essential to the performance-appraisal process. Table 14.2 shows, though, that the judgmental and counseling roles require different skills. Whereas the manager's task in the judgmental role is to judge and evaluate, in the counseling role, it is to help and guide. Success as a counselor, for example, requires the abilities to communicate orally and listen actively. To succeed as an evaluator, the manager needs a good set of performance-measurement techniques in addition to these communication skills.

When done well, performance appraisal facilitates control through both its evaluative and its development purposes. The benefits apply to the individual and the supervisor, as well as the organization as a whole. For example,[6]

1. *The benefits to the individual include improved—*

   ■ *Understanding* Performance appraisal clari-

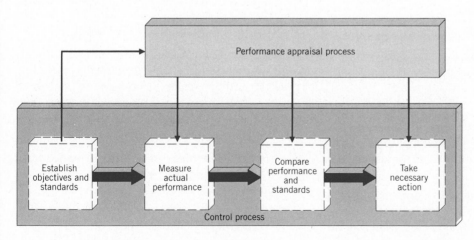

FIGURE 14.8 The role of performance appraisal in the control process.

Table 14.2 Comparison of the Judgmental and Counseling Roles in Performance Appraisal

	Judgmental Role	Counseling Role
Focus	On past performance	On future performance
Purpose	Improve future performance by allocating rewards contingent on past performance	Improve future performance by identifying avenues for learning and personal development
Task of supervisor	To judge and evaluate	To counsel and help
Role of subordinate	Passive, reactive, and even defensive	Active and positive

Source: Based on L. L. Cummings and Donald P. Schwab, *Performance in Organizations: Determinants and Appraisal* (Glenview, Ill.: Scott, Foresman, 1973) p. 5. Used by permission.

fies past achievements, the methods of evaluation, and future expectations.

- *Opportunities* Performance appraisal is a reminder that one's concerns, ideas, needs, and plans should be communicated to supervisors.

- *Confidence* Performance appraisal is a reminder that performance is taken seriously by higher management.

2. *The benefits to the supervisor include improved—*

- *Understanding* Performance appraisal helps identify what support people need.

- *Human-resource planning* Performance appraisal helps identify staff replacement and training needs.

- *Confidence* Performance appraisal is a way of letting people know how well they have done and what is expected of them in the future.

3. *The benefits to the organization include improved—*

- *Performance* Performance appraisal helps improve the predictability of desirable performance.

- *Personnel administration* Performance appraisal provides information that can be stored and used for decision making on matters such as promotions, terminations, or transfers.

- *Training and development* Performance appraisal provides information about personnel strengths and weaknesses that can be used to plan training and development programs.

- *Selection of new personnel* Performance appraisal of current employees helps establish appropriate criteria for the selection of new personnel.

At its best, performance appraisal is a means of gathering information useful for solving problems and making decisions relating to past and future performance. From an evaluative perspective, performance appraisal lets people know where they stand relative to objectives and standards. As such it is an input to decisions that allocate rewards and otherwise administer the personnel function of the organization. From a counseling perspective, performance appraisal facilitates planning for and gaining commitment to the continued training and personal development of subordinates.

Performance Appraisal Methods

Managers use a variety of methods to formally appraise individual performance, including graphic rating scales, behaviorally anchored scales, critical-incident techniques, free-form narratives, and multiperson comparisons. Regardless of the approach used, any appraisal must be[7]

1. *Relevant* The measures of performance must be as closely related to actual job or task requirements as possible.

2. *Unbiased* The measures must be of performance-related factors; they should not be

based on the person or other nonperformance factors.

3. *Significant*   The measures must relate to performance outcomes that are important to the accomplishment of organizational objectives.

4. *Practical*   The measures must be capable of being accurately and efficiently taken in the actual work setting.

Two specific criteria of the strength of a performance-appraisal method are reliability and validity. For a performance-appraisal method to be *reliable*, it must be consistent and stable in yielding the same result over time and/or for different raters. For it to be *valid*, it must be relevant and measure factors that directly relate to actual performance outcomes. Each of these important terms is frequently used in conversation about the performance appraisal process. With this as

background, brief highlights on the major performance-appraisal methods follow.

Graphic Rating Scales

Graphic rating scales list a variety of traits or characteristics that are thought to be related to high performance outcomes in a given job, and that the individual is accordingly expected to exhibit. The scales allow the manager to assign the individual scores on each trait ranging from unsatisfactory at one extreme to outstanding at the other. These ratings are sometimes given point values to allow a summary numerical rating of performance to be given. An example of this common approach to performance appraisal is shown in Figure 14.9. The primary appeal of graphic rating scales is that they are relatively easy to do and are efficient in the use of time and other resources.

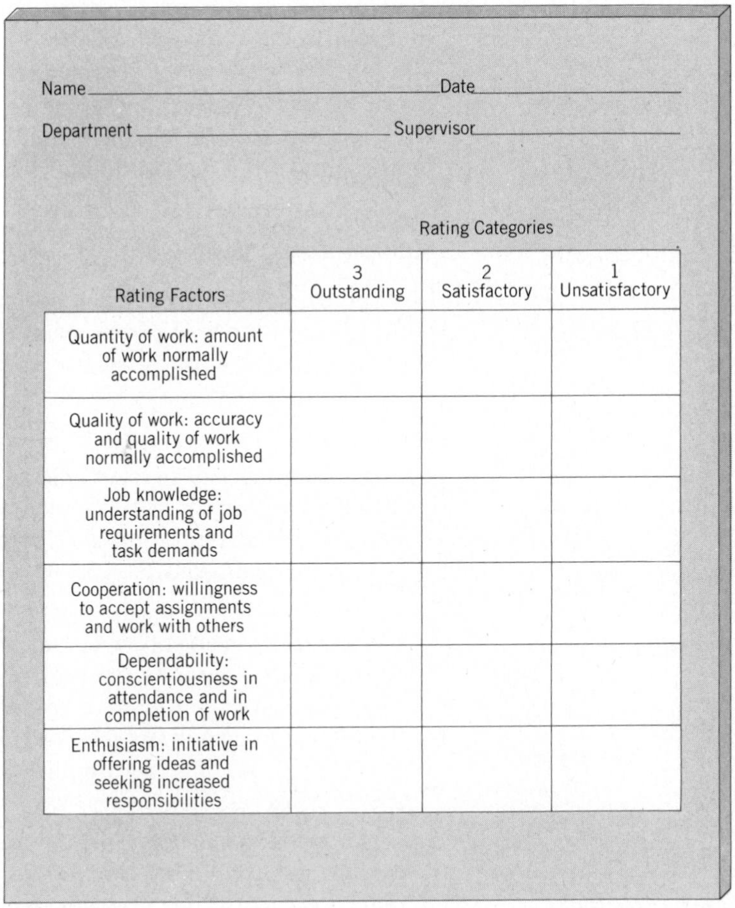

FIGURE 14.9 Typical graphic rating scale for performance appraisal.

Name _____ Date _____

Department _____ Supervisor _____

Rating Categories

Rating Factors	3 Outstanding	2 Satisfactory	1 Unsatisfactory
Quantity of work: amount of work normally accomplished			
Quality of work: accuracy and quality of work normally accomplished			
Job knowledge: understanding of job requirements and task demands			
Cooperation: willingness to accept assignments and work with others			
Dependability: conscientiousness in attendance and in completion of work			
Enthusiasm: initiative in offering ideas and seeking increased responsibilities			

Behaviorally Anchored Rating Scales

A **behaviorally anchored rating scale (BARS)** is based on explicit descriptions of actual behaviors that exemplify various levels of performance achievement. "Extremely poor" performance is illustrated in Figure 14.10 where a customer-service representative can be "expected to treat a customer rudely and with disrespect." Because it is so descriptive, a BARS can be especially helpful in training people to master job skills of demonstrated performance importance. The BARS method of performance appraisal is growing in popularity.

Critical-Incident Techniques

The **critical-incident technique** involves a running log or inventory of effective and ineffective job behaviors. By focusing on recording positive and negative examples of performance, the critical-incident method documents success or failure patterns that can be specifically discussed with the individual. A good critical-incident record is complete and unbiased. This requires the recorder to be observant, diligent, and fair when selecting critical incidents. Examples of positive and negative incidents documented for a customer-service representative follow.

Positive example Took extraordinary care of a customer who had purchased a defective item from a company store in another city.

Negative example Acted rudely in dismissing the complaint of a customer who felt that a "sale" item was erroneously advertised.

Free-Form Narratives

The **free-form narrative** is a written essay description of someone's job performance. The narrative typically includes actual descriptions of performance and an overall evaluation. Free-form narratives are sometimes used in combination with other performance appraisal methods, although they are often used alone as well. Because of their essay character, free-form narratives require good written communication skills on the part of the person doing the evaluation.

Mulitperson Comparisons

Multiperson comparisons compare one person's performance with that of one or more others in order to arrive at a final evaluation. Three of the more common techniques are

1. *Rank ordering* All persons being rated are arranged in order of performance achievement. The best performer goes to the top of the list, and the worst performer goes to the bottom, with no ties allowed.

2. *Paired comparison* Each person is formally compared to every other person and is rated as either the superior or weaker member of the pair. After all paired comparisons are made, each person is assigned a summary ranking based on the number of superior scores achieved.

3. *Forced distribution* Each person is placed into a specified frequency distribution of performance classifications. You know this method

FIGURE 14.10 Behaviorally anchored rating scale for a customer-service representative.

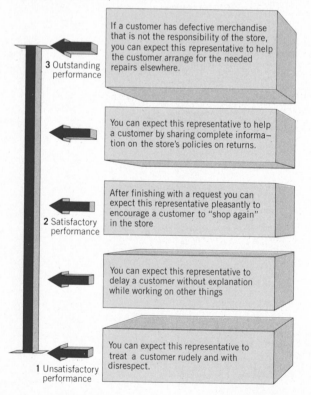

3 Outstanding performance

If a customer has defective merchandise that is not the responsibility of the store, you can expect this representative to help the customer arrange for the needed repairs elsewhere.

You can expect this representative to help a customer by sharing complete information on the store's policies on returns.

After finishing with a request you can expect this representative pleasantly to encourage a customer to "shop again" in the store

2 Satisfactory performance

You can expect this representative to delay a customer without explanation while working on other things

You can expect this representative to treat a customer rudely and with disrespect.

1 Unsatisfactory performance

best from college courses that are "curved" on the basis of X% A's, Y% B's, and so on. In the work setting, a forced distribution might require that 25 percent of the persons being evaluated be given a "superior" rating, 50 percent "average," and 25 percent "poor." All categories must be filled to the assigned percentage, and everyone within a category is considered equal for purposes of the performance appraisal.

Multiperson comparisons can also be combined with one or more of the other performance appraisal methods. They are an additional point of comparative reference that can add rigor to the control process.

Questions and Answers on Effective Performance Appraisal

A good performance appraisal system facilitates managerial control in a positive manner. This includes adequate attention to the needs of individuals as well as the organization. Some questions and answers to keep in mind on the challenges of doing effective performance appraisals are the following.

"Should performance appraisals be done at all?"
The answer to this question is "yes." As indicated earlier, performance appraisals offer numerous benefits that play an important and necessary role in the management process.

"Is any one performance appriasal method uniformly better than the others?"

Table 14.3 shows that all performance appraisal methods have weaknesses. Any system should be designed or chosen to meet the needs of the situation. Often, one involving multiple methods may work best.

"Who should do the performance appraisal?"
At a minimum, the manager should complete a formal performance appraisal for each of his or her immediate subordinates. This establishes a basic performance accountability in the supervisor-subordinate relationship. Some organizations also expand the performance appraisal process to include self-appraisals, peer reviews, and, in some cases, subordinate reviews of the performance of their supervisors. Each of the latter ideas can be useful as a basis of additional constructive dialogue. They do, however, require a high level of trust among the parties involved and should probably stress developmental as opposed to purely evaluative purposes.

"How often should performance appraisals be done?"
Everyone should receive a formal performance appraisal at least once a year. A more frequent schedule of appraisals is appropriate for new employees and for those having performance problems. It is always useful to supplement the formally scheduled appraisal with more frequent informal appraisals. These interim reviews can help reinforce performance targets and modify plans or support activities where appropriate.

"Is there any advice for actually conducting effective performance appraisal interviews?"
The actual performance appraisal interview or

Table 14.3 Potential Weaknesses of the Various Performance-Appraisal Methods

Method	Potential Weaknesses
Graphic rating scale	Traits or factors used in the rating scheme may be poorly chosen and/or fail to cover all relevant aspects of the job; raters may assign different meanings to the same evaluation (i.e., "good" may mean different things to different people).
Behaviorally anchored rating scales (BARS)	Complex to develop; may be cumbersome and lengthy
Critical-incident method	Time consuming; prone to bias from tendencies to "see" or "recognize" only positive or negative incidents; may be incomplete in covering all aspects of job
Free-form essay	Same problems as critical-incident method
Multiperson comparisons	May force the rater to make inappropriate comparisons; hard to use when more than four or five persons must be compared.

Table 14.4 Guidelines for Preparing for and Conducting a Performance-Appraisal Interview

Preparing for the Interview
1. Make sure that everyone understands the performance appraisal system and performance standards being used for their appraisals.
2. Clarify any differences in language between the formal written appraisal and the one you plan to use in the interview.
3. If you are angry with an employee, talk about it before the interview, not during the interview.
4. Be aware of your own biases in judging people.
5. Review the employee's compensation plan and be knowledgeable of his or her salary history.
6. If you have already given the employee a number of negative appraisals, be prepared to take corrective action at this point in time.

Conducting the Interview
1. Be thoroughly prepared.
2. Take enough time for the interview.
3. Focus on positive work performance; don't be overly negative.
4. Remember that strengths and weaknesses usually spring from the same general characteristics.
5. Admit that your judgment of performance contains some subjectivity.
6. Make it clear that the individual holds primary responsibility for development.
7. Be specific when citing examples; never generalize problem behavior.
8. Summarize agreements in writing and file for future reference.

Source: Adapted, by permission of the publisher, from "A Human Factors Approach to Appraisals" by John Cowan, from *Personnel* (November–December 1975), pp. 49–56, © 1975 by AMACOM, a division of American Management Associations. All rights reserved.

meeting may be one of the most difficult events managers must deal with. It can be a stressful, emotional, and even hostile situation. Performance reviews challenge the interpersonal and communication skills of all parties concerned. As a manager, you must take the lead in preparing for and conducting such interviews in an effective manner. Table 14.4 lists several guidelines that should be helpful in this regard.

PAY AND REWARD SYSTEMS

An organization's pay and reward systems serve several purposes. When properly designed and implemented, they (1) attract people to the or-ganization, (2) help motivate them to exert maximum effort in their work, and (3) signify for them the value of their contributions to organizational performance. There is an element of control in each of these purposes. Although we discussed the motivational aspects of pay and rewards in Chapter 12, they deserve special attention here for their role in the overall control process. Let's focus on pay, while recognizing that promotions, honors, and other rewards function in similar ways. We'll begin with an example taken from a perspective offered in the *Wall Street Journal*.

Illustrative Case: High Wages Don't Necessarily Mean High Costs[8]

Most businessmen thought Henry Ford was a madman when he announced, in 1914, that he was raising the minimum wage for plant workers from $2.34 to a hitherto unheard of $5 a day. It simply wouldn't work, the businessmen said. Labor costs would be too expensive. The employees would simply take the extra money and stay drunk. But Ford Motor Co. has lasted longer than most of its detractors. Henry Ford later said: "The payment of the $5 a day for an eight-hour day was one of the finest cost-cutting moves we ever made, and the $6 day was cheaper than the $5."

Unfortunately, Ford's insight into labor costs still eludes many management people today. Low wages do not necessarily mean low costs. In fact, all too often exactly the opposite is true. Today's bankruptcy courts are clogged with firms that have doggedly adhered to the principle of cheap labor.

Consider Eclipse Inc., a Rockford, Illinois-based manufacturer of industrial heating equipment with some 650 employees. In 1978 employee turnover was 95 percent per year, daily absenteeism was running at about 10 percent and there had been a five-year slide in earnings. The company decided to offer wage incentives based on individual and overall company performance, and scheduled merit reviews of all employees, including supervisors. Wages rose by 34 percent over three years, employee turnover was reduced to 20 percent per year and absenteeism to less than 3 percent. Meanwhile, shipping volume per employee rose 65 percent and company profits jumped 600 percent.

For companies the advantages are clear. With good wages accompanied by controls and standards of accountability, a company is in a position to:

- Attract better employees, pay them better than average wages, and expect more from them.
- Motivate people to produce because they want to produce.
- Insist on high productivity and refuse to tolerate anything but good overall quality and performance.

Put another way, for average wages a company will normally obtain average productivity. For high wages a company might expect to get high productivity. But it doesn't. It gets *exceptionally* high productivity.

Incentive Pay and Rewards

By allocating merit pay and/or other rewards on a performance-contingent basis, high performers are reinforced for achievements, while low performers are singled out and reminded of performance deficiencies. On the assumption that the individual understands the basis for the allocation and the message it carries, a framework for performance control is established. High performers can target their efforts on ways to maintain or further improve performance; low performers can be directed toward appropriate performance targets, supported in their efforts to accomplish them, or singled out for replacement.

At the executive level, such incentive plans can include stock options, profit sharing, and bonus plans. At General Motors, for example, 6000+ senior executives participate in a salary bonus plan tied to corporate earnings. The company views the plan as a way of ensuring that it can attract and retain quality talent.[9] At middle-lower management and operating levels, the incentive plans exist mainly in the form of merit pay or promotion systems. But the power of these plans can be just as strong as the attractive executive bonuses just described. Managers should remember, too, that incentive pay and reward plans must be well implemented and that their withdrawal can hurt productivity and morale. One midwest paper mill eliminated a program giving hourly workers twice-yearly bonuses. Productivity dropped 20 percent, turnover among top-performing workers doubled, and job satisfaction of top performers fell. Poor performers ended up liking their jobs better![10]

Base Compensation and Fringe Benefits

Another function of pay in an organization's control system is to attract qualified persons to the job. A large element of performance control can be realized simply by getting the right person placed in a job in the first place. Competency is a major factor in self- or internal control. The more capable a person is, the more self-control one can expect over the task at hand. Unless an organization's prevailing wage and salary structure is attractive and competitive in the labor market, it will be difficult to find and maintain a staff of capable workers. This will increase performance uncertainty among workers and increase the burden on other control systems to monitor results. On the other hand, proper base compensation helps attract a capable workforce and thereby enhances self- or internal control.

The overall employee-benefit program of an organization also plays a role in the attraction and maintenance of a capable work force. Fringe benefits can add 10–40 percent to a person's base salary. Typical benefit packages, such as Exxon's, shown in Figure 14.11, include various options on disability protection, health and life insurance, and retirement plans. When benefits are attractive or at least adequate, the organization is in a better position to employ desirable job applicants and realize the advantages of self-control through staff competency.

One of the more novel approaches to employee-benefit plans is the **cafeteria benefits** program.[11] This program allows employees to select within a given monetary limit that combination of benefits best meeting their needs. Single workers, for example, may well elect different combinations of vacation, insurance, and retirement packages than someone closer to retirement. By providing flexibility, cafeteria benefit plans are designed to appeal to a wider range of individual needs and thus provide further satisfaction in the individual-organization relationship. Two good examples are given in *Newsline 14.2.*

Financial Security Through Exxon Benefits

to meet
all major needs . . . for all employees

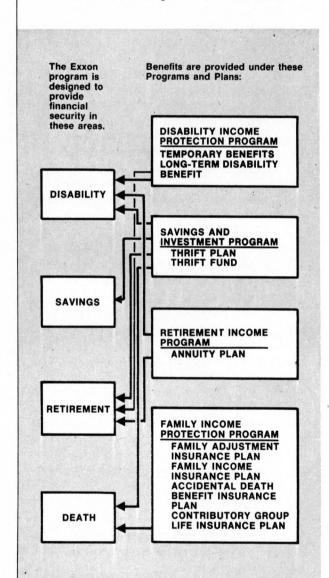

The Exxon program is designed to provide financial security in these areas.

Benefits are provided under these Programs and Plans:

DISABILITY INCOME PROTECTION PROGRAM
TEMPORARY BENEFITS
LONG-TERM DISABILITY BENEFIT

DISABILITY

SAVINGS AND INVESTMENT PROGRAM
THRIFT PLAN
THRIFT FUND

SAVINGS

RETIREMENT INCOME PROGRAM
ANNUITY PLAN

RETIREMENT

FAMILY INCOME PROTECTION PROGRAM
FAMILY ADJUSTMENT INSURANCE PLAN
FAMILY INCOME INSURANCE PLAN
ACCIDENTAL DEATH BENEFIT INSURANCE PLAN
CONTRIBUTORY GROUP LIFE INSURANCE PLAN

DEATH

Of special interest to YOUNGER employees

● up to 8½ years' salary in life insurance protection plus monthly income for surviving dependents.

● programs of basic and major medical insurance, and a dental assistance plan.

● life income while permanently and totally disabled.

● opportunity for employee savings and investment encouraged by substantial Exxon contributions — with loan and withdrawal features.

● continued earnings when off the job because of sickness or injury.

And for LONGER SERVICE employees

● life insurance protection with provision for continued protection into retirement.

● estate accumulation through Thrift Plan savings.

● medical insurance and dental assistance continuing into retirement.

● substantial retirement income through Annuity Plan.

● career savings accumulated in Thrift Plan available as retirement income nest egg.

This folder is a brief summary of the more important provisions of Exxon benefit plans. In all cases the complete official texts of these plans or contracts, which are available in Employee Relations, will govern.

The benefits described on these pages cover regular full-time employees in New York City as provided in the terms of the plans. Many plan provisions are based on the amount of Exxon Benefit Plan Service that an employee has, which generally includes all periods of service in affiliated companies, as defined in the plans and policies concerned.

FIGURE 14.11 Exxon benefit package.

NEWSLINE 14.2

MORE WORKERS ARE GETTING A CHANCE TO CHOOSE BENEFITS CAFETERIA-STYLE

James Bechtel, a 34-year-old senior associate at Morgan Stanley & Co., figures his wife's employer is covering the family's doctor bills so he skips extra medical coverage and loads up on life insurance.

Jean Choffe, an American Can Co. marketing manager, skimps on medical and life insurance to increase company contributions to a capital accumulation plan for employees. Last month, by borrowing against the fund, she was able to buy a house in Fairfield County, Connecticut.

Both employees are taking advantage of a trend toward dishing out fringe benefits cafeteria-style. Workers are given a package of benefits that includes "basic" and "optional" items. Basics might include modest medical coverage, life insurance equal to a year's salary, vacation time based on length of service, and some retirement pay. But then employees can use credits to choose among such additional benefits as full medical coverage, dental and eye care, more vacation time, additional disability income, and higher company payments to the retirement fund.

Source: Excerpted from Deborah Randolph, "More Workers Are Getting a Chance to Choose Benefits Cafeteria-Style," *Wall Street Journal* (July 14, 1981), p. 31. Reprinted by permission of the *Wall Street Journal*. Copyright © 1981 Dow Jones & Company, Inc. All rights reserved.

An organization's overall pay and reward system must include a good benefits plan. Such plans enhance the attractiveness of the organization as a place of employment. In so doing, they can also enhance the level of internal control and self-discipline among the organization's personnel.

EMPLOYEE DISCIPLINE SYSTEMS

Speaking of discipline, did you read the Associated Press news article reporting Jodi Stutz's run-in with an office copying machine? In case you didn't, read on.

Illustrative Case: Secretary Gets Canned[12]

MOLINE, ILL. (AP)—Jodi Stutz says she had no idea that when she put her bare bottom on the Xerox machine, she was putting her job on the line.

"I can't believe I got fired over this," she said Tuesday. "I just can't believe it."

Stutz, a 21-year-old secretary, said that one night after work at Deere & Co. she decided to christen the new copying machine on the floor by sneaking in to the Xerox room and making a picture of her bottom.

"A lot of people were taking pictures of their hands and their faces and fooling around," she said. "So I decided I would take a picture of my bottom, thinking it would be kind of fun just to see what it would look like."

While another secretary stood watch at the door, Stutz pulled down her pants, hopped up on the machine, and pushed the "Print" button.

"It was very, very funny," she said, giggling. "It borderlines on crude, maybe, but it was funny."

Her superiors, however, didn't think so. Word got around after Stutz showed friends in the office her copy.

Jim Coogan, Deere director of advertising, then reportedly got the secretary who had stood watch to confess, and Stutz was called on the carpet.

"They said something like it wasn't in the company's best interest to make a copy of my bottom," she said. "Of course, they never came right out and said it. They were too embarrassed to say what the incident was, but we all knew."

She said she expected a reprimand, but instead she was given two options—quit or be fired.

"I talked to them a long time to get them to change their mind or at least put me on probation," said Stutz, who is now working as a waitress. "My work record was excellent, and they even admitted it was. I told them I was really sorry about it and everything."

A Deere spokesman declined comment.

This case, whether you agree or disagree with the outcome, introduces the role of employee discipline in organizational control systems. **Discipline** can best be defined as influencing behavior through reprimand. Jodi Stutz was disciplined by being fired. Although the dismissal was a most extreme form of discipline in respect to Stutz, it served notice on all other Deere & Co. employees that such behavior would not be tolerated by the company. By disciplining Stutz, Deere was sending a message to other employees about appropriate job behavior. Stutz got fired; other employees were better informed about what they *shouldn't* be doing. Enhanced control through maintenance of an employee-discipline system was the net result.

Progressive Discipline

Serious questions can be raised about how the Jodi Stutz incident was handled. A quick review of the "guidelines to handling punishment" in Chapter 10 puts some of them in perspective. Of predominate concern is the degree of finality represented in the decision to fire her. Most organizations and managers exercise control through discipline in a more systematic and incremental way.

Progressive discipline ties reprimands in the form of penalties or punishments to the severity of the employee's infractions. The reprimand varies in severity according to the number of times a behavior has occurred and/or its significance. For example, the progressive-discipline guidelines of one organization state, "The level of disciplinary action shall increase with the level of severity of behavior engaged in and based on whether the conduct is of a repetitive nature."

Table 14.5 elaborates this organization's progressive-discipline program. It classifies inappropriate employee conduct by levels of significance and associates offenses in each level with alternative progressive-disciplinary actions depending on how many times the offense has occurred. Note that the ultimate penalty of "discharge" is reserved for the most severe behaviors (e.g., any felony crime) or for continual infractions of less severe behaviors. Someone who is continually late for work, for example, would be discharged only after failing to respond to a series of written reprimands and/or suspensions. The goal is always to achieve compliance with organizational expectations through the least extreme reprimand possible—that is, without reaching the more extreme penalties. Progressive-discipline systems seek effective control at minimum cost to individuals and the organization.

Guidelines for Disciplinary Actions

A very good set of guidelines for disciplinary actions, called the "Hot Stove Rules," is attributed to Douglas McGregor. We all know the following rule: "When the stove is hot, don't touch it." We all know, too, that when this rule is violated, we get burned—immediately, consistently, usually not beyond the point of repair, and without regard for who (by name) or what (by personality, race, creed, or sex) we are. The "hot stove rules" of disciplinary action are based on this logic.[13]

1. *The reprimand should be immediate.* The hot stove does not wait until a person has touched it several times before it burns. It responds instantly on the first occasion.

2. *The reprimand should be directed toward one's*

Table 14.5 A Progressive Discipline Program

	Level I	Level II	Level III	Level IV	Level V
	Tardiness Disregard of safety regulations Loafing or wasting time Horseplay or scuffling Insolence	Leaving work without authority Misrepresentation of absence Sleeping during work hours Insubordination Sexual harrassment of co-employee	Falsifications of documents or records Drinking intoxicating beverages Unauthorized or unexcused absence of five through nineteen work days Sexual harrassment by a supervisor	Fighting Immoral or indecent conduct Any criminal misdemeanor	Any criminal felony Theft Bribery Unauthorized and unexcused absence of 20 or more assigned workdays
Disciplinary Actions					
First time	Verbal or written reprimand or warning	Written reprimand or 1–5 workday suspension	1–10 workday suspension	15–20 workday suspension	Discharge
Second time	Written reprimand or 1–5 workday suspension	1–10 workday suspension	15–20 workday suspension	Discharge	
Third time	1–10 workday suspension	15–20 workday suspension	Discharge		
Fourth time	15–20 workday suspension	Discharge			
Fifth time	Discharge				

actions, not one's personality. The hot stove does not degrade the person who touches it. It does not try to "get even" with the offender. It does not care that you did not mean to touch it or that you may be "sorry" that you did. A hot stove simply and directly burns.

3. *The reprimand should be consistent across time and people.* The hot stove burns anyone and everyone who touches it. It is a true equal-opportunity employer. The hot stove is also entirely consistent from one time to another. It does not become more lenient on some days and less lenient on others.

4. *The reprimand should provide important information.* When a person touches a hot stove, it lets him or her know clearly how the behavior can be changed to avoid future punishment.

5. *The reprimand should occur in a warm, supportive setting.* Most people have positive feelings towad a hot stove. It provides warmth and food. The fact that a hot stove has a simple inflexible rule ("don't touch") does not change one's favorable feelings toward it.

6. *Expectations and rules should be realistic.* The don't-touch-a-hot-stove rule is not the result of a whim or fancy of the moment. It is not a symptom of a pathological need to demonstrate power. It is not an issue of control. It is real and necessary. The expectations and rules governing employee behavior should be just as realistic.

MANAGEMENT BY OBJECTIVES: AN INTEGRATED PLANNING AND CONTROL SYSTEM

A basic premise of this chapter is that planning works hand in hand with the other management functions. This is especially evident in the relationship between planning and controlling. One useful technique for integrating these two functions is **management by objectives,** or MBO. As first defined in our discussion of planning in Chapter 5, MBO is a process of joint objective setting between a supervisor and subordinate. MBO is also known by the terms *management by results, management by goals,* and *work planning and review.*

The Concept of MBO

In its simplest terms, MBO involves a formal agreement between a supervisor and subordinate concerning (1) the subordinate's performance objectives for a given time period, (2) the plan(s) through which they will be accomplished, (3) standards for measuring whether or not they have been accomplished, and (4) procedures for reviewing results. Figure 14.12 clarifies this view of MBO in schematic form.

Note the distinction in the figure between "joint" and "individual" responsibilities. The supervisor and subordinate *jointly* establish plans and *jointly* control results in any good MBO action framework. This full participation by subordinates in the MBO process enables and encourages a high degree of self-control. Furthermore, the benefits of joint planning and controlling apply to both parties as the subordinate is facilitated in the work role, while the supervisor is facilitated in the supporting role.

Figure 14.13 shows how the concept of MBO can be applied on an organizationwide basis to facilitate integration in the organization's hierarchy of objectives. This is the rationale under which you were introduced to MBO in Chapter 5. When MBO is done by all superior-subordinate pairs throughout an organization, systemwide coordination of plans and task results is enhanced. Such a comprehensive MBO system helps create the interlocking network of groups

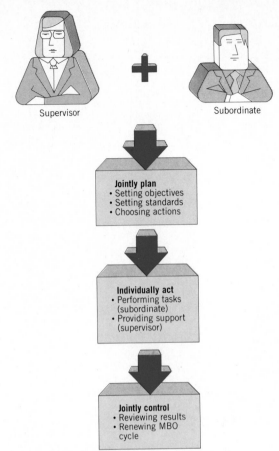

FIGURE 14.12 The MBO process: A planning, action, and controlling cycle.

that organizations depend on for true accomplishment of a common purpose.

MBO in Action

Establishing performance objectives is an essential part of the MBO process. For purposes of MBO, a *good* performance objective is expressed as a desired accomplishment that can be measured as an end product or verified as a set of work activities. Examples of objectives stated in each format follow.

1. *Measurable end product*   "To reduce housekeeping supply costs by 5 percent by July 1, 1984."
2. *Verifiable work activities*   "To improve communications with my subordinates in the next three months by holding weekly group meetings."

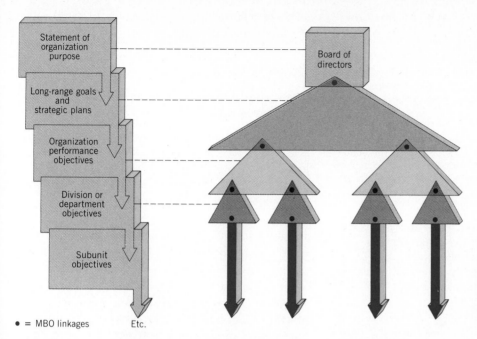

● = MBO linkages   Etc.

Statement of organization purpose

Long-range goals and strategic plans

Organization performance objectives

Division or department objectives

Subunit objectives

Board of directors

FIGURE 14.13 MBO in the hierarchy of organizational objectives. *Source:* Anthony P. Raia, *Managing by Objectives* (Glenview, Ill.: Scott, Foresman, 1974), p. 30. Used by permission.

Each of these objectives is specified so that action outcomes can be evaluated at the end of a stated time period. Any good MBO program involves objectives expressed in similar terms—that is, stated specifically and time defined.

Performance objectives are usually written and formally agreed on by both the superior and subordinate in the MBO process. Three types of objectives may be specified. **Improvement objectives** document a desire to improve a performance factor—for example, "to reduce quality rejects by 10 percent." **Personal development objectives** pertain to personal growth activities, such as "to learn a new computer programming language." Some MBO contracts also include **maintenance objectives,** which formally express intentions to continue performance at existing levels.

The process through which MBO is accomplished is as important as the existence of the objectives themselves. Here's how the MBO sequence works at Alcoa.[14]

Step 1

Individual lists key performance objectives for the coming period with target dates for accomplishing them.

Step 2

Objectives are submitted to the supervisor for

review. Discussions between the supervisor and subordinate result in an agreed set of objectives.

Step 3

The supervisor and subordinate meet on a quarterly basis to review progress and make revisions or update objectives as needed.

Step 4

At the end of the year, the individual prepares a "performance report" that lists major accomplishments and comments on discrepancies between expected and actual results.

Step 5

This self-appraisal is discussed with the supervisor. The reasons for objectives not being met are explored.

Step 6

A new set of objectives is established for the next year, as in Step 1. The MBO cycle begins anew.

Note that the six steps in the Alcoa approach to MBO convey the sense of "participation" referred to earlier. This is a distinct contrast to the "one-way" or "top-down" approach often encountered in management practice. Consider, for example, this observation by Richard Beeson, once president of Canada Dry, about a conversation held with his boss at the time, David Mahoney. It aptly illustrates the type of situations MBO is designed to avoid.[15]

"I had been on the job only a couple of weeks," Beeson says, "when we had a Canada Dry board meeting. I said to Mahoney, 'Dave, we're a little bit below budget now, and I think we can hold that for the rest of the year.'

"Dave looked at me, smiled, and said, 'Be on budget by the six-month mark; be on by the year.'

" 'But Dave,' I said, 'there isn't enough time to get on by the *half*. I inherited this situation, after all.'

"Still smiling, Dave looked at me and said, 'Do I pay you a lot of money? Do I argue with you over what you want to spend? Do I bother you? Then don't tell me what the goals should be. Be on by the half; be on by the end of the year.'

" 'What if I can't, Dave?'

[Mahoney replied] " 'Then clean out your desk and go home.' "

Beeson . . . says he began running through the reasons why he could not meet the goals, but Mahoney said: "Not interested. My board and my stockholders want me to make my numbers. The way I make my numbers is for you guys to make *your* numbers. Make your numbers."

For your information, Beeson stayed! To summarize, then, the end product of MBO is a written agreement that documents agreed work objectives for a subordinate. This document includes a timetable and a set of evaluation criteria. MBO thus offers the advantage of clearly focusing the subordinate's task efforts and the supervisor's support efforts on a specific set of performance objectives. Because the process involves direct face-to-face communication between supervisor and subordinate, MBO also fosters understanding and gives the subordinate a chance to participate in decisions that affect his or her job performance.

MBO Pros and Cons

MBO is one of the most talked about and debated management concepts of the last 25 years. It is the subject of books and a target of research criticism.[16] This criticism is useful because it helps identify things to be avoided and things to do in order to take maximum advantage of MBO as a management technique.

Things to Avoid

Five things above all others seem to detract from the success of MBO.[17]

1. *Tying MBO to compensation* When MBO is linked to pay, there is a tendency for objectives to become ends in themselves; reward maximizing practices by employees, even outright deceit, can sabotage the system.

2. *Focusing attention too much on objectives that are easily quantified* This tends to displace work efforts toward limited and sometimes inappropriate ends.

3. *Focusing too much on written documentation and forms* Excessive paperwork is a characteristic of MBO programs that fail. Although it is important to state objectives in writing, little additional paperwork is required for MBO to work to advantage.

4. *Using a prepackaged program* MBO is often implemented by external consultants who follow standard models used in other organizations. Any MBO "package" usually requires substantial modification to fit the unique needs of a given organization.

5. *Telling subordinates their objectives* This is the top-down approach exemplified earlier in the conversation between Richard Beeson and David Mahoney. It violates the very essence of the MBO concept.

Things to Do

Certain guidelines or things to be done can help make MBO work well for individuals and the organization.

1. *Ensure top management support.* MBO works best when managers from top to bottom in the organization commit themselves to the process, do it right, and reinforce it in their work with subordinates.

2. *Don't let MBO become the responsibility of a personnel director or personnel department.* MBO is a managerial tool and responsibility. Staff personnel cannot *do* MBO for managers elsewhere in

Good MBO involves regular
and face-to-face super-
visor—subordinate com-
munications.

the organization. Managers must *do* MBO for themselves and in direct person-to-person relationships with subordinates.

3. *Emphasize significant and well-stated objectives.* To serve their purpose in MBO, objectives should be specific, time defined, understandable, verifiable, and challenging.

4. *Emphasize regular and direct superior-subordinate interactions.* The essence of MBO is regular task-oriented communication between superior and subordinate. If MBO is to work, this must occur throughout the organization . . . over and over and over again!

MAKING CONTROLS EFFECTIVE

All control systems share the common goal of helping to ensure and coordinate performance contributions within organizations. The managerial emphasis in controlling is on objectives and results. Control is a responsibility of all managers at all levels acting in all types of supervisory capacities in organizations. To make controls ef-

fective, however, managers must recognize potential human reactions to control systems and respond as much as possible to the known characteristics of effective control systems.

Human Reactions to Controls

Not long ago, the Boy Scouts of America revealed that membership figures coming in from the field has been falsified. In response to the pressures of a national membership drive, people within the organization had vastly overstated the number of new Boy Scouts. To their chagrin, the leaders found something that other managers have also discovered: organizational control systems often produced unintended consequences. The drive to increase membership had motivated people to increase the number of new members reported, but it had not motivated them to increase the number of Boy Scouts actually enrolled.[18]

The case of the Boy Scouts poses an interesting dilemma for managers. It shows that at the same time that control systems are designed to ensure performance, human reactions to the controls can render them ineffective and even dysfunctional. Instead of the anticipated results, the measurement emphasis in control systems can result in people acting to "make their numbers" or "play the game." Truly effective control systems channel human energies toward improved work performance instead of toward "beating the system."[19]

Among the human reactions to controls that can lead to such unintended consequences are resentment of the act of measurement, defensiveness about one's true performance, and rejection of the performance targets stated in objectives. These reactions are especially prone to occur in situations of high stress where resources are scarce and/or performance competition is intense.

Characteristics of Effective Control Systems

To help managers avoid such problems with human reactions to control systems, the literature offers a number of guidelines for making controls effective. An effective control system is[20]

1. *Strategic and results oriented* It supports strategic plans and focuses on what needs to be done, not just on the act of measurement itself. The focal points of control are significant activities—that is, activities capable of really making a difference to the accomplishment of organizational objectives.

2. *Information based* It supports problem solving and decision making. A good control system does more than point out variations between actual and desired performance levels. It lends insight as to why the variance occurs and what might be done to correct it.

3. *No more complex than necessary* It complements the task and the plans on which task accomplishment is predicated. Controls should be tailored to fit the people involved, task requirements, and organization structures. A basic rule of thumb is to keep controls as simple as possible. Overcontrol can be costly, and it always raises the prospect of adverse human reactions and tendencies to try to "beat" rather than "support" the system.

4. *Prompt and exception oriented* It reports deviations quickly enough that trends can be corrected before too much harm is done. Ideally, control is triggered before anything actually goes wrong, reports deviations in a manner appropriate to the task at hand, and highlights exceptions instead of standard practices.

5. *Understandable* It presents data in understandable terms. Whether by expert assistance or initial design, good control systems ultimately present data to decision makers in a concise and easy-to-understand fashion. Unnecessarily complex computer printouts and statistics, for example, may detract from, not add to, the usefulness of a given control.

6. *Flexible* It leaves room for individual judgment and is modified to fit new circumstances as they arise. Good control systems allow for sufficient human judgment to respond to unique situations and changing circumstances.

7. *Consistent with the organization structure.* It complements the hierarchy of authority. It gets data into the decision-making system at points where authority to act exists. Until such information gets into the hierarchy at the right place, the probability of corrective action being taken is slight.

8. *Designed to accommodate self-control wherever possible.* It recognizes the capacity for self-control and allows for mutual trust, good communication, and participation among all parties involved. Self-control is enhanced by appropriate job designs and the selection of capable people for the jobs to be performed.

9. *Positive in nature.* It emphasizes development, change, and improvement; it minimizes penalty and reprimand. Commitment to controls is enhanced by a focus on the developmental rather than the punitive side of controls. When punitive measures do become appropriate, it is important that they be done progressively, carefully, well, and with due respect to people involved.

10. *Fair and objective.* It is viewed as impartial and accurate by all parties concerned. When the control system stands above criticisms of partiality and subjectivity, it is likely to be respected for its fundamental purpose—performance enhancement.

SUMMARY

Controlling is the fourth of the management functions. As a process of monitoring performance and taking corrective action, it is a responsibility of all managers at all levels in organizations. This chapter introduced the concept of control, discussed the nature of organizational control systems, and looked in some depth at how control can be facilitated by systems of performance appraisal, pay and rewards, employee discipline, and management by objectives.

There are four elements in the basic control process: (1) establish objectives and standards, (2) measure performance, (3) compare actual performance with standards, and (4) take necessary action as appropriate. These elements are common to each of the control systems discussed in this chapter, as well as those to be discussed in Chapters 15 and 16.

Performance appraisal is an important means for controlling individual behavior in organizations. A manager can use a variety of methods to accomplish performance appraisals, but the process itself will always be challenging. Fortunately, there are some guidelines on how to make performance appraisal a constructive and effective process.

Pay and reward systems contribute to control when properly implemented. Appropriate base pay, for example, brings qualified people capable of considerable self-control to an organization. Incentive pay that is well targeted and contingent on performance can reinforce desirable behaviors on the job. When deviations from standards occur or when basic rules of organizational propriety are broken, a progressive discipline system can serve as an important additional point of control.

Planning and controlling are directly intertwined in management by objectives (MBO), a technique that involves participatory objective setting and performance review between a supervisor and subordinate. MBO helps direct behavior toward important objectives and control results. Because it involves an element of participation, it allows a good deal of self-control to be exercised. This element of participation is one of several characteristics of effective controls pointed out in the last section of this chapter. You should keep these characteristics in mind as you study other control techniques and eventually take action to implement them in management practice.

THINKING THROUGH THE ISSUES

1. Define control as a management function. What is its basic relationship with the other management functions?

2. What is the difference between external and internal control in the work setting?

3. Explain the various steps in the control process.

4. What is the control equation?

5. Define and give examples of three different performance appraisal methods.

6. Explain how often performance appraisals should be accomplished, and in what relationship to annual salary reviews.

7. How can both base compensation and incentive pay be justified as components in a comprehensive organizational control system?

8. What is progressive discipline in the context of managerial control?

9. Is MBO essentially a planning or control technique, or is it both? Why?

10. If you could give someone only three pieces of advice on how to make control systems effective, what would you tell them? Why?

THE MANAGER'S VOCABULARY

Behaviorally anchored rating scale (BARS)	Control process	technique	Discipline
Cafeteria benefits	Controlling	Cybernetic control	External control
	Critical-incident	system	Free-form narrative

Graphic rating scale
Improvement objectives
Input standards
Internal control
Maintenance objectives

Management by exception
Management by objectives (MBO)
Multiperson comparison

Output standards
Performance appraisal
Personal development objectives
Postaction controls

Precontrols
Progressive discipline
Steering controls
Yes/no controls

CAREER PERSPECTIVE: TOUGH-MINDED MANAGERS

A *Wall Street Journal* article reports that managers are getting tougher in dealing with subordinates.[21] The approach often becomes: reward good performers, don't reward poor performers, and don't apologize for expecting people to work hard. Compared with a few years ago, chief executives believe their managers are more likely now to give big raises to their best performers and small raises or none at all to poor performers. These managers also are more likely to fire incompetent workers.

Consider the following survey results as reported in the article.

Question 1

Compared with a few years ago, how likely are your managers to give no raises or small raises to poor performers?

	Large Firms (%)	Medium Firms (%)	Small Firms (%)
More likely	69	59	52
Less likely	16	24	30
No change	12	11	10

Question 2

Compared with a few years ago, how likely are managers in the company you head to fire an incompetent worker?

	Large Firms (%)	Medium Firms (%)	Small Firms (%)
More likely	59	48	39
Less likely	25	38	50
No change	14	13	8

Questions

1. What do these data imply about your future responsibilities as a manager?
2. Can you perform well under such expectations? Why or why not?

CASE APPLICATION: NO-FAULT VERSUS AT-FAULT ABSENTEEISM

Organizations use a variety of means to control absenteeism. Two extremes in this regard are the "no-fault" and "at-fault" approaches.

No-Fault Absenteeism[22]

According to Frank E. Kuzmits, assistant professor of management at the University of Louisville's School of Business, a management approach to no-fault absenteeism "recognizes the inevitability of an occasional absense and avoids the common tendency to blame the employee for not coming to work." Nonjudgmental, the approach does not recognize any difference between excused and unexcused absences. No absence requires explanation; the employee doesn't have to prove the legitimacy of an absence. The no-fault system also frees the manager from the responsibility of differentiating between acceptable and unacceptable absences.

A major feature of the no-fault system is that someone out sick Wednesday through Friday, for example, would only be charged with one absence, while an employee who was out on Wednesday *and* Friday would be charged with two absences. "Why this disparity in recording absences? The procedure," explains Kuzmits, "is designed to achieve two purposes. The first is to avoid penalizing the employee who, on an infrequent basis, is genuinely ill and forced to remain away from work for two or more days. The second is to place a relatively greater penalty upon the 'chronic' absentee who claims large numbers of single-day absences—on Mondays, Fridays, and days preceding and following holidays."

Other special features of the no-fault system include (1) charging employees for double absences when they fail to call in and (2) allowing a bad attendance record to be worked off by deducting one recorded absence for each month of perfect attendance.

At-Fault Absenteeism

A recent headline from the *Wall Street Journal* reads: "AWOL Penalty—GM Workers May Lose Benefits for Certain Absences."[23] The text of the article goes on to introduce a different approach to absenteeism control. It is based on a tentative accord reached between the United Auto Workers union and General Motors in the attempt to help curb GM's $1 billion yearly absenteeism costs.

An employee's benefits will be cut by 20% or more if his or her unexcused absenteeism rate exceeds 20 percent for a six-month period. Among the benefits affected are profit sharing, health insurance, and bereavement pay. Current docking of workers' regular pay would continue.

Huge absences by a few workers account for most of the problem, GM says, but it doesn't know how many would fall into the 20 percent category. UAW chief Douglas Fraser says members don't object to the plan, as he had feared; "they've just had it" with absenteeism. It causes production problems for those who do show up.

Questions

1. What are the strengths and weaknesses of the no-fault and at-fault approaches to absenteeism control?
2. Which approach to absenteeism control do you prefer and why?
3. Is no-fault absenteeism control for everyone? Why or why not?

CLASS EXERCISE: THE MBO CONTRACT

Figure 14.14 shows an MBO contract for a plant manager by the name of John Atkins. Column 1 in the figure lists a number of objectives for Atkins. Column 2 shows their priority as A (higher) or B (lower). Column 3 lists projected completion dates. Column 4 provides space for the results to be documented.

1. Study this MBO contract. In Column 4 write one of the following symbols to identify each objective as an improvement, maintenance, or personal-development objective.

   I = Improvement objective

   M = Maintenance objective

   P = Personal development objective

2. Assume that this MBO contract was actually developed and implemented under the following circumstances. After each statement, write "yes" if the statement reflects proper MBO procedures and write "no" if it reflects poor MBO procedures.

   a. The president drafted the eight objectives and submitted them to Atkins for review.

   b. The president and Atkins thoroughly discussed the eight objectives in proposal form before they were finalized.

   c. The president and Atkins scheduled a meeting in six months to review Atkins's progress on the objectives.

   d. The president didn't discuss the objectives with Atkins again until the scheduled meeting was held.

   e. The president told Atkins his annual raise would depend entirely on the extent to which these objectives were achieved.

3. Share and discuss your responses to parts 1 and 2 of the exercise with a nearby classmate. Reconcile any differences of opinion by referring back to the chapter discussion of MBO. Await further class discussion.

MANAGERIAL JOB OBJECTIVES

John Atkins	7/2	PLANT MANAGER
Prepared by the manager	Date	Manager's job title

J. W. Crawford	7/2	PRESIDENT
Reviewed by supervisor	Date	Supervisor's job title

Statement of Objectives Col. 1	P Col. 2	Date Col. 3	Outcomes or Results Col. 4
1. To increase deliveries to 98% of all scheduled delivery dates	A	6/31	
2. To reduce waste and spoilage to 3% of all raw materials used	A	6/31	
3. To reduce lost time due to accidents to 100 work days/year	B	2/1	
4. To reduce operating cost to 10% below budget	A	1/15	
5. To install a quality-control radioisotope system at a cost of less than $53,000	A	3/15	
6. To improve production scheduling and preventative maintenance so as to increase machine utilization time to 95% of capacity	B	10/1	
7. To complete the UCLA executive program this year	A	6/31	
8. To teach a university extension course in production management	B	6/31	

FIGURE 14.14 An MBO contract. *Source:* Anthony P. Raia, *Managing by Objectives* (Glenview, Ill.: Scott, Foresman, 1974), p. 60. Used by permission.

REFERENCES

[1] The chapter opener is reprinted by permission from *Management in General: A Newsletter for Management from Corporate Personnel–Akron* (Akron, Ohio: General Tire and Rubber, April 1976). Excerpts from *Malice in Blunderland* by Thomas L. Martin. Copyright © 1973 by Thomas L. Martin. Used with the permission of McGraw-Hill Book Company.

[2] Joseph A. Litterer, "Elements of Control in Organizations," in Mariann Jelinek, Joseph A. Litterer, and Raymond E. Miles (eds.), *Organizations by Design: Theory and Practice* (Plano, Texas: Business Publications, 1981), p. 439.

[3] See Ibid.

[4] Douglas McGregor, *The Human Side of Enterprise* (New York: McGraw-Hill, 1960).

[5] See William Newman, *Constructive Control: Design and Use of Control Systems* (Englewood Cliffs, N.J.: Prentice-Hall, 1975); H. Koontz and R. Bradspies, "Managing Through Feedforward Control," *Business Horizons* (June 1972), pp. 25–36.

[6] Adapted from Edgar F. Huse, *Management*, Second Edition (St. Paul: West Publishing, 1982), p. 204.

[7] Patricia Smith, "Behaviors, Results, and Organizational Effectiveness," in Marvin Dunnette (ed), *Handbook of Industrial and Organizational Psychology* (Chicago: Rand McNally, 1976), pp. 745–775.

[8] Excerpted from John A. Patton, "High Wages Don't Necessarily Mean High Costs," *Wall Street Journal* (November 8, 1982), p. 22. Reprinted by permission of the *Wall Street Journal*. Copyright © 1982 Dow Jones & Company, Inc. All rights reserved.

[9] Douglas R. Sease, "GM Asks Holders to Sweeten Terms of Executive Bonuses," *Wall Street Journal* (April 19, 1982), p. 6.

[10] *Wall Street Journal* (November 24, 1982), p. 1.

[11] See Edward E. Lawler III, *Pay and Organization Development* (Reading, Mass.: Addison-Wesley, 1981).

[12] Associated Press, 1980. Used by permission.

[13] The "hot-stove rules" are slightly adapted from R. Bruce McAfee and William Poffenberger, *Productivity Strategies: Enhancing Employee Job Performance* (Englewood Cliffs, N.J.: Prentice-Hall, 1982), pp. 54–55. They are originally attributed to Douglas McGregor, "Hot Stove Rules of Discipline," G. Strauss and L. Sayles (eds.) in *Personnel: The Human Problems of Management*. (Englewood Cliffs, N.J.: Prentice-Hall, 1967). Reprinted by permission of Prentice-Hall, Inc., Englewood Cliffs, New Jersey.

[14] Walter S. Wikstrom, *Managing by-and-with Objectives*, Studies in Personnel Policy, No. 212 (New York: Conference Board, 1968), p. 3.

[15] This conversation is reprinted by permission of *Forbes Magazine*, February 1972 issue, p. 26.

[16] See for example, Dale D. McConkey, *How to Manage by Results*, Third Edition (New York: AMACOM, 1976); Stephen J. Carroll, Jr., and Henry L. Tosi, Jr., *Management by Objectives: Applications and Research* (New York: Macmillan,1973); Anthony P. Raia, *Managing by Objectives* (Glenview, Ill: Scott, Foresman, 1974); Steven Kerr summarizes the criticisms well in "Overcoming the Dysfunctions of MBO," *Management by Objectives*, Vol. 5, No. 1 (1976).

[17] Kerr, op. cit.

[18] Reprinted by permission of the *Harvard Business Review*. Excerpt from Cortlandt Cammann and David A. Nadler, "Fit Control Systems to Your Managerial Style," *Harvard Business Review*, Vol. 54 (January-February, 1976), p. 65. Copyright © 1976 by the President and Fellows of Harvard College; all rights reserved.

[19] Ibid., p. 67.

[20] These characteristics are suggested by Harold Koontz and Cyril O'Donnel, *Essentials of Management* (New York: McGraw-Hill, 1974), pp. 362–365; Howard M. Carlisle, *Management: Concepts, Methods, and Applications*, Second Edition (Chicago: Science Research Associates, 1982), pp. 297–300.

[21] Based on Frank Allen, "Bosses Getting Tougher on Firings and Raises," *Wall Street Journal* (November 21, 1980), p. 25. Reprinted by permission of the *Wall Street Journal*. Copyright © 1980 Dow Jones & Company, Inc. All rights reserved.

[22] Based on "No-fault Absenteeism," *Management Review*, Vol. 70 (November 1981), pp. 6–7.

[23] Information from a report in the *Wall Street Journal* (March 30, 1982), p. 1.

15

BUDGETARY CONTROL AND MANAGEMENT INFORMATION SYSTEMS

DATA GENERAL— LIFE IN THE FAST LANE

"I liked it better in the old days," says Herb Richman, Data General's flamboyant cofounder who is senior vice-president in charge of marketing and sales.[1] "The days when there were only 100 or so people around here and you knew everybody—you could jump up on the lunch table and yell, 'You characters better get the stuff shipped tonight or you won't eat.' Now I'd have to put that in a memo and send it around—it takes a week for everybody to find out I'm ticked off."

In 1968 president Richman, 44, chief executive officer Edson de Castro, 41, and three others started the third largest minicomputer manufacturer in a vacated beauty parlor in a strip shopping center in Hudson, Massachusetts. The beauty parlor is now a pizza joint. Data General is a worldwide enterprise—13,700 employees and over $500 million sales—growing 30 to 35 percent a year.

Here's what planning for 30 percent growth looks like: In 24 months, over half of the people who will be working for Data General haven't been hired yet; most of the minicomputer and microcomputer models it will be selling haven't been introduced yet; a third of the plant space in which they'll be produced hasn't been built yet; over half the customers they'll be sold to haven't been contacted yet; and though Data General will be doing business at an annual rate of $850 million, unit sales will more than double because in the computer industry most prices go down. And if they make an acquisition—Data General is advertising for an acquisitions person—all those numbers will be larger. And that's in 24 months.

Welcome to the world of hypergrowth. It has been like this in the minicomputer industry since it was born in the early 1960s, and the end is not in sight. Every year new technology drops prices 15 to 20 percent—sometimes more—and new users come pouring out of the woodwork. Nobody really knows what the total demand for minicomputers is. The real constraint is not the marketplace but the company's internal capacity to grow—raise enough money, build wisely, find and hire the right people, give them the right training, and produce the right technology at the right price, while keeping it all going at a pace just short of the line where the enterprise will dissolve into chaos because it can't be managed anymore.

"You have to make decisions here a *lot* faster," says product marketing vice-president Rowland Thomas. "You have to move before the optimum time you want to plan everything," he says. "Faster than is desirable. If you decide to do something for the company, you just get a quick okay and go do it. You make more mistakes that way, but they're usually small ones. The trick is you have to remember that half of the people in the company affected by what you did won't know that you did it. You have to remember to go back and tell them."

"There were several reasons why earnings declined in the fourth quarter last year," begins de Castro, starting a well-practiced speech. But . . . the list adds up to a disconcerting loss of control at a company that has always bragged about and absolutely had to have tight, even draconian controls.

PLANNING AHEAD

As organizations like Data General become larger and more complex, and as the environment becomes more dynamic and unpredictable, more formal and systematic methods are needed to ensure effective communication of relevant information among decision makers. This chapter focuses on two of these methods, budgets and management information systems, and examines their contribution to the control process. Key topics include

Budgets
The Budgeting Process
Achieving Budgetary Control
Management Information
Management Information Systems (MIS)
Making MIS Effective

Any control system requires communication of the *right* information at the *right* time and among the *right* people if it is to function effectively. People must know what is expected of them in terms of task performance; managers and other decision makers must have useful information regarding actual performance in order to make plans and take appropriate action. This information-processing component of the managerial role was initially discussed in Chapter 1. Since then it has remained a background theme as we have studied various facets of managerial decision making and problem solving. Figure 15.1 more formally reminds you of the information foundations of the managerial role.

It is now time to look further into the manager's need for information to support the process of control properly. In small organizations, such as early Data General, introduced in the chapter opener, casual methods of gathering and communicating information can allow a control system to function effectively. However, as an organization like Data General grows in size and complexity and as the external environment becomes increasingly dynamic and unpredictable,

more formal methods become necessary. As Herb Richman, Data General's cofounder, said, the manager can neither stay in touch by personally knowing everyone nor communicate what is expected by occasionally "jumping up on the lunch table and yelling." Much more sophisticated mechanisms are needed to gather relevant information and disseminate it in a manner that facilitates problem solving and decision making. Budgets and management information systems are among the available methods that assist managers to fulfill these responsibilities.

Budgets, as introduced in Chapter 4, allocate resources to activities. In one sense they are planning devices that communicate expectations to responsible personnel regarding the utilization of resources. In so doing, budgets also contribute directly to the control process. They not only establish resource-utilization objectives, but also provide a framework for analyzing results and highlighting deviations from plans.

Information systems collect, organize, store, and distribute data regarding activities occurring inside or outside the organization. Because they provide a historical data base, information sys-

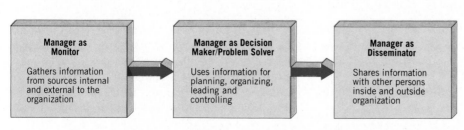

FIGURE 15.1 Information foundations of the managerial role.

tems facilitate planning by assisting in the establishment of objectives and standards, as well as providing support for the formulation of related budgets. Information systems are also essential elements in the control process. They provide the basis for documenting, disseminating, and storing performance results. Depending on their level of sophistication, they may also identify deviations from plans and even suggest what actions should be taken under the circumstances.

Budgets and information systems are interrelated in their mutual support of planning and controlling as management functions. Effective managers will know how to use each to maximum advantage; they will also know how to establish and maintain each as ingredients of a comprehensive organizational control system.

BUDGETS

Budgets are quantitative and usually financial expressions of plans; that is, they allocate resources to activities. Think what this means. As the manager of a work unit—the data-processing department of a bank, for example—an operating budget allocates to you those resources necessary to accomplish the department's day-to-day responsibilities. Without the budget you wouldn't know how much you could or should spend on people, supplies, telephone, equipment, etc.; furthermore, your supervisor wouldn't have a basis for evaluating how efficiently the department performs in terms of resource utilization.

Thus, budgets give managers the resources needed to implement plans in their areas of work responsibility. They also become a foundation for exercising management control over how well resources are utilized to accomplish those plans. As a manager, you must be comfortable working with budgets, supervising people with assigned budgets, and participating in the budgeting processes of the organization as a whole.

In any organization, you can expect to find that[2]

1. *Budgets are stated in monetary terms.* Resources are allocated in specific monetary amounts, even though they may be tied to performance targets stated in nonmonetary amounts (e.g., units sold or produced).

2. *Budgets contain an element of management commitment.* Managers agree to accept the responsibility for attaining the budgeted objectives.

3. *Budgets are based on proposals.* These proposals are usually reviewed and approved by someone in higher authority than the person or unit to which the budgets apply.

4. *Budgets can be changed only under specific conditions.* Budgets are plans that can be modified only after formal review and approval by higher authority.

Budgets and Responsibility Centers

A good budget translates into financial terms the resources assigned by the organization to a specific area of performance responsibility. If you think about it, in fact, managers are persons in organizations who are "responsible" for using resources efficiently and effectively in pursuit of task accomplishments. Look at the manager's challenge depicted in Figure 15.2. It once again acknowledges that every manager is held accountable by a higher-level supervisor for the task performance of a work unit. Now, however, our figure ties this performance responsibility to a budgetary responsibility as well. An effective manager not only gets the task acccomplished; he or she does so within the assigned budget.

From this logic emerges the concept of **responsibility centers,** work units formally charged with budgetary responsibility for carrying out various activities.[3] Any responsibility center includes a manager who is held formally accountable by higher authority for achieving performance objectives while remaining *within the budget*. Responsibility centers may be designated to correspond to any of the subcomponents of organizational structures discussed in Chapters 6 and 7. One way of viewing an organization, in fact, is as a hierarchy of responsibility centers ranging from sections, shifts, or other small units at lower levels to larger aggregations such as departments or divisions at higher levels.

An organizational control system based on the development of interlocking budgets for a hierarchy of responsibility centers is called a **responsibility accounting system.** It is common to find responsibility centers in these systems separated into one or more of the following types,

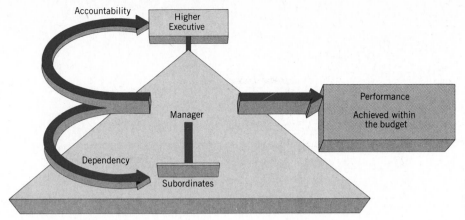

FIGURE 15.2 The manager's challenge and the budget.

depending on the nature of the resource inputs and/or performance targets being measured.

1. *In* **revenue centers** Budgets and performance targets concentrate on the product or service outputs of a responsibility center measured in monetary terms. A revenue center is typically controlled on the basis of sales of products or services.

2. *In* **cost centers or expense centers** The utilization of resource inputs is measured in monetary terms as an expense. No attempt is made to measure outputs in monetary terms. A cost or expense center is controlled on the basis of the cost of resources consumed in day-to-day operations.

3. *In* **profit centers** Budgetary responsibility is measured on the difference between the revenues and expenses of operations—that is, on the amount of profits realized. A profit center is controlled on the basis of contributions made to the overall profit of an organization.

4. *In* **investment centers** Budgetary responsibility includes the expenditure of resources for capital equipment. An investment center is controlled not only on the amount of profits generated, but also on the capital investment required to produce those profits.

Why Budgets Are Important

Budgets, as you can see, help managers plan and control. By encouraging a manager to examine activities critically and creatively relative to avail-able resources and by directing attention toward the future, budgeting facilitates planning. Budgeting also facilitates controlling. Budgets are pre-controls in that they allocate the resources considered necessary to achieve performance objectives. When they allow interim reporting of performance, such as monthly status reports, budgets also serve responsibility-center managers as steering and yes/no controls. Finally, because budgets formally commit the manager to targeted levels of resource utilization and/or performance accomplishment, they serve as benchmarks for postaction controls once actual results are in.

Budgets facilitate controlling on an organization-wide basis as well. The combined operating budget for all responsibility centers, something we will refer to shortly as a *master budget*, provides summary information on expectations held of all the managers in the organization. This helps upper-level managers coordinate the activities of many responsibility centers. A look at Figure 15.3 shows how this might work within the chain of command relating a data-processing department to other units in a bank. This figure also reminds you that a responsibility center is any work unit that operates under the control of an assigned resource budget.

Types of Budgets

Managers become involved with many types of budgets. One way to classify budgets is according to how easily they can be modified over time. We originally discussed this notion in Chapter 4.

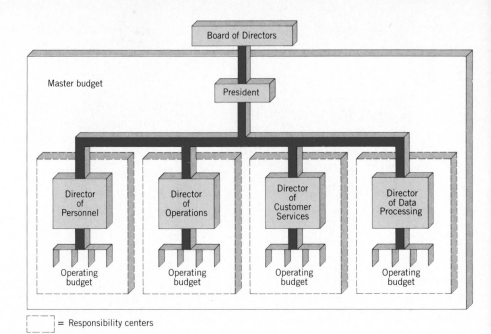

FIGURE 15.3 Multilevel budgetary control in a bank.

[ ] = Responsibility centers

Budgets that do not allow adjustment over time are referred to as **fixed or static budgets. Flexible budgets** can be adjusted over time to accommodate relevant changes in the environment.

Budgets may also be classified according to the time span covered. An important concern of most managers is the **short-range budget** covering periods of one year or less. These are of two general types. **Operating budgets** assign resources to a responsibility center on a short-term basis. **Master budgets** are comprehensive short-term budgets for the organization as a whole. They summarize the approved operating budgets for all the responsibility centers in the organization. Again, both types of short-range budgets are shown in Figure 15.3.

Of course, responsibility centers will also be involved in activities that extend beyond the time horizons of short-term budgets. These longer-term activities, both contemplated and in progress, form the basis of the organization's long-range budgetary system. Because the associated budgets consist of various projects or programs covering periods of more than one year, they are called **long-range budgets.**

Budgets also differ in the extent to which the organization distinguishes between ongoing and new programs or activities. A **zero-based budget,** as defined in Chapter 4, forces both ongoing and newly proposed programs to compete on an equal footing for available resources. Most budgets in organizations don't do this; that is, they are *not* zero-based budgets.

THE BUDGETING PROCESS

All budgeting directs attention to both performance objectives and anticipated resource requirements. The budgeting process itself involves the establishment of budgets that achieve a ''best fit'' between the needs of a work unit or project and the resource capabilities of the organization. In most organizations, this process includes formal procedures for proposing budgets initially, evaluating these proposals, arriving at final budget determinations, and eventually monitoring performance in relation to the budget. Because the demands of budgeting for the long range and short range differ somewhat, we will address them separately.

Budgeting for the Long Range

If a budget is to be used to facilitate and control the allocation of resources to long-term performance programs, the following systematic procedures should be part of the budgeting process. Budgeting for long-range programs should include[4]

1. Procedures that each organizational unit will use to generate program proposals.

2. Procedures for evaluating program proposals, including a set of objective criteria for selecting programs for implementation.

3. Procedures for monitoring the performance of programs.

4. Procedures for periodic zero-based review of ongoing programs and new program proposals.

Let's briefly review each of these requirements in turn. We'll use the Alan Company, a sporting-goods manufacturer, for purposes of illustration.

Generating Program Proposals

Table 15.1 shows four program proposals submitted to the budget committee as part of the Alan Company's long-range budgeting process. In any organization, those subunits serving as designated responsibility centers for long-term programs should submit budget proposals to a budget committee or higher level of management on a regularly scheduled basis. These proposals should describe program objectives, as well as estimated costs and benefits to the organization. While qualitative factors may be important in the eventual decision to accept or reject a program, the proposal should attempt to include as much quantifiable data as possible. This permits the comparative evaluation of alternative programs.

Evaluating Program Proposals

Most organizations are limited in the resources available for allocation to new long-term programs. They thus require decisions that select the most promising proposals for funding—that is, for the assignment of actual resource budgets. Every long-range program proposal should contain a comparison of the expected costs (cash outflows) and expected benefits (cash inflows)

Table 15.1 Long-Range Program Proposals Submitted to Budget Committee of the Alan Company

Originating Subunit	Program Proposal	Estimated Years of Value from Program	Program Objectives
Production	Replace some of the current sporting-goods manufacturing equipment with new equipment	5	To increase the efficiency of the sporting-goods manufacturing process and also to increase the quality of manufactured goods
Marketing	Advertising promotion campaign on national television networks	6	To broaden the market for sporting-goods equipment and thereby increase current and future sales
Personnel	Educational program to allow managerial employees the opportunity of returning to college for their master's degrees	20	To increase the supervisory skills of managers so that they can be more efficient and effective employees
Accounting and electronic data processing	Convert the inventory record-keeping system for sporting goods from batch processing to online, real-time processing[a]	5	To provide more timely reports to management on sporting-goods inventory activities and thereby increase the effectiveness of management's decision-making functions relating to the inventory system

Source: Stephen Moscove and Mark Simkin, *Accounting Information Systems* (New York: Wiley, 1981), p. 65. Used by permission.

[a] Under the Alan Company's present batch-processing system, day-to-day inventory transactions are accumulated (i.e., batched) at week's end and then processed by the computer in order to update the various inventory accounts. With an on-line, real-time processing system, however, each inventory transaction would be immediately processed through the accounts at the time the transactions occurs, thus providing management with continuous updated inventory account balance information.

over its projected life. The anticipated costs and benefits of each program can then be compared, and appropriate provisions made for ensuring future projections are truly comparable in terms of present value.

Monitoring Program Performance

Once a program is approved and funds are allocated to it in a budget, the activities encompassed by the approved program will be assigned to one or more responsibility centers. Any failure by these responsibility centers to fulfill budgetary expectations in terms of realized costs, revenues, and/or profits would be a signal that resources are not being used to the organization's best advantage. Short-term performance monitoring is a way of spotting such difficulties in time to make necessary adjustments. It is at this point that long-range and short-range budgetary systems are substantially interrelated.

Conducting Zero-Based Program Reviews

Approved programs may fail to meet performance expectations even when all responsibility centers carry out activities to the best of their abilities. Errors may have been made in original cost and benefit estimates; original estimates may have been based on assumptions or forecasts of environmental conditions that simply did not come to pass. In such cases the programs may not merit continuation. Thus it is important that all ongoing programs receive periodic zero-based budgetary reviews. Such reviews may result in some ongoing programs being phased out and create opportunities for new ones of greater potential benefit to be budgeted.

Budgeting for the Short Range

Budgeting for the short range is concerned with facilitating and controlling the activities of responsibility centers on an annual or even month-to-month basis. Short-range budgeting provides managers with a means for comparing actual operations with budgeted figures and reporting the results of these comparisons to higher-level managers.

The master budget is the organization's pri-mary short-term budgetary device. This comprehensive budget is often prepared through a standard cycle of events that occur on a specific timetable each year.

Preparation of the Master Budget

The preparation of a master budget is a major event in any organization. This complex process involves the efforts of many people from all levels of management. It also has a major impact on what can and does take place in an organization during any given year.

Master-budget preparation is a negotiation process in which initial proposals by responsibility-center managers are subject to revision as the different components of the budget are brought together and reviewed. All revisions are subject to the same evaluation and review. This process continues until top management is satisfied with the overall master budget plan. Figure 15.4 identifies 12 basic steps in preparing a master budget for a business firm. The following discussion highlights each step.[5]

Step 1

Forecast demand for products and/or services. Master-budget preparation begins with a forecast of sales or demand for the organization's products or services. Such demand forecasts may be developed by organizational personnel alone, or the organization may seek the assistance of outside consultants. The forecast may range from a simple estimate of product demand to complex statistical projections based on the analysis of many factors. We will examine several approaches to demand forecasting in the next chapter.

Step 2

Identify cost patterns for responsibility centers. In the second step of master budgeting, a determination is made as to where responsibility for various cost and revenue components should be assigned. Historical costs and revenues may *not* be a reliable guide for this process, and good judgment is required if it is to be properly completed. For example, if salespersons are allowed to accept rush orders and additional production costs are incurred to meet promised delivery dates, responsibility for the added costs should be as-

Forecast demand
for products and/or services

Identify cost
patterns for responsibility centers

Estimate production costs

Specify operating objectives

Develop sales budget

Develop production budget

Develop purchasing budget

Develop budgets for
responsibility centers

Formulate profit plan

Compare profit plan with
operating objectives

Formulate projected cash budget

Prepare projected statement of
financial position

FIGURE 15.4 Steps in preparation of the master budget of a business firm.

predetermination of the expected materials, labor, and general variable overhead costs of producing the product or service in question. Where standard costs do not exist, similar estimates must still be made. These estimates may be determined through engineering studies of the production/service process or from an analysis of past cost patterns using statistical procedures or personal judgments.

Step 4

Specify operating objectives. Well-managed organizations have carefully prepared strategic plans that include assessments of the external environment as well as of organizational strengths and weaknesses. Against this frame of reference, short-term operating objectives can be specified in support of the strategic plan. Table 15.2 presents operating objectives for a manufacturing company. Note that they are very specific as to what is to be accomplished. They are constrained by the current environmental and organizational factors already reflected in Steps 1, 2, and 3 of the master-budgeting process.

Step 5

Develop a sales budget. If an organization has sufficient capacity to meet forecasted demand for all of its products or services, the sales budget is easily determined by multiplying forecasted sales in units by product or service price per unit. If production capacity is insufficient to satisfy all demand, a decision must be made as to which products or services will be produced with the limited capacity. It is typical to detail sales budgets by each quarter of the budget year, as well as by the year as a whole. If desirable, sales budgets as well as other components in the master budget can be detailed for even shorter intervals.

Step 6

Develop a production budget. The sales budget allows for the required level of production to be specified for the budget period. If production capacity is insufficient to satisfy forecasted sales demand, a decision must be made as to the mix of products or services that will be produced with the limited capacity.

Step 7

Develop a purchasing budget. The production

signed to the sales department, not the production department.

Step 3

Estimate production costs. Given a forecast of demand, the costs of producing the required products and/or services must be determined. In many manufacturing organizations, standard costs are available. These standards represent a

Table 15.2 Operating Objectives for a Manufacturing Company

Profit objectives	1. Over the next 2 years achieve a net income after tax of 12% of reported stockholder's equity at the beginning of the year. 2. Over the next 2 years achieve a net income after tax of 8% on sales.
Market objectives	1. Increase total dollar sales of the company each year by 7%, and for each product at least 5%.

Cost objectives	1. Achieve the following cost targets in 1984:
	    Variable costs of production and sales
	      Small terrariums: $2.50 each
	      Large terrariums: $4.80 each
	      Fixed costs: $220,000 for the year

Inventory objectives	1. Maintain finished goods inventories at a level equal to 50% of the next quarter's production. 2. Maintain raw materials inventory of plastics at a level equal to 10% of the next quarter's usage. Maintain inventory of boxes at the same level as at the beginning of the year.
Personnel objective	1. Move toward a stable work force with no more than 10% turnover through layoffs.

Source: Don DeCoster and Eldon Schafer, *Managerial Accounting: A Decision Emphasis* (New York: Wiley, 1982, p. 499. Used by permission.

budget allows for estimates to be made of the material resources required to achieve production targets. A purchasing budget can then be specified to obtain these resources.

Step 8

Develop budgets for responsibility centers. Budgets for each responsibility center should be assigned, but only in terms of those revenues and/or costs over which the responsibility center has actual control. The manufacturing department of a business firm, for example, should be budgeted as a cost center. The budget for a marketing department in the same firm, however, should reflect a profit center having both revenue and cost responsibilities. An example is in Table 15.3.

Step 9

Formulate a profit plan. At this point in master budgeting, all individual budgets prepared in prior steps are integrated into a profit plan. This plan should reflect the impact of alternative decisions regarding pricing, product mix, and cost standards; it should also show the effect these decisions would have on overall corporate profits. A profit plan can easily be broken out by product line or major program if this is relevant for decision-making and control purposes.

Step 10

Compare profit plan with operating objectives. A profit plan summarizes the overall projected impact of various budget decisions. These anticipated results must be compared with the original operating objectives. A projected failure to achieve desired performance for any operating objective means that the objective should be revised, that changes must be made in one or more of the previously detailed budgets to bring them into conformity with the operating objective, or

Table 15.3 Revenue and Cost Components in a Marketing Department's Budget as a Profit Center

	Quarter				Total for Year
	1	2	3	4	
Budgeted sales revenue	$40,000	$80,000	$240,000	$40,000	$400,000
Less product costs	20,000	30,000	100,000	20,000	170,000
Less cost of marketing	10,000	20,000	30,000	10,000	70,000
Budgeted contribution to corporate profit	$10,000	$30,000	$110,000	$10,000	$160,000

both. This is where the process of master-budget preparation becomes one of negotiation between the managers of responsibility centers and their immediate supervisors. It may take several rounds of negotiation and change in any budget cycle before a satisfactory and final set of operating objectives, supporting budgets, and profit plans is achieved.

Step 11

Formulate a projected cash budget. Based on the profit plan, cash inflows from sales and cash outflows for purchases of raw materials, labor, other expenses, and taxes can be projected. The resulting cash budget specifies the organization's cash balance for the beginning of each budget period and the net requirements for cash during the period. This is an important form of precontrol because such projections reflect the financial viability of the organization for the budget period. A good cash budget helps managers decide whether or not projected cash positions are acceptable or if changes are required in the supporting budgets.

Step 12

Prepare a projected statement of financial position. The master budget is completed with the preparation of a projected statement of overall financial position. This involves a projected balance sheet reflecting the financial impact of all other budget components. Again, precontrol is facilitated when a process of review and revision is initiated because outcomes are less than desirable.

ACHIEVING BUDGETARY CONTROL

Planning facilitates control. Good budgets, like special types of plans, have the potential to help managers effectively fulfill their controlling responsibilities. Achieving budgetary control, however, requires budgets that are both well prepared and well utilized. Three areas of attention are of special managerial significance in this regard: (1) the use of break-even points and financial-ratio analysis, (2) organizing for budgetary control, and (3) the characteristics of effective budgetary control systems.

Break-even Point and Financial-Ratio Analysis

Budgets and the budgeting process make a variety of information available to managers. This information can be used in the control process to identify when a system is not achieving its objectives and is therefore in need of corrective action. Among the techniques managers use to do this, at the subunit and organization-wide levels, is the analysis of break-even points and various financial ratios.

A **break-even point** occurs where total revenue from sales of goods or services is just sufficient to cover total costs. The formula used to calculate a break-even point follows.

In words:

Break-even point = fixed costs divided by (selling price per unit − variable cost per unit)

In mathematical symbols:

$$BEP = \frac{FC}{SP - VC}$$

where,

BEP = break-even point
FC = fixed costs
VC = variable cost per unit
SP = selling price per unit

Break-even analysis is the study of the relationship between budgeted revenues and costs to determine how changes in each affect profit. Suppose a firm can produce 800 units of product during a year and incurs a fixed cost of $5000.[6] The variable costs of production are $5 per unit and units can be sold for $10 per unit. Break-even analysis asks, "Can this firm make a profit during the year?"

Use of break-even analysis in this example proceeds as follows. The first step is calculation of a break-even point. Using data provided in the example, it can be determined that

$$\text{Break-even point} = \frac{\$5000}{\$10 - \$5} = 1000 \text{ units}$$

This means that the firm must sell 1000 units to reach the break-even point and start making a profit.

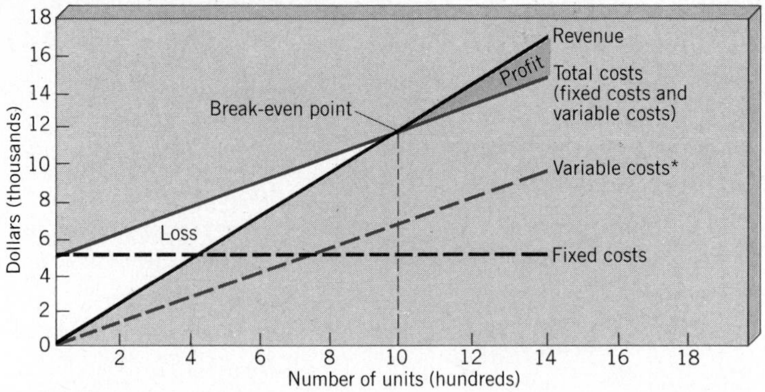

FIGURE 15.5 Break-even analysis. *Source:* Burt Scanlan and Bernard Keys, *Management and Organizational Behavior*, Second Edition (New York: Wiley, 1983), p. 487. Used by permission.

The second step in break-even analysis is to compare the break-even point with projected operations. Because this firm can only produce 800 units, it would be impossible to make a profit. The responsible manager in this case should not proceed with the product under study unless fixed and variable costs can be reduced and/or the selling price increased. It is in this way that break-even analysis facilitates precontrol and helps managers avoid situations where performance objectives will not be realized. A graphic illustration of the problem is shown in Figure 15.5. Break-even analysis is often portrayed in this fashion to facilitate decision making.

The financial projections allowed by the master-budgeting process enable calculation of a number of financial ratios that further facilitate managerial control. Table 15.4 shows common financial ratios relating to profitability, liquidity, debt financing, and operations. Such ratios can be used as benchmarks in evaluating financial performance of a responsibility center over time and in evaluating the potential results associated with various budget projections. Ratios are commonly used in combination with one another; the significance of each varies from one type of organization to the next. Although these ratios are frequently calculated and interpreted by financial staff analysts, managers should be able to interpret and understand them to take advantage of the added performance insights they provide.

Organizing for Budgetary Control

The administration of an organization's budgetary control system often involves the participation of a separate budget department staffed by specialists and headed by a budget director. In addition to the budget department, which serves as a formal staff unit, an organization may have a budget committee consisting of top management and including the chief financial officer or budget director. This committee typically reviews and either approves, disapproves, or adjusts each component in the master budget. Very large organizations have separate budget committees responsible for reviewing the budget submissions of subunits such as departments or divisions.

In addition to approving initial budgets, budget directors and/or budget committees are responsible for approving changes in budgets. Since any budget represents a commitment to action that is part of an organization-wide plan for resource utilization, budget changes should not be made purely at the discretion of the responsibility-center managers. Indeed, such alterations should be carefully analyzed and limited to situations where changing circumstances have made the original budget so unrealistic that it no longer serves a useful purpose as a planning or controlling device.

Characteristics of Effective Budgetary-Control Systems

At the conclusion of Chapter 14, we presented 10 characteristics of effective control systems. This section presents counterpart thoughts on the characteristics of effective *budgetary* control systems. In general, we can say that successful

Table 15.4 Common Financial Ratios Used in Budgetary Control

Ratios	Calculation	Implication
Profitability:		
Percent return on sales	$\dfrac{\text{Net profit after taxes}}{\text{Sales}}$	Shows the efficiency of operations in generating actual or projected profits
Percent return on investment	$\dfrac{\text{Net profit after taxes}}{\text{Total assets}}$	
Liquidity:		
Current ratio	$\dfrac{\text{Current assets}}{\text{Current liabilities}}$	Shows actual or projected financial health in terms of assets that can easily be converted into cash
Debt financing:		
Percent debt to assets	$\dfrac{\text{Total debt}}{\text{Total assets}}$	Shows extent of debt financing used by organization
Percent debt to equity	$\dfrac{\text{Total debt}}{\text{Net worth}}$	
Operations:		
Inventory turnover	$\dfrac{\text{Sales}}{\text{Average inventory}}$	Shows actual or projected efficiency of inventory utilization

budgetary controls share the following characteristics. They are

- Strategic and oriented to results.
- Based on information.
- Simple and understandable.
- Prompt and oriented to exceptions.
- Flexible.
- Based on controllable factors.
- Fair and objective.
- Positive and conducive to self-control.

Brief descriptions of budget systems that satisfy each of these criteria follow.[7]

Strategic and Oriented to Results

The budget is a quantitative presentation of the plans and expected performance of a responsibility center. This is advantageous in that the budget provides a framework for assessing performance. It can be harmful, however, if management focuses too narrowly on budgetary factors to the exclusion of nonmonetary and nonquantifiable factors. For example, an overemphasis on performance measurement in the current period may lead to behavior that is dysfunctional in the long term. This might in-

clude postponement of maintenance expenditures or utilization of cheaper but lower-quality raw materials. Managers must adopt comprehensive and longer-term perspectives on budgets if dysfunctional consequences are to be avoided and strategic directions facilitated for the organization as a whole.

Based on Information

The entire process of budget preparation should be based on information. When managers submit budgets to appropriate authority for approval, any rejections or requests for modification should be accompanied by an explanation. This information will allow the managers to make the necessary corrections in the current budget and also assist them in understanding the process better when doing future budgets. Managers, in turn, should offer information on both budget requirements and appropriate behaviors when reviewing results with subordinates. This helps the subordinate learn what is expected as well as how to go about achieving it.

Simple and Understandable

Budget systems should be no more sophisticated than necessary. Any new or improved method of

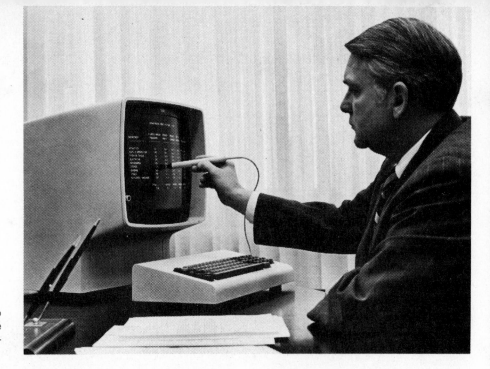

Budgets allocate resources to specific activities and provide ways of monitoring the utilization of these resources.

budgeting should be carefully tested against the existing system to determine its potential effects on the users. Changes should be made only when confidence exists that users will understand the information produced and be motivated to use it.

Prompt and Oriented to Exceptions

Managers need timely information to spot trends and take action before things are too far out of control. Budget reporting should be prompt and allow sufficient lead time for subsequent decision making and action. The system should also highlight deviations from standards and facilitate management by exception.

Flexible

Flexible budgets are usually preferable if an organization's operations and circumstances allow for them. This is especially true for organizations in uncertain environments and for those with new or complex technologies. Managers who adopt an inflexible attitude and evaluate subordinates strictly on short-term budgetary performance may reduce performance and stifle innovation.

Based on Controllable Factors

Budgets should focus on items subject to managerial control. Of course, there are circumstances where it is still desirable to address uncontrollable factors so that managers know how their responsibility centers perform in a comprehensive sense. One way to accomplish this is to separate the budget into controllable and noncontrollable segments.

Fair and Objective

Care must be exercised when specifying the expected levels of performance in a budget. Managers sometimes "pad" their budgets by overestimating costs and underestimating revenues. This is an attempt to cushion themselves against uncertainties and avoid penalties for any failure to meet budget expectations. It is likely to occur in any situation where there is extra heavy pressure to satisfy budgets, especially in the short term. Budgets that are restrictive and demanding to the point of being unfair may lead managers to conclude that meeting expectations is impossible. Frustration and reduced performance may result. A fair and objective budget, on the other hand, still requires some positive "stretching" in order to maintain a desirable performance edge.

Positive and Conducive to Self-Control

If budgets are viewed "negatively" as controls in an organization, they will fail to facilitate desired performance results. Unfortunately, budgets have a high potential for generating negative emotions. They can epitomize the impersonal side of "bureaucratic" control, and are easily identified as things that "tell" managers what they can and cannot do. Because any budget allocates resources among different responsibility centers, and because in most organizations resources are scarce, there is often competition for these resources. This can result in disdain for resulting budgets that allocate fewer resources than desired.

A number of things can be done to make the budgeting system as positive and conducive to self-control as possible. By providing performance information and helpful suggestions to operating management, a budget staff will be viewed more as a means of improving performance than as a reporting or policing function. Keeping the budgeting process truly open and allowing the participation of responsibility-center managers in all stages can further reduce budget-induced anxiety. The result should be improved effectiveness of the initial budget, increased self-control, and greater success for the entire budgetary control process.

MANAGEMENT INFORMATION

"Information enlightens"
"Information aids decision making"
"Information triggers daily activity"[8]

Granted, as the quotes suggest, information is an essential ingredient of the management process. No manager can make good decisions, solve problems, and explore opportunities without having high-quality information to begin with! Up to this point in the book, we have used the term *information* over and over—without ever giving it specific meaning. Let's change that.

Data, Information, and Information Systems

Data consist of raw facts such as figures and other symbols used to represent people, events, and concepts.[9] **Information** is data that have been made meaningful or relevant for the recipient. In the management context, information is data made useful for decision making and problem solving. A true **information system,** accordingly, collects, organizes, and distributes data in such a way that they become meaningful as information.

Figure 15.6 identifies 10 criteria or attributes of true information. It is the role of information systems to process data into information that displays these attributes.

Information Needs of Managers

Users of information systems fall into two general categories. External users are outside parties such as regulators, creditors, suppliers, and stockholders with a vested interest in the organization. Internal users are managers and other persons within the organization who require information in order to fulfill their job responsibilities. Take the case of a retail shoe store.[10]

Among external users

- Customers need to know prices and descriptions of available shoes.
- Suppliers need to know quantities of shoes ordered.
- Bankers need to know the store's financial status.
- The Internal Revenue Service needs to know the store's taxable income.

Among internal users

- Salesclerks need to know the inventory on hand.
- Employees need to know what is withheld from their paychecks.
- The store manager needs to know daily receipts and expenditures.
- The owner needs to know the store's profit position.

A good information system serves the needs of both external and internal users. Our specific concern is with needs of managers as internal users of information. Table 15.5 shows several managerial performance areas on which an information system can report. Note in all cases

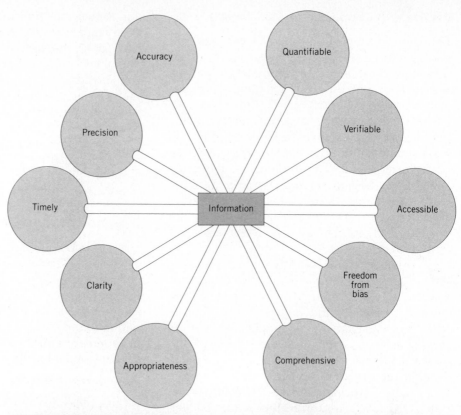

FIGURE 15.6 Basic attributes of information. *Source:* G. Anthony Gorry and Michael Scott Morton, ''A Framework for Management Information Systems,'' *Sloan Management Review* (Fall 1971), p. 6. Reprinted by permission of the Sloan Management Review Association. Copyright © 1971 by the Sloan Management Review Association. All rights reserved.

Timely—The receipt of information within the time frame it is needed by the recipient	Accessible—The ease and speed with which information can be obtained
Precision—The measurement detail used in providing information	Freedom from bias—The absence of intent to alter or modify information in order to influence recipients
Accuracy—The degree of the absence of error in information	Comprehensive—The completeness of the information
Quantifiable—The ability to state information numerically	Appropriateness—How well the information relates to a user's requirement
Verifiable—The degree of consensus arrived at among various users examining the same information	Clarity—The degree to which information is free from ambiguity

that the result is a contribution to improved managerial decision making and problem solving.

The information needs of managers vary by level of responsibility and according to the purpose to be served. Higher-level managers tend to emphasize strategic planning, while middle-level and lower-level managers focus more on operational considerations dealing with the implementation of these plans. Figure 15.7 expands this distinction to show that an information system must serve quite different needs in the two respects.

Failure to satisfy these needs can have important consequences for organizations and their managers. This point was well made in a *Business Week* commentary by Nathaniel H. Leff, a professor at Columbia University's Graduate School of Business. His ideas appeared in an article entitled ''What You Don't Know Can Hurt You.''[11] Leff points out that although effective management requires strategic planning, planning is often neglected because of a high degree of uncertainty faced by firms in today's environment. He goes on to state.[12]

Table 15.5 Examples of Performance Areas That Can Be Reported by an Information System

Performance Areas	Information Reported
Marketing	Sales
	Production margin
	New orders
	Lost customers
Innovation	New products
	New markets
Production	Capacity utilization
	Backlogs
	Backorders
	Manufacturing costs
Resources	Idle equipment
	Obsolete inventory
	Inventory turnover
	Cash flow
Personnel	Absenteeism
	Turnover
	Wage/salary schedules
Social responsibility	Employees in community programs
	Pollution-control expenditures
	Charitable contributions

Source: Adapted from John G. Busch, Jr., Felix R. Strater, and Gary Grudnitski, *Information Systems: Theory and Practice,* Third Edition (New York: Wiley, 1983), p. 69. Used by permission.

In many cases, the antidote is better information. The information that could dispel many uncertainties is often available from outside sources and from within the company. But many businesses have failed to recognize intelligence management as a top managerial job whose effectiveness will determine company performance in many areas.

A well-developed information program can provide the knowledge necessary to reduce areas of uncertainty on some topics, and on other issues, to transform uncertainty into manageable risk. Most important, an improved information system gives companies the quick response capability they need to adjust swiftly as events career from their expected trajectory.

MANAGEMENT INFORMATION SYSTEMS (MIS)

A **management information system,** or MIS, collects, organizes, and distributes data in such a way that it meets the information needs of managers. A good MIS provides information useful to managers in fulfilling their planning, organizing, leading, and controlling responsibilities. It does this through reports that get the right information into the hands of the right persons on a timely and cost-efficient basis. Increasingly, MIS uses the support of computers to fulfill this obligation. Our initial discussion will introduce you to management information systems by examining the evolution and anatomy of MIS and the growing role of computer support of MIS.

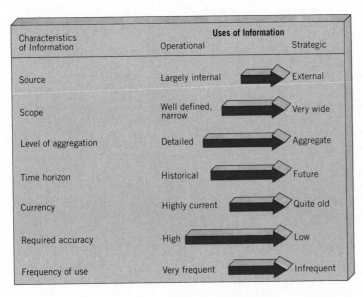

FIGURE 15.7 Information needs for different categories of management decisions. *Source:* G. Anthony Gorry and Michael Scott Morton, "A Framework for Management Information Systems," *Sloan Management Review* (Fall 1971), p. 6. Reprinted by permission of the Sloan Management Review Association. Copyright © 1971 by the Sloan Management Review Association. All rights reserved.

Evolution of MIS

Picture a small business started by an entrepreneur to produce and sell an ingenious new product.[13] Suppose, too, that the product is successful and, as the organization grows, the founder hires assistants and subordinates. A need for coordination and communication systems immediately emerges. Materials that the entrepreneur once ordered may now be ordered by a subordinate. An assistant may make customer commitments and fail to advise others in the company. Obviously, this organization needs a system for gathering and processing information in an accurate and timely way.

Now assume that there are only four managers in the organization. Each manager collects information for decision making from four gen-

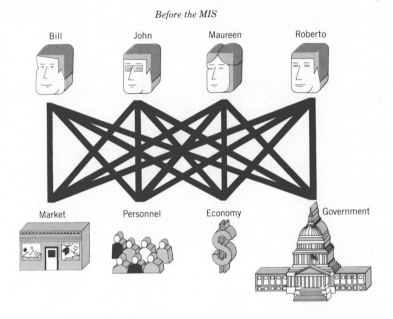

FIGURE 15.8 Information relationships before and after a formal MIS. *Source:* Alan Dalton, "How Management Information Systems Work," *Supervisory Management* (January 1976), pp. 15, 17. Used by permission.

eral information sources (market, personnel, economy, and government). This information is collected, processed (coded, stored, or filed), and retrieved for personal use or delivered to others when needed. In a sense, each manager is his or her own MIS.

This complex information network is depicted in the top half of Figure 15.8. There is a lot of overlap in the situation as each manager deals directly with each information source, as well as with every other manager. Although the information needs of the managers may be met in this situation, it is not accomplished with great efficiency. This information system will become increasingly difficult to maintain as the organization grows and more people become involved.

Figure 15.8 also shows how a formal MIS could coordinate the information-processing requirements of this organization. The new MIS allows for greater efficiency by reducing the complexity of the information networks. It also allows for specific information-processing needs to be identified, standarized, and scheduled as a matter of routine in relation to market, personnel, economy, and government considerations. This true MIS sets the stage for maximum utilization of existing resources, as well as for the further growth that inevitably will accompany the successful product.

Design of MIS

Any management information system operates as a systematic and interrelated set of procedures for gathering data and processing them into information for managerial attention. One can be developed for any aspect of an organization's functions, activities, and operations. The common anatomy of these systems is illustrated by the human-resources or personnel information system shown in Figure 15.9. In the example, personal, financial, and job data are the basic inputs. They are combined into data bases that include wage and salary, fringe benefits, and career and equal employment opportunity files. When accessed and processed, these data files provide information useful to managers who have to make a variety of personnel decisions. Managers have to make these decisions with or without good information. The MIS helps them

make decisions on a timely and efficient basis using accurate and appropriate information.

Computer Utilization in MIS

"Productivity Sold Here" reads a newspaper ad. What is this thing that proposes to enhance a manager's ability to be creative, manage time, and better organize, plan, and analyze work activities? It's the computer, of course, and success stories in computer utilization in MIS are infinite in number and variety. For example,[14]

> Savin Corporation installed in each of its warehouses a computer terminal that keeps track of every item in Savin's inventory and identifies the quantity on hand, the location and movement of stock, and the status of all orders. Employees use the computers to plan logical shipping loads, locate single items in inventory, locate customer records, and identify all the items on hand at any one storage point.

> St. Regis Paper uses computers to keep track of its timber supply—the age of its trees, their species, locations, and other inventory records essential for strategic growing and cutting.

> The R & J Ranch, in Briggs, Texas, keeps computerized breeding files, using computer programs to match the ancestry of bulls and cows for optimal breeding.

Basic Elements of Computer-Based MIS

Advanced management information systems rely on computers to process the large amounts and wide variety of data required to keep a modern organization functioning. The basic components of a computer system are shown in Figure 15.10. We won't go into unnecessary detail here, but you should recognize the following elements central to any computer-based MIS.

Hardware Equipment required to operate a computer system. This includes data-input devices such as terminals and card readers, central processing units, storage devices such as tape drives and disk units, and output devices such as printers and terminals.

Software Instructions in the form of programs that give the computer its capability to perform computational operations on data. These pro-

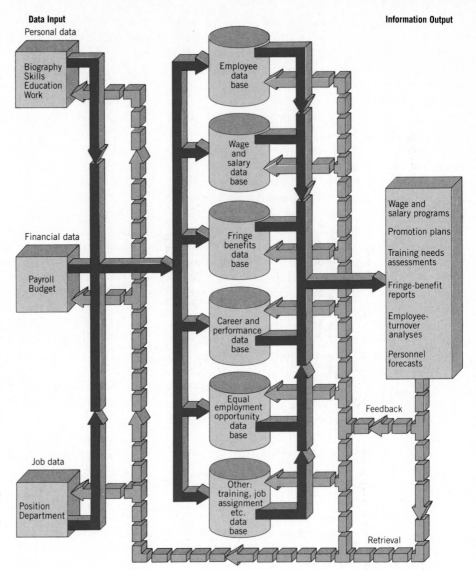

Data Input

Personal data

Biography
Skills
Education
Work

Financial data

Payroll
Budget

Job data

Position
Department

Employee
data
base

Wage
and
salary
data
base

Fringe
benefits
data
base

Career and
performance
data
base

Equal
employment
opportunity
data
base

Other:
training, job
assignment
etc.
data
base

Information Output

Wage and
salary programs

Promotion plans

Training needs
assessments

Fringe-benefit
reports

Employee-
turnover
analyses

Personnel
forecasts

Feedback

Retrieval

FIGURE 15.9 A personnel information system. *Source:* Lawrence J. Gitman and Carl McDaniel, Jr., *Business World* (New York: Wiley, 1983), p. 182. Used by permission.

grams are written in special computer languages such as FORTRAN, COBOL, and BASIC. As described in Table 15.6, one or more of these languages should be part of a modern manager's repertoire of skills and capabilities.

Central processing unit (CPU) The collection of electronic circuitry that controls the computer and allows it to store and perform a variety of computational operations on data according to the instructions of programs. A CPU will include a central memory for storing data and instructions. This memory is often supplemented by external storage on magnetic tapes and disks.

Advances in microelectronics in the 1970s and 1980s have dramatically changed the computer industry and the role of computers in the modern world. Although very large computers are still important, the **personal or microcomputer** is increasingly prominent in management. This small, self-contained computer system is designed to accomplish a variety of data-storage and information-processing tasks in a unit not much larger than a desk typewriter and portable television.

Behind every computerized MIS is a collection of people whose ideas and decisions lead to the original design of the computer-support system, as well as its continuing modification over time. Their goal is to achieve the exact configuration of hardware and software required to meet managers' needs for information. Many organizations employ specialized persons called systems analysts for this purpose. Larger and more complex organizations have entire staffs to provide this expertise to other units.

People are essential to the functioning of a computer-based MIS. The actual running of programs, utilization of magnetic tapes, production of printed outputs, etc., requires people to operate and maintain the computer equipment. People are also needed to prepare inputs, keep track of files and documentation, and deliver outputs to the appropriate users. In addition, people are needed to work with users to determine their

needs and translate these needs into a configuration of hardware, software, personnel, and procedures—that is, to design the information system. Finally, the managers who use the products of computerized information processing are an integral part of the total MIS.

Evolution of Computer-Based MIS

The first use of computers for processing business data took place in the early 1950s. The initial cost of computer hardware and the cost of developing programs and procedures to process data restricted their use to high-volume repetitive accounting transactions relating to payroll, accounts receivable, and inventories. These systems made a variety of reports available to managers for purposes of control and decision

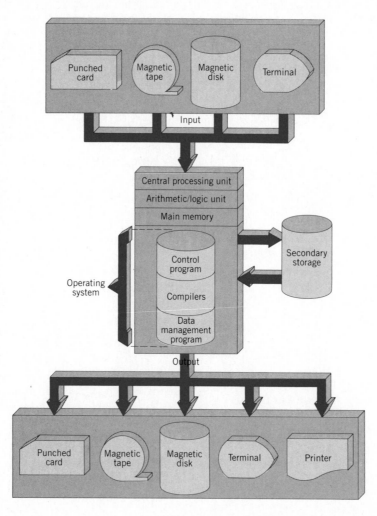

FIGURE 15.10 Components of a computer system. *Source:* Lawrence J. Gitman and Carl McDaniel, Jr., *Business World* (New York: Wiley, 1983), p. 522. Used by permission.

Table 15.6 The Major Computer Programming Languages

FORTRAN   The FORTRAN language was introduced by IBM in 1957 and is short for *FOR*mula *TRAN*slation. The language allows programmers to write processing instructions in formula format. FORTRAN was introduced primarily as a scientific language for use by scientists, mathematicians, and engineers, but it gained fairly wide acceptance for use in business.

COBOL   COBOL means *CO*mmon *B*usiness *O*riented *L*anguage and was designed for use in solving problems common to business. COBOL is a user-developed language introduced in 1960. It relies on the use of an English-like format and eliminates much of the troublesome algebraic notation on which FORTRAN is based.

BASIC   BASIC language is the standard language of time-sharing applications and the microcomputers like the Apple and the TRS-80. BASIC is an acronym for *B*eginners *A*ll-purpose *S*ymbolic *I*nstruction *C*ode and was developed at Dartmouth College for use in academic computing applications. The language is easily learned and widely used for on-line interactive computer applications.

PL/1   This language was developed by IBM for use as a general-purpose language with applications to both business and scientific programming. PL/1 is an extremely powerful and flexible language but hasn't been readily accepted by the business community since it doesn't have many advantages over COBOL.

APL   A language developed in the 1970s that combines the needs of both scientific and business applications is *A Progammer's Language* (APL). APL is a simple language with many features that make it extremely useful for terminal input and output applications. The language hasn't gained widespread use in business; it has been used mainly for its power and brevity in scientific applications.

New Languages   Two new languages that were developed in the late 1970s are Pascal and Ada. Pascal was named for the French mathematician Blaise Pascal. The language was developed for scientific applications and has gained much acceptance in computer science. Pascal has limited input/output capability but handles complex data quite easily. Pascal's suitability for business problems has yet to be evaluated. Ada[a] is a derivation of Pascal and is named for Lady Augusta Ada Lovelace, an important 19th-century computing pioneer. Ada was developed under contracts issued by the Defense Department and went into use in early 1980. Ada is more flexible in its input/output capability, and some observers feel it will gain more acceptance in business than Pascal.

Source: Lawrence J. Gitman and Carl J. McDaniel, Jr., *Business World* (New York: Wiley, 1983), p. 523. Used by permission.
[a] Ada® is a registered-trademark of the U.S. government–Ada Joint Program Office.

making. This utilization of computers continues today and is usually referred to as an **information-reporting system.**

As computer technology continued to advance over time, the ability of computerized information systems to do more than just report information increased. For certain types of decisions, it became possible to write computer programs to identify and analyze alternative solutions to standard types of problems and select the best choice from among them. Such **structured decision systems** relieve managers of the necessity to make routine or programmable decisions.

Continued developments in the high technology of computer hardware and software now allow managers to interact conversationally with the computer to request and process information in the course of solving more complex semistructured problems. The newer **decision-support systems** range from providing information-retrieval capabilities to users, to providing them with access to sophisticated analytical, statistical, and mathematical software.

Overall, improved computer access to large data banks and information-processing routines is having a major impact on management control. Top management in particular is able to stay much better informed about lower-level operations. The result can be enhanced decision making and control. But, as with any control system, it mustbe well used. Improved control is sometimes achieved with other negative ramifications, as the following example from a *Wall Street Journal* article shows.[15]

Managers at Thermo Electron Corporation, Banco Internacional de Colombia, and Northwest Industries Inc. strongly suspect that at their companies, the boss is already pecking away at a computer terminal to monitor the business and, they fear, *to check up on them.* Depending on their boss's style, they are beneficiaries or victims of a new wrinkle in computer technology—executive information systems.

MAKING MIS EFFECTIVE

The power of computer-supported information systems exemplifies the ultimate extension of MIS in organizations. It also highlights the growing responsibility of all levels of management to design and use these systems to the maximum advantage and minimum disadvantage of everyone concerned. This requires an awareness of not only basic MIS ingredients and computer technology, but also their organizational and behavioral implications. Remember, a computer-based MIS should effectively integrate computers, organizations and people.

The purpose of any MIS is to facilitate the accomplishment of organizational objectives through improved problem solving and decision making. The success of MIS in this regard is not, however, guaranteed. To achieve the desired impact, any MIS must be perceived as useful by the persons it is designed to assist. It must be *used* in order for its benefits to be realized. In particular, a number of organizational and behavioral factors can lead to MIS failures, sometimes even before the systems are fully implemented.

Organizational Factors in MIS Success[16]

Prior to initiating a project to develop or enhance an existing MIS application, a manager should evaluate its chances of success. Three categories of organizational factors should be considered in this regard—uncontrollable, partially controllable, and controllable. The status of these factors can influence decisions relating to the implementation and/or design of MIS.

Uncontrollable Factors

Certain organizational factors that affect the success of MIS are beyond short-term control. These include organizational size and structure, as well as factors in the external environment. The time required to modify such factors is simply too long to be of any immediate assistance to an MIS currently under consideration. But if any of these factors are unfavorable, the chances of developing and maintaining a successful MIS are significantly reduced.

In the past, the chances of developing a

The modern manager must be capable of and comfortable working with information processed via computers.

sophisticated computerized information system were greater in larger organizations. These organizations usually have a larger pool of resources to work with and therefore are better able to purchase advanced technologies and attempt riskier projects. They also tend to have more specialized systems staffs to develop and oversee the projects. Smaller organizations, with the absence of these factors, found MIS development more difficult. The advent of microcomputers, however, has changed this. Hardware and software for good basic computerized information systems are now available at reasonable cost.

Information systems, like control systems in general, must conform to the organization structure. Decentralized organizations can find it difficult to develop and implement centralized MIS applications. Divisions and subunits are likely to exercise their independence and develop systems that conform to their unique needs. This is not bad in and of itself, as long as everyone's needs are well served. Simply forcing all information flows through a central organizational unit with little attention to subunit differences could make the centralized information system almost useless.

Organizations in dynamic and uncertain environments can also find it difficult to develop successful MIS. Careful MIS development requires an understanding of the nature of the decisions to be supported and the environment in which those decisions are being made. This can

NEWSLINE 15.1

DON'T EXPECT TOO MUCH FROM YOUR COMPUTER SYSTEM

In a world appropriately filled with glowing promises for computers, managers are well advised to reflect on what computers are not. For more than 20 years, businesses ranging from banking to bookmaking have embraced computer systems with a level of hope and enthusiasm normally reserved for riskfree, high-profit investments.

In the sobering light of actual use, some firms have realized many or all of their high expectations, but others have discovered that computer systems are hardly riskfree and certainly are not a guarantee of higher profits. A computer system represents an expensive, high-technology capital investment, and such investments often promise high returns only for high risk. At a minimum, such investments demand thoughtful and continuing attention from management.

A computer system, no matter how successfully applied to a problem, does not guarantee improvement. For example, a computerized inventory system with poor ordering rules will reorder the wrong quantities of the wrong parts faster and more consistently than its manual counterpart. The computer's outstanding attributes of speed, large memory, consistency, and the ability to follow complex logical instructions are of value only to the extent that they are applied within a good management process. Computers are a complement to, not a substitute for, careful management.

Source: Excerpted from Richard L. Van Horn, "Don't Expect Too Much From Your Computer System," *Wall Street Journal* (October 25, 1982), p. 24. Reprinted by permission of the *Wall Street Journal*. Copyright © 1982 Dow Jones & Company, Inc. All rights reserved.

be difficult in situations where information-processing demands change rapidly.

Partially Controllable Factors

Some factors important to the development of MIS cannot be completely controlled, but are subject to some shorter-term managerial influence. Partially controllable factors include the availability of supporting resources, both financial and personnel, and human expectations relating to the MIS itself.

Sufficient resources must be allocated to develop and support an MIS properly. Systems development and maintenance can be costly in terms of supporting computer technology, specialized staff or consultants, and the commitment of employee time to participate in the entire in-formation-processing cycle. They can be costly, too, in the time required for responsible MIS personnel to understand thoroughly the organizational unit the system is designed to serve and to understand how this unit fits into the entire organization.

Closely related is the set of expectations regarding the role, contributions, and limitations of MIS in the organization. Expectations must be realistic among all personnel who will use and/or be affected by the system. Users must be realistic in their expectations as to what the MIS can do. Specialized MIS personnel must be careful not to promise more than can be delivered and see to it that they understand the limitations of the available system. *Newsline 15.1* suggests that this is especially true in respect to the computer component of an information system.

Some people feel threatened by computers; others expect them to be able to do everything. Both viewpoints are incorrect.

Fully Controllable Factors

Fully controllable factors can be changed to meet the needs of an MIS and its users. Key among them are the organization of the MIS support function and the manner through which MIS utilization is encouraged and monitored over time.

It is often desirable for an organization to employ persons with specialized MIS expertise, and to group them together in an information-systems department. Ideally, this department should be an independent group having no formal identification with any specific functional area, but being available to service the information-processing needs of all others. An independent systems department is less likely to show bias toward any one function or subunit and more likely to be equitable in its treatment of the needs of all functional departments. The executive in charge of the MIS unit should be at the highest management level possible, ideally equivalent to a vice-presidential appointment. A typical MIS department is shown in Figure 15.11,

which also shows the variety of career opportunities available within this field of expertise.

Figure 15.11 includes a steering committee that advises the Manager of Information Systems. This is a group of higher-level managers from throughout the organization who are charged with ensuring that the direction and plans for MIS development are consistent with the overall direction and needs of the organization. Such a group can help sponsor MIS and encourage its complete utilization, as well as maintain some user control over the information-systems group via policies, periodic reviews, and decisions regarding resource allocations.

Behavioral Factors in MIS Success

A well-designed MIS may fail in one organization when it could easily succeed in another. The difference often traces to behavioral factors. People who view an MIS favorably can make it work, even if design flaws exist. By contrast, even the most sophisticated and state-of-the-art MIS will fail if people within the organization don't use it.

Different groups in organizations are affected differently by an MIS. Operating personnel become involved as the MIS places substantial responsibility on them to provide accurate

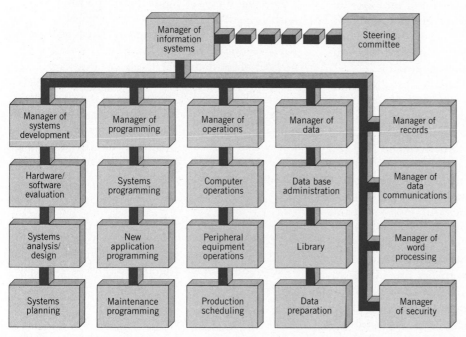

FIGURE 15.11 A management-information systems department. *Source:* John G. Busch, Jr., Felix R. Strater, and Gary Grudnitski, *Information Systems: Theory and Practice* (New York: Wiley, 1983), p. 105. Used by permission.

Table 15.7 Matching Managers' Needs with MIS Capabilities

Management Level	Managerial Responsibilities	Information Needed from MIS	How MIS Information Is Used
Top management	Enhance performance, growth, accumulation, and use of resources; survival of total organization	Environmental data and trends, forecasts, summary reports of operations, exception reports on problems	Set organizational objectives, policies, constraints, make decisions on strategic plans and control of total organization
Middle management	Allocate resources to assigned tasks, establish operating plans, control operations	Summaries and exception reports on operating results; relevant actions and decisions of other middle managers	Set operating plans and policies, control procedures, make exception reports, operating summaries, on resource allocations, actions and decisions related to other middle managers
Lower management	Produce goods or services within budgets, estimate resource requirements, move and store materials	Summary reports of transactions, detailed reports of problems, operating plans and policies, control procedures, actions and decisions of related managers	Create exception and progress reports, identify resource needs, make work schedules

Source: Adapted from Robert G. Murdick, "MIS for MBO," *Journal of Systems Management* (March 1977), pp. 34–40. Used with permission of Robert G. Murdick.

and timely data inputs. This aspect of their jobs can become much more structured and less tolerant of deviation with the advent of a new MIS. If the systems-development group fails to consider the impact of this additional burden, outright resistance to the system is possible.

Managers at all levels are directly affected by any information system. In many ways this group is the focus of the MIS; they are the "users" of a system supposedly designed to meet their needs. An ideal match between an MIS and the needs of top, middle, and lower-level managers is summarized in Table 15.7. In spite of the potential benefits suggested by this table, managers also resist MIS at times. Among the reasons for this is that any MIS changes life for the manager, but not always for the better.[17] An MIS, for example, makes more information available to both the manager and his or her immediate supervisor. Some of this information may not be favorable. An MIS can increase the visibility of the *bad* as well as good decisions. Other sources

of potential discomfort include the fact that an MIS usually allows managers more time to deal with less structured problems. This is not necessarily a plus if the manager must learn new ways of doing things and knows he or she will be held accountable for them in return.

As we have already said, a successful MIS is one that is used. In many cases, minor changes in the design and/or procedures for using an MIS will significantly enhance the perceived compatibility and value of a system for the user. It is always beneficial to have favorable user attitudes. Things to remember include the following.

1. An MIS of higher technical quality produces more favorable user attitudes.

2. Strong management support and participation in MIS development results in more favorable attitudes toward the system and system support staff.

3. User involvement in the design and operation of an MIS results in more favorable attitudes

toward both the MIS system and system support staff.

Common MIS Mistakes

Information systems of many types will be encountered in your career. Sometimes you may be the designer of a new system and you may serve on an MIS steering committee, but always you will be a *user*. The task is to use any MIS well to facilitate your success in all aspects of the management process—and to enhance organizational productivity as a result. As you look forward to this challenge, keep the following six common MIS mistakes in mind. Any MIS is destined to fail if the designers and users act under the following assumptions.[18]

Mistake 1: *Assume more information is always better.* It is common to assume that managers suffer a lack of relevant information. While many managers lack a good deal of information that they should have, they may suffer even more from an overabundance of irrelevant information. Most managers receive much more data (not necessarily "information") than they can possibly absorb even if they spend all of their time trying to do so.

Mistake 2: *Assume managers need all the information they want.* MIS designers typically determine what information is needed by asking managers what they would like to have. This assumes managers know what information they need. But the manager who does not understand a phenomenon is prone to play it safe and, with respect to information, want "everything." The MIS designer, with even less understanding of the phenomenon, can easily increase what is already an overload of irrelevant information by trying to provide even more of everything.

Mistake 3: *Assume that if managers are given all the information they need, their decision making will improve.* It is frequently assumed that managers having the information they need will have no problem using it effectively. This is not necessarily true.

Mistake 4: *Assume more communication means better performance.* An MIS usually provides managers with better current information about what other managers and their departments and divisions are doing. Underlying this provision is the belief that better interdepartmental communication enables managers to coordinate their decisions more effectively and hence improves the organization's overall performance. This is not necessarily so.

Mistake 5: *Assume managers do not have to understand how an MIS works to use it well.* MIS designers try to make the systems as accessible as possible for managers and to assure them that they need to know nothing about it. It is easy for managers to stay ignorant. This leaves them unable to evaluate the MIS as a whole and with a tendency to delegate much of the control process to the system's designers and operators. The MIS users should always be trained to evaluate and control it, instead of the MIS controlling its users.

Mistake 6: *Assume the computer can do everything.* High technology has brought computers directly into the day-to-day world of management. Micro- or personal computers are lending technical sophistication to management and information systems in situations where the costs of such advances were prohibitive until just recently. Along with the growing role of the computer in MIS is the tendency to assume that it can do everything. This is not true; managerial judgment is still a required element in any computer-based information system. Furthermore, interpersonal information sources such as facial expression, gesture, and tone of voice provide additional cues that may give further insight into a complicated problem. Information needs within organizations are much broader than what computers alone can supply.[19]

SUMMARY

Every manager has to deal with budgets and information systems. This chapter has presented an overview of each with particular emphasis on its role in the control process.

A budget both commits resources to plans and establishes the framework through which managers are held accountable for using these resources well for task accomplishment. The responsibility-center concept formalizes this budgetary responsibility for managers at all levels and in all types of subunits within organizations. Responsibility centers can be defined on a revenue, cost/expense, profit, or investment basis. In each case the related budgets tend to encourage activities that improve planning and make control more effective.

Most managers work with short-range operating budgets covering periods of a year or less. The master budget of an organization integrates all operating budgets for the total system. When preparing budgets for the long and short range, careful consideration must be given to the process through which programs or activities are proposed, evaluated, and eventually approved or disapproved as worthy of receiving resource allocations. Ultimately, budgetary control is facilitated by such techniques as break-even point and financial-ratio analysis, proper organization for budget preparation, and adherence to basic characteristics of successful budget systems.

Information, or data made meaningful, is the foundation for all managerial decision making, problem solving, and action. Management information systems (MIS) are designed to collect, organize, and distribute data in such a way that managers' information needs are met.

Computer utilization in MIS includes a variety of hardware and software packages for gathering, storing, and processing data. The personal or microcomputer is increasingly prominent in management as a component in MIS. As the role of computers has evolved over time, the MIS has grown into information-reporting systems, structured decision systems, and decision-support systems. Among the latter, a manager interacts with the computer in a manner that results in advanced analytical problem solving.

Both budgets and MIS require the support of people if they are to serve as effective controls. In each case poor design and/or implementation can discourage, frustrate, and even alienate the persons required to work with the system. Good managers avoid common mistakes in budgetary and MIS design and utilization. User participation in the developmental stage is an essential element in both efforts.

As with all other managerial tools and techniques, MIS can facilitate the management process. But it cannot guarantee your success. Effective managers know how to take maximum advantage of MIS while remaining sensitive to the additional demands and needs of other organizational and behavioral factors in the work setting.

THINKING THROUGH THE ISSUES

1. Identify four types of responsibility centers. Define and give an example of each.

2. Differentiate between fixed and flexible budgets. Which is better? Explain.

3. How does zero-based budgeting differ from flexible budgeting?

4. What is the role of the budget department in the budgetary process?

5. "Budgets represent an implicit contract between the manager of a responsibility center and his or her supervisor. They are agreements to achieve a certain level of performance with the agreed-upon level of resources. A manager's performance should therefore be evaluated solely on his or her ability to meet budgeted figures. Nothing else should be considered." Critically discuss this statement and indicate why you agree or disagree with it.

6. What is the difference between data and information?

7. What is the difference between an information system and a "management" information system?

8. What are the basic elements of a computer-based information system? Briefly describe the function performed by each component.

9. How do structured-decision systems differ from information-reporting systems? . . . from decision-support systems?

10. Computer-based information systems provide useful information to assist managers in solving problems and making better decisions. Assuming this is true, why would managers resist the development and implementation of a new MIS?

THE MANAGER'S VOCABULARY

Break-even analysis
Break-even point
Budget
Central processing unit
Cost center
Data
Decision-support system
Expense center
Fixed or static budget

Flexible budget
Hardware (computer)
Information
Information reporting
system
Information system
Investment center
Long-range budget
Management

information system
Master budget
Operating budget
Personal or
microcomputer
Profit center
Responsibility
accounting system
Responsibility center

Revenue center
Short-range budget
Software (computer)
Structured-decision
system
Zero-based budget

CAREER PERSPECTIVE: COMPUTER ANXIETY HITS MIDDLE MANAGEMENT[20]

Are you one of those hapless people who doesn't know a "byte" from a "baud"? Do you overhear conversations about "apples" and "boards" and immediately think of fruit and wood?

You're not alone. According to Booz, Allen & Hamilton Inc., 90 percent of the roughly 10 million executives and professional managers in the United States today are computer illiterates. Despite the flurry of media attention, computer users are a decided minority. But not for long. As numerous magazine articles pointed out, the product managers of 1990 are sitting in high schools today with Apple Computers beside them.

In their rush to meet the future, computer proponents are pressuring marketing and financial managers to use computers *now*. "You've got a whole generation of middle managers who are being squeezed underneath by people who expect to use the technology to give them an edge," Peter Keen, a Cambridge, Massachusetts, computer consultant, says.

According to consultants and managers, themselves, middle-management reluctance to embrace computers often springs from one source: fear. Computers scare the daylights out of people unfamiliar with them. The technology is foreign. The language is often incomprehensible.

Questions

1. To what extent are you familiar with the operations of computers?
2. Do you have "computer anxiety"? If so, what are its implications for you now and in the future?
3. What steps are you taking or are you prepared to take to ensure that your computer expertise will be sufficient during your managerial career?

The following seven budget games have been observed in various organizations.

The Benevolent King Game In this game the budget is developed by top management (sometimes the controller prepares it for top management) and is then communicated down the line.

The Human Relations Game "Participative decision making" is used as the insightful gimmick that forms the basis of this game. Before budgets are communicated down the line, the employees down the line are requested to submit their estimates of their performance or costs. Other than this participation, the process is essentially the same as the Benevolent King approach. The budgets are still developed and controlled by top management.

The Condescending Game In the Condescending Game, top management achieves a feeling of superiority. Individuals down the line are requested to submit performance or cost estimates, or both. These estimates are then changed and communicated back to the originators with no explanation for the changes. A key strategic factor in this process is to withhold relevant information from those submitting the estimates. This guarantees a disparity between the estimates received and the estimates returned. Several minor tactics can accentuate the feelings of superiority: correct the estimates with a red felt-tip pen, make belittling comments in the margin, and distribute both the original and changed estimates to everyone.

The Guessing Game Someone in top management sets a targeted goal for profit or return on assets. Lower-level managers are then requested to submit their budget estimates; they must guess what would be an acceptable budget recommendation. Unless the submitted estimates are consistent with the targeted goals, they are returned with a simple explanation: "unacceptable—too low" (or "too high—resubmit"). A key factor in the Guessing Game is to withhold information regarding the exact nature of the organization's objectives and acceptable performance levels.

The Ratchet-Encourager Game This is similar to the Guessing Game with one major difference. In this approach, top management does not have a predetermined goal. Lower-level managers are requested to submit an estimate of their costs, performance, or both; regardless of what they submit, it is returned to them with an inspiring note that concludes by asking them to cut their cost and increase their performance. To increase their impact, some notes include several emotional appeals for prosperity, greatness, or the good of the organization. The most effective notes, threaten job security.

The Gallows Game The basic principle of this game is to give subordinates enough rope to hang themselves. This is done by encouraging greater participation in developing the budget than in the other games. All needed information is provided, and subordinates are usually given the freedom to plan, coordinate, and implement the budget on a collective basis. At the end of the period, the budget becomes the gallows to hang substandard performers.

The Dedicated Servant Game The distinction between the Dedicated Servant and the Gallows Games is subtle but significant. Both provide extensive opportunity for participation in the preparation and other aspects of the budgeting process. The difference is that the "hanging" is replaced with nothing—no reward and no punishment. As implied in the name of the game, the participants are required to assume responsibility for planning, organizing, directing, and controlling their own work. In return for accepting this added responsibility and performing the enlarged job, the "dedicated servants" get nothing. They may be told at the outset that their extra efforts will not be rewarded, but the game is more interesting if they are not told.

Questions

1. What dysfunctional behavior would you expect on the part of lower-level managers as a result of each of these budget games?
2. How does the "ideal" budgeting process differ from circumstances described in the games? Explain the significance of the differences.

CLASS EXERCISE: PRIVACY—VICTIM OF COMPUTERIZED PROGRESS?[22]

Not long ago, computers were so huge and costly that only a few of the richest public and private agencies could afford them. Now nearly anyone can. Legally or illegally, almost everybody can also gain access to large computer data banks. We must act quickly, some people insist, to make laws preventing government and private enterprise from gaining too much access to our private lives.

Others believe that information gathering and sharing is vital to our progress and security. They say we must be willing to give up some privacy to improve the quality of our life and live in relative peace and harmony.

1. Take a look at two spheres of activity, education and law enforcement. Each illustrates the dilemma that modern techniques of computerized data storage create.

    Education In a school system of any size, a computer offers great savings in time and money. Student profiles and academic records are easily stored in computers. So, too, are test results. Computerization provides swift access to these records when needed to chart student progress and map out future programs. Computerized records also aid educational research by making it easy to identify student populations with certain common characteristics. Research of this sort is the basis for developing new and better ways to teach.

    Yet as more and more data on students are stored, students' rights—privacy and individuality as well as to learn—are more gravely endangered. The results of achievement, attitudinal, psychological, and personality tests may be made available without their knowledge to potential employers, government officers, or researchers. Mistakes they've made, academic failures they've overcome, and ideas, activities, and attitudes they've long since given up may be attributed to them for the rest of their lives.

    Law Enforcement Through computers, police and other security officers have instant access to arrest and conviction records, state crime reports, and auto-registration information. In hundreds of ways, law-enforcement and intelligence officials use computers to give us the best possible protection. To keep their files confidential, they establish codes for access to specific types of information.

    Still, there's growing concern that these massive files will be subject to misuse. Private enterprises are pressuring for access to them. They want to use them in hiring decisions and in resolving more run-of-the-mill problems such as plant parking-lot infractions.

2. What is your opinion on all this? Do you agree or disagree with the viewpoint that the sophisticated information storage and retrieval capabilities of today's computers can easily invade individual privacy? Why or why not?

3. Share your opinions about the prior questions with a nearby classmate. Discuss and think about any differences of opinion that may exist. Await further class discussion.

REFERENCES

[1] Excerpted from Harold Seneker, "Data General—Life in the Fast Lane," *Forbes* (March 3, 1980), pp. 72–74. Reprinted by permission of *Forbes Magazine* from the March 3, 1980, issue.

[2] Robert Anthony and John Dearden, *Management Control Systems*, Fourth Edition (Homewood, Ill.: Richard D. Irwin, 1980), pp. 368–369.

[3] Ibid.

[4] Stephen Moscove and Mark Simkin, *Accounting Information Systems* (New York: Wiley, 1981), p. 64.

[5] See Don T. DeCoster and Eldon L. Schafer, *Management Accounting: A Decision Emphasis*, Third Edition (New York: Wiley, 1982), pp. 489–514.

[6] This example and subsequent discussion are from Burt Scanlan and Bernard Keys, *Management & Organizational Behavior*, Second Edition (New York: Wiley, 1983), p. 487.

[7] See, for example, Henry Tosi, "The Human Effects of Managerial Budgeting Systems," in J. L. Livingston (ed.), *Managerial Accounting: The Behavioral Foundations* (Columbus, Ohio: Grid, 1975); V. F. Ridgeway, "Dysfunctional Consequences of Performance Measurement," *Administrative Science Quarterly* (September 1956), pp. 240–247; Anthony Hopwood, "Empirical Study of the Role of Accounting Data in Performance Evaluation," *Empirical Research in Accounting—Selected Studies* (1972), Supplement to the *Journal of Accounting Research*, pp. 166–174.

[8] Joseph W. Wilkinson, *Accounting and Information Systems* (New York: Wiley, 1982), p. 3.

[9] John G. Busch, Jr., Felix R. Strater, and Gary Gundnitski, *Information Systems: Theory and Practice*, Third Edition (New York: Wiley, 1983), p. 4.

[10] Wilkinson, op. cit., p. 7.

[11] Nathaniel H. Leff, "What You Don't Know Can Hurt You," *Business Week* (March 14, 1983), p. 12. Reprinted from the March 14, 1983, issue of *Business Week* by special permission of the publisher, © 1983 by McGraw-Hill, Inc., New York, NY 10020. All rights reserved.

[12] Ibid. Used by permission.

[13] This example is adapted from Scanlan and Keys, op. cit. It originally appeared in Alan Dalton, "How Management Information Systems Work," *Supervisory Management* (January 1976), p. 15.

[14] From Henry Weil, "Hooked on Computers," *Air Illinois*, Vol. 26 (October 1982), p. 90. Used by permission.

[15] Mary Bralove, "Some Chief Executives Bypass, and Irk, Staffs in Getting Information," *Wall Street Journal* (January 12, 1983), p. 1. Emphasis added.

[16] See P. Ein-Dor and E. Segev, "Organizational Context and the Success of Information Systems," *Management Science* (June 1978), pp. 1064–1077.

[17] Chris Argyris, "Management Information Sysems: The Challenge to Rationality and Emotionality," *Management Science* (February 1971). pp. 275–292.

[18] Adapted in part from Russell L. Ackoff, "Management Misinformation Systems," *Management Science* (December 1967), pp. 147–156. Used by permission.

[19] Richard L. Daft, *Organization Theory and Design* (St. Paul, Minn.: West Publishing, 1983), p. 329.

[20] Excerpted from Mary Bralove, "Computer Anxiety Hits Middle Management," *Wall Street Journal* (March 7, 1983), p. 20. Reprinted by permission of the *Wall Street Journal*. Copyright © 1983 Dow Jones & Company, Inc. All rights reserved.

[21] Adapted from J. Owen Cherrington, and David J. Cherrington, "Budget Games for Fun and Frustration," *Management Accounting* (January 1976), pp. 28–32. Used by permission.

[22] Adapted from Lawrence J. Gitman and Carl McDaniel, Jr., *Business World* (New York: Wiley, 1983), p. 518. Used by permission.

16

PRODUCTION
AND OPERATIONS
CONTROL

A STAR IS BORN ON THE FACTORY FLOOR

Armed with an MBA from Columbia, Peter Smith landed a prestigious job in General Signal's mergers and acquisitions department, where he worked closely with the chairman.[1] But when he heard that the company was creating a post as director of manufacturing services, he volunteered and got the job. "My peers were aghast," he says.

Smith had his reasons: "There's enormous excitement in manufacturing. You transform raw materials into something of value and deal with a spectrum of people you'd never come across."

In 1977 Smith was appointed manufacturing vice-president of Regina, a $50-million unit that makes floor-care appliances. An erratic performer, the operation had gone through three vice-presidents in five years. Smith found the production floor grueling. "The first thing I noticed was the extraordinary pace," he says. "We worked at a run all day. Manufacturing is unlike any other discipline in the need for immediate decisions."

At age 29, Smith was General Signal's youngest vice-president and the company's first MBA assigned to manufacturing. The union wanted to test his style. "I had only been there a few weeks when a worker struck a supervisor. This was punishable by a one-day suspension or termination. I terminated her on the spot. We had a severe lack of shop-floor discipline."

Smith believes most manufacturing problems arise when management doesn't talk with the workers. "People will flood you with ideas if you let them." He cites his experience with a switch-assembly operation where workers had to twist together five pairs of wires, cap them with nuts, and stuff them into a vacuum-cleaner handle. "We had quality problems with the nuts falling off, and the workers had to wear Band-Aids on their fingers. One suggested we use a switch with push-in connections instead, but the materials cost would double. I calculated how much more productivity we would need to offset the cost and asked the union to help me prove we could get it by using the new switch." The change cut the rejection rate, formerly 20 percent, to less than 1 percent. In three years at Regina, Smith reduced the cost of assembling a vacuum cleaner from $1.56 to $0.88 and generated savings of $12 million.

Smith hasn't done badly for himself in manufacturing. His income has more than quintupled in six years; at 33 he is the company's youngest president and is besieged with job offers.

PLANNING AHEAD

As the chapter opener indicates, how well manufacturing operations are managed often spells the difference between corporate profit or loss. The same is true regarding the management of service operations—banks, for example. In both cases managers are concerned with the production and operations processes through which goods or services are produced. This chapter introduces the key concepts and techniques of production/operations management, and examines how they facilitate managerial control. Major topics include:

Production/Operations Management (P/OM)
Making Forecasts
Establishing Schedules
Controlling Inventories
Controlling Quality
Production and Operations Control in a Managerial Perspective

The chapter opener introduces the central thrust of **production/operations management** (P/OM), a branch of management theory that studies how organizations transform resource inputs (sometimes called the factors of production) into product and service outputs. Whether an organization manufactures a product or provides a service, it must be concerned with the production/operations process that takes raw materials, combines them with people and equipment, and finally produces goods or services. At the Norge Company, for example, people and machines cut, shape, and assemble sheets of steel, nuts, bolts, wire, and other materials into washing machines and dryers as finished products. In a local health clinic, the raw materials are information, medicines, paper forms, and other equipment and supplies. Once again, though, people work with these inputs to provide health-care services to the clinic's clients. Figure 16.1 diagrams the production/operations process with which P/OM is concerned in the setting of a bus line, manufacturing firm, and hospital.

In organizations of all types, production and operations activities must be well managed to ensure that human and material resources are combined in the right amount and at the right time to create a good or service of acceptable quality and in a manner that is as economical as possible. Think for a moment what this means. Abbott Laboratories is a producer of health-care products having sales of $50 million. The company sells 750 different products and employs 650 people at three plants. The production process involves obtaining the raw materials, either liquid or dry, mixing them, filling containers, sterilizing the containers, and packaging. The 2000 customers are primarily hospitals who expect one-day delivery. Imagine trying to coordinate all these activities and still satisfy the one-day delivery time.

To accomplish this challenge, managers at Abbott Labs use a variety of modern production and operations planning and control techniques. These techniques facilitate decision making and problem solving in the various areas critical to planning and controlling the production/operations process. In the remainder of this chapter, you will learn more about these techniques and how they are used either by manufacturing companies like Abbott Labs or by service organizations like the hospitals who buy Abbott's products.

PRODUCTION/OPERATIONS MANAGEMENT (P/OM)

It is important to understand that the elements of production/operations management apply to both industrial and nonindustrial organizations.

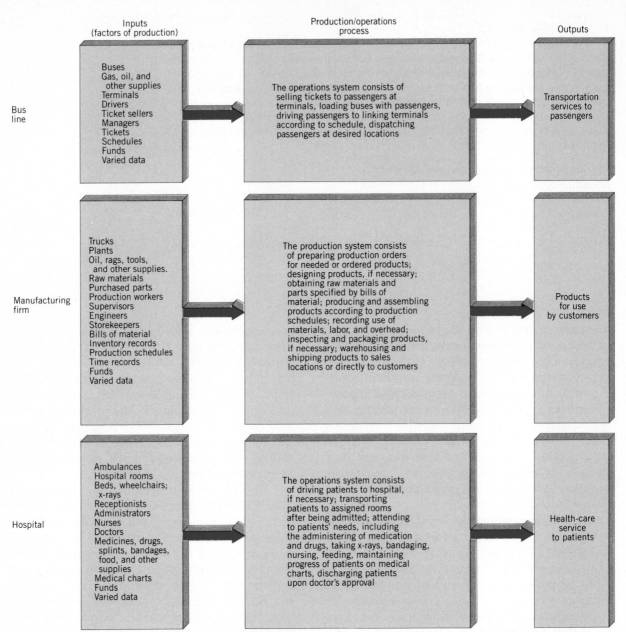

Inputs (factors of production)	Production/operations process	Outputs

Bus line

Buses
Gas, oil, and other supplies
Terminals
Drivers
Ticket sellers
Managers
Tickets
Schedules
Funds
Varied data

The operations system consists of selling tickets to passengers at terminals, loading buses with passengers, driving passengers to linking terminals according to schedule, dispatching passengers at desired locations

Transportation services to passengers

Manufacturing firm

Trucks
Plants
Oil, rags, tools, and other supplies.
Raw materials
Purchased parts
Production workers
Supervisors
Engineers
Storekeepers
Bills of material
Inventory records
Production schedules
Time records
Funds
Varied data

The production system consists of preparing production orders for needed or ordered products; designing products, if necessary; obtaining raw materials and parts specified by bills of material; producing and assembling products according to production schedules; recording use of materials, labor, and overhead; inspecting and packaging products, if necessary; warehousing and shipping products to sales locations or directly to customers

Products for use by customers

Hospital

Ambulances
Hospital rooms
Beds, wheelchairs; x-rays
Receptionists
Administrators
Nurses
Doctors
Medicines, drugs, splints, bandages, food, and other supplies
Medical charts
Funds
Varied data

The operations system consists of driving patients to hospital, if necessary; transporting patients to assigned rooms after being admitted; attending to patients' needs, including the administering of medication and drugs, taking x-rays, bandaging, nursing, feeding, maintaining progress of patients on medical charts, discharging patients upon doctor's approval

Health-care service to patients

FIGURE 16.1 The production/operations process in three types of organizations. *Source:* Joseph W. Wilkinson, *Accounting and Information Systems* (New York: Wiley, 1982), p. 40. Used by permission.

It is just as important for banks, public agencies, hospitals, stores, and schools to manage their service operations as it is for a manufacturing firm to manage its production function. To create a finished good or service by successfully combining labor, materials, and other inputs, any organization must satisfactorily perform three basic activities. These activities or basic components of the production/operations are (1) obtaining and storing raw materials, (2) scheduling people and equipment for the utilization of these materials, and (3) creating finished goods and/or services through the combined efforts of people and equipment.

Illustrative Case: P/OM in Manufacturing and Service Organizations

In any organization, managers must make good decisions to solve the problems and explore the opportunities that arise daily in all aspects of the production/operations process. Let's examine two different organizations, a manufacturing company, the Norge Division of Magic Chef, Inc., and a service organization, the Carbondale Clinic, to illustrate this point.

Obtaining and Storing Raw Materials The Norge Company manufactures washers and dryers, made primarily of steel purchased in sheets from suppliers. Different types of steel are used for different parts. For instance, the cabinet is made of thinner steel than the tub of a washer. Much of this steel is stored outdoors, but some has to be stored indoors to avoid rusting. Steel that is stored outside too long deteriorates badly and becomes useless. Thus it is important that steel not arrive at the plant too far ahead of the time it is needed. Then again, steel that arrives late causes other problems. If the steel used in a given product runs out, production must be shifted to something else or shut down altogether. Both alternatives are costly in time, lost production, and employee morale. Storing the steel also creates problems. Because each type of steel must be separated from every other type, many storage locations are used. When steel of a given type is needed, it must first be determined where it is stored. Good records of all storage locations and inventory levels must be maintained and updated regularly if this process of order and delivery is to work smoothly.

The Carbondale Clinic, by contrast, is a group medical practice of about 30 physicians. It maintains its laboratory and x-ray facilities as well as its own pharmacy. Like Norge, the clinic must also obtain and store raw materials. Instead of steel, its raw materials include cotton swabs, bandages, drugs, and x-ray film. Some of these materials, such as certain drugs and the x-ray film, must be stored under special conditions and may be kept for only specific periods of time before they deteriorate. Others, such as cotton swabs, can last indefinitely. Many drugs and medical supplies must be kept on hand to be available if needed, even though they are used infrequently. The clinic can end up with expensive inventories of seldom-used materials if it's not careful. This requires good systems to order, store, keep track of, and utilize materials if the clinic is to have the supplies necessary to deliver health services to its clients.

Scheduling People and Equipment Norge manufactures several different models of washers and dryers. Each model has unique characteristics that require the use of different parts. Many of these parts are made right at the plant on large hydraulic presses using special "dies" that shape and cut the steel to specifications. For Norge to produce its full line of washers and dryers, a wide variety of presses and dies must be available to make the parts. If too many parts are required from one press, a backlog occurs and production slows. Sufficient people must also be available to operate the presses and move materials and parts from one place to another within the plant. Effective scheduling of these people and equipment is essential to a smooth flow of production in the Norge plant.

Physicians from the Carbondale Clinic use operating rooms at Carbondale Memorial Hospital for performing surgery. These operating rooms contain various pieces of specialized equipment used in different types of operations. A large staff of nurses and technicians assists the physicians and operates the x-ray and laboratory equipment. Again, schedules must be arranged so the right people and equipment are available at the right times for the operations to be done.

Creating Finished Goods and Services Obtaining raw materials and scheduling people and equipment sets the stage for the creation of finished goods and/or services. This transformation process requires a smooth flow of work from the raw materials through to the finished good or service. Figure 16.2 shows two basic types of workflow layouts: (1) the continuous production or product layout, and (2) the intermittent production or job-shop layout. Each type is used by both production and service operations. Any organization, in fact, typically uses both patterns at different points in its transformation process.

Norge builds washing machines on an as-

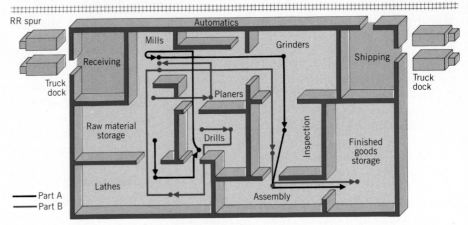

(A) Intermittent or job-shop production

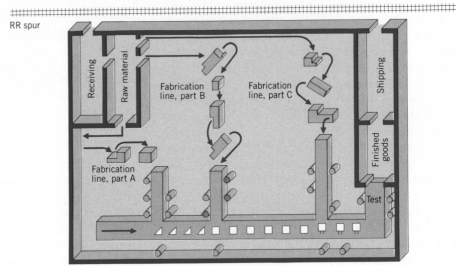

(B) Continuous production

FIGURE 16.2 Workflow layouts. *Source:* Elwood S. Buffa, *Modern Production/ Operations Management*, Sixth Edition (New York: Wiley, 1980). Used by permission.

sembly line, a continuous-production workflow. Parts and components are gathered at the required places along this line. At the beginning, a frame is placed on the line. As it moves down the line, the motor, hoses, and tub all get added in turn until the cabinet is finally put on. At the very end, the washer is filled with water and tested before being boxed and sent to storage.

Two orthopedic surgeons work at the Carbondale Clinic. When they schedule operations, all the necessary people and equipment are gathered together in one room around the operating table. Everyone applies his or her expertise directly to the patient as needed during the operation. Although not an assembly line, the work

is done sequentially by different people performing specialized tasks. The "product" in this case is a medical service, but the concept is the same as the assembly line at Norge. It, too, represents a continuous-production workflow.

All the presses at Norge are grouped in one location; all painting is done in another location; all drilling is done in yet another. Different component parts follow different patterns through these departments. For example, cabinets go directly from the presses to painting, while other parts are routed through the drill department and bypass the presses. This is intermittent production.

The Carbondale Clinic groups physicians

with the same specialty together in one location. Patients entering the clinic are interviewed to assess their problems. They are routed to one or more physicians, the lab, or x-ray. Depending on the problem, each person follows a slightly different pattern through the clinic's service operations. Again, the example is of an intermittent-production layout.

Managerial Implications   By now you should have a picture in your mind of the activities involved in manufacturing and service operations. Both action settings are dynamic; products constantly move through a manufacturing process; clients continually flow through a service operation. Performance success in each case requires that all facets of the production/operations process be well managed. As Figure 16.3 shows, finished goods and services are the result of decisions that exercise good production/operations control. If the environment were always certain and the future always predictable, these decisions would be easy and routine, but this is not the case in today's world. Controlling the production/operations process is thus an essential and exciting managerial task. It places a premium on the manager's ability to plan production and operations activities well enough in the first place so they can be effectively controlled to ensure desired results in the final analysis. As has been noted elsewhere in the text, neither planning nor controlling can succeed without help from the other.

Planning Production/Operations Activities

The role of planning in production/operations management begins with **demand forecasting,** the process of estimating future demand for an organization's products or services. The reason for doing this at all is to get an idea of what will happen in the future. It's a little like driving a car. Your actions will be different if you expect a sharp curve ahead than if you expect a four-lane straightaway. Have you ever tried to adjust the temperature of a shower, turning up the hot water just to find that a second later it got too hot? This is caused by the lag time between when the water leaves the valve until it reaches you. It's hard to anticipate changes if you wait until after you've felt their effect before responding.

The demand forecast in a manufacturing firm may involve projecting the number of prod-

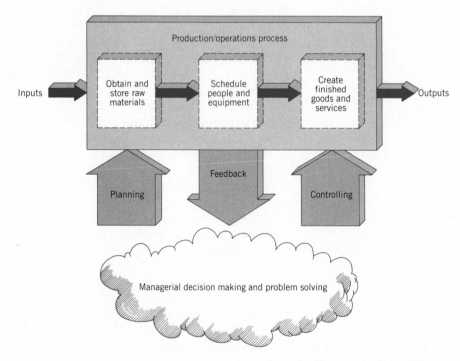

FIGURE 16.3 Managing the production/operations process.

uct units to be made each week. For a hospital the same goal becomes one of projecting how many patients will be served each day. Meeting this demand generates requirements for people, equipment, raw materials, and other resources. A good demand forecast therefore helps develop appropriate plans for production and service operations. The more products to be manufactured or clients served, the greater the resource requirements. If demand is expected to increase, plans must be made to order more materials and supplies, buy more equipment, and hire more people. Then schedules must be prepared through which people and equipment combine to create the finished product or service. Such activities must be well planned because of the lead time involved. It may take several months to hire a new employee; buying parts from a foundry may take several years.

Altogether, the planning side of production/operations activities can be summarized as follows. Demand forecasting projects demand for finished goods and services, which allows planning of production and service operations. When properly done, demand forecasting sets the stage for planning and facilitates production/operations control. Demand forecasts are used by organizations to[2]

1. *Decide whether demand is sufficient to generate the desired returns for the organization.* If demand exists but at too low a "price" to cover the "costs" the organization will incur in producing the output, the organization should reject the opportunity. This is an essential principle in break-even analysis, as discussed in Chapter 15.

2. *Determine long-term capacity needs for facility design.* An accurate projection of demand for a number of years in the future can save the organization great expense in expanding or contracting capacity to accommodate future environmental demands. Because of competitive forces in the environment, even in the not-for-profit sector, an organization that produces inefficiently is courting disaster. This topic will be further discussed later in this chapter.

3. *Identify short-term (1 week–3 months) fluctuations in demand for use in production planning, workforce scheduling, materials planning, and so forth.* These forecasts are of special importance to

P/OM and crucially affect workflow bottlenecks, master scheduling, promised delivery dates, and other such issues of concern to top management and the organization as a whole. This area will also be discussed in this chapter.

Controlling Production/Operations Activities

Planning for production/operations activities without controlling them is like jumping into a hot bath before you've tested the water. You could get burned. Basically, controlling is used to ensure that plans are working. Because forecasts will never be exact, for example, some deliveries will inevitably be late and some machines will inevitably break down, it is essential that an organization have a good production/operations control system. As is the case with other parts of the management process, planning and controlling go hand in hand. Good planning facilitates control and vice versa.

Figure 16.3 shows that planning and controlling of production/operations activities are highly interrelated functions. The feedback paths in the figure are especially important from a control perspective. They represent flows of information about deviations or problems in production or service operations back to the points where decisions can be made and corrective actions taken by appropriate managers. If a materials delivery has been delayed, for instance, the situation must be analyzed to determine what alternatives exist for dealing with the problem. This might involve revising the production schedule, getting substitute parts, or trying to arrange delivery through a different supplier.

There are many points of attention in production operations control systems. Among them, however, three areas of control stand out as of essential importance. To ensure a smooth and effective flow of production and service operations, (1) raw material, work in process, and finished goods inventories must be controlled; (2) production of goods and services must be controlled to ensure they are of acceptable quality; and (3) the schedules that combine the multiple activities of people and equipment must be controlled. In sum, production/operations control centers on inventories, quality, and schedules to ensure success in goods or services produced.

Management of the production/operations process therefore requires simultaneous attention to planning and controlling. Fortunately, the P/OM field offers a number of analytical techniques that assist managers to do just this. In the sections to follow you will learn the basic techniques used by today's managers to make decisions that achieve effective control over production and service operations. A manager's success in these decision areas rests with his or her capability to make forecasts, establish schedules, control inventory, and control quality. We'll begin with a look at forecasting.

MAKING FORECASTS

A demand forecast of product or service outputs sets the stage for planning and controlling production/operations activities. It is now time to talk about various ways of making that forecast. To begin, you should recall our initial discussion of forecasting in Chapter 4 as a fundamental part of the planning process.

Everyone is familiar with all kinds of forecasts, such as forecasts about the weather, the economy, or the future of some industry. In fact, most of our everyday actions are based on forecasts concerning what will happen in the future. You probably wouldn't be a student now if you didn't forecast that a job will be available when you graduate.

In general, we forecast by "extrapolating," or projecting into the future based on what has happened in the past. Weather forecasts are based on what usually happened in the past

when certain atmospheric conditions were present. Managers basically follow the same approach in demand forecasting. They take past data and extrapolate them into the future to project future demand for the products and/or services of an organization or subunit.

Take a look at Figure 16.4. It graphically depicts past sales of air conditioners over a three-year period. How would you project these data into the future? That is, how would you forecast future demand for air conditioners in such a way that production plans could accurately be made?

Time-Series Analysis

One problem in making a forecast from Figure 16.4 is recognizing a pattern. **Time-series analysis** is a method for identifying patterns in data. It is a foundation element in any effective forecast.

Time-series analysis takes historical data and breaks them into individual components—trend, seasonal, cyclical, and random—as shown in Figure 16.5. In general, the four time-series components are used in the following ways.

- *Trend* Reflects the overall upward or downward movement in the variation of data over time.
- *Seasonal* Reflects a wavelike variation of data occurring within a year and following the seasons.
- *Cyclical* Reflects a wavelike variation of data occurring over several years and following business or economic cycles.
- *Random* Reflects an unusual variation of data following irregular occurrences, such as strikes or bad weather.

The principle of time-series analysis is to break historical data into one or more of these components and then analyze each component separately. By focusing on just one component at a time, it is easier to spot key factors and use them as a basis for forecasting. Look again at Figure 16.4. Do you recognize any of these components in the data? Try sketching them in on the data pattern shown in the figure.

Now compare your analysis with the one depicted in Figure 16.6. There seems to be an

FIGURE 16.4 Quarterly air conditioner sales.

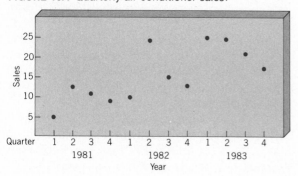

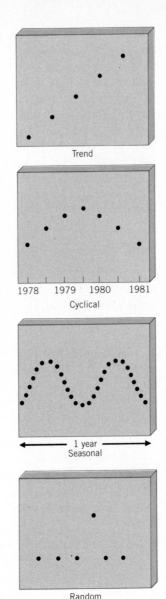

FIGURE 16.5 Four time-series components.

trend, they are leveling off and perhaps entering the downward curve of a cycle.

This example illustrates how time-series analysis helps make preliminary sense from historical data. It is a useful managerial tool. Still, most demand forecasting requires further detail that can be added by techniques such as moving averages, exponential smoothing, and regression analysis. Each of these forecasting methods uses mathematics to extrapolate historical data into the future. Don't be alarmed; the mathematics is straightforward and based on common sense. Because these techniques form the basis for even more sophisticated forecasting methods that are available today, it is important for a modern manager to be informed about them.

Moving Averages

Suppose sales of a company's product had been 1000 units, 1500 units, and 1400 units for each of the last three years, respectively. Given no other information, how would you forecast sales for the next year? One of your first ideas might be to average the three numbers and make that the forecast for fourth-year sales. This is how your calculation would work.

$$\frac{1000 + 1500 + 1400}{3} = 1300 \text{ units/average year}$$

Simple Moving Averages

Computing the average sales was a good idea. In fact, it forms the basis of the **moving-average** method of forecasting, which simply averages past data over a specific time period and uses that result to forecast the future. A 6-month moving average would average the past 6 months of data to project every seventh month; a 12-month moving average would average the past 12 months of data. The reason this method is called a "moving" average is that as time goes by and new data are obtained, the newest value is added and the oldest is dropped to "move" the average forward in time.

Let's take another example. A 6-month moving average for the following data comes out to be 110.17 units per month. Check the calculations to make sure you understand the logic.

upward trend in the data, as indicated by the dashed line in the figure. The solid line shows a seasonal pattern, something we would expect for air conditioners. The circled data point for the first quarter of 1983 falls clearly outside this seasonal pattern. It could be a random component. Careful analysis of this point might reveal that sales were high at that time because of unusually hot weather, a random occurrence for so early in the year. Finally, there seems to be a cyclical pattern present, as shown by the dot-and-dash line. Although sales have been following an upward

Month	Sales
January	100
February	120
March	108
April	130
May	98
June	105

Now, suppose that you learn July's sales are 102. To compute a new 6-month moving average, simply include this new data point in the average and drop January's. The new moving average is

$$\frac{120 + 108 + 130 + 98 + 105 + 102}{6} = 110.5$$

To forecast using moving averages, take the most recent average and use that to forecast the next time period. In the prior example, 110.17 would have been the forecast for July sales; 110.5 becomes the forecast for August sales. Table 16.1

demonstrates this forecasting method for a group of 3-month moving averages.

Weighted Moving Averages

A **weighted moving average** assigns a predetermined weight to each data point and thereby puts more weight on *recent* time periods as a basis for forecasting using the moving-average method. This is logical because more recent time periods may better reflect what will happen in the immediate future.

Using the January–June sales figures presented earlier, a 6-month weighted moving average might look as follows.

$$0.05(100) + 0.05(120) + 0.15(108) + 0.20(130) + 0.25(98) + 0.30(105) = 109.20$$

The "weights" assigned to each month's sales in this computation are 0.05, 0.05, 0.15, 0.20, 0.25,

Table 16.1 Three-Month Moving-Average Forecasts

Month	Sales	3-Month Average	Forecast for Month of
January	100		
February	120		
March	108	109.33	April
April	130	119.33	May
May	98	112.00	June
June	105	111.00	July
July	102	101.67	August

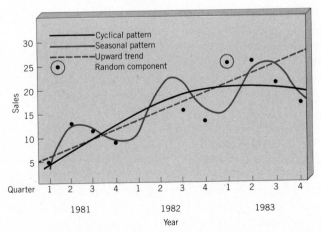

FIGURE 16.6 Time-series analysis of air conditioner sales.

and 0.30. Note two things about these weights. First, the greatest weight is on June sales, the most *recent* time period. Second, the weights all together *add up to 1*. Managers can use whatever weights they desire for a weighted moving-average forecast, as long as these two rules are followed: (1) more recent time periods should be weighted more heavily than more distant time periods, and (2) the sum of all weights should equal 1.0.

The Theory of Moving Averages

To make good managerial decisions regarding the use of moving averages in forecasting, you should understand the theory underlying them. Of the four components of any time series, recall that the only one we *cannot* forecast is the random component. Think for a moment what the random component does. Sometimes it makes demand higher than usual, other times it makes demand lower. In effect, a random component causes variations around some value that demand otherwise would have been if the random event hadn't occurred. A moving-average forecast "averages out" random components to project what would have happened in their absence. The future is forecasted as if past data did not have random components. Of course, this means that forecasts will sometimes be too high and other times too low. But don't be alarmed. This is entirely consistent with the two basic rules of forecasting.

Rule 1 A forecast is never 100 percent accurate.

Rule 2 If it is, something's wrong.

Because random components are inevitable and because they can never be forecasted, a forecast will never be precise. In fact, 10 percent forecasting error is considered good.

Exponential Smoothing

Moving averages require the storage of a lot of historical data. This is a problem. It's not uncommon for organizations to forecast demand for over 1000 end products or services. If just 12-month moving averages were used for forecasting, 12,000 numbers would have to be stored and regularly updated over time. **Exponential** smoothing helps overcome this data-storage problem. This forecasting method uses exponential weights to accomplish the weighted moving average. In so doing it requires fewer historical data.

Exponential smoothing uses a **smoothing constant** alpha (α), which has a value greater than 0 but less than 1. To forecast demand for a future time period (e.g., next week or next month) using exponential smoothing, the original forecast for the present period is added to alpha multiplied by the difference between actual demand in the present period and the original forecast. The *exponential smoothing equation* is expressed as follows.

In words

Forecast for next period = present forecast plus alpha times (actual demand minus present forecast)

In mathematical symbols

$$F_{t+1} = F_t + \alpha(D_t - F_t)$$

where,

$t + 1$	= next time period
t	= present time period
$F_t + 1$	= forecasted demand for next period
F_t	= forecasted demand for present period
D_t	= actual demand for present period
α	= the smoothing constant

Suppose it is April and a manager wants to forecast demand for May. The original forecast for April demand was 105 units ($F_t = 105$); actual demand was only 100 ($D_t = 100$). A smoothing constant of $\alpha = 0.2$ is chosen. Plugging these numbers into the exponential smoothing equation results in a forecasted demand for 104 units in May. Check this answer by working through the example yourself.

From this example you can see that forecasting by exponential smoothing requires only two data points, the original forecast and actual demand for the present time period (F_t and D_t, respectively). This greatly reduces the data-storage requirements compared to the weighted-average methods.

The choice of the smoothing constant or alpha (α) value is critical in exponential smoothing. The more weight desired on recent data, the higher the alpha value that should be used. It is common to choose alpha values between 0.1 and 0.3 in practice. As a rule of thumb, the value of alpha uses the same number of time periods as a moving average of $2/\alpha - 1$ periods. An $\alpha = 0.2$, for example, corresponds roughly to a 9-period moving average.

The *rule of thumb for determining alpha* is expressed as follows.

In words

Alpha = 2 divided by (the number of time periods in a moving average plus 1)

In mathematical symbols

$$\alpha = \frac{2}{n + 1}$$

where,

n = number of time periods in moving average

Regression Analysis

Both the moving-average and exponential-smoothing methods of forecasting work by "averaging out" random components. In the process, however, they can also average out important seasonal, trend, and cyclical time-series components. Thus moving averages and exponential smoothing are best used for short-range forecasting looking a few months and definitely less than a year ahead. **Regression analysis** provides for a medium-range or long-range forecast by comparing past variation in demand against the variation present in another and more pre-dictable variable. Let's illustrate the technique by example.

Consider a company that sells computer programs or software packages. The demand for computer programs probably depends to some extent on the number of computers in use. Note that this assumption nicely fits the basic principle of regression analysis. That is, we should be able to systematically compare past variation in the demand for computer programs with corresponding changes in the numbers of computers in use. This historical comparison, in turn, should allow a forecast of future demand for programs to be made.

In regression analysis the variable whose behavior is being forecasted or predicted for a future period is called the **dependent variable.** Because demand for the computer programs depends on the number of computers in use, it is the dependent variable in our example. An **independent variable** in regression analysis is the one presumed to influence what happens to the dependent variable. In the example, the number of computers in use is an independent variable because it is presumed to influence the demand for computer programs. The essence of regression analysis is to develop a formula that systematically relates the dependent variable to one or more independent variables. This formula can then be used to forecast demand for the dependent variable based on projected values for the independent variables.

Listed in Table 16.2 are hypothetical data for the number of computers in use (in millions) and computer program sales (in ten thousands) for 1977–1983. Figure 16.7 graphs the relationship between these two variables.

Table 16.2 Hypothetical Data for Computers in Use and Computer Program Sales 1977–1983

Year	Computers in Use (millions)	Program Sales (ten thousands)
1977	1	2
1978	2	1
1979	3	4
1980	4	3
1981	5	4
1982	6	6
1983	7	4

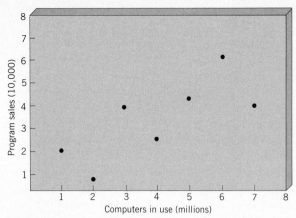

FIGURE 16.7 Computer program sales versus computers in use.

In words

Dependent variable = constant plus another constant multiplied by independent variable

In mathematical symbols

$$Y = a + bX$$

where,

Y = dependent variable (e.g., demand for computer programs)

X = independent variable (e.g., computers in use)

a, b = constants

Actual values for the constants in a straight-line regression equation are determined by statistical methods, often accomplished on computers. For the example in Figure 16.8, $a = 8/7$, $b = 4/7$. Thus the formal regression equation for these data is $Y = 8/7 + 4/7 \, X$. This equation represents the straight line that best describes the historical relationship between computer program sales and numbers of computers in use. To use this equation for forecasting purposes, a manager simply plugs the projected number of computers in use into the equation to generate a forecast for the associated computer program sales. Suppose there will be 8 million computers in use by 1984. Plugging $X = 8$ in the regression equation ($Y = 8/7 + 4/7 \, X$) results in $Y = 5 \, 5/7$. In terms of the example, we would forecast 1984 demand for

In general, you can see that there seems to be a trend or straight-line relationship between these two variables. Regression analysis allows this relationship to be described in a formula that can then be used to forecast the dependent variable into subsequent time periods. A mathematical technique called least-squares analysis helps determine which straight line fits the data best. This is the one that minimizes the deviations from all data points. Use of this technique for these data results in the regression line shown in Figure 16.8. The *equation for a straight-line regression analysis,* such as the one shown in Figure 16.8, follows.

FIGURE 16.8 Least-squares regression line for computer program sales versus computers in use.

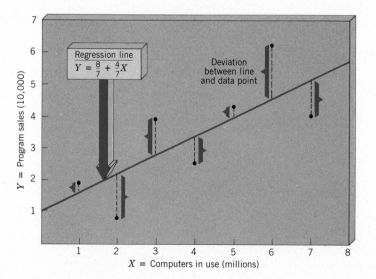

computer programs as about 57,142 (that is, 5 5/7 × 10,000).

A number of sophisticated regression techniques are available. They can accommodate a variety of historical data patterns and forecasting needs, even to the point of making forecasts by the analysis of multiple independent variables. Such multivariate regression analyses accomplished with the aid of computers are increasingly common in forecasting.

ESTABLISHING SCHEDULES

The purpose of forecasting is to enable managers to plan production/operations activities from the start. When activities are well planned initially, control is facilitated in the final result. Given a demand forecast, managers can then establish the schedules through which various material and human-resource inputs will be combined to create the finished good or service. The purpose of scheduling per se is to ensure that the *right things* are done at the *right time* with the *right items and/or people* to create the *desired product or service output* through the most *efficient utilization of resources*.[3]

Many organizations employ specialized personnel with responsibility for scheduling production and/or service operations. In all cases, managers will work with the results of the basic scheduling activities depicted in Figure 16.9. Your familiarity with scheduling should include aggregate and master scheduling, material-requirements planning (MRP), and capacity planning, as well as the special techniques of project scheduling including Gantt charts, CPM, and PERT.

Aggregate Scheduling

Aggregate scheduling is the process of making a rough cut or first approximation to a production/operations schedule based on a demand forecast. Manufacturing organizations, for example, need to decide in general whether to produce early and store products in inventory until demanded, or to delay production until the product is actually demanded and then supply it later. Service organizations such as a hospital must decide if they will staff to meet any demand that occurs (e.g., emergencies) or staff on the basis of de-

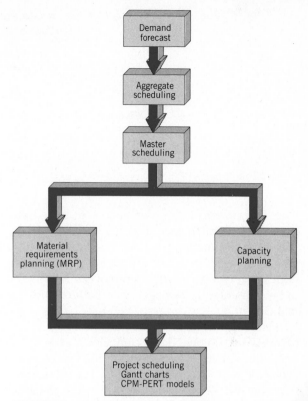

FIGURE 16.9 Basic scheduling activities.

mand that is controlled on the basis of selective admissions policies. In both cases, aggregate planning is a first approximation or approach to making resources available to satisfy forecasted demand.

Because aggregate planning is a first approximation to a production or service schedule, it is not usually very detailed. Yet it does help to set a longer-term perspective on resource utilization that will satisfy product or service demands with minimum cost. To do this, aggregate scheduling focuses on groups of products or services and determines in broad terms what resources will be needed in the associated production/operations processes.

Consider the six bi-monthly demand forecasts shown here for air conditioners. Note that this demand is forecasted for air conditioners as a product group, not as separate models.

Forecasted Air Conditioner Demand

Jan/Feb	Mar/Apr	May/Jun
400	200	500
Jul/Aug	**Sep/Oct**	**Nov/Dec**
700	1000	1400

Table 16.3 Aggregate Production Schedule to Meet Demand for Air Conditioners

Periods	Forecasted Demand	Employees Required	Number Hired	Number Laid Off
Jan/Feb	400	4	—	—
Mar/Apr	200	2	—	2
May/Jun	500	5	3	—
Jul/Aug	700	7	2	—
Sep/Oct	1000	10	3	—
Nov/Dec	1400	14	4	—

One way to meet this demand is to schedule enough production each period to satisfy the demand for air conditioners forecasted for that period. If an employee can produce 100 air conditioners every two months, employees will have to be scheduled in the aggregate pattern shown in Table 16.3.

This approach to production involves a lot of hiring and layoffs. Some companies, especially ones with seasonal products, do follow this approach. Others find it undesirable, and for others it is not even feasible. Instead, they try to keep a constant work force with minimum hiring or layoffs over time. Aggregate schedules allow lead time to anticipate and avoid these ups and downs in staffing. Let's go back, for example, to the company making air conditioners.

Adding the forecasted demand over the 12 months results in a total demand of 4200 units. Dividing this total by six results in an average demand every 2 months of 700 units. A work force of seven employees, therefore, can produce 4200 units in 12 months. Of course, in the early months *more* than are needed will be produced, and in the later months *fewer* will be produced than needed. This is really no problem because excess production can be stored in inventory until needed. When later demand exceeds production, inventory can be drawn on or used to make up the difference.

This new aggregate schedule uses the inventory to smooth or buffer demand and allow for a constant staffing pattern. Another approach yielding a constant work force would be to use overtime to meet periods of increased demand. Aggregate scheduling helps managers look ahead and broadly choose resource-utilization strategies most preferable to the organization as well as capable of satisfying the demand forecasts.

Master Scheduling

Master scheduling specifies in detail exactly what goods or services will be produced during the short term. It makes an aggregate schedule operational on a weekly or even daily basis. Some organizations go even further. The Anheuser-Busch Brewery in St. Louis, for example, plans the production of its beers on an *hourly* basis. Hospitals may also schedule operating rooms, special equipment, and other facilities hourly.

There are really no hard and fast rules for master scheduling. It always involves making trade-offs between different resource requirements and the constraints of various demand forecasts. A look at how master scheduling is done by the Black & Decker Company will give you the flavor of what it entails.[4]

Black & Decker (B&D) makes drills, saws, hedge trimmers, and other power tools. Their Hampstead, Maryland, plant manufactures over $200 million worth of products each year. These products are divided into 120 different tools (some 900 individual models) and 2200 accessories. Some 2500 people are employed in the plant, which covers just under 1 million square feet (about 22 football fields). The company deals with 3500 customers, mostly distributors and wholesalers, the majority of whom demand one-week delivery.

To handle all this, B&D prepares a master schedule on a week-by-week basis for each of the 3100 end products over a 12-month time span. Both marketing and manufacturing are involved in master scheduling. A "logistics group" in mar-

Table 16.4 Master Schedule for Five Weeks Production of Toy Cars

	Master Schedule and Required Components by Week				
	1	2	3	4	5
Finished cars	50	100	25	0	40
Bodies needed	50	100	25	0	40
Wheels needed	200	400	100	0	160
Axles needed	100	200	50	0	80

keting identifies marketplace requirements. The master schedule is the result of their needs being integrated with factory capabilities and constraints. This integration is accomplished by a continuing dialogue between inventory-planning analysts in marketing and production-planning analysts in manufacturing. There are three production-planning analysts at the Hampstead plant—one for tools and two for accessories. These analysts report to a production-planning manager who has overall responsibility for evaluating capacity implications. Marketing needs are viewed by the production-planning analysts in terms of the associated capacity needs, machine loads, and material availabilities. Adjustments in both production quantity and timing are negotiated so that market needs are satisfied and plant profitability is maximized. At the end of each month, a new month is added to the 11 remaining in the master schedule. The production schedule in that month is somewhat imprecise, but becomes more clearly defined as the time draws closer to the present.

Material Requirements Planning (MRP)

The master schedule plans the production of each finished product or service. To fulfill this schedule, all component parts and resources must be brought together at the specified time and in the right place. This is difficult to achieve in practice. A good example is automobile manufacturing, where it takes time to make or order the various components of a final car assembly. This adds additional complication to any production/operations process.

Consider even a toy car whose body is one-piece molded plastic. The iron axles are manufactured by the company, but the plastic body and wheels are bought from an outside supplier. It takes one week of order lead time to obtain the bodies and three weeks for wheels. The axles must be started into production two weeks in advance of actual need. Suppose that the master schedule plans for the assembling of 50 of these cars in a given week. What can the responsible manager do to ensure that he or she has enough, but not too many, component parts regularly on hand to meet this goal?

If your answer includes figuring out how many of each component are needed (50 bodies, 100 axles, etc.), and then planning to produce or order them far enough in advance, you've got the idea behind **material-requirements planning** (MRP). This technique uses a master schedule to determine when and how many component parts or separate resources must be ordered to ensure a smooth and sufficient flow of finished products or services. Once again, we'll proceed by example.

A master schedule for five weeks of production of toy cars is presented in Table 16.4. Since each car has one body, two axles, and four wheels, the weekly requirements for component parts can also be easily determined. These are called gross requirements because they indicate the total number of components needed without taking into consideration any components already in inventory or on order.

Now look at axles. Assume that 230 axles are currently on hand in inventory and that another 100 are scheduled to be completed in week 2. If we subtract axles needed each week (gross requirements) from the on-hand inventory at the

Table 16.5 Availability of Axles for Production of Toy Cars

	Start	Week 1	2	3	4	5
Axles needed (gross requirements)	0	100	200	50	0	80
Scheduled receipts	0	0	100	0	0	0
On-hand inventory	230	130	30	−20	−20	−100

beginning of the week, we find what supply of axles will remain in inventory at the end of the week. The scheduled receipt of axles in week 2 becomes added to inventory. Results of these calculations are found in Table 16.5.

The figures in Table 16.5 indicate that inventory will run out in week 3 unless more axles are ordered. The question is how many to order? One answer is to order as much as the on-hand inventory becomes negative each period. In our example, 20 axles must be ordered to meet gross requirements for week 3. None are required for week 4, and 80 must be ordered for week 5. To differentiate between those weeks when more are needed and more are not, another row labeled "net requirements" can be added to our chart. Net requirements represent any difference between gross requirements and the number available. If enough are on hand, the net requirement is zero; otherwise it is the additional amount needed in that week.

A knowledge of these net requirements along with known order and delivery lead times, two weeks in this case, allows the responsible manager to determine when to order the required axles. To satisfy the net requirement for 20 more axles in week 3, they will have to be ordered two

weeks earlier in week 1 to allow sufficient time. This process of "lead-time offsetting" results in the schedule of planned orders in Table 16.6 that now completes our example. By ordering on this schedule, the right number of axles will always be on hand to meet the master assembly schedule. This assurance is the contribution of MRP to production/operations planning and control.

The prior example may give you the idea that MRP is simple. Actually, you're right; it is! But MRP is also a powerful managerial tool, as *Newsline 16.1* points out. MRP quickly increases in complexity when applied to operations involving the multitude of finished goods or services and component parts suggested earlier in the B&D example. Fortunately, computers make the required calculations easy. They can readily supply the managers of even very complex operations with good MRP information.

Capacity Planning

In the preceding section we were concerned with ensuring a smooth flow of component parts and resources necessary to satisfy forecasted demand. Here our attention shifts to making sure that enough "capacity," or actual production or

Table 16.6 MRP Schedules of Orders for Axles

	Start	Week 1	2	3	4	5	6	7	8
Axles needed (gross requirements)	0	100	200	50	0	80	150	50	100
Scheduled receipts	0	0	100	0	0	0	0	0	0
On-hand inventory	230	130	30	−20	−20	−100	−250	−300	−400
Net requirements	0	0	0	20	0	80	150	50	100
Planned orders	0	20	0	80	150	50	100		

A BIG PAYOFF FROM MRP

Material-requirements planning is almost always referred to in the trade by its initials, MRP. It starts with an annual-sales forecast, usually based on what economists expect. But frequent revisions based on actual sales enable companies to alter the myriad details of ordering and manufacturing to avoid under- or overproduction. In big companies, the interlocking schedules are so complex that the adjustments would be impossible without a computer, explains William E. Mullin, director of systems at Pfizer. When the system works correctly, companies can avert costly ripple effects from either an abrupt drop in sales or problems with deliveries by their suppliers. "In a pinch, the locomotive can be halted much quicker," says Mullin.

A survey by two professors at the University of Minnesota School of Management, John C. Anderson and Roger G. Schroeder, documents the increasing use of MRP. The survey, sponsored by the Inventory Society, went to 1700 companies across the industrial heartland. Of the 679 companies that replied—an unusually high response to a lengthy questionnaire—64 percent said they used some form of MRP and many others said they were considering doing so. Two-thirds of the users had adopted the technique after 1973.

The Minnesota study provides the first statistical evidence of the big payoff companies can bring from sophisticated inventory control. Installation costs ranged from less than $100,000 for small companies to more than $1 million for large ones. But the average increase in annual inventory turnover was an astounding 50.3 percent. For the typical company with $65 million in annual sales, that made possible an inventory reduction of about $8 million, and a saving of $1.8 million per year in carrying costs calculated at recent interest rates. Some companies reported that MRP had enabled them to cut in half the amount of money tied up in inventories for each dollar of sales. The new system also improved service to customers: the average lead time for deliveries declined 18 percent.

Source: Excerpted from Lewis Beman, "A Big Payoff from Inventory Controls," *Fortune*, Vol. 104, No. 2 (July 27, 1981), pp. 76–80. © 1981 Time Inc. Courtesy of *Fortune Magazine*.

service output, is available to meet this forecasted demand. Airlines, for example, measure capacity in available passenger seat miles; hospitals use available beds; manufacturing firms may use available machine time.

The capacity-planning problem for any manager is to have the most economic amount of capacity available to meet production or service demands. This isn't always easy. Thinking back to the description of B&D's master-scheduling efforts, it was mentioned that capacity requirements were constantly being evaluated. Each end product and component part requires a certain amount of "capacity" or time on various machines as well as time for assembly. If too many products are scheduled on one particular machine, the capacity of that machine will be exceeded and the production process can be delayed due to the subsequent lack of parts.

A similar situation holds true in a bank. Sometimes you can walk in and a teller is free or you have to wait only a short time. Those times there is sufficient capacity. There may even be overcapacity if extra tellers are available with no one to wait on. At other times, such as Friday after work or Saturday morning, you've probably experienced the irritation of a long wait just to cash a check or make a deposit. Those times there is insufficient or undercapacity. The bank manager wants to maintain sufficient capacity to meet service demands, and minimize both over- and undercapacity.

The master schedule of any manufacturing or service operation should be established with capacity in mind. It can help managers anticipate and prepare for times when more capacity must be added for too much demand, or excess capacity should be reduced because of too little demand. If a bank manager knows that every Saturday morning will be busy, he or she can plan to add extra tellers and increase capacity. If a hospital administrator expects an emergency room to be busier on holiday weekends, plans can be made to schedule extra staff on those days.

Capacity planning is the scheduling of resource utilization in the production/operations process. It involves two basic ingredients in both manufacturing and service organizations: (1) standard time and (2) capacity requirements.

Standard Time

Before a manager can schedule production or operations capacity, including planned increases or decreases, it must be determined just how much capacity is available. For example, a bank manager may know that each teller can process an average of 40 customers per hour, allowing for breaks and other personal time. This is a measure of **standard time,** a measure of work capacity that takes into account the availability and work efficiency of people and/or equipment. To serve forecasted demand for a certain number of customers in any given day or week, the manager can easily determine how many tellers are needed. If 400 customers are expected to demand banking services on the last business hour of every Friday, 10 tellers will be needed (400 customers divided by a standard time of 40 customers per hour).

The same principle holds true in manufacturing operations. For instance, a production supervisor may have 30 standard hours of drill time available in a given week. This difference between standard time and clock time is because machines cannot run continuously without main-

tenance and because some machine operators work more efficiently than others. Standard time measures both resource availability and efficiency of resource utilization.

Capacity Requirements

The next step in capacity planning is to use standard times to determine the standard hours of capacity available for any given resource. Take the earlier manufacturing example in which MRP has already been used to determine planned orders for component parts of a toy car. For those parts to be manufactured by the company, the planned orders indicate how many of each part must be produced in a given week. This tells us what parts will be using machine capacity during that week. To determine just *how much* machine capacity is needed and *on which* machines, two additional pieces of information are used. The first, usually called a **routing sheet,** indicates which machines or work centers a part must pass through in the various phases of its production. The second, a **bill of capacity,** indicates how much standard time is needed on each machine to make one finished part.

In our example, MRP identified the planned orders for axles over a six-week period. Suppose the routing sheet indicates two operations: a cutting operation that slices the steel rod material to the right length and a stamping operation that shapes it. Suppose, too, that the bill of capacity shows the following standard hours required for each operation.

Operation	Standard hours/units
Cutting	0.02
Stamping	0.01

All the information needed to plan for and schedule capacity on the cutting and stamping machines is now in place. The basic calculation of required capacity is accomplished by multiplying standard time per unit times the number of units required. In week 1 of the example, the capacity needed for cutting the 20 required axles will be 0.4 hours (0.02 hours per unit × 20 units). For stamping it will be 0.2 hours (0.01 hours per unit × 20 units).

You can see that the basic elements of capacity planning, like those in MRP, are simple.

They become more complex when you consider that the demands on the people and/or equipment in any organization will come from many parts and customers. Other products made by the toy-car manufacturer will surely utilize the same equipment and therefore require some of its available capacity. By adding up all standard hours required on each machine and comparing this to time available, a manager can determine whether sufficient capacity is available or if more should be added. This is the process of capacity planning. As with many other aspects of production/operations management, it is facilitated in practice by the growing use of computers in today's organizations.

Gantt Charts, CPM, and PERT[5]

Capacity planning determines how much of a resource is required to satisfy demand. It does not specify the timing by which these resources should be utilized. This latter task is strictly a scheduling problem that requires a determination of how a production or service operation should be routed from start to finish. Among the tools managers use to decide on the most efficient production or operations sequences are Gantt charts and CPM-PERT network models. These project-scheduling techniques relate routing timetables to available resource capacities. They facilitate

control by allowing managers to make sure that all required tasks are completed by the desired dates.[6]

Gantt Charts

Gantt charts, named in honor of the pioneer work of Henry Gantt, were first introduced in Chapter 3 as basic aids to managerial problem solving and decision making. **A Gantt chart** graphically depicts the routing or scheduling of a production/operations sequence from the start to conclusion. Figure 16.10 presents a Gantt chart for a manufacturing project. The left-hand column lists activities required to complete a particular job. To the right, bars are used to schedule the time for each activity.

As the figure shows, the final Gantt chart facilitates both production planning and control by providing a visual measure of the progress of each activity against the time schedule. In the example, scheduling, designing, and ordering are complete; however, the latter two were completed after the date planned. Design started ahead of schedule, while materials delivery has begun but is behind schedule. As of the "starred" review date (October 8), the chart is marked to show that the machine-components activity has not begun and is already behind schedule.

A Gantt chart is most useful in situations where there aren't many tasks, where task times

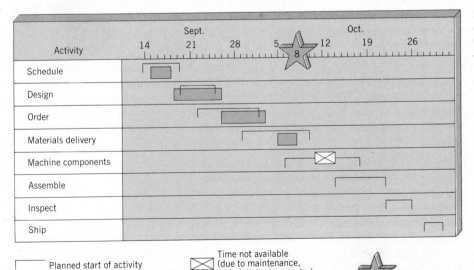

FIGURE 16.10 A Gantt chart. *Source:* Lawrence J. Gitman and Carl McDaniel, Jr., *Business World* (New York: Wiley, 1983), p. 240. Used by permission.

are relatively long (days or weeks rather than hours), and where the job routings are short and relatively simple. Many mechanical and magnetic-board devices are available to facilitate the use of Gantt charts. They are common fixtures in many offices and help managers exercise postaction or feedback control over projects.

CPM-PERT Network Models

One shortcoming of Gantt charts is that they are static devices that cannot accommodate projects involving many separate but interconnected tasks over time. This deficiency is substantially overcome by network models, such as CPM (critical-path method) and PERT (program evaluation and review technique). McDonnell-Douglas, Boeing, General Electric, and other companies connected with the aerospace program were leaders in the development of these approaches. In many instances, government contracts specified that CPM-PERT techniques be used to monitor progress on the projects.

The network chart is fundamental to both CPM and PERT. It is developed by breaking a production/operations project into a series of small subactivities, each of which has a recognizable beginning and ending point. These points in time are called "events," and they are often shown on a network diagram as circles or "nodes." One such diagram is depicted in Figure 16.11. It is drawn to show the necessary relationships among the activities associated with various events. This makes it possible to plan for effective completion of a project by ensuring that activities get done in proper sequence. Because delay or interruption of any activity can affect what will happen in later project stages, CPM and PERT techniques allow for precontrol or feed-forward control as well as post control or feedback control.

In the case of **CPM (critical-path method)**, a single time estimate is developed for each activity. For **PERT (program evaluation and review technique)**, multiple time estimates are developed for each activity in order to take into account time variability. The time required to traverse each path is computed by adding up all required activity times along the path. Among all paths required for the project, the path having

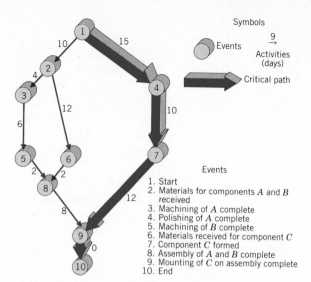

FIGURE 16.11 A PERT network. *Source:* Lawrence J. Gitman and Carl McDaniel, Jr., *Business World* (New York: Wiley, 1983), p. 241. Used by permission.

the longest time is designated the *critical path*. It represents the shortest possible time in which the entire project can be completed. For the sample PERT network in Figure 16.11, the highlighted critical path consists of events (1–4–7–9–10), requiring a total time of 37 days (15 + 10 + 12 + 0).

CPM-PERT network models are best suited to situations in which the interrelationships of activities and reasonable time estimates can be established. One important feature of these models is that they permit the manager to exercise control by determining the overall effects of a delay in the completion of a particular task. It also makes it possible to figure the effect on the schedule of a reallocation of resources from one task to another. Good computer programs are now available to help managers with CPM-PERT schedules for even very complex projects. Computers can be used to determine and draw network paths, and to update these networks as work progresses.

CONTROLLING INVENTORIES

Inventory is the amount of resources or products kept in storage. Organizations keep inventories to maintain flexibility in their production/operations processes, smooth out periods of excess or undercapacity, meet periods of unusual demand, and/or achieve economies from large-scale purchases. Because inventories can represent major resource investments, they must be well managed. The basic objective of inventory control is to maintain inventories sufficient to allow both effective and efficient operations. This means making sure that any inventory is neither too large nor too small for the tasks at hand.

Types of Inventories

It is common for organizations to maintain inventories of raw materials, work in process, and/or finished goods. Recall that in talking about MRP we mentioned that component parts could be kept in inventory. This *raw-materials inventory* is used or "drawn down" when the components are assembled into a finished product. General supplies, such as forms and writing materials, are an important raw-materials component for any organization. *Work-in-process inventories* represent goods in all but the final stage of production. Most manufacturing companies also maintain *finished-goods inventories* of completed but unsold products. The Norge Company, for example, maintains inventories of finished washing machines and dryers.

Although all inventories may seem the same to you, there are big differences among them. The use of finished goods can follow a pattern of **independent inventory demand**. Imagine the demand for cartons of milk in a grocery store. Most customers buy only a few cartons, two or three at the most. As a result, the level of inventory falls gradually over time. There are usually no big drops, and inventory decreases at an approximately uniform rate.

Work-in-process inventory for component parts can easily follow a different pattern. Most manufacturers produce finished products in batches or lots. In the case of the toy cars discussed previously, one week's worth of demand would often be made at a time. Requirements from inventories of the component bodies, axles, and wheels will follow the lot sizes. This is called **dependent inventory demand** because it depends on the production of finished items. Dependent inventory demand follows a "lumpy"

pattern and causes inventory levels to fall in bunches over time.

The dependent and independent demand patterns require different approaches to inventory control. Independent demand can be controlled by orders based on economic-order quantity; dependent demand is controlled via lot-by-lot orders using MRP.

Economic Order Quantity

Two major costs are associated with inventory: ordering costs and carrying or holding costs. **Ordering costs** are the costs of arranging the procurement of items for inventory from outside suppliers as well as the costs of any internal procurement (e.g., manufacture) of such items. They

Control of an organization's investment in inventory is an important managerial responsibility in both manufacturing and service operations.

do *not* include the cost of the items themselves; they only include such things as the cost of labor and materials required to place the orders and arrange for their subsequent shipment and receipt. **Carrying or holding costs,** by contrast, include the costs of storing and insuring the items in inventory against loss plus the opportunity cost or the rate of return that could be realized by investing elsewhere the funds tied up in inventory.

These two inventory costs, carrying and ordering, are constantly balancing each other. If the number of orders per year is high, ordering costs are high and both average inventory and carrying costs tend to be low. Given few orders, average inventory will be high and costs follow the reverse pattern. The total of these two costs is minimized when the two are *equal;* that is, the cost of inventory is minimized when carrying cost equals ordering cost. This principle underlies the control of inventories subject to dependent demand and allows for use of economic order quantities.

The **economic order quantity** (EOQ) is a method of inventory control that involves ordering a fixed number of items every time an inventory level falls to a predetermined point. When this point is reached, a decision is automatically made, more and more frequently now by computer, to place a standard order. The best example is the supermarket, where hundreds of daily orders are routinely made on this basis. These standard order sizes are calculated according to a mathematical formula that results in minimum total inventory cost.

The *formula for determining the economic order quantity (EOQ)* in any situation is expressed as follows.

In words

Economic order quantity = the square root of (two times actual demand for inventory use times ordering cost) divided by carrying cost

In mathematical symbols

$$\text{EOQ} = \sqrt{\frac{2DO}{C}}$$

where,

D = actual demand for inventory use
O = ordering cost of inventory
C = carrying cost of inventory

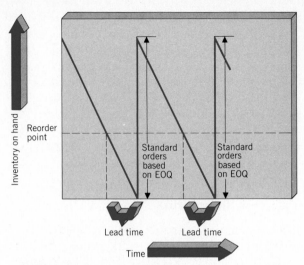

FIGURE 16.12 Inventory controlled by an economic order quantity (EOQ).

Suppose independent demand for inventory is 100 units per year, the cost for each order is $80, and carrying cost is $10 per unit per year. The EOQ in this case comes out to be 40—that is, $\sqrt{2(\$80 \times 100)/10}$. The manager should order 40 units each time to minimize inventory cost. Of course, this order must be placed with sufficient lead time (i.e., time between placing and receiving the order) that enough inventory remains on hand to meet demand in the interim. Figure 16.12 shows the cycle of orders and reorders characteristic of an EOQ-controlled inventory. The objective is always to have new inventory arrive just as old inventory runs out. This minimizes the cost of an independent demand inventory.

Lot-by-Lot Orders

In situations of dependent inventory demand, such as when dealing with in-process inventories of component parts, planned orders are based on the MRP schedule. Recall the example used previously for toy cars. In that case, planned orders were the same as net requirements. They were just offset by the lead time. This approach to inventory control is called **lot-by-lot-ordering** because the planned orders are based on the net requirements in each time period, as they appear "lot by lot" in the MRP schedule.

NEWSLINE 16.2

KANBAN WORKS WONDERS, BUT WILL IT WORK IN U.S. INDUSTRY?

Robert B. Stone, General Motors Corp. vice-president, notes that Japanese companies using "just-in-time" systems require lot sizes to be less than 10 percent of the day's usage.

"The ideal there," he says, "is a lot size of one piece so that every time one vehicle is produced, one of each part in the vehicle is produced."

On a wry note, Stone points out in contrast, that at any one time General Motors has "about $9 billion tied up in inventory."

Many executives, and others who have closely studied Kanban, say the best way to grasp what it is all about is to visit Japanese plants that use it.

Plant visitors to the Toyota Company, for example, say one of the most striking things they first notice is side-loaded trucks of vendors running right into the plant and unloading their materials at designated spots along the production and assembly lines.

Visitors become wide-eyed again when the vendor materials are quickly absorbed into production. There is little or no inventory stockpiling. There is no inspection of the newly arrived materials.

So far, while there has been great enthusiasm among U.S. managers for Kanban, it is apparently not catching on in this country as might be expected—certainly not in terms of total transplants.

"Kanban, or 'just-in-time,' is not for everyone," says George W. Plossl, a leading consultant-educator in production and inventory management.

Source: Adapted from John D. Baxter, "Kanban Works Wonders, But Will It Work in U.S. Industry?" *Iron Age*, Vol. 225, No. 16 (June 7, 1982), pp. 44–48. Used by permission.

Just-in-Time Delivery

The Japanese have recently created quite a stir with something called *kanban,* or **just-in-time delivery** of component parts and supplies. This approach to inventory control involves minimizing carrying costs and maintaining almost no inventories by ordering or producing only as needed. It usually occurs in extremely small lots, possibly even on a unit-by-unit basis. The trade-off, however, is high ordering costs.

Japanese managers who use just-in-time delivery believe it is worth the ordering cost to avoid inventories. General Motors has started using a similar approach, and managers wonder how the concept will work in this country. Some viewpoints are found in *Newsline 16.2*. Richard J. Schonberger, a scholar and consultant in the field

of P/OM, says that the just-in-time approach may be the most important productivity-enhancing management innovation since the turn of the century.[7] All this is true, he says, merely because the system allows production and purchasing to be done in small quantities and no earlier than necessary for use.

Kanban is a Japanese word for the piece of paper that accompanies, for example, a bin of parts in a camera factory.[8] When a worker first takes parts from a new bin, the *kanban* is routed back to the supplier and serves as an order for new parts. Contrast this direct approach to inventory control with the EOQ and lot-by-lot ordering techniques just discussed. It is easy to see the allure in the Japanese system.

Still, it would be unfair not to point out that the just-in-time approach does require special support if it is to work right. Factors that are essential if this system is to succeed include[9]

1. *Geographic concentration* Relatively short transit times from vendor plants to customer plants—less than one day—are necessary to get what is required "just in time." In Japan, for example, Toyota, has most of its suppliers located within 60 miles of its plants.

2. *Dependable quality* The users must be able to receive only *good* parts from suppliers.

3. *Manageable supplier network* A minimum number of suppliers working under long-term contracts helps make just-in-time systems work. Most Japanese auto companies use fewer than 250 parts suppliers; General Motors uses about 3500 suppliers for its assembly operations alone.

4. *Controlled transportation system* The key to this is short, reliable transit lines between suppliers and users.

5. *Efficient receiving and materials handling* Parts must be delivered as close as possible to points of use.

6. *Strong management commitment* Management must make sufficient resources available to ensure that the system works. This commitment must stand firm during periods of conversion to just-in-time systems when the going can be rough and prolonged.

CONTROLLING QUALITY

Every organization should be concerned with the quality of its outputs. **Quality control** is the process of *checking* products or services to ensure that they meet certain standards. The importance of quality control is increasingly evident in the slogans of U.S. companies. Ads for Ford Motor Company say, "If it's not right, we won't ship it."; those of the General Electric Company intone, "Quality is our No. 1 focus."[10]

The purpose of quality control is to ensure that the finished good or service produced by an organization is of high standards. The process of quality control, however, is applied to all aspects of production and operations from the selection of raw materials and supplies right down to the last task performed on the finished good or service. When properly done, quality control improves productivity by reducing waste on the input side and reducing rejects on the output side.

Statistical Quality Control

To illustrate how quality control might work, consider the case of an engine crankshaft for an automobile. These crankshafts are first molded, then machined to the correct dimensions. Because of variations in the parts, wear on the equipment, and/or differences among the skills of machine operators, not all crankshafts will have exactly the same dimensions after machining. That's not totally bad in itself because the crankshaft will still perform properly so long as its dimensions are within certain limits. For instance, the diameter at a certain point on a crankshaft should be 1.28 inches; the part will still function if the diameter is between 1.26 inches (the lower control limit) and 1.30 inches (the upper control limit).

The quality of these crankshafts might be checked by measuring each one as it is completed. If the diameter of a crankshaft is within the upper and lower control limits, it passes; otherwise it fails and must be reworked. An occasional crankshaft falling outside the limits would not be cause for managerial concern, it would simply be rejected. However, several rejects might mean the machining process is out of control and requires correction. It is often helpful to keep track of trends graphically, such as with the **control chart** in Figure 16.13. The basic purpose of a control chart is to display work results on a graph that clearly delineates upper control limits (UCL) and lower control limits (LCL). A process is in or out of control depending on how well results remain within these established limits. The trend shown by the data in Figure 16.13 indicate that the production process should be halted to reset or repair the machine in question.

This same concept can be extended using statistical concepts to set upper and lower control limits and monitor product performance in respect to them. In such cases, instead of checking every part, batches of a product or service are checked by taking a random sample from each. This is called inspection by statistical sampling.

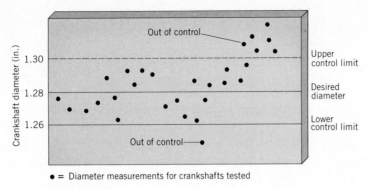

● = Diameter measurements for crankshafts tested

FIGURE 16.13 Control chart for crankshafts.

Because of the inherent difficulty of carefully inspecting every raw-material input or product/service output, most quality control is accomplished via statistical sampling procedures. Using proper methods, the control chart in Figure 16.13 could just as easily represent a statistical sample of 1 percent of crankshafts produced as it could all crankshafts produced. The information made available for managerial control is of equal significance in each case, but the latter is more efficient in larger and more complex production or service operations.

Quality-Control Circles

Statistical methods of quality control have been around for many years. They are good ways of checking for defects, but offer little to indicate how to avoid defects in the first place. **Quality assurance,** the process of *preventing* the production of defective products or services, is among the quality-control concepts that have been given new impetus by the successes of Japanese industry. Some of the hard facts that show how well they do this job include: (1) a new American car is almost twice as likely to have a problem as a Japanese car, (2) an American color television needs repairs twice as often as a Japanese set, (3) American-made computer-memory chips were found in one test to be three times as likely to fail as Japanese-made chips.[11] Interestingly, the ideas on which these accomplishments are based were first introduced to the Japanese over 25 years ago by an American professor and consultant, W. Edwards Deming.[12]

Deming was invited to Japan in 1950 to share the quality-control techniques developed in the United States just prior to World War II. What resulted was a lifelong relationship now epitomized in the "Deming" prize for quality control. This annual award, now in its 34th year, is so important in Japan it is broadcast on national television. The principles Deming taught the Japanese are basically straightforward: tally defects, analyze and trace them to the source, make corrections, and keep a record of what happens afterward. These are good basic precepts for any managerial control system. Consider how the process worked for a U.S. hosiery manufacturer.[13]

The managers of a middle-sized hosiery plant in Tennessee now owned by Genesco decided they had to change the ways they had grown used to in the previous 65 years. A preliminary study showed one source of defects was the "looping" department, which performed the task of closing toes. Inspectors soon found that a few of the workers produced most of the defects. An older worker responsible for 20 percent of the faulty loops was persuaded to take early retirement. A dozen others did fine once they got new glasses. Another said she paid little attention to what she was doing because no one had shown concern for quality; when management did, she easily improved her work. So it went. In seven months, the plant cut its rejects from 11,500 to 2,000 stockings out of a total weekly output of 120,000 pairs. To put it another way, productivity climbed 4 per cent virtually costfree. Until recently few American companies bothered with that kind of analysis.

The essence of Deming's approach to quality control is illustrated in the preceding case. His basic proposition is that the cause of a quality

Japanese products are widely acclaimed for high quality, and the quality control circles present in Japanese companies are frequently given as the reason for the quality achievements.

problem may be some component of the production/operations process, like an employee or a machine, or it may be intrinsic to the production/operations system itself. If it is caused by an employee, that person should be retrained or replaced. Likewise, a faulty machine should be adjusted or replaced. However, if the cause of defects lies within a system, blaming an employee for the problem only produces frustration. Instead, the system must be analyzed and constructively changed. From this notion emerged the "quality-control circle."

A **quality-control circle** is a group of employees (usually no more than 10) who meet periodically (e.g., an hour or so once or twice a month) to discuss ways of improving the quality of their products or services. The objective of using quality-control circles is to build a sense of employee responsibility for quality assurance and to unlock the potential of every employee to contribute useful ideas and information to essential problem-solving and decision-making processes. The quality-control circle is a means of participation that encourages persons to think and talk about the production/operations system. As a result they develop a shared sense of responsibility for how what they do influences the quality of the organization's services or products.

Quality-control circles have achieved rapid popularity in such large firms as RCA, Hughes Aircraft, Ford, General Electric, Bethlehem Steel, and Control Data. Honeywell employs over 300 such teams and anticipates savings of several million dollars as a result.[14] In addition to direct dollar savings, the advantages of quality-control circles include increased morale and commitment among employees. Remarks from one company include[15]

"This is the best thing the company has done in 15 years," an hourly worker told his supervisor.

"The program proves that superiors have no monopoly on brains," an operational employee said.

"It gives me more pride in my work," a female assembler remarked.

As with any managerial technique, the quality-control circle must be carefully analyzed for its applicability in any given work situation. *Newsline 16.3* offers some pros and cons for your consideration.

Illustrative Case: Quality Assurance at American Express[16]

A recent experience of the American Express Company helps pull the various facets of quality control together into a useful managerial per-

QUALITY-CONTROL CIRCLES: THEY WORK AND DON'T WORK

Japan's experience has revealed several preconditions for the success of quality-control or QC circles. Some may be indigenous.

First, the work force must be intelligent and reasonably well educated. Members of the circles must be able to use statistical and industrial engineering analysis. They must know what it takes to make things work on a nuts-and-bolts level, and they must be able to brainstorm together. It is no coincidence that the Japanese companies that have been most successful with these circles and other participatory methods for improving productivity (Hitachi, Teijin, Asahi Glass, and Nippon Kokan) are also well known for their fine recruiting and internal training programs.

Second, management must be willing to trust workers with cost data and important information, and to give them the authority to implement their ideas. At Japanese companies with successful QC programs, managers have tended to work their way up through the ranks. They really believe in their work force. It is no surprise to them that groups of workers, if given information and authority to experiment by trial and error, will be able to reduce downtime, waste, or reworking—the sorts of questions that the circles are most effective in addressing.

Third, workers must be willing and eager to cooperate with each other. Unlike the suggestion box and other worker-incentive programs that reward individuals, QC programs reward groups. A genuine "team spirit" is therefore necessary. Workers must be willing to express themselves and find fulfillment by reaching agreement.

Moreover, if authority in production decisions is to be decentralized down to the level of these circles, the circles have to be able to cooperate with each other lest they work at cross-purposes. Unless there is a spirit of cooperation within the work force—an attitude that talking a problem through with peers is more rewarding than taking it up to management—a company is better off using individual carrots instead of the circles. Otherwise, it may find night shifts undoing the improvements of day shifts.

Quality-control circles don't run themselves. They must be revitalized. Most important is the specific set of goals they are given and a strong manager who coordinates QC circle changes with corporate objectives. In companies that use both the suggestion box and QC circle, management can gather directly from workers ideas that may require significant capital expenditures and at the same time use suggestion-box successes to encourage QC-circle efforts.

Quality-control circles work best when they are part of what the Japanese call total quality control, which embraces concerns about the entire spectrum of a business. And they are one of a number of productivity-improvement techniques that work best when put together. As the Japanese would say, it's like collecting dust to make a mountain. But somebody has to envision the mountain, and know which way the wind is blowing.

Source: Excerpted from Kenichi Ohmae, "Quality Control Circles: They Work and Don't Work," *Wall Street Journal* (March 29, 1982), p. 16. Reprinted by permission of the *Wall Street Journal.* Copyright © 1982 Dow Jones & Company, Inc. All rights reserved.

spective. When the Card Division of American Express undertook the complicated task of devising a quality-measurement system, the initial goal was to ensure consistent delivery of high-quality service. What emerged was a quality-assurance program that allows the company to measure and improve service while at the same time improving workflow and productivity.

Ruth C. Finley, a regional vice-president of the Card Division, started the quality-assurance program because of her strong—but then unsubstantiated—feeling that service to customers was both inadequate and too costly. "For some time, we have been dissatisfied with the traditional approach for evaluating customer service," she explains. "Reports to management were biased because they rarely included customers who had problems but did not complain, or those who were only marginally satisfied with the company's service. Accordingly, management usually got only what it wanted to hear." A cursory examination of obvious problems often led to superficial solutions, such as training programs to teach employees how to be courteous to customers with complaints.

Because the quality-assurance program delved beneath the surface, it found the root causes—as opposed to the manifestations—of customer complaints. "We concluded that the customer-service department is only the catcher's mitt. The real problems arise in other departments: data processing, mail room, new accounts, accounts receivable, etc. The fact that customer service has processed a customer order in two days is not helpful if the order stays in the mail room for four days, and another four days in data processing.

"Similarly, accounts receivable is just concerned about receiving funds. Well, that's fine if customers really owe money. But we had better make sure that they do before sending dunning letters."

Says Finley, "We were then faced with how to measure statistically what, up to then, had been an ephemeral notion of 'quality of service.' By analyzing letters of complaint and telephone calls, we discovered that customers were most concerned with three things: timeliness, accuracy, and responsiveness in fulfilling their requests.

"We felt it was crucial to involve employees in setting standards and improving work procedures, to foster teamwork, and enhance the employees' attitudes," explains Finley. "Employees from various departments joined together to analyze the work of each department, to identify problems—which we called 'business opportunities,' incidentally—and to seek improvements.

"By involving employees, we avoided the 'we've always done it that way' attitude and minimized anxiety and resentment caused by proposed changes. Employees also came to feel responsible for the program and had a clear idea of what was expected of them and the reasons. We discovered what the Japanese have long known: given the opportunity, employees will contribute very good ideas."

Today, customer service at American Express is measured with the same rigor and objectivity as costs and revenues. It is an implicit and important part of each employee's performance appraisal.

PRODUCTION AND OPERATIONS CONTROL IN A MANAGERIAL PERSPECTIVE

Now that we've examined some details involved in planning and controlling production/operations activities, it's time to step back and look at the broad picture again. In its role of transforming raw materials into finished goods or services, the production/operations function is part of the entire managerial framework within an organization. As such, it interfaces with the other functional areas of an enterprise, as shown in Figure 16.14. As you learned in the discussion earlier about Black & Decker, marketing is often involved directly in forecasting and production planning. Because people, raw materials, and equipment cost money, both accounting and finance need to be directly involved. Likewise, because any new product designs or changes in products will affect their production, engineering and P/OM must also interact.

To pull production and operations together in a managerial perspective, it is useful to consider two final topics that highlight contemporary trends in P/OM: (1) the challenges of high technology and (2) the link with corporate strategy.

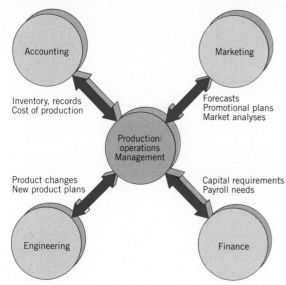

FIGURE 16.14 Functional interfaces of production/operations management.

Challenges of High Technology

One modern side of P/OM that has to be recognized is the increased impact of high technology on the manager's job in general, and on production and operations control in particular. A good way to highlight this point is by example of what is taking place in the manufacturing area of the Du Pont company.[17]

Du Pont is heavily involved in *computer-assisted design* (CAD) and *computer-assisted manufacturing* (CAM). The Engineering Department is developing programs and techniques that eventually will enable them to design and even test entire plants with a computer. Design time may be reduced by four-fifths.

At the Engineering Development and Engineering Physics laboratories in Wilmington, Delaware, engineers apply CAD and CAM techniques in building specialized manufacturing equipment. They have built a computer-controlled machine that can produce a test pack for Du Pont's automatic clinical analyzer several times faster than original machines and have greatly increased the speed at which wire for electronic connectors is plated.

More than 900 process computers are used to control plants in Du Pont, and the number is growing.

Computers do not replace the skill of process operators, but they do augment it by monitoring more temperature, pressure, flow rate, and mix-

ture-control points per second than would otherwise be possible. They give almost continuous reports on what is happening throughout the process. Adjustments can be made promptly—in some cases by the computers themselves—to keep the process running at optimum conditions. Compared to conventional process control, it's the difference between having a computer in your car that gives constant readout on mileage versus having to wait until you fill up the tank to figure out how well you're doing.

At Sabine River Works near Orange, Texas, computer control is saving an estimated $22 million annually.

The growing role of computers in modern management has been mentioned thoughout this book. It has been especially prominent in Chapter 15 and the present chapter. The Du Pont illustration is just one case in point. The impact of high technology is really everywhere. Take, for example, the growing role of robots in production and operations. What is the new breed of industrial robot like? One description follows.[18]

The new robots do not really look like Frankenstein's monster, or like Artoo Deetoo in *Star Wars*, but rather like a row of giant birds. They poke their 9-foot-long, rubber-sheathed necks toward the row of automobile frames. From their beaks, a blinding shower of sparks streams forth. The escape of compressed air creates a loud hissing sound. This is Chrysler's sprawling 145-acre Jefferson plant in East Detroit. Once 200 welders with their masks and welding guns used to work on such an assembly line. Here there are no welders in sight; there are only 50 robots craning forward, spitting sparks. They work two shifts, and the assembly line's output has increased by almost 20 percent since the robots arrived earlier this year.

No modern manager can afford not to be knowledgeable regarding the increased utilization of high technology in all aspects of an organization's manufacturing and service operations. Indeed, the P/OM area may be the one most likely to benefit and experience the greatest challenges from the high-technology developments of the future. Some predictions by the American Society of Manufacturing Engineers and the University of Michigan regarding the use of industrial robots in the United States are worth thinking about in this respect.[19]

- By 1985, 20 percent of the labor in the final assembly of cars will be replaced by automation. In the same year, "scene analysis" will provide enough feedback for robots to select parts scrambled in a bin.

- By 1987, 15 percent of all assembly systems will use robot technology.

- By 1988, 50 percent of the labor in small-component assembly will be replaced by automation.

- By 1990, the development of sensory techniques will enable robots to approximate human capability in assembly.

The Link With Corporate Strategy

A second timely issue relates back to the chapter opener—"A Star Is Born on the Factory Floor." This title is very symbolic. It recognizes that at the heart of any organization lies a core of essential manufacturing or service activities. This was a major point in the Norge and Carbondale Clinic examples that introduced this chapter. During the 1960s and 1970s, Harvard Business School professor Wickham Skinner was a strong and sometimes lonely advocate that businesses in particular give increased attention to the production process. His point was straightforward at the time and remains equally relevant today: manufacturing is an essential ingredient in the successful implementation of any business's corporate strategy. His concern or lament was expressed in 1969.[20]

A company's manufacturing function typically is either a competitive weapon or a corporate millstone. It is seldom neutral. The connection between manufacturing and corporate success is rarely seen as more than the achievement of high efficiency and low costs. In fact, the connection is much more critical and much more sensitive. Few top managers are aware that what appear to be routine manufacturing decisions frequently come to limit the corporation's strategic options, binding it with facilities, equipment, personnel, and basic controls and policies to a noncompetitive posture which may take years to turn around.

Frequently the interrelationship between production operations and corporate strategy is not easily grasped. The notion is simple enough—namely, that a company's competitive strategy at a given time places particular demands on its manufacturing function, and conversely, that the company's manufacturing posture and operations should be specifically designed to fulfill the task demanded by strategic plans. What is more elusive is the set of cause-and-effect factors which determine the linkage between strategy and production operations.

Today Wickham Skinner's appeals have been heard. Shocked by productivity challenges and the increasing loss of sales and opportunities to foreign competition, American businesses are "rediscovering" the factory as a place where the techniques and principles of modern management theory can be applied with success and with a major impact on performance results. John F. Budd, Jr., an Emhart vice-president, calls this the "new pragmatism"; David W. Wallace, chairman and president of Bangor Punta Corporation, calls it the "era of the manufacturing executive."[21]

Whatever the label, the net result is the same. The 1980s is a time when organizations of all types are refocusing on the basics—producing quality products and services quickly and at minimum cost. Executives are increasingly recognizing that the best strategic plans are useless if an organization's products and/or services are too costly or of too poor quality to sell. Today's managers are looking ahead and establishing new directions. Again, the words of Wickham Skinner summarize things well.[22]

Top management was making strategic planning decisions without taking into sufficient account the capabilities and limitations of the manufacturing operation. In reality, production cannot be taken for granted. There is no single most efficient way to make everything. "A factory can only do certain things well," Skinner notes. "There's a constant trade-off, for example, between cost and quality, between short delivery times and controlled inventory. When you recognize that everything is a trade-off you can tell the factory what's most important for it to do. The factory manager has to get dealt in on the company's strategy so he can make structural decisions that match the strategy. If the manufacturing is right, it's a competitive weapon; if it's wrong, it's a corporate millstone."

Skinner's ideas are equally relevant to service organizations. Their focus is on smooth production and provision of customer and client services, not industrial or consumer goods. In this setting it is not the factory that is being rediscovered, it is the service-delivery function. Whatever the setting, the essential argument is that productivity without effective production/operations planning and control is not possible for any organization . . . manufacturing or service, public or private, large or small.

SUMMARY

This chapter introduces the field of production/operations management and the fundamentals of production/operations control. This subject can fill a whole book by itself, and you may well have access to specialized P/OM courses elsewhere in your program of study. For our purposes in the introductory study of management, this chapter gives you an important overview. Even though one chapter certainly cannot cover everything in P/OM, you should now have some idea of the importance, techniques, and problems associated with the role of production and operations management in the control process.

The chapter began by describing the functions that any organization must perform to produce a good or service: (1) obtaining and storing raw materials, (2) scheduling people and equipment, and (3) creating finished goods or services from the combined efforts of people and equipment.

Production/operations management is the management of these resource-transformation processes in organizations. It requires special ef-forts at both planning and controlling production and service operations. Key activities in this regard include forecasting, aggregate scheduling, master scheduling, material-requirements planning, capacity planning and project scheduling, inventory control, and quality control. These activities are essential to any organization. They also make production/operations management an exciting and integral part of an organization's ongoing processes.

Finally, production and operations control in the modern world is heavily influenced by two factors. First, high technology and rapid advances in computers are lending greatly enhanced technical sophistication to production/operations processes and to the analytical capabilities of managers responsible for controlling them. Second, managers of today recognize the critical role of production and service operations in the activities of any organization. Without efficient and effective management of the production/operations function, corporate strategy cannot be fulfilled.

THINKING THROUGH THE ISSUES

1. Explain why production/operations control is extremely important to any organization.

2. List the three major production/operation activities involved in any manufacturing or service operation. Give examples of each in (a) a manufacturing setting and (b) a service setting.

3. Identify and explain two short-range forecasting techniques and one medium- to long-range one.

4. List the four components of a time series and briefly define each.

5. Explain the purpose and focus of aggregate scheduling.

6. What is MRP, or material-requirements planning? Give an example of its application in a manufacturing firm.

7. Explain the difference between standard time and clock time. Of what significance is this to the control of production/operations activities?

8. What is the difference between dependent and independent demand? Of what significance is this to the control of production/operations activities?

9. Explain the linkage between the philosophy of W. Edwards Deming and the concept of a quality-control circle.

10. Why does a modern manager require ever-greater familiarity with computers and their utilization in the production/operations planning and control process?

THE MANAGER'S VOCABULARY

Aggregate scheduling
Bill of capacity
Capacity planning
Carrying costs
Control chart
CPM
Demand forecasting
Dependent inventory demand
Dependent variable

Economic order quantity(EOQ)
Exponential smoothing
Gantt chart
Independent inventory demand
Independent variable
Inventory
Just-in-time delivery
Lot-by-lot ordering

Master scheduling
Material-requirements planning (MRP)
Moving average
Ordering costs
PERT
Production/operations management (P/OM)
Quality assurance
Quality control

Quality-control circle
Regression analysis
Routing sheet
Smoothing constant
Standard time
Time-series analysis
Weighted moving average

CAREER PERSPECTIVE: JOHN LATINI, QUALITY CONTROLLER[23]

WAYNE, Mich.—As the just-built Ford Escort rolled past him on the assembly line, the stocky factory manager opened the door on the driver's side and slammed it. The door cracked against its frame and bounced open. The same thing happened on the next car and the next.

John Latini groaned. The Ford Motor Company executive is well aware that in its advertising Ford touts the Escort's precision engineering and quality standards. And yet here was a flaw that wouldn't even escape notice in a dealer's showroom. As cars with defective doors continued to appear on the 4-mile-long assembly line, Latini retreated to his office to phone Detroit.

As manager of the huge Wayne plant, 54-year-old John Latini is responsible for seeing to it that the new Ford Escort and Mercury Lynx are built as defectfree as possible. "I guess you could say that the buck stops here when it comes to quality," the good-humored Latini says with a smile that spreads widely above his cleft chin. "At least I'm the one whose fanny gets kicked if the cars aren't built right."

A normal day begins for Latini at 7 A.M. as he reviews a stack of 30 reports on the plant's operations during the past 24 hours. But as soon as he can, he heads for the floor, generally stopping first at the end of the assembly line.

Latini makes a point of spending half an hour each day checking cars as they roll off the line. Often he is accompanied by several assistants. Together they swarm over the cars, sticking heads in and out of windows, scribbling notes, and shouting observations above the din of pneumatic wrenches, pounding hammers, and rumbling machinery.

He says the inspection tour is important because it brings small problems to his attention and because it lets workers know that he is interested in the jobs they are doing. "That's the way you get a quality product," he says. "You've got to keep your eye on the little things and you've got to show your employees that you care."

Questions

1. What do you think of Latini's apparent approach to quality control? Is it good or bad?

2. Put yourself in Latini's shoes. How can you avoid getting so bogged down in the details of day-to-day control that the broader and perhaps more strategic issues are missed?

3. Would you like to pursue career opportunities in the quality-control area? Why or why not?

CASE APPLICATION: DAY CITY ROLLERS, INC.

Day City Rollers is a small business that manufactures yo-yos—its only product. The yo-yos are primarily handmade from wood; Day City purchases the string from a supplier. Each yo-yo requires two sides, one dowel rod to connect the sides, and 4 feet of string.

It is now early April and the company is planning its production for the months of June through November. Forecasted sales for the 6 months of concern follow.

June	July	Aug.
3000	5000	6000

Sept.	Oct.	Nov.
2000	2000	3000

Based on past experience, Day City's production manager knows that each employee can make about 500 yo-yos per month. During the year, Day City employs four full-time employees, and during the summer it hires extra college students. As long as Day City guarantees these summer employees a full 3 months of work, it has no trouble hiring them. The summer employees earn $550 per month, while the regular employees earn $750.

The production lead time for all yo-yo parts is 1 month, except for the string, which must be ordered 2 months ahead of time in rolls of 15,000 feet. Day City estimates that it costs $10 to order string and 10¢ per month per 1000 feet to store it. Inventory carrying costs are 10¢ per month per finished yo-yo.

Questions

1. How can Day City meet its forecasted yo-yo demand for the lowest cost? To answer this question: (a) develop an aggregate plan or production schedule (of the form shown in Table 16.3) indicating how many employees will be working each month, and (b) calculate the payroll costs associated with this schedule.

2. When must the component parts be ordered and in what quantities? To answer this question: (a) use your aggregate plan to determine gross requirements for component parts, and (b) use MRP to develop planned orders. Your finished answer should include a chart such as the one presented in Table 16.6.

CLASS EXERCISE: IN OR OUT OF CONTROL?:

This chapter introduced control charts in the discussion of statistical quality control. Good managers will use control charts to spot undesirable trends before too many violations of control limits occur. Problem solving can then be done to correct any production/operations process representing a source of potential trouble.

1. Study the four control charts presented in Figure 16.15.

2. Decide which, if any, of these charts suggest the existence of a problem. Which charts suggest a production or operations process that may be going "out of control"? Why?

3. Share your decisions with a nearby classmate. Be sure to examine the rationale behind each other's conclusions carefully. Await further class discussion.

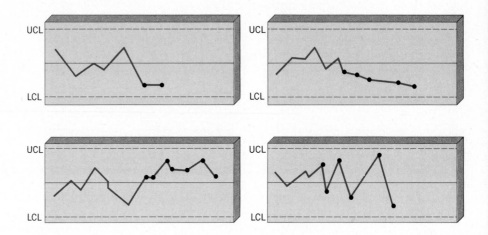

FIGURE 16.15 Four control charts. *Source:* Jack R. Meredith and Thomas E. Gibbs, *The Management of Operations* (New York: 1980), p. 516. Used by permission.

REFERENCES

[1] Lisa Miller Mesdag, "A Star Is Born on the Factory Floor," *Fortune*, Vol. 104, No. 1 (July 13, 1981), p. 60. © 1981 Time Inc. Courtesy of *Fortune Magazine*.

[2] Jack R. Meredith and Thomas E. Gibbs, *The Management of Operations* (New York: Wiley, 1980), pp. 75, 76.

[3] Ibid., p. 296.

[4] William Berry, Thomas Vollmann, and D. Clay Whybark. *Master Production Scheduling: Principles and Practice* (Washington, D.C.: American Production and Inventory Control Society, 1979).

[5] Portions of this section are adapted in part from Lawrence J. Gitman and Carl McDaniel, Jr., *Business World* (New York: Wiley, Inc., 1983), pp. 238–240. Used by permission.

[6] See Meredith and Gibbs, op. cit., pp. 407–408.

[7] Richard J. Schonberger, "A Revolutionary Way to Streamline the Factory," *Wall Street Journal* (November 15, 1982), p. 24.

[8] Urban C. Lehner, "The Nuts and Bolts of Japan's Factories," *Wall Street Journal* (March 31, 1981), p. 20.

[9] Adapted from John D. Baxter, "Kanban Works Wonders, But Will It Work in U.S. Industry?" *Iron Age*, Vol. 225, No. 16 (June 7, 1982), pp. 44–48. Used by permission.

[10] Jeremy Main, "The Battle for Quality Begins," *Fortune* (December 29, 1980), p. 28.

[11] Ibid.

[12] See W. Edwards Deming, "On Some Statistical Aids Toward Economic Production," *Interfaces*, Vol. 5, No. 4 (August 1975), pp. 1–15.

[13] Main, op. cit., p. 30. © 1980 Time Inc. Courtesy of *Fortune Magazine*.

[14] Arnold Kanarick, "The Far Side of Quality Circles," *Management Review*, Vol. 70 (October 1981), pp. 16–17.

[15] Ibid.

[16] Adapted by permission of the publisher, from "How American Express Measures Quality of Its Customer Service" from *Management Review,* Vol. 71 (March 1982), pp. 29–31, © 1982 by AMACOM, a division of American Management Associations. All rights reserved.

[17] *1983 Annual Report of the Du Pont Company,* pp. 3, 6. Used by permission.

[18] "The Robot Revolution," *Time* (December 8, 1980), p. 72.

[19] Ibid.

[20] Reprinted by permission of the *Harvard Business Review.* Excerpt from "Manufacturing—Missing Link in Corporate Strategy" by Wickham Skinner, *Harvard Business Review,* Vol. 47 (May–June 1969), pp. 136–145. Copyright © 1969 by the President and Fellows of Harvard College; all rights reserved.

[21] "Business Refocuses on the Factory Floor," *Business Week* (February 2, 1981), p. 91.

[22] Robert Lubar, "Rediscovering the Factory," *Fortune* (July 13, 1981), pp. 52–64.© 1981 Time Inc. Courtesy of *Fortune Magazine.*

[23] Excerpted from John Koten, "Quality Controller: A Ford Plant Manager Tries to Limit Defects in Escort, Lynx Models," the *Wall Street Journal* (May 15, 1981), p. 1. Reprinted by permission of the *Wall Street Journal.* Copyright © 1981 Dow Jones & Company, Inc. All rights reserved.

Part 5
INTEGRATING CASES

THE SIROCCO COMPANY

The Sirocco Company, located in a large Midwestern city, manufactured and sold hot-air heating equipment for residential installations. Since its incorporation the company had experienced a steady and satisfactory growth. About two years ago several new designs and sizes of both oil and gas furnaces were added to the rather restricted product line that had been adhered to previously. Concurrently, distribution was extended to the Eastern Seaboard and the Southeast, as well as to a wider coverage of the Midwest market.

As a result of these two moves, sales volume increased rapidly until it reached a level about double that of any prior year. Net profits, however, moved in the opposite direction. The president of the company, who was also its principal stockholder, was deeply concerned about this poor showing and set out to determine the reasons for it. He was convinced that while increased taxes and higher wage rates had some bearing on the lower profit margins, there were other more fundamental causes.

Source: Paul E. Holden, Frank K. Schellenberger, and Walter A. Diehm, *Selected Case Problems in Industrial Management*, Second Edition, 1962, p. 329. Reprinted by permission of Prentice-Hall, Inc., Englewood Cliffs, New Jersey.

The president asked his daughter to undertake an investigation of the situation and make recommendations. She had been with the company six years following graduation from college. During this time she had been successively in the Engineering, Manufacturing, Sales, and Accounting departments, learning something of the major phases of the company's operations with a view toward taking over some of the administrative burden from her father.

Although the company had established broad company policies and objectives, it had never instituted any set method of systematic planning and control of company operations. No attempt had ever been made to control expenditures or determine financial requirements for the fiscal periods of the business. There was little or no coordination between any of the departments except that which could be accomplished personally by the president. This problem had not been too serious previously because the company's operations had been small enough for the president to coordinate the activities of the departments on a personal basis through conferences with the various department heads. However, the operations of the company had now grown so large that it was im-

possible for one man to provide this coordination effectively.

An analysis of the cost-accounting system in use showed that only historical costs were provided. Standard costs were considered by the controller to be the lowest costs ever incurred. Therefore, any measurement of current results involved nothing more than a comparison with records of prior periods. The controller agreed that because of the many variables that could enter the picture, this type of comparison was not an adequate measure of performance.

It was discovered that expenditures for administrative expenses, such as officers' salaries, office expenses, credits and collections, accounting, and personnel, were taking up 10 cents out of every sales dollar. Administrative expenses had increased over 200 percent during the period that profits were declining.

Sales estimates had been made in the past by the sales manager on a very unscientific basis. As a matter of fact, his estimates of sales consisted of little more than what he thought his salespeople should sell. Since his estimates had consistently been too optimistic, the head of the Production Department paid little attention to them and produced what he deemed necessary in the light of past experience. As a result, there was little tie-in between sales and production. On several occasions, production of one product had to be discountinued to make way for a customer's order that could not be filled out of stock.

Each year, the sales manager had appropriated a round amount for advertising. Last year, this account was $150,000. Advertising expense was allocated to sales branches on the basis of past sales. The sales manager reasoned that advertising should be directed to those branches that were doing the best job.

Because of the poor coordination between production and sales, the purchasing program of the company had always been largely on a hand-to-mouth basis. For example, when it was decided to undertake the manufacture of oil burners, no accurate estimate of sales had been made. As a result, the purchasing agent had held up his purchase of materials at the request of the production manager until sufficient orders for burners had been received to warrant a production run. Because materials then had to be purchased quickly, top

prices were paid for them. This procedure had been one cause of the low profit margin on oil burners.

The personnel manager had frequently been burdened with the task of hurriedly hiring many new workers in order to speed up production on a certain line for which the demand was larger than had been anticipated by either the sales manager or the production manager.

In the report to her father, the daughter recommended that a system of budgetary control be established. She explained that a sound system of budgetary control would alleviate the company's main problem—namely, that each department head had been working for the good of his or her own department, irrespective of the effect on the other departments.

With this strong representation, the father decided to accept the recommendation and asked the daughter to proceed immediately to install a budget. After the figures had been obtained, an estimate of the results for the next 12 months revealed a net loss of $14,000. Thereupon the

father suggested that all budgetary procedures be discountinued, with the remark, "We do not need a budget to put us into the red; we can find the way ourselves. Instead of sitting around trying to figure out what may or may not happen, instead of dreaming about the future, let's get rid of all this red tape and go to work and get business."

Questions
Put yourself in the position of the daughter.

1. What reasons beyond that mentioned in her final recommendation would you have advanced in support of a plan of budgetary control? What would you have pointed out as the limitations of budgetary control?

2. What steps, preferably in chronological order, would you have taken to set up the budget?

3. What recommendations, in addition to the installation of a budget, would you have made in terms of management controls? Why?

MBO AT AMERICAN DIGITRON

Greg Davis was one of the most vocal opponents of American

Source: This case was prepared by Daniel Robey in collaboration with Alberto de Solo and Todd Anthony. It is found in Daniel Robey, *Designing Organizations: A Macro Perspective* (Homewood, Ill.: Richard D. Irwin, 1982), pp. 431–433. Used by permission.

Digitron's management-by-objectives (MBO) program, but his warnings had not been heeded. Now he found himself having to fire Gus Kaplan, a top salesman, as a result of MBO's implementation.

American Digitron is one of the top seven firms in the rapidly expanding data-processing in-

dustry. It manufacturers, installs, and services information-processing systems worldwide, and carries one of the broadest hardware and software product lines in the industry. Digitron offers a complete line of peripherals, communications networks, data centers, training centers, field maintenance, engineering, and other services.

In 1979 Greg Davis was the ranking administrative manager in American Digitron's Southwest U.S. district. The district was broken down into four departments: sales, systems engineering, field engineering, and administration. The MBO plan was designed to treat each department except administration as an individual profit center. Using a complex formula called the flexible expense budget, the MBO system attempted to balance revenues against expenses in each of these three business areas. Administrative managers, such as Davis, were not subject to this formula, but were evaluated annually according to a different but equally detailed set of objectives. Performance on these objectives was a major criterion in annual performance evaluations of the administrative managers.

Davis was especially upset about his performance on one such measure known as assigned inventory. A few months after American Digitron implemented its MBO program, Gus Kaplan, one of the Southwest district's leading salesmen, had come to Davis to persuade him to keep a very expensive computer system in inventory at that district. Kaplan had assured Davis that a major long-time customer had already signed an order for it. While having such an expensive system on hand would look bad on Davis's assigned inventory performance, he agreed to hold on to the system as a favor to Kaplan.

Unfortunately for both Davis and Kaplan, the proposed sale fell through, and Davis's inventory objectives were not met because of the additional inventory on hand. Upon questioning Kaplan about the order, Davis was told that the customer had never really signed one; Kaplan had only wanted to be sure that the system would be readily available as an additional selling point to the customer. The net result was a lower MBO rating for Davis and the subsequent firing of Kaplan.

Such an occurrence, while having more severe consequences than most, has not been unusual since American Digitron embraced MBO. In the early years of the company's history, when it sold accounting machines, a salesperson wrote the complete order, programmed the machine's tabs and accumulators, and occasionally made minor mechanical adjustments. Today, the computer salesperson depends on an administrative assistant to prepare all the paperwork, a field engineer to install, test, and adjust the equipment, and a systems engineer to get the computer system up and running. At times it was very difficult to find who was to blame when the customer later complained about system malfunctions or other service needs.

Davis predicted all along that the MBO plan and its accompanying rewards system would reduce cooperation among departments in his district, and the Kaplan incident had convinced him. As people sought to meet their own individual objectives, they would become less sensitive to the needs of others, even when they all had to work together to satisfy the customer. Davis was perfectly willing to dismiss disruptive individuals like Kaplan who resorted to outright dishonesty to get their way. But it seemed that MBO had even more problems than just motivating selfishness.

Timeliness of reports was one of the most heavily weighted criteria for judging Davis's performance as a district administrative manager. The Revenue Action Plan was one report that absolutely had to be submitted on time because it was used by upper managment to forecast American Digitron's revenues for each upcoming month. However, it was the *sales manager's* duty to keep track of orders and billing, both of which were required inputs to the report Davis submitted. Timeliness of reports is not among sales managers' performance objectives in the MBO system, though. As a result they often come to Davis's desk late, and the Revenue Action Plan is submitted late. Lately, Davis's own MBO ratings had suffered a great deal because of late filing of these reports.

Davis felt that he and many others had been unjustly victimized by the MBO program. On top of problems like those described, the system multiplied his already substantial load of paperwork. The time had come to voice his complaints. He was certain that other department managers must be experiencing similar difficulties, and he intended to make his views clear at an upcoming meeting of managers at the district level and above. He had already begun to itemize a list of specific complaints.

Questions

1. Why is the MBO system causing difficulty?

2. What specific points do you think Davis will be prepared to voice at the meeting?

3. What modifications should be made to increase the effectiveness of the MBO system? Why?

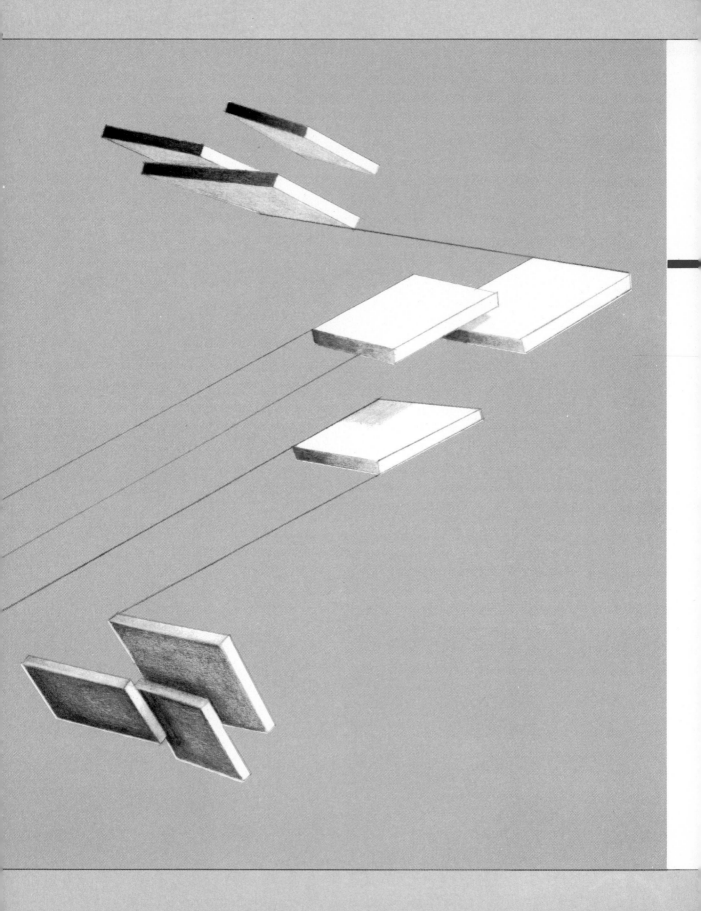

PART
6

PRODUCTIVITY IN THE CONTEMPORARY ENVIRONMENT

Chapters in This Part of the Book

AMC AND CHINA AGREE TO BUILD JEEPS IN PEKING

Unions React to Automation by Stressing Job Security and Retraining

Dow Versus the Dioxin Monster

Each of the above headlines communicates a different challenge faced by managers and organizations in today's complex environment.[1] These challenges involve new technological developments as well as greater international competition and a growing sensitivity to corporate social responsibilities. These are but three examples of the countless problems and opportunities that arise in the contemporary environment. They are among the challenges that futurists predict will only increase in number and variety as we move into the late 1980s and beyond.

Perspective: A New Era for Management

John Naisbitt is one of these futurists. He begins his popular book, *Megatrends*, with the statement,[2]

"As a society, we have been moving from the old to the new. And we are still in motion. Caught between eras, we experience turbulence. Yet, amid the sometimes painful and uncertain present, the restructuring of America proceeds unrelentingly."

Naisbitt could have replaced the word "America" with that of any other country, state, city, or even organization. His statement would remain just as true.

Alvin Toffler, author of *Future Shock, Eco-Spasm, The Third Wave,* and *Previews and Premises,* is another popular futurist. He is well noted for his ability to look ahead into the dynamic and unpredictable world of tomorrow. In a *Wall Street Journal* column, he again presses us to look and think ahead to a world of work in which "revolutionary change is occurring at every level of our social and economic order" and is characterized by "deep changes in organization structure, in scale of operation, in the nature of work and the treatment of workers."[3] High technology, and its growing impact on our

everyday lives, is the force behind these "changes" of which Toffler speaks.

Peter Drucker is even more specific in addressing the new era of management that is now upon us. Earlier in Part 1 we looked at Drucker's perspective of the contemporary work environment. Recall his words: "No job is going to change more in the next decade than that of the first-line supervisor in both factory and office."[4] What are the forces Drucker sees as affecting the managerial role? He mentions the growing presence of automation in the work place and basic changes in the character of industrial relations, particularly the increased transfer of power from supervisor to worker.

Drucker's ideas on what is needed to assist the supervisor in making the necessary transition to achieve success in this contemporary environment are

---

[1] These headlines are from the *Wall Street Journal* (May 3, 1983), pp. 1, 33 and (December 20, 1982) p. 1.
[2] John Naisbitt, *Megatrends: Ten New Directions Transforming Our Lives* (New York: Warner, 1982).

[3] Alvin Toffler, "Reordering Industry as the Era of the Masses Passes," *Wall Street Journal* (June 16, 1983), p. 20.
[4] Peter F. Drucker, "Twilight of the First-Line Supervisor?" *Wall Street Journal* (June 7, 1983), p. 32.

applicable to modern managers functioning at all levels of responsibility in organizations. He says,[5]

"To benefit from the changes—in technology, in industrial relations, in demographics—we need a stronger, more confident, more responsible first-line supervisor. We need to do what IBM did 25 years ago when it determined that the job of its "managers" was to bring out and put to work the strengths of the work force: competence and knowledge and capacity to take responsibility. This is not being permissive; on the contrary, it is being demanding."

To make good decisions and solve problems, managers of tomorrow must be prepared to understand and face up to the many demands of a highly dynamic environment. Success will entail the ability to personally grow, develop, and perform in a manner consistent with changing social trends. From the thoughts of Naisbitt, Toffler, and Drucker we can foresee a world of work subject to the influence of

- High technology
- An information explosion
- Increased worker participation
- Changing labor-management relations
- A global economy
- Heightened environmental awareness
- Greater social responsibility

It all adds up to an era in which the role and function of managers will be stretched to new limits. This will be an era in which the very nature of organizations

themselves will be changing.

Recently, a *Business Week* special report offered further thoughts on how changing times affect the managers of today, and how they will continue to affect managers in the future. Here are some of the ideas the report touches on.

The Impact of Advanced Technology[6]

"The onrushing electronics revolution is changing the role of the middle manager and forcing a radical restructuring of the corporation's middle ranks, shrinking them drastically in the best-managed companies. Just as the industrial revolution changed hierarchies, radicalized labor, realigned political forces, and created widespread social and psychological disruption, the technological revolution is producing pain and strain. The initial impact is being felt by the middle manager, who typically earns $25,000 to $80,000."

The New Demands on Managers[7]

"Companies want flexible 'people-managers' who know how to set goals and motivate other people. They want managers capable of slugging it out in fiercely competitive international markets and who have an understanding of complex financial issues. And they want implementers familiar with computers who

can cope with the impact of technology on their products."

The New Demands on Organizations[8]

"Rigid hierarchical structures have begun to crumble at the best-managed companies. Replacing them are leaner, more fluid organizations, with fewer levels of management and more direct lines of communication between the top and bottom. Instead of relying on entrenched specialist bureaucracies, companies are pulling together a few key managers on an ad hoc basis to solve immediate problems—and disbanding them just as quickly. In place of corporate cultures in which titles determine power—and automatic raises and promotions are built into the system—companies are creating environments in which compensation depends on performance, and freedom to improve performance provides the psychic reward."

Each of the above predictions and viewpoints is but a single glimpse into the world of conflict, change, and development within which the modern manager must be prepared to live. Successful managers recognize that management must be used and managerial skills must be applied to meet these challenges on a day-to-day basis so that they can be mastered. Thus, it is entirely appropriate that Part 6 of this book be devoted to achieving productivity in the contemporary environment.

---

[5] Ibid.

[6] "A New Era for Management," *Business Week* (April 25, 1983), p. 50. Used by permission.
[7] "Who Will Retrain the Obsolete Managers," *Business Week* (April 25, 1983), p. 76. Used by permission.

[8] "The Shrinking of Middle Management," *Business Week* (April 25, 1983), p. 54. Used by permission.

17

MANAGING CONFLICT, CHANGE, AND ORGANIZATION DEVELOPMENT

THEY'RE STRIKING SOME STRANGE BARGAINS AT DIAMOND SHAMROCK

William H. Bricker, president of Diamond Shamrock Corporations, talked to two consultants about ways of helping Shamrock's managers overcome their fears and animosities toward one another and more freely speak their minds.[1] He felt that they would stimulate better communication, decision making, and problem solving. Company performance was expected to improve as a result.

The consultants suggested "organization development" and a specific technique called "role negotiation." The latter was to take place during an "executive retreat." What transpired at the retreat is evident in the following calendar items.

SUNDAY 26:
For three days at a resort in Ohio, 30 managers from Diamond Shamrock's plastics division gathered to negotiate improvements in the way they deal with one another. The first day they took a personality test known as FIRO-B. The tests were handed out by Theron L. Day, manager of employee development, after Richard L. Hill, a consultant, explained the procedure. Though the managers would have preferred watching football on TV, they found themselves answering such questions as whether they "try to get close and personal with people."

MONDAY 27:
A list was posted of the managers' FIRO-B test scores—but not their names. Executives from each of seven departments were asked to figure out which scores belonged to themselves and to other members of the department. In some cases, the intent expressions turned to looks of surprise as the managers discovered such traits in themselves as an urge to dominate.

TUESDAY 28:
Just before they get down to hard bargaining about their roles, the managers exchanged lists of the things they would like each other to do more of, less of, or the same. Each executive then drew up a master list, containing all the requests that were made of him, and posted it on a wall. If a request was puzzling to the recipient, he asked that it be clarified: consultants sat in to keep tempers from flaring up.

WEDNESDAY 28:
After they had a chance to negotiate the requests they were making of one another, the managers drew up written contracts, many of them complete with penalties in case of noncompliance. The head of the operations team, Richard J. Sutch, negotiated two agreements with Harold E. Birr, his special-projects manager, and three more with his two other subordinates. In one of their contracts, Sutch promised to help Birr further plan and develop his career, while Birr agreed in return to improve his own "listening skills."

PLANNING AHEAD

This chapter is about how organizations and their managers cope with and respond to the challenges posed by dynamic and uncertain environments. We will examine a number of specific issues relating to the processes of conflict, change, and development in the manager's work setting. Key topics include

Creativity and Innovation in Organizations
Conflict in Organizations
Conflict Management
Organizational Change
Managing Planned Change
Organization Development (OD)

Organizations and managers must continually adapt to changing situations and be willing to initiate change if they are to prosper and even survive over time. The very nature of the dynamic, complex, and at times unpredictable environment in which we live demands this. People change, their tastes and values change, governments and laws change, technologies change, and knowledge changes. Unless organizations also change, they risk stagnation, decline, and even death. Consider, for example,[2]

- *The small research company* that chose an organization structure too complicated and formal for its young age and limited size. After floundering in rigidity and bureaucracy for several years, it was finally acquired by a larger company.

- *The retail store chain* whose key executives held on to an organization structure long after it had served its purpose, because their power was derived from this structure. The company eventually went into bankruptcy.

- *The large bank* that blamed and disciplined a "rebellious" manager for current control problems, when the underlying cause was centralized procedures that held back expansion into new markets. Many younger managers subsequently left the bank, competition moved in, and profits declined.

Each of the examples is of an organization whose managers thought and acted as if locked into the past, instead of tuned into the present. For one reason or another, key decisions were made without taking changing environmental circumstances into account. The organization suffered as a result.

Another organization that might have easily fallen prey to similar decline is the Girl Scouts. Many environmental changes have occurred since the organization was founded in 1912. But, as *Newsline 17.1* shows, the Girl Scouts organization is a solid one that uses modern management practices. The following observations add further perspective to the example by showing how the Girl Scouts have adapted to environmental changes over time.[3]

Girl Scouts still do sell cookies—an estimated 125 million boxes this year for gross revenues of $219 million. They still camp out in the wilderness. Their motto remains "Be Prepared." But the little green dresses are frequently being replaced by skirt-and-slacks sets or, in many cases, by whatever the scout chooses to wear. Today, girls can become Girl Scouts without joining troops. And Girl Scout "badges," symbols of accomplishment that used to bear such titles as "dressmaker," "homemaker," and "hostess," now are awarded in categories like "aerospace," "business-wise," and "computer fun." Because women increasingly work and live on their own, scouts are emphasizing self-awareness and self-reliance; a "Ms. Fix-It" badge requires projects in home repairs.

Girl Scout officials say nothing has had a more profound effect on their organization than the movement of women into the working world. "Because women's roles are changing, so are girls' roles," says Margaret Lee, the director of programs for a Girl Scout council in Bakersfield, Calif. Linda

NEWSLINE 17.1

GIRL SCOUT OFFICIALS EARN PLAUDITS FOR MANAGEMENT

Girl Scout officials are becoming modern managers.

Each year, the heads of Girl Scout councils from around the country take management seminars taught by Harvard Business School faculty. Peter Drucker, the well-known expert on management, once said he considered Girl Scouts the best-managed organization around. "Tough, hard-working women can do anything," he observed.

Girl Scout workbooks give officials tips on "strategic planning," "feasibility testing," and setting "operating objectives."

Corporate bigwigs are on board, too. The president of Metropolitan Life Insurance Co. and the chairmen of AT&T and IBM are leading a drive to raise funds for a newly opened Girl Scout conference center in Briarcliff, N.Y.

Girl Scouts are no strangers to big money. The 1981 annual report of Girl Scouts U.S.A., certified by Price Waterhouse & Co., shows that the organization had revenues of $22.7 million. Cash and marketable securities on Sept. 30, 1981, totaled $14.7 million.

Source: "Girl Scout Officials Earn Plaudits for Management," *Wall Street Journal* (July 15, 1982), p. 22. Reprinted by permission of the *Wall Street Journal.* Copyright © 1982 Dow Jones & Company, Inc. All rights reserved.

Rogers, field director of a council in Catawba, S.C., says: "We encourage the girl not to think about being the airline stewardess, but about being the pilot. Girl scouting is reaching out into different areas."

There are signs that the changes are paying off. Although last year's total membership, including adults, of 2.8 million was down 28 percent from a record 3.9 million in 1969, it was up 1.6 percent from the 1980 total—the first increase in 12 years. More significantly, the Girl Scouts have been attracting new kinds of members: economically disadvantaged girls, minority-group girls—even pregnant girls.

Both this example and the chapter-opening case of the Diamond Shamrock Corporation illustrate how enlightened management can try to avoid problems and take maximum advantage of environmental opportunities over time. This chapter examines how organizational adaptation is facilitated by sound management of the processes of conflict, change, and development. The central issue involves the capacities of organizations and their members to achieve creativity and innovation in the contemporary environment.

CREATIVITY AND INNOVATION IN ORGANIZATIONS

A healthy organization provides for and stimulates a free flow of information and interchange of criticisms, suggestions, and ideas among its members. The president of Diamond Shamrock, for example, felt that if his managers were more interpersonally comfortable with one another, the whole organization would benefit from more frank and sincere communications. This case represents the positive side—a proactive and concerned top manager willing to take action to promote rather than resist or avoid the challenges of change. The opposite extreme is reflected in the experiences of a Unilever executive who put his frustrations into rhyme.[4]

Along this tree
From root to crown
Ideas flow up
And vetos flow down.

This verse leaves the impression of an organization with the advantages of alertness and imagination at its lower levels, but suffering from resistance to change and a lack of foresight at the top. Whereas Unilever had the internal capability of achieving creativity and innovation, top management was apparently discouraging instead of encouraging it. The ability to facilitate creativity and innovation is among the most basic of a manager's work responsibilities.

Individual Creativity

Creativity—ingenuity and imagination resulting in a novel approach to things or in a unique solution to a problem—was first discussed in Chapter 3. At the time we were interested in creativity as an element in the problem-solving process. You should recall our focus on ways to avoid creativity "blocks" and stimulate both individual and group creativity.

One related issue pertains to the link between people's creative potential and their basic intellectual capabilities. Is the term *creative genius* accurate? Must one have superintellectual powers to achieve creativity? Figure 17.1 summarizes research on these questions and basically concludes that the answer is "no." People do not have to be geniuses to be creative.

Organizational Innovation

Table 17.1 presents several characteristics of creative individuals and creative organizations. Together, the two sets of characteristics establish a capacity for **organizational innovation.** This is the process of taking a new idea and putting it into practice as part of the organization's normal operating routines. An innovative organization is one that is able to[5]

1. *Maintain a continuing influx of new ideas.* Members must be encouraged to scan the environment and watch for new ideas and developments of potential merit to the organization. This involves reaching outside organizational bound-

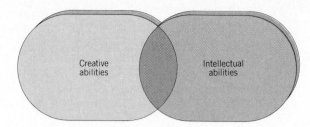

FIGURE 17.1 Relationship of individual creative and intellectual abilities. The degree of overlap between the two sets of abilities—creative and intellectual—is apparently not large. *Source:* H. Joseph Reitz, *Behavior in Organizations* (Homewood, Ill.: Richard D. Irwin, 1977), p. 209. Used by permission.

aries through travel and visits to interact with outsiders, being exposed to consultants, and staying abreast of current events through the written media. Members must stay informed and continually be in contact with sources of new ideas. People who perform this role are often called "information gatekeepers."

2. *Modify new ideas to fit organization needs and circumstances.* Members must be capable of meeting to discuss new ideas to establish their worth, decide on appropriate modifications, and generate enthusiasm for a forthcoming change of practices. Whereas idea generation is stimulated by exposure and external contacts, refinement of these ideas into appropriate forms depends on the organization's internal "climate" and processes. This is the point where leadership styles, corporate cultures, organization structures, and communication skills become extremely relevant to the task at hand.

3. *Implement and reinforce new ideas as part of day-to-day operating routines.* Even the best idea won't benefit anyone or anything until it becomes a part of the organization's standard practice. Not only must the new idea be implemented; it must also be reinforced, and those who use it must be rewarded for their efforts. Then and only then will the full benefits of innovation be experienced over time by the organization and its members.

All managers share the challenge of stimulating innovation in their organizations. This point of view is expressed in *Newsline 17.2* on the "innovative company." The rest of this chapter focuses on how the processes of conflict, planned change, and organization development become

Table 17.1 Characteristics of the Creative Individual and Creative Organization

Creative Individual	Creative Organization
Conceptual fluency, able to produce a large number of ideas quickly	Has "idea persons"; open channels of communication; idea units absolved of other responsibilities; encourages contact with outside sources
Originality, generates unusual ideas	Heterogenous personnel policy; includes marginal, unusual types; assigns nonspecialists to problems; allows eccentricity
Separates source from content in evaluating information; motivated by interest in problem; follows wherever it leads	Has an objective, fact-founded approach; ideas evaluated on their merits; selects and promotes on merit only
Suspends judgment; avoids early commitment; spends more time in analysis, exploration	Lack of financial, material commitment to products, policies; invests in basic research and flexible, long-range planning; experiments with new ideas; everything gets a chance
Less authoritarian; relativistic view of life	More decentralized and diversified; administrative slack; time and resources to absorb errors; risk-taking ethos—tolerates and expects taking chances
Accepts own impulses; playful, undisciplined exploration	Not run as "tight ship"; employees have fun; allows freedom to choose and pursue problems; freedom to discuss ideas
Independent of judgment; shows less conformity; sees self as different	Organizationally autonomous; original and different objectives
Rich, "bizarre" fantasy life *and* superior reality orientation	Security of routine allows innovation; stable, secure environment that allows "creators" to roam; separate units or occasions for generating versus evaluating ideas; separates creative from productive functions

Source: Reprinted from *The Creative Organization*, pp. 16–18, edited by Gary A. Steiner, by permission of The University of Chicago Press, © 1965 by The University of Chicago. All rights reserved.

important to managers in their attempts to achieve the desired ends of individual creativity and organizational innovation.

CONFLICT IN ORGANIZATIONS

Conflict occurs whenever disagreements exist in a social situation over issues of substance and/or emotional antagonisms. **Substantive conflicts** involve disagreements over such things as goals, the allocation of resources, distribution of rewards, policies, and procedures, and job assignments. **Emotional conflicts** result from feelings of anger, distrust, dislike, fear, and resentment, as well as from personality clashes.[6] Both forms may have destructive or constructive implications for organizations and their members.

Destructive Conflict

Destructive conflict works to the disadvantage of the individual(s) and/or organization(s) involved. It occurs, for example, when two employees are unable to work together because of interpersonal hostilities (a destructive emotional conflict) or when the members of a committee fail to act because they can't agree on group goals (a de-

NEWSLINE 17.2

THE INNOVATIVE COMPANY

It is widely believed that large companies cannot innovate. That is simply not true: Merck, Citibank, and 3M are three examples of highly innovative corporate giants. But it is true that to innovate successfully, a company has to be run differently from the typical "well-managed" business, whether large or small.

The innovative company understands that innovation starts with an idea. And ideas are somewhat like babies—they are born small, immature, and shapeless. They are promise rather than fulfillment. In the innovative company executives do not say: "This is a damn-fool idea." Instead they ask: "What would be needed to make this embryonic, half-baked, foolish idea into something that makes sense, that is feasible, that is an opportunity for us?"

Above all, the innovative company organizes itself to abandon the old, the obsolete, the no longer productive. It never says: "There will always be a market for a well-made buggy whip." It knows that whatever human beings have created becomes obsolete sooner or later—usually sooner. And it prefers to abandon its obsolete products itself rather than have them made obsolete by the competition.

We clearly face a period in which the demands and opportunities for innovation will be greater than at any time in living memory—as great perhaps as in the 50 years preceding World War I, during which new technical or social inventions, almost immediately spawning new industries, emerged on average every 18 months.

Telecommunications, automation of manufacturing processes around the microprocessor, the "automated office," rapid changes in banking and finance, medicine, biogenetics, bioengineering, and biophysics—these are only a few of the areas where change and innovation are already proceeding at high speed. To compete in this environment, companies will need to muster large sums of money to boost their research budgets, even in a severe depression. But what will be required above all are the attitudes, policies, and practices of the innovative organization.

Source: Peter F. Drucker, "The Innovative Company," *Wall Street Journal* (February 26, 1982), p. 22. Reprinted by permission of the *Wall Street Journal.* Copyright © 1982 Dow Jones & Company, Inc. All rights reserved.

structive substantive conflict). There are many circumstances under which conflict can be upsetting to the persons experiencing the conflict, to others who may observe its occurrence, and to the organization or subunits in which the conflict situation exists. It can simply be uncomfortable, for example, to be in the same work area where two co-workers are continually hostile toward each other.

The disadvantages of destructive conflicts are many. Some of the more general harm that can be done for the people involved includes unnecessary or overpowering stress, decreased communication and increased suspicion, reduced cooperation, increased competition, and decreased concern for a common goal. Overall, destructive conflicts can reduce the effectiveness of individuals, groups, and organizations by decreasing productivity and satisfaction.

Constructive Conflict

Constructive conflict is quite a different story. It results in benefits instead of disadvantages for the individual(s) and/or organization(s) involved. These benefits include,

1. *Increased creativity and innovation* As a result of the conflict, the people involved end up doing things or behaving in new and better ways.

2. *Increased effort* Conflict takes effort to deal with and can cause the people involved to work harder and achieve new things; conflict helps overcome apathy.

3. *Increased cohesion* Conflict with outsiders can create a greater sense of group identity and cohesion; commitment to the common purpose can increase as a result.

4. *Reduced tension* Conflict can help people drain off interpersonal tensions otherwise held back and causing internal stress.

In its constructive form, conflict helps enhance creativity and innovation in organizations. By offering opportunities to recognize otherwise neglected problems and opportunities, and to increase the creative capacities of individuals and groups in dealing with them, conflict can be of major benefit to organizations. Indeed, the following example illustrates how *too little* conflict can compromise organizational effectiveness.[7]

> The bankruptcy of the Penn Central Railroad has been generally attributed to mismanagement and a failure of the company's board of directors to question actions taken by management. The board was composed of outside directors who met monthly to oversee the railroad's operations. Few questioned the decisions made by the management. Apathy and a desire to avoid conflict allowed poor decisions to stand unquestioned. It can only be postulated how differently things might have turned out for the Penn Central if it had an inquiring board which demanded that the company's management discuss and justify key decisions.

Whether conflict works beneficially for the organization or not depends on two factors: (1) the intensity of the conflict, and (2) how well the conflict is managed. The inverted "U" curve in Figure 17.2 shows that conflict of moderate intensity can be good for the organization, whereas very low- or very high-intensity conflict can be

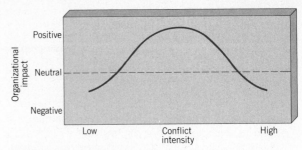

FIGURE 17.2 Conflict intensity and conflict outcomes.

bad. Too much conflict overpowers the organization and its people; too little conflict prevents them from achieving a creative edge. The latter is evidenced by the Penn Central Railroad case.

Types of Conflict Situations

It is reported that managers spend up to 20 percent of their time dealing with conflict situations.[8] On the basis of this time demand alone, developing conflict-management skills is important. Typical conflict situations are (1) conflict within the individual, (2) interpersonal or individual-to-individual conflict, (3) intergroup conflict, and (4) interorganizational conflict. The question now becomes, "How well prepared are you to deal with each type of conflict situation?"

Conflict Within the Individual

Any conflict is a source of stress that can be uncomfortable to the person or persons involved. Among the more potentially upsetting conflicts are those involving the individual alone. In Chapter 11, for example, we discussed conflicts based on role overloads and person-role incompatibilities. Project yourself ahead a few years. Conflict might develop as you "overload" or take on too many responsibilities. Or it might develop as a conflict of values between work activities and family responsibilities.

One perspective on conflict within the individual is shown in Figure 17.3. It presents four individual conflict situations.

1. *Approach-approach conflict* A person must choose between two equally attractive behavioral alternatives.

1. *Approach-approach conflict*—Manager must choose between the equally attractive alternatives of getting a new dictation machine and taking a business trip to Denver.

2. *Avoidance-avoidance conflict*—Manager is forced to give a low-performing employee a bad recommendation on the threat of being negatively evaluated himself. Dashed lines show that escape is not possible.

3. *Approach-avoidance conflict*—Manager desires new important promotion; but isn't sure she/he can handle new responsibilities.

4. *Double (multiple) approach-avoidance conflicts*—Manager wants new job, but is afraid of responsibilities. Job requires transfer to glamorous new locale, but she/he must leave old friends and familiar surroundings.

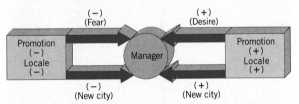

FIGURE 17.3 Four conflicts within the individual. *Source:* Adapted from Thomas V. Bonoma and Gerald Zaltman, *Psychology for Management* (Boston: Kent Publishing Company, 1981), p. 124. Used by permission.

2. *Avoidance-avoidance conflict* A person is forced to make a choice between equally unattractive and undesirable goals.

3. *Approach-avoidance conflict* A person is pushed toward a single goal by a desire to attain it, but is simultaneously pushed away from it by undesirable aspects it also involves.

4. *Multiple approach-avoidance conflict* A person experiences multiple combinations of approach-avoidance conflict.

You can probably identify personal examples that fit into each of these conflict categories. How do you act when you face them? Are the conflicts usually resolved to your satisfaction? Stress is a frequent by-product of within-individual conflict. A special section on stress management in Chapter 21 offers insights that can help you better deal with such conflict situations.

Interpersonal Conflict

Interpersonal conflict occurs among one or more individuals. It can be substantive or emotional in nature, or both. Everyone has experience with interpersonal conflict; it is a major form of conflict faced by managers. We will address this form of conflict in detail when conflict-management strategies are discussed in a later section of this chapter.

Intergroup Conflict

Another conflict situation occurs within the organization as an interlocking network of groups. This topic was first introduced in our look at intergroup relations in Chapter 13. Intergroup conflict is common in organizations, and it makes coordination and integration difficult. A classic example is the contrast in the working relationships between sales and production personnel in two plants of the same manufacturing company.[9] In the Elgin plant, a conflict relationship exists between the two departments; in the Bowie plant the relationship is collaborative. These differences are most apparent in respect to goals and orientation toward decision making, information handling, and attitudes.

Issue Goals and decision-making

At Elgin: Each department emphasizes its own needs and tasks.

At Bowie: Each department stresses common goals and cooperation.

Issue Information handling

At Elgin: Each department ignores the other's problems; distorts its communications with the others.

At Bowie: Each department seeks to understand the other's problems; communicates accurate information.

Issue   Attitudes

> *At Elgin:* Each department develops attitudes supportive of conflict.

> *At Bowie:* Each department develops positive and trusting attitudes regarding the other.

Managers stand at the interface of these intergroup relationships. At times the manager is a liaison directly interfacing his or her work unit with one or more others; at other times the manager is a higher level of authority to whom multiple subunits report. In each case, intergroup relations must be properly managed to maintain collaboration and achieve constructive instead of destructive results from any conflits that occur.

Interorganizational Conflict

Conflict also occurs between organizations. Most commonly, this conflict is thought of in terms of the competition that characterizes firms operating a private enterprise. But interorganizational conflict is a much broader issue. Consider, for example, disagreements between unions and organizations employing their members, between government regulatory agencies and organizations subject to their surveillance, and more generally between organizations and others that supply them with raw materials. In each setting, the potential for conflict involves individuals who represent total organizations, not internal subunits or groups. Although participation in interorganizational conflict is frequently the province of higher-level management, middle-level and lower-level managers can represent their organizations in such relationships with others. Typical examples are a purchasing agent's relationships with suppliers and a supervisor's relationship with union representatives. Again, any resulting conflicts must be managed to the benefit instead of the detriment of the organizations and individuals concerned.

Understanding Conflict Situations

Successful handling of conflict situations requires an ability to understand their underlying processes and elements. Let's proceed by example.[10] The president of a small company is in favor of immediately introducing a new computerized re-

cord-keeping system. The head of the accounting department is opposed to it. There is a definite difference of opinion between the two regarding this possible change of procedures.

The president in this case is a principal party in the conflict. She is also the organizational superior of the other principal party. Although we don't know all the facts, the accountant could feel threatened by the way the president handles the situation. He has already taken some risk to communicate his views upward, and the response of the president may well determine his willingness to do so again in the future. This is a conflict that could prove either constructive in getting the best decision made for the company or destructive by alienating a key employee.

Key factors to be considered in any conflict situation include differences over facts, methods, goals, and values. Table 17.2 shows how differences in these factors could be operating in the case. After such differences are identified, the reasons for them can be established and steps taken to address them. Let's return to the case again and review managerial actions with the potential to resolve the conflict in a constructive manner.

1. *To resolve differences over facts* Information should be shared; steps should be taken to check the validity of the data; more data should be gathered from mutually respected outside sources.

2. *To resolve differences over methods* The common goals of the company's well-being should be remembered; the current disagreement should be viewed as a difference of means, not ends; alternatives to the automated system as proposed should be explored.

3. *To resolve differences over goals* The goals of the president and the accountant should be clarified; each should be discussed and revised relative to the company's goals.

4. *To resolve differences over values* The president and the accountant should share their values on the record-keeping functions; any value differences should be clarified; attempts should be made to find areas where the values overlap and contain consistencies.

Table 17.2 Key Differences of Opinion on the Computerized Record-Keeping System

| | Nature of Differences | | | |
	Over Facts	Over Methods	Over Goals	Over Values
President	"The new system will save money"	"It should be installed at once"	"We want rapid and accurate data retrieval on demand"	"Efficiency is the key"
Head of accounting department	"The new system will be more expensive"	"Let's move slowly"	"We need a flexible system managed by accountants who can solve unexpected problems"	"We must consider the welfare of loyal workers"

Source: Adapted by permission of the *Harvard Business Review.* Excerpt from "Management of Differences" by Warren H. Schmidt and Robert Tannenbaum, *Harvard Business Review,* Vol. 38 (November-December 1960), p. 110. Copyright © 1960 by the President and Fellows of Harvard College; all rights reserved.

If steps such as these are successful, the original conflict may prove constructive for the company. Perhaps a new computerized system will be implemented, with resulting cost savings. Or the manual system might be retained and a costly "mistake" avoided. In either event, proper understanding of the conflict situation would result in the best interests of the company being served.

Another way to analyze conflict is according to the stages through which it develops. Figure 17.4 shows that these stages include antecedent conditions, perceived and felt conflict, manifest conflict, conflict resolution or suppression, and conflict aftermath.[11] The antecedents of conflict are often found in role ambiguities, competition for scarce resources, task interdependencies, communication barriers, unresolved prior conflicts, and individual differences in perceptions, personality, needs, values, and goals. When these conditions exist, the stage is set for conflict to develop. Their presence indicates a situation of high conflict potential.

Perceived conflict occurs when the antecedents are recognized as a basis for substantive or emotional differences between people. Of course, this perception may or may not be shared among the persons involved. When conflict is felt, it achieves meaning in the sense that sufficient tension exists that there is a desire to reduce the discomfort. Sometimes people feel conflict, but can't pin down its source or cause.

Conflict that is openly expressed is said to be manifest. A manifest conflict can be resolved, in the sense that the antecedent conditions are corrected, or suppressed, in that although no change in antecedent conditions occurs, conflict behaviors are controlled.

Finally, the aftermath of how a given conflict is handled can affect future conflicts. Unresolved conflicts continue to fester and promote future conflicts over similar issues. True conflict resolution establishes conditions that reduce the potential for future conflicts of a similar nature and/or set the stage for other conflicts to also be resolved in a constructive fashion.

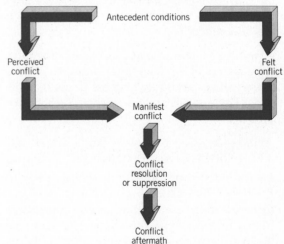

FIGURE 17.4 The stages of conflict. *Source:* John R. Schermerhorn, Jr., James G. Hunt, and Richard N. Osborn, *Managing Organizational Behavior* (New York: Wiley, 1982), p. 461. Used by permission.

CONFLICT MANAGEMENT

Managers can be principal parties to conflicts, that is, as persons actively involved in the conflict situation. They may also be called on to act as mediators in the conflicts of others. In each case the manager must be a *skilled* participant in conflict dynamics if constructive and not destructive results are to be realized.

Conflict Resolution

Conflict can be addressed through nonattention, suppression, or resolution. Nonattention means what it says: there is no direct attempt to deal with a manifest conflict. The conflict is left on its own to emerge as a constructive or destructive force. Suppression decreases the negative consequences of a conflict, but it does not address or eliminate root causes. It is a surface solution that allows the antecedent conditions constituting the original reasons for conflict to remain in place. **Conflict resolution** only occurs when the underlying reasons for a conflict are removed and no lingering conditions or antagonisms are left to rekindle things in the future.

Conflict-Management Styles

A person's "style" or approach to a conflict situation can be described in terms of relative emphasis on cooperativeness and assertiveness.[12]

Cooperativeness is the desire to satisfy the other party's needs and concerns;

assertiveness is the desire to satisfy one's own needs and concerns.

Figure 17.5 shows five conflict-management styles that result from various combinations of cooperativeness and assertiveness in conflict situations. These styles and the intentions each represents are[13]

1. **Avoidance** Being uncooperative and unassertive; downplaying disagreement, failing to participate in the situation, and/or staying neutral at all costs.

2. **Competition** *or* **authoritative command** Being uncooperative but assertive; working against the wishes of the other party, fighting

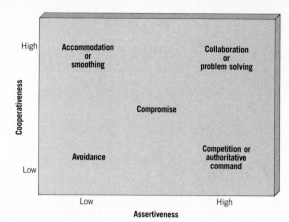

FIGURE 17.5 Five conflict-management styles.

to dominate in win-lose competition, and/or forcing things to a favorable conclusion through the exercise of authority.

3. **Accommodation** *or* **smoothing** Being cooperative but unassertive; letting the other's wishes rule; smoothing over differences to maintain superficial harmony.

4. **Compromise** Being moderately cooperative and assertive, but not to either extreme; working toward partial satisfaction of everyone's concerns; seeking "acceptable" rather than "optimal" solutions so that no one totally wins or loses.

5. **Collaboration** *or* **problem solving** Being both cooperative and assertive; seeking true satisfaction of everyone's concerns by working through differences; finding and solving problems so everyone gains as a result.

Conflict Outcomes

One of the obvious things about Figure 17.5 is that the conflict-management styles vary in the outcomes they are likely to produce. In particular, they vary in the creation of lose-lose, win-lose, and win-win outcomes. This is significant because true conflict resolution only occurs in the win-win case.[14]

Lose-Lose Conflict

Lose-lose conflict occurs when no one achieves his or her true desires, and the underlying reasons for conflict remain unaffected. Although a lose-lose conflict may appear settled or even seem to disappear for a while, it has a tendency to reoccur in the future. Lose-lose outcomes are common when conflict is managed by avoidance, accommodation, smoothing, and/or compromise.

Avoidance is an extreme form of nonattention. Everyone pretends that conflict doesn't really exist and hopes that it will simply go away. Accommodation or smoothing plays down differences among the conflicting parties and highlights similarities and areas of agreement. Peaceful coexistence through a recognition of common interests is the goal. Smoothing, as suggested by "we run a happy ship here" and "nice people don't fight," may ignore the real essence of a given conflict. "Let's compromise" is another phrase frequently heard in conflict settings. Compromise occurs when accommodations are made such that each party to the conflict gives up something of value. As a result, neither party gains its full desires, and the antecedent conditions for future conflicts are established.

Win-Lose Conflict

In **win-lose conflict**, one party achieves its desires to the exclusion of the other party's desires. This may result from competition, where a victory is achieved through force, superior skill, or domination. It may also result from authoritative command, when a formal authority simply dictates a solution and specifies what is to be gained and lost and by whom. When the authority figure is an active party to the conflict, it is easy to predict who will be the winner and the loser. Because win-lose strategies also fail to address the root causes of conflict, future conflicts over the same issues are likely.

Win-Win Conflict

Win-win conflict is resolved to the mutual benefit of all conflicting parties. This is typically achieved by confrontation of the issues and use of problem solving to reconcile differences. This positive approach to conflict involves a recognition by the conflicting parties that something is wrong and needs attention. Win-win conditions eliminate reasons for continuing or resurrecting the conflict, because nothing has been avoided or suppressed. All relevant issues are raised and openly discussed. The ultimate test for a win-win solution may be whether or not the conflicting parties are willing to say two things to each other.

1. "I want a solution that achieves your goals and my goals and is acceptable to both of us."
2. "It is our collective responsibility to be open and honest about facts, opinions, and feelings."

Problem solving and collaboration are often the most successful approaches to conflict resolution. Still, there are times when all of the five conflict-management styles are of potential value to the practicing manager. Examples of when the chief executives of several organizations report using them are in Table 17.3.

The Manager as Mediator

By definition a manager is someone in an organization who has one or more subordinates. This means that any manager is likely to become involved in conflicts as a third-party mediator. Acting as a third party, for example, the manager can help subordinates work out interpersonal conflicts or resolve intergroup conflicts involving subunits under his or her supervision. The mediator role is critically important but extremely difficult to fulfill. It can be constructively approached from two different directions—active intervention and facilitation.

Active Intervention

Managers can do a variety of things to intervene actively in an attempt to resolve conflict situations.[15] There are times when an *appeal to superordinate goals* can focus the attention of conflicting parties on one mutually desirable end state. This offers all parties a common frame of reference against which to analyze differences and reconcile disagreements. Conflicts whose antecedents lie in competition for scarce resources can also be resolved by *expanding the resources* available to everyone. Although costly, this technique removes the reasons for the continuing conflict. By *altering one or more human variables* in a situation— that is, by replacing or transferring one or more

Table 17.3 Situations in Which Chief Executives Use the Five Conflict-Management Styles

Style	Application
Avoidance	When an issue is trivial, or more important issues are pressing. When you perceive no chance of satisfying your concerns. When potential disruption outweighs the benefits of resolution. To let people cool down and regain perspective. When others can resolve the conflict more effectively. When issues seem tangential or symptomatic of other issues.
Authoritative command	When quick, decisive action is vital (emergencies). On important issues where unpopular actions such as costcutting, enforcing unpopular rules, and discipline need implementing. On issues vital to company welfare, when you know you're right.
Smoothing	When you find you are wrong—to allow a better position to be heard, to learn, and to show your reasonableness. When issues are more important to others than yourself—to satisfy others and maintain cooperation. To build social credits for later issues. To minimize loss when you are outmatched and losing. When harmony and stability are especially important.
Compromising	When goals are important, but not worth the effort or potential disruption of more assertive modes. When opponents with equal power are committed to mutually exclusive goals. To achieve temporary settlements to complex issues. To arrive at expedient solutions under time pressure. As a backup when problem solving or authoritative command is unsuccessful.
Problem solving	To find an integrative solution when both sets of concerns are too important to be compromised. When your objective is to learn. To merge insights from people with different perspectives. To gain commitment by incorporating concerns into a consensus. To work through feelings that have interfered with a relationship.

Source: Adapted from Stephen P. Robbins, " 'Conflict Management' and 'Conflict Resolution' Are Not Synonymous Terms!" in John F. Veiga and John N. Yanouzas, *The Dynamics of Organization Theory.* Copyright © 1979, West Publishing Company. All rights reserved.

of the conflicting parties—conflicts caused by poor interpersonal relationships can be eliminated. The same holds true if a manager can *alter structural variables*, such as by rearranging the physical work setting or putting incompatible persons on different work shifts.

Facilitation

Another approach to mediation is through a facilitator role. This approach is heavily interpersonal in nature and requires the successful use of communication skills. Active listening is especially helpful here because dysfunctional emotions must be drawn off and a free flow of communications encouraged in order to get at the root of a problem.

Interpersonal conflicts are often complicated by high emotions which result in behavior that seems quite unreasonable, irrational, and illogical to the outside observer. Outside attempts to intervene might be met with hostility, aggression,

"Harbrucker, you're upsetting the rest of the staff."

The manager often becomes involved in conflicts as a third-party mediator.

and verbal or physical attack; or the response might be just the opposite and involve withdrawal, silence, and fear. In such situations a manager's goal as mediator should be to facilitate the flow of communication between the parties involved. Some advice on this demanding task follows.[16]

1. Select a supportive, quiet situation for a discussion; give your full attention; avoid interruptions.

2. Expect and prepare yourself to hear negative, critical, sometimes unpleasant, confused, distorted talk, or silence and reluctance to speak; don't act shocked or surprised.

3. Draw off and release these emotions, feelings, and sentiments; don't disagree or argue, don't agree either.

4. Listen, especially to feelings, attitudes, sentiments, values, perceptions, and beliefs, as well as to more objective data.

5. Restrain your emotions; remain neutral; don't correct or deny; don't blame or criticize; don't judge.

6. Try in all the preceding steps to understand, feel, and empathize with the other party.

ORGANIZATIONAL CHANGE

The study of conflict leads directly to a companion subject—change. "Change is inevitable," as the saying goes. But is it necessarily so? Consider these almost forgotten bits of British history.[17]

- The British created a civil-service job in 1803 calling for a man to stand on the cliffs of Dover with a spyglass. He was supposed to ring a bell if he saw Napoleon coming. The job was abolished in 1945.

- The Royal Artillery was giving a demonstration to some visiting Europeans on Salisbury Plain in the 1950s. The visitors were most impressed with the speed and precision of the light artillery crew, but one of them asked what was the duty of the man who stood at attention throughout the whole demonstration.

  "He's number six," the adjutant explained.

  "I too can count. But why is he there?"

  "That's his job. Number six stands at attention throughout."

  "But why then do you not have five."?No one knew. It took a great deal of research through old training manuals, but finally they discovered his duty. He was the one who held the horses.

Perhaps the introduction of a little well-managed conflict into each of the previous situations would have facilitated much-needed change long before it actually occurred.

The Manager's Role as Change Agent

A **change agent** is a person or group taking responsibility for changing the existing pattern of behavior of another person or social system. Change agents make things happen. In the examples just given, the British civil service and Royal Artillery lacked change agents. Part of every manager's job is to act as a change agent in the work setting. This means being alert to situations or people needing change, open to good ideas, and able to support the implementation of new ideas into actual practice. Change agents facilitate creativity and innovation in organizations.

Figure 17.6 shows six phases through which change may occur in organizations. In this figure top management plays a key role as change agent. The potential for change also exists at all levels of management and operating responsibil-

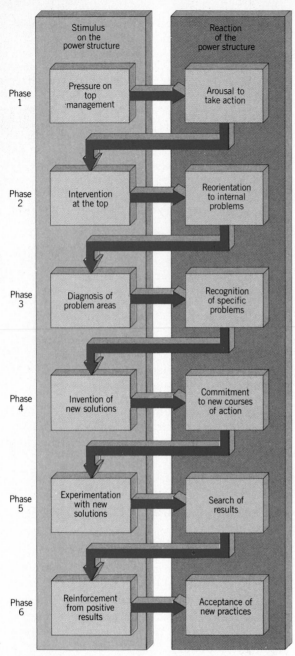

	Stimulus on the power structure	Reaction of the power structure
Phase 1	Pressure on top management	Arousal to take action
Phase 2	Intervention at the top	Reorientation to internal problems
Phase 3	Diagnosis of problem areas	Recognition of specific problems
Phase 4	Invention of new solutions	Commitment to new courses of action
Phase 5	Experimentation with new solutions	Search of results
Phase 6	Reinforcement from positive results	Acceptance of new practices

FIGURE 17.6 Phases of organizational change. *Source:* Reprinted by permission of the *Harvard Business Review*, "Patterns of Organizational Change," by Larry E. Greiner, *Harvard Business Review*, Vol. 45 (May–June 1967). Copyright © 1967 by the President and Fellows of Harvard College: all rights reserved.

ity in organizations. Figure 17.6 depicts change taking a "top-down" pattern; it may also occur from "bottom-up" or "middle-outward" patterns. In each case, managers play key change-agent roles.

Planned and Unplanned Change

Not all change in organizations happens at a change agent's direction. **Unplanned changes** occur spontaneously or at random and without a change agent's attention. They may be disruptive, such as a wildcat strike that results in a plant closure, or beneficial, such as an interpersonal conflict that results in a new procedure or rule being established to guide interdepartmental relations. The appropriate goal in managing unplanned change is to act immediately once it is recognized so as to minimize any negative consequences and maximize any possible benefits.

We are particularly interested in **planned change** that happens as a result of specific efforts by a change agent. Planned change is a direct response to someone's perception of a **performance gap**—that is, a discrepancy between the desired and actual state of affairs. Performance gaps may represent problems to be resolved or opportunities to be explored. In each case, managers as change agents should spot performance gaps and initiate planned changes to close them.

Consider the following problem situation described in a newspaper article.[18]

> NORTHAMPTON, Mass.—The midmorning sunshine darted through the windows as Jerry Hathaway, his wife, and this three-year-old daughter ("she's a great little camper") prepared for a weekend outing along the shimmering Quinebaug River.
>
> With their gear assembled, one detail remained. Hathaway's wife, Donna, had to telephone a message to the local boxboard plant of Tenneco Inc.'s Packaging Co. of America. The message: "Jerry will be out sick today."
>
> This popular lie plus legitimate absences adds up to a monumental headache for U.S. industry. Statistics suggest that absenteeism costs workers and the economy $20 billion a year in lost pay alone. In addition, industry spends $10 billion a year in sick pay and $5 billion on fringe benefits that continue whether or not the worker is there.

Absenteeism also can cripple production and profits. A computer analysis at the University of Nebraska for a major manufacturer showed that a 1 percent rise in absences could slash profits by 4 percent. Once when Hathaway and six co-workers failed to report for the 40-person night shift at the packaging company plant here, the evening's target of 1 million square feet of corrugated boxboard was sliced by 20 percent.

The performance gap in this case is a high absenteeism rate. It prompted Eli Kwartler, the plant manager, to initiate a problem-solving and planned-change effort in response. He surveyed workers in the plant and found that night workers wanted a four-day week of ten-hour shifts Monday through Thursday, instead of a five-day week of eight-hour shifts. The company changed work schedules to a four-day night shift with the result that absences fell and the shift's production climbed 9 percent. Even Jerry Hathaway took fewer days off after the changeover. He no longer had to skip Fridays to take long weekends.

This case illustrates how a planned change in working hours was initiated by management to resolve a performance gap in one company. It is useful to think of most planned changes as problem-solving efforts initiated by managers on behalf of the organization and its members.

Organizational Targets for Change

Organizational change involves some modification in the various components that constitute the essence of the organization. These targets of change, as shown in Table 17.4 include organizational purpose and objectives, strategy, tasks, technology, people, and structure. Most often planned organizational change will involve more than one of these targets. Just as these components are closely intertwined in the day-to-day functioning of organizations, so will they be intertwined in any change process. At the very least,[19]

A change in the basic *tasks* performed by an organization—that is, a modification in what it is the organization does—is almost inevitably accompanied by a change in *technology*—that is, a modification in the way in which tasks are accomplished. Changes in tasks and technology usually require alterations in the *structure* of the organization, including changes in the patterns of authority and

Table 17.4 Organizational Targets for Change

Targets	Possible Methods
Purpose and objectives	Clarify overall mission; modify existing objectives; use management by objectives
Strategy	Modify strategic plans; modify operational plans; modify policies and procedures
Tasks	Modify job designs; use job enrichment
Technology	Improve equipment and facilities; improve methods and workflows
People	Modify selection criteria; modify recruiting practices; use training and development programs; clarify roles and expectations
Structure	Modify job descriptions; modify organizational design; adjust coordination mechanisms; modify distribution of authority

communication as well as in the roles of members. These technological and structural changes can, in turn, necessitate change on the part of *members*—the basic components of the organization. For example, members may have to acquire additional knowledge and develop new skills to perform their modified roles and to work with the new technology.

MANAGING PLANNED CHANGE

Change is a complicated phenomenon at the heart of which lie people. But, as our earlier examples from British history showed, people have a tendency to act habitually and in stable ways over time. That is, they may tend *not* to change even when circumstances warrant. As a manager, you will need to recognize and deal with such inertia in the work setting. To begin, it helps to understand the basic process of planned change.

The Planned-Change Process[20]

Kurt Lewin, a noted psychologist, recommends that any planned-change effort be viewed as a three-phase process: unfreezing, changing, and refreezing.[21] This process is diagrammed in Figure 17.7.

FIGURE 17.7 The three steps in the change process. *Source:* Adapted from John R. Schermerhorn, Jr., James G. Hunt, and Richard N. Osborn, *Managing Organizational Behavior* (New York: Wiley, 1982), p. 495. Used by permission.

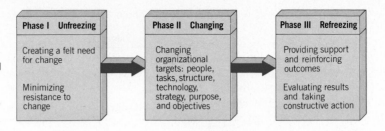

The Unfreezing Phase

Unfreezing is the stage of preparing a situation for change. It involves disconfirming existing attitudes and behaviors to create a felt need for something new. Unfreezing is facilitated by environmental pressures, declining performance, the recognition of a problem, and awareness of opportunity or a better way, among other things. Conflict is an important unfreezing force in organizations. The stress it involves often helps people break old habits and recognize alternative ways of thinking about or doing things.

The Changing Phase

The changing phase involves the actual modification in organizational targets for change, including purpose, strategy, people, task, structure, and/or technology. Lewin feels that many change agents enter the changing phase prematurely, are too quick to change things, and therefore end up creating resistance to change in a situation that is not adequately unfrozen. When managers implement change before felt needs for change exist in the minds of the people involved, there is an increased likelihood that the change attempts will fail.

The Refreezing Phase

The final stage in the planned-change process is refreezing. Designed to maintain the momentum of a change, refreezing efforts include positively reinforcing desired outcomes and providing extra emotional and resource support when difficulties are encountered. Evaluation and feedback are key elements in this final step. They provide data on the costs and benefits of a change, and offer opportunities to make constructive modifications in the change over time. Improper refreezing re-

sults in changes that are easily abandoned or incompletely implemented.

Choosing a Change Strategy

Managers use various strategies for getting other persons to adopt a desired change. Figure 17.8 summarizes these as force-coercion, empirical-rational, and normative-reeducative change strategies.[22]

Force-Coercion Strategies

A **force-coercion strategy** uses the power bases of legitimacy, rewards, and punishments as primary inducements to change. The change agent acts unilaterally to "command" change through the formal authority of his or her position, induce change via an offer of special rewards, or bring about change via threats of punishment. Most people comply with this strategy out of fear of punishment or desire for reward. This compliance with the change agent's desires is usually temporary and continues only so long as the opportunity for rewards and punishments remains obvious. For this reason, force-coercion is most useful as an unfreezing device that helps people break old patterns of behavior and gain initial impetus to try new ones.

Think about this strategy as part of your managerial style. Here's what it might mean in practice.[23]

As a change agent using a force-coercion strategy You believe that people who run things are basically motivated by self-interest and what situations offer in terms of potential personal gains or losses. Since you feel people change only in response to such motives, you try to find out where their vested interests lie and then put the pressure on. If you have formal authority you use it; if not, you resort to whatever possible rewards and punishments you have access to and do not hesitate to threaten others with these weapons. Once you find a weakness you exploit it and are always wise to work "politically" and by building supporting alliances wherever possible.

Empirical-Rational Strategies

Change agents using an **empirical-rational strategy** attempt to bring about change through persuasion backed by special knowledge and rational argument. Use of this strategy assumes that rational people will be guided by reason and self-interest in deciding whether or not to support a change. Expert power is mobilized to convince others that the cost/benefit value of a proposed change is high and that the change will leave people better off than before. Expertise can be brought to bear by the manager's personal credibility as an "expert," by bringing in "outside experts" to give testimony (e.g., consultants), or by a demonstration project. When successful, this strategy helps unfreeze and refreeze a change situation. It results in a more longer-lasting and internalized change than does force-coercion. Once again, let's apply this strategy to you.

As a change agent using an empirical-rational strategy. You believe that people are inherently rational and guided by reason in their actions and decision making. Once a specific course of action is demonstrated to be in a person's self-interest, you assume that reason and rationality will cause the person to adopt it. Thus you approach change

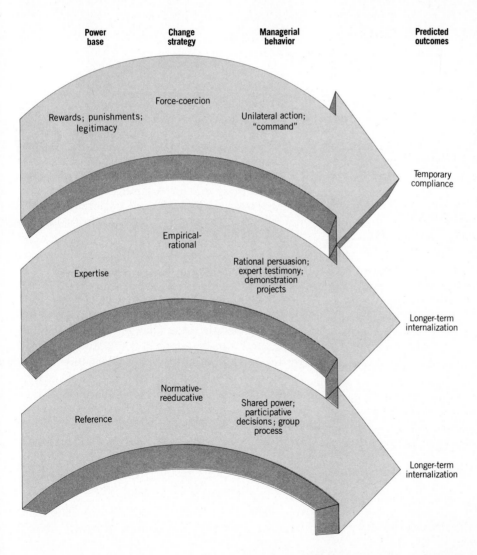

FIGURE 17.8 Power bases, change strategies, managerial behavior, and predicted change outcomes. *Source:* John R. Schermerhorn, Jr., James G. Hunt, and Richard N. Osborn, *Managing Organizational Behavior* (New York: Wiley, 1982), p. 496. Used by permission.

Changing technology has had a major impact on the nature of work in newsrooms.

with the objective of communicating through information and facts the essential "desirability" of change from the perspective of the person whose behavior you seek to influence. If this logic is effectively communicated, you are sure that the person(s) will adopt the proposed change.

Normative-Reeducative Strategies

A **normative-reeducative strategy** identifies or establishes values and assumptions from which support for a proposed change will naturally emerge. This strategy focuses on the building of essential foundations in personal values, group norms, and shared goals to support change in all of its phases. Managers using normative-reeducative approaches emphasize reference power and willingness to allow other persons to participate in the decisions through which changes are planned and implemented. Given this high level of involvement, the strategy is likely to result in a longer-lasting and internalized change. From your perspective this might mean the following.

> *As a change agent using a normative-reeducative change strategy.* You believe that people have complex motivations. You feel that people behave as they do as a result of sociocultural norms and commitments to these norms. You also recognize that

changes in normative orientations involve changes in attitudes, values, skills, and significant relationships, *not* just changes in knowledge, information, or intellectual rationales for action and practice. Thus when seeking to change others you are sensitive to the supporting or inhibiting effects of any group pressures and norms that may be operating. In working with people you try to find out their side of things and to identify their feelings and expectations.

Dealing With Resistance to Change

"Resistance" is usually viewed as something to be overcome in order for change to be successful. But when people resist change, they are defending something important that appears threatened by the change attempt. Thus resistance can be considered feedback that the informed change agent may use to modify the planned change effort in a constructive way. Take the computer, for example. Its growing impact on the work setting has been a frequent reference in this book. As *Newsline 17.3* shows, it is also a technological change that often results in resistance from the people whose work routines it affects.

Table 17.5 uses the example of a new management practice to further illustrate typical

NEWSLINE 17.3

COMPUTER PSYCHOLOGIST

Some call her work "tech psych," but social psychologist Shoshana Zuboff of the Harvard Business School prefers to label her research "the study of computer-mediated work." Whatever the title, it's a whole new field of psychology that deals with the not always smooth relationship between person and computer in the workplace.

Zuboff has interviewed nearly 400 workers whose jobs have been affected by computers, and is struck by their almost uniform uneasiness. She cautions management to "listen to the resistance" of people forced to deal with technology. "There are lots of things in this conversion that motivate people toward resentment," says Zuboff. "They may be afraid it demands skills they don't have. Their relationships with co-workers are being altered, and they are uncomfortable. Then there's the abstraction, the intangibility of computers that leaves people feeling frustrated."

Source: Forbes (May 23, 1983), p. 78. Used by permission.

sources of resistance to change in the work setting. The table also shows that an informed change agent can take steps to deal with such resistance constructively, if it is recognized early enough in the change process. All things considered, six general approaches for dealing with resistance can be identified.[24]

1. *Education and communication* Use of one-on-one discussions, presentations to groups, memos, reports, and demonstrations to educate people beforehand about a change and to help them see the logic of the change.

2. *Participation and involvement* Allowing others to help design and implement the change; asking individuals to contribute ideas and advice, or forming task forces or committees to work on the change.

3. *Facilitation and support* Providing socioemotional support for the hardships of change, actively listening to problems and complaints, providing training in the new ways, and helping overcome performance pressures.

4. *Negotiation and agreement* Offering incentives to actual or potential resistors; working out trade-offs to provide special benefits in exchange for assurance that the change will not be blocked.

Table 17.5 Potential Sources of Resistance to a New Management Practice and Suggested Change-Agent Responses

Source of Resistance	Suggested Response
Fear of the unknown	Information and encouragement
Need for security	Clarification of intentions and methods
No felt need to change	Demonstrate problem or opportunity
Vested interests threatened	Enlist key people in change planning
Contrasting interpretations	Disseminate valid information, facilitate group sharing
Poor timing	Await better time
Lack of resources	Provide supporting resources and/or reduced performance expectations

Source: John R. Schermerhorn, Jr., James G. Hunt, and Richard N. Osborn, *Managing Organizational Behavior* (New York: Wiley, 1982), p. 497. Used by permission.

5. *Manipulation and co-optation* Use of covert attempts to influence others; selectively providing information and consciously structuring

Table 17.6 Methods for Dealing with Resistance to Change

Approach	Commonly Used in Situations	Advantages	Drawbacks
Education and communication	Where there is a lack of information or inaccurate information and analysis	Once persuaded, people will often help with the implementation of the change.	Can be very time-consuming if lots of people are involved.
Participation and involvement	Where the initiators do not have all the information they need to design the change, and where others have considerable power to resist.	People who participate will be committed to implementing change, and any relevant information they have will be integrated into the change plan.	Can be very time-consuming if participants design an inappropriate change.
Facilitation and support	Where people are resisting because of adjustment problems.	No other approach works as well with adjustment problems.	Can be time-consuming, expensive, and still fail.
Negotiation and agreement	Where someone or some group will clearly lose out in a change, and where that group has considerable power to resist.	Sometimes it is a relatively easy way to avoid major resistance.	Can be too expensive in many cases if it alerts others to negotiate for compliance.
Manipulation and co-optation	Where other tactics will not work, or are too expensive.	It can be a relatively quick and inexpensive solution to resistance problems.	Can lead to future problems if people feel manipulated.
Explicit and implicit coercion	Where speed is essential, and the change initiators possess considerable power.	It is speedy, and can overcome any kind of resistance.	Can be risky if it leaves people mad at the initiators.

Source: Reprinted by permission of the *Harvard Business Review.* Excerpt from "Choosing Strategies for Change" by John P. Kotter and Leonard A. Schlesinger, Vol. 57 (March-April 1979), p. 111. Copyright © 1979 by the President and Fellows of Harvard College. All rights reserved.

events so that the desired change receives maximum support.

6. *Explicit and implicit coercion* Use of force to get people to accept change; threatening resistors with a variety of undesirable consequences if they don't go along as planned.

The advantages and disadvantages of these approaches are further described in Table 17.6. Managers using them must understand that resistance to change is something to be recognized and constructively addressed instead of feared. The presence of resistance typically suggests that something can be done to achieve a better "fit" between the change, the situation, and the people the change will affect. A manager should "listen" to such feedback and act accordingly.

ORGANIZATION DEVELOPMENT (OD)

Behavioral scientists have been working since the early 1960s with a comprehensive approach to planned change that is designed to improve the overall effectiveness of organizations. Called **organization development** (OD), this planned-change approach is defined as the application of behavioral science knowledge in a long-range effort to improve an organization's ability to cope with change in its external environment and increase its internal problem-solving capabilities.[25] OD quite clearly belongs in our study of conflict and change as forces impacting organizational productivity in the contemporary environment.

The essence of OD is suggested in the chapter-opening example of the development efforts taken by Diamond-Shamrock Corporation. Underlying OD as a planned-change framework is a strong human-resource focus and an allegiance to several relatively well-established behavioral science principles. These principles apply to individuals, groups, and organizations as follows.[26]

1. *Principles regarding individuals*

   - Individual needs for growth and development are most likely to be satisfied in a supportive and challenging work environment.
   - Most people are capable of assuming responsibility for their own actions and of making positive contributions to organizational performance.

2. *Principles regarding groups*

   - Groups help people satisfy important needs.
   - Groups can be either helpful or harmful in supporting organizational objectives.
   - People can increase the effectiveness of groups in meeting individual and organizational needs by working in collaboration.

3. *Principles regarding organizations*

   - Changes in one part of an organization will affect other parts as well.
   - The culture of the organization will affect

the nature and expression of individual feelings and attitudes.

   - Organizational structures and jobs can be designed to meet the needs of individuals and groups as well as the organization.

A General Model of OD

Figure 17.9 depicts a general model of OD and shows its relationship to the phases of planned change. The OD process begins with *diagnosis*, gathering and analyzing data to assess a situation and set appropriate change objectives. From a planned-change perspective, good diagnosis helps to unfreeze an existing situation as well as pinpoint appropriate action directions. Diagnosis leads to active *intervention* wherein change objectives are pursued through a variety of specific activities. This equates to the changing phase of the planned-change process. In the *reinforcement* stage of OD, changes are monitored, reinforced, and evaluated. Refreezing of change occurs at this point, and foundations for future replication of similar diagnosis-intervention-reinforcement cycles are set. For one business firm the three stages in this general model of OD evolved as follows.

1. *Diagnosis*   Management perceived a performance gap and hired a consultant. The con-

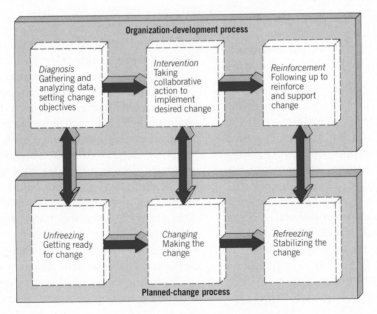

FIGURE 17.9 The organization development and planned change processes.

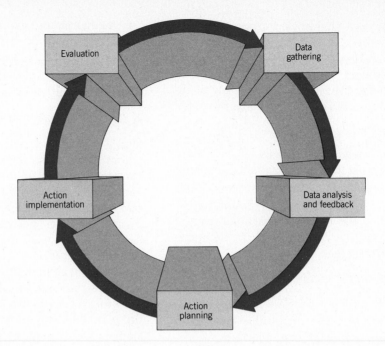

FIGURE 17.10 A general action research model.

sultant interviewed key people and planned a workshop where managers could analyze the interview results in a problem-solving format.

2. *Intervention* The workshop was held. Participants were coached on how to analyze the data and determine appropriate action directions; they also received advice on the effectiveness of the group process.

3. *Reinforcement* The consultant continued to meet periodically with the group to review progress; additional help was given when things "bogged down"; problem-solving workshops became annual events for the firm.

Although OD is a planned-change process, the example suggests that it is also something more. Think of OD as "planned change *plus*" if you'd like. That "plus" is the goal of creating change in a way that organization members develop a capacity for continual self-renewal by learning how to implement similar diagnosis-intervention-reinforcement cycles in the future. True OD seeks more than the successful accomplishment of one planned change. OD seeks to achieve change in such a way that organization members become more active and confident in taking similar steps to maintain longer-run organizational effectiveness. A large part of any OD

program's success in this regard rests with the strength of its action-research foundations.

Action Research

Action research is a process of systematically collecting data on an organization, feeding it back to the members for action planning, and evaluating results by collecting and reflecting on more data after the planned actions have been taken.[27] It is a data-based and collaborative approach to problem solving and organizational assessment. Action research helps identify action directions that may enhance organizational effectiveness.

A typical action-research sequence is diagrammed in Figure 17.10. You first became acquainted with this technique as part of the team-building process introduced in Chapter 13. The sequence is initiated when someone senses a performance gap and decides to analyze the situation systematically for the problems and opportunities it represents. The process continues with data gathering, data feedback, data analysis, and action planning. It continues to the point where action is taken and results evaluated. The evaluation or reassessment stage may or may not generate another performance gap. If it does, the action-research cycle begins anew.

Table 17.7 A Comparison of Different Methods of Data Collection

Method	Major Advantages	Major Potential Problems
Interviews	1. Adaptive—allow data collection on a range of possible subjects 2. Source of "rich" data 3. Empathic 4. Process of interviewing can build rapport	1. Can be expensive 2. Interviewer can bias responses 3. Coding/interpretation problems 4. Self-report bias
Questionnaires	1. Responses can be quantified and easily summarized 2. Easy to use with large samples 3. Relatively inexpensive 4. Can obtain large volume of data	1. Nonempathic 2. Predetermined questions may miss issues 3. Data may be overinterpreted 4. Response bias
Observations	1. Collect data on behavior rather than reports of behavior 2. Real-time, not retrospective 3. Adaptive	1. Interpretation and coding problems 2. Sampling is a problem 3. Observer bias/reliability 4. Costly
Secondary data/ unobtrusive measures	1. Nonreactive—no response bias 2. High face validity 3. Easily quantified	1. Access/retrieval possibly a problem 2. Potential validity problems 3. Coding/interpretation

Source: From David A. Nadler, *Feedback and Organizational Development: Using Data-Based Methods*, p. 119. Copyright © 1977 Addison-Wesley, Reading, Mass. Reprinted with permission.

Data gathering is a major element in the action-research process. Table 17.7 describes several methods available for this, including the major advantages and problems associated with each. Interviews and written questionnaires are common means of gathering data in action research. Formal written surveys of employee attitudes and needs are growing in popularity. Many available survey forms have been tested for reliability and validity. Some have even been used to the extent that "norms" are available so that one organization can compare its results with those from a broader sample of organizations.

OD Interventions

OD interventions are activities initiated by consultants or managers in support of a comprehensive OD program. They are ways of facilitating the action-research process and ways of taking action in response to the problems and opportunities it brings to the surface. A list of popular OD interventions focusing on the individual, group, and organizational levels of action follows. The various interventions reflect management theories and concepts discussed throughout this book. Some, like team building and management by objectives, are techniques you are already familiar with; others are new. In all cases a brief synopsis of the intervention technique is provided to give you a more complete feel for the range of ways OD can be implemented in actual practice.

1. *OD interventions to improve individual effectiveness*

   ■ *Sensitivity training (T-groups)* Unstructured group sessions where participants learn interpersonal skills and increased sensitivity to other persons.

   ■ *Management training* Structured educational opportunities for developing managerial skills and capabilities.

   ■ *Role negotiation* Structured interactions to

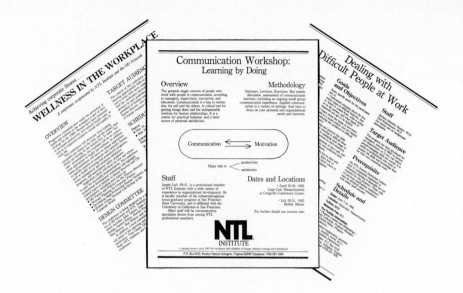

Educational opportunities to develop managerial skills are important components of many organization development (OD) programs.

clarify and negotiate role expectations among persons who work together.

- *Job redesign* Realigning task components to fit the needs and capabilities of the individual better.

- *Career planning* Structured advice and discussion sessions to plan for career development.

2. *OD interventions to improve group effectiveness*

- *Team building* Structured experiences to help group members set goals, improve interpersonal relations, and become a better-functioning team.

- *Process consultation* Third-party observation of critical group processes (e.g., communication and decision making), and giving advice on how to improve these processes.

- *Intergroup team building* Structured experiences to help two or more groups set shared goals, improve intergroup relations, and become better coordinated and mutually supportive.

3. *OD interventions to improve organizational effectiveness*

- *Survey feedback* Comprehensive and systematic data collection to identify attitudes

and needs, analyze results, and plan for constructive action.

- *Confrontation meeting* One-day intensive meeting of a sample of employees to gather data on their attitudes and needs, analyze results, and plan for constructive action relevant to the organization as a whole.

- *Structural redesign* Realigning the organization structure to meet the needs of environmental and contextual forces.

- *Management by objectives* Formalizing an MBO framework throughout the organization so that individual-subunit-organizational objectives are clearly linked to one another in means-ends chains.

OD in a Managerial Perspective

OD is an exciting application of behavioral science theory to management practice. It includes a set of tools with which any manager concerned about achieving and maintaining high levels of productivity will want to be familiar. Because of its comprehensive nature and scientific foundations, OD is frequently done with the aid of an external consultant or internal professional staff member.

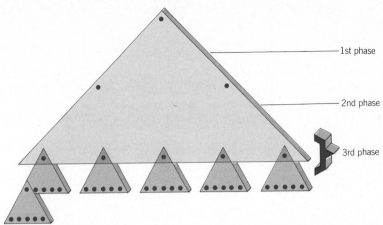

1st phase. Data gathering, feedback, and diagnosis—consultant and top executive only.

2nd phase. Data gathering, feedback, and revised diagnosis—consultant and two or more key staf or line people

3rd phase. Data gathering and feedback to total top executive team in "team-building" laboratc with or without key subordinates from level below

4th and additional phases. Data gathering, and team-building sessions with second- or third-level teams

Subsequent phases. Data gathering, feedback, and interface problem-solving sessions across groups

Simultaneous phases. Several managers may attend "stranger" T-groups; courses in the management development program may supplement this learning

FIGURE 17.11 Organization-development phases in a hypothetical organization. *Source:* Copyright © 1969 by the Regents of the University of California. Reprinted from *California Management Review*, Volume XII, p. 27, by permission of the Regents.

Still, the basic concept of OD as a comprehensive approach to planned change can and should be routinely used by managers to help guide day-to-day problem-solving activities. Just as "human-resource development" must be a continuing management concern, so too must "organizational development." There are times when every organization or subunit needs to reflect systematically on its strengths and weaknesses—and on the problems and opportunities it faces. The concepts and ideas of OD can assist managers to do just that.

Figure 17.11 gives you a final example of what a comprehensive OD effort can look like when done throughout the organization. Note the involvement of all organizational levels along with the use of data feedback, T-groups, team-building, and management training sessions. As this illustration shows, organization development is an important integrating resource for managers interested in working comprehensively, collaboratively, and regularly over time to introduce planned changes and improve organizational productivity.

SUMMARY

This chapter approached the challenges of managing in the contemporary environment from the perspectives of conflict, planned change, and organization development. Each of these processes is an opportunity for managers to facilitate organizational creativity and innovation and thereby adapt to changing environmental circumstances over time. A good manager makes sure that conflict, planned change, and organization development processes work to the advantage of those areas of organizational responsibility under his or her control.

Conflicts can be constructive or destructive. To manage conflict successfully, a manager must be able to understand conflict situations for the substantive and/or emotional differences they represent. Then the reasons for these differences can be identified and appropriate actions taken. People attend to conflict in different ways, including avoidance, competition, smoothing, compromise, and problem solving. Only the problem-solving approach leads to true conflict resolution. As mediators, managers also employ active intervention techniques and facilitation to control conflict situations.

The process of conflict ultimately involves an opportunity for change. Managers have the responsibility to act as change agents bringing about planned changes in their work settings. To be successful at change, managers must be aware of the unfreezing, changing, and refreezing phases of change, as well as the force-coercion, empirical-rational, and normative-reeducative change strategies. Resistance frequently occurs during change and should be carefully handled to lend support to any planned-change effort.

Finally, the process of planned change is extended to the total system level in the form of organization development (OD), a comprehensive approach to implementing change and fostering organizational effectiveness. Based on action research foundations and drawing on a wide range of possible interventions, OD is a relatively new and promising application of behavioral science principles to management practice. Its basic goal is to help organizations keep pace with their environment and achieve productivity while maintaining high-quality work lives for their members.

THINKING THROUGH THE ISSUES

1. What is "organizational innovation"? Why are individual creativity and organizational innovation necessary ingredients of organizational productivity in the contemporary environment?

2. What is the difference between constructive and destructive conflict? Give an example of each from an organizational situation with which you are familiar.

3. Name five possible causes of conflict in organizations. Give examples of each.

4. Identify five conflict styles a manager might use. Which one(s) are most prone to result in conflict resolution? Why?

5. What can a manager do to resolve conflict when acting as a third-party mediator?

6. Why is a manager a change agent?

7. What are Lewin's three phases in the planned-change process? Give examples of what managers can do to accomplish each stage successfully.

8. Define the three basic change strategies and give examples of how a manager might use them in practice.

9. Describe how action research works as a foundation element in organization development (OD).

10. List and give examples of two OD interventions that address problems at each of the following levels of action: (1) individual, (2) group, (3) organization as a whole.

THE MANAGER'S VOCABULARY

Accommodation	Conflict resolution	Normative-reeducative	Smoothing
Action research	Constructive conflict	change strategy	Substantive conflict
Authoritative	Creativity	Organizational change	Unplanned change
command	Destructive conflict	Organizational	Win-lose conflict
Avoidance	Emotional conflict	innovation	Win-win conflict
Change agent	Empirical-rational	Organization	
Collaboration	change strategy	development (OD)	
Competition	Force-coercion change	Performance gap	
Compromise	strategy	Planned change	
Conflict	Lose-lose conflict	Problem solving	

CAREER PERSPECTIVE: HELP WANTED— DIRECTOR OF ORGANIZATIONAL DEVELOPMENT[28]

The following advertisement appeared one day in the help-wanted section of the *Wall Street Journal*.

Director
Organizational
Development

Major fortune 1000 Company is seeking a Director of Organizational Development for its headquarters office staff. This newly created position has high visibility and reports to the Vice President–Human Resources.

The individual selected will be responsible for the development and implementation of all employee developmental programs (includes a heavy emphasis on team building) to improve organizational effectiveness throughout a multi-plant company. Additional responsibilities would include developing innovative programs for implementation in long-range Human Resource plans.

Headquarters office is located in a Midwestern community where quality of life is next to ideal. We have experienced a very rapid growth rate over the last 10 years, and future growth plans are aggressive. In addition to stability, we offer a most challenging opportunity, competitive salary, comprehensive benefit package, and a lucrative incentive bonus program.

Questions

1. What would an organization hope to gain from this newly created position?
2. What special attributes and capabilities should an individual have in order to succeed as the director of organizational development? Why?
3. Would you be interested in this type of position at some point in your career? Why or why not?

CASE APPLICATION: DASHMAN COMPANY[29]

The Dashman Company is a large concern making many types of equipment for the armed forces of the United States. It has over 20 plants, located in the central part of the country, whose purchasing procedures had never been completely coordinated. In fact, the head office of the company had encouraged each of the plant managers to operate with their staffs as separate independent units in most matters. Late in the year, when it began to appear that the company would face increasing difficulty in securing certain essential raw materials, Mr. Manson, the company's president, appointed an experienced purchasing executive, Mr. Post, as vice-president in charge of purchasing—a position especially created for him. Manson gave Post wide latitude in organizing his job, and assigned Mr. Larson as Post's assistant. Larson had served the company in a variety of capacities for many years, and knew most of the plant executives personally. Post's appointment was announced through the formal channels usual in the company, including a notice in the house organ published by the company.

One of Post's first decisions was to centralize the company's purchasing procedure immediately. As a first step he decided that he would require each of the executives who handled purchasing in the individual plants to clear with the head office all purchase contracts they made in excess of $10,000. He felt that if the head office was to do any coordinating in a way that would be helpful to each plant and to the company as a whole, he must be notified that the contracts were being prepared at least a week before they were to be signed. He talked his proposal over with Manson, who presented it to his board of directors. They approved the plan.

Although the company made purchases throughout the year, the beginning of its peak buying season was only three weeks away at the time this new plan was adopted. Post prepared a letter to be sent to the 20 purchasing executives of the company. The letter follows:

Dear _____,

The board of directors of our company has recently authorized a change in our purchasing procedures. Hereafter, each of the purchasing executives in the several plants of the company will notify the vice-president in charge of purchasing of all contracts in excess of $10,000 which they are negotiating at least a week in advance of the date on which they are to be signed.

I am sure that you will understand that this step is necessary to coordinate the purchasing requirements of the company in these times when we are facing increasing difficulty in securing essential supplies. This procedure should give us in the central office the information we need to see that each plant secures the optimum supply of materials. In this way the interests of each plant and of the company as a whole will best be served.

Yours very truly,

Post showed the letter to Larson and invited his comments. Larson thought the letter an excellent one, but suggested that since Post had not met more than a few of the purchasing executives, he might like to visit all of them and take the matter up with each one personally. Post dismissed the idea at once because, as he said, he had so many things to do at the head office that he could not get away for a trip. Consequently, he had the letters sent out over his signature.

During the two following weeks replies came in from all except a few plants. Although a few executives wrote at greater length, the following reply was typical.

Dear Mr. Post,

Your recent communication in regard to notifying the head office a week in advance of our intention to sign contracts has been received. This suggestion seems a most practical one. We want to assure you that you can count on our cooperation.

Yours very truly,

/s/

During the next six weeks the head office received no notices from any plant that contracts were being negotiated. Executives in other departments who made frequent trips to the plants reported that the plants were busy, and the usual routines for that time of year were being followed.

Questions

1. Who is the change agent in this case? What did the change agent do right? . . do wrong?

2. What should have been done? Why?

3. What are the implications of this case for the management of planned change in organizations?

CLASS EXERCISE: MANAGING A CONFLICT SITUATION

Assume that you are a supervisor in charge of a manufacturing operation. A recent change in company procedures now makes it possible for employees to engage in job rotation. In a staff meeting held to discuss the possibility, it becomes immediately apparent that two of your subordinates want to change to a job rotation schedule, while one does not.

1. Listed here are several styles you might follow to manage this conflict situation: (1) avoidance, (2) authoritative command, (3) smoothing, (4) compromise, and (5) problem solving. In the spaces below write the name of the conflict-management style that best corresponds to the approach being described.

   _____ Simply tell all three subordinates that job rotation will begin immediately.

   _____ Convince all three that their good feelings toward one another are more important than any job design; get them to agree to rotate jobs or not, depending on what will maintain harmony in the group.

   _____ Work out an arrangement where job rotation occurs for a while, is stopped for a while, and so on; this allows each person to have his or her way part of the time.

   _____ Drop the idea about making any job design changes; forget you ever raised the possibility in the first place.

2. Which of the four described approaches would you choose to follow in this situation? Or would you prefer to do something else? If the latter, briefly describe the approach here and label it with one of the listed conflict management styles.

3. Share your results with a nearby classmate. Discuss any differences of opinion. Await further class discussion led by your instructor.

REFERENCES

[1] Arthur M. Louis, "They're Striking Some Strange Bargains at Diamond Shamrock," *Fortune* (January 1976), pp. 142–156. © 1981 Time Inc. Courtesy of *Fortune Magazine*. Calendar items slightly modified and used by permission.

[2] Reprinted by permission of the *Harvard Business Review*. Excerpt from "Evolution and Revolution as Organizations Grow," by Larry E. Greiner, *Harvard Business Review*, Vol. 50 (July–August 1972), pp. 37, 38. Copyright © 1972 by the President and Fellows of Harvard College; all rights reserved.

[3] Mario Shar, " 'Be Prepared': The Girl Scouts Make Many Changes to Stay Viable in the 1980's," the *Wall Street Journal* (July 15, 1982), p. 1. Reprinted by permission of the *Wall Street Journal*. Copyright © 1982 Dow Jones & Company, Inc. All rights reserved.

[4] Cited in Peter F. Drucker, *Management: Tasks, Responsibilities and Practices* (New York: Harper and Row, 1973), p. 797.

[5] See James M. Utterback, "Innovation in Industry and the Diffusion of Technology," *Science* (February 15, 1974), pp. 620–626; Gerald Zaltman, Robert B. Duncan, and Jonny Holbeck, *Innovation in Organizations* (New York: Wiley, 1974); James F. Stoner, *Management*, Second Edition (Englewood Cliffs, N.J.: Prentice-Hall, 1982).

[6] Richard E. Walton, *Interpersonal Peacemaking: Confrontations and Third-Party Consultation* (Reading, Mass.: Addison-Wesley, 1969), p. 2.

[7] © 1978 by the Regents of the University of California. Reprinted from Stephen P. Robbins, " 'Conflict Management' and 'Conflict Resolution' are not Synonymous Terms!" *California Management Review*, Vol. XXI (Winter 1978), p. 70, by permission of the Regents.

[8] Kenneth W. Thomas and Warren H. Schmidt, "A Survey of Managerial Interests with Respect to Conflict," *Academy of Management Journal*, Vol. 19 (1976), pp. 315–318.

[9] Developed from John M. Dutton and Richard E. Walton, "Interdepartmental Conflict and Cooperation: Two Contrasting Studies," in Jay W. Lorsch and Paul R. Lawrence (eds.), *Managing Group and Intergroup Relations* (Homewood, Ill.: Richard D. Irwin, 1972), pp. 300, 301.

[10] Slightly adapted by permission of the *Harvard Business Review*. Excerpt from "Management of Differences" by Warren H. Schmidt and Robert Tannenbaum, *Harvard Business Review*, Vol. 39 (November-December 1960), pp. 107–115. Copyright © 1960 by the President and Fellows of Harvard College; all rights reserved.

[11] These stages are generally consistent with the conflict models described by Alan C. Filley, *Interpersonal Conflict Resolution* (Glenview, Ill.: Scott, Foreman, 1975); Louis R. Pondy, "Organizational Conflict: Concepts and Models," *Administrative Science Quarterly*, Vol. 12 (September 1967), pp. 269–320.

[12] Thomas L. Ruble and Kenneth W. Thomas, "Support for a Two-Dimensional Model of Conflict Behavior," *Organizational Behavior and Human Performance*, Vol. 16 (1976), pp. 143–155.

[13] Developed from Ibid and Robert R. Blake and Jane Strygley Mouton, "The Fifth Achievement," *Journal of Applied Behavioral Science*, Vol. 6 (1970), p. 418.

[14] The following discussion is based on Filley, op. cit., pp. 21–30.

[15] See Robbins, op. cit.

[16] Based on Earl Planty, "Handling Problems (Communicating) Where Emotions Are High and Conflicts Exist," Senior Seminar in General Management (January 1970).

[17] Reported in Robert Townsend, *Up the Organization; How to Stop the Corporation from Stifling People and Strangling Profits* (New York: Knopf, 1970), p. 93; Anthony Jay, *Management and Machiavelli: An Inquiry Into The Politics of Corporate Life* (New York: Holt, Rinehart, 1967), p. 96.

[18] Excerpted from James Robins, "Firms Try Newer Way to Slash Absenteeism as Carrot and Stick Fail," *Wall Street Journal* (March 14, 1979). Reprinted by permission of the *Wall Street Journal*. Copyright © 1979 Dow Jones & Company, Inc. All rights reserved.

[19] Robert A. Cooke, "Managing Change in Organizations," in Gerald Zaltman (ed.), *Management Principles for Nonprofit Organizations* (New York: American Management Association, 1979).

[20] This section is adapted in part from John R. Schermerhorn, Jr., James G. Hunt, and Richard N. Osborn, *Managing Organizational Behavior* (New York: Wiley, 1982), pp. 492–498. Used by permission.

[21] Kurt Lewin, "Group Decision and Social Change," in G. E. Swanson, T. M. Newcomb, and E. L. Hartley (eds.), *Readings in Social Psychology* (New York: Holt, Rinehart, 1952), pp. 459–473.

[22] Robert Chin and Kenneth D. Benne, "General Strategies for Effecting Changes in Human Systems," in Warren G. Bennis, Kenneth D. Benne, Robert Chin, and Kenneth E. Corey (eds.), *The Planning of Change*, Third Edition (New York: Holt, Rinehart, 1969), pp. 22–45.

[23] This and each of the following applications is developed from an exercise reported in J. William Pfeiffer and John E. Jones, *A Handbook of Structured Experiences for Human Relations Training*, Vol. II (La Jolla, Calif.: University Associates, 1973). Used by permission.

[24] John P. Kotter and Leonard A. Schlesinger, "Choosing Strategies for Change," *Harvard Business Review*, Vol. 57 (March-April 1979), pp. 109–112.

[25] Edgar F. Huse, *Organization Development and Change*, Second Edition (St. Paul: West Publishing, 1980), p. 508.

[26] Adapted from Huse, op. cit., pp. 30, 31.

[27] Wendell L. French and Cecil H. Bell, Jr., *Organization Development*, Second Edition (Englewood Cliffs, N.J.: Prentice-Hall, 1978), p. 88.

[28] The *Wall Street Journal* (March 10, 1982), p. 21. Reprinted by permission of the *Wall Street Journal*. Copyright © 1982 Dow Jones & Company, Inc. All rights reserved.

[29] Adapted from a case copyright © by the President and Fellows of Harvard College. Reprinted by permission.

18

MANAGING
LABOR-MANAGEMENT
RELATIONS

ANATOMY OF AN AUTO-PLANT RESCUE

One after another the big old Chrysler plants in Detroit shut down.[1] Hamtramck Assembly, Eight Mile Stamping, and Huber Foundry closed in 1980, Lynch Road Assembly and part of Mack Stamping in 1981. It was the same each time. First the rumors on the factory floor. Then the stark announcement of the closing. That was it. Labor and management never tried to work together to keep a plant open. A year ago the familiar rumors flitted through the Detroit Trim plant, which makes seat covers for Chrysler cars. Figures shown to managers said Detroit Trim was hopelessly noncompetitive, and the plant seemed doomed. Surprisingly, not only is the plant still functioning today, but its productivity is up by more than 25 percent and it has prospects of enjoying prolonged good health.

This time, when the rumors started, the United Auto Workers went to Chrysler's management to find out if they were true, and if so, to see what the union could do to help. And this time Chrysler was responsive. Without any of the belligerent rhetoric that has characterized union-management relations in the auto industry, the two sides worked out an agreement that completely altered the economics of the plant, the way it works, and the way it is managed. By March 1 the plant met the productivity goals Chrysler had set as a condition for keeping it open.

When finally drawn together by a mutual threat, labor and management discovered they both thought the plant's 709 employees, blue- and white-collar alike, were not putting in much of a day's work. Many sewing-machine operators were finishing their quotas an hour or more before the whistle signaled the end of the day shift at 2:30 P.M. The two sides agreed that the plant's roster could be cut by 25 percent and the remaining employees given new quotas to keep them busy for a full 8 hours—or 7½ hours to be more accurate, since the 8 hours include two 12-minute breaks and a 5-minute wash-up period.

Old work rules have been swept aside along with the old work standards. A foreman doesn't have to call a plant electrician to unplug a sewing machine. Anyone can unplug it.

While they haven't become bosom buddies, management and labor have achieved a measure of trust and mutual respect that has been conspicuously missing in Detroit. Joe Zappa, 57, president of the once-powerful UAW Local 212 that encompasses Detroit Trim, says of Moe Teodosic, 43, the kinetic plant manager, "Without him, we would never have done it." Teodosic says the same of Zappa. Indeed, it almost seemed as if the plant management and union leaders formed an alliance aimed at dragging along their respective constituencies—corporate managment and labor rank and file.

PLANNING AHEAD

What happened at Detroit Trim is part of a growing trend for organized labor and management to work together for mutual gain. The labor-management relationship is a complex one, however, and it places special demands on the manager. Increased familiarity with the following topics will prepare you to be a more informed participant in the labor-management relationship.

Labor Unions in Society
The Legal Environment of Labor-Management Relations
How Organizations Become Unionized
Collective Bargaining
Managerial Implications of Collective Bargaining
Improving Labor-Management Relations

A **labor union** is an organization to which workers belong and which collectively deals with employers on their behalf. Two examples of labor unions frequently in the news are the United Auto Workers (UAW) and the Teamsters. **Labor-management relations** is the ongoing relationship between a group of employees represented by a union and management in the employing organization.[2] The foundation for any labor-management relationship is **collective bargaining,** the process of negotiating, administering, and interpreting a formal agreement or labor contract between a union and the employing organization. Labor contracts specify the rights and obligations of employees and management in respect to wages, work hours, work rules, and other conditions of employment. They constitute a major influence on the management process and the managers who implement it in unionized work settings.

Figure 18.1 depicts how the presence of a labor union and collective bargaining can intervene in the relationship between a manager and his or her immediate subordinates. As the following headlines suggest, this situation is made more complicated when labor-management relations become emotionally charged.[3]

> Labor Relations in the
> Steel Industry Turn
> Hostile as Firms
> Get Tougher

> Brown & Sharpe Strikers
> Resist Givebacks as
> Eight-Month Walkout
> Grows Violent

Unions are important forces in today's environment. They have the potential to impact the productivity of organizations and their members significantly. Any manager in any organization—small or large and public or private—must be prepared to deal successfully with unions. This chapter is designed to increase your understanding of unions and the challenges they add to the management process. We'll begin by examining labor unions in general and their role in contemporary society.

FIGURE 18.1 A manager's view of labor-management relations.

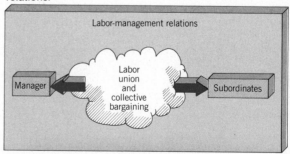

LABOR UNIONS IN SOCIETY

We live in a society where labor unions are frequently in the news. Such unions as the UAW, UMW (United Mine Workers), and the Teamsters have tremendous power to impact our daily lives. All we need is a strike by automobile workers, airline pilots, or truckers, for example, to feel these effects. As citizens, as potential union members, and as managers, it helps to understand unions and their implications.

Evolution of the Labor Movement

Labor unions headquartered in the United States represent over 20 million persons. A sample of large labor organizations is presented in Table 18.1. A growing number of unions are now found in occupations not traditionally unionized, such as public employees (teachers, police officers, and government workers) and professional athletes.

Early History

Labor unions have a strong base in American society, and the roots of this strength trace well into the past. Although the first American unions were established around 1800, the labor movement remained small until the 1930s. Before the Great Depression, probably no more than 10 percent of the labor force belonged to unions. The early resistance of workers to unionization is generally attributed to several factors related to the social, political, and economic environments of the day.

1. *The absence of a well-entrenched class system* The United States was a country of many opportunities for upward mobility. Wage earners were less apt to see themselves as permanently a part of the working class and therefore less prone to seek the support of organized labor.

2. *The massive influx of immigrants* Prior to the early 1900s, immigration to the United States

Table 18.1 Labor Organizations Reporting 100,000 Members or More, 1980

Labor Organization	Members (× 1000)	Labor Organization	Members (× 1000)
Teamsters (Ind.)	1891	Retail, Wholesale	215
National Education Association (Ind.)	1684	Government (NAGE) (Ind.)	200
Automobile Workers (Ind.)	1357	Transportation Union	190
Food and Commercial	1300	Iron Workers	184
Steelworkers	1238	Nurses Association (Ind.)	180
State, County	1098	Railway Clerks	180
Electrical (IBEW)	1041	Fire Fighters	178
Carpenters	784	Painters	164
Machinists	754	Transit Union	162
Service Employees	650	Electrical (UE) (Ind.)	162
Laborers	608	Sheet Metal	161
Communication Workers	551	Bakery, Confectionary, Tobacco	160
Teachers	551	Oil, Chemical	154
Clothing and Textile Workers	455	Rubber	151
Operating Engineers	423	Police (Ind.)	150
Hotel	400	Boilermakers	145
Plumbers	352	Bricklayers	135
Ladies' Garment	323	Transport Workers	130
Musicians	299	Postal and Federal Employees	125
Paperworkers	275	Printing and Graphic	122
Government (AFGE)	255	Woodworkers	112
Postal Workers	251	Office	107
Mine Workers (Ind.)	245	California	105
Electrical (IUE)	233	Maintenance of Way	102
Letter Carriers	230		

Source: Bureau of Labor Statistics, based on reports to the Bureau of Labor Statistics.
Note: All organizations not identified as (Ind.) are affiliated with the AFL-CIO.

created an ethnically and racially mixed labor force. Cultural differences, ethnic hostilities, and the absence of a common language often made it difficult to organize unions.

3. *Relatively high wages and standards of living* Immigrants, in particular, found themselves generally better off than they were in their countries of origin. As a result, they often lacked the motivation to join unions.

4. *Employers' resistance to unions* Employers of the day were very strong, and violence was not an uncommon result when unionization attempts occurred. Employers were also generally supported by a court system that issued injunctions against a variety of union activities.

The Growth Period

By the early 1930s, union membership was declining and many believed that the labor movement was all but dead. Then a number of important environmental changes resulted in a dramatic rebound of the labor movement and ushered in the modern era of labor-management relations. Figure 18.2 shows the general trend in union membership from 1935 to the present. The number of union members grew rapidly to a peak of approximately 36 percent of the nonfarm work force during World War II.

Behind this increase in union membership stood a number of trends. The transformation of the American economy from agricultural to one based on heavy industry and manufacturing created an industrial working class conscious of limited opportunities for upward mobility. Declining immigration and the passage of time increased the number of workers who spoke a common language and shared a cultural heritage. Social barriers that had restricted union growth in earlier times were greatly reduced. In addition, economic pressures of the depression added impetus to unionization as a result of increased worker discontent and a tarnished image for business.

Perhaps even more important, changes in public policy created a legal environment more supportive and protective of unions. Congressional action in the 1930s resulted in laws protecting the right of workers to join unions and engage in strikes, and requiring employers to bargain in

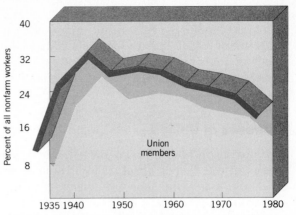

FIGURE 18.2 Union share of the U.S. work force. The union share of the work force, in decline since World War II, is now pegged at about 22%. This figure—based on unaudited membership reports to the Labor Department—is surely inflated. *Source:* Daniel Seligman, "Who Needs Unions?" *Fortune* (July 12, 1982), p. 64. © 1982 Time Inc. Courtesy of Fortune Magazine.

good faith with certified unions and refrain from interfering with union activities or discriminating against union members. This new legal environment for labor-management relations helped unions to grow and prosper.

Changing Times

Union membership has declined from its World War II peak to a level of about 22 percent of today's work force. This decline is partly the result of structural changes in the American economy since the war. Industries traditionally unionized (e.g., manufacturing, construction, and mining) have declined somewhat in importance relative to the emerging financial, service, and high-technology industries, which have been more resistant to unionization efforts.

Changing characteristics of the labor force have also contributed to the decline of the labor movement. Women and younger workers have historically been less apt to belong to unions; professional and white-collar workers have been less inclined toward unions than blue-collar workers. As each of these groups has increased in importance in the labor force, the proportion of workers holding union membership has declined.

Finally, organized labor shares in the responsibility for declining union membership. Unions have been slow to react to changing social and economic conditions. As a result, many of their programs and goals fail to adequately address the needs of contemporary workers. Modern union leaders are working hard to correct this situation.

Purposes of Unions

A major distinction between present-day labor unions in the United States and those in most other countries is the generally conservative nature of U.S. union goals; the dominant ideology is often characterized as "business" or "bread-and-butter" unionism. U.S. unions focus almost exclusively on the economic concerns of their members and generally avoid involvement in activities designed to alter the basic fabric of society. U.S. unions are generally supportive of the capitalist system, although they see conflict with management over the terms and conditions of employment as inevitable. Political action is typically directed at advancing the economic interests of workers or at providing legal protection for unions and members. This is a marked contrast with European unions, which are often associated with socialist political parties and are concerned with greater worker participation in the management process. For example, the German labor movement, in association with the Social Democratic Party, has secured passage of codetermination laws that require employee participation on corporate boards of directors.

The legacy of Samuel Gompers (1850–1924) remains a dominant force in the U.S. labor movement. Gompers served as president of the American Federation of Labor (AFL) during 1886–1924. Under his leadership, the AFL successfully organized many separate labor organizations by applying a set of principles that still articulate the guiding philosophy of the U.S. labor movement. In Gompers's words,[4]

> The ground-work principle of America's labor movement has been to recognize that first things must come first. The primary essential in our mission has been the protection of the wage-workers, now; to increase wages; to cut hours off the long workday; . . . to improve the safety and the sanitary conditions of the workshop; to free workers from the tyrannies, petty or otherwise, which

served to make their existence a slavery. These . . . are the primary objectives of trade unionism.

The primary purpose of labor unions remains, in the eyes of most union leaders, the representation of the employee in the workplace—much the same goal that Gompers espoused nearly a century ago. Of course, the specific issues have changed to some extent since Gompers's time. Today's unions, for example,

- Seek retirement and fringe-benefit systems to minimize the impact of plant closings and relocations.
- Try to reduce employment practices that discriminate against minorities.
- Become directly involved in the political process by endorsing the campaigns of preferred candidates for offices at all levels of government.
- Become involved in efforts to support free trade unionism abroad—such as the Solidarity trade union in Poland.

The purposes of unions are also evolving as the environment changes. Problems with the U.S. economy in the 1980s increased the pressure for unions to assist their members in times of unemployment and personal hardship. The United Steelworkers, for example, established food banks to help its laid-off members feed their families; the Sheet Metal Workers Association went so far as to offer to pay all or part of laid-off members' car loans, mortgages, or rents when they faced foreclosure or eviction.[5]

In addition to stimulating more personal services for members, difficult economic times also foster greater cooperation between labor and management. This point is evident in the chapter-opening example of cooperation between the UAW and Chrysler at Detroit Trim. Among these developments has been the increased willingness of unions to accept wage and benefit cuts, as well as other concessions, in return for increased job security. Such "give-backs" by unions have been rare in the past. Joint labor-management committees have also been formed in a variety of industries to work cooperatively to solve problems that adversely affect both firms and their employees, and to resolve differences between

Local unions are the fundamental building blocks of national and international union organizations.

unions and management before instead of after strikes.

Types of Unions

The earliest U.S. labor organizations were composed exclusively of persons in skilled trades. These **craft unions** represented workers in single crafts or occupations—for example, carpenters, plumbers, and electricians. Workers were successful in organizing craft unions because they possessed skills that employers could not easily replace. Since craft unions were concerned with protecting their members' jobs from the competition of other crafts and less skilled workers, agreements among craft unions established fairly well-defined **jurisdictions** or task domains within which each craft union retained autonomy to organize and represent workers. Craft unions agreed not to organize workers outside their respective jurisdictions and negotiated agreements with employers requiring that only members of a particular craft union be assigned to particular types of jobs. They dominated the labor movement prior to the 1930s and still remain powerful forces in such areas as construction and transportation.

The organization of unions by crafts was less practical in large factories employing individuals

in dozens of different but highly interdependent jobs. Consequently, as the labor movement has grown after the depression, **industrial unions** have become increasingly prominent. They typically serve a single industry and represent both skilled and less skilled workers in a wide variety of occupations. Although industrial unions often organize in many different areas, most limit their organizing activities to a few primary industrial jurisdictions. The UAW, for example, primarily represents employees in the automobile-manufacturing and aerospace industries, while the UMW's primary jurisdiction is coal mining. In terms of total membership, industrial unions currently dominate the U.S. labor movement.

Some unions are organized in a variety of unrelated industries. They are referred to as **general unions** because they lack a specific craft or industry focus. Perhaps the best example in the United States is the Teamsters. It is the largest union in the country and represents workers in a wide variety of industries and occupations. The future is likely to see a reduction in the total number of unions as those with overlapping jurisdictions merge and others with dwindling memberships are absorbed into stronger unions. Although the emergence of a great number of truly general unions is unlikely, we should see an increase in the number of multi-jurisdictional unions over time.

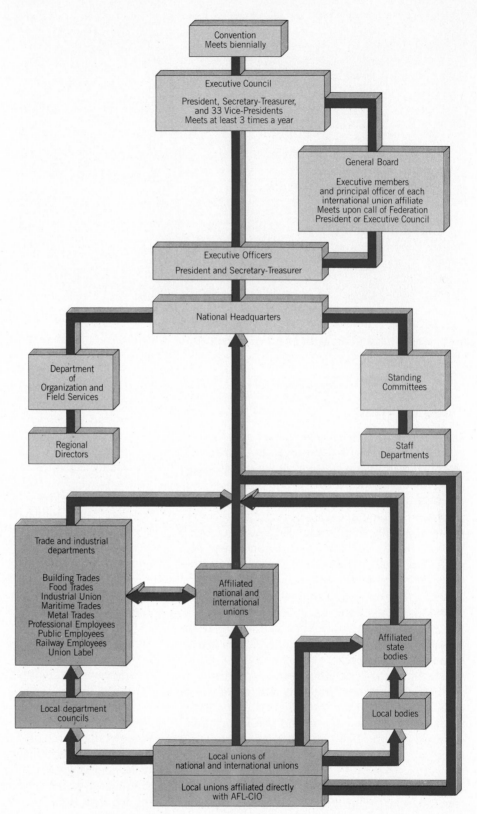

FIGURE 18.3 Structure of the AFL-CIO. *Source: Director of National Unions and Employee Associations,* Bulletin 2044, Bureau of Labor Statistics, 1977, p. 2.

Unions as Organizations

The basic organizational unit of the U.S. labor movement is the national or international union. National unions have members throughout the United States; international unions also have members outside the United States. There are now about 170 national or international unions and about 35 professional and state employee associations active in the United States. Most are affiliated with the AFL-CIO (American Federation of Labor–Congress of Industrial Organizations).

The AFL-CIO

The AFL-CIO is not a trade union itself. It is an association that provides services to its affiliated but independent unions. With an affiliated membership of about 18 million workers, the AFL-CIO is a dominant force in the American labor movement. Its actions are far-reaching in scope and impact. The structure of the federation is shown in Figure 18.3.

Among other things, the AFL-CIO is active in the political arena. Its Committee on Political Education works to elect pro-labor candidates to political office, while its Legislative Department is primarily involved in lobbying activities. Other departments and committees of the AFL-CIO assist affiliate unions in organizing campaigns for new members, preparing for contract negotiations, resolving disputes with other unions, and coordinating with other unions having similar interests.

Unions affiliated with the AFL-CIO retain autonomy in negotiating contracts and administering their internal affairs. While the federation may make recommendations, individual unions are free to conduct their own affairs. However, affiliated unions that engage in activities the AFL-CIO considers contrary to the interests of organized labor can be suspended or expelled from the federation. The Teamsters union was expelled from the AFL-CIO in 1957 for corrupt activities.

National and International Unions

The building block of virtually all national and international unions is the **local,** an administra-

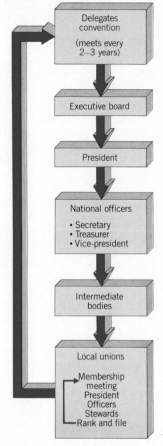

FIGURE 18.4 Key elements in a national or international union.

tive unit that services at the local level a particular group of workers represented by the union. The affairs of the local union are normally administered by elected officers or, in some cases, full-time business agents. Their duties typically include negotiating new contracts, administering existing contracts, and handling contract disputes. As shown in Figure 18.4, the president and other officers of locals are normally assisted by **union stewards,** employees who are union officials and who represent fellow workers in resolving disputes with management. The union steward is a person with whom managers frequently interact as part of day-to-day practice in a unionized work setting.

The next level of authority above the local union is the intermediate body, which coordinates and facilitates the activities of locals. At the upper level of the union organizational structure are the national or international president, offi-

NEWSLINE 18.1

AFTER WILLIAMS: UNION LOOKS AHEAD

The executive board of the troubled Teamsters union will choose an interim president this week after bidding a bittersweet farewell to Roy Lee Williams.

U.S. District Judge Prentice H. Marshall of Chicago agreed to stay a provisional 55-year prison sentence handed to Williams, convicted of conspiring to bribe a U.S. senator, when Williams's attorneys said the Teamster leader would resign and sever his ties with the nation's largest union.

Williams had been convicted of conspiring to bribe Senator Howard W. Cannon (D–Nevada) in connection with trucking deregulation. Cannon, who was never charged in the case, was defeated last November.

In an April 6 speech on the floor of the Senate, Orrin G. Hatch (R–Utah), who heads the Labor and Human Resources Committee, demanded Williams's resignation and implored the Teamster executive board to "take advantage of this opportunity to finally clean house and do something about the future of the union, its image and the protection of the hard-working people."

Teamsters for a Democratic Union, an 8000-member dissident faction, has demanded that Williams's successor be chosen by the rank-and-file.

"This would be the kind of revitalization that this union needs right now," dissident spokesman Bob Master said Friday. "We don't particularly have a preference."

Source: Excerpted from "After Williams: Union Looks Ahead," the *Southern Illinoisan* (April 17, 1983), p. 7. Used by permission.

---

cers, and executive council. The national officers, in turn, are normally accountable to the delegate's convention at which rank-and-file members are generally represented by delegates chosen by the locals. This convention is a counterpart to the stockholders' meeting for a corporation; the executive board of the union serves a function similar to a corporation's board of directors.

Management Problems in Unions

Two management problems relating to the administration of national and local unions have plagued the U.S. labor movement over the years. First, a small minority of unions have been influenced and in some instances dominated by organized crime. Labor "racketeers" use their control of such unions to extort money from employers in return for special labor contracts, and to extort money from members in return for work opportunities. Corrupt union officials may also conspire with criminals to use union funds to finance illicit activities and/or to "launder" the profits from illegal activities.

A second management problem relates to the tendency for some unions to become excessively centralized as they grow and mature. As the union leaders become more distant from and less accountable to the rank and file, they may act in self-serving ways that are inconsistent with the desires of the members.

Senate hearings in the late 1950s highlighted such management problems and led to the passage of the Landrum-Griffin Act of 1959 to regulate the internal affairs of unions. This act requires unions to file annual financial statements with the Department of Labor, to guarantee members certain rights, and to hold periodic elections of union officials. The act also mandates standards for these elections, restricts national and international unions from assuming direct control over local unions, and prohibits corrupt practices by union officers. As *Newsline 18.1* suggests, however, corruption problems still appear on occasion. Fortunately, the legal system is now diligent and well prepared in monitoring these illicit practices.

THE LEGAL ENVIRONMENT OF LABOR-MANAGEMENT RELATIONS

The preceding discussion highlights the importance of the legal environment of labor-management relations. The cornerstone of this law is the **National Labor Relations Act (NLRA).**

National Labor Relations Act

The NLRA as we know it today is a composite of the Wagner Act of 1935 as amended by the Taft-Hartley Act of 1947 and the Landrum-Griffin Act of 1959. This important element in the legal environment of labor-management relations seeks to protect both employee and employer rights.[6]

The Wagner Act of 1935 sets forth a number of employee rights with regard to unions. It specifically gives employees the right to join or form unions, to bargain collectively, and to undertake "concerted" activities (i.e., strikes) in pursuit of their bargaining objectives. As shown in Table 18.2, the Wagner Act is also specific in prohibiting several unfair labor practices applicable to employers.

Under the Wagner Act, the **National Labor Relations Board (NLRB)** was created to conduct elections through which employees decide whether or not to unionize, investigate any charges of unfair labor practice, and generally administer the provisions of the act. Only nonsupervisory personnel working in the private sector are covered by the act. Agricultural workers, persons employed in companies that do not engage in appreciable levels of interstate commerce, railway and airline employees (separately protected under the Railway Labor Act of 1926), and independent contractors are excluded. Coverage was extended to private-sector health-care workers in 1974.

Table 18.2 Selected Unfair Labor Practices Subject to Provisions of the NLRA

Employee Rights: **Wagner Act (1935)** prohibits *employers* from
- Interfering with the right of employees to join unions (*Example:* Threatening to fire employees who join unions)
- Discriminating against employees to discourage union membership (*Example:* Denying a pay increase to a union activist)
- Refusing to bargain in good faith with a certified union (*Example:* Changing wage levels without discussing the matter with union representatives.)

Employer Rights: **Taft-Hartley Act (1947)** prohibits *unions* from
- Coercing or restraining employees in the exercise of their rights under the NLRA (*Example:* Mass picketing with the intention of intimidating strikebreakers)
- Engaging in certain types of strikes (*Example:* A jurisdictional strike to compel the employer to give work to members of one union as opposed to another)
- Refusing to bargain in good faith with an employer's representatives (*Example:* Striking over something other than wages, hours, and conditions of employment)

A rash of strikes after World War II and some perception that the Wagner Act was biased against employers led Congress to pass the Taft-Hartley Act of 1947. The Taft-Hartley amendments to the NLRA prohibit unions from engaging in such unfair labor practices as those listed in Table 18.2. In addition, they set forth procedures through which employees can "decertify" or revoke a union's right to represent them, individual states can enact "right-to-work" laws that prohibit union membership from being used as a condition for employment, and the U.S. president can seek temporary injunctions to suspend otherwise legal strikes that threaten national health or safety.

The final component in NLRA is the Landrum-Griffin Act passed in 1959. As noted earlier, this act regulates internal affairs of unions relating to certain financial matters and administrative procedures.

A number of other laws complement the NLRA as part of the legal regulation of labor-management relations. Some states have passed "little" Wagner Acts that govern collective bargaining and union organizing in sectors not covered by the NLRA (e.g., agriculture and small business). State and local government employees

Better wages and job security are frequent issues in labor contract negotiations.

have also been granted bargaining rights in several states and, beginning with the Kennedy administration, a series of presidential executive orders have extended such rights to federal employees. The U.S. Civil Service Act was amended in 1978 to incorporate a number of provisions similar to the NLRA. Federal employees are still prohibited from striking, however. Probably the most famous recent test of this provision in the law came during the federal air-traffic controllers' strike of 1981. The law prevailed in that case when President Reagan summarily dismissed all strikers after efforts to bring them back to work proved fruitless. His actions were legally upheld through a number of court appeals, and new air-traffic controllers were hired to replace the fired strikers.

National Labor Relations Board

The unfair labor practices defined by the NLRA are not crimes. But when an unfair labor practice is alleged to have occurred, the NLRB investigates. If the allegation is substantiated, remedial action will be prescribed. The most common order by the NLRB is for the offending party to refrain from such actions in the future and post public notices to that effect. In cases where someone has been injured as the result of an unfair

labor practice, the board may require restitution. For example, if the board determines that an employee was discharged for joining a union, it will normally order that the employee be reinstated and paid any lost wages. If one of the parties involved in an unfair labor practice case disagrees with the board's findings, it may appeal the decision through the federal court system.

HOW ORGANIZATIONS BECOME UNIONIZED

Most unions employ a staff of organizers whose function is to assist employees in establishing a collective-bargaining agreement with their employer. *Newsline 18.2* introduces the unorthodox tactics of one of the more successful union organizers of recent years.

Although union organizers may occasionally attempt to initiate interest in unionization among employees in a nonunion company, more often a group of employees concerned about wages or other employment conditions will approach a union and request help in forming a local union and obtaining collective-bargaining rights. They usually do so with a specific issue or goal as their rallying point. **Comparable worth,** for example, is the principle that persons doing jobs equiva-

NEWSLINE 18.2

ROGERS'S TOUGH, UNORTHODOX TACTICS PREVAIL IN STEVENS ORGANIZING FIGHT

Ray Rogers engineered a lengthy national campaign against J. P. Stevens Company that ended this weekend. On behalf of the Amalgamated Clothing and Textile Workers Union, Rogers put pressure on companies that do business with Stevens or that have Stevens directors on their own boards. The object: To prod, harrass, and embarrass the companies until they pressed for a change in Stevens's policies. With the collective-bargaining agreement reached between Stevens and the union, Rogers may finally have succeeded in winning some credibility for his unorthodox way of fighting for workers' power.

Most recently, Rogers threatened to contest the election of directors at Metropolitan Life Insurance Company, one of Stevens's major lenders. That prospect inspired Richard Shinn, chairman of the big mutual insurer, to do some behind-the-scenes maneuvering shortly before the final settlement between Stevens and the union.

Source: Adapted from Gail Bronson and Jeffrey H. Birnbaum, "Rogers' Tough, Unorthodox Tactics Prevail in Stevens Organizing Fight," *Wall Street Journal* (October 21, 1980), pp. 31, 36. Reprinted by permission of the *Wall Street Journal.* Copyright © 1980 Dow Jones & Company, Inc. All rights reserved.

lent in skill and importance should receive equal pay. Women have historically been disadvantaged in this respect, and the issue now has organizing appeal in work settings employing a substantial percentage of females. Since only 6 million of the 38 million U.S. female workers belonged to labor organizations in 1980, they represent a substantial target for union organizers.[7]

Northeast Color Research, Inc. in Somerville, Mass., began as a nonunionized firm owned by Joanne and Les Frederick. What happened to them is a further introduction into the process through which organizations become unionized.[8]

> As Northeast Color Research Inc. expanded from a two-person shop in 1960 to a 25-person organization in the 1970s, the Fredericks failed to define pay policies or work rules. In addition, their production supervisor, with no experience or training in supervision, never learned how to communicate with employees. The company's dozen production workers finally rebelled. They petitioned for an NLRB-sponsored election and voted nine

to three to be represented by the United Food and Commercial Workers Union. As a result, the Fredericks had to negotiate their first labor contract.

The Decision to Seek Union Representation

The preceding example introduces some of the reasons why workers may decide to unionize and the process through which this can legally be achieved. We'll look first at the decision to unionize.

A great deal of research has been done in recent years on both the determinants of union growth and attitudes of employees toward unionization.[9] Economists have shown that union growth is related to the business cycle. When other things are equal, unions tend to grow more in periods of high inflation and economic expansion. In periods of inflation, workers see unions as likely to protect their earnings; in periods of economic expansion, employers are less likely to resist unionization efforts.

Psychological studies find that employee attitudes toward unions are more favorable when job satisfaction is low. But the nature of this relationship varies according to the occupational status of the employee. White-collar and professional workers are more likely to favor unionization when dissatisfied with intrinsic rewards of their jobs (e.g., personal autonomy, self-fulfillment); blue-collar workers are more likely to favor unionization when dissatisfied with the extrinsic rewards of their jobs (e.g., pay, fringe benefits, quality of supervision, work conditions). This latter point may have been the deciding factor, for example, in the Northeast Color Research case just described. In addition, employees are more likely to favor unionization when (1) they perceive of themselves as having little power to change work conditions for the better, (2) they expect a union to be effective in changing work conditions, and (3) they have only limited employment opportunities elsewhere.

Employer resistance to union organizing activities has clearly increased in recent years, and associated with this trend has been the emergence of management-consulting firms that specialize in "preventive-labor relations." They help employers develop strategies to avoid a decision by employees to seek union representation. Many executives simply act on their own to protect their organizations from unionization. One study of 26 large nonunionized firms found that many of their personnel policies reflected the objective of maintaining nonunion status.[10] These firms implemented modern personnel systems, with considerable emphasis on employee participation (e.g., quality circles), progressive compensation and benefits programs, employment security, and promotion from within. The central ingredient at Emerson Electric is good communication.[11] Emerson's president personally monitors annual employee-attitude surveys and is known to replace plant managers who allow employee relations to deteriorate.

Certification of Unions

The U.S. legal system defines a clear process by which workers can choose a union to be their representative in negotiating the terms and conditions of work with an employer. This is accomplished in the private sector by a **certification election** held under provisions of the NLRA and supervised by the NLRB. Public-sector organizing is governed by federal executive orders and various state labor laws. Because the public-sector process is modeled after the NLRB procedures shown in Figure 18.5, we will examine and use it as a more general example.

The process of certifying a union formally begins when a petition for an election is filed with the NLRB. This petition must be signed by at least 30 percent of the employees in a potential **bargaining unit**—that is, the organization or subunit of an organization that would eventually be subject to union representation. There may be disagreement between a union and the employer

FIGURE 18.5 Steps in the union certification procedure under the National Labor Relations Act.

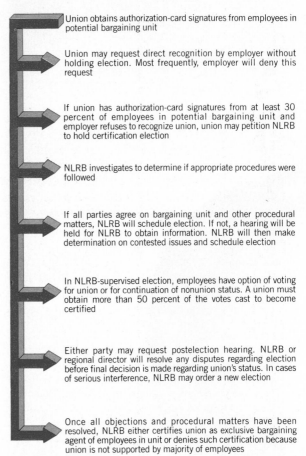

Union obtains authorization-card signatures from employees in potential bargaining unit

Union may request direct recognition by employer without holding election. Most frequently, employer will deny this request

If union has authorization-card signatures from at least 30 percent of employees in potential bargaining unit and employer refuses to recognize union, union may petition NLRB to hold certification election

NLRB investigates to determine if appropriate procedures were followed

If all parties agree on bargaining unit and other procedural matters, NLRB will schedule election. If not, a hearing will be held for NLRB to obtain information. NLRB will then make determination on contested issues and schedule election

In NLRB-supervised election, employees have option of voting for union or for continuation of nonunion status. A union must obtain more than 50 percent of the votes cast to become certified

Either party may request postelection hearing. NLRB or regional director will resolve any disputes regarding election before final decision is made regarding union's status. In cases of serious interference, NLRB may order a new election

Once all objections and procedural matters have been resolved, NLRB either certifies union as exclusive bargaining agent of employees in unit or denies such certification because union is not supported by majority of employees

as to the appropriateness of a proposed bargaining unit because the composition of the unit may influence the outcome of the election. Thus prior to any election, the NLRB may have to determine if the employees in the proposed unit share a "community of interests" and if all of them fall under the jurisdiction of the law. Supervisors, for example, are not covered by the NLRA and may not vote in certification elections. The criteria used by the NLRB in determining if a community of interests exists include

1. The extent to which workers share similar skills, employment interests, work duties, and working conditions.
2. The employer's organizational structure (including the functional integration of departments, the nature of the supervisory system, the interchange of employees among departments, and the geographic distribution of the employer's operations).
3. The history of bargaining in the company or industry.
4. The preferences of the employees regarding the structure of the bargaining unit.

Once the bargaining unit has been determined and any other issues resolved, a date is set for the secret-ballot certification election. Prior to the election, the union and company normally attempt to influence workers to vote either for or against unionization. Pre-election campaigns are monitored and closely regulated by the NLRB. Both unions and employers are prohibited by law from threatening or bribing employees. They may provide persuasive information to the employees regarding what they believe to be the advantages or disadvantages of unionization, but campaign literature and speeches may not contain misrepresentations of fact.

The NLRA requires that a union establish its "majority status" in an election in order to be recognized. This means that a union must receive at least 51 percent of the votes cast to become certified as the employee's bargaining agent. Should a union lose an election, it may not petition for a new election for at least one year.

Figure 18.6 shows the percentage of certification elections won by unions since 1936. Note

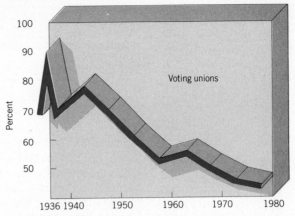

FIGURE 18.6 Percent of certification elections won by unions since 1936. *Source:* Daniel Seligman, "Who Needs Unions?" *Fortune* (July 12, 1982), p. 56. © 1982 Time Inc. Courtesy of Fortune Magazine.

the downward trend. Unions are currently winning less than half of the NLRB supervised certification elections. At their peak in 1937, unions won the right to represent employees 94 percent of the time.

The NLRA also provides employees with a procedure for **decertification**—that is, a means for revoking the certification of a union previously certified as their bargaining agent. A showing of interest by 30 percent or more members of the bargaining unit is required for a decertification election to be held by the NLRB. Decertification elections are sometimes initiated by a union that wants to replace an existing union. Such "raiding" is less common today than it was in the 1940s and early 1950s before the merger of the AFL and CIO. Most decertification elections today involve only the employees' choice between remaining unionized and returning to nonunion status.

Although employers may express opinions during a preelection campaign for decertification, they may neither initiate a decertification campaign nor encourage employees to do so. As *Newsline 18.3* shows, however, the process of decertification is often controversial.

The number of decertification elections held in the United States now runs over 1000 per year. Unions are losing almost 75 percent of them.[12]

THE JEFFERSON ELECTRIC CLASH

Here at Jefferson Electric, situated in a predominantly nonunion area 95 miles south of Nashville, the Aluminum Workers union and plant management clashed from the outset after the union representation victory of 1980. Contract negotiations dragged on for 17 months and then broke off last November. The union filed 120 charges of unfair labor practices against the company. It alleged, among other things, that Jefferson Electric fired, suspended, or otherwise punished employees because they supported the union. A federal judge temporarily restrained the concern from engaging in such actions. The union later settled some charges when Jefferson Electric agreed to pay 22 workers about $59,000. Mr. Gant, the plant manager, contends that the union would have sought a full NLRB hearing rather than settle "if they thought the charges were legitimate."

Because many of the dismissed union sympathizers agreed to accept cash payments rather than demand their old jobs back, the settlements had the effect of eroding the union's base of support. And by the time that anti-union employees began the first of three decertification attempts in mid-1981, layoffs had shrunk the plant staff to 109 from 210.

Some former union supporters backed the decertification drive, declaring that "the union has done nothing for us," says long-time union opponent Betty Harper, a coil winder. But pro-union workers say that many people signed the decertification petition out of fear they would otherwise lose their jobs. One man, they say, was fired without cause after he refused repeated petition-signing requests from a woman who even waited for him for two hours in the plant parking lot. Company officials say they dismissed the man because he wouldn't work overtime.

The final straw may have been two speeches given to employees last summer by Jefferson Electric's president, Carl Zeminick. In each, he said he couldn't pay them their annual raise on the usual August 1 date. "He told us if the union was voted in again, they'd have to negotiate a raise," recalls Addie Cosby, a union backer, "but if the union was voted out, management soon would meet and find out how much they could afford to give." Even without a contract, the union had won a wage increase of about 8 percent the previous August. Zeminick says he couldn't bargain for another raise before the August 12 decertification election because management already had stopped recognizing the union.

Source: Excerpted from Joann S. Lublin, "Labor Reverses: Pugnacious Companies and Skeptical Workers Cost Unions Members," *Wall Street Journal* (October 21, 1982), pp. 1, 25. Reprinted by permission of the *Wall Street Journal.* Copyright © 1982 Dow Jones & Company, Inc. All rights reserved.

COLLECTIVE BARGAINING

Collective bargaining, as noted earlier, stands at the heart of the labor-management relationship. The process of negotiating, interpreting, and administering a labor contract establishes the conditions of employment under which managers and their subordinates work together in the unionized setting. Collective bargaining involves a formal, written, legally binding contract that has a major impact on day-to-day as well as longer-term managerial activities in an organization. The *Chicago Tribune* cartoon depicts the tricky balance between the interests of the employee and employer that collective bargaining tries to maintain.

Reprinted by permission of the Tribune Company Syndicate, Inc.

What the Bargaining Is All About

Labor contracts are complex and often lengthy agreements between the management of an organization and the union(s) representing its employees. A recent agreement between the United Auto Workers and General Motors was 350 pages long. Although the specific provisions of these contracts vary from one organization to the next, the collective-bargaining process and labor agreement generally address the following issues.[13]

Union Security

An important issue in most labor negotiations is union security. This is an agreement that imposes some form of union membership on employees or requires the payment by employees of a service fee to the union. The most restrictive form of union security is called a **closed shop.** Under this arrangement a person must be a union member in good standing *before* being hired as an employee. The Taft-Hartley Act made the closed shop illegal. The most common union-security clause is the **union shop,** wherein all employees must belong to the union and newly hired employees must join the union within a certain number of days. A third form of union security, the **agency shop,** requires all employees to pay a service fee to the union even though they don't officially have to join.

Management Rights

Unionization obviously poses a challenge to management's authority and decision making, and management may seek some security of its own in a labor contract. Approximately 70 percent of all labor contracts have some form of **management rights** provision. A typical clause formally gives the employer all rights to manage the operation except as these rights are modified through specific terms of the labor agreement. For instance, the labor contract might modify the employer's promotion policy by specifying that seniority be considered in making promotion decisions. A common management-rights provision is a lengthy list of specific areas not subject to collective bargaining, such as the right to (1) schedule working hours, (2) hire and fire workers, (3) set production standards, (4) promote, demote, and transfer workers, and (5) determine the number of supervisors in each department.

Wages and Benefits

Much time and effort in arriving at a labor contract are devoted to provisions for wage increases and fringe-benefit improvements for employees. Wage increases are often stated as (1) immediate across-the-board percentage or cents-per-hour increases, (2) deferred increases based on productivity improvements, and (3) cost-of-living adjustments (COLA). Besides wage increases, unions often demand improvements in various fringe benefits, including (1) wage rates for overtime and holiday work, (2) insurance programs (life, health and hospitalization, dental care), (3) vacation and sick-leave privileges, and (4) pensions. In some industries, such as steel and auto manufacturing, fringe benefits make up to 40 percent of the total compensation package.

Job Security

Job security is assurance that workers will keep their jobs over time and regardless of economic conditions. **Seniority,** or length of continuous service with an employer, is discussed in about 90 percent of all labor contracts. It plays several roles in establishing job security for the employee. One of these is to determine eligibility for benefits such as vacations, holiday privileges, and pensions. It may also be used to determine job assignments where seniority becomes a criterion for selecting among workers for higher-paying jobs, shift work, overtime work, and job transfers.

Other Major Issues

Among other important bargaining issues are the duration of the labor contract and the no-strike and no-lockout clauses. In private industry the most typical labor contracts have a three-year duration; contracts in the public sector are generally for shorter periods. Under a no-strike clause, the union agrees not to strike during the term of the contract. In turn, the employer gives a no-lockout pledge, which means business will not be shut down and workers forced off their jobs in an attempt to get the union to change its position on some crucial issue.

The Bargaining Process

The NLRB oversees the entire collective-bargaining process, from negotiating a new labor contract to resolving any disputes that arise under an existing one. In each case the bargaining takes place in face-to-face meetings between labor and management representatives during which a variety of demands, proposals, and counterproposals are exchanged by both parties. Several rounds of bargaining may be required before an issue or contract is eventually decided.

Labor contracts cover fixed time periods and are renegotiated as the expiration dates approach. Such negotiations frequently take place under the threat of a strike deadline—that is, a threatened refusal by union members not to work beyond a certain date unless a new contract is agreed on. Bargaining frequently goes down to the deadline. The newspaper report on one new contract between the UAW and Chrysler read, "Negotiators reached the settlement, which calls for a two-year contract on noneconomic terms, at about 6:15 a.m. CDT yesterday after they had bargained 30 hours past the UAW's original strike deadline of midnight Tuesday."[14]

Most bargaining begins with a statement of position by both management and the union on a given issue. If the initial differences in the two positions are too great, the *bargaining zone* may be too wide to produce any meaningful discussions. The example depicted in Figure 18.7 describes bargaining between the Carpenters union and U.S. Homes on a wage issue.[15] The union starts with an initial demand of $0.90 per hour wage increase, knowing full well that a "final offer" from management of a $0.60 per hour increase is likely and feeling that anything less than $0.40 per hour would be totally unacceptable. The bargaining representative for U.S. Homes, by contrast, starts by offering $0.20 per hour, would be glad to settle a "final offer" at $0.40 per hour, and in no way will give more than $0.60 per hour for the wage increase.

If both management and labor restrict their demands to the initial offers, no zone exists for realistic bargaining and a strike is possible. Once "final-offer" points are reached in the negotiations, however, true bargaining can take place, with the likelihood that some compromise and agreement will be reached. In this case the likely compromise would be a $0.50 per hour increase. This is why you frequently find that both unions and management settle disputes at something different from their stated "final-offer" points.

Grievances and Arbitration

The typical labor contract prohibits or severely limits the union's right to strike during the life of the agreement. Thus a procedure is needed to resolve disputes that arise regarding the implementation and interpretation of a contract in day-

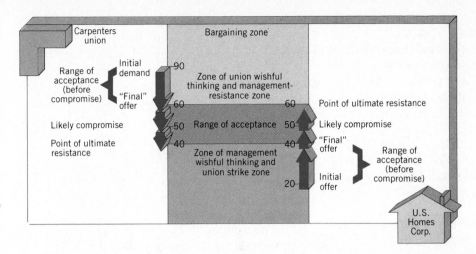

Fig. 18.7 Bargaining between the Carpenters Union and U.S. Homes.

to-day labor-management relations. In fact, this is the point where a labor contract can have the most direct impact on a manager—as a constraint on the day-to-day working relationship between the manager and subordinates. Two terms are most significant in this regard for their managerial implications—grievance and arbitration.

Grievances

A **grievance** is a complaint from an employee regarding treatment he or she has received in respect to a condition of employment. Most grievances allege that a manager or management in general has violated some provision of the labor contract. The union's mechanism for airing such disputes and policing the terms of the collective-bargaining agreement is a formal grievance procedure specified in the labor contract.

Figure 18.8 illustrates the grievance procedure specified in the UAW contract with International Harvester.[16] The first step in the procedure is taken when the employee discusses a complaint with the supervisor. Things may be resolved here. If not, the procedure passes to the next step where the complaint is formally presented as a written grievance to the supervisor. It is typical for a union steward to be present at this meeting. If the dispute is not resolved at this level, further discussions take place between the employee and a chief steward (or other union officials), and the employee's supervisor and other management officials. At this point in the procedure the latter might include a labor-rela-

tions specialist on the management staff and the plant manager. If the problem is still not resolved, it goes to the next stage where higher-level union and management officials become involved. This might include the president of the local union and a representative from the national union, as well as the plant manager and a top corporate executive. If there is still no agreement, the matter passes into arbitration.

FIGURE 18.8 Processing a grievance at International Harvester.

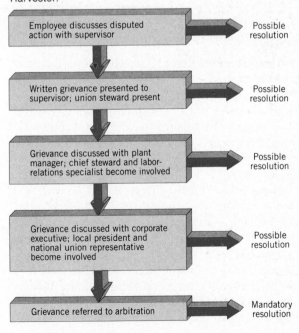

Arbitration

Arbitration is the process by which parties to a labor-management dispute agree to abide by the decision of a neutral and independent third party called an arbitrator.[17] Arbitrators settle issues for which bargaining impasses have been reached during contract negotiations or, as in Figure 18.8, they settle grievances unable to be resolved at earlier steps in the grievance procedure. The courts have granted arbitrators wide powers, and their decisions are usually considered final and binding.

Mediation and conciliation might be employed to help resolve a dispute prior to the point of formal arbitration. Both approaches also bring in neutral third parties, but they do not have the arbitrator's power to make final and binding decisions. In **conciliation** the neutral tries to keep the parties to a dispute focused on the issues of disagreement. He or she acts as a channel of communication for the exchange of information between the parties. In **mediation,** a stronger form of intervention, the neutral engages in substantive discussions with union and management negotiators in separate meetings and in joint sessions. He or she makes suggestions to the parties in the hope that concession and compromise will result.[18]

Illustrative Case:
Jack Pritchard's Attendance Record[19]

Most grievances don't go to arbitration. But some problems just can't be settled without it. One such problem for Labconco, a small Kansas City manufacturer of laboratory equipment, involved a worker's attendance record. The company's discipline procedure for workers with attendance problems involves four progressive steps—a verbal warning, a written warning, a three-day suspension, and finally firing. Before a worker is given a warning, though, the company offers counseling. After the disciplinary process has begun, it can be canceled if the worker's attendance improves.

When Jack Pritchard, an assembler, left work early one day to appear as a defendant in court, he was fired. Pritchard filed a grievance the next day. Supporting the grievance, the union claimed

he had been fired unjustly because his absence was unavoidable. It asked that he be reinstated. Three months later, having passed unresolved through earlier stages of the grievance procedure, the case was presented before a professional arbitrator, a college dean paid by the company and the union and chosen by them from a list supplied by the Federal Mediation and Conciliation Service. At issue in this case was the discharge clause in the labor contract between the company and the union that says "no employee shall be discharged, suspended, or disciplined without just cause."

The arbitration hearing began with opening statements by the company and the union. The company called its witnesses—the director of administrative services, production manager, and Pritchard's supervisor. Through testimony and exhibits, the company's lawyer presented the following case. Labconco's attendance rules had been formulated with the union's cooperation and implemented with the union's approval. In accordance with the rules, Pritchard had been counseled often, had received many verbal and written warnings, and had even twice been suspended for three days before he'd finally been fired.

The union's witnesses—Pritchard and the union steward for his department—didn't refute the company's testimony. They focused on his personal problems—an invalid wife, a large family, and seemingly unending health and financial problems. All these, they argued, made it hard for him to meet the demands of his job. "With all the problems that this person has had," asked the union representative, "why did the company have to take the day to terminate the man when they knew full well he had to be in court?"

The company's position was that the absence was part of a pattern Pritchard apparently was unable to change. So many allowances had been made for him already, explained the production manager, that "we were on the cliff-edge of discriminating against other employees." Further, Pritchard hadn't tried to change the court date or inform the company of it until the day before it was scheduled to take place.

The arbitrator's decision was released more than a month after the hearing. It held that the company's attendance rules were reasonable and

The strike of the air traffic controllers ended when strikers were fired under the law that prevents strikes by U.S. Government employees.

that the company had the right to enforce them reasonably, even when absences might seem beyond the employee's control. The union had produced no evidence to show the company had enforced the rules in a "capricious or discriminatory manner." Though Pritchard's problems invited sympathy, "leniency or clemency is the prerogative of the employer rather than of the arbitrator." The company's action was upheld.

MANAGERIAL IMPLICATIONS OF COLLECTIVE BARGAINING

Modern labor contracts influence both the operational and strategic aspects of management. Look, for example, at Table 18.3, which lists issues typically covered. In nonunion settings, managers make decisions and take action in respect to things like wages, work hours, rest periods, vacations, and disciplinary rules on personal prerogative—always, one hopes, while exercising good judgment. In unionized settings, however, all or much of that is changed. Union and management representatives collectively bargain for a labor contract that stipulates what managers and employees are to do at work and what is to be done when they don't. Simply put, collective bargaining places limits on managerial decision making.

Table 18.3 Issues Often Covered in a Labor Contract

Hours of work	Sick leave
Rest periods	Vacations
Wages	Fringe benefits
Incentive pay	Pensions
Disciplinary rules	Grievance procedures
Layoff procedures	Management rights
Promotions and transfers	Contract duration
Seniority rights	Union dues

Wages and Wage Adjustments

The presence of a union and collective bargaining generally reduces the ability of managers in an organization to tie worker performance to compensation. Incentive and piece-rate wage systems, for example, are less common among unionized firms; when they do exist, they tend to be closely regulated by contract language. Unions also tend to look unfavorably on merit-pay plans in which wage or salary increases are tied to performance measures. In general, collective bargaining narrows earnings differentials among individual workers within an organization. In place of pay rates and increases that are specific to the individual, unions normally negotiate standard rates for particular job categories and across-the-board annual increases for all employees of a bargaining unit. The final result is to limit a manager's discretion over wages and wage adjustments for individual subordinates.

Promotions, Transfers, and Layoffs

Job security is an important issue in most collective bargaining. Unions generally believe that employees acquire, through service to an organization, a vested interest in their jobs and acquire something akin to property rights with respect to employment. Labor contracts therefore usually define job rights on the basis of seniority and other terms that limit the discretion of managers in making promotion, transfer, and layoff decisions. Seniority instead of performance may be the governing criterion in unionized settings. Managers in such settings must understand the complexities of rules governing the allocation of job opportunities as specified in the labor contract, and also know where and when they have personal discretion on such matters.

The rules governing job rights may vary somewhat between the practices of craft and industrial unions. Craft unions largely assume the responsibility for training new members to a craft through apprenticeship programs. The union selects job candidates and refers them to a prospective employer. Employers may find this system beneficial because they do not have to incur the costs of screening applicants, but such arrangements usually give management only limited rights to refuse to hire an individual referred by the union to fill a job vacancy.

In industrial union settings, management usually has complete discretion in the initial hiring of employees. When it comes to movement beyond the entry level, however, most labor contracts specify a bidding system through which employees are considered for promotion or transfer based on both seniority and ability. The contracts vary in terms of the weight assigned to seniority versus ability. One survey of labor contracts found that nearly 70 percent specify seniority as a factor to be taken into consideration in promotion decisions; only 33 percent, however, required that it be the determining factor and fewer than 10 percent required that it be the sole factor in such decisions.[20] Nonetheless, managers in unionized firms may be constrained by the bidding system to the point where they are re-

quired by contract to assign a job opening to a less capable but more senior person.

Seniority rules play an even greater role in layoff decisions. It is taken into account for such purposes in 83 percent of all labor contracts and is the sole determining factor for layoffs in 46 percent of them.[21] This can create managerial problems if more capable employees are lost through layoff when less capable ones are retained. Such seniority provisions can also create difficulties for organizations implementing affirmative action. Minority and female workers hired under such programs generally have lower seniority than other employees, and a disproportionate number of them may lose their jobs during a layoff. Some contracts, however, have provisions protecting such employees so that an organization's efforts to comply with the law will not be undermined by poor economic conditions.

Work Assignments

Decisions through which work is assigned to individuals or groups are frequently an issue in labor-management relations. Conflicts over work assignments most often arise in craft-union settings in the form of jurisdictional disputes. For example, a construction-site supervisor may assign a general laborer the task of driving a truck to pick up supplies. The Teamsters union (to which many truckers belong) may see this as an infringement of its jurisdiction.

In industrial union settings, conflicts over work assignments are more likely to result from management decisions to subcontract to outsiders work that traditionally is done by union members. The work may be subcontracted to a nonunion source, or possibly even to a foreign producer. If such subcontracting has the potential of adversely affecting union employees, such as threat of temporary or permanent layoff, the decision to subcontract becomes a mandatory topic for labor-management negotiation. It is not a decision that can be made by management alone.

Employee Discipline

Because there will be times when employees view the disciplinary decisions of their supervisors as arbitrary, inequitable, or both, most labor

UNIONS REACT TO AUTOMATION BY STRESSING JOB SECURITY AND RETRAINING

The Machinists and Aerospace Workers union adopts a workers' bill of rights to guide coming contract talks with Boeing and Lockheed, among others. It calls for sharing savings from automation with workers, not just stockholders and the boss, a tax on robots that replace people, and worker participation in workplace changes.

Communications Workers of America reiterates its call for a similar bill of rights and promotes retraining. This week, the union opens an Indianapolis training center to teach office automation, computer literacy, and career planning to phone-company workers. Four more centers plan to open by year end. Some 3000 idle auto workers begin retraining funded by car makers as a result of 1982 contracts.

But some labor leaders fear the new age holds "potential for disruption and discontent." The AFL-CIO studies its negative social and economic effect.

Source: "Labor Letter," the *Wall Street Journal* (May 3, 1983), p. 1. Reprinted by permission of the *Wall Street Journal.* Copyright © 1982 Dow Jones & Company, Inc. All rights reserved.

contracts try to limit the disciplinary powers of managers. Actions subject to discipline, as well as the penalties to be assessed, are often incorporated into the labor contract in detail. This was the case, for example, in the Jack Pritchard case described earlier. The Labconco corporation had a labor contract that clearly prescribed progressive discipline for unexcused absences from work.

The principle of **just cause** is central to employee discipline in most collective-bargaining situations. It holds that an employee should not be disciplined without sufficient justification ("cause") and that the penalty imposed should not be excessive compared to the offense. If a disciplinary case ends up in a formal grievance or arbitration, management has the obligation of establishing just cause for its actions. While the personnel procedures of many nonunion organizations also mandate that supervisors establish just cause in disciplinary cases, this is not required by law. Disciplinary procedures in nonunion settings consequently afford managers greater freedom of action, although the potential for discipline to be misused is increased as well.

Technological Change

Job displacement as a possible result of increased automation and other forms of technological change is a continuing concern of organized labor. This is especially true with the rising use of robotic and computer technologies. Since technological change can affect employment opportunities and conditions of work, management is normally obligated by labor contracts to bargain over the decision to implement new technologies in the workplace.

Efforts by unions to restrict technological change, while often successful in the short run, usually fail in the long term. Either domestic or foreign competitors of unionized firms eventually create pressures necessitating accommodation to the realities of new technology by unions. As *Newsline 18.4* indicates, unions turn their attention to softening the blow of technological change by negotiating contract provisions requiring organizations to retrain displaced workers and/or help them find work elsewhere. Displaced workers often receive substantial severance pay; in return for accepting the changes, unions may expect the remaining employees to share in the financial benefits of increased productivity.

The longshoring industry is a good example. The development of containerized freight systems substantially reduced the need for dock workers, since the loading and unloading of ships is now automated. Unions representing longshore workers initially resisted implementation of container systems. As U.S. shipping suffered, however, the unions agreed to compromise. In return for reductions in the size of the work force, the employers increased benefits and made annual-income guarantees to the remaining workers. Special incentives were paid to employees who either accepted early retirement or moved to other jobs.

IMPROVING LABOR-MANAGEMENT RELATIONS

The traditional side of labor-management relations is reflected in the adversarial relationship shown in Figure 18.9. Labor and management are viewed as adversaries, destined to conflict and possessed of certain weapons with which to fight the other. Times are changing to some extent. Recall the chapter-opening example of Chrysler and the UAW working together to save Detroit Trim from closing. The list of similar examples goes on. Until recently, for example, members of the United Rubber Workers union at a B. F. Goodrich plant in Akron, Ohio, worked in two separate areas. Their contract specified that under most conditions, workers in one area couldn't be asked to do the same job in the other area—no matter how busy things were. Now that rule is gone. Gone, too, is the "bottleman's" job at McLouth Steel Products Company in Detroit. Previously, a designated worker, the "bottleman," carried a bottle-shaped ladle of cast iron from the furnace to another part of the plant. It took a total of two hours to make the trip twice in an eight-hour shift. It was the only task the "bottleman" was allowed to do under the old labor contract. Now the job is assigned part-time to other workers, just as it should be.[22] This all has happened because of increased cooperation in labor-management relations.

The Trend Toward Cooperation

The stimulus underlying the transition away from traditional adversarial roles and toward greater labor-management cooperation is in part economically determined. Cooperation is one way for both parties to survive the hardships of downturns such as the one experienced in the world economy of the early 1980s. But there is more to this transition than pure economic necessity. The shift toward greater cooperation is also prompted by the emergence of labor leaders who feel unions must change if they are to prosper in the years ahead, and by the changing perceptions of managers who are more likely to view labor leaders as equal "partners" in the world of work.[23]

In a word, times are changing and labor-management relations are changing, too. Both labor and management are feeling the pressure and uncertainty of learning how to succeed under new circumstances. One labor leader notes, "We've been teaching our local leaders and our members all these years to be aggressive and militant, now we have to undo all that." From a management perspective, Lee Iacocca remarks as chairman of Chrysler Corporation, "As long as the golden goose kept getting bigger and bigger, it was okay to have a shootout every three years. But now that it's getting smaller, we have to develop a new relationship based on cooperation. We are in uncharted waters."[24]

What the Manager Can Do

The manager stands in the middle of the uncertainty and great challenge associated with these transitions in labor-management relations. Since you might someday serve as a manager in a unionized setting, it is appropriate to point out how the individual manager can help maintain labor-management cooperation. In addition to practicing good day-to-day management, the following personal efforts by managers can foster improved labor-management relations.

1. *Effective communication* A manager should work hard to establish good communication with his or her subordinates and with their union representatives, including union stewards and other local officials.

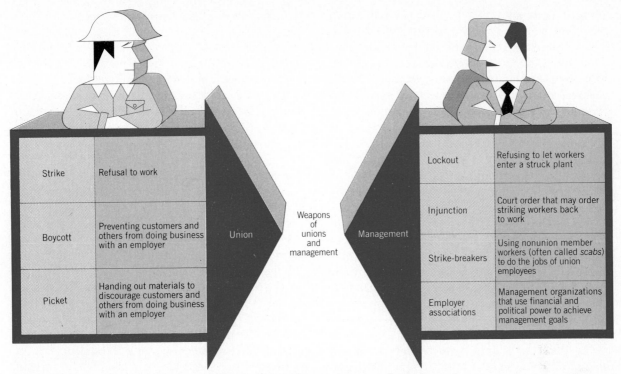

Union		Weapons of unions and management	Management	
Strike	Refusal to work		Lockout	Refusing to let workers enter a struck plant
Boycott	Preventing customers and others from doing business with an employer		Injunction	Court order that may order striking workers back to work
Picket	Handing out materials to discourage customers and others from doing business with an employer		Strike-breakers	Using nonunion member workers (often called *scabs*) to do the jobs of union employees
			Employer associations	Management organizations that use financial and political power to achieve management goals

FIGURE 18.9 Adversaries in labor-management relations. *Source:* Lawrence J. Gitman and Carl McDaniel, Jr., *Business World* (New York: Wiley, 1983), p. 218. Used by permission.

2. *Respect for the labor contract* A manager should know the provisions of the labor contract and how they apply to the work unit; a manager should also work sincerely with union members to administer the contract on a day-to-day basis.

3. *Support for the grievance procedure* The grievance procedure, like it or not, is the basic mechanism for resolving disputes relating to a labor contract. A manager should make every effort to resolve problems short of a formal grievance being filed. Once filed, however, a grievance should be handled promptly and in strict conformity to procedures.

4. *Sponsorship of the labor-management "team"* A manager is uniquely positioned to sponsor greater labor-management cooperation; by taking advantage of any and all opportunities to promote shared goals, a manager's efforts can help bridge the gap between contest and cooperation in labor-management relations.

Even managers in a nonunion setting can take advantage of this advice. Remember, unions fill a need for their members. This need most typically relates to a deficiency in the treatment they are receiving at work. Good management can go a long way toward reducing such deficiencies and thereby decreasing the need for a union to be certified as a bargaining agent for employees. The final point, then, is straightforward. In unionized work settings, successful managers practice good management within the labor contract; in nonunion settings, successful managers practice good management.

SUMMARY

Labor unions are an important force in the contemporary work environment. Although union membership has been declining as a percent of the total U.S. labor force, some 200 national and international unions represent U.S. workers to their employers. The majority of these unions are affiliated with the AFL-CIO, a labor federation that provides services to its member unions. Most national and international unions are broken down into locals, which provide services directly to members and represent them in the workplace. The union steward is the local union representative with whom line managers most frequently interact.

Labor-management relations within the United States are governed by an elaborate labor-law system, the cornerstone of which is the National Labor Relations Act (NLRA). Originally the Wagner Act of 1935, the NLRA has been modified by the Taft-Hartley (1947) and Landrum-Griffin (1959) laws to specify a number of unfair labor practices applicable both to management and unions. In addition, the NLRA establishes basic employee rights with respect to unionization, and provides systems through which employees can choose to certify a particular union to represent them for purposes of collective bargaining and to decertify a union which they no longer desire to have represent them. The NLRA is administered by the National Labor Relations Board (NLRB).

Collective bargaining is the process of negotiating, interpreting, and administering a labor contract. The labor contract, in turn, is a formal written agreement stipulating the wages, hours, and other terms of employment for union members working for an organization. During the life of a contract, employees who feel they are being mistreated on a contract issue may file a grievance. This begins a grievance procedure for resolving the dispute that may go as far as formal arbitration.

Modern labor contracts set constraints on the prerogatives of managers in dealing with their subordinates. The typical contract limits a manager's decision making in respect to wages and compensation practices, promotions, transfers, layoffs, work assignments, employee discipline, and even the implementation of technological changes.

Recent trends evidence greater cooperation in labor-management relations. Adversarial roles are giving way to enhanced cooperation as a mutual accommodation to present economic and social realities. While emerging trends support improved labor-management relations in general, the individual manager in both union and nonunion settings can do a great deal to support these improvements in day-to-day dealings with subordinates.

THINKING THROUGH THE ISSUES

1. Define and clarify the distinction between a labor union, labor-management relations, and collective bargaining.

2. Why do people join unions? Are these reasons as relevant today as they were in the early 1900s? Explain your answer.

3. What is the basic difference between a craft union and an industrial union?

4. State and explain two management problems that unions may face.

5. What is the National Labor Relations Act (NLRA) and what purpose does it serve?

6. Explain the steps employees would go through to certify a union as their bargaining agent in a business firm.

7. Can employees remove a union as their bargaining agent? Explain your answer.

8. What are the major issues with which collective bargaining is typically concerned?

9. What is arbitration, and when will a grievance normally end up in formal arbitration?

10. How does collective bargaining affect the individual manager on a daily basis? Use examples to explain your answer.

THE MANAGER'S VOCABULARY

Agency shop
Arbitration
Bargaining unit
Certification election
Closed shop
Collective bargaining
Comparable worth
Conciliation

Craft unions
Decertification
General unions
Grievance
Industrial unions
Just cause
Jurisdiction

Labor-management
relations
Labor union
Local
Management rights
Mediation
National Labor

Relations Act (NLRA)
National Labor
Relations Board
(NLRB)
Seniority
Union shop
Union stewards

CAREER PERSPECTIVE: LABOR LEADERS RISE BY DEGREES[25]

The rise of specialized education for managers, exemplified in undergraduate business degrees and M.B.A.'s, has a parallel on the other side of the bargaining table. Labor leaders of today are generally better educated than their predecessors, and more people with specialized degrees in labor studies are coming to the fore in the union movement. An increasing number of four-year colleges and universities are offering academic programs in labor history, labor and politics, collective bargaining, and labor law.

One example of this new breed of labor leader is Ray Rogers, the union organizer whose tactics in the campaign against J. P. Stevens & Company were the subject of *Newsline 18.2*. An astronomy major who switched into sociology the last year he attended the University of Massachusetts, Rogers says he got his ''basic training'' working as a VISTA volunteer in the Appalachian Mountains of Tennessee. This two-year exposure to extreme poverty and illiterate people taught him profound lessons about economics and politics.

As the founder of Corporate Campaign, Inc., his ten-person consulting firm, Rogers only makes $425 a week. In his previous capacity as member of the Amalgamated Clothing and Textile Workers Union, he wouldn't accept money from the other unions he counseled. ''I'm happy if my consulting gains AC-TWU support,'' he said. ''I'm not in this to get rich. I'd rather have their help than their money.''

Questions

1. Have you ever thought seriously about a career in the labor-union movement? Why or why not?
2. What are the implications of the increasing professionalization of the labor movement for managers who work in unionized settings? Explain your answer.

CASE APPLICATION: NORGE ASKS EMPLOYEES TO HELP PLANT SAVE MONEY[26]

For the first time in recent history, if ever, Norge union employees are being asked to make concessions in midcontract. Company officials have submitted a list of 14 proposals to the union members asking for approval in order to help the company save money. A union committee and business representatives have made a response asking to see several documents concerning the company's financial situation before any contract concessions are considered.

Norge's director of administration, Jon Nicholas, said it would be "detrimental at this point to comment" on the proposals, but said they were made as a cost-cutting maneuver. "The industry has deteriorated in terms of sales," he said, "and everybody is cost-conscious." Union business representative David Garner also expressed concern at the proposals being made public. "I'm sorry the newspaper is involved in this," he said. "It can't do either side any good."

However, Garner did consent to talk about the concession proposals and the union's response to date. In brief, some of the items being asked by Norge are:

- A one-year extension of the present contract.
- Deferment for one year of wage increases scheduled for May (those increases, according to the contract, are 24 cents per hour for incentive workers and 40 cents per hour for nonincentive workers).
- Elimination of a $20-per-week vacation bonus for the duration of the agreement.
- Elimination of future cost-of-living increases for the duration of the agreement. (Workers are given a five-cent-per-hour cost-of-living increase each six months at present.)
- Permit the company to appoint union members as temporary supervisors.
- Give only one day (instead of three) off for the death of grandparents, grandchildren, or in-laws.
- Combine and eliminate several worker classifications.

According to a report distributed to union members, the union's response to these proposals will be "that we are prepared to listen to their problems but before we can seriously consider any changes in the current agreement, the company must open its books to us." The union has asked for several documents such as the company's federal income tax forms, Securities and Exchange Commission reports, and other internal company documents "which could prove or disprove the company's claim." Those kinds of reports are normally not available to union officials, Garner said, but when the company calls its financial ability into question, the union has a legal right to see the documents. The information would then be sent to the international union's central Research Department for verification.

The report said, "Regardless of what the company says or does or what their documents show, we will not take any action on company proposals unless and until these things happen: The company takes serious steps to reduce administrative costs, such as shutting off air conditioning in the offices, reduce nonunion employees' salaries and benefits, and get rid of some of the very management officials whose mistakes got us into this mess."

Garner said the union has bargained for many, many years for wages, fringe benefits, and contract language, and "we're not going to give them up easily." But, he emphasized, the union is willing to listen and give consideration after the company provides the requested documents. He said he has been told the documents will be provided but has not seen them yet.

Questions

1. Is the union's request for documents a reason-

able one to make of Norge management? Why or why not?

2. What should Norge management be doing in order to ensure maximum employee support for the proposed concessions?

3. What are the potential disadvantages to the company of opening its books to the union? Would you make the books available if you were Jon Nicholas? Why or why not?

CLASS EXERCISE: YOU BE THE ARBITRATOR[27]

1. The following incident actually happened at the American Telephone & Telegraph Company. Read and think about it.

Mary is a senior operations clerk. She works in a test room for an operations manager and coordinates administrative duties for the office. Her job requires working with others in the office. She is responsible for processing vouchers and employee phone bills, answering the office phone, making out time reports, maintaining the vacation schedule, forwarding payroll inquiries, and performing other duties related to the administration of the office.

Although Mary is considered an efficient worker, she has developed a reputation for being rude and uncooperative. Employees have complained that she is impossible to work with. On several occasions when her fellow employees have asked for information she has scolded them for asking such "dumb questions."

Her appraisals in the past have been satisfactory in every category except "sense of cooperation." Her supervisor characterizes her as a good, productive worker on jobs that do not require her contact with others. However, in her most recent appraisal she receives a "limited" in the category of "sense of cooperation." Her supervisor informs her that improvement is expected in this area or she could face discipline. Mary replies that if employees would stop asking so many stupid questions she wouldn't be so provoked. Her supervisor responds that answering inquiries is part of the job.

A few days later a customer calls to complain about service. At the time, Mary was busy typing a report and she told the customer everyone in the office was busy, so call back later. When the customer later tracks down the operations manager, the customer complains about the rudeness of the clerk. Her supervisor asks Mary about the incident and she acknowledges the conversation but says she couldn't find anybody to talk to the customer. After making other inquiries, the supervisor finds that Mary made no effort to ask anyone in the office about assisting the customer. Consequently, the supervisor suspends Mary for three days for unsatisfactory job performance.

In the following months a series of incidents were documented. Employees continued to complain that Mary was slow to respond to their questions. In one incident, a supplier was not paid promptly because Mary didn't like the supplier's agent. Mary was subsequently given two more suspensions and finally warned that unless her cooperation improved to a satisfactory level, she would be terminated. A few weeks later her supervisor asked her to update a time report. Mary said she was tired of making changes and if the supervisor wanted the change to make it himself.

Mary was fired for poor work performance demonstrated by her repeated lack of cooperation with others. Despite satisfactory performance in all other areas, Mary's continued lack of cooperation was unacceptable.

The union contended in a grievance that Mary worked hard and knew her job and the company could not dismiss an employee for lack of cooperation when all other work performance categories were satisfactory.

2. This case went to an arbitrator who had to decide if Mary's dismissal was with "just cause." If you were the arbitrator in this case, how would you decide?

3. Share your decision with a nearby classmate. Discuss the rationales for each of your decisions. Await further class discussion.

REFERENCES

[1] Excerpted from Jeremy Main, "Anatomy of an Auto-Plant Rescue," *Fortune* (April 4, 1983), p. 108. © 1983 Time Inc. Courtesy of Fortune Magazine.

[2] Adapted from William F. Glueck, *Personnel: A Diagnostic Approach*, Revised Edition (Dallas: Business Publications, 1978), p. 637.

[3] The headlines are from the *Wall Street Journal* (June 23, 1982), p. 25; (August 27, 1982), p. 15.

[4] Samuel Gompers, *Labor and the Common Welfare*, as cited in E. Wight Bakke, Clark Kerr, and Charles Amrod (eds.), *Unions, Management and the Public*, Third Edition (New York: Harcourt, Brace & World, 1967), p. 42.

[5] *Business Week* (February 7, 1983), p. 37.

[6] An excellent nontechnical description of the NLRA, entitled *A Guide to Basic Law and Procedures under the National Labor Relations Act*, is available from any regional office of the NLRB (or may be ordered through the Government Printing Office).

[7] Joann S. Lublin, "Big Fight Looms Over Gap in Pay for Similar 'Male,' 'Female' Jobs," the *Wall Street Journal* (September 16, 1982), p. 29.

[8] Reported in Robert C. Wood, "The Decline and Fall of a Union," *Inc.* (October 1982), pp. 134–136.

[9] See Thomas Kochan, *Collective Bargaining and Industrial Relations*, (Homewood, Ill.: Richard D. Irwin, 1980), pp. 124–150; Jack Fiorito and Charles Greer, "Determinants of U.S. Unionism: Past Research and Future Needs," *Industrial Relations*, Vol. 21 (Winter 1982), pp. 1–32.

[10] Fred K. Foulkes, *Personnel Policies in Large Nonunion Companies* (Englewood Cliffs, N.J.: Prentice-Hall, 1980).

[11] *Business Week* (April 4, 1983), p. 60.

[12] Daniel Seligman, "Who Needs Unions?" *Fortune* (July 12, 1982), pp. 54–66.

[13] Adapted from Lawrence J. Gitman and Carl McDaniel, Jr., *Business World* (New York: Wiley, 1983), pp. 214–216. Used by permission.

[14] Dale D. Buss, "Chrysler, UAW Tentatively Set One-Year Pact," the *Wall Street Journal* (September 17, 1982), p. 4.

[15] This example is from Gitman and McDaniel, op. cit., p. 213.

[16] Ibid., p. 216.

[17] Adapted from Glueck, op. cit., p. 677.

[18] Gitman and McDaniel, op. cit., p. 219.

[19] Adapted from ibid., p. 217. Used by permission.

[20] *Basic Patterns in Union Contracts* (New York: Bureau of National Affairs, 1979).

[21] Ibid.

[22] Both examples are cited in Robert S. Greenberger, "Work-Rule Changes Quietly Spread as Firms Try to Raise Productivity," the *Wall Street Journal* (January 25, 1983), p. 33.

[23] Adapted from Raymond L. Hilgert, "Union/Management Relations: Era of Mutual Interdependence," *The Collegiate Forum* (Spring 1983), pp. 6, 18.

[24] Both quotes are from Robert L. Simison, "UAW Struggles With a New Idea: Cooperation," the *Wall Street Journal* (April 14, 1981), p. 22.

[25] Information from "Trends: Labor Leaders Now Rise by Degrees," *Nation's Business* (March 1981), p. 24; Gail Bronson and Jeffrey H. Birnbaum, "Rogers' Tough, Unorthodox Tactics Prevail in Stevens Organizing Fight," the *Wall Street Journal* (October 21, 1980), p. 36; *Forbes* (July 18. 1983), p. 149.

[26] Excerpted from Bonnie Marx, "Norge Employees Asked to Help Plant Save Money," *Southern Illinoisan* (August 15, 1982), p. 4. Used by permission.

[27] Reported in *Mgr.* (No. 1, 1978), p. 19. Used by permission.

19

MANAGING IN
AN INTERNATIONAL
ARENA

IN NIGERIA, PAYOFFS ARE A WAY OF LIFE

LAGOS, Nigeria—Many of the intersections in crowded downtown Lagos are blocked by police barricades.[1]

Ostensibly, the roadblocks are there to help the government uncover arms and other smuggled goods. In reality, their purpose is to enable the poorly paid local militia to participate in one of Nigeria's most flourishing businesses: graft and corruption.

For the foreign visitor, payoffs start right at the airport. Nigeria still demands evidence of smallpox vaccination, even though the disease has been eradicated worldwide. Experienced travelers say the requirement is just a device to extract money from visitors who don't have the necessary vaccination documents. Without papers or a payoff of about $40, the traveler is quarantined for days or sent back home on the first flight.

"This is the most corrupt country I have ever worked in," declares the German manager of a large construction project. Other foreigners who do business here echo this sentiment. Nevertheless, most are resigned to making the payoffs.

The German construction boss, for example, was told by a Nigerian bureaucrat it would cost him an extra $10,000 to have the government process previously approved plans for a stone quarry. The German telexed the demand to his home office and was told to go along with it.

Then to the German's surprise he was asked by a second Nigerian official to pay an additional $7000 for permission to begin the actual digging at the quarry. With a tight deadline to meet on the project, he paid again. "We don't have any choice if we want to get the work done," he explains.

The largest payoffs are the commissions paid to gain major contracts. All Western businessmen agree the practice is widespread; they disagree only as to the amount. Figures of as much as 25 percent of the contract price are mentioned frequently.

In fact, Nigerian business standards are generally so shady that most Western embassies have started preparing lists of Nigerian firms to be avoided by foreign companies seeking to do business here. The U.S. embassy list contains 2500 names and is growing steadily, and U.S. officials are currently assembling a master roster combining the blacklisted names from the lists of all the embassies.

It isn't only the Nigerians who are guilty of questionable practices, however. Many foreigners take to the Nigerian way of doing business. For example, an English restaurant owner here discovered that "hotel notice boards," or bulletin boards, were among the items that could be imported without restriction. Because the Scotch steaks he wants to serve his customers fall under an import ban, "I'm bringing in all my Scotch steaks as 'hotel notice boards.' "

One of the most fascinating of all management challenges is working in the
international arena. The chapter-opening example shows just how "foreign"
and difficult this arena of action can be. We'll examine many facets of international management in this chapter. The topics include

International Management
International Business
Multinational Corporations (MNCs)
Environmental Constraints on International Operations
The Management Functions in an International Perspective
Comparative Management Practices

There is no doubt about it; we live in an international world. The supersonic Concorde flies
from New York to London or Paris in just over 3
hours. It is possible to board a plane in Chicago
and get off in Japan in less than a day's time.
These are incredible opportunities for a person
to see and become involved in all of the splendor
and variety of our world.

It is not only through travel that the average
person is increasingly becoming a citizen of the
world, but in everyday living as well. Just think
how many of your favorite consumer products
are made outside the United States. We have cars
and cameras from Japan, wines from France, and
coffee from Colombia, to name but a few. Think,
too, how many nights pass without the evening
television news reporting on international events
and even turmoil—not many.

Into this growing sense of worldwide citizenry steps the modern manager. As the world
shrinks and the operations of organizations more
and more frequently span national boundaries, a
new action dimension emerges to challenge a
manager's skills and capacities. This is the fascinating international arena for the practice of management.

INTERNATIONAL MANAGEMENT

International management is a term used to describe management that involves the conduct of
business or other operations in foreign countries.
Scholars study international management to
learn how the management process applies

across cultural and national boundaries; practicing managers benefit from these efforts when
they learn how to transfer management practices
successfully from one cultural setting to another.

Perhaps you are asking at this point, "But
when and where will I ever get involved in this
thing called 'international management'? I fully
expect to work for a domestic organization." The
response is twofold.

1. *You will always be affected by international
events in day-to-day living.* A familiarity with international management can help you to put
these worldwide events in perspective and better
understand them. The study of international
management can help you become a more informed citizen of the world.

2. *The likelihood is high that international management responsibilities will someday enter into your
career.* Two opportunities to become involved in
international management include working overseas in the foreign operation of a domestic firm
and working overseas as an expatriate employee
of a foreign firm. *Newsline 19.1* offers a third example of how you might encounter international
management without ever leaving home—as a
domestic employee of a foreign firm operating in
your country. These and other opportunities may
well come your way someday. The issues and
ideas offered in this chapter will help you in the
event they do.

This chapter focuses primarily on international management from the perspective of businesses and their international operations. This

NEWSLINE 19.1

HONDA'S ACCORD: HOW AUTO FIRM FARES IN DEALING WITH U.S. WORKERS

MARYSVILLE, Ohio—At a motorcycle plant here 37 miles northwest of Columbus, employees take pride in their ability to compete with the Japanese.

"Our quality is higher than Japan's," boasts William Bumgarner, the paint-room supervisor. "I can take you to our showroom and show you the bikes we make in America and the ones made in Japan. There is a difference; ours are much better. I am proud of that."

Bumgarner should know. Not only does he compete with the Japanese; he also works for them. The Marysville plant is the U.S. manufacturing beachhead of Honda of America, a subsidiary of Japan's Honda Motor Co., and Honda executives here say that the plant is indeed turning out more defect-free bikes than Honda's plants in Japan produce. With its motorcycle production going smoothly, Honda is proceeding with plans to put up an auto-assembly plant here, too. When that opens, probably late next year, it will be the first Japanese auto plant in the United States.

That American workers would be able to produce quality products wasn't self-evident to Honda when it began operations here two years ago. Japanese manufacturers generally have a low opinion of American labor. For Honda, resolving doubts about quality before proceeding with the auto plant was especially important, because the Marysville auto plant initially will turn out just 144,000 Honda Accords a year, and Honda will still need to export some Japanese-made Accords to the U.S.

Source: Excerpted from Masayoshi Kanabayashi, "Honda's Accord: How Auto Firm Fares in Dealing with U.S. Workers," *Wall Street Journal* (October 2, 1981), p. 1. Reprinted by permission of the *Wall Street Journal*. Copyright © 1981 Dow Jones & Company, Inc. All rights reserved.

focus was chosen because businesses are visible and active in the international arena, and because they have been studied the most by scholars. As has consistently been true throughout the book, however, the concepts, issues, and guidelines to be developed in the business context readily apply to other types of organizations.

INTERNATIONAL BUSINESS

International business is just what the label implies: it is the conduct of for-profit transactions of goods and services across national boundaries. It is the foundation for world trade and the movement of raw materials, finished products, and specialized services from one country to another around the globe. Have you ever considered just how international most major business firms have become? Take the Coca-Cola Company, for example.

Illustrative Case: Coca-Cola Company[2]

The Coca-Cola Company has been in business for about 90 years. It has annual sales of over $3 billion and operates in about 150 countries. Over 50 percent of its profits typically come from foreign operations. Much of the company's growth is due to its secret formula for producing Coke. The formula is the basis for a syrup that is sold to wholesalers and bottlers around the world.

Cola-Cola also owns Taylor and Great Western Wines, Tab, Fresca, and Sprite. It produces orange juice and instant coffee and tea products, including the brands Minute Maid and Butter-Nut.

The organization structure of Coca-Cola divides the world into three parts, with an executive vice-president in charge of each. One part involves operations in the United States and Central and South America. Another involves Europe, Africa, Southeast Asia, and the Indian subcontinent. The third involves Canada, the Pacific, and the Far East.

Dealing in worldwide markets requires decisions and strategies considerably different from those appropriate for organizations operating in only one country. For example, when Coca-Cola gave an Israeli firm a franchise to bottle and sell Coke in Israel in 1967, Coke was promptly boycotted in the Arab countries. However, Coca-Cola has technology and know-how that the Arab countries need. Coca-Cola's food division has expertise in agriculture, and the Arabs are interested in developing their agricultural know-how. Consequently, the company has reason to hope that this expertise will maintain sales of Coke in the Arab world.

Another international market decision made by Coca-Cola involved India. The Indian government insists that all multinationals transfer some of their knowledge and ownership to Indian nationals. Coca-Cola refused to make its secret formula known and thus lost the lucrative Indian market. Management decided that disclosure of the secret formula would be even more adverse to the company's interests than losing India's business.

Even if Coca-Cola had no foreign sales or production facilities, its operations would still be greatly affected by the international environment. Imports are essential for two of the company's major products—soft drinks and coffee. Almost all coffee must be imported, and about half the sugar used in soft drinks comes from foreign sources.

Reasons for Going International

The Coca-Cola example shows how strongly even one of our most common day-to-day products is tied to international business operations. It also shows how complex international management can become once a business or any other organization crosses a national boundary in the course of its operations.

Business firms engage in international activities for many reasons. In general, the impetus is a quest for opportunities not otherwise available in domestic markets, or to solve problems that can't be solved through domestic operations alone. More specifically, international business offers firms the potential for[3]

1. *Profits* Profit is a major reason for an organization becoming global in operation; organizations often initiate international operations to expand their profit potential.

2. *Expanded markets* Greater sales can result when a firm focuses on a global marketing base; a worldwide orientation means that goods can be sold successfully to many markets.

3. *Raw materials* International activities can increase access to needed raw materials; businesses operating in many countries have broader bases of raw-materials.

4. *Financial resources* Greater capital is available to international firms, since they can draw on the financial resources of many nations.

5. *Lower labor costs* Labor costs vary greatly around the world; international corporations can concentrate labor-intensive operations in countries with lower labor costs.

When you think of these potential benefits of international business, you might picture them as sought most aggressively by large U.S.-based firms such as Exxon, IBM, Ford, and others. The giants of international business, however, include many large enterprises based outside the United States. Names familiar to you may include Royal Dutch/Shell, Mitsubishi, and British Petroleum. Also, foreign firms are increasingly making large direct investments in the United States. Table 19.1 shows the top 10 of these in 1983. As the number of foreign firms establishing sizeable operations in the United States grows, the chances also increase for you to become involved in international management as the domestic employee of a foreign-owned firm.

Table 19.1 Large Foreign Direct Investments in the United States

Foreign Investor	Country	U.S. Company	Percent Owned	Industry
1. Seagram Co. Ltd.	Canada	Joseph E. Seagram & Sons	100	Spirits and wines
		E. I. du Pont de Nemours	21	Chemicals, energy
2. Anglo American Corp. of	South	Phibro-Salomon	26	Metal trading, brokerage
So. Africa Ltd. Minerals	Africa	Englehard Corp.	27	Metals
and Resources	Bermuda	Adobe Oil & Gas	28	Energy
		Inspiration Consol Copper	50	Copper
		Terra Chemicals	100	Fertilizer
Charter Consolidated	UK	National Mine Service	51	Mining equipment
3. Royal Dutch/Shell Group	Netherlands	Shell Oil	69	Energy
	UK	Scallop Corp.	100	Energy
		Billiton Exploration	100	Metals
		Billiton Metals	100	Metals
		Ocean Minerals	30	Metals
4. British Petroleum Plc.	UK	Standard Oil of Ohio	53	Energy
		BP North America	100	Energy
5. Mitsui & Co. Ltd.	Japan	Alumax	45	Aluminum
		Mitsui & Co. USA	100	Multicompany
6. Flick Group	Germany	W. R. Grace	28	Multicompany
7. B.A.T. Industries Plc.	UK	BATUS	100	Paper, retailing, tobacco
8. Generale Occidentale	France	Grand Union	100	Supermarkets
		Diamond International	100	Packaging, lumber
9. Tengelmann Group	Germany	Great A&P Tea Co.	51	Supermarkets
10. Regie Nationale des	France	American Motors	46	Automotive
Usines Renault		Mack Truck	20	Automotive

Source: Information reprinted by permission of Forbes Magazine from "Here Come the Canadians," *Forbes* (July 4, 1983), pp. 101, 102.

Forms of International Business

International businesses exchange goods, services, technologies, and capital across national boundaries. Just how international business gets transacted varies among the alternative forms shown in Figure 19.1. International business takes place as

- *Importation/exportation* of goods and services.
- *Licensing agreements* for producing or selling goods or services in another country.
- *Management contracts* for operating foreign companies or facilities.
- *Joint ventures* that establish operations in a foreign country through mutual ownership with local partners.
- *Foreign subsidiaries or branches* that establish a

wholly owned subsidiary operation in a foreign country.

Each of these options is a strategic alternative available to firms pursuing international business activities. In general, the commitment to international business in terms of resource investments and potential complications from foreign operations increases as the choice moves from import/export at one extreme to the establishment of foreign subsidiaries or branches at the other.

MULTINATIONAL CORPORATIONS (MNCs)

A **multinational corporation,** or MNC, is a business firm with extensive international operations

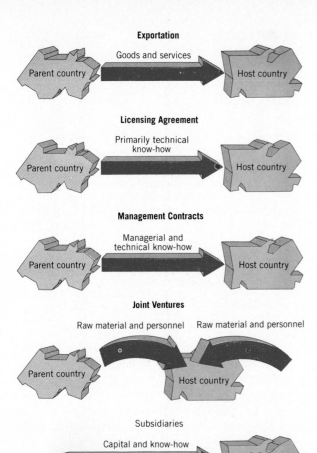

Exportation

Goods and services

Parent country → Host country

Licensing Agreement

Primarily technical know-how

Parent country → Host country

Management Contracts

Managerial and technical know-how

Parent country → Host country

Joint Ventures

Raw material and personnel   Raw material and personnel

Parent country   Host country

Subsidiaries

Capital and know-how

Parent country   Host countries

Capital and know-how

FIGURE 19.1 Forms of international business. *Source:* From *Essentials of Management* by Harold Koontz, Cyril O'Donnell, and Heinz Weihrich, p. 51. Copyright 1982 by Harold Koontz, Cyril O'Donnell, and Heinz Weihrich. Used with the permission of the McGraw-Hill Book Company.

in more than one foreign country. MNCs are more than companies that just do "business abroad." They become heavily involved in direct capital expenditures, joint ventures, and formal subsidiaries that allow the manufacture and distribution of products or the provision of services in foreign countries. MNCs are global concerns that often get very large, powerful, and aggressive in their international operations.

MNCs and the World Economy

Many of the premier businesses in the world are found in any listing of MNCs. Table 19.2 shows the top 10 MNCs headquartered in the United States and the top 10 headquartered elsewhere in the world in 1983. In a time when consumer tastes and raw-materials markets increasingly span national boundaries, the actions of multinational firms can substantially impact the world economy and the affairs of individual nations as well. Decision makers in MNCs, accordingly, bear a responsibility that moves beyond the productivity of their business operations to encompass issues of major global significance.

It is in the latter context that the complexities and controversies of international business in general, and MNCs in particular, come into special focus. To provide you with some perspective on the issues, let's take a brief look at how MNCs are criticized for their roles in the world economy.

Table 19.2 The Ten Largest U.S. and Foreign Multinational Corporations in 1983

Rank	Company
U.S.	
1	Exxon
2	Mobil
3	Texaco
4	Standard Oil of California
5	Phibro-Salomon
6	Ford
7	IBM
8	General Motors
9	Gulf Oil
10	E.I. du Pont de Nemours
Foreign	
1	Royal Dutch/Shell Group (Netherlands)
2	Mitsubishi Corp. (Japan)
3	Mitsui & Co. Ltd. (Japan)
4	C. Itoh & Co. Ltd. (Japan)
5	Marubeni (Japan)
6	British Petroleum (United Kingdom)
7	Sumitomo (Japan)
8	Nissho-Iwai Corp. (Japan)
9	ENI-Ente Nazionale Idrocarburi (Italy)
10	IRI-Istituto Ricostruzione Industriale (Italy)

Source: Information reprinted by permission of Forbes Magazine from "Hard Times in Any Language," *Forbes* (July 4, 1983), p. 114; "The Japanese Try Harder," *Forbes* (July 4, 1983), p. 124.

MNC/Host-Country Relations

Among the critics are those who are concerned that MNCs have an adverse impact on the host countries in which they operate. This is particularly true for MNCs operating in developing countries. Consider this one "tongue-in-cheek" description of the MNC as published in the London *Economist*.[4]

> It fiddles its accounts. It avoids or evades its taxes. It rigs its intracompany transfer prices. It is run by foreigners, from decision centres thousands of miles away. It imports foreign labour practices. It doesn't import foreign labour practices. It overpays. It underpays. It competes unfairly with local firms. It is in cahoots with local firms. It exports jobs from rich countries. It is an instrument for rich countries' imperialism. The technologies it brings to the third world are too old-fashioned. No, they are too modern. It muddles. It bribes. Nobody can control it. It wrecks balances of payments. It overturns economic policies. It pays off governments against each other to get the biggest investment incentives. Won't it please come and invest? Let it bloody well go home.

The description includes both negative and positive points of view on MNC/host-country relations. Figure 19.2 shows how the interests of MNCs and their host countries can and should overlap. International business offers host countries a variety of potential advantages including expanded tax bases, more revenue, access to special industries, and reduced local unemployment. Ideally, the goals of the MNC and host country complement rather than contradict each other. When the MNC prospers, so too should the host country.

If Figure 19.2 represents what should happen in MNC/host-country relations, a logical question to ask is, "What goes wrong?" There are many answers to this question, far more than we can hope to cover here. Among the more general concerns are fears that MNCs will operate in host countries in ways that[5]

- Extract excessive profits.
- Fail to help domestic firms develop.
- Divert the most talented of local personnel from domestic enterprises.
- Fail to transfer advanced technologies and know-how into local hands.

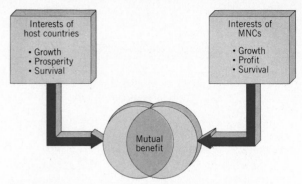

FIGURE 19.2 Overlapping interests of MNCs and host countries.

- Fail to respect local customs, needs, and government objectives.
- Dominate the local economy.
- Interfere with the local government.

One of the most provocative and emotional of the themes in the preceding list is the suspicion that MNCs exercise too much influence over the internal political and economic affairs of their host countries. One side of the argument depicts the MNC as simply being insensitive to local needs and considerations. Another side depicts the MNC as outrightly aggressive in trying to manipulate local conditions into a posture most favorable to its own operations—that is, MNCs are viewed as placing their own interests above those of any nation. A dramatic example is the case of International Telephone & Telegraph Corporation's (ITT) apparent interventions during the 1970s into the national politics of Chile. In 1973 testimony before the Senate Foreign Relations Committee, ITT executives admitted they schemed to prevent the election of Marxist Salvador Allende as Chile's president and to disrupt the country's economy. Their apparent goal was to prevent the expropriation of ITT's Chilean subsidiary.[6]

Please keep in mind that MNC/host-country relations can be harmonious and mutually beneficial. We have focused on the negative here. One of the challenges of international management is to ensure that such controversies and criticisms as those pointed out here are exceptions instead of the rule. *Newsline 19.2* is one further reminder of the broad range of contributions MNCs can and do make to their local hosts.

NEWSLINE 19.2

MULTINATIONAL LARGESSE

American multinationals give a broad range of aid to employees and their families in less-developed countries, says a new report by the New York–based Conference Board, and it is not simple altruism. The study of more than 200 companies in 12 countries (including Costa Rica, Egypt, Indonesia, Pakistan, Sri Lanka, and Peru) says that the help is motivated by local laws, operating needs, and plain public relations. Free medical exams were provided by 90 percent, and by 25 percent for employees' families. Nearly 50 percent operated clinics, and about 25 percent (most agri-business firms) ran hospitals. About half provided grants to colleges and about 25 percent to secondary schools in countries where they operated. Nor was this all in-house. Fewer than half of the 15,000 students at 50 schools built in Indonesia by Caltex, the board says, are children of employees. About two-thirds gave scholarships for employees and their families, and a third lent engineers and other specialists to local schools as teachers. Nearly two-thirds also provided housing aid, usually free or subsidized homes, and half offered mortgages at less than market rates.

Source: Reprinted by permission of Forbes Magazine from "Multinational Largesse," *Forbes* (July 18, 1983), p. 10.

MNC/Home-Country Relations

Another aspect of the MNC story deals with the home country's point of view. This is the country in which the MNC is headquartered and from which its international operations are largely directed and controlled. In fact, this "home" affiliation underlies some of the criticisms levied against MNCs from the host-country perspective—that is, feelings that their foreign priorities are sometimes targeted to serve the interests of the home country more than those of the host country. Even in their home countries, however, MNCs are subject to criticism. Among those are concerns that MNCs

- Export jobs by diverting labor-intensive operations to cheaper foreign labor markets.
- Divert capital investments away from domestic opportunities to those abroad.
- Lose touch with domestic needs and priorities.
- Allow and even encourage corrupt practices in their overseas dealings.

The last item on the list deserves special elaboration. The subject of foreign corrupt practices is a source of continuing controversy in the United States. In 1977 the Foreign Corrupt Practices Act became law. This act made it illegal for firms and their managers to engage in a variety of "corrupt" practices, such as giving bribes and excessive commissions in return for business favors abroad. At the time the law was passed, over 300 companies were linked to corrupt foreign practices. The ITT case is just one of these.

Think back to the chapter opener, "In Nigeria Payoffs Are a Way of Life." The implied message is that one must expect to make payoffs to do business there. This is exactly the argument that by 1982 had led to substantial lobbies to get the 1977 antibribery law repealed. Critics of the law felt that it failed to recognize the "reality" of business as practiced in many foreign nations. The end result is continuing debate on the issue. On one side of the debate stand those who advocate retaining the antibribery law; on the other side stand critics who feel the law contradicts international business practices. Read on to capture the flavor of these contrasting positions.

Argument: We Should Not Relax the Corporate Antibribery Law[7]

Amid pious assurances that no one wants to go back to the bad old bribery days, business spokespersons argue that the 1977 Foreign Corrupt Practices Act imposes too much expensive red tape on companies and inhibits exports. It is an unconvincing argument, not least because U.S. exports in fact have increased substantially since enactment of the law.

The need to keep the strict 1977 law is underscored by a recent report of a panel of outside directors of International Telephone & Telegraph Corp. The ITT directors, as a result of a court order, conducted exhaustive investigations into bribery practices by units of the worldwide corporation and internal efforts to end bribery. Their report isn't altogether reassuring, despite an apparently sincere effort by top management to prevent bribery.

To begin with, the scale of past bribery by ITT units was bigger than corporation officials thought. In 1976, the director's panel first estimated that payments of bribes to win contracts totaled $3.8 million during 1971–1975. In 1978, another investigation increased the estimate to $8.7 million. This year [1982] the directors reported discovering seven new cases of bribery, raising the estimate of questionable payments to $14 million.

There is a barely disguised argument that only naive moral Puritans care whether U.S. corporations bribe foreigners in strange lands. Payoffs are a necessary way of doing business in many countries, the argument runs, so U.S. companies shouldn't be put at a competitive disadvantage.

This argument ignores evidence that many U.S. companies have succeeded in selling abroad without ever resorting to bribery. It ignores the steady rise of U.S. exports since the antibribery law was passed. And it ignores the dangers to U.S. foreign policy interests of bribery by U.S. companies; in the mid-1970s the bribery scandal destabilized governments in Japan, South Korea, the Netherlands, and other nations.

The 1977 antibribery law is an effective deterrent. There is not good reason to relax it.

Argument: The Antibribery Law Clashes with Practices Overseas[8]

The single most noticeable splash in the pool of controversy over the questions of "proper" international business conduct has been produced by the Foreign Corrupt Practices Act (FCPA) of 1977. This law attempts to curb bribery by prohibiting firms from making or authorizing payments, offers, promises, or gifts for the purpose of "corruptly" influencing actions by governments or their officials in order to obtain or retain business for a company.

Much of the world's business is conducted in an arena of kickbacks, bribery, and shakedowns. Should business be allowed and encouraged to play this game? Or should it be compelled to wash its hands entirely, leaving the spoils to competitors in other lands?

A major problem of any single nation's antibribery law is that one person's corruption is another's business routine. What some Westerners might regard as commercial corruption of government and business has always been looked upon as an inescapable fact of everyday life in the less-developed world. The arrangements for giving and taking payments are often "legal" under local law and custom. Nevertheless, officials usually design schemes to hide the transactions as much as possible and are unwilling to publicly admit taking the payoff.

One could plausibly argue that, much like a legal covenant a business might have with a foreign country to operate within its domain, businesses implicitly take part in a social contract to honor the ethical standards of that culture as well. This means that an American multinational firm ought to at least comply with the standards of common morality of the country in which it operates.

Therefore, for those doing business in other cultures, we propose this definition of a "moral" act: *that which persons of good intentions and honorable standards in the host country recognize as proper conduct.* This specification supposes a willingness and ability of serious and sensitive people to continue the investigation into the "morality" of countries with which they would do business. It also recognizes the fact that morals vary between countries. This approach parallels the "marketing concept" which calls for researching the needs of target consumers, in order to devise an appropriate response.

The greatest problem to date has been generated not so much by American imposition of its own high (in theory, if not always in practice) standards, but rather by a ready and often blatant disregard for standards of moral conduct in the

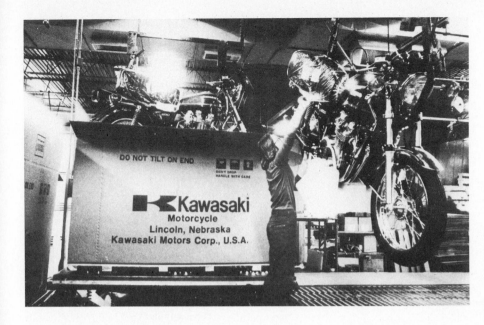

An increasing number of foreign firms are establishing subsidiaries within the United States to manufacture and distribute their products.

host culture. We contend there is room for a "moral pragmatism" that gets right things done by doing things right.

ENVIRONMENTAL CONSTRAINTS ON INTERNATIONAL OPERATIONS

The environment is an important influence on any organization, be it domestic or international in focus. Chapter 7 identifies the external environment as a strategic factor in organization design and highlights the point that more complex environments place greater challenges on organizations than do simpler ones. Managers must respond to this complexity by designing organizational structures and adopting management practices capable of handling it successfully. Nowhere is this environmental challenge greater than in the arena of international management.

Organizations with international operations face a great range of diversity in the environments of the various countries in which and with which they do business. Fortunately, we have a framework for looking at the external environments of organizations and singling out important factors for managerial attention. Called the "general environment" in Chapter 7, that framework includes the cultural values, economic, legal-political, and educational conditions common

to a given geographic region. In the present context we can define that "region" as a "country," and use the four components of the general environment to target attention on some of the key environmental constraints on international management that can be expected to vary from one country to the next.

Figure 19.3 presents the situation schematically. Because of cross-national differences in the general environment, the task of international management is never easy. The following example attests to this fact. As you read the case, keep in mind that international management must accommodate environmental constraints to achieve productivity.

Illustrative Case: GM's Overseas Drive

General Motors' lack of success in its international operations has concerned the large automaker for years. The problem is well evidenced by this headline from a *Wall Street Journal* article.[9]

> GM's European Sales Starting to
> Increase After Recent Losses,
> But Ford Still Leads

Excerpts from another article add further detail to GM's lackluster overseas performance.[10]

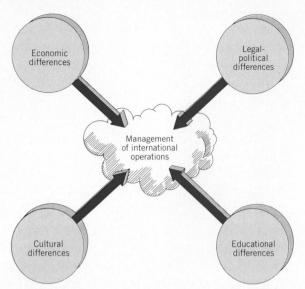

FIGURE 19.3 General environment factors influencing management of international operations.

The reasons for GM's lack of international success are something of a mystery. Some GM historians believe that the conservative business policies laid down by Alfred Sloan, the former GM chairman, have made the risks of doing business abroad unattractive.

Others argue that GM's overseas subsidiaries have suffered from a Detroit-always-knows-best syndrome. As a result of constant interference from engineers and designers in the United States, foreign products always seemed to wind up looking more American than European. "The joke was that whenever we'd start out to build a Mercedes, we'd end up with a Cadillac," says David Lewis, a University of Michigan professor who once worked in the chairman's office at GM.

For years, GM treated its foreign subsidiaries like undeserving orphans, forcing them to finance their own expansion through earnings and local borrowings. But the practice, says David Healey, an auto analyst at Drexel Burnham Lambert Inc., not only inhibited foreign growth but also resulted in "some pretty weird items" on GM's worldwide balance sheet. "They had debts in one place at 15 percent interest and debts in another at 10 percent," he says. "It made no sense at all."

GM has had a particularly tough time, for instance, persuading bright young managers to accept overseas assignments. Because the company formerly used its foreign operations as a dumping

ground for washed-up executives, some employees still attach that stigma to foreign transfers. "International was like the black hole," says James Bowling, who worked on GM's worldwide staff. "People were sent abroad, and you never heard from them again."

A long-term consequence of GM's inability to groom executives overseas is a shortage of international savvy at the top of the corporation. None of the five members of GM's powerful executive committee have ever served abroad (one did work in Canada), and none speak a foreign language. By comparison, five of the seven top executives at Ford have put in time abroad, and several are fluent in more than one foreign language.

"GM has yet to become a truly multinational corporation," says Peter Drucker, whose organizational study of GM, "Concept of the Corporation," has served as a model for a number of major U.S. companies. "They are an American concern with overseas affiliates" that aren't integrated into the company.

Peter Drucker's closing comments are an interesting commentary on the case. He implies that for an organization to be truly "multinational," it must understand and successfully accommodate the intricacies of operating in different countries. Things like language barriers, governmental practices, consumer preferences, and cultural biases—all things which the article implies GM had a hard time dealing with—are but a few of the environmental differences to which international management must adapt. Let's examine some of these differences in more detail.

Economic, Legal-Political, and Educational Differences

To operate successfully in a foreign country, a wise manager requires answers to many questions. They include[11]

- What is the political structure of the country?
- Is the political structure stable?
- Under what type of economic system does the country operate?
- Does the government view foreign capital as being in competition or in partnership with local enterprises?

- In what ways does the government control private enterprise?
- What is the supply of local labor?

Because the differences in these factors are so numerous across countries, our discussion will be generally descriptive. Your goal at this point is to recognize that a wide variety of environmental differences must be systematically considered if decision making and problem solving in international management are to be properly tailored to the demands of local situations.

Economic Differences

Looking around the world, we can see many shared economic concerns, needs, and problems. But there are important differences as well, including a major distinction in the economic environments of developed and developing countries. Firms operating in developing countries, for example, may find special challenges in[12]

1. *Quality-of-life concerns* Increasing population, urbanization, and industrialization put great pressures on local economies and living conditions in developing nations. International operations must adapt to local conditions; they may also be asked to help enhance quality of life by counterbalancing some of the negative trends as well.

2. *Technological deficiencies* Especially in the less-developed economies, there may be a lack of modern and sophisticated technologies. This often means that the international operation becomes a source of technology transfer; it also means the operation must frequently adapt to locally available technology.

3. *Capital shortages* The availability of local capital for investment purposes may be severely limited. International operations in such economies may be required to allow local government participation in ownership and/or become involved to some extent with outside lenders.

These are a few examples of economic differences that one might watch for when moving from developed to less-developed countries. Another more basic economic issue from one country to the next relates to the nature of the foreign economic system itself. In broadest terms, the economic systems of the world fall on a continuum of two extremes—free-market economies and centralized-planning economies. Each presents a different set of challenges to the foreign firm that must operate under its constraints.

Free-market economies characterize most Western nations such as the United States. They operate under an economic system governed by laws of supply and demand. Although government policies will influence the free-market system, they do so to a far lesser extent than in **centralized-planning economies.** The latter, characterized by the Soviet Union and Eastern bloc nations, require a central government body to make basic economic decisions for an entire nation. Such centralized systems may determine allocations of raw materials, set product or service output quotas, regulate wages and prices, and even distribute qualified personnel among alternative employers. To be successful in each setting, organizations must adapt to the differing constraints of free-market and centrally planned economies.

Legal-Political Differences

The legal-political system of any nation is closely tied to its economic system. Figure 19.4 broadly relates the two economic extremes just discussed to two political extremes—democratic or representative government and totalitarianism. In between both sets of extremes, of course, are the multiple and varied combinations that actually represent the countries of the world at any point in time.

Democratic systems rely on free elections and representative assemblies of the population to establish a government for the society as a whole. **Totalitarian systems** govern by restricted representation in the affairs of government through dictatorship, single-party rule, or preferred-membership group rule. As international operations vary between countries governed at these political extremes, they encounter very different constraints. Figure 19.4 shows that more restrictions on international operations are to be expected under totalitarian rule and centralized economies than under democratic rule and free-market economies.

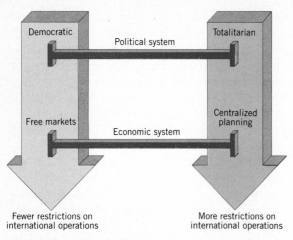

Democratic ← Political system → Totalitarian

Free markets ← Economic system → Centralized planning

Fewer restrictions on
international operations

More restrictions on
international operations

FIGURE 19.4 Extremes in political and economic systems among countries of the world.

The legal systems of the nations of the world also vary widely. This is significant because an international operation is expected to abide by the laws of the host country. The more host-country laws differ from those of the home country and/or from other countries in which international operations are conducted, the more difficult and complex adaptation to local ways may be. Did you know, for example, that it is difficult to lay off workers in most Western European countries? Did you know that the retirement age is 55 in Japan? Or did you know that some jobs in South Africa are restricted to persons of certain race? Each of these examples is of a legal standard quite different from, say, standard U.S. personnel practices. Thus U.S. managers working in these countries would require substantial adjustments in their standard ways of thinking; the same would hold true for managers from these countries called on to operate in the United States.

Another legal issue in international operations deals with incorporation practices. The United States has a private-enterprise system based on private ownership and control of business. Many other countries of the world emphasize government ownership of enterprise to greater or lesser extents. A U.S. firm cannot establish operations in Egypt, for example, without allowing at least 51 percent ownership by local control. Another example is France. In the 1982 French national elections the socialist François

Mitterand was elected president. He ushered in a trend to nationalize major French enterprises, even those involving foreign investments. ITT, for example, was forced to negotiate the sale of its telecommunications unit there to the French government. The ultimate legal risk in such cases is when a host country expropriates foreign assets without payment. As noted earlier, this is presumably what ITT executives feared in Chile in the early 1970s.

Educational Differences

Educational systems also vary from one country to the next, and the level and quality of education achieved by the local populations varies as well. Whereas illiteracy is a minor problem in most Western nations, it is still a major problem in less-developed areas of the world. Since international operations usually employ the local labor force to some extent, literacy and the level of technical education are important environmental factors. For those operations needing more skilled employees, the better the educational system and the greater the availability of trained persons, the better things will be for the employing organization.

Great pressures are often placed on international operations to train and upgrade the skills of local citizens. At the same time, a firm may have to import qualified personnel from the home or other countries to compensate for local deficiencies, on a short-term or long-term basis. This creates complex situations within the firm and in firm/host-country relations. U.S. and European firms operating in Tanzania, for example, employ large numbers of Asian expatriates to staff certain technical positions, such as accounting and engineering. The Tanzanian government, in turn, exerts continued pressure for the firms to replace these expatriates as soon as possible with local nationals.

Cultural Differences

It was said in Chapter 7 that "cultural values are very *subtle* aspects of the general environment." This is truly an understatement. "Culture" is indeed subtle, but it is complex and elusive as well. What does the word mean to you?

A formal definition is a good place to begin this look at cultural differences as additional environmental constraints on international operations. **Culture** is a shared set of beliefs, values, and patterns of behavior common to a group of people. Some aspects of culture that make it significant to international management are that it[13]

- Is difficult to change.
- Changes slowly, if at all.
- Exists in the minds of people.
- Is shared by a number of people.
- Is crystallized in the institutions people have built together (e.g., family, education, religion, law, literature).
- Represents the national character.

When managers and even management theorists deal with culture, they are prone to stereotypes and generalizations. Among international management consultants, for example, it may be heard that[14]

- The French hate MBO.
- Family is vital to Norwegians.
- Success in Asia is family first.
- Organizational loyalty is the clue to Japan.

There is a pressing need for more systematic guidelines on cultural patterns and differences across nations. One recent advance in this area of management research has been made by Geert Hofstede, a Dutch scholar and international consultant to organizations.

National Culture in Four Dimensions

Hofstede studied national culture in four dimensions. Examples of each dimension, shown in Table 19.3, are[15]

- *Power distance*   The degree to which a society accepts a hierarchical or unequal distribution of power in organizations.
- *Uncertainty avoidance*   The degree to which a society perceives ambiguous and uncertain situations as threatening and as things to be avoided.
- *Individualism-collectivism*   The degree to which a society focuses on individuals or groups as

resources for work and social problem solving.
- *Masculinity*   The degree to which a society emphasizes often stereotyped "masculine" traits (e.g., assertiveness, independence, and insensitivity to feelings) as dominant values.

Using formal measures of these four dimensions, Hofstede studied over 116,000 personnel from a U.S.-based MNC operating in 40 countries. From the results of this study, he argues that management practices must be tailored to fit local cultures, and that management theories developed in one culture should be seriously questioned when transferred to another. Consider how U.S. managers in his sample scored on the cultural dimensions relative to managers from the other countries. Comparative data on selected other countries are provided for your further interest.

- *Power distance*   U.S. managers ranked 15 out of 40 countries, reflecting a moderate tolerance of unequal power distribution; Singapore and Hong Kong ranked much higher, showing less tolerance.
- *Uncertainty avoidance*   U.S. managers ranked 9 out of 40, reflecting above-average tolerance for uncertainty; France and Italy scored higher with a greater tendency toward uncertainty avoidance.
- *Individualism-collectivism*   The United States ranked 40 out of 40, being the most individualistic country in the sample, Colombia and Venezuela ranked among the least individualistic.
- *Masculinity*   The United States ranked 28 out of 40, reflecting generally strong "masculine" values; Sweden and Norway fell substantially to the other extreme.

Although Hofstede's research is relatively recent and somewhat controversial, it does point out that there are important differences in national culture and that these differences can affect the management of international operations.

Culture in the More Popular Dimensions

Anyone who travels from one country to the next knows that cultural differences exist, and that many of them must be mastered to succeed in

Table 19.3 Examples of Four Dimensions of National Culture

Power-Distance Dimension

Small Power Distance	Large Power Distance
Superiors consider subordinates to be "people like me"	Superiors consider subordinates to be a different kind of people
Superiors are accessible	Superiors are inaccessible
All should have equal rights	Power holders are entitled to privileges

Uncertainty-Avoidance Dimension

Weak Uncertainty Avoidance	Strong Uncertainty Avoidance
Time is free	Time is money
There is more willingness to take risks in life	There is great concern with security in life
There should be as few rules as possible	There is a need for written rules and regulations

Individualism-Collectivism Dimension

Collectivist	Individualist
"We" consciousness holds sway	"I" consciousness holds sway
Identity is based in the social system	Identity is based in the individual
Belief is placed in group decisions	Belief is placed in individual decisions

Masculinity Dimension

Feminine	Masculine
Sex roles in society are more fluid	Sex roles in society are clearly differentiated
Interdependence is the ideal	Independence is the idea
Small and slow are beautiful	Big and fast are beautiful

Source: Developed from Geert Hofstede, "Motivation, Leadership, and Organization: Do American Theories Apply Abroad?" *Organizational Dynamics*, Vol. 9 (Summer 1980), pp. 46–49.

the foreign environment. Hofstede provides a researcher's view; there are also any number of more popular and still valid generalizations that can guide your thinking. We close this section on culture with two illustrations. In a foreign culture, one should be at least prepared for

1. *Language differences* Languages vary dramatically around the world; even the same basic language (such as English) varies in usage from one country to the next (e.g., from America to England to Australia). A classic example of how even the best-intentioned use of a foreign language may flop is President Carter's 1977 visit to Poland. In his arrival speech he said, "I am interested in the Polish people's desires for the future." Unfortunately, his remarks caused a national uproar when translated as, "I am interested in your lusts for the future."[16]

2. *Etiquette and custom differences* Local customs vary in terms of dress and interpersonal

habits, as well as protocols of time. One must learn in a given culture whether to be on time or to be late, how to dress for business, and how close to get in interpersonal relationships. What is standard and polite in one country may be considered impolite somewhere else.

THE MANAGEMENT FUNCTIONS IN AN INTERNATIONAL PERSPECTIVE

It goes without saying that the basic management functions—planning, organizing, leading, and controlling—apply to the international arena. It also holds true, though, that international management must accommodate the great diversity among national environments. Figure 19.5 depicts how the challenges of implementing the management functions vary between the domestic and international arenas of action. Additional thoughts on these challenges follow.

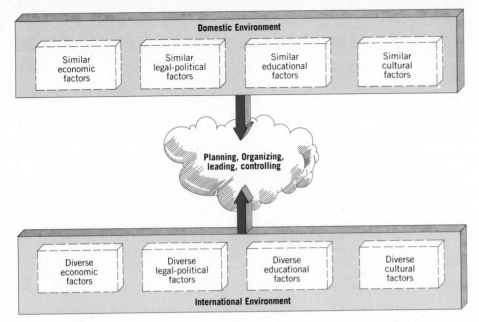

FIGURE 19.5 Domestic and multinational environments of management.

Planning and Controlling

The diversity of the international operating environment makes planning and controlling, already substantial tasks, even more difficult for managers. Let's look at some of the more pressing issues.

Strategic Planning and Control

Central to the strategic-planning model presented in Chapter 5 is analysis of (1) the external environment and (2) the organization's internal strengths and weaknesses. A second look at Figure 19.5 reveals how complex the first of these tasks becomes in the international environment. The great diversity from one nation to the next stresses the planning function in accommodating differences in government policies, economic factors, technological sophistication, resource supplies, and cultural variations, among others. Table 19.4 is even more specific in this regard.

Planning in the international arena requires a worldwide perspective. Picture a home office somewhere in the United States, say Chicago. Foreign operations are scattered around the globe—Asia, Africa, South America, and Europe. Somehow the strategic-planning process must link the home office and foreign affiliates, while taking into account the diversity in environments and needs facing the foreign operations, as well as the home office. These same factors add considerable pressure to control systems. Normal routines involving budgets, information systems, and other comprehensive controls are more difficult to maintain and implement in the face of this environmental complexity. Geographic distance, alone, adds a significant burden to the control requirements of any international operation.

A difficult scenario has just been described. It is logical that local management *should* make decisions consistent with the host country's environment, and that local managers *should* supply adequate information to corporate headquarters so that top management can systematically make strategic decisions and maintain overall control.[17] Perhaps closer to the truth of what often happens is that top management in corporate headquarters makes the strategic choices and sets policy for foreign operations with only sketchy planning inputs from the field. In short, planning for strategic matters becomes a corporate prerogative, while implementation occurs locally, and control may well be left to chance. Under these circumstances, managers located in the foreign or host country are likely to remain frustrated by the lack of individual attention to their needs by home-

Table 19.4 Domestic Versus International Planning Constraints

Domestic Planning Done in Context of	International Planning Done in Context of
Single language	Multiple and varied languages
Single political system	Multiple and varied political systems
Single currency	Multiple currencies of different and fluctuating values
One set of government regulations	Multiple and varied government regulations
Known business climate	Multiple and varied business climates
Known cultural values	Multiple and varied cultural values
Localized sources of information	Diverse and distant sources of information

Source: Adapted, by permission of the publisher, from "Motivation, Leadership, and Organization: Do American Theories Apply Abroad?" by Geert Hofstede, *Organizational Dynamics*, Vol. 9 (Summer 1980), pp. 46–49. Copyright © 1980, AMACOM, a division of American Management Associations. All rights reserved.

office executives. It is unlikely, for example, that any strategic decision made in Chicago on the basis of limited information and perspective can optimally serve the needs of operations located in Asia, or anywhere else in the world.

Strategic planning and control in the international arena require major investments in information systems and sensitivity to all of the environmental issues discussed earlier in this chapter. Good multinational organization structures and leadership practices can help greatly. We'll discuss some of them in a moment. Another effort that can assist planning and controlling in the international arena is the global forecast, particularly those involving political-risk analysis.

Political-Risk Analysis

Forecasting is a useful planning tool. Organizations that operate seriously in the international arena typically have planning staffs specially trained and assigned to forecast and follow worldwide trends. Table 19.5 gives you some ideas of the global trends forecasted for the 1980s.

Political risk analysis involves forecasting the probability of various events that can threaten the security of a foreign investment. This is a high-level and even glamorous form of forecasting. Many ex-diplomats become private consultants in the field, Henry Kissinger (ex-U.S. sec-

retary of state) is one that comes immediately to mind.

The stakes of political risk are high. It is obvious, for example, that foreign investors suffered in the political turmoil accompanying the fall of the Shah of Iran and the overthrow of Nicaraguan governments. It is less obvious that in one day in February 1982, it was possible for a firm to lose 28 percent of its foreign assets overnight. How? Simply because the Mexican government made a decision to allow its currency, the peso, to float in the international money markets. The net result was a 28 percent loss in the value of Mexican assets valued in U.S. dollars. Not all multinationals were caught by surprise in this case; some took protective measures ahead of time and benefited accordingly.[18] They were the firms that had done their political-risk analysis well.

Among the basic factors that would be considered in a political-risk analysis for operations in a particular foreign country are the following.[19]

1. *Social instability*   Potential for local rebellions, subversion, riots, strikes, and spontaneous violence.

   Example: The continuation of violence in Lebanon makes it a risky location for foreign investment.

2. *Foreign conflict*   Potential for the host country to enter into armed or diplomatic conflicts with other nations.

Table 19.5 Global Forecasts for the 1980s

Issue	Forecast
Expansion and growth	It will become increasingly difficult to grow without risk of retrenchment caused by shifting national political and economic forces; local capital will be harder to come by to finance expansion; the demands on foreign firms will increase accordingly.
Automation	Increasing trend toward robotics in manufacturing may decrease the attractiveness of countries with large unskilled labor supplies.
Consumer tastes	Consumer tastes will become more global and less local in orientations, but marketing strategies will have to adjust to local cultures in order to sell a product successfully from one country to the next.
Disaggregation of production	Specialization of production among foreign operations will be tempered by political and economic uncertainties; firms will disaggregate into several countries to spread the risks of operating in any one.
Foreign exchange	International money markets will remain volatile; this will require sophisticated techniques for managing and protecting foreign liquid assets.

Source: See Jagjit Brar, R. David Ramsey, and Peter Wright, "Six Challenges to Global Corporations," *Collegiate Forum* (Spring 1982), p. 14.

Example: U.S. interests in Argentina were hurt when Great Britain and Argentina went to war in 1982 over the Falkland (Malvinas) Islands.

3. *Governmental system* Potential for the governmental system of the country to shift from one extreme to another, or drastically revise its policies toward foreign investors and other nations.

Example: The election in 1981 of a socialist government in France changed the political climate and ushered in substantial nationalization of industry.

4. *Economic climate* Potential for the local economy to surge or decay, and for economic components such as labor forces, capital structures, and regulatory bodies to change in positive or negative directions.

Example: The loss in foreign assets in 1982 when the Mexican government allowed the peso to float in international money markets.

Organizing and Leading

The same factors that challenge the planning and controlling functions in the international arena also influence organizing and leading. Three areas of special attention can be highlighted in the General Motors case cited earlier in this chapter. If you recall

The article stated: "GM has yet to become a truly multinational corporation. They are an American concern with overseas affiliates that aren't integrated into the company."

The implication is: GM's *organization structure* is not well suited to international operations.

The article stated: "GM has had a particularly tough time, for instance, persuading bright young managers to accept overseas assignments."

The implication is: GM has a *staffing* problem in its international operations.

The article stated: "A long-term consequence of GM's inability to groom executives overseas is a shortage of international savvy at the top of the corporation."

The implication is: GM has a *leadership* problem in its international operations.

Multinational Organization Structures

A basic principle of organization design holds in the international as well as the domestic setting: structure should match environment and context (size, technology, strategy, and people). Multinational organization structures are not all that different from others; they are just more complex. The Sidney Harris cartoon carries this point to the extreme.

The usual pattern for an emerging international business is simply to set aside a vice-presidential function and give it the responsibility for overseeing all international operations. This structure may be fine for a single foreign country and single product or business line. As operations expand into multinational settings, however, the demands on the organization and the international division manager can easily overload the structure.

Two structures better adapted to worldwide operations are the multinational geographic and product structures shown in Figures 19.6 and 19.7, respectively. Each encourages decentralization and flexibility in responding to varying needs and conditions on a worldwide basis.[20] In the multinational geographic structure (Figure 19.6), any given country becomes simply one of a number of world markets. Producing and selling functions are grouped under separate geographic units. Responsibility for all products in a given area is assigned to a single line executive who reports to corporate management. In the multinational product structure (Figure 19.7), worldwide product responsibility is assigned to separate line-product group managers; area specialists coordinate product activity in a given area from the corporate staff level. Each product group has operational responsibility on a worldwide basis for its products or services, but operates in any given area under the guidance of the area specialist.

As with all organization structures, there are disadvantages as well as advantages to each of the prior choices. Moving to a multinational product structure may result in difficulty coordinating multiple product groups, and/or having product-group executives who lack expertise or the willingness to listen to expert advice on certain areas of the world. The multinational geographic structure, by contrast, facilitates area ex-

"IT'S NOT SURPRISING. THE PRODUCTION DEPARTMENT IS IN SPAIN, THE WAREHOUSE IS IN KOREA, THE ACCOUNTING DIVISION IS IN BOLIVIA, THE BOARD OF DIRECTORS IS IN CANADA..."

pertise but can make it cumbersome to coordinate product developments and technology transfers from one area to the next.

Staffing International Operations

The General Motors example also points out how difficult it can be to staff international operations properly. The company apparently has had trouble in the past getting good executives to transfer overseas because the assignments are considered "dead ends"—that is, bad for one's career. In 1980 Thomas Murphy, the GM's chairman, attempted to change this. He circulated a memo saying the route to the top of the company included stints abroad. He also persuaded Robert Stempel, a rising corporate star and the head of GM's Pontiac division, to accept command of Adam Opel in Germany to serve as an example.

Organizations operating internationally should have some home-country staff in foreign locations. At the executive level this helps facilitate planning and control through better corporate staff–foreign affiliate linkages. The experiences gained in the process offer further long-term value to the organization as a whole. Any firm that is truly international in orientation should have people with foreign experience in key decision-making positions within the corporate headquarters staff. Only in this way can the international arena, with all of its peculiarities and unique demands, be truly represented in strategic decision making. Peter Drucker directly attributes some of GM's continuing overseas difficulties to this problem. "They have little understanding of international markets," he says. "And you'll never really understand a foreign country until you've been drunk there."[21]

From an organization's point of view, one fact of this matter is that it is costly not only to transfer home-office personnel abroad, but also to pay moving expenses, cost-of-living allowances, overseas salary supplements, special vacation privileges, and other family support and benefits necessary to maintain an overseas assignment. Such compensation and benefit packages are designed to make an overseas assignment as attractive as possible to the employee and his or her family. Even then, success in over-

FIGURE 19.6 A multinational geographic structure. *Source:* Reprinted by permission of the *Harvard Business Review*. Excerpt from "Organizing a Worldwide Business" by Gilbert H. Clee and Wilbur M. Sachtjen, *Harvard Business Review*, Vol. 42 (November–December 1964), p. 102. Copyright © 1964 by the President and Fellows of Harvard College, all rights reserved.

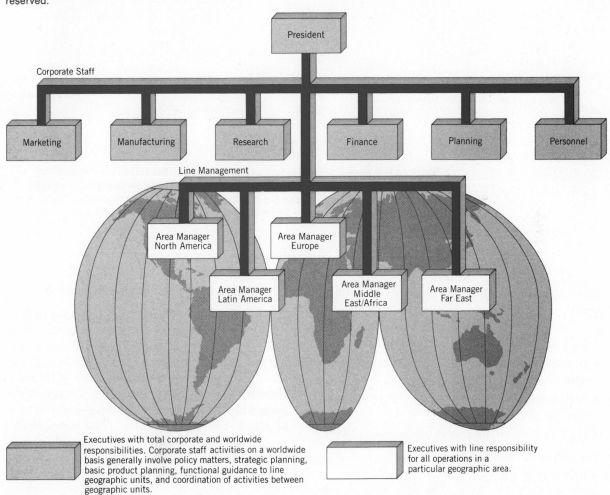

Executives with total corporate and worldwide responsibilities. Corporate staff activities on a worldwide basis generally involve policy matters, strategic planning, basic product planning, functional guidance to line geographic units, and coordination of activities between geographic units.

Executives with line responsibility for all operations in a particular geographic area.

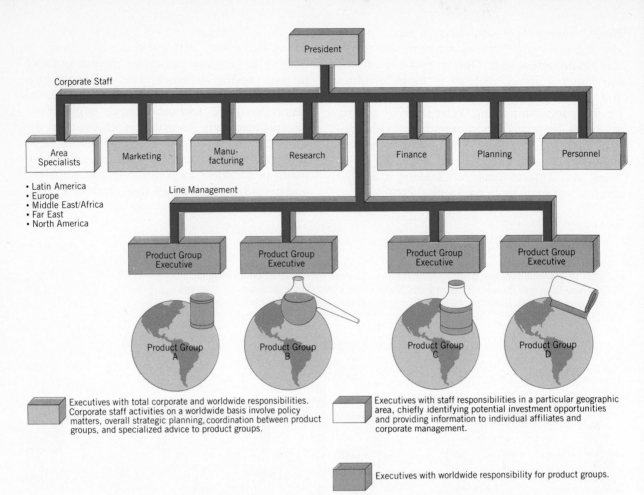

FIGURE 19.7 A multinational product structure. *Source:* Reprinted by permission of the *Harvard Business Review*. Excerpt from "Organizing a Worldwide Business" by Gilbert H. Clee and Wilbur M. Sachtjen, *Harvard Business Review*, Vol. 42 (November–December 1964), p. 107. Copyright © 1964 by the President and Fellows of Harvard College, all rights reserved.

seas assignments generally requires at a minimum

- Real desire to work in a foreign country.
- Active encouragement and support from spouse and family.
- Adaptability and flexibility on the part of self, spouse, and family.
- High degree of cultural awareness/sensitivity.
- Technical competence.
- Leadership ability.

Leadership in the International Setting

The last item on the preceding list is fundamental. Good management involves successful leadership, and there is continuing debate on how the practice of leadership applies across cultures. Our discussion on environmental differences from one country to the next clearly suggests that leadership in international management should be highly contingent as well. That is, leadership practices should fit the unique demands of local cultures and situations as much as possible.

But what does this last statement really

mean? Does it mean that our prevailing theories of contingency leadership, expectancy motivation theory, and group dynamics really do apply across cultures? Or does it mean that the theories don't universally apply and that new theories, specific to alternative cultures, must be developed in their place? These are among the most challenging of all questions facing management theorists today. One of the best ways to address the questions and put the leadership function into an international management perspective is through a look at research into what is called comparative management practices.

COMPARATIVE MANAGEMENT PRACTICES

Comparative management, as a field of inquiry, is the study of how management practices systematically differ from one country and/or culture to the next. As the worldwide focus of management expands, the significance of comparative management studies expands as well. A central research question of primary interest is whether or not a management practice that works well in one country or culture can be successfully transferred to another.

Do American Practices Apply Abroad?

For much of the twentieth century, the United States has been a major source of research on management. U.S. management practices have also been frequently used as appropriate models by managers from other nations around the world. *Newsline 19.3* indicates that this is true even in the U.S.S.R.—it appears that more and more Soviet factory directors are going to business school in the traditional American sense!

Against this background, however, lies a significant academic question: "Do American theories apply abroad?" Geert Hofstede, whose research was mentioned earlier, feels that they don't; at least he feels they don't apply universally and without modification.[22] Some of his specific concerns deal with leadership, motivation, and organization design.

Leadership Across Cultures

Hofstede critiques popular leadership theories according to how U.S. workers score on the four dimensions of national culture reviewed earlier. He argues, for example, that the U.S. focus on "participation" in the practice of leadership reflects a moderate position on the power-distance scale. France, a country with a higher score, shows less concern for participative management in the U.S. style. Countries with still lower scores, such as Sweden and Israel, are characterized by even more "democratic" management initiatives than the U.S. style.

Another example involves a prestigious U.S. consulting firm that analyzed decision-making practices in a large Scandinavian firm. The report criticized the corporation's decision-making style, which was described as "intuitive" and

Comparative management is the study of how management practices systematically differ from one country and/or culture to the next.

NEWSLINE 19.3

SOVIET FACTORY DIRECTORS GO TO BUSINESS SCHOOL

Since the late 1960s, the Soviet Union has engaged in a large-scale effort to import and disseminate Western management concepts, training thousands of managers in dozens of programs around the country. Last year as an exchange student in Moscow, I spent three months observing the training of factory directors at one such program, at the Plekhanov Institute of the National Economy.

Much of the curriculum looks familiar to Western business school students. Soviet managers are now taught organizational design, management psychology, information processing, and managerial decision making, and much of the instruction is drawn directly out of Western textbooks.

The most popular course by far among trainees was management psychology. Soviet factory directors tend to come from narrow technical backgrounds; their formal higher education has usually consisted of four years in some engineering specialty. In the training programs, they therefore show a great interest in general managerial problems.

In some respects, Western management thought represents an ethic alien to Soviet ideology. Its capitalist origins are suspect, and many of its philosophical foundations contradict Marxism-Leninism.

When speaking of employee motivation, for instance, Soviet management scientists grudgingly admit that the theories of informal group behavior they now preach do not coincide with Marx's teachings about the primary role of class in motivating individual behavior. A quarter of a century after Stalin's death, controversy still rages over whether Marxism-Leninism permits a theory of personal leadership. But I was told by management scientists that executives are now expected to learn these controversial theories because the Party considers them "useful."

This isn't the first time the Soviet regime has tried to import Western managment thought. Back in the 1920s, Lenin thought Frederick Winslow Taylor's time-and-motion studies would help Soviet socialism surpass the achievements of capitalism in a few short decades. Today's Soviet leaders are likewise infatuated with Western "scientific management," believing it contains some secret formula for transmitting the efficiency of capitalism.

Source: Excerpted from Mark R. Beissinger, "Soviet Factory Directors Go to Business School," *Wall Street Journal* (November 2, 1981), p. 22 Reprinted by permission of the *Wall Street Journal.* Copyright © 1981 Dow Jones & Company, Inc. All rights reserved.

"consensus based." The consultants compared these tendencies with examples of practices in other companies evidently taken from their U.S. clients. Their comparisons emphasized fact-based instead of intuitive management, and fast decisions based on clear responsibilities instead of the use of informal, personal contacts and the concern for consensus.

Hofstede questions whether or not this consulting firm is doing its Scandinavian clients a service. In particular, the consultants appear to have overlooked that decisions have to be made in a way that corresponds to the values of the environment in which they are to be implemented. This doesn't mean that the Scandinavian corporation's management need not improve its decision making and could not learn from the consultants' experience. But it does suggest that all of this should be done through a mutual recognition of cultural differences, not by ignoring them.

Motivation Across Cultures

Hofstede's critique of the cross-culture applications of motivation theories focuses largely on the assumptions underlying U.S.-based theories. He sees these theories as value-laden and heavily tied to cultures that stress willingness to accept risk and high concern for performance. Hofstede's data show this pattern consistent only with Anglo-American countries such as the United States, Canada, and the United Kingdom.

One of Hofstede's examples acknowledges that even a common value, such as the desire for increased humanization of work, has evolved into different management strategies in the American and European traditions. U.S. practice emphasizes job enrichment and a focus on restructuring *individual* jobs; autonomous work groups and restructuring jobs for groups or *teams* are the major focus of European practices.

Organization Design Across Cultures

A third focus for comparative management studies is organization design. Two of Hofstede's propositions on the application of basic structural design alternatives across cultural boundaries follow.

1. *Greater centralization* of decision making is preferred in countries with higher power-distance scores (*example:* France).
2. *Greater formalization* in the form of added rules and procedures is preferred in countries with higher uncertainty-avoidance scores (*example:* Germany).

An interesting insight into these patterns is found in the responses of a group of European MBA students when asked how they would resolve a common organizational problem—a conflict within one company between the sales and production departments. French students would refer the problem to higher authority, while German students would establish written policies

governing sales/production relationships. British students by contrast, would use some form of group training to improve interpersonal skills among sales and production personnel.

Commentary

You have just experienced a heavy dose of one person's point of view on the transferability of management practices and theories across cultures. It is a useful review because Hofstede has studied the issue more rigorously than most scholars and his thoughts are both recent and provocative. They are not however, without fault.

Let's concede that there are important differences across cultures, just as the general environment itself varies substantially from one nation to the next. Hofstede's work is worthwhile because he approaches cultural differences in a systematic and empirical fashion. He then uses apparent variations in cultural patterns to explain the different preferences and practices of management in various countries. Cross-cultural research is difficult, though, and Hofstede's work is criticized for methodological shortcomings. He is also criticized for making his arguments on the failure of American management theories abroad too extensive and too general, given the data at hand.[23]

Still, more work like Hofstede's is needed so that comparative management questions can be pursued more extensively and with ever-increasing precision in the future. Hofstede's research also sensitizes us to cultural differences at the very time that interest is high in seeing what managers in one country can learn from the theories and successes of managers in other countries. Nowhere is this more evident than current worldwide interest in Japanese management practices.

American and Japanese Management Practices

Two of the most popular management books of 1980s are based on a comparison of Japanese and U.S. management practices. *Theory Z* by William Ouchi and *The Art of Japanese Management* by Richard Tanner Pascale and Anthony G. Athos have already been referenced in this book.[24] They are highly recommended reading and are on the bookshelves of most informed executives today.

The authors of the two books feel that looking at Japanese practices and comparing them with American practices can enlighten managers as to the essential ingredients of business and organizational success. Fundamental to this success is a strong bond between organization and individual. This involves shared loyalties—loyalty of the organization to the needs of the individual employee and loyalty of the individual to the objectives of the organization. Some of the specific Japanese practices that are viewed with special interest are the following.

1. *Lifetime employment* Many Japanese join a company with the expectation of working there for an entire career. Both the organization and individual grow and mature together over time.

2. *Job rotation* Many Japanese managers are rotated through several types of jobs and functions over time. This broadens their perspectives on the organization as a whole. Consider this description of what happens to a typical university graduate joining a Japanese bank as a management trainee.[25]

> Under the guidance of a mentor, he will be exposed in this first 10 years to almost all the bank's operations. He will be given jobs in commercial banking, retail lending to customers, personnel, back-of-the-office clerical work. He will work at both branches and headquarters, and he will have to learn how to manage tellers, and to deal with both individual customers and large company clients. After 10 years, it's typical to gain the first promotion, perhaps to another branch in charge of new business. A few years later, it may be back to headquarters, this time in the international division.

3. *Collective decisions* The Japanese often use a complex decision process that spreads responsibility for results and creates a team feeling among all parties involved. Called the *ringi system*, a typical decision sequence is

   - After discussing a proposed solution to a problem, members of a work group arrive at a consensus and draft a plan of action.

- The plan circulates among persons at the same or lower levels if they will be eventually affected; each affixes a formal seal after the review.
- The plan is passed up the hierarchy gathering more seals at each stop until it reaches the level of final approval.

4. *Quality-control circles* The Japanese make good use of periodic group meetings to discuss possible quality improvements. We discussed the "QC-circle" concept in some detail in Chapter 16.

You can see in these examples some interesting departures from what might be considered standard American practice. Table 19.6 goes further in detailing common differences between the organization structures and management systems of U.S. and Japanese firms.

Do Japanese Practices Apply Abroad?

There is a tendency when reading and thinking about Japanese management practices to view them as highly desirable for application in other countries and cultures. This tendency is basically the same one that we cautioned against when critiquing the transfer of American management theories abroad a bit earlier. Perhaps Hofstede's words can again help you to put this issue of culture and the transfer of management practices among cultures in a realistic perspective.[26]

> The way Americans look to Japan these days closely resembles the way the French, British, and Germans used to look to America 30 years ago. What the Japanese are doing with American ideas resembles what the Americans were doing earlier with European ideas. In several respects, history repeats itself. Disregard of other cultures is a luxury only the strong can afford. . . . [The] consequent increase in cultural awareness represents an intellectual and spiritual gain. And as far as management theories go, cultural relativism is an idea whose time has come.

The final answer on how well management practices such as lifetime employment, the ringi system, and even quality-control circles work in the United States and other countries remains to be determined. For now, it appears that we should use books like *Theory Z* and *The Art of*

Table 19.6 Traditional U.S. and Japanese Organization and Management Systems

Characteristics	Traditional U.S. System	Traditional Japanese System
Organization structure	Hierarchical bureaucracy with specialized and highly structured functions and positions; duties and responsibilities clearly defined in writing for each individual. Organization built around individual.	Hierarchical organization with loose, broad general functions and informal job descriptions with strong reliance on internalized work-group norms of cooperation, consensus seeking, and high group achievement standards. Organization built around groups.
Management systems Management philosophy and expectations	Maximized return on investment through technological and individual efficiency. Employees dislike work but may be motivated by money if tasks are closely supervised. Organization goals therefore believed to be incongruent with employee goals.	People seen as most valuable asset in order to achieve company goals—that is, increasing their share of international markets. Organization and employee group goals are therefore seen as congruent to group goals.
Decision-making system	Decision-making system is highly centralized, top-down, and written, with extensive postdecision verbal communication to seek compliance.	Decision-making system is highly decentralized, bottom-up, and informal, with verbal communications used to seek consensus and written system (Ringi) used as postconfirmation.
Management-employee relationship and control system	Management-employee relationship centered on formal work relationship. Employment commitment dependent on economic conditions and performance. Employee oriented to occupation or profession rather than organization. Individual, formal performance standards and controls. Advisory management/employee relationship predominates.	Paternalistic relationship with employees and their families. Lifetime employment with reciprocal employee-company dependency and loyalty. Reliance on high group motivation and standards with social work controls. Joint management-employee problem solving used as way of reinforcing common goals.
Selection, compensation, and promotion	Employees selected primarily on basis of job-related formal education and/or practical experience and skills for specialized specific job with little or no employment security. Promotion and rewards primarily based on productivity as determined by management.	Employees selected directly from school based on academic achievement, corporate examinations, and extensive screening program including familial relationships and school ties for lifetime. Promotion and compensation function of education, tenure, sex, and family responsibility until age 55. Broad group-evaluation criteria.
Human-resources training development	Human-resource potential seldom fully recognized. Human-resource training and development not carefully planned but intermittent with high levels of functional and technological orientation to improve individual performance. High career/job specialization.	Human resources seen as invaluable lifetime investment. Continuous in-house training and development key to both organization loyalty and technical development. Less job and career specialization with broader skills and management development as team member. Technical adaptation and development traditionally very well developed.

Source: From Robert R. Rehder, "What American and Japanese Managers are Learning from Each Other," *Business Horizons*, Vol. 24 (1981), p. 67. Copyright 1981 by the Foundation for the School of Business at Indiana University. Reprinted by permission.

Japanese Managment for provocation and dialogue, but not necessarily for prescriptions. The same holds true for many of the ideas on Japanese management practice shared elsewhere in this book. Some of the perspectives offered in the part openers, such as "The Long and Short of Japanese Planning" and "A Japanese Pilgrimage," stimulated our thinking in regard to fundamental management issues, but they gave no definitive answers. Their function, like much of the current writing on Japanese management, is to help develop creative and critical thinking about the way we do things and about whether or not we can and should be doing them better.

Future research on Japanese management practices will clarify their similarities and differences with American practices. Eventually, many more nations and cultures will surely be systematically integrated into this comparative-research scheme. Managers around the world have much to share with and learn from one another. This is the point being made in Figure 19.8.

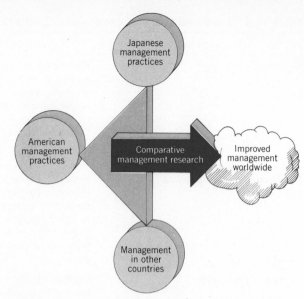

FIGURE 19.8 Future research directions in comparative management.

SUMMARY

International management involves the management of organizations with operations in more than one country. As businesses in particular become more and more global in outlook and operations, the challenges of international management are becoming increasingly clear to practitioners and researchers alike. Lessons learned from this setting of international business are therefore a useful foundation for considering the special demands of managing organizations of all types in an international arena.

Multinational corporations (MNCs) are the epitomy of the complex global organization. With operations in several different countries, MNCs are important elements in the world economy. They are controversial for their potential influence on the economies and politics of both their home and host countries.

MNCs, like all organizations operating internationally, face a variety of external environmental constraints. These include economic, legal-political, educational, and cultural differences that are most typically encountered when national boundaries are crossed. Each of these differences can create special pressures on plan-

ning, organizing, leading, and controlling international operations. Managers with international responsibilities must remain sensitive to these external constraints and adjust their practices accordingly.

Comparative management is the study of how management practices differ and transfer across cultures. One of the most timely questions currently being asked in the comparative management framework is, do American theories apply abroad? In this chapter we used the empirical research of Geert Hofstede to examine some of the insights and debate on the cross-cultural applicability of theories of leadership, motivation, and organizational design. We also reviewed the popular comparison of American and Japanese management practices. Our conclusion was that Japanese practices should be carefully studied and evaluated before being universally applied in other cultures. While we await further research on these and other important comparative topics, the best advice is for every manager to remain alert and sensitive to environmental and cultural differences when managing in the international arena.

THINKING THROUGH THE ISSUES

1. What is international business? Why is it a useful point of reference for studying the key issues of international management?

2. What are the major forms of international business?

3. Why would a business firm want to operate abroad?

4. Explain and give examples of how MNCs (multinational corporations) cause controversies in their relationships with their host countries.

5. Explain and give examples of how MNCs cause controversies in their relations with their home countries.

6. Identify and give examples (at least two each) of economic, legal-political, and educational differences that might be encountered between the United States and (1) France and (2) Mexico.

7. What is "culture"? Why is it important to international management?

8. Draw organization charts that show two different ways a corporation might structure itself for worldwide operations. Explain when and why each form might be preferable to the other.

9. Do U.S. management theories apply abroad? Defend your answer.

10. As it was described in this chapter, what do you consider the most appealing aspect of Japanese management practice? Why?

THE MANAGER'S VOCABULARY

Centralized-planning economy
Comparative management
Culture
Democratic system
Foreign subsidiary
Free-market economy
International business
International management
Joint venture
Multinational corporation (MNC)
Political-risk analysis
Totalitarian system

CAREER PERSPECTIVE: OVERSEAS WORK

In one of its weekly "Labor Letter" columns, the *Wall Street Journal* carried the following report on the career implications of an overseas work assignment.[27] It suggests that overseas work is appealing more to U.S. managers as a wise career move.

"Kenny, Kindler & Hunt, a New York recruiter, says more fast-track executives seek these assignments as a quick way to get overall management experience. In charge of whole divisions, they can show they can deal with labor, foreign exchange, political, and other areas. A Kenny study of 125 managers finds 37 percent willing to take these jobs; 10 years ago, it estimates, the figure was about 10 percent.

"Heidrick & Struggles, another recruiter, adds that many foreign companies making U.S. acquisitions look for top executives with international experience. In the past, many U.S. managers worried that being overseas would get them 'two-yeared into oblivion,' or forgotten at headquarters, say Heidrick & Struggles. Now, particularly at banks and consumer-oriented firms, managers seek these jobs.

"Edmund Piccolin, vice-president at PepsiCo's international division, says his group is the 'primary farm team' for top company talent."

1. Do you agree or disagree with the viewpoint that an overseas assignment could be a "fast track" to career advancement in the management ranks? Why or why not?

2. Are you willing to consider an opportunity to work overseas for a time?

3. What personal development efforts may be appropriate to increase your future potential to succeed in an international management assignment?

CASE APPLICATION: THE CASE OF THE MISSING ADS[28]

When several Americans came to work as department heads at one of the largest Japanese automotive firms in the United States, they had all been reading extensively on Japanese methods. Most of them had come from a major American automotive company, and all had had long experience in the industry. Inevitably, under the pressure of business in this fast-growing organization, they turned instinctively to their accustomed Western management techniques. They looked to the Japanese nationals at the top levels of the organization to give them direction, objectives, and priorities. But nothing was forthcoming; the Japanese were waiting patiently for initiatives from them.

After a time, on the Americans' initiative, an organization chart was drawn up in an effort to settle where the authority and responsibility for decisions rested. It was a thoroughly American document, showing in neat boxes the various departments—parts, service, sales, marketing, planning, and so on—and the vertical relationships, with the Japanese president at the top and the lowest subdepartment on the bottom. The Japanese, who rarely draw up organization charts (and who, if they do, invariably make them read horizontally, like a flowchart), tolerated the American version as a "when in Rome" accommodation. But the chart did not solve the problems; the organization was not functioning well, and decisions were not being made.

For example, there was the simple problem of timing the availability of advertising media for the introduction of new models each year. In the U.S. market this occurs in October; in Japan, new models are introduced in January. From the parent company in Japan, the advertising materials consistently arrived two to three months late for the introduction of new models. Year after year, the U.S. distributors complained about the delay. The American heads of the sales and advertising departments took the problem up the chain of command and requested their Japanese president to contact Japan and straighten the matter out. He did contact Japan—but the problem remained.

By chance, other departments in the organization provided an opportunity for overcoming the difficulty. Beginning in the early 1970s top management began to assign a Japanese "coordinator" to each American department head. The coordinators, usually promising young executives in training for international assignments, were to become acquainted with U.S. business practices. It was not long before they began observing with dismay that the American managers tended to concentrate on their functional roles and to expect coordination between functions to occur at the senior management levels—as is the practice in many U.S. companies. To the Japanese, it appeared, as one put it, "as if the various departments were separate companies, all competing against each other."

As inveterate communicators, some coordinators began to pick up problems that cropped up in one department and share them with their counterparts in other departments. In this roundabout way, the Americans learned what their colleagues were doing. Coordination between departments improved.

Soon the Japanese coordinators became aware of the difficulties typified by the late arrival of the advertising materials. True to their training in the U.S. companies, the Americans were sending a report on every problem up the chain of command. Japanese top management in the United States would listen to each complaint, then send the American manager back for "more information." Translated, this meant "Come back with a proposal." Not comprehending, the Americans became increasingly impatient and frustrated. Occasionally, as in the case of the ads, the problems became so serious that the Americans insisted they be reported to Japan. The Japanese president obliged them, but the parent company remained unresponsive. The reason was simple: since Japanese organizations are unaccustomed to dealing with problems from the top down, the Tokyo organization did not know how to handle the letter from the president of the Japanese subsidiary in the United States to the president of the parent company in Japan.

Once the coordinators understood the nature of the difficulty, remedying the advertising-materials lag and similar problems was easy. A coordinator would simply pick up the telephone and call somebody at his managerial level in Tokyo. In a few days an answer would come back—and in this manner the matter of the ads was resolved.

The coordinators took some time—and the American department heads a somewhat longer time—to realize that the neat boxes in the organization chart were not interacting. By U.S. standards, the Americans were doing a good job. But without American superiors to make decisions and weave the organization together, they found that their effectiveness was diminished. To bridge the gap in managerial styles, the coordinators created a shadow organization. In this manner they not only solved the coordination problem but also involved the parent organization.

Questions

1. Is the "problem" in this case due to poor structure, poor management practice (on whose part?), or both? Defend your answer.

2. What environmental factors have affected the American managers in this case?

3. Is the stated solution a good one? Why or why not?

CLASS EXERCISE: NISSAN, U.S.A.

In June 1983, Marvin T. Runyon drove a pickup truck off the assembly line at an auto plant in Smyrna, Tennessee.[29] When he did so, it represented the first result of an expensive attempt to transplant an efficient Japanese production system to the United States. Runyon is president and chief executive officer of Nissan Motor Manufacturing Corporation, U.S.A.

Three years earlier Runyan had just retired as vice-president of Ford Motor Company after 38 years of service. Then, at the age of 55, he was challenged by Nissan's offer to start the $500-million operation in Tennessee. A key feature of the plant was to be the utilization of many successful Japanese management techniques in the new U.S. setting.

1. What follows are portions of an interview with Runyon.[30] Certain words in Runyon's responses to the interviewer's questions have been deleted. Read the questions, read Runyon's responses, and fill in the missing words based on your understanding of Japanese management practices.

Q. According to published media reports, you and other Nissan officials have indicated that Japanese management techniques will be employed at the Smyrna plant. How similar in structure and operation will the plant here be to Nissan's Kyushu plant?

Runyon. Actually, what we're doing here is taking what we think is the best of Japanese management and what we think is the best of American management and combining them to come up with a hybrid-type management that is not Japanese management and not American management, but Nissan Motor Manufacturing Corporation, U.S.A., management.

We are reducing the management _____ that are customarily found in U.S. auto manufacturing companies. A lot of companies are very tiered. We're going to have five _____ of management—president, vice-president, plant manager, operations manager, and supervisor.

We're going to have a very _____ management style. What I mean is everybody _____ in what is done in this company. It will be more of a _____ management than top-down. The top fellow decides everything that's going to happen, tells everybody, then expects everybody to march to that drumbeat. Japanese don't work that way. They work from a _____ technique. And that's what we plan to do.

Q. *In view of the basic cultural differences between Japanese and Americans, what makes you believe and Nissan believe that the style of management that works very successfully in Japan also will be successful in this country?*

Runyon. The long-term approach will _____ work in any country. A lot of companies in the United States operate very effectively. They employ these same types of management techniques. Actually, if you'll go back and check maybe 20 years ago, you'll find that the management styles that we had here then are what's being done in Japan now. The Japanese just kept doing it and a lot of our companies didn't.

Q. *What specific Japanese management techniques are you using at the Smyrna plant? In particular, will the concept of quality circles be utilized?*

Runyon. We intend to have quality circles after we start building our product. It's very difficult to have a quality circle until you have a product. There again, that's part of this _____ management the Japanese have. Quality circles consist of technicians—people who actually work on the product—who

_____ and _____ mutual problems and concerns and then come up with _____.

Another thing about Japanese management style that we're going to have is that decisions are made at the _____ level possible. What happens is that the people who have the idea—the quality circle—present the idea to each level of managment or to the level that has approval. They make their own presentations. Now if the approval level can be handled by the supervisor, then that's the end of it—the supervisor handles it. Decisions are forced to the _____ level possible. Again, the idea is communication.

Q. *Do you hire employees then with the idea of trying to provide lifetime employment for them, or do you have to take more of an American approach, realizing that an employee may only be here for a few years?*

Runyon. Our approach is that we feel we offer very good employment. We have very good benefits. We feel that we offer very good job _____ to employees to participate in improving the company. We look for people who are interested in working here and who have a sense of _____, a sense of _____, of being involved and participating in what we do. If we are not productive in this company in every way, we will not be successful. Again, our own objective is to produce the best ____ truck sold in North America. _____ and productivity go hand in hand. Our people understand that it's really up to _____ to make this company successful. There's no one person who is going to make this company successful. It's going to take _____ and everybody knows that.

2. Compare your responses to the missing words with those of a nearby classmate. Discuss and reconcile any differences of opinion.

3. Discuss with this classmate your feelings and opinions regarding Runyon's responses to the interviewer's questions.

4. Do you feel the Nissan, U.S.A. approach will succeed? Why or why not? Await further class discussion led by your instructor.

REFERENCES

[1] Excerpted from Jonathan Spivak, "In Nigeria, Payoffs Are a Way of Life," *Wall Street Journal* (July 12, 1982), p. 16. Reprinted by permission of the *Wall Street Journal*. Copyright © 1982 Dow Jones & Company, Inc. All rights reserved.

[2] Adapted by permission from *Management*, Second Edition, by Edgar F. Huse, p. 596, copyright © 1982 by West Publishing Company.

[3] See Gerald A. Silver, *Introduction to Management* (Minneapolis: West Publishing, 1979), pp. 484–486.

[4] Controlling the Multinationals," *Economist* (January 24, 1976), p. 68. Used by permission.

[5] Adapted from R. Hall Mason, "Conflicts Between Host Countries and Multinational Enterprise," Vol. XVII, *California Management Review* (1974), pp. 6, 7.

[6] "The Questions the ITT Case Raises," *Business Week* (March 31, 1973), p. 42.

[7] Excerpted from Norman C. Miller, "We Should Not Relax the Corporate Anti-Bribery Law," *Wall Street Journal* (July 15, 1982), p. 26. Reprinted by permission of the *Wall Street Journal*. Copyright © 1982 Dow Jones & Company, Inc. All rights reserved.

[8] Excerpted from Brad Reid and Ed Zimmerman, "Marketing, Morality and Multinational Firms," *Collegiate Forum* (Spring 1982), p. 5. Reprinted by permission of the *Wall Street Journal*. Copyright © 1982 Dow Jones & Company, Inc. All rights reserved.

[9] *Wall Street Journal* (April 25, 1983), p. 27.

[10] Excerpted from John Koten, "Innocents Abroad: GM's Overseas Drive Continues to Sputter After Three-Year Push," *Wall Street Journal* (July 19, 1982), pp. 1, 10. Reprinted by permission of the *Wall Street Journal*. Copyright © 1982 Dow Jones & Company, Inc. All rights reserved.

[11] Developed from John D. Daniels, Ernest W. Ogram, Jr., and Lee H. Radebaugh, *International Business: Environment and Operations*, Second Edition (Reading, Mass.: Addison-Wesley, 1979), p. 51.

[12] Ibid., pp. 54–56.

[13] Geert Hofstede, "Motivation, Leadership, and Organization: Do American Theories Apply Abroad?" *Organizational Dynamics*, Vol. 9 (Summer 1980), p. 43.

[14] John W. Hunt, "Applying American Behavioral Science: Some Cross-Cultural Problems," *Organizational Dynamics*, Vol. 10 (Summer 1981), p. 68.

[15] Hofstede, op. cit., pp. 43–46; Leonard D. Goodstein, "American Business Values and Cultural Imperialism," *Organizational Dynamics*, Vol. 10 (Summer 1981), p. 50.

[16] *New York Times* (July 28, 1978), p. 27.

[17] See David H. Holt, "Changing Planning Roles, Strategy Formulation and Host-Country Managers," *Collegiate Forum* (Spring 1982), p. 8.

[18] These examples are from Donald A. Ball and Wendell McCulloch, Jr., "Country-Risk Analysis," *Collegiate Forum* (Spring 1982), p. 12.

[19] See, for example, Dan Haendel, *Foreign Investments and the Management of Political Risk* (Boulder, Col.: Westview Press, 1979).

[20] Gilbert H. Clee and Wilbur M. Sachtjen, "Organizing a Worldwide Business," *Harvard Business Review*, Vol. 42 (November-December 1964), pp. 55–67.

[21] Koten, op. cit.

[22] Research critique is based on Hofstede, op. cit.

[23] See Leonard D. Goodstein, "American Business Values and Cultural Imperialism," *Organizational Dynamics*, Vol. 10 (Summer 1981), pp. 49–54; Hunt, op. cit.

[24] William Ouchi, *Theory Z: How American Business Can Meet the Japanese Challenge* (Reading, Mass.: Addison-Wesley, 1981); Richard Tanner Pascale and Anthony G. Athos, *The Art of Japanese Management: Applications for American Executives* (New York: Simon and Schuster, 1981).

[25] William Ouchi, "The Broad Career Path of Japanese Executives," *Wall Street Journal* (April 6, 1981), p. 20. Reprinted by permission of the *Wall Street Journal*. Copyright © 1981 Dow Jones & Company, Inc. All rights reserved.

[26] Geert Hofstede, "A Reply to Goodstein and Hunt," *Organizational Dynamics*, Vol. 10 (Summer 1981), p. 68.

[27] "Labor Letter: Overseas Work Appeals to More U.S. Managers as a Wise Career Move," *Wall Street Journal* (July 19, 1983), p. 1. Reprinted by permission of the *Wall Street Journal*. Copyright © 1983 Dow Jones & Company, Inc. All rights reserved.

[28] This case is reprinted by permission of the *Harvard Business Review*. Excerpt from "Made in America (under Japanese Management)" by Richard Tanner Johnson and William G. Ouchi, *Harvard Business Review*, Vol. 52 (September-October 1974), pp. 67–68. Copyright © 1974 by the President and Fellows of Harvard College; all rights reserved.

[29] Information from John Holusha, "Japan Meets Tennessee at Auto Plant," *Southern Illinoisan* (June 19, 1983) p. 26; Charles E. Dole, "Nissan Trucks from Hills of Tennessee,"*The Christian Science Monitor* (June 30, 1983), p. 15; and "Theme and Variation," *The Owen Manager* (Spring/Summer 1983), pp. 2–7.

[30] Excerpted from "Theme and Variation," *The Owen Manager*, op. cit. Published by the Owen Graduate School of Management, Nashville, TN 37203, in cooperation with the Office of Alumni Publications. © Copyright by Vanderbilt University. Used by permission.

20

MANAGING WITH ETHICS AND SOCIAL RESPONSIBILITY

INDUSTRIAL ESPIONAGE
AT THE HARVARD B-SCHOOL

This case has not been written up at the Harvard Business School yet, but it probably will be soon.[1]

Dan Friedman, president of Corporation 2, is working on a plan to protect his company's market share in the shire industry when his executive vice-president informs him that the confidential computer code of Corporation 6, one of their most aggressive competitors, has fallen into their hands. (A shire is a cross between a shirt and a tire.) Since the six companies in the shire business share a central computer, the code could give Friedman instant access to the secret decisions made by Corporation 6, a go-go concern challenging Corporation 2's industry leadership.

Production planning and market timing are all-important in the cutthroat shire business. Knowing what a competitor is up to ahead of time would be a significant advantage. As it is, companies in the industry spend heavily to buy market studies and other publicly available intelligence, called snoop reports, on such things as who's floating bonds or investing in new technology in which regions. For that matter, with Corporation 6's code, Friedman could order all the snoop reports he wanted and simply charge them to his competitor.

The fortuitous discovery comes at a critical time: an unforeseen depression looms over the economy, threatening an imminent shakeout in the shire industry that could well determine market position for a decade.

Friedman has only two days to use the code—if he decides to do so. What should he do as president of Corporation 2?

PLANNING AHEAD

We'll return to the chapter-opening case shortly. Make sure, though, that you have made up your mind what Friedman should do as president of Corporation 2. Should he use the confidential computer code to access the secret decisions of competitors or not? This chapter is about how a manager's decisions and actions are affected by a sense of ethics and social responsibility. Specific topics of study include

What Is Ethical Behavior?
Managerial Ethics
Maintaining High Ethical Standards Among Managers
Corporate Social Responsibility
Government Regulation of Business
Ethics, Social Responsibility, and the Manager's Challenge

The introductory case is based on events that occurred when a group of MBA students participated in a computer simulation at the Harvard Business School. This "game" is designed to integrate various parts of the graduate curriculum. When we left the case, Dan Friedman was trying to decide what he should do as president of Corporation 2 now that he possessed Corporation 6's secret computer code. Here's what happened.

■ Corporation 2 used the code to access Corporation 6's decisions during the game and to charge extra expenses to Corporation 6's financial accounts.

■ Corporation 2 passed on information about Corporation 6 to other companies in the game; the other companies used the information to disadvantage Corporation 6.

■ Based on an anonymous tip, Corporation 6 discovered the sabotage and publicly exposed Corporation 2 just minutes before the game ended.

■ Corporation 2 was assessed a penalty by the course instructor and finished in last place for the game competition.

The whole incident might have ended at this point, but the conduct and "ethics" of the student players became a controversial issue. Consider these contrasting viewpoints on what took place.[2]

Corporation 2 members

■ "We couldn't believe we had the other company's password; it was such a joke."

■ "We never had a meeting over whether it was right or wrong to use the password. In the context of the game, once you have access to information, it would not make sense not to use it."

■ "It wasn't as though we were cheating. I thought part of the fun was doing things like espionage or collusion."

Corporation 6 members

■ "We felt let down. . . . This is a professional business school and these were the people we'd been in class with for an entire year."

■ "My question was, if there was nothing on the line here and they did this, what would they do when there was money riding on it?"

■ "One of the concerns I have . . . is how the cold, unimpassioned monetary values we learn at Harvard can be applied. If you look at risks against costs in such a case—the possible penalties against the possible gains—you may come out with a positive net present value. That means it may be unethical but it is economically justifiable. I'd hate to read about some classmate in jail ten years down the road who justified his crime by the kind of analysis he learned at the Harvard Business School."

Dan Friedman, President of Corporation 2, in retrospect

■ "One of the things that the Harvard Business School teaches is that there are no truths. There are some broad issues here, and a variety of different opinions, and we got a chance to think about them."

This chapter asks you to think about issues related to those Dan Friedman speaks about. Throughout this book our focus has been on the manager's basic goal of performance accomplishment—that is, to help the organization and its members achieve high productivity. Our thoughts, principles, and suggestions regarding how best to accomplish this goal have been many. Now it is time to think about mastering this challenge while acting ethically and in a socially responsible fashion. These issues are important, timely, and real.

WHAT IS ETHICAL BEHAVIOR?

We will use three words with frequency in the coming discussion—*ethics, moral,* and *ethical.* Let's turn to the dictionary for initial clarity in their respective meanings.[3]

Ethics (éth-iks) *n.pl.* The system or code of morals of a particular person, religion, group, profession, etc.

moral (mor-l) *adj.* Relating to, dealing with, or capable of making the distinction between right and wrong in conduct; good or right in conduct or character.

ethical (éth-ik-l) *adj.* Having to do with ethics or morality; of or conforming to moral standards; conforming to the standards of conduct of a given profession or group.

Ethics is a difficult word when it comes to specifying its meaning. The dictionary definition is a good point of departure. We will consider **ethics** to be the code of morals of a person or group that sets standards as to what is good or bad or right or wrong in one's conduct. **Ethical behavior,** in turn, is what is morally accepted as "good" or "right" in the context of a governing moral code.

There is clearly a legal component to ethical behavior. That is, any behavior considered ethical should also be legal in a just and fair society. This does *not* mean, however, that just because an action is *not* illegal it is necessarily ethical. Think

about this last statement. Is it truly ethical, for example, for an employee to

- Take longer than necessary to do a job?
- Do personal business on company time?
- Call in sick to take a day off for leisure?
- Fail to report violations of company rules by a co-worker?

None of the prior acts are strictly illegal. But many people (perhaps you) would consider one or more of them to be unethical.

To thus establish whether a given behavior is ethical or not, we must inquire beyond its legality and probe into whether it is right or wrong in a broader moral sense.[4] The following equation figuratively expresses this expanded view of ethical behavior.

$$\text{Ethical behavior} = \text{legal behavior} + \text{"something else"}$$

"Something else" in this equation represents behavior that conforms to the moral standards governing the situation. These moral standards, in turn, are usually based on society's prevailing norms and values.

Figure 20.1 places the equation, ethical behavior = legal behavior + "something else," in a social context that serves as the source of the norms and values that give meaning to a moral code. Depending on the situation, the relevant social context might be defined at the group, organizational, societal, or even broader levels. Think back to the Harvard Business School case. Perhaps the actions of Corporation 2's members could be considered ethical according to standards governing the conduct of business-simulation games at the school. That is, perhaps the social context of the game made them both legal and morally acceptable. This was one of Dan Friedman's arguments, in fact. Then again, it may be upsetting for you to recognize that ethical standards governing a learning situation in such a prestigious school are different from those we would like managers to live by in actual business practice. It can be argued even further that the ethical standards of both management education and management practice should be congruent with the norms and values of society as a whole.

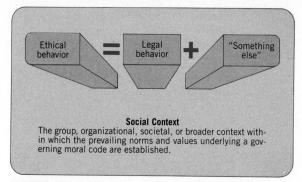

FIGURE 20.1 The social context of ethical behavior.

A classic business quote goes, "Ethical business is good business." The same can be said for all persons and institutions in all aspects of society.

MANAGERIAL ETHICS

Managerial ethics are standards and principles that guide the actions and decisions of managers, and determine if the actions and decisions are "good or bad" or "right or wrong" in a moral sense. Managerial ethics are of great social importance because they influence the actions and decisions that influence the social impact of organizational performance.

Ethical managerial behavior is behavior that conforms not only to law, but also to a broader set of moral principles common to society. Managers who act ethically and with a sense of social responsibility can have a positive impact on the social good performed by their organizations. Managers who fail in this regard make it more difficult for their organizations to perform in a moral and socially acceptable sense.

Ethical Dilemmas Faced by Managers

An **ethical dilemma** occurs every time a manager must choose whether or not to pursue a course of action that, although offering the potential of personal or organizational benefit or both, is also unethical and/or illegal in the broader social context. Every so often, a case of illegal managerial behavior makes the news. A sensational example was John Z. DeLorean's 1982 arrest on drug-trafficking charges. He was purportedly trying to set up a multimillion-dollar cocaine deal to raise cap-

ital to save his bankrupt Delorean Motor Company.

Not all illegal acts by corporate leaders are as sensational as DeLorean's. But you will find an increasing number of media reports on white-collar crime and a corresponding debate on how these "corporate criminals" should be treated. Consider the case of Bob Rowan who, as president and chief executive officer of Fruehauf Corporation, became involved in a scheme to defraud the United States government of $12 million in excise taxes.[5] He was caught and convicted. Instead of being sent to prison, he was sent to work for four months at the Sacred Heart Rehabilitation Center for alcoholics. During this time Rowan was on unpaid leave from his $403,193-a-year job as company president. But he approached the assignment with motivation and purpose. He worked hard to upgrade management of the center. About the task, Rowan said, "My objective was not only to help Sacred Heart, but to show that a [convicted] business executive can make a greater contribution to society by working than by sitting in some country-club jail reading books." Bob Rowan's prosecutors didn't agree with his latter comment. They argued that jail was more appropriate than a public-service sentence.

Set the obviously illegal acts aside for the moment. Managers are still left with many dilemmas that involve the choice among alternatives of questionable ethical qualities. What would you do as president of a company, for example if[6]

Case 1 The minister of a foreign nation asks you to pay a $200,000 consulting fee? Extraordinary payments to lubricate the decision-making machinery are common in this country. In return for the money, the minister promises special assistance in obtaining a $100-million contract that would produce at least a $5-million profit for your company. The contract would probably go to a foreign competitor if not won by your company

Case 2 You learn that a competitor in a highly competitive industry, has made an important scientific discovery that will substantially reduce, but not eliminate, your profit for about a year. There is a possibility of hiring one of the competitor's employees who knows the details of the discovery.

Case 3 You learn that an executive in your company who earns $50,000 a year has been padding his expense account by about $1500 a year.

These cases were raised in a survey of *Harvard Business Review* subscribers. The 1227 respondents replied as follows.

Case 1 Foreign payment: Forty-two percent would refuse to pay; 22 percent would pay, but consider it unethical; 36 percent would pay and consider it ethical in the foreign context.

Case 2 Competitor's employee: Fifty percent probably would hire the person; 50 percent would not.

Case 3 Expense account Eighty-nine percent feel padding is okay if superiors know about it; only 9 percent feel it is unacceptable regardless of the circumstances.

Table 20.1 summarizes the experiences of this same sample of executives regarding conflicts between company interests and their personal ethics. Note that most of the ethical dilemmas developed in the managers' relationships with superiors, customers, and employees. Superiors, in particular, were singled out as sources of pressure to support incorrect viewpoints, sign false documents, overlook their wrongdoing, and do business with their friends. The most frequent issues underlying the ethical dilemmas involved honesty in communications through advertising and with top management, clients, and government agencies, as well as the receipt of special gifts, entertainment, and kickbacks. Specific examples of ehtical dilemmas faced by these executives follow.

The vice-president of a California industrial manufacturer "Being required as an officer to sign corporate documents which I knew were not in the best interest of minority stockholders."

A manager of product development from a computer company in Massachusetts "Trying to act as though the product [computer software] would correspond to what the customer had been led by sales to expect, when, in fact, I knew it wouldn't."

A manager of corporate planning from California "Acquiring a non-U.S. company with two sets of books used to evade income taxes—standard

Table 20.1 Executive Views of Conflicts Between Company Interests and Personal Ethics

	Percentage
Conflicts in Relation with	
Superiors	12.8
Customers	12.0
Employees	11.5
Agents and customers	9.5
Competitors	4.8
Law, government, and society	4.8
Suppliers	2.5
Potential investors	0.5
Other and unspecified	41.6
Conflicts with Regard to	
Honesty in communication	22.3
Gifts, entertainment, and kickbacks	12.3
Fairness and discrimination	7.0
Miscellaneous law breaking	5.8
Honesty in executing contracts and agreements	5.5
Firings and layoffs	4.8
Price collusion and pricing practices	2.3
Other and unspecified	40.1

Source: Adapted by permission of the *Harvard Business Review.* Excerpt from "Is the Ethics of Business Changing?" by Steven N. Brenner and Earl A. Mollander, *Harvard Business Review* (January-February 1977), p. 60. Copyright © 1977 by the President and Fellows of Harvard College; all rights reserved.

practice for that country. Do we (1) declare income and pay taxes, (2) take the "black money" out of the country (illegally), or (3) continue tax evasion?"

The president of a real-estate property-management firm in Washington "Projecting cash flow without substantial evidence in order to obtain a higher loan than the project can realistically amortize."

A Texas insurance manager "Being asked to make policy changes that produced more premium for the company and commission for an agent but did not appear to be of advantage to the policyholder."

Factors Affecting Managerial Ethics

As interesting as the preceding examples may be, we must be careful. It is almost too easy to confront ethical dilemmas in the safety of a textbook or college classroom. In practice, managerial ethics are influenced by a number of forces present

Table 20.2 Factors Influencing Ethical Standards of Managers

	Respondents Listing Factor (%)
Factors Causing Higher Standards	
Public disclosure, publicity, media coverage, better communication	31
Increased public concern; public awareness, consciousness, and scrutiny; better-informed public; societal pressures	20
Government regulations, legislation, and intervention; federal courts	10
Education of business managers, increase in manager professionalism and education	9
New social expectations for the role business is to play in society, young adults attitudes, consumerism	5
Business's greater sense of social responsibility and greater awareness of the implications of its acts; business responsiveness, corporate policy changes, top management emphasis on ethical action	5
Other	20
Factors Causing Lower Standards	
Society's standards are lower; social decay; more permissive society; materialism and hedonism have grown; loss of church and home influence; less quality, more quantity desires	34
Competition, pace of life, stress to succeed, current economic conditions, costs of doing business, more businesses compete for less	13
Political corruption, loss of confidence in government, Watergate, politics, political ethics and climate	9
People more aware of unethical acts, constant media coverage, TV, communications create atmosphere for crime	9
Greed, desire for gain, worship the dollar as measure of success, selfishness of the individual, lack of personal integrity and moral fiber	8
Pressure for profit from within the organization from superiors or from stockholders; corporate influences on managers, corporate policies	7
Other	21

Source: Reprinted by permission of the *Harvard Business Review.* Excerpt from "Is the Ethics of Business Changing?" by Steven N. Brenner and Earl A. Mollander, *Harvard Business Review* (January-February 1977), 57–71. Copyright © 1977 by the President and Fellows of Harvard College; all rights reserved.

Note: Some respondents listed more than one factor, so there were 353 factors in all listed as causing higher standards and 411 in all listed as causing lower ones. Categories may not add up to 100 because of rounding errors.

in the actual situation within which the manager must perform. Table 20.2 shows some of the factors practicing managers see as causes of higher and lower ethical standards. At the personal level, greed lowers standards, while professionalism and management education are sources of higher standards. Pressure for profit from within an organization draws standards down, while a sense of social responsibility raises them. Competition, political corruption, media coverage of unethical acts, and social decay are felt to cause lower standards. Increased public exposure and concern, government regulation, and new social expectations, by contrast, are sources of higher standards.

In between these many and sometimes conflicting forces stands the individual manager. He or she must choose courses of action that dem-

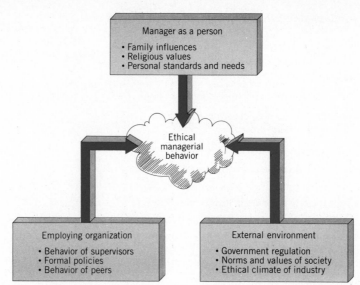

FIGURE 20.2 Factors affecting ethical managerial behavior.

onstrate acceptable managerial ethics in situations where the pressures among these various forces may be contradictory and great. Increased awareness of the sources of pressure may help you to deal with them better in your managerial future. Figure 20.2 divides these forces into influences emanating from (1) the manager, (2) the organization, and (3) the environment.

The Manager as a Person

Managerial ethics are affected by the personal experiences and background of the manager. Family influences, religious values, personal standards, and personal needs (financial and otherwise) will help determine the ethics influencing a manager's conduct in any given circumstance. Although other factors are also important, the power of these individual factors as determinants of personal ethical standards is certainly great.

The Employing Organization

The organization is another important factor with the capability to influence managerial ethics. Formal organizational policies and rules are often established to guide behavior and decision making in situations prone to create ethical dilemmas for the persons involved. IBM, for example,

states two basic guidelines for its employees regarding tips, gifts, and entertainment.[7]

- No IBM employee, or any member of his or her immediate family, can accept gratuities or gifts of money from a supplier, customer, or anyone in a business relationship. Nor can they accept a gift of consideration that could be perceived as having been offered because of the business relationship. "Perceived" simply means this: If you read about it in your local newspaper, would you wonder whether the gift just might have had something to do with a business relationship?

- No IBM employee can give money or a gift of significant value to a customer, supplier, or anyone if it could reasonably be viewed as being done to gain a business advantage.

We noted earlier that managers consider their immediate supervisors as important influences on their behavior. Just exactly what a supervisor requests of a manager, and which of a manager's actions are rewarded or punished, will certainly impact the personal ethical standards that emerge. The expectations and reinforcement of peers and other insiders are likely to have similar impact. Within any organization, both stated policies and the day-to-day actions of people establish the social context for ethical behavior.

The External Environment

Organizations are influenced by an external environment composed of competitiors, government laws and regulations, and social norms and values among others. Laws interpret social values to define appropriate behaviors for organizations and their members; regulations help governments to monitor these behaviors and keep them within acceptable standards. But the climate of competition in an industry also sets a standard of behavior for those who hope to prosper within it. Sometimes the pressures of competition contribute further to the ethical dilemmas of managers. One day early in 1982, for example, Robert Crandall, president of American Airlines, telephoned Howard Putnam, president of Braniff International Airlines. Both companies were suffering from money-losing competition on routes from their home base of Dallas. A portion of their conversation follows.[8]

Putnam.   Do you have a suggestion for me?

Crandall.   Yes, I have a suggestion for you. Raise your fares 20 percent. I'll raise mine the next morning.

Putnam.   Robert, we ...

Crandall.   You'll make more money and I will, too.

Putnam.   We can't talk about pricing.

Crandall.   Oh, Howard. We can talk about anything we want to talk about.

The U.S. Justice Department alleges that Crandall's suggestion of a 20 percent fare increase amounts to an illegal attempt to monopolize airline routes. The matter is now under a civil lawsuit. This example introduces the topic of government regulation of business to be discussed later in this chapter.

MAINTAINING HIGH ETHICAL STANDARDS AMONG MANAGERS

A recent survey of business students indicated that 88 percent expected to encounter pressures to compromise their ethics in future jobs; 50 per-

"YOU'LL HAVE TO MAKE A CHOICE, LEWIS. EITHER YOU QUIT THIS COMMITTEE OR YOU QUIT THE ETHICS COMMITTEE."

An ethical dilemma occurs whenever a manager must choose whether or not to pursue a course of action that, although offering potential gain, is unethical in a broader social context.

cent implied that they would have no recourse but to conform to the lower standards.[9] Given such expectations, ones that you may in fact share, it is especially appropriate to examine ways of maintaining high ethical standards in management. Our thoughts will focus on (1) exposing unethical practices, (2) top management support for high ethical standards, and (3) a managerial code of ethics.

Exposing Unethical Practices

Ray Palmateer, a foreman in International Harvester Company's East Moline, Illinois, tractor works reported to police that a fellow employee tried to sell him stolen tools.[10] Instead of getting a pat on the back from his employer, Palmateer was fired as a "whistle blower." The Illinois Supreme Court allowed him to sue the company for "retaliatory discharge." All signs are that the courts are growing increasingly supportive of efforts by employees to report unethical acts by their co-workers and to avoid engaging in unethical acts on behalf of their employers. Michigan's Whistle Blowers' Protection Act of 1981 pursues this issue to the ultimate. The act makes it illegal "for an employer to discharge or threaten a worker or to discriminate in salary, benefits, privileges, or location of employment because an employee has reported a violation of law or regulation to any public body."

Notwithstanding such legal support, managers and other organizational employees may face barriers that make it hard for them to expose unethical behavior in the workplace. This problem is highlighted by conclusions of a study released by the Merit Systems Protection Board of the federal service: "Numerous federal employees are aware of fraud and abuse in federal agencies and departments but are afraid to come forward." Three important organizational blocks to exposing unethical behaviors are:[11]

1. *Strict chain of command* Most organizations operate in some allegiance to the chain-of-command principle, which states that one should not bypass a level when communicating upward or downward in a hierarchy of authority. This makes it difficult to expose unethical practices of one's boss to higher-level management because the chain of command must be violated to bring it to their attention. It is even more difficult to do this when the risk exists that you may have misperceived the situation (i.e., nothing wrong is really taking place) or that the boss may be acting on orders from above. The chain of command can also interfere with exposing unethical behavior when one's boss is aware of an unethical practice among subordinates, but refuses to take action. Once again, the only route for exposing things is to bypass the boss and communicate to a higher management level, perhaps at substantial personal risk.

2. *Task-group cohesiveness* Chapter 13 points out that group norms are powerful influences on the behaviors of members. There may be times, however, when group norms support behaviors that violate a member's personal standards of ethics; violating the norms may result in social ostracism and subsequent loss of group-membership privileges. The resulting tendency to go along with the group and avoid "blowing the whistle" is especially great in groups where a high degree of coehsion, loyalty, and interpersonal harmony exist.

3. *Ambiguous priorities* It is not always clear what is "right" or "wrong" according to the internal policies of an organization. Formal policy statements may be inconsistent with what appears as acceptable day-to-day practice; official directives may differ from standard ways for "getting the job done." For example, company policy may require the solicitation of competitive bids on all major purchases. In practice, purchasing agents may be told by their supervisors to continue working with a preferred supplier. Such ambiguities make it difficult to pinpoint whether a behavior is unethical or not, let alone expose it.

Top Management Support for High Ethical Standards

The persons serving in management capacities play crucial roles in the maintenance of high ethical standards in any organization. The individual worker may be honest and of the highest moral character. Yet forces emanating from higher levels of authority might cause them to overlook the unethical practices of others and even to adopt some themselves. We noted earlier that executives in one survey consider the behavior of their superiors as the single most important factor influencing unethical decisions. The implication is that top management sets an ethical tone for the organization as a whole. This point is evident in the following examples.[12]

- "If the boss winks," someone once stated, "he or she will find the employees winking back" with illegal, corner-cutting behavior.
- Communications from the top can explicitly apply pressure to "get the business at all costs."
- Communication from the top can also subtly suggest that it doesn't want to know about deceptive or illegal practices among employees.
- When the top management takes advantage of company resources for purely personal pleasures (e.g., taking the company plane on pleasure trips, or taking pleasure trips to vacation

spots on ostensibly legitimate business purposes), lower-level employees may be expected to do likewise.

There is no doubt that top management has the power to shape an orgnization's policies and set its moral tone as well. As a result, top managers have a major responsibility to serve as models of appropriate ethical behavior for the entire organization. Not only must they be the epitomy of high ethical conduct, top managers must also communicate similar expectations throughout the organization . . . and reinforce results!

This general appeal easily extends to all levels of management. Every manager is in a position to influence subordinates. Care must be taken to do so in a positive and informed manner. The important supervisory act of goal setting and communication of performance expectations is but one example. A supervisor may unknowingly encourage unethical practices by exerting *too* much pressure for the accomplishment of goals that are *too* difficult. A surprising 64 percent of 238 executives in one study reported feeling under pressure to compromise personal standards to achieve company goals; a survey of Pitney-Bowes employees revealed 59 percent felt that pressure to compromise personal ethics to achieve corporate goals was a problem. A *Fortune* magazine survey reports that 34 percent of its respondents felt that a company president can have a real impact on the ethical climate of the organization by setting reasonable goals "so that subordinates are not pressured into unethical actions."[13]

Codes of Managerial Ethics

Formal codes of ethical conduct guide members of such professions as engineering, medicine, law, and public accounting. Indeed, the existence of such codes is part of the very definition of a profession. The codes channel individual behavior in directions consistent with the historical and shared norms of the professional group. The National Association of Accountants, for example, has a code of ethics for companies' internal accountants. Among other things, the code requires an accountant to report to superiors within the company any improper behavior that may be observed. Association officials feel the code will give managment accountants a standard to point to if asked to "cook the books" or overlook accounting abuses. One says[14]

Those who call themselves professional will welcome the support provided by this code of conduct in helping them to resist inappropriate demands of a superior or of anyone else.

There are growing feelings that formal codes of ethical conduct would benefit the practice of management as well. Those in favor see them as means for clarifying expectations regarding appropriate means of accomplishing performance goals, for giving managers a point of outside reference when they want to refuse unethical requests, and for offering increased management quality as persons adhering to the codes rise to the top of corporate ladders. Arguments against the codes express fears that it will be impossible to specify codes to cover all possible situations and actions, that codes will be overly restrictive of individual freedom, and that codes will prove difficult to enforce.

Many organizations establish their own codes of ethics to govern the expected behavior of employees. While less encompassing than the general or professional codes just discussed, they do serve an important internal purpose. The code of ethics of the Whirlpool Corporation is shown in Figure 20.3.

Managers at all levels in organizations must work together to support high ethical standards in the workplace. Through policies and actions higher-level managers can clarify, reinforce, and reward ethical behavior. But individual responsibility for high ethical standards must be felt by each manager as well; the maintenance of high ethical standards in management begins with having honest and moral people serve in managerial roles. Think about this as a personal challenge and remember that the maintenance of high ethical standards will not always be easy. "Expediency" may often pressure against doing what is "right." John DeLorean, in fact, may have anticipated his future difficulties in this passage from his 1979 best-selling book, *On a Clear Day You Can See General Motors*.[15]

Business in America . . . is impersonal. This is particularly true of large American multinational corporations. . . . They have no personality. The

Whirlpool has a simple, yet comprehensive code of ethics.

It represents an irrevocable commitment to our customers and stockholders that our actions will be governed by the highest personal and professional standards in all activities relating to the operation of this business.

The following statement is the foundation for all written policies dealing with ethical business conduct. It places the ultimate responsibility for ethical behavior precisely where it belongs in any organization...on the shoulders of the person in charge.

No employee of this company will ever be called upon to do anything in the line of duty that is morally, ethically or legally wrong.

Furthermore, if in the operation of this complex enterprise, an employee should come upon circumstances of which he or she cannot be personally proud, it should be that person's duty to bring it to the attention of top management if unable to correct the matter in any other way.

Written policies dealing with specific matters such as conflicts of interest, political activities, fair employment practices, business entertainment, gifts, and substantiation of advertising and promotion claims have been communicated throughout the company. Such policies are periodically reviewed as necessary, and recommunicated.

"The system works."

In any business enterprise, ethical behavior must be a tradition, a way of conducting one's affairs that is passed on from generation to generation of employees at all levels of the organization. It is the responsibility of management, starting at the very top, to both set the example of personal conduct and create an environment that not only encourages and rewards ethical behavior, but which also makes anything less totally unacceptable.

I believe this has been achieved at Whirlpool. The men who founded this company back in 1911 were individuals possessed of great integrity and honor. They fostered a tradition of ethical conduct in their business practices, and they perpetuated that tradition through careful selection of the people who would one day fall heir to leadership of the company.

The system works. Time and time again I have witnessed its efficacy. It shows no hospitality whatsoever to those not willing to abide by its standards, and unerringly identifies and purges them.

Benton Harbor, Michigan 49022

JOHN H. PLATTS
Chairman of the Board
Whirlpool Corporation

FIGURE 20.3 The Whirlpool Corporation's code of ethics.

ultimate measure of success and failure of these businesses is not their effect on people but rather their earnings. . . . In such a completely impersonal context, business decisions of questionable personal morality are easily justified. The unwavering devotion to the bottom line brings this about. . . . Too often the only questions asked are: What is the expedient thing to do to save the system? How can we increase profits?

CORPORATE SOCIAL RESPONSIBILITY

It's now time to shift our examination of ethical behavior from the level of the individual to the organization. We begin by recognizing that all organizations exist in complex relationship with elements in their external environments. Figure 20.4 depicts how this environment takes meaning for a business firm as a network of other organizations and institutions with which it must interact. Against this action framework **corporate social responsibility** is defined as an obligation of the organization to act in ways that serve both its own interests and the interests of its many external publics.

One of the major consumer scares of the recent past occurred when seven deaths resulted from cyanide maliciously placed in capsules of Extra-Strength Tylenol. Johnson & Johnson (J&J), the maker of this popular aspirin substitute, moved quickly to remove all Tylenol from distri-

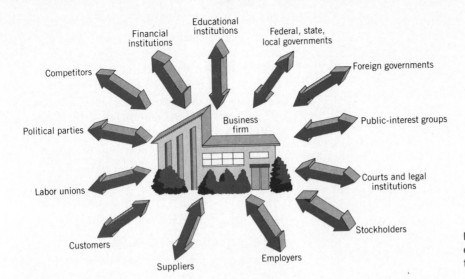

FIGURE 20.4 The external environment of a business firm.

bution. This was done at great expense to the company, even though it was immediately determined that the cyanide got into the capsules after they left J&J manufacturing and distribution control. A socially responsible company delivers reasonable and safe products to its customers. By deciding to withdraw Tylenol from the market, J&J executives acted in a socially responsible way to protect consumers as well as corporate interests.

The Concept of Social Responsibility

Organizations fulfill their social responsibilities in many ways. See, for example, if you can guess what the following four people have in common.[16]

Helen Olson works at Save the Children Federation. She has traveled to Honduras and to the Dominican Republic in her capacity as financial adviser.

Eric Grey works in a program to train physically disabled high-school students at the Rusk Institute for Rehabilitation Medicine at New York University Medical Center.

Marv Silvern works with ninth and tenth graders as an assistant director of the New York City Comprehensive Math and Science program. Its objective is to train minority students in science and mathematics to prepare them for engineering studies.

Norman Steele is an adjunct professor of international marketing at Baruch College in New York. He is working on a plan for an executive MBA program and heads a program that places students in jobs related to their business studies.

The common element is that each of these people is an IBM employee working in the company's "community-service" program. IBM spent $20 million in 1981 on this program, which loans employees to other institutions serving the public interest. The typical loan is for one year, and IBM pays the employee's full salary. The person on leave is guaranteed a job at the same level upon return.

"Why," you might ask, "do companies maintain expensive social-service leave programs? What are the benefits?" Answers to your questions are found in the responses of persons involved in a similar program offered by the Xerox Corporation.[17]

"I came back super-charged-up and proud of the company. I think it helped my career." —Xerox employee.

"The hope and expectation is that we get back a better employee—one better equipped at problem solving and a lot of other things." —Xerox vice-president.

"More companies are going to have to be doing this, because you have to put something back into the communities—you can't just extract profits. And this is not bad for business, either." — Xerox manager.

Both IBM and Xerox can be considered as acting in socially responsible ways by making paid social-service leaves available to their employees. Other examples abound. Hueblein, the marketeer of Smirnoff Vodka and Kentucky Fried Chicken, announced in 1982 that it would spend $180+ million over the next five years to create jobs and promote the black business community.[18] Mobil, the giant oil firm, regularly sponsors public-service advertisements in popular magazines. One subject is alcoholism. Along with an appeal to support the National Council on Alcoholism, one ad offers the following facts for public consumption.

- Alcoholism is a disease, not a decision.
- Prevention programs can reduce the risk of developing alcoholism.
- To conquer alcoholism without help is extraordinarily difficult.

Remember that the obligation to act in a socially responsible fashion is not reserved for businesses alone. Every organization, public or private, has a basic responsibility to protect and enhance the public welfare. Labor unions, universities, hospitals, government agencies, and others are no more exempt from social responsibility than are business firms such as General Foods, Dow Chemical, or General Motors. A common obligation to act in ethical and socially responsible ways is shared by all.

Areas of Social Responsibility

Listed in Table 20.3 are major areas of social responsibility that apply to business firms and other types of organizations. These include ecology and environmental quality, consumerism, community needs, governmental relations, corporate giving, minorities and disadvantaged persons, labor relations, stockholder relations, and economic activities. The table conveys a widening circle of corporate social responsibility that, for a business firm, includes employees, share-

FIGURE 20.5 An excerpt from a Johnson & Johnson recruiting brochure.

Our Credo

We believe our first responsibility is to the doctors, nurses and patients, to mothers and all others who use our products and services ■ In meeting their needs everything we do must be of high quality ■ We must constantly strive to reduce our costs in order to maintain reasonable prices ■ Customers' orders must be serviced promptly and accurately ■ Our suppliers and distributors must have an opportunity to make a fair profit ■

We are responsible to our employees, the men and women who work with us throughout the world ■ Everyone must be considered as an individual ■ We must respect their dignity and recognize their merit ■ They must have a sense of security in their jobs ■ Compensation must be fair and adequate, and working conditions clean, orderly and safe ■ Employees must feel free to make suggestions and complaints ■ There must be equal opportunity for employment, development and advancement for those qualified ■ We must provide competent management, and their actions must be just and ethical ■

We are responsible to the communities in which we live and work and to the world community as well ■ We must be good citizens—support good works and charities and bear our fair share of taxes ■ We must encourage civic improvements and better health and education ■ We must maintain in good order the property we are privileged to use, protecting the environment and natural resources ■

Our final responsibility is to our stockholders ■ Business must make a sound profit ■ We must experiment with new ideas ■ Research must be carried on, innovative programs developed and mistakes paid for ■ New equipment must be purchased, new facilities provided and new products launched ■ Reserves must be created to provide for adverse times ■ When we operate according to these principles, the stockholders should realize a fair return ■

Wherever You Start, You Can Make A Difference

Early responsibility, diversity, and growth characterize the array of functional career opportunities at Johnson & Johnson. Some of our professionals, shown here, discuss their careers later in this brochure.

Johnson & Johnson is the largest and most diversified health care products company in the world. We rank among the top 100 of the Fortune 500 U.S. industrial corporations, with sales of about $5 billion. Our products range from the well-known BAND-AID Brand Adhesive Bandage to the most advanced medical diagnostic imaging equipment.

We are a highly decentralized family of 150 companies—each with responsibility for charting its own course for the future. When you work for a Johnson & Johnson

company—whether in marketing, sales, engineering, finance, research, or another function—you're part of a relatively small, highly autonomous organization, rich with the vast resources of Johnson & Johnson. That makes you a vital contributor from the beginning. And that's the Johnson & Johnson difference.

We can offer you a unique opportunity to play an important part in an important company—and in an atmosphere in which bright, talented people can make a difference wherever they start.

Table 20.3 Possible Areas of Corporate Social Responsibility

Ecology and Environmental Quality
Cleanup of existing pollution
Design of processes to prevent pollution
Aesthetic improvements
Noise control
Dispersion of industry
Control of land use
Required recycling

Consumerism
Truth in lending, in advertising, and in all business activities
Product warranty and service
Control of harmful products

Community Needs
Use of business expertise and community problems
Reduction of business's role in community power activities
Aid with health-care facilities
Aid with urban renewal

Governmental Relations
Restrictions on lobbying
Control of business political action
Extensive new regulation of business
Restrictions on international operations

Business Giving
Financial support for artistic activities
Gifts to education
Financial support for assorted charities

Minorities and Disadvantaged Persons
Training of hard-core unemployed

Minorities and Disadvantaged Persons
Equal employment opportunity and quotas for minority employment
Operation of programs for alcoholics and drug addicts
Employment of persons with prison records
Building of plants and offices in minority areas
Purchasing from minority businesses
Retraining of workers displaced by technology

Labor Relations
Improvement of occupational health and safety
Prohibition of "export of jobs" through operations in nations with low labor costs
Provision of day-care centers for children of working mothers
Expansion of employee rights
Control of pensions, especially vesting of pension rights
Impatience with authoritarian structures; demand for participation

Stockholder Relations
Opening of boards of directors to public members representing various interest groups
Prohibition of operations in nations with "racist" or "colonial" governments
Improvement of financial disclosure
Disclosure of activities affecting the environment and social issues

Economic Activities
Control of conglomerates
Breakup of giant industry
Restriction of patent use

Source: From *Business and Society: Environment and Responsibility,* Third Edition, by Keith Davis and Robert L. Blomstrom, Copyright © 1975 Keith Davis and Robert L. Blomstrom. Used with the permission of the McGraw-Hill Book Company.

holders, actual and potential customers, and eventually the general citizenry, or public at large. The Johnson & Johnson credo presented in Figure 20.5 is consistent with this viewpoint.

While your attention is focused on these many areas of social responsibility, two specific points must be considered: the relationship between social responsibility and business profit and social responsibility and managerial ethics.

Social Responsibility and Business Profit

"Business giving," or corporate philanthropy in the public service, falls within the arena of social responsibility. What is your reaction to the following case?[19]

> From October 1 to November 30, 1982, the American Express Company donated to the Atlanta Arts Alliance the following amounts based on con-

sumer usage of Amex services in 15 surrounding counties.

- 5¢ for each time an Amex charge card was used or traveler's check purchased.
- $2 for each new charge card issued.
- $5 for each time travel arrangements in an amount exceeding $500 were booked by Amex travel services.

Most typically you hear the bad side of corporate social responsibility. That is, you hear about the dumping of dangerous industrial waste, marketing of unsafe products, and overpricing. It is easy to develop the impression that the quest for profits is incompatible with public service and social responsibility. But there is no reason why profits and social responsibility can't go hand in hand. The Amex case shows how a company can benefit from socially responsible acts, at the same time that the public interest is

NEWSLINE 20.1

MANY WORKERS OPPOSE EMPLOYERS' PRESSURES TO GIVE TO CHARITIES

Terri Ware got the message from her boss: Give to the United Way, or else.

The part-time bank teller refused to give, so her boss fired her. "I've had 100 percent participation from my employees for years," says Richard Deckerhoff, the president of First Federal Savings & Loan in Cumberland, Md., "and I'll be damned if one person is going to come along and change that." He offered her the job back only after the firing received publicity.

Many companies still exert strong, though subtle, pressure in support of the United Way. Many workers at Chase Manhattan Bank, for instance, fill out their contribution cards in front of a supervisor, who often reads the donation amounts in the employes's presence. Office workers at American Telephone & Telegraph Co. get suggested contribution levels, and their bosses are rewarded if those levels are reached. A middle manager at Chicago & North Western Transportation Co. feels pressure from her bosses above to raise money from the workers below.

The United Way says it discourages coercion, but it leaves on-the-job solicitation to the companies and acknowledges that it doesn't have any control over how the money is raised. "We're aware that the problem exists," a United Way spokesman says, "but there's nothing we can really do about coercion beyond opposing it." The agency also puts out a memo to companies about coercion, though it doesn't suggest specific ways to prevent it.

Source: David J. Blum, "Donor's Backlash: Many Workers Oppose Employers' Pressures to Give to Charities," *Wall Street Journal* (January 12, 1982), p. 1. Reprinted by permission of the *Wall Street Journal.* Copyright © 1982 Dow Jones & Company, Inc. All rights reserved.

served. The company used charitable giving as a marketing tool; it tied a creative marketing program to a local community need for outside assistance to the arts. Surely, other innovative programs targeted at any of the areas of responsibility identified in Table 20.3 can offer similar benefits to organizations and society. Profit and social responsibility *can* go hand in hand.

Social Responsibility and Managerial Ethics

It may be easy for managers to get so wrapped up in their organization's pursuit of a social cause that personal ethics become compromised in the process. *Newsline 20.1* points out how this might happen even in the context of such praiseworthy programs as United Way campaigns. A recent survey done for the United Way, in fact, found that 15 percent of respondents felt they had been coerced into giving at work. As the director of the National Committee for Responsive Philanthropy, a watchdog group, comments: "Companies can apply the pressure more than anyone, since they have power over your job and future.[20] It hardly makes sense for corporate social responsibility to be pursued at the expense of responsible and ethical action toward employees. Somewhere in between such conflicting forces, good managers will make the difference.

Levels of Social Responsibility

Organizations respond to their external social obligations with varying degrees of commitment.

Table 20.4 Examples of a Three-Stage Scheme for Classifying Corporate Behavior

Dimension of Behavior	Stage One: Social Obligation	Stage Two: Social Responsibility	Stage Three: Social Responsiveness
Response to social pressures	Maintains low public profile, but if attacked, uses PR methods to upgrade its public image; denies any deficiencies; blames public dissatisfaction on ignorance or failure to understand corporate functions; discloses information only where legally required	Accepts responsibility for solving current problems; will admit deficiencies in former practices and attempt to persuade public that its current practices meet social norms; attitude toward critics conciliatory; freer information disclosures than state one	Willingly discusses activities with outside groups; makes information freely available to public; accepts formal and informal inputs from outside groups in decision making; is willing to be publicly evaluated for its various activities
Philanthropy	Contributes only when direct benefit to it clearly shown; otherwise, views contributions as responsibility of individual employees	Contributes to noncontroversial and established causes; matches employee contributions	Activities of state two, *plus* support and contributions to new, controversial groups whose needs it sees as unfulfilled and increasingly important

Source: Excerpted from S. Prakash Sethi, "A Conceptual Framework for Environmental Analysis of Social Issues and Evaluation of Business Response Patterns," *Academy of Management Review*, Vol. 4 (January 1979), p. 68. Used by permission.

Three levels or stages of socially responsible corporate behavior can be identified.[21]

1. *Social obligation* Corporate behavior at this level conforms only to legal requirements and competitive market pressures.
2. *Social responsibility* Corporate behavior at this level is congruent with prevailing norms, values, and expectations of society.
3. *Social responsiveness* Corporate behavior at this level takes preventive action to avoid adverse social impacts from company activities and even anticipates or takes the lead in future movement beyond current expectations.

Implied in this framework is a desirable progression of corporate behavior from social obligation on one extreme to social responsiveness at the other. Table 20.4 elaborates on the distinctions among these levels of social responsibility using examples relating to external social pressures and philanthropic giving.

Arguments "Against" and "For" Social Responsibility

Throughout our discussion so far runs an underlying theme that businesses and other organizations *should* act in a socially responsive fashion.

There are really two sides to this argument. Milton Friedman, widely recognized advocate of classic free-market economics, argues against social responsibility. He contends that "few trends could so thoroughly undermine the very foundations of our free society as the acceptance by corporate officials of a social responsibility other than to make as much money for their stockholders as possible." Paul Samuelson, another distinguished economist, disagrees. He states that "a large corporation these days not only may engage in social responsibility, it had damn well better try to do so."[22] To help you develop a truly informed perspective, the cases against and for corporate social responsibility are now summarized.[23]

The Case "Against" Corporate Social Responsibility

Major arguments against the assumption of social responsibility by business include

- *Loss of profit maximization* Diverting resources to social-responsibility programs undermines the principles of a competitive marketplace and deprives stockholders of economic gain.
- *Cost* Social obligations can become costly for firms, with the result that some may be driven

from business and others forgo attractive investments.

- *Lack of skills*   Many businesses lack the necessary personnel skills to work successfully with social issues.

- *Dilution of purpose*   Pursuit of social goals may dilute the economic productivity of business; society may suffer as both economic and social goals are poorly accomplished.

- *Too much power*   Business already has enough power as a social institution; there is no need to allow it to develop even greater social influence.

- *Lack of accountability*   Business has no direct line of accountability to the people; thus, it is unwise to give it further discretion to act where it cannot be held accountable for outcomes.

- *Lack of broad support*   Society is divided in its position on business social involvement; actions in face of such divided support are predisposed to fail.

The Case "For"
Corporate Social Responsibility

Major arguments supporting the assumption of social responsibility by business include

- *Public expectations*   Public opinion in support of business social involvement runs deep; productivity goals are expected to co-exist with quality-of-life goals.

- *Long-run viability*   If business fails to act, other groups will eventually step in to assume the responsibilities and the power that goes with them.

- *Public image*   Socially responsible behaviors improve the public image of business.

- *Better environment*   To the extent business can improve the environment, the environment will be more conducive to future business prosperity.

- *Avoidance of government regulation*   Government regulation of business is costly and restrictive; the more socially responsible business is, the less government regulation can be expected.

- *Balance of responsibility and power*   Because business has so much social power, its sense of social responsibility should be equally large.

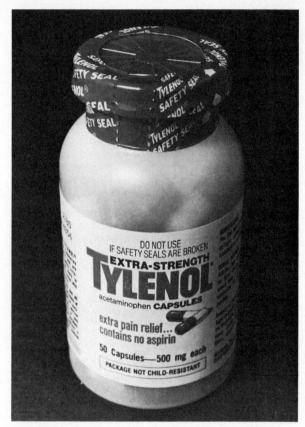

One result of the criminal contamination of Tylenol capsules with cyanide is the increased availability of medicines in safety-sealed packages.

- *Let business try*   Other institutions have failed in handling many social problems; it makes sense to let business try to solve them.

- *Business has the resources*   There is a pool of expertise and capital in business that can be used in social service; it is logical to let it try.

- *Problems can become profits*   If the innovative capability of business can be applied to social problems, many might be handled profitably in a traditional business sense.

- *Prevention is better than curing*   Any delays in addressing the social problems of today may magnify problems in the future.

- *Stockholder interests*   In almost all the prior respects, businesses can prosper and benefit from an improved environment; socially responsive behavior is in the best long-run interest of the shareholder.

Keith Davis is a management theorist who has thought seriously about this debate.[24] He concludes that because business has already assumed some social responsibility, the only legitimate question to ask is, "Will business assume a much more significant role, or will it not?" Although Davis feels the public at large must eventually answer this question, the evidence is that socially responsible behavior is a growing public expectation of business. It seems reasonable, therefore, to conclude that businesses and other types of organizations can and should integrate expanded social responsibility into their activities and values. These final comments by Davis sum it up best.

> Society wants business as well as all other major institutions to assume significant social responsibility. Social responsibility has become the hallmark of a mature, global civilization. . . . The business which vacillates or chooses not to enter the arena of social responsibility may find that it gradually will sink into customer and public disfavor.

GOVERNMENT REGULATION OF BUSINESS

One argument in favor of corporate social responsibility is to avoid costly and restrictive government regulations. If businesses don't act responsibly on their own, the argument goes, government will step in and attempt to regulate the desired behavior. This is but one example of the many ways government regulations constrain and impact the practice of management. This fact led C. L. Brown, chairman of the board of the American Telephone & Telegraph Company (AT&T), to send a special letter to all AT&T shareholders. Excerpts from that letter follow.[25]

Dear Share Owner:

This special message is to alert you to the effort now under way in the House of Representatives to pass legislation that in our view poses a very serious threat to your investment as well as to the security of Bell System employees and the cost of telephone service in this country.

Specifically, I am urging you to write or call your Congressman to say in no uncertain terms that H.R. 5158, a bill introduced by Rep. Timothy Wirth, should be rejected. . . .

From time to time in the past, AT&T share owners who felt that their company was being misused by government regulations or proposed legislation have urged us to mount a letter-writing campaign.

We have always been reluctant to do that. But we are now convinced that the stakes are too high, the risks too great and the time too short for such reluctance on our part.

Beyond that, I believe I would be neglecting my personal responsibilities to share owners if I failed to tell you how contrary to your interests I believe this legislation to be. . . .

In short, the time has come for the owners of this business to make their concerns heard among all the other voices being listened to in Congress. Your investment, your savings are at stake. It is your company, your money. I urge you to let your Congressman know it.

Sincerely
C. L. Brown
C. L. Brown
Chairman of the Board

The tone of C. L. Brown's letter conveys dissatisfaction with potential Congressional legislation. Basically, he is trying to mobilize AT&T shareholders to take political action to protect what he feels is the company's best interest. That action is to convince legislators *not* to support H.R. 5158.

The Complex Legal Environment

Government regulations are an important influence on all organizations. The legal environment of business, in particular, is most complex. Although many laws and regulations are certainly beneficial, business executives often complain that others are overly burdensome. *Newsline 20.2* is but one example. Specific business concerns are that regulations increase costs by creating the need for increased paperwork and staff to maintain compliance, and that the paperwork consumes so much managerial time that attention is diverted from more important productivity concerns.

Table 20.5 highlights a few of the laws regulating business activity that were passed between 1960 and 1975. This is the way things were in 1975. In reality, the legal environment is constantly changing, and managers must always re-

NEWSLINE 20.2

MANY BUSINESSES BLAME GOVERNMENTAL POLICIES FOR PRODUCTIVITY LAG

AKRON, Ohio—Goodyear Tire & Rubber Co. produces things made of rubber. But like many companies, it has developed a big sideline—paper.

One recent week, the company's computer center cranked out 345,000 pages of jargon-filled paper, weighing 3200 pounds—all to meet one new regulation of the Occupational Safety and Health Administration. The regulation required that employees have access to data on exposure to chemicals used in their plants. That huge stack of reports was divided into 70 smaller piles for distribution to Goodyear manufacturing facilities.

Goodyear figures that complying with regulations of six of the more demanding federal agencies cost $35.5 million last year and that just filling out the required reports chewed up 34 employee-years. A study by the Business Roundtable, a corporate executives' group, of compliance costs for 48 major companies for 1977 shows that they laid out $2.6 billion over and above what good corporate citizens normally would have spent on environmental protection, employee health and safety, and other matters if the six government agencies hadn't intervened. Some economists projected from those figures that the extra cost for all businesses exceeded $100 billion.

Source: Excerpted from Ralph E. Winter, "Paper Weight: Many Businesses Blame Government Policies for Productivity Lag," *Wall Street Journal* (October 28, 1980), p. 1. Reprinted by permission of the *Wall Street Journal.* Copyright © 1980 Dow Jones & Comapny, Inc. All rights reserved.

main informed about new and pending laws as well. Listed here are four of the cases with fundamental business issues that went before the Supreme Court in its 1982 term.[26]

- Guardians Association vs. Civil Service Commission
  Issue Do the civil-rights laws allow unintentional discrimination against blacks or other minorities?

- White vs. Massachusetts Council of Construction Employers
  Issue May a city force its contractors to hire local residents?

- Weyerhaeuser Co. vs. Lyman Lamb
  Issue When does it become illegal price fixing for a company to copy its competitor's pricing moves?

- Bowsher vs. Merck & Co.

Issue What cost and pricing records can federal auditors get from government contractors?

Among the recent trends in goverment legislation is a growing interest in quality-of-life issues. Another look at Table 20.5, in fact, reveals several themes we have already discussed as key social-responsibility areas—water pollution, air pollution, consumer protection, and noise control, among others. When we hear or read about such regulations in the news, the report is usually negative. That is, we either hear business complaints about the costs of compliance with the laws, or we hear public outcries protesting spectacular business violations of the laws. Underneath it all, though, legislation is accomplishing some good in all areas of corporate social responsibility. As a reminder of this positive side of government regulation, consider these brief

Table 20.5 Some Significant Legislation Regulating Business, 1960–1975

Civil Rights Act of 1960	Radiation Control for Health and Safety Act of 1968
Federal Hazardous Substances Labeling Act of 1960	Cigarette Smoking Act of 1969
Fair Labor Standards Amendments of 1961, 1966, and 1974	Child Protection and Toy Safety Act of 1969
Federal Water Pollution Control Act Amendments of 1961	Federal Coal Mine Health and Safety Act of 1969
Oil Pollution Act of 1961 and Amendments of 1973	Natural Environmental Policy Act of 1969
Food and Agriculture Act of 1962	Tax Reform Act of 1969
Air Pollution Control Act of 1962	Bank Holding Act Amendments of 1970
Antitrust Civil Process Act of 1962	Bank Records and Foreign Transactions Act of 1970
Drug Amendments of 1962	Economic Stabilization Act of 1970 and Amendments of 1971 and 1973
Clean Air Act of 1963 and Amendments of 1966 and 1970	Environmental Quality Improvement Act of 1970
Equal Pay Act of 1963	Fair Credit Reporting Act of 1970
Civil Rights Act of 1963	Investment Company Amendments of 1969
Food Stamp Act of 1964	Noise Pollution and Abatement Act of 1970
Automotive Products Trade Act of 1965	Occupational Safety and Health Act of 1970
Federal Cigarette Labeling and Advertising Act of 1965	Securities Investor Protection Act of 1970
Water Quality Act of 1965	Water and Environmental Quality Improvement Act of 1970
Clean Water Restoration Act of 1966	Export Administration Finance Act of 1971
Fair Packaging and Labeling Act of 1966	Consumer Product Safety Act of 1972
Federal Coal Mine Safety Act Amendments of 1966	Equal Employment Opportunity Act of 1972
Financial Institutions Supervisory Act of 1966	Federal Environment Pesticide Control Act of 1972
Oil Pollution of the Sea Act of 1966	Noise Control Act of 1972
Age Discrimination in Employment Act of 1967	Agriculture and Consumers Protection Act of 1973
Air Quality Act of 1967	Emergency Petroleum Allocation Act of 1973
Agricultural Fair Practices Act of 1968	Highway Safety Act of 1973
Consumer Credit Protectors Act of 1968	Water Resources Development Act of 1974
Natural Gas Pipeline Safety Act of 1968	

Source: From Albert Seelye, "Societal Change and Business-Government Relationships," *MSU Business Topics* (Autumn 1975), pp. 5–13. Reprinted by permission of the publisher, Division of Research, Graduate School of Business Administration, Michigan State University.

examples of the quality-of-life protection currently held by citizens of the United States.[27]

1. *Occupational and public safety* Government plays an active role in seeking to make the workplace and the work environment safe and healthy for the worker. The passage of the Occupational Safety and Health Act (OSHA) in 1970 put business clearly on notice that the government was concerned with employee safety. Concerns for public safety have resulted in legislation dealing with such issues as children's toys, flammable fabrics, public smoking, packaging of poisonous products, safe drinking water, and highway speed limits.

2. *Pollution protection* The major environmental pollution acts, which began with the Air Pollution Control Act in 1962, are intended to eliminate pollution of the air, water, and land in the United States. These regulations have led to an increased awareness by the business community that the Environmental Protection Agency (EPA) is serious about ending useless and careless pollution of the environment. Many companies have taken steps, in cooperation with governmental agencies, to reduce pollution and clean up their operations.

3. *Fair labor practices* Legislation and regulations that prohibit discrimination in labor prac-

tices by business have been passed by Congress. These regulations were designed to reduce barriers to employment based on race, sex, age, national origin, and marital status.

4. *Consumer protection*   The rise in consumerism has led to government regulation of business relationships with customers. One such regulation is the Consumer Credit Protection Act of 1969, which requires that consumers be fully informed about the rates they are paying for borrowed money. Another is the Consumer Product Safety Act of 1972—a broad-based law that gives the government authority to examine, and to force a business to withdraw from sale, any product that it feels is hazardous to the consumer. An example of the application of this regulation was the required withdrawal of all hairdryers with asbestos insulation after it was determined that lab animals exposed to asbestos had developed cancer.

Government Agencies as Regulators

It may not be too farfetched to say that behind every piece of legislation is a government agency charged with the responsibility of monitoring and ensuring compliance to its mandates. You know these agencies best by their acronyms; FAA (Federal Aviation Administration), EPA (Environmental Protection Agency), OHSA (Occupational Health and Safety Administration), and FDA (Food and Drug Administration) are a few examples. Figure 20.6 shows that all such agencies stand at the interface between the public interest, as reflected in laws and legislation, and the activities of organizations and their members. The agencies are staffed and supported from the federal budget to make sure that the public interest is best served.

Take one case in point. When you fly, you want to be secure in knowing that you are flying in a safe aircraft and according to safe procedures. The FAA was established to regulate the air-traffic industry with just this goal in mind. Backed by a myriad of legislation, the FAA works daily in the public interest. *Newsline 20.3* is a good example of the way all of us hope and expect such agencies to work in our behalf.

As with the underlying legislation itself, the activities of government agencies are subject to

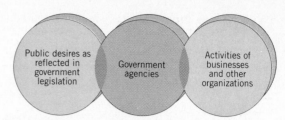

FIGURE 20.6 The government agency at the interface.

criticism. Public outcries and political slogans to "dismantle the bureaucracy" and/or "deregulate business" reflect concerns that specific agencies and their supportive legislation are not functional. Many times, it is the agency's interpretation of a law and manner of seeking compliance that is criticized, not the law itself. Businesses sometimes feel that regulating agencies are unclear in telling them how to comply with the laws, require unnecessary paperwork to document compliance, and/or are inconsistent in enforcing the laws.

There will always be conflict in a relationship where one party oversees the activities of another. In the case of business-government relationships such "give-and-take" is a part of day-to-day routine. Just as businesses must be sincere in their social responsibility, government agencies should be sincere in applying laws fairly and

FIGURE 20.7 The mutual exchange of influence between government and business.

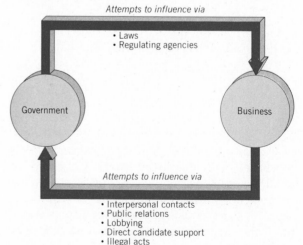

Attempts to influence via

• Laws
• Regulating agencies

Government

Business

Attempts to influence via

• Interpersonal contacts
• Public relations
• Lobbying
• Direct candidate support
• Illegal acts

NEWSLINE 20.3

FAA IS MAKING STIFF DEMANDS ON BOEING TO PROVE THE SAFETY OF ITS NEW 767 JETLINER

SEATTLE—With the debut of Boeing Co.'s new 767 imminent, the Federal Aviation Administration is winding up its most rigorous job of clearing a jetliner for takeoff.

Prodded by critics to get tougher with plane makers, the FAA has made stiff demands for proof of the safety of this next-generation airliner. The agency has required unusual tests of the plane's resistance to stress and its safeguards. It has asked for mountains of data, including some 157 major documents that, taken together, are 35 feet thick. And it has imposed many more design requirements than those on earlier planes.

The licensing effort is "the most demanding in FAA history," says Charles Foster, the director of the agency's Seattle office. Boeing officials agree. "The FAA has been a lot more stringent and is asking for a lot more data than in past certifications," says Douglas Clifford, a Boeing chief engineer. Complete compliance, he adds, is "somewhat exasperating." And sometimes Boeing has balked at the agency's demands.

Source: Excerpted from Albert R. Karr, "FAA is Making Stiff Demands on Boeing to Prove the Safety of Its New 767 Jetliner," *Wall Street Journal* (July 23, 1982), p. 30. Reprinted by permission of the *Wall Street Journal.* Copyright © 1982 Dow Jones & Company, Inc. All rights reserved.

with an understanding of the operating problems they may pose to the organizations they affect.

Political Action by Businesses

Government directly influences business through both laws and the regulating efforts of agencies such as the EPA and FAA. But, as the letter to shareholders from AT&T's C. L. Brown suggests, the line of influence between government and business is not a one-way arrow. Just as government takes a variety of actions to influence organizations, organizations can and do take a variety of actions to influence government.

Figure 20.7 lists five ways in which representatives of businesses attempt to influence government. Such influence takes place[28]

1. *Through interpersonal contacts* Business executives can persuade government officials or politicians to support probusiness and oppose antibusiness legislation; this requires that executives get to know important people in government and develop positive interpersonal relationships with them.

2. *Through public-relations (PR) campaigns* Businesses can build positive images among the general public that lead to public support for them on legislative matters. Many firms are aggressive in their PR efforts. Note how frequently, for example, you see Mobil explaining through television or magazine ads how hard the company works for the social good. Presumably, a better-informed public will pass this feeling along to their elected officials.

3. *Through lobbying* Businesses can hire professional staff or consultants to communicate their preferences directly to legislators. These *lobbyists* are always active in trying to convince congressional representatives and senators to vote probusiness in new legislation, modify existing legislation in business's favor, and/or to sponsor

supportive legislation. The "deregulation" theme popular in the early years of the Reagan administration was backed by considerable lobbying for reduced power of "watchdog" government agencies.

4. *Through direct candidate support* Business executives can endorse preferred candidates running for public office; they may also run for public office themselves or accept political appointments when offered by elected officials. A recent trend is the creation of **political action committees,** or PACs, which are organized to assist in the election of candidates who favor the interests of the organizers. Under the law, PACs are allowed to collect money and donate it to the election campaigns of favored candidates. PACs have grown in popularity in the 1980s, and are used not only by businesses but by trade associations and labor unions as well. Business executives feel that PACs increase their political influence.

5. *Through illegal acts* Business representatives can gain special favors from corrupt officials who accept bribes or illicit financial campaign contributions and/or who succumb to threats of blackmail. The U.S. Corrupt Practices Act prohibits both business and organized labor from making donations to political campaigns from corporate or union funds. Still, violations do occur. While we must acknowledge that illegal acts exist, they are certainly contrary to the high standards of ethical practice and social responsibility that managers should follow.

Living with Regulations as a Manager

The constraints established by laws, regulations, and their interpretations by representatives of government agencies will result in both social advantages and disadvantages. The public will benefit when irresponsible or naive firms are led to act in more acceptable ways. The public will suffer when the governing laws and regulating agencies become overly burdensome and too costly in their demands on legitimate business practices.

In the middle of these multiple and sometimes conflicting forces, as usual, stands the manager. The arena of regulated action will continue to test a manager's ethics and sense of social responsibility. But, as we have already said, there is no reason that high ethical standards and social responsibility need be inconsistent with the manager's quest for productivity. The argument holds true for managers in any organizational setting, public or private, small or large, located in the United States or anywhere else in the world.

ETHICS, SOCIAL RESPONSIBILITY, AND THE MANAGER'S CHALLENGE

Throughout this book we have focused on the manager's challenge as depicted, with one new modification, in Figure 20.8. That modification now makes the manager's performance objective subject to qualification by the two themes of the present chapter—high ethical standards and social responsibility. Although it has been fairly easy to talk about these themes, and even though it may be easy to gain agreement as to their positive values, it can be difficult for managers to reconcile the many conflicting viewpoints they may bring to an actual decision situation.

Emerging Managerial Values

Values are the underlying beliefs and attitudes that help determine individual behavior. Trends in the evolution of managerial values over time suggest that managerial decisions in general will increasingly reflect quality-of-life as well as performance values. Three historical phases in the evolution of managerial values are[29]

Phase I Profit-maximizing managers The profit motive was viewed as the predominate managerial focus in the late nineteenth and early twentieth centuries. Concerns for social welfare in the form of working conditions, preservation of the environment, and consumer protection were secondary. The capitalist business system was guided by beliefs in profit maximization and an emphasis on economic growth. The good manager was one who worked hard and contributed to profit maximization and the maintenance of economic growth.

Phase II Trusteeship managers Fundamental changes in business institutions and society during the 1920s and 1930s ushered in an era of

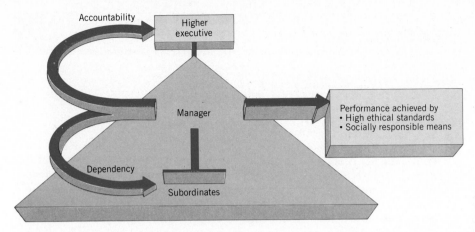

FIGURE 20.8 Ethics, social responsibility, and the manager's challenge.

trusteeship management with a broadened sense of managerial responsibility. Managers became agents of stakeholders, including stockholders, employees, customers, suppliers, and the local community. The task of trusteeship was multiple in focus. Profit maximization was asked to find its way along with such external interests as those represented by labor unions and government regulations.

Phase III "Quality-of-life" managers The affluent society of the 1950s allowed attention to shift further away from the production of goods and services, and toward consideration of the social impact of these goods and services . . . and the organizations producing them. Poverty, deteriorating cities, air and water pollution, defacement of the landscape, and disregard for consumers reflected an emerging set of priorities that today call on managers not only to achieve economic success, but also to solve basic social problems.

This profile of contemporary management values as "quality-of-life" oriented may be somewhat idealistic, but it does reflect an increasing willingness of managers to subject their decisions and actions to the scrutiny of ethical and social as well as performance criteria. Once again, the manager stands on the boundary as *the* person who must accommodate each of these criteria in his or her decisions and actions. The argument is not that the decisions are getting any easier, but that managers are becoming more willing to increase the weight given to ethical and social responsibility considerations.

Social Responsibility and the Management Functions

Ethical and social challenges of the types we have been discussing cut across each of the management functions. To help you to put this point into a final managerial perspective, the essence of these implications is briefly highlighted here.

Planning

Planning identifies desired goals and the actions required to accomplish them. *Newsline 20.4* shows that some firms are investing in specialized staffs of *issues managers* to help accomplish planning in an increasingly complex social environment. The desired benefit from such investments is to anticipate future problems or opportunities with sufficient lead time that actions may be taken in the organization's, as well as society's, best advantage. Managers can and should incorporate an awareness of relevant social issues into their planning activities.

Organizing

Organizing mobilizes resources to accomplish the actions and directions made explicit through plans. Top managers must monitor the environment, establish policies, and commit resources in ways that contribute to socially responsible behaviors. Staff managers can assist top managers to fulfill the environmental-scanning and policy-formulation roles. Operating managers ultimately implement policies and apply resources

NEWSLINE 20.4

FIRMS HIRING NEW TYPE OF MANAGER TO STUDY ISSUES, EMERGING TROUBLES

In the late 1970s, Arco and a few other large oil, banking, and insurance concerns set up special trend-spotting departments, assigning them a task previously done somewhat haphazardly by top executives, government-relations people, planners, and public-relations staffs. "They were fed up with unpleasant surprises," says Richard Drobnick of the University of Southern California business school. Today about 70 companies have issues managers.

Some corporations emphasize legislative and governmental issues. Others, like Northwestern National Bank in Minneapolis, use issues managers to spot emerging concerns for their community and philanthropic programs.

Arco does both. Its system is organized around five clusters of issues: resources, environments, corporate and planning (including tax, antitrust, and labor matters), manufacturing processes, and Arco's participation in its many trade associations. Managers of the five clusters earn from $48,000 to $77,000 a year.

Source: Excerpted from Earl C. Gottschalk, Jr., "Firms Hiring New Type of Managers to Study Issues, Emerging Troubles," *Wall Street Journal* (June 10, 1982), p. 21. Reprinted by permission of the *Wall Street Journal.* Copyright © Dow Jones & Company, Inc. All rights reserved.

responsibly and in the organization's behalf. Finally, an organization's staffing practices can result in hiring people consistent with the organization's social policies and goals.

Leading

The leadership role is as important to social responsibility as it is to any other objective of organizational importance. Top management assumes special importance because of its power to set the operating tone and climate for the organization as a whole. Socially responsive top managers will be broadminded, socially aware, and sensitive to the environment in the model they offer subordinates. Managers at all levels serve as role models for their subordinates and peers. To the extent that managers lead through actions exemplifying high ethical and social standards, other persons in the organization are likely to reflect similar standards of behavior in their conduct. This is a good illustration of the power of leadership by example.

Controlling

Effective control should always result in information feedback that helps managers make decisions that maintain or even enhance the organization's social contributions. Irresponsible personnel should be identified at performance-appraisal time and be either removed from the situation or counseled. Responsible personnel, by contrast, should be singled out for praise, recognition, and even formal reward.

A **social audit** is a systematic assessment and reporting of an organization's resource and action commitments, and performance accomplishments in areas of social responsibility.[30] You might think of social audits as attempts to assess the social performance of organizations, much as financial audits assess their performance in an economic sense. They offer the potential benefits of improved internal resource allocations, more complete evaluations of corporate social accomplishments, and documentation of these accomplishments for public-relations efforts. But they also suffer from the difficulties of accurately measuring the effectiveness of social programs.

Social auditing will most likely increase in popularity and sophistication in the future. A natural counterpart to business's growing sense of corporate social responsibility is the corresponding desire for a means of measuring costs and documenting results. One company's experience with social auditing follows.[31]

> The board of directors determined that a social responsibility committee should be appointed by the board chairman to make a social audit for the firm. The committee consisted of two company officers and one public member. It found very few audit guidelines and had to develop its own program with the counsel of persons both inside and outside the company. Early in the program the committee recognized that the audit needed to be more comprehensive than anticipated and that social effects of company operations were more extensive then expected.
>
> Eventually six areas for audit were developed as follows: social importance of regular activities, consumerism, community service, environment, equal employment, and fixing responsibility within the firm for social performance. Audit programs were developed for each area, and both qualitative and quantitative data were sought to measure results. The entire process helped management translate vague ideas about social performance into hard realities.

SUMMARY

This chapter began with an ethical dilemma that emerged during a computer simulation game at the Harvard Business School. It went on to consider a wide variety of issues, examples, and challenges faced by managers as they strive to meet performance expectations in a complex and demanding environment. Ultimately, our goal was to learn more about achieving productivity while maintaining high ethical standards and a sense of corporate social responsibility.

Ethical behavior by managers both meets legal obligations and conforms to guiding social principles of what is "right or wrong" or "good or bad." There is and probably always will be a lingering philosophical debate on ethics in all reaches of human behavior. Nevertheless, our definition helps to identify ethical dilemmas faced by managers and understand how the resolution of these dilemmas is influenced by a variety of personal, organizational, and environmental factors. Although no precise guidelines exist, managers appear increasingly allegiant to high ethical standards. The efforts of some to establish a universal code of managerial ethics is one illustration.

Organizations are also increasingly subject to social evaluation of their conduct. A socially responsible corporation, for example, acts in ways that serve public interests as well as economic interests of the firm. Social responsibility extends to all segments of society, including customers, employees, stockholders, and local communities. It is often regulated in whole or part by government agencies acting under mandates granted by legislation. All organizations operate under the umbrella of a complex legal environment that causes them to complain at times about the burdens of regulation. Our review of government regulation also recognizes, though, that the public welfare is often well served through the legislation of social responsibility.

The resolution of ethical dilemmas and conflicting social responsibility in any decision situation will never be easy or clear-cut. Underneath it all, the personal value systems of managers will determine how well their decisions and actions satisfy performance, ethical, and social-responsibility criteria. These values, although observed to be evolving in a direction supportive of "quality-of-life" management, remain dynamic and individualized in the contemporary world.

THINKING THROUGH THE ISSUES

1. What was the central issue raised in the opening Harvard Business School case? Can you identify similar issues in your personal experiences? Give examples.

2. Define in your own words: ethics, morals, ethical behavior.

3. State three factors that may influence managers toward unethical practices.

4. What can managers do to promote high ethical standards for themselves? For subordinates?

5. Why aren't more unethical practices exposed in organizations? What should be done to correct this situation? Why?

6. What is the relationship between the ethics of managers and the social responsibility of organizations? Explain your answer.

7. Identify three major areas of corporate social responsibility. Explain how one can argue "against" social responsibility in these areas of corporate influence on society.

8. What do we mean by the "legal environment of business?" How does it impact corporate social responsibility?

9. Give four examples of how businesses seek to influence government. State whether or not you consider these practices legitimate, and why.

10. Describe the major differences one could expect to find between managers who reflect "profit-maximizing," "trusteeship," and "quality-of-life" values.

THE MANAGER'S VOCABULARY

Corporate social responsibility	Ethical managerial behavior	Managerial ethics	Social audit
Ethical behavior	Ethics	Political action committees (PACs)	Values
Ethical dilemma			

CAREER PERSPECTIVE: ARE BUSINESS ETHICS A JOKE?[32]

A survey of the ethical orientations of 131 business majors (93 MBA and 38 undergraduates) was conducted at a major mideastern university. The researcher reported, "The major finding . . . appears to seriously challenge the contention that today's business students are prepared or inclined to improve the climate for ethical decision making in the firms they join." Some findings from the survey include

■ Sixty-five percent of the students perceived the current business climate as essentially unethical.

■ Forty-seven percent perceived a negative ethical trend in the business climate.

■ Eighty-eight percent expected to encounter pressures to compromise personal ethics in future jobs.

■ Fifty percent felt that they would have no alternative but to compromise their ethics in such circumstances.

The researcher offered the following quotes to support a claim that the "vast majority of these students . . . seemed all too willing to compromise their code of ethics."

■ "I'll be as unethical as the next guy. Why should I let someone get ahead of me by doing unethical things?"

- "I'm aggressive and seek success, so I'll mold my ethical standards to that of the company in which I'm employed."
- "You've got to do what others do to get somewhere."
- "I'll play the game to achieve."
- "Almost all of us will compromise our ethics to resist failure."
- "I just want to fit in and find my place in business."
- "I'll go with the crowd and use unethical practices if they are generally in use."
- "I'll do as I'm told as long as I get paid."
- "If there is a need to be unethical, I will be so."

Questions

1. How do you perceive ethical standards in today's business environment?

2. Do you anticipate work situations that may challenge your personal ethics?

3. Are you willing, as most students in the preceding survey appear to be, to compromise your ethics to get ahead? Why or why not?

CASE APPLICATION: THE EXPENSE ACCOUNT[33]

Sam Swanson was in a predicament. Last week Sam went down to the branch plant in Baltimore. When he came back, he filled in his expense sheet and was about to hand it in when Bill Wilson and Jack Martin stopped by. The following conversation took place.

Bill: Come on, wrap it up. It's time for some coffee.

Jack: Sam, we've given you the honor of buying us coffee today.

Sam: Okay, fellows, I accept the honor—but wait until I add that 30 cents to my "swindle sheet" so that I can get paid for it.

Bill: How much are you charging the company for that Baltimore trip?

Sam: Wait, let's see—it comes out to a total of $142.

Jack: $142! My gosh, Sam, you've made some boner. Let's see what you have there.

Sam (handing sheet to Jack): What should it be?

I thought I put everything down.

Bill: Seven of us have been going to Baltimore for over three years now, and none of us has ever been lower than $150—and most of the time, it's above $160.

Jack: To start off with, Sam, you have only $2.75 for limousine to the airport. Most of us put down the taxicab rate of $5.50. You don't have any transportation back from the airport—what about that? Those two items alone add up to $11.00. That'll make your total $150.25.

Sam: Betty picked me up at the airport. The regulations on the back say I can't charge for that.

Bill: She had to buy gas, and there's wear and tear on the car.

Jack: Didn't you buy someone lunch or dinner while you were there? Your expense account will stand one or two of those.

Sam: Actually, fellows, everyone was buying

me lunch or dinner. I didn't get much of a chance to spend money.

Bill: Gosh, Sam, do something with that expense account—don't turn in $142. That'll make the rest of us look pretty bad. Bring it up to $150 anyway, or we'll be in for a rough time.

Jack: I agree; fix it up, Sam. But first let's get that cup of coffee.

While drinking coffee, Jack and Bill explained their philosophy: While away from home on business you are really spending 24 hours a day on the job and only getting paid for 8 hours; therefore, the extra expenses are warranted. They also pointed out that there are some hidden costs to the individual—getting clothes cleaned, maintaining luggage, the cost of a babysitter so your spouse can leave the house while you are away, and other little items that add up.

When Sam came back from coffee, he reexamined his expenses. If he charged $5.50 taxi fare to and from the airport, he would be just above the $150 mark. But he really didn't spend this money, so it didn't seem right to put that on the expense sheet.

Sam was new with the company—three months. He was getting along very well with the other workers. He also recognized that if they did not like him, they could make his work rough—maybe get him into a spot where he couldn't do his job.

Questions

1. What should Sam do? (Choose only one response.)
   a. Charge $11.00 for cab fare to and from the airport, so that the total is $150.25.
   b. Charge cab fare from the airport (when his wife picked him up), making a total of $147.50.
   c. Charge limousine fare from the airport to make a total of $144.75.
   d. Make no change; hand in the expense account for $142.
   e. Ask his supervisor what he should do.
   f. Something else. (explain)

2. Why?

CLASS EXERCISE: RESPONDING TO ETHICAL PRESSURES[34]

1. Answer the following question by circling the appropriate response. Be as realistic as possible.

   The Setting   Your first full-time job after graduation.

   The Question   If confronted at work by pressures from the organization to engage in behavior you consider unethical, would you (choose only one of the alternatives):
   a. Change yourself to bring your ethics into line with those of the organization?
   b. Attempt to change the organization?
   c. Withdraw from the organization as a place of employment?
   d. Resist changing your personal ethical code while remaining employed by the organization?

2. Share your response with a neighbor and discuss your respective viewpoints.

3. Await further class discussion when the instructor will
   a. Poll the class for its responses.
   b. Share how students in another university answered the same question.
   c. Open the floor to general class discussion on the subject of ethical pressures in the work setting.

REFERENCES

[1] Thomas Moore, "Industrial Espionage at the Harvard B-School," *Fortune* (September 6, 1982), p. 70. © 1982 Time Inc. Courtesy of Fortune Magazine.

[2] Ibid.

[3] All definitions are from *Webster's New World Dictionary of the American Language,* Second College Edition, David B. Juralnik (ed.)(New York: World Publishing, 1972).

[4] For a good discussion of business ethics, see George K. Saul, "Business Ethics: Where Are We Going?" *Academy of Management Review,* Vol. 6 (April 1981), pp. 269–276.

[5] *Fortune* (August 1979), p. 42. © 1979 Time Inc. Courtesy of Fortune Magazine.

[6] The cases and subsequent discussion are reprinted by permission of the *Harvard Business Review.* Excerpt from "Is the Ethics of Business Changing?" by Steven N. Brenner and Earl A. Molander, *Harvard Business Review,* Vol. 55 (January-February 1977), p. 57. Copyright © 1977 by the President and Fellows of Harvard College; all rights reserved.

[7] Frank Cary, *Business Conduct Guidelines*, International Business Machines, publisher. Cited in Burt Scanlan and Bernard Keys, *Management and Organizational Behavior,* Second Edition (New York: Wiley, 1983), p. 597.

[8] William M. Carley, "Antitrust Chief Says CEOs Should Tape All Phone Calls to Each Other," *Wall Street Journal* (February 1983), p. 23.

[9] John A. Pearce, II, "Newcomer's Need for a Code of Business Ethics," *Collegiate Forum* (Fall 1978), p. 12.

[10] "Armor for Whistle Blowers," *Business Week* (July 6, 1981), pp. 97, 98.

[11] Adapted from James A. Waters, "Catch 20.5: Morality as an Organizational Phenomenon," *Organizational Dynamics,* Vol. 6 (Spring 1978), pp. 3–15.

[12] Harold L. Johnson, "Ethics and the Executive," *Business Horizons,* Vol. 24 (1981), pp. 53–59.

[13] All reported in Charles D. Pringle and Justin G. Longnecker, "The Ethics of MBO," *Academy of Management Review,* Vol. 7 (April 1982), p. 309.

[14] David B. Hilder, "Accountants' Code Calls Whistle-Blowing Inappropriate Unless the Law Requires It," *Wall Street Journal* (July 21, 1983), p. 6.

[15] Quoted in *Fortune* (November 29, 1982), p. 38.

[16] Elisabetta Di Cagno, "IBM: One Corporation's Contribution," *Hermes,* Vol. 8 (Winter 1982), p. 18. The discussion that immediately follows is also based on this article.

[17] Jeffrey A. Tannenbaum, "Paid Public-Service Leaves Buoy Workers, But Return to Old Jobs Can Be Wrenching," *Wall Street Journal* (May 6, 1981), p. 27.

[18] "Pushing Ahead: Heublein's Pact with Blacks," *Fortune* (April 19, 1982), p. 7; *Success* (February 1982), p. 37.

[19] "AmEx Shows the Way to Benefit from Corporate Giving," *Business Week* (October 18, 1982), pp. 44, 45.

[20] David J. Blum, "Donor's Backlash: Many Workers Oppose Employer's Pressures to Give to Charities," *Wall Street Journal* (January 12, 1982), p. 1.

[21] S. Prakash Sethi, "A Conceptual Framework for Environmental Analysis of Social Issues and Evaluation of Business Response Patterns," *Academy of Management Review,* Vol. 4 (January 1979), pp. 63–74.

[22] The Friedman quote is from Milton Friedman, *Capitalism and Freedom* (Chicago: University of Chicago Press, 1962); Samuelson quote is from Paul A. Samuelson, "Love that Corporation," *Mountain Bell Magazine* (Spring 1971). Both are cited by Keith Davis, "The Case For and Against Business Assumption of Social Responsibilities," *Academy of Management Journal* (June 1973, pp. 312–322.

[23] This discussion is developed from Keith Davis and Robert L. Blomstrom, *Business and Society: Responsibility,* Third Edition (New York: McGraw-Hill, 1975), pp. 23–36; Davis, op. cit.

[24] The quotes and substance of this section are drawn from Davis, op. cit., p. 322.

[25] Reprinted by permission of the American Telephone & Telegraph Company.

[26] *Business Week* (October 11, 1982), p. 34.

[27] Adapted from Lawrence J. Gitman and Carl McDaniel, Jr., *Business World* (New York: Wiley, 1983), p. 11. Used by permission.

[28] Adapted from Glueck, op. cit., pp. 108–110; Davis and Blomstrom, op. cit., pp. 207–213.

[29] Robert Hay and Ed Gray, "Social Responsibilities of Business Managers," *Academy of Management Journal,* Vol. 18 (March 1974), pp. 135–143.

[29] Robert Hay and Ed Gray, "Social Responsibilities of Business Managers," *Academy of Management Journal,* Vol. 18 (March 1974), pp. 135–143.

[30] See Raymond A. Bauer and Dan H. Fenn, Jr., "What is a Corporate Social Audit?" *Harvard Business Review,* Vol. 51 (January-February 1973), pp. 37–48.

[31] © 1973 by the Regents of the University of California. Reprinted from Barry Richman, "New Paths to Corporate Social Responsibility," *California Management Review,* Vol. 15 (Spring 1973), pp. 23, 24; by permission of the Regents.

[32] These data are reported by John A. Pearce II, "Newcomer's Need for a Code of Business Ethics," *Collegiate Forum* (Fall 1978), p. 12. Reprinted by permission of the *Collegiate Forum.* Copyright © 1978 Dow Jones & Company, Inc. All rights reserved.

[33] Rossall J. Johnson, "Conflict Avoidance through Acceptable Decision" (research project on decision making), *Human Relations,* Vol. 27, No. 1 (1974). Reproduced with the author's permission.

[34] Based on Pearce, op. cit.

Part 6
INTEGRATING CASES

LATINO GLASS, S.A.

Production superintendent Angel Ramos obviously was upset. Ramos had been with Latino since the company began its operations in his country 12 years ago. He had worked hard during these years and had been recognized for his efforts with numerous promotions. He had counted heavily on replacing Roy Webster as plant manager at Latino Glass when he heard that Webster was being promoted to president. Now he waited outside Webster's office, having just learned that an "outsider" was being brought in as the new plant manager. He was unaware that Webster himself was concerned about Ramos's predicament, and that he was discussing it with the company controller at that very moment.

Background

Latino Glass was founded as a joint venture in Latino, South America. The parent United States company, Stateside Glass Company, produced a wide variety of glass products for both domestic and foreign markets. Latino Glass, unlike most glass plants, which specialize in a sin-

gle product, produced two products. Therefore, managers could acquire experience in two product areas simultaneously. The Latino operation was considered by ambitious middle-level managers in Stateside Glass as a good opportunity to gain valuable managerial experience. In addition to the two-product experience, the Latino operation was thought to provide decision-making opportunities that comparable level managers in Stateside did not have. On the other hand, it was generally believed that many of the decisions made by Latino managers were reviewed by corporate-level managers at the home office of Stateside Glass.

Latino's primary product was black-and-white television picture tubes. Competition in the area had been limited for some time as a result of a government decree prohibiting the importation of picture tubes into the country. One Japanese firm did build and operate a similar plant in Latino, however, and gained about 20 percent of the total market. In addition, recent trade agreements among several Latin American countries allowed a Mexican producer of picture tubes to market its product in Latino. To date, Latino has not been hurt seriously by the Mexican competition, and sales outside the country are on the increase.

Approximately one year ago, the company decided to expand its present production and add a line of picture tubes for color television. However, a government declaration made shortly after the decision caused the parent company to hold up any action of the addition on the new line. The original plan had called for Stateside Glass to form a second joint-venture company in Latino for the express purpose of producing the color-television picture tubes. The government declaration stated that all new enterprises begun in Latino must have at least 51 percent Latino ownership. A final decision as to whether or not the company's plans will be nullified by the declaration has not yet been made by the local government.

Roy Webster's Observations

"When Angel Ramos found out, by way of the grapevine, that we were bringing in Joe Kent to be plant manager, he was quite upset, even somewhat emotional. Indirectly, he threatened to quit. Ramos is a good man and has performed well as production superintendent for three years. He's only 32 years old."

"When I was plant manager, I never had any trouble with him—we always got along pretty well, though he tends to be a lit-

Source: Donald D. White and H. William Vrooman (eds.), *Action in Organizations,* Second Edition (Boston: Allyn and Bacon, 1977), pp. 367–369. Used by permission.

tle impulsive. I guess when I moved up to president from plant manager, he assumed he would replace me as plant manager. While I was never free to tell him, he was my choice for the job, even though I knew he would have some problems because of lack of experience in the areas reporting to him—plant accounting and industrial relations, especially. I guess Paul Moore (vice-president of Latin American operations for Stateside) felt Ramos's lack of experience would create too many problems. That's on our agenda of topics to be discussed on my next trip to the states. It is the policy of Stateside Glass to promote nationals as rapidly as they are capable of assuming greater responsibility—and we follow it. Of the 250 people employed by Latino Glass, there are only three Americans—the project manager who is coordinating the introduction of the lab-products line in terms of production and sales, the plant manager, and myself, the president. Besides, we can't do much without government permission, and the industry department likes to see Latinos in high company positions—it improves our image with the government. But Joe Kent was assigned the job by Moore, and that's the way it will have to stay.

"There is another aspect of the Ramos problem that must be considered. The heads of the departments reporting to the plant manager are used to having an American over them. When the time comes to move a Latino person into the job of plant manager, we might have problems with the Latino people who report to him. It's all right if an American is the plant manager, but as soon as a Latino native is

in that job, each of the other Latino people will feel that he or she should have had the job. I'm not sure they're ready to accept another Latino guy as their boss. When Joe Kent's time is up here and he returns to Stateside Glass, in about three years, I think Angel Ramos will be ready for the plant manager's job. I can't promise him anything because I'll be leaving Latino Glass about that time myself. But I wouldn't be surprised if he were the next plant manager.

"Latino Glass has progressed nicely in the past five years. We've had some problems, but I think we're really sailing now. Joe Kent worries me a little. His confidential file indicates he has a short temper, lets everybody know it when things don't go right—or so his file indicates. He spent the first four weeks after being assigned here in an intensive Spanish course—he's actually been on the job less than two weeks. I've noticed that he never uses his Spanish. I guess he's afraid or embarrassed to make mistakes. Our home-office personnel committee reviewed the records of the top production superintendents in the Stateside plants, and Joe, evidently, came out as the strongest prospect. Before coming to Latino, he was production superintendent in a color-television tube plant. He has been with Stateside Glass for 15 years—almost all of them in line positions in production. Two years ago he was offered a promotion to plant manager in an overseas operation, in Asia to be exact, but he turned it down. Some people feel that if he had turned down a second promotion, namely plant manager here in Latino, he'd never be offered another chance. I don't think

Stateside really operates like that—but Joe might think so. I just hope that he and Angel Ramos get the job done and don't crash head on. If those two don't work together, they will make us all look bad.

"I've suggested to Joe, subtly of course, that he use the work-objectives program that I started when I was plant manager. It worked for me. It should work for him if I can just get him to try it. I don't know when I'll get around to starting it with the people who report to me. The work-objectives program (some call it 'management by results') consisted of my sitting down with each of my subordinates, individually, and discussing what goals they should strive to reach in the forthcoming six-week period. Then we got together as a group, my subordinates and I, and each subordinate would tell the others what he was going to achieve in the coming period. We discussed each person's objectives as a group because sometimes they can help each other achieve their objectives. I like to see them set objectives that are a little higher than what is likely they can achieve—something to shoot at, so to speak. As I said, though, I haven't had time since I've been president to start it with my immediate subordinates. I wish Joe Kent would continue the work-objectives program in his area. It could help him do a better job; but if he and Ramos don't get along and don't support each other, we're all going to look bad."

Questions

1. What major changes are affecting Latino Glass?
2. What conflicts and problems

1. are likely to be associated with Joe Kent's arrival to take Roy Webster's place?
3. As an external consultant, what do you recommend

should be done if Stateside Glass is to build an effective Latino operation that serves local needs as well as those of the parent company?

4. What special advice would you give Joe Kent to increase his chances of success in this new international management assignment? Why?

CHIEFLAND MEMORIAL HOSPITAL

James A. Grover, retired land developer and financier, is the current president of Chiefland Memorial Hospital Board of Trustees. Chiefland Memorial is a 200-bed voluntary short-term general hospital serving an area of approximately 50,000 persons. Grover has just begun a meeting with the administrator of the hospital, Edward M. Hoffman. The purpose of the meeting is to seek an acceptable solution to an apparent conflict-of-authority problem within the hospital between Hoffman and the chief of surgery, Dr. Lacy Young.

The problem was brought to Grover's attention by Young during a golf match between the two men. Young had challenged Grover to the golf match at the Chiefland Golf and Country Club, but it turned out that this was only an excuse for Young to discuss a hospital problem with Grover.

The problem that concerned Young involved the operating-room supervisor, registered nurse Geraldine Werther. Werther

schedules the hospital's operating suite in accordance with policies that she "believes" to have been established by the hospital's administration. One source of irritation to the surgeons is her attitude that maximum utilization must be made of the hospital's operating rooms if hospital costs are to be reduced. She therefore schedules in such a way that operating-room idle time is minimized. Surgeons complain that the operating schedule often does not permit them sufficient time to complete a surgical procedure in the manner they think desirable. More often than not, insufficient time is allowed between operations for effective preparation of the operating room for the next procedure. Such scheduling, the surgical staff maintains, contributes to low-quality patient care. Furthermore, some of the surgeons have complained that Werther shows favoritism in her scheduling, allowing some doctors more use of the operating suite than others.

The situation reached a crisis when Young, following an explosive confrontation with Werther, told her he was firing her. Werther then made an appeal to Hoffman, the hospital administrator, who in turn informed Young that discharge of nurses was an administrative preroga-

tive. In effect Young was told he did not have authority to fire Werther. Young asserted that he did have authority over any issue affecting medical practice and good patient care in Chiefland Hospital. He considered this a medical problem and threatened to take the matter to the hospital's board of trustees.

As the meeting between Grover and Hoffman began, Hoffman explained his position on the problem. He stressed the point that a hospital administrator is legally responsible for patient care in the hospital. He also contended that quality patient care cannot be achieved unless the board of trustees authorizes the administrator to make decisions, develop programs, formulate policies, and implement procedures. While listening to Hoffman, Grover recalled the position belligerently taken by Young, who had contended that surgical and medical doctors holding staff privileges at Chiefland would never allow a "layperson" to make decisions impinging on medical practice. Young also had said that Hoffman should be told to restrict his activities to fund raising, financing, maintenance, and housekeeping—administrative problems rather then medical problems. Young had then requested that Grover clarify in a

Source: Reprinted with permission from John M. Champion and John H. James, Critical Incidents in Management, Third Edition (Homewood, Ill.: Richard D. Irwin, 1975), pp. 40–41. Copyright © 1975. Used by permission of Richard D. Irwin, Inc.

definitive manner the lines of authority at Chiefland Memorial.

As Grover ended his meeting with Hoffman, the severity of the problem was unmistakably clear to him, but the solution remained quite unclear. Grover knew a decision was required—and soon.

Questions

1. What are the major "conflicts" at issue in this case? Who is involved in each? Who or what is to blame in each conflict situation and why?

2. What should Grover do? Why?

3. Is the current situation at Chiefland Memorial "ripe" for a union organizing campaign among nurses? Explain your answer.

PART

7

CONCLUSION

MANY EXECUTIVES COMPLAIN OF STRESS, BUT FEW WANT LESS-PRESSURED JOBS

Problems of Dual-Career Families Start Forcing Businesses to Adapt

This is the final part of the book. It consists of only one chapter, "Management for Productivity: A Career Perspective." The purpose of Part 7 is to help you anticipate future decisions that must be successfully faced if you are to achieve a productive and satisfying managerial career. Each of the preceding headlines is suggestive of the issues involved—job stress, proving yourself as a manager, and working a career into family responsibilities.[1] These are but a few of many personal challenges to come.

Throughout this book we have emphasized the acquisition of knowledge and the mastery of basic skills in order to succeed in the management process. This emphasis is appropriate and necessary if you are to establish the foundations for career success. True success, however, requires that knowledge and skills be accompanied by personal qualities that lend strong character to your work efforts. This is the final topic we will now address— putting your knowledge and

skills together with who you are as a person so that you can play a significant role in the continued development of our modern and global society.

In his book *No Easy Victories,* John Gardner speaks of a similar challenge.[2] Read his words twice in the following quote—once as written; then once again substituting the word *manager* for *leader* and *organization* for *society.*[3]

"Leaders have a significant role in creating the state of mind that is the society. They can serve as symbols of the moral unity of the society. They can express the values that hold the society together. Most important, they can conceive and articulate goals that lift people out of their petty preoccupations, carry them above the conflicts that tear a society apart, and unite them in the pursuit of objectives worthy of their best efforts."

Chapter 21 is designed to help you probe deeper into the personal challenges of meeting

these responsibilities of leaders and managers in contemporary society. Before starting this concluding chapter, think about the following advice offered by Ralph Z. Sorenson, past president of Babson College and current president and chief executive officer of Barry Wright Corporation, a manufacturer of computer-related accessories and other diversified industrial products. He speaks wisely about the specific qualities required for a manager to achieve success in the future you face.

Perspective: A Lifetime of Learning to Manage Effectively[4]

"Years ago, when I was a young assistant professor at the Harvard Business School, I thought that the key to developing managerial leadership lay in raw brain power. I thought the role of busi-

---

[1]These headlines are from the *Wall Street Journal* (September 29, 1982), p. 27; (July 15, 1981), p. 23.

[2]John Gardner, *No Easy Victories* (New York: Harper, 1968).
[3]James L. Hayes, "A Manager of Quality," *Management Review,* Vol. 17 (April 1982), pp. 2, 3.

[4]Excerpted from Ralph Z. Sorenson, "A Lifetime of Learning to Manage Effectively," *Wall Street Journal* (February 28, 1983), p. 18. Reprinted by permission of the *Wall Street Journal.* Copyright © 1983 Dow Jones & Company, Inc. All rights reserved.

ness schools was to develop future managers who knew all about the various functions of business; to teach them how to define problems succinctly, analyze these problems and identify alternatives in a clear, logical fashion, and, finally, to teach them to make an intelligent decision.

"My thinking gradually became tempered by living and working outside the United States and by serving seven years as a college president. During my presidency of Babson College, I added several additional traits or skills that I felt a good manager must possess. The first is the *ability to express oneself* in a clear, articulate fashion. Good oral and written communication skills are absolutely essential if one is to be an effective manager.

"Second, one must possess that amorphous and intangible set of qualities called *leadership skills.* To be a good leader one must understand and be sensitive to people and be able to inspire them toward the achievement of common goals.

"Next I concluded that effective managers must be *broad human beings* who not only understand the world of business but also have a sense of the cultural, social, political, historical, and (particularly today) international aspects of life and society. This suggests that exposure to the liberal arts and humanities should be part of every manager's education.

"Finally, as I pondered the lessons of Watergate and the almost daily litany of business and government-related scandals that have occupied the front pages of newspapers throughout the 70s and early 80s, it became abundantly clear that a good manager in today's world must have *courage and a strong sense of integrity.* He or she must know where to draw the line between right and wrong.

"That can be agonizingly difficult. Drawing a line in a corporate setting sometimes involves having to make a choice between what appears at first glance to be conflicting 'rights.' For example, if one is faced with a decision whether to close an ailing factory, whose interests should prevail? Stockholders? Employees? Customers? Or those of the community in which the factory is located? It's a tough choice. And the typical manager faces many others.

"Sometimes, these choices involve simple questions of honesty or truthfulness. More often, they are more subtle and involve such issues as having to decide whether to 'cut corners' to meet 'bottom-line' profit objectives that may be expedient in the short run, but that are not in the best long-term interests of the various constituencies being served by one's company. Making the right choice in situations such as these clearly demands integrity and the courage to follow where one's integrity leads.

"But now I have shed the cap and gown of a college president and donned the hat of chief executive officer. As a result of my experience as a corporate CEO, my list of desirable managerial traits has become still longer.

"It now seems to me that what matters most in the majority of organizations is to have reasonably intelligent, hard-working managers who have a sense of pride and loyalty toward their organization; who can get to the root of a problem and are inclined toward action; who are decent human beings with a natural empathy and concern for people; who possess humor, humility, and common sense; and who are able to couple drive with stick-to-it-iveness and patience in the accomplishment of a goal.

"It is the *ability to make positive things happen* that most distinguishes the successful manager from the mediocre or unsuccessful one. It is far better to have dependable managers who can make the right things happen in a timely fashion than to have brilliant, sophisticated, highly educated executives who are excellent at planning, analyzing, and dissecting, but who are not so good at implementing. The most cherished manager is the one who says 'I can do it,' and then does."

21

MANAGEMENT FOR PRODUCTIVITY: A CAREER PERSPECTIVE

SOME HAPPY EMPLOYEES AT DELTA WANT TO BUY A BIG GIFT FOR THE BOSS

Atlanta—In its third fiscal quarter, ended March 31, Delta Air Lines ran up an $18.4 million loss, its biggest ever. But that didn't keep the airline from giving its employees an unexpectedly generous pay raise of some 8.5 percent in September.[1]

Ginny Whitfield, a flight attendant, and others were impressed. "A bunch of us were sitting around one day saying how wonderful this company was," she says. "So someone said, 'Let's buy them an airplane.' "

A $30 million Boeing 767 airplane, no less.

With two other flight attendants, Ginny Whitfield organized a campaign to raise the purchase price from Delta's 36,000 employees, who are nonunion. With this week's paychecks, the employees will be asked to sign a pledge card voluntarily committing 2.5 percent of one year's pay to the airplane purchase. Delta has 20 Boeing 767s on order. The employees' gifts would pay for the first one to go into service.

Delta officials emphasize that the idea is entirely the employees', not Delta's, but "if they buy the jet, I guarantee you we'll accept it," a spokesman for the airline says. At Delta headquarters, he says, "Everybody is just a wee bit overwhelmed."

It remains to be seen whether employees will pledge enough money. The campaign organizers expect 80 percent of the employees to go along, and that should be enough to provide the needed $30 million. In any case, Delta will get whatever money does get pledged.

Some employees already have responded favorably to the idea of buying Delta an airplane. "I think this is fantastic," says Ken Mabry, a Delta mechanic. "I've never been so excited in my life about giving back a portion of my salary." He figures his pledge toward the airplane purchase will cost him about $875 on his $34,000 yearly earnings.

PLANNING AHEAD
Wouldn't it be nice if someday your subordinates felt as positive about you as Delta's employees appear to feel toward it? This chapter puts the practice of management into a final career perspective. It is hoped that your managerial career will be rewarding and productive—for you, for others who work for you, and for your organization. Key topics in the chapter include

A Manager's Look to the Future
Stress and the Manager
Managing a Managerial Career
Management for Productivity: A Recap

Delta's employees, noted in the chapter opener, finally did present a new Boeing 767 to the company as a gift. Delta's management, as the saying goes, must have been doing something right! Having now read and studied *Management for Productivity,* you should also be prepared to do things "right" as a manager. The Delta example clearly shows that organizational productivity and employee satisfaction are entirely compatible with each other. Doing things "right" as a manager essentially means to facilitate both.

This final chapter helps put the many ideas, theories, and concepts of the book into a final perspective. It is time to take the initiative to look ahead to your managerial future and anticipate the challenges, excitement, and opportunities to come. Please think seriously about the future you face, the stress you'll experience, the career you will have, and how *Management for Productivity* has helped prepare you to master each of these challenges to the best of your ability.

A MANAGER'S LOOK TO THE FUTURE

In these classic words from his great novel *A Tale of Two Cities,* Charles Dickens described the world of 1775.[2]

> It was the best of times, it was the worst of times, it was the age of wisdom, it was the age of foolishness, it was the epoch of belief, it was the epoch of incredulity, it was the season of Light, it was the season of Darkness, it was the spring of hope, it was the winter of despair, we had everything before us, we had nothing before us.

Robert Fulmer, a noted management theorist, points out that Dickens's words may apply equally well today.[3]

> Dickens saw the marked contrasts that surrounded the early days of the Industrial Revolution. Today, as we near the end of the Industrial Revolution, we find our world marked by contrasts equally as dramatic. An analysis of the probabilities associated with this decade reveals that it is indeed both the best of times and the worst of times.

While it may be easy to agree with this last statement, it is harder to be precise as to just what the latter part of the 1980s and beyond will offer to managers of the future. Still, those who think seriously about the future find themselves in general agreement on a number of trends. Let's review these trends to help put your developing thoughts on management into a futuristic frame of reference.

Trends in the Environment

The general environment was defined in Chapter 6 as a set of background educational-political-economic-cultural forces with the potential to influence organizations and their members. Throughout this book, and especially in Part 6, we have explored key factors in the environment of major significance to managers. The modern manager, though, must be prepared to master the challenges of tomorrow as well as those of today. *Future shock* is a phrase popularly used to describe the discomfort that comes when times of rapid and uncertain change make this very difficult to accomplish. Yet, a manager's responsibility is to look ahead and achieve productivity as circumstances change over time.

Let's brainstorm just a bit as general background to the remainder of this chapter. Several projections on emerging environmental trends with implications for managers in the United States in the 1990s and beyond.[4]

- Inflation will not disappear, although it may moderate.

- Shortages of energy and natural resources will continue and even intensify on a worldwide basis.

- Foreign competition will increase, especially in the technologically mature industries such as textiles, steel, and autos.

- The annual growth in the labor force will decrease slightly.

- The shift in population from the Northeast and Midwest to the South and West will continue; over 50 percent of the population will live in the South and West by the end of the decade.

- The average age of the population will continue to rise; there will be 27 million persons over 65 by 1990.

- Employment will shift increasingly out of agriculture and manufacturing, and toward service occupations.

- Continued employment gains will be made by females and members of minority groups.

- Computers and robots will continue to increase the technological sophistication of industry and office systems.

- Legal pressures and government regulation of business will continue to grow, although conservative politicians may slow the trend at times.

There are many potential implications of such trends should the forecasts prove accurate. One, for example, relates to the availability of jobs in the economy of the future. Figure 21.1 projects that there will be plenty of jobs in 1990, but they will be spread unevenly across the marketplace. Consistent with some of the prior trends, many of the new jobs will go to persons in service industries and with skills appropriate to the information age now upon us.

Trends in People

Trends in the environment can be associated with complementary trends among people in the work force. Managers of the future will have to deal with new demands and concerns in their human-resource management activities. Supervisor-subordinate relationships of the future, in particular, are likely to reflect the following specific changes over time.[5]

1. *Pressures for self-determination* People will seek greater freedom to determine *how* to do their jobs and *when* to do them. Pressures for increased worker participation in the forms of job enrichment, autonomous work groups, flexible working hours, and compressed workweeks will grow.

2. *Pressures for employee rights* People will expect their rights to be respected on the job as well as outside of work. These include the rights of individual privacy, due process, and freedom from sexual harassment, as well as protection against discrimination on the basis of age, sex, ethnic background, or handicap.

3. *Pressures for security* People will expect their security to be protected, both in respect to their physical well-being (i.e., occupational safety and health matters) and economic livelihood (e.g., guaranteed protection against layoffs and cost-of-living increases).

4. *Pressures for equity of earnings* People will expect to be compensated for the comparable worth of their work contributions. What began as a concern for earnings differentials between women and men doing the same jobs will be extended to cross-occupational comparisons. Questions such as why a nurse receives less pay than a carpenter and why a maintenance worker is paid more than a secretary will be asked with increasing frequency. They will require answers other than the fact that certain occupations (such as nursing) have traditionally been dominated by women, while others (such as carpentry) have been dominated by men.

5. *Pressures to achieve and maintain a high quality of life* People will expect to live and work in conditions that protect, foster, and respect the dignity of the human being. This includes expanded opportunities for participation in the

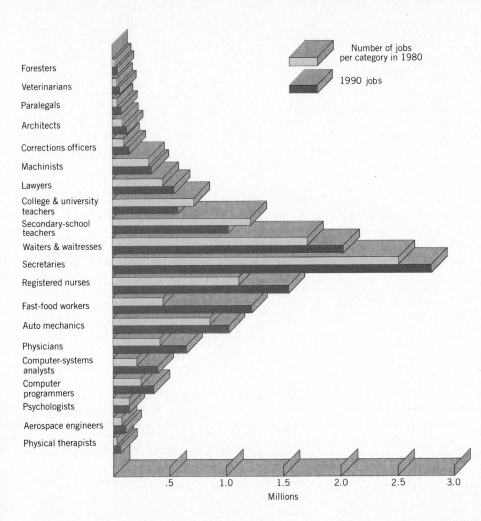

Number of jobs per category in 1980

1990 jobs

Foresters
Veterinarians
Paralegals
Architects
Corrections officers
Machinists
Lawyers
College & university teachers
Secondary-school teachers
Waiters & waitresses
Secretaries
Registered nurses
Fast-food workers
Auto mechanics
Physicians
Computer-systems analysts
Computer programmers
Psychologists
Aerospace engineers
Physical therapists

.5   1.0   1.5   2.0   2.5   3.0
Millions

FIGURE 21.1 Winners and losers among 1990 jobs. *Source:* Jeremy Main, "Work Won't Be the Same Again," *Fortune* (June 28, 1982), p. 61. © 1982 Time Inc. Courtesy of Fortune Magazine.

workplace and protection of rights, as well as freedom from physical or mental harm at work or by the by-products of work (e.g., industrial waste).

Managers of the future will have to address and respect people as the human resources of organizations in the broader sense and legal context of a maturing society. The successful and respected managers will be the ones best able to cope with and find opportunity in pressures such as those just reviewed.

Trends in Technology

Another undeniable aspect of our environment is the emergence of high technology as a dominant force in our lives. "With computers and high technology," as the saying goes, "work won't be the same again!" This theme has emerged several times throughout this book. Without doubt, the greatest technological forces of the present decade are the computer, electronic information processing, and the robot. Each, in its own way, has the capability to transform future work radically. By 1990 over 100,000 robots will be at work in the United States; between 1982 and 1990 the number of work stations using microcomputers and electronic word-processing equipment will increase from 4 million to 25 or 30 million.[6] The resulting changes in the nature of work and in the relationship between the worker and the task will be revolutionary. Consider this description of how the growing use of the computer affects work.[7]

Work becomes abstract, the electronic manipulation of symbols. Different jobs become similar. The

Doonesbury cartoon (show-
ing personal computer .

bank auditor who once dropped in unannounced at branch offices and the pulp-mill operator who walked the line with wrench in hand now both sit in front of computer screens monitoring on-line information.

Managers of the future must be prepared to utilize and successfully adapt to the opportunities made available by these advances in computer, robot, and electronic information-processing technologies. This challenge includes helping employees who must work at the interface with these complex machines. The Doonesbury cartoon conveys the sense of uncertainty that may be experienced when someone is asked to deal with new technology.

A brief glimpse of the electronic office follows.[8] The setting is Westinghouse Electric Corporation's construction group in Pittsburgh. The goal is to create a well-integrated electronic information-processing system that will enable the group to increase productivity while sustaining a projected growth in overall workload.

> Secretaries typically used to spend 30 percent of their time typing, but in February, executive vice-president William Coates had all the typewriters removed (except for one near his office, with a log beside it for the user to sign). Secretaries and their bosses now have computer terminals on which they can write and send memos, edit letters, store and recall information, design charts, and perform all manners of electronic marvels. They now dictate to a communications center.

> The secretaries are delighted with their freed-up time, which they use for more productive tasks, such as doing research or arranging meetings. The bosses seem pleased, too, because they spend less time on routine chores.

Selected Paradoxes to Come[9]

Robert Fulmer warns against treating these trends in environment, people, and technology as if they were singular themes. He sees a need to assess and assimilate the implications of sometimes contrasting trends. He offers the following paradoxes as potential complications in the managerial experience that you may face in the future.

Paradox 1: The Decline of Traditional Incentives, with Increased Popularity of Financially Rewarded Careers

The incentives that once encouraged people to work—namely, money and fear—are less effective today than in the past. According to a Daniel Yankelovich poll, money and job security fail to motivate 44 percent (mostly younger members) of the work force. Of these, 27 percent are described as "hedonistic, live-for-today, turned off, sensation seeking." The other 17 percent, mostly young managers, are hungry for but frustrated by not receiving "responsibility, challenge, autonomy, informality" from their jobs.[10] Fulmer points out that just as financial incentives seem to be losing some of their prior clout, however, interest in the more financially oriented occupations is growing. College enrollments in the liberal arts and humanities decline, while those in business, engineering, and preprofessional programs grow. One argument is that such choices are motivated by the prospect of financial rewards such as those projected in Table 21.1 for a variety of managerial positions in business and industry for 1985–1987. Even though "challenge" and "responsibility" will remain key components

Table 21.1 Projected Average Annual Salaries for Various Managerial Jobs in Business and Industry, 1985–1987

	1985	1986	1987
Accounting manager	$42,356	$46,592	$51,251
Auditing manager	43,806	48,187	53,005
Cost accounting manager	39,135	43,049	47,353
Payroll supervisor	29,633	32,596	35,856
Credit and collection manager	36,398	40,038	44,042
Personnel director	46,383	51,021	56,123
Employment manager	35,592	39,151	43,066
Customer service manager	37,203	40,923	45,016
Compensation manager	43,001	47,301	52,031
Manager—administrative services	39,619	43,581	47,939
Manager—electronic data processing	47,188	51,907	57,097
Branch manager	37,364	41,100	45,210
Sales manager	47,993	52,792	58,072
Advertising manager	43,967	48,364	53,200
Warehouse manager	35,592	39,151	43,066
Plant manager	51,053	56,158	61,774
Supervisor	34,304	37,734	41,508
General supervisor	39,619	43,581	47,939
Purchasing agent	40,263	44,289	48,718
Buyer	32,532	35,785	39,364

Source: Projections for 1985 based on the 1981 Administrative Management Society's *1981 AMS Guide to Management Compensation.* Reprinted by permission.
Note: Projections assume a 10 percent rate of inflation.

in job and career satisfaction, money will be important, too. Workers of tomorrow are likely to be disappointed when or if these financial rewards are not forthcoming.

Paradox 2: Increased Competition for Promotions, But More Flexibility in Work Positions

Projections place more than half the labor force in the 25–44 age group by 1990. This means greater competition for jobs, perhaps to the extent of 20 workers competing for each middle-management position that opens up. The promotion rate will fall dramatically; at the same time, the number of entry-level workers will shrink as a result of the declining fertility rate that has been in evidence since the mid-1960s. Greater flexibility in work positions will be needed to attract and accommodate people to these jobs. One can expect, for example, that job sharing, flexible working hours, permanent part-time work, and "work-at-home" programs will grow in frequency. Such programs are attempts

to accommodate the often-conflicting pressures of work and family life. As a result, they have the capability to bring to the workplace an otherwise unavailable employee.

Paradox 3: More Ability and Need to Centralize Decisions, But More Pressure to Decentralize

Rapid advancements in computers and other electronic technologies offer managers greater access to information, as well as an ability to process this information better and more rapidly. This makes it easier to centralize decision making and improve management controls. In the computer-assisted office of the future, for example, the loss ratio in a loan officer's portfolio or the number of calls handled by a phone operator can be monitored constantly and compared with norms. So while the boss may not be around much, employees will be tied more tightly to performance standards. Still, counterpressures toward increased worker participation and rights of self-determination will also increase. While in-

Offices of the future will become increasingly computerized and influenced by high technology.

formation technology offers the benefits of increased efficiency and perhaps enhanced technical quality of decision making, expanded work-participation schemes offer the advantages of greater employee commitment and motivation to implement decision outcomes. Managers in the future will travel a narrow and difficult road while walking between these parallel and possibly conflicting trends.

Paradox 4: The Triumph of Worker Participation, Yet a Revival of Scientific Management

The "quality-of-life" concerns of the 1970s and 1980s will enhance the move toward more worker participation in the affairs and decisions of the workplace. We have already noted where autonomous work groups, quality-control circles, and job-enrichment programs exemplify such trends. There is also widespread recognition of the need for production and operations improvements in organizations in general, and basic industries in particular. This theme was clearly in evidence in our treatment of production and operations control in Chapter 16. Among the many improvement efforts will be a return to some of the basic principles of scientific management. This return

will reemphasize work efficiency, but not to the extreme where workers are treated as minor cogs in the production process. Managers of the future will be called to meet the challenge of achieving high productivity with dignity, respect, and satisfaction on the part of all members of the work force.

Paradox 5: Continued Progress for Women at Work, But Lingering Inequality

Dramatic gains have been made in the past 20 years by women in the workplace. Women are increasingly found in occupations traditionally dominated by males, and women are increasingly accepted as equal working partners in the managerial ranks. In 1950, women held only 12 percent of all management positions; by 1980 this figure was 26 percent. By the year 2000 it is anticipated that women will hold 10 percent of the top positions in the 500 largest U.S. companies, and *Newsline 21.1* is one example of the growing number of women achieving entrepreneurial success in smaller businesses. Still, Fulmer notes, "that's progress, but hardly equality." The fact that women MBA graduates tend to earn less than their male counterparts seems consistent with his guarded point of view.[11]

NEWSLINE 21.1

MORE WOMEN START UP THEIR OWN BUSINESSES WITH MAJOR SUCCESSES

When Sandra Kurtzig went into business for herself 10 years ago, she operated out of a room in her home and stashed all her business funds in a shoebox. If there was more money in the shoebox at the end of the month than the beginning, her company made a profit.

"I had no management experience," she recalls. "My long-range plans were figuring out where to go for lunch." Her business was simple enough: She developed computer software that let weekly newspapers keep track of their newspaper carriers.

These days Kurtzig has more complicated matters on her mind. Her little business, named ASK Computer Systems Inc., has grown to $22 million a year in sales, 200 employees, $2.3 million of profits, and a reputation as one of the most successful computer software companies around. Sandra Kurtzig, founder and president, owns $66.9 million of ASK stock.

Source: Excerpted from Earl C. Gottschalk, Jr., "Distaff Owners: More Women Start Up Their Own Businesses With Major Successes," *Wall Street Journal* (May 17, 1983), p. 1. Reprinted by permission of the *Wall Street Journal.* Copyright © 1983 Dow Jones & Company, Inc. All rights reserved.

Paradox 6: More People Working, Yet Higher Unemployment

The U.S. Bureau of Labor Statistics projects that the labor force will grow from 105 million in 1980 to 122–128 million in 1990. Table 21.2 shows how the professional business employment outlook is expected to change for this same time period. Increased employment opportunities will occur mainly in the technical areas such as computers and electronics. Chronic unemployment problems can be expected to accompany this shift in opportunity toward the high-technology and service sectors. Workers displaced from lagging industries such as steel and autos may find themselves without the skills required to shift occupations. Many people may find themselves underemployed or working in jobs for which they are not suited. This includes persons who stumble into jobs for which they have little training or aptitude, and those who are highly trained and can't find employment in their areas of expertise.

An Age of Transition

The phrase is often used, but it is quite appropriate to say that the future is sure to be an "age of transition." Although no one can say for sure what lies ahead, we are able to describe likely trends and analyze the paradoxes they represent. It is ultimately up to the manager to understand future circumstances and adjust effectively to them when making decisions and taking action. The astute managers will succeed; the less informed ones will not.

STRESS AND THE MANAGER

The prior discussion clearly suggests that the pressures of the managerial role and all of the responsibilities it entails will be great. We first addressed this issue in depth when examining conflict in Chapter 17. The following cases of Mary, Bob, and Ray are good reminders of the challenges you may someday face. Although

Table 21.2 Professional Business-Occupation Employment Outlook for 1990

Occupation	Employment (×1000) in 1990	Change 1978–1990 (%)
Computer specialists	754	93.94
Computer programmers	361	77.22
Computer systems analysts	392	112.38
Social scientists	248	41.26
Economists	42	56.30
Accountants and auditors	1,055	35.83
Appraisers, real estate	48	49.79
Assessors	38	28.26
Buyers, retail and wholesale trade	298	25.13
Cost estimators	108	34.94
Personnel and labor-relations specialists	208	22.86
Purchasing agents and buyers	202	23.69
Tax examiners, collectors, and revenue agents	60	19.61
Tax preparers	51	77.93
Travel agents and accommodations appraisers	70	56.06
Underwriters	90	28.98
Managers, officials, and proprietors	10,677	21.31
Auto-parts department managers	59	23.28
Construction inspectors, public administration	61	37.62
Inspectors (excluding construction), public administration	125	20.82
Restaurant, cafe, and bar managers	650	30.27
Sales managers, retail trade	323	23.93
Store managers	1,107	19.52
Wholesalers	284	21.42
Salesworkers	8,079	25.40
Real-estate brokers	49	44.47
Sales agents and representatives, real estate	400	56.74
Sales agents and representatives, insurance	405	30.81
Sales agents and representatives, security	88	60.70
Clerical workers	22,519	26.37
Bank tellers	606	37.51
New accounts tellers	66	36.57
Tellers	540	37.62
Bookkeepers and accounting clerks	2,014	23.72
Accounting clerks	845	20.74
Claims examiners, insurance	58	52.29
Clerical supervisors	526	30.81
Collectors, bill and account	113	32.26

Source: From Max L. Carey, "Occupational Employment Growth through 1990," *Monthly Labor Review* (August 1981), pp. 48–53. Used by permission.

working in different managerial jobs and organizational settings, each person shares something in common with the others—high levels of job-related stress.[12]

1. *Mary* Mary, a recent Wharton MBA, spent a sleepless night contemplating her first presentation before the executive committee of her new employer. She had spent much of the last 6 months preparing the report for her presentation and felt it was the first real test of her managerial potential. Mary's presentation lasted 5 minutes and was followed by about 10 minutes of questions from committee members. Mary was thanked for making a fine presentation and dismissed from the meeting by the firm's president. She quickly went to the nearest lounge and in a release of tension shook uncontrollably.

2. *Bob* Bob's wife, Jane, is becoming increasingly worried about her husband. Several months ago Bob was passed over for a promotion

to plant supervisor that he felt he deserved after 15 years of loyal service to the company. Bob used to come home from work tired but cheery and spent an hour or so playing with their two boys. Lately, however, Bob walks into the house, grabs a can of beer, and plops down in front of the television. Except for dinner, he spends his evenings watching television and drinking beer. He has little to do or say to either Jane or the kids. Jane is at wit's end. She has begged Bob to go to the doctor, but he says, "Nothing is wrong with me. It's your imagination."

3. *Ray* Ray, a successful advertising account executive, was finishing his typical "two-martini" lunch with a potential client, but Ray's mind wasn't on business as usual. He was thinking about the pain in his stomach and the diagnosis the doctor had given him yesterday. Ray's doctor had told him he had a spastic colon induced by his life-style. Ray, recently divorced, knows his gin consumption, smoking habit, and 12-hour workdays aren't good for him, but his job is now the most important thing in his life, and the advertising business just happens to be highly stressful. Ray doesn't know what to do and resolves not to worry about his health and to concentrate on selling his luncheon partner one fantastic contract.

Stress is a state of tension experienced by individuals facing extraordinary demands, constraints, or opportunities. In Mary's case, stress resulted from an opportunity to make an important presentation. Bob's stress emerged from a constraint—inability to gain promotion. Ray is torn between the demands of a doctor's advice and the potential opportunity of a successful business luncheon. Stress, again, is the result.

Job-related stress goes hand in hand with the dynamic and sometimes uncertain nature of the managerial role. *Newsline 21.2* attests to this fact, but it also indicates that many managers experience satisfaction from facing and conquering the stress associated with their jobs.

Any look ahead toward your managerial future would be incomplete without confronting stress as something you are sure to encounter along the way. For a start, think about this statement by a psychologist who works with top-level managers having severe drinking problems: "All executives deal with stress. They wouldn't be executives if they didn't. Some handle it well, others handle it poorly."[13] If you understand stress and how it operates in the work setting, you should be more likely to handle it well. This goes both for the personal stress you may experience and for the stress experienced by persons you supervise.

Sources of Stress

Stressors are the things that cause stress. It is important for a manager to understand and be able to recognize stressors because they cause job-related stress, which influences work attitudes and behavior.

Figure 21.2 shows three categories of stressors that can act in this fashion—work, personal, and nonwork factors. Of these, the work factors have the most obvious potential to create stress. Such stress can result from excessively high or low task demands, role conflicts or ambiguities, poor interpersonal relations, or career progress that is too slow or too fast. A look back to the examples of Mary, Bob, and Ray shows how these factors can act alone or in combination to cause job stress.

A variety of personal factors are also sources of potential stress for people at work. Such individual characteristics as needs, capabilities, and personality can influence how one perceives and responds to the work situation. Some researchers, for example, identify a Type A personality for which stressful behavior patterns such as the following are commonplace.[14]

- Always moves, walks, and eats rapidly.
- Feels impatient with the pace of things, hurries others, dislikes waiting.
- Does several things at once.
- Feels guilty when relaxing.
- Tries to schedule more and more in less and less time.
- Uses nervous gestures such as clenched fist, banging hand on table.
- Doesn't have time to enjoy life.

The achievement orientation, impatience, and perfectionism of individuals with Type A personalities may create stress in work circumstances other persons find relatively stress-free.

NEWSLINE 21.2

MANY EXECUTIVES COMPLAIN OF STRESS, BUT FEW WANT LESS-PRESSURED JOBS

Over 40 percent of top executives sometimes or often lie awake at night thinking about business problems. But fewer than one in five thinks he or she would be happier in a less stressful job.

Those are some of the findings of a Gallup Organization poll of business leaders conducted for the *Wall Street Journal*. It shows that highly placed executives and business owners commonly feel stress—and that they have developed a great range of techniques to cope with it.

Of executives who do complain of stress, a disproportionate number are young. In medium-sized companies, for instance, 48 percent of the chiefs under age 45 find stress a problem, compared with only 29 percent among those aged 45 or more. "As you grow older, you learn to handle stress and don't feel it," says the chairman of a manufacturing concern. The president of a beverage concern adds, "I'm less strained at 54 than I was at 35—I've had to work on it."

Executives commonly have specific strategies to cope with this stress. A large majority—79 percent at the big companies, 73 at the medium-sized, and 61 percent at the small—say they engage in physical exercise to relieve stress. Golf was the most commonly mentioned sport, followed by tennis, hunting or fishing, and running or jogging.

Source: Excerpted from Roger Ricklefs, "Many Executives Complain of Stress, But Few Want Less-Pressured Jobs," *Wall Street Journal* (September 29, 1982), p. 27. Reprinted by permission of the *Wall Street Journal*. Copyright © 1982 Dow Jones & Company, Inc. All rights reserved.

Type A personalities, in this sense, bring stress on themselves.

Finally, nonwork factors may "spill over" and impact the stress an individual experiences at work. Such things as family events (e.g., the birth of a new child), economics (e.g., sudden loss of extra income), and personal affairs (e.g., preoccupation with a hobby) can add to the stress otherwise associated with work and/or personal factors.

Constructive and Destructive Stress

This preliminary discussion may give the impression that stress always acts as a negative influence on our lives. There are actually two faces to stress, as shown in Figure 21.3–one constructive and one destructive.

Constructive stress acts in a positive way for the individual and/or the organization. Figure 21.3 shows that low to moderate levels of stress act in a constructive or energizing way that increases effort, stimulates creativity, and encourages diligence in one's work. You may know such stress as the tension that causes you to study hard before exams, pay attention in class, and complete assignments on time. The same positive results of stress can be found in the workplace, and in respect to all three categories of stressors. Individuals of the Type A personality, for example, are likely to work long hours and be less satisfied with poor performance. High task demands imposed by a supervisor may draw forth higher levels of task accomplishment. Even nonwork stressors such as new family responsibilities may cause an individual to work harder in

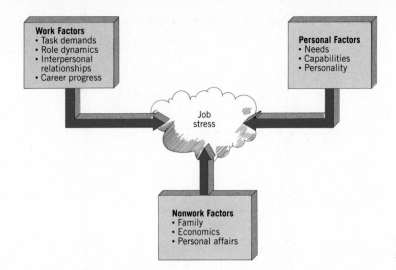

FIGURE 21.2 Potential sources of job stress.

anticipation of greater financial rewards.

Destructive stress, on the other hand, is dysfunctional for the individual and/or the organization. Whereas low to moderate levels of stress can enhance productivity, excessively high stress can overload and break down a person's physical and mental systems. Productivity can suffer as people react to very intense stress through absenteeism, turnover, errors, accidents, dissatisfaction, and reduced performance.

Managers must know how to maintain the positive edge offered by constructive stress. They must also be concerned about destructive stress and its potential to impact people and their work performance adversely. Among the latter concerns is a most fundamental one—the possible negative impact of destructive stress on individual health.

FIGURE 21.3 Constructive and destructive stress.

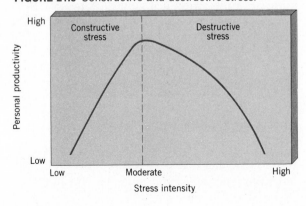

Stress and Health

Table 21.3 shows risk factors associated with 10 leading causes of death. Overall, 51 percent of the risk factors are life-style related; an additional 19 percent are found in the environment. Stress is an important factor in both columns. Excessive stress from life-style and/or environmental sources can reduce resistance to disease and increase the likelihood of physical and/or mental illness. Job stress can lead to severe health problems in the form of heart attack, stroke, hypertension, ulcers, drug-alcohol-tobacco abuse, overeating, depression, and muscle aches, among others.

Managers should be alert to signs of excessive stress in themselves and persons with whom they work. The symptoms are multiple and varied. Table 21.4 offers one checklist of stress indicators. Other signs to watch for include[15]

- Change in eating habits.
- Unhealthy feeling—aches and pains.
- Restlessness, inability to concentrate.
- Tense, uptight, fidgety, or nervous feelings.
- Increase in drinking or smoking.
- Feelings of being disoriented or overwhelmed.
- Sleeping problems.
- Depression or irritability.
- Upset stomach.
- Dizziness, weakness, lightheadedness.

Table 21.3 Leading Causes of Death and Their Determinants

| Leading Causes of Death | Estimated Contribution to Cause of Death (%) | | | |
	Lifestyle	Environment	Health-Care Services	Biology
Heart disease	54	9	12	25
Cancer	37	24	10	29
Stroke	50	22	7	21
Motor vehicle accidents	69	18	12	1
All other accidents	51	31	14	4
Homicide	63	35	0	2
Suicide	60	35	3	2
Cirrhosis	70	9	3	18
Influenza/pneumonia	23	20	18	39
Diabetes	34	0	6	60
Total	51	19	10	20

Source: Slightly adapted from John D. Adams, "Health, Stress, and the Manager's Life Style," *Group and Organization Studies,* Vol. 6 (September 1981), p. 293. Copyright © 1981 by International Authors, B.V. Used by permission.

Increasingly, and rightly so, the modern manager is likely to adopt an expanded view of the social responsibility of serving in a managerial role; that is, a view that accepts responsibility for job-related influences on the health of one's colleagues and subordinates. This position is defended on the basis of the following arguments.[16]

1. *Humanitarianism* To the extent that managerial awareness and action can enhance employee health, managers have a humanitarian responsibility to do so.

2. *Productivity* Healthy employees are absent less, make fewer errors, and must be replaced less frequently than less healthy ones; even rough estimates place the cost of lost productivity because of poor employee health at $75–90 billion per year.

Table 21.4 Checklist of Stress Symptoms for People at Work

Original behavior	*changes to* New behavior
Regular attendance	Absenteeism
Good decisions	Errors in judgment
Diligence	Carelessness
Quality work	Mistakes, errors
Good humor	Poor humor
Positive attitude	Negative attitude
Openness to change	Resistance to change
Punctuality	Tardiness
Good interpersonal relations	Poor interpersonal relations

3. *Creativity* Persons in poor health are less creative and less prone to take reasonable risks than their healthy counterparts.

4. *Return on investment* Organizations invest substantial amounts of time and money in the development of employees; when poor health reduces or removes the individual's contribution to the organization, return on the human-resource investment is lost.

Effective Stress Management

You can see that the role of stress in the work setting is complex. We know that constructive stress may facilitate productivity, but it is also true that destructive stress can reduce productivity and even impair a person's health. Thus a good manager will find a healthy fit between the individual, the work environment, and the amount of job stress it involves. A healthy fit is one that stimulates productivity without damaging health. It is achieved through effective stress management, the ability to (1) prevent stress, (2) cope with stress, and (3) maintain personal wellness.

Stress Prevention

It is always best to manage stress by preventing it from reaching excessive levels in the first place. Stressors emerging from personal and nonwork factors must be recognized so that action can be taken to prevent them from adversely affecting the work experience. Persons with Type A personalities, for example, may exercise self-discipline; managers of Type A employees may try to model a lower-key, more relaxed approach to work. At another level, family difficulties may be relieved by a change of work schedule, or the anxiety they cause may be reduced by knowing that one's supervisor understands.

Among work factors with the greatest potential to cause excessive stress are role ambiguities, conflicts, and overloads. Role clarification through a management-by-objectives (MBO) approach can work to good advantage here. By bringing supervisor and subordinate together around task-oriented communications, MBO is an opportunity to spot stressors and take action to reduce or eliminate them.

Stress Coping

We have already identified some of the symptoms indicating that excessive stress may already be affecting an individual at work. These include uncharacteristic irritability, nervousness or hostility, complaints of spontaneous illnesses, as well as any deviation from customary behavior patterns. When these symptoms are recognized, it is time to take action to maintain the desired healthy fit. Among the suggested guidelines individuals may follow to cope with stress by maximizing its benefits and minimizing its destructive effects are the following.[17]

1. *Control the situation*   Avoid unrealistic deadlines. Do your best, but know your limits. You cannot be everything to everyone. Learn to identify and limit your exposure to stressors that trigger a strong stress response within you.

2. *Open up to others*   Freely discuss your problems, fears, frustrations, and sources of uptightness with those who care about you. When in doubt, smile! A sincere smile often can defuse emotion and build a bridge of goodwill.

3. *Pace yourself*   Plan your day on a flexible basis. Don't try to do two or more things at the same time. Counter unproductive haste by forcing yourself to slow down. Think before reacting to negative situations or people. Live on a day-to-day basis instead of a minute-by-minute basis.

Stress is a state of tension experienced by individuals facing extraordinary demands, constraints, or opportunities.

NEWSLINE 21.3

EMPLOYERS TRY IN-HOUSE FITNESS CENTERS TO LIFT MORALE, CUT COST OF HEALTH CLAIMS

A lot of huffing and puffing emanates these days from the basement of the one-and-a-half-year-old Federal Reserve Bank building in Boston. The exertion comes from Fed employees intent on restraining the growth of their waistlines, not the money supply.

The Boston Fed has spent $25,000 to convert a 4000-square-foot storage room into an employee fitness center, complete with a ten-station universal gym, ballet bars, a punching bag, exercise mats, showers, and lockers.

At first glance, it might seem that such facilities are a poor use of space and a drain on corporate profits. But proponents of fitness centers say that they can improve employee morale and save money by getting a company's "walking time bombs," those with cardiovascular problems, on a proper exercise schedule and diet.

Source: Excerpted from Robert Guenther, "Employers Try In-House Fitness Centers to Lift Morale, Cut Cost of Health Claims," *Wall Street Journal* (November 10, 1981), p. 31. Reprinted by permission of the *Wall Street Journal*. Copyright © 1981 Dow Jones & Company, Inc. All rights reserved.

4. *Exercise and relax* Engage in regular noncompetitive physical activity such as jogging, swimming, riding a bike, or playing tennis, handball, or racquetball. (See your doctor when in doubt about your physical condition.) When feeling uptight, relax for a few minutes by following these simple steps: (a) Sit comfortably with eyes closed in a quiet location; (b) Slowly repeat a peaceful word or phrase over and over to yourself in your mind; (c) Take complete but comfortable breaths, inhaling through the nose and exhaling through the mouth; (d) Avoid distracting thoughts by keeping a passive mental attitude.

Personal Wellness

Personal wellness is a term used to describe the pursuit of one's physical and mental potential through a personal health-promotion program.[18] This concept recognizes individual responsibility to enhance personal health through a disciplined approach to such things as smoking, weight gain and alcohol use, maintenance of a nutritious diet, and engaging in a regular exercise and physical-fitness program. The essence of personal wellness is a life-style that reflects a true commitment to health.

Because stress has the potential to impact health, personal wellness makes a great deal of sense as a stress-management strategy. The manager who aggressively maintains his or her health should be better prepared to deal with the inevitable stresses of the managerial role. It may well be that these managers will be able to take constructive advantage of levels of stress that would otherwise take on destructive characteristics.

Managers can and should encourage personal wellness among subordinates. This extends the concept of personal wellness into the supervisory responsibility. Some organizations sponsor physical-fitness programs among their employees. One example is described in *Newsline 21.3.*

MANAGING A MANAGERIAL CAREER

The stress about which we have been talking is highlighted in the context of one's overall career aspirations. It is in this respect that success and failure on the job take on special meaning. A **career** is a sequence of jobs and work pursuits constituting what a person does for a living. For many of us, a career begins on an anticipatory basis with our formal education. From there it progresses into an initial job choice and any number of subsequent choices that may involve changes in task assignments, employing organizations, and even occupations.

A **career path** is a sequence of jobs held over time during a career. Career paths vary between those that are pursued internally within the same organization and those that involve changes among employing organizations over time. Many organizations encourage internal career paths by making long-term career opportunities available to their employees. Delta Airlines, the company in our chapter-opening example, is a case in point. Figure 21.4 shows the top of Delta's 1981 organization chart. Note that the top managers have been with the company an average of 26 years, and have followed primarily internal ca-

reer paths. Delta's president is a good example. Starting at the entry level as a reservation agent in 1946, David C. Garrett, Jr. rose through the ranks to become chief executive by 1981.

Career Planning and Development

Careers inevitably mix together the needs of people and organizations. Edgar Schein, a noted management theorist and consultant on careers, states,[19]

> Organizations are dependent on the performance of their people, and people are dependent on organizations to provide jobs and career opportunities. . . . The problem for society, for organizations, and for people is how to match their respective needs, not only at the point of entry into the organization, but also throughout the career or life history of the person in the organization.

Because of the commitment of time and physical and emotional energy it involves, the career is an important component of a person's total life experience. The following quotes from a recent study about people and their careers should cause you to think about your career, as well as the careers of those persons who will someday become your subordinates.[20]

FIGURE 21.4 Career paths of top managers at Delta Airlines. *Source:* "Delta: The World's Most Profitable Airline," *Business Week* (August 31, 1981), pp. 70, 71. Reprinted from the August 31, 1981 issue of *Business Week* by special permission. Copyright © 1981 by McGraw-Hill, Inc., New York, N.Y. 10020. All rights reserved.

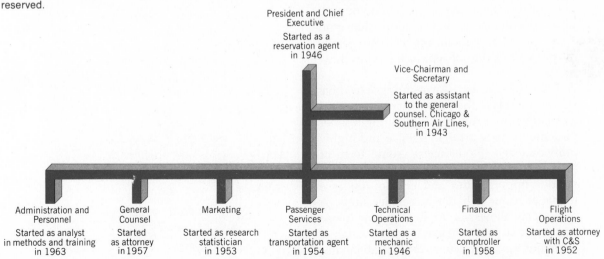

"Years ago I made a bad mistake, and now I'm paying for it; I'm trapped in this job."

"I should have found out how this firm was run before taking their offer. I had other good prospects at the time."

"They led me down the garden path, and I was fool enough to be taken in."

Such pessimistic statements suggest that everyone should think seriously about their careers, and think ahead! **Career planning** is the process of systematically matching career goals and individual capabilities with opportunities for their fulfillment. Advice varies on just how this should be done, as the following thoughts of two successful executives show.[21]

1. *Harlan Cleveland* A career as an executive is not something you plan for yourself. It's a series of accidental changes of job and shifts of scenery on which you look back later, weaving through the story retroactively some thread of logic that was not visible at the time.

If you try too carefully to plan your life, the danger is that you will succeed—succeed in narrowing your options and closing off avenues of adventure that cannot now be imagined, perhaps because they are not yet technologically possible. When a student asks me for career advice, I can only suggest that he or she opt for the most exciting "next step" without worrying where it will lead, and then work hard on the job in hand, not pine for the one in the bush. When your job no longer demands of you more than you have, go and do something else. Always take by preference the job you *don't* know how to do.

2. *William O. Grabe* An aspiring executive should not make the personal investment in a career without some basic planning. Career planning is more art than science and highly individualized. Nonetheless, some form of plan can greatly enhance the evaluation of various opportunities and enable you as a manager to make better career decisions. A career plan allows you to identify how to use your basic strengths to maximum advantage, set major career objectives, and establish im-

mediate milestones to measure personal development and advancement.

A fundamental requirement of successful career planning is self-awareness—the ability to bring out your own best effort. The path to the top can be hard. So you as a manager should assess your physical and mental strengths and your willingness to concentrate on the fulfillment of your career plan.

Cleveland and Grabe offer contrasting viewpoints. While Cleveland suggests a career should be allowed to progress in a somewhat random but always opportunistic way, Grabe sees a career as something to be rationally planned and pursued in a logical step-by-step fashion. Interestingly, each man found executive success in his own way. In fact, it is best not to look on the two points of view as "either-or" alternatives. A well-managed career will probably include elements of each. The carefully thought-out plan can point you in a general career direction; an eye for opportunity can fill in the details along the way.

Figure 21.5 summarizes a basic framework for formal career planning. It has a lot in common

FIGURE 21.5 Steps in formal career planning.

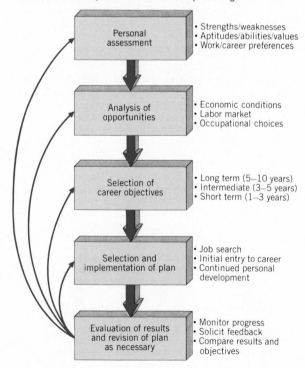

Personal assessment
• Strengths/weaknesses
• Aptitudes/abilities/values
• Work/career preferences

Analysis of opportunities
• Economic conditions
• Labor market
• Occupational choices

Selection of career objectives
• Long term (5–10 years)
• Intermediate (3–5 years)
• Short term (1–3 years)

Selection and implementation of plan
• Job search
• Initial entry to career
• Continued personal development

Evaluation of results and revision of plan as necessary
• Monitor progress
• Solicit feedback
• Compare results and objectives

Doonesbury cartoon (showing job interview).

with the process of strategic planning covered in Chapter 5. The five steps in the framework begin with personal assessment and then progress through analysis of opportunities, selection of career objectives, and implementation of strategies until the point of evaluation of results is reached. Then the process is recycled as necessary to allow constructive revision of the career plan over time. Success in each of these steps entails a good deal of self-awareness and frank assessment. The message is clear—a successful career begins with sufficient insight to make good decisions about matching personal needs and capabilities with job opportunities over time.

As with personal wellness, your managerial responsibility in respect to career planning and development is twofold. It includes both the responsibility to plan and manage your career, and the responsibility to assist in the career planning and development of subordinates. Some ideas on meeting each set of responsibilities follow.[22]

1. *To take charge of his or her personal career, a manager should*

   ■ Establish a personal career plan; be willing to modify this plan as opportunities develop.

   ■ Take and maintain a personal-skills inventory; try to match job responsibilities and skills.

   ■ Set specific personal development objectives.

   ■ Maintain a career-oriented dialogue with higher-level managers.

   ■ Take advantage of all training and development opportunities.

   ■ Evaluate and constructively modify personal development efforts over time.

2. *To assist in the career planning and development of subordinates, a manager should*

   ■ Establish a human-resource plan for the work unit.

   ■ Take and maintain a human-resource inventory for the work unit.

   ■ Establish human-resource development objectives for the work unit.

   ■ Maintain a career-oriented dialogue with subordinates.

   ■ Encourage and support subordinates' participation in training and development activities.

   ■ Evaluate and constructively modify all efforts to meet the development needs of subordinates over time.

Initial Entry to a Career

The most fundamental prerequisite to any successful career, no matter how well planned, is for a person to be good at his or her work. The potential to advance most frequently arises through a record of performance accomplishment. Thus one of the best pieces of career advice that can be given to anyone is to work hard and try to perform well on the job. We can only wonder, for example, what chance the job applicant has in the Doonesbury cartoon. He hardly seems to be communicating a sense of desire and capability to perform!

Initial entry to a new job and/or organization is the first point at which the individual and the organization begin to learn if they have chosen

Table 21.5 A Production Manager's Balance Sheet for Present Position

	Positive Anticipations	Negative Anticipations
Tangible gains and losses for *self*	1. Satisfactory pay 2. Plenty of opportunities to use my skills and competencies 3. For the present, my status in the organization is okay (but it won't be for long if I am not promoted in the next year)	1. Long hours 2. Constant time pressures—deadlines too short 3. Unpleasant paperwork 4. Poor prospects for advancement to a higher-level position 5. Repeated reorganizations make my work chaotic 6. Constant disruption from high turnover of other executives I deal with
Tangible gains and losses for *others*	1. Adequate income for family 2. Spouse and children get special privileges because of my position in the firm	1. Not enough time free to spend with my family 2. Spouse often has to put up with my irritability when I come home after bad days at work
Self-approval or Self-disapproval	1. This position allows me to make full use of my potentialities 2. Proud of my achievements 3. Proud of the competent team I have shaped up 4. Sense of meaningful accomplishment when I see the products for which we are responsible	1. Sometimes feel I'm a fool to continue putting up with the unreasonable deadlines and other stupid demands made by the top managers
Social approval or disapproval	1. Approval of people on my team, who look up to me as their leader and who are good friends 2. Approval of my superior who is a friend and wants me to stay	1. Very slight skeptical reaction of my spouse, who asks me if I might be better off in a different firm 2. A friend in another firm who has been wanting to wangle something for me will be disappointed

Source: Irving Janis and Dan Wheeler, "Thinking Clearly About Career Choices," *Psychology Today* (May 1978), p. 75. Reprinted from *Psychology Today.* Copyright © 1978 Ziff-Davis Publishing Company.

well in the sense of achieving a good person-job-organization fit. As we discussed in our review of staffing in Chapter 9, "misfits" can occur because of breakdowns in procedures and decisions during the selection process. The result is that turnover sometimes occurs shortly after persons assume new jobs. Good advice to the manager is to do a thorough job in all phases of the staffing process—job analysis through recruitment, selection, orientation, and training. Providing applicants with realistic job previews is most helpful in clarifying expectations so that they can make truly informed choices about whether or not to accept a new job.

The job applicant also shares the responsibility for success or failure in the selection process. Choosing a job and joining an organization are difficult decisions that inevitably exert a lot of influence over our lives. Whenever a new job is being contemplated, the best advice is to know yourself and learn as much about the job and organization as you can. One example of such an assessment is shown in Table 21.5.

Adult Transitions During a Career

As people mature, they pass through various adult life stages. Each entails somewhat different problems and prospects, some of which can have a career impact. It can be helpful for you to recognize these transitions and prepare to face them in the course of your managerial career. It is also useful to recognize the effects of these transitions as experienced by the people with whom you work. Understanding the special problems and pressures encountered by other persons at various stages of the adult life cycle may help you work better with them in a managerial capacity.

Figure 21.6 is one portrayal of the development periods of adulthood. Note the three transition points: early-adult transition, mid-life transition, and late-adult transition. Although they may not always occur exactly as indicated in the figure, the logic of each transition involves unique challenges of interest to you.[23]

1. *The move to early adulthood*   Early adulthood is a period of completing one's education, entering an occupation, and getting married. Parenthood follows, with new family and job responsibilities. It is a time of vitality, self-determination, and perhaps one or more job changes.

2. *Mid-life transition*   In the late 30s and early 40s, the career is all-important. Family complications stress this orientation, and personal crisis can occur. Some frustrations in the career may occur and bring with them added questions and confidence, goals, and identity. For the first time health and age become relevant concerns.

3. *Middle and later adulthood*   Settling in begins here, with a knowledge of the "system" and a mellowing of goals. Concerns turn toward making a real impact at work, being a mentor to others, and balancing goals and reality. This is a time of consolidating personal affairs and accepting career limitations. The next step is retirement and, perhaps, a new career.

When you think about adult life stages or transitions, you should note that sooner or later the careers of most people level off. A **career plateau** is a position from which someone is not likely to move to a higher level of work responsibility. Three reasons account for many career plateaus.[24]

1. *Personal choice*   Some people plateau by personal choice, basically because they like their jobs. This may involve feeling that the job continues to be challenging, or it may mean that one is comfortable with existing competencies and insecure about moving on to test new ones.

2. *Limited ability*   Other persons plateau because they have reached the limits of their ability. Even though they do their present jobs well, they are not considered to have the abilities and/or the desire to learn the abilities required for promotion.

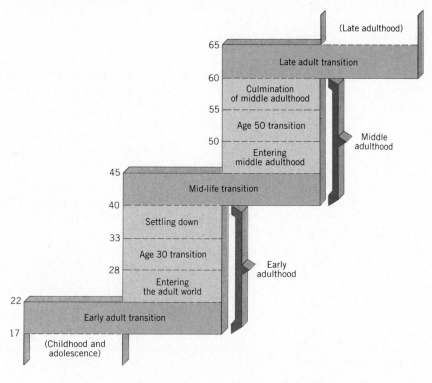

FIGURE 21.6 Developmental periods in early and middle adulthood. *Source:* Daniel J. Levinson, *The Seasons of a Man's Life* (New York: Knopf, 1978), p. 57. Used by permission.

3. *Limited opportunity* A third reason for career plateaus is a lack of opportunity for promotion or transfer. An individual may want to move, but be blocked from doing so because all the desired alternative jobs are filled.

It takes imagination and effort to maintain the productivity and job satisfaction of someone who is on a career plateau. For some people the plateau may occur at a life stage when it is a comfortable fit with individual needs. For others the plateau may occur too early or at a time when other significant adult transitions highlight the importance of continuing success in one's career. In both cases, a clear understanding of the plateaued employee's needs can assist in the selection of appropriate managerial strategies.

Table 21.6 shows how the work-related needs of persons may vary from one career stage to the next. These ideas can help you to understand your needs and reactions to opportunities, problems, and plateaus encountered over the course of a career. They can also be used to understand the special needs of your subordinates as they pass through various adult and career transitions.

Dual-Career Families

In more and more families, both spouses are participating in the work force and seeking rewarding careers. The chances are that you will become or already are part of such a working team. Individual career problems and prospects become magnified in these cases because of the added challenge of managing the separate careers of both partners. A recent survey of corporate chief executives identified problems typical to dual-career couples.[25]

In one of every ten of the survey cases, the executive's spouse is employed full-time outside the home. Among couples in that category, about 18 percent report that the wife or husband of the survey respondent turned down a promotion or job offer from another organization within the past two years. Most often, the reason cited was conflict with the other partner's career.

Table 21.6 Developmental Needs in Early, Middle, and Late Career

Stage	Task Needs	Social and Emotional Needs
Early career	1. Develop action skills 2. Develop a specialty 3. Develop creativity, innovation 4. Rotate into new area after 3–5 years	1. Support 2. Autonomy 3. Deal with feelings of rivalry, competition
Middle career	1. Develop skills in training and coaching others (younger employees) 2. Training for updating and integrating skills 3. Develop broader views of work and organization 4. Job rotation into new job requiring skills	1. Opportunity to express feelings about mid-life (anguish, defeat, limited time, restlessness) 2. Reorganize thinking about self (mortality, values, family, work) 3. Reduced self-indulgence and competitiveness 4. Support and mutual problem-solving for coping with midcareer stress
Late career	1. Shift from power role, to one of consultation, guidance, wisdom 2. Begin to establish self in activities outside the organization (start on part-time basis)	1. Support and counseling to help see integrated life experiences as a platform for others. 2. Acceptance of one's one and only life cycle 3. Gradual detachment from organization

Source: From Douglas T. Hall, *Careers in Organizations*, p. 90. Copyright © 1976 by Goodyear Publishing Co. Inc. Reprinted by permission.

How are career conflicts resolved? About 42 percent of the respondents who have experienced such a conflict said the career with the higher compensation takes priority. Another solution mentioned frequently gives precedence to the career that offers a greater long-term potential.

As a result of such conflicts, the working partners in dual-career families can easily find themselves living and working under considerable stress. Two examples of basic day-to-day pressures follow.[26]

> "If I were in top management, I'd be in a pickle," says Robert Adams, whose career as a marketing manager for Door-Oliver Inc. doesn't require senior management's customary workload and 14-hour days. But Adams has a wife with a career of her own and a six-month-old son, and he worries that some companies still measure career dedication by "what time your car leaves the parking lot."

> A magazine editor remembers the time her boss dropped by her desk at 5:45 p.m. for a conference. She said matter-of-factly that she would be right with him. When he walked down the hall to his office, she frantically phoned her husband and told him he would have to get home to relieve the babysitter, who was scheduled to leave for an appointment. "What was I going to tell my boss?" she asks. "Sorry, I can't meet with you because I've got to relieve my babysitter? He already thinks women are flaky."

Dual-career couples present problems to organizations as well. Some employers worry that the pressures felt by employees in dual-career families may harm productivity and morale. Then, too, the dual-career family sometimes makes it difficult to recruit new employees or transfer existing ones to new places.

The "trailing-spouse" problem is the need to find employment for the partner who leaves a job to make a move to a new location benefiting the other partner's career. In fact, that trailing spouse is often the woman. Wives still tend to relocate for the benefit of their husband's careers, and one reason is that the couple follows the route of higher compensation. Even though women have made recent strides in gaining equal employment and career opportunity, the pay of women managers still generally lags behind that of their male counterparts. This disparity in pay

remains despite the fact that women are now getting the recognition they deserve as capable and responsible managers. *Newsline 21.4* makes this latter point quite well.

Final Advice

Many problems and prospects await you in your managerial career. The issues previously discussed merely set the stage for the excitement to come. By way of final advice, consider the following suggested career tactics.[27]

1. *Perform* The basic foundation of success in any job is good performance. A record of high performance will please your superiors, earn respect from your peers and subordinates, and call attention to you as a person of high potential.

2. *Stay visible* Don't hesitate to make sure others recognize your hard work, and the performance results achieved. This is a public-relations task to be done in a professional manner and without becoming known as a braggart. When the performance record is there, project memos, progress reports, and even requests for more frequent evaluation and feedback sessions with superiors can enhance the visibility of your success.

3. *Be willing to move* Don't get locked into a job that you have already mastered and/or that is narrow and limited in the visibility or opportunity it offers. Take advantage of promotion opportunities within the organization. Be willing to change organizations for similar reasons. Don't be afraid to nominate yourself when appropriate for new and challenging changes of assignment.

4. *Find a mentor* It is always beneficial to have a senior executive who acts as a mentor you can learn from and who sponsors your career interests. Ideally, this will be a person who can create mobility and opportunity for you as his or her own career progresses over time.

5. *Manage your career* Stay active in thinking seriously and systematically about your career. Prepare and maintain a career plan even if it is only a broad frame of reference for directing your efforts and evaluating opportunities as

NEWSLINE 21.4

BUSINESS VOTES "YES" ON WOMEN AS EXECUTIVES . . .

Q. *Here are a series of statements about women in the workplace. Do you agree or disagree?*

	Percent	
	Agree	**Disagree**
A. Contributions of women executives in the company are more positive than negative	94%	2%
Women executives are performing on the job as well as or better than expected	86	5
Quite a number of women use sex and guile to get ahead ..	7	87
Some men now can't get ahead in certain jobs because they are being saved for women	8	89

. . . but still finds it hard to accept them as bosses

Q. *Do you agree or disagree with these statements?*

	Percent	
	Agree	**Disagree**
A. It has been harder to promote women to high-level positions than we thought it would be	41%	52%
Men don't like to take orders from women	41	49
Women don't like to take orders from other women	39	45

Source: Business Week/Harris Poll, *Business Week* (June 28, 1982), p. 10. Reprinted from the June 28, 1982 issue of *Business Week* by special permission. Copyright © 1982 by McGraw-Hill, Inc., New York, NY 10020. All rights reserved.

they arise. Don't let success at any one stage distract you from taking advantage of new appointments with further growth potential. Take charge of your career, and stay in charge.

6. *Continue your education* Lifelong learning is

both a responsibility and a prerequisite of long-term managerial success. In today's dynamic and challenging environment, the manager who fails to continue to learn and develop appropriate skills will not succeed. Maintain the yearn to learn—that is, make a commitment to take advantage of all opportunities for continuing education and ongoing development of your knowledge and skills in the management area.

MANAGEMENT FOR PRODUCTIVITY: A RECAP

Before leaving this final chapter, let's clarify for one last time the basic theme of this book. To begin, a manager is anyone to whom one or more others report in an organization. The manager's job is to make good decisions and solve problems in such a way that organizational productivity is enhanced. To do this, managers must foster both high performance and satisfaction among the members of their work units.

Figure 21.7 presents a comprehensive view of management as it is addressed in this book. The premise underlying the figure is clear-cut. The insights available in the knowledge base we know as the field of "management" can help managers do their jobs well. This knowledge can help you, in particular, make appropriate decisions, solve difficult problems, and take advantage of day-to-day opportunities in a managerial career. Managers of all types—such as marketing managers, accounting managers, personnel managers, and finance managers—and managers working in all types of organizations—large or small, public or private—can and should draw

on "management" as a knowledge base to help achieve productivity.

Figure 21.7 also points out three basic elements in the practice of management through which performance results can be achieved: (1) developing the essential managerial skills—technical, human, conceptual; (2) implementing the management functions—planning, organizing, leading, controlling; (3) enacting the managerial roles—interpersonal, informational, and decisional.

The ultimate value of this book to the practicing manager and to students of management is further summarized in Figure 21.8. This figure should help you review the entire book and integrate its many insights as they relate to the practice of management in the demanding world of tomorrow.

As you look ahead to this exciting future, reflect on these comments from a book with the title, *Productivity: Prospects for Growth*.[28] They ask you to accept a great deal of responsibility as a manager, and to fulfill this responsibility well. The task is clear; the rest is up to you!

The potential gains from increased productivity for any individual, organization, or nation are great. Such gains, however, can be realized only if positive steps are taken to improve productivity. Fundamentally, each of us has an inherent responsibility to apply, in the most effective manner possible, the resources with which we are endowed or entrusted. We must always seek a better

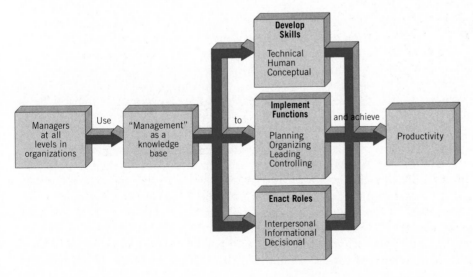

FIGURE 21.7 A comprehensive view of management.

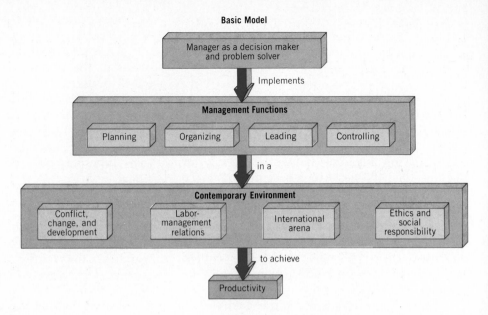

Basic Model

Manager as a decision maker and problem solver

Implements

Management Functions

| Planning | Organizing | Leading | Controlling |

in a

Contemporary Environment

| Conflict, change, and development | Labor-management relations | International arena | Ethics and social responsibility |

to achieve

Productivity

FIGURE 21.8 A framework for studying management.

way and try to leave things better than we found them. Improved productivity requires awareness, commitment, ingenuity, action, and perseverance. The opportunity is there—what we do with it depends upon ourselves.

SUMMARY

The manager's quest for productivity includes a concern to facilitate both high performance and satisfaction within the work unit and organization as a whole. Trends suggest that managers of the late 1980s and beyond will be held accountable for achieving productivity in an extremely challenging environment. We look ahead to a world in which international competition, energy shortages, and growing economic complexity will be but a few of the conditions with which managers must successfully deal. When these trends are coupled with emerging pressures in supervisor-subordinate relations and the increased application of high technology in the workplace, the work setting of future managers appears complicated indeed.

Stress—the state of tension that accompanies exposure to extraordinary demands, constraints, and/or opportunities—will certainly accompany the managerial role. Managers must tolerate high levels of personal and job-related stress; they must also be prepared to recognize and understand the impact of stress on others with whom they work. Although the destructive side of

stress is sometimes reflected in reduced productivity and perhaps even ill health, stress has a more positive side that can stimulate creativity and high performance. The effective manager of the future will be able to work well under stress.

Career planning and development is another important managerial responsibility. Managers must take charge of their personal careers in order to ensure success. This can involve deliberate and close adherence to a formal career plan, or it may involve having a clear sense of career direction, but being ready and able to respond to unforeseen opportunities as they occur. Because of a manager's supervisory responsibilities, he or she will also be involved in assisting subordinates in their career planning and development activities. Looking ahead to a managerial career involves anticipating such things as the pressures of initial entry to a career, dual-career families, transitions through various adult life stages, and even the potential career plateau. Through it all, good managers will remain aware of how their needs and those of others must inevitably work in harmony with those of the organization.

Managers perform a most important social task. Productivity is the cornerstone of a healthy, prosperous, and gainful society. If high productivity is to be achieved in the future, good managers will have to lead the way. *Management for Productivity* was written to help you make this important and positive contribution to our world.

THINKING THROUGH THE ISSUES

1. What is the significance of the behavior of Delta's employees as shown in the chapter-opening example?

2. Identify three environmental trends that can be predicted for the future. Why do you think they are important to managers?

3. Identify three trends in people that will affect management in the future. How do you think they will impact managerial work?

4. What will the growing revolution in high technology mean to managers of the future?

5. What is job stress, and what are some of the potential stressors that can cause it to occur?

6. How can stress be constructive for the individual?

7. What can a manager do in a high-pressure work or career situation to minimize the destructive potential of stress?

8. What is the advantage of a systematic approach to career planning?

9. Identify what are likely to be the special problems of persons who are at transitions in early, middle, and late adulthood. How should persons experiencing these problems be handled by their supervisors?

10. Review the list of career suggestions provided in the section of the chapter entitled "final advice." What is your evaluation of this advice? Why?

THE MANAGER'S VOCABULARY

Career	Career plateau	Destructive stress	Personal wellness
Career path	Constructive stress	Stress	Stressors
Career planning			

CAREER PERSPECTIVE: FAST TRACK AT BETHLEHEM STEEL[29]

It has been tough to convince bright young college graduates to join the steel industry. Steel companies have reputations for stodgy management, dirty plants, declining profits, and big problems. David Mengel, a 21-year-old graduate of Pennsylvania State University, took the challenge. He was happy to sign up with Bethlehem Steel Corporation for the opportunity of participating in Bethlehem's Loop class of 1980. This unusual recruiting and training program puts college graduates on the fast track in management from the first day they join the company. The program offers the new graduate a guaranteed shot at management from the beginning. From Bethlehem's perspective, the program is a way of competing with companies that offer higher salaries in more appealing industries, but can't offer the immediate challenge and responsibility.

A trainee "loops" through all of the company's operations, from steelmaking to accounting to public relations in three phases. The first phase is a two-week orientation session at headquarters. It provides an overall look at the company and thorough exposure to the steel-making process. The second phase involves extensive movement through the recruit's assigned plant or office. This leads to phase three, on-the-job training for two years. Participants receive quarterly evaluations. The goal is for them to rise at least as high as department heads during their careers.

The company started this program in 1922 and 56 percent of its current top managers were participants. The percentage is even higher in some middle-management levels. One outcome of the program appears to be high loyalty. The company has a high retention rate of 70 percent through the first five years of employment for Loop participants.

Participants in the Loop classes consider themselves unique. Elton J. Deleune, a graduate of Duke University, says, "We're bombarded with the fact that we're special; it's hard not to start thinking that 'maybe I am better.' " But the program breeds feelings of both camaraderie and competition. On the cooperative side, participants help one another out during technical study sessions. For example, an engineer in the program may explain to an accountant how steel is rolled into sheets in the mills while receiving an explanation of the company's need for faster depreciation to offset inflation in return. On the competitive side, participants vie for the attention of top executives. M. Tracey Carlson, a Mount Holyoke graduate, wants to be Bethlehem's first woman sales manager. She says that aim is modest compared to the goals of her colleagues. "One guy has already said he's going to be chairman one day," she says. "I don't think he'll make it, though."

Questions

1. What are the apparent strengths and weaknesses of Bethlehem's Loop management-development program?

2. Would you like to join a "fast-track" management-development program? Why or why not?

3. Would you take a risk to join such a program in the steel industry as opposed to accepting a job offer with less initial responsibility in a high-technology field? Explain your answer.

CASE APPLICATION: CAN COMPANIES KILL?[30]

This case is real. It is based on information in a legal complaint filed with the courts. Only names and certain details have been changed to protect the identities of the parties involved.

Roger Berman joined the company as a manage-

ment trainee soon after he graduated from high school. A hard worker, he put himself through college at night while rising steadily through the ranks of the giant corporation. Eventually he became manager of a large department, with a salary of about $50,000, plus substantial fringe benefits. In time, however, the job became increasingly difficult for him, demanding more and more of his evening and weekend hours. The pressure became so great that he asked several times to have his workload lightened. His superiors promised to ease up on him, but nothing changed.

Approaching 50, with 30 years of service to the company, Berman decided in 1978 to take early retirement, largely to escape from the strain of his job. His superiors talked him into staying on, promising to ease his work load. Relying on those promises, he agreed, but again, the complaint charges, no relief came. Some time after that Berman discovered that he would not become eligible again for early retirement and pension for another five years.

With escape by retirement thus effectively blocked, Berman became increasingly anxious about his ability to accomplish his work. His company doctor referred him to an outside psychiatrist. The psychiatrist reported back to the company, warning that Berman's mental health was "precarious" and would be "further impaired" without some relief in the conditions of his work. Still, apparently, nothing changed.

On January 10, 1979, Berman's colleagues found him sitting at his desk in a dazed stupor. They could not snap him out of it, nor could the company doctor. During this "catatonic" episode, according to the complaint, he was not sent to a hospital; he was not sent home; no one called his wife. After a few hours, he came out of it on his own. He stayed in the office for the rest of that day, and left for home, alone.

On the morning of January 31, 1979, Roger Berman left for work early, as usual, and drove into the city to his office at the corporate headquarters of a large international conglomerate. Instead of putting in his customary long day, however, he left the office abruptly during the morning. He may have driven around for some time, but eventually he went home and pulled into his garage. With the motor still running, he got out of the car, closed the garage door, and apparently sat down to wait. His body was found there later, slumped on the floor.

The autopsy report listed carbon monoxide as the cause of death, but in this case "cause" is a matter of some dispute. Berman's widow is suing his former employer for $6 million, claiming it caused her husband's death by failing to respond to his repeated complaints of overwork and by displaying a "callous and conscious disregard" for his mental health. The case raises the question of whether an employer can, in effect, by its own action or inaction, kill with stress.

Questions

1. How do you explain Roger Berman's suicide based on the situation as presented in the case?

2. What could/should have been done by Roger and/or his superiors to manage the stress he seemed to have experienced?

3. Do you support the widow's lawsuit? Why or why not?

CLASS EXERCISE: BEHAVIOR QUIZ[31]

1. Complete the following behavior quiz. Circle the number on the scale that best characterizes your behavior for each trait.

a. Casual about appointments	1 2 3 4 5 6 7 8	Never late for appointments
b. Not competitive	1 2 3 4 5 6 7 8	Very competitive
c. Never feel rushed	1 2 3 4 5 6 7 8	Always feel rushed
d. Take things one at a time	1 2 3 4 5 6 7 8	Try to do many things at once.
e. Slow doing things	1 2 3 4 5 6 7 8	Fast doing things
f. Express feelings	1 2 3 4 5 6 7 8	"Sit" on feelings
g. Many outside interests	1 2 3 4 5 6 7 8	Few outside interests

2. Now total your scores for the seven items. Multiply this total by 3 to arrive at a final number of points.

Score : _____ × 3 = _____ final points

3. In Chapter 21 we discuss a Type A personality as prone to stress-related illnesses. The Type A person creates self-induced stress as a result of constant striving for achievement. Circle the personality profile determined in the prior quiz by locating your total point score on the following list.

Number of points	Type of Personality
Less than 90	B
90 to 99	B+
100 to 105	A−
106 to 119	A
120 or more	A+

4. Think about the accuracy of this personality profile and its potential implications regarding your work-stress-health relationships. Share and discuss your results with a nearby class-mate. Await further class discussion led by the instructor.

REFERENCES

[1] Margaret Loeb, "Some Happy Employees at Delta Want to Buy a Big Gift for the Boss," *Wall Street Journal* (September 28, 1982), p. 31. Reprinted by permission of the *Wall Street Journal.* Copyright © 1982 Dow Jones & Company, Inc. All rights reserved.

[2] Charles Dickens, *A Tale of Two Cities,* in *The Works of Charles Dickens* (New York: P. F. Collier, 1880), p. 343.

[3] Robert M. Fulmer, "Eight Paradoxes for the 1980s," Working paper #0-003, School of Business Administration, Emory University, Atlanta, Ga.

[4] Based in part on George Strauss, "Personel Management: Prospect for the Eighties," in K. M. Rowland and G. R. Ferris (eds.), *Personnel Management* (New York: Allyn and Bacon, 1982), pp. 504–513.

[5] Ibid. John Naisbitt, *Megatrends: Ten New Directions Transforming Our Lives* (New York: Warner, 1982).

[6] Jeremy Main, "Work Won't Be the Same Again," *Fortune* (June 28, 1982), p. 58.

[7] Ibid. p. 59.

[8] Ibid., pp. 64, 65.

[9] This section is adapted from Fulmer, op. cit. Used by permission.

[10] Cited by Strauss, op. cit., p. 514.

[11] "Boosting the Careers of B-School Grads," *Business Week* (October 11, 1982), p. 72; and Roy Rowan, "How Harvard's Women MBA's Are Managing," *Fortune* (July 11, 1983), pp. 58–72.

[12] Adapted from Arthur P. Brief, Randall S. Schuler, and Mary Van Sell, *Managing Job Stress* (Boston: Little, Brown, 1981), pp. 7, 8.

[13] Michael Weldholz, "Stress Increasingly Seen as Problem with Executives More Vulnerable," *Wall Street Journal* (September 28, 1982), p. 31.

[14] Meyer Freidman and Ray Roseman, *Type A Behavior and Your Heart* (New York: Knopf, 1974).

[15] See John D. Adams, "Health, Stress, and the Manager's Life Style," *Group and Organization Studies,* Vol. 6 (September 1981), pp. 291–301.

[16] See John M. Ivancevich and Michael T. Matteson, "Optimizing Human Resources: A Case for Preventive Health and Stress Management," *Organizational Dynamics,* Vol. 9 (Autumn 1980), pp. 6–8.

[17] Adapted from Robert Kreitner, "Personal Wellness: It's Just Good Business," *Business Horizons,* Vol. 25 (May–June 1982), pp. 28–35. Copyright 1982 by the Foundation for the School of Business at Indiana University. Reprinted by permission.

[18] Ibid.

[19] Edgar H. Schein, *Career Dynamics: Matching Individual and Organizational Needs* (Reading, Mass.: Addison-Wesley, 1978), p. 1.

[20] Irving Janis and Dan Wheeler, "Thinking Clearly About Career Choices," *Psychology Today* (May 1978), p. 67.

[21] These viewpoints are found in the *Advanced Management Journal* (Summer 1975). Adapted, by permission of the publisher, from *Advanced Management Journal* (Summer 1975), © 1975 by *AMACOM,* a division of American Management Associations. All rights reserved.

[22] Kae H. Chung and Leon C. Megginson, *Organizational Behavior: Developing Managerial Skills* (New York: Harper & Row, 1981), pp. 539–540; Schein, op. cit., pp. 189–199.

[23] Based on Daniel J. Levinson, *The Seasons of a Man's Life* (New York: Knopf, 1978), pp. 56–63.

[24] This and subsequent discussion is based on Kirby Warren, "Reflections," *Senior Seminar Newsletter* (Bloomington, Ill.: Fall 1982); see also Thomas P. Ference, James A. F. Stoner, and E. Kirby Warren, "Managing the Career Plateau," *Academy of Management Review,* Vol. 2 (October 1977), pp. 602–612.

[25] Frank Allen, "Mobile Managers Get Greater Pay,

Especially if They Join New Firms," *Wall Street Journal* (October 6, 1980), p. 31. Reprinted by permission of the *Wall Street Journal.* Copyright © Dow Jones & Company, Inc. All rights reserved.

26 From Mary Bralove, "Problems of Two-Career Families Start Forcing Businesses to Adapt," *Wall Street Journal* (July 15, 1981), p. 23. Reprinted by permission of the *Wall Street Journal.* Copyright 1981 Dow Jones & Company, Inc. All rights reserved.

27 Based on Ross A. Webber, "13 Career Commandments," *MBA* (May 1975), p. 47; Alan N. Schoonmaker, *Executive Career Strategy* (New York: American Management Association, 1971).

28 Robert M. Ranftl, "Making Research and Develop-ment Work," in Jerome M. Rosow (ed.), *Productivity: Prospects for Growth* (New York: Van Nostrand, 1981), pp. 225, 239.

29 Information from Douglas Sease, "Grads Trained for Fast Track at Bethlehem," *Wall Street Journal* (July 29, 1980), p. 31. Adapted by permission of the *Wall Street Journal.* Copyright © 1980 Dow Jones & Company, Inc. All rights reserved.

30 From Berkeley Rice, "Can Companies Kill?" *Psychology Today,* Vol. 15 (June 1981), p. 77. Reprinted from *Psychology Today.* Copyright © 1981, Ziff-Davis Publishing Company.

31 This quiz is slightly adapted from Brief, et al., op. cit., p. 87. Used by permission.

Part 7
INTEGRATING CASES

PRODUCTIVITY IMPROVEMENT AT MOTOROLA

In the decade of the 70s, U.S. electronics companies were hard hit by rising imports of foreign-built consumer electronics products. Despite that, Motorola Inc., Chicago, did well. It began the previous decade at a respectable $700 million annual sales, and grew to 70,000 employees and sales at $3 billion per year.

It moved out of consumer electronics to concentrate in high-technology industrial and commercial electronics equipment. As the 1980s began, besides its threefold growth in a decade, it could point to a 17 percent return on stockholder equity, a 14 percent return on invested capital, and a 6 percent return on sales.

So when Motorola says it can grow in the 80s, it's worth a listen. And where U.S. industrial productivity has been falling in recent years, Motorola believes—as do a number of other U.S. companies—that by attacking the twin areas of productivity and quality control, U.S. products can be more competitive in both domestic and foreign markets.

There are countless ideas as to how to get U.S. productivity up. Motorola lists four elements

Source: Excerpted from Keith W. Bennett, "Motorola Focus on Productivity & Quality Is Worth a Look," *Iron Age* (February 10, 1982), pp. 61–64. Used by permission.

it wanted in its program. First, it would begin with product design, and the goal of instituting the best design at a minimal cost. Second, it would buy the newest and best equipment for its plants. Third, it would ensure that people in the company understand and believe in the policies and methods used in the plants. The fourth element is what Ralph Elsner, vice-president of the company, calls "the crucial element": getting people involved and motivated.

If you've been following the history of productivity-improvement programs in the United States, you certainly are well aware that most of them contain many of the same elements. Usually, you'll find the work-team concept. Less frequently, you find a direct relation between setting and reaching output and quality goals, and attaching a direct cash compensation to that goal. There also has to be a strong management involvement, from top to bottom. There has to be idea feedback from the line people back to their managers, and it has to function rapidly.

Motorola, though, seems to have been moving fairly deliberately in putting all these elements together throughout its total plant system in its Participative Management Program (PMP).

"There are really two plans,"

Elsner notes. "Plan I is the operating and manufacturing force. Based on a kind of 'line-of-sight' idea, the teams are kept to about 75 per shift, or a total three-shift team of approximately 250 persons. The PMP team can be as small as 35 persons.

The Plan I team tracks its own performance and sets its own goals. The feedback comes in measurement of some six cost elements: current cost, quality (as measured by deliveries and returns and factory quality reports), delivery of product against schedules, inventory controls, housekeeping and safety records, and cost improvement.

Bonuses are calculated and paid monthly. A steering committee meets monthly to discuss reports and suggestions from the working committee. This steering group is another avenue for managers to meet with an organizational cross section and to maintain open communication between the working committees and other parts of the company. The steering committee also reviews performance data from the work groups.

"Once a week, everybody meets with the supervisor in a session that can be as short as five minutes, but may go as long as two hours," Elsner says. "Generally, the meetings tend to get shorter as the program matures and the original problems get honed down. Despite this, however, some sections meet daily, and the loss of that much time in a group doesn't interfere with the gains in productivity."

Plan II is in the area of supporting services—for example, design, financial, and sales and marketing elements of the company. Results in these groups have traditionally been harder to measure. Here again, a system of steering committees (which include Plan I representatives) reviews annual plans set by the working committees of engineers and office workers. The Plan II groups are fewer in number—generally, one per business center.

Motorola holds that measured cash rewards are a necessary part of the PMP program (unlike the quality circles used in Japan). So it was necessary to measure the output of the Plan II groups, and that is related to the level of profit earned by the business center in which the Plan II group is working. The Plan II bonus is based on the profit return above a minimum, and against goals set by the group itself.

Ralph Elsner agrees with the charge leveled by some veterans of other productivity plans that a PMP program can make a manager's job tougher. Supervisors have to keep open communication with the work force, and have to be able to suggest—often—where they used to command. They have to listen. And that has often been the downfall of many such programs.

To keep the consciousness of the manager, "We've also developed a questionnaire that each manager can send out as a blind question to his or her own people. The results—which give a picture of how the workers feel

about him or her—are for the manager's use only."

The PMP program at Motorola began in the chief executive office. Chairman Robert Galvin brought in Ralph Elsner as the operating executive and vice-president reporting directly to the executive office. Elsner has only one staff member and a secretary. Each plant has its own PMP manager, reporting to the plant manager in the same way that Elsner reports to the chief executive, as deputy to the president.

PMP is a communications program. It brings people and data together at every level. Production results, for example, are posted regularly on display boards. Every member of every team can see the results, as well as talk about them at daily and weekly meetings. Some of the information is apparently pretty strategic stuff—for example, the loss or acquisition of a large account. Good or bad, the news goes up for everybody to consider.

It also rises along with a streamlined version of the old, and often ignored, suggestion box. This, however, is another display board. It's the "I Recommend" board, posted in each team area. There are forms on the board. Anybody with an idea that he or she feels will help the team along posts it on the board. It's the job of the manager and committees to see that an action report is back on the board within 72 hours.

As has been said here, this kind of management is tough for some managers. It takes getting used to. Raph Elsner admits that this could be a problem sometimes. "But since we've realized that PMP is the way we have to go, we've also realized we have

to help managers in using the program."

A PMP training program for vice-presidents and managers who report to them is going into its pilot stages, and there have already been courses for middle managers—thousands of them as the program developed.

Motorola has moved pretty carefully at this point, as the history shows, in expanding this program. By the end of 1983, of 45,000 domestic employees, it is hoped that 25,000 will be working with the Plan I groups, and 20,000 will be in Plan II groups.

With this rapid acceleration in the use of PMP at home, Motorola appears to be at least looking at its application in its overseas operations—but again appears to move with the same caution that it did in expanding and testing the program in its domestic plants in the 1970s.

The idea behind participative management is that there is a lot of talent out in the shop.

Elsner recalls the woman on an assembly line who turned out to have a master's degree in physics, but took an assembly-line job because teaching jobs were sparse. "Today's worker seems like a new kind of person. They won't take guff from management; they are well educated, well schooled, observant, often critical. They tend to challenge their bosses."

This is just the resource that PMP could tap, though it's not unique and other companies with somewhat similar participative management programs have enjoyed the same discovery.

"You still have failures," concedes Elsner. "But where we found a group that was failing, it tended to be where the boss had abdicated. This program isn't self-sustaining. The boss has to get along with people, and they have to work at group participation."

PMP is, it appears, a people-oriented communications program, with the important difference that it has a built-in cash component that is both an incentive to participation and an early-warning device that tells managers in advance when something is going wrong.

Questions

1. To what extent does Motorola's PMP program reflect good use of the fundamentals of planning, organizing, leading, and controlling? Explain your answer.

2. Do you agree with the statement by Ralph Elsner, a Motorola vice-president, that "a PMP program can make a manager's job tougher"? Why or why not?

3. How consistent with anticipated future trends in environment, people, and technology is the Motorola PMP approach? Explain your answer.

PRODUCTIVITY PROFILES

An extensive study by the Hughes Aircraft Company sought to identify useful techniques for optimizing productivity in technology-based organizations. Much of the study dealt with traditional research and development (R&D) efforts, although it also involved examination of key interfacing activities such as marketing, finance, procurement, manufacturing, and information systems. The study involved 28 consultants, more than 3500 R&D managers, and more than 59 industry, government, and education organizations. Two results of the study are the productivity profiles that follow.

The Productive Employee

1. *Is well qualified for the job.* Without the proper job qualifications, high productivity is out of the question. The well-qualified employee

   - Is intelligent and learns quickly.
   - Is professionally and technically competent, keeps abreast of the field.
   - Is creative and innovative, shows ingenuity and versatility.
   - Knows the job thoroughly.
   - Works "smart," uses common sense, organizes work efficiently, uses time effectively, doesn't get bogged down.

2. *Is highly motivated.* A "turned-on" employee is well on the road to high productivity. The highly motivated employee

   - Is self-motivated, takes initiative, and has a strong sense of commitment.
   - Is persevering, gets the job done in spite of obstacles.
   - Displays constructive discontent—"thinks" improvement into everything.
   - Is goal/achievement/results-oriented.
   - Has a high energy level and directs that energy effectively.
   - Gets satisfaction from a job well done.

3. *Has a positive job orientation.* A person's attitude toward work assignments greatly affects his or her work performance. The employee with a positive job orientation

   - Enjoys the job and is proud of it.
   - Sets high standards.
   - Has good work habits
   - Has good rapport with higher management.
   - Is flexible and adaptive to change.

4. *Is mature.* A mature employee displays consistent performance and requires minimal supervision. The mature employee

   - has high integrity, is genuine, honest, and sincere.
   - Has a strong sense of responsibility and self-respect.
   - Knows personal strengths and weaknesses.
   - Learns from experience.
   - Has healthy ambition— wants to grow professionally.

5. *Interfaces effectively with others.* The ability to establish positive interpersonal relationships is an asset that does much to enhance productivity. The employee who interfaces effectively

   - Exhibits social intelligence.
   - Is personable, is accepted

Source: The productivity profiles are from Robert M. Ranftl, "Making Research and Development Work," in Jerome M. Rosow, *Productivity: Prospects for Growth* (New York: Van Nostrand, 1981), pp. 205–239. Used by permission.

by and works well with superiors and colleagues.
- Communicates effectively, expresses thoughts well, is a good listener.
- Works well in team efforts, is cooperative, shares ideas.
- Exhibits a positive attitude and displays enthusiasm.

The Productive Manager

1. *Is competent at staffing.* To achieve high productivity, an organization must be staffed by capable personnel. The manager who is competent at staffing
   - Has high recruiting standards.
   - Is skilled at recognizing talent.
   - Attracts and holds capable people.
   - Is not afraid to hire top people, does not feel threatened by them.
   - Regularly introduces "new blood" into the organization.

2. *Directs work efforts effectively.* Good direction is essential for ensuring high productivity. The manager who is good at giving directions
   - Responds to the organization's current and long-range needs.
   - Exhibits conceptual skills, keeps everything in proper perspective.
   - Is results-oriented and sets a good example.
   - Delegates effectively, clearly defines assignments, responsibilities, and authority, and tries not to second-guess subordinates.
   - Is competent in dealing with people.

- Always keeps things under control, continually monitors performance.

3. *Is competent at handling complex problems and dealing with new concepts.* Skill in handling uncertainty and complexity in problem solving is an important asset for achieving high productivity. The manager capable of handling complexity and new concepts
   - Has a good understanding of the work to be done.
   - Is skilled at improvising, easily identifies and removes roadblocks and bottlenecks.
   - Is willing to take calculated risks.
   - Handles emergencies decisively, is not prone to "crisis management."

4. *Is a skillful communicator.* Productivity depends on people in the work setting. The manager with strong communication skills
   - Maintains an effective flow of two-way communication with properly informed superiors, peers, and subordinates.
   - Is readily accessible.
   - Is skillful at oral and written communication, conveys ideas clearly, concisely, and persuasively, makes effective presentations.
   - Conducts meetings skillfully.

5. *Supports subordinates in their work performance and encourages their full participation in the work environment.* Productivity can be achieved only when a manager's subordinates contrib-

ute optimally to performance objectives. A supportive and encouraging manager
   - Knows subordinates, their capabilities, and their aspirations, respects individual differences.
   - Makes everyone involved a party to the action, involves employees in decisions that affect them, makes all members feel they are important to the team effort.
   - Provides clear assignments and background information necessary for performance of those assignments.
   - Holds subordinates responsible for performance, provides performance feedback, appraises performance skillfully.
   - Gives appropriate credit, rewards fairly, praises publicly, criticizes privately.

Questions

1. Is the list of characteristics in the profile of a productive employee complete? What would you add, delete, and/or change in the profile? Why?

2. Is the list of characteristics in the profile of a productive manager complete? What would you add, delete, and/or change in the profile? Why?

3. Can a manager achieve productivity without productive subordinates? Explain your answer.

4. What characteristics do the productive employee and productive manager share in common? Why is this overlap important to you in your managerial career?

APPENDIX

QUANTITATIVE DECISION TECHNIQUES: AN INTRODUCTION TO MANAGEMENT SCIENCE

Management science and operations research are terms first introduced in Chapter 2 in a discussion of the quantitative approaches to management. These are terms used interchangeably to describe the same thing. Basically, management science/operations research (MS/OR) involves the use of mathematics to *help* managers analyze decision alternatives in a rational and scientific manner. Note that the word *help* is emphasized. These techniques can never make decisions by themselves. If used properly, however, MS/OR can be very useful in providing a manager with additional information to be used in decision-making and problem solving.

All MS/OR techniques may be classified into two large categories: deterministic or stochastic. *Deterministic methods* treat all values as fixed or known. For instance, the economic order quantity (EOQ) formula presented in Chapter 16 is deterministic. It involves a forecast of future demand, inventory carrying cost, and ordering cost, each of which is treated as a fixed value.

Stochastic methods, on the other hand, take variability into consideration. They include probability estimates of each possible value. For example, the Emperor Products case in Chapter 3 involved risk and uncertainty. To help the company president reach a decision, a decision matrix or payoff table was developed that explicitly included the probability of each possible outcome. This payoff table approach is part of the stochastic technique called *decision theory.*

Some problems are easily solved by deterministic methods, while others are more appropriately addressed using stochastic techniques. This Appendix discusses some of the most useful MS/OR techniques in each category and shows how they can be applied to various problem situations. Together with other quantitative decision-making techniques examined in Chapter 3 and Chapter 16, this overview provides you with a good introduction to management science. Still, you should realize that there are many more MS/OR techniques available than those discussed here. These are covered in specialized MS/OR courses most likely available at your college or university. They can also be reviewed by consulting books such as those by Wagner[1] or Anderson, Sweeney, and Williams.[2]

LINEAR PROGRAMMING

Linear programming is one of the most widely known and frequently used MS/OR techniques. Like all other MS/OR methods, it is based on formulating a problem in mathematical terms. The basic purpose of linear programming is to help the manager decide how to best allocate scarce resources among competing uses.

Consider the case of Ajax Computer Products. Ajax produces "floppy" disks for microcomputers in two sizes: 5¼ and 8 inches. Ajax is planning the production of disks for the coming week. Each disk requires both manufacturing and testing time, as shown in Table A.1. In the manufacturing process time can be considered a scarce resource. This week 1200 minutes of manufacturing time and 1500 minutes of testing time will be available. Each 5¼-inch disk contributes $3 of profit, and each 8-inch disk contributes $5.

Every linear programming problem consists of two basic parts: the *objective function* and the *constraints.* In this problem, Ajax's objective is to maximize its profit. The constraints are the manufacturing and testing times which limit how many disks can be produced. The problem is to decide how many disks of each size to make.

Objective Function

The objective function can be formulated for this case by letting the variable X represent the number of 5¼-inch disks to produce and the variable Y represent the number of 8-inch disks. If Ajax earns $3 profit per 5¼-inch disk, then total profit from that size disk will be $3X$. Likewise, total profit from 8-inch disks will be $5Y$. Thus, the objective function is

Maximize $3X + 5Y$

In other words, Ajax wants to maximize its total profit from producing both the 5¼- and the 8-inch disks.

Constraints

Since the objective function represents profit, it would certainly be attractive to make profit as

Table A.1 Ajax Computer Products: "Floppy" Disk

	Disk Size		Time Available (minutes)
	5¼ inches	8 inches	
Manufacturing time	2	3	1200
Testing time	2	5	1500
Profit	$3	$5	

large as possible. However, the constraints on time available for manufacturing and testing limit how many disks can be made during this week.

Recall from Table A.1 that each 5¼-inch disk requires 2 minutes of manufacturing time. Thus, the manufacturing time needed to produce 5¼-inch disks is $2X$, where X again represents the number of 5¼-inch disks produced. The manufacturing time for 8-inch disks is $3Y$. Thus, total manufacturing time for both size disks will be $2X + 3Y$. Since only 1200 minutes of manufacturing time is available this week, the total manufacturing time used to produce disks must be "less-than-or-equal-to" ($\leq$) 1200. In mathematical terms this is stated as the following equation.

$$2X + 3Y \leq 1200$$

A similar constraint can also be formulated for the amount of testing time available. It turns out to be

$$2X + 5Y \leq 1500$$

Still one more constraint must be added to the problem. Although it may seem obvious to you, we must also specify that the number of disks to be produced of either size cannot be negative. This *nonnegativity restriction* is stated mathematically as

$$X, Y \geq 0$$

In words, this equation says that X and Y must both be "greater-than-or-equal-to" zero.

LP Formulation of the Problem

The following linear programming (LP) formulation of the Ajax production problem is obtained by combining the objective function and all constraints.

Objective function: Maximize $3X + 5Y$

Subject to constraints: $2X + 3Y \leq 1200$
$2X + 5Y \leq 1500$
$X, Y \geq 0$

Before we move on to solve this problem, there are two additional things you should notice. First, the mathematical functions (objective function and constraints) are *linear*. That is, if you graph them they appear as straight lines. They do not include any nonlinear terms like $X \cdot Y$ or X^2. The technique we are discussing is called *linear* programming because it deals with *linear* functions. Another field called *nonlinear programming* does deal with nonlinear objective functions and constraints. It is beyond the scope of this Appendix. If interested, you may consult the book by Bradley, Hax, and Magnanti.[3]

A second thing to note is that, although Ajax's problem involved only two variables and three constraints, complex linear programming problems may actually involve thousands of variables and hundreds of constraints. Fortunately, they are made relatively easy to solve by the assistance of computers.

Graphic Solution

At this point you may have your own ideas about the optimal (profit maximizing) solution to Ajax's problem. If so, jot it down in the margin now so we can compare results later.

Because the Ajax problem involves only two variables, X and Y, Ajax's management decided to solve the problem graphically. To begin, they plotted the constraint $2X + 3Y \leq 1200$, as shown in Figure A.1. While $2X + 3Y$ may be less than 1200, the largest value it can assume is $2X + 3Y = 1200$. As graphed in Figure A.1, this line sets the limit for the constraint. The line and the entire shaded area below it thus represent all possible values of X and Y that satisfy the constraint $2X + 3Y \leq 1200$.

The other constraint ($2X + 5Y \leq 1500$) and the nonnegativity restriction ($X, Y \geq 0$) can be

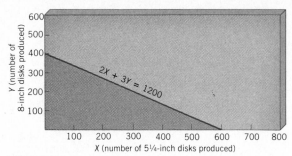
FIGURE A.1 Ajax problem constraint.

added to the graph as shown in Figure A.2. This time, though, the shaded area includes only values that satisfy all the constraints and restrictions. It is called the *feasible region* because any feasible solution—that is, one that satisfies all the constraints—must lie either in this shaded area or on the lines that bound it.

The question to be answered now is: "Which point in the feasible region will maximize profit?" To find that point, the objective function must be added to the graph. Since the objective function is stated as maximize $3X + 5Y$, the line which represents it should be moved out to the farthest location where at least one point is still in the feasible region. Figure A.3 shows that this occurs where the two constraint lines meet. This mathematically occurs at

$$2X + 3Y = 1200$$
$$2X + 5Y = 1500$$

By mathematically solving these two equations, we find the optimal point occurs at $X =$

FIGURE A.2 Ajax problem feasible region.

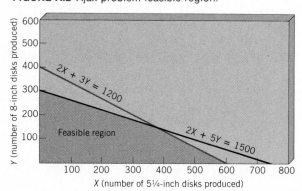

375 and $Y = 150$, and the maximum profit is $1875. In other words, Ajax should produce 375 of the 5¼-inch disks and 150 of the 8-inch ones to arrive at maximum profit of $1875.

Mathematical Programming

Linear programming is actually part of a larger component of MS/OR called *mathematical programming*. This technique uses more sophisticated mathematics, frequently with the aid of a computer, to solve more complex problems. For example, as you have probably realized by now, the graphic approach used here only works for problems with two variables. Since one axis of the graph is needed for each variable, it is difficult to handle problems with three variables and it is impossible to solve graphically a linear programming problem involving four or more variables. For such problems, a mathematical programming approach called the *simplex method* is applied. Again, a discussion of the simplex method is beyond the scope of this Appendix, but is presented in the book by Anderson, Sweeney, and Williams.[4]

The linear programming solution in the Ajax problem turned out in whole numbers. But what if it had been $X = 375¼$ and $Y = 150⅞$? Ajax cannot produce one-fourth or seven-eights of a disk, but simply rounding the solution to the nearest integer (whole number) may not provide the optimal solution. In fact, such a solution may not even be feasible! To handle problems in which the solution must be in terms of whole numbers, *integer programming* is used. If you are interested in learning more about this or other mathematical programming methods, Bradley, Hax and Magnanti is an excellent reference.[5]

MINIMUM SPANNING TREE PROBLEMS

Chapter 16 introduced PERT (Program Evaluation and Review Technique) and CPM (Critical Path Method) as techniques for handling network problems. These are problems that can be depicted as an interconnected series of events or activities that must be completed in sequential

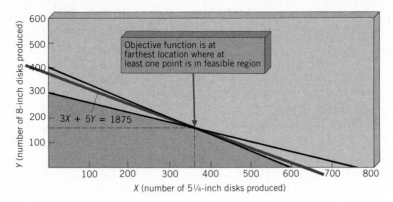

FIGURE A.3 Ajax problem solution.

combinations for a solution or finished task to be achieved.

PERT and CPM are valuable tools for managers. They can help you plan a project and make sure it stays on schedule. It turns out that many other important managerial problems can be solved as network problems, even some you would not think of in network terms. As a future manager, you should at least be aware of some of these.

Consider the case of the Rolling Greens Country Club. The club's board of directors has decided to install a water sprinkler system on the back nine holes of the golf course. Because the cost of the system will be directly proportional to the amount of pipe used, the board wants to minimize the amount of pipe needed to connect all nine holes to the sprinkler network. Table A.2 gives a matrix of distances between all nine greens.

This is a *minimum spanning tree* problem. Think of each circle and sprinkler connection in Figure A.4 as a "node," with "arcs" being all

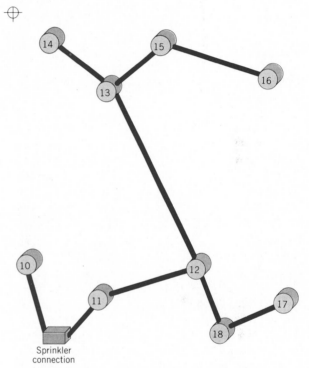

FIGURE A.4 Rolling Greens minimum spanning tree.

Table A.2 Matrix of Distances (ft)

	Connection	10	11	12	13	14	15	16	17	18
Connection	—	220	125	325	475	555	600	700	510	315
10	220	—	280	430	410	400	560	745	660	480
11	125	280	—	205	400	525	510	580	400	210
12	325	430	205	—	350	530	390	400	230	130
13	475	410	400	350	—	210	165	400	560	480
14	555	400	525	530	210	—	325	590	760	655
15	600	560	510	390	165	325	—	260	550	530
16	700	745	580	400	400	590	260	—	430	510
17	510	660	400	230	560	760	550	430	—	190
18	315	480	210	130	480	655	530	510	190	—

possible lines connecting these nodes. To solve the Rolling Greens problem you must find those arcs that connect all nodes in the shortest total distance. Laying the pipe in conformance to this network will minimize the cost of pipe required in the sprinkler system.

To do that, begin at the sprinkler connection and link it to the nearest green. Based on Table A.2, that is Green 11 with a distance of 125 feet. Now find the green closest to either 11 *or* the sprinkler connection. Be sure *not* to include 11 or the sprinkler connection because they are already connected. The shortest will be from 11 to 12 with a distance of 205. Continue by finding the shortest distance from any connected node to any unconnected node. These will be 12 to 18, 18 to 17, sprinkler connection to 10, 12 to 13, 13 to 14, 13 to 15, and 15 to 16. The final solution is shown in Figure A.4.

There are many other network problems of the minimum spanning tree type. For example, you can use network methods to find the shortest route for trucks to take between cities or to decide when an assembly line should be changed to produce a different product. MS/OR offers a variety of mathematical approaches to complex minimum spanning tree problems. Again, the computer is an important resource for solving these problems efficiently and effectively.

QUEUING THEORY

Place yourself in the following situation. The Mid-Continent Bank is building a drive-up window to serve customers who wish to transact business from their cars. The bank's manager is trying to decide whether to staff the window with one teller or two. Two tellers will cost more, but they can handle customers at a faster rate than one teller.

To help solve this problem, the responsible manager can use the stochastic MS/OR technique known as *queuing theory*. A queue is simply a waiting line. The goal of queuing theory is to compute the number of service personnel or work stations needed to minimize customer waiting time and service cost. The ideas underlying queuing theory include recognition that 1) customers arriving at a service facility will have to wait in line (as shown in Figure A.5), 2) the rate at which these customers arrive is variable, and 3) the time it takes for each customer to be serviced is also variable.

For most queuing problems it is necessary to develop a probability distribution for the number of arrivals per time period, such as arrivals per hour. In general, queuing systems have been found to approximate the Poisson probability distribution for arrivals during a given time period. The equation for this distribution is

$$P(n) = \frac{e^{-\lambda t}(\lambda t)^n}{n!}$$

where,

n = number of customers arriving (1, 2, . . .)
t = time period (minute, hour, etc.)
λ = mean number of arrivals per time period t
e = constant, approximately 2.72

FIGURE A.5 A Queuing problem.

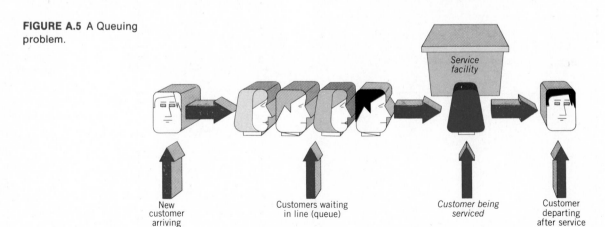

New customer arriving

Customers waiting in line (queue)

Customer being serviced

Customer departing after service

Service facility

It has also been found that the time to service each customer usually follows an exponential probability distribution. Its equation is

$$P\ (t)\ =\ \mu e^{-\mu t}$$

where,

t = service time

μ = mean number serviced per given time period (minute, hour, etc.)

e = constant, approximately 2.72

Fortunately, these two probability distributions need not be dealt with directly. Using them as a basis, mathematicians have developed the following set equations that can give you extremely useful information on a queuing problem.

λ/μ = proportion of time the service facility is busy

$$\frac{\lambda^2}{\mu\ (\mu\ -\ \lambda)} = \text{mean length of the queue}$$

$$\frac{\lambda}{\mu\ (\mu\ -\ \lambda)}\ \text{waiting} = \text{mean customer time spent}$$

where,
λ = mean number of arrivals during a given time period (minute, hour, day)

μ = mean service rate (in terms of same time period as λ)

Let's return now to the Mid-Continent Bank and apply these formulas to the facts at hand. Suppose the bank manager expects that the mean arrival rate (λ) will be 20 cars per hour. With one teller, the mean service rate (μ) is 30 cars per hour and with two it is 40 per hour. Using this information and the prior formulas, the following computations can be made to facilitate the decision of whether to use one teller or two.

One Teller Case

Facts:

$\lambda\ =\ 20$
$\mu\ =\ 30$

Computations

Proportion of time busy   = 66.7 percent
Mean length of queue   = $1\frac{1}{3}$
Mean time spent waiting = 4 minutes
                                (.067 hours)

Two Teller Case

Facts:
$\lambda\ =\ 20$
$\mu\ =\ 40$

Computations:

Proportion of time busy = 50 percent
Mean length of queue   = 1/2 car
Mean waiting time   = 1.5 minutes
                                (.025 hours)

Armed with this information provided by queuing theory, the manager is now in a better position to decide whether to add the second teller.

SIMULATION

In the case of Mid-Continent Bank you were able to use some fairly simple formulas to obtain useful information on the queuing problem. These formulas were based on the Poisson and exponential probability distributions and they made your work much easier than if you had to deal directly with the equations for those probability distributions. But what if the number of arrivals per time period at the bank did not follow the Poisson distribution, or what if the service times were not exponential? In these cases you could not have used the formulas presented.

Indeed, there are often problem situations in real life that do not match any standard mathematical formula. In such cases the MS/OR approach of *simulation* can be a useful decision-making technique.

The purpose of simulation is essentially to develop a mathematical model that resembles as closely as possible the real-life decision situation, and then use a computer to solve the problem many times under various decision circumstances. For example, suppose the manager of Mid-Continent Bank found that the number of arrivals per hour did *not* match the Poisson probability distribution and that service time also did *not* match the exponential distribution. Instead, the manager observed the actual flow of cars through the drive-up window for a time. Table A.3 presents the data collected from this observation.

Table A.3 shows that in 20 percent of the cases there was 0 to 2 minutes observed between each new customer arrival; in 60 percent of the cases there was 2 to 4 minutes between arrivals; and in another 20 percent there was a 4 to 6 minute interval. Similarly, service time was between 0 to 1 minute in 10 percent of all cases, and so on, as shown in Table A.3.

These data can be used to develop a probability model of the drive-up window service. T do this, however, we need some way of generating time between arrivals of 0 to 2 minutes 20 percent of the time, and so on, to match the real-life situation. This can be done by using *random numbers*.

Nearly any statistics book includes a table of random numbers. The idea behind such a table is that the probability of any number occurring is the same as that for any other number. Thus, for the 10 digits zero through nine, the probability of any particular number being found at a given location in the table is 1/10.

The way random numbers are used for simulation purposes is as follows. Look again at the data collected by Mid-Continent Bank. The probability of 0 to 2 minutes lapsing between arrivals is 0.2—that is, a 20 percent probability. This corresponds to the probability of finding two numbers (say 0 and 1) in a table of random numbers (0.1 + 0.1 = 0.2). For a probability of 0.6 we can use six different numbers (say 2 through 7). In this way we can relate the occurrence of certain digits in a random number table to probabilities of various arrival times shown in Table A.3. Thus if a 4 is drawn from the random number table, it corresponds either to a time between arrivals of 2 to 4 minutes or a service time of 1 to 2 minutes.

Using this scheme the staff of Mid-Continent Bank was able to simulate the drive-up window.

Table A.3 Flow of Cars Through Service Window of Mid-Continent Bank

Time Between Arrivals	Percentage of Arrivals	Random Digits
0–2	20	0, 1
2–4	60	2–7
4–6	20	8, 9

Service Time (minutes)	Service Time Percentage	Random Digits
0–1	10	0
1–2	40	1–4
2–3	40	5–8
3–4	10	9

Table A.4 Simulation of Mid-Continental Bank

Arrival No.	Arrival Time	Random No.	Time Before Next Arrival (minutes)	No. in Line	Time Enter Service	Random No.	Service Time (minutes)	Depart Service
1	0:00	7	3	0	0:00	9	3.5	0:03.5
2	0:03	1	1	1	0:03.5	4	1.5	0:05
3	0:04	0	1	1	0:05	9	3.5	0:08.5
4	0:05	4	3	1	0:08.5	0	0.5	0:09
5	0:08	8	5	1	0:09	4	1.5	0:10.5
6	0:13	0	1	0	0:13	3	1.5	0:14.5
7	0:14	8	5	1	0:14.5	1	1.5	0:16
8	0:19	1	1	0	0:19	2	1.5	0:20.5
9	0:20	7	3	1	0:20.5	7	2.5	0:23
10	0:23	8	5	0	0:23	3	1.5	0:24.5

They used the midpoint of each range of times to represent the whole range (e.g., 1 minute for 0 to 2 minutes between arrivals). Part of their results are shown in Table A.4. For each car that arrives, if the service facility is free, it enters. Otherwise, it waits in line until the window is free.

The same approach can be used to simulate many other situations, from traffic flow on a highway to the operation of a coal mine. Most simulations are done via computer. Like all the other MS/OR approaches discussed, they assist you in making managerial decisions.

REFERENCES

[1] Harvey M. Wagner, *Principles of Operations Research* (Englewood Cliffs, N.J.: Prentice-Hall, 1975).

[2] David R. Anderson, Dennis J. Sweeney, and Thomas A. Williams, *An Introduction to Management Science* (St. Paul: West Publishing, 1982).

[3] Stephen P. Bradley, Arnoldo C. Hax, and Thomas L. Magnanti, *Applied Mathematical Programming* (Reading, Mass.: Addison-Wesley, 1977).

[4] David R. Anderson, Dennis J. Sweeney, and Thomas A. Williams, *Linear Programming* (St. Paul: West Publishing, 1974).

[5] Bradley et al., op. cit.

GLOSSARY

The numbers in parentheses after the term indicate the chapters in which the term was defined.

Accommodation (in conflict management) (17)   Playing down differences among conflicting parties, and highlighting similarities and areas of agreement.

Accountability (6)   The requirement for the subordinate to answer to the supervisor for results accomplished in the performance of any assigned duties.

Action Research (17)   A process of systematically collecting data on an organization, feeding it back for action planning, and evaluating results by collecting and reflecting on more data after the planned actions have been taken.

Active Listening (11)   Taking action to help the source of a message to say what he or she really means.

Activities (13)   The verbal and nonverbal behaviors in which group members engage.

Administrator (1)   A manager who works in a public or nonprofit organization as opposed to a business concern.

Affirmative-Action Programs (9)   Programs designed to increase employment opportunities for women and other minorities including veterans, the aged, and the handicapped.

Agency Shop (18)   A labor-management agreement that requires all nonsupervisory employees of an organization to pay a service fee to a union, even though they don't officially have to join.

Aggregate Scheduling (16)   The process of making a rough cut or first approximation to a production/operations schedule based on a demand forecast.

Apprenticeship (9)   A special form of training that involves formal assignment to serve as understudy or assistant to a person already having the desired job skills.

Arbitration (18)   The process by which parties to a labor-management dispute agree to abide by the decision of a neutral and independent third party called an arbitrator.

Assessment Center (9)   A selection technique that engages job candidates in a series of experiential activities over a one- or two-day period.

Authoritative Command (in conflict management) (17)   When formal authority dictates a conflict solution and specifies what is gained or lost and by whom.

Authority (or Formal Authority) (1)   The right to "command" other persons.

Authority-and-Responsibility Principle (6)   Authority should equal responsibility when work is delegated from supervisor to subordinate.

Authority Decision (10)   A decision made by the manager and then communicated to the group.

Autocratic (or Directive) Leadership (10)   A leadership style displaying a high concern for the task and low concern for people.

Autonomous Work Groups (8)   Self-managed work teams with responsibility for accomplishing defined performance objectives, and with discretion to decide how tasks will be distributed among individuals and at what pace work will progress in order to meet these objectives.

Automation (8)   The total mechanization of a job.

Autonomy (8)   The degree to which a job gives the individual substantial freedom, independence, and discretion in scheduling the work and in determining the procedures to be used in carrying it out.

Avoidance (in conflict management) (17)   Pretending that a conflict doesn't really exist; hoping that a conflict will simply go away.

Bargaining Unit (18)   The organization or subunit of an organization that would eventually be subject to union representation.

Behavioral Decision Theory (3)   A view of decision making that assumes managers act only in terms of what they perceive about a given situation.

Behaviorally Anchored Rating Scale (BARS) (14)   A performance-appraisal method based on explicit descriptions of actual behaviors that exemplify various levels of performance achievement.

Bill of Capacity (16)   A document showing how much standard time is needed on each machine to make one finished part in a manufacturing operation.

Bottom-Up Planning (4)   Planning that begins with plans developed at lower management levels without constraints, that are then passed up the hierarchy to top management lvels.

Brainstorming (3)   A group technique for generating a large quantity of ideas by freewheeling contributions being made without criticism.

Break-even Analysis (15)   The study of the relationship between budgeted revenues and costs to determine how changes in each affect profit.

Break-even Point (15)   The point where total revenue from sales is just sufficient to cover total costs. Break-even point equals fixed costs divided by selling price per unit minus variable cost per unit of production.

Budgets (4, 15)   A plan that commits resources to projects or programs; a formalized way of allocating resources to specific activities.

Bureaucracy (2, 7)   An intentionally rational and efficient form of organization founded on principles of logic, order, and legitimate authority.

Cafeteria Benefits (14)   An employee-benefits program that allows workers to select within a given monetary limit a combination of benefits that best meets their needs.

Capacity Planning (16)   The scheduling of resource

utilization in the production/operations process.

Career (21)   A sequence of jobs and work activities constituting what a person does for a living.

Career Path (21)   A sequence of jobs held over time during a career.

Career Planning (21)   The process of systematically matching career goals and individual capabilities with opportunities for their fulfillment.

Career Plateau (21)   A position from which someone is not likely to move to a higher level of work responsibility.

Carrying or Holding Costs (16)   The actual cost of items going into inventory, as well as the cost of storing and insuring them against loss.

Central Processing Unit (CPU) (15)   The collection of electronic circuitry that controls the computer and allows it to store and perform a variety of computational operations on data according to the instructions of programs.

Centralization (6)   The concentration of authority for most decisions at the top levels of an organization.

Centralized Planning Economy (19)   A market system where basic economic decisions for an entire country are made by a central government body.

Certainty (3)   A problem environment in which the information is sufficient to predict the results of each alternative in advance of implementation.

Certification Election (18)   An election, held under the provisions of the National Labor Relations Act and supervised by the National Labor Relations Board, through which employees secretly ballot on whether or not a union should represent them with an employer.

Chain of Command (6)   An unbroken line of authority that vertically links all persons in an organization with successively higher levels of authority.

Change Agent (17)   A person or group taking responsibility for changing the existing pattern of behavior of another person or social system.

Choice Making (3)   The process or evaluating and selecting among alternative solutions to a problem.

Classical Decision Theory (3)   A view of decision making that assumes managers act on the basis of complete certainty about a given situation.

Closed Shop (18)   A labor-management agreement that requires a person to be a union member in good standing *before* being hired.

Closed System (2)   A system that does not interact with its environment.

Coaching (9)   The communication of specific technical advice to an individual.

Coercive Power (10)   The capability to punish or withhold positive outcomes as a means of controlling other people.

Cohesiveness (13)   The degree to which members are attracted to a group and are motivated to remain part of it.

Collaboration (in conflict management) (17)   Seeking true satisfaction of everyone's concerns; working through differences and solving problems so everyone wins as a result.

Collective Bargaining (18)   The process of negotiating, administering, and interpreting a formal agreement or labor contract between a union and the employing organization.

Combination Strategy (5)   A strategy that involves stability, growth, and retrenchment in one or more combinations.

Communication (11)   An interpersonal process of sending and receiving symbols with meanings attached to them.

Communication Channel (11)   The medium through which a message is conveyed from sender to receiver.

Comparable Worth (18)   The principle that persons doing jobs equivalent in skill and importance should receive equal pay.

Comparative Management (19)   The study of how management practices systematically differ from one country and/or culture to the next.

Competition (in conflict management) (17)   When a conflict victory is achieved through force, superior skill, or domination of one party by another.

Compressed Workweek (8)   Any work schedule that allows a full-time job to be completed in less than the standard five days of eight-hour shifts.

Compromise (in conflict management) (17)   When accommodations are made such that each party to the conflict gives up something of value to the other.

Conceptual Skill (1)   The ability to view the organization or situation as a whole and solve problems to the benefit of everyone concerned.

Conciliation (18)   A process of intervention in labor-management disputes through which a neutral party tries to keep the parties to a dispute focused on the issues of disagreement.

Conflict (17)   A disagreement in a social situation over issues of substance and/or emotional antagonism.

Conflict Resolution (17)   The removal of the reasons—substantial and/or emotional—for a conflict.

Constructive Conflict (17)   Conflict which results in benefits instead of disadvantages for the individual(s) and/or organization(s) involved.

Constructive Stress (21)   Stress that acts in a positive or energizing way to increase effort, stimulate creativity, and encourage diligence in one's work.

Consultative Decision (10)   A decision for which each group member provides information, advice, or opinion, which is then used by the manager to make a final decision on behalf of the group.

Content Theories (12)   Motivation theories that offer ways to profile or analyze individuals to identify their needs.

Contingency (2)   An approach of modern management theory that there is no one best way to manage, and that what is best depends in any given circumstance on the nature of the situation.

Continuous-Process Technology (7)   A technology involving the continuous feeding of raw materials into an automated system of production.

Continuous Reinforcement (12)   Administering a reward every time a desired behavior occurs.

Contributions (8)   Work activities of value the individual offers to the organization in return for inducements.

Control Chart (16)   A graphic display of work results that clearly delineates upper control limits (UCL) and lower control limits (LCL).

Control Process (14)   The process of establishing performance objectives and standards, measuring actual performance, comparing actual performance with objectives and standards, and taking necessary action.

Controlling (14)   The process of monitoring performance and taking action to ensure desired results.

Coordination (6)   The process of linking the specialized activities of individuals and groups to one another, and ensuring that a common purpose is served.

Corporate Culture (5)   The predominant value system for the organization as a whole.

Corporate Social Responsibility (2)   An obligation of an organization to act in ways that serve both its own interests and the interests of its many external publics.

Cost-Benefit Analysis (3)   Comparing the costs and benefits of each potential course of action.

Cost or Expense Center (15)   A responsibility center where budgets and performance targets concentrate on the utilization of resource inputs measured in monetary terms as expenses.

Critical-Path Method (CPM) (16)   A network-modeling technique that breaks the various phases of a production/operations project into a sequence of events and the activities leading to those events.

Craft Unions (18)   Labor unions that represent workers in single crafts or occupations—for example, carpenters, plumbers, or electricians.

Creativity (3, 17)   An application of ingenuity and imagination that results in a novel approach or unique solution to a problem.

Critical-Incident Technique (14)   A performance-appraisal method that involves a running log or inventory of effective and ineffective job behaviors.

Culture (19)   A shared set of beliefs, values, and patterns of behavior common to a group of people.

Cybernetic Control System (14)   A control system that is entirely self-contained in its performance-monitoring and correction capabilities.

Data (15)   Raw facts such as figures and other symbols used to represent people, events, and concepts.

Decentralization (6)   The dispersion of authority to make decisions throughout all levels of management by extensive delegation.

Decertification (of unions) (18)   A means through which employees can revoke the certification of a union previously certified as their bargaining agent.

Decision Making (3)   The process that encompasses all activities ranging from the identification of a problem through the actual choice of a preferred problem-solving alternative.

Decision Matrix or Payoff Table (3)   An extension of decision-tree analysis to display the possible outcomes of various alternatives while taking the probabilities of their occurrence into account.

Decision-Support System (15)   A computerized MIS in which managers conversationally interact with the computer to request and process information in the course of solving complex and semistructured problems.

Decision Tree (3)   A graphic illustration of the alternatives available to solve a problem.

Deficit Principle (12)   Maslow's principle, which holds that a satisfied need is not a motivator of behavior.

Delegation (6)   The process of distributing and entrusting work to other persons.

Delphi Technique (4)   A forecasting technique wherein a panel of experts respond sequentially to a survey questionnaire soliciting opinions on future events.

Demand Forecasting (16)   The process of estimating future demand for an organization's products or services.

Democratic (or Participative) Leadership (10)   A person whose leadership style displays high concerns for both people and task.

Democratic Systems (19)   Legal-political systems that rely on free elections and representative assemblies of the population to establish a government for the society as a whole.

Departmentation (6)   The creation of work units or groups by placing several jobs under the authority of a common manager.

Departmentation by Division (6)   The formation of departments based on products, clients, territories, time, or projects.

Departmentation by Function (6)   The formation of

departments based on people performing similar or closely related activities.

Dependent-Inventory Demand (16) Demand, such as for component parts, that follows a "lumpy" pattern and causes inventory levels to fall in "bunches" over time.

Dependent Variable (16) A variable whose behavior depends on another variable (an independent variable); a variable whose behavior is being predicted or forecasted for some future period by regression analysis.

Destructive Conflict (17) Conflict that works to the disadvantage of the individual(s) and/or organizations(s) involved.

Destructive Stress (21) Stress that is dysfunctional for the individual and/or the organization.

Differentiation (7) The difference observed between the structures and managerial orientations of various departments or other subunits of an organization.

Directive (or Autocratic) Leadership (10) A person whose leadership style displays a high concern for the task and low concern for people.

Discipline (14) Influencing behavior through reprimand.

Displacement of Objectives (5) When the means become more important than the ends they were originally intended to serve.

Division of Labor (1) The process of breaking work into smaller components and allocating them as individual or group tasks designed to fit together in service of the organization's purpose.

Downward Communication (11) Communication flowing from higher to lower levels in an organization's hierarchy of authority.

Economic Environment (5) Consists of customers, suppliers, and competitors whose actions have the potential to affect demand for goods or service and resource availabilities.

Economic Order Quantity (16) A method for controlling inventory by ordering a fixed number of items each time inventory level falls to a predetermined point.

Effective Communication (11) When the intended meaning of the source and the perceived meaning of the receiver are one and the same.

Effective Group (13) A group that achieves and maintains high levels of *both* task performance and membership satisfaction over time.

Efficient Communication (11) Communication that occurs at minimum cost in terms of resources expended.

Emergent Behaviors (13) What group members do in addition to or in replacement of what is asked by the organization.

Emotional Conflict (17) Conflict resulting from feelings of anger, distrust, dislike, fear, and resentment, as well as from personality clashes.

Empirical-Rational Change Strategy (17) A change strategy where the change agent attempts to bring about change through persuasion backed by special knowledge and rational argument.

Environmental Uncertainty (7) The rate and predictability of change associated with important environmental elements.

Equal Employment Opportunity (EEO) (9) The right of people to employment and advancement without regard to race, sex, religion, color, or national origin.

Equifinality (2) The ability of a system to achieve the same end state from a variety of paths.

Ethical Behavior (20) Behavior that is accepted as "right" or "good" in the context of a governing moral code.

Ethical Dilemma (20) A situation in which a manager must choose whether or not to pursue a course of action that, although offering the potential of personal or organizational benefit or both, is also unethical and/or illegal in the broader social context.

Ethical Managerial Behavior (20) Behavior by managers that conforms not only to law, but also to a broader set of moral principles common to society.

Ethics (20) The code of morals of a person or group that sets standards as to what is good or bad, or right or wrong in one's conduct.

Existence Needs (12) Desires for physiological and material well-being in Alderfer's ERG theory (discussed in Chapter 12).

Expectancy (12) The person's belief that working hard will enable various levels of task performance to be achieved.

Excepted Problems (3) Those problems that are anticipated as a basis for future decisions.

Expected Value (3) The dollar value of the predicted outcomes for an alternative course of action times the probability of its occurrence.

Expert Power (10) The capability to control other people because of specialized knowledge.

Exponential Smoothing (16) A special form of weight moving average that uses exponential weights and requires less historical data to make forecasts.

External Control (14) Control that occurs through direct supervision or administrative systems such as rules and procedures.

External Recruitment (9) The process of attracting job candidates from sources external to the organization.

Extinction (12) Decreasing the frequency of or eliminating an undesirable behavior by making the removal of a desirable consequence contingent on the occurrence of the behavior.

Feedback (in a systems sense) (2)   Information about system performance that can be used for purposes of adaptation, control, and constructive change.

Feedback (in an interpersonal sense) (11)   The process of telling someone else how you feel about something that person did or said, or about the situation in general.

Feedback (from the job itself) (8)   The degree to which carrying out the work activities required by the job results in the individual obtaining direct and clear information on the results of his or her performance.

Firing (9)   The act of involuntary and permanent dismissal of an employee.

Fixed (or Static) Budget (4, 15)   A budget that allocates resources on a single estimate of costs; a budget that does not allow adjustment over time.

Flexible Budget (4, 15)   A budget that allows the allocation of resources to projects to vary in proportion with various levels of activity; a budget that can be adjusted over time to accommodate relevant changes in the environment.

Flexible Working Hours (or Flextime) (8)   Any work schedule that gives employees some choice in the pattern of daily work hours.

Force-Coercion Change Strategy (17)   A change strategy where the change agent acts unilaterally to try to "command" change through the formal authority of his or her position, to induce change via an offer of special rewards, or to bring about change via threats of punishment.

Forecast (4, 16)   An attempt to predict outcomes; a projection into the future based on historical data combined in some scientific manner.

Formal Communication Channels (11)   Those communication channels that follow the chain of command established by an organization's hierarchy of authority.

Formal Group (13)   A group created by the formal authority within the organization to help transform resource inputs into product or service outputs.

Formal Leadership (10)   When a manager leads through the exercise of formal authority.

Formal Structure (6)   The structure of the organization in its pure or ideal state.

Free-Form Narrative (14)   A performance-appraisal method that involves a written description of someone's job performance.

Free-Market Economy (19)   A market system where economic activities are generally governed by laws of supply and demand.

Functional Authority (6)   The authority to act within a specified area of expertise and in relation to the activities of other persons or units lying outside the formal chain of command.

Functional Manager (1)   A manager who has responsibility for one area of activity such as finance, marketing, production, personnel, accounting, or sales.

Gantt Chart (4, 16)   A bar graph or diagram that shows the allocation of time allowed to the various activities comprising a project; a chart that graphically depicts the routing or scheduling of a production/operations sequence from beginning to conclusion.

General Environment (7)   The cultural, economic, legal-political, and educational conditions in the locality where an organization operates.

General Manager (1)   A manager who has responsibility for a complex organizational subunit that includes many areas of functional activity.

General Unions (18)   Labor unions that are organized in a variety of unrelated industries and lack a specific craft or industry focus.

Graphic Rating Scale (14)   A performance-appraisal method that lists a variety of traits or characteristics, thought to be related to high performance outcomes in a given job, that the individual is accordingly expected to exhibit.

Grievance (18)   A complaint from an employee regarding treatment he or she has received in respect to a condition of employment specified in a labor contract.

Group (13)   A collection of people who regularly interact with one another over time and in respect to the pursuit of one or more common goals.

Group Decision (10)   A decision where all group members participate with the manager and finally agree by consensus on the course of action to be taken.

Group Dynamics (13)   Forces operating groups that affect task performance and membership satisfaction.

Group Process (13)   The means through which multiple and varied resource inputs are combined and transformed into group outputs.

Groupthink (13)   A tendency for highly cohesive groups to lose their critical evaluative capabilities.

Growth Needs (12)   Desires for continued psychological growth and development in Alderfer's ERG theory (discussed in Chapter 12).

Growth-Need Strength (8)   The individual's desire to achieve a sense of psychological growth—that is, higher-order need satisfaction—in his or her work.

Growth Strategy (5)   A strategy that involves expansion of the organization's current operations.

Halo Effect (11)   When one attribute is used to develop an overall impression of a person or situation.

Hardware (computer) (15)   Equipment required to operate a computer system.

Hawthorne Effect (2)   The tendency of persons who are singled out for special attention to perform as anticipated merely because of the expectancies created by the situation.

Hierarchy of Authority (1, 6)   The arrangement of work positions in order of increasing formal authority in an organization.

Hierarchy of Needs (2, 12)   Five levels of human needs defined by Abraham Maslow as becoming activated in order of prepotency—physiological, safety, social, ego, and self-actualization needs.

Hierarchy of Objectives (5)   A series of objectives linked to one another at the various levels of management such that each higher level objective is supported by one or more lower-level ones.

Higher-Order Needs (12)   Esteem and self-actualization needs in Maslow's hierarchy.

Horizontal Coordination (6)   The process of coordinating the activities of individuals or groups working at, or close to, the same level in the hierarchy.

Human Relations (or Supportive) Leadership (10)   A person whose leadership style displays a high concern for people but low concern for task.

Human Resource Audit (9)   A systematic inventory of the strengths and weaknesses of existing personnel.

Human Resource Inventory Chart (Replacement Chart) (9)   A chart that shows the promotability of persons in key positions within the organization.

Human Resource Maintenance (13)   A group's ability to maintain its social fabric and capabilities of its members to work well together over time.

Human Resource Planning (Personnel Planning) (9)   A process of identifying staffing needs, forecasting the available personnel, and determining what additions or replacements are required to maintain a staff of the desired size and quality.

Human Resources (1)   The people, individuals, and groups that help organizations produce goods or services.

Human Skill (1)   The ability to work well in cooperation with other persons.

Hygiene Factors (8)   Factors in the work setting such as working conditions, interpersonal relations, organizational policies and administration, supervision, and salary.

Improvement Objectives (14)   Objectives that document intentions to improve performance in different areas.

Independent Inventory Demand (16)   A demand for inventory that follows a uniform pattern and causes inventory to decrease at a gradual rate over time.

Independent Variable (16)   A variable whose behavior influences the behavior of another variable (a dependent variable); a variable whose behavior is used by regression analysis to predict or forecast the behavior of some other variable in a future time period.

Inducements (8)   Things of value the organization gives to the individual in return for valued contributions.

Industrial Unions (18)   Labor unions that serve a single industry and represent workers across a wide variety of occupations.

Informal Communication Channels (11)   Communication channels that exist outside of the formal channels and do not adhere to the organization's hierarchy of authority.

Informal Group (13)   A group that emerges within an organization and that exists without being formally specified by someone in authority for a performance purpose.

Informal Leadership (10)   When a person without formal authority proves influential in directing the behavior of other persons.

Informal Structure (6)   The undocumented and officially unrecognized structure that coexists with the formal structure of an organization.

Information (15)   Data that have been made meaningful or relevant for the recipient.

Information-Reporting System (15)   A computerized MIS that processes data relating to standard accounting transactions and makes a variety of reports available to managers.

Information System (15)   A system that collects, organizes, and distributes data regarding activities occurring inside and outside the organization.

Input Standards (14)   Standards that measure work efforts that go into a performance task.

Inside-Out Planning (4)   Creates plans that focus efforts on doing what one already does, but trying to do it better.

Instrumentality (12)   The person's belief that various work-related outcomes will occur as a result of task performance.

Integration (7)   The level of coordination achieved among subsystems in an organization.

Intensive Technology (7)   A technology where there is uncertainty as to how to produce desired outcomes, and high interdependence among members of the work force.

Interactions (13)   Behaviors that group members direct toward other persons.

Intermediate (or Medium-Range) Plan (4)   A plan that covers one to five years.

Intermittent Reinforcement (12)   Administering a reward only periodically upon the appearance of desired behavior.

Internal Control (14)   Self-control that occurs through self-discipline and the personal exercise of individual or group responsibility.

Internal Recruitment (9)   The process of making employees aware of job vacancies through job posting and personal recommendations.

International Business (19)   The conduct of for-profit transactions of goods and services across national boundaries.

International Management (19)   Management that involves the conduct of business or other operations in foreign countries.

Intuitive Thinker (3)   A person who approaches problems in a flexible and spontaneous fashion.

Inventory (16)   The amount of resource inputs or product outputs kept in storage.

Inventory Control (14)   A control system that monitors raw material, work in process, and finished-good inventories to make sure workflows are properly maintained.

Inventory of Alternatives (3)   A list of all possible solutions to a problem along with a summary of the favorable and unfavorable points of each.

Investment Center (15)   A responsibility center where budgets and performance targets concentrate not only on profits but also on the amount of capital investment required to produce those profits.

Job (8)   The collection of tasks a person performs in support of organizational objectives.

Job Analysis (9)   An orderly study of job requirements and facets that can influence performance results.

Job Depth (8)   The extent of planning and evaluating duties performed by the individual worker rather than the supervisor.

Job Description (8)   A written statement that details the duties and responsibilities of any person holding a particular job.

Job Design (6, 8)   The allocation of specific work tasks to individuals and groups; the process through which jobs are defined as collections of specific tasks.

Job Enlargement (8)   A job-design strategy that increases task variety by combining into one job two or more tasks that were previously assigned to separate workers.

Job Enrichment (8)   A job-design strategy that builds satisfier factors into job content; a job-design strategy that increases job depth by adding to a job some of the planning and evaluating duties normally performed by the supervisor.

Job Rotation (8)   A job-design strategy that increases task variety by periodically shifting workers among jobs involving different tasks.

Job Satisfaction (8)   The degree to which an individual feels positively or negatively about various aspects of the job, including assigned tasks, work setting, and relationships with co-workers.

Job Scope (8)   The number and combination of tasks an individual or group is asked to perform.

Job Sharing (8)   When one full-time job is split between two persons.

Job Simplification (8)   A job-design strategy that involves standardizing work procedures and employing people in clearly defined and very specialized tasks.

Job Specification (9)   A list of the qualifications required of any job occupant.

Joint Ventures (19)   Forms of international business that establish operations in a foreign country through mutual ownership with local partners.

Jurisdictions (18)   Task domains within which craft unions retain autonomy to organize and represent workers.

Just Cause (18)   A principle, often specified in labor contracts, holding that an employee should not be disciplined without sufficient justification ("cause") and that the penalty imposed should not be excessive compared to the offense.

Just-in-Time Delivery (16)   An approach to inventory control that involves minimizing carrying costs and maintaining almost no inventories by ordering or producing components only as needed; sometimes called the "Kanban" system.

Labor-Management Relations (18)   The ongoing relationship between a group of employees represented by a union and management in the employing organization.

Labor Union (18)   An organization to which workers belong and that collectively deals with employers on their behalf.

Laissez-Faire (or Abdicative) Leadership (10)   A person whose leadership style displays low concern for both people and task.

Lateral Communication (11)   Communication among persons working at the same level in the hierarchy of authority, but typically representing different departments or work units.

Law of Contingent Reinforcement (12)   In order for a reward to have maximum value, it must be delivered only if the desired behavior is exhibited.

Law of Effect (12)   Behavior that results in a pleasant outcome is likely to be repeated; behavior that results in an unpleasant outcome is not likely to be repeated.

Law of Immediate Reinforcement (12)   The more immediate the delivery of a reward after the occurrence of a desirable behavior, the greater the reinforcing value of the reward.

Leader-Member Relations (10)   A term used in Fiedler's contingency leadership theory to describe the degree to which the group supports the leader.

Leadership (10)   The manager's use of power to influence the behavior of other persons in the work setting.

Leadership Style (10)   The recurring pattern of behaviors exhibited by a leader.

Leading (10)   The process of directing human-resource efforts toward organizational objectives.

Learning (1)   Any change in behavior that occurs as a result of experience.

Legitimate Power (10)   The capability to control other people by virtue of the rights of office.

Line Manager (1)   A manager who has direct responsibility for the production of the organization's basic product or service.

Local (18)   An administrative unit of a national or international union that services at the local level a particular group of workers represented by the union.

Logical Incrementalism (5)   Views organizational strategies emerging over time as a series of incremental changes to existing patterns of behavior.

Long-Linked Technology (7)   A mass-production or assembly-line technology relying on highly specialized jobs performed in a closely controlled sequence to create a final product.

Long-Range Budget (15)   A budget covering periods of more than one year.

Long-Range Plan (4)   A plan covering five years or more.

Lose-Lose Conflict (17)   When no one achieves their true desires, and the underlying reasons for conflict remain unaffected.

Lot-by-Lot Ordering (16)   A method for controlling inventory by ordering with sufficient lead time the net requirements specified in a Material Requirements Planning (MRP) schedule.

Lower-Order Needs (12)   Physiological, safety, and social needs in Maslow's hierarchy.

Maintenance Activities (13)   Actions by group members that support the emotional life of the group as an ongoing social system.

Maintenance Objectives (14)   Objectives that formally express intentions to continue performance at existing levels.

Management (1)   A body of knowledge and field of academic inquiry based on scientific principles and serving as an important foundation for any manager.

Management by Exception (14)   Focusing managerial attention on situations in which differences between actual and desired performance are substantial.

Management by Objectives (MBO) (14)   A process of joint objective-setting between a superior and subordinate that can be done on an organizationwide basis.

Management Development (9)   Training directed toward improving a person's knowledge and skills in the fundamentals of management.

Management Functions (1)   Planning, organizing, leading, and controlling—the basic activities performed by all managers.

Management Information System (15)   A system that collects, organizes, and distributes data in such a way that the information meets the needs of managers.

Management Process (1)   The process of planning, organizing, leading, and controlling the utilization of resources to accomplish the organization's purpose.

Management Rights (18)   The rights of an employer to manage the work operation but only as those rights are modified through specific terms of labor agreement.

Management Science (Operations Research; Quantitative Analysis) (2)   A scientific approach to management that uses mathematical techniques to analyze and solve problems.

Management Theory (2)   A set of concepts and ideas that systematically explains and predicts the behaviors of organizations and their members.

Manager (1)   A person in an organization who is responsible for the work performance of one or more other persons.

Managerial Ethics (2)   Those standards and principles that guide the actions and decisions of managers, and determine if those actions and decisions are "good or bad" or "right or wrong" in a moral sense.

Manager's Job (1)   To help the organization achieve a high level of performance through the utilization of its human and material resources.

Mass Production (7)   The production of a large number of one or a few products with an assembly-line type of system.

Master Budget (15)   A comprehensive short-term budget for the organization as a whole.

Master Scheduling (16)   Specifies in detail exactly what goods or services will be produced during the short term—for example, on a weekly or even daily basis.

Material Requirements Planning (MRP) (16)   A technique that uses a master schedule to determine when and how many component parts or separate resources must be ordered to ensure a smooth and sufficient flow of finished products or services.

Material Resources (1) The information, equipment, raw materials, facilities, and other physical inputs that organizations employ in the production of goods or services.

Matrix Departmentation (Matrix Organization) (6) A form of organization that combines functional and divisional forms of departmentation to take best advantage of each.

Means-End Chain (4) A chain of efforts and objectives that sequentially links the work of individuals and groups of various levels of the organization to a common purpose.

Mechanistic Structures (7) Organizational structures that are highly bureaucratic in form; they employ centralized authority, rules and procedures, a clear-cut division of labor, narrow spans of control, and formal impersonal means of coordination.

Mediating Technology (7) A technology that links together parties seeking a mutually beneficial exchange of values.

Mediation (18) A process in which a neutral party engages in substantive discussions with union and management negotiators in separate meetings and in joint sessions in the hope that concession and compromise will curtail a labor-management dispute.

Mentoring (9) The act of sharing experiences and insights between a seasoned and junior manager.

Mixed Message (11) When a person's words communicate one message and actions, body language, or appearance communicate something else.

Modeling (9) The process of demonstrating through personal behavior that which is expected of others.

Motion Study (2) The science of reducing a job or task to its basic physical motions.

Motivation to Work (12) The forces within the individual that account for the level, direction, and persistence of effort expended at work.

Moving Average (16) Averages of past data over a specific time period that are used to forecast the future.

Multinational Corporation (MNC) (19) A business firm with extensive international operations in more than one foreign country.

Multi-Person Comparison (14) A performance appraisal method that involves a comparison of one person's performance with that of one or more persons.

National Labor Relations Act (NLRA) (18) The cornerstone of American labor law that protects employer and employee rights in labor-management relations; consists of the Wagner Act (1935), Taft-Hartley Act (1947), and Landrum-Griffin Act (1959).

National Labor Relations Board (NLRB) (18) A board created by the NLRA to administer the provisions of the act.

Need (2, 12) A physiological or psychological deficiency a person feels the compulsion to satisfy.

Need for Achievement (nAch) (12) The desire to do something better or more efficiently, to solve problems, or to master complex tasks.

Need for Affiliation (nAff) (12) The desire to establish and maintain friendly and warm relations with other persons.

Need for Power (nPower) (12) The desire to control other persons, to influence their behavior, or to be responsible for other people.

Negative Entropy (2) The tendency toward system continuity and survival.

Negative Reinforcement (12) A means for increasing the frequency of or strengthening a behavior by making the avoidance of an undesirable consequence contingent on the occurrence of the behavior.

Noise (11) Anything that interferes with the effectiveness of the communication process.

Nominal Group (3) A group technique for generating ideas by following a structured format of individual response, group sharing without criticism, and written balloting.

Nonprogrammed Decisions (3) Specific solutions arrived at by the creative and unstructured process of problem solving for nonroutine problems.

Nonroutine Problems (3) Those problems that are unique and new and for which standard responses are not available.

Norm (13) A behavior expected of group members.

Normative-Reeducative Change Strategy (17) A change strategy where the change agent attempts to identify or establish values and assumptions such that support for a proposed change naturally emerges.

Official Objective (5) The organization's formal purpose or mission as stated in a report to shareholders, article of incorporation, or other similar official documents.

Off-the-Job Training (9) Training that is accomplished in an area away from the actual work setting.

On-the-Job Training (9) Training that is accomplished in the work setting and during performance of an actual job.

Open System (1, 2) A system that interacts with its environment and transforms resource inputs into outputs.

Operant Conditioning (12) The process of controlling behavior by manipulating its consequences.

Operating Budget (15) A budget that assigns resources to a responsibility center on a short-term basis.

Operating Objectives (5)   The specific ends toward which organizational resources are actually allocated.

Operational Plans (4)   Plans of limited scope that address those activities and resources required to implement strategic plans.

Operations Research (also called Management Science or Quantitative Analysis) (2)   A scientific approach to management that uses mathematical techniques to analyze and solve problems.

Ordering Costs (16)   The costs of arranging the procurement of items for inventory from outside sources, as well as the costs of any internal procurement (e.g., manufacture of such items).

Organic Structures (7)   Organizational structures that have decentralized authority, few rules and procedures, more ambiguous division of labor, wide spans of control, and informal and more personal means of coordination.

Organization (1)   A collection of people working together in a division of labor to achieve a common purpose.

Organization Chart (6)   A diagram that describes the basic arrangement of work positions within an organization.

Organization Development (OD) (17)   The application of behavioral science knowledge in a long-range effort to improve an organization's ability to cope with change in its external environment and increase its internal problem-solving capabilities.

Organizational Behavior Modification (OB Mod) (12)   The application of operant conditioning techniques to influence human behavior in work settings.

Organizational Change (17)   Change involving some modification in the goals, structure, tasks, people, and technology that constitute the essence of the organization.

Organizational Communication (11)   The process through which information is exchanged in interactions among persons inside the organization.

Organizational Context (7)   Strategy, size, technology, and people characterizing the organization.

Organizational Design (7)   The process of choosing and implementing an appropriate structural configuration for the organization.

Organizational Innovation (17)   The process of taking a new idea and putting it into practice as part of the organization's normal operating routines.

Organizational Objectives (5)   Ends the organization seeks to achieve by its existence and operations.

Organizing (6)   The process of dividing work into manageable components and coordinating results to serve a purpose.

Orientation (9)   Activities through which new employees are made familiar with their jobs, co-workers, and the policies, rules, objectives, and services of the organization as a whole.

Output Standards (14)   Standards that measure performance results in terms of quantity, quality, cost, or time.

Outside-In Planning (4)   Creates plans that reflect an analysis of the external environment and then make the internal adjustments necessary to exploit opportunities and minimize problems posed by it.

Participative (or Democratic) Leadership (10)   A leadership style that displays high concern for both people and task.

Payoff Table (or Decision Matrix) (3)   An extension of decision-tree analysis to display the possible outcomes of various alternatives while taking the probabilities of their occurrence into account.

Perception (11)   The process through which people receive, organize, and interpret information from the environment.

Performance (8)   The quantity and quality of task contributions from an individual or group doing a job.

Performance Appraisal (14)   A process of formally evaluating performance and providing feedback on which performance adjustments can be made.

Performance Effectiveness (1)   An output measure of task or goal accomplishment.

Performance Efficiency (1)   A measure of the resource cost associated with goal accomplishment—that is, outputs realized compared to inputs consumed.

Performance Gap (17)   A discrepancy between the desired and actual status of affairs.

Performance Objective (14)   A desired performance accomplishment that can be expressed as a measurable end product or verifiable set of work activities.

Permanent Groups (13)   Work groups that retain their presence over time.

Personal Development Objectives (14)   Objectives that formally express intentions to engage in personal growth activities.

Personal or Microcomputer (15)   A small, self-contained computer system designed to accomplish a variety of data-storage and information-processing tasks in a unit not much larger than a desk typewriter and portable television.

Personal Staff (6)   "Assistant-to" positions that provide special administrative support to higher-level positions.

Personal Wellness (21)   The pursuit of one's physical and mental potential through a personal-health–promotion program.

Plan (4)   A statement of intended means for accomplishing a desired result.

Planned Change (17)   Change that occurs as a result of specific efforts in its behalf by a change agent.

Planning (4)   The process of setting obejctives and determining what should be done to accomplish them.

Planning Objective (4)   The desired future state or end result to be accomplished through implementation of a plan.

Policy (4)   A standing plan that communicates broad guidelines for making decisions and taking action.

Political Action Committees (PACs) (20)   Committees organized by companies and other organizations to assist in the election of candidates who favor their interests.

Political Environment (5)   Includes governmental units at regional, state, national, and international levels, special-interest groups and other political entities, and the legal-judicial framework of society.

Political-Risk Analysis (19)   Forecasting the probability of various events that can threaten the security of a foreign investment.

Position Power (10)   The degree to which a position in the organization's hierarchy of authority gives a person the power to reward and punish subordinates; a term used in Fiedler's contingency leadership theory.

Positive Reinforcement (12)   A means for strengthening or increasing the frequency of a behavior of making a desirable consequence contingent on the occurrence of the behavior.

Postaction Controls (14)   Controls that take place after an action is completed; sometimes called feedback controls.

Power (10)   The ability to get someone else to do something you want done; the ability to make things happen the way you want.

Precontrols (14)   Controls that are initiated prior to the start of a production or service activity; sometimes called *feed-forward controls.*

Probability (3)   The degree of likelihood that an event will occur.

Problem (3)   A difference between an actual situation and a desired situation.

Problem Finding (3)   Identifying gaps between actual and desired states, and determining their causes.

Problem Solving (3)   The process of identifying a discrepancy between an actual and desired state of affairs, and then taking action to resolve the discrepancy.

Problem-Solving (in conflict management) (17)   Seeking true satisfaction of everyone's concerns; working through differences and solving problems so everyone wins as a result.

Procedures (and Rules) (4)   Standing-use plans that precisely describe what actions are to be taken in specific situations.

Process Theories (12)   Motivation theories that address the thought processes through which individuals give meaning to rewards and allow them to influence their behavior.

Production/Operations Management (P/OM) (16)   A branch of management theory that studies how organizations transform resource inputs into product and service outputs.

Productivity (1)   A summary measure of the quantity and quality of work performance with resource utilization considered.

Profession (2)   An organization or network in which membership is limited to persons sharing expertise in a specialized body of knowledge and that is governed by a universal code of ethics.

Profit Center (15)   A responsibility center where budgets and performance targets concentrate on the amount of profits realized—that is, on the difference between revenues and expenses.

Profit Plan (15)   A primary document in any operating budget that details revenues and costs and projects the resulting net income in the form of an income statement.

Program Evaluation and Review Technique (PERT) (16)   A network-modeling technique that breaks the various phases of a production/operations project into a sequence of events and the activities leading to those events.

Programmed Decisions (3)   Specific solutions determined by past experience as appropriate for the problem at hand.

Progression Principle (12)   Maslow's principle, which holds that five human needs exist in a strict hierarchy of prepotency such that a need at one level doesn't become activated until the next lower-level need is already satisfied.

Progressive Discipline (14)   The process of tying reprimands in the form of penalties or punishments to the severity of the employee's infractions.

Projection (11)   The assignment of personal attributes to other individuals.

Promotion (9)   Movement of a person to a higher-level position within the organization.

Psychological Contract (8)   The shared set of expectations held by the individual and the organization, specifying what each expects to give to and receive from the other in the course of their working relationship.

Psychological Group (13)   A group whose members are aware of one another's needs and potential resource contributions, and achieve high levels of interaction and mutual identification in pursuit of a common purpose.

Punishment (12)   A means for decreasing the frequency of or eliminating an undesirable behavior by making an unpleasant consequence contingent on the occurrence of that behavior.

Purpose (of an organization) (1)   To produce a good or service.

Qualitative Forecasting Technique (4)   The use of expert opinions to predict the future.

Quality Assurance (16)   The process of *preventing* the production of defective products or services.

Quality Control (16)   The process of *checking* goods or services to ensure that they meet certain standards.

Quality-Control Circle (16)   A group of employees who meet periodically to discuss ways of improving the quality of their products or services.

Quality of Working Life (1)   The overall quality of human experiences in the workplace.

Quantitative Analysis (also called Operations Research or Management Science) (2)   A scientific approach to management that uses mathematical techniques to analyze and solve problems.

Quantitative Forecasting Techniques (4)   The use of statistical analyses and mathematics to predict the future.

Rational Choices (3)   Those decisions that are logical and optimal based on economic decision criteria.

Realistic Recruitment (9)   A recruitment philosophy that seeks to provide the job candidate all pertinent information without distortion.

Recruitment (9)   A set of activities designed to attract a qualified pool of job applicants to an organization.

Reference Power (10)   The capability to control other people because of their desires to identify personally and positively with the power source.

Regression Analysis (16)   A mathematical technique that provides a forecast by comparing past variation in one variable (the dependent variable)—for example, demand—against variation in another and more predictable variable (the independent variable).

Reinforcement Theory (12)   A motivation theory that examines how people learn patterns of behavior based on environmental reinforcements.

Relatedness Needs (12)   Desires for satisfying interpersonal relationships.

Reliability (9)   A measure of the extent to which a test will yield approximately the same results over time if taken by the same person.

Replacement (9)   The act of removing a person from an assigned job.

Required Behaviors (13)   Those things the organization requests from group members by way of job performance and in return for the right of continued membership and support.

Responsibility (6)   The obligation to perform that results from accepting assigned tasks; a commitment by the subordinate to the supervisor to carry out assigned duties as agreed.

Responsibility Accounting System (15)   An organizational control system based on the development of interlocking budgets for a hierarchy of responsibility centers.

Responsibility Center (15)   A work unit formally charged with budgetary responsibility for carrying out various activities.

Retrenchment Strategy (5)   A strategy that involves slowing down, cutting back, and seeking performance improvement through greater efficiencies in operations.

Revenue Center (15)   A responsibility center where budgets and performance targets concentrate on product or service outputs measured in monetary terms as revenues.

Reward (12)   A work outcome of positive value to the individual.

Reward Power (10)   The capability to offer something of value—a positive outcome—as a means of controlling other people.

Risk (3)   A problem environment in which information is not certain but probabilities can be associated with the outcomes of problem-solving alternatives.

Role (11)   A set of activities expected of a person in a particular job or position within the organization.

Role Ambiguity (11)   When the person in a role is uncertain about what others expect in terms of his or her behavior.

Role Conflict (11)   When the person in a role is unable to respond to the expectations held by one or more others.

Role Overload (11)   When too many role expectations are being communicated to a person at a given time.

Routine Problems (3)   Those problems that arise on a regular basis and can be addressed through standard responses.

Routing Sheet (16)   A document that shows which machines or work centers a part must pass through in the various phases of its production.

Rules (and Procedures) (4)   Standing-use plans that precisely describe what actions are to be taken in specific situations.

Satisficing (3)   In problem solving, choosing the first satisfactory alternative that comes to your attention.

Satisfier Factors (8)   Factors in job content such as sense of achievement, recognition, responsibility, advancement, or personal growth experienced as a result of task performance.

Scalar Principle (6)   There should be a clear and unbroken chain of command linking every person in the organization with successively higher levels of authority up to and including the chief executive officer; this chain of command should be followed when orders are conveyed from higher to lower levels of authority.

Schedules (4)   Single-use plans that tie activities to specific time frames or targets.

Science (2)   A body of knowledge systematically created via the steps in the scientific method.

Scientific Management (2)   As advocated by Frederick W. Taylor, involves developing a science for every job including rules of motion and standardized work instruments, careful selection and training of workers, and proper supervisory support for workers.

Selection (9)   The process of choosing from a pool of applicants the person or persons best meeting job specifications.

Selective Perception (3, 11)   The tendency of people to define problems from their own points of view; the tendency to single out for attention those aspects of a situation or attributes of a person that reinforce or appear consistent with one's existing beliefs, values, or needs.

Seniority (18)   The length of an employee's continuous service with an employer.

Sentiments (13)   Feelings, attitudes, beliefs, or values held by group members.

Shaping (12)   The creation of a new behavior by the positive reinforcement of successive approximations to the desired behavior.

Short-Range Budget (15)   A budget covering periods of one year or less.

Short-Range Plans (4)   A plan covering one year or less.

Single-Use Plan (4)   A plan that is used only once.

Situational Control (10)   A term used in Fiedler's contingency leadership theory to describe the extent to which a leader can determine what a group is going to do, and what the outcomes of its actions and decisions are going to be.

Size (of an organization) (7)   The number of persons employed by an organization; sometimes measured by total assets, sales, or revenues.

Skill (1)   The ability to translate knowledge into action that results in the desired performance.

Skill Variety (8)   The degree to which a job requires a variety of different activities in carrying out the work and involves the use of a number of different skills and talents of the individual.

Small-Batch Production (7)   A variety of custom products that are tailor made, usually with considerable craftsmanship, to fit customer specifications.

Smoothing (in conflict management) (17)   Playing down differences among conflicting parties, and highlighting similarities and areas of agreement.

Smoothing Constant (α, alpha) (16)   A constant between 0 and 1 that determines how much weight is put on data in exponential smoothing.

Social Audit (20)   A systematic assessment and reporting of an organization's resource and action commitments, and performance accomplishments in areas of social responsibility.

Social Environment (5)   Consists of the value systems, sociodemographic characterisitics, and other characteristics of persons comprising the society.

Socialization (9)   The process of systematically changing the expectations, behavior, and attitudes of a new employee in a manner considered desirable by the organization.

Software (computer) (15)   Instructions in the form of programs that give the computer its capability to perform computational operations on data.

Span of Control (6)   The number of subordinates reporting directly to a manager.

Span-of-Control Principle (6)   There is a limit to the number of persons one manager can effectively supervise; care should be exercised to keep the span of control within manageable limits.

Specialization (6)   The process through which multiple work tasks are defined in a division of labor.

Specialized Staff (6)   Positions that perform a technical service or provide special problem-solving expertise for other parts of the organization.

Specific Environment (7)   The actual organizations, groups, and persons with whom the focal organization must interact in order to survive and prosper.

Stability Strategy (5)   A strategy that maintains the present course of action.

Staffing (9)   The process of filling jobs with appropriate persons.

Staff Manager (1)   A manager who uses special technical expertise to support the production efforts of line managers.

Staff Planners (4)   Persons who take responsibility for leading and coordinating the planning function for the total organization or a major subsystem.

Standard Time (16)   A measure of work capacity that takes into account the availability and work efficiency of people and/or equipment.

Standing-Use Plan (4)   A plan that is used more than once.

Steering Controls (14)   Controls that act in anticipation of problems and focus primarily on what happens during the work process; sometimes called concurrent controls.

Stereotype (11)   When an individual is assigned to a group or category, and then the attributes commonly associated with the group or category are assigned to the individual in question.

Strategic Management (5)   The managerial responsibility for formulating, implementing, and evaluating strategies that lead to longer-term organizational success.

Strategic Plan (4)   A comprehensive plan that reflects the longer-term needs and directions of the organization or subunit.

Strategic Planning (5)   The process of determining the major objectives of an organization and defining the strategies that will govern the acquisition and utilization of resources to achieve those objectives.

Strategic Planning Principle No. 1 (5)   Strategy and objectives must direct effort toward accomplishment of the organization's basic mission and overall purpose.

Strategic Planning Principle No. 2 (5)   Strategy and objectives should target effort on specific results that will solve key problems and exploit key opportunities in the organization's external environment.

Strategic Planning Principle No. 3 (5)   Strategy and objectives should build on strengths and minimize weaknesses in the organization.

Strategic Planning Principle No. 4 (5)   Strategy and objectives should be consistent with prevailing managerial values and the corporate culture.

Strategic Plan (4)   A plan that is comprehensive in scope and reflects the longer-range needs of the organization or subunit.

Strategy (5)   A comprehensive plan or action orientation that sets critical direction and guides the allocation of resources for an organization.

Stress (21)   A state of tension experienced by individuals facing extraordinary demands, constraints, or opportunities.

Stressors (21)   Things that cause stress.

Structure (6)   The formal system of working relationships that both divide and coordinate the tasks of people and groups to serve a common purpose.

Structured Decision System (15)   Computerized MIS that creates and analyzes alternative solutions to standard types of problems and selects the best or optimal choice among them.

Suboptimization (5)   When some subunits accomplish their objectives at the expense of other subunits in the organization.

Substantive Conflicts (17)   Disagreements over such things as goals, the allocation of resources, distribution of rewards, policies, and procedures, and job assignments.

Substitutes for Leadership (10)   Factors in the work setting that encourage and direct work efforts toward organizational objectives without the direct involvement of a leader.

Subsystem (2, 7)   A smaller component in a larger system; department or work unit headed by a manager but is a smaller part of a total organization.

Superordinate Goal (5)   A goal statement that conveys and represents the overall purpose of the organization to its members and interested outsiders.

Supportive (or Human-Relations) Leadership (10)   A leadership style with a high concern for people, but low concern for task.

Synergy (6)   The creation of a whole that is greater than the sum of its individual parts.

System (2)   A collection of interrelated parts that function together to achieve a common purpose.

Systematic Thinker (3)   A person who approaches problems in a rational and analytical fashion.

System Boundary (2)   The point of separation between a system and its external environment.

Task Activities (13)   Actions by group members that contribute directly to the group's performance purpose.

Task Identity (8)   The degree to which the job requires completion of a "whole" and identifiable piece of work—that is, one that involves doing a job from beginning to end with a visible outcome.

Task Significance (8)   The degree to which the job has a substantial impact on the lives or work of people elsewhere in the organization or in the external environment.

Task Structure (10)   A term used in Fiedler's contingency leadership theory to describe the extent to which task goals, procedures, and guidelines are clearly spelled out.

Team Building (13)   A sequence of planned activities to gather and analyze data on the functioning of a group and implement constructive changes to increase its operating effectiveness.

Technical Skill (1)   The ability to use a special proficiency or expertise relating to a method, process, or procedure.

Technological Environment (5)   Includes the available technologies and the related capability of society to develop or acquire appropriate technologies in the future.

Technological Imperative (7)   The viewpoint that technology is a major influence on organizational structure.

Technology (7)   The combination of equipment,

knowledge, and work methods that allows an organization to transform inputs into outputs.

Temporary Groups (13)   Work groups that are created for a specific purpose and typically disband with its accomplishment.

Temporary Systems (7)   Adaptive, rapidly changing task forces organized around problems.

Theory (2)   A set of concepts and ideas that systematically explains and predicts physical and social phenomena.

Theory X (2)   A set of managerial assumptions that people in general dislike work, lack ambition, are irresponsible and resistant to change, and prefer to be led than to lead.

Theory Y (2)   A set of managerial assumptions that people in general are willing to work and accept responsibility, and are capable of self-direction, self-control, and creativity.

Time-Series Analysis (16)   A method for identifying patterns in data by breaking historical data into components—trend, seasonal, cyclical, and random.

Top-Down Planning (4)   Planning that begins with broad objectives set by top management and then allows lower management levels to make plans within these constraints.

Totalitarian Systems (19)   Legal-political systems that involve restricted representation in the affairs of government through dictatorship, single-party rule, or preferred-membership group rule.

Training (9)   A set of activities that provide learning opportunities through which people can acquire and improve job-related skills.

Transfer (9)   Movement of a person to a different job at the same or similar level of responsibility in the organization.

Uncertainty (3)   A problem environment in which the information is such that managers are unable to associate probabilities with the outcomes of problem-solving alternatives.

Unexpected Problems (3)   Those problems that are not anticipated.

Union Shop (18)   A labor-management agreement that requires all employees of an organization to join a union.

Union Stewards (18)   Employees who are union officials and who represent workers in resolving disputes with management.

Unity-of-Command Principle (6)   Each person in an organization should report to one and only one supervisor.

Unplanned Change (17)   Change that occurs spontaneously or at random and without a change agent's direction.

Upward Communication (11)   Communication flowing from lower to higher levels in an organization's hierarchy of authority.

Valence (12)   The value the individual assigns to work-related outcomes.

Validity (9)   The degree to which a test measures exactly what it intends to relative to a job specification.

Values (5, 20)   Broad beliefs about what is or is not appropriate; the underlying beliefs and attitudes that help determine the behavior an individual displays.

Vertical Coordination (6)   The process of coordinating the activities of individuals and groups up and down the hierarchy of authority.

Weighted Moving Average (16)   A moving average that assigns a predetermined weight to each data value and thereby puts more weight on certain time periods when making forecasts.

Win-Lose Conflict (17)   When one party achieves its desires at the expense and exclusion of the other party's desires.

Win-Win Conflict (17)   When conflict is resolved to the mutual benefit of all concerned parties.

Work (1, 8)   An activity that produces value for other people.

Yes/No Controls (14)   Controls that are similar to steering controls except they represent formal checkpoints that must be successfully passed if an activity is to proceed.

Zero-Based Budget (4, 15)   A budget that allocates resources to a project or activity as if it were brand new; forces both ongoing and newly proposed programs to compete on an equal footing for available resources.

Zone of Indifference (10)   The range of directives and requests that people consider appropriate to their basic employment or psychological contract with the organization.

PHOTO CREDITS

Chapter 14

Opener: Ken Karp. Page 449: Courtesy General Tire. Page 467: Ken Karp.

Chapter 15

Opener: Gilles Peress/Magnum. Page 488: Richard Wood/Taurus. Page 497: Courtesy IBM.

Chapter 16

Opener: Ken Karp. Page 531: Sarah Putman/The Picture Cube. Page 536: Eiji Miyazawa/Black Star.

Chapter 17

Opener: Christopher Morrow/Stock, Boston. Page 547: Left, Courtesy The New York Times; right, John Blaustein/Woodfin Camp. Page 580: Courtesy NTL Institute.

Chapter 18

Opener: Majorie Pickens. Page 595: Ellis Herwig/Stock, Boston. Page 600: Abigail Heyman/Archive Pictures.

Page 605: VCR Chicago Tribune. Page 609: Joan Liftin/Archive Pictures.

Chapter 19

Opener: Bernard Pierre Wolff/Photo Researchers. Page 631: UPI. Page 640: Sidney Harris. Page 643: Georg Gerster/Photo Researchers.

Chapter 20

Opener: Nick de Gregory/Leo deWys. Page 663: Sidney Harris. Page 666: Courtesy Whirlpool Corp. Page 668: Courtesy Johnson & Johnson. Page 672: Mark Antman/The Image Works.

Chapter 21

Opener: Ellis Herwig/Stock, Boston. Page 700: Copyright, 1982. G.B. Trudeau. Reprinted with permission of Universal Press Syndicate. Page 702: Courtesy Exxon Corp. Page 709: Ann Chwatsky/Leo deWys. Page 713: copyright, 1982, G.B. Trudeau. Reprinted with permission of Universal Press syndicate.

NAME INDEX

Califano, Joseph A., Jr., 176
Cammann, Cortlandt, 473nn. 18, 19
Cannon, Howard W., 598
Carey, Max L., 704
Carley, William M., 685n.8
Carlisle, Arthur Elliott, 430–433
Carlisle, Howard M., 202n.2, 272, 473n.20
Carlson, Ed, 362–363
Carlson, Eugene, 164n.15
Carlson, M. Tracey, 722
Carrington, Tim, 396n.1
Carroll, Stephen J., 30n.11, 233n.2, 273, 473n.16
Carter, Jimmy, 636
Cartwright, Darwin, 331n.7
Cary, Frank, 685n.7
Castelli, Leo, 236
Champagne, Paul J., 262n.14
Champion, John M., 688
Chance, Susan, 283
Chandler, Alfred, Jr., 223, 233n.18
Chemers, Martin M., 320, 332n.16
Cherrington, David J., 506n.21
Cherrington, J. Owen, 506n.21
Chin, Robert, 586n.22
Ching, Frank, 210
Choffel, Jean, 461
Christensen, Kathryn, 262n.2, 263n.23
Chung, Kae H., 724n.22
Churchman, C. West, 63n.16
Clay, Donald, 249
Clee, Gilbert H., 641, 642, 653n.20
Cleveland, Harlan, 712
Clifford, Douglas, 677
Coates, William, 700
Cobb, Hattie, 249
Cohen, Allan R., 262nn. 20, 21
Connor, Michael J., 312
Considine, Frank W., 151
Coogan, Jim, 462
Cooke, Robert A., 586n.19
Corey, Kenneth E., 586n.22
Cosby, Addie, 604
Costello, Timothy W., 366n.15
Coulson, Robert, 293n.18
Cowan, John, 458
Cox, William, 260, 261
Craft, Robert E., Jr., 262n.9
Crandall, Robert, 663
Cressey, Donald, 179, 202n.3
Cressor, Bob, 328–329
Cummings, Larry L., 62n.3, 454
Curley, John, 275, 292n.1
Cushing, Byrant, 288
Cushing, Carole, R., 288

Daft, Richard L., 233n.17, 506n.19
Dalton, Alan, 492, 506n.13
Damm, Alexander, 76, 77

Daniels, Derick J., 267
Daniels, John D., 653nn. 11, 12
Davis, Edward E., Jr., 218
Davis, Evan M., 313
Davis, Keith, 202n.5, 359, 669, 673, 685nn. 22, 23, 24
Davis, Stanley M., 202nn. 8, 9
Day, Theron L., 556
Deal, Terrence, 154
Dearden, John, 505nn. 2, 3
de Castro, Edson, 476
Deci, Edward L., 397n.12
Deckerhoff, Richard, 670
DeCoster, Don T., 484, 505n.5
Deitzer, Bernard, 203n.17
Delbecq, André L., 93n.16, 133n.14
Deleune, Elton J., 722
DeLorean, John Z., 659, 665–666
Deming, W. Edwards, 535–536, 544n.12
de Solo, Alberto, 547
Dessler, Gary, 293n.14
Devries, David L., 397nn. 18, 20
Di Cagno, Elisabetta, 685n.16
Dickens, Charles, 697, 724n.2
Dickson, William J., 63n.12
Diehm, Walter A., 546
Dill, William, 61
Dobbins, James, 336
Doktor, Robert H., 57
Dole, Charles E., 653n.29
Douglas, Martin, 440–441
Dowling, William F., 262n.16
Downey, Kirk, 262n.9
Driver, Michael J., 93n.4
Drobnick, Richard, 680
Drucker, Peter F., 3n.2; 7; 30nn. 1, 38; 120; 133n.12; 144–145; 163nn. 4, 9, 10, 12; 177; 199–200; 203n.16; 552–553; 558; 561; 585n.4; 632; 641
Duncan, Robert B., 585n.5
Dunnette, Marvin, 473n.7
du Pont, Pierre, 173
Dutton, John M., 585n.9
Dyer, William D., 429n.18

Eicher, Steve, 125
Ein-Dor, P., 506n.16
Eisner, Ralph, 726–728
Engdahl, Gordon W., 224
Engle, Clarence, 247
English, Jon, 30n.8
Evereklian, Alicia, 221

Farace, Richard V., 365n.9
Farson, Richard E., 366n.21
Fayol, Henri, 42–46; 63nn. 9, 10; 107
Fenn, Dan H., Jr., 685n.30
Ferrence, Thomas P., 724n.24
Ferris, G. R., 724nn. 4, 5, 10

Fiedler, Fred, 318–321, 326, 332n.16
Filhe, Ellsworth, Jr., 349
Filley, Alan C., 586nn. 11, 14
Finercane, Robert E., 332n.22
Finley, Ruth C., 538
Fiorito, Jack, 618n.9
Flippo, Edwin B., 282, 293n.10
Foley, Patrick, 336, 337
Follett, Mary Parker, 43, 44, 62n.8
Ford, Henry, 3, 40–41, 137–138, 254, 458
Ford, Henry, II, 288
Ford, Henry, III, 138
Forst, C. Dale, 206
Foster, Charles, 677
Foster, Gene, 406
Foulkes, Fred K., 618n.10
Fowble, Lowell, 266
Fox, Henry, 312
Fraser, Douglas, 471
Frederick, Joanne, 601
Frederick, Les, 601
Freidman, Meyer, 724n.14
Friedman, Dan, 656–658
Friedman, Milton, 671, 685n.22
French, John R. P., 331n.7
French, Wendell L., 586n.27
Fry, Ronald E., 332n.24
Fulmer, Robert, 697, 700, 702, 724nn. 3, 9

Gadon, Herman, 262nn. 20, 21
Galbraith, Jay R., 30n.4, 228, 233nn. 8, 21
Gallese, Liz Roman, 76
Galvin, Robert, 727
Gant, Mr., 604
Gantt, Henry, 529
Gardner, John, 692
Garino, David P., 155
Garner, David, 616
Garrett, David C., Jr., 169, 711
Gebo, James, 244
Geneen, Harold S., 154, 363, 425
Geschow, George, 163n.1, 164n.31
Getty, J. Paul, 35–36, 62n.2
Ghiselli, E. E., 331n.11
Gibbs, Thomas E., 544, 544nn. 2, 3, 6
Gilbreth, Frank, 42, 43, 62n.7, 447
Gilbreth, Lillian, 42, 43, 447
Gitman, Lawrence J., 31n.18; 93n.5; 133n.6; 181; 190; 271; 352; 494–496; 506n.22; 529; 530; 544n.5; 607; 613; 618nn. 13, 15, 16, 18, 19; 685n.27
Glueck, William F., 133n.4; 139–142; 146; 163nn. 5, 6; 164nn. 20, 25; 293n.8; 618nn. 2, 17; 685n.28
Goldman, Emanuel, 141
Golembiewski, Robert T., 262–263n.21
Gompers, Samuel, 594, 618n.4

SUBJECT INDEX

Comparative management practices, 643–648
Comparative standards, 447
Compensation, 459–461
  collective bargaining affecting, 605–606, 609–610
  in future, 698, 701
  high, as reducing costs, 458–459
  incentive, 459
  Japanese *vs.* U.S., 647
  management by objectives tied to, 466
  for managers, 13, 701
  merit, problems of, 381
  see also Fringe benefits; Pay and reward systems
Competition:
  in conflict management, 566, 568
  intergroup, 422–423
  for promotions, in future, 701
Competitive forecasts, 122
Complexity:
  controls as coping with, 445
  of people, in modern management approaches, 54
Comprehensive controls in organizational control systems, 453–457
Comprehensive strategic planning, 156–157
Compressed workweeks, 256, 257
Compromise in conflict management, 566, 568
Computer anxiety, 503
Computer-assisted design (CAD), 539
Computer-assisted manufacturing (CAM), 539
Computer-based management information systems, 493–501
Computer hardware, 493
Computer programming, 53, 530, A2–A4
Computer programming languages, 494, 496
Computer software, 493–494
Computers:
  central processing unit of, 494
  in decision-support systems, 496
  executive training in, 221
  in information-reporting systems, 495–496
  in management, 539
  personal (micro), 494
  in structured decision systems, 496
  work affected by, 699–700
Conceptual skills, 24
Conciliation in grievance procedure, 608
Concurrent controls, 450
Conflict:
  active intervention in, 567–568
  antecedents of, 565
  defined, 560

facilitation in, 568–569
  within individuals, 562–563
  managers as mediators of, 567–569
  between organizations, 564
  in organizations, 560–569
  outcomes of, 565–567
  suppression of, 565, 566
  types of:
    approach-approach, 562–563
    approach-avoidance, 563
    avoidance-avoidance, 563
    constructive, 561–562
    destructive, 560–561
    emotional, 560
    felt, 565
    foreign, in political-risk analysis, 638–639
    intergroup, 563–564
    interorganizational, 564
    interpersonal, 563
    lose-lose, 566, 567
    manifest, 565
    perceived, 565
    role, 356
    substantive, 560
    win-lose, 567
    win-win, 567
Conflict management, 566–569
Conflict resolution, 565, 566
Conflict situations, 562–565
Confrontation meetings, 580
Consensus, achievement of, 323
Constructive conflict, 561–562
Constructive stress, 706, 707
Consultative decision making, 87, 88, 323–325
Consumer Credit Protection Act of 1969, 676
Consumer forecasts, 122
Consumer Product Safety Act of 1972, 676
Consumer protection by government, 676
Contact(s):
  direct, for integration, 228
  interpersonal, government influenced by, 676–677
Content theories of motivation, 374–380, 392. *See also* Hierarchy-of-needs theory (Maslow)
Context, job, 240, 241, 243, 271
Contextual forces in organizational design, 215, 220–226
Continental Airlines, 76, 77
Contingency, planning for, 125
Contingency approaches:
  to leadership, 317–326
  to management, 57–58
  to organizational design, 211, 214
Contingency strategies, 139
Contingent reinforcement, law of, 387
Continuous-process technology, 221–222

Continuous reinforcement, 389
Contracts:
  defined, 239
  management, in international business, 626
  psychological, 239
Contributions, defined, 239
Control(s):
  in control process, 448–450
  in control systems, 453–457
  effectiveness of, 467–468
  human reactions to, 467–468
  purposes of, 445–446
  span of, 192–193
  types of, 450
    comprehensive, 453–457
    external, 448–450
    internal (self-), 448–449
    inventory, 530–534
    quality, *see* Quality control; Quality-control circles
    situational (Fiedler), 318–319
Control charts in quality control, 534, 535
Controlling, 443–468
  communication in, 339
  defined, 445
  Fayol rule resembling, 44
  importance of, 445–446
  in international environment, 637–639
  and leading, 452
  as management function, 20, 21, 44, 445–450
  and management levels, 21
  and organizing, 452
  and planning, 109, 121–122, 451. *See also* Management by objectives (MBO)
  problem solving in, 71–72
  in production/operations management, 516–517. *See also* Production/operations management (P/OM)
  social responsibility in, 680–681
  see also Leading; Organizing; Planning
Control process, 446–450. *See also* Performance
Control systems:
  characteristics of, 468
  components of, 451–453. *See also* Controlling; Leading; Organizing; Planning
  comprehensive controls in, 453–457
  cybernetic, 446
  Japanese *vs.* U.S., 647
  and planning systems, integrated (MBO), 143–145, 464–467, 547–549, 580, 709
Cooperation:
  in conflict management, 566
  in labor-management relations, 612

Disciplinary procedures and systems, 461–463, 610–611
Discrimination in employment, 274–275, 675–676. *See also* Equal employment opportunity (EEO)
Disobedience, 311–313
Displacement:
    job, automation as causing, 611–612
    of objectives, 143
Dissatisfaction, job, 240–241
Disseminator role of managers, 337, 338
Distractions, physical, as communication barrier, 343–344
Distributed leadership, 419
Distribution, forced, in multiperson comparisons, 456–457
Divisional departmentation, 187–188
Division of labor, 11, 177
Division of work, 180
Dorsey Corporation, 161
Double approach-avoidance conflict, 563
Downward communication, 353
Drives, *see* Need(s)
Dual-career families, 76, 716–717
Du Pont Company, 539
Dynamic environments, 139
Dysfunctional activities, 419

Earnings, *see* Compensation
Eclipse Inc., 458
Econometric modeling, 124
Economic environment, 150, 152
    international, 633, 639
    organizations affected by, 218–219
    in political-risk analysis, 639
Economic forecasts, 122
Economic order quantity (EOQ), 531–532
Economic values, 153
Economy(ies):
    centralized-planning *vs.* free-market, 633, 634
    world, multinational corporations in, 627–631
Education:
    conditions of, affecting organizations, 218, 219
    continuing, as career tactic, 718–719
    in dealing with resistance to change, 575, 576
    in international environment, 634
    of labor leaders, 615
    see also specific Work entries; Working
Effect, law of (Thorndike), 386
Effective communication, 340–344, 357–361, 612
Effective groups, 407, 408, 410. *See also* Effectiveness, group
Effectiveness:
    group, 407, 408, 410, 419–420, 580
    individual, 579–580

organizational, 580
performance, 17–18
Efficiency:
    in communication, 340
    performance, 17–18
Elaborating as task activity, 418
Electronic information processing, 699, 700. *See also* Computers; *specific Computer entries*
Emergent behaviors, 411–412
Emerson Electric Company, 128
Emotional blocks, overcoming, 80
Emotional conflicts, 560
Empirical-rational change strategies, 573–574
Employees:
    advisory councils of, 356
    compensation of, *see* Compensation; Fringe benefits
    health of, 708
    in Japan, 102–103, 125. *See also* Japanese companies
    and management, relations of, *see* Labor-management relations
    meetings of, 355–356
    new:
        orientation of, 283–284
        socialization of, 283
    participation by, *see* Participation by employees
    productive, *see* Productive managers; Productivity
    replacement of, 269, 285–289, 610. *See also* Promotions
    rights of, 599–600, 698
    selection of, 269, 279–282, 647
    in unions; *see* Union(s); *specific Union entries*
    women, 601, 702, 703. *See also* Women managers; Women's groups
    see also Labor; *specific Labor entries*
Employers:
    rights of, 599–600, 605
    union organizing resisted by, 602
    see also Corporations; Organizations
Employment:
    discrimination in, 274–275, 675–676
    equal opportunity in, 274–275, 281
    lifetime, in Japan, 646, 647
    1990 outlook for, 704
    see also Unemployment in future
Employment policies, 113–115
Employment tests, 280–281
Encoding errors in communication, 340–341
Encouraging as maintenance activity, 418
Engineered standards, 447
Enlargement of jobs, 246–247
Enrichment of jobs, 247–252, 376–377
Ento International, 127

Environmental Protection Agency (EPA), 675
Environments of organizations, 215–220
    analysis of, in strategic planning, 147, 150, 152
    and forecasting, 152, 638–639
    for problem solving, 81–82
    and strategies, 138–139
    and subsystems, 226
    types of:
        certain, 81–82
        dynamic, 139
        external, *see* External environment
        general, 218–220, 697–698
        international, 631–636, 639
        legal, *see* Legal environment of organizations
        political, 150, 152, 219–220
        risky, in problem solving, 82
        social, 150, 152
        specific, 219, 220
        stable, 139
        technological, 150, 152
        uncertain, 82, 139, 217–218
Equal employment opportunity (EEO), 274–275, 281. *See also* Discrimination in employment
Equifinality, defined, 56
Equipment, scheduling of, 513
Equity of earnings in future, 698
Equity theory of motivation, 380–381
ERG theory of Alderfer, 376–377
Esteem needs of Maslow, 375, 377
Ethical, defined, 658
Ethical behavior (conduct), 658–659, 665–666
Ethical dilemmas of managers, 161, 659–660
Ethical managerial behavior, defined, 659. *See also* Ethics, managerial
Ethics:
    defined, 658
    managerial, 659–666, 670
Etiquette differences in international environment, 636
Existence needs of Alderfer, 376
Expanded markets in international business, 625
Expectancy theory of motivation, 382–385
Expected problems, 76
Expected value, 84–85
Expense centers, 479
Expert power, 310
Explicit coercion in dealing with resistance to change, 576
Exponential smoothing in demand forecasting, 520–521
Exportation/importation of goods and services, 626
External control in control process, 448–450

External environment:
  components of, 150–152
  effects of:
    on human-resource planning, 274–276
    on managerial ethics, 663
    on organizational design, 216–217
    on organization structure, 184
  strategies for, 139
External recruitment, 277–278
External users of information systems, 489
Extinction in behavior modification, 386, 388
Exxon Benefit Plan Service, 459, 460
Evaluation:
  in budgeting process, 481–482
  in performance appraisal, 453
  in planning process, 118, 146
Evans Products Company, 109–110, 144, 145

Facilitation:
  in conflict mediation, 568–569
  in dealing with resistance to change, 575, 576
Facilities plans, 111
Factory foremen, worker problems with, 304. *See also* Labor-management relations; Lower-level managers
Fair labor practices, legislation and regulations affecting, 675–676. *See also* Unfair labor practices under NLRA
Families, dual-career, 76, 716–717
Feasible region in linear programming, A4
Federal Aviation Administration (FAA), 676, 677
Federal Reserve Bank of Boston, 710
Feedback, 57
  absence of, as communication barrier, 341
  defined, 56, 358
  effective, 358–360
  in job enrichment, 248, 250–252
  survey, 580
Feedback controls, 450
Feed-forward controls, 450
Felt conflict, 565
Final-offer points in collective bargaining, 606, 607
Financially rewarded careers in future, 700–701
Financial plans, 111
Financial position, projected statements of, 485
Financial ratios in budgetary control, 486, 487
Financial resources in international business, 625

Finished goods and services in production/operations management, 513–515
Finished-goods inventories, 531
Firestone, 163
Firings, dealing with, 287–289
Fixed budgets, 115, 480
Flat organizations, 192
Flexibility in future work positions, 701
Flexible budgets, 115, 480, 488
Flexible strategies, 139
Flexible working hours (flextime), 257
Following as maintenance activity, 418
Force-coercion change strategies, 572–573
Forced distribution in multiperson comparisons, 456–457
Ford Motor Company, 3, 83, 117, 138, 196, 458
Forecasting:
  defined, 122
  of demand, 482, 515–523
  and environmental components, 152, 638–639
  errors in, 124
  human-resource, 271–274
  as international planning tool, 638–639
  for 1990s and beyond, 698
  as quantitative management technique, 53
  techniques of, 122–124, 517–518
  types of, 122
Foreign branches of corporations, 626
Foreign conflict in political-risk analysis, 638–639
Foreign Corrupt Practices Act of 1977, 629–631
Foreign direct investments in U.S., 626
Foreign subsidiaries of corporations, 626
Foremen, factory, worker problems with, 304. *See also* Labor-management relations; Lower-level managers
Formal authority, 11–12
Formal communication channels, 351. *See also* Hierarchy of authority
Formal groups, 401–403. *See also* Informal groups
Formal leadership, 305–306
Formal organization structure, 180–182
Formal planning, 117–118, 157–158
Forming stage of group development, 408–409
Four-day workweeks, 256, 257
Free-form narratives in performance appraisal, 456, 457
Free-market economies, 633, 634
Fringe benefits, 459–461, 605–606, 609–610. *See also* Compensation
Fullfeder Pen Company case, 200–201
Functional authority, 195, 197

Functional departmentation, 185–187
Functional managers, 14, 15
Functions supervised and span of control, 192
Future:
  managerial outlooks for, 697–703
  in planning process, 118. *See also* Forecasting
Future shock, 697–698

Gantt charts, 116, 529–530
Gatekeeping as maintenance activity, 418
General Electric Company, 163, 217
General environment of organizations, 218–220, 697–698
General Foods Corporation, 254–256
General managers, 14–15
General Motors, 471, 631–632, 639–641
General Signal, 510
General systems theory of Bertalanffy, 55–56
General Tire management newsletter, 444
General unions, 595
Girl Scouts organization, 557–558
Goal orientation, differences in, 227
Goals:
  management by (MBO), 143–145, 464–467, 547–549, 580, 709
  superordinate, 149
  see also Objectives; Path-goal theory of leadership (House)
Goods and services:
  finished, in production/operations management, 513–515
  importation/exportation of, 626
Goodyear Tire & Rubber Co., 674
Government agencies, regulation by, 676, 677
Government legislation and regulations affecting organizations, 274–275, 279–281, 629–631, 664, 673–678
Government systems:
  democratic and totalitarian, 633
  in political-risk analysis, 639
Grapevines as informal communication channels, 351–353
Graphic rating scales, 455, 457
Grievance procedures, 607, 608, 613
Group cohesiveness, 412–418, 664. *See also* Groupthink
Group decision making, 87, 88, 323–325
Group dynamics, 410–412
  defined, 410
  Homan's model of, 410–412, 418
  intergroup, 421–423
  leading through, 399–423
Group effectiveness, 407, 408, 410, 419–420, 580

Information-reporting systems, 496. *See also* Computers; *specific Computer entries*

Information systems, 477–478, 489–492 management, 491–501 *see also* Budgetary control systems; Budgets

Initial integration stage of group development, 409–410

Initial screening in recruitment process, 276, 277

Initiating as task activity, 418

Innovation in organizations, 143, 559–561. *See also* Creativity; Intuitive thinkers

Inputs, group, transformed into group outputs, 409

Input standards, 447

Inside-out planning, 118–119

Institute for the Future (IFF), 123

Instrumentality in expectancy theory, 382, 385

Integer programming, A4

Integrated planning and control system (MBO), 143–145, 464–467, 547–549, 580, 709

Integration: in group development, 409–410 official objectives in, 142 in subsystem design, 226–228

Intellectual blocks, overcoming, 80

Intelligence as leadership trait, 315

Intelligence tests, 280

Intensive technology, 220

Interactions in group dynamics, 411–412

Intergroup competition, 422–423

Intergroup conflict, 563–564

Intergroup dynamics, 421–423

Intergroup team building, 580

Intermediate-range plans, 110

Intermittent reinforcement, 389

Internal control in control process, 448–449

Internal recruitment, 266, 277, 278

Internal Revenue Service (IRS), 217

Internal users of information systems, 489–492

International business, 624–626, 629–631. *See also* Multinational corporations (MNCs)

International Business Machines Corporation (IBM), 149, 154, 198, 283, 662, 667, 668

International economic environment, 633, 639

International Harvester Company, 663

International management, 623–649

International Telephone & Telegraph Corporation (ITT), 154, 425, 628, 630

International unions, 596–598

International Woodworkers of America (IWA), 395

Interorganizational conflict, 564

Interpersonal conflict, 563

Interpersonal contact, government influenced by, 676–677

Interpersonal orientation in differentiation, 227

Intervention phase of organization development, 577, 578

Interviews: as data-gathering method, 579 performance-appraisal, 457–458 in selection process, 279–280

Intuition in planning, 157–158

Intuitive thinkers, 70–71. *See also* Creativity

Inventories: of alternatives, 82, 84 of materials, 530–532. *See also* Material-requirements planning (MRP)

Inventory charts, human-resource, 273, 274, 286

Inventory control, 530–534

Inventory modeling, 53

Investment, return on, and employee health, 708

Investment centers, 479

Involvement in dealing with resistance to change, 575, 576

ITT (International Telephone & Telegraph Corporation), 154, 425, 628, 630

Japanese companies: corporate culture of, 154–155 just-in-time delivery systems of, 533 management systems of, 645–648, 650–652 organization structure of, 172–173 participatory planning in, 102–103 quality-control circles at, 404, 441, 535, 537, 646 in U.S., 624, 650–652 *vs.* U.S. companies, 301–302, 645–648, 650–652 worker treatment by, 125 work ethic approach of, 301–302

J. C. Penney Company, 162

Jefferson Electric, 604

Job advertisements, 276, 277

Job analysis for staffing needs, 271, 272

Job applicants, advice for, 714

Job-application forms, 279

Job burnout, 394–395

Job characteristics, core, in job enrichment, 248, 250–252

Job content, 241, 243

Job context, 183, 240, 241, 243, 244, 271

Job depth, 247–248

Job descriptions, 237, 238, 271

Job design: assembly-line, 245–247, 253–254 alternatives to, 254, 260–261 in concept and practice, 243–248 as control function, 452 defined, 243 for groups, 253–257. *See also* Work groups for individuals, 236–252 specialization by, 184 strategies for, continuum of, 245–248. *See also* Job enrichment; Job rotation; Job simplification task attributes of, 243–245 team-assembly, 245, 247 work-setting attributes of, 243, 244 *see also* Job redesign; Organizational design

Job displacement, 611–612

Job dissatisfaction, 240–241

Job enlargement, 246–247

Job enrichment, 247–252, 376–377

Job performance, 240. *See also* Task performance

Job redesign, 580. *See also* Job design

Job-related stress, 703–710

Job-related tangibles and intangibles, 271

Job rotation, 246–247, 285, 646

Jobs: defined, 237 feedback from, 248, 250–252

Job satisfaction, 239–243 group cohesiveness in, 414–415 *see also* Satisfaction

Job scope, 243

Job security, 606, 610, 698

Job sharing, 257

Job simplification, 246. *See also* Automation

Job specialization, 184, 243–245

Job specifications, 271

Job transfers, 286, 610

Joint ventures, 626

J. P. Stevens Company, 601, 615

Judgmental roles in performance appraisal, 453, 454

Jurisdiction of the law in union organizing, 603

Just-cause principle, 611

Just-in-time delivery, 533–534

Kanban delivery systems, 533

Kawasaki Motor Corporation, 125

Labconco Company, 608–609

Labor: division of, 11, 177 organized; *see* Union(s); *specific Union entries*

problems of, 78
structure created by, 182
Midlife transition, 715
Mid-Ohio Electric Company, 56–57
Miller Brewing Company, 141
Minimum spanning tree problems, A4–A6
Minnesota Mining & Manufacturing Co. (3M), 224
Mission in strategic planning, 147–151
Mixed messages, 342
Mobil Oil, 151
Modeling:
  econometric, 124
  inventory, 53
  as training device, 285
Modern approaches to management, 41, 54–59
Modern managers, 3
Modified assembly-line jobs, 245–247
Money as motivator, 383–384, 395
Monitoring program performance, 482
Monitor role of managers, 337, 338
Monsanto Company, 180
Moral, defined, 658
Morgan Stanley & Co., 461
Morris, Philip, Inc., 141
Motorola, Inc., Chicago, 726–728
Motion study, 43, 644
Motivation:
  cognitive explanation of, 385
  concept of, 371–372
  integrated approach to, 392–393
  leading through, 369–393
  money in, 383–384, 395
  parables of, 373, 380, 392
  and rewards, 372–374
  theories of:
    acquired-needs (McClelland), 377–380
    content, 374–380, 392
    across cultures, 645
    equity, 380–381
    expectancy, 382–385
    hierarchy-of-needs (Maslow), see Hierarchy-of-needs theory (Maslow)
    process, 374, 380–385, 392
    reinforcement, 374, 385–392
  to work, 372
Motives, see Needs
Moving as career tactic, 717
Moving averages, 518–520
Multilevel strategic planning, 156–157
Multinational corporations (MNCs), 626–631, 640–642. See also International business; International management
Multinational geographic structure of organizations, 640, 641
Multinational product structure of organizations, 640, 642

Multiperson comparisons in performance appraisal, 456–457
Multiple approach-avoidance conflict, 563
Multiple outcomes in expectancy theory, 382–383
Multiplier effect in expectancy theory, 382
Murphy's laws, 444

nAch (need for achievement) of McClelland, 377–379
nAff (need for affiliation) of McClelland, 377–379
National Aeronautics and Space Administration (NASA), 217
National culture, dimensions of, 635–636. See also Cultural differences
National Labor Relations Act (NLRA), 599–600
National Labor Relations Board (NLRB), 599, 600, 606
National unions, 596–598
Need(s):
  for achievement, 315
    of McClelland (nAch), 377–379
  acquired (McClelland), 377–380
  for affiliation, of McClelland (nAff), 377–379
  defined, 48, 374
  existence, of Alderfer, 376
  groups as satisfying, 403, 404, 406–407
  growth, of Alderfer, 376. See also Growth-need strength
  hierarchy of, see Hierarchy-of-needs theory (Maslow)
  higher-order, 375, 377
  individual, 374–380
  lower-order, 375, 377
  for power, of McClelland (nPower), 377–379
  relatedness, of Alderfer, 376
  staffing, 271
Negative entropy, 56
Negative reinforcement, 386, 388
Negotiation in dealing with resistance to change, 575, 576
Network models as quantitative management technique, 53
Network problems, 529, 530, A4–A6
Networks, communication, 215–216. See also Communication channels
Nigeria, corruption in, 622
Nissan Motor Manufacturing Corporation, U.S.A., 651–652
No-fault absenteeism, 471
Noise, sources of, 340–344
No-lockout pledges, 606
Nominal groups in problem solving, 81
Nonlinear programming, A3

Nonprogrammed decisions, 75
Nonroutine problems, 75
Nonverbal communication, 342–343
Norge Division of Magic Chef Inc., 513–515, 616
Normative-reeducative change strategies, 574
Northeast Color Research Inc., 601
Northside Child Health Care Center case, 294–296
No-strike clauses, 606
nPower (need for power) of McClelland, 377–379

Objectives:
  defining, 118
  displacement of, 143
  evaluating, 118
  hierarchy of, 143–145
  management by, 143–145, 464–467, 547–549, 580, 709
  in planning process, 118, 120–121. See also Objectives, types of, planning
  types of:
    imprecise, 121
    maintenance, 465
    official, 142
    operating, 142–143, 483–485
    organizational, 142–147
    performance, 447, 448
    personal development, 465
    planning, 110
    precise, 120–121
  see also Goal orientation; Goals
OB Mod (organizational behavior modification), 386–392
Observations in data gathering, 579
Occupational achievement, need for, 315, 377–379
Occupational safety, government regulation of, 675
OD interventions, 579–580
OD (organization development), 576–581. See also Planned change
Official objectives, 142
Off-the-job training, 285
One-way communication, 341
On-the-job training, 284–285
Open office hours, 355
Open offices, 244
Open systems:
  defined, 55
  groups as, 407–408
  organizations as, 11, 54–55
Open-systems view of organizations, 56–57, 211–212
Operant conditioning, 386
Operating budgets, 480
Operating management, 155–157
Operating objectives, 142–143, 483–485
Operational plans, 111–113

Operations and production, controlling, *see* Production/operations management (P/OM)

Operations research, 41, 51–54, A1–A9

Opinion giving as task activity, 418

Opinion pools in forecasting, 124

Opportunity, limited, in careers, 716

Opportunity situation in control process, 448

Oral communications, 338–339, 341–343

Ordering, rank, in multiperson comparisons, 456

Ordering costs of inventory, 531–532

Orders, lot-by-lot, 532

Organic structures of organizations, 212–216, 222, 223, 225–229

Organization:
  analysis of, 147, 152–153
  bureaucratic, 44–46. *See also* Bureaucracies
  defined, 177
  matrix (departmentation), 188–190. *See also* Matrix organizations and personality, Argyris theory of, 49–51
  see also Organizations; Organizing

Organizational behavior modification (OB Mod), 386–392

Organizational change, 569–576. *See also* Organization development (OD)

Organizational communication, 351–356. *See also* Communication

Organizational context, 215, 220–226

Organizational control systems, *see* Control systems

Organizational design, 205–229
  contextual forces in, 215, 220–226
  contingency approach to, 211, 214
  across cultures, 645
  defined, 207
  environmental factors in, 215–220. *See also* Environments of organizations
  guidelines for, 217, 222, 223, 226–228
  human resources in, 225–226
  information processing in, 214–216
  organizational size in, 222–224. *See also* Organizational size
  strategies in, 139–140, 212–216, 222–223, 225–229
  subsystem design in, 226–229
  see also Bureaucracies; Job design

Organizational development, 576–581

Organizational effectiveness, 580

Organizational factors in management information system success, 497–499

Organizational identities, 149–151

Organizational innovation, 143, 559–561. *See also* Creativity; Intuitive thinkers

Organizational objectives, 142–147. *See also* Operating objectives

Organizational performance and planning, 126. *See also* Performance; Planning; Plans; *specific Performance entries*

Organizational policies, 113–115

Organizational size, 184, 222–224

Organizational structure, *see* Organization structures

Organizational subsystems, 55, 226–229

Organization charts, 180–182, 237, 238, 650, 651

Organization development (OD), 576–581. *See also* Planned change

Organization development interventions, 579–580

Organizations:
  characteristics of, 8–12
  conflict between, 564
  conflict in, 560–569
  division of labor in, 11
  effects on:
    of cultural values, 218
    of economic conditions, 218–219
    of educational conditions, 218, 219
    of legal-political conditions, 219–220
    of legislation and regulations, 274–275, 279–281, 629–631, 664, 673–678
  environments of, *see* Environments of organizations
  flat, 192
  groups in, *see* Groups
  hierarchy of authority in, 11–12
  human resources of, *see* Human resources of organizations
  ingredients of, 10–12
  managerial ethics affected by, 662
  managers in, *see* Management; Managers; *specific Managerial entries*
  material resources of, 7, 17–19
  matrix, 228. *See also* Matrix departmentation (organization)
  as open systems, 11, 54–55
  open-systems view of, 56–57, 211–212
  outputs of, 8
  purposes of, 10–11
  sizes of, 184, 222–224
  social responsibility in, 143, 666–673, 679–681, 708
  society composed of, 6
  tall, 192
  unionizing of, 600–604
  unions as, 596–598
  see also Organization; Organizing

Organization structures, 180–185
  design of, as control function, 452
  differences in, 227
  Japanese *vs.* U.S., 647
  from managerial perspective, 182–185, 207
  of multinational corporations, 640–642
  specialization in, *see* Specialization
  and strategies, 184, 223
  types of:
    formal, 180–182
    informal, 181–182
    mechanistic and organic, 212–216, 222, 223, 225–229
    task, 319, 321
  see also Coordination

Organized crime, 178–179, 598

Organized labor, *see* Union(s); *specific Union entries*

Organizing, 175–198
  communication in, 339
  and controlling, 425
  as decision process, 179–180
  defined, 177
  Fayol rule resembling, 44
  importance of, 178
  in international environment, 639–643
  as management function, 20, 21, 44, 177–180
  and management levels, 21
  for planning, 128
  planning affecting, 109
  problem solving in, 71–72
  social responsibility in, 679–680
  see also Controlling; Leading; Planning

Orientation of employees, 269, 282–284

Outcomes, multiple, in expectancy theory, 382–383

Outputs, group, 409

Output standards, 447

Outside-in planning, 119

Overspecialization in bureaucracies, 209

Paired comparisons, 456

Parables of motivation, 373, 380, 392

Participation of employees:
  in dealing with resistance to change, 575, 576
  in decision making, 102–103, 322, 326–327, 702

Participative leadership style, 316, 317, 322, 326–327. *See also* Leader-participation theory (Vroom and Yetton)

Participative Management Program (PMP) at Motorola, 726–728

Path-goal theory of leadership (House), 321–323, 326, 385

PATH (People Associated for Tomorrow's Highways), 220
Pay, *see* Compensation; Fringe benefits
Pay and reward systems, 458–461
Payoff tables, 84–85
Penney, J. C., Company, 162
Penn Manor, 381
People, *see* Groups; Human resources; Individuals
PepsiCo, Inc., 162
Perceived conflict, 565
Perception:
  and communication, 345–351
  selective, 79, 349
Perception process, 350–351
Perceptual blocks, overcoming, 80
Performance:
  actual, measuring, 447
  defined, 240
  good, as career tactic, 717
  group cohesiveness and satisfaction related to, 414–415
  job, 240
  job satisfaction related to, 241–243
  organizational, and planning, 126. *See also* Planning; Plans
  program, monitoring, 482
  and rewards, 242, 373–374
  and staffing, 269–270
  task, 240, 243, 267, 407, 408. *See also* Job content; Job design
Performance-appraisal interviews, 457–458
Performance-appraisal systems, 453–458
Performance areas, reports by, 491
Performance art, 236
Performance effectiveness, 17–18
Performance efficiency, 17–18
Performance gaps, 570–571
Performance norms in work groups, 413–416
Performance objectives, 447, 448
Performance standards, 271, 447, 448
Permanent groups, 402
Personal computers, 494
Personal development objectives, 465
Personality and organization, Argyris theory of, 49–51
Personality tests, 280
Personal power, 310
Personal requirements in job analysis, 271
Personal staff, 197
Personal wellness in stress management, 707–708, 710
Personnel departments, 269–270
Personnel planning, 111, 269–276, 279–281
Personnel specialists, 270
PERT (program evaluation and review technique), 529, 530, A4–A5
Philip Morris, Inc., 141

Phillips Petroleum Corporation, 312
Physical distractions in communication, 343–344
Physical examinations, 281–282
Physiological needs of Maslow, 375, 377
Planned change, 570–576. *See also* Organization development (OD)
Planners, staff, 128
Planning, 105–129
  approaches to, 118–121
  benefits of, 124–126
  centralization of, for economies, 633, 634
  communication in, 339
  and controlling, 109, 121–122, 451. *See also* and review, of work (MBO)
  defined, 107
  Fayol rule resembling, 44
  forecasting in, *see* Forecasting
  guidelines for, 126–129
  with imprecise objectives, 121
  for integration, 228
  in international environment, 637–639
  leading affected by, 109
  limits of, 127–128
  as management function, 20, 21, 44, 108–117
  and management levels, 21, 112, 128–129
  and organizational performance, 126
  organizing affected by, 109
  organizing for, 128–129
  with precise objectives, 120–121
  and problem solving, 71–72, 118
  in production/operations management, 515–516. *See also* Production/operations management (P/OM)
  purpose of, 125
  and review, of work (MBO), 143–145, 464–467, 547–549, 580, 709
  social responsibility in, 679, 680
  types of:
    capacity, 526–529
    career, 580, 711–713
    directional, 121
    formal, 117–118, 157–158
    human-resource (personnel), 111, 269–276, 279–281
    intuitional, 157–158
    material-requirements, *see* Material-requirements planning (MRP)
    strategic, *see* Strategic planning
    supervisory, 128, 129
    total posture (Quinn), 159
  worker participation in, 102–103, 702
  see also Controlling; Leading; Organizing
Planning groups, staff, 128

Planning objectives, 110
Planning process, 117–122
Plans:
  defined, 109–110
  dimensions of, 110–112
  in planning process, 118
  types of, 111–113
Polaroid Corporation, 163
Policies, organizational, 113–115
Political action by businesses, government influenced by, 676–678
Political action committees (PACs), 677
Political environment of organizations, 150, 152
  and legal environment, 219–220, 633–634
Political-risk analysis in international environment, 638–639
Political values, 153
Pollution protection by government, 675
Portsmouth Naval Shipyard, 406
Position power, 309, 310, 319, 321
Positive reinforcement, 386–391
Postaction controls, 450
Postponement strategy, 85, 86
Power:
  acceptance theory of (Barnard), 310–311
  acquiring and using, 314
  connotations of, 308
  defined, 305
  inventory of, 310
  as leadership resource, 308–314
  limits to, 310–313
  need for, of McClelland (nPower), 377–379
  sources of, 309–310
  types of:
    coercive, 309, 310
    expert, 310
    legitimate, 309, 310
    managerial, 310, 314
    personal, 310
    position, 309, 310, 319, 321
    reference, 310
    reward, 309, 310
Power distance in national culture, 635, 636
Precise objectives in planning, 120–121
Precontrols, 450
Preferred solutions, choosing, 73, 74, 85–88. *See also* Decision making
Preliminary contact in recruitment process, 276–277
Premises regarding future conditions, 118. *See also* Forecasting
Priorities, ambiguous, 664
Proactive problem solving, 70
Probability of occurrence of outcomes, 84–85
Problem avoiders, 70

Reinforcement theory of motivation, 374, 385–392
Rejection of job candidates, 282
Relatedness needs of Alderfer, 376
Relationship-oriented leadership style, 319, 321
Reliability of performance-appraisal methods, 455
Reliable employment tests, 281
Religious values, 153
Replacement of employees, 269, 286–289, 610. *See also* Promotions
Required behaviors, 411–412
Research:
  action, 578–579
  operations, 41, 51–54, A1–A9
Resistance to change, dealing with, 574–576
Resources of organizations:
  financial, in international business, 625
  human, *see* Human resources of organizations
  material, 7, 17–19, 152
  as operating objective, 142–143
Responsibility:
  in delegation process, 194
  social, 143, 666–673, 679–681, 708
Responsibility accounting systems, 478–479
Responsibility centers, 478–479, 482–484
Results:
  management by (MBO), 143–145, 464–467, 547–549, 580, 709
  in planning process, 118
Résumés, 279
Retirement, preparing for, 287
Retrenchment strategies, 139, 141
Return on investment and employee health, 708
Revenue centers, 479
Revitalization, official objectives in, 142
Reward power, 309, 310
Rewards:
  and incentive pay, 459
  in job satisfaction, 242
  and motivation, 372–374, 380–384, 387, 389
  and performance, 242, 373–374
  see also Positive reinforcement
Reward systems, 458–461
Right-to-work laws, 599
Rights:
  employee, 599–600, 605
  employer (management), 599–600, 698
Ringi system in Japan, 646, 647
Risk:
  of death, 707, 708
  defined, 82
  political, in international environment, 638–639

Risky environments in problem solving, 82
Robots:
  in assembly-line jobs, 247
  in future, 699
  in production and operations, 539–540
Role ambiguity, 356
Role conflict, 356
Role dynamics, 356
Role negotiation, 579–580
Role overload, 356
Roles:
  communication of, 356
  counseling, 453, 454
  defined, 356
  managerial, 23–24, 337–338, 569–576
Rotation of jobs, 246–247, 285, 646
Routine problems, 75
Routing sheets, 528–529
Rubik's cube, 69, 82
Rules:
  in integration, 227–228
  as standing-use plans, 114, 115
Rutland (Vermont) Hospital, 407

Saab automobile plant, 260–261
Safety needs of Maslow, 375, 377
Salaries, *see* Compensation
Sales budgets, 483
Satisfaction:
  job, 239–243
    group cohesiveness in, 414–415
  of needs, groups in, 403, 404, 406–407. *See also* Need(s)
Satisficing in problem solving, 87
Satisfier factors in two-factor theory of Herzberg, 241
Scalar principle in chain of command, 191
Schedules:
  in production/operations management, 513, 523–530, 532. *See also* Critical-path method (CPM); Program evaluation and review technique (PERT)
  reinforcement, 389
  as single-use plans, 116–117
  work, 116, 256–257
Science:
  defined, 37
  management as, 37, 39. *See also* Management science; Management science/operations research
Scientific management, 42–43, 644, 702
Scientific method, steps in, 37
Scope, job, 243
Scope dimension of plans, 111
Scot Lad Foods Inc., 405
Secondary data/unobtrusive measures, 579
Security:
  as future pressure on managers, 698

informal groups as providing, 403
job, 606, 610, 698
union, 605
Selection of employees, 269, 279–282, 647
Selective perception, 79, 349
Self-actualization in behavioral approaches to management, 46–51
Self-actualization needs of Maslow, 375, 377
Self-assurance as leadership trait, 315
Self-control in control process, 448–449
Self-determination as future pressure on managers, 698
Semantic barriers to communication, 340–341
Senders in communication process, 339–340
Seniority:
  as collective-bargaining issue, 606, 610
  promotions by, 286
Sensitivity training, 579
Sentiments in group dynamics, 411–412
Services, *see* Goods and services
Sex discrimination in employment, 275
Sex stereotypes, 348
Shaping in positive reinforcement, 388
Short-range budgets, 480, 482. *See also* Master budgets
Short-range plans, 110
Simple moving averages, 518–519
Simulation as management technique, 53, A7–A9
Single-use plans, 111–112, 114–116
Sirocco Company case, 546–547
Situational control (Fiedler), 318–319
Sizes of organizations, 184, 222–224
Skills:
  conceptual, 24
  human, 24
  leadership, 419
  managerial, 24–26
  technical, 24
Skill variety in job enrichment, 248, 250–252
Small-batch production technology, 221, 222
Smoothing (accommodation), 520–521, 566, 568
Snow removal in New York, 51–52
Social audits, 680–681
Social environment, 150, 152
Social instability in political-risk analysis, 638
Socialization:
  in behavioral approaches to management, 46–51
  of new employees, 283
Social needs of Maslow, 375, 377
Social responsibility, 143, 666–673, 679–681, 708